New Perspectives on

Microsoft® Office Professional for Windows® 95

A Document-Centric Approach

INTRODUCTORY

The New Perspectives Series

The New Perspectives Series consists of texts and technology that teach computer concepts and the programs listed below. Both Windows 3.1 and Windows 95 versions of these programs are available. You can order these New Perspectives texts in many different lengths, software releases, bound combinations, Custom Books, and CourseKits™. Contact your CTI sales representative or customer service representative for the most up-to-date details.

The New Perspectives Series

Computer Concepts

dBASE

Internet, Netscape Navigator, and the World Wide Web

Lotus 1-2-3

Microsoft Access

Microsoft Excel

Microsoft Office Professional

Microsoft PowerPoint

Microsoft Windows 3.1

Microsoft Windows 95

Microsoft Word

Microsoft Works

Novell Perfect Office

Paradox

Presentations

Quattro Pro

WordPerfect

New Perspectives on

Microsoft® Office Professional for Windows® 95

A Document-Centric Approach

INTRODUCTORY

Judy Adamski

Joseph J. Adamski

Grand Valley State University

A DIVISION OF COURSE TECHNOLOGY

ONE MAIN STREET, CAMBRIDGE MA 02142

an International Thomson Publishing company I(T)P

Albany • Bonn • Boston • Cincinnati • London • Madrid • Melbourne • Mexico City
New York • Paris • San Francisco • Singapore • Tokyo • Toronto • Washington

New Perspectives on Microsoft Office Professional for Windows 95 — Introductory: A Document-Centric Approach is published by CTI.

Managing Editor	Mac Mendelsohn
Series Consulting Editor	Susan Solomon
Senior Product Manager	Barbara Clemens
Developmental Editor/Product Manager	Kathleen Finnegan
Production Editor	Nancy Ray
Text and Cover Designer	Ella Hanna
Cover Illustrator	Nancy Nash

For more information contact:

Course Technology
One Main Street
Cambridge, MA 02142

International Thomson Publishing Europe
Berkshire House 168-173
High Holborn
London WCIV 7AA
England

Thomas Nelson Australia
102 Dodds Street
South Melbourne, 3205
Victoria, Australia

Nelson Canada
1120 Birchmount Road
Scarborough, Ontario
Canada M1K 5G4

International Thomson Editores
Campos Eliseos 385, Piso 7
Col. Polanco
11560 Mexico D.F. Mexico

International Thomson Publishing GmbH
Königswinterer Strasse 418
53227 Bonn
Germany

International Thomson Publishing Asia
211 Henderson Road
#05-10 Henderson Building
Singapore 0315

International Thomson Publishing Japan
Hirakawacho Kyowa Building, 3F
2-2-1 Hirakawacho
Chiyoda-ku, Tokyo 102
Japan

ISBN 0-7600-3579-2

Printed in the United States of America

10 9 8 7 6 5 4 3 2

From the New Perspectives Series Team

At Course Technology, we have one foot in education and the other in technology. We believe that technology is transforming the way people teach and learn, and we are excited about providing instructors and students with materials that use technology to teach about technology.

Our development process is unparalleled in the higher education publishing industry. Every product we create goes through an exacting process of design, development, review, and testing.

Reviewers give us direction and insight that shape our manuscripts and bring them up to the latest standards. Every manuscript is quality tested. Students whose backgrounds match the intended audience work through every keystroke, carefully checking for clarity and pointing out errors in logic and sequence. Together with our own technical reviewers, these testers help us ensure that everything that carries our name is error-free and easy to use.

We show both *how* and *why* technology is critical to solving problems in college and in whatever field you choose to teach or pursue. Our time-tested, step-by-step instructions provide unparalleled clarity. Examples and applications are chosen and crafted to motivate students.

As the New Perspectives Series team at Course Technology, our goal is to produce the most timely, accurate, creative, and technologically-sound product in the entire college publishing industry. We strive for consistent high quality. This takes a lot of communication, coordination, and hard work. But we love what we do. We are determined to be the best. Write us and let us know what you think. You can also e-mail us at info@course.com.

The New Perspectives Series Team

Joseph J. Adamski
Judy Adamski
Roy Ageloff
David Auer
Rachel Bunin
Joan Carey
Patrick Carey
Barbara Clemens
Kim Crowley
Jessica Evans
Kathy Finnegan
Robin Geller
Chris Greacen
Roger Hayen
Charles Hommel
Chris Kelly
Terry Ann Kremer
Melissa Lima
Mac Mendelsohn
Dan Oja
June Parsons
Sandra Poindexter
Mark Reimold
Ann Shaffer
Susan Solomon
John Zeanchock
Beverly Zimmerman
Scott Zimmerman

Preface The New Perspectives Series

What is the New Perspectives Series?

Course Technology's **New Perspectives Series** combines text and technology products that teach computer concepts and microcomputer applications. Users consistently praise this series for its innovative pedagogy, creativity, supportive and engaging style, accuracy, and use of interactive technology. The first New Perspectives text was published in January of 1993. Since then, the series has grown to more than thirty titles and has become the best-selling series on computer concepts and microcomputer applications. Others have imitated the New Perspectives features, design, and technologies, but none have replicated its quality and its ability to consistently anticipate and meet the needs of instructors and students.

How is the New Perspectives Series different from other microcomputer applications series?

The **New Perspectives Series** distinguishes itself from other series in at least four substantial ways: sound instructional design, consistent quality, innovative technology, and proven pedagogy. The texts in this series consist of two or more tutorials, which are based on sound instructional design. Each tutorial is motivated by a realistic case that is meaningful to students. Rather than learn a laundry list of features, students learn the features in the context of solving a problem. This process motivates all concepts and skills by demonstrating to students *why* they would want to know them.

Instructors and students have come to rely on the high quality of the New Perspectives Series and to consistently praise its accuracy. This accuracy is a result of Course Technology's unique multi-step quality assurance process that incorporates student testing at three stages of development, using hardware and software configurations appropriate to the product. All solutions, test questions, and other CourseTools (see below) are tested using similar procedures. Instructors who adopt this series report that students can work through the tutorials independently, with a minimum of intervention or "damage control" by instructors or staff. This consistent quality has meant that if instructors are pleased with one product from the series, they can rely on the same quality with any other New Perspectives product.

The **New Perspectives Series** distinguishes itself with its innovative technology. This series innovated truly *interactive* learning applications—Course Labs. These applications have set the standard for interactive learning.

How do I know that the New Perspectives Series will work?

Some instructors who use this series report a significant difference between how much their students learn and retain with this series as compared to other series. With other series, instructors often find that students can work through the book and do well on homework and tests, but still not demonstrate competency when asked to perform particular tasks outside the context of the text's sample case or project. With the **New Perspectives Series**, however, instructors report that students have a complete, integrative learning experience that stays with them. They credit this high retention and competency to the fact that this series incorporates critical thinking and problem solving with the computer skills mastery.

How does the book I'm holding fit into the New Perspectives Series?

New Perspectives microcomputer applications books are available in the following categories:

Brief books are about 100 pages long and are intended to teach only the essentials of the particular microcomputer application.

Introductory books are about 300 pages long and consist of 6 or 7 tutorials. An Introductory book is designed for a short course on a particular application or for a one-term course to be used in combination with other introductory books.

Comprehensive books consist of all of the tutorials in the Introductory book, plus 3 or 4 more tutorials on more advanced topics. They also include the Brief Windows tutorials, 3 or 4 Additional Cases, and a Reference Section.

Intermediate books take the 3 or 4 tutorials at the end of four Comprehensive books and combine them. Reference Sections and Additional Cases are also included.

Advanced books begin by covering topics similar to those in the Comprehensive books, but cover them in more depth. Advanced books then go on to present the most high-level coverage in the series.

Four-in-One books and **Five-in-One** books combine a Brief book on Windows with 3 or 4 Introductory books. An Essential Computer Concepts section is also included.

Concepts and Applications books combine the *New Perspectives on Computer Concepts* book with various Brief and Introductory microcomputer applications books.

Custom Books, including CourseKits and Custom Editions, offer even more flexibility, so schools can customize texts to match course content exactly.

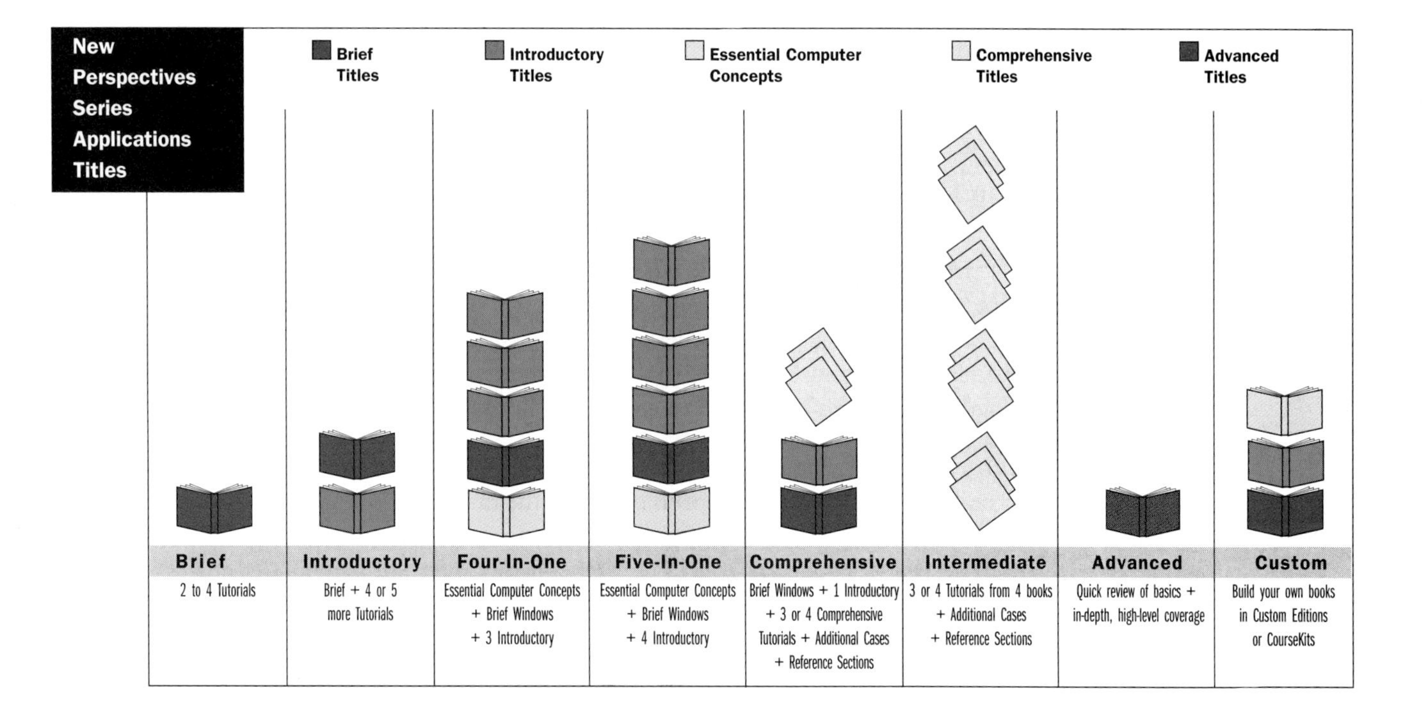

In what kind of course could I use this book?

This book can be used in any course in which you want students to learn all the most important topics of Microsoft Office for Windows 95 programs, and want to emphasize integration throughout the course, in keeping with Microsoft's document-centric approach.

How do the Windows 95 editions differ from the Windows 3.1 editions?

Larger Page Size If you've used a *New Perspectives* text before, you'll immediately notice that the book you're holding is larger than the Windows 3.1 series books. We've responded to user requests for a larger page, which allows for larger screen shots and associated callouts. Look on page OF 23 for an example of how we've made the screen shots easier to read.

Sessions We've divided the tutorials into sessions. Each session is designed to be completed in about 45 minutes to an hour (depending, of course, upon student needs and the speed of your lab equipment). With sessions, learning is broken up into more easily-assimilated chunks. You can more accurately allocate time in your syllabus. Students can more easily manage the available lab time. Each session begins with a "session box," which quickly describes what skills the student will learn in the session. Furthermore, each session is numbered, which makes it easier for you and your students to navigate and communicate about the tutorial. Look on page OF 37 for the session box that opens Session 1.2.

Quick Checks Each session concludes with meaningful, conceptual questions—called Quick Checks—that test students' understanding of what they learned in the session. The answers to all of the Quick Check questions are at the back of the book preceding the Index. You can find examples of Quick Checks on pages OF 36 and OF 56.

New Design We have retained a design that helps students easily differentiate between what they are to *do* and what they are to *read*. The steps are easily identified by their shaded background and numbered steps. Furthermore, this new design presents steps and screen shots in a larger, easier-to-read format. Some good examples of our new design are on pages OF 30 and OF 59.

What features are retained in the Windows 95 editions of the New Perspectives Series?

"Read This Before You Begin" Page This page is consistent with Course Technology's unequaled commitment to helping instructors introduce technology into the classroom. Technical considerations and assumptions about software are listed in one place to help instructors save time and eliminate unnecessary aggravation. The "Read This Before You Begin" page for this book is on page OF 2.

Tutorial Case Each tutorial begins with a problem presented in a case that is meaningful to students. The problem turns the task of learning how to use an application into a problem-solving process. The problems increase in complexity with each tutorial. These cases touch on multicultural, international, and ethical issues—so important to today's business curriculum.

1.
2.
3.

Step-by-Step Methodology This unique Course Technology methodology keeps students on track. They click or press keys always within the context of solving the problem posed in the tutorial case. The text constantly guides students, letting them know where they are in the course of solving the problem. In addition, the numerous screen shots include callouts that direct students' attention to what they should look at on the screen. On almost every page in this book, you can find an example of how steps, screen shots, and callouts work together.

TROUBLE?

TROUBLE? Paragraphs TROUBLE? paragraphs anticipate the mistakes that students are likely to make and help them recover from these mistakes. By putting these paragraphs in the book, rather than in the Instructor's Manual, we facilitate independent learning and free the instructor to focus on substantive conceptual issues rather than on common procedural errors. Two representative examples of TROUBLES? are on pages OF 18 and OF 24.

Reference Windows Reference Windows appear throughout the text. They are short, succinct summaries of the most important tasks covered in the tutorials. Reference Windows are specially designed and written so students can refer to them for their reference value when doing the Tutorial Assignments and Case Problems, and after completing the course. Page OF 371 contains the Reference Window for Using AutoFormat.

Task Reference The Task Reference is a summary of how to perform common tasks using the most efficient method, as well as helpful shortcuts. It appears as a table at the end of the book. In this book the Task Reference is on pages OF 523 through OF 528.

Tutorial Assignments, Case Problems, and Lab Assignments Each tutorial concludes with Tutorial Assignments, which provide students with additional hands-on practice of the skills they learned in the tutorial. The Tutorial Assignments are followed by four Case Problems that have approximately the same scope as the tutorial case. In the Windows 95 applications texts, there is one Case Problem in the book and one in the Instructor's Manual that require students to solve the problem independently, with minimal guidance. Finally, if a Lab (see next page) accompanies the tutorial, Lab Assignments are included. Look on pages OF 128 through OF 129 for the Tutorial Assignments for Tutorial 2. An example of a Lab Assignment is on page OF 133.

Exploration Exercises The Windows environment allows students to learn by exploring and discovering what they can do. Exploration Exercises can be Tutorial Assignments or Case Problems that might challenge students to explore the capabilities of the program they are using, and extend their knowledge using the Windows Help facility and other reference materials. Page OF 337 contains Exploration Exercises for Tutorial 5.

The New Perspectives Series is known for using technology to help instructors teach and administer, and to help students learn. What CourseTools are available with this textbook?

All of the teaching and learning materials available with the **New Perspectives Series** are known as CourseTools. Most of them are available in the Instructor's Resource Kit.

Course Labs Computer skills and concepts come to life with the New Perspectives Course Labs—highly interactive online tutorials that guide students step by step, present them with Quick Check questions, allow them to explore on their own, and test their comprehension. Lab Assignments are also included in the book at the end of each relevant tutorial. The labs available with this book and the tutorials in which they appear are:

Using a Keyboard	Using a Mouse	Using Files	Peripheral Devices	User Interfaces	Word Processing	Spread-sheets	Databases
Windows Tutorial 1	Windows Tutorial 1	Windows Tutorial 2	Essential Concepts	Essential Concepts	Office Tutorial 2	Office Tutorial 3	Office Tutorial 4
	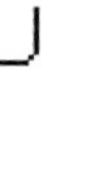				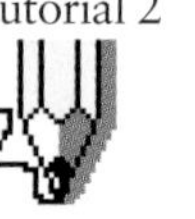	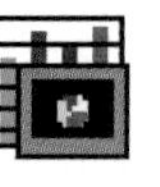	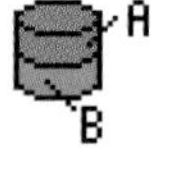

Course Test Manager Course Test Manager is cutting-edge Windows-based testing software that helps instructors design and administer pre-tests, practice tests, and actual examinations. The full-featured program provides random test generation of practice tests, immediate online feedback, and generation of detailed study guides for questions that are incorrectly answered. Online pretests help instructors assess student skills and plan instruction. Also, students can take tests at the computer; tests can be automatically graded and can generate statistical information for the instructor on individual and group performance. Instructors can also use Course Test Manager to produce printed tests.

Course Presenter Course Presenter is a CD-ROM-based presentation tool that provides instructors with a wealth of resources for use in the classroom, replacing traditional overhead transparencies with computer-generated screenshows. Course Presenter gives instructors the flexibility to create custom presentations, complete with matching student notes and lecture notes pages. (Instructors can also use Course Presenter to create traditional transparencies.) The presentations integrate closely with the Table of Contents of the relevant New Perspectives book and other CourseTools, and provide instructors with another resource to use so they can teach the way they want to teach.

Online Companions When you use a New Perspectives product you can access Course Technology's faculty and student sites on the World Wide Web. You may browse the password-protected Faculty Online Companion to obtain all of the materials you need to prepare for class. Please see your Instructor's Manual or call your Course Technology customer service representative for more information. Students may access their Online Companion in the Student Center at http://www.vmedia.com/cti/.

Instructor's Manual Instructor's Manuals are written by the authors and are quality-assurance tested. They are available in printed form and through the Course Technology Faculty Online Companion. Call your customer service representative for the URL and your password. Each Instructor's Manual contains the following items:

- Instructor's Notes for each tutorial prepared by the authors and based on their teaching experience. Instructor's Notes contain a tutorial overview, tutorial outline, troubleshooting tips, and lecture notes.
- Printed solutions to all of the Tutorial Assignments and Case Problems.
- An Additional Case Problem for each tutorial to augment teaching options.
- Solutions disk(s) containing every file students are asked to create or modify in the Tutorials, Tutorial Assignments, and Case Problems.

Student Files Disks Student Files Disks contain all of the data files that students will use for the Tutorials, Tutorial Assignments, and Case Problems. A README file includes technical tips for lab management. These files are also available online. See the inside covers of this book and the "Read This Before You Begin" page before Tutorial 1 for more information on student files.

Instructor's Resource Kit

You will receive the following CourseTools in the Instructor's Resource Kit:

- Course Labs Setup Disks
- Course Test Manager Test Bank Disks
- Course Presenter CD-ROM
- Instructor's Manual and Solutions Disks
- Student Files Disks

Acknowledgments

We want to thank the many individuals who contributed to the successful completion of this book. These include all the reviewers of this book, Dan Combellick, Scottsdale Community College, Wade Graves, Grayson County College, Linda Wise Miller, University of Idaho, and Steve St. John, Rogers State College; all the Course Technology staff, particularly the production team of Nancy Ludlow and Nancy Ray; and the quality assurance team of Jim Valente, Leonard Emma, Gina Griffiths, Timothy Marks, and Patrick Reilly; Cary Prague at Cary Prague Books and Software for permission to use icons from Picture Builder Wizard; and all the staff at Gex; and the editorial team of Mac Mendelsohn and Barbara Clemens. Special thanks to Susan Solomon for entrusting this book to us and for her friendship and support, and to Kathy Finnegan for her energy, spirit, and superior editorial talents.

Judy Adamski
Joe Adamski

Brief Contents

From the New Perspectives Team	**v**
Preface	**vi**
Essential Computer Concepts	**EC 1**
Brief Windows 95 Tutorials	**WIN95 1**
1 Exploring the Basics	WIN95 3
2 Working with Files	WIN95 29
Read This Before You Begin	**OF 2**
Introductory Office Professional for Windows 95 Tutorials	**OF 3**
TUTORIAL 1 A Tour of Microsoft Office Professional for Windows 95	**OF 3**
Using the Tutorials Effectively	**OF 4**
Session 1.1	OF 5
Session 1.2	OF 37
Session 1.3	OF 56
Tutorial Assignments	OF 73
Case Problems	OF 74
TUTORIAL 2 Word Basics and Embedding a WordArt Object	**OF 78**
Session 2.1	OF 79
Session 2.2	OF 100
Session 2.3	OF 114
Tutorial Assignments	OF 128
Case Problems	OF 129
Word Processing Lab Assignment	OF 133
TUTORIAL 3 Excel Basics and Embedding a Worksheet	**OF 134**
Session 3.1	OF 135
Session 3.2	OF 161
Session 3.3	OF 182
Tutorial Assignments	OF 195
Case Problems	OF 196
Spreadsheets Lab Assignment	OF 199
TUTORIAL 4 Access Basics and Importing an Excel Worksheet	**OF 201**
Session 4.1	OF 202
Session 4.2	OF 222
Session 4.3	OF 237
Session 4.4	OF 258
Tutorial Assignments	OF 276
Case Problems	OF 279
Databases Lab Assignment	OF 284
TUTORIAL 5 PowerPoint Basics and Embedding an Excel Chart in a Presentation	**OF 285**
Session 5.1	OF 286
Session 5.2	OF 302
Session 5.3	OF 321
Tutorial Assignments	OF 330
Case Problems	OF 332
TUTORIAL 6 Enhancing an Excel Workbook and Creating and Linking a Chart to Word	**OF 340**
Session 6.1	OF 341
Session 6.2	OF 365
Session 6.3	OF 383
Session 6.4	OF 402
Tutorial Assignments	OF 418
Case Problems	OF 419
TUTORIAL 7 Querying and Enhancing an Access Database	**OF 425**
Session 7.1	OF 426
Session 7.2	OF 454
Session 7.3	OF 472
Tutorial Assignments	OF 496
Case Problems	OF 498
QUICK CHECK ANSWERS	**OF 505**
INDEX	**OF 513**
TASK REFERENCE	**OF 523**

Table of Contents

From the New Perspectives Team	**v**
Preface	**vi**
Essential Computer Concepts	**EC 1**
Brief Windows 95 Tutorials	**WIN95 1**
1 Exploring the Basics	**WIN95 3**
2 Working with Files	**WIN95 29**
Introductory Office Professional for Windows 95 Tutorials	**OF 1**
Read This Before You Begin	**OF 2**

TUTORIAL 1

A Tour of Microsoft Office Professional for Windows 95 — OF 3

Using the Tutorials Effectively	**OF 4**
Session 1.1	**OF 5**
What Is Office 95?	**OF 5**
Word	OF 6
Excel	OF 7
Access	OF 8
PowerPoint	OF 8
Other Office 95 Tools	OF 9
Office Shortcut Bar	**OF 11**
Viewing an Integrated Word Document	**OF 13**
Locating and Storing Documents on Your Student Disk	OF 14
Opening an Existing Word Document	OF 16
The Word Window	**OF 18**
Saving a Document with a New Filename	**OF 19**
Navigating a Document	**OF 22**
Editing a Word Document	**OF 23**
Inserting Text	OF 23
Deleting Text	OF 24
Copying Text	OF 25
Moving Text	OF 26
Formatting a Word Document	**OF 27**
Aligning Paragraphs	OF 28
Changing Font Type and Size	OF 29
Changing the Font Style	OF 30
Saving a Document with the Same Filename	**OF 31**
Getting Help	**OF 31**
Using the Help Contents	OF 32
Using the Answer Wizard	OF 33
Using Context-Sensitive Help	OF 34
Printing a Document	**OF 35**
Exiting Word	**OF 36**
Session 1.2	**OF 37**
Changing Copied Access Data	**OF 37**
What Is a Database?	**OF 38**
Primary Access Objects	**OF 39**
Copying an Access Database	**OF 40**
Opening an Existing Access Database	**OF 42**
The Access and Database Windows	**OF 43**
Working with Access Tables	**OF 43**
Opening an Access Table	OF 44
Navigating an Access Datasheet	OF 45
Updating an Access Table	OF 46
Printing a Table	**OF 47**
Exiting Access	**OF 48**
Linking and Embedding Objects	**OF 48**
Updating an Embedded Excel Worksheet	**OF 50**
Opening an Existing Excel Workbook	**OF 53**
Editing an Excel Worksheet	**OF 54**
Session 1.3	**OF 56**
Opening an Existing PowerPoint Presentation	**OF 57**
Using My Computer to Open an Existing Presentation	OF 57
Saving a Presentation with a New Filename	OF 59
The PowerPoint Window	**OF 59**
Viewing a Presentation Using Slide View	**OF 60**
Viewing a Presentation Using Slide Sorter View	**OF 61**
Changing the Slide Order	**OF 61**
Adding a New Slide	**OF 62**
Linking an Excel Chart	**OF 66**
Viewing a Slide Show	**OF 71**
Printing a Slide	**OF 72**
Tutorial Assignments	**OF 73**
Case Problems	**OF 74**

TUTORIAL 2

Word Basics and Embedding a WordArt Object — OF 78

Session 2.1	**OF 79**
Developing Effective Word Documents	**OF 79**
Planning a Document	**OF 80**
Starting a New Word Document	**OF 81**
Entering Text in a Document	**OF 83**
Typing Text	OF 83
Displaying Nonprinting Characters	OF 85
Correcting Text	OF 86
The AutoCorrect Feature	OF 87
Using Undo	OF 88
Organizing Document Windows	**OF 89**
Opening an Existing Document	OF 89
Switching Between Open Documents	OF 90
Tiling Document Windows	OF 91
Saving and Naming a Document	OF 93
Editing a Document	**OF 94**
Navigating a Document	OF 94
Inserting Text	OF 96
Selecting and Replacing Text	OF 96
Deleting Text	OF 99
Session 2.2	**OF 100**
Changing Character Formats	**OF 100**
Changing Font Type and Size	OF 100
Using Bold, Italic, and Underlining	OF 103
Using Tabs	**OF 105**
Copying and Moving Text	**OF 107**
The Clipboard	OF 108
Copying and Pasting Text	OF 108
Moving Text	OF 109
Creating Numbered and Bulleted Lists	**OF 111**
Formatting Text as a Numbered List	OF 112
Formatting Text as a Bulleted List	OF 112
Session 2.3	**OF 114**
Embedding and Changing a WordArt Object	**OF 114**

Embedding a WordArt Object OF 116
Resizing a WordArt Object OF 119
Changing a WordArt Object OF 121

Checking the Spelling in a Document **OF 122**

Previewing and Printing a Document **OF 125**

Tutorial Assignments **OF 128**

Case Problems **OF 129**

Word Processing Lab Assignment **OF 133**

TUTORIAL 3

Excel Basics and Embedding a Worksheet OF 134

Session 3.1 OF 135

Developing Effective Worksheets **OF 135**
Planning a Worksheet OF 136

Starting a New Excel Workbook **OF 138**

The Excel Window **OF 138**

Renaming a Worksheet **OF 140**

Entering and Correcting Labels **OF 140**

Navigating a Worksheet **OF 145**

Entering and Correcting Numbers and Dates **OF 146**
Working with Numbers OF 146
Working with Dates OF 148

Saving a New Workbook **OF 149**

Entering and Correcting Formulas **OF 149**
Formulas and Functions OF 149
Entering Arithmetic Formulas OF 151
Copying and Pasting Formulas OF 152
Entering Formulas Containing Functions OF 154
Using Logical Functions OF 158

Closing a Workbook and Exiting Excel **OF 160**

Session 3.2 OF 161

Opening an Existing Workbook **OF 161**

Working with Ranges **OF 162**
Naming Ranges and Cells OF 162
Moving to a Named Range or Cell OF 164

Inserting and Deleting Columns and Rows **OF 165**
Inserting Columns and Rows OF 165
Deleting Columns and Rows OF 167

Moving the Contents of Cells **OF 168**
Cutting and Pasting Cell Contents OF 168
Dragging Cell Contents OF 169

Changing Number and Date Formats **OF 171**

Adjusting Column Widths **OF 175**

Adding and Removing Borders **OF 177**

Splitting the Worksheet Window **OF 180**

Session 3.3 OF 182

Inserting and Sizing an Embedded Picture **OF 182**

Clearing Cell Contents **OF 185**

Printing a Worksheet **OF 186**

Embedding an Excel Worksheet in a Word Document **OF 187**
Editing an Embedded Excel Worksheet OF 192

Tutorial Assignments **OF 195**

Case Problems **OF 196**

Spreadsheets Lab Assignment **OF 199**

TUTORIAL 4

Access Basics and Importing an Excel Worksheet OF 201

Session 4.1 OF 202

Introduction to Database Concepts **OF 202**
Organizing Data OF 202
Databases and Relationships OF 203
Relational Database Management Systems OF 204

Guidelines for Designing Databases **OF 205**

Creating a Database **OF 207**

Guidelines for Designing Access Tables **OF 209**
Naming Fields and Objects OF 209
Assigning Field Data Types OF 210
Assigning Field Sizes OF 212

Creating a Table **OF 212**
Defining Fields OF 213
Specifying the Primary Key OF 217
Saving the Table Structure OF 218

Adding Records to a Table **OF 219**

Saving a Database **OF 221**

Session 4.2 OF 222

Modifying the Structure of an Access Table **OF 222**
Moving a Field OF 222
Adding a Field OF 223
Changing Field Properties OF 224

Copying Records from Another Access Database **OF 226**

Updating a Database **OF 228**
Deleting Records OF 229
Changing Records OF 229

Importing Excel Data to a New Table **OF 231**

Deleting a Field from a Table Structure **OF 235**

Printing a Datasheet **OF 236**

Session 4.3 OF 237

Creating a Form with an AutoForm Wizard **OF 237**

Saving a Form **OF 238**

Navigating a Form **OF 239**

Finding Data Using a Form **OF 239**

Printing Selected Form Records **OF 242**

Creating a Form Using the Form Wizard **OF 243**

Changing a Form's AutoFormat **OF 246**

Maintaining Table Data Using a Form **OF 248**

Defining Table Relationships **OF 251**
One-to-Many Relationships OF 252
Referential Integrity OF 252
Defining a Relationship Between Two Tables OF 253

Creating a Form with a Main Form and a Subform **OF 255**

Session 4.4 OF 258

Creating a Report Using the Report Wizard **OF 258**

Introduction to Queries **OF 266**

The Query Window **OF 266**

Creating and Running a Query **OF 268**

Specifying a Condition in a Query **OF 270**

Sorting Data in a Query **OF 271**

Saving a Query OF 273
Querying More Than One Table OF 273
Changing Data Using a Query OF 275
Tutorial Assignments OF 276
Case Problems OF 279
Databases Lab Assignment OF 284

TUTORIAL 5
PowerPoint Basics and Embedding an Excel Chart in a Presentation OF 285

Session 5.1 OF 286
Developing Effective PowerPoint Presentations OF 286
Planning a Presentation OF 287
Starting a New Presentation OF 288
Entering Text on a Slide OF 290
Adding Slides OF 292
Adding Slides in Slide View OF 292
Adding Slides in Outline View OF 294
Viewing a Slide Show OF 299
Working in Outline View OF 299
Deleting a Slide OF 299
Moving Text Up and Down OF 300
Promoting and Demoting Text OF 301

Session 5.2 OF 302
Changing the Template OF 302
Working in Slide View OF 303
Adding and Deleting Text OF 303
Rearranging Text OF 305
Formatting Text OF 306
Working with Objects on the Drawing Toolbar OF 308
Creating and Changing a Shape OF 308
Changing the Slide Layout OF 312
Inserting Slides from Another Presentation OF 313
Inserting Clip Art OF 314
Adding Animation Effects OF 319

Session 5.3 OF 321
Embedding an Excel Chart OF 321
Rearranging Slides OF 322
Annotating Slides During a Slide Show OF 324
Working with Speaker's Notes OF 326
Inserting Speaker's Notes OF 326
Checking Spelling OF 328
Printing a Presentation OF 329
Printing Multiple Slides per Page OF 329
Printing Speaker's Notes OF 329
Tutorial Assignments OF 330
Case Problems OF 332

TUTORIAL 6
Enhancing an Excel Workbook and Creating and Linking a Chart to Word OF 340

Session 6.1 OF 341
Effective Workbook Organization OF 341
Completing the Documentation Sheet OF 342
Displaying and Formatting the Date Using the TODAY Function OF 343
Creating a Series with AutoFill OF 344
Working with Formulas OF 347
Using the AutoSum Button OF 347
Using the Fill Handle to Copy a Formula OF 348
Relative and Absolute References OF 350
Automatic Recalculation OF 357
Adding a Text Note OF 358
Testing a Worksheet OF 359
Using Percentage Formats OF 362
Sorting Rows OF 363

Session 6.2 OF 365
Changing Character Formats OF 365
Changing Font Type and Font Size OF 365
Using Bold, Italic, and Underlining OF 366
Applying Patterns and Colors OF 367
Adjusting Row Heights OF 369
Changing Alignments OF 370
Changing Cell Alignment OF 370
Centering Text Across Columns OF 371
Using AutoFormat OF 371
Changing the Printed Appearance of a Worksheet OF 373
Portrait and Landscape Orientations OF 373
Changing Headers and Footers OF 374
Centering a Printed Worksheet OF 377
Working with Printed Gridlines OF 377
Printing Worksheets OF 378
Displaying and Printing Formulas OF 381

Session 6.3 OF 383
Developing Effective Charts OF 383
Planning a Chart OF 384
Creating an Excel Chart OF 384
Excel Chart Types OF 385
Creating a Column Chart OF 386
Revising the Chart Data Series OF 390
Modifying an Excel Chart OF 391
Selecting and Activating a Chart OF 391
Changing the Plot Area OF 393
Editing, Adding, and Removing Chart Text OF 393
Moving and Resizing a Chart OF 395
Using Pictures in a Column Chart OF 396
Stacking Pictures OF 398
Displaying the Title in a Colored Box with a Shadow OF 399
Previewing and Printing a Worksheet and Chart OF 400

Session 6.4 OF 402
Analyzing Data with Charts OF 402
Creating a Pie Chart OF 403
Changing the Chart to a 3-D Pie Chart OF 405

Pulling Out a Wedge on a 3-D Pie Chart OF 406
Changing the Elevation and Rotation of a 3-D Chart OF 408
Changing the Colors on a Chart OF 409
Changing Chart Patterns OF 410
Formatting the Chart Labels OF 411
Adding a Border Around a Chart OF 413

Linking an Excel Chart to a Word Document OF 414
Updating a Linked Chart OF 415

Tutorial Assignments OF 418

Case Problems OF 419

TUTORIAL 7

Querying and Enhancing an Access Database OF 425

Session 7.1 OF 426

Viewing the Relationships of Database Tables OF 426
One-To-Many Relationships OF 427
Many-To-Many Relationships OF 428

Defining Record Selection Criteria for Queries OF 433
Specifying an Exact Match OF 433
Changing a Datasheet's Appearance OF 436
Using a Comparison Operator to Match a Range of Values OF 437
Using a Pattern Match OF 439

Defining Multiple Selection Criteria for Queries OF 441
The And Logical Operator OF 442
The Or Logical Operator OF 444

Sorting Data OF 445
Sorting One Field Using a Toolbar Sort Button OF 445
Sorting Multiple Fields Using a Toolbar Sort Button OF 446
Selecting Multiple Sort Fields in Design View OF 448

Filtering Data OF 450
Using Filter By Selection OF 450
Using Filter By Form OF 452

Session 7.2 OF 454

Performing Calculations in a Query OF 455
Using Calculated Fields OF 455
Changing Query Field Properties OF 458
Using Record Calculations OF 459
Using Record Group Calculations OF 462

Creating a Parameter Query OF 463

Creating a Top Values Query OF 467

Creating an Action Query OF 468

Session 7.3 OF 472

Customizing Forms OF 472

The Form Window in Design View OF 473
Controls OF 474
Form Sections OF 476

Adding Fields to a Form OF 476

Viewing and Saving a Form OF 477

Resizing Controls OF 478

Moving Controls OF 479

Selecting and Aligning Multiple Controls OF 480

Using Captions OF 481

Placing a Rectangle Around Controls OF 483

Adding a Combo Box Using Control Wizards OF 485

Embedding and Changing a Graphic Image on a Form OF 488

Modifying a Graphic Image in Paint OF 491

Resizing a Form OF 493

Compacting a Database OF 495

Tutorial Assignments OF 496

Case Problems OF 498

Reference Windows

Displaying and Docking the Office Shortcut Bar OF 11
Opening an Existing Document OF 16
Saving a Document With a New Filename OF 21
Copying or Moving Text OF 26
Printing a Document OF 35
Copying an Access Database OF 41
Opening an Access Object OF 44
Opening an Existing Document Using My Computer OF 57
Starting a New Word Document OF 81
Moving Text Within a Document OF 109
Checking the Spelling in a Document OF 122
Correcting Mistakes Using Edit Mode OF 142
Moving to a Cell Using the Cell Reference OF 146
Entering a Formula OF 151
Copying and Pasting a Cell or Range of Cells OF 153
Using the Function Wizard OF 156
Naming a Range or Cell OF 163
Moving to a Named Range or Named Cell OF 164
Inserting Columns or Rows OF 166
Deleting Columns or Rows OF 167
Cutting and Pasting Cell Contents OF 168
Dragging a Cell or Range OF 169
Formatting Numbers and Dates Using the Format Menu OF 172
Adjusting Column Width Using AutoFit OF 175
Adjusting Column Width Using the Format Menu OF 175
Adding a Border OF 177
Removing a Border OF 180
Embedding a Picture OF 182
Clearing Cell Contents OF 186
Embedding an Excel Worksheet in Word OF 188
Defining a Field in a Table OF 213
Specifying a Primary Key for a Table OF 218
Finding Data OF 240
Starting a New Presentation OF 288
Selecting a Slide in Outline View OF 300
Changing a Design Template OF 302
Inserting Slides from Another Presentation OF 313
Changing the Order of Slides OF 323
Using AutoFill to Complete a Series OF 344
Copying Cell Contents with the Fill Handle OF 349
Adding a Text Note OF 358
Sorting Rows OF 363
Changing Row Height with the Row Resizing Pointer OF 369
Changing Row Height with the Row Height Dialog Box OF 370
Using AutoFormat OF 371
Using the ChartWizard OF 384
Selecting Non-Adjacent Cells OF 387
Revising the Chart Data Series OF 391
Activating a Selected Chart OF 391
Using a Picture in a Column or Bar Chart OF 397
Sorting a Query Datasheet OF 448
Using Filter By Selection OF 451
Using Filter By Form OF 452
Using Expression Builder OF 456
Creating a Parameter Query OF 464
Creating and Running an Action Query OF 469
Embedding an Existing Graphic Image OF 489

New Perspectives on

Essential Computer Concepts

Credits

Figure 1: Computer Advertisement – Midwest Micro Home System, EC 4 MidWest Micro computer system photographs provided courtesy of MidWest Micro, Fletcher Ohio; Computer Advertisement – Laser Printer, EC 4 Photo courtesy of Hewlett-Packard Company. **Figure 2**: Office workers at their computers – AS400, EC 4 Courtesy of International Business Machines Corporation. **Figure 4**: desktop with a printer: Epson Direct Endeavor Pro, EC 6 Courtesy of EPSON Americas, Inc. **Figure 5**: Desktop with tower system: Pavillon 5000, Series PC, EC 6 Photo courtesy of Hewlett-Packard Company. **Figure 6**: A notebook computer – IBM Thinkpad 701C/CS, EC 7 Courtesy of International Business Machines Corporation. **Figure 7**: A mini-computer – AS400, EC 7 Courtesy of International Business Machines Corporation. **Figure 8**: A mainframe computer – IBM 3080, EC 8 Courtesy of International Business Machines Corporation. **Figure 12**: An Ergonomically designed mouse, EC 10 Courtesy of Logitech Inc. **Figure 13**: An Intel Pentium microprocessor, EC 11 Courtesy of Intel Corporation. **Figure 18**: A color monitor – IBM (Helpcenter), EC 16 Courtesy of International Business Machines Corporation. **Figure 20**: Dot-matrix printer: Epson's FX-870 & FX-1170, EC 17 Courtesy of EPSON Americas, Inc. **Figure 22**: Ink-jet printer: Stylus Color II, EC 18 Courtesy of EPSON Americas, Inc. **Figure 23**: Laser printer: HP Laser Jet 4MV, EC 19 Photo courtesy of Hewlett-Packard Company. **Figure 28**: A 3.5" hard disk drive, EC 21 Courtesy of Conner Peripherals, Inc. **Figure 35**: Microsoft Word for Windows 95, EC 30 Compliments of Microsoft Corporation. **Figure 36**: Microsoft Excel for Windows 95, EC 31 Compliments of Microsoft Corporation. **Figure 37**: Microsoft Access for Windows 95, EC 32 Compliments of Microsoft Corporation. **Figure 38**: A PowerPoint for Windows 95, EC 33 Compliments of Microsoft Corporation.

ESSENTIAL COMPUTER CONCEPTS

Essential Computer Concepts

OBJECTIVES

In this chapter you will learn:

- The major components of a computer system
- The terms used to specify the capacity and the speed of computer memory, processors, and storage
- How data is represented by the binary number system and the ASCII code
- The common types of network interface cards and network software
- How peripheral devices are connected to a computer system
- The basic concepts of data communications
- The difference between systems software and applications software

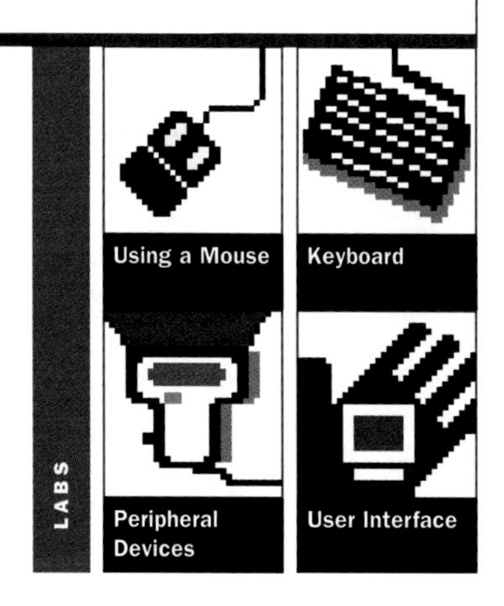

International ComAir

Today Tenzing Lu begins her first job. She just graduated with a degree in business, and she has been hired as a trainee in International ComAir's management development program. Her main responsibility will be to work on special projects for the vice president of Operations, Ms. Thompson.

When Tenzing meets with Ms. Thompson to discuss her first project, Ms. Thompson explains that she is concerned that International ComAir may not be using computers as effectively as it could. She mentions that the company has large computers to handle reservations, but that other operations are being handled manually. She also observes that recent graduates beginning their careers at International ComAir are out-producing some veteran employees. She thinks one of the reasons for this very welcome boost in productivity has been the everyday use of personal computers.

Ms. Thompson asks Tenzing to investigate how the average employee at International ComAir could benefit from the use of personal computers. Tenzing is to research this matter and recommend to management what the average employee should have for hardware and software.

Tenzing is most enthusiastic about her new assignment. Although she knows that she is not an expert on computing, she did have an excellent introductory course on computers in college that she thinks will be very useful for this assignment. Because she knows computers are constantly changing, she decides to evaluate the type of computing tools currently available that would fit the company's needs. Tenzing goes to the company library to begin her research. She has asked you to help her with her task.

As you and Tenzing begin work, she explains the types of questions you will attempt to answer. Tenzing found the ad shown in Figure 1 in a computer mail-order magazine. Does the computer shown in the ad represent a viable system configuration? How much should the system cost? What capabilities should it have? What training will be required of the user in order to take advantage of the capabilities of the system? The information in this chapter will help you answer these questions by developing your understanding of computer technology and terminology.

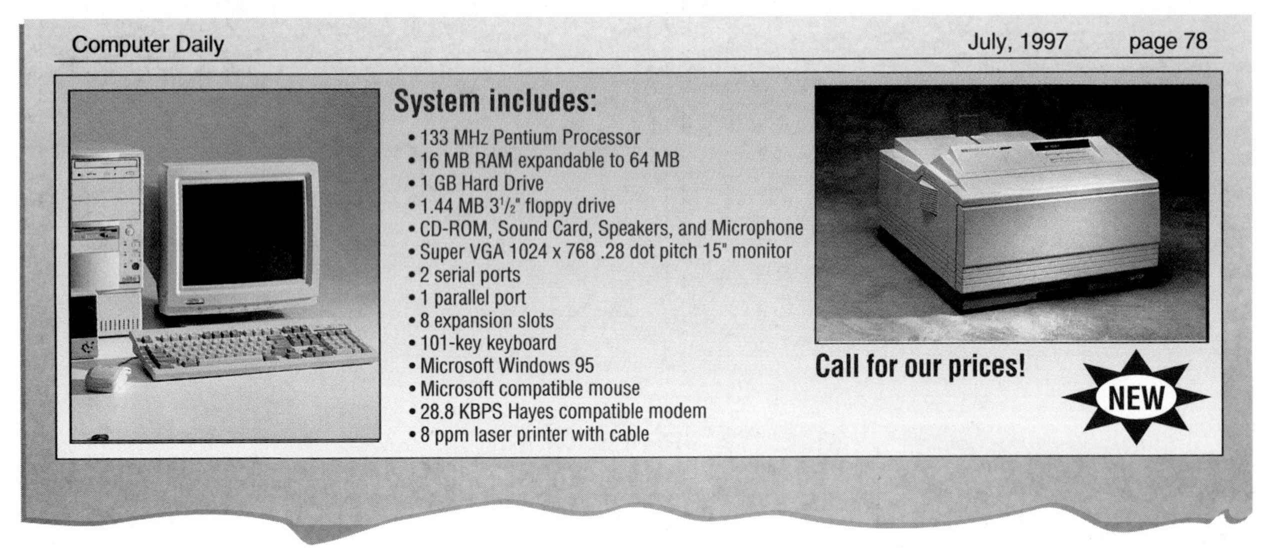

Figure 1 Computer advertisement

What Is a Computer?

Computers have become essential tools in almost every type of activity in virtually every type of business (Figure 2). A computer can be defined as an electronic device that accepts information, manipulates it, and then produces the required results. It is a versatile tool with the potential to perform many different tasks.

Figure 2 Office workers at their computers

A **computer system** is composed of the computing device and additional devices such as a printer. A computer system can manage financial information, create and manipulate graphs, record day-to-day business transactions, help managers make critical business decisions, maintain inventories, display photographs and video productions, conduct and participate in video conferencing, and perform many other tasks to help business associates be more efficient and productive.

The tangible components of a computer system are referred to as **hardware**. Some examples of hardware are keyboards, screens, disk drives, printers, scanners, digital cameras, and circuit boards. The selection of hardware components that make up a particular computer system is referred to as the **configuration**. The technical details about the speed, capacity, or size of each component are called **specifications**. For example, a computer system might be *configured* to include a printer; a *specification* for that printer might be a print speed of eight pages per minute or that it has the capacity for color.

Software refers to the intangible components of a computer system, particularly the **programs**, or lists of instructions, that are needed to make the computer perform a specific task. Software is the key to a computer's versatility. When your computer is using word processing software—for example, the Microsoft Word program—you can type memos, letters, and reports. When your computer is using accounting software, such as the Intuit QuickBooks accounting program, you can maintain information about what your customers owe you and display a graph showing the timing of customer payments.

The hardware and the software of a computer system work together to process **data**—the words, figures, sounds, and graphics that describe people, events, things, and ideas.

Figure 3 shows how you, the computer, the data, and the software interact to get work done. Let's say you want to write a report. First, you instruct the computer to use the word processing program. Once the word processing program has been activated, you begin to type the text of your report. What you type into the computer is called **input**. You might also need to issue commands that tell the computer exactly how to process your input. Perhaps you want the title to be centered and the text to be double-spaced. You use an input device, such as a keyboard or a mouse, to input data and issue commands.

Figure 3 Data is input, processed, stored, and output

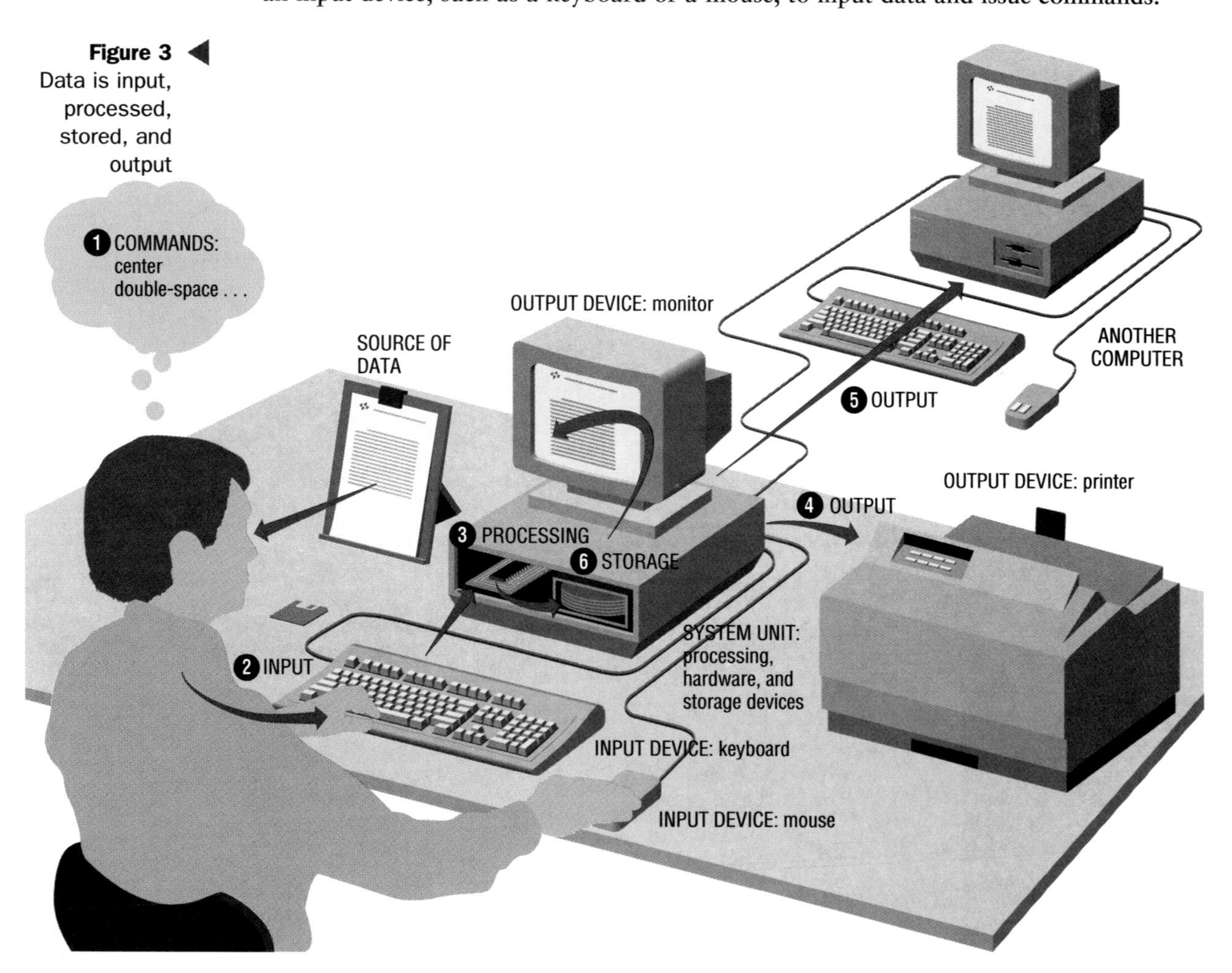

The computer processes the report according to your commands and the instructions contained in the software—the title becomes centered and all the text double-spaced. **Processing** changes the data you have input, for example, by moving text, sorting lists, or performing calculations. Or, you might choose to import an illustration, or text or numeric information such as stock prices from a source on another computer. This processing takes place on the **main circuit board** of the computer, also referred to as the **motherboard,** which contains the computer's major electronic components. The electronic components of the main circuit board are referred to as **processing hardware**.

After you have written your report, you may want to print it. The result produced by computer processing is called **output**, which is displayed on an **output device** such as a printer or screen. Instead of printing output, you might want to send the report electronically to a coworker. Sending data from one computer to another is referred to as **data communications.** To send your report to a coworker's computer you use a **communications device.**

When you have finished working, you use a **storage device**, such as a disk drive, to save your report on some sort of **storage medium**, such as a floppy disk. The text of your report is stored on the disk as a **file** under the filename of your choice. You might also choose to save your document to a network where it will be available to other workers as well. (You'll learn more about networks later in this chapter.)

Types of Computers

In her research, Tenzing has found that personal computers are not the only way to compute; there are other types of computers, which are classified by their size, speed, and cost. **Microcomputers**, also called **personal computers** (PCs), are relatively inexpensive—$500 to $10,000—and small enough to fit on a desk. Two typical desktop microcomputer configurations are shown in Figure 4 and Figure 5. Figure 4 shows a standard horizontal system unit. The vertical system unit in Figure 5 is referred to as a **tower case.** Desktop computers receive their power from a wall outlet, which limits where you can use them. They are most often used in the home and at the office.

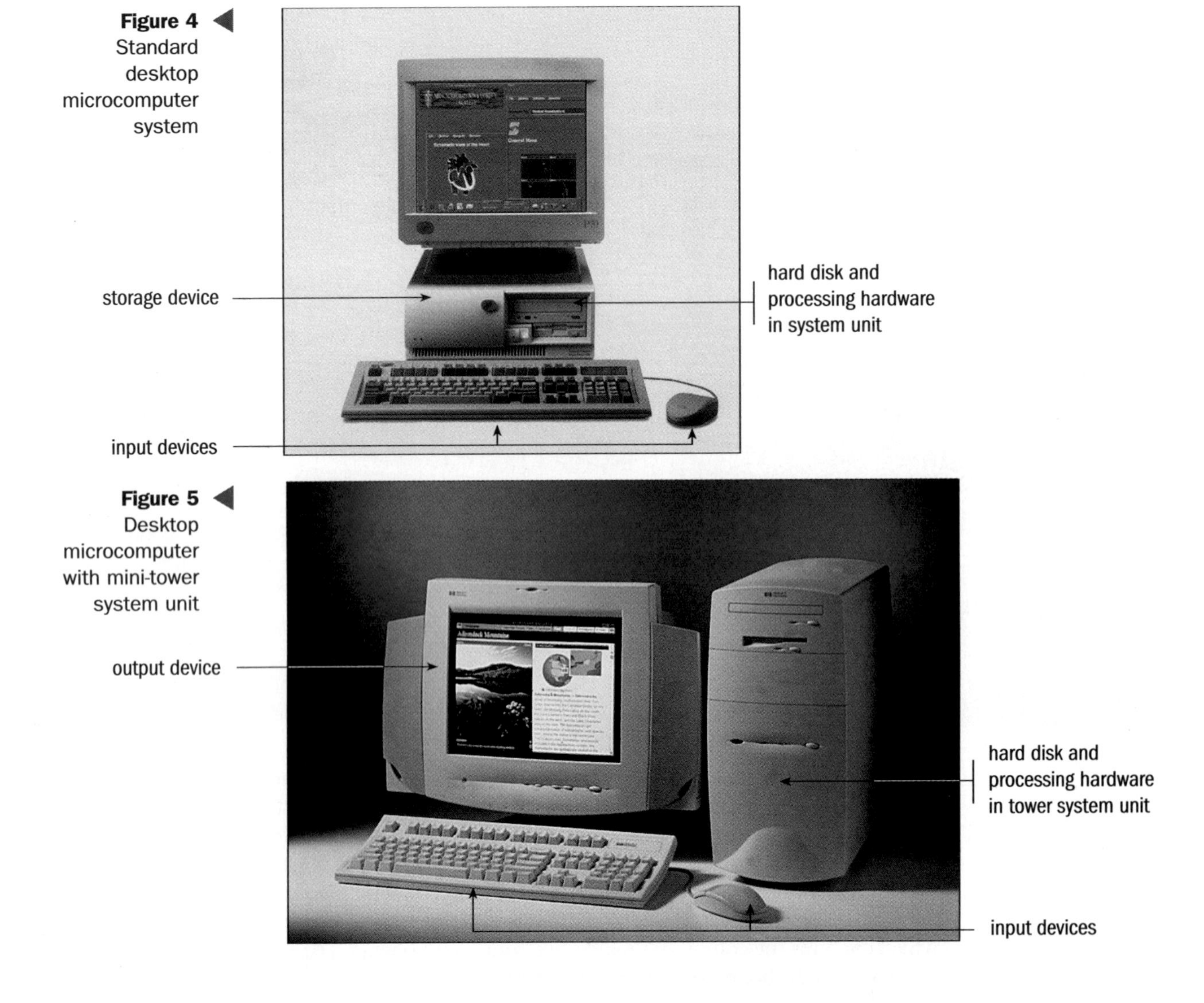

Figure 4 Standard desktop microcomputer system

Figure 5 Desktop microcomputer with mini-tower system unit

Notebook microcomputers, such as the one in Figure 6, are transportable. They are smaller and lighter than desktop microcomputers and use power from electrical outlets or rechargeable batteries. Though smaller in size, a notebook computer generally costs more than a desktop microcomputer with equivalent specifications, because miniature components often cost more than traditional hardware.

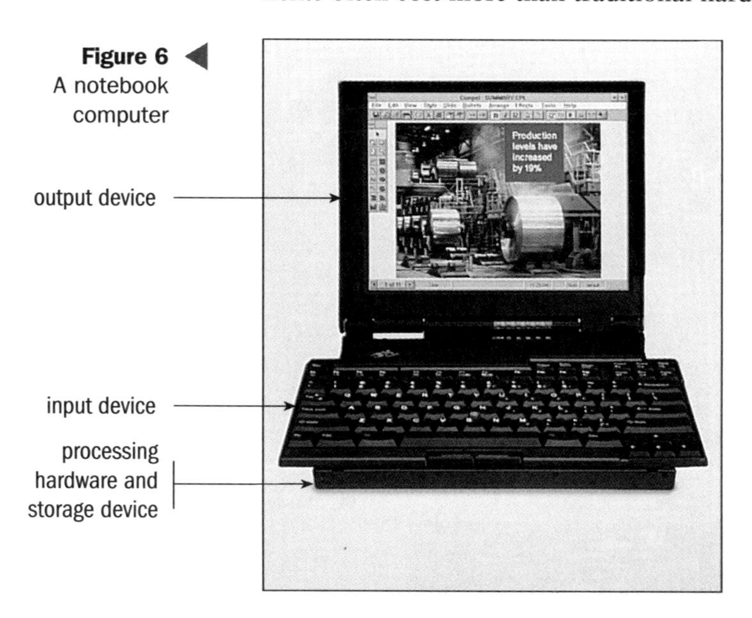

Figure 6 A notebook computer

Microcomputers are used extensively in small and large businesses. But some businesses, government agencies, and other institutions also use larger and faster types of computers: minicomputers, mainframes, and supercomputers. Unlike most microcomputers, these can have multiple input and output devices so that more than one person can work simultaneously.

Minicomputers, like the one in Figure 7, are somewhat larger than microcomputers. They operate three to ten times faster than microcomputers and cost anywhere from $10,000 to $500,000. **Mainframe computers**, like the one shown in Figure 8, are larger and more powerful than minicomputers. Mainframes have large capacities for storing and manipulating data, operate 10 to 40 times faster than microcomputers, and cost between $100,000 and $2 million.

Figure 7 A minicomputer

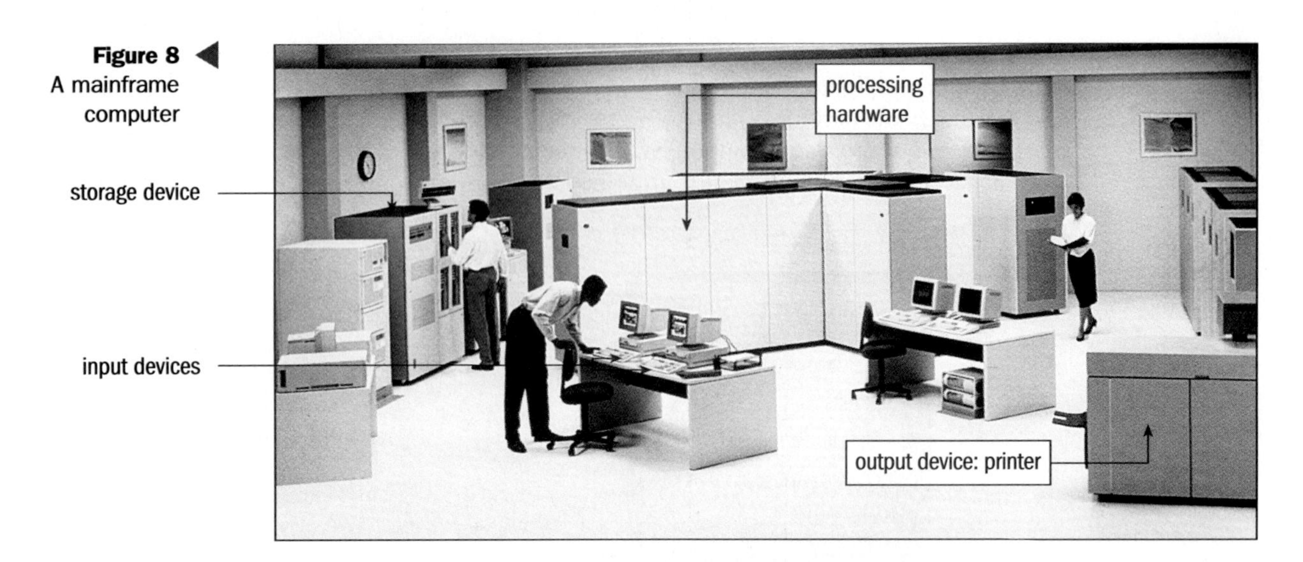

Figure 8 A mainframe computer

The largest and fastest computers, called **supercomputers**, are so expensive that only the largest companies, government agencies, and universities can afford them. Supercomputers, such as the one shown in Figure 9, operate 50 to 1,500 times faster than microcomputers.

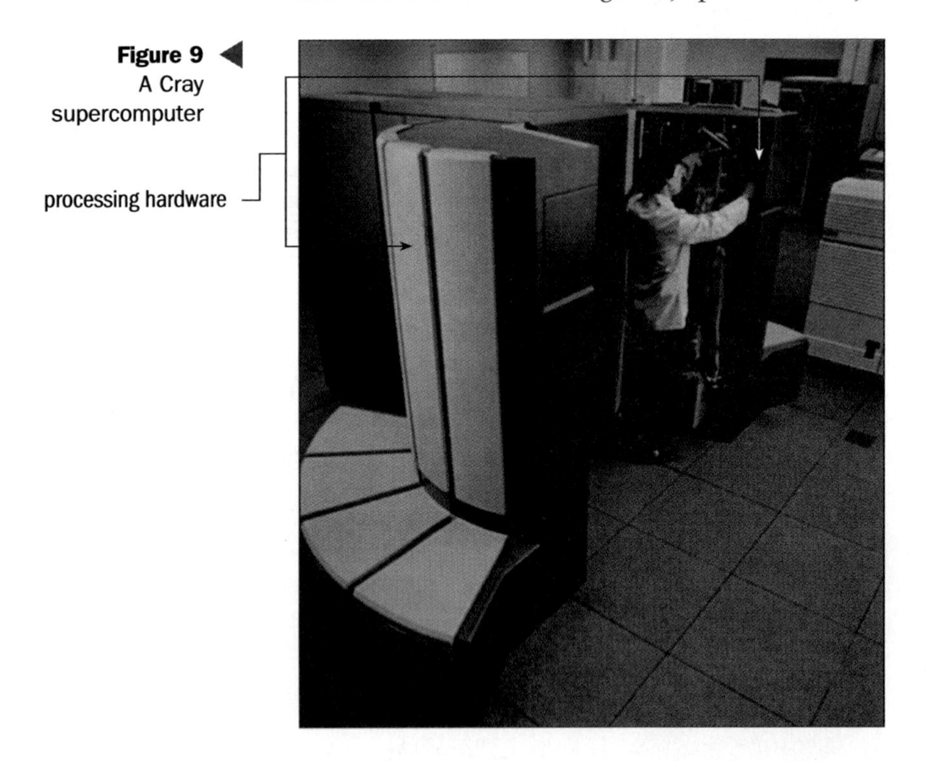

Figure 9 A Cray supercomputer

With the accelerated development of newer and better computers, the guidelines for classifying types of computers have become fuzzy. For example, some recently developed microcomputers operate at higher speeds than some minicomputers. Some minicomputer systems may have more workstations than some smaller mainframe installations.

How would Tenzing classify the computer in the advertisement shown in Figure 1 at the beginning of the chapter? If your answer is "a desktop microcomputer" you are correct. The computer in that ad fits on a desk, is not portable, and probably costs $1,000 to $2,500.

The remainder of this chapter will focus on microcomputer hardware and software concepts. These concepts will help you successfully use software to accomplish tasks both in school and at work.

Computer Hardware

As you've already learned, computer hardware can be defined as the components of a computer you can see and touch. Let's now look at the hardware you might use in a typical microcomputer system.

Input Devices

As you have already learned, you input data and commands by using an input device such as a keyboard or a mouse. The computer can also receive input from a storage device. This section takes a closer look at the input devices you might use. Storage devices are covered in a later section.

The most frequently used input device is a keyboard. Figure 10 shows a standard 101-key keyboard, and Figure 11 shows an ergonomically designed 101-key keyboard. Ask your instructor which keyboard you'll be using. Keyboards consist of three major parts: the main keyboard, the keypads, and the function keys. The design of the keyboard makes it easier to do some editing and input tasks.

Figure 10 Traditional 101-key keyboard

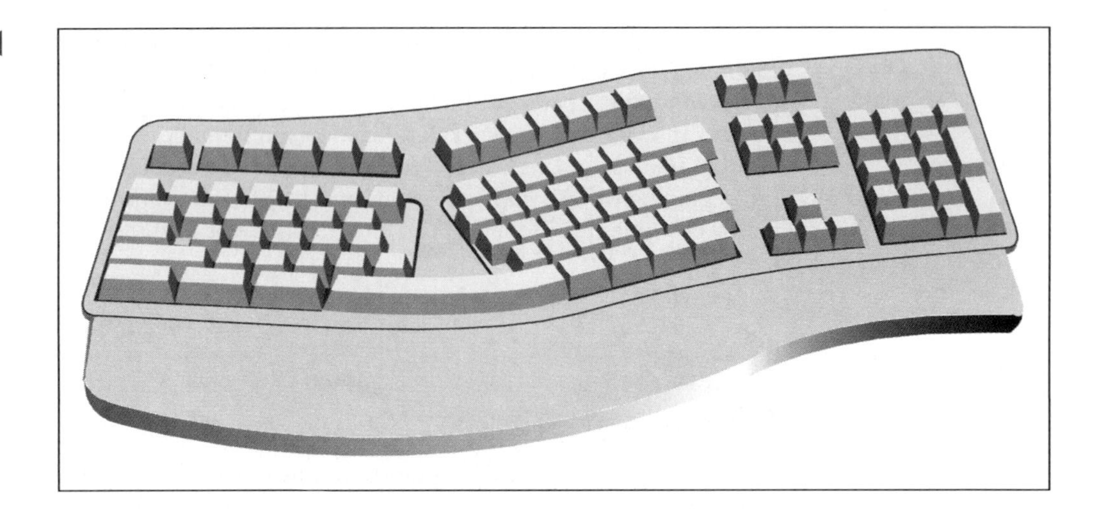

Figure 11 An ergonomically designed 101-key keyboard

Your computer also should be equipped with a pointing device called a **mouse**, as shown in Figure 12. As you push or pull the mouse on the surface of your desk or on a mouse pad, a **pointer** moves on the screen. Using the mouse, you can position the pointer anywhere on the screen, manipulate text or pictorial objects on the screen, and select commands.

Figure 12 A mouse

Programs such as Microsoft Windows are specifically designed to be used with a mouse. If a mouse is not included with your computer system, you can probably add one very inexpensively.

Now that you have read about input devices, refer back to the computer advertisement shown in Figure 1 at the beginning of the chapter. Can you list the input devices included with the advertised system? If you said that the system comes with at least two input devices, a mouse and a keyboard, you are right. You also might have noted that the keyboard is a standard 101-key keyboard.

Processing Hardware

The two most important components of microcomputer hardware are the **microprocessor**, a silicon chip designed to manipulate data sometimes called the **central processing unit (CPU)**, and the **memory**, which stores instructions and data. You should know what type of microprocessor is in your computer and its memory capacity. These factors directly affect the price of a computer and its performance.

THE MICROPROCESSOR The microprocessor is an **integrated circuit**—an electronic component often called a "chip"—on the main circuit board of the computer. The most popular microprocessors in IBM-compatible computers are the Intel 80486 and Pentium 80586, as shown in Figure 13. These numbers are simply model numbers designated by the manufacturer, and they are often abbreviated as 486 and Pentium. Faster chips, such as the 80686, are already in the testing stage. The higher the model number, the more powerful the microprocessor; this means that the microprocessor can handle larger chunks of data faster.

Figure 13 An Intel Pentium microprocessor, found in many IBM-compatible computers

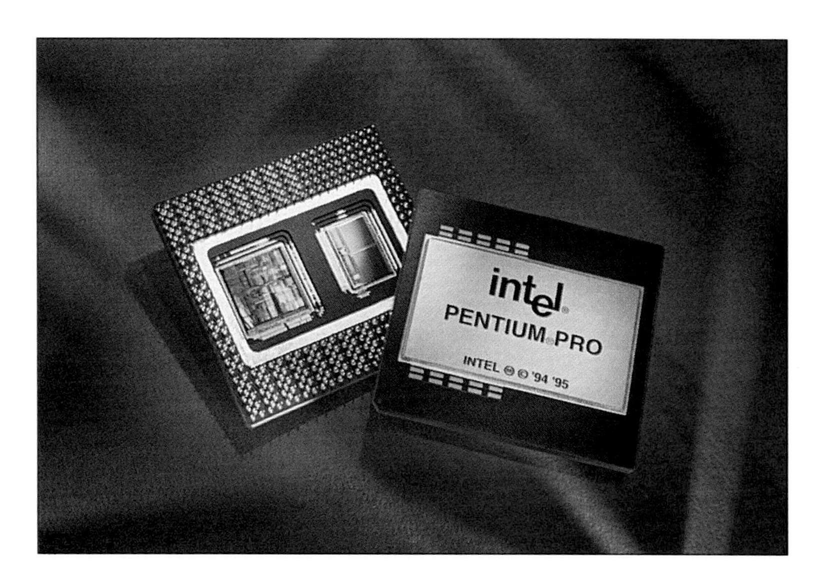

The speed of a microprocessor is determined by its **clock speed**. The computer clock is part of a group of circuits associated with the microprocessor. Think of the clock speed as the heartbeat or the pulse of the computer. The higher the clock speed, the faster the computer. Clock speed is measured in millions of cycles per second, or **megahertz (MHz)**. The Intel 8088 microprocessor on the first IBM PC models operated at only 4.77 MHz. The newer Intel Pentium microprocessor typically operates at 133 MHz.

Let's take another look at the computer advertisement in Figure 1. What is the type and speed of the microprocessor? Your answer should be that it is a Pentium microprocessor, which can operate at 133 MHz. Since the Pentium microprocessor is a recent model, you would expect it to be more costly than computers with older microprocessors such as the 80486.

DATA REPRESENTATION Within a computer, data is represented by microscopic electronic switches that can be either off or on. The off switch is designated by a 0 and the on switch by a 1. Each 1 or 0 is called a **binary digit**, or **bit** for short. Bits are very handy for representing numbers in the binary number system. A series of eight bits represents character data, such as a digit, a letter or a punctuation mark. These patterns of 1s and 0s are similar to the patterns of dots and dashes used to represent the letters of the alphabet in Morse code.

Microcomputers commonly use the **ASCII code** to represent character data. ASCII (pronounced "ask-ee") stands for American Standard Code for Information Interchange.

A string of eight bits is called a **byte**. As Figure 14 shows, the byte that represents the integer value 0 is 00000000, with all eight bits "off" or set to zero. The byte that represents the integer value 1 is 0000001, and the byte that represents 255 is 11111111.

Figure 14 Binary representation of the numbers 0 through 255

Number	Binary Representation
0	00000000
1	00000001
2	00000010
3	00000011
4	00000100
5	00000101
6	00000110
7	00000111
8	00001000
⋮	⋮
14	00001110
15	00001111
16	00010000
17	00010001
⋮	⋮
253	11111101
254	11111110
255	11111111

Each byte can also represent a character such as the letter A or the symbol $. For example, Figure 15 shows that in ASCII code the letter A is represented by the byte 01000001, the letter B by 01000010, and the letter C by 01000011. The symbol $ is represented by 00100100. The phrase "Thank you!" is represented by 10 bytes—each of the eight letters requires one byte, and the space and the exclamation point also require one byte each. To find out how many bits are needed to represent the phrase "Thank You!", multiply the number of bytes by eight, since there are eight bits in each byte.

Figure 15 ◀ ASCII code representing the letters A to Z and the symbols # $ % &

Character	ASCII
A	01000001
B	01000010
C	01000011
D	01000100
E	01000101
F	01000110
G	01000111
H	01001000
I	01001001
J	01001010
K	01001011
L	01001100
M	01001101
N	01001110
O	01001111
P	01010000
Q	01010001
R	01010010
S	01010011
T	01010100
U	01010101
V	01010110
W	01010111
X	01011000
Y	01011001
Z	01011010
#	00100011
$	00100100
%	00100101
&	00100110

As a computer user you don't have to know the binary representations of numbers, characters, and instructions, because the computer handles all the necessary conversions internally. However, because the amount of memory in a computer and the storage capacity of disks are expressed in bytes, you should be aware of how data is represented so you will understand the capacity and the limitations of your computer.

MEMORY Computer **memory** is a set of storage locations on the main circuit board. Your computer has two types of memory: read-only memory and random-access memory.

Read-only memory (ROM) is the part of memory reserved for a special set of commands that are required for the internal workings of the computer. The microprocessor can read these commands but cannot erase or change them. When you turn off your computer, the commands in ROM remain intact and ready for use when you turn the computer on again.

Random-access memory (RAM) temporarily stores data and program instructions. RAM is measured in kilobytes (K or KB) and megabytes (MB). The prefix kilo (pronounced "kee-lo") means one thousand, but for historical and technical reasons a kilobyte is actually 1024 bytes. The prefix "mega" usually means one million, but a **megabyte** is precisely 1,024 x 1,024 or 1,048,576 bytes. As shown in Figure 16, each RAM storage location can hold one character of data. Most IBM-compatible microcomputers have a minimum of 4 MB of RAM. A 4 MB computer can hold the equivalent of 4,096,000 (4,000 x 1,024) characters in RAM.

Figure 16 A conceptual model of how data (DEAR [space] MS. [space] JONES) is stored in RAM in ASCII code

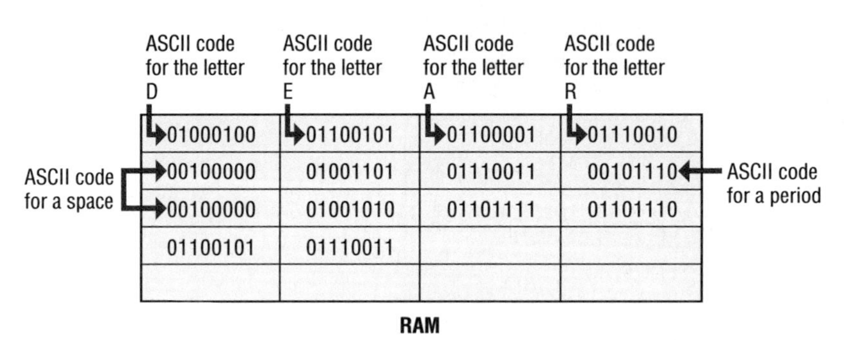

RAM is one of the most critical elements of a computer system. To use an analogy, we could say that RAM is the major traffic hub of the micro world, where data and instructions wait until it is time to travel elsewhere to be processed or stored.

Figure 17 illustrates the flow of data in and out of RAM. When you first switch on your computer, operating system instructions are loaded into an area of RAM, where they remain until you turn the computer off (1). The **operating system** controls many essential internal activities of the computer system. When you want to use an application program, such as a word processor, all or part of the application program is loaded into RAM (2). When you input data from a device such as the keyboard, the data is temporarily stored in RAM (3).

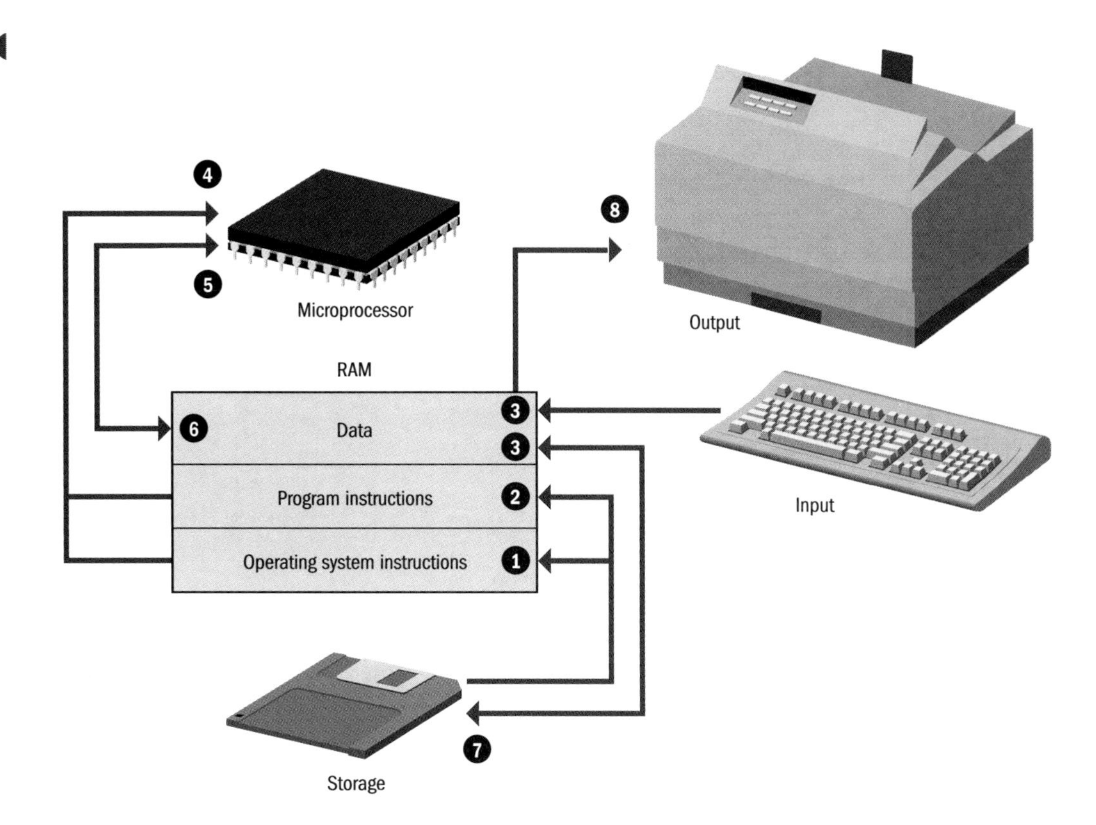

Figure 17 RAM is a temporary storage area for data, programs, and the operating system

Operating system instructions and program instructions are sent from RAM to the microprocessor for processing (4). Any data needed for the processing indicated by these instructions is fetched from RAM (5). After the data has been processed, the results are sent back into RAM (6). If you want a permanent record of the results, the data is stored (7) or output (8). When you have finished using an application, RAM is freed up for the next program you want to use. When you turn your computer off, all the data in RAM disappears.

Modern **graphical user interface (GUI)** programs that communicate through the use of graphics (boxes, menus and windows) instead of just text require large amounts of RAM. The amount of RAM required for an application program usually is specified on the package or in the program documentation. Computers configured with more RAM typically cost more than those with smaller amounts of RAM. It may be possible to expand the amount of RAM in a computer up to a specified limit.

Take another look at the computer advertisement shown in Figure 1 at the beginning of the chapter. How much RAM is included with the computer? What is the maximum amount of RAM that can be installed? You are correct if you said that 16 MB of RAM are included and that the RAM can be expanded to a maximum of 64 MB.

Output Devices

Output is the result of processing data; **output devices** show you those results. The most commonly used output devices are monitors and printers.

A **monitor** is the TV-like video screen that displays the output from a computer, as shown in Figure 18. Most desktop computer monitors use **cathode ray tube (CRT) technology**, whereas notebook computers use a flat-panel display technology such as a **liquid crystal display (LCD)**.

Figure 18 ◀ A color monitor

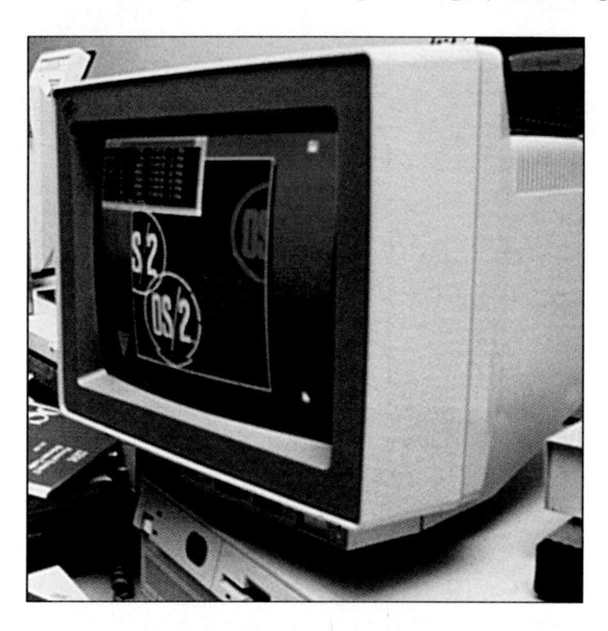

Figure 19 shows how text and graphics displayed on computer monitors are created with little dots of light called **pixels**, short for "picture elements." The entire monitor screen is a grid of pixels that combine to create the illusion of a continuous image. A basic **video graphics array (VGA)** monitor has a 640 x 480 grid, and a **super VGA** monitor has a maximum grid size of 800 x 600 or 1,024 x 768. As the number of pixels in the grid increases, the resolution of the monitor increases. Monitors with higher resolution have displays that are clearer, sharper, and easier to read.

Figure 19 ◀ Pixels combining to form the word "output"

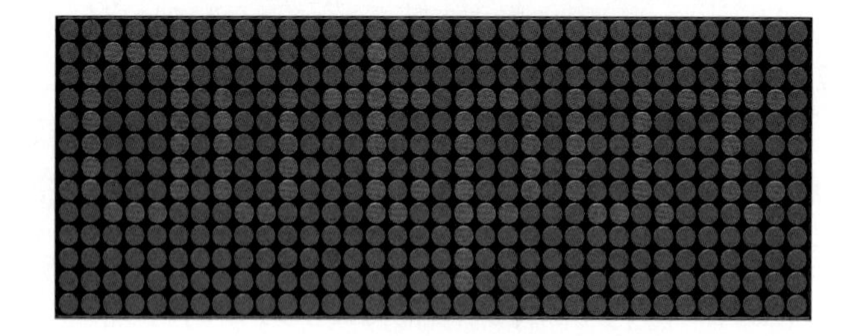

A **display card**—also called a **display adapter**, **video controller**, or **graphics adapter**–connects the monitor to the main circuit board of the computer. The display card must match the monitor through **software drivers**. For example, suppose you have purchased a super VGA monitor to add to your current computer system. You need to check the specification sheet that accompanied your old display card to see if it is accompanied by a software driver that will perform successfully with the new monitor. If the specification sheet indicates that the original display card is not compatible with your new monitor, you might need to update your software driver and/or hardware. Sometimes you can use the telecommunications capability of your computer to download a software driver from the vendor's computerized bulletin board connected to a dial-up telephone line.

A **printer** produces a paper copy of the text or graphics processed by the computer. A paper or acetate transparency copy of computer output is called **hard copy**, because it is more tangible than the electronic or magnetic copies found on a disk, in the computer memory, or on the monitor.

The three most popular types of printers are dot-matrix, ink-jet, and laser printers. **Dot-matrix printers**, like the one shown in Figure 20, form text and graphic images by producing tiny dots of ink on the printer paper. The dots are formed when pins strike an inked ribbon. Less expensive dot-matrix printers have nine pins. More expensive models have 24 pins and produce higher-quality output. Figure 21 shows text that was output in two different modes: draft mode and near-letter-quality mode. **Draft mode** prints very quickly but produces relatively low-quality print, while **near-letter-quality (NLQ) mode** prints more slowly but produces higher-quality print. The speed of a dot-matrix printer usually is measured in characters per second (cps).

Figure 20 A dot-matrix printer

Figure 21 Sample output from a dot-matrix printer

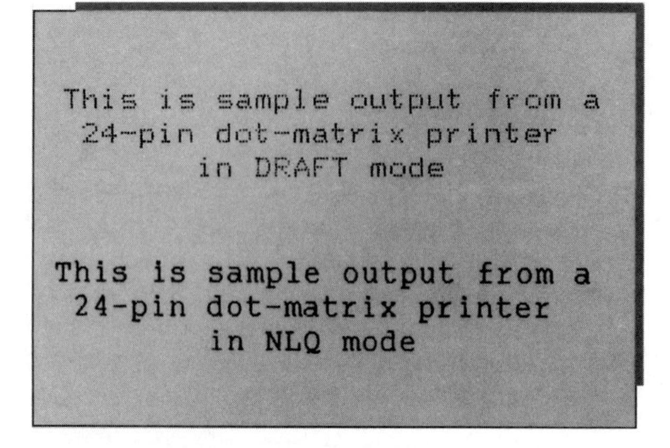

Ink-jet printers, like the one in Figure 22, spray tiny dots of ink onto the paper to form text and graphics. Ink-jet printers are quieter than dot-matrix printers and produce graphics of reasonable quality and text of high quality. The speed of an ink-jet printer is comparable to that of a dot-matrix printer.

Figure 22 An ink-jet printer

Laser printers, such as the model in Figure 23, use laser beams to bond a powder substance, called **toner**, to the paper. The technology is similar to that used in copy machines. The speed of a laser printer is usually indicated in pages per minute (ppm). Laser printers are quiet and fast and produce the highest-quality printing of any type of printer. Laser printers are available that can print in full color or in black and white. For all these reasons laser printers are becoming the standard type of printer in the business world.

Figure 23
A laser printer

Return to the beginning of the chapter and list the output device(s) included with the computer system in the computer advertisement. If you listed a monitor and a laser printer that prints 8 pages per minute, you are correct.

Storage Devices and Media

Because RAM retains data only while the power is on, your computer must have a more permanent storage option. As Figure 24 shows, a **storage device** receives data from RAM and writes it on a storage medium, such as a disk. Later the data can be read and sent back to RAM. So a storage device is used not only to store data but also for data input and output.

Figure 24
A storage device receives information from RAM, writes it on the storage medium, and reads and sends it back to RAM

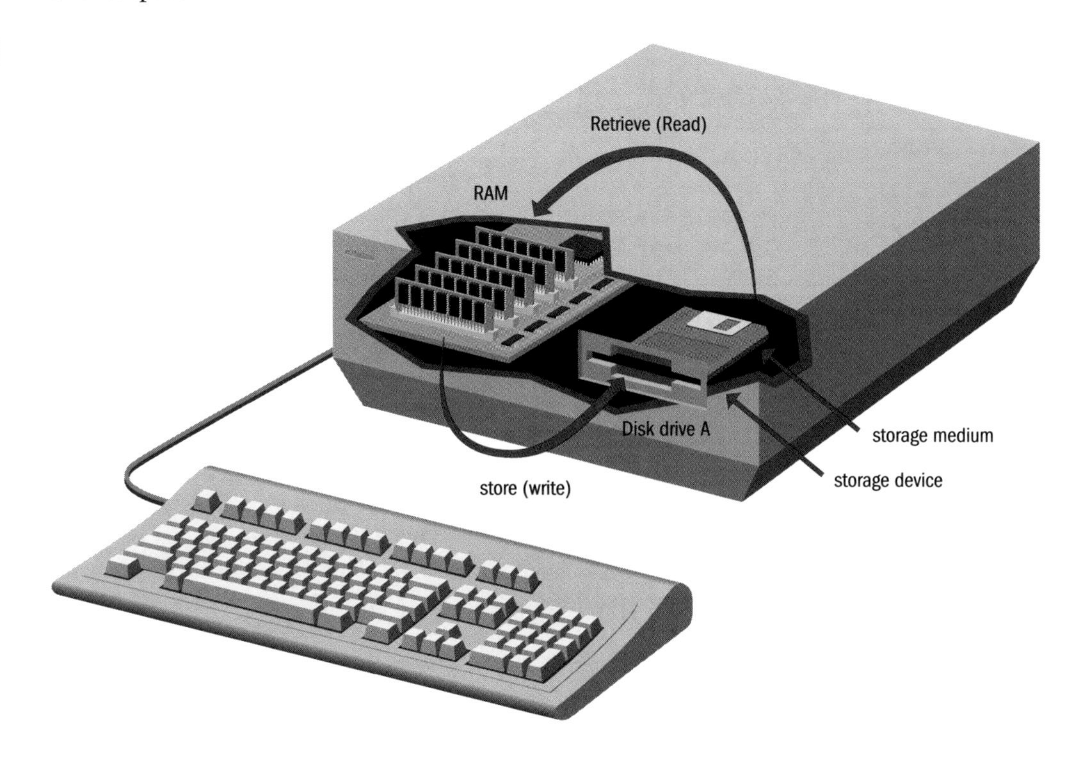

There are a variety of microcomputer storage devices, each using a particular storage medium, as shown in Figure 25. Hard-disk drives store data on hard disks, and floppy-disk drives store data on floppy disks; tape drives store data on tape cartridges or cassettes; and CD-ROM drives store data on compact discs.

Figure 25 Storage devices and their associated media

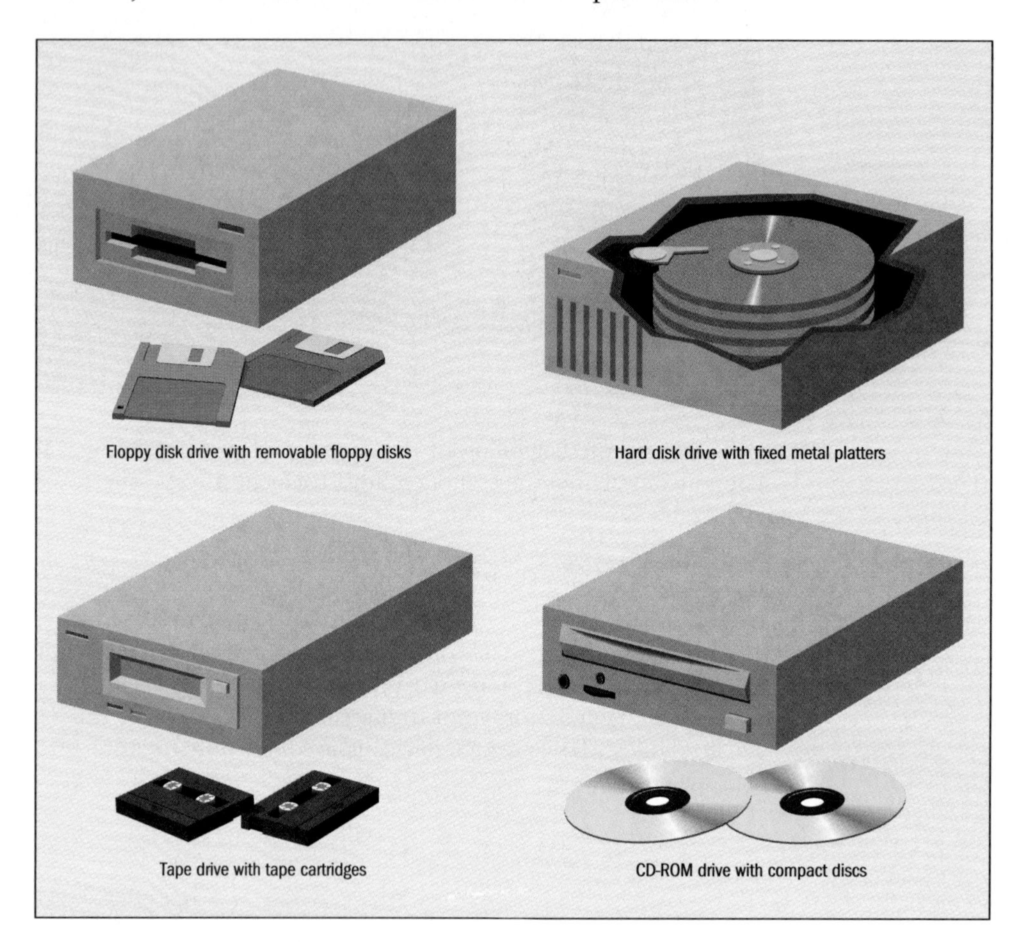

Floppy disks, sometimes called diskettes, are flat circles of iron oxide-coated plastic enclosed in a square case called a **disk case**. The most common size of disks for microcomputers is 3½" (shown in Figure 26) which has a storage capacity of 1.44 MB. They are usually double-sided, high-density disks that have a movable metal plate that protects the surface of the disk when it's not in use.

Figure 26 3½" disk

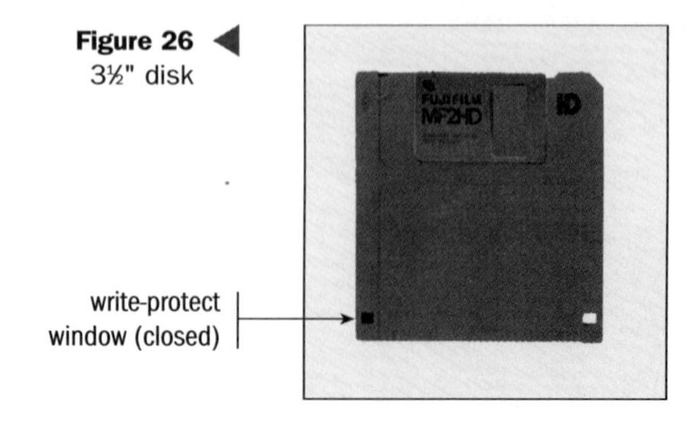

You can write-protect a disk to prevent any changes to the data on it. **Write protection** prevents additional data from being stored on the disk, and any data from being erased from the disk. To write protect a 3½" disk, you would open the write-protect window, as shown in Figure 27.

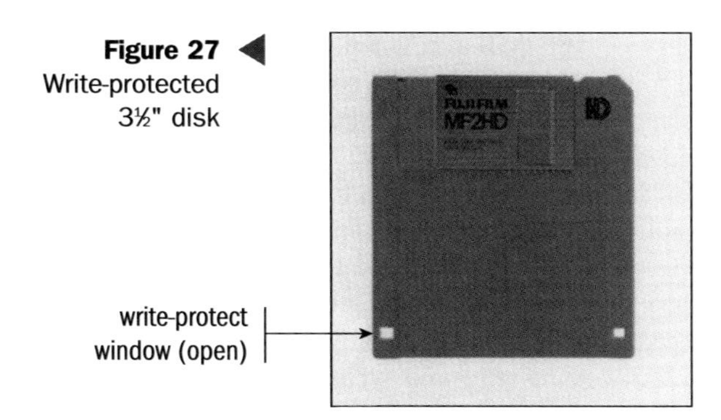

Figure 27 ◀ Write-protected 3½" disk

Hard disks, also called **fixed disks**, are iron oxide-covered metal platters that are usually sealed inside a hard disk drive, as shown in Figure 28. Hard-disk storage has two advantages over floppy disks: speed and capacity.

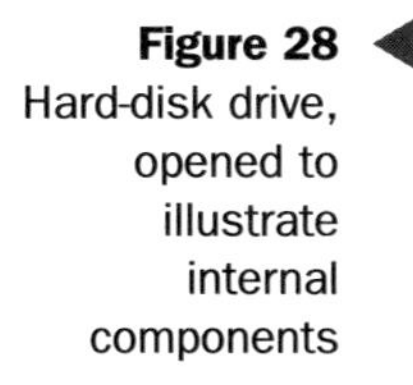

Figure 28 ◀ Hard-disk drive, opened to illustrate internal components

The speed of a disk drive is measured by its **access time**, the time required to read or write one record of data. Access time is measured in milliseconds (ms), one-thousandth of a second. A hard disk drive typically has an access time in the range of 8 to 20 ms, the 8-ms access time being the fastest. Floppy disk drives have much slower access times.

The capacity of microcomputer hard disks is between 100 and 1,000 MB, or 1 GB (gigabyte). A hard disk with a capacity of 100 MB can store the equivalent of about 144,000 pages of single-spaced text, compared to only 440 pages on a 1.44 MB 3½" floppy disk. Large hard-disk storage capacity is becoming increasingly important for the new graphics-based computing environments. For example, to install the complete Microsoft Windows 3.11 program, you must have a minimum of 20 MB or more of free disk space. Microsoft Windows 95 requires 40 to 80 MB or more depending on the complexity of the installation. Each additional application you add to the Windows environment adds to the space required because of additional system files. The WordPerfect for Windows word processing program needs a minimum of 35 MB of disk space.

Optical storage devices use laser technology to read and write data on compact discs (CDs) or laser discs. The advantages of optical storage include reliability and capacity. Unlike data stored on magnetic media, such as floppy disks and hard disks, data stored on optical discs is less susceptible to environmental problems such as dirt, dust, and magnetic fields. Typical storage capacities for optical drives begin at 128 MB and can exceed 1 GB. CD-ROM drives are the most common type of optical storage for microcomputers. Most popular CD-ROM drives operate in a read-only mode, meaning that your computer can read information from it, but cannot change anything on it.

Tape drives provide inexpensive archival storage for large quantities of data. Tape storage is much too slow to be used for day-to-day computer tasks; therefore, tapes are used to make backup copies of data stored on hard disks. If a hard disk fails, data from the backup tape can be reloaded on a new hard disk with minimal interruption of operations.

You generally will have a number of storage devices on your computer, each labeled with a letter. Your floppy disk drive usually will be drive A, and your hard-disk drive usually will be drive C. Figure 29 shows some common configurations of storage devices.

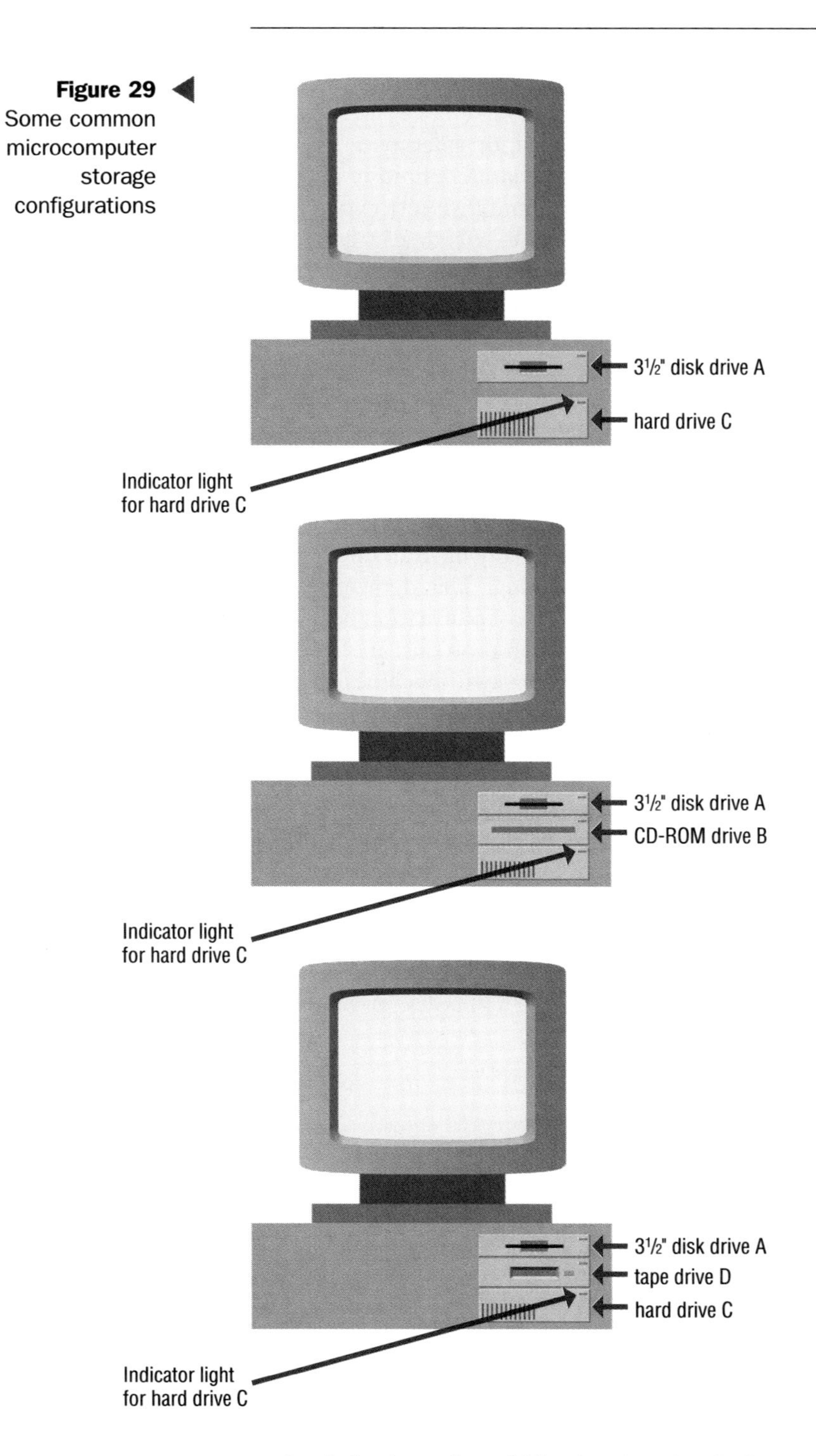

Figure 29 Some common microcomputer storage configurations

Look back at the ad Tenzing is using in her research; how many storage devices are included? How would you describe the type and capacity of each? Your answer should be that the computer comes with three drives: a hard disk drive with 1 GB capacity, a 3½" disk drive with 1.44 MB capacity, and a CD-ROM drive.

Data Communications

The transmission of text, numeric, voice, or video data from one machine to another is called **data communications**. This broad-based definition encompasses many critical business activities, such as sending a fax or sending electronic mail messages and accessing the information super-highway—the **Internet**—which is a collection of local, regional, and national computer networks that are linked together to exchange data. Data communications also refers to the process of sending data between two computers.

The four essential components of data communications are a sender, a receiver, a channel, and a protocol. The machine that originates the message is the **sender**. The message is sent over some type of **channel**, such as a twisted-pair phone cable, a coaxial cable, a microwave channel, or an optical fiber. The machine that is designated as the destination for the message is called the **receiver**.

The rules that establish an orderly transfer of data between the sender and the receiver are called **protocols**. For example, when you are talking on the phone, you and the person with whom you are communicating generally have an implied agreement that while one of you is speaking, the other one is listening. This agreement could be called a protocol, because it assists in the orderly exchange of information between you and the person at the other end of the line. Data communication protocols are handled by hardware devices and by software. Usually this means that for two machines to communicate, each machine requires a communication device and appropriate communication software.

The World Wide Web has added a new dimension to data communications. The **World Wide Web** consists of **home pages**, like the one shown in Figure 30, which are graphical representations of data and electronic links to information contained at different locations on the Internet. The graphic images used in the World Wide Web require a higher rate of data transfer than traditional text displays. Tenzing notes that she will need to ask Ms. Thompson if employees will need modems with sufficient speed, or any other other hardware, to allow employees to efficiently access the World Wide Web.

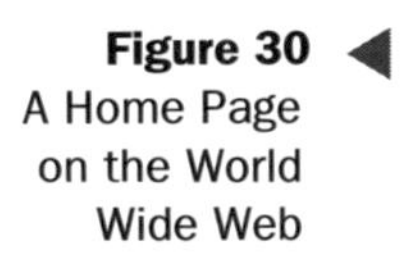

Figure 30 ◀
A Home Page on the World Wide Web

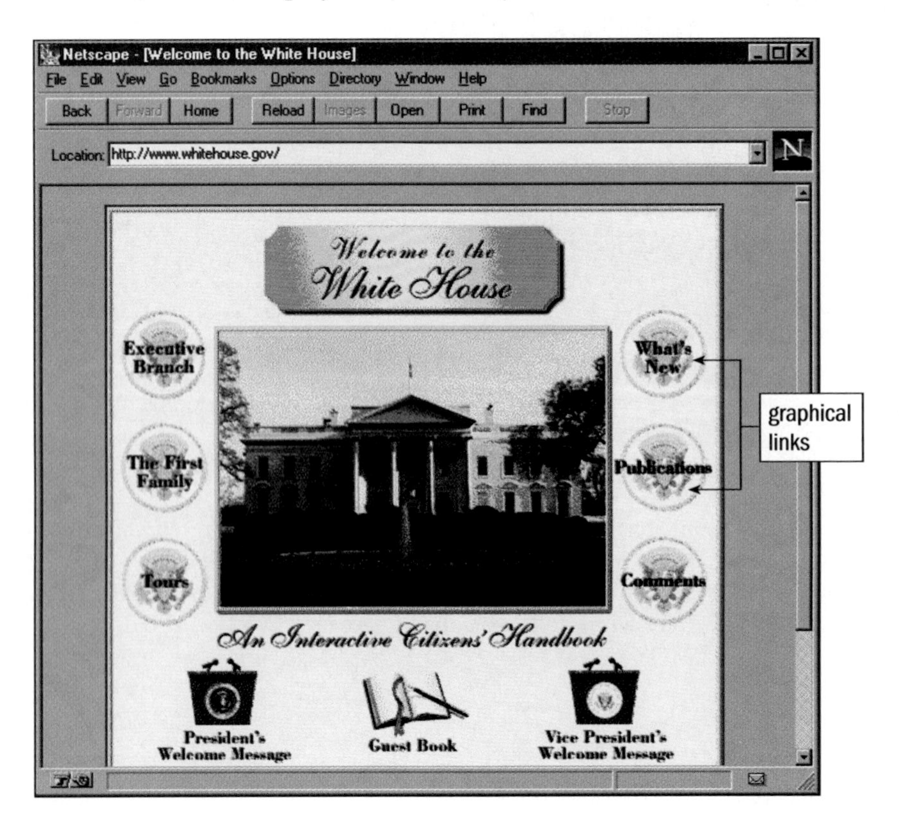

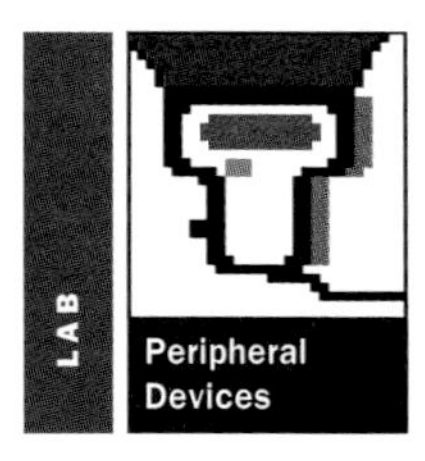

Peripheral Interfaces

Input and output devices sometimes are referred to as **peripherals**. Communication between your computer and its peripherals is essential. Without it you would not be able to print or to use your mouse. This communication between the computer and its peripheral devices is sometimes referred to as **interfacing**. If you are going to set up a computer, move it, or add peripheral devices, you should have some understanding of interfacing.

Figure 31 shows the components of a device interface. A cable connects the peripheral, in this case, a printer, to the computer. The cable plugs into a connector called a **port**, usually located in the back of the system unit. The port is connected to circuitry that controls the transmission of data to the device. This circuitry either is part of the main computer circuit board or is on a **controller card**. Controller cards are also referred to as **interface cards** or **expansion cards**. These cards, which provide an electrical connection to a variety of peripheral devices, plug into electrical connectors on the main board called slots or **expansion slots**. The transmission protocol is handled by a **device driver**, a computer program that can establish communication because it contains information about the characteristics of your computer and of the device.

Figure 32 The components necessary to connect a printer to a computer

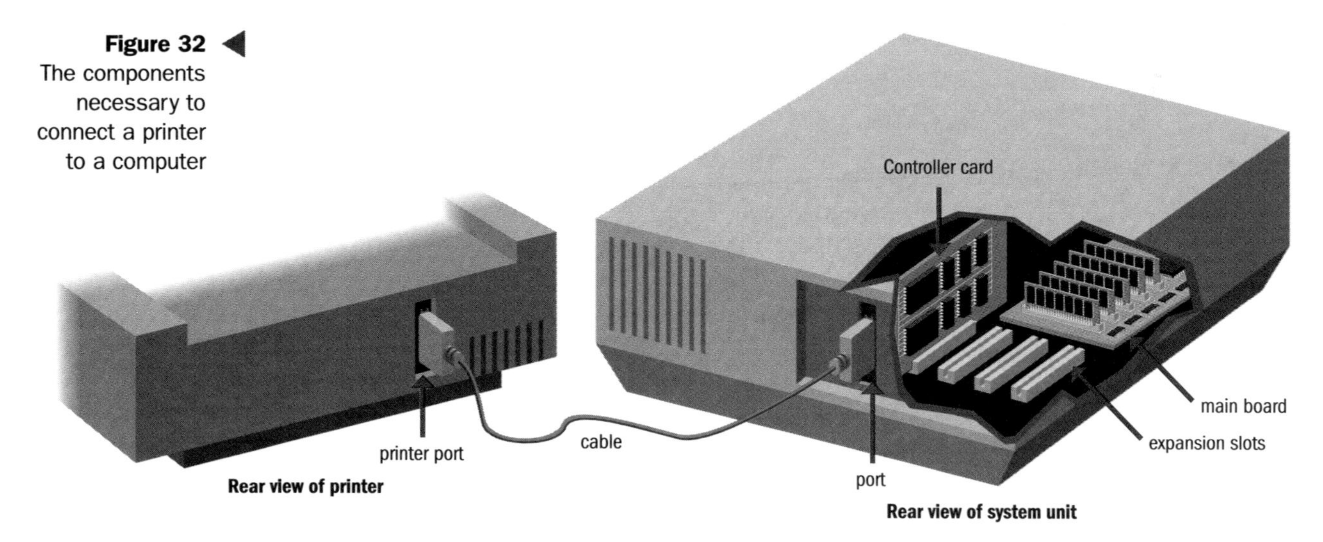

Microcomputers can have several types of ports, including keyboard, video, serial, parallel, MIDI, and SCSI , as shown in Figure 32. A **serial port** sends one bit of data at a time. Typically a mouse, a laser printer, a modem, a digital camera, and speech hardware require a serial port. Serial ports are designated COM1, COM2, COM3, and COM4.

Figure 32 Ports in the back of the system unit

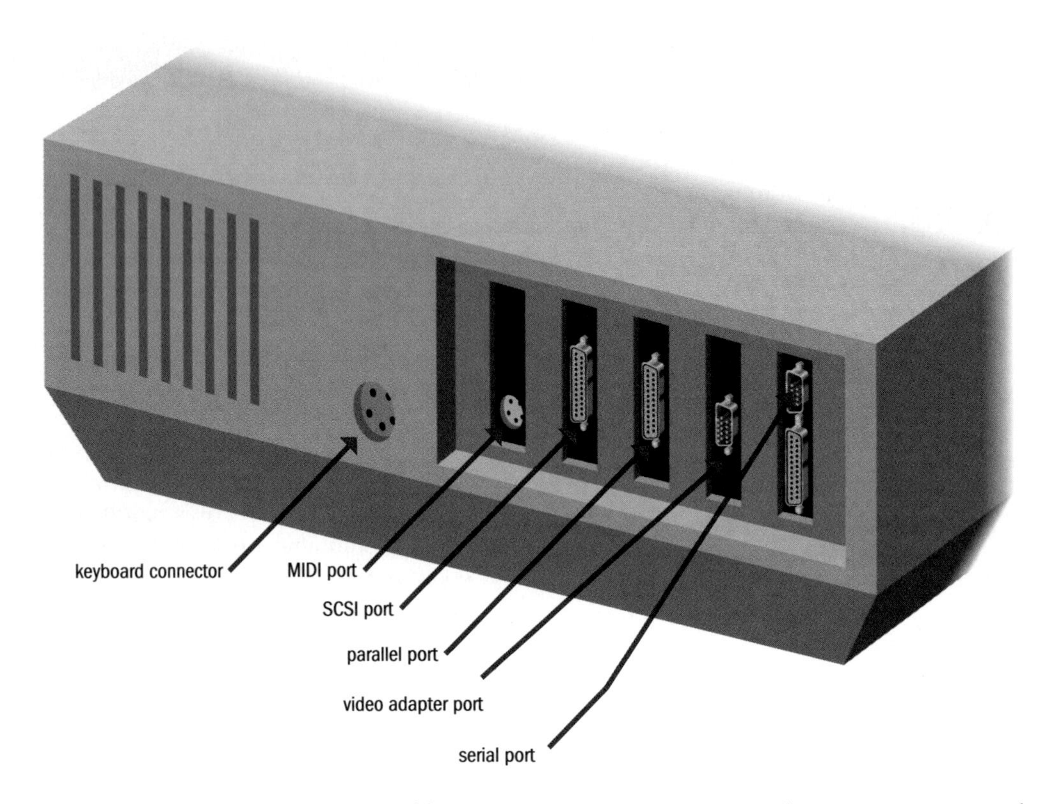

A **parallel port** sends a group of bits at a time. Most printers and scanners use a parallel port. Parallel ports are designated LPT1 and LPT2.

A **SCSI port** is a variation of the parallel port. SCSI (pronounced "scuzzy") stands for small computer system interface. First popularized for Apple Macintosh computers, SCSI has also become established in the IBM-compatible market. Some tape devices, hard-disk drives, and CD-ROM drives use a SCSI port. One of the advantages of the SCSI port is that it has the potential to provide a connection for more than one peripheral device at a time, unlike a standard parallel or serial port, which provides a connection for only one device at a time.

MIDI ports were originally used in the music industry to send data efficiently between devices that create and play electronic music. MIDI (pronounced "middy") stands for musical instrument digital interface. Today, MIDI ports are used to connect computers to electronic instruments and recording devices.

This discussion of ports and interfacing may seem a bit technical, but it pertains to an important aspect of computing—expandability. New innovations in computing appear every day, and you probably will want to use some of the new technology without having to purchase a new computer system. Expansion slots make this possible. All other factors being equal, computers with many expansion slots are a better investment than those with only a few.

Now refer back to the ad at the beginning of this chapter. What types of ports are included with the computer system described in the ad? Is this computer system expandable? How? Your answer is correct if you said that there are two serial ports and one parallel port. The system also appears to have an adequate number of expansion slots. The ad says there are eight, but it does not indicate if all of them are available. It may be that some of the slots already are filled with expansion cards for devices such as the modem, the disk-drive controller, and the video controller. Tenzing should find out how many of the expansion slots are empty.

Network Communication

In the business world you usually don't work alone but rather as part of a team. As a team member you'll probably use a computer which is part of a network. A **network** connects your computer to the computers of other team members, enabling you to share data and peripheral devices, such as printers, modems, and fax machines.

There are a variety of networks, too many to discuss thoroughly here. We will focus our discussion on some of the basic concepts pertaining to a local-area network, one of the network types commonly found in businesses.

In a **local-area network (LAN)**, computers and peripheral devices are located relatively close to each other, generally in the same building. If you are using such a network, it is useful to know three things: the location of the data, the type of network card in your computer, and the software that manages the communications protocols and other network functions.

Some networks have one or more **file servers**, as shown in Figure 33; these are computers that act as the central repositories for application programs and that provide mass storage for most of the data used on the network. A network with a file server is called a **client/server** network. This type of network is partially dependent on the file server because it contains most of the data and software. Most systems include multiple file servers for redundancy and therefore are not totally dependent on one file server. Some networking software allows a user logged in to one server to use other servers automatically. When a network does not have a file server, all the computers essentially are equal, and the task of storing files and programs is distributed among them. This is called a **peer-to-peer network.**

Figure 33 A file server is the central repository for data and applications programs

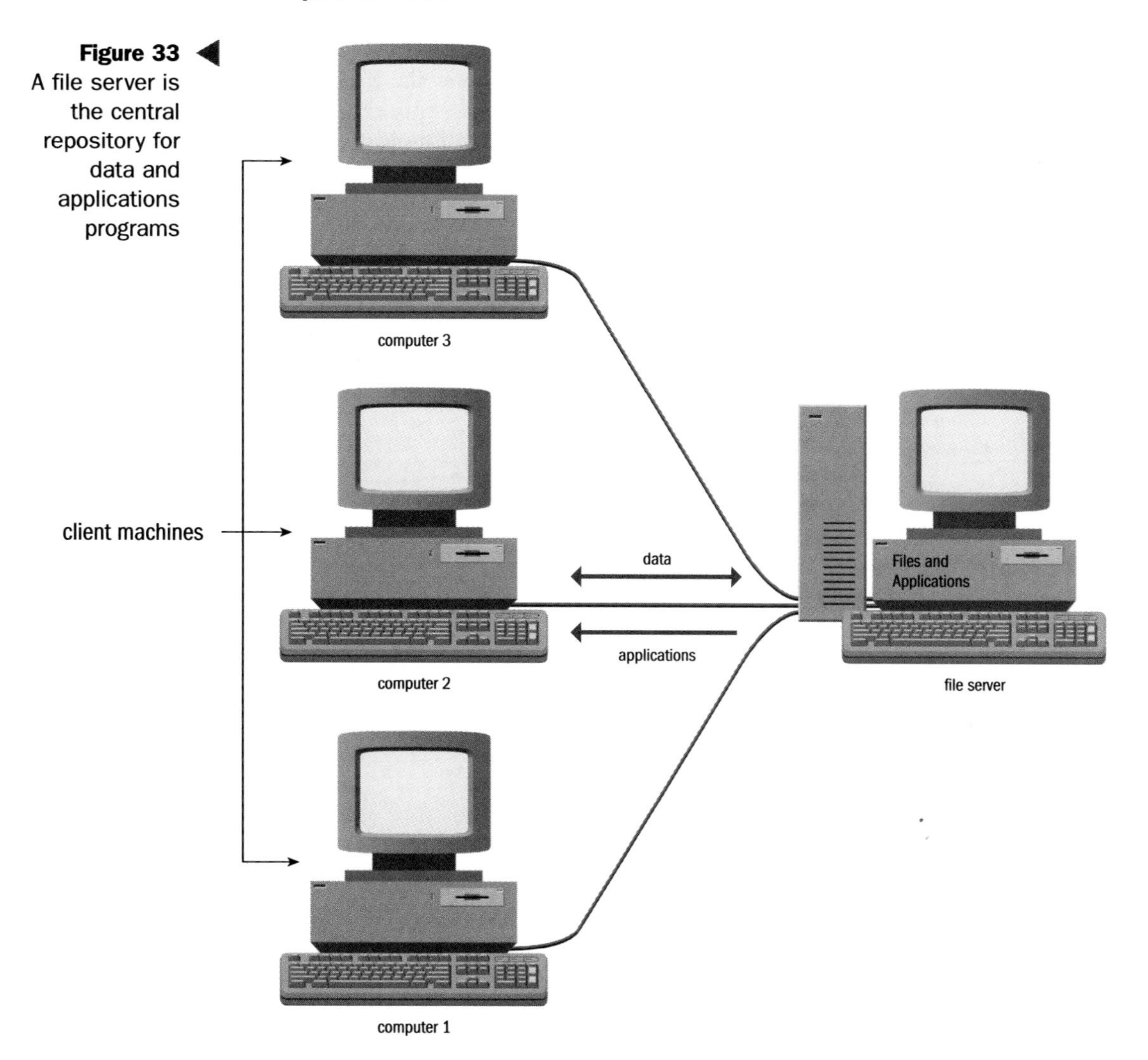

The type of network card you have in your computer must be compatible with the topology of the network. The **topology** is a description of the electronic layout and media used internally in the network and affects many aspects of the network including the transmission speed of your data. The network card is plugged into one of the expansion slots in your computer. The most common network topologies are Ethernet, Token-Ring, and FDDI (fiber optic topology).

Network software establishes the communications protocol for the network. Your network software resides on a disk in drive A or on your hard-disk drive. Additional network software might be stored on the file server. The most common microcomputer networking software packages include Microsoft NT, Novell NetWare, IBM LAN Server, Banyan Vines, and Microsoft Windows for Workgroups. Why is it important to know the type of network software you are using? Some software is designed to be used on specific types of networks. If you have a network, before you purchase software, read the packaging or documentation to determine whether the software is designed to work with your network. In addition, some hardware is tested specifically for compatibility with particular networks. The term "NetWare compatible," for example, indicates that the hardware should work on a Novell NetWare network.

Turn once again to the computer ad at the beginning of the chapter and think about these questions: Is this computer networked? Can it be networked? Why or why not? Your answer should be that the computer is not currently part of a network and is not shipped with a network card. However, it should be possible to connect this computer to a Novell, Microsoft, or IBM network with the appropriate network card and software, which would have to be purchased separately.

Telecommunications

Telecommunications means communicating over a comparatively long distance. Telecommunications enables you to send data over the phone lines to another computer and to access data stored on computers located in another city, state, or country.

The telecommunications process requires a communications device called a *mo*dulator-*dem*odulator, or **modem**, which connects your computer to a standard phone jack. The modem converts the **digital**, or stop-start, signals your computer uses into **analog**, or continuous wave, signals, which can traverse ordinary phone lines. An external modem connects to the serial port in the back of the computer, while an internal modem plugs into one of the expansion slots on the computer's main board. Figure 34 shows the telecommunications process, in which a modem converts digital signals to analog signals at the transmitting site and a second modem converts the analog signals back to digital signals at the receiving site.

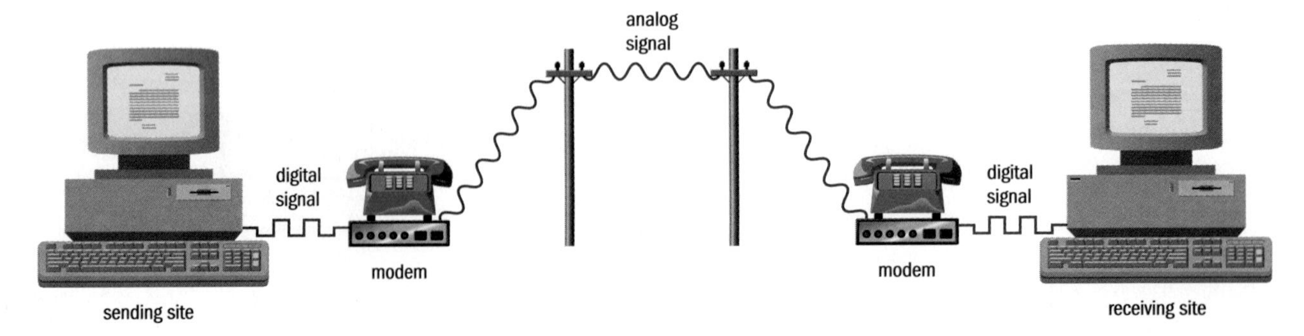

Figure 34 Using modems to send and receive a memo

To use a modem for telecommunications, you also must have **communications software** to handle the transmission protocols. When you initiate a telecommunications call, you are required to provide specifications about your modem and the destination computer. To do this, you need to know the **baud rate** (speed) of your modem and the port it uses (COM1, COM2, COM3, or COM4). Speed is measured in units called a baud, most of the time (but not always) equivalent to one bit per second (bps). A thousand bits per second would be a kilobit per second (KBPS). You also need to know how the destination computer's modem is expecting to receive data: the number of data bits, the number of start/stop bits, and the type of parity, a way of confirming that the data was not damaged in transit. To obtain this information, you often need to call the technical support group for the destination computer.

Look again at the computer advertisement shown in Figure 1 at the beginning of the chapter. What do the specifications tell you about its telecommunications capabilities? Your answer should be that the computer system comes with a 28.8 KBPS modem, which should be more than adequate if International ComAir employees want to access the World Wide Web. Communications software is not mentioned; however, Microsoft Windows contains a telecommunications package called Terminal or HyperTerminal.

Computer Software

Just as a tape recorder or a compact-disc player is worthless without tapes or compact discs, computer hardware is useless without computer software. The types of software you use determine what you can do with your computer. For example, word processing software enables you use a computer to prepare documents; graphics software lets you use a computer to create graphs and illustrations. Software can be divided into two general types: systems software and applications software.

Systems Software

Systems software includes the programs that run the fundamental operations in your computer, such as loading programs and data into memory, executing programs, saving data on a disk, displaying information on the screen, and sending information through a port to a peripheral.

A special type of systems software is the **operating system**, which works like an air-traffic controller to coordinate the flow of activities within the computer. The most popular operating system for IBM-compatible microcomputers is usually referred to as the disk operating system, or DOS (rhymes with "boss"). DOS has been sold under the trade names PC-DOS and MS-DOS. Both systems were developed primarily by Microsoft Corporation, so they are essentially the same.

DOS has gone through several revisions since its introduction in 1981. The original version, numbered 1.0, has been followed by versions 2.0, 3.0, 3.1, 3.2, 3.3, 4.0, 4.1, 5.0, 6.0, and 6.2, 6.22. Early versions of DOS lack some of the capabilities of later versions. Consequently, some newer software will not run on computers that use older versions of DOS. You can upgrade the version of DOS on your computer if the computer meets certain memory, processor, and storage requirements.

As an operating system, DOS has several drawbacks. It was originally designed for computers with limited amounts of memory and small storage capacities that performed only one task at a time and serviced only one user. Another drawback of DOS is the complexity of commands you must use to specify tasks. To use most versions of DOS, you must memorize a list of command words and understand the punctuation and spacing rules for constructing valid command "sentences." DOS users often complain that the DOS **user interface**, or the way they communicate with the software, is difficult for them because they forget the command words and because typing mistakes or punctuation errors in commands sometimes produces unexpected results.

In response to user complaints, several companies have designed easy-to-use **operating environments**—software that provides a sort of protective layer between the user and DOS. The goal of operating an environment such as Microsoft's Windows is to provide an easier way for users to issue DOS commands. Once the operating environment is installed, you basically can forget that you're using DOS. More recent operating environments have a "friendlier" user interface because their screen appearance helps direct users in their interactions with the computer.

Microsoft has expanded on the concept of operating environments. With Windows versions 2.0, 2.11, 3.0, 3.1, 3.11, and Windows 95 it has tried to make an environment that simplifies the use of any program and provides users with some of the features they need for the newer, more powerful computers.

The first versions of Microsoft Windows were operating environments that supplemented the DOS operating system. More recent versions of Windows, Windows NT and Windows 95, are complete operating systems that do not require DOS. However, these operating systems do allow you to use software written for DOS as well as software written for Windows.

As an alternative to DOS and Windows, IBM has developed an operating system called **OS/2**, which is specifically designed for the large amounts of RAM and very large disk capacities of today's more powerful microcomputer systems. To take advantage of the capabilities of OS/2, you must use applications software specifically written to operate in this environment. Because OS/2 is a relative newcomer to the market, the selection of OS/2 applications software is somewhat limited. You can use many of the programs designed for DOS and Windows, but they will function in essentially the same way as on a computer that uses DOS for the operating system.

Another type of system software, which relates to the security of data stored in computers, is **virus protection software**. Unfortunately, there are unscrupulous programmers who deliberately construct **viruses** or **Trojan horses**, programs designed to destroy stored software. Several companies, including McAfee and Symantec, produce virus protection software programs designed to detect viruses and cleanse a disk containing a data-destroying virus.

Applications Software

A wide variety of software exists to help you accomplish many different tasks using your computer. This type of software is called **applications software** because it enables you to apply your computer to accomplish specific goals. Five major types of applications software are word processing, spreadsheet, database management, graphics and presentation, and personal information management.

Word processing software enables you to electronically create, edit, format, and print documents. The advantages of a word processor over a typewriter are numerous. With a word processor you can move paragraphs, check spelling, create tables and columns, modify margins, correct typos, import graphics and database information, and view how a document will appear before you print it. A wide selection of word processing software is available for the Windows environment, including Microsoft Word for Windows, WordPerfect for Windows, and Lotus Development Corporation's Word Pro. An example of a screen from a word processing program is shown in Figure 35.

Figure 35 A Microsoft Word for Windows 95 screen

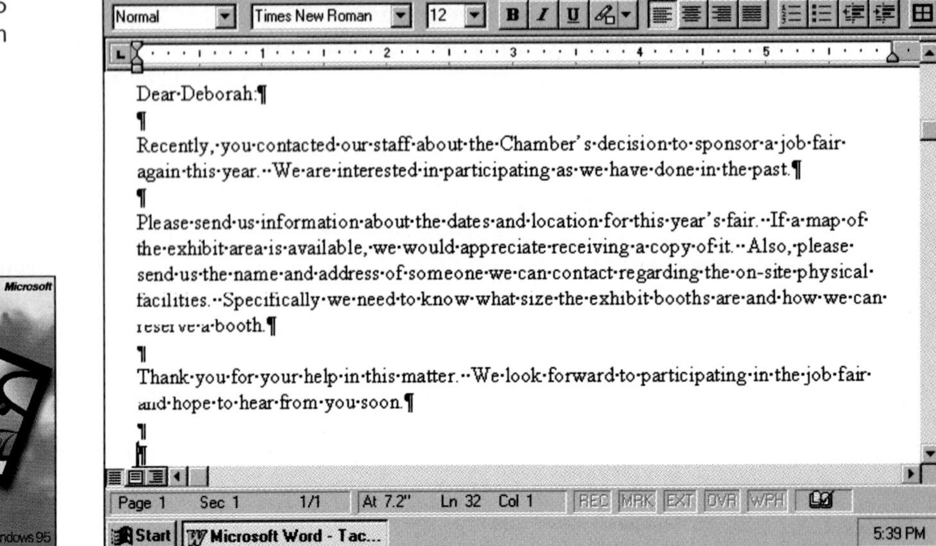

An **electronic spreadsheet** enables you to perform calculations with numbers arranged in a grid of rows and columns on the computer screen. You type numbers into the grid, then create formulas that perform calculations using those numbers. In many ways a spreadsheet is the ultimate calculator. Once your numbers are on the screen, you don't have to reenter them when you want to redo a calculation with revised or corrected numbers. As an additional benefit, spreadsheet software provides you with excellent printouts of the raw data or of graphs created from the data.

With the appropriate data and formulas, you can use an electronic spreadsheet to prepare financial reports, analyze investment portfolios, calculate amortization tables, examine alternative bid proposals, and project income, as well as perform many other tasks involved in making informed business decisions. Three of the top-selling spreadsheets for Windows are Microsoft Excel, Quattro Pro for Windows, and Lotus Development's Lotus 1-2-3 for Windows. An example of a spreadsheet screen is shown in Figure 36.

Figure 36 ◀ A Microsoft Excel for Windows 95 screen

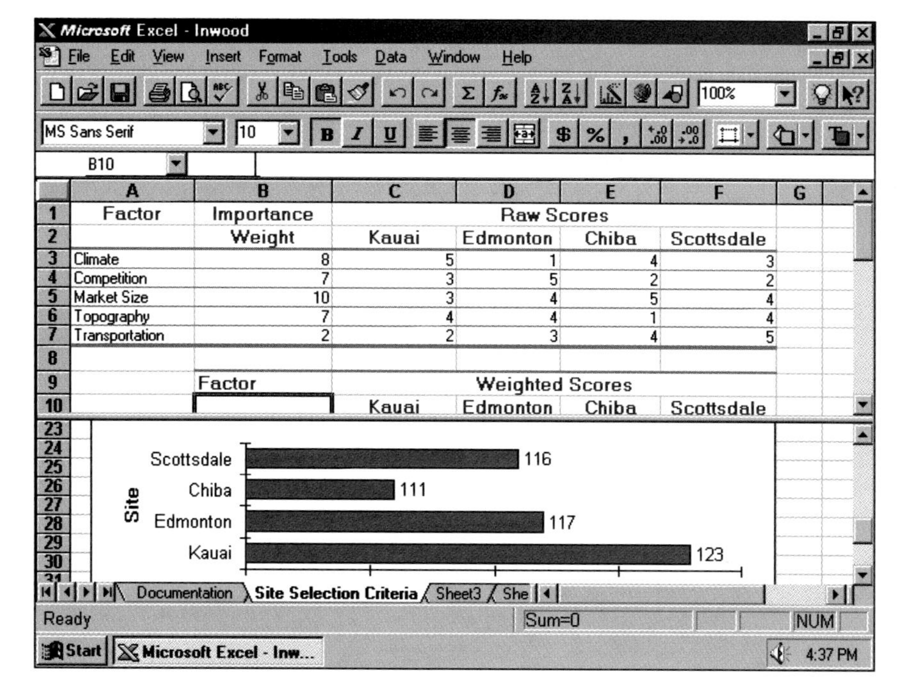

Database software helps you manage and manipulate information you previously might have stored in file cabinets or on rolodex cards or index cards. Information about employees, clients, schedules, supplies, and inventory can be managed effectively with a database. Database software lets you easily search, sort, select, delete, and update your file of information. Versatile reporting capabilities also are offered. Microsoft Access, Lotus Approach, and Borland Paradox for Windows are examples of database management software available for the Windows environment. An example of a database screen is shown in Figure 37.

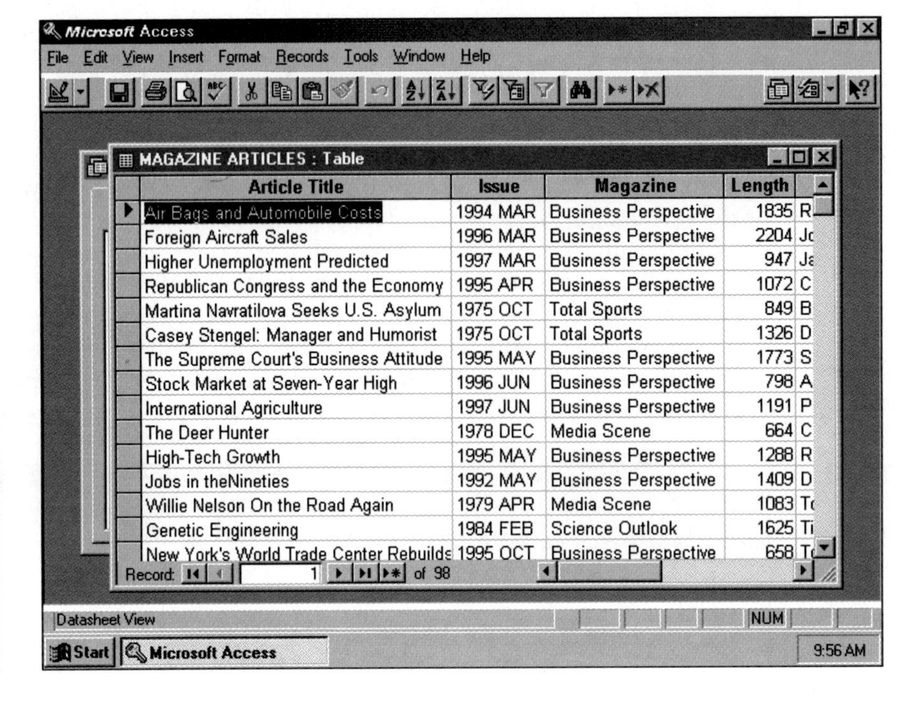

Figure 37 ◀ An Access for Windows 95 screen

Graphics and presentation software makes it possible for you to create presentations with illustrations, diagrams, graphs, and charts. Some products assist you in creating a presentation that can be delivered directly from your laptop computer complete with color visuals and hard-copy handout material. Many graphics programs also provide collections of predrawn pictures, known as clipart, that you can use as is or incorporate in other drawings. Adobe Acrobat and Aldus Freehand are popular graphics programs, and Microsoft's PowerPoint and Lotus Freelance Graphics are popular Windows presentations graphics programs. A screen from a popular presentation graphics program is shown in Figure 38.

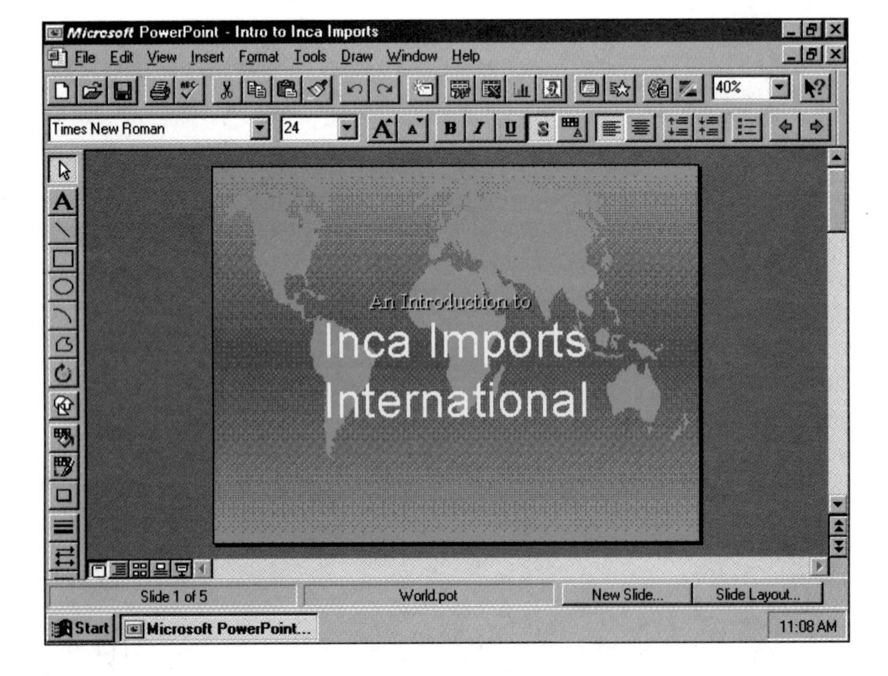

Figure 38 ◀ A PowerPoint for Windows 95 screen

Personal information management systems or **contact management systems** help some individuals to perform their tasks more efficiently, whether for business or personal use. Some common features are an appointment scheduler database, name and address database, a planning calendar, prioritized to-do list generators, and a notepad filing system. Telecommunications modules assist travelers in dialing calls from hotel rooms and provide documentation as to content and length of the telephone call. The most popular packages are Lotus Organizer, Microsoft Schedule+ and Starfish Software's SideKick.

What types of software are included with the computer described in the ad that Tenzing found? What operating system is provided? Is there an operating environment? Is there any applications software? You are correct if you said the only software included with the system is the Windows 95 operating system. No applications software is included.

Now that you have completed this chapter on essential computer concepts, you should have a basic understanding of the hardware and software components of a computer system. You should also be able to understand the terminology in a computer ad, such as the one at the beginning of the chapter. You have seen that the computer system in the ad Tenzing found includes all the components necessary for a basic computer system, though network hardware and software are not included. Would this be a good system for Tenzing to recommend for purchase at International ComAir? To answer that question, you must become familiar with current microcomputer pricing. You will have an opportunity to do some comparison shopping as you work through the questions at the end of this chapter.

Questions

1. What is the key to a computer's versatility?
   a. software
   b. hardware
   c. price
   d. super VGA
2. Keyboards, screens, hard disk drives, printers, and main circuit boards are all examples of which of the following?
   a. input devices
   b. output devices
   c. peripherals
   d. hardware
3. Moving text, sorting lists, and performing calculations are examples of which of the following?
   a. input
   b. output
   c. processing
   d. storage
4. What telecommunications hardware is needed to convert digital signals to analog signals?
   a. mouse
   b. device driver
   c. modem
   d. slot
5. What do you call a collection of data stored on a disk under a name that you assign it?
   a. a file
   b. the operating system
   c. a protocol
   d. a pixel

6. Which one of the following would not be considered a microcomputer?
   a. desktop
   b. notebook
   c. PC
   d. mainframe
7. The selection of components that make up a particular computer system is referred to as:
   a. the configuration
   b. the specification
   c. the protocol
   d. the device driver
8. Which of the following maintains data only on a temporary basis?
   a. ROM
   b. a disk
   c. RAM
   d. a hard disk
9. Which one of the following microprocessors is fastest?
   a. 66 MHz 80486
   b. 50 MHz 80486
   c. 75 MHz Pentium
   d. 133 MHz Pentium
10. What do you call each 1 or 0 used in the representation of computer data?
    a. a bit
    b. a byte
    c. an ASCII
    d. a pixel
11. What usually represents one character of data?
    a. a bit
    b. a byte
    c. an integer
    d. a pixel
12. What is a kilobyte?
    a. 100 megabytes
    b. 1,024 bytes
    c. one-half a gigabyte
    d. one million bits
13. Which one of the following would you *not* expect to find in RAM while the computer is on?
    a. operating system instructions
    b. data the user has entered
    c. applications program instructions
    d. write-protect window
14. What connects a monitor to a computer?
    a. a parallel port
    b. a network card
    c. a graphics adapter
    d. near letter-quality mode
15. Which one of the following statements best defines a peer-to-peer network?
    a. A central file server acts as a repository for all files and applications programs used on the network.
    b. Your messages travel to a mainframe computer and then are routed to their destinations.
    c. The task of storing data and files is distributed among all the computers that are attached to the network.
    d. The messages travel around a ring until they reach their destination.

16. Which one of the following is systems software?
    a. Lotus 1-2-3
    b. DOS 6.22
    c. WordPerfect for Windows
    d. Corel Draw
17. Which one of the following is an operating environment but not an operating system?
    a. DOS 6.22
    b. Windows 3.11
    c. Windows NT
    d. OS/2
18. Random-access computer memory is measured in ______________________.
19. Floppy disk, hard disk, and tape storage capacity is measured in ______________________.
20. Disk access time is measured in ______________________.
21. The resolution of computer monitors is measured in ______________________.
22. The microprocessor clock speed is measured in ______________________.
23. The transmission of text, numeric, voice, or video data from one computer to another is called ______________________.
24. Connecting a computer to peripheral devices is called ______________________.
25. List the four essential components of data communication.
26. For each of the following data items, indicate how many bits and how many bytes of storage would be required:

Data Item	**Bits**	**Bytes**
North		
Scissors		
CEO		
U.S.A.		
General Ledger		
123 N. Main St.		

27. Read the following requirements for using Microsoft Windows 95 (taken from the documentation that accompanies the Microsoft Windows 95 program). Then turn back to the computer advertisement shown in Figure 1 at the beginning of the chapter and determine if the computer specifications listed in the ad are sufficient to run Windows 95.
    Windows 95 requires:
    - For 386 enhanced mode, a personal computer with an 80386 processor (or higher)
    - 4MB of RAM (although 8 MB is recommended)
    - 40-80 MB of free disk space (100 MB is recommended)
    - floppy-disk drive
    - a display adapter that is supported by Windows
    - a printer that is supported by Windows
    - Hayes, Multi-tech, Trail Blazer, or compatible modem, if you want to use HyperTerminal, the Windows communication application
    - a mouse that is supported by Windows. Although not required, a mouse is highly recommended so that you can take full advantage of the easy-to-use Windows graphical interface.

28. Using the Windows 95 specifications in Question 27, look through a recent computer magazine and find the least expensive computer that will run this operating environment. Make a photocopy of the ad showing the specifications, price, and vendor. Write the name of the magazine and the issue date on the top of the ad.
29. Look through the ads in a computer magazine to find a variety of peripheral devices. Note the type of port to which they connect, then add the devices to the appropriate column of the following chart:

Types of Port	Connecting Devices
Serial Port	
Parallel Port	
MIDI Port	
SCSI Port	

Lab Assignments

The following Lab Assignments are designed to accompany the interactive Course Labs. To start each Course Lab, click the Start button on the Windows 95 taskbar, point to Programs, point to Course Labs, point to New Perspectives Applications, and click the name of the Lab (for example, Using a Mouse). If you do not see Course Labs on your Program menu, see your instructor or technical support person.

Course Lab: Using a Mouse A mouse is a standard input device on most of today's computers. You need to know how to use a mouse to manipulate graphical user interfaces and to use the rest of the Labs.

1. The Steps for the Using a Mouse Lab show you how to click, double-click, and drag objects using the mouse. Click the Steps button and begin the Steps. As you work through the Steps, answer all of the Quick Check questions that appear. When you complete the Steps, you will see a Summary Report that summarizes your performance on the Quick Checks. Follow the directions on the screen to print the Summary Report.
2. Click the Explore button. Demonstrate your ability to use a mouse and to control a Windows program by creating a poster. To create a poster, select a graphic, type the caption for the poster, then select a font, font style and size, and a border. Print your completed poster.

Course Lab: Using a Keyboard To become an effective computer user, you must be familiar with your primary input device—the keyboard.

1. The Steps for the Using a Keyboard Lab provide you with a structured introduction to the keyboard layout and the function of special computer keys. Click the Steps button and begin the Steps. As you work through the Steps, answer all of the Quick Check questions that appear. When you complete the Steps, you will see a Summary Report that summarizes your performance on the Quick Checks. Follow the directions on the screen to print the Summary Report.
2. Click the Explore button to start the typing tutor. You can develop your typing skills using the typing tutor in Explore. Take the typing test and print out your results.

3. Click the Explore button. Try to improve your typing speed by 10 words per minute. For example, if you currently type 20 words per minute, your goal would be 30 words per minute. Practice each typing lesson until you see a message that indicates you can proceed to the next lesson. Create a Practice Record as shown here to keep track of how much you practice. When you have reached your goal, print out the results of a typing test to verify your results.

Practice Record

Name:____

Section:______________________________________

Start Date:__________ Start Typing Speed:__________wpm

End Date:__________ End Typing Speed:__________wpm

Lesson #:__________ Date/Time Practiced __________

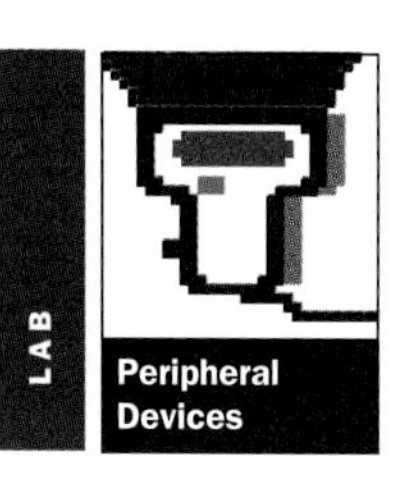

Course Lab: Peripheral Devices A wide variety of peripheral devices provide expandability for computer systems and provide users with the equipment necessary to accomplish tasks efficiently. In the Peripheral Devices Lab you will use an online product catalog of peripheral devices.

1. Complete the Steps to find out how to use the online product catalog. Click the Steps button and begin the Steps. As you work through the Steps, answer all of the Quick Check questions that appear. When you complete the Steps, you will see a Summary Report that summarizes your performance on the Quick Checks. Follow the directions on the screen to print the Summary Report.
2. After you know how to use the product catalog to look up products, features, and prices, use Explore to create an outline that shows the way peripheral devices are categorized in the catalog.
   a. List the characteristics that differentiate printers.
   b. List the factors that differentiate monitors.
   c. Describe the factors that determine the appropriate type of scanner for a task.
   d. List the peripheral devices in the catalog that are specially designed for notebook computers.
3. Suppose that the company that produces the peripheral devices catalog selected your name from its list of customers for a free scanner. You can select any one of the scanners in the catalog. Assume that you own a notebook computer to which you could attach any one of the scanners. Click the Explore button and use the catalog to help you write a one-page paper explaining which scanner you would select, why you would select it, and how you would use it.
4. Suppose you are in charge of informations systems in a metropolitan hospital. Twenty nursing stations need printers. The printers will be used for a variety of reports. High print quality is not essential, but, of course, the reports must be readable. Some reports require more than one copy. Because they will be situated near patients, the printers must be quiet. Use the catalog in the Explore portion of the Lab to write a one-page paper in which you recommend a printer from the catalog for the nursing stations. Support your recommendation by explaining the advantages of the printer you selected and the disadvantages of the other printers available.
5. Suppose you a own a basic computer system, such as the one in Figure 4 of this chapter. You have an idea that you can earn the money for your college tuition by using your computer to help other students produce spiffy reports with color graphics and scanned images. Your parents have agreed to "loan" you $1,000 to get started. Click the Explore button and look through the online peripheral devices catalog. List any of the devices that might help you with this business venture. Write a one-page paper explaining how you would spend your $1,000 to get the equipment you need to start the business.

LAB User Interfaces

Course Lab: User Interfaces You have learned that the hardware and software for a user interface determine how you interact and communicate with the computer. In the User Interfaces Lab, you will try five different user interfaces to accomplish the same task—creating a graph.

1. Begin with the Steps to find out how each interface works. Click the Steps button and begin the Steps. As you work through the Steps, answer all of the Quick Check questions that appear. When you complete the Steps, you will see a Summary Report that summarizes your performance on the Quick Checks. Follow the directions on the screen to print the Summary Report.
2. Click the Explore button. Use each Interface to make a 3-D pie graph using data set 1. Title your graphs "Bike U.S. Sales." Use the percent style to show the percentage of each slice of the pie. Print each of the five graphs (one for each interface).
3. Click the Explore button. Select one of the user interfaces. Write a one to two-page step-by-step set of instructions for how to produce a line graph using data set 3. This line graph should show lines and symbols, and have the title "Home Budget."
4. Using the user interface terminology you learned in this Lab and in this chapter, write a description of each of the interfaces you used in the Lab. Then, suppose you worked for a software publisher and you were going to create a software package for producing line, bar, column, and pie graphs. Which user interface would you use for the software? Why?

Index

A

Access, Microsoft, EC 31–32
Access time, EC 22. *See also* Hard disks
Analog signals, EC 28
Applications, EC 30–33. *See also* Software
  database, EC 31–32
  graphics/presentations, EC 32
  personal information management, EC 33
  spreadsheet, EC 31
  word processing, EC 30
ASCII code, EC 12–13, EC 14

B

Baud rate, EC 28
Binary digits, EC 12
Binary system, EC 12–13, EC 14
Bits, EC 12
Bytes, EC 12

C

Cathode ray tube (CRT), EC 16. *See also* Monitors
CD-ROM drives, EC 20
Channels, EC 24. *See also* Data communications
Chips, EC 11
Client-server networks, EC 27. *See also* Networks
Clipart, EC 32
Clock speed, EC 11. *See also* Microprocessors
COM1–4, EC 25
Communications
  data, EC 6, EC 24–29
  devices, EC 6
  software, EC 28
  telecommunications, EC 28–29
Compatibility
  of monitors, EC 16
  in networks, EC 28
Computers
  and data communications, EC 6, EC 24–29
  data representation in, EC 12–13
  definition of, EC 4
  expandibility of, EC 25
  hardware for, EC 9–23
  memory in, EC 14–15
  music and, EC 22
  networking, EC 27–29
  parts of, EC 4–6
  speed of, EC 11
  software for, EC 29–33
  types of, EC 6–9
Configuration, EC 4. *See also* Hardware
Contact management software, EC 33
Controller cards, EC 25
CPUs (central processing units), EC 11–12

D

Data. *See also* Data communications
  definition of, EC 6, EC 24
  flow through RAM, EC 14–15
  protecting, EC 20, EC 30
  storage of, EC 19–23
Database software, EC 31–32
Data communications, EC 6, EC 24–29
  components of, EC 24
  and networks, EC 27–29
  peripheral interfaces and, EC 25–26
  telecommunications and, EC 28
Device drivers, EC 25
Digital signals, EC 28
Disk case, EC 20
Diskettes, EC 19–21
Display adapter, EC 17
Display cards, EC 17
DOS, EC 29–30
Draft mode, EC 17. *See also* Printers
Drivers
  device, EC 25
  software, EC 17

E

Electronic mail, EC 24
Excel, Microsoft, EC 31
Expansion cards, EC 25
Expansion slots, EC 25–26

F

Faxing, EC 24
Files, EC 6
File servers, EC 27. *See also* Networks
Fixed disks, EC 21–22
Floppy disks, EC 20–22
  vs. hard disks, EC 22
  protecting data on, EC 20, 21

G

Graphics adapter, EC 17
Graphics software, EC 32
Graphics user interface (GUI), EC 15

H

Hard disks, EC 20–21
Hardware
  definition of, EC 4
  processing, EC 5, EC 11–15
Home pages, EC 24

I

Input
  definition of, EC 5
  devices, EC 6, EC 9–15
  keyboards, EC 5, EC 9
  mouse, EC 5, EC 9–10
  storage devices, EC 9
Integrated circuits, EC 11. *See also* Microprocessors
Intel processors, EC 11
Interface cards, EC 25
Interfacing, EC 25–26
Internet, the, EC 24

K

Keyboards, EC 5, EC 9
  using, EC 36

L

Laser discs, EC 22
Liquid crystal displays (LCDs), EC 16. *See also* Monitors
LANs (local-area networks), EC 27
LPT1–2, EC 26

M

Main circuit board, EC 5
Mainframe computers, EC 7–8
Megabytes, EC 14

Megahertz (MHz), EC 11
Memory, EC 11, EC 13–14. *See also* Storage devices
MHz (megahertz), EC 11
Microcomputers, EC 6–7
  notebook, EC 7
Microprocessors, EC 11
Microsoft software
  Access, EC 31–32
  Excel, EC 31
  PowerPoint, EC 32
  Windows, EC 29–32
  Word, EC 30
MIDI ports, EC 26
Minicomputers, EC 7
Modems, EC 28
Monitors, EC 16–17
Motherboard, EC 5
Mouses, EC 5, EC 10
  using, EC 36

N

Near-letter quality (NLQ) mode, EC 17
Networks, EC 27–28
  software for, EC 28
  topologies, EC 28
  types of, EC 27–28
Notebook computers, EC 7

O

Operating environments, EC 29–30
Operating systems, EC 14, EC 29–30
Optical storage devices, EC 22
OS/2, EC 30
Output
  definition of, EC 6, EC 16
  devices, EC 6, EC 16–19

P

Parallel ports, EC 26
Parity, EC 29
Peer-to-peer networks, EC 27. *See also* Networks
Pentium processors, EC 11
Peripherals, EC 37
  definition of, EC 25
  interfacing, EC 25–26
Personal computers (PCs), EC 6–7
Personal information management software, EC 32
Pixels, EC 16
Ports, EC 25
PowerPoint, Microsoft, EC 32
Presentation software, EC 32
Printers, EC 6, EC 16–19
  dot-matrix, EC 17–18
  ink-jet, EC 18
  laser, EC 18–19
Processing, EC 5
  hardware, EC 5
Programs. *See* Applications; Software
Protocols, EC 24. *See also* Data communications
  and device drivers, EC 25
  telecommunications, EC 28

R

RAM (random-access memory), EC 14
  amount required, EC 15
  storage devices and, EC 19
Receivers, EC 24. *See also* Data communications
ROM (read-only memory), EC 13

S

SCSI ports, EC 26
Senders, EC 24. *See also* Data communications
Serial ports, EC 25
Servers, file, EC 27. *See also* Networks
Software, EC 29–33
  applications, EC 30–33
  communications, EC 28
  definition of, EC 5
  drivers, EC 17
  network, EC 27–28
  operating system, EC 14, EC 29–30
  systems, EC 29–30
  virus protection, EC 30
Specifications, definition of, EC 4
Spreadsheet software, EC 31
Storage devices, EC 6, EC 19–23
  floppy disks, EC 20, EC 21
  hard disks, EC 21–22
  labeling of, EC 22
  optical, EC 22
  tape drives, EC 22
Storage media, EC 6, EC 19–23
Supercomputers, EC 8

T

Tape drives, EC 22
Telecommunications, EC 28–29
Toner, EC 18
Topology, EC 28. *See also* Networks
Tower case, EC 6

U

User interfaces, EC 29, EC 38

V

Video controller, EC 17
Video graphics arrays (VGA), EC 16. *See also* Monitors
Virus protection, EC 30

W

Windows, Microsoft, EC 29–32
Word, Microsoft, EC 30
Word processing software, EC 30
World Wide Web, EC 24
Write protection, EC 21

New Perspectives on

Microsoft® Windows® 95

BRIEF

TUTORIALS

TUTORIAL 1

Exploring the Basics

Your First Day in the Lab 3

TUTORIAL 2

Working with Files

Your First Day in the Lab—Continued 29

Read This **Before You Begin**

TO THE STUDENT

To use this book, you must have a Student Disk. Your instructor will either provide you with a Student Disk or ask you to make your own by following the instructions in the section called "Creating Your Windows 95 Student Disk" in Tutorial 2. See your instructor or lab manager for further information.

USING YOUR OWN COMPUTER

If you are going to work through this book using your own computer, you need:

- **The Student Disk** Ask your instructor or lab manager for details on how to get the Student Disk. *You will not be able to complete the tutorials or exercises in this book using your own computer until you have the Student Disk.*
- **Labs** Some of the assignments at the end of each tutorial require the Course Labs. These Labs should be available on the computers in your school computer lab. If you would like to install these Labs on your home computer, ask your instructor or technical support person for assistance.
- **Computer system** Microsoft Windows 95 must be installed on your computer.

TO THE INSTRUCTOR

MAKING THE STUDENT DISK FILES AVAILABLE

To complete the tutorials in this book, your students must use a set of files on a Student Disk. To make these files available to them, you should use the New Perspectives Windows 95 Brief Setup Disk to install the software on your server or standalone computers, following the instructions on the setup disk label to install the CTI Windows 95 Applications software. Your students can then use the Windows 95 Start menu to run the program that will create their student disks. Tutorial 2 contains steps that instruct your students how to generate student disks.

If you prefer to provide student disks yourself rather than letting students generate them, install the New Perspectives Windows 95 Brief Setup Disk (following the instructions on the disk label), then generate Student Disk copies using the Make a Student Disk program (following the instructions in Tutorial 2).

COURSE LABS

Some of the assignments at the end of each tutorial provide an opportunity for students to reinforce their understanding and skills by using Course Labs. The software for these labs is included on the Setup Disk. The Labs are automatically installed on your server or standalone computer when you install the Setup Disk software. Students run the Labs from the Windows 95 Start menu. Instructions are included in each Lab Assignment.

INSTALLING THE NEW PERSPECTIVES WINDOWS 95 BRIEF SETUP DISK

Follow the instructions on the Setup Disk label. By adopting this book, you are granted the license to install this software on any computer or computer network used by you or your students.

README FILE

A Readme.doc file located on the Setup Disk provides additional technical notes, troubleshooting advice, and tips for using the software in your school's computer lab. You can view the Readme file using WordPad.

SYSTEM REQUIREMENTS:

The CTI Windows 95 Applications software for this New Perspectives book is designed to run on a typical Windows 95 computer. You will need at least the following:

- Microsoft Windows 95 on a local hard drive or on a network drive
- A 386 (or higher) processor with a minimum of 4 MB RAM (8 MB RAM or more is strongly recommended)
- A mouse supported by Windows 95
- A printer supported by Windows 95
- A VGA 640 x 480 256-color display is recommended; an 800 x 600, 1024 x 768 SVGA or 16-color VGA display is also acceptable
- 5 MB of free hard disk space
- If you wish to install the Setup Disk on a network drive, your network must support Microsoft Windows 95

TUTORIAL 1

Exploring the Basics

OBJECTIVES

In this tutorial you will learn to:

- Identify the controls on the Windows 95 desktop
- Use the Windows 95 Start button to run software programs
- Identify and use the controls in a window
- Switch between programs using the taskbar
- Use Windows 95 controls such as menus, toolbars, list boxes, scroll bars, radio buttons, tabs, and check boxes

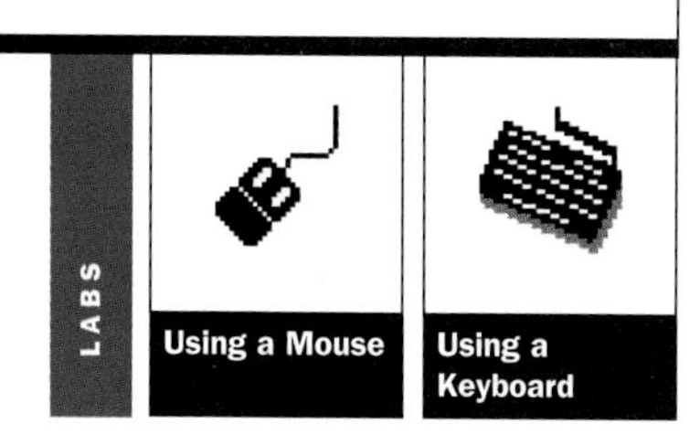

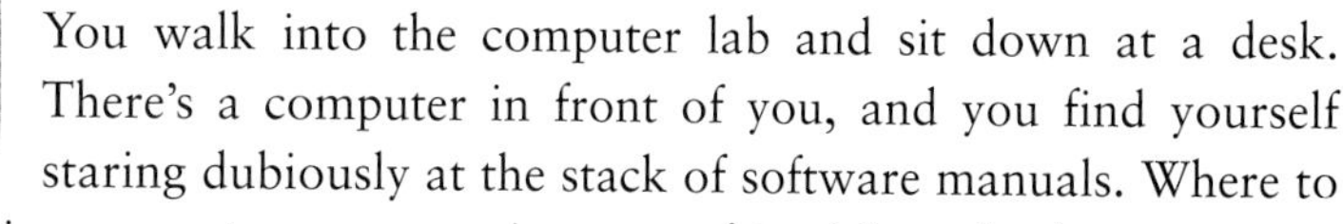

CASE

Your First Day in the Lab

You walk into the computer lab and sit down at a desk. There's a computer in front of you, and you find yourself staring dubiously at the stack of software manuals. Where to start? As if in answer to your question, your friend Steve Laslow appears.

Gesturing to the stack of manuals, you tell Steve that you were just wondering where to start.

"You start with the operating system," says Steve. Noticing your slightly puzzled look, Steve explains that the **operating system** is software that helps the computer carry out basic operating tasks such as displaying information on the computer screen and saving data on your disks. Your computer uses the **Microsoft Windows 95** operating system—Windows 95, for short.

Steve tells you that Windows 95 has a "gooey" or **graphical user interface (GUI)**, which uses pictures of familiar objects, such as file folders and documents, to represent a desktop on your screen. Microsoft Windows 95 gets its name from the rectangular-shaped work areas, called "windows," that appear on your screen.

Steve continues to talk as he sorts through the stack of manuals on your desk. He says there are two things he really likes about Windows 95. First, lots of software is available for computers that have the Windows 95 operating system and all this software has a standard graphical user interface. That means once you have learned how to use one Windows software package, such as word-processing software, you are well on your way to understanding how to use other Windows software. Second, Windows 95 lets you use more than one software package at a time, so you can easily switch between your word-processing software and your appointment book software, for example. All in all, Windows 95 makes your computer an effective and easy-to-use productivity tool.

Steve recommends that you get started right away by using some tutorials that will teach you the skills essential for using Microsoft Windows 95. He hands you a book and assures you that everything on your computer system is set up and ready to go.

You mention that last summer you worked in an advertising agency where the employees used something called Windows 3.1. Steve explains that Windows 3.1 is an earlier version of the Windows operating system. Windows 95 and Windows 3.1 are similar, but Windows 95 is more powerful and easier to use. Steve says that as you work through the tutorials you will see notes that point out the important differences between Windows 95 and Windows 3.1.

Steve has a class, but he says he'll check back later to see how you are doing.

Using the Tutorials Effectively

These tutorials will help you learn about Windows 95. The tutorials are designed to be used at a computer. Each tutorial is divided into sessions. Watch for the session headings, such as Session 1.1 and Session 1.2. Each session is designed to be completed in about 45 minutes, but take as much time as you need. It's also a good idea to take a break between sessions.

Before you begin, read the following questions and answers. They are designed to help you use the tutorials effectively.

Where do I start?

Each tutorial begins with a case, which sets the scene for the tutorial and gives you background information to help you understand what you will be doing in the tutorial. Read the case before you go to the lab. In the lab, begin with the first session of the tutorial.

How do I know what to do on the computer?

Each session contains steps that you will perform on the computer to learn how to use Windows 95. Read the text that introduces each series of steps. The steps you need to do at a computer are numbered and are set against a color background. Read each step carefully and completely before you try it.

How do I know if I did the step correctly?

As you work, compare your computer screen with the corresponding figure in the tutorial. Don't worry if your screen display is somewhat different from the figure. The important parts of the screen display are labeled in each figure. Check to make sure these parts are on your screen.

What if I make a mistake?

Don't worry about making mistakes—they are part of the learning process. Paragraphs labeled "**TROUBLE?**" identify common problems and explain how to get back on track. Follow the steps in a **TROUBLE?** paragraph *only* if you are having the problem described. If you run into other problems:

- Carefully consider the current state of your system, the position of the pointer, and any messages on the screen.
- Complete the sentence, "Now I want to...." Be specific, because you are identifying your goal.
- Develop a plan for accomplishing your goal, and put your plan into action.

How do I use the Reference Windows?

Reference Windows summarize the procedures you learn in the tutorial steps. Do not complete the actions in the Reference Windows when you are working through the tutorial. Instead, refer to the Reference Windows while you are working on the assignments at the end of the tutorial.

How can I test my understanding of the material I learned in the tutorial?

At the end of each session, you can answer the Quick Check questions. The answers for the Quick Checks are at the end of the book.

After you have completed the entire tutorial, you should complete the Tutorial Assignments. The Tutorial Assignments are carefully structured so you will review what you have learned and then apply your knowledge to new situations.

What if I can't remember how to do something?

You should refer to the Task Reference at the end of the book; it summarizes how to accomplish commonly performed tasks.

What are the 3.1 Notes?

The 3.1 Notes are helpful if you have used Windows 3.1. The notes point out the key similarities and differences between Windows 3.1 and Windows 95.

What are the Interactive Labs, and how should I use them?

Interactive Labs help you review concepts and practice skills that you learn in the tutorial. Lab icons at the beginning of each tutorial and in the margins of the tutorials indicate topics that have corresponding Labs. The Lab Assignments section includes instructions for how to use each Lab.

Now that you understand how to use the tutorials effectively, you are ready to begin.

SESSION 1.1

In this session, in addition to learning basic Windows terminology, you will learn how to use a mouse, to start and stop a program, and to use more than one program at a time. With the skills you learn in this session, you will be able to use Windows 95 to start software programs.

Using a Keyboard

Starting Windows 95

Windows 95 automatically starts when you turn on the computer. Depending on the way your computer is set up, you might be asked to enter your user name and password. If prompted to do so, type your assigned user name and press the Enter key. Then type your password and press the Enter key to continue.

To start Windows 95:

1. Turn on your computer.

The Windows 95 Desktop

In Windows terminology, the screen represents a **desktop**—a workspace for projects and the tools needed to manipulate those projects. Look at your screen display and locate the objects labeled in Figure 1-1 on the following page.

Because it is easy to customize the Windows environment, your screen might not look exactly the same as Figure 1-1. You should, however, be able to locate objects on your screen similar to those in Figure 1-1.

TROUBLE? If the Welcome to Windows 95 box appears on your screen, press the Enter key to close it.

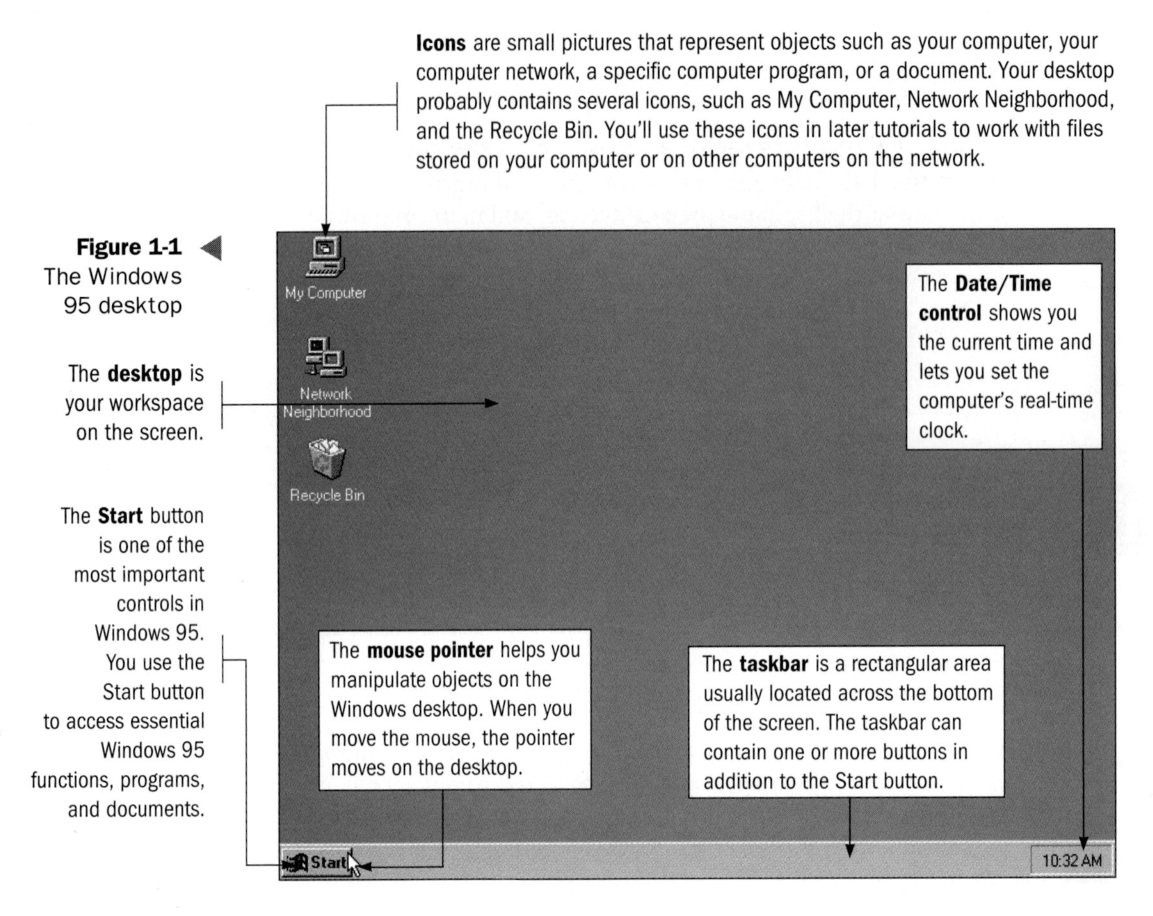

Figure 1-1 The Windows 95 desktop

TROUBLE? If the screen goes blank or starts to display a moving design, press any key to restore the image.

Using the Mouse

A **mouse**, like those shown in Figure 1-2, is a pointing device that helps you interact with objects on the screen. In Windows 95 you need to know how to use the mouse to point, click, and drag. In this session you will learn about pointing and clicking. In Session 1.2 you will learn how to use the mouse to drag objects.

You can also interact with objects by using the keyboard; however, the mouse is much more convenient for most tasks, so the tutorials in this book assume you are using one.

Pointing

The **pointer**, or **mouse pointer**, is a small object that moves on the screen when you move the mouse. The pointer is usually shaped like an arrow. As you move the mouse on a flat surface, the pointer on the screen moves in the direction corresponding to the movement of the mouse. The pointer sometimes changes shape depending on where it is on the screen or the action the computer is completing.

Find the arrow-shaped pointer on your screen. If you do not see the pointer, move your mouse until the pointer comes into view.

Figure 1-2 ◀
The mouse

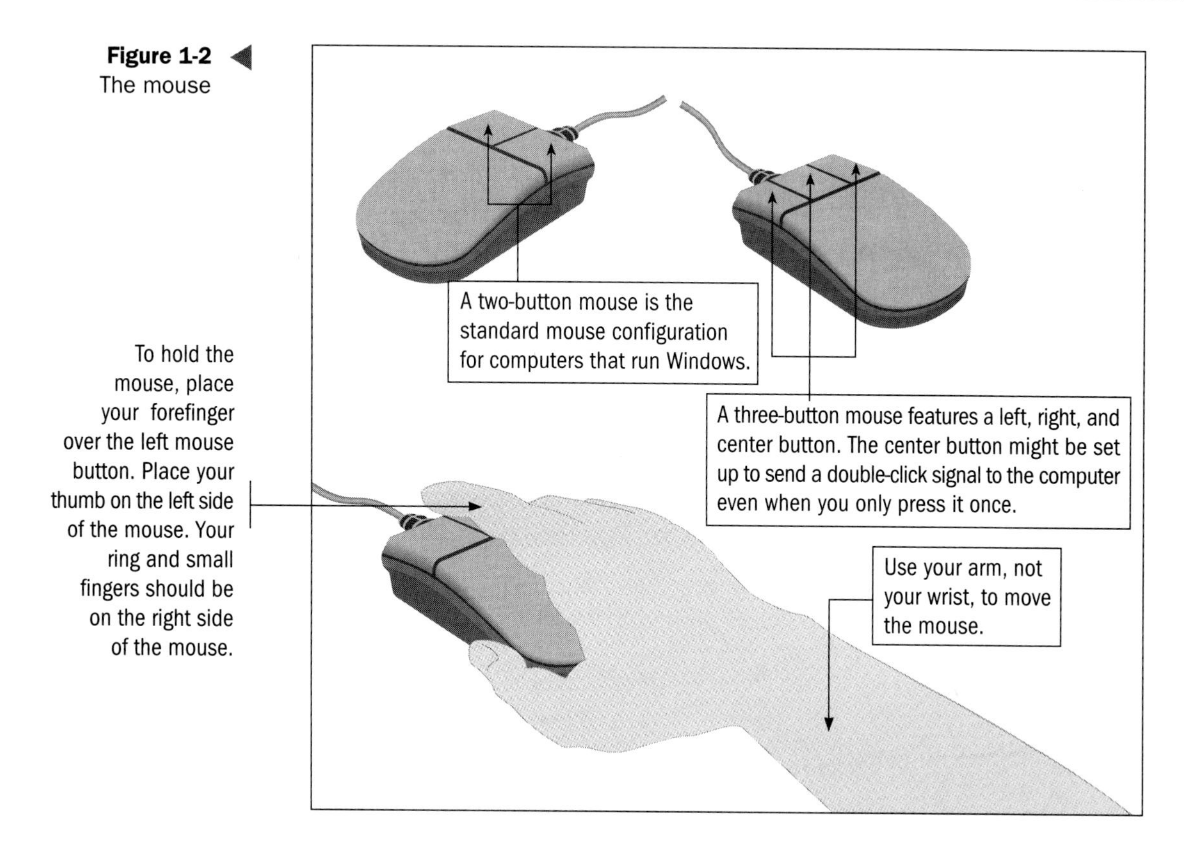

Basic "mousing" skills depend on your ability to position the pointer. You begin most Windows operations by positioning the pointer over a specific part of the screen. This is called **pointing**.

To move the pointer:

1. Position your right index finger over the left mouse button, as shown in Figure 1-2. Lightly grasp the sides of the mouse with your thumb and little finger.

   TROUBLE? If you want to use the mouse with your left hand, ask your instructor or technical support person to help you use the Control Panel to change the mouse settings to swap the left and right mouse buttons. Be sure you find out how to change back to the right-handed mouse setting, so you can reset the mouse each time you are finished in the lab.

2. Locate the arrow-shaped pointer on the screen.

3. Move the mouse and watch the movement of the pointer.

If you run out of room to move your mouse, lift the mouse and move it to a clear area on your desk, then place the mouse back on the desk. Notice that the pointer does not move when the mouse is not in contact with the desk.

When you position the mouse pointer over certain objects, such as the objects on the taskbar, a "tip" appears. These "tips" are called **ToolTips**, and they tell you the purpose or function of an object.

To view ToolTips:

1. Use the mouse to point to the **Start** button Start. After a few seconds, you see the tip "Click here to begin" as shown in Figure 1-3 on the following page.

Figure 1-3
Viewing ToolTips

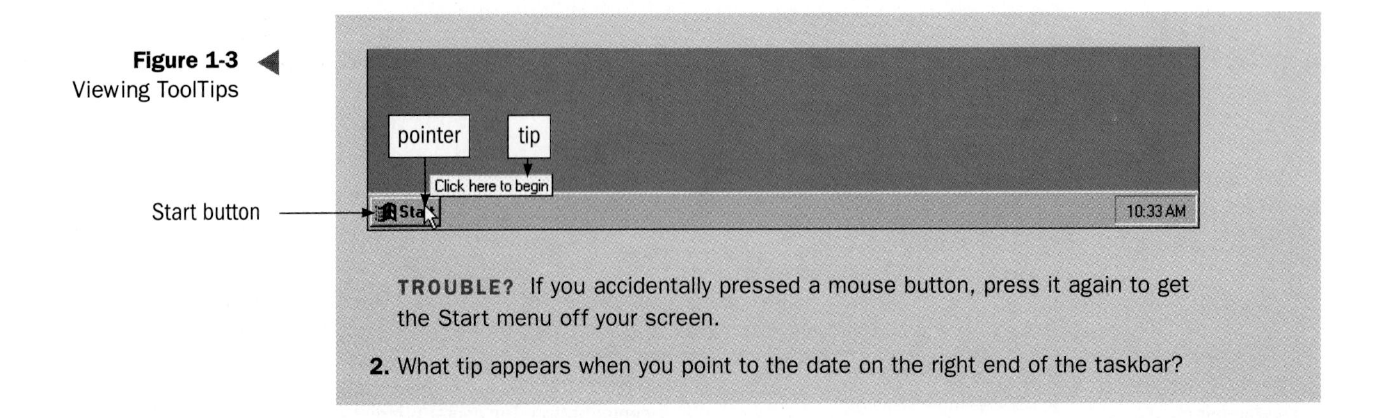

TROUBLE? If you accidentally pressed a mouse button, press it again to get the Start menu off your screen.

2. What tip appears when you point to the date on the right end of the taskbar?

Clicking

3.1 NOTE

Windows 3.1 users frequently double-click the mouse to accomplish tasks. Double-clicking means pressing the mouse button twice in rapid succession. Many people had trouble learning how to double-click, so Windows 95 does not require double-clicking.

When you press a mouse button and immediately release it, it is called **clicking**. Clicking the mouse selects an object on the desktop. *You usually click the left mouse button, so* unless the instructions tell you otherwise, always click the left mouse button.

Windows 95 shows you which object is selected by highlighting it, usually by changing the object's color, putting a box around it, or making the object appear to be pushed in, as shown in Figure 1-4.

Figure 1-4
Selected objects

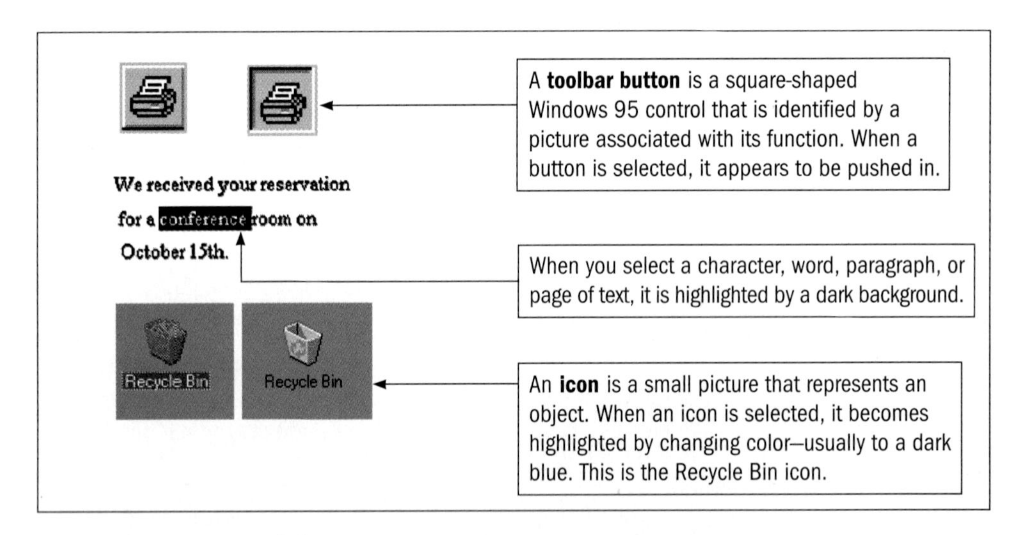

To select the Recycle Bin icon:

1. Position the pointer over the **Recycle Bin** icon.
2. Click the mouse button and notice how the color of the icon changes to show that it is selected.

Starting and Closing a Program

The software you use is sometimes referred to as a **program** or an **application**. To use a program, such as a word-processing program, you must first start it. With Windows 95 you start a program by clicking the Start button. The Start button displays a menu.

A **menu** is a list of options. Windows 95 has a **Start menu** that provides you with access to programs, data, and configuration options. One of the Start menu's most important functions is to let you start a program.

The Reference Window below explains how to start a program. Don't do the steps in the Reference Window now; they are for your later reference.

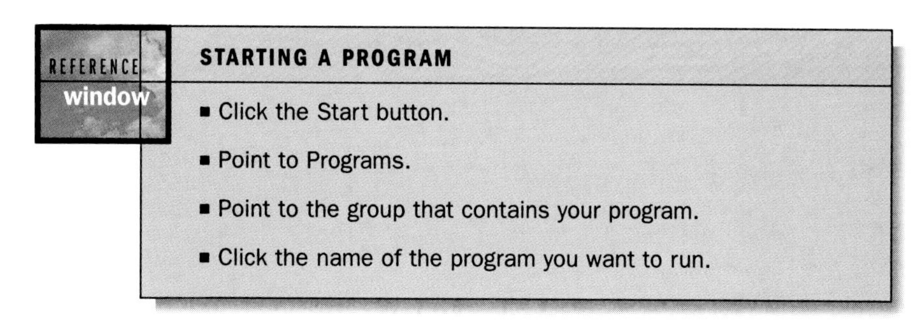

REFERENCE window

STARTING A PROGRAM

- Click the Start button.
- Point to Programs.
- Point to the group that contains your program.
- Click the name of the program you want to run.

3.1 NOTE

WordPad is similar to Write in Windows 3.1.

Windows 95 includes an easy-to-use word-processing program called WordPad. Suppose you want to start the WordPad program and use it to write a letter or report.

To start the WordPad program from the Start menu:

1. Click the **Start** button **Start** as shown in Figure 1-5. A menu appears.

Figure 1-5 ◀ Starting the WordPad program

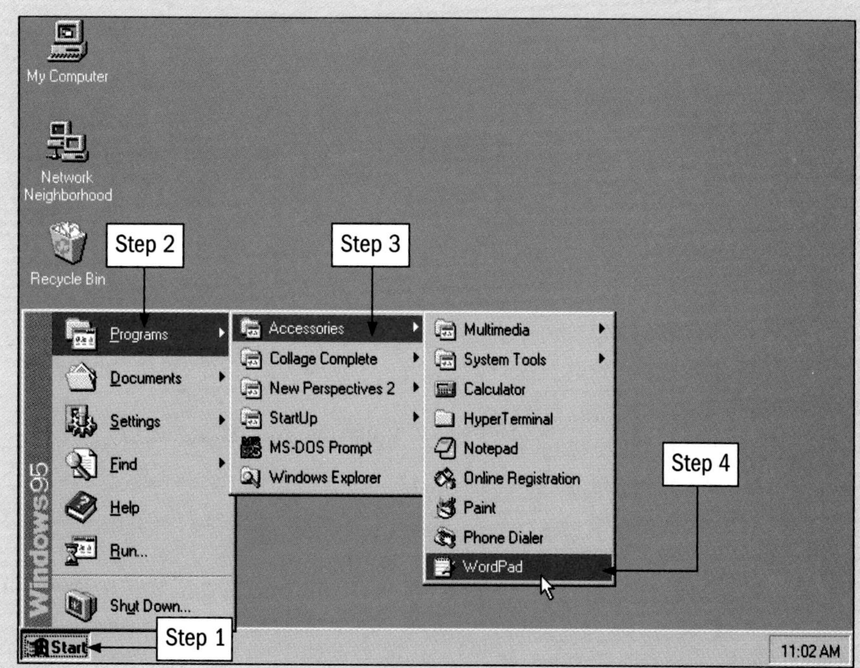

2. Point to **Programs**. After a short pause, the next menu appears.

   TROUBLE? If you don't get the correct menu, go back and point to the correct menu option.

3. Point to **Accessories**. Another menu appears.
4. Click **WordPad**. Make sure you can see the WordPad program as shown in Figure 1-6 on the following page.

Figure 1-6 The WordPad program

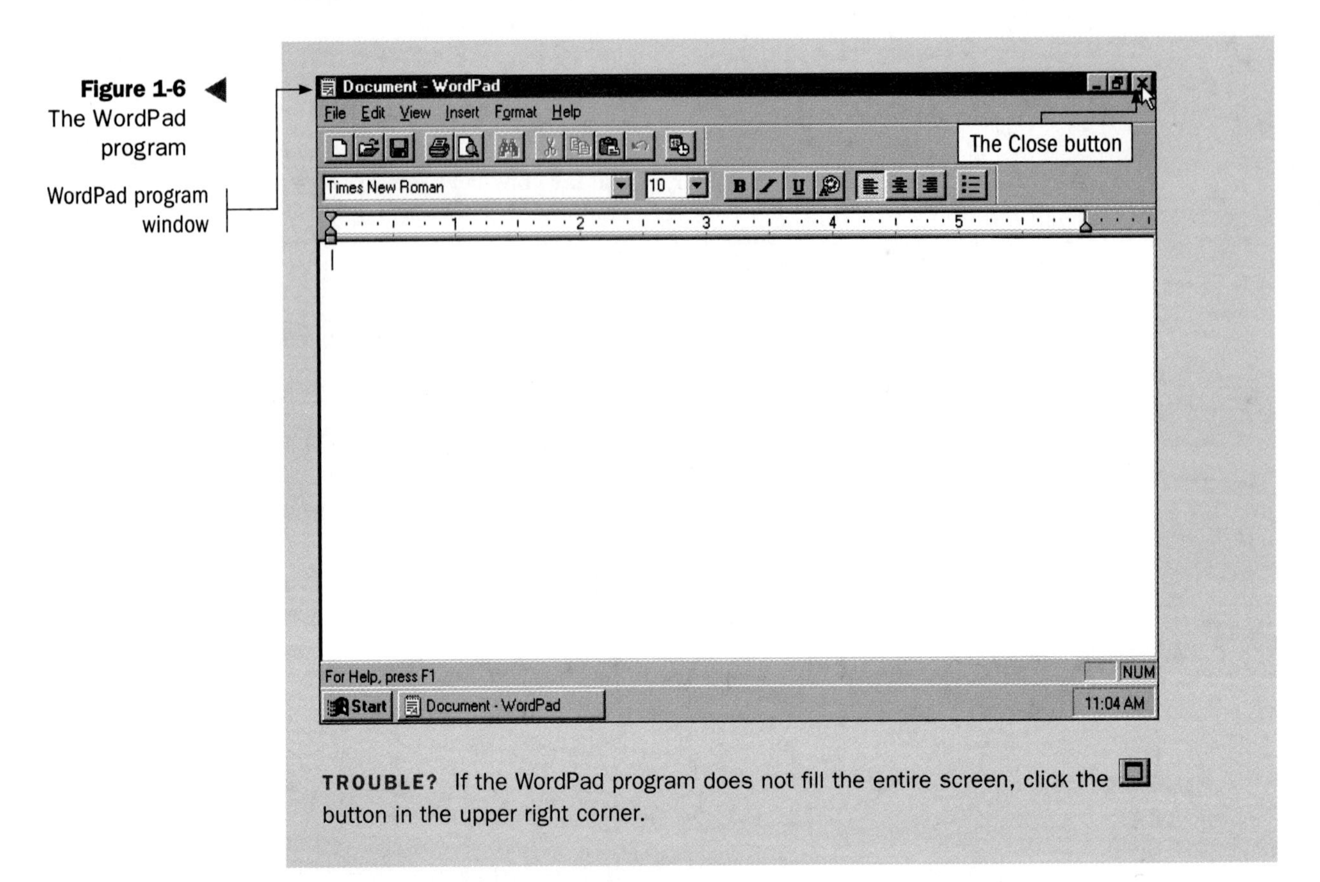

TROUBLE? If the WordPad program does not fill the entire screen, click the button in the upper right corner.

3.1 NOTE

As with Windows 3.1, in Windows 95 you can also exit a program using the Exit option from the File menu.

When you are finished using a program, the easiest way to return to the Windows 95 desktop is to click the Close button.

To exit the WordPad program:

1. Click the **Close** button. See Figure 1-6. You will be returned to the Windows 95 desktop.

Running More than One Program at the Same Time

3.1 NOTE

Paint in Windows 95 is similar to Paintbrush in WIndows 3.1.

One of the most useful features of Windows 95 is its ability to run multiple programs at the same time. This feature, known as **multi-tasking**, allows you to work on more than one task at a time and to quickly switch between tasks. For example, you can start WordPad and leave it running while you then start the Paint program.

To run WordPad and Paint at the same time:

1. Start WordPad.

   TROUBLE? You learned how to start WordPad earlier in the tutorial: Click the Start button, point to Programs, point to Accessories, and then click WordPad.

2. Now you can start the Paint program. Click the **Start** button again.
3. Point to **Programs**.
4. Point to **Accessories**.
5. Click **Paint**. The Paint program appears as shown in Figure 1-7. Now two programs are running at the same time.

TROUBLE? If the Paint program does not fill the entire screen, click the ▢ button in the upper right corner.

Figure 1-7 ◀ The Paint Program

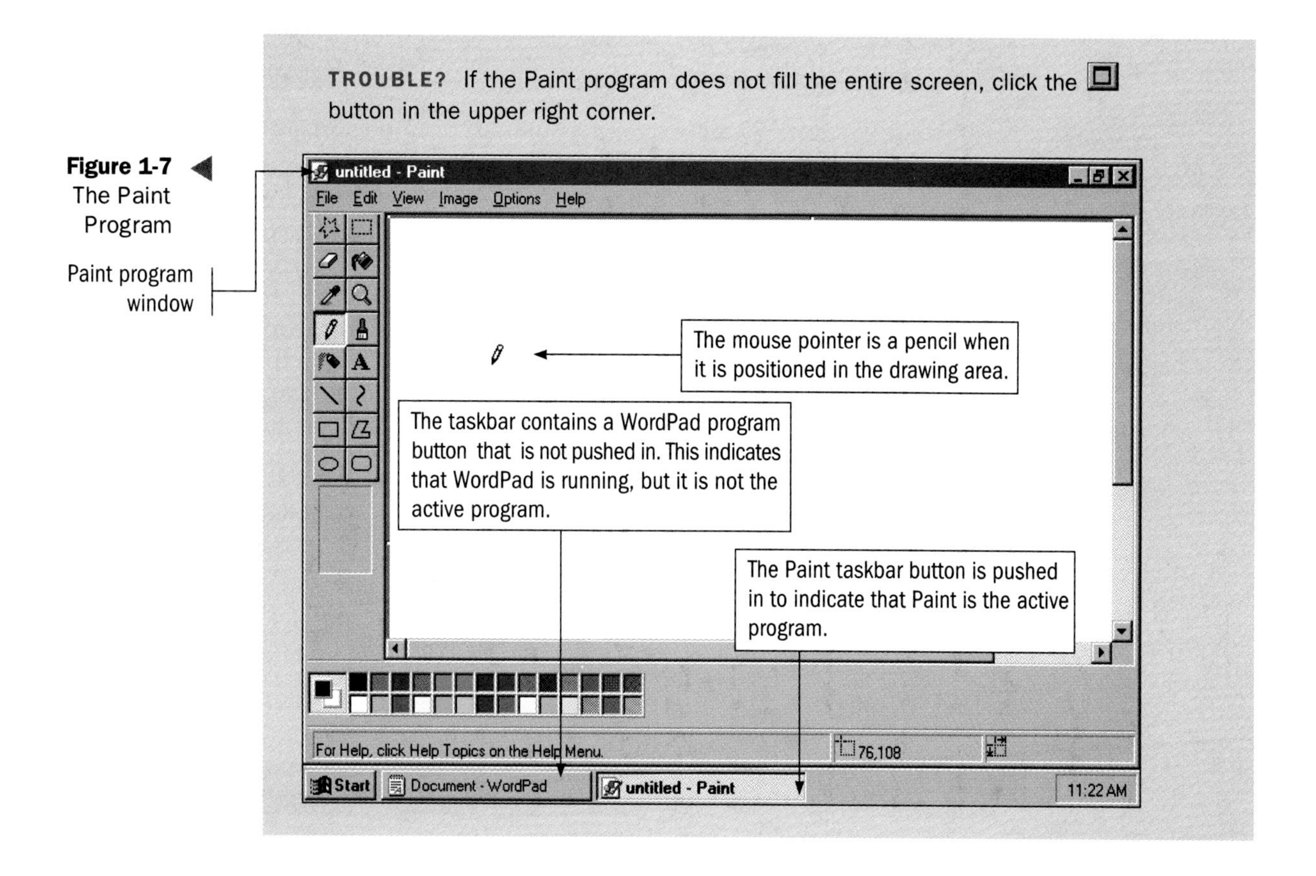

3.1 NOTE

With Windows 3.1, some users had difficulty finding program windows on the desktop. The buttons on the Windows 95 taskbar make it much easier to keep track of which programs are running.

What happened to WordPad? The WordPad button is still on the taskbar, so even if you can't see it, WordPad is still running. You can imagine that it is stacked behind the Paint program, as shown in Figure 1-8.

Figure 1-8 ◀ Programs stacked on top of a desk

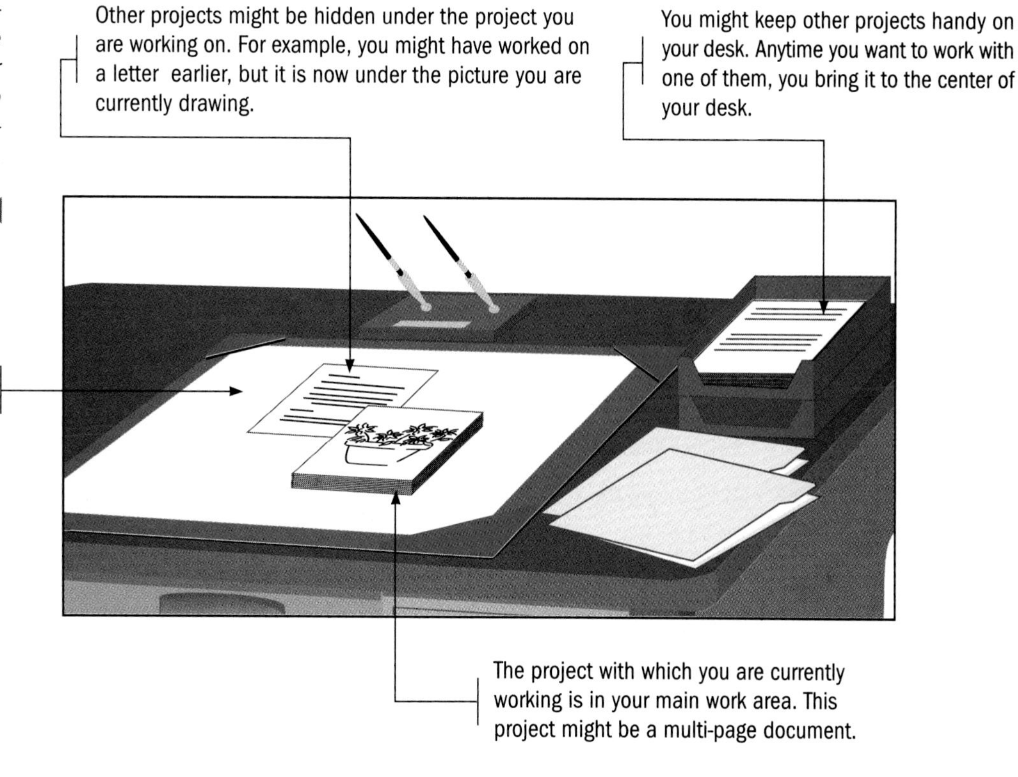

Switching Between Programs

3.1 NOTE

In Windows 95, you can still use Alt-Tab to switch between programs. You can also click on any open window to switch to it.

Although Windows 95 allows you to run more than one program, only one program at a time is active. The **active** program is the program with which you are currently working. The easiest way to switch between programs is to use the buttons on the taskbar.

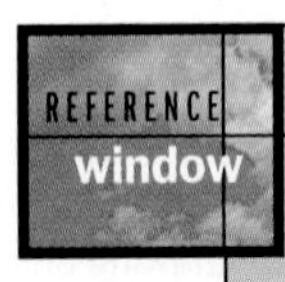

SWITCHING BETWEEN PROGRAMS

- Click the taskbar button that contains the name of the program to which you want to switch.

To switch between WordPad and Paint:

1. Click the button labeled **Document - WordPad** on the taskbar. The Document - WordPad button now looks like it has been pushed in to indicate it is the active program.
2. Next, click the button labeled **untitled - Paint** on the taskbar to switch to the Paint program.

Closing WordPad and Paint

It is good practice to close each program when you are finished using it. Each program uses computer resources such as memory, so Windows 95 works more efficiently when only the programs you need are open.

To close WordPad and Paint:

1. Click the **Close** button ☒ for the Paint program. The button labeled "untitled - Paint" disappears from the taskbar.
2. Click the **Close** button ☒ for the WordPad program. The WordPad button disappears from the taskbar, and you return to the Windows 95 desktop.

Shutting Down Windows 95

It is very important to shut down Windows 95 before you turn off the computer. If you turn off your computer without correctly shutting down, you might lose data and damage your files.

To shut down Windows 95:

1. Click the **Start** button Start on the taskbar to display the Start menu.
2. Click the **Shut Down** menu option to display the Shut Down Windows options screen.
3. Make sure the **Shut down the computer?** option is selected.
4. Click the **Yes** button.
5. Wait until you see a message indicating it is safe to turn off your computer, then switch off your computer.

You should typically use the option "Shut down the computer?" when you want to turn off your computer. However, other shut-down options are available. For example, your school might prefer that you select the option to "Close all programs and log on as a different user." This option logs you out of Windows 95, leaves the computer turned on, and allows another user to log on without restarting the computer. Check with your instructor or technical support person for the preferred method for your school's computer lab.

Quick Check

1 Label the components of the Windows 95 desktop in the figure below:

Figure 1-9

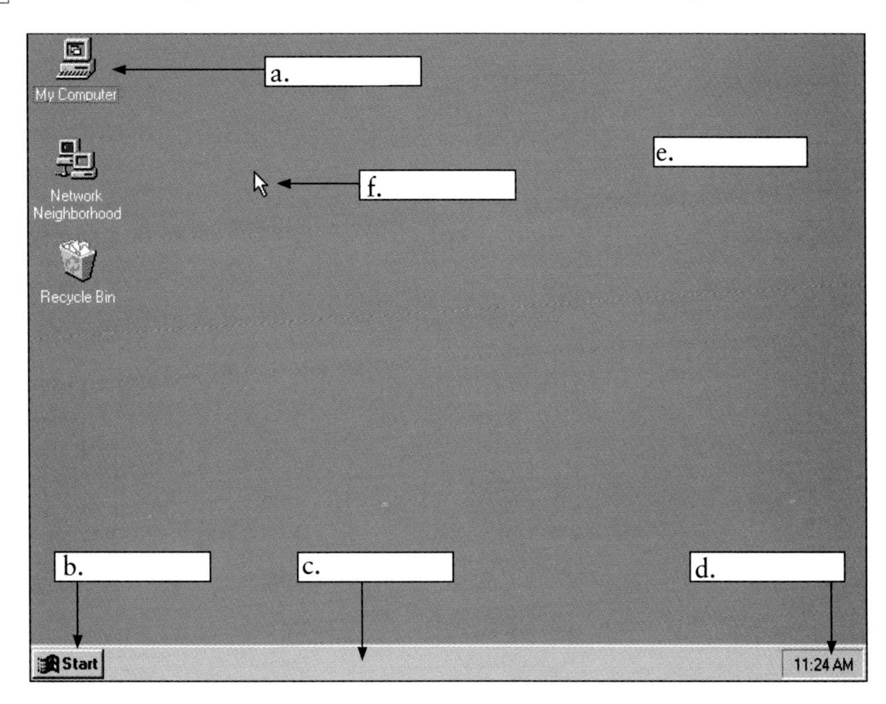

2 The ____________ feature of Windows 95 allows you to run more than one program at a time.

3 The ____________ is a list of options that provides you with access to programs, data, and configuration options.

4 What should you do if you are trying to move the pointer to the left edge of your screen, but your mouse runs into the keyboard?

5 Windows 95 shows you that an icon is selected by ____________ it.

6 Even if you can't see a program, it might be running. How can you tell if a program is running?

7 Why is it good practice to close each program when you are finished using it?

8 Why do you need to shut down Windows 95 before you turn off your computer?

SESSION 1.2

In this session you will learn how to use many of the Windows 95 controls to manipulate windows and programs. You will learn how to change the size and shape of a window and to move a window so that you can customize your screen-based workspace. You will also learn how to use menus, dialog boxes, tabs, buttons, and lists to specify how you want a program to carry out a task.

Anatomy of a Window

When you run a program in Windows 95, it appears in a window. A **window** is a rectangular area of the screen that contains a program or data. A window also contains controls for manipulating the window and using the program. WordPad is a good example of how a window works.

Windows, spelled with an uppercase "W," is the name of the Microsoft operating system. The word "window" with a lowercase "w" refers to one of the rectangular windows on the screen.

To look at window controls:

1. Make sure Windows 95 is running and you are at the Windows 95 desktop screen.
2. Start WordPad.

   TROUBLE? To start WordPad, click the **Start** button, point to Programs, point to Accessories, and then click **WordPad**.
3. Make sure WordPad takes up the entire screen.

   TROUBLE? If WordPad does not take up the entire screen, click the button in the upper right corner.
4. On your screen, identify the controls labeled in Figure 1-10.

Figure 1-10 Window controls

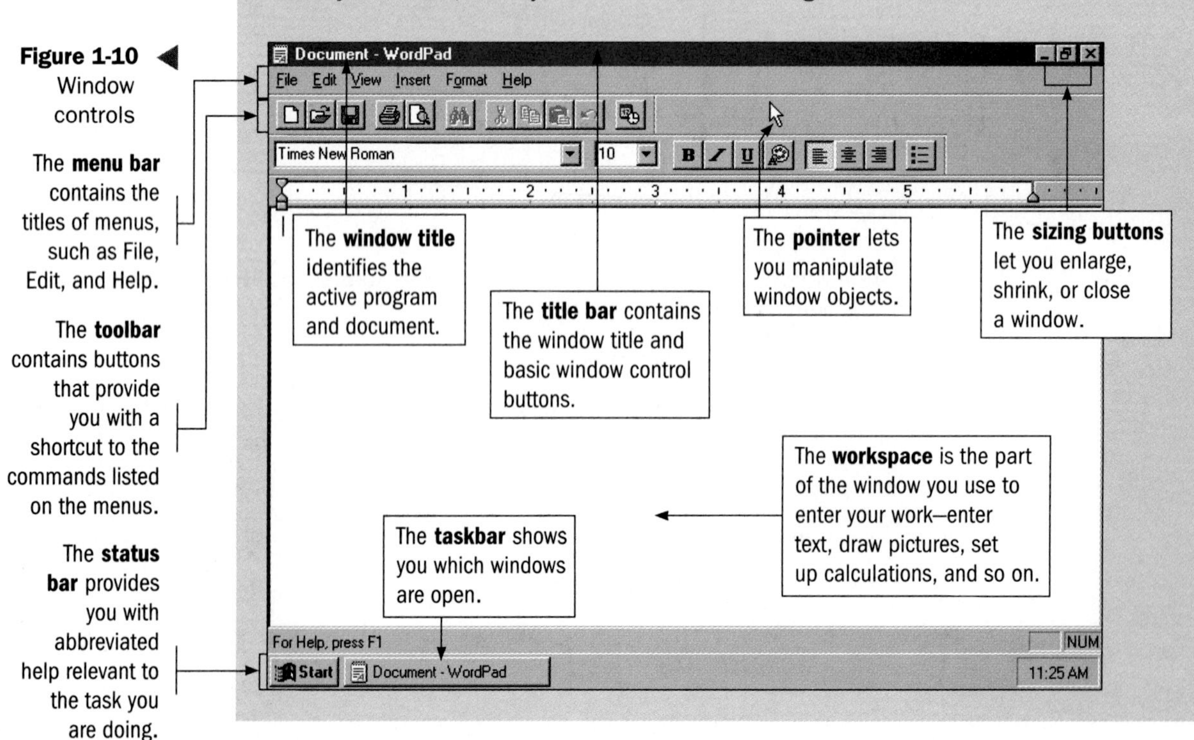

The **menu bar** contains the titles of menus, such as File, Edit, and Help.

The **toolbar** contains buttons that provide you with a shortcut to the commands listed on the menus.

The **status bar** provides you with abbreviated help relevant to the task you are doing.

Manipulating a Window

There are three buttons located on the right side of the title bar. You are already familiar with the Close button. The Minimize button hides the window. The other button either maximizes the window or restores it to a predefined size. Figure 1-11 shows how these buttons work.

Figure 1-11 Minimize, Maximize and Restore buttons

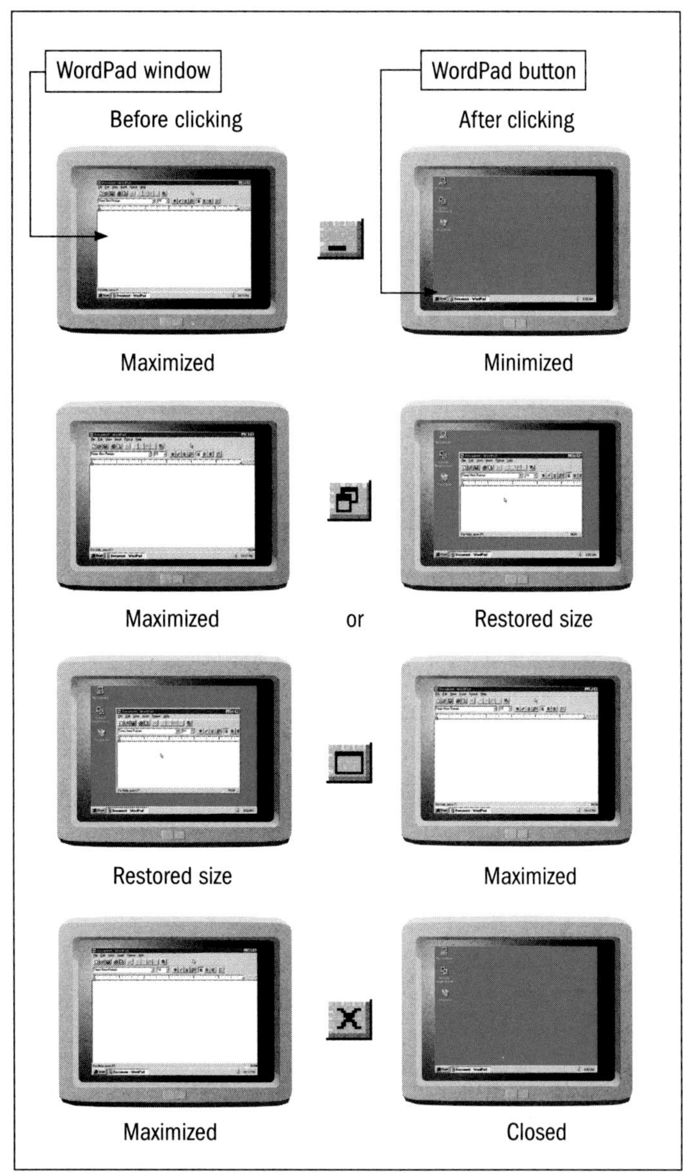

The **Minimize button** shrinks the window, so you only see its button on the taskbar.

The middle button appears as a **Restore button** or a **Maximize button.** When the window is maximized, the Restore button appears. It can be used to reduce the size of the window to a predetermined or "normal" size. When the window does not fill the entire screen, the Maximize button appears. Clicking the Maximize button enlarges the window to fill the screen.

The **Close button** closes the window and removes its button from the taskbar at the bottom of the screen.

Minimizing a Window

The **Minimize button** shrinks the current window so that only the button on the taskbar remains visible. You can use the Minimize button when you want to temporarily hide a window but keep the program running.

To minimize the WordPad window:

1. Click the **Minimize** button. The WordPad window shrinks so only the Document - WordPad button on the taskbar is visible.

   TROUBLE? If you accidentally clicked the Close button and closed the window, use the Start button to start WordPad again.

Redisplaying a Window

You can redisplay a minimized window by clicking the program's button on the taskbar. When you redisplay a window, it becomes the active window.

To redisplay the WordPad window:

1. Click the **Document - WordPad** button on the taskbar. The WordPad window is restored to its previous size. The Document - WordPad button looks pushed in as a visual clue that it is now the active window.

Restoring a Window

The **Restore** button reduces the window so it is smaller than the entire screen. This is useful if you want to see more than one window at a time. Also, because of its small size, you can drag the window to another location on the screen or change its dimensions.

To restore a window:

1. Click the **Restore** button on the WordPad title bar. The WordPad window will look similar to Figure 1-12, but the exact size of the window on your screen might be slightly different.

Figure 1-12 WordPad after clicking the Restore button

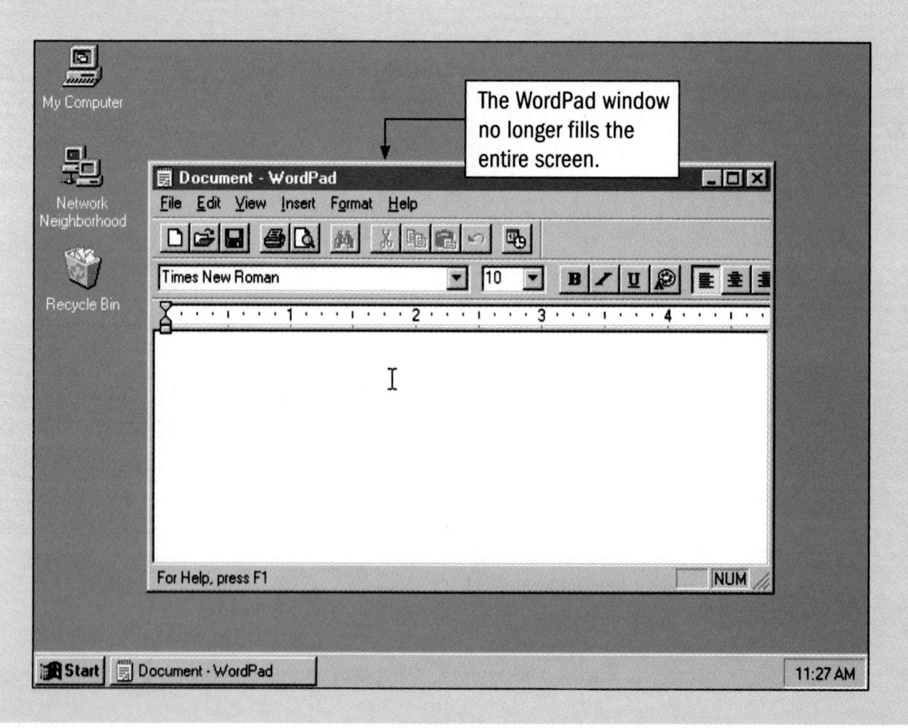

Moving a Window

You can use the mouse to **move** a window to a new position on the screen. When you hold down the mouse button while moving the mouse, it is called **dragging**. You can move objects on the screen by dragging them to a new location. If you want to move a window, you drag its title bar.

To drag the WordPad window to a new location:

1. Position the mouse pointer on the WordPad window title bar.
2. While you hold down the left mouse button, move the mouse to drag the window. A rectangle representing the window moves as you move the mouse.
3. Position the rectangle anywhere on the screen, then release the left mouse button. The WordPad window appears in the new location.
4. Now drag the WordPad window to the upper-left corner of the screen.

Changing the Size of a Window

3.1 NOTE

You can also change the size of a window by dragging the top, bottom, sides, and corners of the window, as you did in Windows 3.1.

You can also use the mouse to change the size of a window. Notice the sizing handle at the lower right corner of the window. The **sizing handle** provides a visible control for changing the size of a current window.

To change the size of the WordPad window:

1. Position the pointer over the sizing handle. The pointer changes to a diagonal arrow.
2. While holding down the mouse button, drag the sizing handle down and to the right.
3. Release the mouse button. Now the window is larger.
4. Practice using the sizing handle to make the WordPad window larger or smaller.

Maximizing a Window

The **Maximize button** enlarges a window so that it fills the entire screen. You will probably do most of your work using maximized windows because you can see more of your program and data.

To maximize the WordPad window:

1. Click the **Maximize** button on the WordPad title bar.

Using Program Menus

Most Windows programs use menus to provide an easy way for you to select program commands. The **menu bar** is typically located at the top of the program window and shows the titles of menus such as File, Edit, and Help.

Windows menus are relatively standardized—most Windows programs include similar menu options. It's easy to learn new programs, because you can make a pretty good guess about which menu contains the command you want.

Selecting Commands from a Menu

When you click any menu title, choices for that menu appear below the menu bar. These choices are referred to as **menu options.** To select a menu option, you click it. For example, the File menu is a standard feature in most Windows programs and contains the options related to working with a file: creating, opening, saving, and printing a file or document.

To select Print Preview from the File menu:

1. Click **File** in the WordPad menu bar to display the File menu.

   TROUBLE? If you open a menu but decide not to select any of the menu options, you can close the menu by clicking its title again.

2. Click **Print Preview** to open the preview screen and view your document as it will appear when printed. This document is blank because you didn't enter any text.

3. After examining the screen, click the button labeled "Close" to return to your document.

Not all menu options immediately carry out an action—some show submenus or ask you for more information about what you want to do. The menu gives you hints about what to expect when you select an option. These hints are sometimes referred to as **menu conventions.** Study Figures 1-13a and 1-13b so you will recognize the Windows 95 menu conventions.

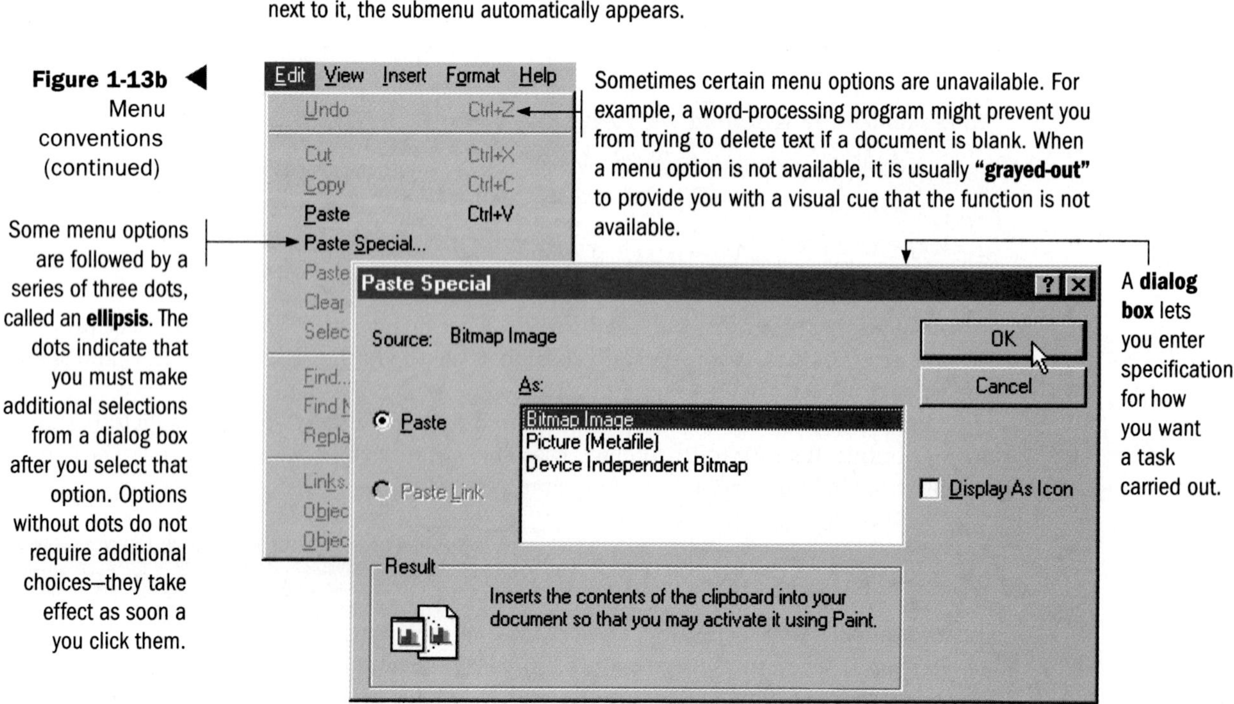

Figure 1-13a Menu Conventions

Figure 1-13b Menu conventions (continued)

Using Toolbars

A **toolbar** contains buttons that provide quick access to important program commands. Although you can usually perform all program commands using the menus, the toolbar provides convenient one-click access to frequently-used commands. For most Windows 95 functions, there is usually more than one way to accomplish a task. To simplify your introduction to Windows 95 in this tutorial, you will learn only one method for performing a task. As you become more accomplished using Windows 95, you can explore alternative methods.

In Session 1.1 you learned that Windows 95 programs include ToolTips that indicate the purpose and function of a tool. Now is a good time to explore the WordPad toolbar buttons by looking at their ToolTips.

To find out a toolbar button's function:

1. Position the pointer over any button on the toolbar, such as the Print Preview icon. After a short pause, the name of the button appears in a box and a description of the button appears in the status bar just above the Start button.
2. Move the pointer to each button on the toolbar to see its name and purpose.

You select a toolbar button by clicking it.

To select the Print Preview toolbar button:

1. Click the **Print Preview** button.
2. The Print Preview dialog box appears. This is the same dialog box that appeared when you selected File, Print Preview from the menu bar.
3. Click Close to close the Print Preview dialog box.

Using List Boxes and Scroll Bars

As you might guess from the name, a **list box** displays a list of choices. In WordPad, date and time formats are shown in the Date/Time list box. List box controls include arrow buttons, a scroll bar, and a scroll box, as shown in Figure 1-14.

Figure 1-14 List Box

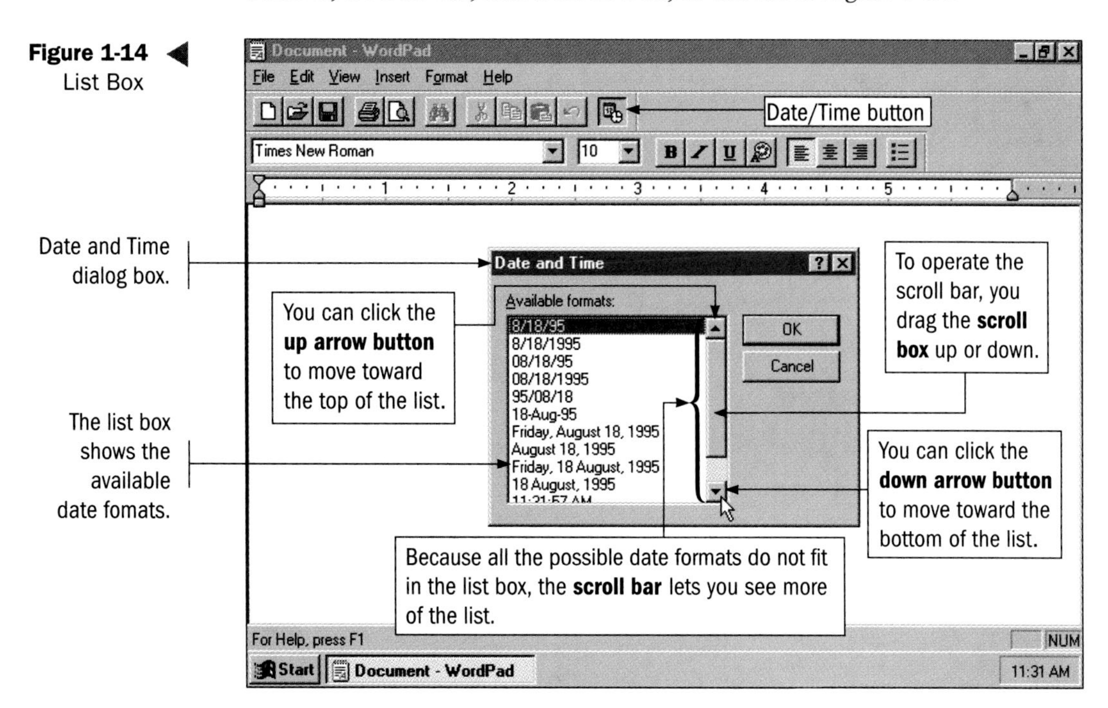

To use the Date/Time list box:

1. Click the **Date/Time** button to display the Date and Time dialog box. See Figure 1-14.
2. To scroll down the list, click the **down arrow** button. See Figure 1-14.
3. Find the scroll box on your screen. See Figure 1-14.
4. Drag the **scroll box** to the top of the scroll bar. Notice how the list scrolls back to the beginning.
5. Find a date format similar to "October 2, 1997." Click that date format to select it.
6. Click the **OK** button to close the Date and Time list box.This inserts the current date in your document.

A variation of the list box, called a **drop-down list box**, usually shows only one choice, but can expand down to display additional choices on the list.

To use the Type Size drop-down list:

1. Click the **down arrow** button shown in Figure 1-15.

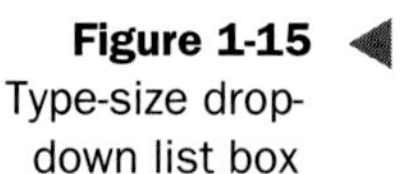
Figure 1-15 Type-size drop-down list box

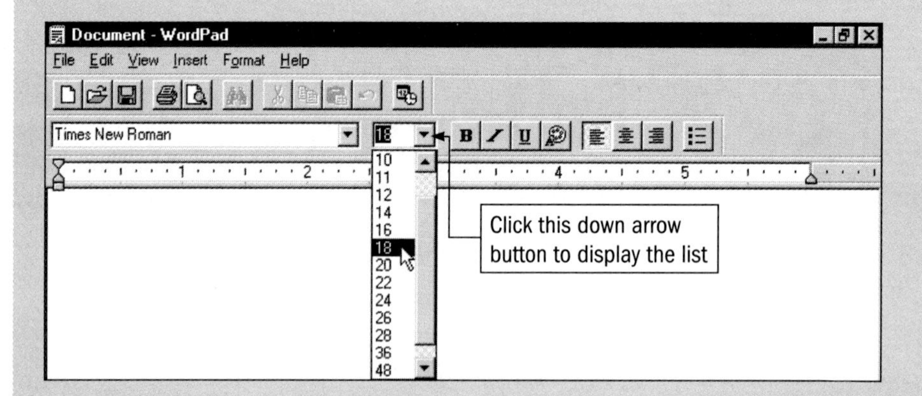

2. Click **18**. The drop-down list disappears and the type size you selected appears at the top of the pull-down list.
3. Type a few characters to test the new type size.
4. Click the **down arrow** button in the Type size drop-down list box again.
5. Click **12**.
6. Type a few characters to test this type size.
7. Click the **Close** button to close WordPad.
8. When you see the message "Save changes to Document?" click the **No** button.

Using Tab Controls, Radio Buttons, and Check Boxes

Dialog boxes often use tabs, radio buttons, or check boxes to collect information about how you want a program to perform a task. A **tab control** is patterned after the tabs on file folders. You click the appropriate tab to view different pages of information or choices. Tab controls are often used as containers for other Windows 95 controls such as list boxes, radio buttons, and check boxes.

Radio buttons, also called **option buttons**, allow you to select a single option from among one or more options. **Check boxes** allow you to select many options at the same time. Figure 1-16 explains how to use these controls.

Figure 1-16 Tabs, radio buttons, and check boxes

A **tab** indicates an "index card" that contains information or a group of controls, usually with related functions. To look at the functions on an index card, click the tab.

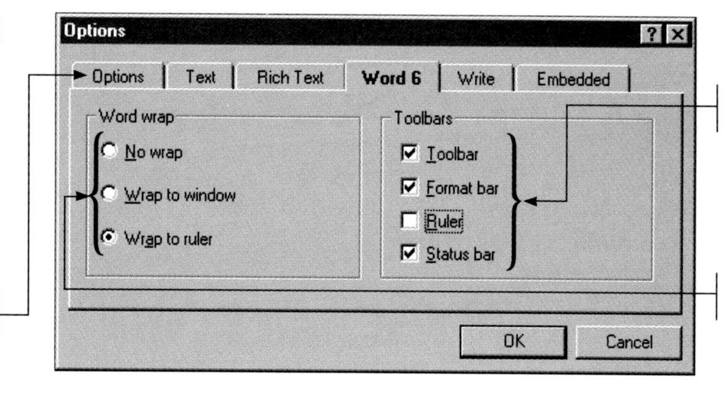

Check boxes allow you to select one or more options from a group. When you click a check box, a check mark appears in it. To remove a check mark from a box, click it again.

Radio buttons are round and usually come in groups of two or more. You can select only one radio button from a group. Your selection is indicated by a black dot.

Using Help

Windows 95 **Help** provides on-screen information about the program you are using. Help for the Windows 95 operating system is available by clicking the Start button on the taskbar, then selecting Help from the Start menu. If you want Help for a program, such as WordPad, you must first start the program, then use the Help menu at the top of the screen.

STARTING WINDOWS 95 HELP

- Click the Start button.
- Click Help.

To start Windows 95 Help:

1. Click the **Start** button.
2. Click **Help.**

Help uses tabs for each section of Help. Windows 95 Help tabs include Contents, Index, and Find as shown in Figure 1-17 on the following page.

Figure 1-17 ◀ Windows 95 Help

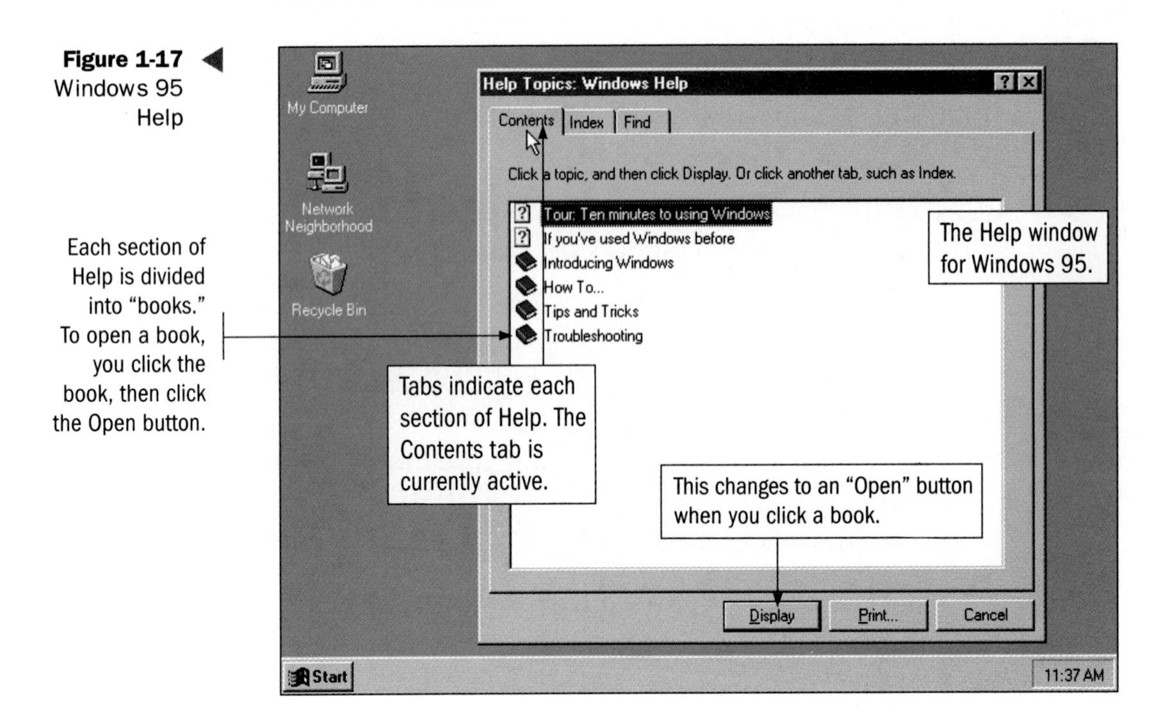

The **Contents tab** groups Help topics into a series of books. You select a book, which then provides you with a list of related topics from which you can choose. The **Index tab** displays an alphabetical list of all the Help topics from which you can choose. The **Find tab** lets you search for any word or phrase in Help.

Suppose you're wondering if there is an alternative way to start programs. You can use the Contents tab to find the answer to your question.

3.1 NOTE

You can also double-click to select and open a topic in a single step.

To use the Contents tab:

1. Click the **Contents** tab to display the Contents window.
2. Click the **How To...** book title, then click the **Open** button. A list of related books appears below the book title. See. Figure 1-18.

Figure 1-18 ◀ Help Window

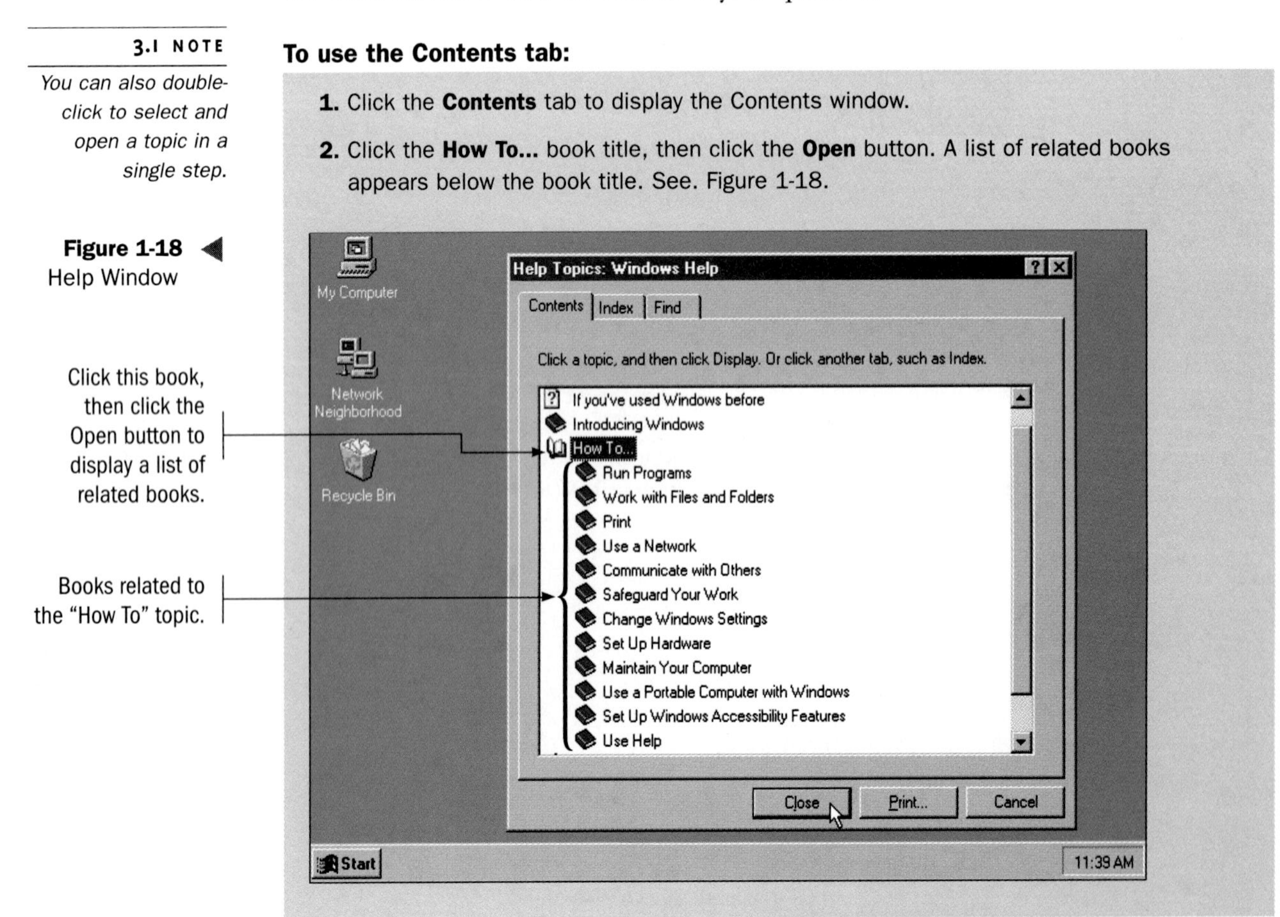

3. Click the **Run Programs** book, then click the **Open** button. The table of contents for this Help book is displayed.
4. Click the topic **Starting a Program**, then click the **Display** button. A Help window appears and explains how to start a program.

Help also provides you with definitions of technical terms. You can click any underlined term to see its definition.

To see a definition of the term "taskbar":

1. Point to the underlined term, **taskbar** until the pointer changes to a hand. Then click.
2. After you have read the definition, click the definition to deselect it.
3. Click the **Close** button on the Help window.

The **Index tab** allows you to jump to a Help topic by selecting a topic from an indexed list. For example, you can use the Index tab to learn how to arrange the open windows on your desktop.

To find a Help topic using the Index tab:

1. Click the **Start** button.
2. Click **Help**.
3. Click the **Index** tab.
4. A long list of indexed Help topics appears. Drag the scroll box down to view additional topics.
5. You can quickly jump to any part of the list by typing the first few characters of a word or phrase in the line above the Index list. Type **desktop** to display topics related to the Windows 95 desktop.
6. Click the topic **arranging open windows on** in the bottom window.
7. Click the **Display** button as shown in Figure 1-19.

Figure 1-19 Displaying a Help Topic

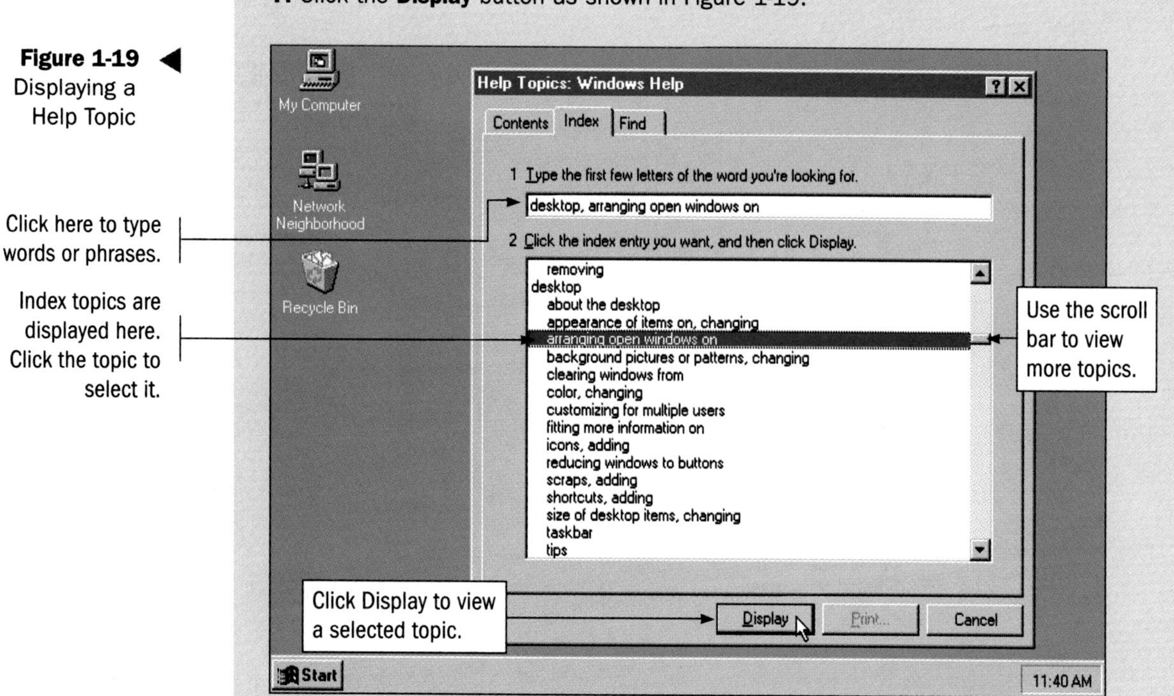

8. Click the **Close** button [X] to close the Windows Help window.

The **Find tab** contains an index of all words in Windows 95 Help. You can use it to search for Help pages that contain a particular word or phrase. For example, suppose you heard that a screen saver blanks out your screen when you are not using it. You could use the Find tab to find out more about screen savers.

To find a Help topic using the Find tab:

1. Click the **Start** button [Start].
2. Click **Help**.
3. Click the **Find** tab.

   TROUBLE? If the Find index has not yet been created on your computer, the computer will prompt you through several steps to create the index. Continue with Step 4 below after the Find index is created.

4. Type **screen** to display a list of all topics that start with the letters "screen."
5. Click **screen-saver** in the middle window to display the topics that contain the word "screen-saver."
6. Click **Having your monitor automatically turn off**, then click the **Display** button.
7. Click the **Help window** button shown in Figure 1-20. The screen saver is shown on a simulated monitor.

   TROUBLE? If you see an error message, your lab does not allow students to modify screen savers. Click the OK button and go to Step 9.

Figure 1-20 Clicking a Button in Help

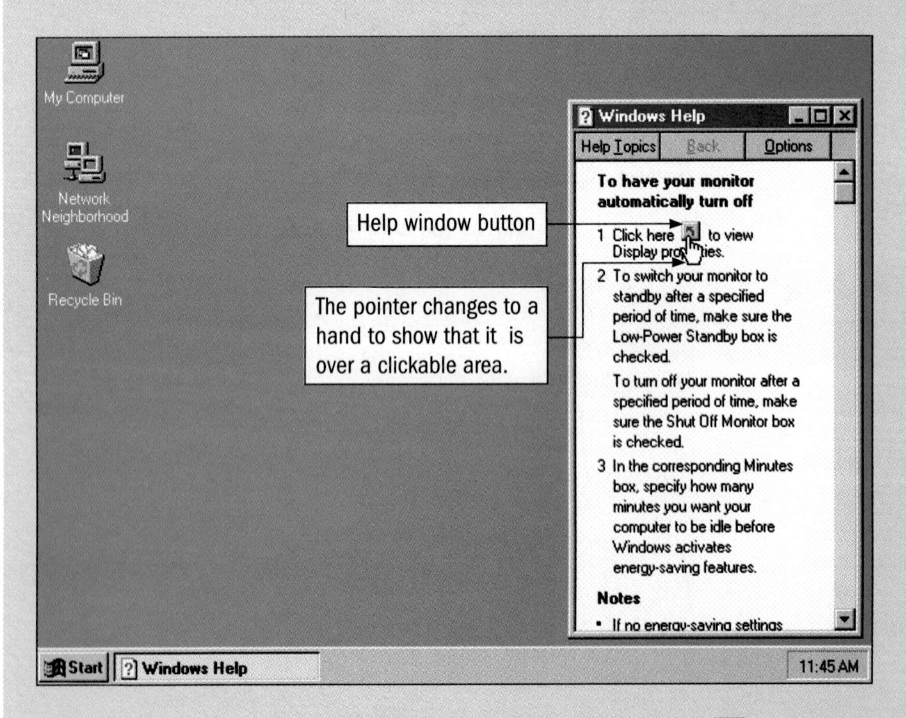

8. To close the Display properties window, click the **Close** button [X] in the Display Properties window.
9. Click the **Close** button [X] to close the Help window.

Now that you know how Windows 95 Help works, don't forget to use it! Use Help when you need to perform a new task or when you forget how to complete a procedure.

Quick Check

1 Label the parts of the window shown in Figure 1-21.

Figure 1-21

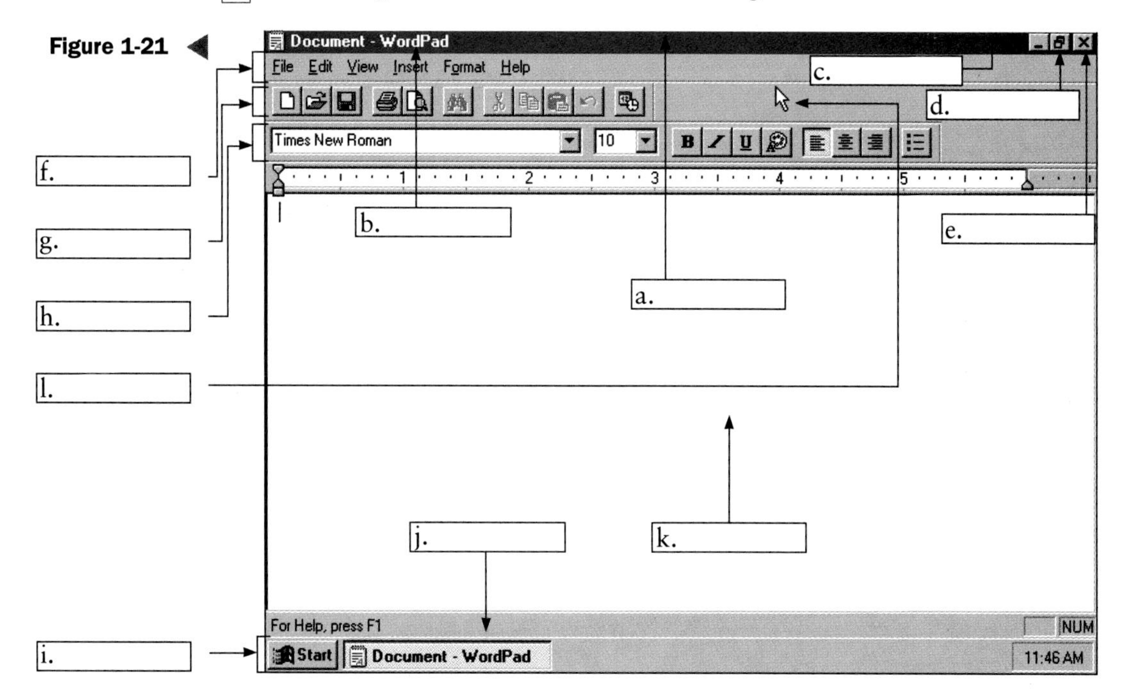

2 Provide the name and purpose of each button:
a.
b.
c.
d.

3 Explain each of the following menu conventions:
a. Ellipsis...
b. Grayed out
c. ▶
d. ✔

4 A(n) ___________ consists of a group of buttons, each of which provides one-click access to important program functions.

5 Label each part of the dialog box below:

Figure 1-22

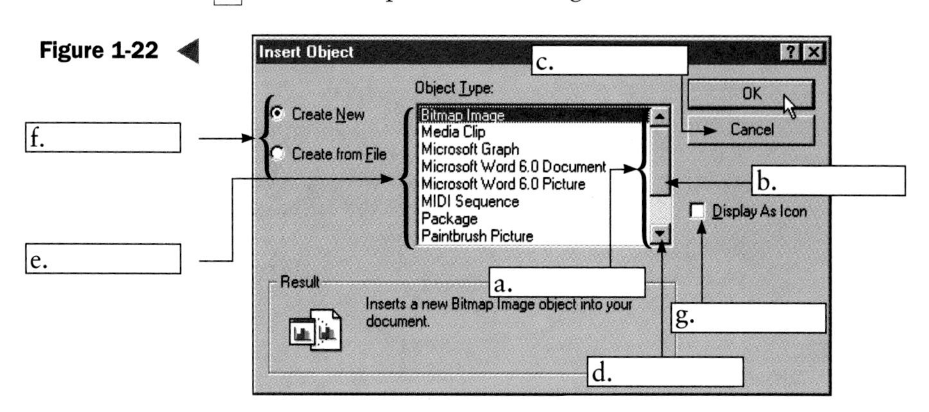

6 Radio buttons allow you to select __________ option(s) at a time, but __________ allow you to select one or more options.

7 It is a good idea to use __________ when you need to learn how to perform new tasks, simplify tedious procedures, and correct actions that did not turn out as you expected.

End Note

You've finished the tutorial, but Steve Laslow still hasn't returned. Take a moment to review what you have learned. You now know how to start a program using the Start button. You can run more than one program at a time and switch between programs using the buttons on the taskbar. You have learned the names and functions of window controls and Windows 95 menu conventions. You can now use toolbar buttons, list boxes, drop-down lists, radio buttons, check boxes, and scroll bars. Finally, you can use the Contents, Index, and Find tabs in Help to extend your knowledge of how to use Windows 95.

Tutorial Assignments

1. Running Two Programs and Switching Between Them In this tutorial you learned how to run more than one program at a time using WordPad and Paint. You can run other programs at the same time, too. Complete the following steps and write out your answers to questions b through f:

a. Start the computer. Enter your user name and password if prompted to do so.
b. Click the Start button. How many menu options are on the Start menu?
c. Run the program Calculator program located on the Programs, Accessories menu. How many buttons are now on the taskbar?
d. Run the Paint program and maximize the Paint window. How many application programs are running now?
e. Switch to Calculator. What are the two visual clues that tell you that Calculator is the active program?
f. Multiply 576 by 1457. What is the result?
g. Close Calculator, then close Paint.

2. WordPad Help In Tutorial 1 you learned how to use Windows 95 Help. Just about every Windows 95 program has a help feature. Many computer users can learn to use a program just by using Help. To use Help, you would start the program, then click the Help menu at the top of the screen. Try using WordPad Help and complete steps a, b, and c:

a. Start WordPad.
b. Click Help on the WordPad menu bar, then click Help Topics.
c. Using WordPad help, write out your answers to questions 1 through 3.
   1. How do you create a bulleted list?
   2. How do you set the margins in a document?
   3. What happens if you hold down the Alt key and press the Print Screen key?

3. Using Help to Explore Paint In this assignment, you will use the Paint Help to learn how to use the Paint program. Your goal is to create and print a picture that looks like the one in Figure 1-23.

Figure 1-23

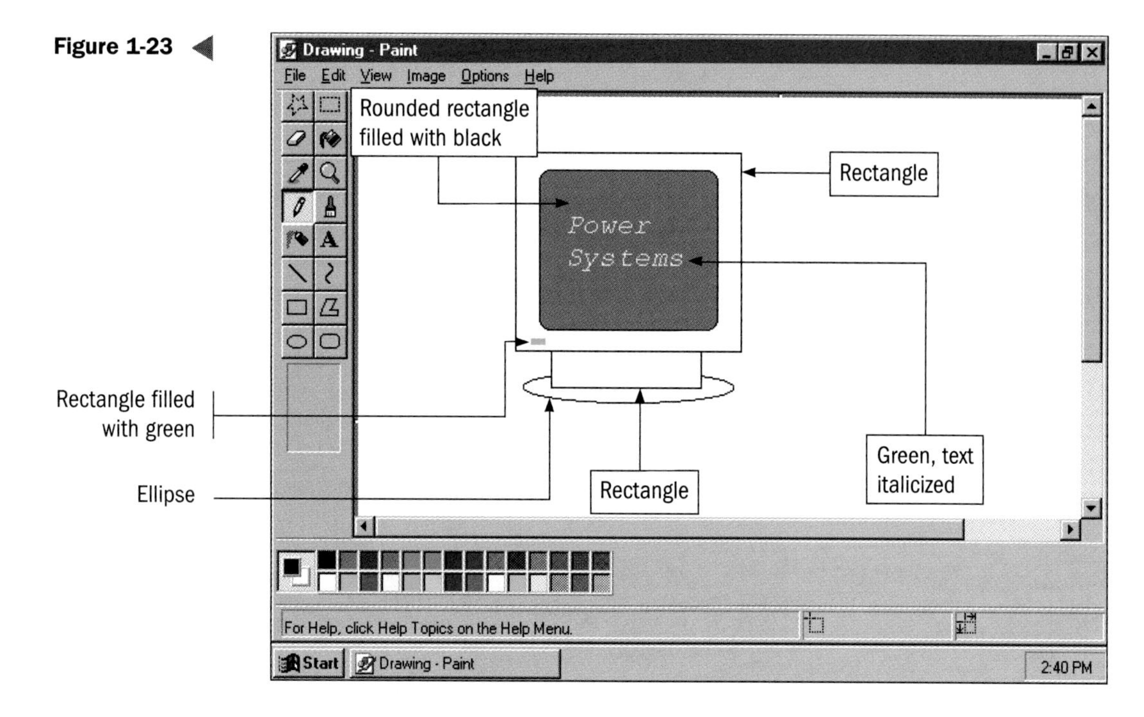

a. Start Paint.
b. Click Help, then click Help Topics.
c. Use Paint Help to learn how to put text in a picture and how to draw rectangles and circles.
d. Draw a picture of a monitor using rectangles, circles, and text as shown in Figure 1-23.
e. Print your picture.

4. The Windows 95 Tutorial Windows 95 includes a five part on-line tutorial. In Tutorial 1 you learned about starting programs, switching windows, and using Help. You can use the on-line Windows 95 Tutorial to review what you learned and pick up some new tips for using Windows 95. Complete the following steps and write out your answers to questions f, g, and h:

a. Click the Start button to display the Start menu.
b. Click Help to display Windows help.
c. Click the Contents tab.
d. From the Contents screen, click Tour: Ten minutes to using Windows.
e. Click the Display button. If an error message appears, the Tour is probably not loaded on your computer. You will not be able to complete this assignment. Click Cancel, then click OK to cancel and check with your instructor or technical support person.
f. Click Starting a Program and complete the tutorial. What are the names of the seven programs on the Accessories menu in the tutorial?
g. Click Switching Windows and complete the on-line tutorial. What does the Minimize button do?
h. Click Using Help and complete the tutorial. What is the purpose of the ? button?
i. Click the Exit button to close the Tour window.
j. Click the Exit Tour button to exit the Tour and return to the Windows 95 desktop.

Lab Assignments

1. Learning to Use the Keyboard If you are not familiar with computer keyboards, you will find the Keyboard Lab helpful. This Lab will give you a structured introduction to special computer keys and their function in Windows 95. As you work through the Lab, you will be asked to answer Quick Check questions about what you have learned. At the end of the lab, you will see a summary report of your answers. If your instructor wants you to print out your answers to these questions, click the Print button on the summary report screen.

a. Click the Start button.
b. Point to Programs, then point to CTI Windows 95 Applications.
c. Click Windows 95 New Perspectives Brief.
d. Click Using a Keyboard. If you cannot find Windows 95 New Perspectives Brief or Using a Keyboard, ask for help from your instructor or technical support person.

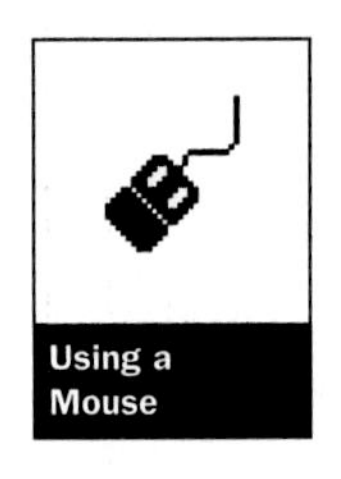

2. Mouse Practice If you would like more practice using a mouse, you can complete the Mouse Lab. As you work through the Lab, you will be asked to answer Quick Check questions about what you have learned. At the end of the lab, the Quick Check Report shows you how you did. If your instructor wants you to print out your answers to these questions, click the Print button on the summary report screen.

a. Click the Start button.
b. Point to Programs, then point to CTI Windows 95.
c. Point to Windows 95 New Perspectives Brief.
d. Click Using a Mouse. If you cannot find Windows 95 New Perspectives Brief or Using a Mouse, ask for help from your instructor or technical support person.

TUTORIAL 2

Working with Files

OBJECTIVES

In this tutorial you will learn to:

- Format a disk
- Enter, select, insert, and delete text
- Create and save a file
- Open and edit a file
- Print a file
- Create a Student Disk
- View the list of files on your disk
- Move, copy, delete, and rename a file
- Make a backup of your floppy disk

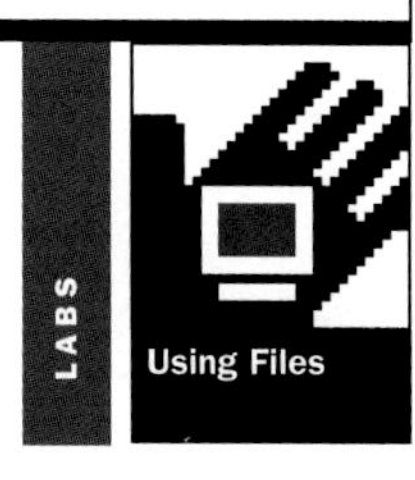

CASE

Your First Day in the Lab—Continued

Steve Laslow is back from class, grinning. "I see you're making progress!"

"That's right," you reply. "I know how to run programs, control windows, and use Help. I guess I'm ready to work with my word-processing and spreadsheet software now."

Steve hesitates before he continues, "You could, but there are a few more things about Windows 95 that you should learn first."

Steve explains that most of the software you have on your computer—your word-processing, spreadsheet, scheduling, and graphing software—was created especially for the Windows 95 operating system. This software is referred to as **Windows 95 applications** or **Windows 95 programs**. You can also use software designed for Windows 3.1, but Windows 95 applications give you more flexibility. For example, when you name a document in a Windows 95 application, you can use descriptive filenames with up to 255 characters, whereas in Windows 3.1 you are limited to eight-character names.

You typically use Windows 95 applications to create files. A **file** is a collection of data that has a name and is stored in a computer. You typically create files that contain documents, pictures, and graphs when you use software packages. For example, you might use word-processing software to create a file containing a document. Once you create a file, you can open it, edit its contents, print it, and save it again—usually using the same application program you used to create it.

Another advantage of Windows 95 is that once you know how to save, open, and print files with one Windows 95 application, you can perform those same functions in *any* Windows 95 application. This is because Windows 95 applications have similar controls. For example, your word-processing and spreadsheet software will have identical menu commands to save, open, and print documents. Steve suggests that it would be worth a few minutes of your time to become familiar with these menus in Windows 95 applications.

You agree, but before you can get to work, Steve gives you one final suggestion: you should also learn how to keep track of the files on your disk. For instance, you might need to find a file you have not used for a while or you might want to delete a file if your disk is getting full. You will definitely want to make a backup copy of your disk in case something happens to the original. Steve's advice seems practical, and you're eager to explore these functions so you can get to work!

Tutorial 2 will help you learn how to work with Windows 95 applications and keep track of the files on your disk. When you've completed this tutorial, you'll be ready to tackle all kinds of Windows 95 software!

SESSION 2.1

In Session 2.1 you will learn how to format a disk so it can store files. You will create, save, open, and print a file. You will find out how the insertion point is different from the mouse pointer, and you will learn the basic skills for Windows 95 text entry, such as inserting, deleting, and selecting.
For this session you will need two blank 3 ½-inch disks.

Formatting a Disk

Before you can save files on a disk, the disk must be formatted. When the computer **formats** a disk, the magnetic particles on the disk surface are arranged so data can be stored on the disk. Today, many disks are sold preformatted and can be used right out of the box. However, if you purchase an unformatted disk, or if you have an old disk that you want to completely erase and reuse, you can format the disk using the Windows 95 Format command.

The following steps tell you how to format a 3 ½-inch high-density disk using drive A. Your instructor will tell you how to revise the instructions given in these steps if the procedure is different for your lab equipment.

All data on the disk you format will be erased, so don't perform these steps using a disk that contains important files.

To format a disk:

1. Start Windows 95, if necessary.
2. Write your name on the label of a 3 ½-inch disk.
3. Insert your disk in drive A. See Figure 2-1.

Figure 2-1 Inserting a disk into the disk drive

TROUBLE? If your disk does not fit in drive A, put it in drive B and substitute drive B for drive A in all of the steps for the rest of the tutorial.

4. Click the **My Computer** icon to select it, then press the **Enter** key. Make sure you can see the My Computer window. See Figure 2-2.

TROUBLE? If you see a list instead of icons like those in Figure 2-2, click View. Then click Large Icon.

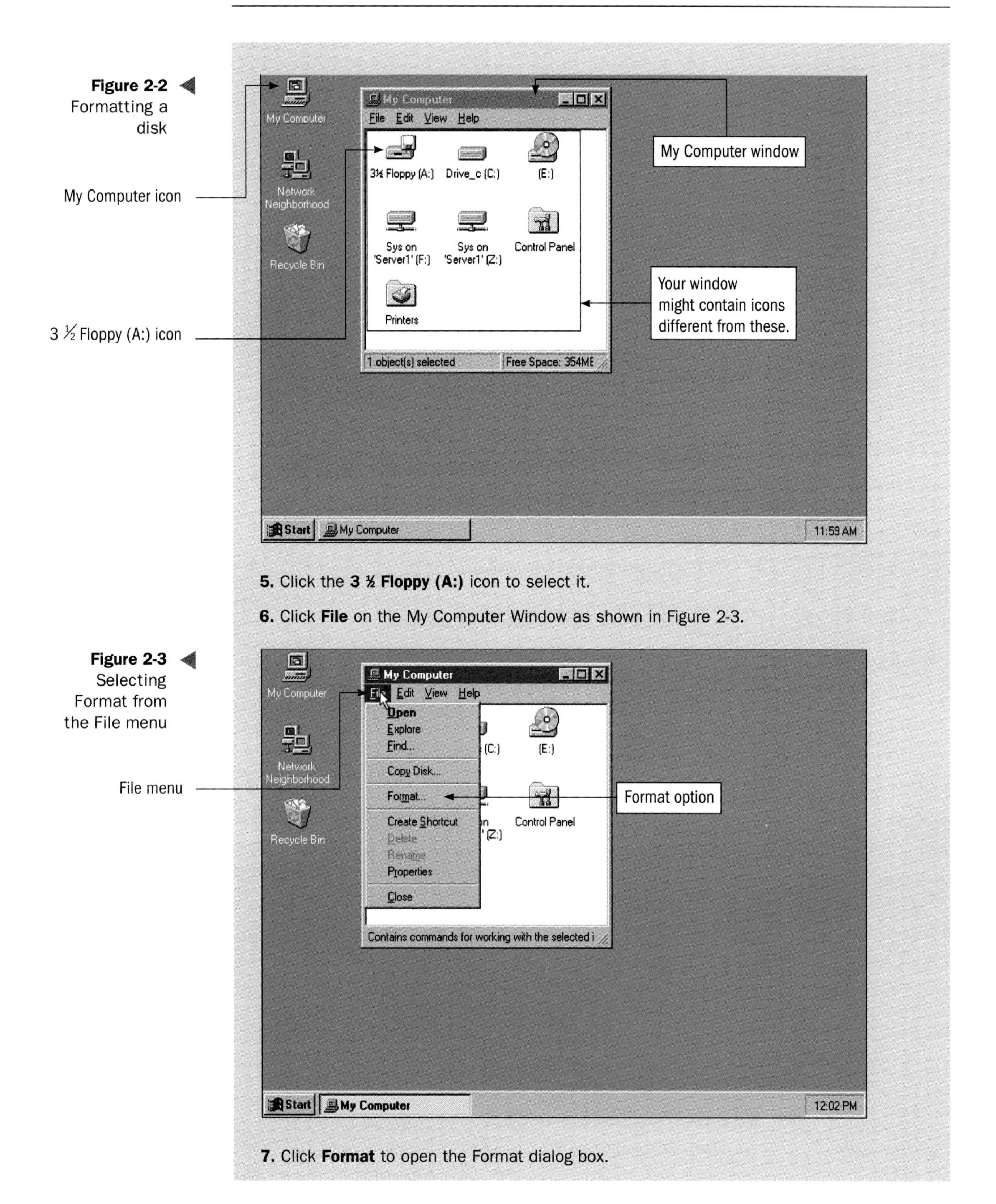

Figure 2-2 Formatting a disk

5. Click the **3 ½ Floppy (A:)** icon to select it.

6. Click **File** on the My Computer Window as shown in Figure 2-3.

Figure 2-3 Selecting Format from the File menu

7. Click **Format** to open the Format dialog box.

8. Make sure the dialog box settings on your screen match those in Figure 2-4.

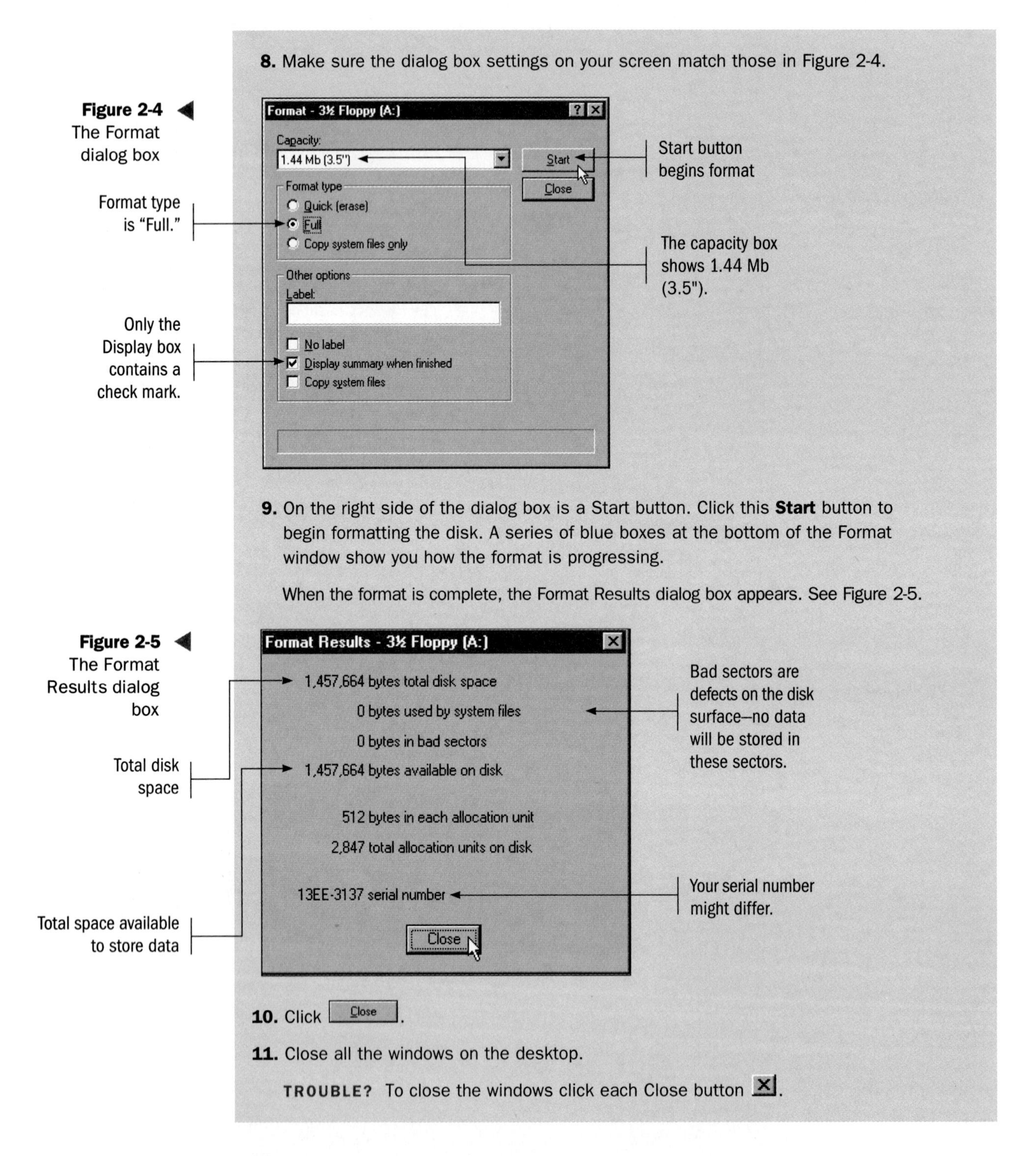

Figure 2-4 The Format dialog box

9. On the right side of the dialog box is a Start button. Click this **Start** button to begin formatting the disk. A series of blue boxes at the bottom of the Format window show you how the format is progressing.

   When the format is complete, the Format Results dialog box appears. See Figure 2-5.

Figure 2-5 The Format Results dialog box

10. Click Close.

11. Close all the windows on the desktop.

    TROUBLE? To close the windows click each Close button.

Working with Text

To accomplish many computing tasks, you need to type text in documents and text boxes. Windows 95 facilitates basic text entry by providing a text-entry area, by showing you where your text will appear on the screen, by helping you move around on the screen, and by providing insert and delete functions.

When you type sentences and paragraphs of text, do *not* press the Enter key when you reach the right margin. The software contains a feature called **word wrap** that automatically continues your text on the next line. Therefore, you should press Enter only when you have completed a paragraph.

If you type the wrong character, press the Backspace key to backup and delete the character. You can also use the Delete key. What's the difference between the Backspace and the Delete keys? The Backspace key deletes the character to left. The Delete key deletes the character to the right.

Now you will type some text using WordPad to learn about text entry.

To type text in WordPad:

1. Start WordPad.

   TROUBLE? If the WordPad window does not fill the screen, click the Maximize button.

2. Notice the flashing vertical bar, called the **insertion point**, in the upper-left corner of the document window. The insertion point indicates where the characters you type will appear.

3. Type your name, using the shift key to type uppercase letters and using the space bar to type spaces, just like on a typewriter.

4. Press the **Enter** key to end the current paragraph and move the insertion point down to the next line.

5. As you type the following sentences, watch what happens when the insertion point reaches the right edge of the screen:

This is a sample typed in WordPad. See what happens when the insertion point reaches the right edge of the screen.

TROUBLE? If you make a mistake, delete the incorrect character(s) by pressing the Backspace key on your keyboard. Then type the correct character(s).

The Insertion Point versus the Pointer

The insertion point is not the same as the mouse pointer. When the mouse pointer is in the text-entry area, it is called the **I-beam pointer** and looks like I. Figure 2-6 explains the difference between the insertion point and the I-beam pointer.

Figure 2-6 The insertion point vs. the pointer

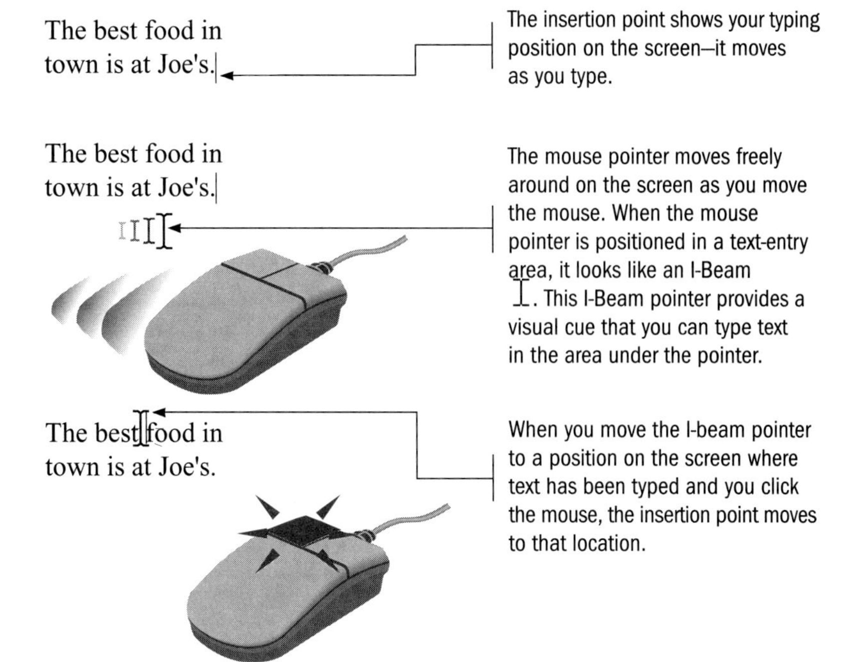

To move the insertion point:

1. Check the location of the insertion point and the I-beam pointer. The insertion point should be at the end of the sentence you typed in the last set of steps.

   TROUBLE? If you don't see the I-beam pointer, move your mouse until you see it.

2. Use the mouse to move the I-beam pointer to the word "sample," then click the left mouse button. The insertion point jumps to the location of the I-beam pointer.

3. Move the I-beam pointer to a blank area near the bottom of the work space and click the left mouse button. *Notice that the insertion point does not jump to the location of the I-beam pointer.* Instead the insertion point jumps to the end of the last sentence. The insertion point can move only within existing text. It cannot be moved out of the existing text area.

Selecting Text

Many text operations are performed on a **block** of text, which is one or more consecutive words, sentences, or paragraphs. Once you select a block of text, you can delete it, move it, replace it, underline it, and so on. As you select a block of text, the computer highlights it. If you want to remove the highlighting, just click in the margin of your document.

Suppose you want to replace the phrase "See what happens" with "You can watch word wrap in action." You do not have to delete the text one character at a time. Instead you can highlight the entire phrase and begin to type the replacement text.

To select and replace a block of text:

1. Move the I-beam pointer just to the left of the word "See."

2. While holding down the left mouse button, drag the I-beam pointer over the text to the end of the word "happens." The phrase "See what happens" should now be highlighted. See Figure 2-7.

Figure 2-7 Highlighting text

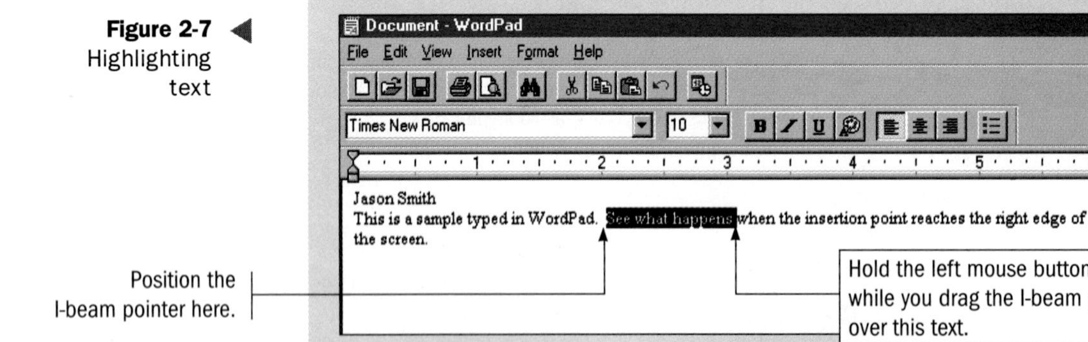

3. Release the left mouse button.

   TROUBLE? If the phrase is not highlighted correctly, repeat Steps 1 through 3.

4. Type: **You can watch word wrap in action**

   The text you typed replaces the highlighted text. Notice that you did not need to delete the highlighted text before you typed the replacement text.

Inserting a Character

Windows 95 programs usually operate in **insert mode**—when you type a new character, all characters to the right of the cursor are pushed over to make room.

Suppose you want to insert the word "sentence" before the word "typed."

To insert characters:

1. Position the I-beam pointer just before the word "typed," then click.
2. Type: **sentence**.
3. Press the **spacebar**.

Notice how the letters in the first line are pushed to the right to make room for the new characters. When a word gets pushed past the right margin, the word-wrap feature pushes it down to the beginning of the next line.

3.1 NOTE

When you save a file with a long filename, Windows 95 also creates an eight-character filename that can be used by Windows 3.1 applications. The eight-character filename is created by using the first six non-space characters from the long filename, then adding a tilde (~) and a number. For example, the filename Car Sales for 1997 would be converted to Carsal~1.

Saving a File

As you type text, it is held temporarily in the computer's memory. For permanent storage, you need to save your work on a disk. In the computer lab, you will probably save your work on a floppy disk in drive A.

When you save a file, you must give it a name. Windows 95 allows you to use filenames containing up to 255 characters, and you may use spaces and punctuation symbols. You cannot use the symbols \ ? : * " < > | in a filename, but other symbols such as &, -, and $ are allowed.

Most filenames have an extension. An **extension** is a suffix of up to three characters that is separated from the filename by a period, as shown in Figure 2-8.

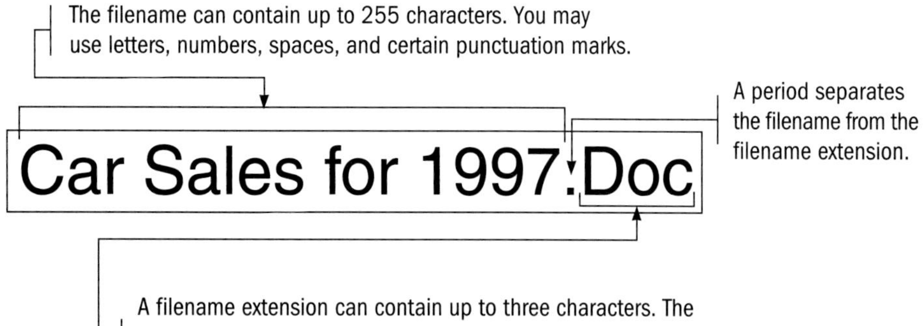

Figure 2-8 Filename and extension

The file extension indicates which application you used to create the file. For example, files created with Microsoft Word software have a .Doc extension. In general, you will not add an extension to your filenames, because the application software automatically does this for you.

Windows 95 keeps track of file extensions, but does not always display them. The steps in these tutorials refer to files using the filename, but not its extension. So if you see the filename Sample Text in the steps, but "Sample Text.Doc" on your screen, don't worry—these are the same files.

Now you can save the document you typed.

To save a document:

1. Click the **Save** button on the toolbar. Figure 2-9 shows the location of this button and the Save As dialog box that appears after you click it.

Figure 2-9 The Save button

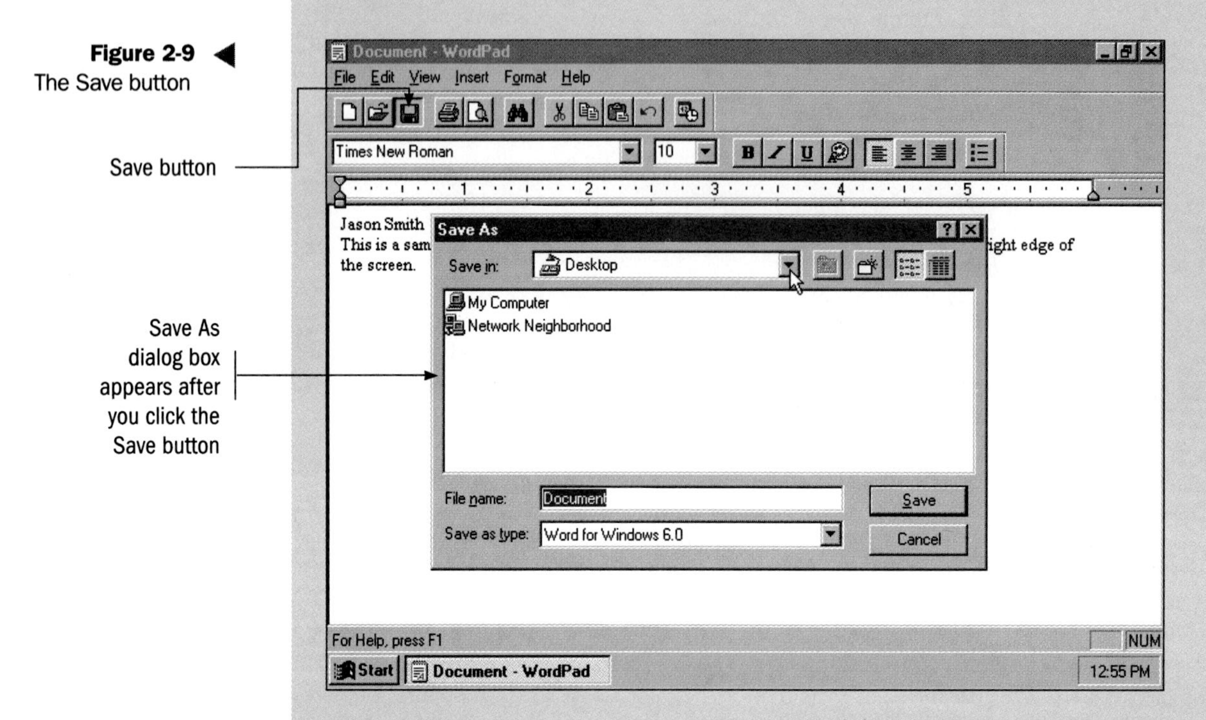

2. Click on the side of the Save in: box to display a list of drives. See Figure 2-10.

Figure 2-10 Selecting the drive

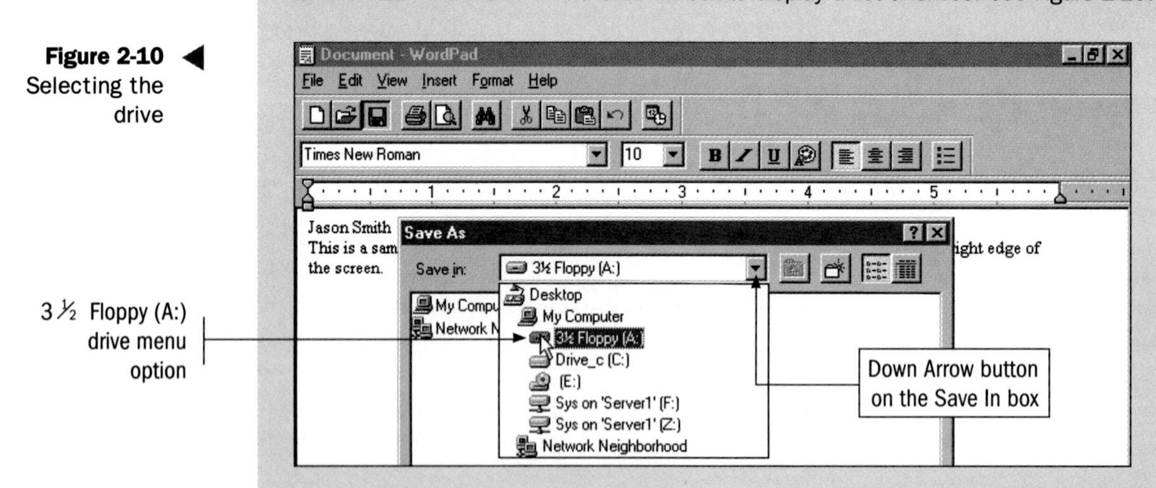

3. Click **3½ Floppy (A:)**.
4. Select the text in the File Name box.

   TROUBLE? To select the text, position the I-beam pointer at the beginning of the word "Document." While you hold down the mouse button, drag the I-beam pointer to the end of the word.

5. Type **Sample Text** in the File Name box.
6. Click the **Save** button. Your file is saved on your Student Disk and the document title, "Sample Text," appears on the WordPad title bar.

What if you tried to close WordPad *before* you saved your file? Windows 95 would display a message—"Save changes to Document?" If you answer "Yes," Windows displays the Save As dialog box so you can give the document a name. If you answer "No," Windows 95 closes WordPad without saving the document.

After you save a file, you can work on another document or close WordPad. Since you have already saved your Sample Text document, you should continue this tutorial by closing WordPad.

To close WordPad:

1. Click the **Close** button [X] to close the WordPad window.

Opening a File

Suppose you save and close the Sample Text file, then later you want to revise it. To revise a file you must first open it. When you **open** a file, its contents are copied into the computer's memory. If you revise the file, you need to save the changes before you close the application or work on a different file. If you close a revised file without saving your changes, you will lose the revisions.

Typically, you would use one of two methods to open a file. You could select the file from the Documents list or the My Computer window, or you could start an application program and then use the Open button to open the file. Each method has advantages and disadvantages. You will have an opportunity to try both methods.

3.1 NOTE

Document-centric features are advertised as an advantage of Windows 95. But you can still successfully use the application-centric approach you used with Windows 3.1 by opening your application, then opening your document.

The first method for opening the Sample Text file simply requires you to select the file from the Documents list or the My Computer window. With this method the document, not the application program, is central to the task; hence this method is sometimes referred to as *document-centric*. You only need to remember the name of your document or file—you do not need to remember which application you used to create the document.

The Documents list contains the names of the last 15 documents used. You access this list from the Start menu. When you have your own computer, the Documents list is very handy. In a computer lab, however, the files other students use quickly replace yours on the list.

If your file is not in the Documents list, you can open the file by selecting it from the My Computer window. Windows 95 starts an application program that you can use to revise the file, then automatically opens the file. The advantage of this method is its simplicity. The disadvantage is that Windows 95 might not start the application you expect. For example, when you select Sample Text, you might expect Windows 95 to start WordPad because you used WordPad to type the text of the document. Depending on the software installed on your computer system, however, Windows 95 might start the Microsoft Word application instead. Usually this is not a problem. Although the application might not be the one you expect, you can still use it to revise your file.

To open the Sample Text file by selecting it from My Computer:

1. Click the **My Computer** icon. Press the **Enter** key. The My Computer window opens.
2. Click the **3½ Floppy (A:)** icon, then press the **Enter** key. The 3½ Floppy (A:) window opens.
3. Click the **Sample Text** file icon, then press the **Enter** key. Windows 95 starts an application program, then automatically opens the Sample Text file.

   TROUBLE? If Windows 95 starts Microsoft Word instead of WordPad, don't worry. You can use Microsoft Word to revise the Sample Text document.

Now that Windows 95 has started an application and opened the Sample Text file, you could make revisions to the document. Instead, you should close all the windows on your desktop so you can try the other method for opening files.

To close all the windows on the desktop:

1. Click [X] on each of the windows.

   TROUBLE? If you see a message, "Save changes to Document?" click the No button.

The second method for opening the Sample Text file requires you to open WordPad, then use the Open button to select the Sample Text file. The advantage of this method is that you can specify the application program you want to use—WordPad in this case. This method, however, involves more steps than the method you tried previously.

To start WordPad and open the Sample Text file using the Open button:

1. Start WordPad.
2. Click the **Open** button on the toolbar. Figure 2-11 shows the location of this button and the dialog box that appears after you click it.

Figure 2-11 The Open button and dialog box

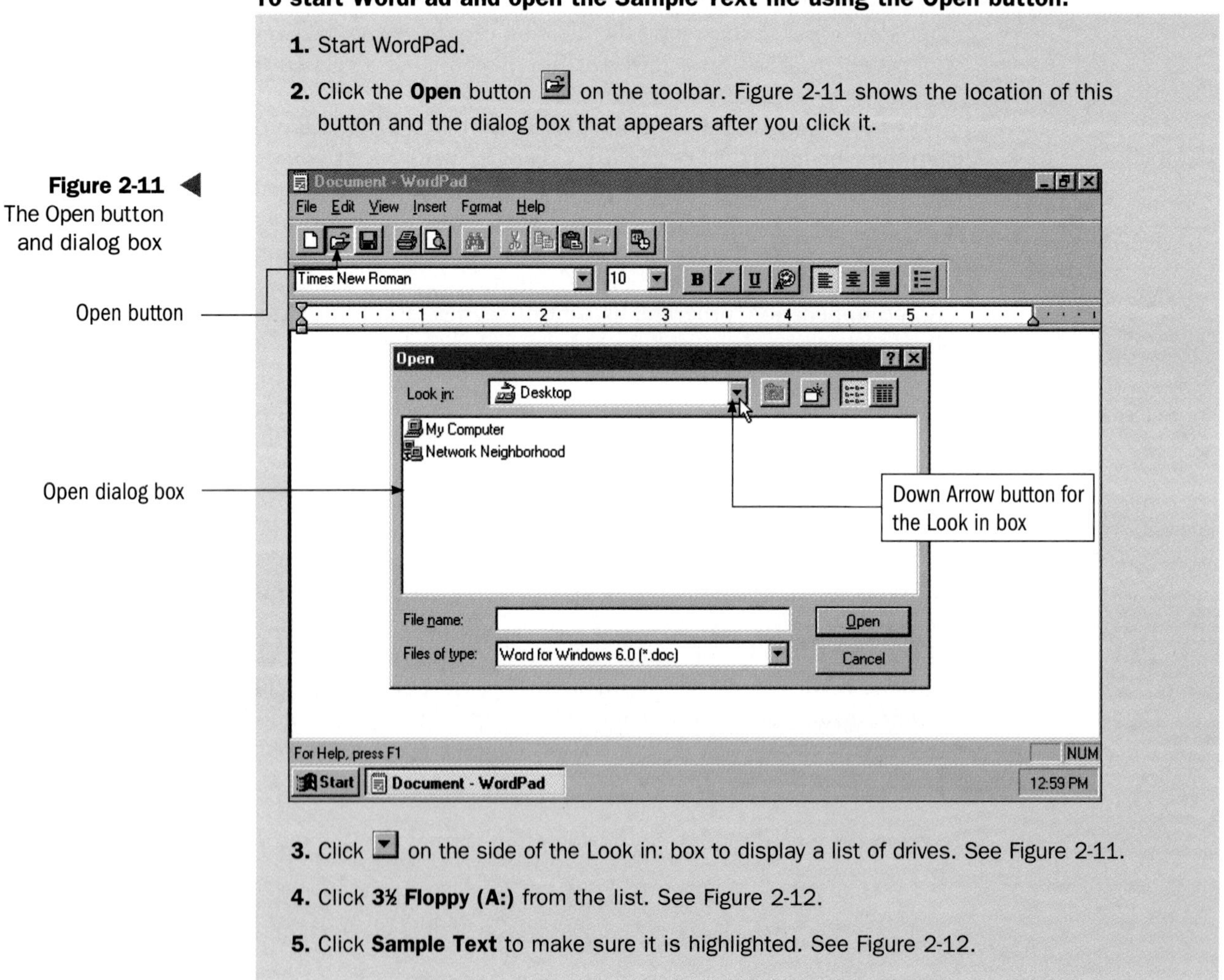

3. Click on the side of the Look in: box to display a list of drives. See Figure 2-11.
4. Click **3½ Floppy (A:)** from the list. See Figure 2-12.
5. Click **Sample Text** to make sure it is highlighted. See Figure 2-12.

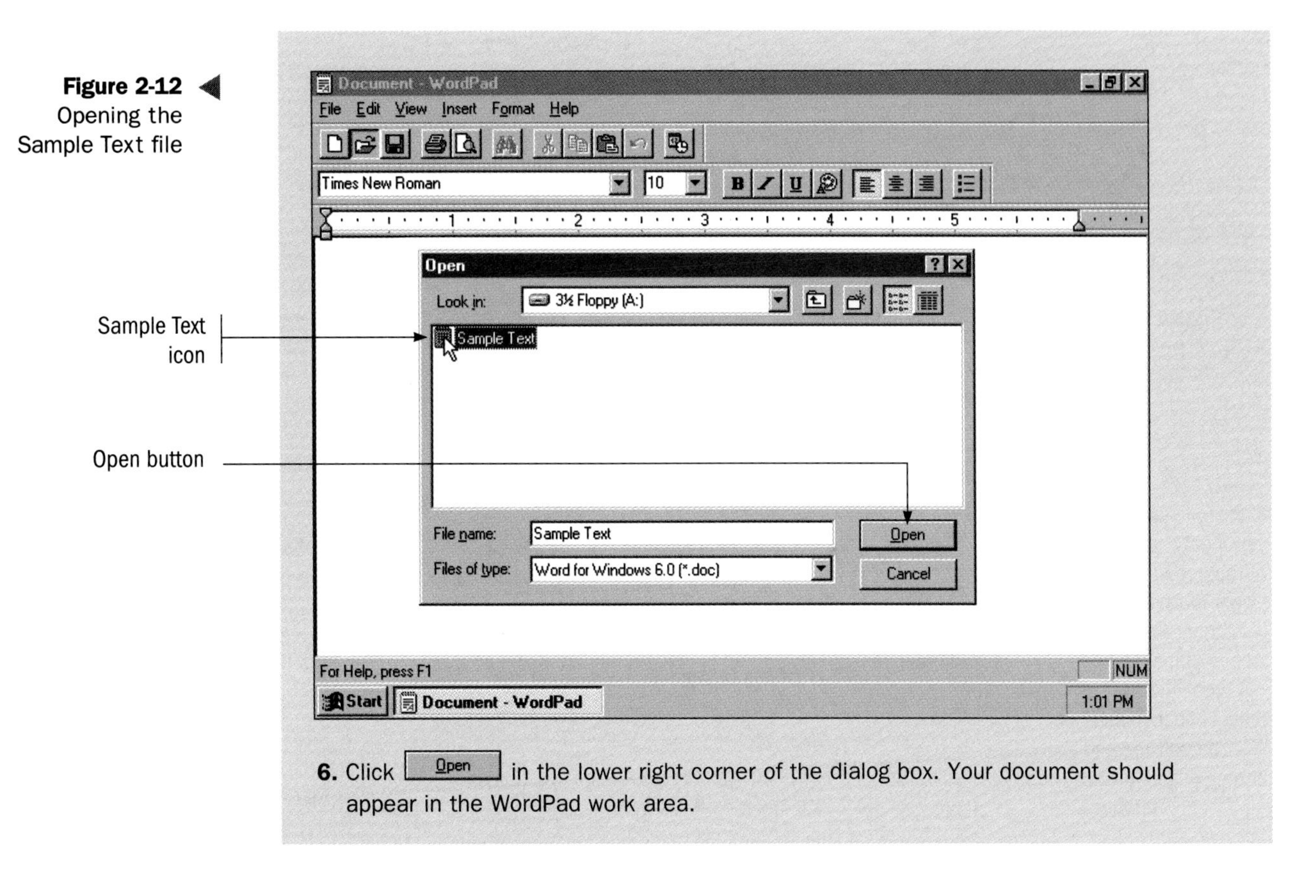

Figure 2-12 Opening the Sample Text file

6. Click Open in the lower right corner of the dialog box. Your document should appear in the WordPad work area.

Printing a File

Now that the Sample Text file is open, you can print it. It is a good idea to use Print Preview before you send your document to the printer. **Print Preview** shows on screen exactly how your document will appear on paper. You can check your page layout so you don't waste paper printing a document that is not quite the way you want it. Your instructor or technical support person might supply you with additional instructions for printing in your school's computer lab.

To preview, then print the Sample Text file:

1. Click the **Print Preview** button on the tool bar.
2. Look at your print preview. Before you print the document and use paper, you should make sure that the font, margins, and other document features look the way you want them to.

   TROUBLE? If you can't read the document text on screen, click the Zoom In button.
3. Click the **Print** button. A Print dialog box appears.

4. Study Figure 2-13 to familiarize yourself with the controls in the Print dialog box.

Figure 2-13 ◀ The Print dialog box

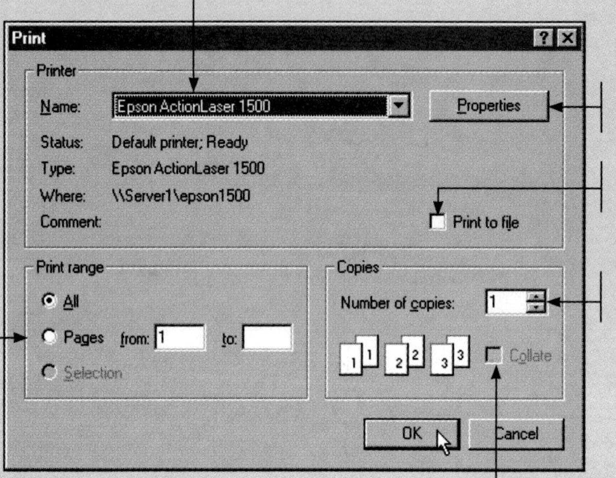

5. Make sure your screen shows the Print range set to "All" and the number of copies set to "1."

6. Click the **OK** button to print your document.

   TROUBLE? If your document does not print, make sure the printer has paper and the printer on-line light is on. If your document still doesn't print, ask your instructor or technical support person for help.

7. Close WordPad.

   TROUBLE? If you see the message "Save changes to Document?" click the "No" button.

Quick Check

1. A(n) __________ is a collection of data that has a name and is stored on a disk or other storage medium.

2. __________ erases all the data on a disk and arranges the magnetic particles on the disk surface so the disk can store data.

3. When you are working in a text box, the pointer shape changes to a(n) __________.

4. The __________ shows you where each character you type will appear.

5. __________ automatically moves text down to the beginning of the next line when you reach the right margin.

6. Explain how you select a block of text: __________.

7. Which of these characters are not allowed in Windows 95 file names: \ ? : * " < > | ! @ # $ % ^ & ; + - ( ) /

8 In the filename New Equipment.Doc, .Doc is a(n) ____________.

9 Suppose you created a graph using the Harvard Graphics software and then you stored the graph on your floppy disk under the name Projected 1997 Sales - Graph. The next day, you use Harvard Graphics to open the file and change the graph. If you want the new version of the file on your disk, you need to ____________.

10 You can save ____________ by using the Print Preview feature.

SESSION 2.2

In this session, you will learn how to manage the files on your disk—a skill that can prevent you from losing important documents. You will learn how to list information about the files on your disk; organize the files into folders; and move, delete, copy, and rename files.

Creating Your Student Disk

For this session of the tutorial, you must create a Student Disk that contains some sample files. *You can use the disk you formatted in the previous session.*

If you are using your own computer, the CTI Windows 95 Applications menu selection will not be available. Before you proceed, you must go to your school's computer lab and find a computer that has the CTI Windows 95 Applications installed. Once you have made your own Student Disk, you can use it to complete this tutorial on any computer you choose.

To add the sample files to your Student Disk:

1. Write "Windows 95 Student Disk" on the label of your formatted disk.
2. Place the disk in Drive A.

   TROUBLE? If your 3½-inch disk drive is B, place your formatted disk in that drive instead, and for the rest of this session substitute Drive B where ever you see Drive A.

3. Click the **Start** button Start. See Figure 2-14.

Figure 2-14

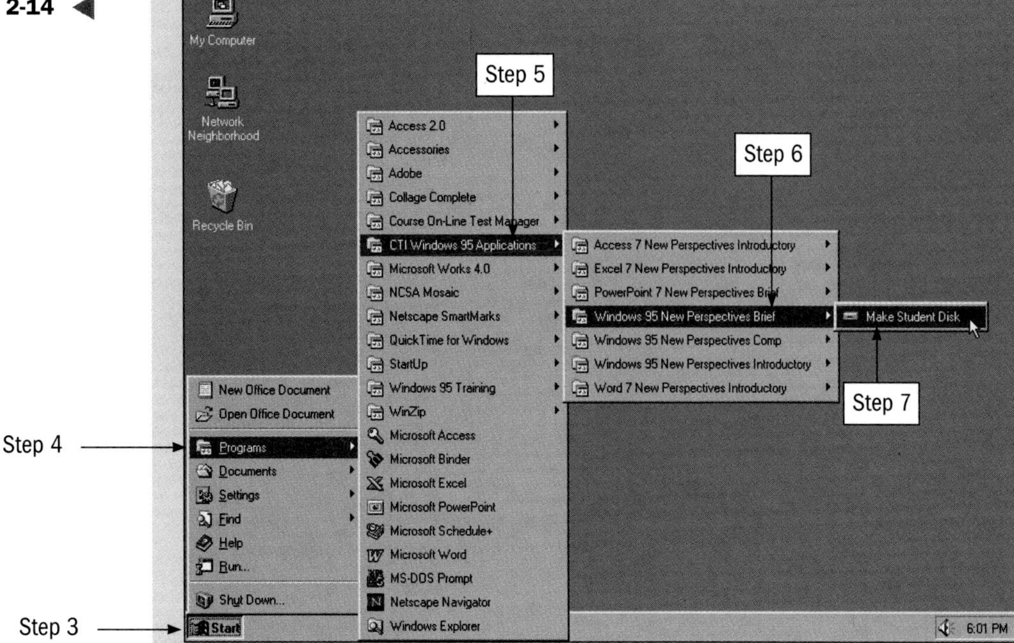

4. Select **Programs.**
5. Select **CTI Windows 95 Applications.**

   TROUBLE? If CTI Windows 95 Applications is not listed, contact your instructor or technical support person.

6. Click **Windows 95 New Perspectives Brief.**
7. Select **Make Student Disk.**

   A dialog box opens, asking you to indicate the drive that contains your formatted disk.

8. If it is not already selected, click the Drive radio button that corresponds to the drive containing your student disk.
9. Click the **OK** button.

   The sample files are copied to your formatted disk. A message tells you when all the files have been copied.

10. Click **OK.**
11. Close all the open windows on your screen.

Your Student Disk now contains sample files that you will use throughout the rest of this tutorial.

My Computer

The **My Computer icon** represents your computer, its storage devices, and its printers. The My Computer icon opens into the My Computer window, which contains an icon for each of the storage devices on your computer. On most computer systems the My Computer window also contains Control Panel and Printers folders, which help you add printers, control peripheral devices, and customize your Windows 95 work environment. Figure 2-15 on the following page explains more about the My Computer window.

You can use the My Computer window to keep track of where your files are stored and to organize your files. In this section of the tutorial you will move and delete files on your Student Disk in drive A. If you use your own computer at home or computer at work, you would probably store your files on drive C, instead of drive A. However, in a school lab environment you usually don't know which computer you will use, so you need to carry your files with you on a floppy disk that you use in drive A. In this session, therefore, you will learn how to work with the files on drive A. Most of what you learn will also work on your home or work computer when you use drive C.

In this session you will work with several icons, including My Computer. As a general procedure, when you want to open an icon, you click it and then press the Enter key.

Figure 2-15 Information about My Computer

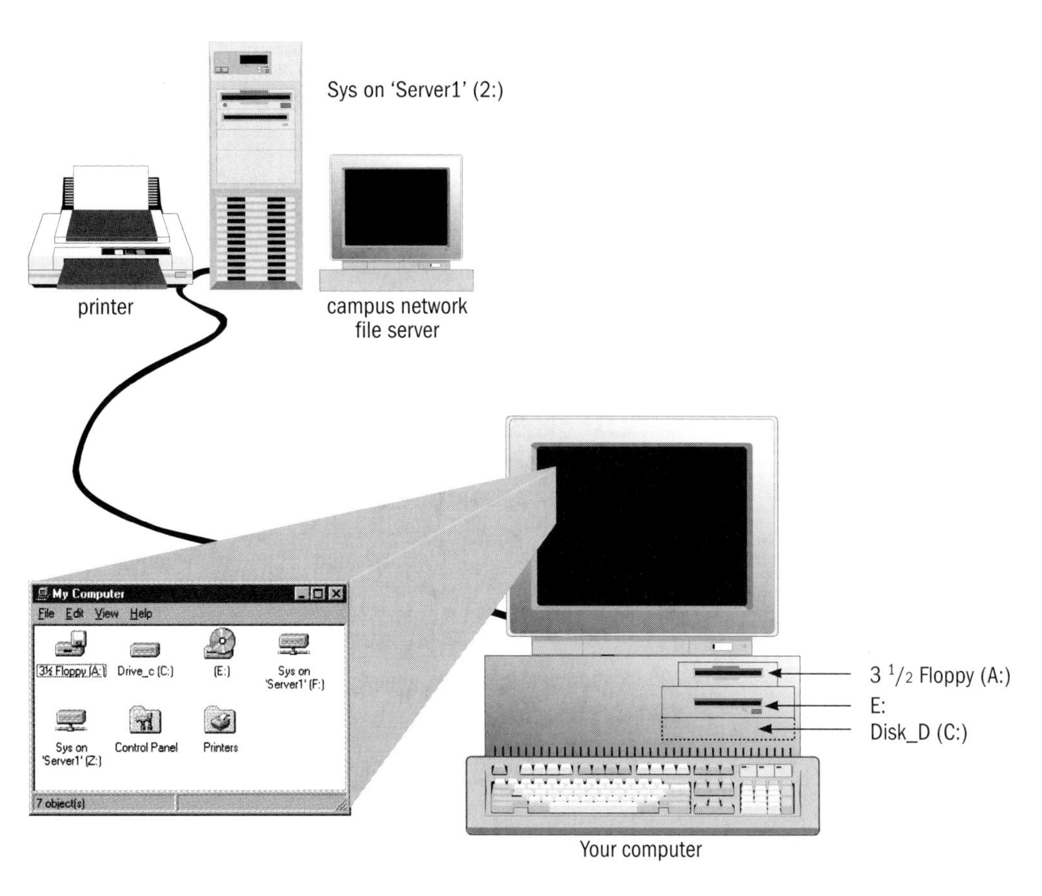

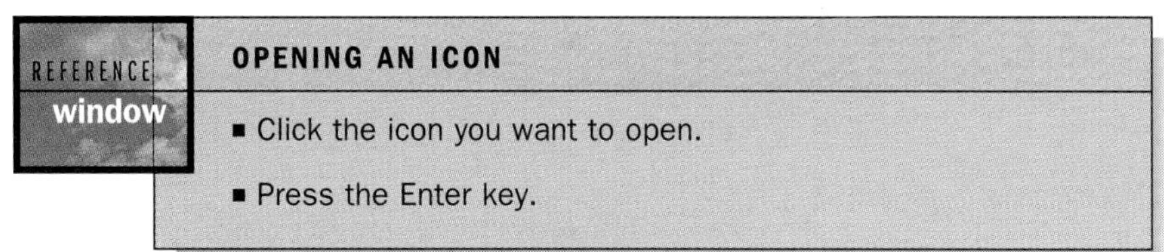

OPENING AN ICON

- Click the icon you want to open.
- Press the Enter key.

Now you should open the My Computer icon.

To open the My Computer icon:

1. Click the **My Computer** icon to select it.
2. Press the **Enter** key. The My Computer window opens.

Now that you have opened the My Computer window, you can find out what is on your Student Disk in drive A.

To find out what is on your Student Disk:

1. Open the **3½ Floppy (A:)** icon by clicking it, then pressing the **Enter** key. A window appears showing the contents of drive A:. See Figure 2-16.

Figure 2-16 Contents of Student Disk

3 ½ Floppy (A:) window

Maximize button

View menu

Icons show contents of drive A

Your screen might not show file extensions.

TROUBLE? If you see a list of file names instead of icons, click View, then click Large icons.

2. Click the **Maximize** button if the window is not maximized.

Windows 95 provides four ways to view the contents of a disk—large icons, small icons, list, or details. The standard view, shown on your screen, displays a large icon and title for each file. The icon provides a visual cue to the type and contents of the file, as Figure 2-17 illustrates.

Figure 2-17 Program and file icons

Text files that you can open and read using the WordPad or NotePad software are represented by notepad icons.

WordPad Document

Netlog

Exchng32

The icons for Windows programs usually depict an object related to the function of the program. For example, an icon that looks like a calculator signifies the Windows Calc program; an icon that looks like a computer signifies the Windows Explorer program.

Explorer

Calc

Many of the files you create are represented by page icons. Here the page icon for the Circles file shows some graphics tools to indicate the file contains a graphic. The Page icon for the Access file contains the Windows logo, indicating that Windows does not know if the file contains a document, graphics, or data base.

Access.mdb

Circles

Folders provide a way to group and organize files. A folder icon contains other icons for folders and files. Here, the System folder contains files used by the Windows operating system.

System

Non-Windows programs are represented by this icon of a blank window.

Command

The **Details** view shows more information than the large icon, small icon, and list views. Details view shows the file icon, the filename, the file size, the application you used to create the file, and the date/time the file was created or last modified.

To view a detailed list of files:

1. Click **View** then click **Details** to display details for the files on your disk as shown in Figure 2-18.

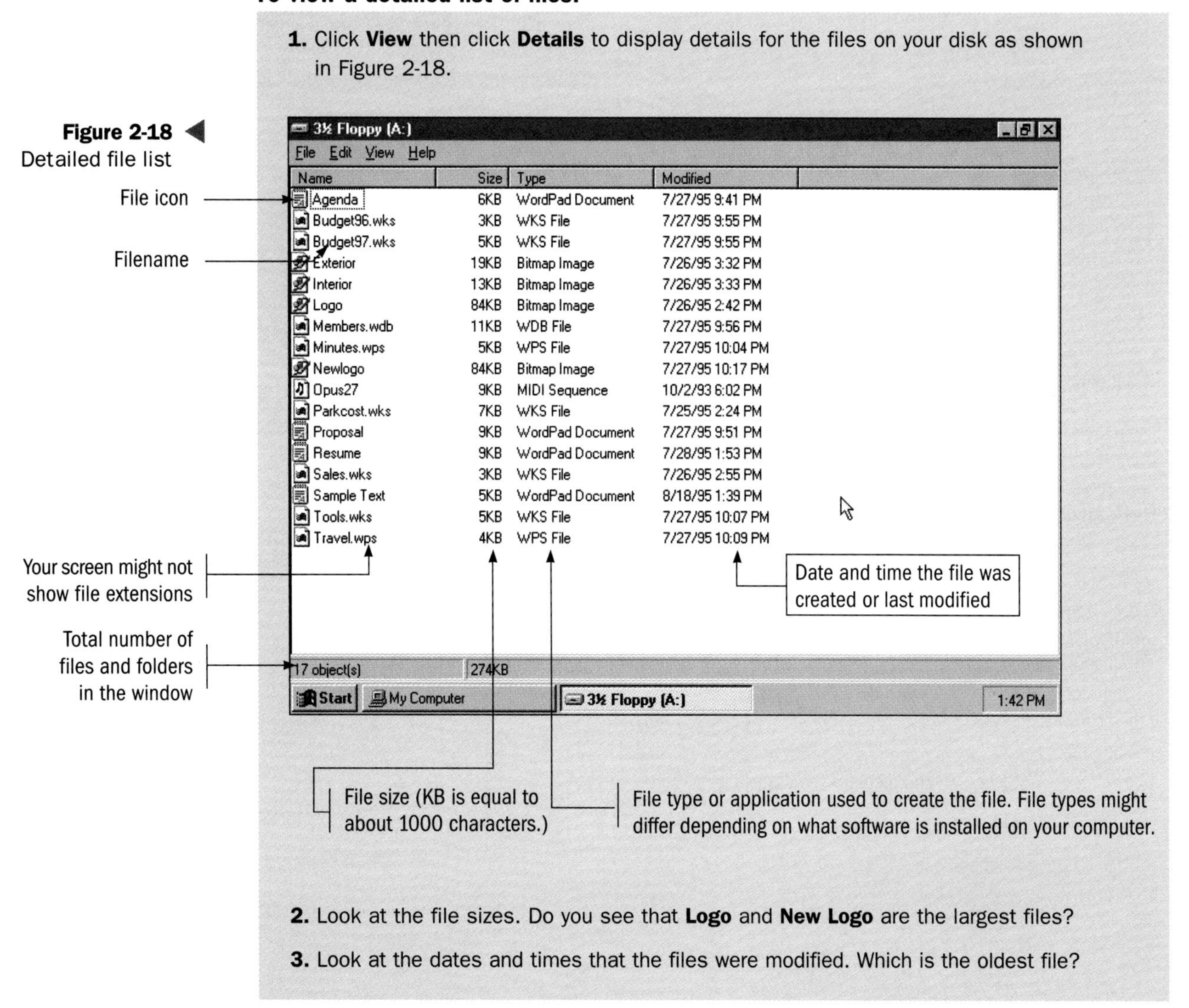

Figure 2-18 Detailed file list

2. Look at the file sizes. Do you see that **Logo** and **New Logo** are the largest files?
3. Look at the dates and times that the files were modified. Which is the oldest file?

Now that you have looked at the file details, switch back to the large icon view.

To switch to the large icon view:

1. Click **View** then click **Large Icons** to return to the large icon display.

Folders and Directories

A list of files is referred to as a **directory**. The main directory of a disk is sometimes called the **root directory**. The root directory is created when you format a disk and is shown in parentheses at the top of the window. For example, at the top of your screen you should see "3 ½ Floppy (A:)." The root directory is A:. In some situations, the root directory is indicated by a backslash after the drive letter and colon, such as A:\. All of the files on your Student Disk are currently in the root directory.

If too many files are stored in a directory, the directory list becomes very long and difficult to manage. A directory can be divided into **folders** (also called **subdirectories**), into which you group similar files. The directory of files for each folder then becomes much shorter and easier to manage. For example, you might create a folder for all the papers you write for an English 111 class as shown in Figure 2-19.

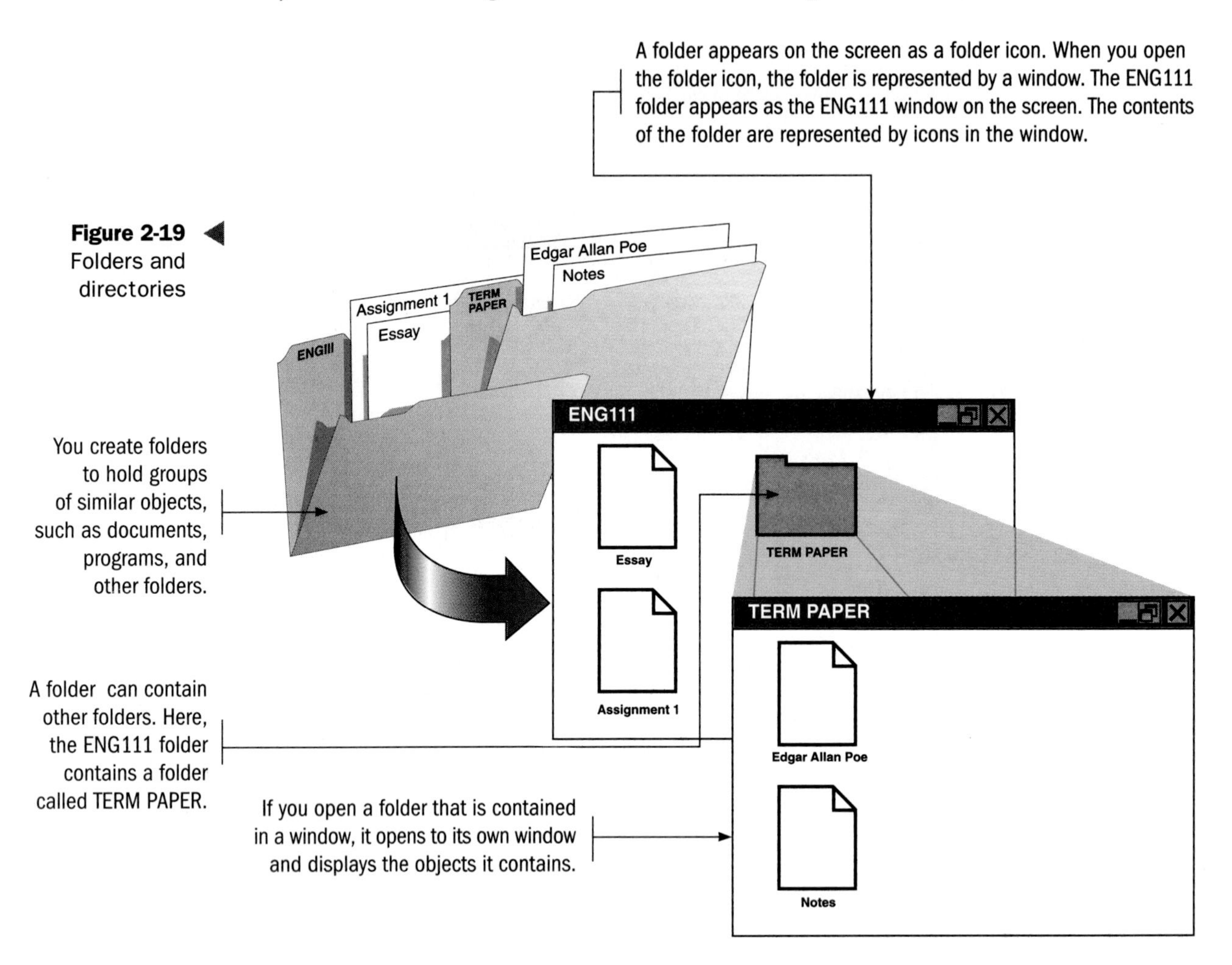

Figure 2-19 Folders and directories

Now, you'll create a folder called My Documents to hold your document files.

To create a My Documents folder:

1. Click **File** then point to **New** to display the submenu.
2. Click **Folder**. A folder icon with the label "New Folder" appears.
3. Type **My Documents** as the name of the folder.
4. Press the **Enter** key.

When you first create a folder, it doesn't contain any files. In the next set of steps you will move a file from the root directory to the My Documents folder.

CREATING A NEW FOLDER

- Open the My Computer icon to display the My Computer window.
- Open the icon for the drive on which you want to create the folder.
- Click File then point to New.
- From the submenu click Folder.
- Type the name for the new folder.
- Press the Enter key.

Moving and Copying a File

You can move a file from one directory to another or from one disk to another. When you move a file it is copied to the new location you specify, then the version in the old location is erased. The move feature is handy for organizing or reorganizing the files on your disk by moving them into appropriate folders. The easiest way to move a file is to hold down the *right* mouse button and drag the file from the old location to the new location. A menu appears and you select Move Here.

You can also copy a file from one directory to another, or from one disk to another. When you copy a file, you create an exact duplicate of an existing file in whatever disk or folder you specify. To copy a file from one folder to another on your floppy disk, you use the same procedure as for moving a file, except that you select Copy Here from the menu.

Suppose you want to move the Minutes file from the root directory to the My Documents folder. Depending on the software applications installed on your computer, this file is either called Minutes or Minutes.wps. In the steps it is referred to simply as Minutes.

To move the Minutes file to the My Documents folder:

1. Click the **Minutes** icon to select it.
2. Press and hold the right mouse button while you drag the **Minutes** icon to the My Documents folder. See Figure 2-20.

Figure 2-20 Moving a file

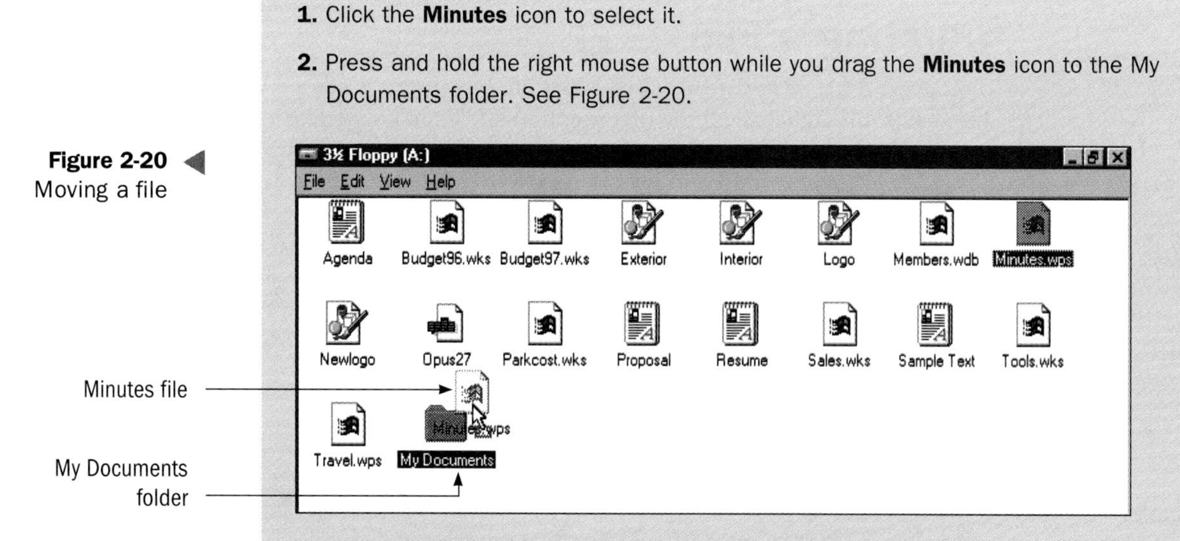

3. Release the left mouse button. A menu appears.
4. Click **Move Here**. A short animation shows the Minutes file being moved to My Documents. The Minutes icon disappears from the window showing the files in the root directory.

MOVING A FILE

- Open the My Computer icon to display the My Computer window.
- If the document you want to move is in a folder, open the folder.
- Hold down the *right* mouse button while you drag the file icon to its new folder or disk location.
- Click Move Here.
- If you want to move more than one file at a time, hold down the Ctrl key while you click the icons for all the files you want to move.

3.1 NOTE

Windows 3.1 users be careful! When you delete or move an icon in the Windows 95 My Computer window you are actually deleting or moving the file. This is quite different from the way the Windows 3.1 Program Manager worked.

Anything you do to an icon in the My Computer window is actually done to the file represented by that icon. If you move an icon, the file is moved; if you delete an icon, the file is deleted.

After you move a file, it is a good idea to make sure it was moved to the correct location. You can easily verify that a file is in its new folder by displaying the folder contents.

To verify that the Minutes file was moved to My Documents:

1. Click the **My Documents** folder, then press **Enter**. The My Documents window appears and it contains one file—Minutes.
2. Click the My Documents window **Close** button.

TROUBLE? If the My Computer window is no longer visible, click the My Computer icon, then press Enter. You might also need to open the 3 ½ Floppy (A:) icon.

Deleting a File

You delete a file or folder by deleting its icon. However, be careful when you delete a *folder*, because you also delete all the files it contains! When you delete a file from the hard drive, the filename is deleted from the directory but the file contents are held in the Recycle Bin. If you change your mind and want to retrieve the deleted file, you can recover it by clicking the Recycle Bin.

When you delete a file from a floppy disk, it does not go into the Recycle Bin. Instead it is deleted as soon as its icon disappears. Try deleting the file named Agenda from your Student Disk. Because this file is on the floppy disk and not on the hard disk, it will not go into the Recycle Bin.

To delete the file Agenda:

1. Click the icon for the file **Agenda**.
2. Press the **Delete** key.
3. If a message appears asking, "Are sure you want to delete Agenda?", click **Yes**. An animation shows the file being deleted.

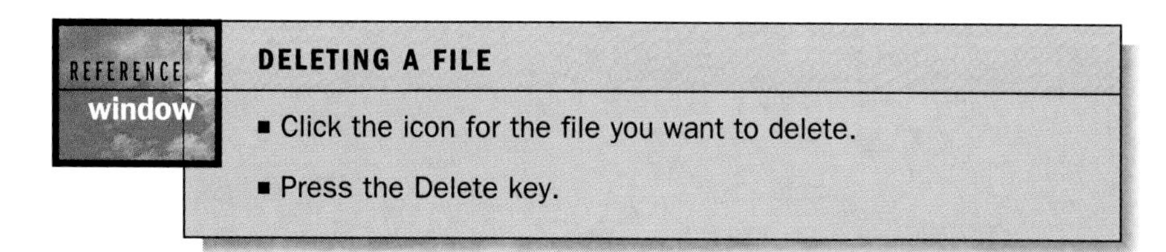

Renaming a File

You can easily change the name of a file using the Rename option on the File menu. Remember that when you choose a filename it can contain up to 255 characters, including spaces, but it cannot contain \ ? : " < > | characters.

Practice using this feature by renaming the Sales file to give it a more descriptive filename.

To rename Sales:

1. Click the **Sales** file to select it.
2. Click the label "Sales". After a short pause a solid box outlines the label and an insertion point appears.
3. Type **Preliminary Sales Summary** as the new filename.
4. Press the **Enter** key.
5. Click the **Close** button ☒ to close the 3 ½-inch Floppy (A:) window.

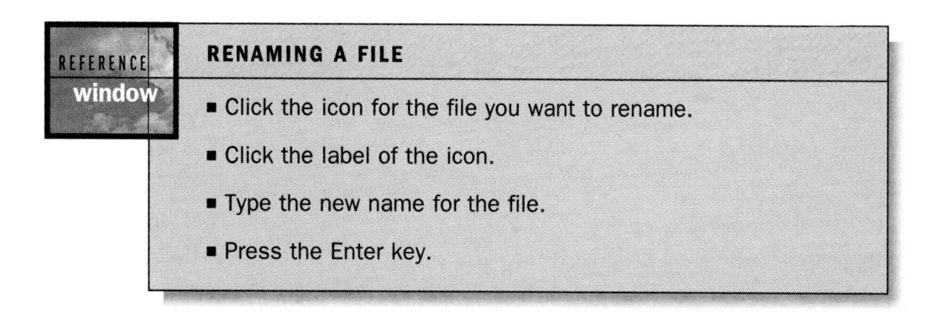

Copying an Entire Floppy Disk

You can have trouble accessing the data on your floppy disk if the disk gets damaged, exposed to magnetic fields, or picks up a computer virus. If the damaged disk contains important files, you will have to spend many hours to try to reconstruct those files. To avoid losing all your data, it is a good idea to make a copy of your floppy disk. This copy is called a **backup** copy.

If you wanted to make a copy of an audio cassette, your cassette player would need two cassette drives. You might wonder, therefore, how your computer can make a copy of your disk if you have only one disk drive. Figure 2-21 illustrates how the computer uses only one disk drive to make a copy of a disk.

Figure 2-21 Using one disk drive to make a copy of a disk

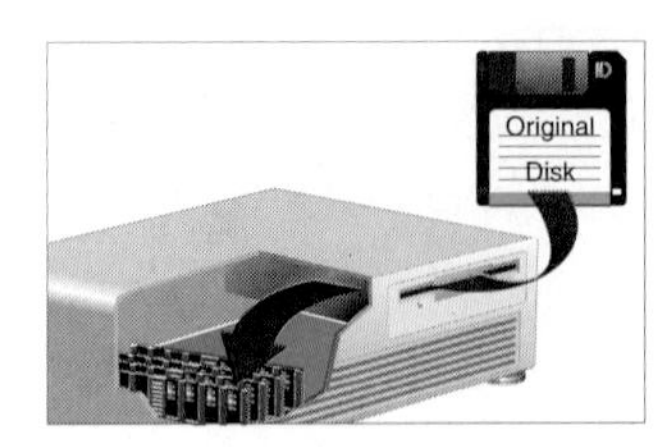

1. First, the computer copies the data from your original disk into memory.

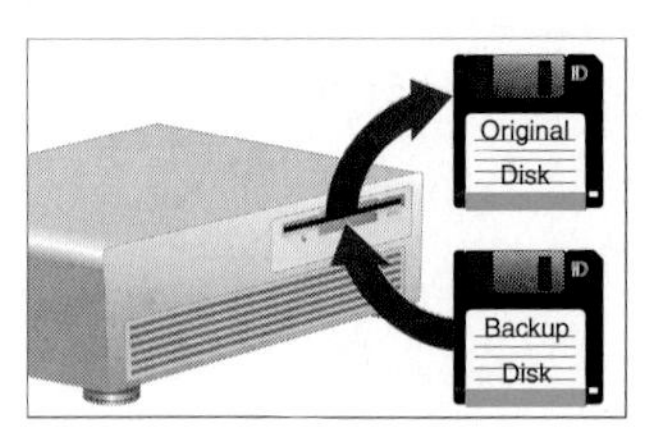

2. Once the data is in memory, you remove your original disk from the drive and replace it with your backup disk.

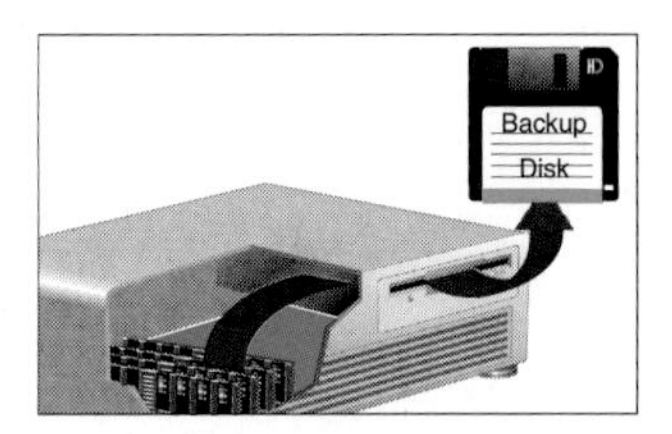

3. The computer moves the data from memory onto your backup disk.

REFERENCE window

MAKING A BACKUP OF YOUR FLOPPY DISK

- Click My Computer then press the Enter key.
- Insert the disk you want to copy in drive A.
- Click the 3 ½ Floppy (A:) icon (3½ Floppy (A:)) to select it.
- Click File then click Copy Disk to display the Copy Disk dialog box.
- Click Start to begin the copy process.
- When prompted, remove the disk you want to copy. Place your backup disk in drive A.
- Click OK.
- When the copy is complete, close the Copy Disk dialog box.
- Close the My Computer dialog box.

If you have two floppy disks, you can make a backup of your Student Disk now. Make sure you periodically follow the backup procedure, so your backup is up-to-date.

To back up your Student Disk:

1. Write your name and "Backup" on the label of your second disk. This will be your backup disk.
2. Make sure your Student Disk is in drive A.
3. Make sure the My Computer window is open. See Figure 2-22.

Figure 2-22 ◀ The My Computer window

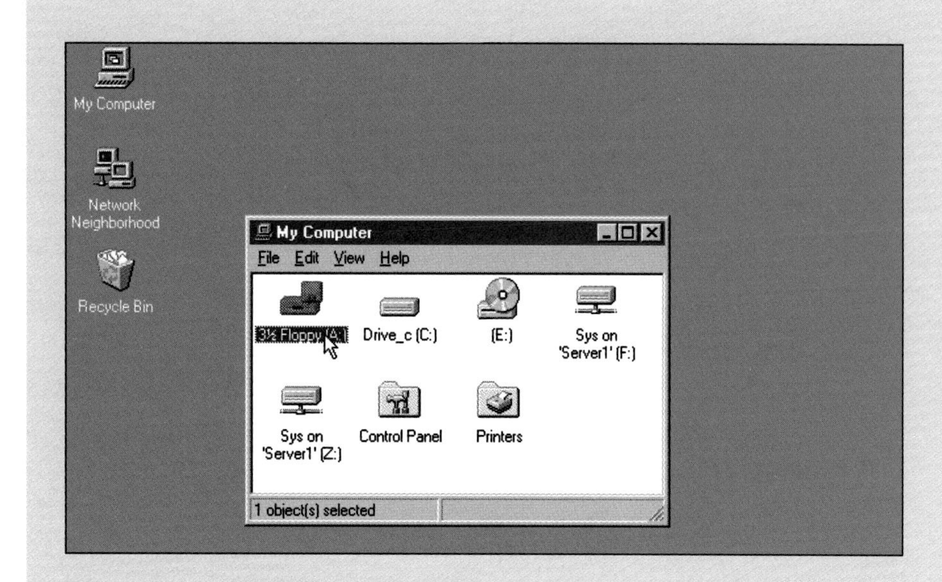

4. Click the **3 ½ Floppy (A:)** icon to select it.

   TROUBLE? If you mistakenly open the 3½ Floppy (A:) *window*, click ☒.

5. Click **File**.

6. Click **Copy Disk** to display the Copy Disk dialog box as shown in Figure 2-23.

Figure 2-23 ◀ The Copy Disk dialog box

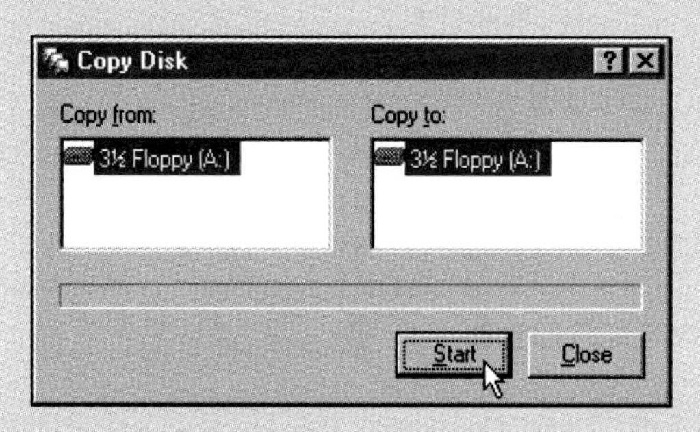

7. On the lower right side of the dialog box, you'll see a Start button. Click this **Start** button to begin the copy process.

8. When the message "Insert the disk you want to copy to (destination disk)..." appears, insert your backup disk in drive A.

9. Click the **OK** button. When the copy is complete, you will see the message "Copy completed successfully."

10. After the data is copied to your backup disk, click ☒ on the blue title bar of the Copy Disk dialog box.

11. Click ☒ on the My Computer window to close the My Computer window.

12. Remove your disk from the drive.

Each time you make a backup, the data on your backup disk is erased, and replaced with the data from your updated Student Disk. Now that you know how to copy an entire disk, make a backup whenever you have completed a tutorial or you have spent a long time working on a file.

Quick Check

1. If you want to find out about the storage devices and printers connected to your computer, click the ___________ icon.
2. If you have only one floppy disk drive on your computer, it is identified by the letter ___________.
3. The letter C: is typically used for the ___________ drive of a computer.
4. What are the five pieces of information that the Details view supplies about each of your files?
5. The main directory of a disk is referred to as the ___________ directory.
6. You can divide a directory into ___________.
7. If you delete the icon for a file, what happens to the file?
8. If you have one floppy disk drive, but you have two disks, can you copy a file from one floppy disk to another?

End Note

Just as you complete the Quick Check for Session 2.2, Steve appears. He asks how you are doing. You summarize what you remember from the tutorial, telling him that you learned how to insert, delete, and select text. You also learned how to work with files using Windows 95 software—you now know how to save, open, revise, and print a document. You tell him that you like the idea that these file operations are the same for almost all Windows 95 software. Steve agrees that this makes work a lot easier.

When Steve asks you if you have a supply of disks, you tell him you do, and that you just learned how to format a disk and view a list of files on your disk. Steve wants you to remember that you can use the Details view to see the filename, size, date, and time. You assure him that you remember that feature—and also how to move, delete, and rename a file.

Steve seems pleased with your progress and agrees that you're now ready to use software applications. But he can't resist giving you one last warning—don't forget to back up your files frequently!

Tutorial Assignments

1. Opening, Editing, and Printing a Document In this tutorial you learned how to create a document using WordPad. You also learned how to save, open, and print a document. Practice these skills by opening the document on your Student Disk called Resume, which is a résumé for Jamie Woods. Make the changes shown in Figure 2-24, and then print the document. After you print, save your revisions.

Figure 2-24

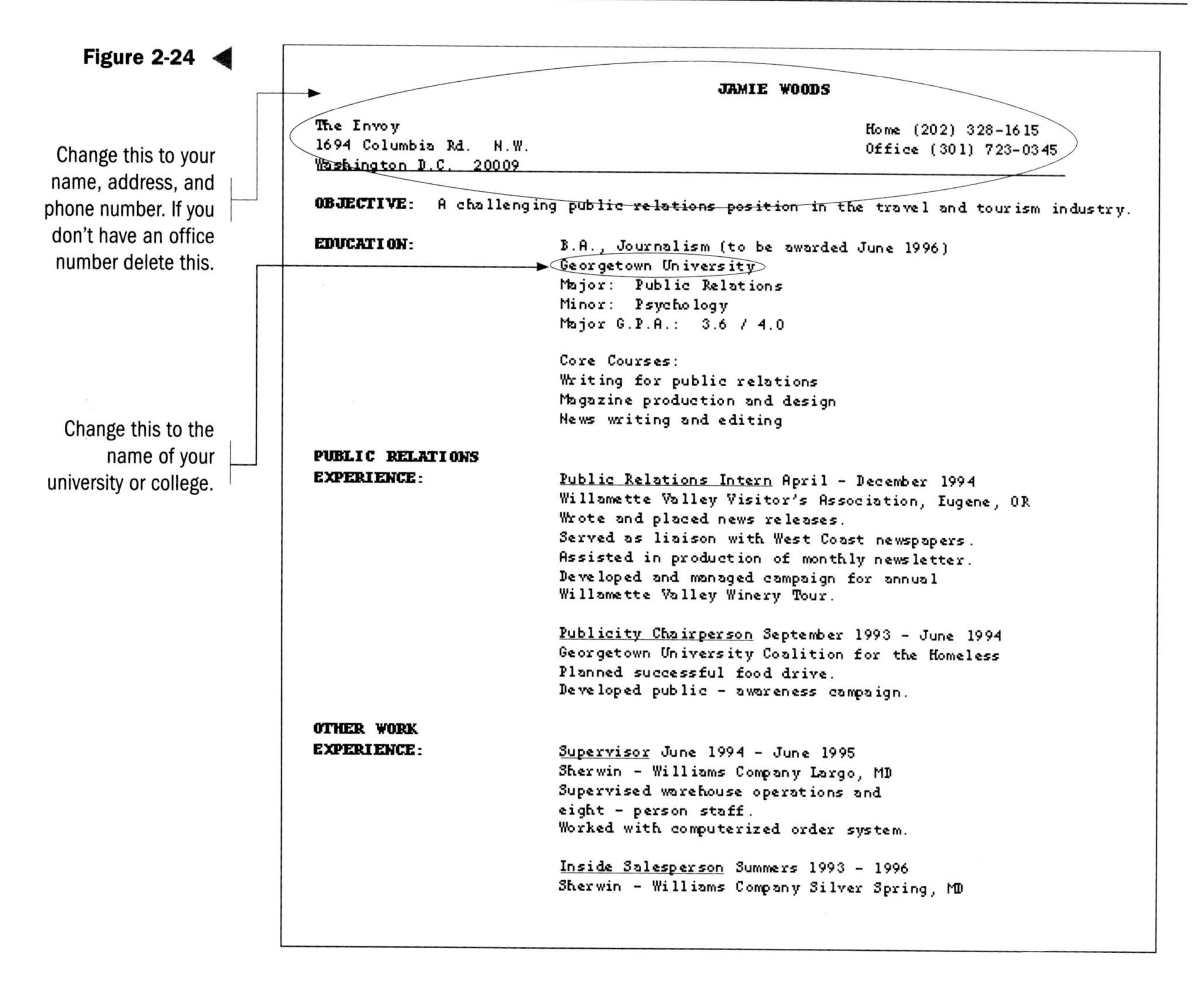

JAMIE WOODS

The Invoy
1694 Columbia Rd. N.W.
Washington D.C. 20009

Home (202) 328-1615
Office (301) 723-0345

OBJECTIVE: A challenging public relations position in the travel and tourism industry.

EDUCATION: B.A., Journalism (to be awarded June 1996)
Georgetown University
Major: Public Relations
Minor: Psychology
Major G.P.A.: 3.6 / 4.0

Core Courses:
Writing for public relations
Magazine production and design
News writing and editing

PUBLIC RELATIONS EXPERIENCE: Public Relations Intern April - December 1994
Willamette Valley Visitor's Association, Eugene, OR
Wrote and placed news releases.
Served as liaison with West Coast newspapers.
Assisted in production of monthly newsletter.
Developed and managed campaign for annual
Willamette Valley Winery Tour.

Publicity Chairperson September 1993 - June 1994
Georgetown University Coalition for the Homeless
Planned successful food drive.
Developed public - awareness campaign.

OTHER WORK EXPERIENCE: Supervisor June 1994 - June 1995
Sherwin - Williams Company Largo, MD
Supervised warehouse operations and
eight - person staff.
Worked with computerized order system.

Inside Salesperson Summers 1993 - 1996
Sherwin - Williams Company Silver Spring, MD

2. Creating, Saving, and Printing a Letter Use WordPad to write a one-page letter to a relative or a friend. Save the document in the My Documents folder. Use the Print Preview feature to look at the format of your finished letter, then print it, and be sure you sign it.

3. Managing Files and Folders Earlier in this tutorial you created a folder and moved the file called Minutes into it. Now complete a through g below to practice your file management skills.

a. Create a folder called Spreadsheets.
b. Move the files ParkCost, Budget96, Budget97, and Preliminary Sales Summary into the Spreadsheets folder.
c. Create a folder called Park Project.
d. Move the files Proposal, Members, Tools, Logo, and New Logo into the Park Project folder.
e. Move the ParkCost file from the Spreadsheets folder to the Park Project folder.
f. Delete the file called Travel.
g. Switch to the Details view and answer the following questions:

Write out your answers to questions a through e.

a. What is the largest file in the Park Project folder?
b. What is the newest file in the Spreadsheets folder?
c. How many files are in the root directory?
d. How are the Members and Resume icons different?
e. What is the file with the most recent date on the entire disk?

4. More Practice with Files and Folders For this assignment, you will format your disk again and put a fresh version of the Student Disk files on it. Complete a through h below to practice your file management skills.

a. Format a disk.
b. Create a Student Disk. Refer to the section "Creating Your Student Disk" in Session 2.2.
c. Create three folders on your new Student Disk: Documents, Budgets, and Graphics.
d. Move the files Interior, Exterior, Logo, and NewLogo to the Graphics folder.
e. Move the files Travel, Members and Minutes to the Documents folder.
f. Move Budget96 and Budget97 to the Budgets folder.
g. Switch to the Details view.

Answer questions a through f.

a. What is the largest file in the Graphics folder?
b. How many WordPad documents are in the root directory?
c. What is the newest file in the root directory?
d. How many files in all folders are 5KB in size?
e. How many files in the Documents folder are WKS files?
f. Do all the files in the Graphics folder have the same icon?

5. Finding a File Microsoft Windows 95 contains an on-line Tour that explains how to find files on a disk without looking through all the folders. Start the Windows 95 Tour (if you don't remember how, look at the instructions for Tutorial Assignment 1 in Tutorial 1), then click Finding a File, and answer the following questions:

a. To display the Find dialog box, you must click the __________ button, then select __________ from the menu, and finally click __________ from the submenu.
b. Do you need to type in the entire filename to find the file?
c. When the computer has found your file, what are the steps you have to follow if you want to display the contents of the file?

6. Help with Files and Folders In Tutorial 2 you learned how to work with Windows 95 files and folders. What additional information on this topic does Windows 95 Help provide? Use the Start button to access Help. Use the Index tab to locate topics related to files and folders. Find at least two tips or procedures for working with files and folders that were not covered in the tutorial. Write out the tip in your own words and indicate the title of the Help screen that contains the information.

Lab Assignments

1. Using Files Lab In Tutorial 2 you learned how to create, save, open, and print files. The Using Files Lab will help you review what happens in the computer when you perform these file tasks. To start the Lab, follow these steps:

a. Click the Start button.
b. Point to Programs, then point to CTI Windows 95 Applications.
c. Point to Windows 95 New Perspectives Brief.
d. Click Using Files. If you can't find Windows 95 New Perspectives Brief or Using Files, ask for help from your instructor or technical support person.

Answer the Quick Check questions that appear as you work through the Lab. You can print your answers at the end of the Lab.

Answers to Quick Check Questions

SESSION 1.1

1 a. icon b. Start button c. taskbar d. Date/Time control e. desktop f. pointer

2 Multitasking

3 Start menu

4 Lift up the mouse, move it to the right, then put it down, and slide it left until the pointer reaches the left edge of the screen.

5 Highlighting

6 If a program is running, its button is displayed on the taskbar.

7 Each program that is running uses system resources, so Windows 95 runs more efficiently when only the programs you are using are open.

8 Answer: If you do not perform the shut down procedure, you might lose data.

SESSION 1.2

1 a. title bar b. program title c. Minimize button d. Restore button e. Close button f. menu bar g. toolbar h. formatting bar i. status bar j. taskbar k. workspace l. pointer

2 a. Minimize button—hides the program so only its button is showing on the taskbar.
b. Maximize button—enlarges the program to fill the entire screen.
c. Restore button—sets the program to a pre-defined size.
d. Close button—stops the program and removes its button from the taskbar.

3 a. Ellipses—indicate a dialog box will appear.
b. Grayed out—the menu option is not currently available.
c. Submenu—indicates a submenu will appear.
d. Check mark—indicates a menu option is currently in effect.

4 Toolbar

5 a. scroll bar b. scroll box c. Cancel button d. down arrow button e. list box f. radio button g. check box

6 one, check boxes

7 On-line Help

SESSION 2.1

1 file

2 formatting

3 I-beam

4 insertion point

5 word wrap

6. You drag the I-beam pointer over the text to highlight it.
7. \ ? : * < > | "
8. extension
9. save the file again
10. paper

SESSION 2.2

1. My Computer
2. A (or A:)
3. Hard (or hard disk)
4. Filename, file type, file size, date, time
5. Root
6. Folders (or subdirectories)
7. It is deleted from the disk.
8. Yes

Windows 95 Brief Tutorials **Index**

Special Characters
- \ (backslash), 45
- ~ (tilde), 35
- () (parentheses), 45
- ... (ellipsis), 18
- triangles, 18

A

active program
- taskbar buttons, 6
- window title, 14

active window, displaying, 16
adding files to disks, 41–42
applications. *See also* WordPad application
- active. *See* active program
- closing, 10, 12, 37
- exiting, 10
- extensions, 35
- finding program windows, 9
- multiple, running at same time. *See* multitasking
- starting, 8–10
- switching between, 12
- used to create file, 45
- Windows 3.1, 29
- Windows 95, 3, 29

arrow buttons, 19

B

backslash (\), root directory, 45
Backspace key, error correction, 32
backup copies, 49–51
bad sectors, 32
blocks of text, selecting, 34
books, Help, 22–23
buttons. *See also specific buttons*
- desktop, 6
- sizing, 14
- taskbar. *See* taskbar buttons
- toolbars. *See* toolbar buttons

C

changing. *See also* switching
- closing files without saving changes, 37
- filenames, 49
- printer setup, 40
- size of windows, 14–15, 17

characters
- filenames, 29, 35, 49
- inserting, 35

check boxes, 21
check marks, menu options, 18
clicking, 8–9
- menu options, 17

clock, setting, 6
Close button, 10
closing
- applications. *See* closing applications
- files, without saving changes, 37
- Windows 95, 12–13
- windows, 14
- WordPad, 9, 37

closing applications, 8, 12
- before saving files, 37

collating pages,40
commands
- menus. *See* menus
- toolbar buttons, 14, 19

computer, turning off, 12–13
Contents tab, Help, 22–23
Control Panel, 42
controls
- tab controls, 20, 22–24
- windows, 14–15

copies, specifying number, 40
Copy Disk dialog box, 51
Copy Here, copying files, 47
copying
- entire floppy disks, 49–51
- files, 47

correcting errors, 32–33

D

data loss
- backup copies to prevent, 49–51
- formatting disks, 30
- turning off computer, 12

date
- of file creation or revision, 45
- setting, 6, 23–24

Date and Time dialog box, 19–20
Date/Time control, 6
Date/Time list box, 19–20
definitions, technical terms, 23
Delete key, error correction, 32–33
deleting
- files, 48
- folders, 48
- icons, 48

desktop, 5–6
buttons, 6
returning to, 11
Details view, disk contents, 45
dialog boxes. *See also specific dialog boxes*
check boxes, 20–21
ellipsis (...), 18
radio (option) buttons, 21
tab controls, 21
use, 18
directories, 45–46
folders, 45–46
subdirectories, 45–46
disk drives, selecting, 36
disks
adding files, 41–42
bad sectors, 32
copying, 49–51
deleting files, 48–49
formatting. *See* formatting disks
listing files, 42–45
sending printout to, 40
space, 32
displaying
files, 42–45
functions, with tab controls, 20, 22–24
Help topics, 21, 22–24
list box options, 19–20
printers, 40
Tooltips, 7
windows, 15
.Doc extension, 35
documents. *See also* text
previewing, 39
printing selected pages, 39–40
saving, 36
double-clicking, 8, 27
down arrow button, 19
dragging
files, 47–49
scroll box, 19
windows, 16–17
drives, selecting, 36
drop-down list boxes, 19–20

E

ellipsis (...), menu options, 18
Empty Recycle Bin option, 48
enlarging windows, 15
entering text in WordPad, 32–33
errors. *See* mistakes
exiting. *See* closing
extensions, filenames, 35–36

F

File menu, 31
Rename option, 49
filenames, 29, 35–36
characters, 29, 35, 49
extensions, 35
renaming files, 49
Windows 3.1, 35
Windows 95, 35
files, 29. *See also* documents
adding to disks, 41–42
closing applications before saving, 37
closing without saving changes, 37
copying, 47
date and time of creation or revision, 45
deleted, retrieving, 48
deleting, 48
directories, 45–46
listing, 44–45
moving, 47–48
naming. *See* filenames
opening, 39
organizing, 45–46
printing, 39–40
saving, 36, 37, 38
size, 45
turning off computer, 12
type, 45
verifying location, 47–48
finding
program windows, 10
words and phrases in Help, 21, 22–24
Find tab, Help, 24, 26
floppy disks. *See* disks
folders, 45–46
creating, 46
deleting, 48–49
Format dialog box, 31–32
Format option, 32
Format Results dialog box, 32
formatting disks, 30–32
root directory, 45

G

graphical user interface (GUI), 3
grayed-out menu options, 18
GUI (graphical user interface), 3

H

hard disk. *See* disks
Help , 21–24
    books, 22–23
    listing topics, 22, 23–24
    selecting topics, 21–24
    starting, 21
    status bar, 22
    tab controls, 22–23
Help window, 22, 23
hiding windows, 15, 16
highlighting
    selected icons, 8
    selected objects, 8
    selected text, 8, 34

I

icons, 6, 9. *See also specific icons*
    actions on, effects, 48, 49
    deleting, 48
    large icon view, 45
    My Computer window, 42
    opening, 43
    printers, 43
    selecting, 8
    storage devices, 42
Index tab, Help, 23, 27–28
inserting characters, 35
insertion point, 33
    moving, 34
Interactive Labs, 5

J

jumping to Help topics, 21–22

K

keyboard, 6
    copying files, 47–48
    error correction, 32–33

L

Labs, 28, 54
    Using a Keyboard, 28
    Using a Mouse, 28
    Using Files, 54
large icon view, disk contents, 45
left-handed use of mouse, 7
list boxes, 19–20
    drop-down, 20
    moving in, 19
    viewing options, 19
listing. *See* displaying
lost data. *See* data loss

M

main directory, 45–46
Maximize button, 15
maximizing windows, 17
menu bar, 14, 17
menu conventions, 17, 18
menu options, 17, 18
    check marks, 18
    ellipsis (...), 18
    grayed-out, 18
    triangles, 18
menus, 8, 17–18. *See also specific menus*
    conventions, 18
    options. *See* menu options
    selecting commands, 17–18
    starting applications, 9–11
    submenus, 18
    titles, 17
Microsoft Windows 3.1. *See* Windows 3.1
Microsoft Windows 95. *See* Windows 95
Minimize button, 15, 16
minimizing windows, 15
mistakes
    correcting in text, 32–33
    in using tutorials, 4
modifying. *See* changing
mouse, 6–9
    clicking. *See* clicking
    double-clicking, 8
    dragging. *See* dragging
    left-handed use, 7
    pointing with, 7. *See also* mouse pointer
    room to move, 7
mouse pointer, 6, 11
    insertion point compared with, 33
    moving, 7–8

moving. *See also* switching
- files, 47–48
- insertion point, 33
- in list boxes, 23
- mouse, room for, 7
- mouse pointer, 7–8
- scroll box, 23
- windows, 16–17

multitasking, 3, 10–12
- closing applications, 12
- switching between applications, 12
- WordPad and Paint applications, 10–12

My Computer icon, 42
- opening, 43

My Computer window, 50
- opening, 42, 43

N

naming files. *See* filenames

O

objects, selecting, 8
on-line Help. *See* Help
Open button, 38, 39
Open dialog box, 38
opening
- books in Help, 22
- files, 38–39
- My Computer icon, 42
- windows, 41, 42

open windows, taskbar, 23
operating systems, 3. *See also* Windows 3.1; Windows 95
option buttons, 21
organizing files, 47

P

pages
- collating, 40
- selected, printing, 40

Pages radio button, 40
Paint application
- closing, 12
- running WordPad at same time with, 10–12

parentheses (()), root directory, 45
phrases, searching for in Help, 22, 24, 29–30
pointer. *See* mouse pointer
pointing with mouse, 6–7
previewing documents, 39
Print dialog box, 39–40
printers
- icons, 42
- modifying setup, 40
- selecting, 40
- viewing, 40

Printers folders, 42
printing
- collating pages, 40
- files, 39–40
- number of copies, 40
- parts of documents, 40

Print Preview, 39
Print range box, 40
programs. *See* active program; applications
properties button, 40

R

radio buttons, 20–21
Recycle Bin
- emptying, 48
- retrieving files, 48

Reference Windows, 4
Rename option, 49
renaming files, 49
replacing text, 34
Restore button, 15
restoring windows, 16
retrieving deleted files, 48
root directory, 45

S

Save As dialog box, 36
Save button, 36
Save Changes to Document? message, 36
saving files, 36
scroll box, moving, 19
searching. *See* finding
sectors, bad, 32
selecting
- commands from menus, 17–18
- disk drives, 36

Help topics, 22–24
icons, 6
multiple items with checkboxes, 21
number of copies to print, 40
objects, 6
printers, 40
single items with radio buttons, 21
text, 8, 34
toolbar buttons, 19
setting clock, 6
setup, printer, 40
shrinking windows, 15
Shut down the computer option, 12
shutting down Windows 95, 12
size, files, 45
sizing buttons, 15
sizing handle, 17
sizing windows, 15–17
software. *See* active program; applications
speaker icon, 6
Start button, 8, 9
starting
Help, 26
programs, 8–10
Windows 95, 5–6
Start menu, starting programs, 9–10
status bar, 14
storage devices. *See also* disks
icons, 42
Student Disk
adding files, 41–42
backing up, 50–51
listing files, 44–46
subdirectories, 45–46
submenus, 18
switching. *See also* changing
to desktop, 11
to large icon view, 45
between programs, 12

T

tab controls, 20–21
Help, 26–27
taskbar, 6
buttons. *See* taskbar buttons
taskbar buttons, 6, 12–13
active program, 12
open windows, 17
Task References, 4
technical terms, definitions, 23
text, 32–34. *See also* documents
blocks, 34
error correction, 32–33
inserting characters, 35
insertion point, 33–34
replacing, 34
selecting, 8, 34
typing in WordPad, 32–33
word wrap, 32
3½ Floppy (A:) icon, 31
3.1 Notes, 5
tilde (~), filenames, 35
time of file creation or revision, 45
setting, 6
title bar, 14
titles
menus, 14, 17
windows, 14
toggle switches, 18
toolbar buttons, 8, 14, 19
finding out function, 22
selecting, 23
toolbars, 19
buttons. *See* toolbar buttons
Tooltips, 7–8, 19
triangles, menu options, 18
TROUBLE paragraphs, 4
turning off computer, 12–13
tutorials, using effectively, 4–5
Type Size drop-down list box, 20
typing text in WordPad, 33

U

underlined terms, definitions, 23
up arrow button, 19

V

verifying file location, 47–48
viewing. *See* displaying

W

windows, 16–17. *See also specific windows*
- active, 12
- controls. *See* controls
- displaying, 16
- Help, 21
- hiding, 11
- moving, 16–17
- multiple, at one time, 10–11
- open, 17
- opening, 42, 43
- Reference Windows, 4
- restoring, 15
- sizing, 17

Windows 3.1, 4
- deleting icons, 48
- double-clicking, 8, 27
- filenames, 35
- finding program windows, 11
- switching between programs, 12
- 3.1 Notes, 5
- using applications with Windows 95, 29

Windows 95, 3
- applications, 3, 29. *See also* WordPad
- desktop. *See* desktop
- Help. *See* Help
- shutting down, 12
- similarities and differences between Windows 3.1 and. *See* Windows 3.1
- software available for, 3
- starting, 5–6
- Windows 3.1 applications, 29

Windows 95 Student Disk. *See* Student Disk

window title, 14

WordPad application
- closing, 14, 37
- exiting, 10
- running Paint at same time with, 10–12
- starting, 9
- typing text, 32–33

word-processing application. *See* WordPad application

words
- definitions, 28
- searching for, in Help, 22, 24

word wrap, 32, 33

workspace, 11

Windows 95 Brief **Task Reference**

TASK	PAGE #	RECOMMENDED METHOD	NOTES
Character, delete	33	Press Backspace	
Check box, de-select	21	Click the check box again	Tab to option, press Spacebar
Check box, select	21	Click the checkbox	Tab to option, press Spacebar
Detailed file list, view	45	From My Computer, click View, Details	
Disk, copy your	50	Place disk in drive A:, from My Computer click 3½ Floppy (A:), click File, Copy Disk, Start	See "Making a Backup of Your Floppy Disk."
Disk, format	30	Click My Computer, click 3½ Floppy (A:), press Enter, click File click Format, click Start	
Drop-down list, display	20	Click	
File, copy		From My Computer, right-click the file, drag to the new location, press C	
File, delete	49	From My Computer, click the file, press Delete, click Yes	See "Deleting a File."
File, move	48	From My Computer, use the left mouse button to drag the file to the desired folder or drive	See "Moving a File."
File, open	37	Click	
File, print	39	Click	
File, print preview	39	Click	
File, rename	49	From My Computer, click the file, click File, click Rename, type new name, press Enter	See "Renaming a File."
File, save	35	Click	
Folder, create	46	From My Computer, click File, New, Folder	See "Creating a New Folder."
Help topic, display	23	From the Help Contents window, click the topic, then click Open	
Help topic, open	23	From the Help Contents window, click the book, then click Display	
Help, start	21	Click Start, then click Help	F1, See "Starting Windows 95 Help."
Icon, open	43	Click the icon, then press Enter or double-click the icon	See "Opening an Icon."

Windows 95 Brief **Task Reference**

TASK	PAGE #	RECOMMENDED METHOD	NOTES
Icons, view large	45	From My Computer, click View, Large Icons	
Insertion point, move	34	Click the desired location in the document Use arrow keys	
List box, scroll	20	Click [▲] or [▼], or drag the scroll box	
Menu option, select	17	Click the menu option	
Menu, open		Click the menu option	Alt-underlined letter
Program, quit	10	Click [X]	Alt-F4
Program, start	9	Click the Start button, point to Programs, point to the program option, click the program	See "Starting a Program."
Radio button, de-select	21	Click a different radio button	Tab to option, press Spacebar
Radio button, select	21	Click the radio button	Tab to option, press Spacebar
Start menu, display			Ctrl-Esc
Student data disk, create	41	Click [Start], click Programs, CTI Win95, Windows 95 Brief, Make Windows 95 Student Disk, press Enter	
Text, select	34	Drag the pointer over the text	
Tooltip, display	19	Position pointer over the tool	
Window, change size	17	Drag [resize handle]	
Window, close	10	Click [X]	Ctrl-F4
Window, maximize	17	Click [□]	
Window, minimize	15	Click [_]	
Window, move	17	Drag the title bar	
Window, redisplay	16	Click the taskbar button	
Window, restore	16	Click [restore]	
Window, switch	12	Click the taskbar button of the program	Alt-Tab, See "Switching Between Programs."
Windows 95, shut down	12	Click [Start], click Shut Down, Click Yes	
Windows 95, start	5	Turn on the computer	

New Perspectives on

Microsoft® Office Professional for Windows® 95

A Document-Centric Approach

INTRODUCTORY

TUTORIALS

TUTORIAL 1
A Tour of Microsoft Office Professional for Windows 95 OF 3

TUTORIAL 2
Word Basics and Embedding a WordArt Object OF 78

TUTORIAL 3
Excel Basics and Embedding a Worksheet OF 134

TUTORIAL 4
Access Basics and Importing an Excel Worksheet OF 201

TUTORIAL 5
PowerPoint Basics and Embedding an Excel Chart in a Presentation OF 285

TUTORIAL 6
Enhancing an Excel Workbook and Creating and Linking a Chart to Word OF 340

TUTORIAL 7
Querying and Enhancing an Access Database OF 425

Read This **Before You Begin**

TO THE STUDENT

STUDENT DISKS

To complete the tutorials, Tutorial Assignments, and Case Problems in this book, you need nine Student Disks. Your instructor will either provide you with Student Disks or ask you to make your own.

If you are supposed to make your own Student Disks, you will need nine blank, formatted disks. You will need to copy a set of folders from a file server or standalone computer onto your disks. Your instructor will tell you which computer, drive letter, and folders contain the folders you need. The following table shows you which folders go on each of your disks, so that you will have enough disk space to complete all the tutorials, Tutorial Assignments, and Case Problems:

Student Disk	Write this on the disk label	Put these folders on the disk
1	Tutorial 1 Tutorial	Tutorial.01 from Disk 1 folder
2	Tutorial 1 Tutorial Assignments	Tutorial.01 from Disk 2 folder
3	Tutorial 1 Case Problems	Tutorial.01 from Disk 3 folder
4	Tutorials 2 & 3	Tutorial.02, Tutorial .03
5	Tutorial 4 Tutorial and Tutorial Assignments	Tutorial.04 from Disk 5 folder
6	Tutorial 4 Case Problems	Tutorial.04 from Disk 6 folder
7	Tutorial 5	Tutorial.05
8	Tutorial 6	Tutorial.06
9	Tutorial 7 Tutorial	Tutorial.07 from Disk 9 folder
10	Tutorial 7 Tutorial Assignments	Tutorial.07 from Disk 10 folder
11	Tutorial 7 Cases 1 & 2	Tutorial.07 from Disk 11 folder
12	Tutorial 7 Cases 3 & 4	Tutorial.07 from Disk 12 folder

When you begin each tutorial, be sure you are using the correct Student Disk. See the inside front or inside back cover of this book for more information on Student Disks, or ask your instructor or technical support person for assistance.

COURSE LABS

This book features interactive Course Labs to help you understand some important concepts. There are Lab Assignments in the Windows and Essential Concepts sections, and at the end of Office Tutorials 2, 3, and 4 that relate to these Labs. To start the Labs, click the Start button on the Windows 95 taskbar, point to Programs, point to Course Labs, point to New Perspectives Applications, and click the name of the Lab.

USING YOUR OWN COMPUTER

If you are going to work through this book using your own computer, you need:

- **Computer System** Microsoft Windows 95 and Microsoft Office Professional for Windows 95 must be installed on your computer. This book assumes a complete installation of Office.
- **Student Disks** Ask your instructor or lab manager for details on how to get the Student Disks. You will not be able to complete the tutorials or exercises in this book using your own computer until you have Student Disks.
- **Course Labs** See your instructor or technical support person to obtain the Course Labs for use on your own computer.

VISIT OUR WORLD WIDE WEB SITE

Additional materials designed especially for you are available on the World Wide Web. Go to http://www.vmedia.com/cti/.

TO THE INSTRUCTOR

To complete the tutorials in this book, your students must use a set of student files. These files are stored on the Student Files Disks that are included in the Instructor's Resource Kit. Follow the instructions on the disk labels and the Readme.doc file to copy them to your server or standalone computer. You can view the Readme.doc file using WordPad.

Once the files are copied, you can make Student Disks for the students yourself, or tell students where to find the files so they can make their own Student Disks. Make sure the files get correctly copied by following the instructions in the Student Disks section above, which will ensure that students have enough disk space to complete all the tutorials, Tutorial Assignments, and Case Problems.

SPREADSHEET COURSE LAB SOFTWARE

Several tutorials feature online Course Labs that introduce basic concepts. This software is distributed on the Course Labs Setup Disk, included in the Instructor's Resource Kit. To install the Lab software, follow the setup instructions on the disk label and in the Readme.doc file. Once you have installed the Course Lab software, your students can start any Lab from the Windows 95 desktop by clicking Start, pointing to Programs/Course Labs/New Perspectives Applications, and clicking the name of the Lab.

CTI SOFTWARE AND STUDENT FILES

You are granted a license to copy the Student Files and Course Labs to any computer or computer network used by students who have purchased this book. The files and software are included in the Instructor's Resource Kit and may also be obtained electronically over the Internet. See the inside front or inside back cover of this book for more details.

TUTORIAL 1

A Tour of Microsoft Office Professional for Windows 95

Reviewing a Seminar Schedule and a Seminar Presentation

OBJECTIVES

In this tutorial you will:

- Learn about the features and programs of Office 95
- Display and use the Office Shortcut Bar
- Open, navigate, edit, format, save, and print a Word document
- Use the Help system for Office 95 programs
- Copy, open, navigate, and update an Access database
- Open, update, and save an Excel workbook
- Open, save, update, and print a PowerPoint presentation
- Update an embedded Excel worksheet in a Word document
- Link and update an Excel chart in a PowerPoint presentation

CASE

Valle Coffee

Ten years ago Leonard Valle became the president of Algoman Imports, a small distributor of inexpensive coffee beans to supermarkets in western Michigan. At that time the company's growth had leveled off, so during his first three years Leonard took several dramatic, risky steps in an attempt to increase sales and profits. First, he changed the inexpensive coffee bean varieties that Algoman Imports had been distributing to a selection of gourmet varieties from Central and South America, Africa, and several island nations. Second, he purchased facilities and equipment so that the company could roast, grind, flavor, and package the coffee beans instead of buying them already roasted and packaged whole. Because the company could now control the quality of the finest gourmet coffees, Leonard stopped distributing to supermarkets and shifted sales to restaurants and offices in the area.

Within two years, company sales and profits soared; consequently, five years ago Leonard took over ownership of the company. He changed the company name to Valle Coffee, continued expanding into other markets and geographic areas, and expanded the company's line of coffee flavors and blends.

Valle Coffee today stresses quality, price, and service. The company continues to sell imported gourmet regular and decaffeinated (decaf) coffees. In addition, the company produces and sells regular and decaf flavored coffees, such as Caramel Creme, French Vanilla, Hazelnut Creme, and Swiss Chocolate Almond; and regular and decaf blended coffees, such as Dutch Breakfast, Kona Blend, San Francisco Blend, and Valle Gourmet Blend.

For its restaurant and office customers located throughout Michigan, Ohio, and Indiana, Valle Coffee roasts, grinds, and vacuum-seals the coffee in single-batch packages. For its rapidly expanding mail-order business, which the company started three years ago, customers purchase whole roasted beans. At its headquarters location, Valle Coffee has one retail outlet, which is a combination store and coffee shop, where it sells whole and ground coffee, as well as prepared coffee, espresso, and cappuccino. Also at its headquarters Valle Coffee periodically offers three types of seminars to introduce prospective customers to gourmet coffees.

Part of Valle Coffee's success can be credited to its use of computers in all aspects of its business, including financials, inventory control, shipping, receiving, production, and sales. Several months ago the company upgraded to Microsoft Windows 95 and Microsoft Office Professional for Windows 95 (or simply Office 95), two software products from Microsoft Corporation. Belinda Jones, a seminar instructor, used these products to prepare a seminar schedule handout and a presentation for the Coffee I seminar, which is an introduction to coffee growing and processing. In this tutorial, you will work with the seminar schedule and presentation as you learn to use Office 95.

Using the Tutorials Effectively

The tutorials in this book will help you learn about Office 95. These tutorials are designed to be used at a computer. Each tutorial is divided into sessions. Watch for the session headings, such as Session 1.1 and Session 1.2. Each session is designed to be completed in about 45 minutes, but take as much time as you need. It's also a good idea to take a break between sessions.

Before you begin, read the following questions and answers. They are designed to help you use the tutorials effectively.

Where do I start?

Each tutorial begins with a case, which sets the scene for the tutorial and gives you background information to help you understand what you will be doing in the tutorial. Ideally, you should read the case before you go to the lab. In the lab, begin with Session 1.1.

How do I know what to do on the computer?

Each session contains steps that you will perform on the computer to learn how to use Office 95. Read the text that introduces each series of steps. The steps you need to do at a computer are numbered and are set against a colored background. Read each step carefully and completely before you try it.

How do I know if I did the step correctly?

As you work, compare your computer screen with the corresponding figure in the tutorial. Don't worry if your screen display is somewhat different from the figure. The important parts of the screen display are labeled in each figure. Check to make sure these parts are on your screen.

What if I make a mistake?

Don't worry about making mistakes—they are part of the learning process. Paragraphs labeled "**TROUBLE?**" identify common problems and explain how to get back on track. Follow the steps in the **TROUBLE?** paragraph *only* if you are having the problem described. If you run into other problems:

- Carefully consider the current state of your system, the position of the mouse pointer, and any messages on the screen.
- Identify your goal. Completing the sentence, "Now I want to...." will help you to be specific.
- Develop a plan for accomplishing your goal, and put your plan into action.

How do I use the Reference Windows?

Reference Windows summarize the procedures you learn in the tutorial steps. Do not complete the actions in the Reference Windows when you are working through the tutorial. Instead, refer to the Reference Windows when you are working on the assignments at the end of the tutorial.

How can I test my understanding of what I learned in the tutorial?

At the end of each session, you can answer the Quick Check questions. The answers for the Quick Checks are at the end of the book.

After you have completed the entire tutorial, you should complete the Tutorial Assignments and Case Problems. They are carefully structured so that you will review what you have learned and then apply your knowledge to new situations.

What if I can't remember how to do something?

You can use the Task Reference at the end of the tutorials; it summarizes how to accomplish tasks using the most efficient method.

Before you begin the tutorials, you should know how to use the menus, dialog boxes, toolbars, Help facility, and My Computer in Windows 95. You'll have the necessary skills and knowledge you need if you've worked through the two Brief Windows 95 tutorials.

Now that you know how to use the tutorials effectively, you are ready to begin.

SESSION 1.1

In this session you'll learn how to use the Office Shortcut Bar, recognize common program window components, open and work with an existing Word document, save a Word document, make simple editing and formatting changes to a Word document, and use the Help system.

What Is Office 95?

Office 95 (Professional version) is a collection of software programs developed by Microsoft to work specifically with Windows 95. The core programs in this collection, or **suite**, are Word, Excel, Access, and PowerPoint. A Standard version of Office 95, which does not include Access, is also available.

The Office 95 programs are consistent with Windows 95, having similar-looking windows and dialog boxes and many common features, such as file saving, file printing, and spell checking. Consequently, when you learn to use a common feature in one program, you'll know how to use that feature in the other programs. The programs also automate many common tasks—for example, in Word if you type "teh," the typing error is immediately corrected to "the"; in Excel if you enter a series of numbers, the program can perform calculations for you automatically.

Office 95's data-sharing capabilities make it easy for you to use and share, or **integrate,** the same data in all four programs, which saves time and ensures consistent information. You can also focus on the documents you have to complete instead of on the programs you have to use. As shown in Figure 1-1, **data integration** and a **document-centric approach** let you concentrate more on the work you are trying to accomplish and less on the computer technology you are using.

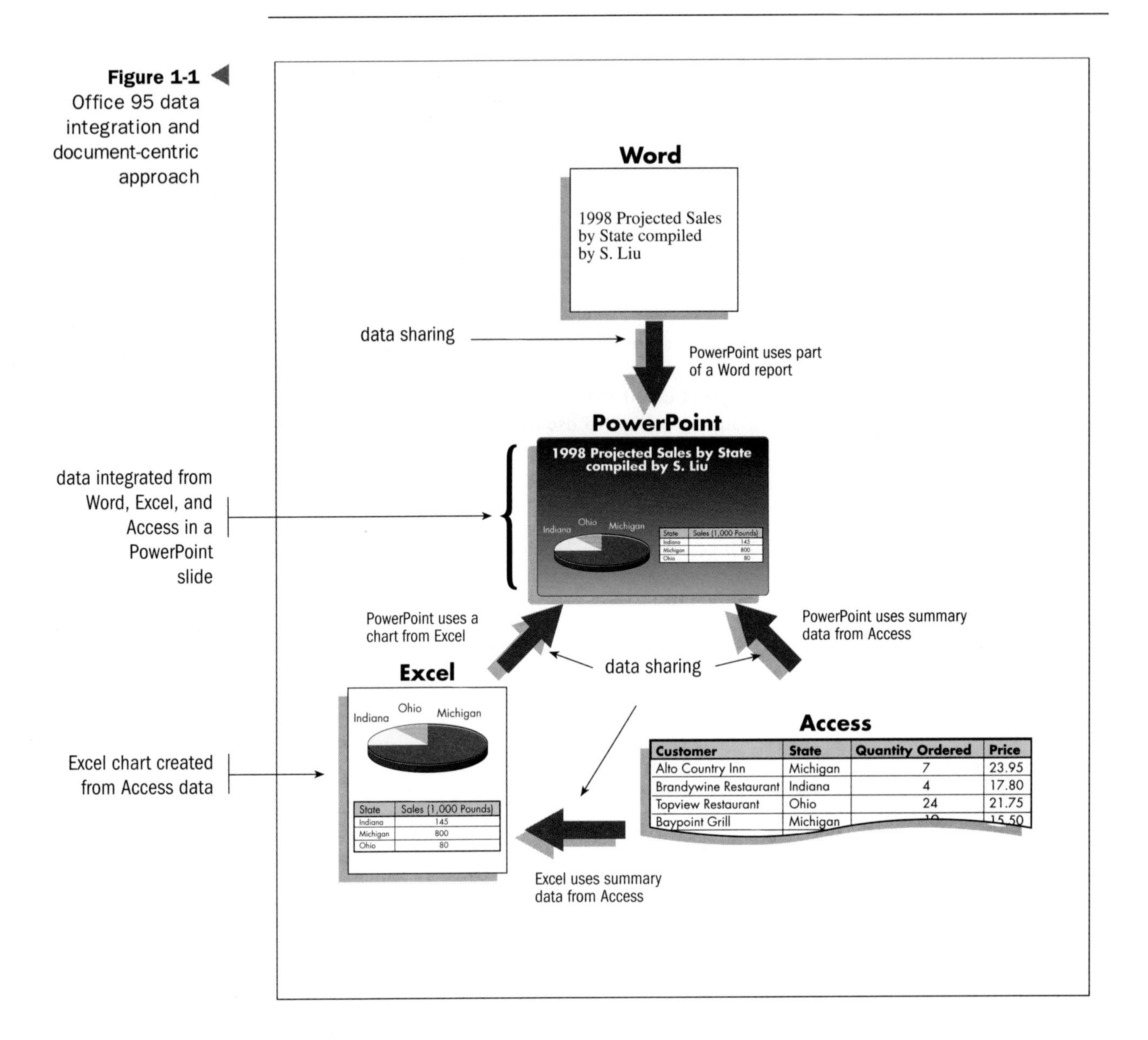

Figure 1-1 Office 95 data integration and document-centric approach

Each Office 95 program provides you with valuable tools to accomplish many tasks, such as writing reports and analyzing data, much more easily and efficiently than if you did these tasks by hand. Using these programs saves you time and allows you to produce more professional-looking documents. Let's take a brief look at each of these Office 95 programs and how Valle Coffee might use them.

Word

Microsoft Word for Windows 95 Version 7, or simply **Word**, is a word-processing program that you use to create documents such as letters, forms, memos, newsletters, and reports. Word offers many features that help you write, edit, and format documents in an attractive way. You can also create, insert, and position diagrams, graphics, tables, and other objects that enhance the appearance of your documents. Valle Coffee uses Word to create documents such as the seminar schedule shown in the Word window in Figure 1-2.

Figure 1-2 Word window

Valle Coffee's seminar schedule document

Excel

Microsoft Excel for Windows 95 Version 7, or simply **Excel**, is a worksheet program that you use to manipulate, analyze, and display numerical information. In Excel you can perform calculations easily, and you can display data visually using charts, such as pie charts and bar charts, to highlight significant information and relationships. Valle Coffee uses Excel to create worksheets and charts such as the ones shown in the Excel window in Figure 1-3.

Figure 1-3 Excel window

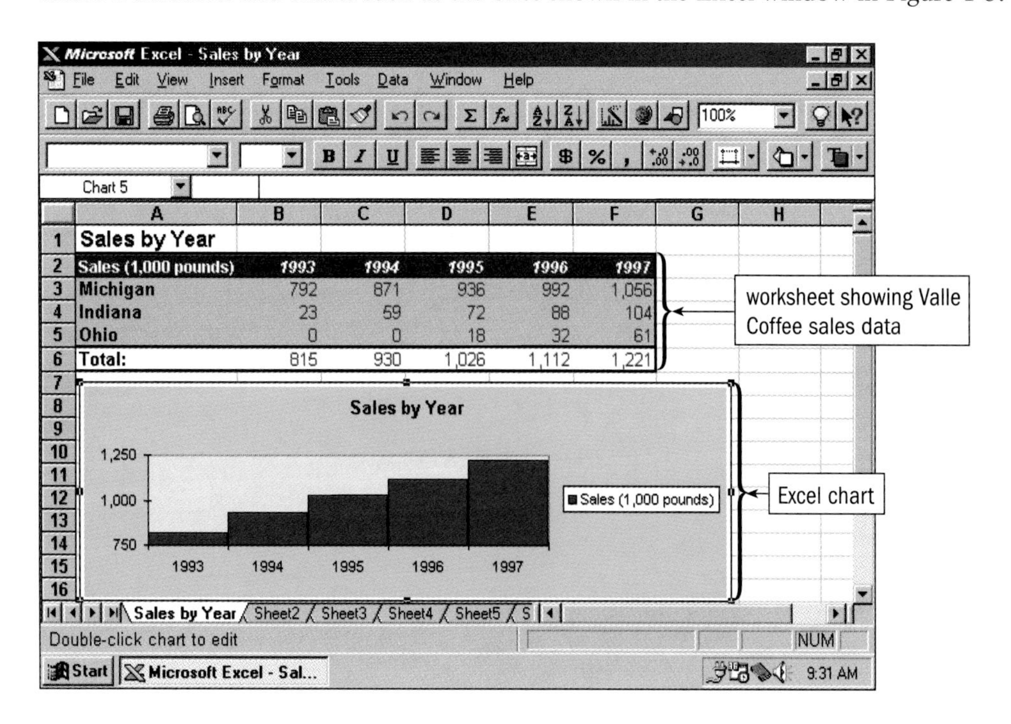

Access

Microsoft Access for Windows 95 Version 7, or simply **Access**, is a database management program that you use to enter, maintain, and retrieve related data in a database. With Access you can retrieve and sort information in many ways, create your own forms to facilitate data entry and data analysis, and create professional-looking reports. Valle Coffee uses Access to enter, maintain, and retrieve data such as the customer data shown in the Access window in Figure 1-4.

Figure 1-4
Access window

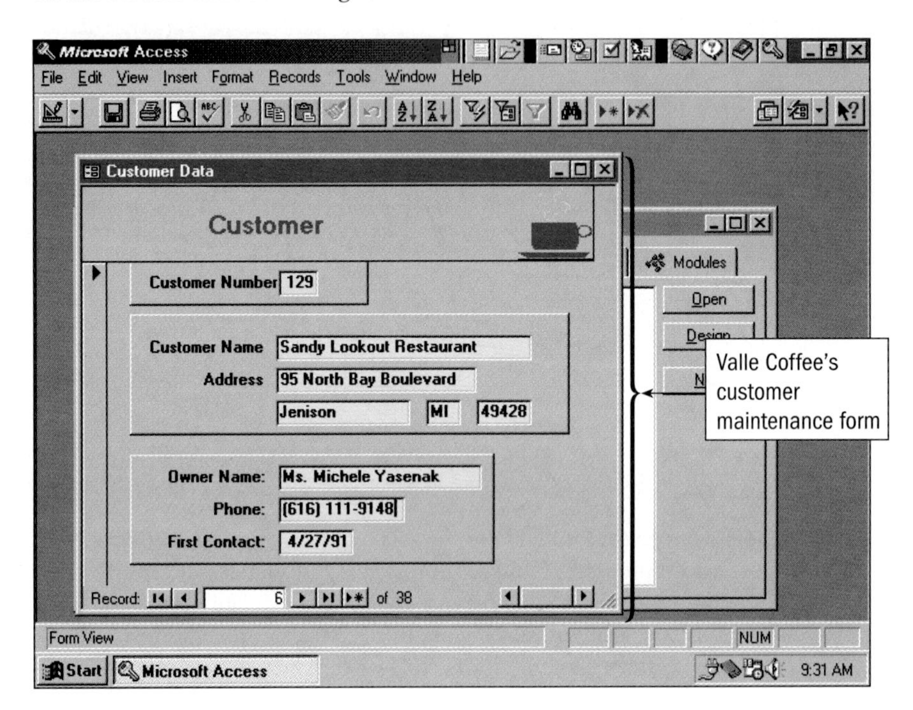

PowerPoint

Microsoft PowerPoint for Windows 95 Version 7, or simply **PowerPoint**, is a presentation graphics program that you use to create professional-looking and effective presentations containing text, graphics, charts, and so on. You can show a presentation on a computer screen, project it onto a screen as a slide show, or use it as the basis for overhead transparencies and 35mm slides. You can also create audience handouts, outlines, and speaker's notes. Valle Coffee uses PowerPoint to create slide presentations such as the one shown in the PowerPoint window in Figure 1-5.

Figure 1-5 PowerPoint window

Other Office 95 Tools

Office 95 provides additional tools you can use with the four main programs to create and change special objects. Figure 1-6 describes the seven primary Office 95 tools and shows how Valle Coffee might use them.

Figure 1-6 ◀ Office 95 tools

Office Tool	Example
ClipArt Gallery organizes clip art images, which are familiar (and fun) graphic illustrations that you can insert into your documents in any size you choose. Office 95 comes with hundreds of clip art images. Valle Coffee might use the image of the coffee cup, for example, in the ClipArt Gallery to create a logo.	
Data Map lets you insert geographical maps based on tabular data, like this map of coffee sales by state at Valle Coffee.	
Equation Editor lets you add mathematical symbols and complex equations to a document. The president of Valle Coffee might add an equation like this one to a document about investment maturities.	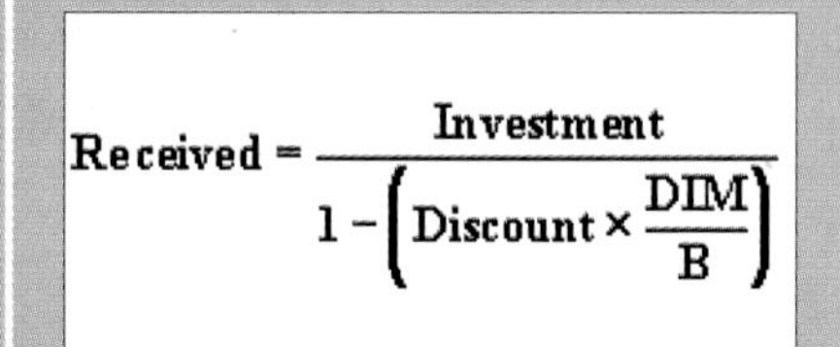 $\text{Received} = \dfrac{\text{Investment}}{1 - \left(\text{Discount} \times \dfrac{\text{DIM}}{\text{B}}\right)}$
Graph lets you insert charts based on tabular data in a variety of visual displays, like this 3-D column chart showing coffee sales by year at Valle Coffee.	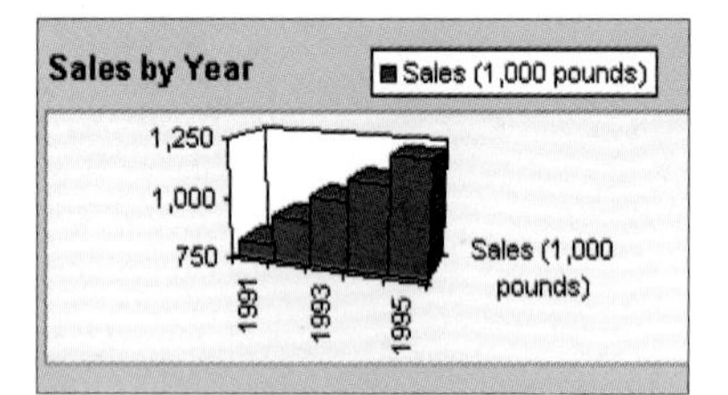
Organization Chart lets you create a flowchart showing, for example, the personnel and reporting structure at Valle Coffee.	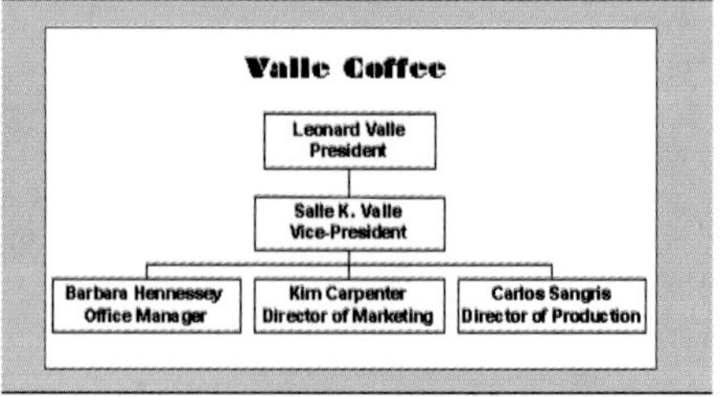
Paint is a Windows 95 program that lets you create and modify your own full-color graphic images. Valle Coffee might use Paint to create a logo, such as this stylized coffee cup.	
WordArt lets you display and shape text using a variety of visual effects. You can enhance text by applying interesting combinations of shading, color, dimension, and rotation. Valle Coffee might use WordArt to design a trademark company name.	

Now that you know the programs and tools you'll be using in these tutorials, you are ready to use the Office Shortcut Bar to work with the Valle Coffee documents.

Office Shortcut Bar

The **Office Shortcut Bar** is a toolbar that gives you access to your Office 95 documents. You use the Office Shortcut Bar to start new documents and open existing documents for the Office 95 programs, and you can customize it to include other programs. When you use the Office Shortcut Bar along with the taskbar, you can start and navigate through your Office 95 documents and programs easily.

If the Office Shortcut Bar does not appear on your Windows 95 desktop, you need to know how to display and dock it. A **docked** toolbar is one that is attached to an edge of the screen. The figures in this book show the Office Shortcut Bar docked at the top of the screen and placed within the title bar area. Docking at the top and on the right of the screen are the most common positions for the Office Shortcut Bar. Your school's lab should have the Office Shortcut Bar in a standard position on all its computers, and you should not move it from this position unless instructed to do so by your instructor or technical support person.

If the Office Shortcut Bar is not available on the computer you're using, you can still start and work with the Office 95 programs and tools by using the Programs menu, which is available by clicking the Start button on the taskbar. You can also use the options New Office Document and Open Office Document on the Start menu to work with your Office 95 documents.

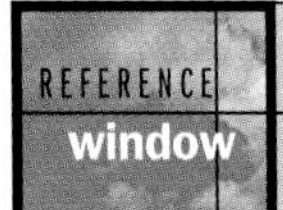

DISPLAYING AND DOCKING THE OFFICE SHORTCUT BAR

- Click the Start button on the taskbar, point to Programs, then click Microsoft Office Shortcut Bar.
- Click any position on the Office Shortcut Bar that is not occupied by a button, then drag the Office Shortcut Bar to the standard docked position for your lab, using the outline that appears as a guide.

If the Office Shortcut Bar does not appear docked on the Windows 95 desktop in your lab's standard position, follow the steps in this section.

To display and dock the Office Shortcut Bar:

1. Make sure Windows 95 is running on your computer and the Windows 95 desktop appears on your screen.

   TROUBLE? If the Welcome to Windows 95 dialog box appears on your screen, click the Close button to close it.

2. If the Office Shortcut Bar is not displayed, click the **Start** button on the taskbar, point to **Programs**, then point to **Microsoft Office Shortcut Bar**. See Figure 1-7. Depending on how your computer is set up, your desktop might contain different icons and your menus might show different options.

Figure 1-7 Displaying the Microsoft Office Shortcut Bar

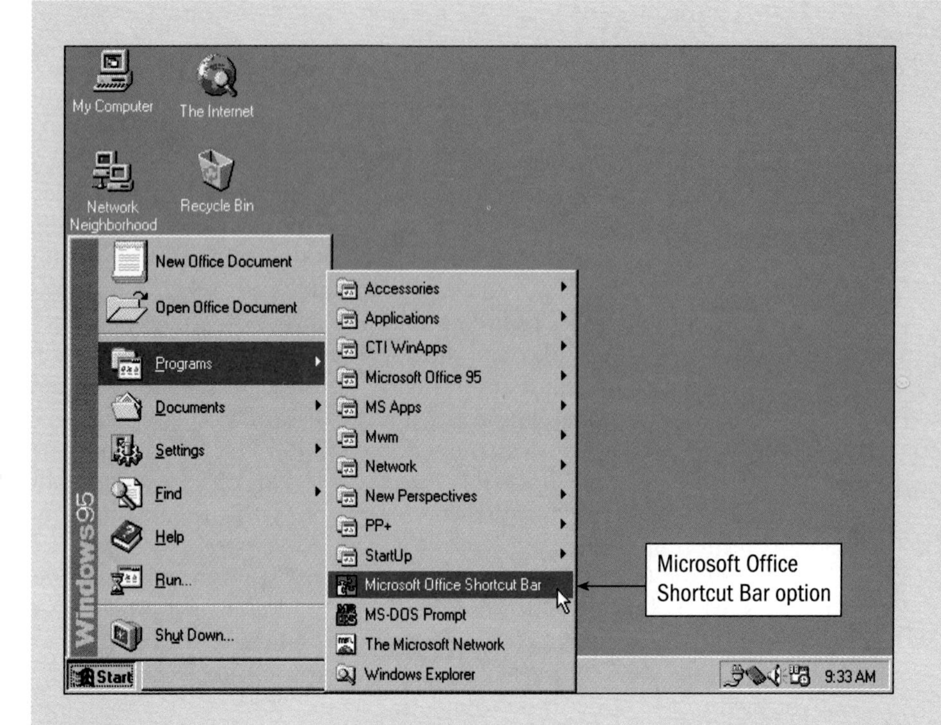

TROUBLE? If you do not see the option "Microsoft Office Shortcut Bar" on the Programs menu, point to Microsoft Office 95 or any other similarly worded menu option, then point to Microsoft Office Shortcut Bar on the menu that appears. If you cannot find the Microsoft Office Shortcut Bar option, ask your instructor or technical support person for assistance.

3. To display the Office Shortcut Bar, click **Microsoft Office Shortcut Bar**. See Figure 1-8. Depending on how Office 95 is set up on your computer, your Office Shortcut Bar might contain different buttons.

Figure 1-8 Office Shortcut Bar on the Windows 95 desktop

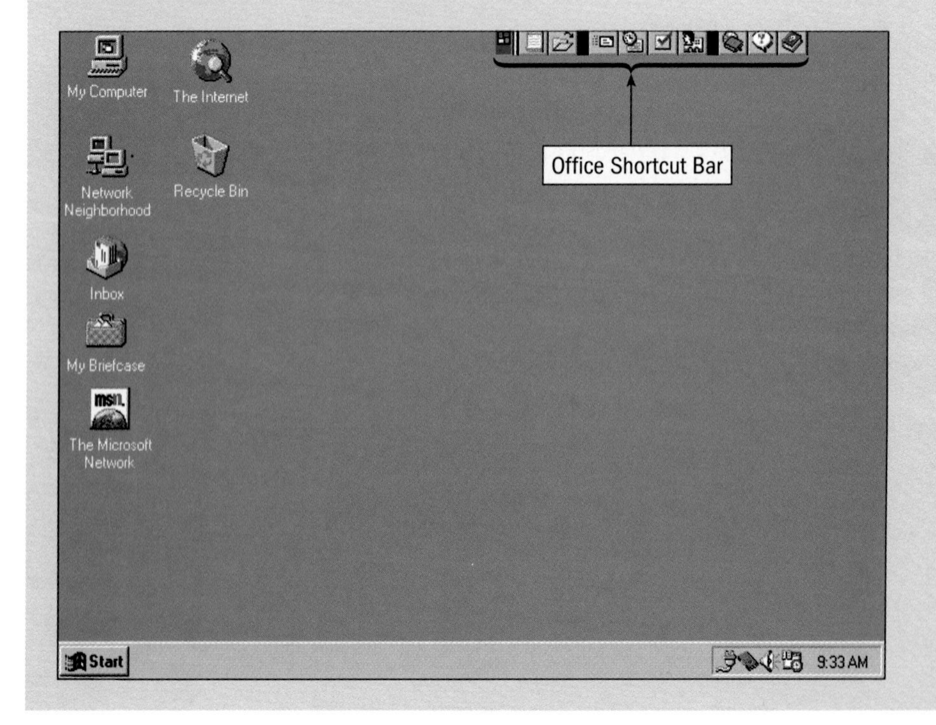

TROUBLE? If a dialog box or program window appears on your screen, you probably clicked the wrong menu option. Click the Close button for that dialog box or window, then repeat Steps 2 and 3. If your Office Shortcut Bar appears in a location different from the standard location for your lab, point to any position on the Office Shortcut Bar that is not occupied by a button, then click and drag the Office Shortcut Bar to the correct location.

TROUBLE? If you want your Office Shortcut Bar to appear in the same location as the one in the figures, drag the bar to the docked position at the top of the screen. To place the Office Shortcut Bar in the title bar area, click the colored squares at the far left of the bar to display the menu, then click Customize. In the Customize dialog box, make sure the View tab is the selected tab, then click the check box for Auto Fit into Title Bar area. Click the OK button. Check with your instructor or technical support person to make sure that you're allowed to change the Office Shortcut Bar's position in your lab.

The Office Shortcut Bar stays in the same position on your screen no matter what windows and dialog boxes you open. You can move, hide, and modify the buttons on the Office Shortcut Bar, but it's best to use the default location and buttons until you have more experience using Office 95 programs. When you point to a button on the Office Shortcut Bar or any Office 95 toolbar and pause for a moment, a ToolTip box appears with the name of the button. **ToolTips** tell you the purpose or function of toolbar buttons.

To display ToolTips for the Office Shortcut Bar buttons:

1. Point to the second button from the left on the Office Shortcut Bar. After a few seconds, the Open a Document ToolTip appears. See Figure 1-9.

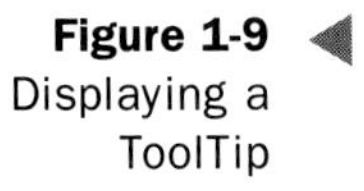

Figure 1-9 Displaying a ToolTip

2. Point to the leftmost button on the Office Shortcut Bar until the Start a New Document ToolTip appears.

   The two leftmost buttons are the ones you will use in these tutorials. However, if you want you can take a moment to view the ToolTips for the other buttons on the Office Shortcut Bar.

3. Point to each of the other buttons on the Office Shortcut Bar to view their ToolTips.

Now that you have access to the Office Shortcut Bar, you can begin your work with Office 95 documents. Belinda asks you to look at the seminar schedule she has prepared and make some changes before she prints and distributes it.

Viewing an Integrated Word Document

Belinda's seminar schedule, shown in Figure 1-10, is a Word document that lists and briefly describes the free seminars offered by Valle Coffee in May. The document includes text formatted in different ways, a graphic image created in Paint, and three tables. The first two tables contain data from an Access database, and the third table contains data from an Excel worksheet. Because the Word document contains data from other programs, it is called an **integrated document**.

Figure 1-10 Valle Coffee's seminar schedule

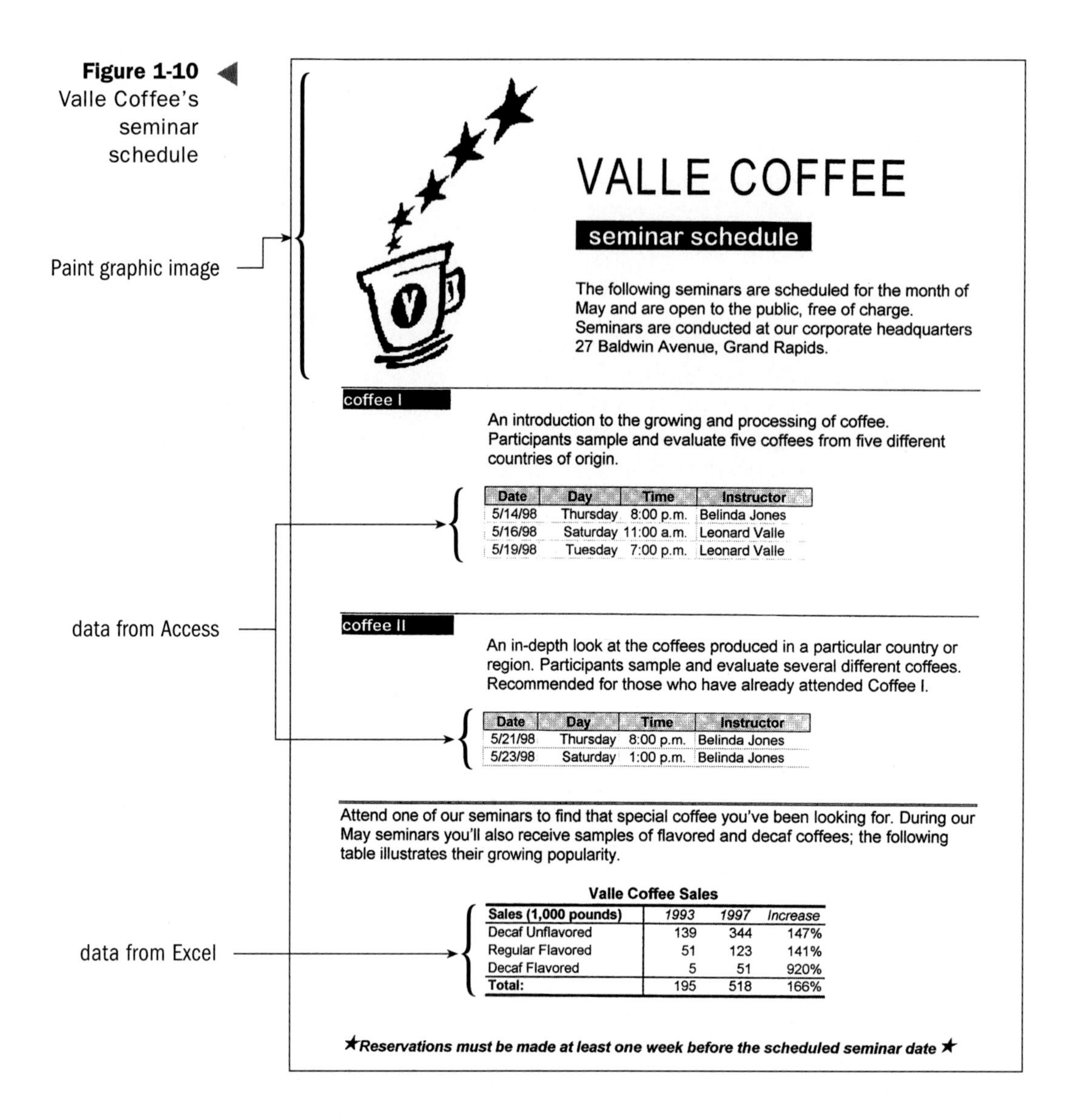

VALLE COFFEE

seminar schedule

The following seminars are scheduled for the month of May and are open to the public, free of charge. Seminars are conducted at our corporate headquarters 27 Baldwin Avenue, Grand Rapids.

coffee I

An introduction to the growing and processing of coffee. Participants sample and evaluate five coffees from five different countries of origin.

Date	Day	Time	Instructor
5/14/98	Thursday	8:00 p.m.	Belinda Jones
5/16/98	Saturday	11:00 a.m.	Leonard Valle
5/19/98	Tuesday	7:00 p.m.	Leonard Valle

coffee II

An in-depth look at the coffees produced in a particular country or region. Participants sample and evaluate several different coffees. Recommended for those who have already attended Coffee I.

Date	Day	Time	Instructor
5/21/98	Thursday	8:00 p.m.	Belinda Jones
5/23/98	Saturday	1:00 p.m.	Belinda Jones

Attend one of our seminars to find that special coffee you've been looking for. During our May seminars you'll also receive samples of flavored and decaf coffees; the following table illustrates their growing popularity.

Valle Coffee Sales

Sales (1,000 pounds)	1993	1997	Increase
Decaf Unflavored	139	344	147%
Regular Flavored	51	123	141%
Decaf Flavored	5	51	920%
Total:	195	518	166%

★*Reservations must be made at least one week before the scheduled seminar date*★

The seminar schedule is a Word document file on your Student Disk. Before starting your work with the seminar schedule, you need to know how to find the Word document file, and all other files, on your Student Disk.

Locating and Storing Documents on Your Student Disk

To find a document you must know its filename (or document name), the folder that contains that document, and the disk that contains that folder. Belinda's seminar schedule document is named Schedule and is located on the Student Disk. This book assumes that your Student Disk is in drive A. You also need to know the folder name that contains the document. Figure 1-11 illustrates the folder and document structure for your Student Disk.

Figure 1-11
Structure of a tutorial folder

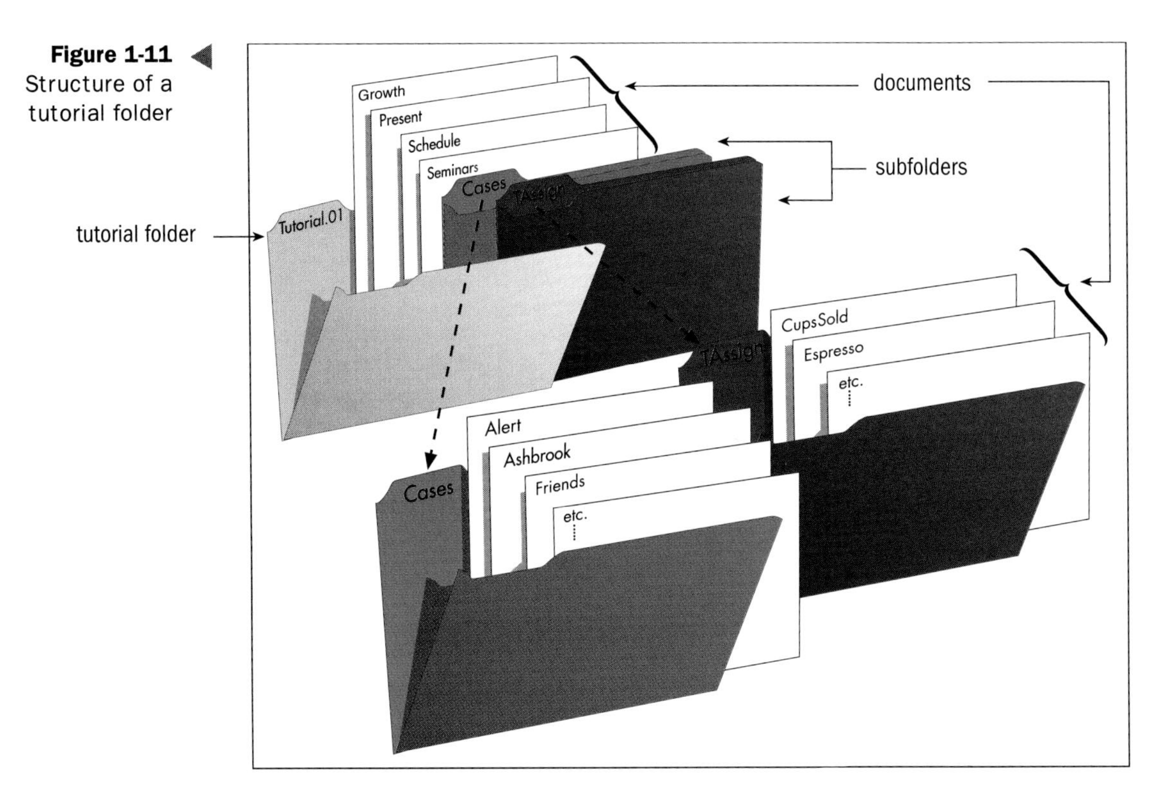

Each tutorial has its own folder on your Student Disk. For example, documents for Tutorial 1 appear in the Tutorial.01 folder, documents for Tutorial 2 appear in the Tutorial.02 folder, and so on. Therefore, Belinda's Schedule document is in the Tutorial.01 folder on your Student Disk.

Because you might complete part of a tutorial but then want to start the tutorial over again, the tutorials instruct you to first save each document with a different filename. This allows you to work with a copy of the document and leave the original intact. Later in this tutorial, for example, you will save a copy of Belinda's seminar schedule document with a filename of Seminar Schedule in the Tutorial.01 folder on your Student Disk.

In addition to documents, each tutorial folder also contains two folders, or subfolders, for the work you do in the exercises at the end of the tutorial. These two folders are named TAssign and Cases. The documents you need to complete the Tutorial Assignments are located in the TAssign folder, and the documents you need to complete the Case Problems are located in the Cases folder. For some tutorials, the TAssign and Cases subfolders will not be on the same disk as the tutorial files. The subfolders are sometimes placed on separate disks to ensure that you will have enough disk space to complete the tutorial and all the Tutorial Assignments and Case Problems. See the Read This Before You Begin page at the beginning of these tutorials for the distribution of files on the Student Disks.

For most of your work in Office 95, you will not need to know a filename's extension. In case you do need to know a filename extension, Figure 1-12 shows some extensions and the programs that use them. For example, the extension for Belinda's Schedule document is "doc," which indicates the file is a Word document.

Figure 1-12
Office 95 extensions and programs

Extension	Program	Extension	Program
bmp	Paint	ppt	PowerPoint
doc	Word	wmf	ClipArt
mdb	Access	xls	Excel

Now that you know where your documents are stored, you are ready to open Belinda's seminar schedule.

Opening an Existing Word Document

To work with Belinda's seminar schedule, you need to open the file named Schedule in the Tutorial.01 folder on your Student Disk. Because this is an existing document, you'll open it by using the Open a Document button on the Office Shortcut Bar.

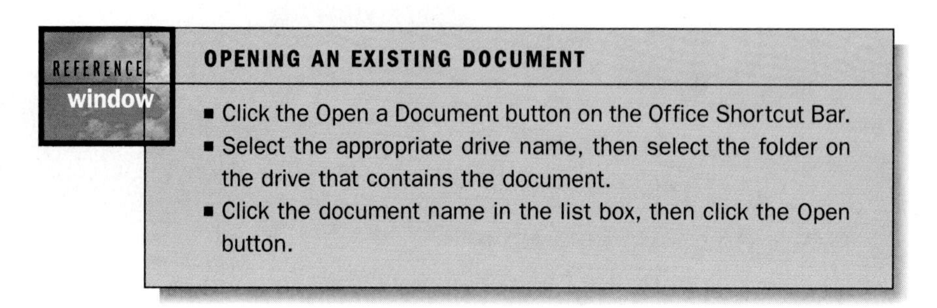

REFERENCE window

OPENING AN EXISTING DOCUMENT

- Click the Open a Document button on the Office Shortcut Bar.
- Select the appropriate drive name, then select the folder on the drive that contains the document.
- Click the document name in the list box, then click the Open button.

When you open a document that already exists, Windows 95 first starts the program that was used to create the document and then opens the document itself. In this case, Windows 95 will start Word, then open the Schedule document.

To start Word and open the Schedule document:

1. Place your Student Disk in the disk drive.
2. Click the **Open a Document** button on the Office Shortcut Bar. The Open dialog box opens. See Figure 1-13.

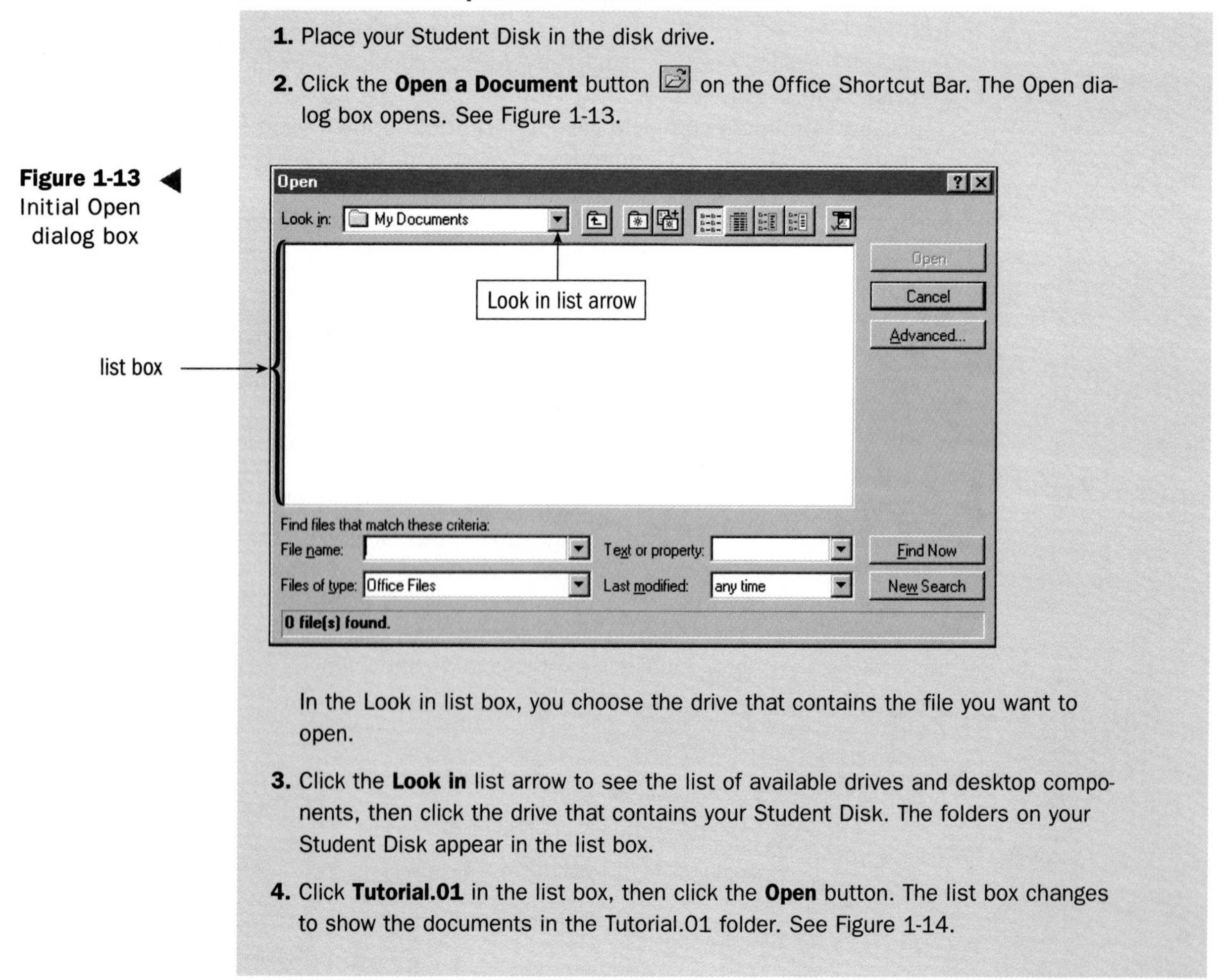

Figure 1-13 Initial Open dialog box

In the Look in list box, you choose the drive that contains the file you want to open.

3. Click the **Look in** list arrow to see the list of available drives and desktop components, then click the drive that contains your Student Disk. The folders on your Student Disk appear in the list box.
4. Click **Tutorial.01** in the list box, then click the **Open** button. The list box changes to show the documents in the Tutorial.01 folder. See Figure 1-14.

Figure 1-14 Open dialog box showing contents of the Tutorial.01 folder

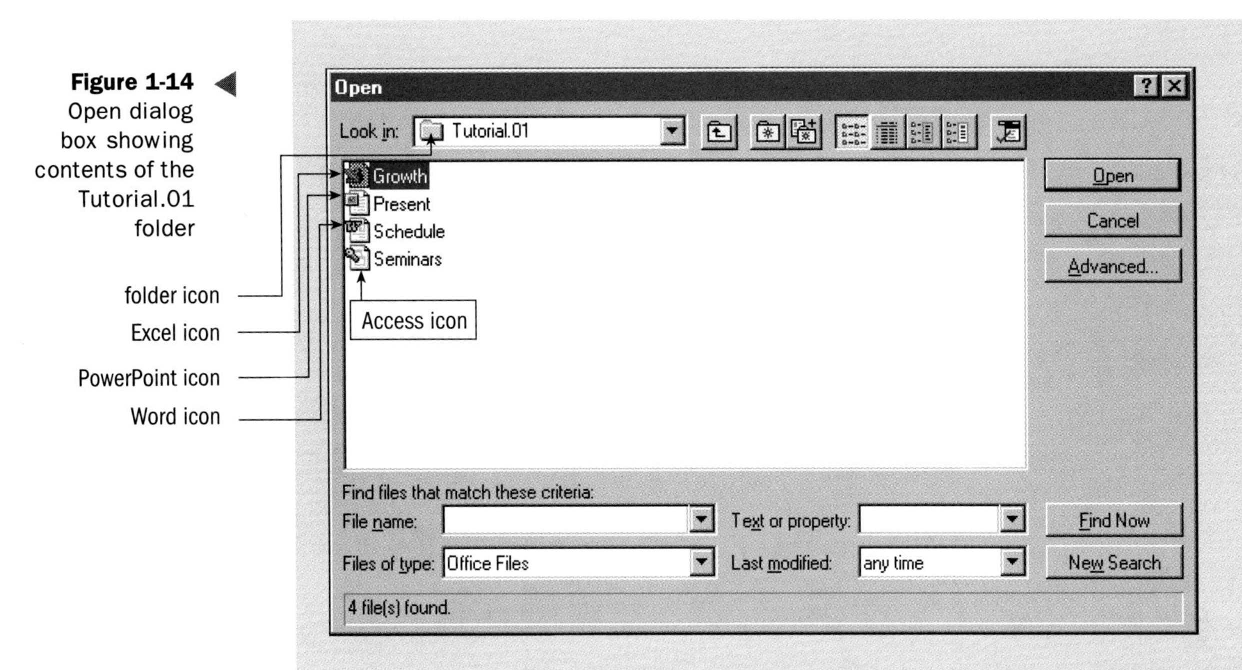

TROUBLE? Your list box might show the extensions for the documents if your computer lab was set up with this Windows 95 option. If that is the case, the extensions will appear on your screens for all programs.

In the list box, an icon precedes each name to identify it as either a folder name or a document name, and to indicate which program was used to create the file. The programs used to create the four documents shown in the list box in Figure 1-14 are Excel for Growth, PowerPoint for Present, Word for Schedule, and Access for Seminars.

5. Click **Schedule** in the list box, then click the **Open** button. A title screen (also called a splash screen) appears briefly, Word starts, then the document appears in the Word window. See Figure 1-15. Don't worry if your screen doesn't look exactly the same as Figure 1-15. You are ready to continue when you can see the Word title bar.

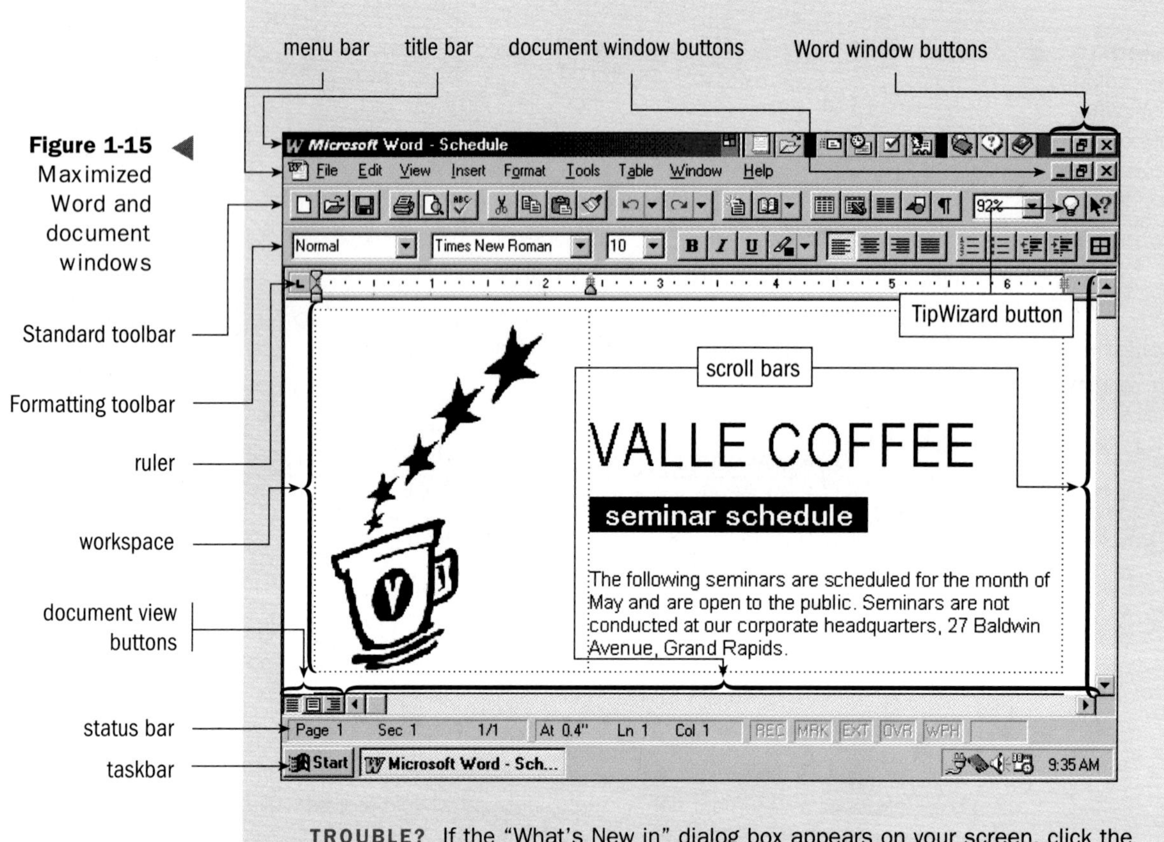

Figure 1-15 Maximized Word and document windows

TROUBLE? If the "What's New in" dialog box appears on your screen, click the dialog box's Close button to close it. If your Word window is not maximized, click the Word window's Maximize button. Your screen might display a little more or less than the document shown in Figure 1-15 if you are using a display type that is different from the one used to produce the figures in the tutorials or if your Word startup options are different. This screen variation should not be a problem as you continue with the tutorial.

TROUBLE? If the TipWizard button is selected, click it to deselect the TipWizard option. (See Figure 1-15 for the location of the TipWizard button.) The TipWizard displays information about the Word program in the area between the Formatting toolbar and the ruler. Turning the TipWizard off gives you more workspace for your document. You can work with the TipWizard on, if you prefer, but keep in mind that your screen will vary slightly from the figures in the tutorials.

Before you can make Belinda's changes to the document, you must become familiar with the components of the Word window and their use.

The Word Window

Word operates like other Windows 95 programs. The Word screen in Figure 1-15 shows several familiar Windows controls, such as the title bar, menu bar, scroll bars, and taskbar. Figure 1-16 describes the function of each component on the Word screen. You need to become familiar with each component's location and function to use Word properly. You will learn to use all of them in these tutorials, so don't be concerned if some of the terminology and features are unfamiliar to you now. Carefully read through the function of each screen component listed in Figure 1-16 and note the location of that component on the Word screen shown in Figure 1-15.

Figure 1-16 ◀ Word screen components and their functions

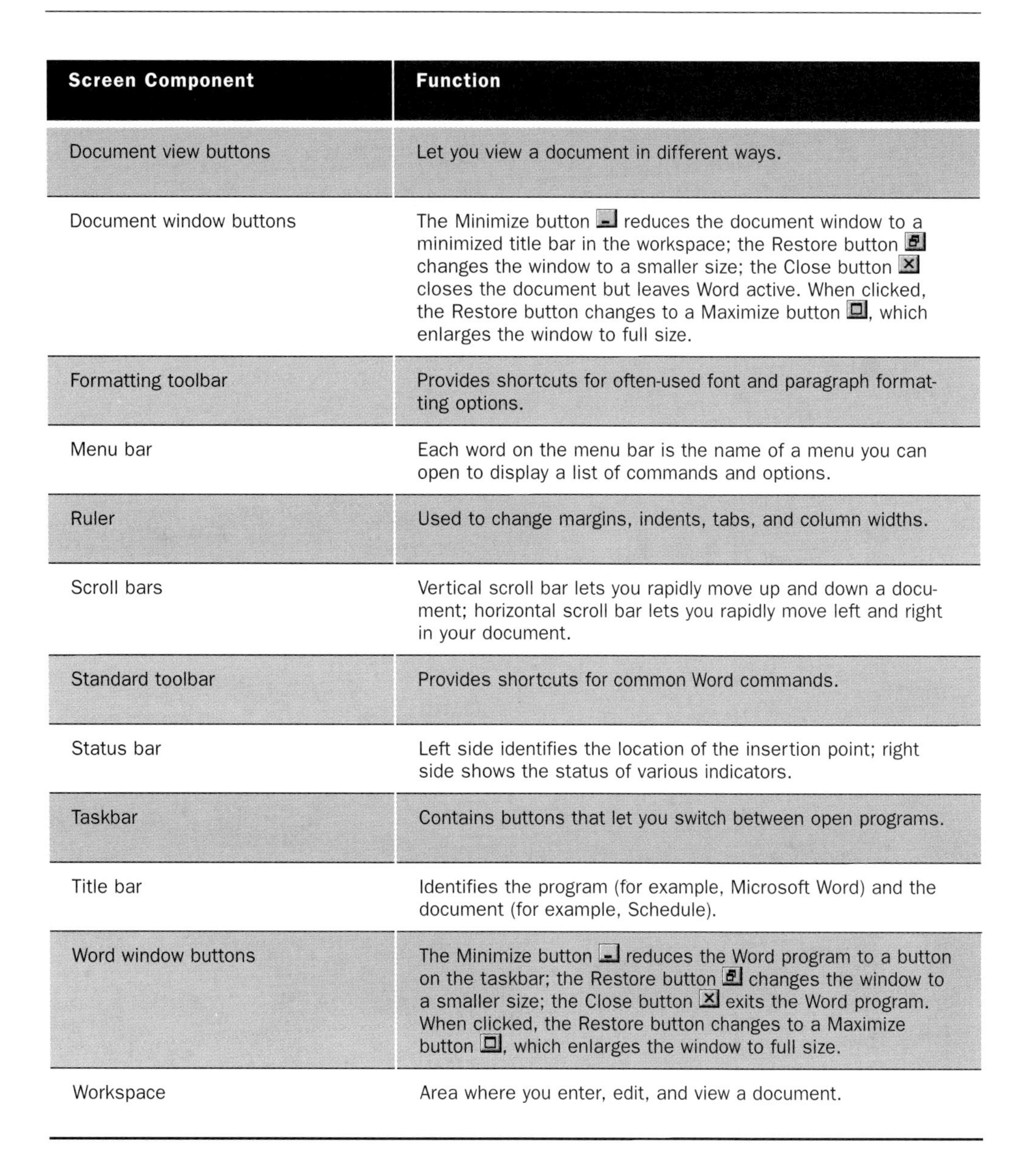

Screen Component	Function
Document view buttons	Let you view a document in different ways.
Document window buttons	The Minimize button reduces the document window to a minimized title bar in the workspace; the Restore button changes the window to a smaller size; the Close button closes the document but leaves Word active. When clicked, the Restore button changes to a Maximize button, which enlarges the window to full size.
Formatting toolbar	Provides shortcuts for often-used font and paragraph formatting options.
Menu bar	Each word on the menu bar is the name of a menu you can open to display a list of commands and options.
Ruler	Used to change margins, indents, tabs, and column widths.
Scroll bars	Vertical scroll bar lets you rapidly move up and down a document; horizontal scroll bar lets you rapidly move left and right in your document.
Standard toolbar	Provides shortcuts for common Word commands.
Status bar	Left side identifies the location of the insertion point; right side shows the status of various indicators.
Taskbar	Contains buttons that let you switch between open programs.
Title bar	Identifies the program (for example, Microsoft Word) and the document (for example, Schedule).
Word window buttons	The Minimize button reduces the Word program to a button on the taskbar; the Restore button changes the window to a smaller size; the Close button exits the Word program. When clicked, the Restore button changes to a Maximize button, which enlarges the window to full size.
Workspace	Area where you enter, edit, and view a document.

The Word screen contains two windows: the Word program window and the document window. The **Word window** opens automatically when you start Word or open a Word document. The **document window** opens within the Word window when you open a document. Because both windows are maximized and share the same title bar and borders, they appear as one window.

Before you can begin to work on Belinda's document, you must save the document with a new filename.

Saving a Document with a New Filename

When you opened the Schedule document, a copy of the original document on your Student Disk was transferred into memory (RAM) and a portion of the copy was displayed on your screen. Making changes to the document changes only the copy in memory; the original document on your disk remains unchanged. A default feature of Word, **AutoSave**, automatically saves the document you are working on, at preset intervals that you can specify, to a temporary file on disk. That way, in case of a power failure or other mechanical problem, you will not lose all your work. To store the document in its changed form permanently on disk, however, you must manually save the document. **Saving** a document transfers the most recent version of the document from memory to disk. After you manually save a document, the temporary file that was created by AutoSave is deleted.

You can save a document using either the same filename or a new filename. As shown in Figure 1-17, saving with the same filename transfers a copy of the most recent version of the document in memory to your disk, *replacing the original document on disk*. If you then realize you made changes you had not intended to make and you need to retrieve the original version, you will not be able to; the original document will have been overwritten by the new version.

Figure 1-17 Saving a document with the same filename or a new filename

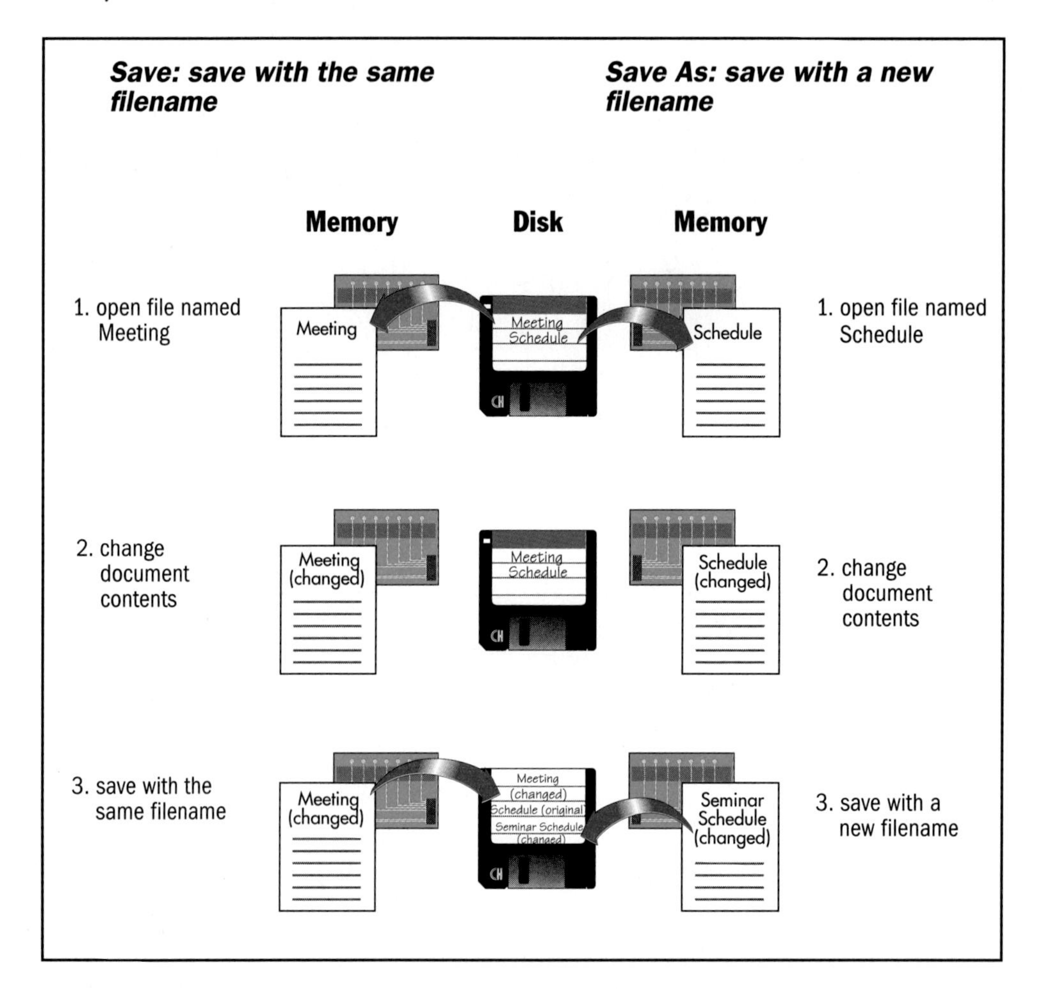

However, if you want to save the new version and the original document as separate files, you can do so by saving the new version with a new name. The Save As option on the File menu transfers a copy of the changed document to your disk without overwriting the original document. Both the original document *and* the changed document are stored with separate filenames on the disk, as shown in Figure 1-17. Now, if you need to refer back to the original document, you can do so, because it still exists.

Often you will not need to keep the original versions, so you will save edited documents with the same filename as the originals. Before you save, however, ask yourself two questions: Am I comfortable that my changes are correct? and Do I have a compelling reason to keep the original document? If you are comfortable with your changes and you no longer need the original, then save the document with the same filename.

Learning a new program like Word requires practice, experimentation, and trial and error. You should feel free to make mistakes and to experiment with the program. Therefore, you'll save Belinda's Schedule document with a new filename in case you want to restart the tutorial at a later time.

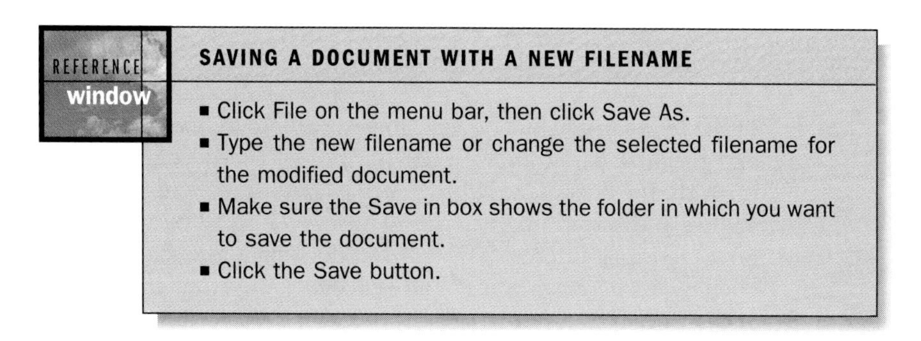

REFERENCE window

SAVING A DOCUMENT WITH A NEW FILENAME

- Click File on the menu bar, then click Save As.
- Type the new filename or change the selected filename for the modified document.
- Make sure the Save in box shows the folder in which you want to save the document.
- Click the Save button.

You'll save Belinda's Schedule document with the new filename of Seminar Schedule in the Tutorial.01 folder on your Student Disk.

To save the document with a new filename:

1. Position the mouse pointer on the **File** menu and click, then click the **Save As** option. The Save As dialog box opens. See Figure 1-18.

Figure 1-18 Save As dialog box

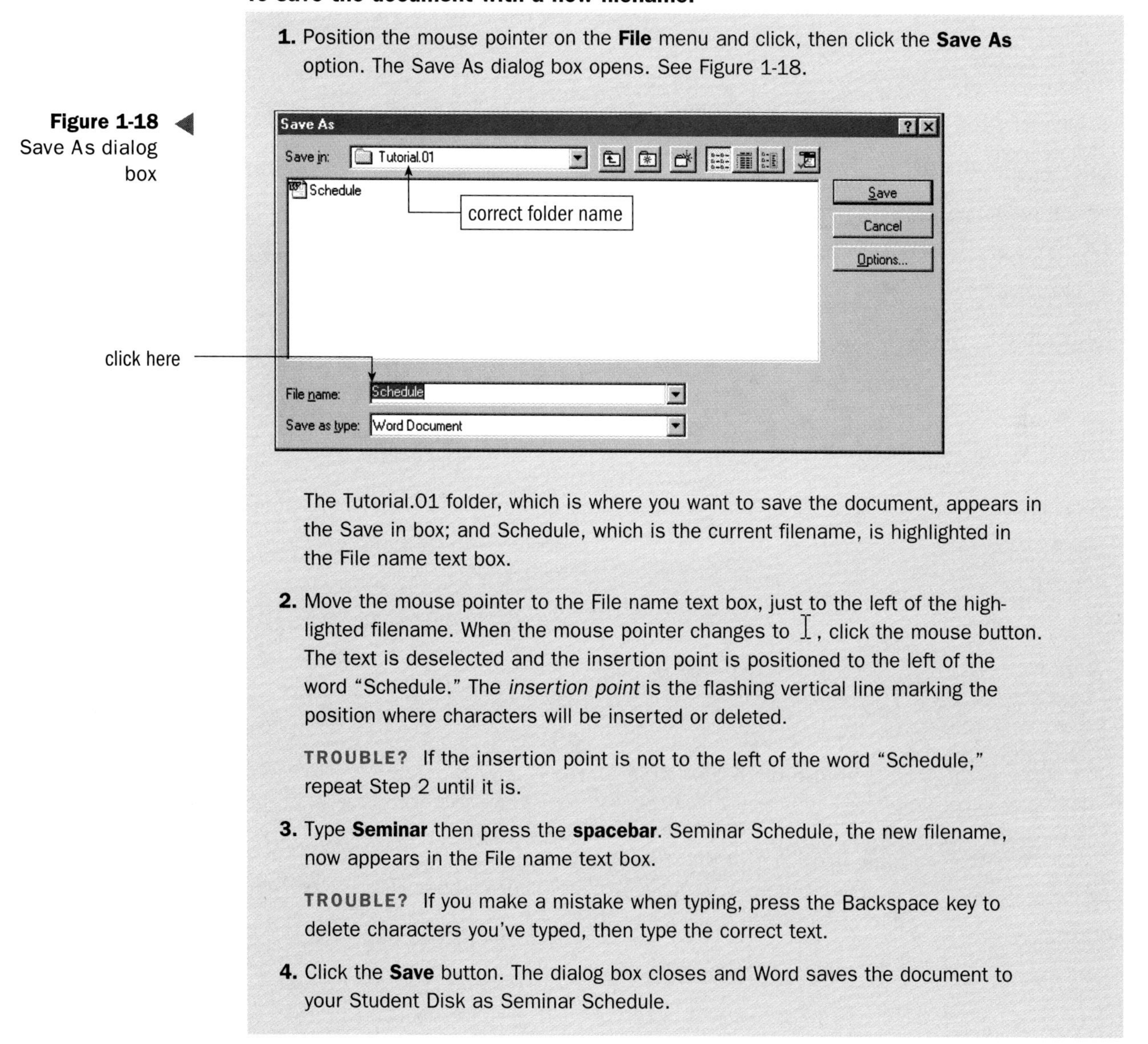

   The Tutorial.01 folder, which is where you want to save the document, appears in the Save in box; and Schedule, which is the current filename, is highlighted in the File name text box.

2. Move the mouse pointer to the File name text box, just to the left of the highlighted filename. When the mouse pointer changes to I, click the mouse button. The text is deselected and the insertion point is positioned to the left of the word "Schedule." The *insertion point* is the flashing vertical line marking the position where characters will be inserted or deleted.

   TROUBLE? If the insertion point is not to the left of the word "Schedule," repeat Step 2 until it is.

3. Type **Seminar** then press the **spacebar**. Seminar Schedule, the new filename, now appears in the File name text box.

   TROUBLE? If you make a mistake when typing, press the Backspace key to delete characters you've typed, then type the correct text.

4. Click the **Save** button. The dialog box closes and Word saves the document to your Student Disk as Seminar Schedule.

The Word window title bar now shows Seminar Schedule as the document name.

Belinda wants to verify the changes that must be made in the document, so she asks you to scroll through the different parts of the document on the screen.

Navigating a Document

Take a moment to look at the document on your screen. You can see only the top portion of the seminar schedule, which consists of a logo, the company name, the document title, and the first paragraph. To see the rest of the document, you must **navigate**, or move through, the document. Word's vertical and horizontal scroll bars contain the same scroll arrows and scroll boxes as the Windows 95 scroll bars. You can use the scroll bars and boxes to bring different parts of your document into view. When you see the place in your document where you want to move to, click the mouse pointer to place the insertion point at that location.

Belinda wants to verify that the company name is formatted correctly, so she asks you to move the insertion point there.

To position the insertion point:

1. Move the mouse and position the mouse pointer I between the **C** and **O** in "COFFEE," then click. Word places the insertion point at the position you clicked. See Figure 1-19.

Figure 1-19 Insertion point in new position

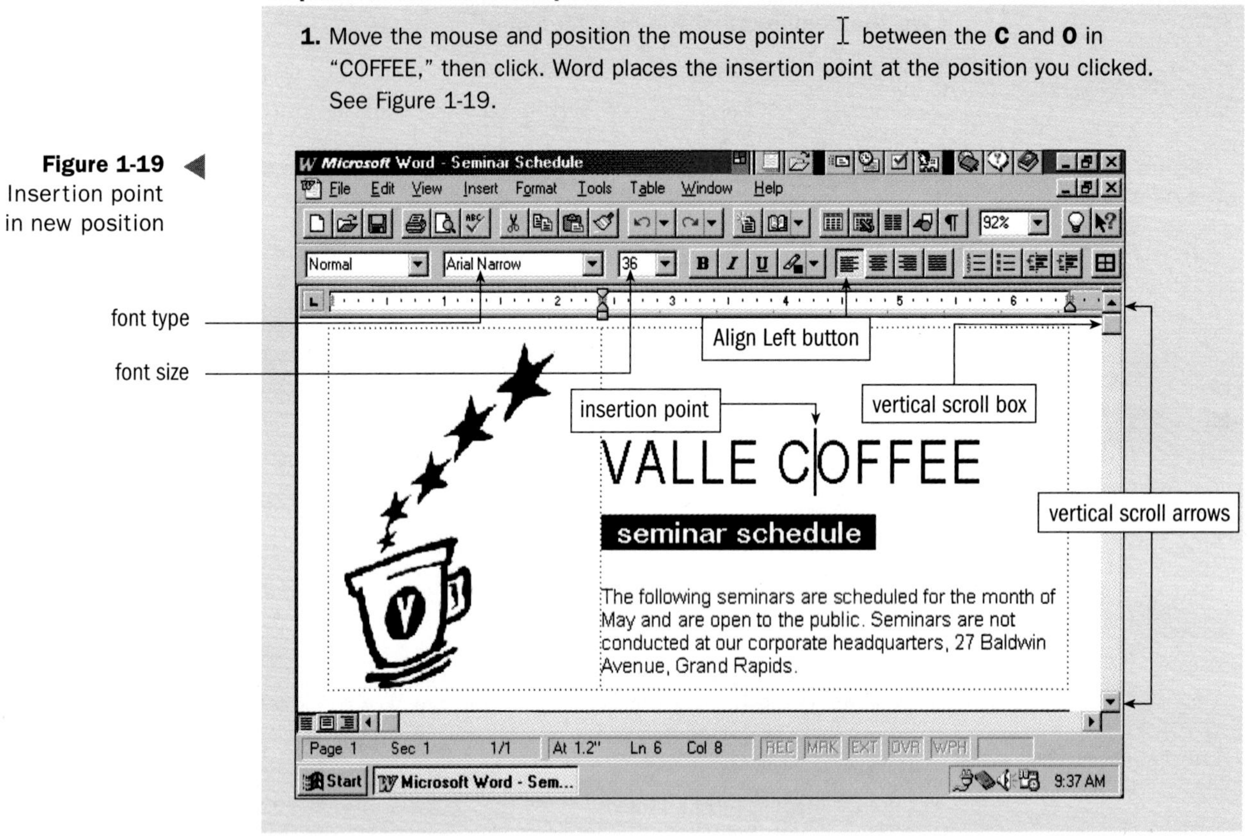

Notice the term "Arial Narrow" and the number "36" on the Formatting toolbar. These represent the shape (font type) and size of the letters in the company name. Notice also that the Align Left button on the Formatting toolbar is selected; this indicates that the first letter of the company name starts at the left edge of its designated area.

The company name is formatted correctly, so Belinda asks you to display the remaining portions of the document.

To navigate the document:

1. Click the down scroll arrow on the vertical scroll bar three times. Notice that the location of the insertion point does not change. You can use the down scroll arrow and the up scroll arrow on the vertical scroll bar to move through a document line by line.

2. Click once below the vertical scroll box. When you click below or above the scroll box, you scroll one *window* of text at a time.

3. Drag the scroll box to the bottom of the vertical scroll bar to move quickly to the end of the document. You can no longer see the insertion point, because it remains on the company line at the top of the document. Notice the small horizontal bar at the end of the document. This is called the *end mark* because it indicates the end of the document.

   TROUBLE? If the scroll box moves back up the vertical scroll bar a short distance, don't be concerned as long as the end of the document appears on the screen.

4. Position the mouse pointer after the word "Reservations" in the last line of text on the screen, then click. The location of the insertion point changes to the position you clicked. See Figure 1-20.

Figure 1-20 The end of the Seminar Schedule document

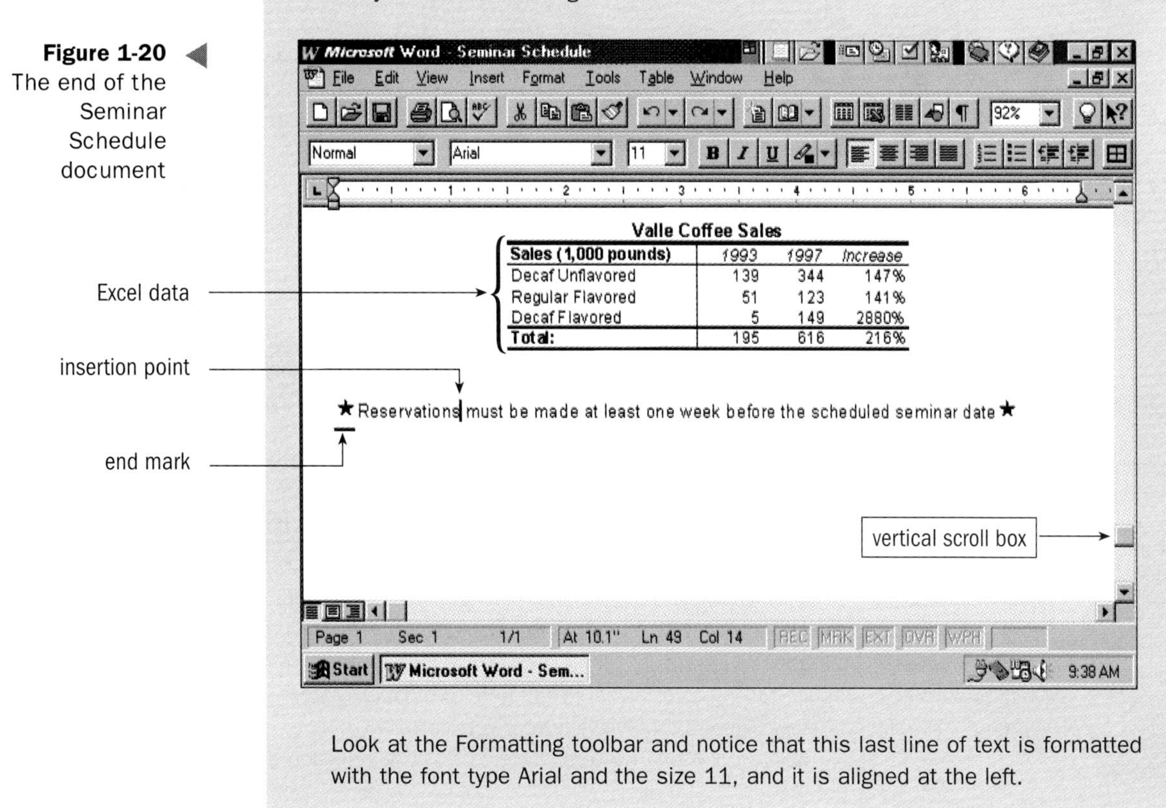

Look at the Formatting toolbar and notice that this last line of text is formatted with the font type Arial and the size 11, and it is aligned at the left.

Belinda has identified the changes she wants you to make to the document, so you now need to edit the document.

Editing a Word Document

Editing a document involves changing its content by inserting, deleting, copying, or moving text.

Inserting Text

To insert new text, you place the insertion point at the appropriate position and then type the new text. As you type, Word moves any existing text to the right and adjusts line endings to accommodate the inserted text.

Belinda wants the text ", free of charge" inserted at the end of the first sentence in the document.

To insert the text:

1. Drag the scroll box to the top of the vertical scroll bar, then place the insertion point in the first sentence, immediately after the word "public" and before the period.
2. Type **, free of charge**. As you type the new text, the existing text moves to the right. See Figure 1-21. Note that your text might break differently across lines, depending on the type of monitor you're using.

Figure 1-21 Document after inserting text

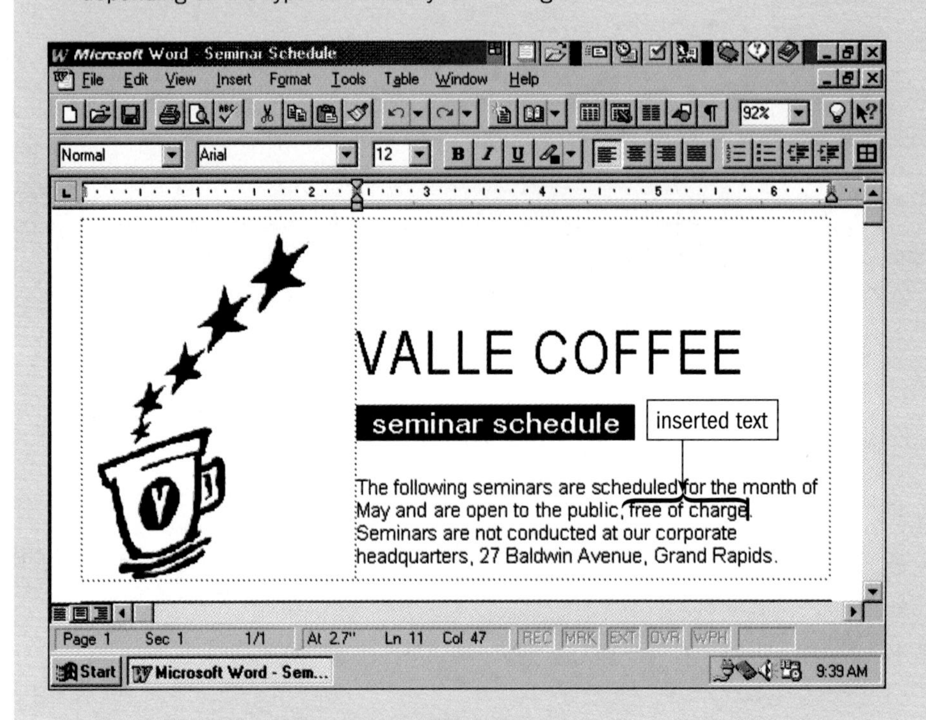

TROUBLE? If the text you type replaces existing text, check to see if the indicator "OVR" appears in the status bar. If it does, this means that Word is in Overtype mode. You need to switch back to Insert mode by pressing the Insert key or double-clicking OVR in the status bar. Then type the text that was replaced, using Figure 1-21 as a guide. If you make a typing error, press the Backspace key to delete characters to the left of the insertion point, then type the correct text.

TROUBLE? If a red, wavy line appears under text you type, this indicates that Word does not recognize the text, perhaps because a word is misspelled. Use the Backspace key to remove the incorrect text, then type the correct text. Don't be concerned about the red, wavy lines at this point; you'll learn how to check the spelling in a document later in this book.

Next, Belinda asks you to delete the word "not" in the second sentence.

Deleting Text

You can delete characters by using the Backspace or Delete keys. The Backspace key deletes the character to the left of the insertion point, whereas the Delete key deletes the character to the right of the insertion point.

To delete the text:

1. Place the insertion point in the second sentence, immediately after the "n" in "not."
2. Press the **Delete** key twice to delete the letters "o" and "t." Notice that the text closes up after the characters are deleted.
3. Press the **Backspace** key twice to delete the "n" and the space. See Figure 1-22.

Figure 1-22 ◀ Document after deleting text

Belinda next wants you to copy text from the coffee I section of the document to the coffee II section of the document.

Copying Text

When editing a document, you might need to copy text to another part of the document or to a completely different document. You can accomplish this easily by using the **copy-and-paste** technique. This technique is a four-step process: select the text you want to copy, click the Copy button, position the insertion point where you want the copy placed, then click the Paste button. The selected text remains in its original position, and a copy of it is inserted at the insertion point.

Belinda wants the phrase "Participants sample and evaluate" copied from the coffee I section and pasted at the beginning of the second sentence in the coffee II section.

To copy the text:

1. Scroll down the document until both the coffee I and coffee II sections are on the screen.
2. In the text of the coffee I section, position the pointer to the left of the "P" in "Participants," click and hold down the mouse button, drag the mouse pointer to the right to select the text **Participants sample and evaluate**, then release the mouse button. Be sure to include the space that follows the word "evaluate." See Figure 1-23.

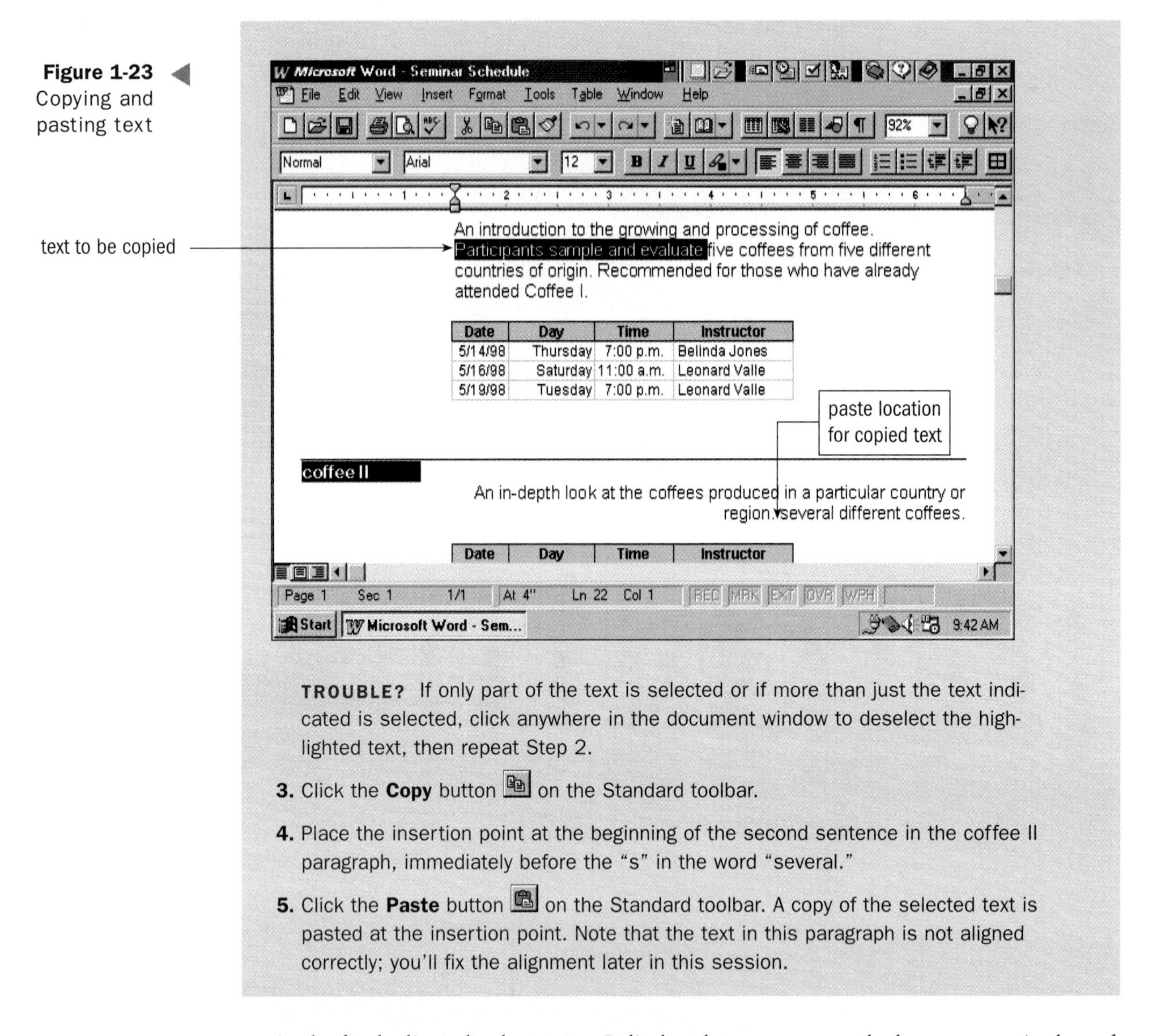

Figure 1-23 Copying and pasting text

TROUBLE? If only part of the text is selected or if more than just the text indicated is selected, click anywhere in the document window to deselect the highlighted text, then repeat Step 2.

3. Click the **Copy** button on the Standard toolbar.
4. Place the insertion point at the beginning of the second sentence in the coffee II paragraph, immediately before the "s" in the word "several."
5. Click the **Paste** button on the Standard toolbar. A copy of the selected text is pasted at the insertion point. Note that the text in this paragraph is not aligned correctly; you'll fix the alignment later in this session.

As the final edit to the document, Belinda asks you to move the last sentence in the coffee I section to the end of the coffee II section.

Moving Text

To move text from one position to another, you can use the **cut-and-paste** technique, which is a four-step process similar to the copy-and-paste technique. With the cut-and-paste technique, you click the Cut button instead of the Copy button after selecting the text you want to move. Unlike when copying text, the selected text is *deleted* from its original position and moved to the new location.

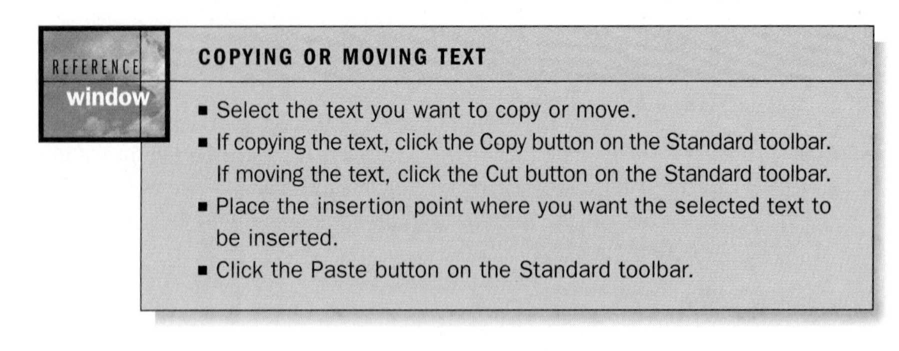
REFERENCE window

COPYING OR MOVING TEXT

- Select the text you want to copy or move.
- If copying the text, click the Copy button on the Standard toolbar. If moving the text, click the Cut button on the Standard toolbar.
- Place the insertion point where you want the selected text to be inserted.
- Click the Paste button on the Standard toolbar.

You'll use the cut-and-paste technique to move the text as Belinda requested.

To move the text:

1. If the coffee I and coffee II paragraphs are not both visible on your screen, scroll until they are.
2. In the coffee I paragraph, position the mouse pointer to the left of the space preceding the word "Recommended," click and hold down the mouse button, drag the mouse pointer to the right and down to select the entire sentence, then release the mouse button. See Figure 1-24.

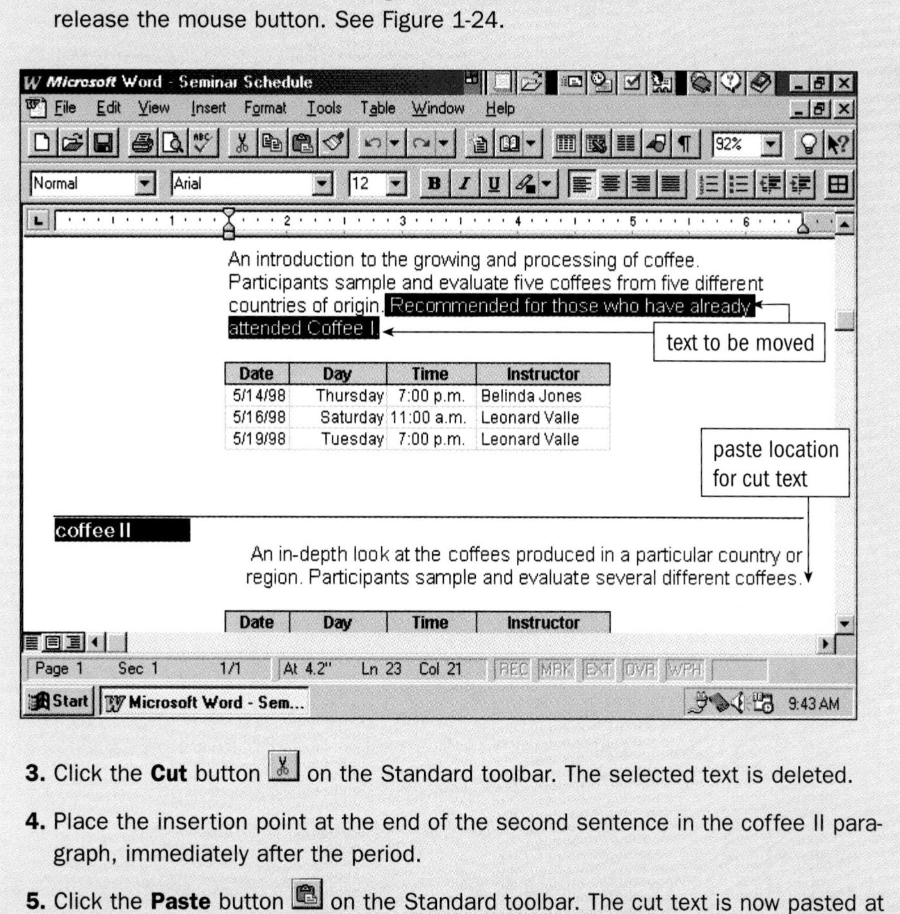

Figure 1-24 Cutting and pasting text

3. Click the **Cut** button on the Standard toolbar. The selected text is deleted.
4. Place the insertion point at the end of the second sentence in the coffee II paragraph, immediately after the period.
5. Click the **Paste** button on the Standard toolbar. The cut text is now pasted at the end of the coffee II paragraph.

You have finished Belinda's edits to the document. Next, Belinda asks you to make several formatting changes to the document.

Formatting a Word Document

When you **format** a document, you improve the document's appearance and readability to better convey the message you are communicating. Common formatting options include font type, font size, font style, and paragraph alignment. The three most popular font styles used to emphasize text are bold, italic, and underline. The four paragraph alignment options are left, centered, right, and justified. Because you use these formatting options frequently, Word provides buttons for them on the Formatting toolbar.

Belinda notices that the coffee II paragraph is right-aligned, but it should be left-aligned. You need to reformat this paragraph.

Aligning Paragraphs

Paragraph alignment determines how the lines of text in a paragraph are aligned horizontally on the left and right. With **left alignment**, which is the default setting, all paragraph lines are even on the left and ragged on the right; with **centered alignment**, all paragraph lines are centered horizontally; with **right alignment**, all paragraph lines are even on the right and ragged on the left; and with **justified alignment**, all paragraph lines are even on both the left and right. See Figure 1-25. The Formatting toolbar provides buttons for each of these alignment options.

Figure 1-25 Paragraph alignment options

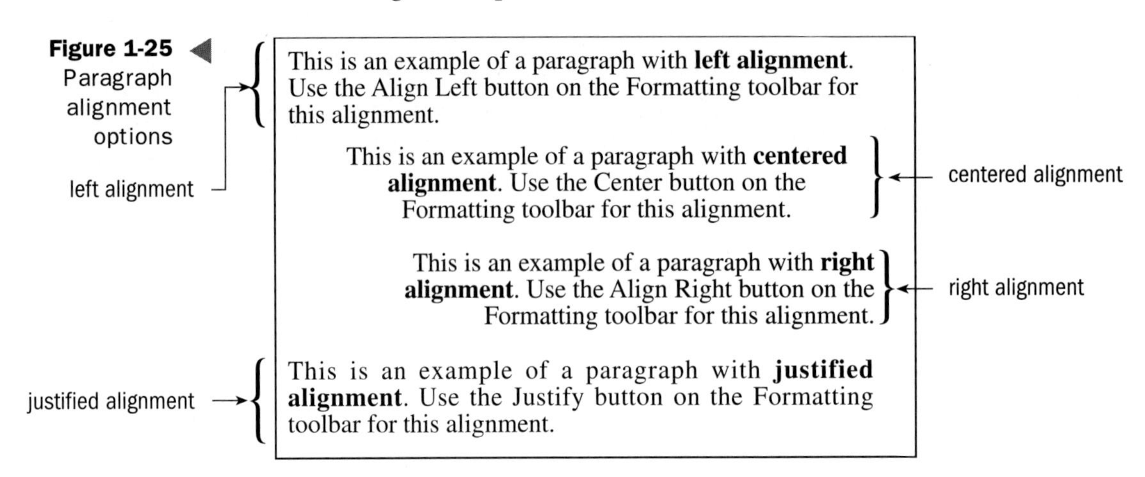

You need to change the paragraph alignment for the coffee II paragraph from right alignment to left alignment.

To change the paragraph alignment:

1. The insertion point should still be in the coffee II paragraph and the Align Right button on the Formatting toolbar should be selected. If you have moved the insertion point, click anywhere in the coffee II paragraph.
2. Click the **Align Left** button on the Formatting toolbar. The text is now even on the left and ragged on the right. See Figure 1-26.

Figure 1-26 Changing the paragraph alignment

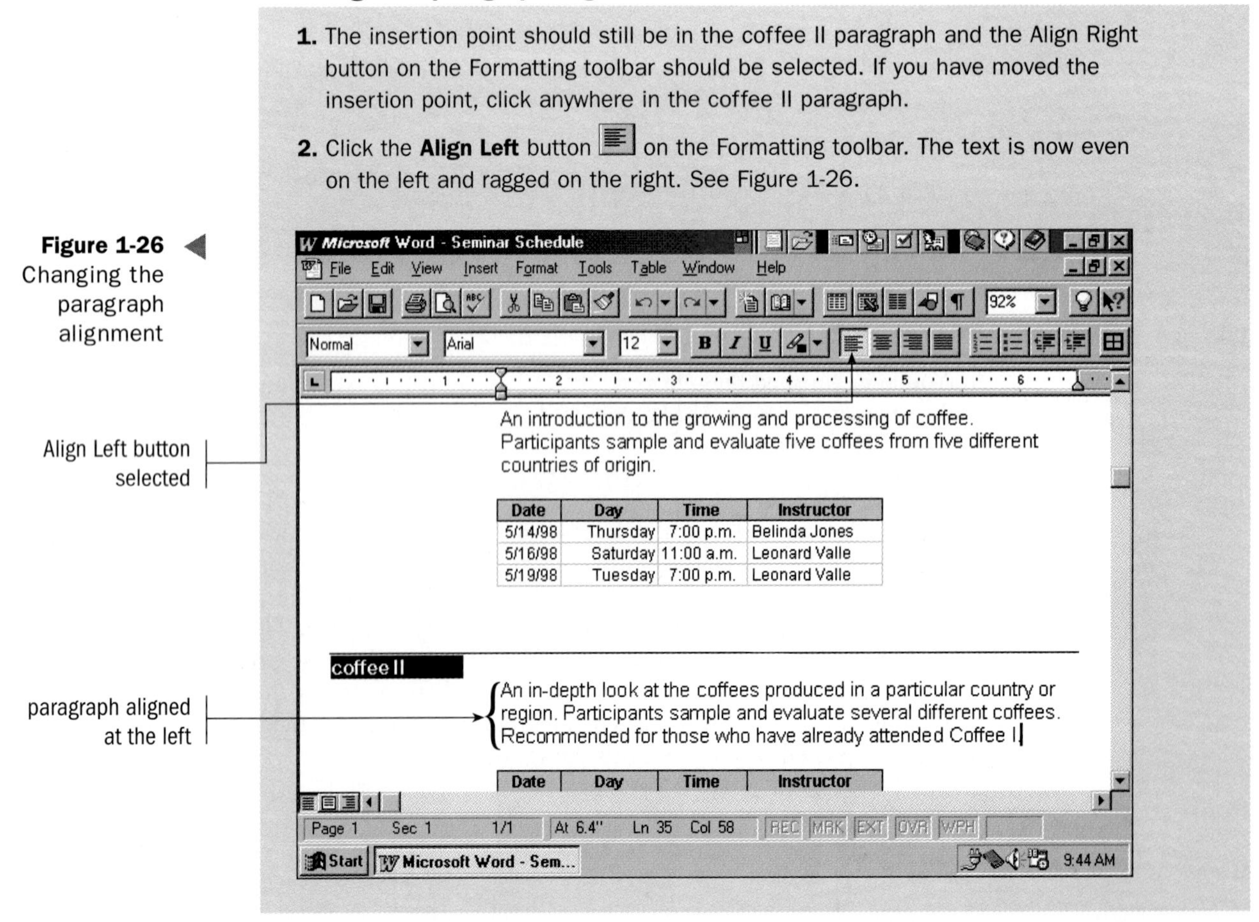

Belinda also noticed that the next full paragraph is formatted with the wrong font style and size, and she asks you to change them.

Changing Font Type and Size

Like other Office 95 programs, Word has many different font types and sizes you can use in your documents. However, for readability it's best to use only two or three different font type/size combinations in the same document. The Formatting toolbar provides options for choosing a font type and a font size to format selected text. If you want to apply a font option to an entire paragraph, for example, you must first select that paragraph.

The first three paragraphs in the seminar schedule are formatted with a font type of Arial and a font size of 12. You need to change the fourth paragraph, which is formatted with a font type of Times New Roman and a font size of 13, to the same font type/size combination as the other paragraphs.

To change the font type and size of the fourth paragraph:

1. Click once below the vertical scroll box to scroll down to the next window of text. The fourth paragraph, which begins, "Attend one of our seminars," should be visible on your screen.
2. Move the mouse pointer to the left of the paragraph. When the mouse pointer changes to ↗, double-click to select the entire paragraph.

   TROUBLE? If only part of the paragraph is selected, or if more than just the paragraph is selected, click anywhere in the paragraph to deselect the highlighted text, then repeat Step 2.

3. Click the **Font** list arrow on the Formatting toolbar. The Font list box opens, as shown in Figure 1-27. Your list might contain different fonts from those shown in the figure.

Figure 1-27 Changing the font type

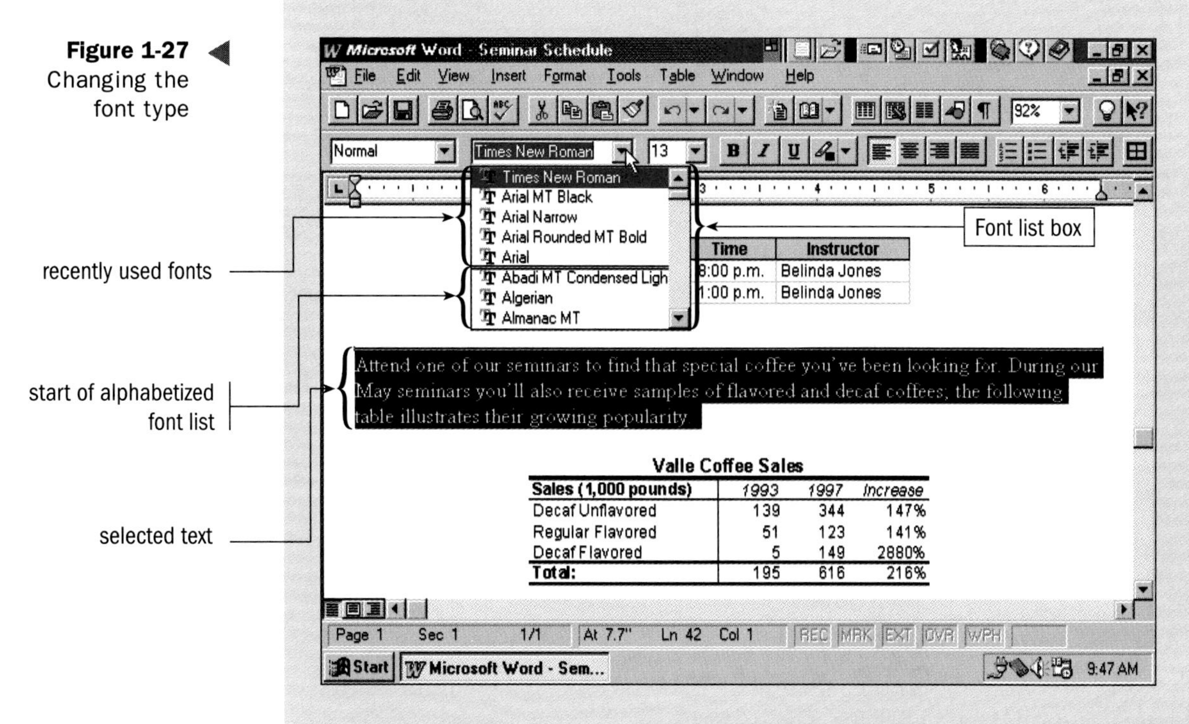

In the Font list box, recently used font types appear above the double line, and all font types appear alphabetically below the double line.

4. If necessary, scroll until you see Arial in the Font list box.

5. Click **Arial**. The font type for the entire selected paragraph changes to Arial.
6. Make sure the paragraph remains selected, click the **Font Size** list arrow, then click **12** in the Font Size list box. The font size for the entire selected paragraph changes to 12.

As a final formatting change, Belinda wants you to change the document's last sentence to a font style of bold and italic in order to draw attention to this text.

Changing the Font Style

The Formatting toolbar provides buttons for applying the bold, italic, and underline font styles to selected text. You'll apply both the bold and italic font styles to the last sentence in the seminar schedule.

To change the font style of the last sentence:

1. If the document's last sentence is not visible on your screen, scroll until it is.
2. Move the mouse pointer to the left of the sentence. When the mouse pointer changes to ↗, click to select the entire sentence.
3. On the Formatting toolbar, click the **Bold** button **B** then click the **Italic** button *I*.
4. Click anywhere in the last sentence to deselect the highlighted text. See Figure 1-28.

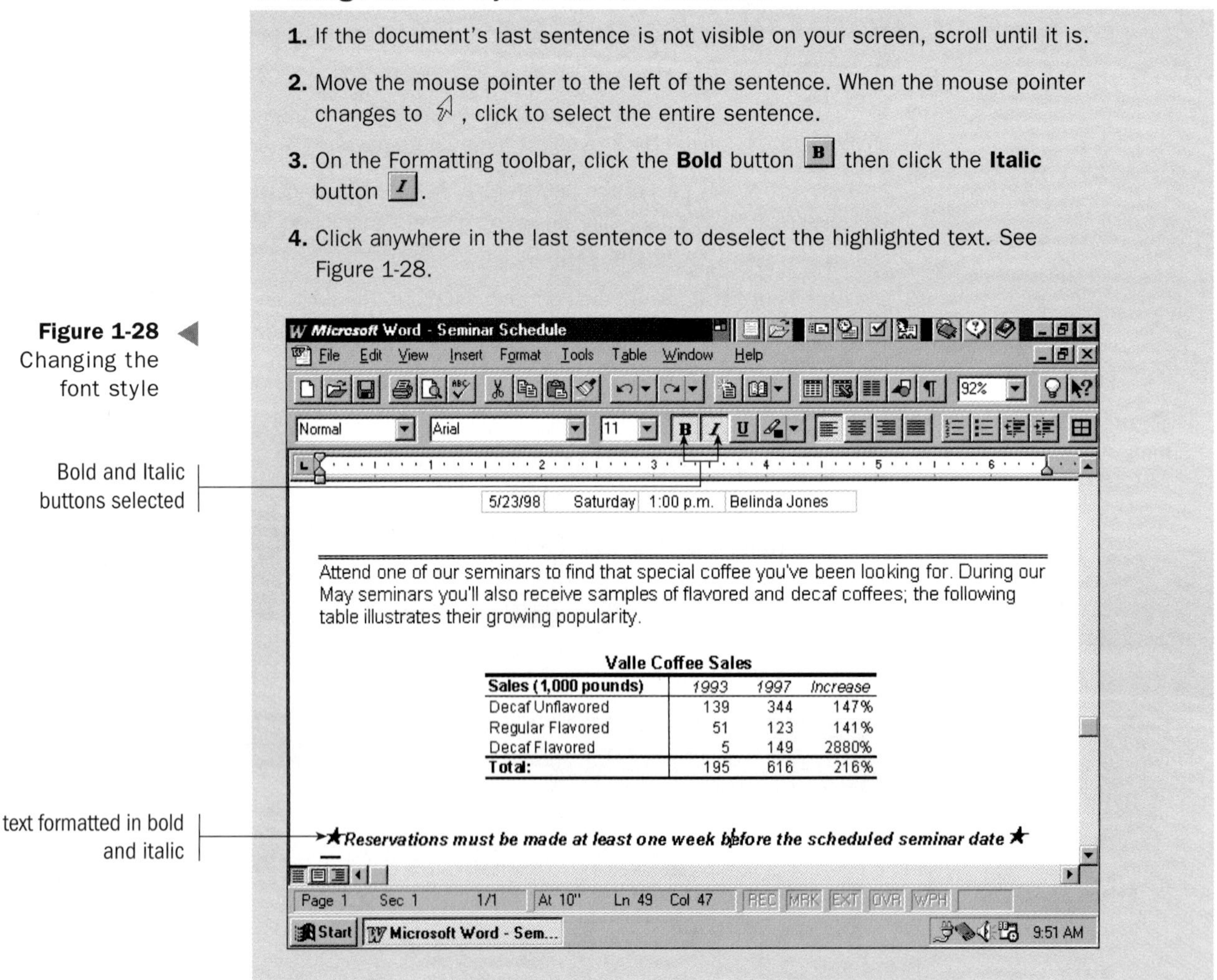

Figure 1-28 Changing the font style

You have completed all of Belinda's editing and formatting changes to the document. Because Belinda has to leave for a meeting, she asks you to save and then print the new version of the document. She wants to review a hardcopy of the seminar schedule for content and appearance before she has it photocopied and distributed.

Saving a Document with the Same Filename

You must save a document after you've changed it to store the document permanently on your disk. You'll save this document, Seminar Schedule, with the same filename. (The original Schedule document is still intact on your Student Disk.) To save a document with the same filename, you could use the Save option on the File menu. However, a quicker method is to use the Save button on the Standard toolbar.

To save the document with the same filename:

1. Click the **Save** button on the Standard toolbar. Word saves the document to your Student Disk using the current filename, Seminar Schedule, and replaces the previous version of the document.

Belinda wants a printed copy of the document, but you are not sure how to produce one. Word's Help system can help you learn how to print a document.

Getting Help

When you are using Word or another Office 95 program, you might need to find information on how to complete a certain task. Or, you might need to clarify a definition, learn more about a particular feature, or investigate more advanced capabilities. In these situations you can use the program's Help system to get the information you need. A **Help system** provides on-screen information about the program you are using. The Help system for each Office 95 program works in the same way as the Windows 95 Help system.

The Help Topics: Microsoft Word window (Figure 1-29), which you open from the Help menu on the Word window, gives you access to the on-line Help topics for Word. The other Office 95 programs have a similar Help Topics window.

Figure 1-29 Help Topics: Microsoft Word window

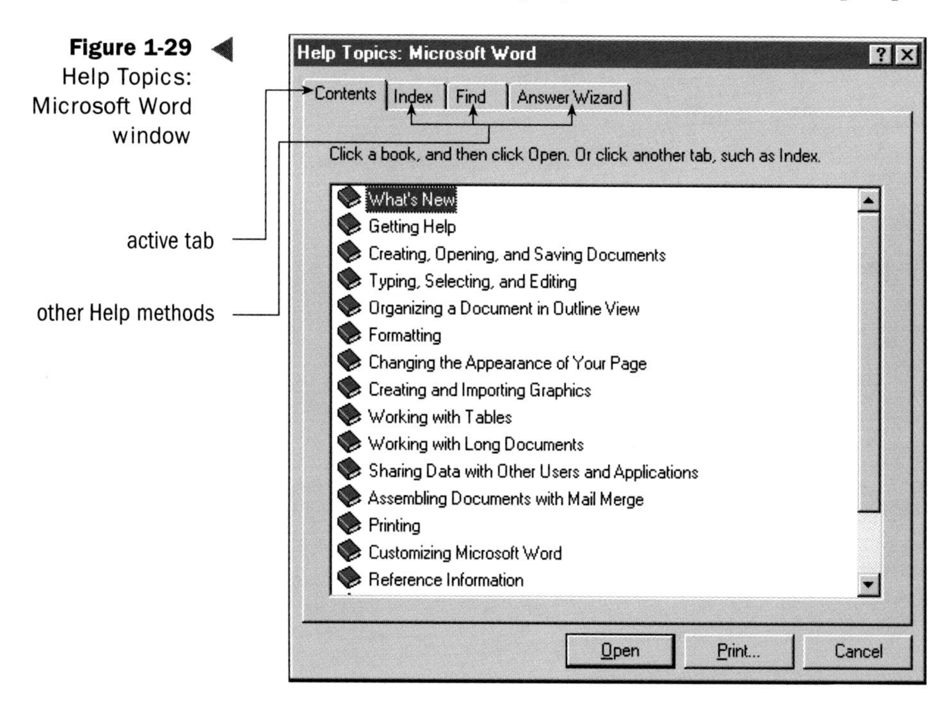

Each Office 95 program's Help Topics window contains four tabs, each representing a specific method for obtaining on-screen Help. The four tabs are Contents, Index, Find, and Answer Wizard. Their functions are described below:

- The **Contents** tab displays a set of books, each of which contains a particular category of information. When you open a book, Help displays the topics in that category. Selecting a topic displays the detailed information for that topic.

- The **Index** tab displays an alphabetical list of topics, just like a typical index in the back of a book. You can either select a topic from the list or type a topic to find information about it.
- The **Find** tab contains an index of all words in the program's Help system. You can enter one or more words you want to find. In response, Help displays topics that contain those words.
- The **Answer Wizard** tab lets you type a request for information in your own words and then provides a list of topics that will answer your request. The Answer Wizard also walks you through the steps for completing the specified task.

Using the Help Contents

First you'll use the Contents tab to review how to use the Help system.

To use the Contents tab:

1. Click **Help** on the menu bar, then click **Microsoft Word Help Topics**. The Help Topics: Microsoft Word window opens.
2. If necessary, click the **Contents** tab to make it the active tab in the window.
3. Click **Getting Help** then click the **Open** button. The Getting Help book opens and the list of topics for this book is displayed.
4. Click **Getting assistance while you work** then click the **Display** button. Help displays the "Getting assistance while you work" topic. See Figure 1-30.

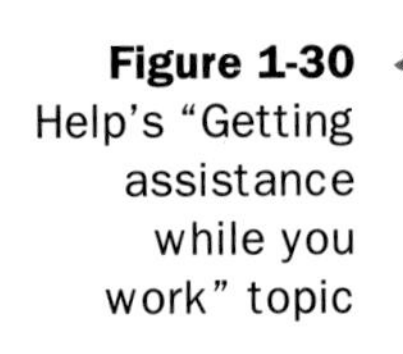

Figure 1-30 Help's "Getting assistance while you work" topic

The topic contains five labels, each of which you can click to display an explanation about the labeled topic. To remove a displayed explanation, click anywhere on the screen.

5. Click **Screen Tips** and read the displayed explanation.
6. Click **Answer Wizard** and read the displayed explanation.
7. Click each of the other three labels and read the displayed explanations.
8. Click the **Help Topics** button. Help closes the topic and redisplays the Help Topics: Microsoft Word window.

Next you'll use the Answer Wizard to find out how to print a document.

Using the Answer Wizard

The Answer Wizard is easy to use. Simply type your request in the form of a question or a series of key words, and the Answer Wizard will display a list of topics that answer your request.

You need to ask the Answer Wizard the question, "How do I print?"

To use the Answer Wizard:

1. Click the **Answer Wizard** tab to make it the active tab in the window.
2. In the text box, type **how do I print** then click the **Search** button. The Help system searches for answers to your question, then displays the topics that relate to your question. See Figure 1-31.

Figure 1-31 Using the Answer Wizard

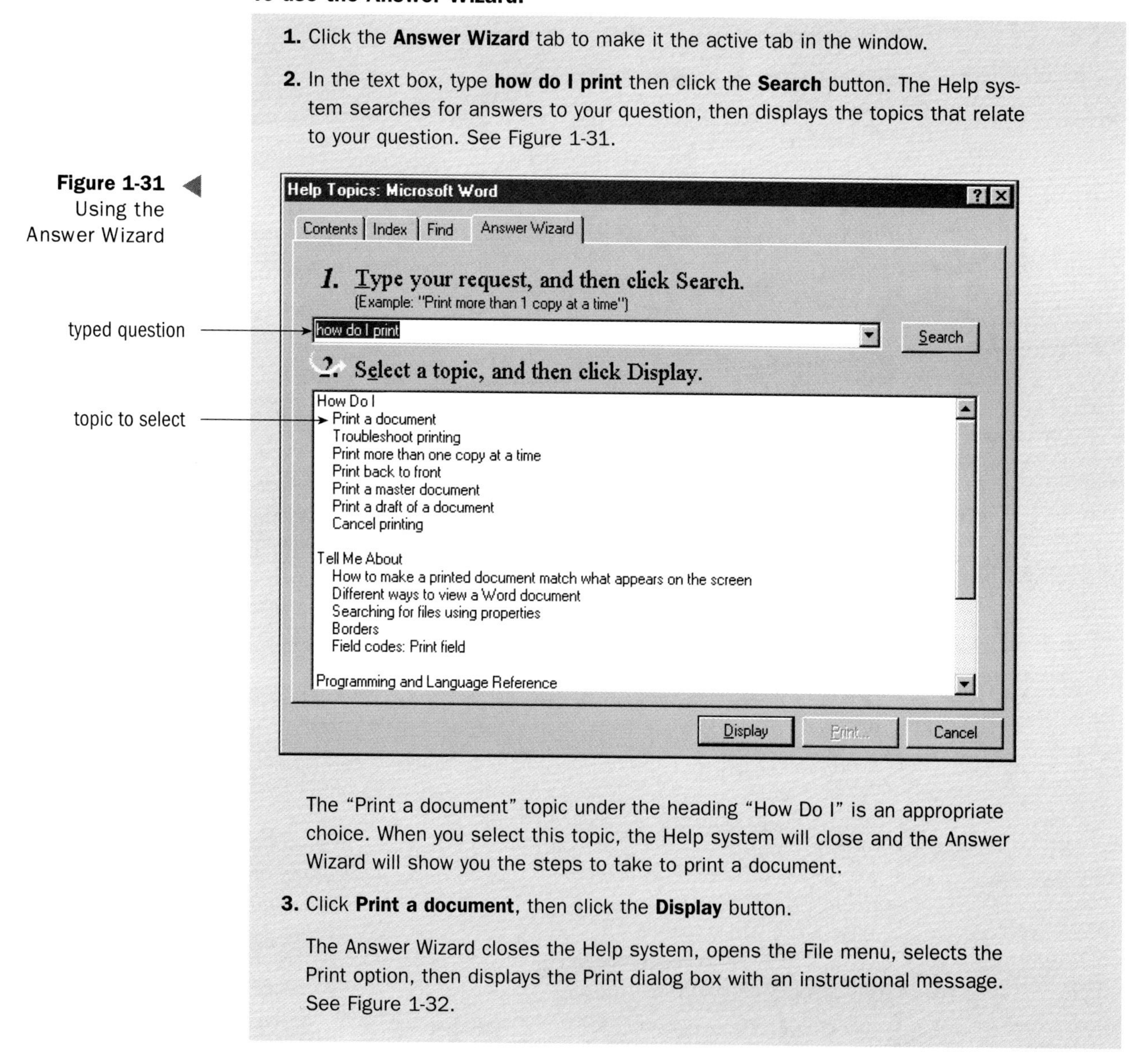

The "Print a document" topic under the heading "How Do I" is an appropriate choice. When you select this topic, the Help system will close and the Answer Wizard will show you the steps to take to print a document.

3. Click **Print a document**, then click the **Display** button.

The Answer Wizard closes the Help system, opens the File menu, selects the Print option, then displays the Print dialog box with an instructional message. See Figure 1-32.

Figure 1-32 Printing steps demonstrated and explained by Answer Wizard

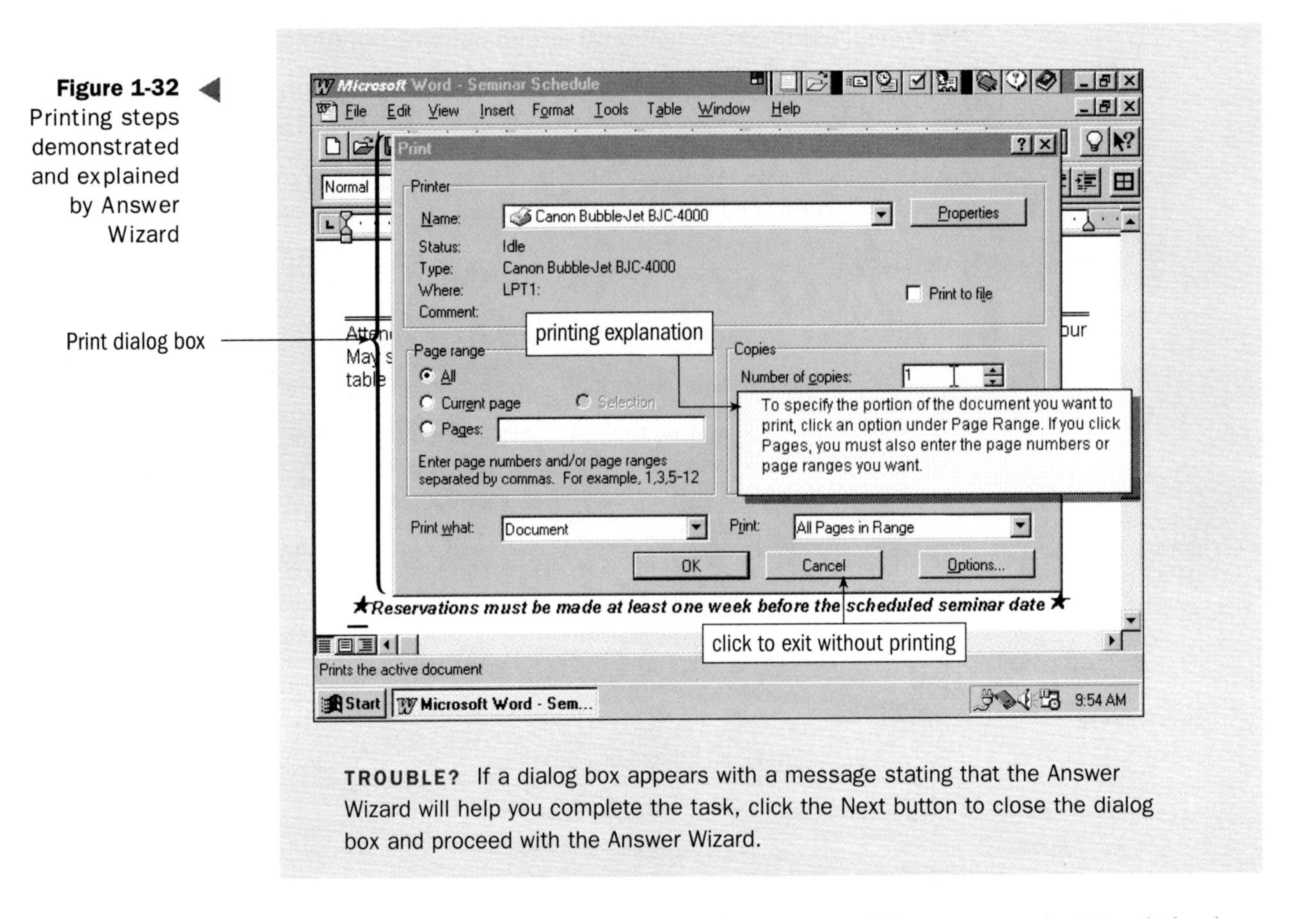

TROUBLE? If a dialog box appears with a message stating that the Answer Wizard will help you complete the task, click the Next button to close the dialog box and proceed with the Answer Wizard.

The Answer Wizard has shown you the steps you follow to open the Print dialog box. You could print the active document by clicking the OK button in this dialog box. Before printing the document and finishing your work with the Help system, however, you'll use context-sensitive Help to learn how to print a document using the Print button on the Standard toolbar.

Using Context-Sensitive Help

If you have a question about a particular component of a program window or a particular menu option, you can use the Help button on the Standard toolbar to ask for context-sensitive Help. **Context-sensitive Help** displays information about the component or option you click. When you click the Help button, the mouse pointer changes to ?, the Help pointer. When you click the Help pointer on the window component or option you want information about, Help displays the information on the screen. This information is called a **ScreenTip**.

You'll view context-sensitive Help information about the Print button on the Standard toolbar after closing the Print dialog box.

To obtain context-sensitive Help about the Print button:

1. Click the **Cancel** button on the Print dialog box to close it without printing the document.

2. Click the **Help** button on the Standard toolbar. The mouse pointer changes to ?.

3. Use the tip of the arrow in the Help pointer to point to the **Print** button on the Standard toolbar.

4. Click the **Print** button. Help displays a boxed explanation about the Print button. See Figure 1-33.

Figure 1-33 Using context-sensitive Help

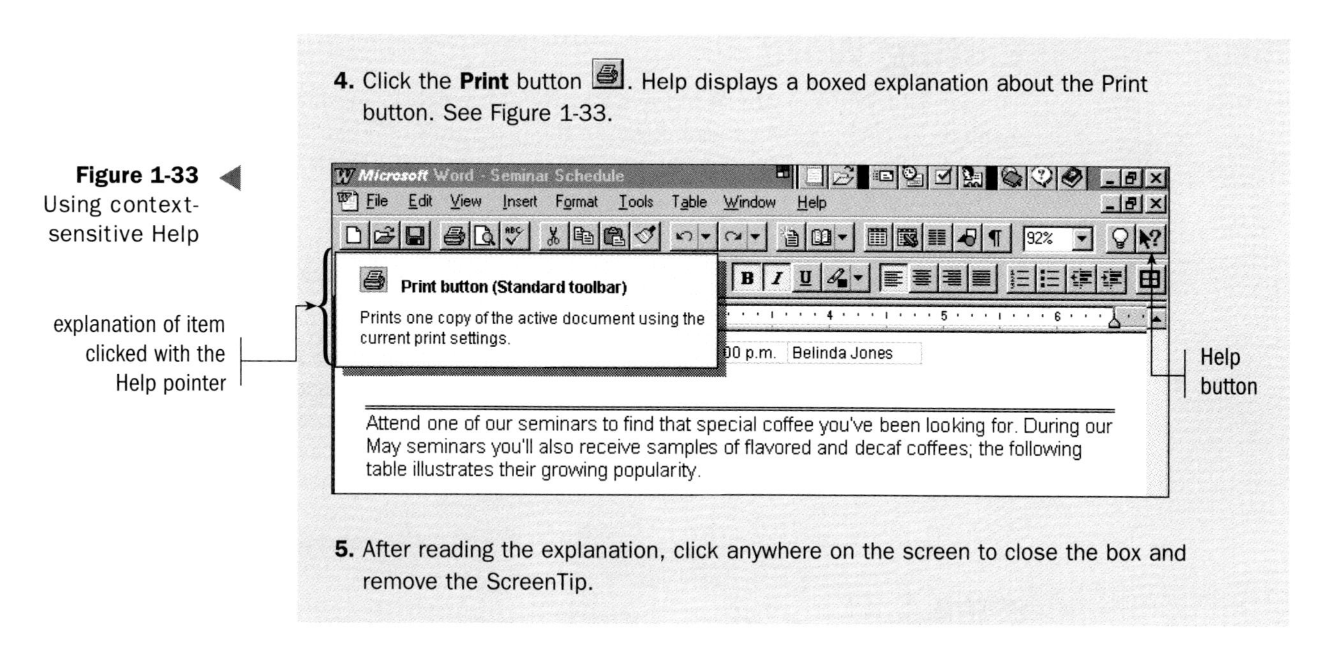

5. After reading the explanation, click anywhere on the screen to close the box and remove the ScreenTip.

Now that you've used the Help system to learn how to print a document, you're ready to print the seminar schedule document for Belinda.

Printing a Document

When you finish working with a Word document, you usually want to print one or more copies of the document. You can print using the File menu or the Print button. If you print using the Print command on the File menu, a dialog box lets you specify which pages of the document you want to print, the number of copies you want to print, and the printer you will use. If, instead, you use the Print button, Word prints one copy of the entire document immediately using the current settings.

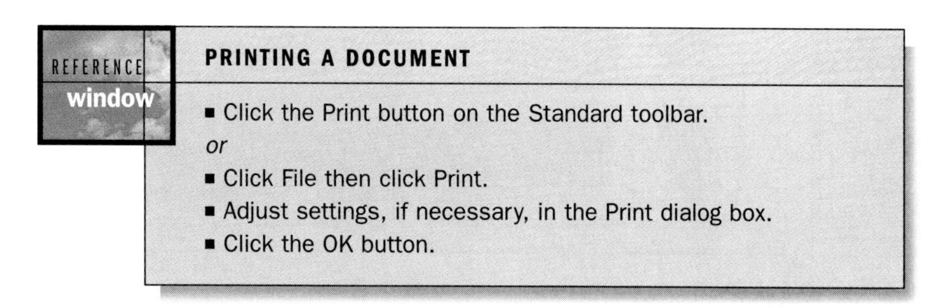

PRINTING A DOCUMENT

- Click the Print button on the Standard toolbar.

or

- Click File then click Print.
- Adjust settings, if necessary, in the Print dialog box.
- Click the OK button.

In later tutorials, you will print documents using a variety of options in the Print dialog box. For now, you'll use the Print button on the Standard toolbar to print one copy of the entire document, which fits on a single page.

To print the document:

1. Click the **Print** button on the Standard toolbar to print one copy of the entire document.

   TROUBLE? If the document does not print, see your instructor or technical support person for assistance.

Now that you have finished your initial work with the Word document, you can exit Word.

Exiting Word

You can exit Word or any Windows 95 program by choosing the Exit option on the File menu or by clicking the Close button on the program's title bar. Because the Close button method is faster, you'll use this method throughout the tutorials.

To exit Word:

1. Click the **Close** button on the title bar. Word closes and you return to the Windows 95 desktop.

   TROUBLE? If a dialog box opens with the message "Do you want to save changes to Seminar Schedule?" you must have modified the document since last saving it. Because any changes since your last save would have been unintentional, click the No button to exit Word without saving these changes.

You leave the printed document in Belinda's office for her review.

Quick Check

1. Name the four programs that make up the Office 95 suite.
2. The __________ is a toolbar that gives you access to your Office 95 documents.
3. A(n) __________, which appears when you point to a toolbar button, tells you the button's purpose or function.
4. The files for each tutorial are stored on your Student Disk in three folders named __________, __________, and __________.
5. Label the components of the Word window shown in Figure 1-34:

Figure 1-34

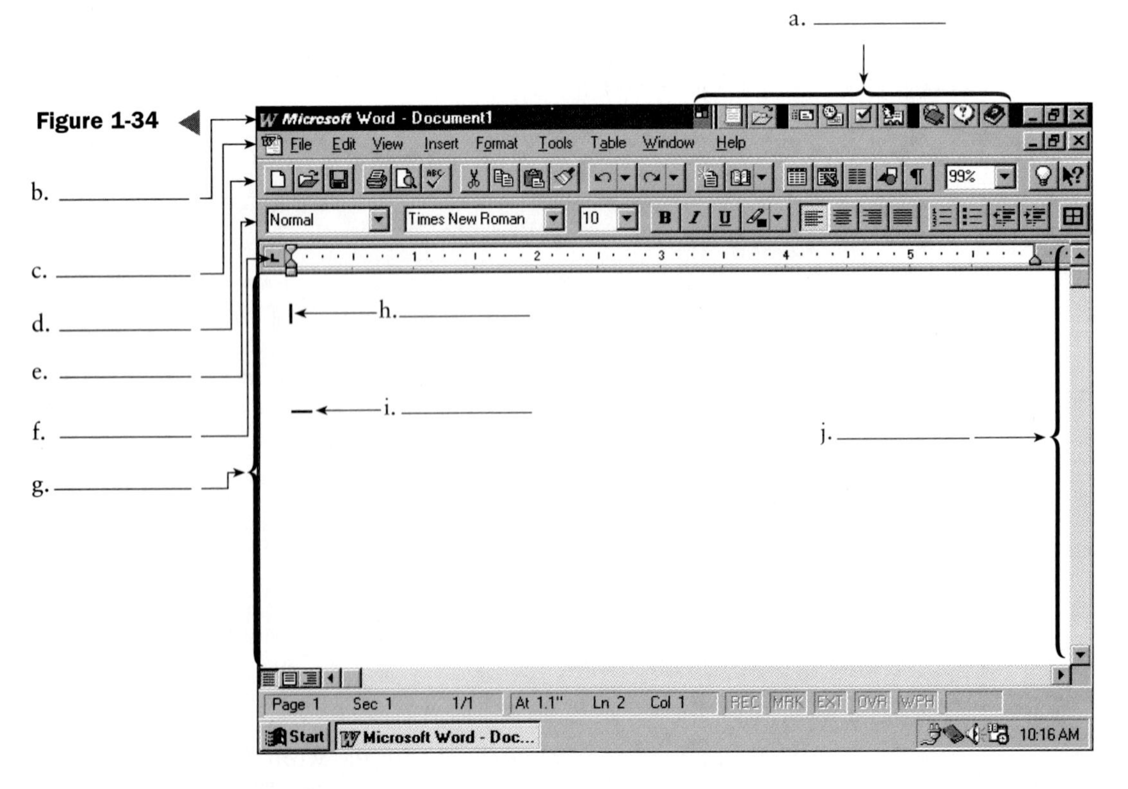

6. What happens to an existing file on a disk when you save the file with the same filename?

7 Which character is deleted when you use the Backspace key? the Delete key?

8 What are the differences between the copy-and-paste technique and the cut-and-paste technique?

9 What are some common formatting options for text, and how do you apply them?

10 Describe how you use each of the four tabs in the Help Topics window—Contents, Index, Find, and Answer Wizard.

11 Describe the difference between printing a document using the Print button on the Standard toolbar and using the Print command on the File menu.

12 What are the two ways in which you can exit Word?

SESSION 1.2

In this session you will learn how to open and work with an existing Access database, update data in an Access database, change embedded Excel data, change data in an existing Excel worksheet, and switch between open programs. The session also introduces you to Object Linking and Embedding (OLE).

Changing Copied Access Data

When she reviewed the printout of the seminar schedule, Belinda noticed that one of the times in the Coffee I seminar schedule is incorrect and that one of the sales numbers in the Valle Coffee Sales table needs to be changed. The values in the seminar schedule were copied from an Access database, and the sales numbers were embedded from an Excel worksheet. Copying and embedding are both ways to integrate data among programs.

Belinda asks you to change the two values in the Seminar Schedule document. First, you must open the document.

To start Word and open the Seminar Schedule document:

1. Place your Student Disk in the disk drive.
2. From the Windows 95 desktop, click the **Open a Document** button on the Office Shortcut Bar.
3. In the Open dialog box, click the **Look in** list arrow, then click the drive that contains your Student Disk.
4. Click **Tutorial.01** in the list box, then click the **Open** button to see a list of the folders and files in the Tutorial.01 folder.
5. Click **Seminar Schedule** in the list box, then click the **Open** button. Word starts and then opens the Seminar Schedule document in the document window.
6. If necessary, click the **Maximize** button on the title bar to maximize the Word and document windows.

   TROUBLE? If the TipWizard button is selected, click it to deselect the TipWizard option.

The data for each of the two seminars is organized as a Word table. A **table** is data arranged horizontally in rows and vertically in columns. The intersection of a row and column is called a **cell**. For simple changes, you can edit data in a Word table just as you edit text. The types of table edits you can perform include inserting, deleting, copying, and moving data.

Belinda wants you to change the time for the first Coffee I seminar from 7:00 p.m. to 8:00 p.m.

To change the value in the table:

1. Scroll the document to display the Coffee I seminar table in the document window.
2. Place the insertion point between the 7 and the colon (:) in the Time column for the 5/14/98 Coffee I seminar.
3. Press the **Backspace** key to delete the 7, then type **8**. The time now shows 8:00 p.m.

Because the seminar table data was copied from an Access database, the change you just made is not reflected in the database. You'll open the Access database to verify that it still contains the original data. Before you do, you'll save the Word document with the change you made. However, you won't exit Word because after your work with Access you still need to change the sales number.

To save the document with the same filename:

1. Click the **Save** button on the Standard toolbar. Word saves the document to your Student Disk, using the current filename, Seminar Schedule, and replaces the previous version of the document.

Before starting your work with the Access database, you need to have a basic understanding of databases. Later in this book, you'll learn these concepts in more detail.

What Is a Database?

A **database** is a collection of data organized to allow efficient entry, maintenance, and retrieval of that data. A **database management system** (**DBMS**), such as Access, is a program designed to manage and control databases. An Access database consists of a collection of tables. One of Valle Coffee's databases, shown in Figure 1-35, consists of three tables: the Topic table contains data about the types of seminars offered by Valle Coffee, the Instructor table contains data about the seminar instructors, and the Seminar table contains data about each seminar.

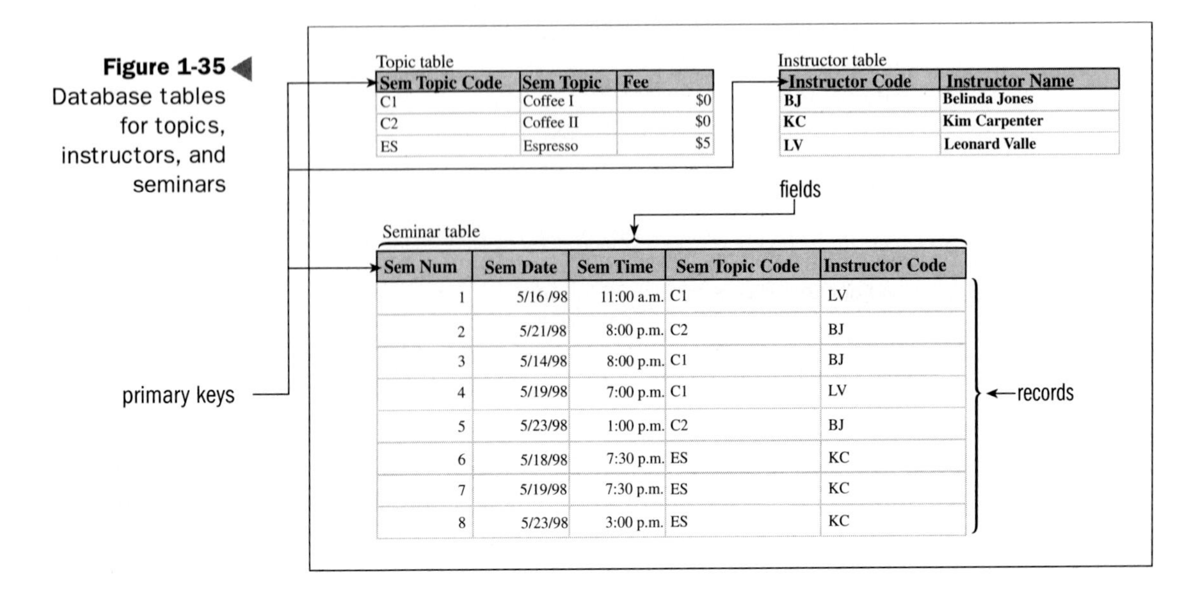

Topic table

Sem Topic Code	Sem Topic	Fee
C1	Coffee I	$0
C2	Coffee II	$0
ES	Espresso	$5

Instructor table

Instructor Code	Instructor Name
BJ	Belinda Jones
KC	Kim Carpenter
LV	Leonard Valle

Seminar table

Sem Num	Sem Date	Sem Time	Sem Topic Code	Instructor Code
1	5/16 /98	11:00 a.m.	C1	LV
2	5/21/98	8:00 p.m.	C2	BJ
3	5/14/98	8:00 p.m.	C1	BJ
4	5/19/98	7:00 p.m.	C1	LV
5	5/23/98	1:00 p.m.	C2	BJ
6	5/18/98	7:30 p.m.	ES	KC
7	5/19/98	7:30 p.m.	ES	KC
8	5/23/98	3:00 p.m.	ES	KC

Figure 1-35 Database tables for topics, instructors, and seminars

The rows in the tables are called **records**, and the columns in the tables are called **fields**. The first field in the Topic table is the Seminar Topic Code, abbreviated Sem Topic Code. This field is a unique code, which means that no two records in the Topic table have the same value for the Sem Topic Code field. Having a unique field ensures that each record in the table can be distinguished from all other records in the table. For example, a table containing personnel information might use the Social Security number to distinguish each employee record. The field that contains unique values is called the **primary key** in the table. Thus, Sem Topic Code is the primary key for the Topic table, Instructor Code is the primary key for the Instructor table, and Sem Num is the primary key for the Seminar table.

Primary Access Objects

Tables, which contain all the data in a database, are the fundamental objects in an Access database. Other significant objects in an Access database are queries, forms, and reports.

A **query** is a question you ask about the data stored in a database. In response to a query, Access displays the specific records and fields that answer your question. As examples of queries, Belinda might want to know when the next Coffee I seminar is scheduled, when she is next scheduled to instruct a seminar, or which seminars are scheduled after May 20. Figure 1-36 shows the results of a query that asked for all scheduled seminars in order by date.

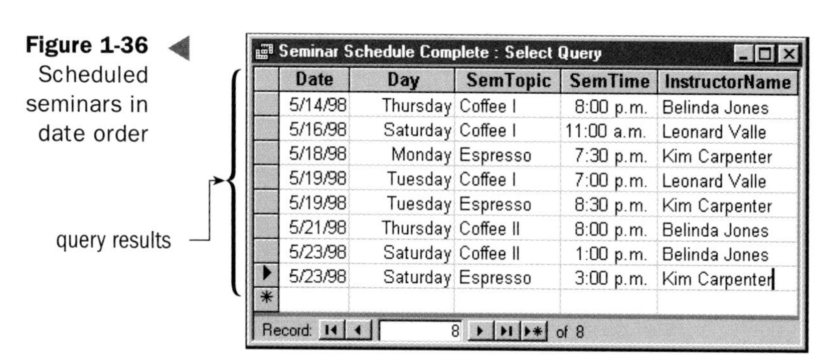

Figure 1-36 Scheduled seminars in date order

Seminar Schedule Complete : Select Query

Date	Day	SemTopic	SemTime	InstructorName
5/14/98	Thursday	Coffee I	8:00 p.m.	Belinda Jones
5/16/98	Saturday	Coffee I	11:00 a.m.	Leonard Valle
5/18/98	Monday	Espresso	7:30 p.m.	Kim Carpenter
5/19/98	Tuesday	Coffee I	7:00 p.m.	Leonard Valle
5/19/98	Tuesday	Espresso	8:30 p.m.	Kim Carpenter
5/21/98	Thursday	Coffee II	8:00 p.m.	Belinda Jones
5/23/98	Saturday	Coffee II	1:00 p.m.	Belinda Jones
5/23/98	Saturday	Espresso	3:00 p.m.	Kim Carpenter

Forms are objects you create to maintain, view, and print records of data from a database. Although you can perform these same functions with tables and queries, forms can present data in customized and useful ways. For example, the form shown in Figure 1-37 allows you to add, change, delete, view, and print one seminar record at a time while displaying visual verification of the related data in the Topic and Instructor tables.

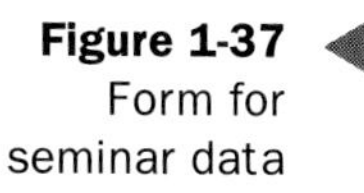

Figure 1-37 Form for seminar data

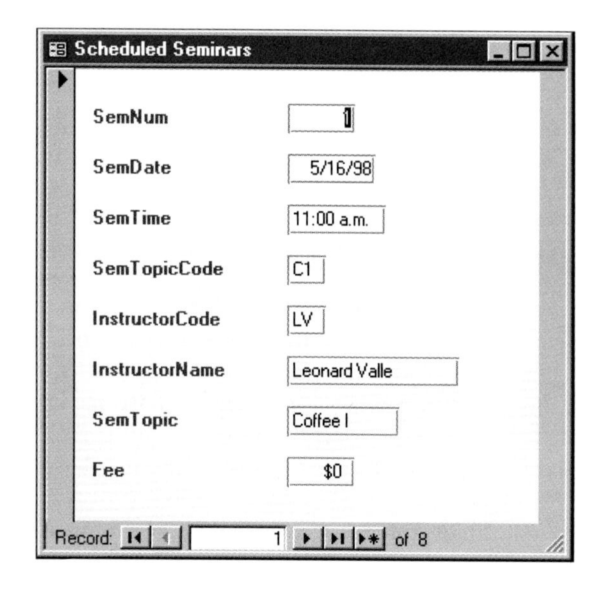

Scheduled Seminars

SemNum: 1
SemDate: 5/16/98
SemTime: 11:00 a.m.
SemTopicCode: C1
InstructorCode: LV
InstructorName: Leonard Valle
SemTopic: Coffee I
Fee: $0

Record: 1 of 8

Reports are formatted printouts (or screen displays) of the contents of one or more tables in a database. Although you can print data from tables, queries, and forms, reports allow you the greatest flexibility for formatting printed output. For example, you can print reports showing membership lists, billing statements, and mailing labels. Figure 1-38 shows a report listing all seminars scheduled at Valle Coffee.

Figure 1-38 Report of scheduled seminars

Valle Coffee
Complete Seminar Schedule

Date	Day	Seminar Topic	Seminar Time	Instructor Name
5/14/98	Thursday	Coffee I	8:00 p.m.	Belinda Jones
5/16/98	Saturday	Coffee I	11:00 a.m.	Leonard Valle
5/18/98	Monday	Espresso	7:30 p.m.	Kim Carpenter
5/19/98	Tuesday	Coffee I	7:00 p.m.	Leonard Valle
5/19/98	Tuesday	Espresso	8:30 p.m.	Kim Carpenter
5/21/98	Thursday	Coffee II	8:00 p.m.	Belinda Jones
5/23/98	Saturday	Coffee II	1:00 p.m.	Belinda Jones
5/23/98	Saturday	Espresso	3:00 p.m.	Kim Carpenter

Before you begin working in Access, you'll make a copy of Belinda's database in order to keep the original database intact. That way, you can start this session over from the beginning if you want to.

Copying an Access Database

Unlike Word, Excel, and PowerPoint, which provide a Save As option that allows you to save an open file with a different filename, Access does not provide an option for saving a database file with a different filename. To create your own copy of a database and preserve the original database, you must copy the database using Windows Explorer, My Computer, or some other software tool. Because you can perform a copy operation only when the file you are copying is closed, make sure the database is closed before you try to copy it.

Access stores all the tables, queries, forms, and reports for a database in a single file; consequently, database files are large files. You should monitor the size of a database file carefully and always make sure you have sufficient room on your destination disk before making a copy of an existing database.

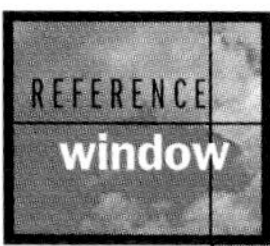

COPYING AN ACCESS DATABASE

- Using the right mouse button, click the Start button on the taskbar.
- On the shortcut menu, click Explore.
- Scrolling as necessary, click the drive, then click the folder that contains the database you want to copy.
- Click the filename of the database, click Edit on the menu bar, then click Copy.
- If necessary, change to the drive and folder that will contain the copy of the database.
- Click Edit on the menu bar, then click Paste.

Belinda's database is named Seminars. You'll copy this database, then rename the copied file as Valle Seminars.

To copy the Seminars database:

1. Using the right mouse button, click the **Start** button on the taskbar. A shortcut menu opens next to the Start button.

   When you click a screen component, such as a button, icon, or filename, with the right mouse button, a shortcut menu opens. A *shortcut menu*, also called a *context menu*, is a context-sensitive list of options available for the object you clicked. You select an option on a shortcut menu just as you select any menu option, by clicking the left mouse button on that option. If you open a shortcut menu by mistake, click outside the shortcut menu with the left mouse button to close it.

2. Click **Explore** on the shortcut menu. The Exploring window opens.

3. Scrolling as necessary, click the plus symbol to the left of the drive that contains your Student Disk in the All Folders list box, then click **Tutorial.01**. The list of files in the Tutorial.01 folder on your Student Disk appears in the Contents of 'Tutorial.01' list box.

4. Click **Seminars** in the list box, click **Edit** on the menu bar, then click **Copy**.

   TROUBLE? The filename on your screen might be Seminars.mdb instead of Seminars, depending on the default settings on your computer. The extension "mdb" identifies the file as an Access database.

5. Click **Edit** then click **Paste**. A copy of the Seminars database with a default filename of Copy of Seminars is added to the Contents of 'Tutorial.01' list box.

6. Using the right mouse button, click **Copy of Seminars** in the Contents of 'Tutorial.01' list box. A shortcut menu opens. See Figure 1-39.

Figure 1-39 Shortcut menu for a selected file

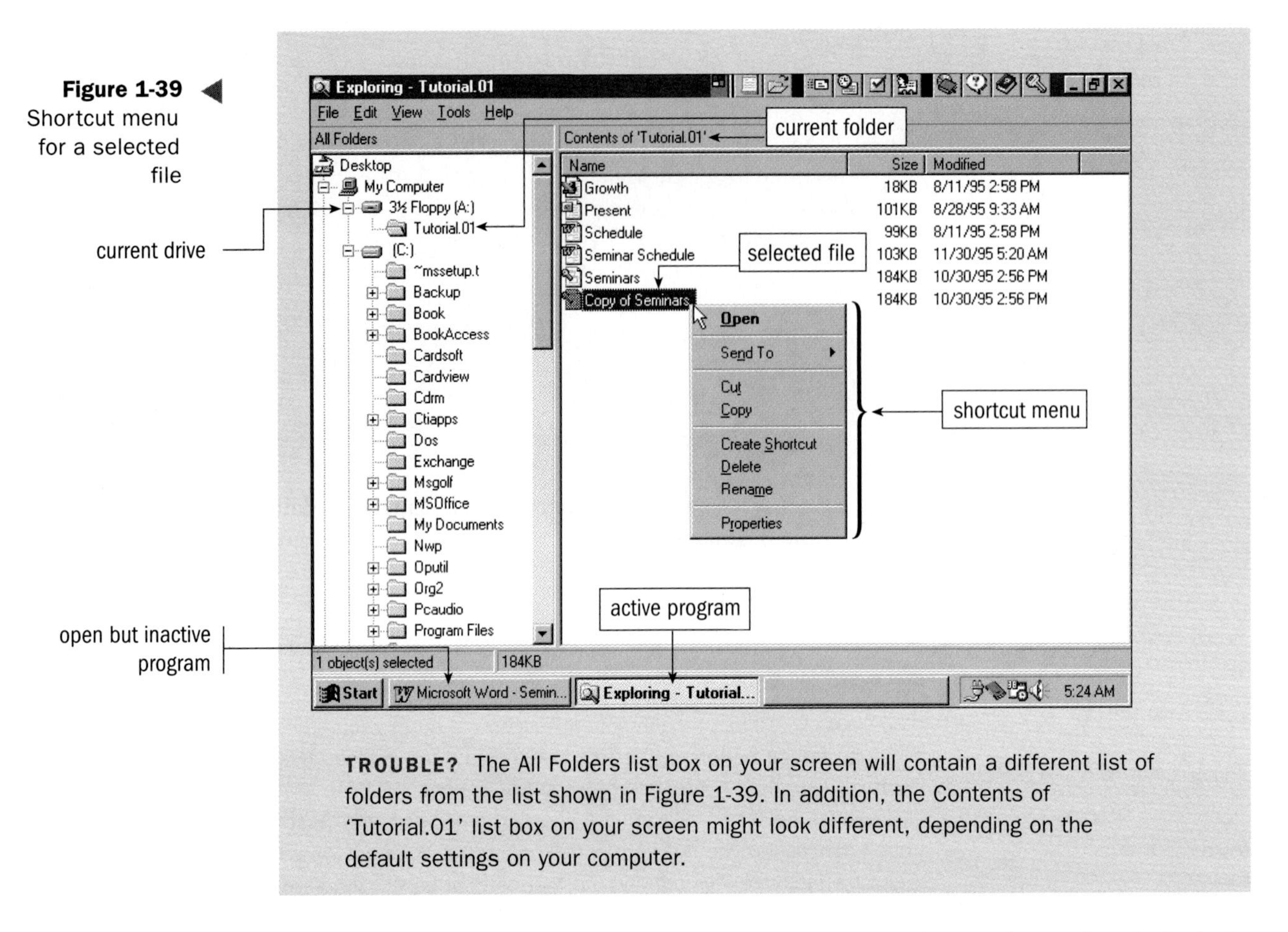

TROUBLE? The All Folders list box on your screen will contain a different list of folders from the list shown in Figure 1-39. In addition, the Contents of 'Tutorial.01' list box on your screen might look different, depending on the default settings on your computer.

The shortcut menu shown in Figure 1-39 lists options that can be used with the highlighted Copy of Seminars file.

To rename the database:

1. Click **Rename** on the shortcut menu. The filename appears highlighted inside a box to indicate that it is selected for editing.
2. Place the insertion point to the left of the word "Copy" in the filename, then press the **Delete** key seven times to remove "Copy of" and leave a space followed by the word "Seminars."
3. Type **Valle** then press the **Enter** key. The filename is now Valle Seminars, which remains highlighted.
4. Click the **Close** button on the Exploring title bar to close Windows Explorer.

Your screen once again displays the Seminar Schedule document in the Word window. Next, you'll open the Valle Seminars database on your Student Disk to examine its contents.

Opening an Existing Access Database

You open an Access database in the same way you open a Word document. When you open the database, you also start Access.

To start Access and open the Valle Seminars database:

1. Click the **Open a Document** button on the Office Shortcut Bar.

2. If necessary, click the **Look in** list arrow, then click the drive that contains your Student Disk.
3. If necessary, click **Tutorial.01** in the list box, then click the **Open** button to see a list of the files in the Tutorial.01 folder.
4. Click **Valle Seminars** in the list box, then click the **Open** button. A title screen appears briefly, Access starts, and then the Valle Seminars database appears in the Access window. See Figure 1-40.

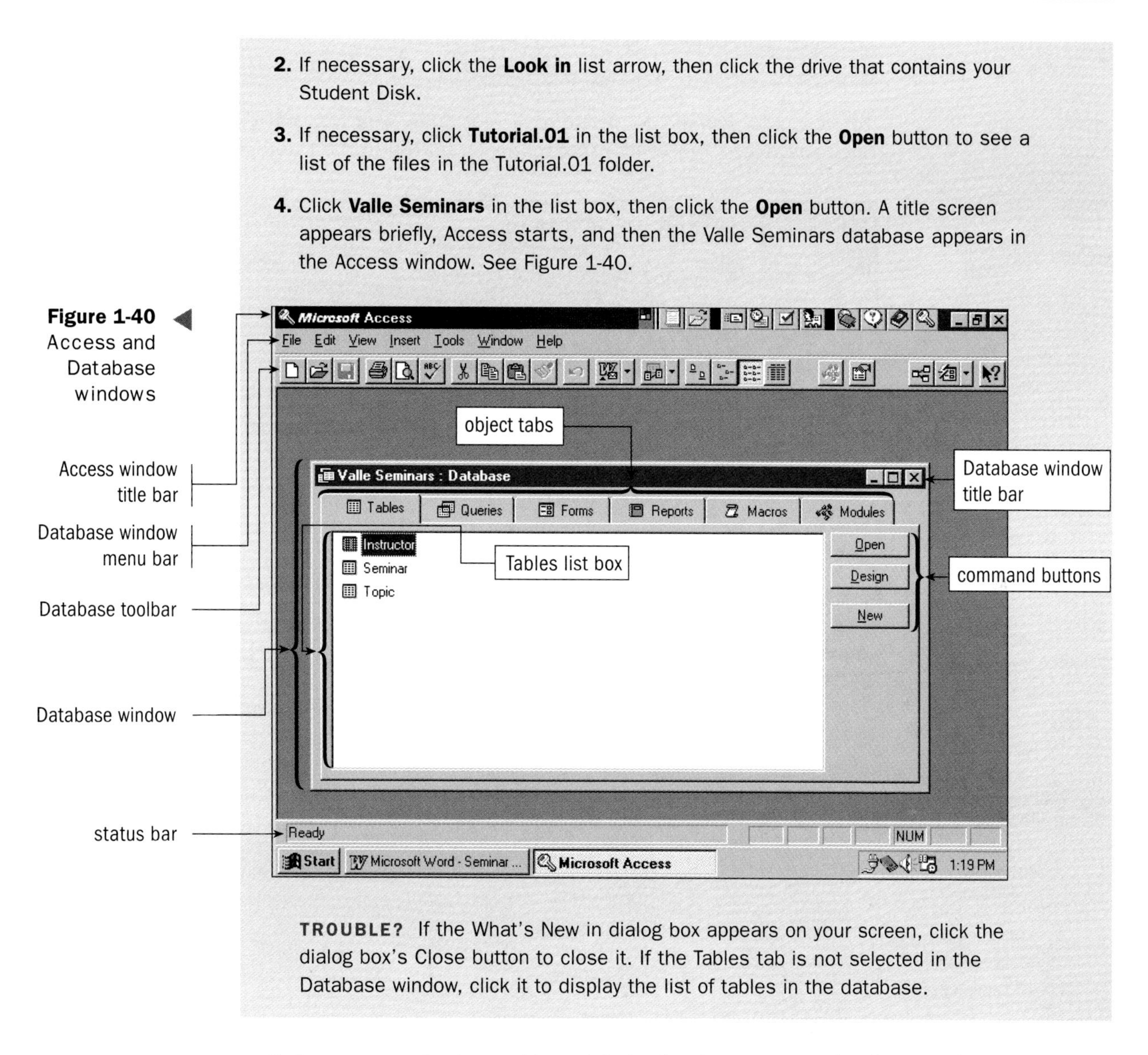

Figure 1-40
Access and Database windows

TROUBLE? If the What's New in dialog box appears on your screen, click the dialog box's Close button to close it. If the Tables tab is not selected in the Database window, click it to display the list of tables in the database.

Before you can begin working with the database, you need to become familiar with the components of the Access and Database windows and their use.

The Access and Database Windows

The **Access window** is the program window that appears when you start the program. The **Database window** appears when you open a database; this window is the main control center for working with an open Access database. Except for the Access window title bar, all other screen components now on your screen are associated with the Database window. Most of these screen components—including the title bars, title bar buttons, menu bar, toolbar, and status bar—are the same as the components in the other Office 95 core programs.

The Database window contains six object tabs. Each **object tab** controls one of the objects—such as tables, forms, and queries—in an Access database.

Belinda has several changes that she wants you to make to the Valle Seminars database.

Working with Access Tables

As noted earlier, tables contain all the data in a database. Tables are the fundamental objects for your work in Access.

Opening an Access Table

To view, add, change, or delete data in a table, you first must open the table. You can open any Access object by using the Open button in the Database window.

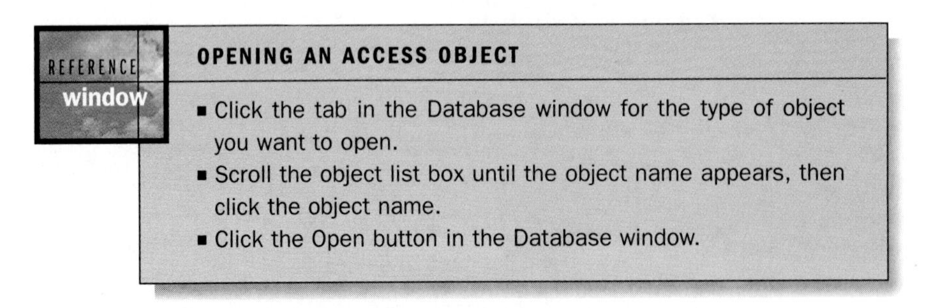

REFERENCE window

OPENING AN ACCESS OBJECT

- Click the tab in the Database window for the type of object you want to open.
- Scroll the object list box until the object name appears, then click the object name.
- Click the Open button in the Database window.

First, you'll open the Instructor table.

To open the table:

1. If the Instructor table is not highlighted, click **Instructor** to select it.
2. Click the **Open** button in the Database window. The Instructor table opens in Datasheet view on top of the Database and Access windows. See Figure 1-41.

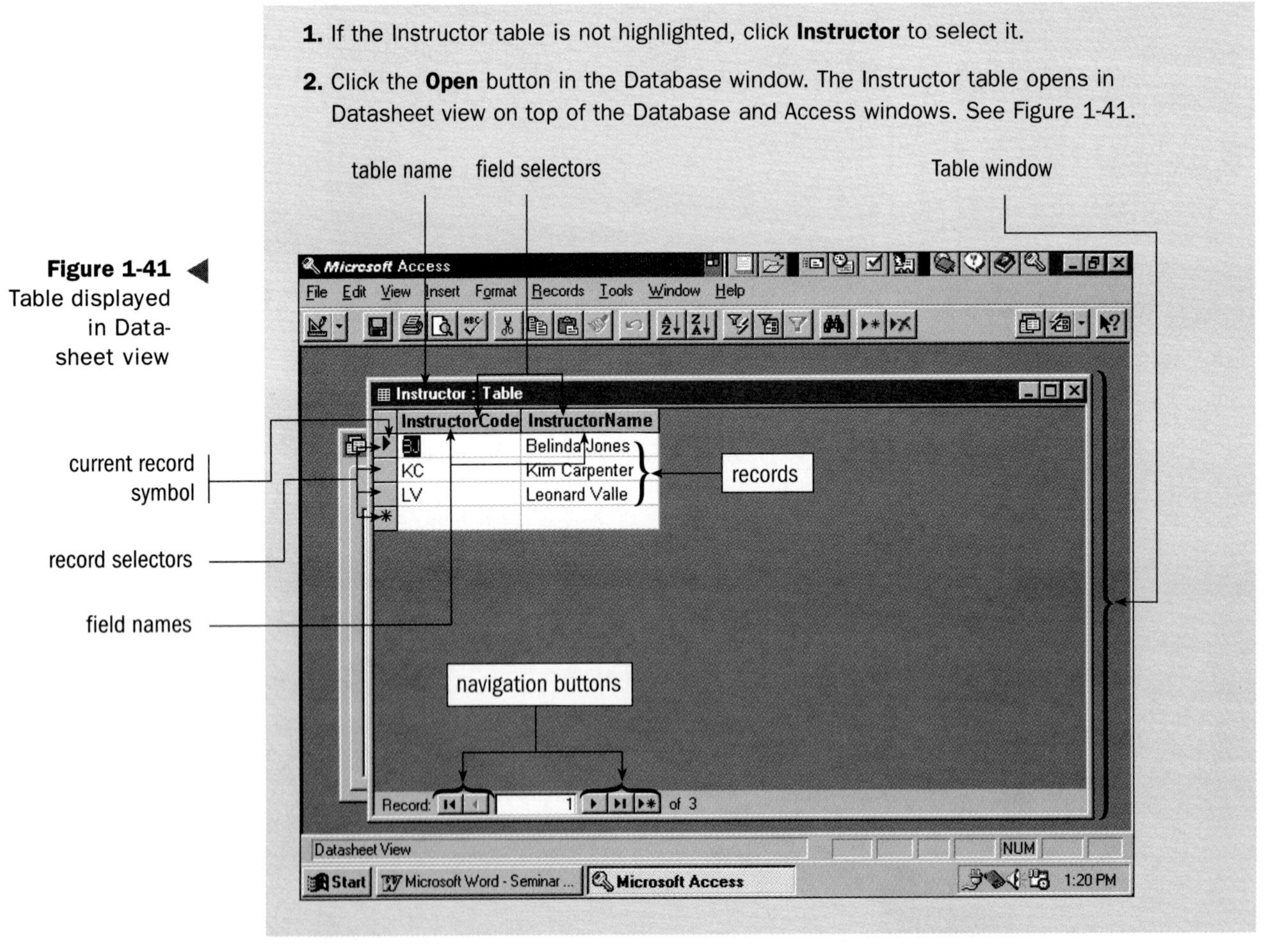

Figure 1-41 Table displayed in Datasheet view

Datasheet view shows a table's contents as a **datasheet** in rows and columns, similar to a table or worksheet. Each row is a separate record in the table, and each column contains the field values for one field in the table. Each column is headed by a field name inside a field selector, and each row has a record selector to its left. Clicking a **field selector** or a **record selector** selects that entire column or row respectively, which you can then manipulate. A field selector is also called a **column selector**, and a record selector is also called a **row selector**.

Navigating an Access Datasheet

When you first open a datasheet, Access selects the first field value in the first record. Notice that this field is highlighted and that a darkened triangle symbol, called the current record symbol, appears in the record selector to the left of the first record. The **current record symbol** identifies the currently selected record. Clicking a record selector or field value in another row moves the current record symbol to that row. You can also move the mouse pointer over the data on the screen and click one of the field values to position the insertion point.

Unlike the Instructor table, which fits comfortably in a small portion of the Table window, most tables contain dozens of fields and hundreds or thousands of records. For larger tables, Access provides horizontal and vertical scroll bars to help you navigate through the data. Using the **navigation buttons**, shown in Figure 1-41, is another way to move vertically through the records. Figure 1-42 shows which record becomes the current record when you click each navigation button. The current record number appears between the two sets of navigation buttons, and the total number of records in the table appears to the right of the navigation buttons.

Figure 1-42 Navigation buttons

Navigation Button	Record Selected	Navigation Button	Record Selected
⏮	First record	⏭	Last record
◀	Previous record	▶*	Blank (new) record
▶	Next record		

Now that you've viewed the contents of the Instructor table, you can close its datasheet. Then you can open the Seminar table and navigate through its datasheet. This is also the table in which you need to make changes for Belinda, including updating the time for the May 14 Coffee I seminar.

To open and navigate the Seminar datasheet:

1. Click the **Close** button ☒ on the Table window title bar. The datasheet closes and the Database window becomes the active window.
2. Click **Seminar** in the Tables list box, then click the **Open** button. The Seminar table opens in Datasheet view.
3. Click the **Next record** navigation button ▶. The second record is now the current record, as indicated by the current record symbol in the second record selector. Also, notice that the second record's value for the SemNum field is highlighted, and "2" (for record number 2) appears between the sets of navigation buttons.
4. Click the **Last record** navigation button ⏭. The eighth record is now the current record.
5. Click the **Previous record** navigation button ◀. The seventh record is now the current record.
6. Click the **First record** navigation button ⏮. The first record is now the current record.

In the Seminar table, Belinda wants you to change one of the InstructorCode values, add one record, delete one record, and update the time for the May 14 seminar.

Updating an Access Table

Updating, or **maintaining**, a database is the process of adding, changing, and deleting records in database tables to keep them current and accurate. To update a table, you must open the table, move to the appropriate table location, then apply the update.

Because the changes Belinda wants you to make involve the open Seminar table, you only need to navigate and apply each update. First, Belinda wants you to change the InstructorCode value in the sixth record from KC to BJ.

To change the InstructorCode value:

1. In the sixth record, position the insertion point to the right of KC in the InstructorCode column.
2. Press the **Backspace** key twice to delete both characters, then type **BJ**.

Next you need to add a new record for a new seminar being offered on 5/16/98.

To add the new record:

1. Click the **Blank (new) record** navigation button ▶*.

   Access moves the current record symbol to the ninth record, which is the next available row for adding a new record. The SemNum value, which is highlighted, is a special type of field for which Access automatically supplies a value. Access does not allow you to enter a value for this field.

2. Press the **Tab** key. Access advances the insertion point to the next field.
3. Type **5/16/98**, press the **Tab** key, type **10:00**, press the **spacebar**, type **a.m.**, press the **Tab** key, type **ES**, press the **Tab** key, type **BJ**, then press the **Tab** key.

   Access moves to the tenth record and *immediately* adds the ninth record to the database table. Unlike most programs, such as Word, Excel, and PowerPoint, Access does not require that you save your updates to a database because the updates are applied to the database file as you make them.

   TROUBLE? If you make a typing mistake, position the insertion point where you made the mistake, use the Backspace or Delete keys to remove the incorrect text, then retype the correct value.

Next, you'll delete the seventh record, which contains data about a seminar that has been canceled.

To delete the record:

1. Move the mouse pointer to the record selector for the seventh record. When the mouse pointer changes to ➡, click to select the entire row.
2. Click the **Delete Record** button ▶✕ on the Table Datasheet toolbar. Access deletes the record and displays a dialog box asking if you are sure you want to delete the record.
3. Click the **Yes** button to confirm the deletion and close the dialog box. Notice that Access does not renumber the records after you delete a record.
4. Click the **First record** navigation button |◀ to move back to the beginning of the table.

Finally, you need to update the time for the May 14 Coffee I seminar, which is the third record in the table. Recall that you changed the time for this seminar in the copied Access data in the Word document. Notice that the change was not made automatically to the record in the Access table. Because the data was *copied* from the Access table to the Word document, any changes made in one location are not made automatically in the other. To have the data updated automatically, you would need to *link* the two occurrences of the data. (You will learn more about linking data later in this session.)

To update the time of the May 14th seminar:

1. For the third record, click between the **7** and the colon (**:**) in the SemTime field.
2. Press the **Backspace** key, then type **8**. The time is updated to 8:00 p.m. You've completed all the changes Belinda requested. See Figure 1-43.

Figure 1-43 After updating the Seminar table

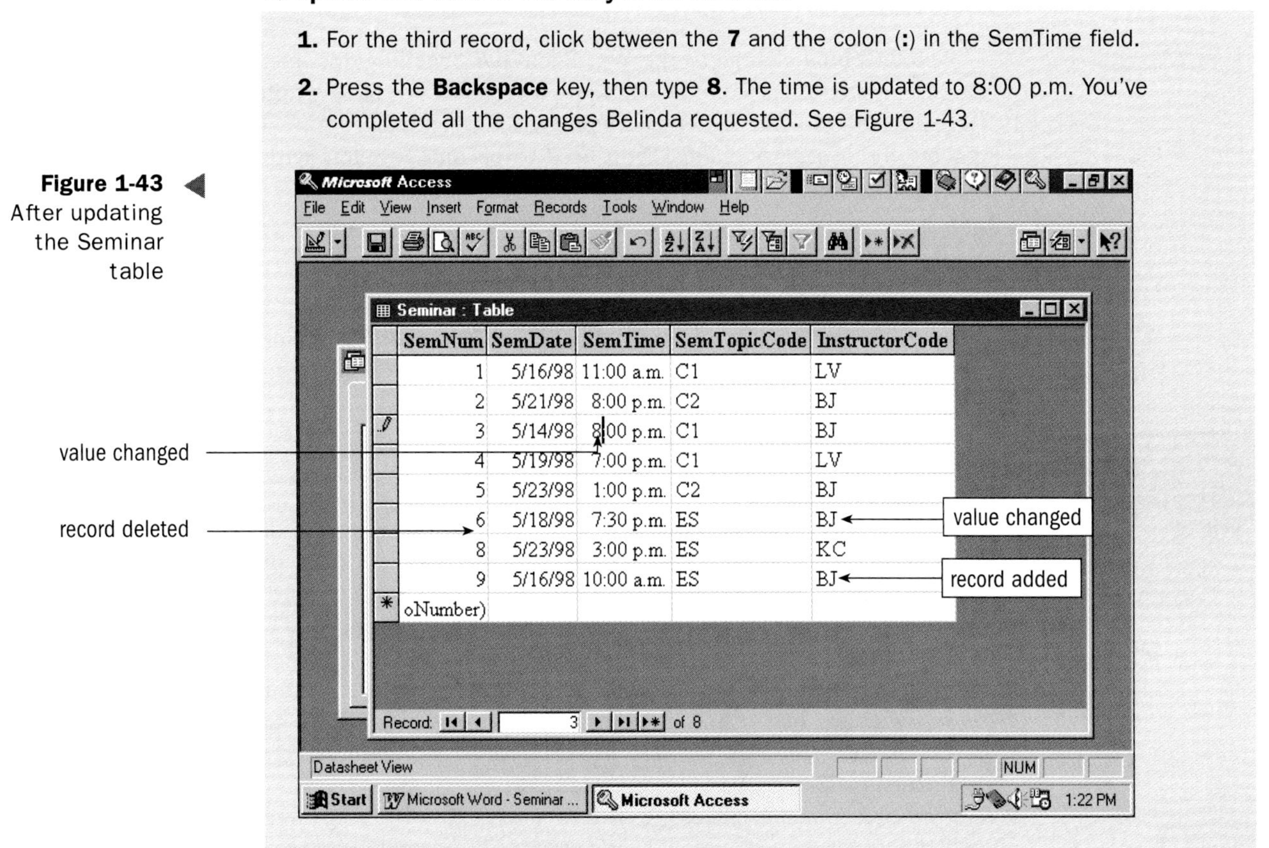

Now that you've updated the table, you'll print it for Belinda so that she can verify the changes you've made.

Printing a Table

Like other Office 95 programs, Access allows you to print using either the Print command on the File menu or the Print button on the toolbar. The Print command displays a dialog box in which you can specify print settings. The Print button prints the table using the current settings. You'll use the Print button to print the Seminar table.

To print the table:

1. Click the **Print** button on the Table Datasheet toolbar.

You have completed your work with the Access database, and you give the printout to Belinda for her review. Belinda asks you to exit Access and make one more change to the Word document.

Exiting Access

As you did when exiting Word, you'll simply click the Close button on the title bar to exit Access. When exiting, Access closes the database before closing the program.

To exit Access:

1. Click the **Close** button [X] on the title bar. The database is closed, Access closes, and the Word window becomes the active window.

Belinda's final change to the Word Seminar Schedule document is to correct the 1997 Decaf Flavored sales value by changing it from 149 to 51. As noted earlier in this session, the sales table in the Word document was embedded from an Excel worksheet. Before making the necessary change, you need to become familiar with the concepts of linking and embedding.

Linking and Embedding Objects

Integration is the combining of data from two or more programs into one document. Copying or moving data from one program to another is a simple form of integration. When you copy or move data, the original and copied data are independent of each other, as you saw earlier with the data copied from Access to Word. To update the data, you had to make the same change twice—updating the copied data in the Word document, then updating the original data in the Access database. This is not always the most efficient way to maintain data.

Linking and embedding are two efficient ways to integrate data. Unlike copying and moving, linking and embedding retain a connection between programs. You embed or link data, or objects, using the features of Object Linking and Embedding (OLE). An **object** is a chart, graphic, worksheet, table, or other "package" of data or information. **OLE** (pronounced oh-LAY) lets you embed or link an object from one program into another. For example, you can embed or link a worksheet from Excel and place it in a Word document. The program containing the original object is called the **source** program (Excel in this example), and the program in which you embed or link the object is the **destination** program (Word in this example).

If an object is **embedded**, it exists as a separate object in the destination program. An embedded object is not linked to the source object, which means that changes to a source object are not made automatically to the embedded object and vice versa. Figure 1-44 shows an example of embedding an object and then changing it using Excel as the source program and Word as the destination program.

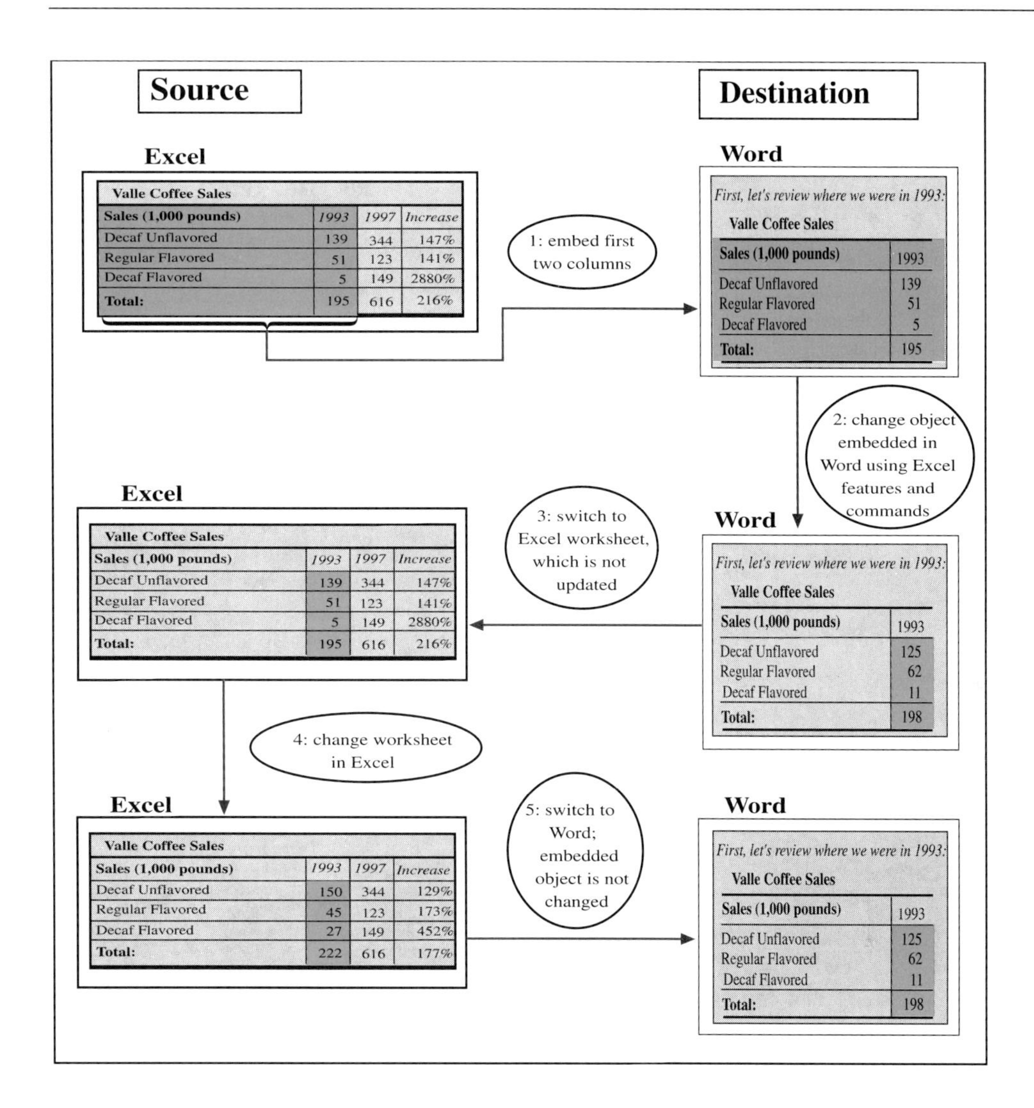

Figure 1-44 Embedding data from Excel to Word

When you change an embedded object, the menus and toolbars of the destination program (Word in this example) change to those of the source program (Excel in this example). That is, you use the source program (Excel) to change the embedded object. After changing the embedded object, the menus and toolbars revert to those for the destination program (Word), which you use for any other document edits.

The advantage of embedding an object over copying data is that you can use the features and commands of the *source program* to change the object. For copied data, you can use only the features and commands of the program into which you copied the data; therefore, you are limited in the types of changes you can make.

You can also use OLE to link objects between two programs. Linking objects provides a more direct connection between the data in two programs than embedding does. When you **link** an object, any changes you make to the object in one program—source or destination—are made *automatically* to the corresponding object in the other program. As shown in Figure 1-45, a linked object does not exist as a separate object in the destination program. Instead, OLE creates a connection, or link, between the object in the source program and the destination program. This link ensures that any changes to the object initiated from either the source or destination program are reflected in the other program.

Figure 1-45 Linking data from Excel to Word

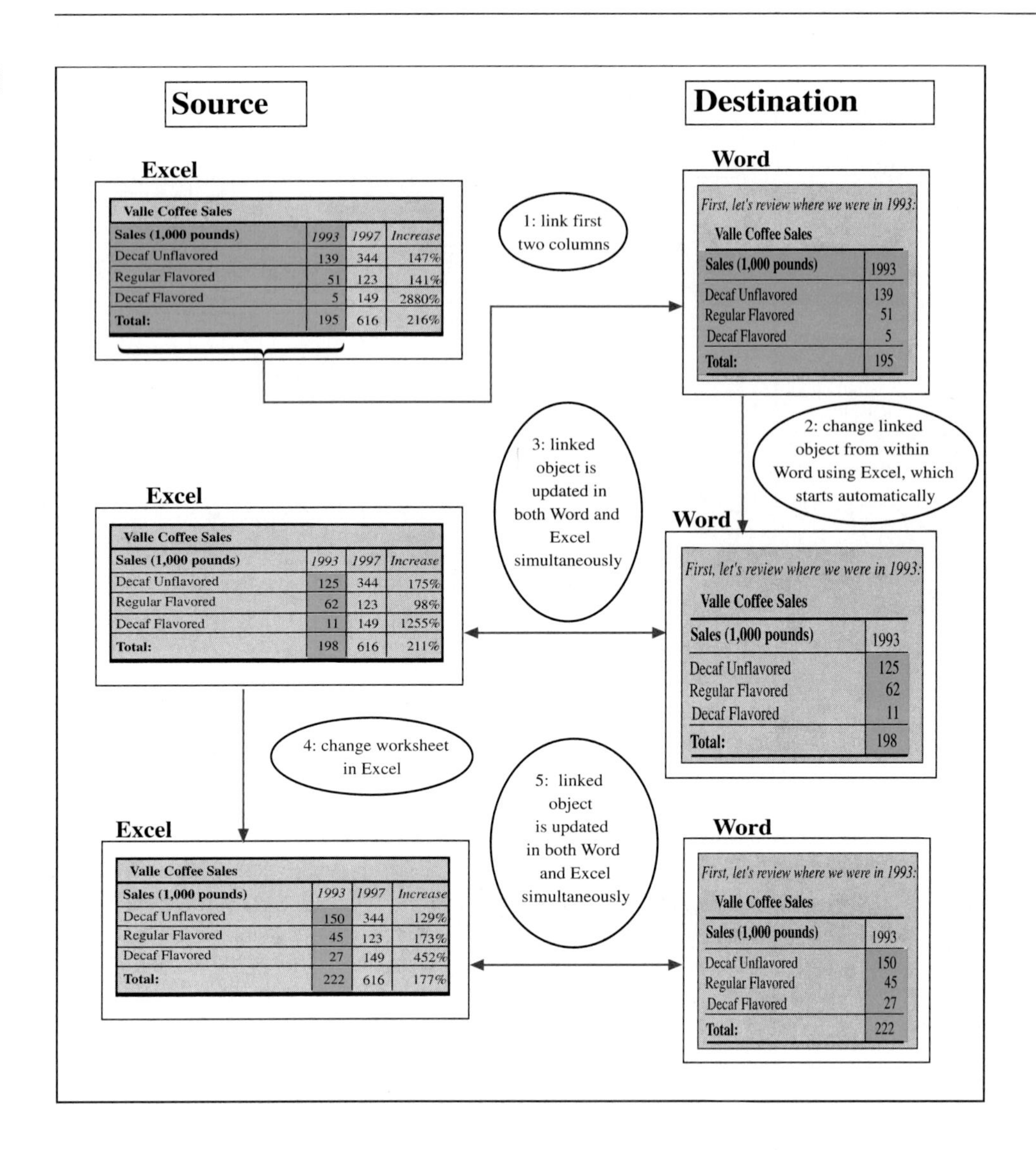

When you change a linked object from the destination program, the source program (Excel in this example) starts and becomes the active program. When finished with the changes, you resume working in the destination program.

Because a linked object does not exist as a separate object in the destination program, linking does not increase the size of the document in the destination program. In contrast, an embedded object does increase the size of the document in the destination program.

How you choose to integrate data—copying, embedding, or linking—depends on how you plan to use the data. If you want to take a "snapshot" of certain data at a particular point in time, you would either copy or embed the data so that any future updates would not affect it. If you want objects in both the source and destination programs to be updated automatically each time you make a change, you would link the objects.

Belinda wants you to edit the embedded Excel worksheet by changing the 1997 Decaf Flavored sales value from 149 to 51.

Updating an Embedded Excel Worksheet

To change data in an embedded object, you must first select the object then make the change using the features and commands of the source program. The sales value you need to change is in the embedded Excel worksheet, which is near the bottom of the Seminar Schedule document.

To select the embedded worksheet object:

1. Scroll until the entire Valle Coffee Sales table is on your screen.
2. Position the insertion point immediately to the left of the value 149 in the 1997 column and the Decaf Flavored row. A box appears around the table and the insertion point does not appear inside the boxed area. See Figure 1-46.

Figure 1-46 Selecting an embedded object

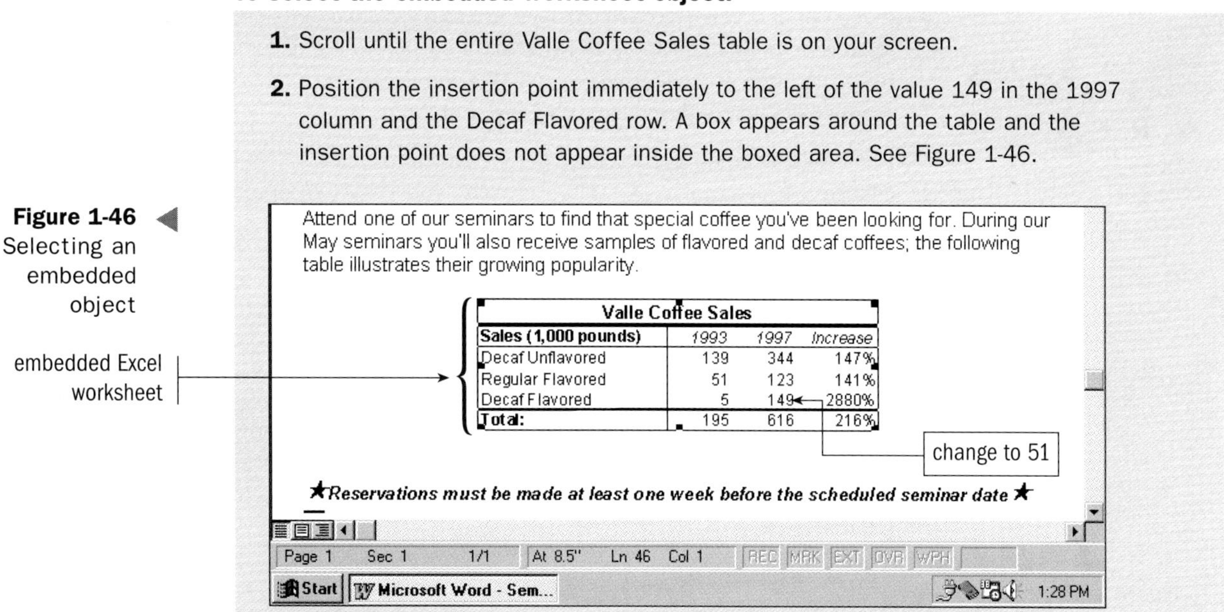

When you click any part of an object, a selection box appears around the object. A **selection box** indicates that the entire object is selected. You can use the object's shortcut menu to display a list of options available for the selected object.

To start updating the embedded Excel worksheet:

1. Right-click anywhere inside the object. The object's shortcut menu opens.
2. Click **Edit Worksheet** on the shortcut menu. After several seconds, some of the Word components on the screen change to Excel components. See Figure 1-47.

Figure 1-47 Excel activated from Word for an embedded worksheet

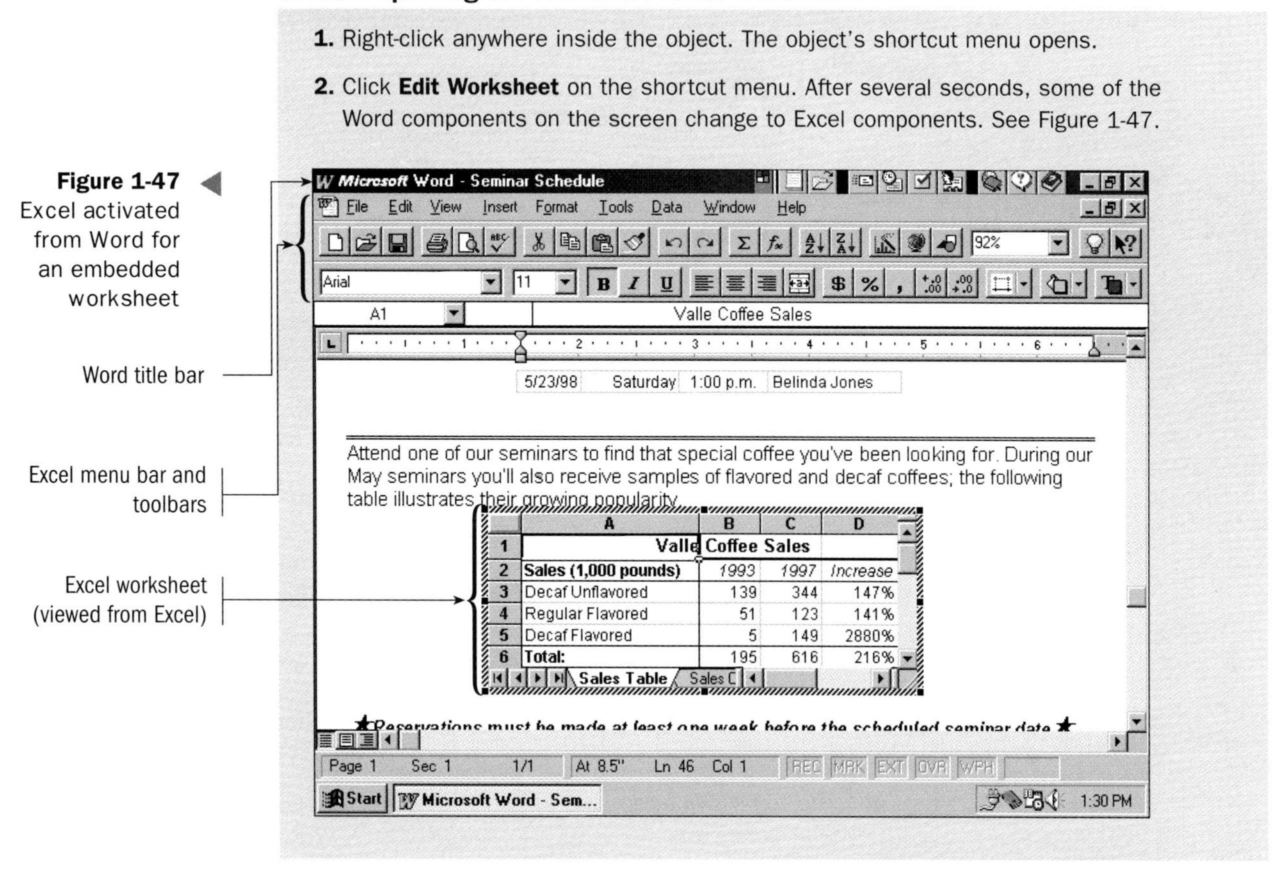

The title bar, ruler, and status bar are still those for the Word window, but the menu bar and toolbars have changed to Excel's components. The Word document window is still displayed. However, a portion of the document window contains the Excel worksheet. When you click the Excel worksheet, the menu bar, or the toolbars, you are working with Excel, not Word.

Don't be concerned about all the details on your screen at this time. After you change the sales value and return to Word, you'll start Excel to make some changes to an existing worksheet.

Now you need to edit the embedded Excel worksheet.

3. Click **149** in the 1997 column and the Decaf Flavored row of the Excel worksheet. A box appears around the value to indicate it is selected. The boxed area is called a *cell*.

4. Type **51** then press the **Enter** key. The value changes from 149 to 51. Also, notice that three other values are recalculated automatically—the total 1997 sales value, the percentage increase value for Decaf Flavored coffee, and the total percentage increase value. See Figure 1-48.

Figure 1-48 After changing the Excel worksheet

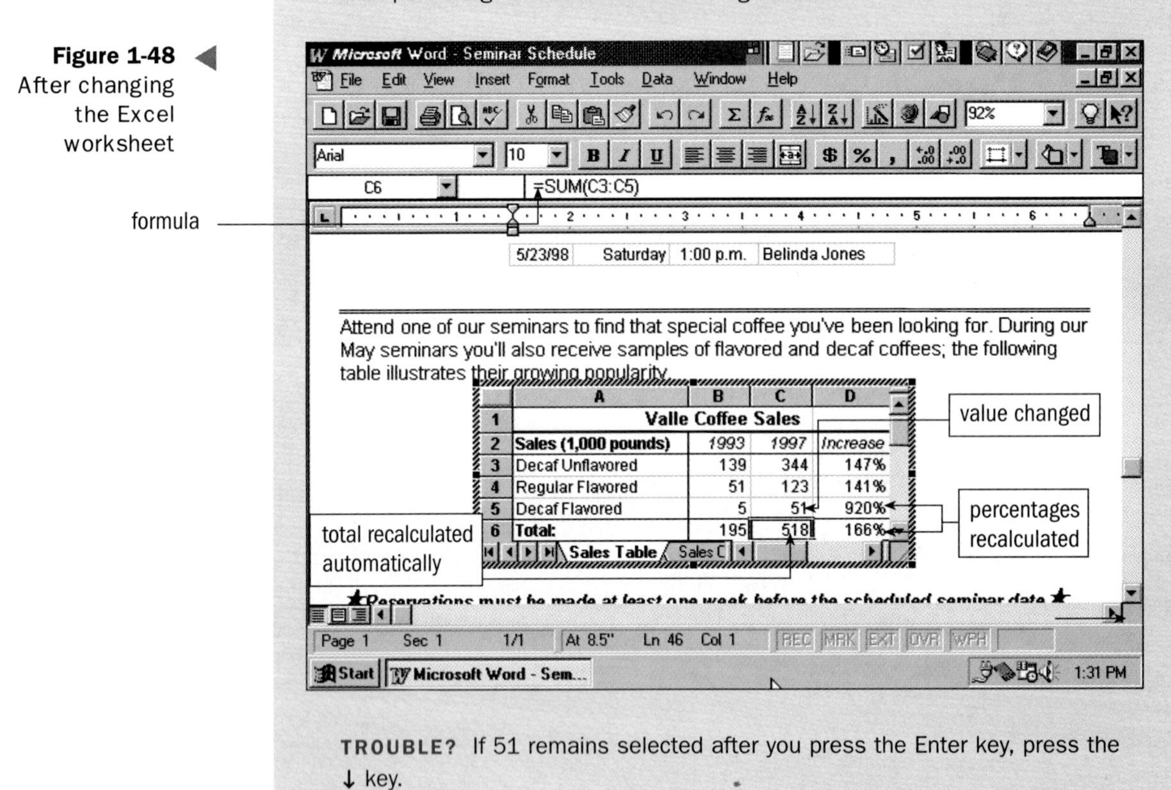

TROUBLE? If 51 remains selected after you press the Enter key, press the ↓ key.

When you pressed the Enter key, the selection moved down one cell. That cell contains a **formula**, which is a calculation you want Excel to perform. The formula automatically sums the values in the three cells above the selected cell.

After changing the Excel data, you can return to the Word and document windows.

To return to the destination program after changing the embedded object:

1. Click anywhere in the document outside the Excel worksheet. The changes are applied to the embedded object, and all Excel screen components are replaced by their Word counterparts.

2. Click the **Save** button on the Standard toolbar to save the revised Word document.

Next, Belinda asks you to open the Excel document containing the data that was embedded in the Word document.

Opening an Existing Excel Workbook

An Excel document is called a **workbook**, which consists of one or more individual **worksheets** (or simply **sheets**). Belinda's Growth workbook was the basis for the embedded worksheet that you just updated in the Seminar Schedule document. She wants you to open this workbook and change some of its data.

To start Excel and open the Growth workbook:

1. Click the **Open a Document** button on the Office Shortcut Bar.
2. If necessary, click the **Look in** list arrow, click the drive that contains your Student Disk, click **Tutorial.01** in the list box, then click the **Open** button to see a list of the files in the Tutorial.01 folder.
3. Click **Growth** in the list box, then click the **Open** button. A title screen appears briefly, Excel starts, and then the Growth workbook appears in the Excel window. See Figure 1-49.

Figure 1-49 Excel window

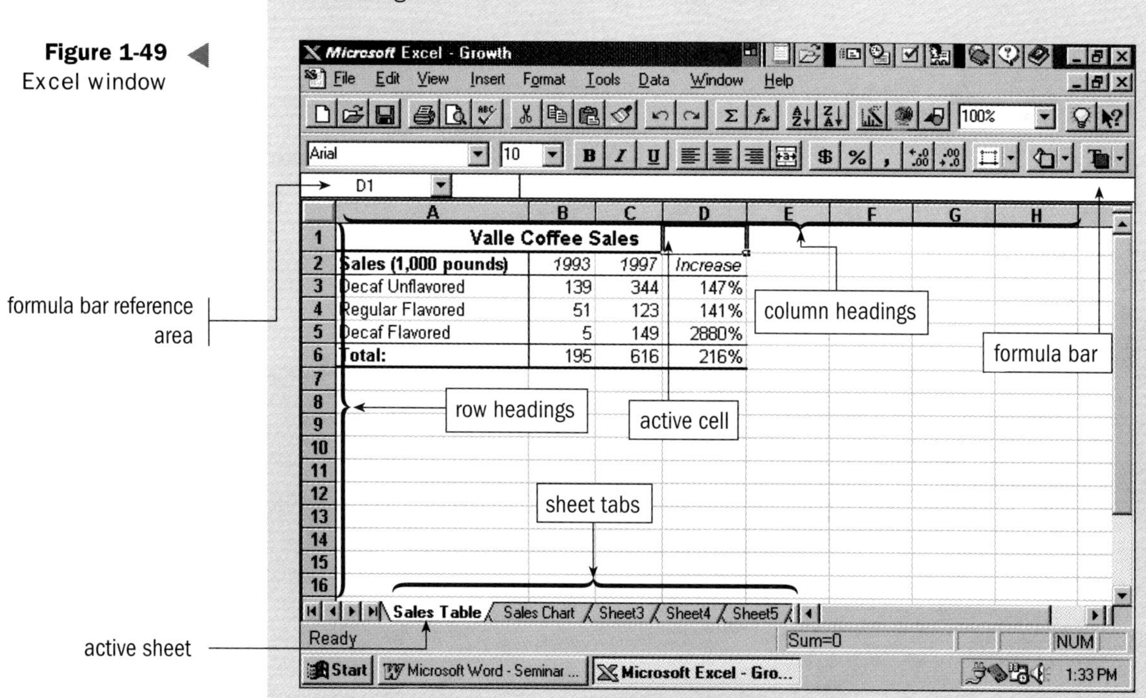

TROUBLE? If the What's New in dialog box appears on your screen, click the dialog box's Close button to close it. If your Excel window is not maximized, click the Excel window's Maximize button. If your document window is not maximized, click the document window's Maximize button.

The Excel window has a title bar, menu bar, Standard and Formatting toolbars, and status bar similar in appearance and location to the Word and Access windows. The Excel document window is divided into rows and columns—the rows are identified by numbers to the left and the columns are identified by letters at the top. A **cell** is a rectangular box at the intersection of a column and row and is referenced by its column and row location. For example, in Figure 1-49 the **active cell**, which is the currently selected cell, is cell D1.

Each sheet in a workbook is identified by a tab in the row above the status bar. The Growth workbook, for example, has sheets named Sales Table, Sales Chart, Sheet3, and so on. The Sales Table sheet is the active sheet because its tab is selected. You will work with the Sales Chart sheet in the next session.

Belinda points out that the sales value for 1997 Decaf Flavored coffee was not changed in the worksheet when you changed the value in the embedded worksheet in Word. Belinda wants you to edit the Sales Table sheet by changing this sales value and by inserting one new row in the worksheet. However, you first need to save the Growth workbook with the new filename of Sales Increase in the Tutorial.01 folder on your Student Disk.

To save the workbook with a new filename:

1. Click **File** then click **Save As**. The Save As dialog box opens.

   The Tutorial.01 folder, which is where you want to save the document, appears in the Save in box; and Growth, which is the current filename, is highlighted in the File name text box.

   TROUBLE? If the Save As dialog box on your screen shows a different folder or filename, enter the correct folder or filename in the appropriate box.

2. Type **Sales Increase** in the File name text box, then click the **Save** button. The dialog box closes and Excel saves the workbook to your Student Disk as Sales Increase.

   The Excel window title bar now shows Sales Increase as the workbook name.

You can now edit the worksheet for Belinda.

Editing an Excel Worksheet

To make changes in a worksheet you first must be able to navigate the workbook. You can use the scroll bars and the navigation buttons, which are located to the left of the sheet tabs, to navigate a workbook. Because the entire Sales Table sheet fits between cells A1 and D6, you won't need to use either of these navigation tools at this time. To move to a cell that is visible on your screen, you simply click the cell.

To edit the sales value in the Excel worksheet:

1. Click cell **C5**, which has a value of 149, to make it the active cell. You will change this cell's value to 51, which is the same change you made to the embedded object in Word.

2. Type **51** then press the **Enter** key. The value in cell C5 changes from 149 to 51, cell C6 becomes the active cell, and the total in cell C6 changes from 616 to 518. The values in cells D5 and D6 are also recalculated.

Next, Belinda asks you to insert a row between rows 3 and 4 and to add the values for Regular Unflavored sales.

To insert the row and add the new values:

1. Click cell **A4** because you want one new row to be inserted at the location above this location.
2. Click **Insert** on the menu bar, then click **Rows**. Excel inserts a blank row below row 3 and shifts all other rows down one row.
3. Type **Regular Unflavored** then press the **Tab** key. Cell B4 becomes the active cell.

   TROUBLE? When you start typing, you might see text appear in the cell. Simply ignore this text and continue typing.
4. Type **620** then press the **Tab** key. The total in cell B7 is updated automatically.
5. Type **703** then press the **Tab** key. The total in cell C7 is updated automatically. See Figure 1-50.

Figure 1-50 Changing the Excel worksheet

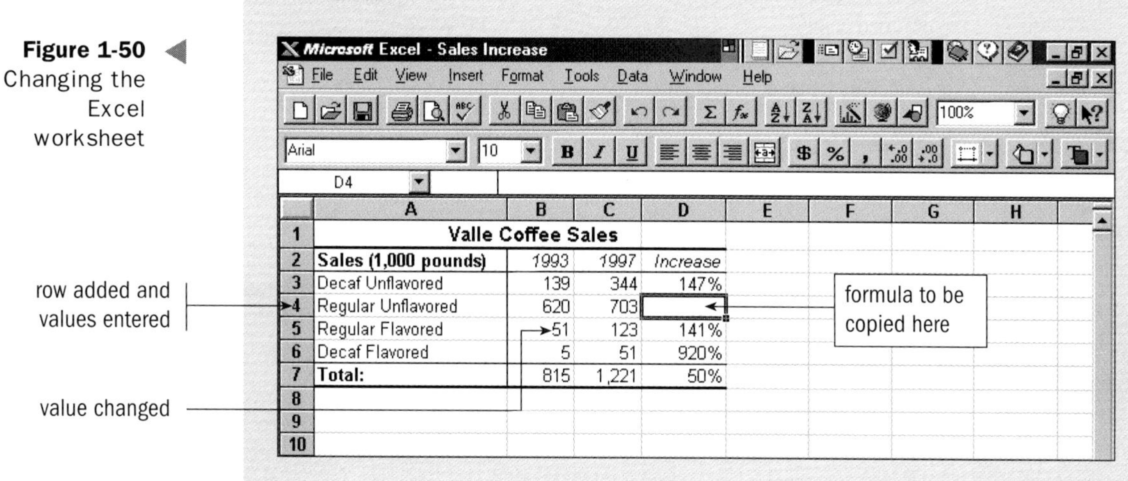

Notice that cell D4 has not been changed; that is, it does not contain a value showing the percentage of increase in Regular Unflavored sales from 1993 to 1997. Belinda asks you to copy the formula from cell D3 to cell D4, then switch to Word to see if any of your changes affected the embedded worksheet.

To copy the formula:

1. Right-click cell **D3**. The shortcut menu opens.
2. Click **Copy** on the shortcut menu. A rotating dashed line surrounds cell D3 to indicate that the copy action is active for this cell.
3. Right-click cell **D4**, then click **Paste** on the shortcut menu. The formula in cell D3 is copied to cell D4, and the value 13% appears in cell D4.

   TROUBLE? If you paste the formula in the wrong cell, click Edit on the menu bar and click Undo Paste. Then repeat Steps 1 through 3.

   Now switch to Word to see if your changes are reflected in the embedded Excel worksheet.
4. Click the **Microsoft Word - Seminar** button on the taskbar. Word becomes the active program.

As expected, your changes are not reflected in the embedded worksheet. In this case, you don't want them to be, because the new row that you inserted contains data about regular unflavored coffee. The text in the Seminar Schedule document describing the embedded worksheet pertains only to flavored and decaf coffees.

The document is now complete and ready to be printed.

5. Click the **Print** button on the Standard toolbar to print one copy of the finished document.

TROUBLE? If the document does not print, see your instructor or technical support person for assistance.

You're finished working with the Seminar Schedule document and can now exit both Word and Excel.

To exit the active programs:

1. Click the **Close** button on the Word title bar. A dialog box opens, asking you if you want to save your changes.
2. Click the **Yes** button. Word saves your document with the same filename, closes the document, and then exits. Excel becomes the active program.
3. Click the **Save** button on the Standard toolbar, then click the **Close** button on the Excel title bar.

Quick Check

1. In an Access database table, the rows are called _________ and the columns are called _________.
2. How do you open a shortcut menu?
3. _________ buttons allow you to move vertically through records in an Access database and through worksheets in an Excel workbook.
4. The _________ identifies the selected record in an Access table.
5. What are the differences between linking and embedding? between copying and embedding?
6. Describe a situation in which embedding would be a better way to integrate data than linking.
7. An Excel document is called a(n) _________ and contains one or more _________.
8. What screen components change when you edit an embedded object?
9. A(n) _________ is a rectangular box at the intersection of a column and row in an Excel worksheet.

SESSION 1.3

In this session you will learn how to open, navigate, edit, and print a PowerPoint presentation. You will also learn how to link an Excel chart to a PowerPoint slide and how to change the linked chart.

Opening an Existing PowerPoint Presentation

Belinda has printed and distributed the completed Seminar Schedule document. Now she wants to finish a PowerPoint document she started. She asks you to help her finish the document, which is called a **presentation** in PowerPoint. Figure 1-51 shows the first two completed slides in Belinda's PowerPoint presentation.

Figure 1-51 First two presentation slides for the coffee I seminar

slide 1

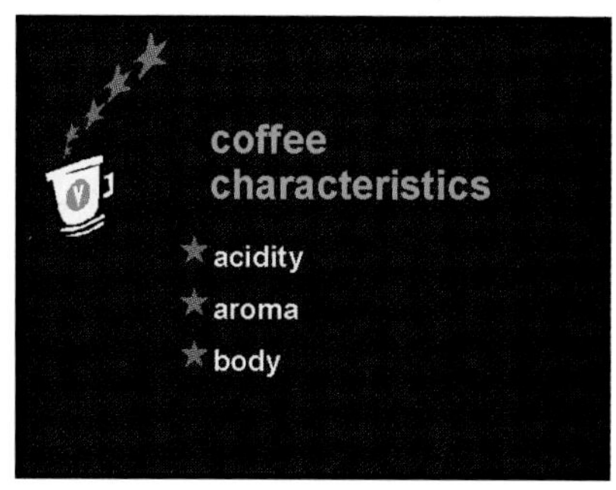

slide 2

Belinda's seminar presentation, which Valle Coffee will use for the coffee I seminar, currently contains nine slides with the following characteristics:

- All nine slides have the same background color and a graphic image of a coffee cup.
- The first slide is a title slide for the presentation.
- The second slide lists three general coffee characteristics, and slides three through seven list the characteristics of coffee from five countries.
- The eighth slide contains space in which you will link an Excel chart.
- The last slide is a blank slide, which is left on the screen for the question-and-answer portion of the seminar.

Belinda asks you to open the presentation, which is named Present in the Tutorial.01 folder on your Student Disk.

Using My Computer to Open an Existing Presentation

To open the PowerPoint presentation, you could use the Open a Document button on the Office Shortcut Bar, which you used to open all previous documents. However, you might encounter situations when the Office Shortcut Bar is not on the screen and you want to use another method of opening a document. The My Computer icon on the Windows 95 desktop also gives you access to your documents.

OPENING AN EXISTING DOCUMENT USING MY COMPUTER

- Right-click the My Computer icon on the Windows 95 desktop, then click Open on the shortcut menu.
- Right-click the name of the drive that contains your document, then click Open on the shortcut menu.
- Right-click the folder that contains your document, then click Open on the shortcut menu.
- Repeat the previous step for any subfolders.
- Right-click your document's icon, then click Open on the shortcut menu. The program in which you created the document starts, then that program opens the selected document.

You'll open Belinda's Present presentation using the My Computer icon on the Windows 95 desktop.

To open the document using the My Computer icon:

1. Place your Student Disk in the disk drive.
2. From the Windows 95 desktop, right-click the **My Computer** icon, then click **Open** on the shortcut menu. The My Computer group window opens.
3. Right-click the **3½ Floppy (A:)** icon, then click **Open** on the shortcut menu.

   TROUBLE? If your disk is in a different drive, right-click that drive's icon instead.
4. Right-click the **Tutorial.01** icon, then click **Open** on the shortcut menu.
5. Right-click the **Present** icon, then click **Open** on the shortcut menu. After a short delay, PowerPoint starts then opens the Present presentation. See Figure 1-52.

Figure 1-52 PowerPoint window

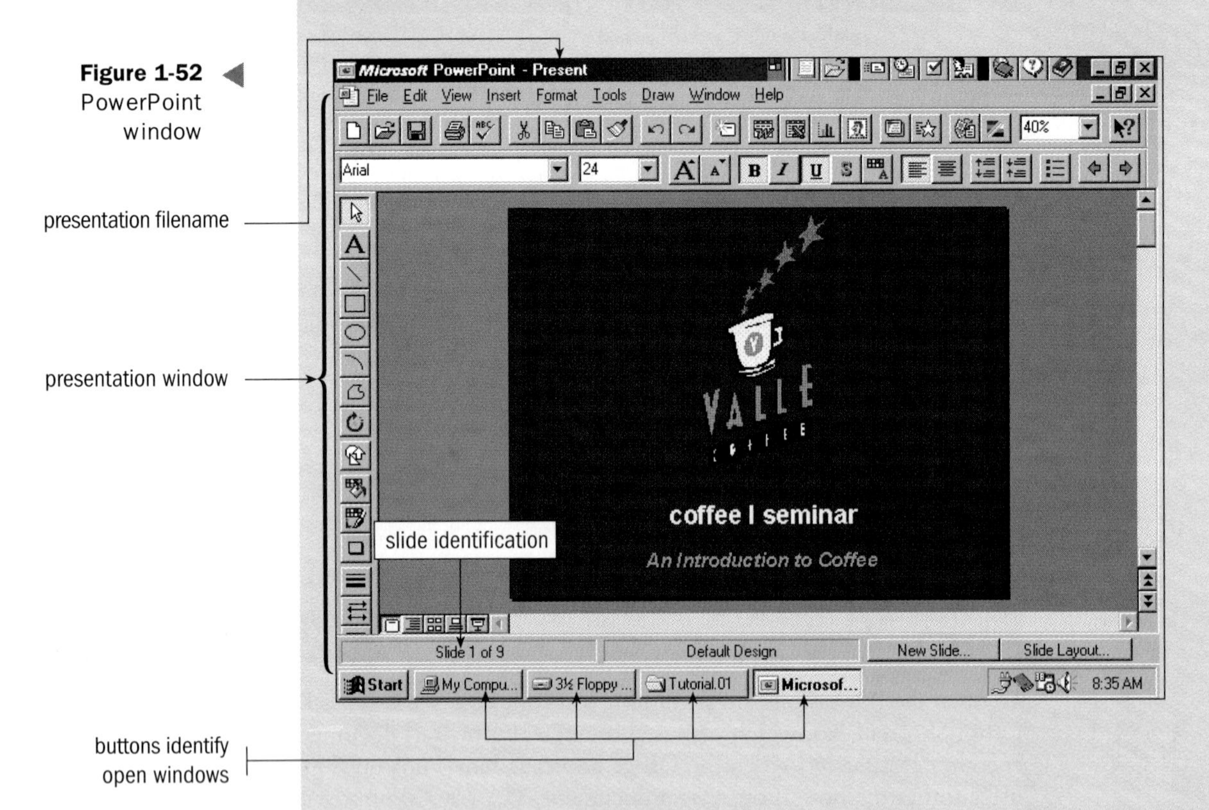

   TROUBLE? If the What's New in dialog box appears on your screen, click the dialog box's Close button to close it. If necessary, maximize the PowerPoint window.

   Notice the four buttons to the right of the Start button on the taskbar. These buttons identify the four windows that are now open. Because you need to have only the PowerPoint window open, you should close the other three windows. These three windows all belong to the My Computer program. If you click one of the three buttons and then click that window's Close button, you close only one window and must repeat these steps for the other two buttons. A quicker method is to close all three windows at one time by pressing and holding down the Shift key while you click the Tutorial.01 window's Close button. This technique closes all open windows associated with the same program.
6. Click the **Tutorial.01** button on the taskbar. The Tutorial.01 window opens.

7. Press and hold down the **Shift** key, then click the **Close** button on the Tutorial.01 title bar. The Tutorial.01, 3½ Floppy (A:), and My Computer windows close at the same time. Only the PowerPoint document remains open.

Before you begin your work in the presentation, you'll save the presentation with the filename Coffee I Presentation so that the original document remains unchanged in case you need to start the session over again.

Saving a Presentation with a New Filename

As you did with Word and Excel documents earlier, you'll save the PowerPoint document using another filename. The procedure is exactly the same as the one you used previously.

To save the presentation with a new filename:

1. Click **File** on the menu bar, then click **Save As** to open the Save As dialog box. Present is highlighted in the File name text box, and Tutorial.01 appears in the Save in box.
2. Type **Coffee I Presentation** then press the **Enter** key. Note that pressing the Enter key has the same effect as clicking the Save button. The dialog box closes and Word saves the presentation to your Student Disk as Coffee I Presentation.

The PowerPoint window title bar now shows Coffee I Presentation as the presentation filename.

The PowerPoint Window

The PowerPoint window, shown in Figure 1-53, is similar in many ways to the Word window. For example, both have many of the same components in the same positions: title bar, menu bar, Standard toolbar, Formatting toolbar, scroll bars, document view buttons, status bar, and taskbar.

Figure 1-53 PowerPoint window

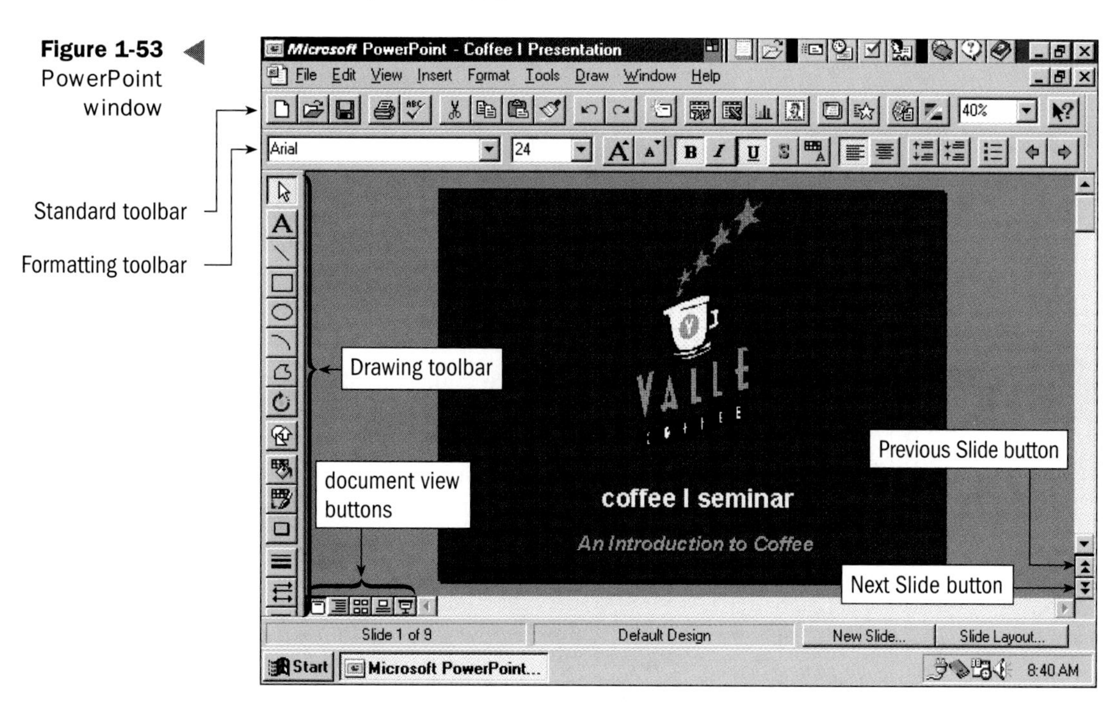

There are several differences between the Word and PowerPoint windows. In PowerPoint, the **presentation window** contains the central workspace; in Word, the document window is the comparable window. The PowerPoint status bar indicates the slide number displayed on the screen and the total number of slides in the presentation. Because PowerPoint presentations make more extensive use of drawings than do Word documents, the Drawing toolbar appears on the PowerPoint window automatically. You use the **Drawing toolbar** to draw lines and shapes on your slides. At the bottom of the vertical scroll bar are the **Previous Slide** and **Next Slide** buttons, which you click to move through the slides in the presentation.

The five document view buttons on the left end of the horizontal scroll bar allow you to change the way you look at a slide presentation. They switch you to slide view, outline view, slide sorter view, notes pages view, and slide show view. Figure 1-54 shows and describes each document view button. You can also select the view you want to use from the View menu.

Figure 1-54 PowerPoint document view buttons

Document View	Button	How To Use
Slide		Work on one slide at a time to view, enter, and edit text, drawings, and graphics
Outline		View and edit the titles and text on slides in outline format
Slide Sorter		View miniature images of several slides at a time, change the order of slides, and set special features for a slide show
Notes Pages		View, enter, and edit speaker's notes on individual slides
Slide Show		Present a slide show with its special effects; each slide fills the screen

Belinda suggests that you look through the presentation, using different views, to become familiar with the content of the presentation and with PowerPoint.

Viewing a Presentation Using Slide View

First you'll use slide view to review Belinda's entire presentation, one slide at a time.

To view the presentation in slide view:

1. Read the first slide, then click the **Next Slide** button on the vertical scroll bar. PowerPoint advances from slide 1 to slide 2.
2. Read the slide, then click the **Next Slide** button to advance to the next slide.
3. Repeat Step 2 until you reach slide 8. The blank space in this slide is where you will link an Excel chart later in this session.
4. Click the **Next Slide** button to advance to the last slide in the presentation.

The last slide is blank, except for the coffee cup image and the color background. Placing a blank slide like this one at the end of a presentation is a good idea, because it signals the end of the presentation and does not distract the audience while the presenter conducts a question-and-answer session.

Once you reach the last slide, the Next Slide button does not advance you further. Likewise, if you are viewing slide 1, clicking the Previous Slide button keeps slide 1 on the screen.

Viewing a Presentation Using Slide Sorter View

Next you'll use slide sorter view to see several slides at once so that Belinda can verify their order. To switch to this view you use the Slide Sorter View button on the horizontal scroll bar.

To view the presentation in slide sorter view:

1. Click the **Slide Sorter View** button on the horizontal scroll bar. PowerPoint switches to slide sorter view. See Figure 1-55.

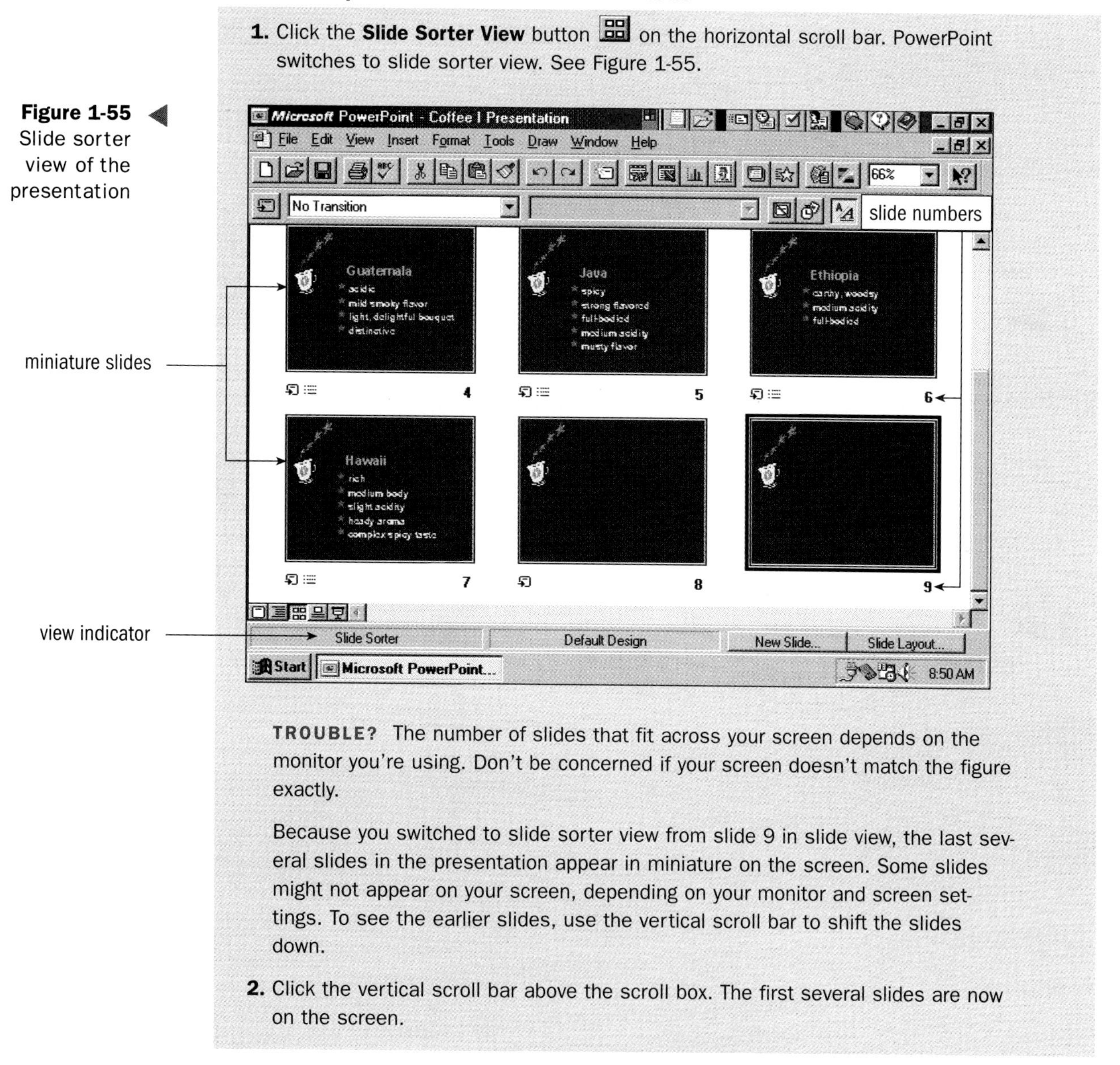

Figure 1-55 Slide sorter view of the presentation

TROUBLE? The number of slides that fit across your screen depends on the monitor you're using. Don't be concerned if your screen doesn't match the figure exactly.

Because you switched to slide sorter view from slide 9 in slide view, the last several slides in the presentation appear in miniature on the screen. Some slides might not appear on your screen, depending on your monitor and screen settings. To see the earlier slides, use the vertical scroll bar to shift the slides down.

2. Click the vertical scroll bar above the scroll box. The first several slides are now on the screen.

Belinda decides that slide 6, Ethiopia, should precede slide 4, Guatemala, and asks you to make this change. Also, she asks you to add a slide after slide 1 with some information about coffee bean types.

Changing the Slide Order

To change the order of slides, you use the mouse to drag a slide to a new location. The other slides in the presentation adjust to the new slide order.

You need to reposition slide 6 before slide 4.

To change the order of the slides:

1. Click slide **6**. A heavy black box appears around slide 6 to indicate it is selected.
2. Click slide **6** and, while holding down the mouse button, drag the mouse pointer to the left of slide 4. As you drag the mouse pointer, it changes to . When you drag the mouse pointer far enough to the left of slide 4, a solid black vertical line to the left of slide 4 indicates the new position for slide 6. See Figure 1-56.

Figure 1-56 Moving a slide

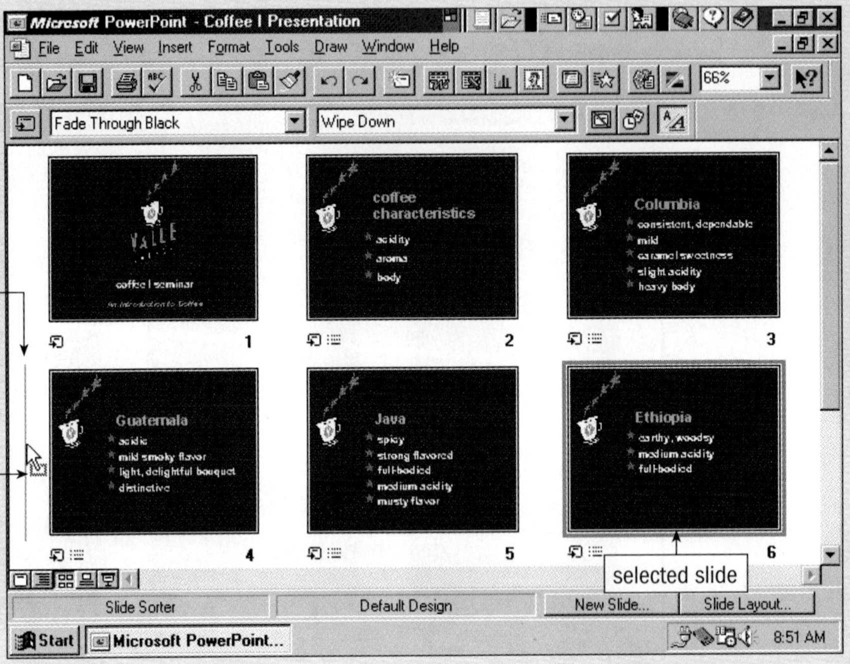

marks selected slide's new position

pointer shape while dragging the slide

selected slide

3. Release the mouse button. Slide 6 changes to slide 4, slide 4 changes to 5, and slide 5 changes to 6.

Belinda wants you to insert a new slide 2 with information about coffee bean types.

Adding a New Slide

To add a new slide, you can use the Insert New Slide button on the Standard toolbar or the New Slide command on the Insert menu. You can add the slide while you are still in slide sorter view so that you can easily verify its correct placement.

To add the new slide:

1. Click slide **1** to select it.
2. Click the **Insert New Slide** button on the Standard toolbar. The New Slide dialog box opens. See Figure 1-57.

Figure 1-57
New Slide dialog box

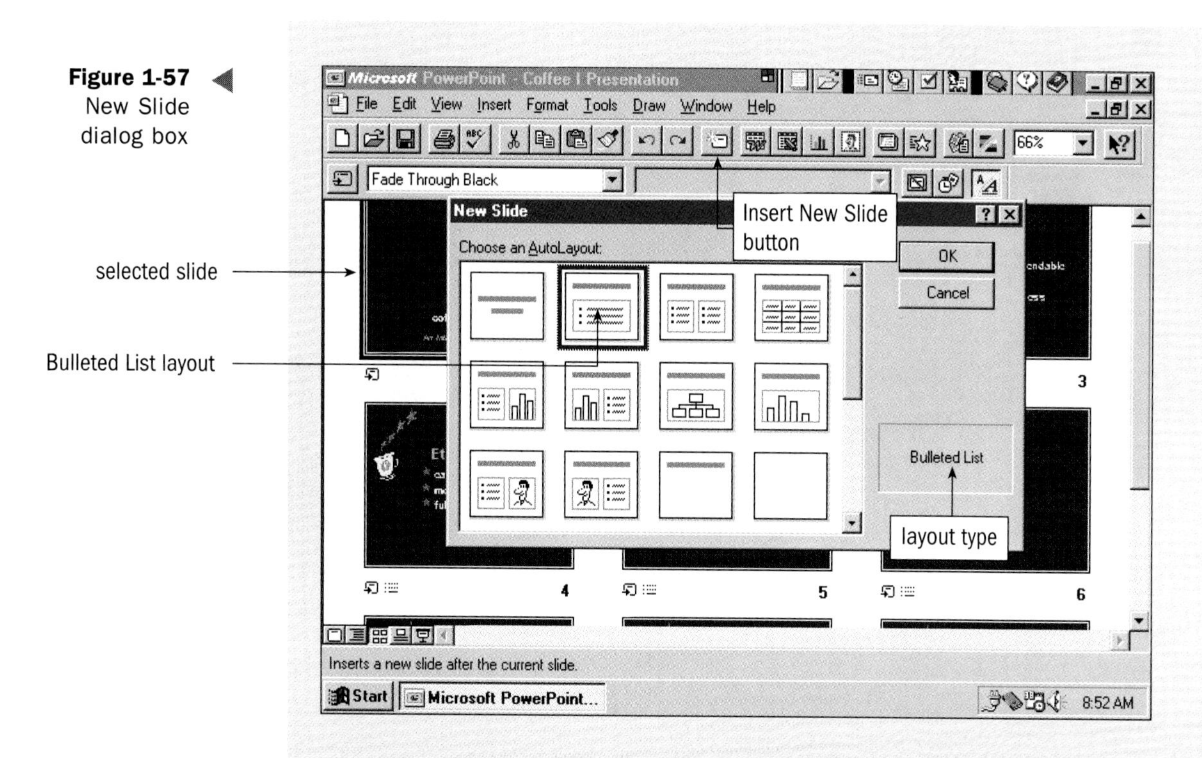

When you add a slide, you must decide what text and graphics will be included and how they will be arranged on the slide. The slide arrangement is called the *layout.* You assign a layout to the slide by choosing an *AutoLayout,* a predefined format for a slide. The name of the AutoLayout appears in the lower-right box in the dialog box.

3. If it is not already selected with a heavy black box around it, click the **Bulleted List** layout (the second slide from the left, in the top row). Be sure that "Bulleted List" appears in the lower-right box.
4. Click the **OK** button. PowerPoint inserts a new slide after slide 1. The new slide has the same background color as the other slides and is blank except for the coffee cup logo. All slides in the presentation will share these two characteristics, because the layout for the slides was designed to include them.

To add the title and bulleted items to the new slide, you need to switch to slide view. The new slide will have two placeholders, one for the title and the other for the bulleted items. A **placeholder** is an area of a window reserved for entering text or graphics.

To add text to the new slide:

1. Click the **Slide view** button on the horizontal scroll bar. PowerPoint changes to slide view and shows a blank slide (except for the logo and background color) with two placeholders. See Figure 1-58.

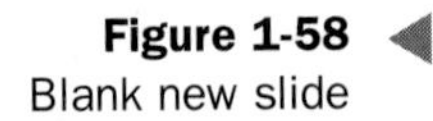

Figure 1-58
Blank new slide

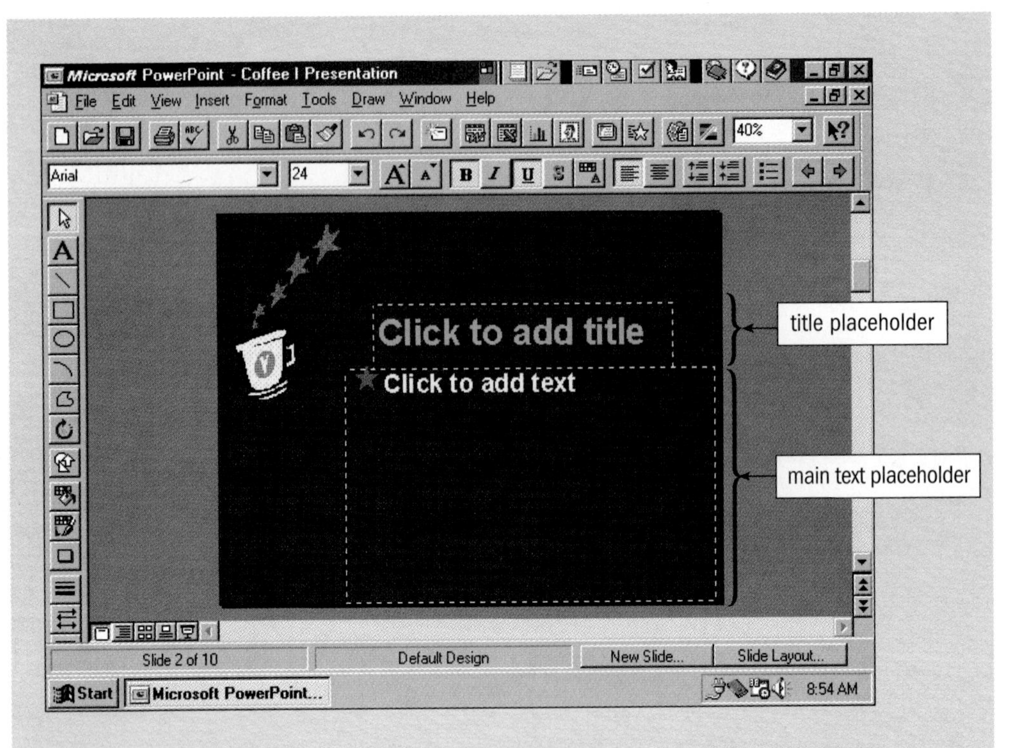

2. Click the **title placeholder** then type **coffee bean types.**

3. Click the **main text placeholder**. The insertion point appears following a star bullet in the main text placeholder.

4. Type **Robusta** then press the **Enter** key. The insertion point moves to the next line, following a star bullet.

5. Type **Arabica**.

6. Click anywhere outside the two placeholders to deselect the main text placeholder. The bulleted text partially overlaps the title, so you need to move the bulleted text down slightly.

7. Click one of the bulleted items to display the main text placeholder, then click the thick, main text placeholder border. Eight small boxes, called *sizing handles*, appear on the border. You use these handles to change the size of the selected object.

8. Position the mouse pointer on the center sizing handle at the top of the box. The mouse pointer changes to ↕. See Figure 1-59.

Figure 1-59 Moving bulleted items

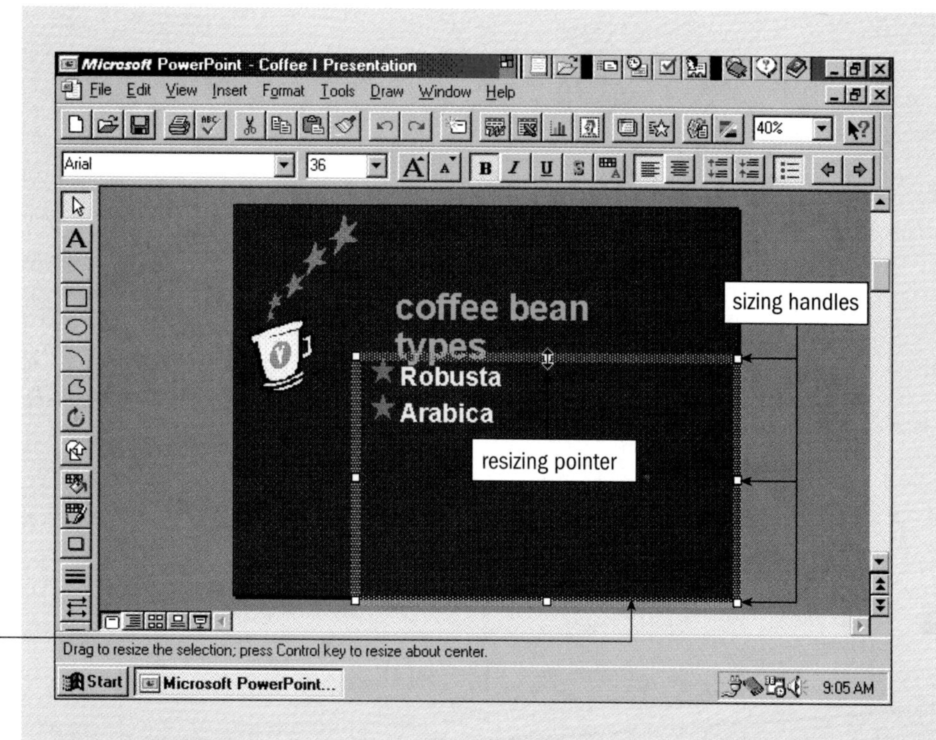

main text placeholder border

The bulleted items need to be just below the bottom of the coffee cup.

9. Click and drag the center sizing handle down to shorten the box, then release the mouse button.

10. Click anywhere outside the two placeholders to deselect the main text placeholder. Make sure your slide 2 looks like Figure 1-60.

Figure 1-60 Completed new slide 2

TROUBLE? If the bulleted items are too high or low, repeat Steps 7 through 10 to adjust the position of the items.

Belinda wants you to link an Excel chart to slide 9 in the presentation. The chart shows Valle Coffee sales data for each category of coffee. The chart is on the Sales Chart sheet in the Sales Increase workbook, which you worked with in the previous session.

Before you link the chart, you should save the presentation because you've made changes to it.

To save the presentation and move to slide 9:

1. Click the **Save** button on the Standard toolbar. PowerPoint saves the presentation with the same filename.
2. Click and hold the mouse button down on the vertical scroll box. A *ScrollTip* appears and displays the current slide number and title in a box. As you drag the vertical scroll box, the ScrollTip changes to display your location in the presentation.
3. Drag the vertical scroll box to slide 9.

With the correct slide displayed, you're ready to link the Excel chart to the PowerPoint presentation.

Linking an Excel Chart

As you learned in the previous session, linking an object in one program to another program establishes a connection between the two programs. Any changes you make to the object in one program are automatically reflected in the other program.

Belinda wants you to link a chart showing sales data to the presentation. Because this data might change, or Belinda might change the format of the chart, she wants to link the data so that any changes will be made automatically in the destination program—in this case, the PowerPoint presentation. Belinda doesn't want you to create a link to the entire Sales Increase workbook, but just to the chart in this workbook. Therefore, you need to open the Sales Increase workbook, select the Sales Chart sheet, select the chart, and then copy the chart in preparation for linking it.

First you need to open the workbook and select the Sales Chart sheet.

To open the Excel workbook and select the sheet:

1. Click the **Open a Document** button on the Office Shortcut Bar.
2. If necessary, click the **Look in** list arrow, click the drive that contains your Student Disk, click **Tutorial.01** in the list box, then click the **Open** button to see a list of the files in the Tutorial.01 folder.
3. Click **Sales Increase** in the list box, then click the **Open** button. Excel starts and opens the Sales Increase workbook with the Sales Table sheet displayed in the Excel window.
4. Click the **Sales Chart** tab on the horizontal scroll bar. The Sales Chart sheet is displayed in the Excel window. See Figure 1-61.

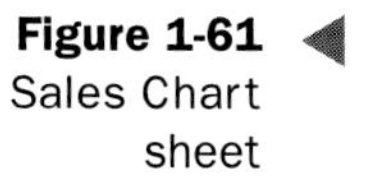

Figure 1-61
Sales Chart sheet

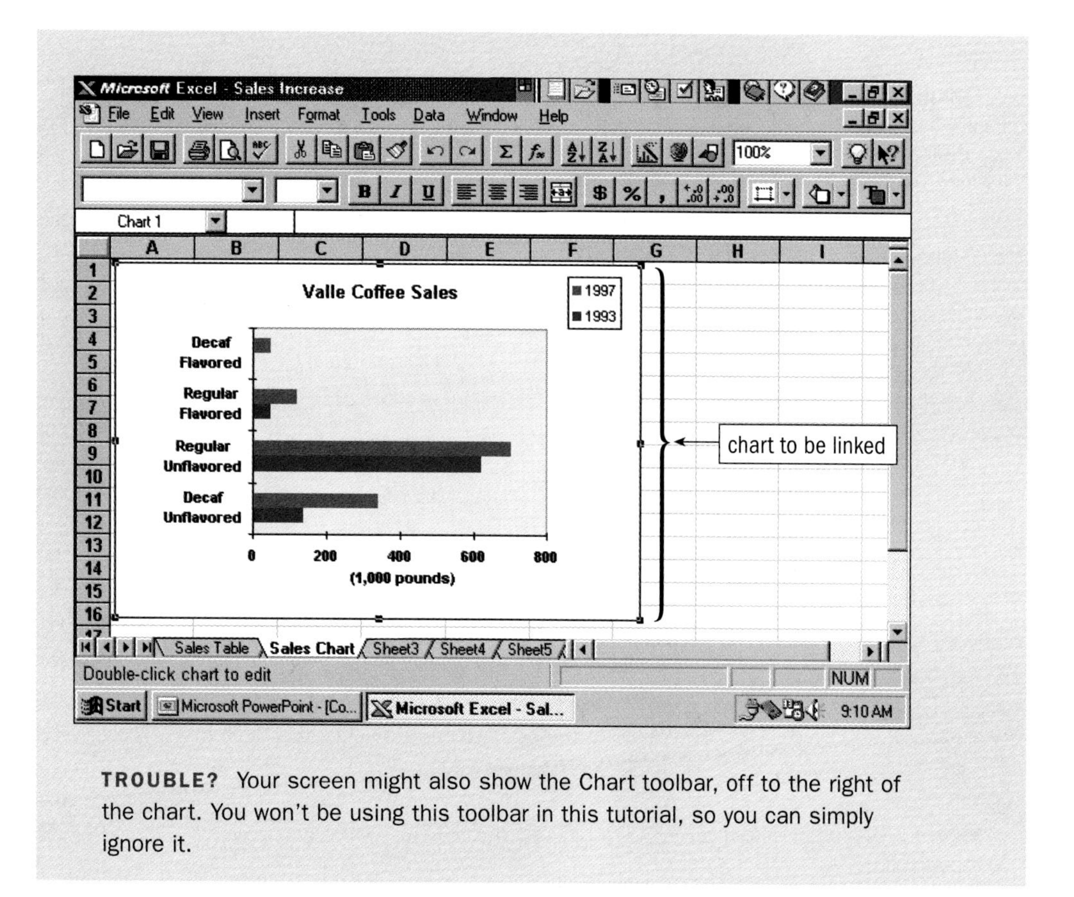

TROUBLE? Your screen might also show the Chart toolbar, off to the right of the chart. You won't be using this toolbar in this tutorial, so you can simply ignore it.

A **chart** is a graphical representation of data. The chart in the Sales Chart sheet is based on the data in the Sales Table sheet. As you update the data in the Sales Table sheet in Excel, the chart is updated automatically. Recall that you added a row for Regular Unflavored coffee in the Sales Table sheet during the previous session. That new row of data appears as the pair of Regular Unflavored bars in the chart.

The sizing handles on the border of the chart indicate that the chart is already selected. You need to copy the chart, switch to PowerPoint, and then paste the chart in slide 9. To create a link to the chart, however, you need to use the Paste Special option on the Edit menu, instead of the Paste button on the Standard toolbar.

To link the Excel chart:

1. If it is not already selected on your screen, click inside the chart to select it. You should see eight sizing handles around the border of the chart when it is selected.

2. Click the **Copy** button on the Standard toolbar.

3. Click the **Microsoft PowerPoint - (Co...** button on the taskbar. The PowerPoint window is now on the screen and slide 9 is displayed in the presentation window.

   TROUBLE? If another slide is displayed on your screen, change slides until slide 9 is displayed. Your taskbar might display more or less of "Microsoft PowerPoint - (Co...," depending on what applications are running on your computer.

4. Click **Edit** on the menu bar, then click the **Paste Special** option. The Paste Special dialog box opens. See Figure 1-62.

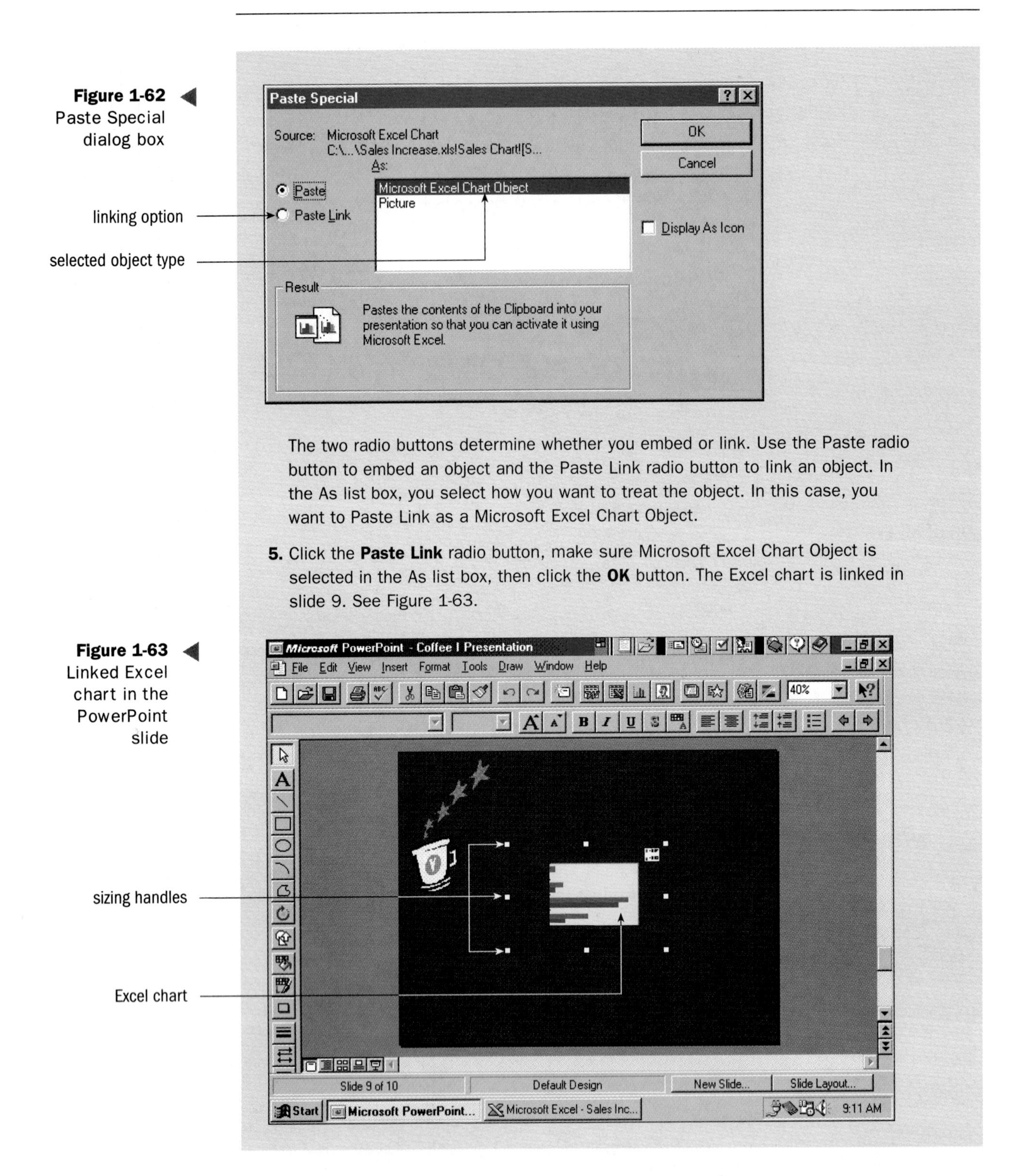

Figure 1-62 Paste Special dialog box

The two radio buttons determine whether you embed or link. Use the Paste radio button to embed an object and the Paste Link radio button to link an object. In the As list box, you select how you want to treat the object. In this case, you want to Paste Link as a Microsoft Excel Chart Object.

5. Click the **Paste Link** radio button, make sure Microsoft Excel Chart Object is selected in the As list box, then click the **OK** button. The Excel chart is linked in slide 9. See Figure 1-63.

Figure 1-63 Linked Excel chart in the PowerPoint slide

Although the link is successful, Belinda is not pleased with the results. The chart is too small and the slide background color makes it impossible to read the text on the chart. She asks you to fix these problems. First, you'll resize the chart on the slide.

To resize the linked Excel chart:

1. Move the mouse pointer to the lower-right sizing handle. When the mouse pointer changes to ↘, click and drag the handle down and to the right until the outline of the chart touches the right border of the slide; then release the mouse button.

2. Move the mouse pointer to the upper-left sizing handle. When the mouse pointer changes to ↘, click and drag the handle up and to the left until the left outline of the chart is just to the right of the coffee cup logo; then release the mouse button. See Figure 1-64.

Figure 1-64 After resizing the linked Excel chart

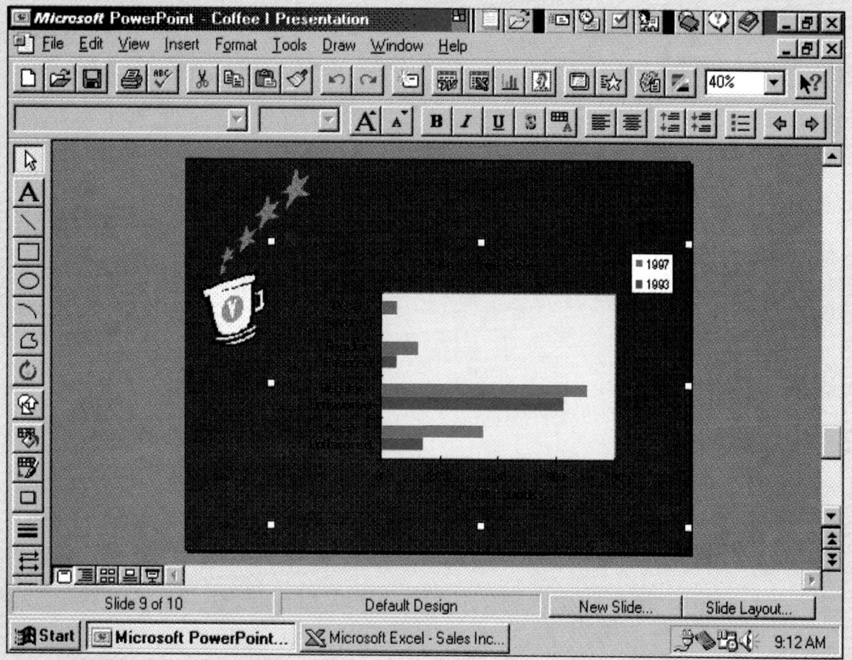

TROUBLE? If the resized chart on your screen is not approximately the same size as the one shown in Figure 1-64, use the same sizing handles to increase or decrease the size of your chart.

Although the size of the chart might not seem large enough, Belinda knows from past experience that the chart will look fine during a slide show. She thinks the text on the chart would be more readable if you colored the chart background, rather than change the slide background. To recolor or otherwise change a linked object, you must edit the object using the source program, in this case, Excel.

To change the linked Excel worksheet:

1. Right-click the chart to open its shortcut menu.
2. Click **Edit Worksheet Link** on the shortcut menu. The linked Excel chart is displayed in the Excel window.
3. Right-click the chart, then click **Edit Object** on the shortcut menu. The chart's size increases, and it appears raised on the Excel window. See Figure 1-65.

Figure 1-65 Editing a chart

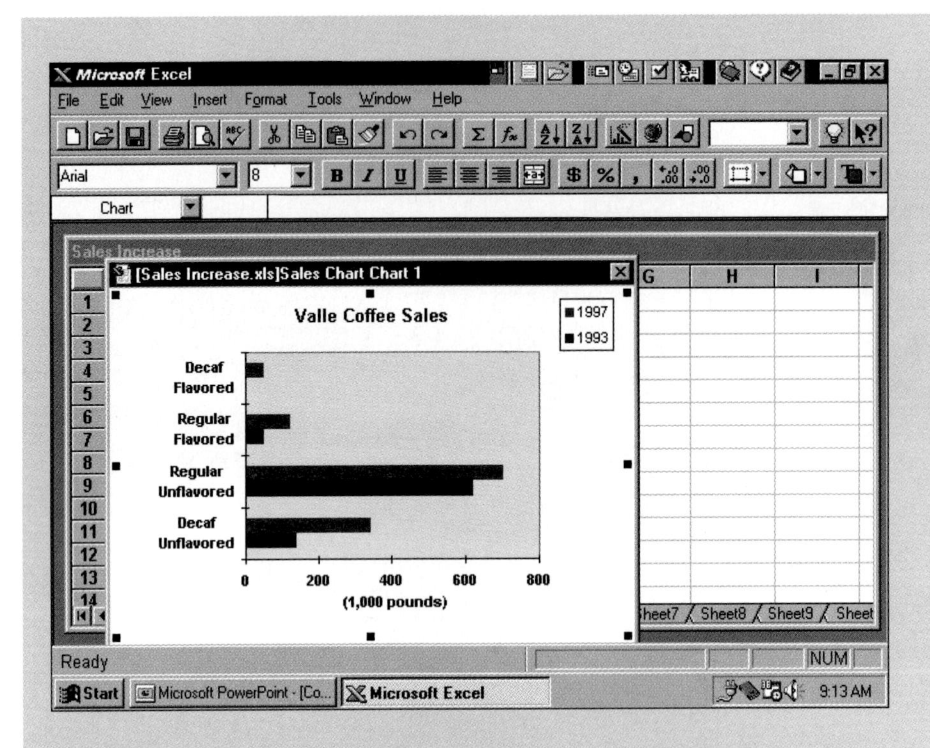

4. Right-click the white background color on the chart, then click **Format Chart Area**. The Format Chart Area dialog box opens. See Figure 1-66.

Figure 1-66 Format Chart Area dialog box

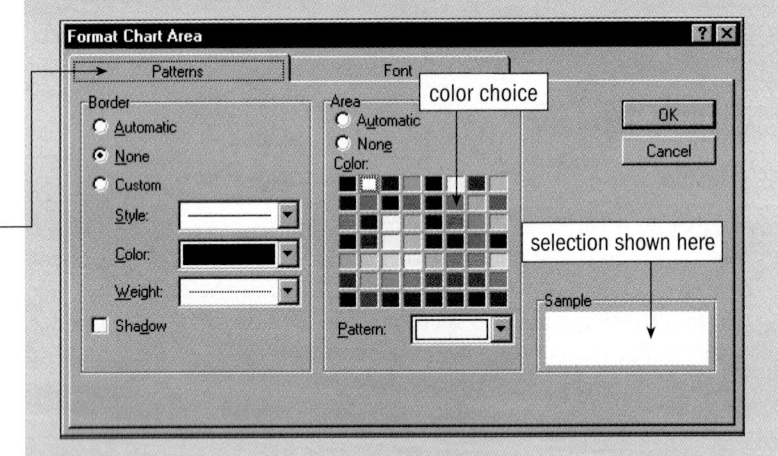

5. If it is not selected, click the **Patterns** tab in the dialog box.

   Belinda wants to change the Area color from white to green, which will mask out the background color of the slide.

6. Click the **green color** (second row, third from the right) in the palette. The Sample box in the lower right displays the selected color.

7. Click the **OK** button. The dialog box closes and the chart in the Excel window now has green as an area color.

8. Click the **Microsoft PowerPoint - (Co...** button on the taskbar. The PowerPoint window displays slide 9 in the presentation window. Because the chart is linked to Excel and any changes are reflected automatically in PowerPoint, the chart now has the green area color. See Figure 1-67.

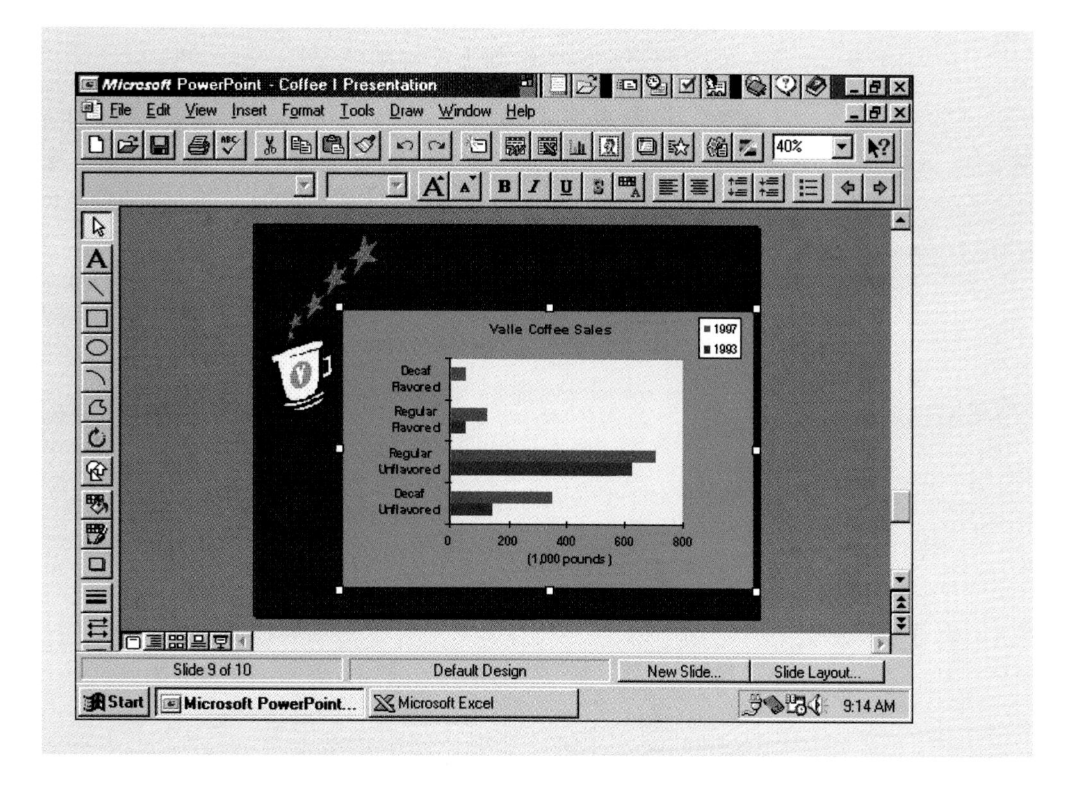

Figure 1-67 Chart area color changed

Belinda thinks slide 9 looks fine and asks you to run the slide show from the beginning, so that she can evaluate the quality and content of the presentation.

Viewing a Slide Show

Before exiting PowerPoint, you should run the slide show as it would be presented at the seminar. You use the Slide Show button on the horizontal scroll bar to start the slide show. Once you are viewing the slide show, you click the left mouse button or press the spacebar to advance to the next slide. To go back to the previous slide, press the ← key.

When you run a slide show, the first slide that appears on the screen is the slide that is selected; therefore, you have to select slide 1 if you want to run the slide show from the beginning.

To view the slide show:

1. Drag the vertical scroll box to the top of the vertical scroll bar to display slide 1.
2. Click the **Slide Show** button on the horizontal scroll bar. Slide 1 appears, filling the entire screen.
3. Click the left mouse button or press the spacebar. PowerPoint advances from slide 1 to slide 2.

   TROUBLE? If a button containing two icons appears in the lower-left corner of any slide during the slide show, ignore it for now.

4. Click the left mouse button or press the spacebar. PowerPoint advances from slide 2 to slide 3. You might have noticed that there was a brief "fade to black" during the transition from slide 2 to slide 3. This is one of the many transition effects available with PowerPoint. Some of the other slides in the presentation use this same effect.

   TROUBLE? If the fade-to-black transition effect is not noticeable on your computer, the speed of your computer might be too fast to show this effect.

Slide 3 displays a title but not the text, because this is a "build slide." A *build slide* is a special effect that adds the text list one point at a time or one group at a time. In the case of this slide, PowerPoint displays each list item one after the other as the spacebar is pressed.

5. Click the left mouse button or press the spacebar three times to see the items on slide 3 display one at a time.
6. Click the left mouse button or press the spacebar. PowerPoint advances from slide 3 to slide 4, using the fade-to-black transition. Slide 4 is also a build slide, but in this case the entire list appears at once.
7. Click the left mouse button or press the spacebar. The entire list appears at a time.
8. Continue through the presentation, observing the transitions and build-slide effects, until you see the PowerPoint window on the screen.

Belinda asks you to print slide 9 so that she can verify if it would be suitable as a handout at the Coffee I seminars.

Printing a Slide

You can print one or more slides in a presentation using the Print command on the File menu. Like the other Office 95 programs, PowerPoint provides a Print button on the Standard toolbar for printing one copy of the entire document. You'll use the Print command to print slide 9 of the presentation, then you'll exit PowerPoint and Excel.

To print slide 9, then exit PowerPoint:

1. Click **File** then click **Print**. The Print dialog box opens. See Figure 1-68.

Figure 1-68 Print dialog box

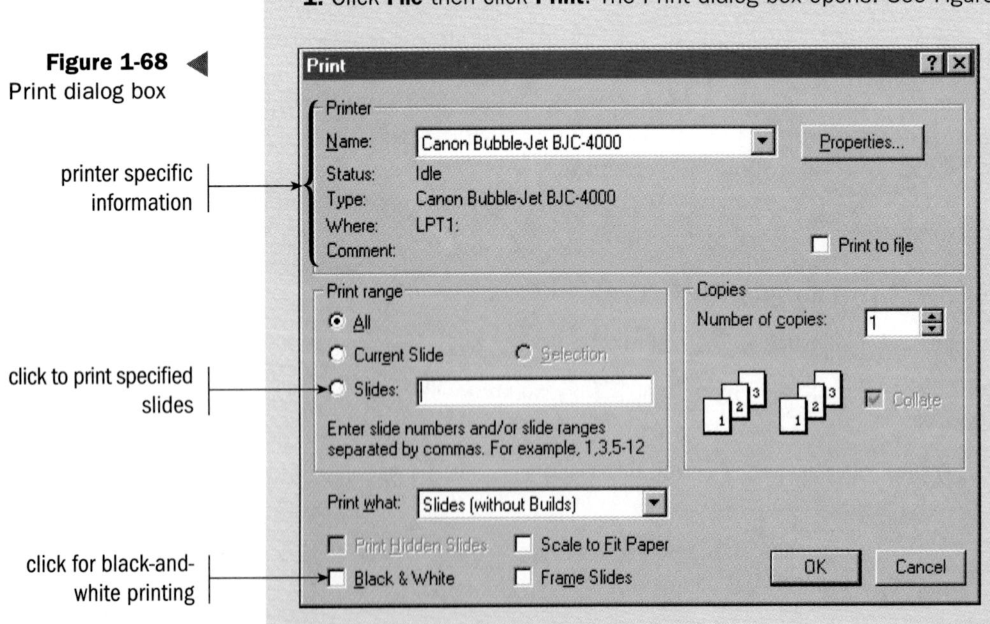

2. Make sure that **Slides (without Builds)** is selected in the Print what box. This box also provides options for printing handouts, speaker notes, and an outline of the presentation.
3. Click the **Slides** radio button, then type **9** in the Slides box to select only slide 9 for printing.
4. To print on a black-and-white printer, click the **Black & White** check box.

5. Click the **OK** button to print slide 9.
6. Click the **Close** button [X] on the program's title bar. PowerPoint displays a dialog box asking if you want to save your changes.
7. Click the **Yes** button. PowerPoint saves the presentation and then exits. The Excel window is now displayed on your screen.
8. Click outside the chart to deselect it, then click the **Close** button [X] on the program's title bar. Excel displays a dialog box asking if you want to save your changes.
9. Click the **Yes** button. Excel saves the workbook and then exits. You return to the Windows 95 desktop.

You have now completed your initial work with Word, Access, Excel, and PowerPoint. Belinda is satisfied with both the finished seminar schedule document and the presentation for the Coffee I seminar. You're ready to use the Office 95 programs in future tutorials, both separately and in integrated tasks, to produce other documents for Valle Coffee.

Quick Check

1. When the Office Shortcut Bar is not available, describe an alternative method for opening an existing document.
2. Explain the differences between slide view, slide sorter view, and slide show view in PowerPoint.
3. How do you change the order of slides in a presentation?
4. A(n) __________ is a predefined format for a slide.
5. What is a placeholder?
6. Explain the difference between the Paste and Paste Link options in the Paste Special dialog box.
7. What is a build slide?

Tutorial Assignments

Belinda Jones has started a schedule announcement and a presentation for the Espresso seminar. She asks you to finish these documents by completing the following steps.

1. Make sure your Student Disk is in the disk drive. Open the Word Espresso document in the TAssign folder within the Tutorial.01 folder.
2. Save the document as Espresso Schedule in the same folder.
3. Edit the document:
   a. The two sentences in the espresso paragraph, which is above the schedule, are in the wrong order. Use the cut-and-paste technique to switch them.
   b. In the second bulleted sentence following the schedule, add the word "differences" between "the" and "between."
   c. Copy the text "Do you want to" in the third bulleted sentence and paste it at the beginning of the fourth bulleted sentence.
4. Format the document as follows:
   a. Change the font style of the third and fourth bulleted sentences to italic.
   b. Change the font type and size of the paragraph following the bulleted sentences from Times New Roman 16 to Arial 12.
5. Change the time of the May 16 seminar in the table from 11:30 a.m. to 10:00 a.m.
6. Save the changes you've made so far.

7. Copy the Access Seminars database in the TAssign folder within the Tutorial.01 folder using the filename Espresso Seminars, then open the Espresso Seminars database.
8. Update the database as follows:
   a. In the Seminar table, change the time of the May 16 seminar from 11:30 a.m. to 10:00 a.m.
   b. In the Seminar table, add a record for a new seminar being offered on June 6, 1998, at 2:00 p.m. with a topic of ES and an instructor of KC.
9. Print the Seminar table, then exit Access. (*Hint:* Use the Print button on the Standard toolbar.)
10. Open the Excel CupsSold workbook in the TAssign folder within the Tutorial.01 folder, then save the workbook as Espresso Sales in the same folder.
11. Change the value for 1995 Caffe latte sales from 77 to 88.

12. Use the Excel Help system to learn how to rename a worksheet, then rename the Cups Data sheet to "Specialty Coffee Sold."
13. Update the embedded Excel worksheet near the bottom of the Espresso Schedule Word document by changing the value for 1995 Caffe latte sales to 88.
14. Save the Espresso Schedule document, print the document, then exit Word.
15. Open the PowerPoint Slides presentation in the TAssign folder within the Tutorial.01 folder, then save the presentation as Espresso Presentation in the same folder.
16. Switch the order of slides 2 and 3, so that the cappuccino slide follows the caffe latte slide.
17. Add a new slide after slide 1. Add a title of "espresso" and add the three bulleted items: "strong," "bittersweet," and "lemon optional."
18. Link the Excel chart from the Espresso Sales workbook to slide 5, then resize the chart on the slide to a larger, more readable size.
19. Save the presentation, then view the slide show of the presentation.

20. Print the entire presentation, selecting the "Handouts (6 slides per page)" option in the Print what box. Make sure the Black & White option is also selected.
21. Save the Espresso Presentation file, then exit PowerPoint.
22. Save the Espresso Sales workbook, then exit Excel.

Case Problems

1. Ashbrook Mall Information Desk Ashbrook Mall is a large, modern mall located in Phoenix, Arizona. Everything that happens within the mall and anything that affects the mall's operation are the responsibility or concern of the Mall Operations Office. Among the independent operations that report to the Mall Operations Office are the Maintenance Group, the Mall Security Office, and the Information Desk. You will be helping the personnel at the Information Desk.

The Information Desk provides many varied services. For example, strollers, wheelchairs, and motorized carts are available at the Information Desk; users are required to show identification and give their zip codes, which are used for monthly market analysis reports. Information Desk personnel also collect mail; distribute maps; give directions to stores, restaurants, and nearby accommodations; provide first aid; and make announcements over the mall's public-address system. In addition, they maintain a catalog of current job openings at stores within the mall. Candidates pick up application forms and leave completed forms and resumes at the Information Desk.

You'll finish a flyer document started by Tuan Huynh, an Information Desk employee, by completing the following steps:

1. Make sure your Student Disk is in the disk drive. Open the Word Alert document in the Cases folder within the Tutorial.01 folder.

2. Save the document as Job Announcement in the same folder.
3. Edit the document as follows:
   a. In the second paragraph, which begins "Wouldn't you rather," change the first occurrence of the word "rather" to the words "like to."
   b. In the third paragraph, which begins "There are many job opportunities," correct the spelling of the word "Ashbook."
   c. In the same paragraph, add the word "Mall" following the word "Ashbrook."
   d. In the same paragraph, delete the word "partial."
4. Format the document as follows:
   a. Change the alignment of the first paragraph, "Shopper alert!!," from left to centered alignment.
   b. In the second paragraph, underline the words "make" and "spend."
   c. For the last line in the document, change the font size from 8 to 14 and change the font style to bold and italic.
5. For the Book Emporium entry in the table, which consists of copied Access data, change the position from "Stock" to "Stock Clerk."
6 Save the Job Announcement document, print the document, then exit Word.
7. Copy the Access Ashbrook database in the Cases folder within the Tutorial.01 folder using the filename Ashbrook Jobs, then open the Ashbrook Jobs database.
8. Update the Job table in the database as follows:
   a. For the Book Emporium entry in the table, change the position from "Stock" to "Stock Clerk."
   b. Delete the record for Taco City's Server position.
   c. Add a record for a new job opportunity for a "Salesclerk" at "Balloons+" for "15-25" hours/week.
9. Print the Job table, then exit Access. (*Hint*: Use the Print button on the Standard toolbar.)

2. Professional Litigation User Services Professional Litigation User Services (PLUS) is a company that creates all types of visual aids for judicial proceedings. Clients are usually private law firms, although the district attorney's office has occasionally contracted for their services. PLUS creates graphs, maps, timetables, and charts, both for computerized presentations and in large-size form for presentation to juries. PLUS also creates videos, animations, presentation packages, slide shows—in short, anything of a visual nature that can be used in a judicial proceeding to make, clarify, or support a point.

Kevin Levinson, one of the founding partners of PLUS, is preparing a four-page brochure that describes the services offered by PLUS. He has completed the first three pages and asks you to complete the back page of the brochure by completing the following steps:

1. Make sure your Student Disk is in the disk drive. Open the Word PLUS document in the Cases folder within the Tutorial.01 folder.
2. Save the document with the filename PLUS Back Page in the same folder.
3. Edit the document:
   a. Put the words "Show" and "Evidence" on the same line.
   b. In the line "Clearly, and Dramatically & Realistically," delete the word "and."
   c. In the line "For further information," add "about our services" to the end of the line.
   d. In the telephone number, change "905" to "590."
4. Format the document:
   a. In the line "Legal Visualization PLUS" near the top of the document, change the font size from 11 to 16 and change the font style to italic.
   b. Change the alignment of the last two lines to centered.

Because the data used to generate the chart in the center of the page was not embedded along with the chart, the chart cannot be updated. You must replace the embedded chart with a linked chart by completing the following steps.

5. Open the Excel MedIndex workbook in the Cases folder within the Tutorial.01 folder, then save the workbook as Medical Care Change in the same folder.
6. Change the numbers in the worksheet under the years for 1989 to 1992 to 7.7, 9.0, 8.7, and 9.8, respectively.
7. Link the chart and place it in the same position as the embedded chart in the PLUS Back Page document.
8. Select and delete the embedded chart from the document. (*Hint:* Use the shortcut menu.)
9. Save the PLUS Back Page document, print the document, then exit Word.
10. Save the Medical Care Change workbook, print the workbook, then exit Excel.

3. Best Friends Best Friends is a not-for-profit organization that trains hearing and service dogs for people with disabilities. Established in 1989 in Boise, Idaho, by Noah and Sheila Warnick, Best Friends is modeled after Paws With A Cause®, the original and largest provider of hearing and service dogs in the United States.

While visiting relatives in Byron Center, Michigan, Noah and Sheila heard about the good work done by Paws With A Cause®. They visited the training facility, read all their literature, and then talked with Michael Sapp, Sr., the founder of Paws®. Soon after, Noah and Sheila quit their high-pressure jobs on Wall Street, moved their family to Idaho, and established Best Friends.

Like Paws With A Cause® and other such organizations, Best Friends strives to provide "Dignity Through Independence." Best Friends hearing dogs are trained to understand sign language commands and to respond to such sounds as doorbells, telephones, alarm clocks, and smoke alarms. Service dogs are trained for tasks such as pulling wheelchairs, opening and closing doors, turning lights on and off, bracing, and retrieving. Both types of dogs first complete a basic training course before they receive their specialized training.

Noah and Sheila need a PowerPoint presentation, giving an overview of the services their dogs provide, that they can present to area businesses and organizations for fund solicitation purposes. They have started preparing the presentation and ask you to finish it for them by completing the following steps:

1. Make sure your Student Disk is in the disk drive. Open the PowerPoint Friends presentation in the Cases folder within the Tutorial.01 folder.
2. Save the document as Best Friends Presentation in the same folder.
3. Using the Title Slide layout, insert a new slide after slide 1. Type "Prepared by" in the title placeholder, then type your name in the main text placeholder. The presentation should now contain three slides.
4. Following the title slide you just created, add two or three slides, using the Bulleted List layout, that summarize the services offered by Best Friends. Type meaningful titles for the slides in the title placeholders and concise bulleted items in the main text placeholders.

5. A Design Template determines the appearance of the slides in a presentation. Use the Help Contents method to open the "Changing the Appearance of Your Presentation" book and the topic "Using Design templates to give my presentations a consistent look." Read the topic thoroughly. Then use the Help Index to find and display information on Design Templates; read the topic "Use a template to apply the format of another presentation to this presentation."

6. Using what you learned in the previous step, change the presentation design template from Soaring to Side Bar.
7. Open the Excel Placed workbook in the Cases folder within the Tutorial.01 folder, then save the workbook as Best Friends Placements in the same folder.
8. In the workbook, change the number in cell D3 for 1992 Hearing dogs from 2 to 4.

9. Use the Answer Wizard in the Excel Help system to learn how to insert a column, then insert a column between the 1993 and 1995 columns. From top to bottom, enter 1994, 6, and 7 as values for the new column.
10. Link the chart in the workbook and place it on the last slide of the presentation.
11. Resize the linked chart to a larger, more readable size.
12. Add a new last slide, which will remain blank, using the Blank layout.
13. Save the presentation with the same filename, print the entire presentation, then exit PowerPoint. *Note*: In the Print dialog box, select Handouts (6 slides per page) and, if you do not have a color printer, select Black & White.
14. Save the workbook with the same filename, print the workbook, then exit Excel.

4. Wandzell Tool and Die Wandzell Tool and Die (WTD) works with small companies in the aeronautical and automotive industries to design and create the tools and dies used in these companies' manufacturing processes. WTD has dozens of PCs, wants to standardize on a single application suite, and asks you to prepare a presentation giving an overview of Office 95. Prepare a presentation for WTD by completing the following steps:

1. Review the Office 95 material in this tutorial and sketch, on paper, four to six slides to use in the presentation. For each slide, create a title and two to six concise bulleted items. Your presentation should briefly describe Office 95 and the programs and tools it provides.
2. Make sure your Student Disk is in the disk drive. Open the PowerPoint WTD presentation in the Cases folder within the Tutorial.01 folder.
3. Save the document as Wandzell Presentation in the same folder.
4. For slide 1, type a title for the presentation in the title placeholder, and type your name in the main text placeholder.
5. For the remaining slides, type the entries from your paper sketch. You'll need to add new slides after slide 1; use the Bulleted List layout for these slides. Do not use the second of the two slides provided to you; you'll use this slide later in this case.
6. Open the Excel PCCost workbook in the Cases folder within the Tutorial.01 folder, then save the workbook as Wandzell PC Cost in the same folder.
7. In the workbook, change the number of PCs in the worksheet from 24, 32, and 47 to 26, 35, and 52, respectively.
8. Link the chart in the workbook and place it on the last slide of the presentation.
9. Resize the linked chart to a larger, more readable size.
10. Add a new last slide, which will remain blank, using the Blank layout.
11. Save the presentation with the same filename, print the entire presentation, then exit PowerPoint. *Note*: In the Print dialog box, select Handouts (6 slides per page) and, if you do not have a color printer, select Black & White.
12. Save the workbook with the same filename, print the workbook, then exit Excel.

TUTORIAL 2

Word Basics and Embedding a WordArt Object

Creating a Letter Outlining Promotional Goals

OBJECTIVES

In this tutorial you will:

- Learn how to develop and plan effective Word documents
- Start, name, and save a new document
- Enter and correct text
- Switch and tile open documents
- Insert, select, replace, delete, copy, and move text
- Change character formats, use tabs, and create numbered and bulleted lists
- Embed and change a WordArt object
- Spell check a document
- Preview and print a document

LABS

Word Processing

Valle Coffee

Kim Carpenter is the director of marketing for Valle Coffee. Her primary responsibilities are to conceive, plan, design, track, and evaluate Valle Coffee's advertising and promotional efforts.

Media Consultants is a new, local firm that assists clients in media and market research. In an effort to increase their customer base and make themselves known among local businesses, agents from Media Consultants occasionally visit companies, offering a free consultation and evaluation of the company's promotional efforts. Maria Herrera of Media Consultants made such a call on Valle Coffee and met briefly with Kim. After conferring with Leonard Valle, Kim has decided to accept the Media Consultants offer of a free evaluation. Kim's next step is to send Maria a letter that includes a specific statement of Valle Coffee's promotional objectives and provides a detailed breakdown of the most recent month's promotional expenditures.

In this tutorial you will use Word to help Kim create the letter that she needs to send to Maria. You'll learn how to develop, edit, and format a document, and how to add special effects to text using WordArt.

SESSION 2.1

In this session you'll learn how to develop and plan effective documents; enter and correct text; organize document windows; select, insert, replace, and delete text; and save a new Word document.

Developing Effective Word Documents

In Office 95, any file you create using one or more of the Office 95 programs is considered a **document**. The seminar schedule and the seminar presentation you worked with in Tutorial 1 are both documents.

Documents you create using Word more closely fit the standard sense of "document"—that is, they include words, sentences, and paragraphs of text. Letters, memos, and reports are typical Word documents.

As you learned in Tutorial 1, **Word** is a word-processing program that allows you to create professional-looking documents quickly and easily. By using a word-processing program such as Word, you can work more efficiently by revising and reusing text in documents you have already created and saved. You can also use Word's formatting features to enhance the appearance of your documents.

The recommended procedure for developing a Word document is shown in Figure 2-1.

Figure 2-1 Developing a Word document

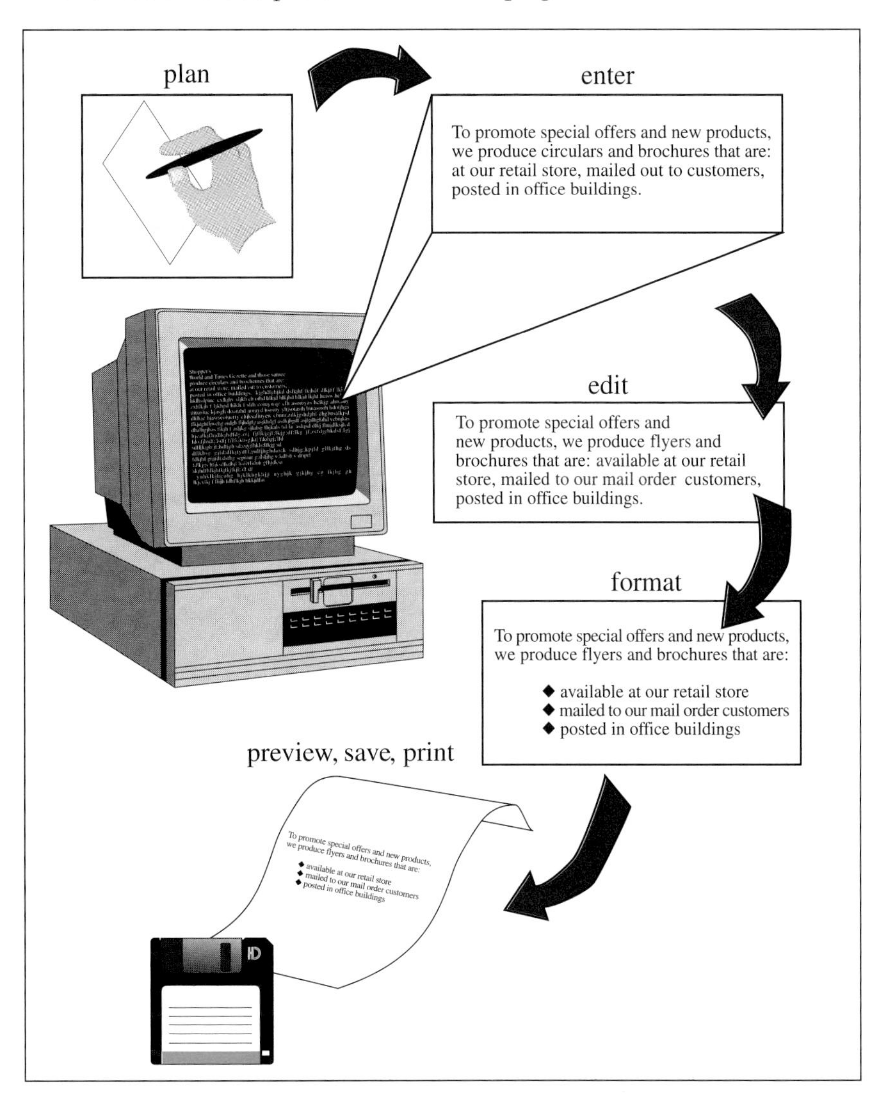

To develop a Word document, follow these guidelines:

- Plan the document by determining its purpose and what it will include.
- Enter (type) the text.
- Edit the document by inserting, deleting, and moving text, as needed.
- Format the document to make it more attractive and readable.
- Preview, save, then print the completed document.

Planning a Document

Before you begin to create a document, you should first plan and organize what you intend to say in it. Determining what you need to write before you actually begin to write it will help to ensure that your document is organized logically, makes all the points you want to make, and does not lack any important information.

Kim wants to print the letter to Media Consultants on Valle Coffee's letterhead stationery, and she wants the letter to include all the standard parts of a letter: date, inside address, salutation, body, closing, and signature block, as shown in Figure 2-2. The body of the letter will contain an introductory paragraph followed by a brief statement of Valle Coffee's promotional objectives. Then the letter will include one short paragraph describing the intent and desired results for each of the general promotional categories. Kim also wants you to embed an Excel worksheet that details last month's promotional expenses (covered in Tutorial 3). Finally, a short paragraph concludes the body of the letter.

Figure 2-2 The letter to Media Consultants Page 1 of 2

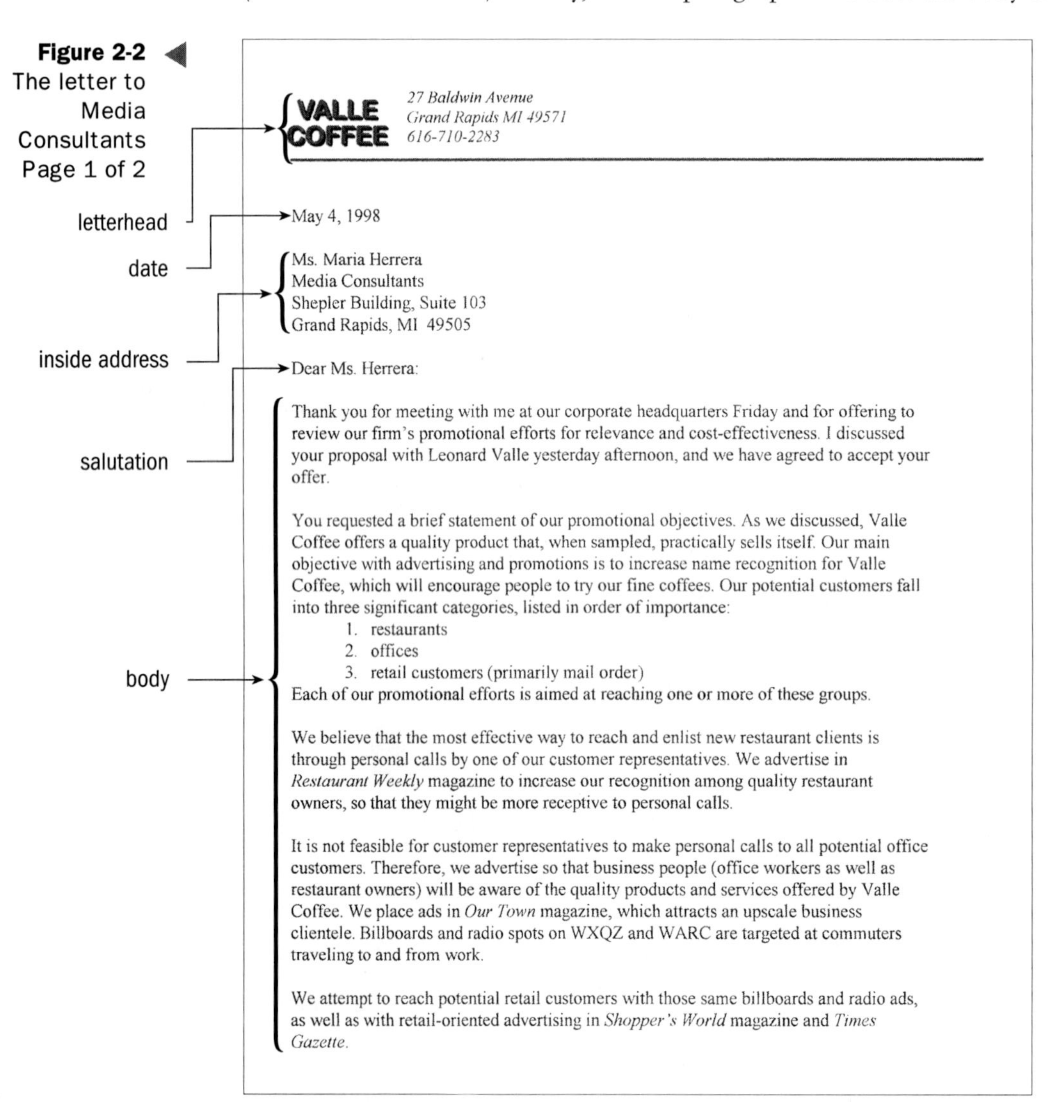

VALLE COFFEE
27 Baldwin Avenue
Grand Rapids MI 49571
616-710-2283

May 4, 1998

Ms. Maria Herrera
Media Consultants
Shepler Building, Suite 103
Grand Rapids, MI 49505

Dear Ms. Herrera:

Thank you for meeting with me at our corporate headquarters Friday and for offering to review our firm's promotional efforts for relevance and cost-effectiveness. I discussed your proposal with Leonard Valle yesterday afternoon, and we have agreed to accept your offer.

You requested a brief statement of our promotional objectives. As we discussed, Valle Coffee offers a quality product that, when sampled, practically sells itself. Our main objective with advertising and promotions is to increase name recognition for Valle Coffee, which will encourage people to try our fine coffees. Our potential customers fall into three significant categories, listed in order of importance:

1. restaurants
2. offices
3. retail customers (primarily mail order)

Each of our promotional efforts is aimed at reaching one or more of these groups.

We believe that the most effective way to reach and enlist new restaurant clients is through personal calls by one of our customer representatives. We advertise in *Restaurant Weekly* magazine to increase our recognition among quality restaurant owners, so that they might be more receptive to personal calls.

It is not feasible for customer representatives to make personal calls to all potential office customers. Therefore, we advertise so that business people (office workers as well as restaurant owners) will be aware of the quality products and services offered by Valle Coffee. We place ads in *Our Town* magazine, which attracts an upscale business clientele. Billboards and radio spots on WXQZ and WARC are targeted at commuters traveling to and from work.

We attempt to reach potential retail customers with those same billboards and radio ads, as well as with retail-oriented advertising in *Shopper's World* magazine and *Times Gazette*.

Figure 2-2 The letter to Media Consultants Page 2 of 2

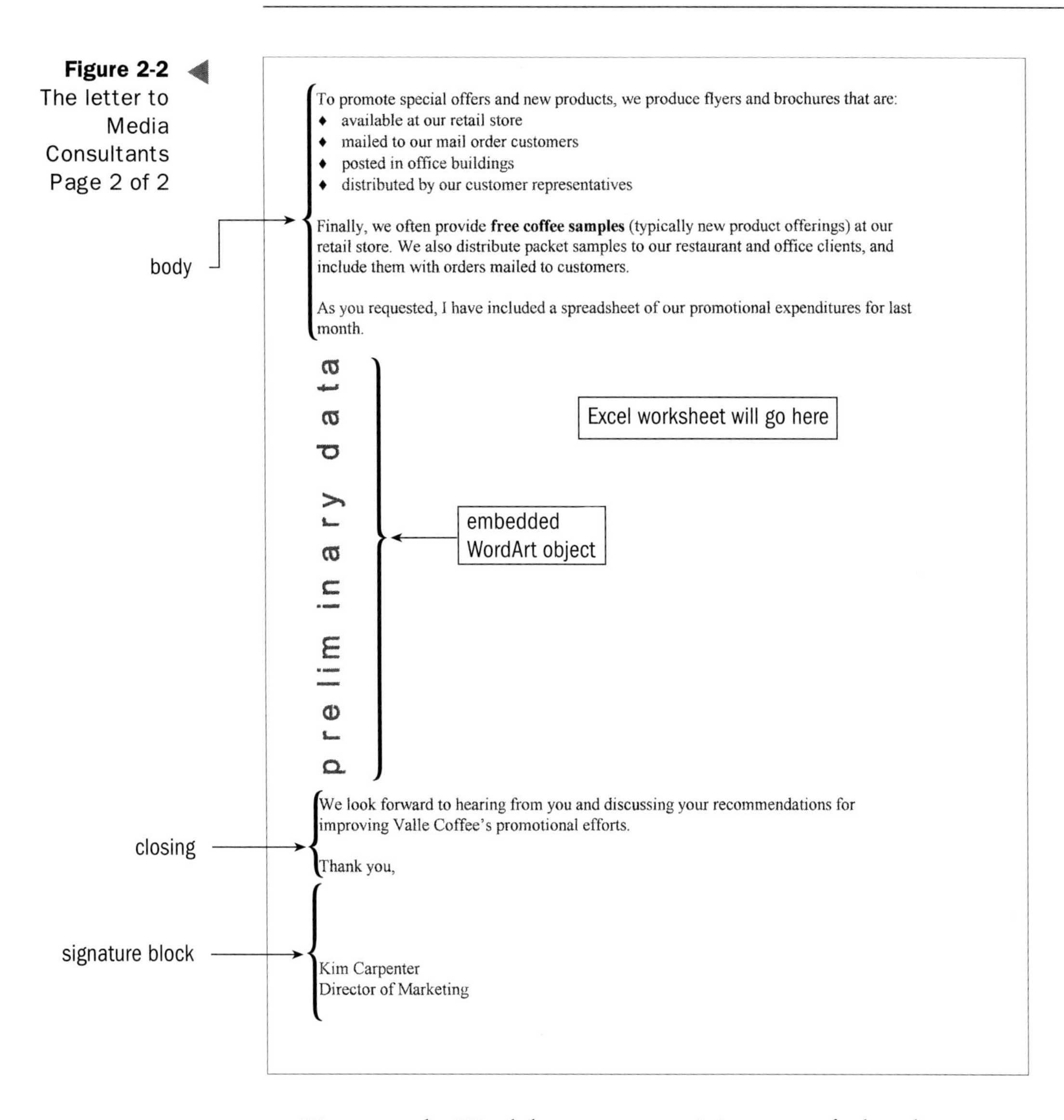
To promote special offers and new products, we produce flyers and brochures that are:
- available at our retail store
- mailed to our mail order customers
- posted in office buildings
- distributed by our customer representatives

Finally, we often provide **free coffee samples** (typically new product offerings) at our retail store. We also distribute packet samples to our restaurant and office clients, and include them with orders mailed to customers.

As you requested, I have included a spreadsheet of our promotional expenditures for last month.

We look forward to hearing from you and discussing your recommendations for improving Valle Coffee's promotional efforts.

Thank you,

Kim Carpenter
Director of Marketing

Kim created a Word document containing most of what she wants to include in the letter. She asks you to enter the date, inside address, salutation, and first paragraph into a new document while she finds the file containing her document.

To help Kim create the letter, you first need to start a new Word document.

Starting a New Word Document

Having planned the organization of the letter, you are now ready to enter the text for the letter. First, you must start a new Word document.

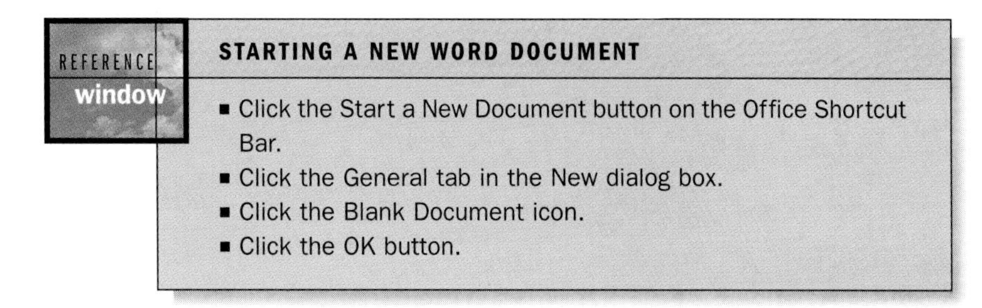

STARTING A NEW WORD DOCUMENT

- Click the Start a New Document button on the Office Shortcut Bar.
- Click the General tab in the New dialog box.
- Click the Blank Document icon.
- Click the OK button.

To start a new Word document:

1. Start Windows 95 and make sure the Office Shortcut Bar is displayed.

   TROUBLE? If you don't see the Office Shortcut Bar, click the Start button on the taskbar, point to Programs, then click Microsoft Office Shortcut Bar. If you don't see the Microsoft Office Shortcut Bar option on the Programs menu, ask your instructor or technical support person for help.

2. Insert your Student Disk in the disk drive.

3. Click the **Start a New Document** button on the Office Shortcut Bar. The New dialog box opens.

4. If necessary, click the **General** tab to make it the active tab in the New dialog box. See Figure 2-3.

Figure 2-3
New dialog box

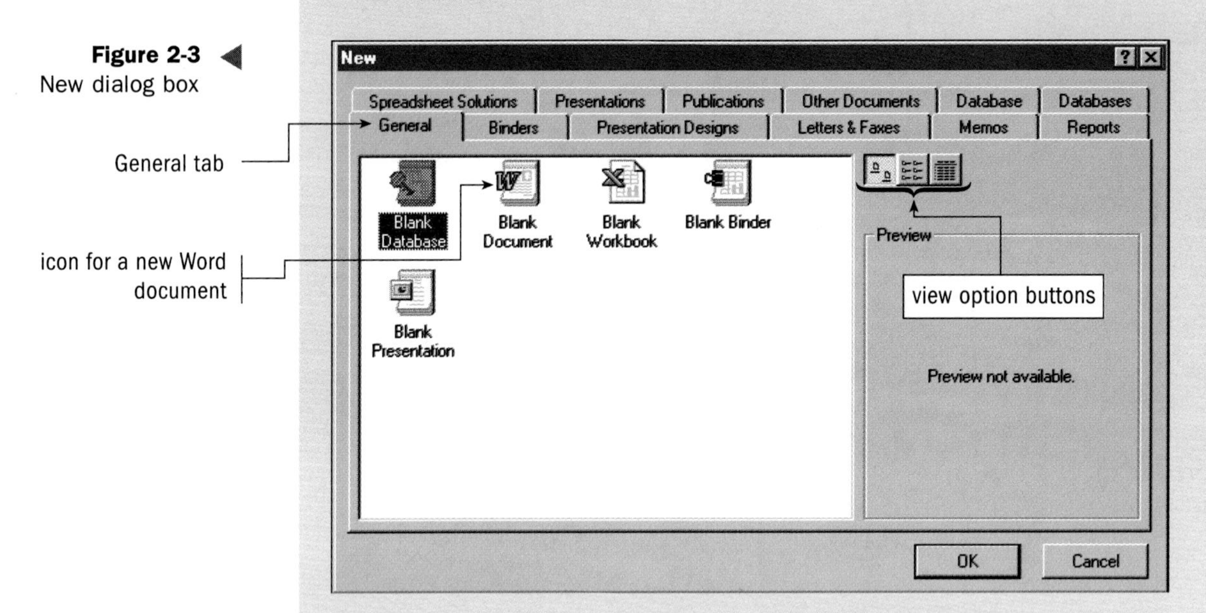

   The New dialog box lets you choose the type of document you want to create, such as a Word document, Excel workbook, or PowerPoint presentation. For some types of documents, a sample of the document appears in the Preview box.

   TROUBLE? If one of the other two view option buttons is selected, your screen will show small icons in a columnar format (on the left of the dialog box).

5. Click the **Blank Document** icon.

6. Click the **OK** button. The Word window opens.

7. Make sure the Word and document windows are both maximized.

   Your screen should now look like Figure 2-4.

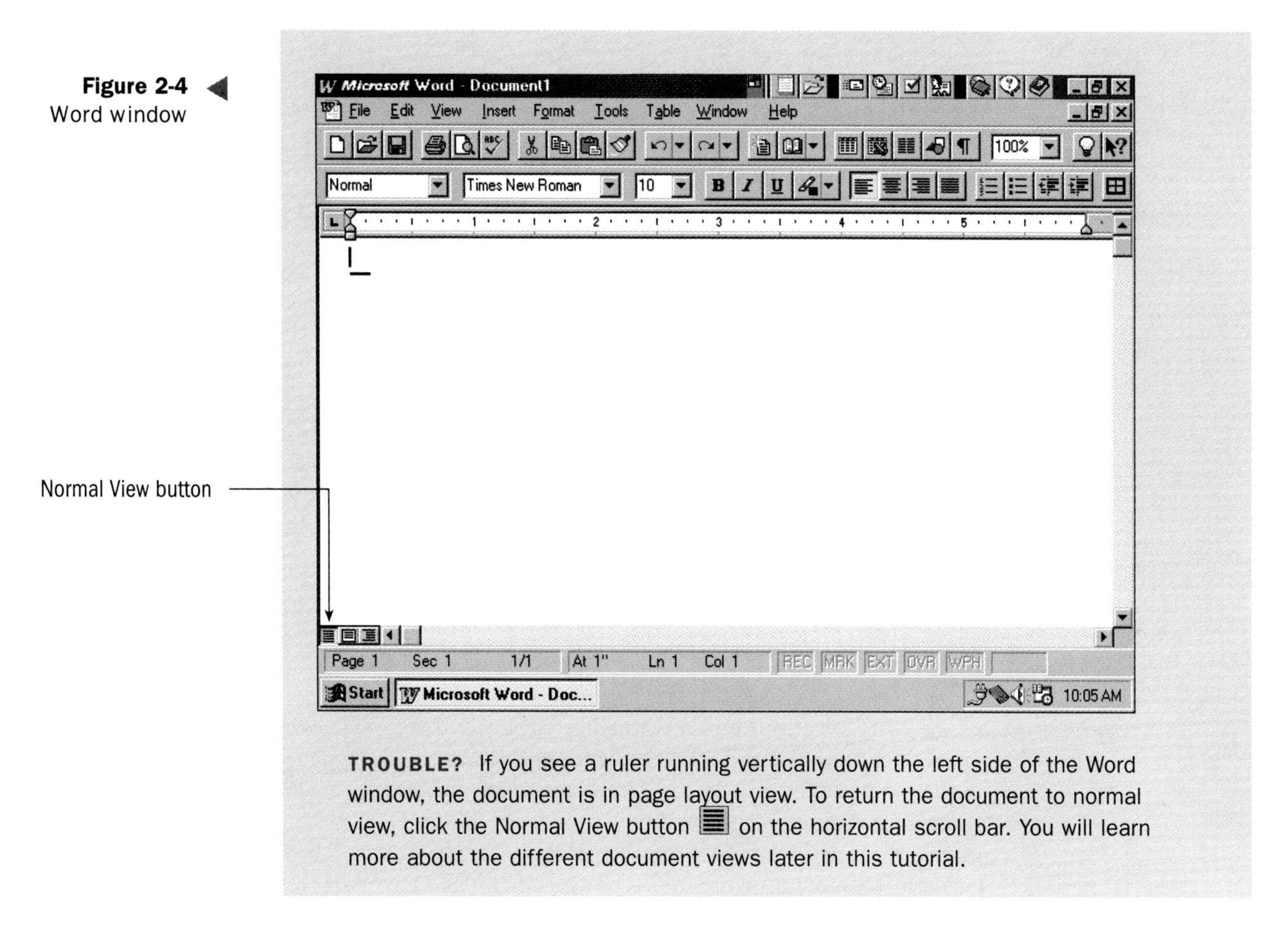

Figure 2-4 Word window

TROUBLE? If you see a ruler running vertically down the left side of the Word window, the document is in page layout view. To return the document to normal view, click the Normal View button on the horizontal scroll bar. You will learn more about the different document views later in this tutorial.

Now you're ready to start entering the text of the letter to Media Consultants.

Entering Text in a Document

First, you need to enter the date, inside address, and salutation for the letter. Figure 2-5 shows the text you will enter and the appropriate spacing.

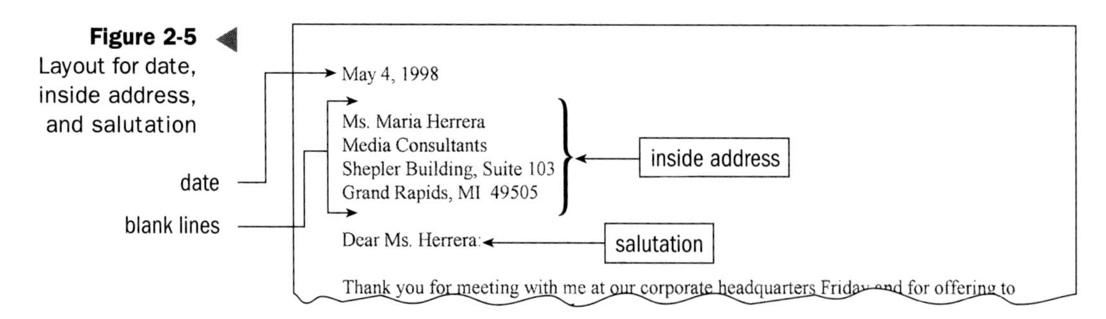

Figure 2-5 Layout for date, inside address, and salutation

Typing Text

To enter text in a Word document, you simply move the insertion point to the location you want and then start typing. The insertion point currently is located at the first position of the new document, which is right above the end mark. You can verify this by checking the status bar near the bottom of the screen, which shows that the insertion point's location is on page 1, section 1, line 1, and column 1, as shown in Figure 2-6. As you enter text, the status information changes to reflect the new position of the insertion point.

Figure 2-6 After starting a new Word document

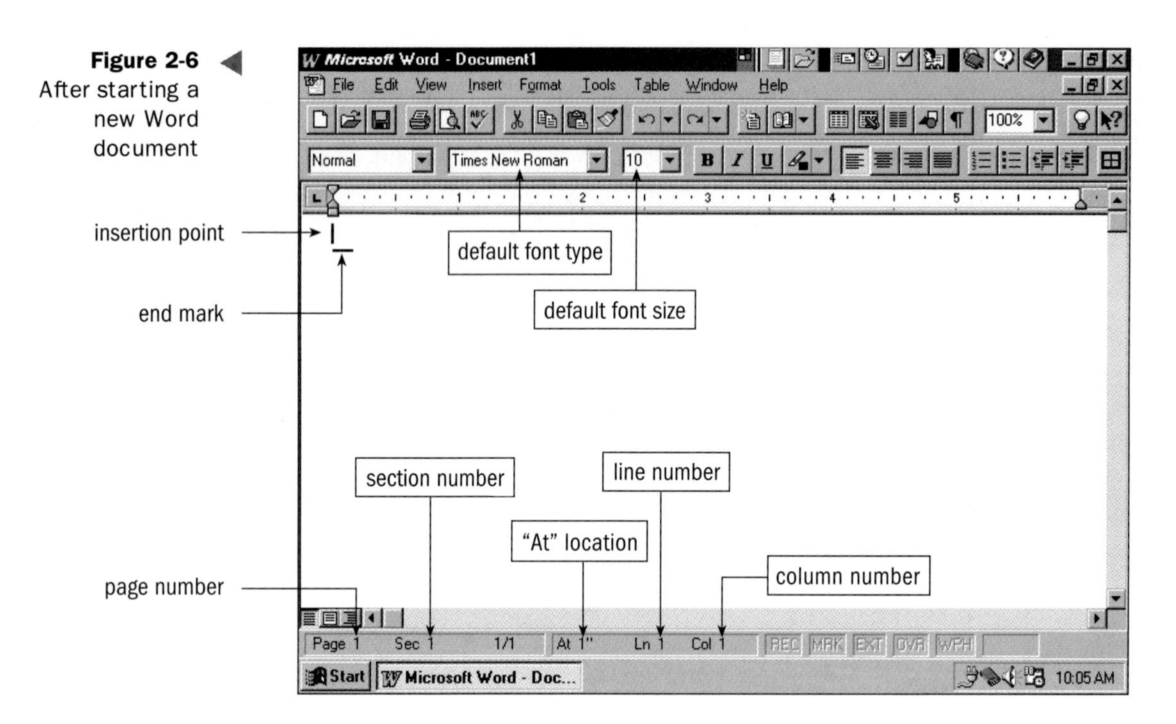

The "At" location on the status bar currently displays 1", which indicates a top margin of one inch for the document. Settings such as the document margins are determined by the template used to create the document. A **template** is a set of predefined styles and formatting options. Whenever you choose the Blank Document icon to start a new document, Word assigns the Normal template to the document. The **Normal template** provides a general document format that is not specific to any particular document type. Word also provides other templates you can use to create specific types of documents, such as memos, reports, resumes, and so on.

The first item you need to type is the date. To allow room for the Valle Coffee letterhead, you need to position the date at least 1.8 inches from the top edge of the paper. One way to move the insertion point down to 1.8 inches is to enter a series of blank lines.

To insert blank lines to accommodate the letterhead:

1. Press the **Enter** key five times.
2. Verify that the status bar now indicates that the insertion point is positioned at 1.8", on line 6, column 1.

   TROUBLE? If your status bar indicates that the insertion point is on line 6, column 1, but the "At" position is something other than 1.8", make sure that the font type is Times New Roman and the font size is 10. (See Figure 2-6 for the location of the font type and size options.) Change either or both of these options, if necessary. If your status bar still indicates something other than 1.8" for the "At" position, the difference is probably due to the type of printer connected to your computer and you should not be concerned. Just keep in mind that your screen will look slightly different from the figures in this tutorial.

   If your status bar does not display the information shown in Figure 2-6, you might be pointing your mouse at one of the toolbar buttons and displaying a ToolTip. To see how this works, first you'll display a ToolTip then move the pointer into the document window to remove the ToolTip and display the status bar information.

3. Point to the **Help** button on the Standard toolbar, hold for a few seconds, but do not click. The button's ToolTip appears and the status bar changes to display an explanation of that button.

4. Move the pointer into the document window. The ToolTip disappears and the status bar information is redisplayed.

Now that you have moved the insertion point down, you are ready to type the date.

To type the date:

1. Type **May 4, 1998**. Notice that the insertion point is now located in column 12.
2. Press the **Enter** key to move the insertion point to the beginning of the next line.

To help you recognize the format of your document as you are working in it, Kim suggests that you display special characters called nonprinting characters.

Displaying Nonprinting Characters

Word allows you to display **nonprinting characters**, which represent formatting items such as paragraph marks, tabs, and spaces. When you activate the Show/Hide button on the Standard toolbar, Word displays the nonprinting characters. The symbol ¶ is a paragraph mark that appears at the end of every paragraph; the symbol · indicates each blank space you enter with the spacebar; and the symbol → indicates each tab you enter with the Tab key. Whether you display nonprinting characters is a matter of personal preference, but it is generally a good idea to display them when you are entering and editing text.

To display nonprinting characters:

1. Click the **Show/Hide** button ¶ on the Standard toolbar. Word displays the paragraph marks and space marks.

   When it is activated, the Show/Hide button appears pushed in and is a lighter gray. The Show/Hide button works as a *toggle*, which means that you click it to turn it on, then click it again to turn it off.

2. Click the **Show/Hide** button ¶ again. Notice how the display changes.
3. Click the **Show/Hide** button ¶ one more time to redisplay the nonprinting characters.

In your plan for the letter, the inside address follows the date. You need a blank line before and after the inside address to separate it from the date above it and the salutation that follows it.

To type the inside address:

1. Press the **Enter** key to insert a blank line.
2. Type **Ms. Maria Herrera** then press the **Enter** key. The words "Maria" and "Herrera" are each underlined with a wavy red line. Word checks spelling automatically as you type. When Word encounters a word that it does not recognize, a wavy red line appears under the word. For now, don't worry about any possible spelling or typing errors; you'll correct errors later in the tutorial.

   TROUBLE? If you do not see wavy red lines under "Maria" and "Herrera," the option for automatic spell checking has been turned off. This is not a problem, because you will correct all spelling errors later in this tutorial.

TROUBLE? If Word activates the TipWizard button on your Standard toolbar automatically, the Word option for selecting the TipWizard is active and the TipWizard appears between the Formatting toolbar and the ruler. Read the tip displayed, then click the TipWizard button to turn off the option. If you would prefer to display the TipWizard, you can leave the option on, but your screen will look slightly different from the figures in this tutorial.

3. Refer to Figure 2-7 and type the text of the inside address. Press the **Enter** key twice after typing the address to insert a blank line.

Figure 2-7 The letter with date and inside address entered

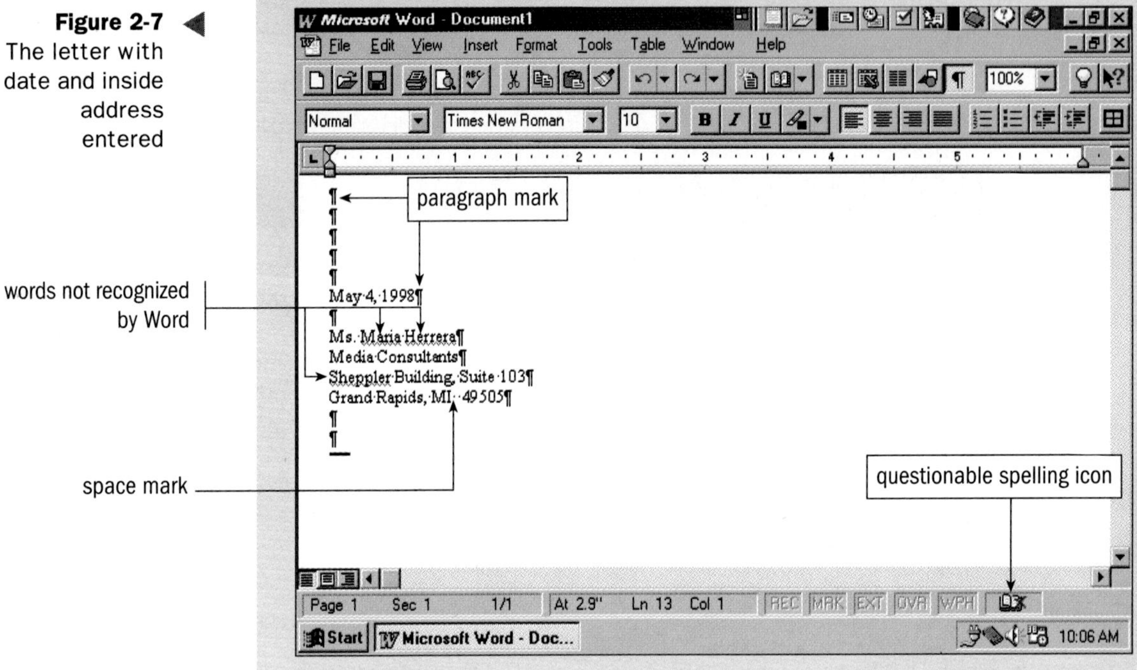

As you type, Word displays the questionable spelling icon in the right of the status bar. See Figure 2-7. This icon indicates potential spelling errors by displaying a red "x." You can double-click the icon to display a list of alternative spellings for a word in question and to correct errors as you go. You'll correct any spelling errors later in this tutorial when you use Word's spell check feature.

TROUBLE? If you see wavy red lines under any words in addition to "Maria," "Herrera," and "Sheppler," don't worry about it for now. You'll correct all typing and spelling errors later in this tutorial.

Correcting Text

Word allows you to correct typing errors at any time. If you notice a typing error shortly after making it, you can press the Backspace key up to and including the error, then type the correct text. Pressing the Backspace key deletes the character or nonprinting character immediately to the left of the insertion point. Pressing the Delete key deletes the character or nonprinting character immediately to the right of the insertion point. You can also use Word's spell check feature to find spelling errors in your document. (You learn more about spell checking later in this tutorial.)

In the next set of steps, you'll make an intentional error then correct it using the Backspace key.

To enter the salutation for the letter and correct an error using the Backspace key:

1. Type **Deer Ms** (do not type a period). Notice that Word did not mark the word "Deer" as a possible spelling error, because "deer" is a word that Word recognizes.
2. Press the **Backspace** key five times to delete all the characters, including the nonprinting space character, back to the first "e."
3. Type **ar Ms. Herrera:** then press the **Enter** key twice to finish the salutation and to insert a blank line following it.

The AutoCorrect Feature

Word's **AutoCorrect** feature automatically corrects common typing errors as you make them. For example, AutoCorrect will change "adn" to "and" automatically after you type the incorrect word and press the spacebar. AutoCorrect also automatically capitalizes the first letter in a sentence and the names of days, and it corrects capitalization if you type two capital letters at the beginning of a word.

To view the AutoCorrect options:

1. Click **Tools** on the menu bar, then click **AutoCorrect**. The AutoCorrect dialog box opens. See Figure 2-8.

Figure 2-8 AutoCorrect dialog box

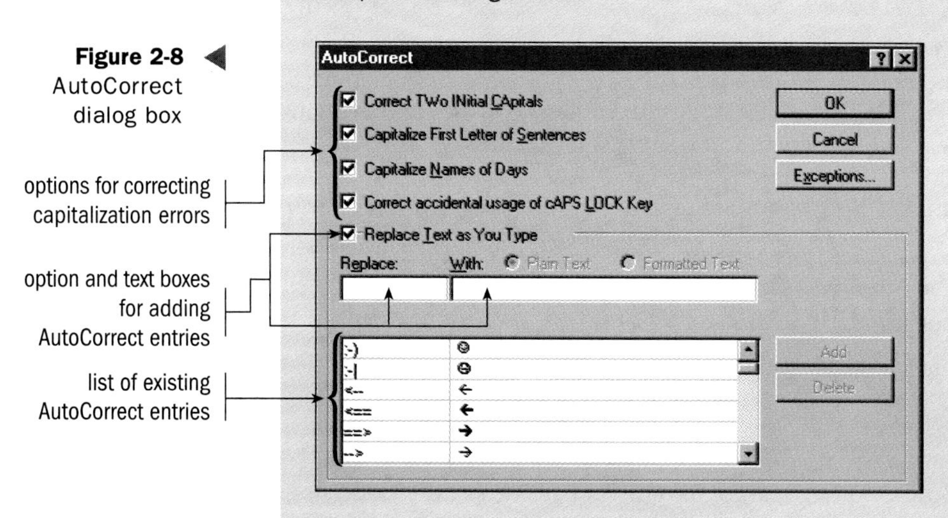

The top four check boxes allow you to correct capitalization errors automatically. The Replace Text as You Type option and related text boxes allow you to add AutoCorrect entries for the typing errors you typically make. Word will automatically correct the text you type in the Replace text box with the text you type in the With text box for each entry you add. The list at the bottom of the dialog box shows the existing AutoCorrect entries.

2. If any of the first four check boxes does not contain a check mark, click the check box to select that option.
3. Scroll through the list box at the bottom of the AutoCorrect dialog box to see the existing AutoCorrect entries. Notice that "adn" is corrected to "and" and "teh" is corrected to "the" automatically.
4. Click the **OK** button to close the AutoCorrect dialog box.

Next you'll enter the first paragraph in the body of the letter. As shown in Figure 2-9, you will make a few intentional typing errors to see how AutoCorrect works.

Figure 2-9 Using AutoCorrect

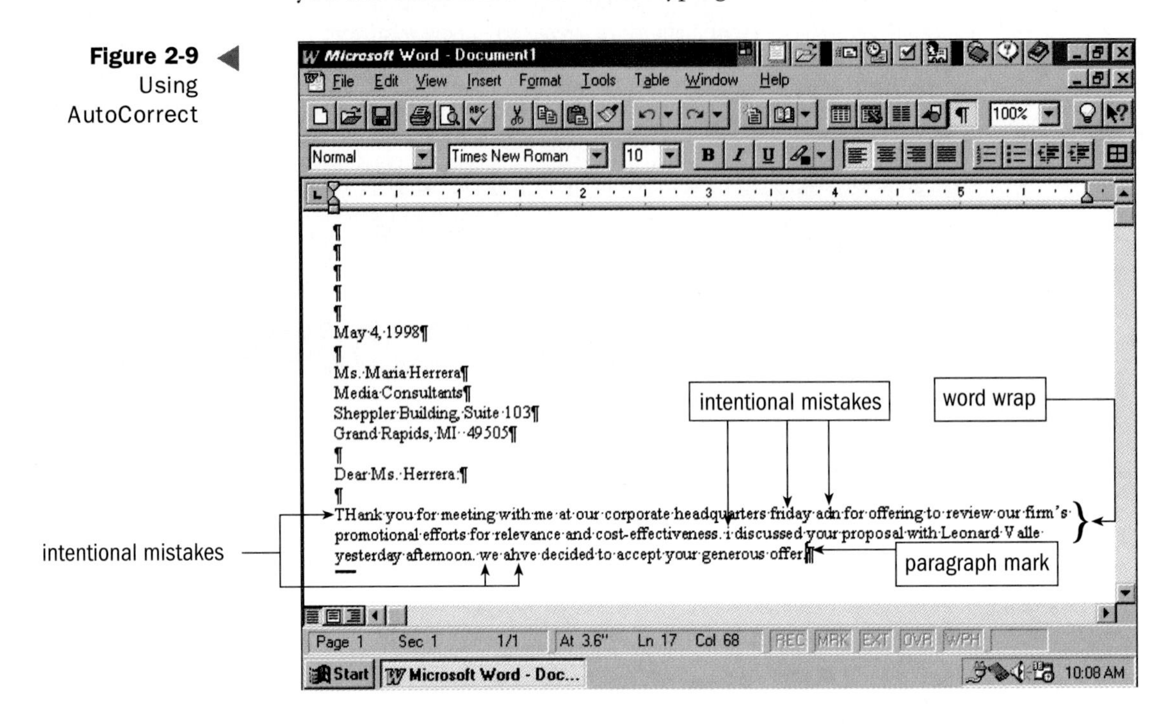

When you type the first paragraph, you do not have to press the Enter key at the end of the line as you did when you typed the date, inside address, and salutation. As you enter text, if a word does not fit completely on a line, Word moves it to the beginning of the next line for you automatically. This feature is known as **word wrap**.

To type the first paragraph and see how AutoCorrect works:

1. Type **THank** then press the **spacebar**. AutoCorrect changes the two initial capital letters in the word "THank" to "Thank."

2. Refer to Figure 2-9 and type the first paragraph. Do not press the Enter key at the end of a line. AutoCorrect changes "friday" to "Friday," "adn" to "and," "i" to "I," "we" to "We," and "ahve" to "have."

Another editing feature for correcting errors is the Undo option, which allows you to undo your most recent action.

Using Undo

Word provides the **Undo** button, which allows you to cancel your most recent action. Undo is especially useful to restore text you accidentally deleted, but you can also use it to delete text you typed by mistake, or to cancel the last action taken by Word.

Word also provides the **Redo** button, which allows you to restore an action that you've undone.

Now start entering the next paragraph, then use the Undo and Redo buttons to see their effects.

To use the Undo and Redo features:

1. Press the **Enter** key twice then type **You requested**.
2. Click the **Undo** button on the Standard toolbar. Word deletes "You requested" and the paragraph mark, the last entry you made.

   Notice the down arrow button to the right of the Undo button. You can click the down arrow button to display a list of all the changes you've made since opening the document, so you can undo one or more changes.
3. Click the **Redo** button to reverse the undo action and redisplay the text. Notice that the Redo button has a down arrow button you can click to display a list of changes you can redo.
4. Click the **Undo** button again to remove the text.

The Undo and Redo features are useful options, especially when you delete, move, or copy large blocks of text. These features allow you to experiment easily with different options, because you can always return to the previous point in your editing.

Kim has found her document containing the bulk of the letter to Media Consultants. She wants you to add the text from her document to the end of your document.

Organizing Document Windows

With Word you can have two or more documents open at a time. The Window menu helps you keep track of all open documents and allows you to move back and forth between them.

Kim's document is named Promote. You need to open the Promote document, while keeping your document open, and then copy text from Promote to your open document.

Opening an Existing Document

You currently have one document open: the letter you created as a new document at the beginning of this session. When you create a new document, Word automatically assigns a name that consists of the word "Document" followed by a number. The Word title bar shows that your current document is "Document1." (If the document name in your title bar has a different number, you accidentally created a new document at some point in this session. That will not cause a problem; just continue with the tutorial.)

You need to open Kim's Promote document so that you can copy text from it to your document. The Promote document is an existing document located in the Tutorial.02 folder on your Student Disk.

To open the Promote document:

1. Click the **Open** button on the Standard toolbar. Word displays the Open dialog box.
2. Click the **Look in** list arrow to display the list of available drives and desktop components.
3. Click the drive that contains your Student Disk. The display changes to reflect the selected drive. The main list box displays the folders on your Student Disk.
4. Click **Tutorial.02** then click the **Open** button. The main list display changes to show you all the folders and files in the Tutorial.02 folder.

TROUBLE? If you cannot find a folder named Tutorial.02, make sure the Look in text box contains the location of your Student Disk. If the drive is correct and you are using the correct Student Disk but you still cannot locate the Tutorial.02 folder, check with your instructor or technical support person.

5. Click **Promote**, if necessary, then click the **Open** button. The document Promote opens as the active document. The Promote document is the letter that Kim created and wants you to combine with your document.

TROUBLE? If you cannot find a file named Promote, make sure the Look in text box contains the folder Tutorial.02. If the folder is correct but you still cannot find the Promote file, check with your instructor or technical support person.

To copy text from Kim's letter to your letter, you need to switch between the two open documents.

Switching Between Open Documents

You now have two documents open, but you can see only one of them. The document that is visible, Promote, is the **active** document. Document1 is still open, even though it is hidden from view at the moment. Figure 2-10 illustrates the relationship between the active document and other open documents.

Figure 2-10 Open documents and the active document

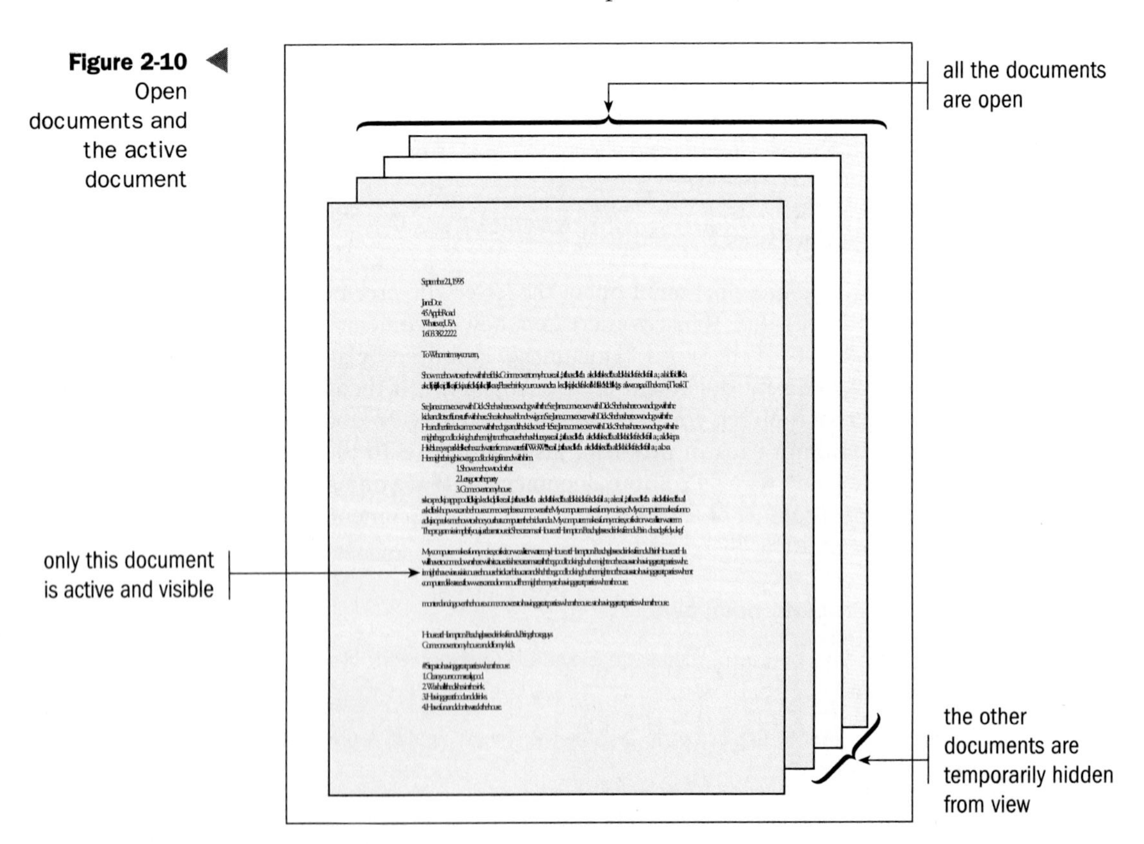

If you want Document1 to be the active document, you need to switch to that document. You use the Window menu, a standard menu for all Windows 95 programs, to switch back and forth among all open documents for a program.

You need to switch to your document so you can determine where you should add the text from Kim's document.

To switch between the two open documents:

1. Click **Window** on the menu bar. Word displays the Window menu, the bottom part of which lists all your open Word documents. See Figure 2-11. The check mark in front of Promote indicates that it is the active document.

Figure 2-11 Window menu

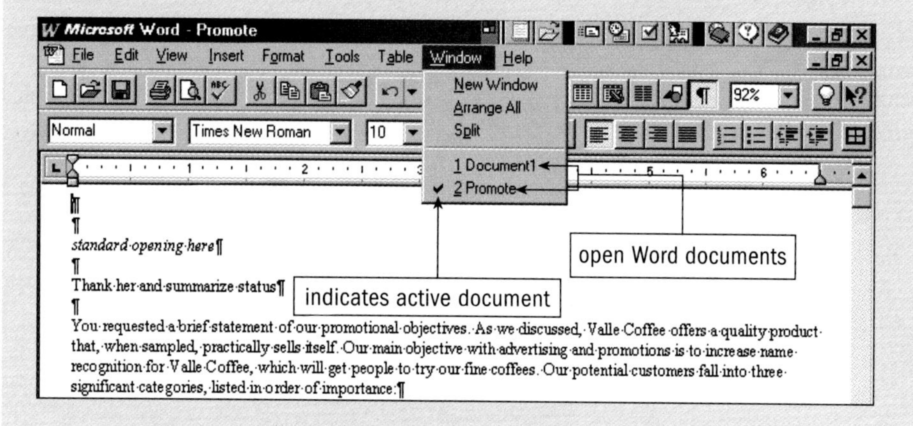

TROUBLE? If you have a third document listed, you accidentally created an extra document earlier in this session. Simply ignore this extra document for now.

2. Click **Document1** in the list. The Window menu closes and Document1 becomes the active document.

   The text in Kim's document should be placed after the text you entered, so you need to insert a blank line in preparation for copying Kim's text.

3. Press the **Enter** key twice to add a blank line and place the insertion point on the following line.

4. Click **Window** then click **Promote** to make that document the active document again.

When you switch between two open documents, you are able to view only one document at a time. Word provides a way for you to display both documents at once by tiling the documents.

Tiling Document Windows

Tiling means to arrange windows so that no window overlaps another and all windows are visible. The Arrange All option on the Window menu tiles all your open Word documents.

Because you need to copy the text of Kim's document into your letter, you'll tile the two document windows so that you can see both at the same time. To copy the text you'll use the copy-and-paste technique, which is covered in greater detail later in this tutorial.

To tile the two document windows:

1. Click **Window** on the menu bar, then click **Arrange All**. The document window divides into two parts. Each part has a title bar containing the name of the document. The active document, Promote, appears in the upper window. Its title bar is colored, and the Minimize, Maximize, and Close buttons are visible on the right side of the title bar. The other open document, Document1, is visible in the lower window. Its title bar is gray, indicating that the window is not active.

2. Scroll through the Promote window, using the vertical scroll bar, until the Promote window looks similar to Figure 2-12; click the **Document1** window to make it the active document; then scroll through the Document1 window until your screen looks similar to Figure 2-12.

Figure 2-12 Two tiled document windows

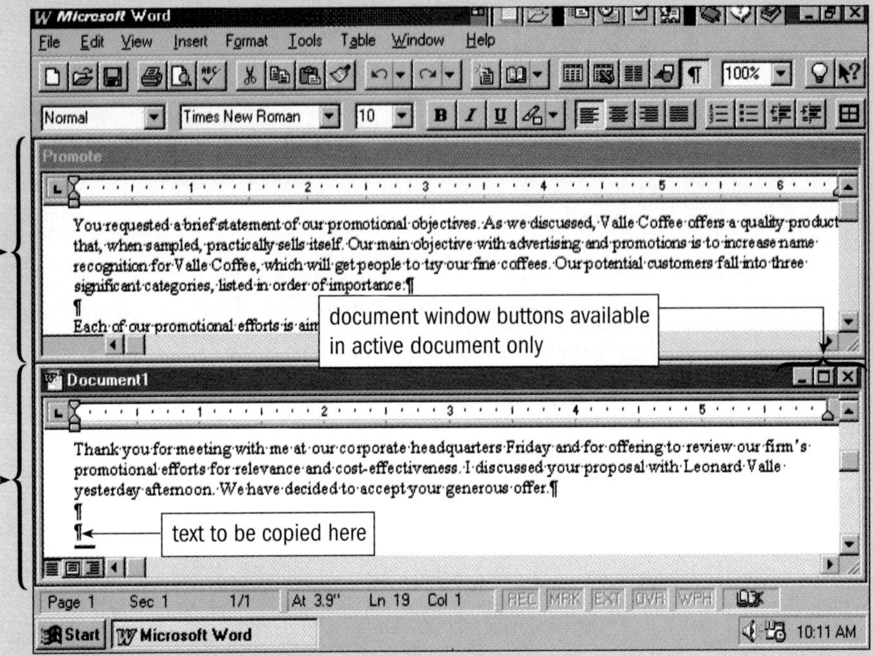

the inactive document

the active document

document window buttons available in active document only

text to be copied here

Next, you need to select all the text from Kim's document, so you first must make Promote the active window.

3. Click anywhere within the Promote window. Promote becomes the active window, and it now contains the document window buttons.

4. Click **Edit** on the menu bar, then click **Select All**. All the text in the Promote document is selected, which is indicated by the highlighted text in the Promote window.

   You need to make a copy of the selected text in preparation for placing the copy at the end of your document.

5. Click the **Copy** button on the Standard toolbar.

   Next, you must make the Document1 window the active window in order to paste the copied text at the end of your document.

6. Click anywhere within the Document1 window, make sure the insertion point is still at the end of the document, then click the **Paste** button on the Standard toolbar. The text from Kim's Promote document is added to the end of your document.

7. Click the **Maximize** button on the Document1 title bar. The two documents are no longer tiled, and Document1 is now the active document.

Now that you've copied the text from Kim's document, you need to save and name your document.

Saving and Naming a Document

You entered text into your document and copied several paragraphs of text from Kim's document into yours. Before you continue, you should save your document and name it. A document name can consist of multiple words and can include spaces between words. The following characters are *not* permitted in document names: **/ \ > < * ? " | : ;**. You'll save your document as "Promotion Letter."

To save and name the document:

1. Click the **Save** button on the Standard toolbar. Because you have not saved this file before, Word displays the Save As dialog box. Notice that "May 4" is highlighted in the File name text box. The first time you save a document, Word constructs a suggested filename using the first sentence of the document. In this case, the suggested name is not suitable, and you need to replace it with a more appropriate name.
2. Type **Promotion Letter**. *Do not press the Enter key.* Because the suggested filename was highlighted, typing a new name replaces all the highlighted text. If you pressed the Enter key at this point, Word would save the document in the selected folder and drive, which might not be where you want to save the document.
3. If Tutorial.02 is not displayed in the Save in text box, click the **Save in** list arrow, click the drive containing your Student Disk, click **Tutorial.02**, then click the **Open** button.
4. Click the **Save** button in the dialog box. Word saves the document as Promotion Letter on your Student Disk and closes the Save As dialog box.

When working with multiple open documents, it's a good idea to close those documents you no longer need. Closing a document removes the document from your computer's memory, which frees up more memory for Word and other open programs to do their work.

You no longer need Kim's document, Promote, so you can close it.

To close the Promote document:

1. Click **Window** on the menu bar, then click **Promote**. Promote becomes the active document.

   You want to close the document but leave Word and the Promotion Letter document open. Therefore, you must use the Close button on the menu bar, not the Close button on the title bar. (You could also use the Close option on the File menu to close the document and leave Word open.)

2. Click the **Close** button on the Word window menu bar. Word closes the Promote document. Your letter remains open and becomes the active document.

   TROUBLE? If a dialog box opens asking if you want to save changes to the Promote document, click the No button to close the dialog box and the Promote document without saving changes you might have made accidentally to the document.

Kim would like you to make some changes to the letter before she sends it to Maria at Media Consultants. To make the changes, you need to edit the document.

Editing a Document

Editing a document involves changing it by inserting, deleting, replacing, copying, or moving text. Before you can make any such changes, you need to know how to navigate through a document and move the insertion point to a specific location.

Navigating a Document

Recall that the insertion point is that location in the document indicated by the flashing vertical line. Any character you type will be placed at the insertion point position. When you create a new document, as you did earlier in this session, the insertion point is always located at the end of the document.

As you learned in Tutorial 1, you can use the vertical and horizontal scroll bars to view different parts of a document. In a multipage document, such as the letter you're working with, when you click and drag the scroll box in the vertical scroll bar, a box appears to the left of the scroll bar. This box, called a **ScrollTip**, displays the current page number as you scroll through the document. Remember that the insertion point doesn't change location when you use the scroll bars to navigate through a document.

You can move the insertion point using the keys shown in Figure 2-13. To perform a movement involving two keys, hold down the first key while pressing the second key. For example, hold down the Ctrl key and press the Home key to move the insertion point to the beginning of the document.

Figure 2-13 Keyboard navigation techniques

To move the insertion point:	Press:
Left or right one character	← or →
Left or right one word	Ctrl + ← or Ctrl + →
To the beginning or end of the line	Home or End
To the beginning or end of the document	Ctrl + Home or Ctrl + End
Up or down one line	↑ or ↓
Up or down one paragraph	Ctrl + ↑ or Ctrl + ↓
Up or down one screen	Page Up or Page Down
To the top or bottom of the screen	Ctrl + Page Up or Ctrl + Page Down

Next, try navigating through the letter and moving the insertion point using the keyboard.

To position the insertion point using the keyboard:

1. Hold down the **Ctrl** key and press the **Home** key. The insertion point moves to the beginning of the document. Notice that the status bar changes to reflect the current location of the insertion point.

2. Hold down the **Ctrl** key and press the **End** key to move the insertion point to the end of the document.

3. Press the **Page Up** key. The display and the insertion point move up one screen.
4. Hold down the **Ctrl** key and press the **Page Down** key. The text displayed on the screen does not change, but the insertion point moves to the last position on the screen.
5. Hold down the **Ctrl** key and press the **Home** key. The insertion point moves to the beginning of the document.
6. Press the ↓ key until the insertion point is positioned in front of the word "Thank," the first word in the body of the letter.
7. Hold down the **Ctrl** key and press the → key. The insertion point moves one word to the right.
8. Press the **End** key. The insertion point moves to the end of the current line.

You can also use the mouse to move the insertion point. If you can see the position you want to move to on the screen, the fastest way to move the insertion point is to move the mouse pointer to the position then click the mouse button. When you move the mouse pointer, its shape changes to I.

If you can't see the location you want to move to, first use the scroll bar to bring the location into view; then click the mouse button when the pointer is located where you want the insertion point.

To use the mouse to position the insertion point and scroll the document:

1. Move the mouse so that the pointer is immediately in front of the "C" in "Consultants" in the inside address, then click the mouse button. The status bar indicates that the insertion point is positioned at line 9, column 7.

   TROUBLE? Your status bar might display different numbers from those mentioned in steps or shown in figures. Use the numbers as guidelines and don't be concerned if your numbers differ slightly.

2. Click once in the middle of the vertical scroll bar on the right of the screen. The display moves down one screen.
3. Place the insertion point so that it is positioned between the "o" and the "u" in the word "You" (which begins a paragraph). The status bar changes to identify the new insertion point in your document.

   TROUBLE? If the text described in Step 3 is not on your screen, scroll the screen until the text is visible.

4. Position the mouse pointer on the scroll box in the vertical scroll bar. The pointer changes to ↖.
5. Click and drag the scroll box in the vertical scroll bar to the bottom of the scroll bar. Notice the displayed ScrollTip indicating the page number. Click and drag the vertical scroll box back up to the top of the scroll bar.

You can also use a combination of keyboard and mouse techniques to position the insertion point. For example, you could press the Page Down key to move down one screen at a time until the location you want is visible, then use the mouse to point and click at the location.

Kim has several editing changes she wants you to make to your document, as shown in Figure 2-14.

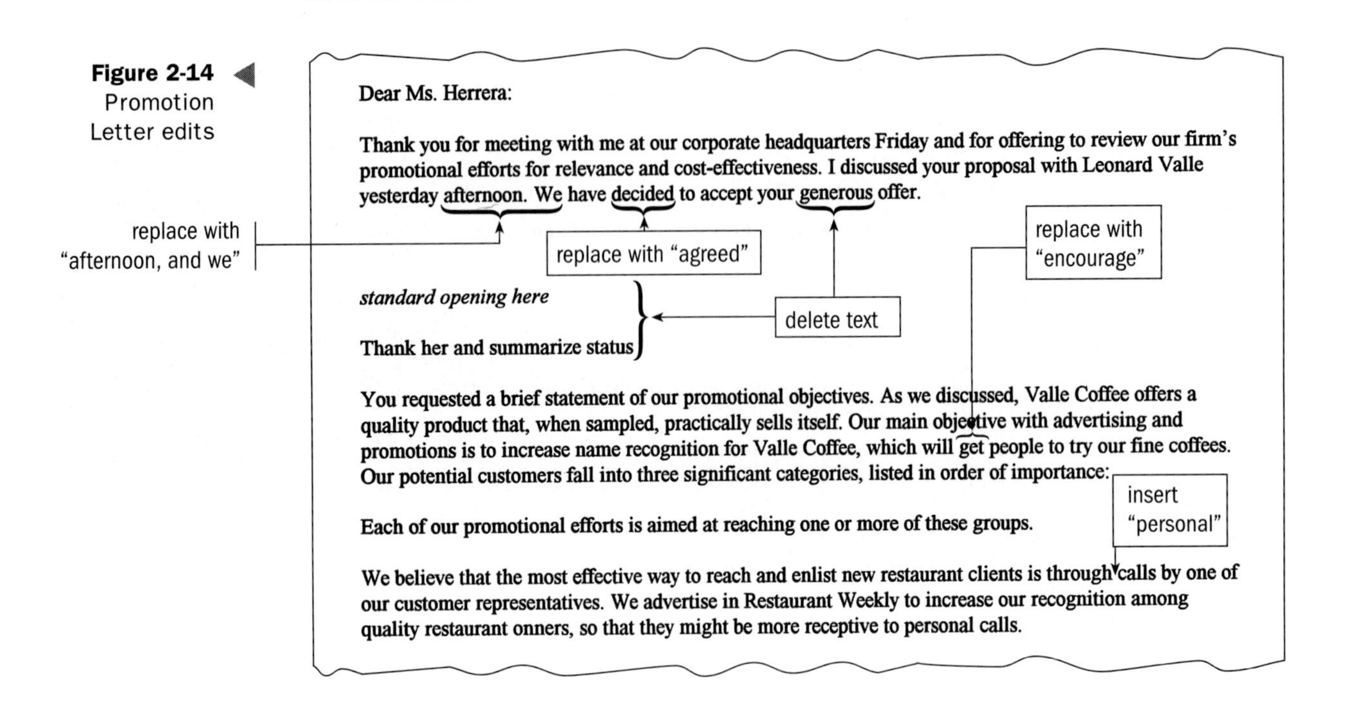

Figure 2-14 Promotion Letter edits

Inserting Text

Now that you know how to position the insertion point, you can insert the text Kim wants in your document. To insert new text, you move the insertion point to the appropriate position and then simply type the new text. As you type, Word moves existing text to the right and adjusts line endings to accommodate the inserted text.

Kim wants the word "personal" inserted before the word "calls" in the paragraph that starts "We believe," as shown in Figure 2-14.

To insert the text:

1. Press the **Page Down** key to move the display down one screen. The paragraph beginning "We believe" should now be visible on the screen.

   TROUBLE? If that paragraph is not visible, scroll up or down the document until you can see the paragraph.

2. Place the pointer immediately to the left of the word "calls" in the first line of the paragraph, then click the mouse button to position the insertion point.

3. Type **personal** then press the **spacebar**. As you type the new text, the existing text moves to the right.

   TROUBLE? If your typing overwrites existing text, check the status bar to see if the indicator "OVR" is on. This means that Word is in Overtype mode. You need to switch back to Insert mode, by pressing the Insert key or by double-clicking OVR in the status bar, so that text you type will not overwrite existing text.

As shown in Figure 2-14, Kim has identified three places in your document where she wants you to replace text.

Selecting and Replacing Text

If you need to replace or delete text, you could position the insertion point at the beginning of the text and then press the Delete key as many times as necessary to remove the text. To replace the deleted text, you could then type the new text. If you need to delete or replace more than a few characters, however, this method is inefficient. A better method is to select all the text you want to replace or delete, and then process the selected text all at once.

Most Word editing and formatting techniques require that you first select the text you want to change. You can select text using the keyboard or the mouse. Because the mouse is easier to use and more efficient, you will concentrate on mouse techniques for text selection.

Before making Kim's changes, you'll practice different ways of selecting text.

To select text using the click-and-drag technique:

1. Hold down the **Ctrl** key and press the **Home** key to position the insertion point at the beginning of the document.
2. Position the pointer in front of the "C" in "Consultants" in the inside address, click the mouse button and hold it down as you drag the mouse to the right until the pointer is located after the last character in the word, then release the mouse button. The word "Consultants" is selected and highlighted.
3. Click the mouse button anywhere in the document workspace. The word "Consultants" is no longer highlighted, meaning it has been *deselected.* Any time you want to deselect text, you simply click the mouse button anywhere in the document workspace.
4. Position the pointer in front of the first "s" in "Consultants" in the inside address, click the mouse button and hold it down as you drag the mouse to the right until the pointer is located after the second "n" in that word, then release the mouse button. The characters "sultan" in the middle of the word "Consultants" have been selected and are highlighted.
5. Position the pointer in front of the "n" in "Thank" in the first line of the letter body, click and drag the mouse to the right until the pointer is located between the "d" and "q" in headquarters, then release the mouse button. The first ten words in the line are selected.

   TROUBLE? If your screen doesn't show the letters "Tha" in "Thank" and "quarters" in "headquarters" highlighted, the Automatic Word Selection option is not activated. To turn this option on, click Tools on the menu bar, then click Options to display the Options dialog box. Click the Edit tab, click the check box for Automatic Word Selection, then click the OK button. As you become more experienced using Word, you might prefer to work with this option off so that you can select only portions of a word when selecting multiple words.
6. Position the pointer in front of the "M" in "Ms." in the inside address, click and drag the mouse down and to the right until the pointer is located within the zip code, then release the mouse button. The entire inside address is selected, because the Word default is to select an entire word when you select the first part of a word.

In addition to the click-and-drag technique you just used to select text, Word provides several additional selection techniques. Some of these techniques involve positioning the pointer in the **selection bar**, which is the area along the left margin of the document. When the pointer is positioned in the selection bar, its shape changes to ↗. These additional selection techniques are summarized in Figure 2-15.

Figure 2-15 Selection techniques

To select:	Do this:
A word	Double-click the word
A sentence	Press the Ctrl key then click within the sentence
A line	Click in the selection bar next to the line
Multiple lines	Click in the selection bar next to the first line, then drag down through the last line
A paragraph	Double-click in the selection bar next to the paragraph
Multiple paragraphs	Click in the selection bar at the start of the first paragraph, then drag down through the last paragraph
Entire document	Triple-click in the selection bar, or click Edit then click Select All

Now try selecting text using the techniques described in Figure 2-15.

To select text:

1. Hold down the **Ctrl** key and press the **Home** key to position the insertion point at the beginning of the document.
2. Position the pointer anywhere within the word "headquarters" in the first paragraph, then double-click the mouse button. The entire word is selected.
3. Position the pointer anywhere within the first sentence of the letter, then press and hold the **Ctrl** key as you click the mouse button. The entire sentence is selected.
4. Move the pointer into the selection bar next to the first paragraph of the letter, then double-click the mouse button. The entire first paragraph is selected.
5. Position the pointer anywhere in the salutation then click. The insertion point moves to that position, and the first paragraph of the letter is deselected.

Now that you know how to select text, you can replace text. To do so, you select the text to be replaced and then type the new text. Word replaces all the highlighted text with the new text.

Refer to Figure 2-14 as you next make the replacements to text in your document, as requested by Kim.

To select and replace text:

1. Select the word **decided** in the last line of the first paragraph by double-clicking the word.
2. Type **agreed**. The new text replaces the selected word.

   TROUBLE? If the new text did not replace the selected text, you need to turn on the Typing Replaces Selection option. Click Tools on the menu bar, then click Options to display the Options dialog box. Click the Edit tab of the dialog box, then click the Typing Replaces Selection text box to select this option. Click the OK button to close the dialog box.

3. Use the click-and-drag technique to select the characters **. We** in the third line of the first paragraph.
4. Type **,** and press the **spacebar**, then type **and we**. The new text replaces the selected text.
5. If necessary, scroll the display so that you can see the entire paragraph that begins "You requested a brief statement."
6. Select the word **get** in that paragraph by double-clicking the word.
7. Type **encourage**. The new text replaces the selected word.

Next you'll make Kim's final two editing changes, which require you to delete text from your document.

Deleting Text

The process for deleting text is similar to that for replacing text. To delete text, you first select the text, and then you press the Delete key.

Kim wants you to delete the first several lines that you copied from her document and the word "generous" in the first paragraph.

To delete the text:

1. Scroll until you see the first paragraph of the letter on your screen.
2. Select the word **generous** in the last line of the first paragraph.
3. Press the **Delete** key. The selected text disappears.
4. Scroll until you see the entire paragraph that begins "You requested a brief statement" at the bottom of your screen.
5. Move the pointer into the selection bar next to the paragraph mark below the first paragraph of the letter, click and drag the mouse down to the line "Thank her and summarize status," then release the mouse button. Four paragraph marks and two lines are selected. See Figure 2-16.

Figure 2-16 Deleting text

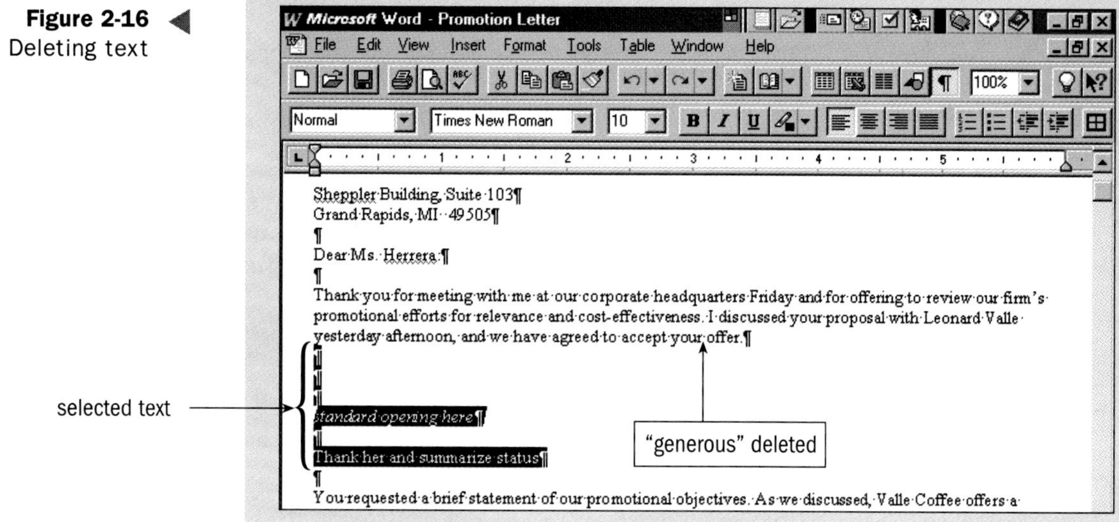

Microsoft Word - Promotion Letter

File Edit View Insert Format Tools Table Window Help

Normal | Times New Roman | 10 | 100%

Sheppler Building, Suite 103¶
Grand Rapids, MI 49505¶
¶
Dear Ms. Herrera:¶
¶
Thank you for meeting with me at our corporate headquarters Friday and for offering to review our firm's promotional efforts for relevance and cost-effectiveness. I discussed your proposal with Leonard Valle yesterday afternoon, and we have agreed to accept your offer.¶
¶
¶
¶
standard opening here¶
¶
Thank her and summarize status¶
¶
You requested a brief statement of our promotional objectives. As we discussed, Valle Coffee offers a

selected text

"generous" deleted

6. Press the **Delete** key. The selected text disappears.

You've completed Kim's editing changes, so you should save your document before continuing.

To save your edited document:

1. Click the **Save** button on the Standard toolbar to save the changes you've made to the document.

Quick Check

1. What is the recommended procedure for developing Word documents?
2. How do you start a new Word document?
3. What does the Show/Hide button on the Standard toolbar control, and why is this button called a toggle?
4. Describe three types of corrections AutoCorrect can make for you automatically.
5. Explain when you would use the Undo and Redo buttons.
6. What is the difference between an active document and an open document?
7. Describe the steps you would follow to select and delete all the text in a single paragraph.
8. Where is the selection bar and what is its purpose?

Now that you've completed Session 2.1, you can exit Word or you can continue to the next session.

SESSION 2.2

In this session you will learn how to change character font types and sizes; use tabs to format text; move, copy, and paste blocks of text; and create numbered and bulleted lists.

Now that you've finished editing Kim's letter to Media Consultants, you're ready to start formatting it.

Changing Character Formats

You format a document to improve its appearance and make it easier to read. For example, you can increase the font size to draw attention to a word; use bold, italics, or underlining for emphasis; and create bulleted or numbered lists to group related items.

Changing Font Type and Size

A **font type**, or **font**, is a set of letters, numbers, and symbols, all with a single, consistent design. Some fonts are **serif** fonts, which means they include a short line at the ends of the strokes of a letter. Fonts that do not have these short lines are called **sans serif** fonts. In general, serif fonts are used for the body of text, and sans serif fonts are used for titles and other headings. Fonts also differ from one another in the thickness of the strokes, the height and width of the characters, and the style of the characters.

The Font list box lists all the fonts available to you. A partial list of fonts is shown in Figure 2-17. (Your computer's list of fonts might differ from the list shown in the figure.)

Figure 2-17 Font list box

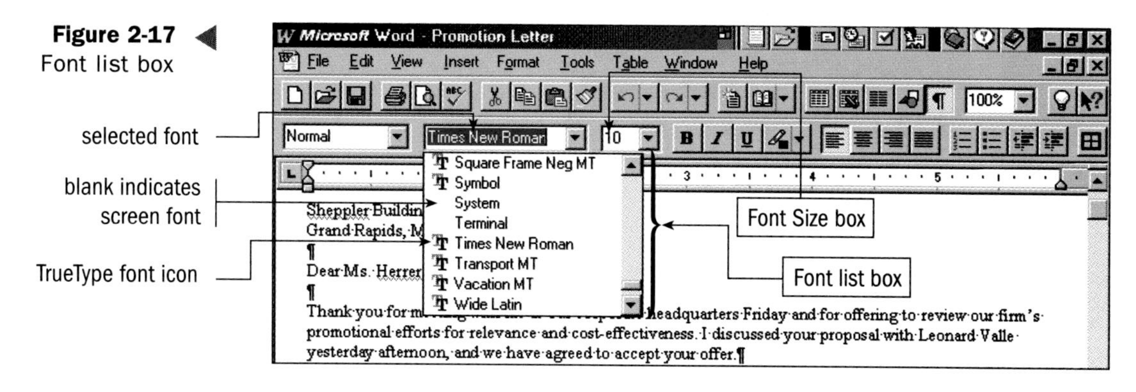

The fonts in the list with no icon next to them are **screen fonts**; if you use a screen font, the way your document looks when printed might be different from the way it appears on the screen. Your font list might include a font marked with a printer icon. Such fonts, called **printer fonts**, are built into your specific printer. Fonts in the list with a double "T" icon are TrueType fonts. **TrueType fonts** work on every printer and can be printed in almost any size; most importantly, a TrueType font has a consistent appearance on every screen and every printer. For these reasons, it is best to use only TrueType fonts for documents.

The set of available fonts can differ from computer to computer, or installation to installation. Figure 2-18 illustrates some of the TrueType fonts that might be included in your font list.

Figure 2-18 Examples of some TrueType fonts

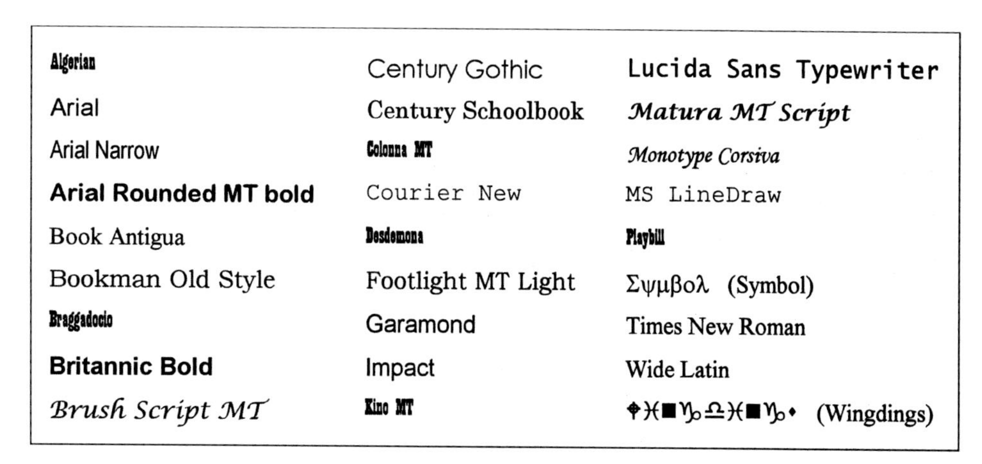

Type size, or **font size**, refers to the physical height of the font measured in points. A **point** is 1/72 inch. Available font sizes for screen and printer fonts vary, depending on the font; TrueType fonts are available in any size from 4 points to hundreds of points. A point size of 10 or 12 is suitable for most documents. Figure 2-19 illustrates some font size samples for Times New Roman, a popular TrueType font.

Figure 2-19 Sample Times New Roman font sizes

This is 10 point

This is 12 point

This is 24 point

This is 36 point

You can apply different font types and sizes to individual paragraphs, words, or characters in a document. However, it's best not to use more than two or three different fonts in a single document. The appearance of a document with many different fonts can be jarring and distracting, lessening the impact of the document's contents.

Kim has several formatting changes she wants you to make to your document, as shown in Figure 2-20.

Figure 2-20 Initial Promotion Letter formatting changes

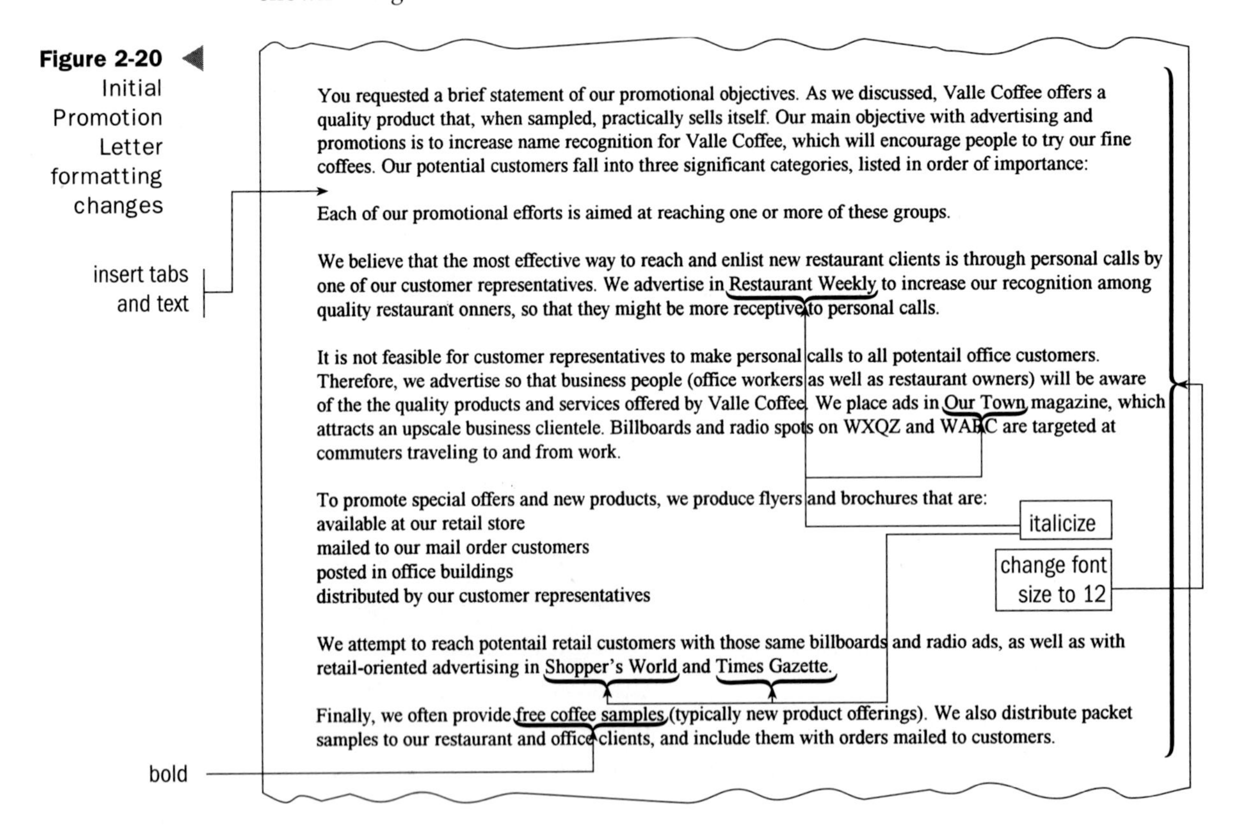

You requested a brief statement of our promotional objectives. As we discussed, Valle Coffee offers a quality product that, when sampled, practically sells itself. Our main objective with advertising and promotions is to increase name recognition for Valle Coffee, which will encourage people to try our fine coffees. Our potential customers fall into three significant categories, listed in order of importance:

Each of our promotional efforts is aimed at reaching one or more of these groups.

We believe that the most effective way to reach and enlist new restaurant clients is through personal calls by one of our customer representatives. We advertise in Restaurant Weekly to increase our recognition among quality restaurant onners, so that they might be more receptive to personal calls.

It is not feasible for customer representatives to make personal calls to all potentail office customers. Therefore, we advertise so that business people (office workers as well as restaurant owners) will be aware of the the quality products and services offered by Valle Coffee. We place ads in Our Town magazine, which attracts an upscale business clientele. Billboards and radio spots on WXQZ and WABC are targeted at commuters traveling to and from work.

To promote special offers and new products, we produce flyers and brochures that are:
available at our retail store
mailed to our mail order customers
posted in office buildings
distributed by our customer representatives

We attempt to reach potentail retail customers with those same billboards and radio ads, as well as with retail-oriented advertising in Shopper's World and Times Gazette.

Finally, we often provide free coffee samples (typically new product offerings). We also distribute packet samples to our restaurant and office clients, and include them with orders mailed to customers.

Your first formatting task is to change the font size of the entire promotion letter from 10 to 12. Before making this change, therefore, you need to select all the text in the document.

To change the font size of all the text in the letter:

1. Click **Edit** on the menu bar, then click **Select All** (or triple-click in the selection bar) to select all the text in the document. Font type and size changes are applied to whatever text is selected.

The current font size is 10 point, which is the value displayed in the Font Size text box on the Formatting toolbar. Kim thinks that this type size might be too small for comfortable reading and wants you to try a larger size.

2. Click the **Font Size** list arrow to open the Font Size list.
3. Click **12**. The text changes from 10 point to 12 point.

Next, you'll change the font type from Times New Roman to Arial to see if this change improves the appearance of the letter.

To change the font type of all the text in the letter:

1. Make sure the text of the letter is still selected.
2. Click the **Font** list arrow to open the font list. All the available fonts are listed in alphabetical order in the bottom part of the list. Word keeps track of recently used fonts and repeats them at the top of the list to make them easier to find. A double line separates the two parts of the list. Scroll the list, if necessary, until you see the font named Arial.
3. Click **Arial**. All the text in the letter changes to Arial, which is a sans serif font. Times New Roman, the default font originally used for the letter, is more appropriate for this letter, so you need to change the font type back to Times New Roman.
4. Click the **Undo** button on the Standard toolbar. Your last action, changing the font type from Times New Roman to Arial, is canceled. The entire letter is redisplayed in Times New Roman.
5. Click anywhere in the workspace of the document to deselect the text of the document.

As shown in Figure 2-20, you also need to italicize and bold selected text in the document.

Using Bold, Italic, and Underlining

The most popular formatting techniques for emphasizing a particular word or phrase are to print the text in boldface, in italics, or underlined. Italics are also used for the titles of books, magazines, newspapers, movies, and so on. You can apply each of these styles with a button on the Formatting toolbar. Each of these buttons is a toggle you use to turn that style on or off for the selected text. Although you can use two or even all three of these formatting techniques in combination, it's generally best to apply only one of them to selected text.

Kim wants the phrase "free coffee samples" on page two of the letter to appear in bold so that it stands out from the rest of the text.

To bold the text:

1. Scroll until you see the entire paragraph that begins "Finally, we often provide free coffee samples" at the bottom of your screen. See Figure 2-21.

Figure 2-21 ◀ Formatting text in bold

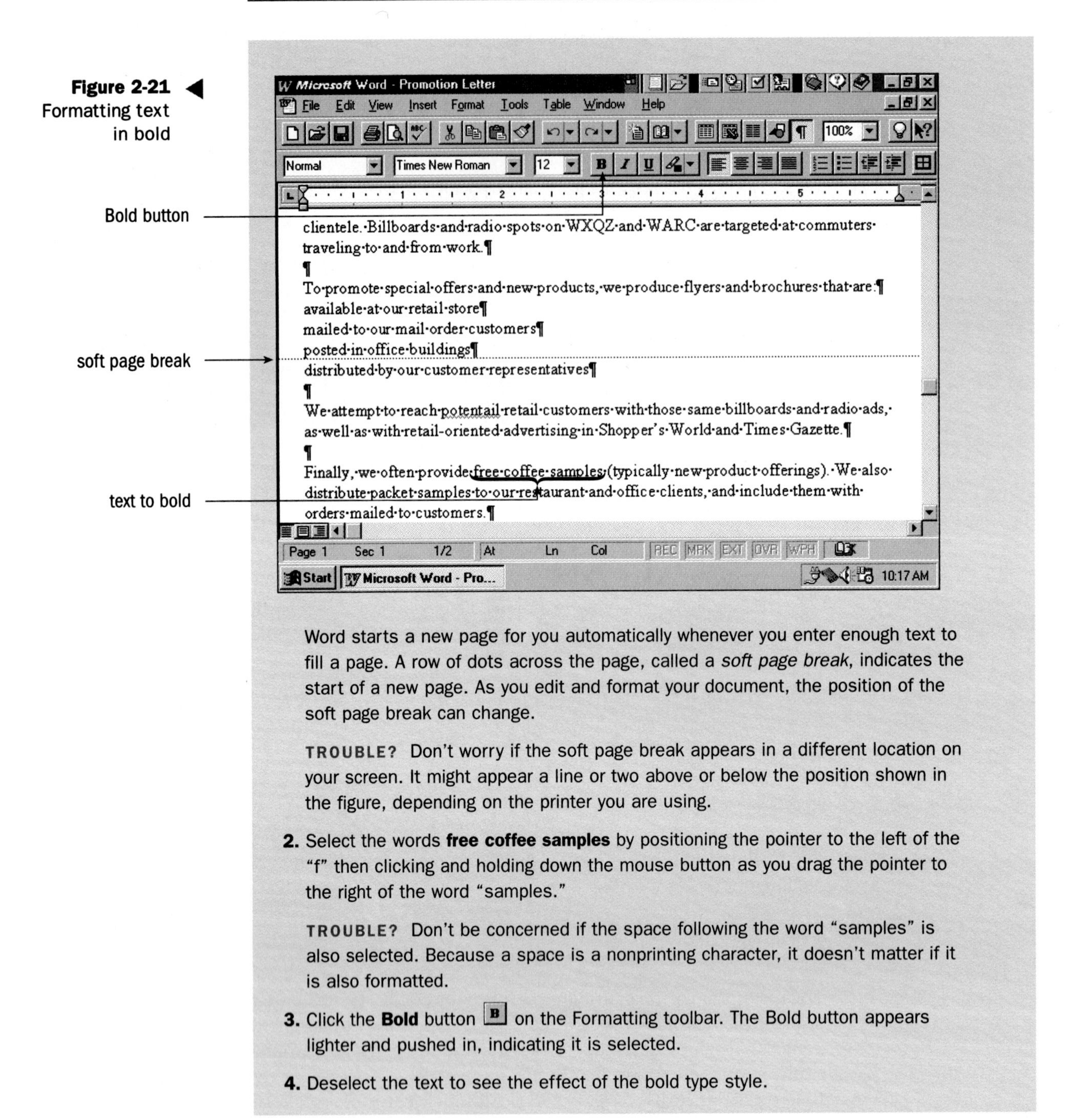

Word starts a new page for you automatically whenever you enter enough text to fill a page. A row of dots across the page, called a *soft page break*, indicates the start of a new page. As you edit and format your document, the position of the soft page break can change.

TROUBLE? Don't worry if the soft page break appears in a different location on your screen. It might appear a line or two above or below the position shown in the figure, depending on the printer you are using.

2. Select the words **free coffee samples** by positioning the pointer to the left of the "f" then clicking and holding down the mouse button as you drag the pointer to the right of the word "samples."

   TROUBLE? Don't be concerned if the space following the word "samples" is also selected. Because a space is a nonprinting character, it doesn't matter if it is also formatted.

3. Click the **Bold** button **B** on the Formatting toolbar. The Bold button appears lighter and pushed in, indicating it is selected.
4. Deselect the text to see the effect of the bold type style.

Kim noted that the names of the newspapers and magazines should be italicized, so you need to apply the italic style to this text in your document.

To italicize the names of the newspapers and magazines:

1. Select the title **Shopper's World** in the location indicated in Figure 2-20.
2. Click the **Italic** button *I* on the Formatting toolbar. The Italic button appears lighter and pushed in.
3. Deselect the text to see the effect of the italic type style.

4. Repeat Steps 1 through 3 for the text **Times Gazette** and **Our Town** in the locations indicated in Figure 2-20. (You'll use a different technique to format the text "Restaurant Weekly.")

   If any of the text you need to select extends from one line to the next, you can use the same click-and-drag technique you learned earlier to select the text.

You can also use the Format Painter button on the Standard toolbar to change the format of selected text. The **Format Painter** copies the format of selected text and applies it to other text you select. If you want the copied format applied to two or more different selections, double-click the Format Painter button, then click the button once to turn it off when you are done copying the format. The Format Painter is particularly useful when you want to copy the format of text that has had multiple formats applied to it; this saves you from having to apply each of the formats individually to other text you want to format in the same way.

You'll use the Format Painter to apply the italic style to "Restaurant Weekly" in your document.

To use the Format Painter to apply formatting:

1. If it is not selected, select **Our Town** in the location shown in Figure 2-20. You will copy the italic format of this selected text and apply it to "Restaurant Weekly."

2. Click the **Format Painter** button on the Standard toolbar. The Format Painter button appears lighter and pushed in.

3. Select **Restaurant Weekly** in the location indicated in Figure 2-20. The italic style is applied to this newly selected text, and the Format Painter is turned off.

   TROUBLE? If the text "Restaurant Weekly" had been split across two lines and is now on the same line, you have not made a mistake. Formatting changes can cause text to wrap differently.

4. Deselect the text to see the effect of the italic type style.

   TROUBLE? If text other than the words "Restaurant Weekly" has been italicized, click the Undo button on the Standard toolbar, then repeat Steps 1 through 4.

Kim forgot to enter three category lines following the second paragraph of the letter. She asks you to insert these categories and use the Tab key to indent them.

Using Tabs

A **tab stop** is a predefined stopping point along a document line. Each time you press the Tab key, the insertion point moves to the next tab stop. If the Show/Hide button on the Standard toolbar is activated, a tab character → appears on the screen at the location of the insertion point when you press the Tab key. Word's default tab stops are set at every 0.5 inch, but you can use the ruler to position and create new tab stops. Word has four different types of tabs that are identified by their corresponding tab markers on the ruler (Figure 2-22).

Figure 2-22 Word tabs

Alignment	Button	Description
Left	L	Text aligns at the left and extends to the right of the tab stop
Center	⊥	Text aligns at the middle of the tab stop, extending an equal distance to the left and right of the stop
Right	┘	Text aligns at the right and extends to the left of the tab stop
Decimal	⊥.	Decimal points in number align at the tab stop; text or numbers without decimals extend to the left of the tab stop

Tabs are most useful for aligning text and decimal numbers, as illustrated in Figure 2-23. You can use the Tab Alignment button on the left side of the ruler to select the type of tab you want to use, then click at the point on the ruler where you want to set that tab stop.

Figure 2-23 Aligning with tabs

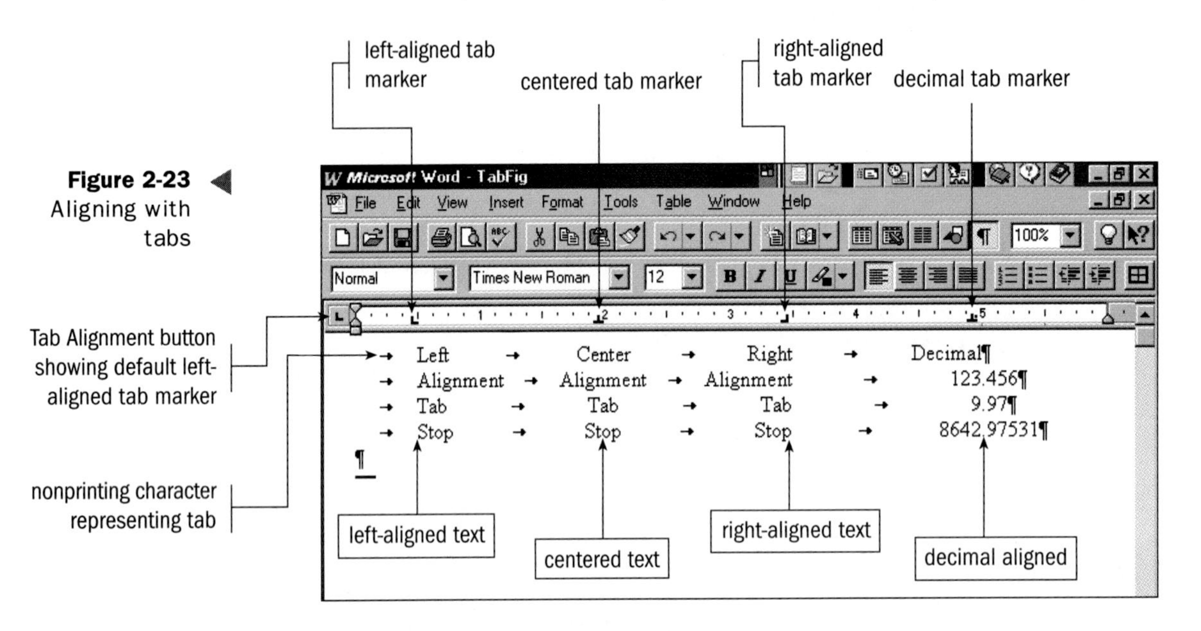

Next, you'll enter the three category lines in the location indicated in Figure 2-20 and use the Tab key to indent each line.

To insert tabs and text:

1. Refer to Figure 2-20 and position the insertion point to the left of the paragraph mark that follows the second paragraph of the letter.
2. Press the **Tab** key. The tab character → appears, and the insertion point moves to the 0.5-inch mark on the ruler, the location of the next tab stop.
3. Type **restaurants** then press the **Enter** key.
4. Press the **Tab** key, type **offices** then press the **Enter** key.
5. Press the **Tab** key then type **retail customers (primarily mail order)**. See Figure 2-24.

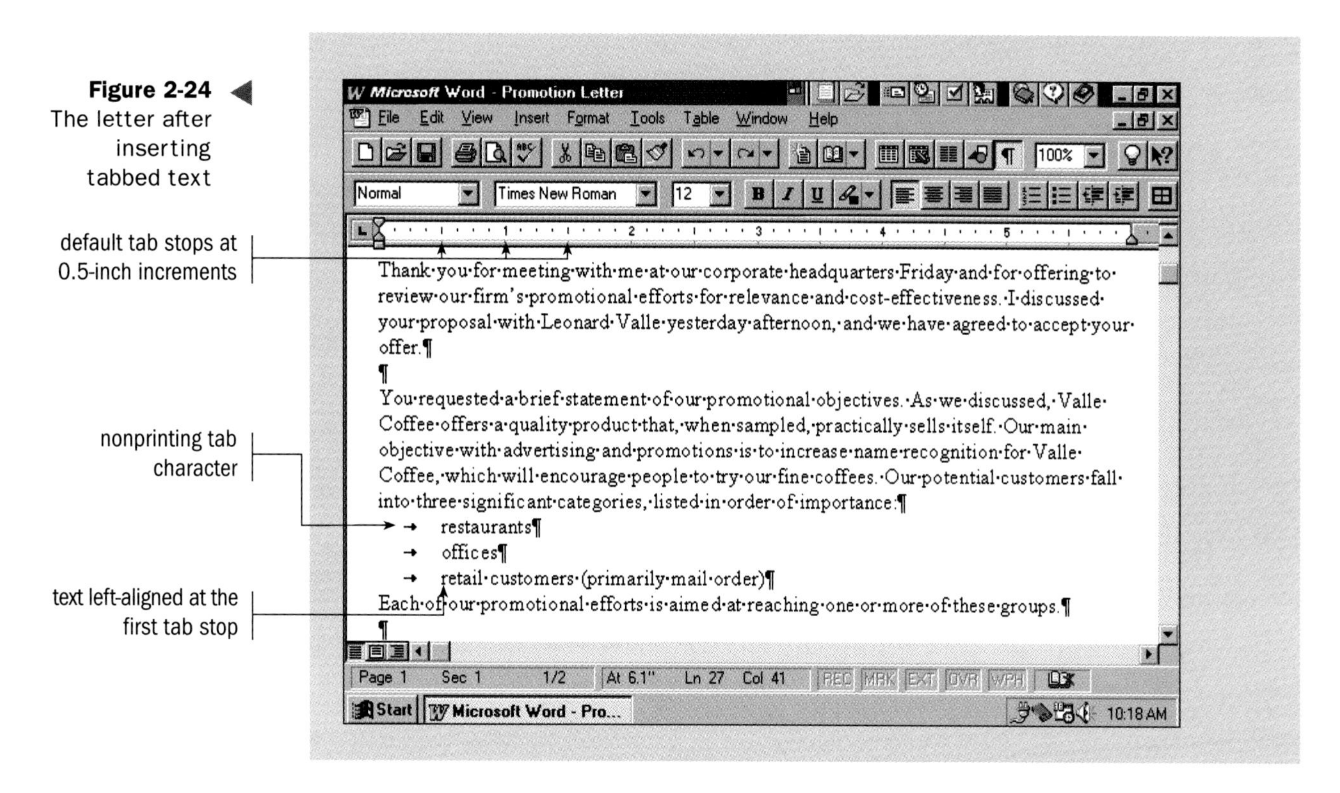

Figure 2-24 The letter after inserting tabbed text

You have completed Kim's initial formatting changes. Now you need to copy and move selected text in your document, as shown in Figure 2-25.

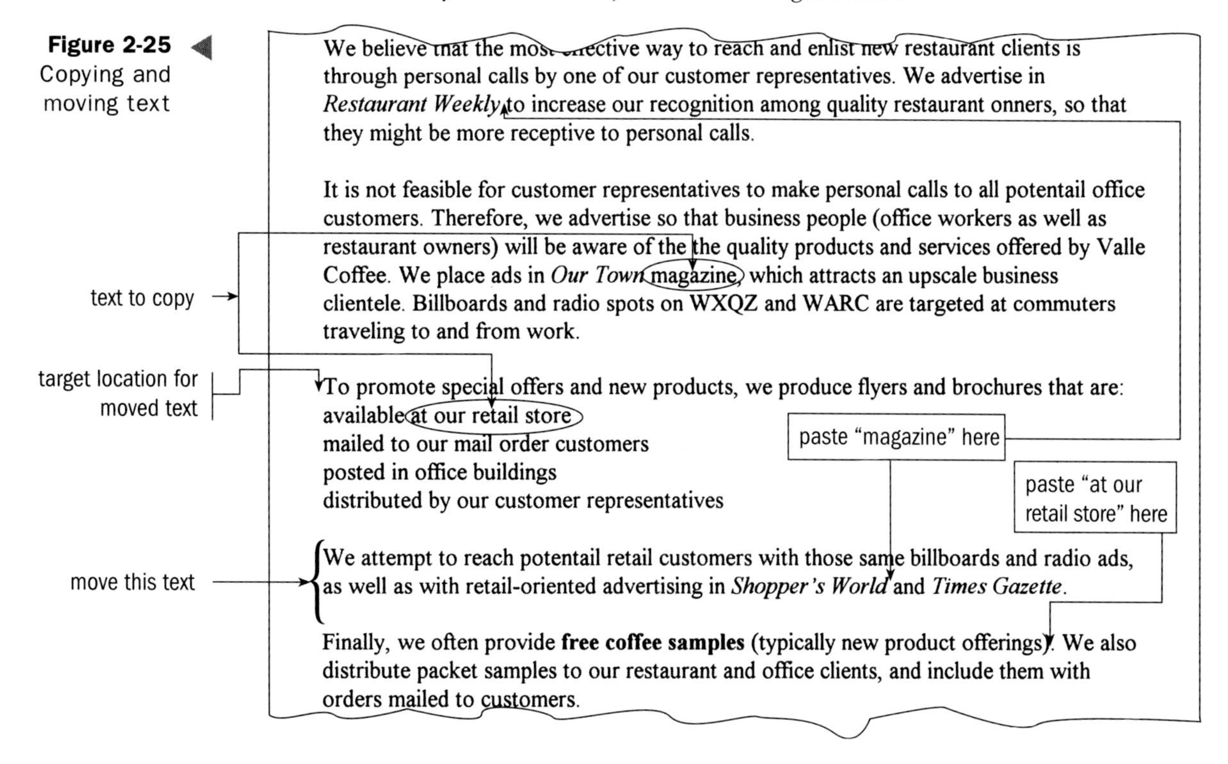
We believe that the most effective way to reach and enlist new restaurant clients is through personal calls by one of our customer representatives. We advertise in *Restaurant Weekly* to increase our recognition among quality restaurant onners, so that they might be more receptive to personal calls.

It is not feasible for customer representatives to make personal calls to all potentail office customers. Therefore, we advertise so that business people (office workers as well as restaurant owners) will be aware of the the quality products and services offered by Valle Coffee. We place ads in *Our Town* magazine, which attracts an upscale business clientele. Billboards and radio spots on WXQZ and WARC are targeted at commuters traveling to and from work.

To promote special offers and new products, we produce flyers and brochures that are:
available at our retail store
mailed to our mail order customers
posted in office buildings
distributed by our customer representatives

We attempt to reach potentail retail customers with those same billboards and radio ads, as well as with retail-oriented advertising in *Shopper's World* and *Times Gazette*.

Finally, we often provide **free coffee samples** (typically new product offerings). We also distribute packet samples to our restaurant and office clients, and include them with orders mailed to customers.

Figure 2-25 Copying and moving text

Copying and Moving Text

Often you'll need to work with a whole section, or **block**, of text within your document, perhaps to format, delete, move, or copy it. You worked with a block of text earlier, when you selected the entire letter and changed the font size from 10 to 12. Here you need to copy and move blocks of text to make the changes Kim wants in the document.

When you **copy** information, the original text stays in its current location and a duplicate of it is placed in a new location. In contrast, when you **move** information, the original text is removed from its current location and placed in a new location. Most methods for copying and moving text involve the Clipboard.

The Clipboard

The **Clipboard** is a standard feature in Windows 95 programs that provides a temporary area for storing information you need to copy or move from one location to another. Clipboard operations include the Cut, Copy, and Paste commands, which are available in every Windows 95 program. Once you have placed selected information on the Clipboard by cutting (removing) it or copying it, you can then paste that information as many times as you want, into any document you want. However, when you subsequently cut or copy new text, the contents of the Clipboard are overwritten with the new text and are no longer available.

Copying and Pasting Text

You can use the Copy and Paste buttons on the Standard toolbar, or the Copy and Paste commands on the shortcut menu or the Edit menu, to copy and paste text within a document or between documents.

Kim wants to make clear in your letter that *Restaurant Weekly* and *Shopper's World* are magazines. She asks you to copy the word "magazine," which occurs after *Our Town*, immediately following the two magazine names. She also wants you to copy the phrase "at our retail store," as shown in Figure 2-25.

To copy and paste the text:

1. Refer to Figure 2-25 and scroll the document until the paragraphs containing *Restaurant Weekly* and *Our Town* are visible on your screen.
2. Select the word **magazine** that follows *Our Town*, then click the **Copy** button on the Standard toolbar. A copy of the selected text is placed on the Clipboard.
3. Position the insertion point immediately after *Restaurant Weekly*, then click the **Paste** button on the Standard toolbar. A copy of the Clipboard contents is pasted at the current location.
4. Refer to Figure 2-25 and, if necessary, scroll until the paragraph containing *Shopper's World* is visible on your screen.
5. Position the insertion point immediately after *Shopper's World*, then click the **Paste** button on the Standard toolbar. A copy of the Clipboard contents is pasted at the current location.
6. Referencing their locations in Figure 2-25, scroll your document until the paragraphs containing the phrase "at our retail store" and the bolded phrase "free coffee samples" are both visible on your screen. This time you'll use the shortcut menu to copy and paste text.
7. Select the phrase **at our retail store**.
8. With the pointer in the highlighted area, click the right mouse button to display the shortcut menu, then click **Copy**. A copy of the selected text is placed on the Clipboard and replaces the previous text on the Clipboard.
9. Position the insertion point immediately after the closing parenthesis in the target paragraph, click the right mouse button to display the shortcut menu, then click **Paste**. A copy of the Clipboard contents is pasted at the current location.

Next Kim asks you to move a paragraph that she had positioned incorrectly, as shown in Figure 2-25.

Moving Text

One significant advantage of a word-processing program is the ability to rearrange your document by moving blocks of text from one location to another. This feature is so important that Word provides several different techniques for moving text within a document: the drag-and-drop technique, in which you select the text and use the mouse to move it; the F2 function key; and the Cut and Paste buttons on the Standard toolbar (or the Cut and Paste commands on the shortcut menu or the Edit menu).

REFERENCE window

MOVING TEXT WITHIN A DOCUMENT

- Select the text to be moved.
- Use the mouse to drag and drop the text to the new location.

or

- Press [F2], position the insertion point at the new location, then press the Enter key.

or

- Click the Cut button on the Standard toolbar, position the insertion point at the new location, then click the Paste button on the Standard toolbar.

or

- With the pointer in the highlighted area, right-click to display the shortcut menu, then click Cut. Place the insertion point at the new location, right-click to display the shortcut menu, then click Paste.

When you use the **drag-and-drop** method, you drag the selected text to a new location and then drop it in place by releasing the mouse button. This technique works well when you need to move text only a short distance.

To move text within a document using drag and drop:

1. Refer to Figure 2-25 and scroll the document until the paragraph that starts "We attempt to reach" is visible on your screen, then select that entire paragraph and the paragraph mark that follows it.
2. Scroll the document so that the selected text and the target location for the move are both visible on your screen. See Figure 2-26.

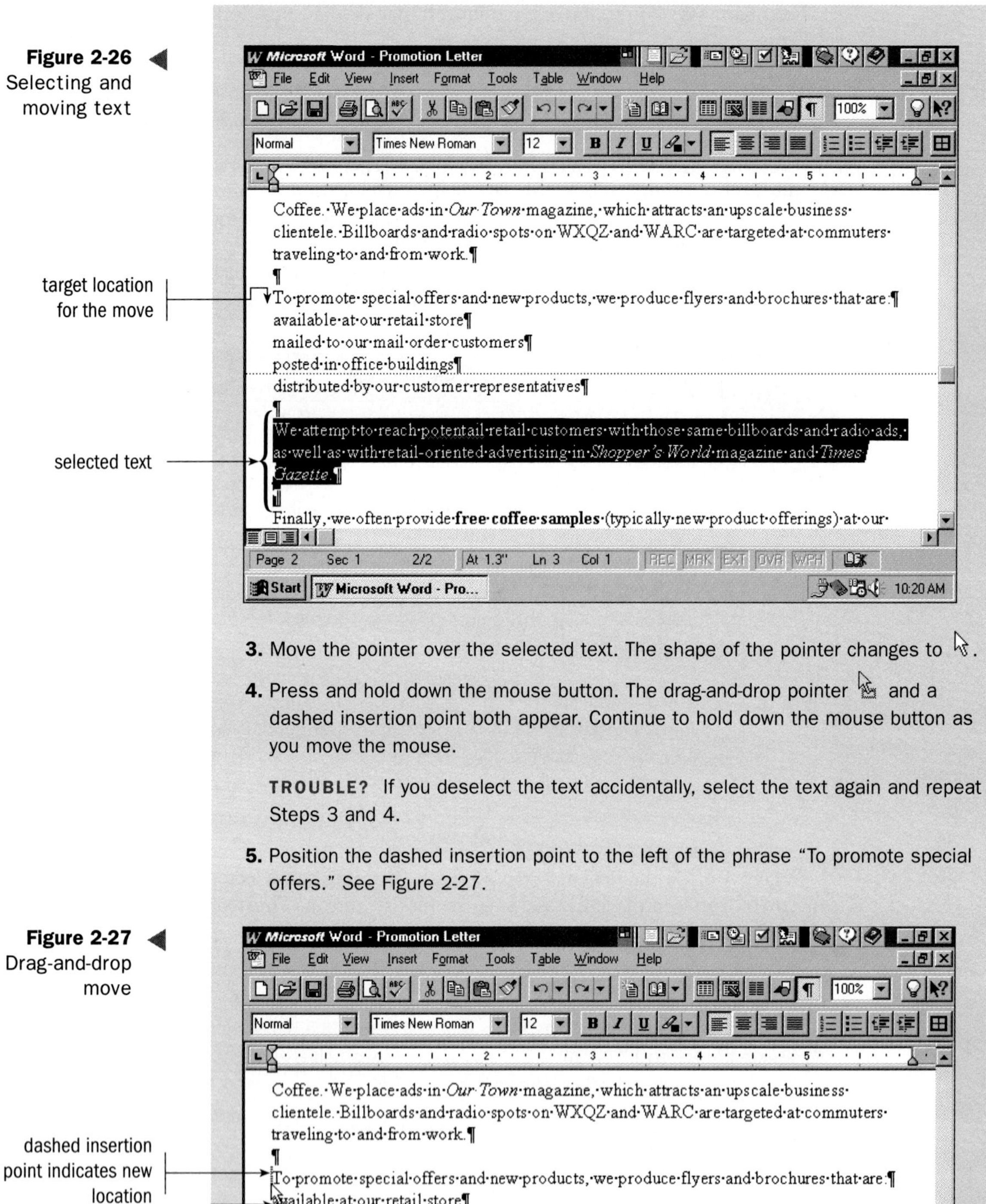

Figure 2-26 Selecting and moving text

3. Move the pointer over the selected text. The shape of the pointer changes to ↖.

4. Press and hold down the mouse button. The drag-and-drop pointer and a dashed insertion point both appear. Continue to hold down the mouse button as you move the mouse.

TROUBLE? If you deselect the text accidentally, select the text again and repeat Steps 3 and 4.

5. Position the dashed insertion point to the left of the phrase "To promote special offers." See Figure 2-27.

Figure 2-27 Drag-and-drop move

6. Release the mouse button. The selected text moves to the new location.

7. Deselect the highlighted text.

TROUBLE? If the text you moved is not in the correct location, click the Undo button on the Standard toolbar. Repeat Steps 1 through 7, making sure you do not release the mouse button until the dashed insertion point is located to the left of the "T" in "To promote special offers."

Kim's next changes involve formatting selected text as numbered and bulleted lists, as shown in Figure 2-28.

Figure 2-28 Text to format as numbered and bulleted lists

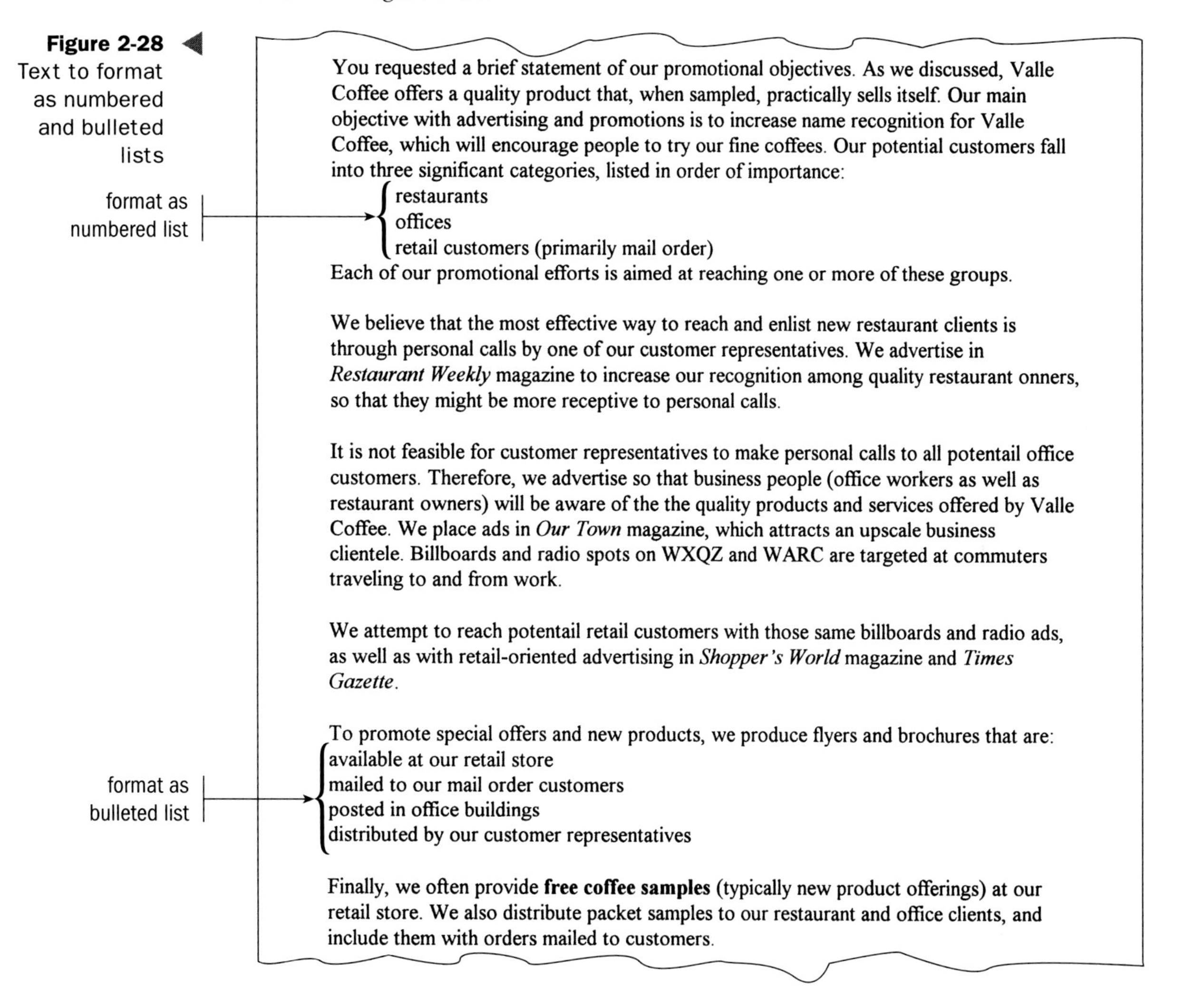

You requested a brief statement of our promotional objectives. As we discussed, Valle Coffee offers a quality product that, when sampled, practically sells itself. Our main objective with advertising and promotions is to increase name recognition for Valle Coffee, which will encourage people to try our fine coffees. Our potential customers fall into three significant categories, listed in order of importance:
restaurants
offices
retail customers (primarily mail order)
Each of our promotional efforts is aimed at reaching one or more of these groups.

We believe that the most effective way to reach and enlist new restaurant clients is through personal calls by one of our customer representatives. We advertise in *Restaurant Weekly* magazine to increase our recognition among quality restaurant onners, so that they might be more receptive to personal calls.

It is not feasible for customer representatives to make personal calls to all potentail office customers. Therefore, we advertise so that business people (office workers as well as restaurant owners) will be aware of the the quality products and services offered by Valle Coffee. We place ads in *Our Town* magazine, which attracts an upscale business clientele. Billboards and radio spots on WXQZ and WARC are targeted at commuters traveling to and from work.

We attempt to reach potentail retail customers with those same billboards and radio ads, as well as with retail-oriented advertising in *Shopper's World* magazine and *Times Gazette*.

To promote special offers and new products, we produce flyers and brochures that are:
available at our retail store
mailed to our mail order customers
posted in office buildings
distributed by our customer representatives

Finally, we often provide **free coffee samples** (typically new product offerings) at our retail store. We also distribute packet samples to our restaurant and office clients, and include them with orders mailed to customers.

Creating Numbered and Bulleted Lists

If your document contains a list of items, you might choose to format the list as either a numbered or a bulleted list. In a **numbered list**, the first item is numbered 1, the second 2, and so on. An optional form of the numbered list indicates the first item as A, the second B, and so on. In a **bulleted list**, a heavy dot or other shape called a **bullet** appears to the left of each item in the list. Use a numbered list when the items specify a sequence of steps or other ordered group, such as items listed in order by size, age, or importance. Otherwise, use a bulleted list for items listed in no specific sequence or order.

The process is similar for creating either type of list. You can use the Numbering button or the Bullets button on the Formatting toolbar to apply the default numbering or bullet format, respectively. If you want to choose a different numbering or bullet format, you can select the Bullets and Numbering option from the Format menu. Like other toolbar buttons, the Numbering and Bullets buttons on the Formatting toolbar are both toggles. You can remove numbering or bullets from a list simply by selecting the list, then clicking the Numbering or Bullets button.

Your letter contains two lists: a list of potential customers and a list of flyer and brochure usage, as shown in Figure 2-28.

Formatting Text as a Numbered List

First, you'll format the list of potential customers as a numbered list because, as stated in the paragraph above the list, the customers are shown in order of importance.

To format the text as a numbered list:

1. Select the list of potential customers in the location indicated in Figure 2-28.
2. Click the **Numbering** button on the Formatting toolbar. Numbers appear to the left of each item in the list. See Figure 2-29.

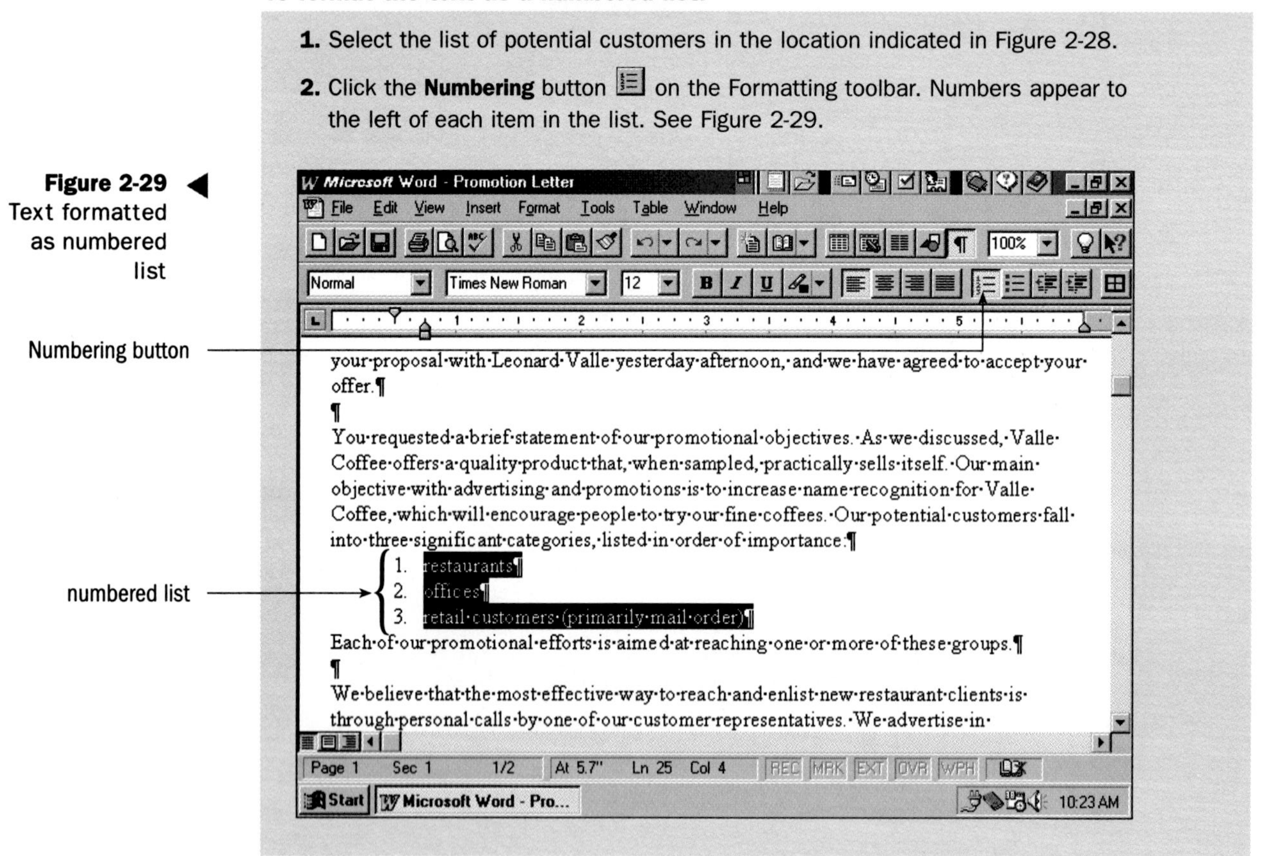

Figure 2-29 Text formatted as numbered list

Kim next wants you to format the list describing flyer and brochure usage, shown in Figure 2-28, as a bulleted list.

Formatting Text as a Bulleted List

Kim wants the list of flyer and brochure usage formatted as a bulleted list, but she isn't sure which bullet format you should use. She asks you first to format the list with the default bullets, then look at the other available bullet formats.

To format the text as a bulleted list:

1. Select the list describing flyer and brochure usage in the location indicated in Figure 2-28.
2. Click the **Bullets** button on the Formatting toolbar. Bullets appear to the left of each item in the list. See Figure 2-30.

Figure 2-30 Text formatted as bulleted list

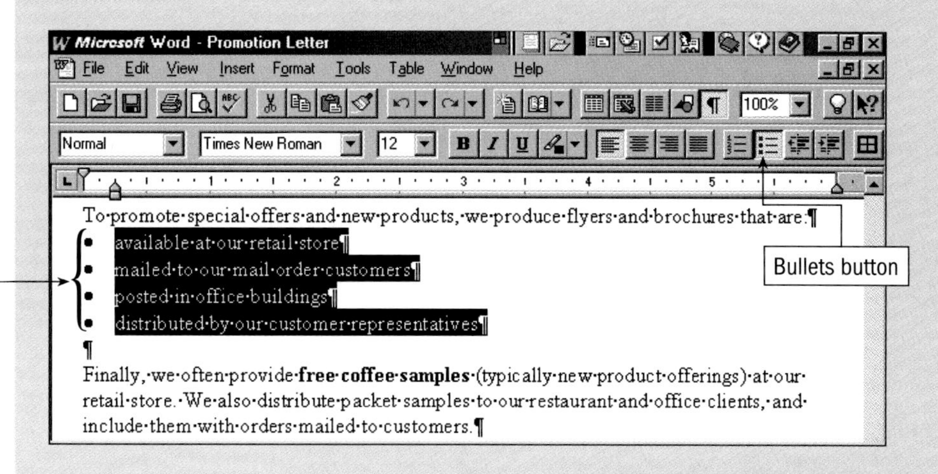

To see the other bullet formats, you use the Bullets and Numbering option from the Format menu.

3. Click **Format** on the menu bar, then click **Bullets and Numbering**. The Bullets and Numbering dialog box opens. See Figure 2-31.

Figure 2-31 Bullets and Numbering dialog box

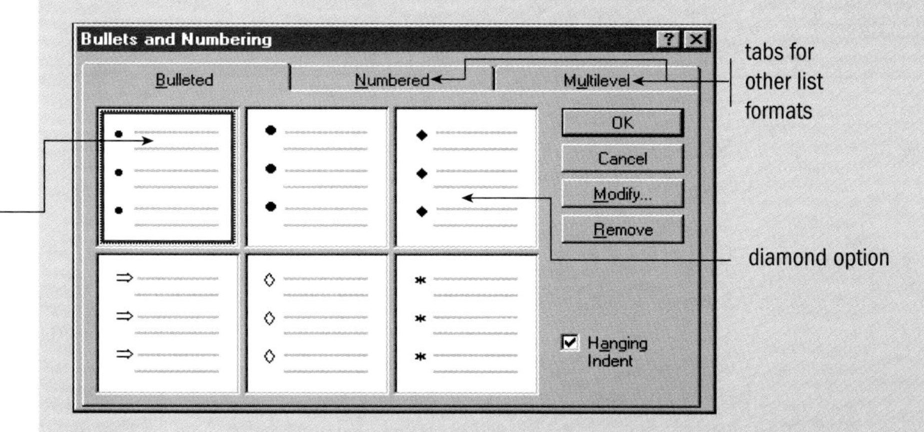

Word provides six different formats for bulleted lists, including diamonds, arrows, and stars. Kim thinks that the diamond option would be appropriate for the bulleted list.

4. Click the third sample in the first row to select the diamond-shaped bullets.
5. Click the **OK** button to close the Bullets and Numbering dialog box. Word displays the list with the diamond bullet format.
6. Deselect the list.

   You have completed Kim's editing and formatting changes, so you should save the document at this point.

7. Click the **Save** button on the Standard toolbar.

Quick Check

1. In general, when do you use serif fonts? sans serif fonts?
2. Font size is measured in multiples of a(n) __________, which equals 1/72 inch.
3. The Bold button on the Formatting toolbar is a(n) __________, which turns that style on or off for the selected text.
4. What are the three most commonly used formatting options for emphasizing a particular word or phrase?
5. What are the four different types of tabs available in Word?
6. Name the three buttons on the Standard toolbar that are associated with the Clipboard, and describe how they work with the Clipboard.
7. When is it best to use the drag-and-drop technique for moving text?
8. When should you format a list as a numbered list rather than a bulleted list?

Now that you've completed Session 2.2, you can exit Word or you can continue to the next session.

SESSION 2.3

In this session you will learn how to embed and modify a WordArt object, check spelling, and preview and print your document.

Now that you've finished editing and formatting Kim's letter to Media Consultants, she wants you to embed a WordArt object on the second page of the document.

Embedding and Changing a WordArt Object

As shown in Figure 2-32, Kim wants the letter to Media Consultants to include an embedded Excel worksheet that details last month's promotional expenses. (You'll insert the worksheet in Tutorial 3.) April's promotional expenses won't be finalized until all the charges for the month have been received. Because it is early in May, not all the final charges are known. Kim has decided to send the April data anyway and asks you to note somehow within the letter that the worksheet figures are preliminary. She suggests that you use WordArt to add this notation.

Figure 2-32
Second page of the letter to Media Consultants

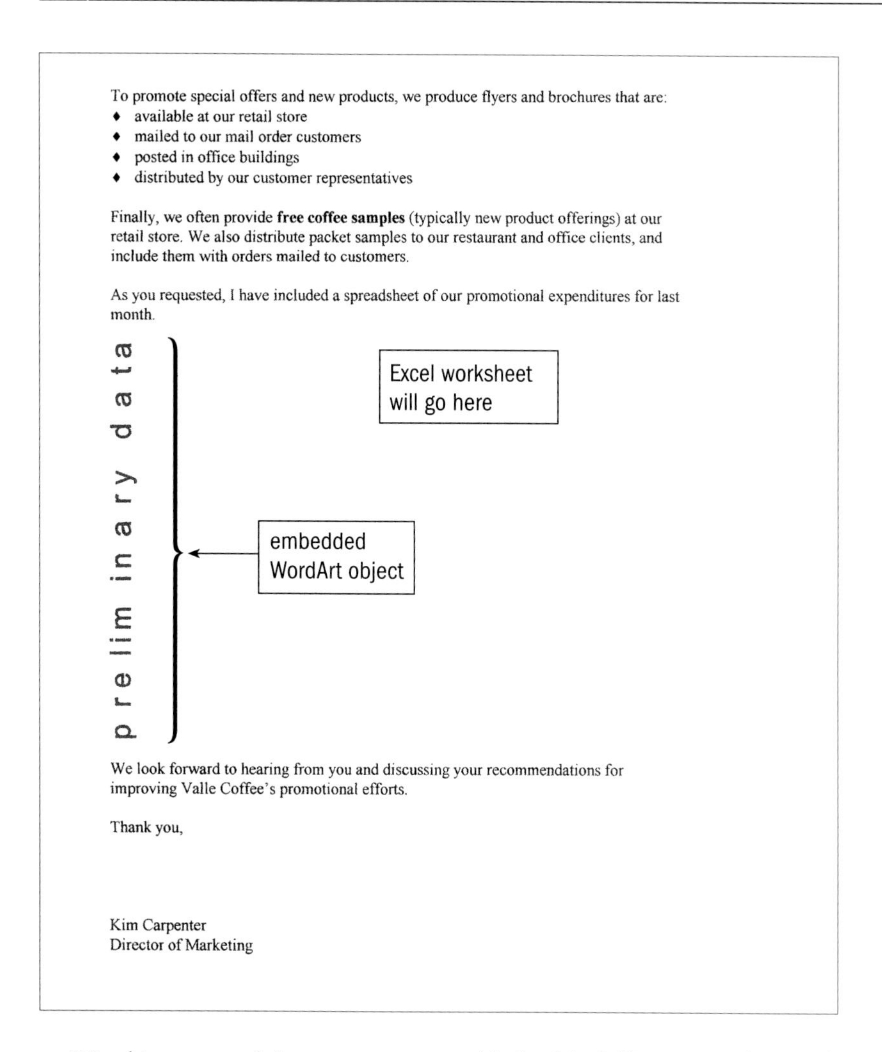
To promote special offers and new products, we produce flyers and brochures that are:
- available at our retail store
- mailed to our mail order customers
- posted in office buildings
- distributed by our customer representatives

Finally, we often provide **free coffee samples** (typically new product offerings) at our retail store. We also distribute packet samples to our restaurant and office clients, and include them with orders mailed to customers.

As you requested, I have included a spreadsheet of our promotional expenditures for last month.

We look forward to hearing from you and discussing your recommendations for improving Valle Coffee's promotional efforts.

Thank you,

Kim Carpenter
Director of Marketing

WordArt, one of the programs provided with Office 95, is designed to work with the core programs such as Word and Access. **WordArt** allows you to create special effects with text. For example, you can apply any one of 36 shapes to the text you enter; curve, fade, and slant text; and flip, stretch, rotate, slide, shade, and shadow text, as shown in Figure 2-33.

Figure 2-33
Sample WordArt shapes and special effects

Shape Name	Shape	Special Effect	Special Effect Applied to Plain Text Shape
PlainText	VALLE COFFEE	Flip	VALLE COFFEE
Bottom to Top	VALLE COFFEE	Stretch	VALLE COFFEE
Arch Down (Curve)	VALLE COFFEE	Rotate 180°	VALLE COFFEE
Deflate	VALLE COFFEE	Slider 100%	VALLE COFFEE
Fade Left	VALLE COFFEE	Special Shading	VALLE COFFEE
Slant Up	VALLE COFFEE	Yellow Shadow	VALLE COFFEE

You'll use WordArt to create an object stating that the data is preliminary, and then embed the object into the letter in the location indicated in Figure 2-32.

Embedding a WordArt Object

To create a new WordArt object, you must start the WordArt program. You can do this from within Word while Word is still active. This is an example of **multitasking**, which is the process of running two or more programs at the same time. Recall that in Tutorial 1 you used Excel to update an embedded worksheet while Word was active and to update a linked Excel chart while PowerPoint was active. These are additional examples of multitasking.

To start WordArt:

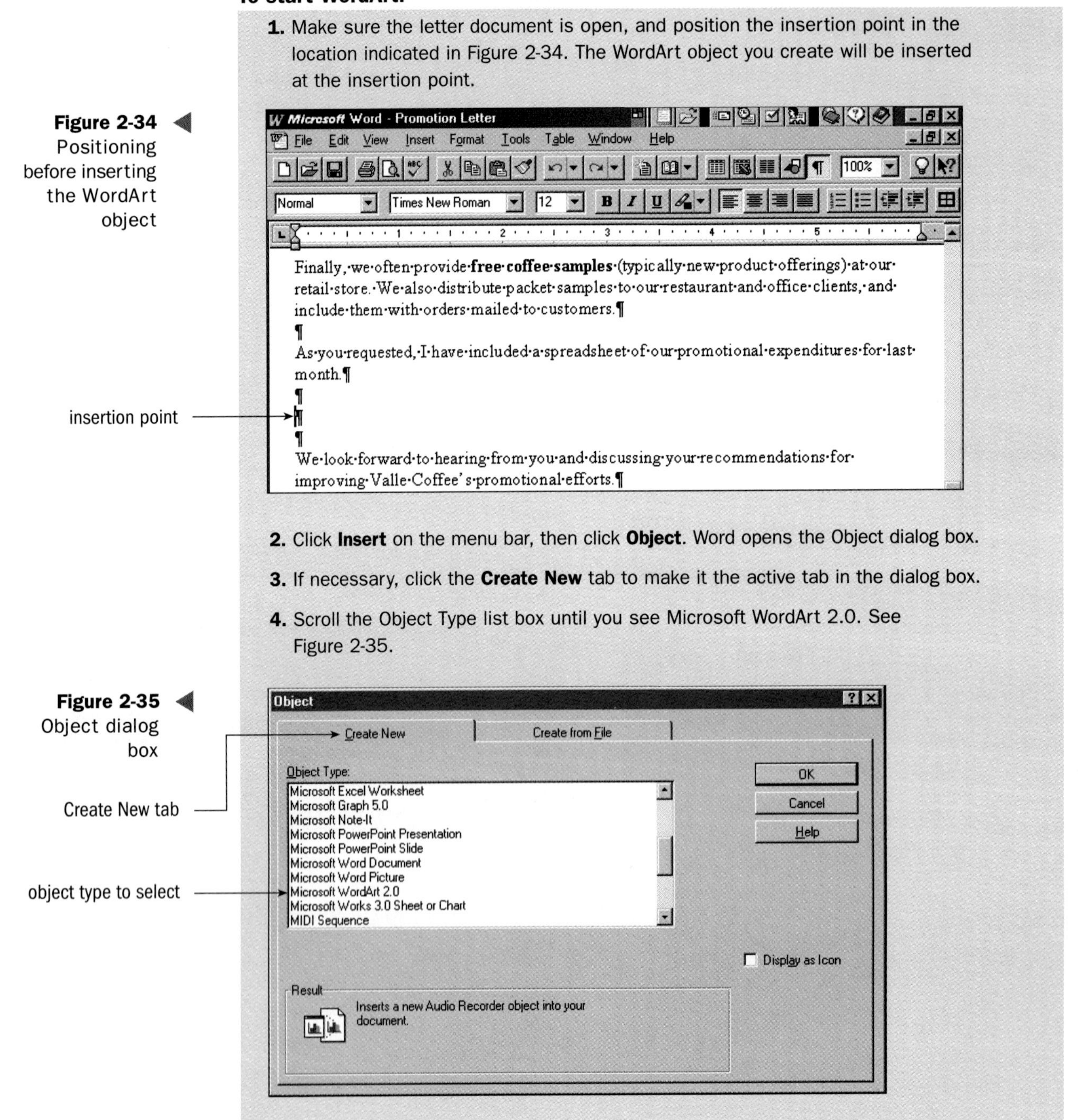

1. Make sure the letter document is open, and position the insertion point in the location indicated in Figure 2-34. The WordArt object you create will be inserted at the insertion point.

Figure 2-34 Positioning before inserting the WordArt object

2. Click **Insert** on the menu bar, then click **Object**. Word opens the Object dialog box.

3. If necessary, click the **Create New** tab to make it the active tab in the dialog box.

4. Scroll the Object Type list box until you see Microsoft WordArt 2.0. See Figure 2-35.

Figure 2-35 Object dialog box

TROUBLE? If Microsoft WordArt 2.0 isn't listed in your Object Type list box, your computer doesn't have this program installed. Ask your instructor or technical support person if it's possible to install Microsoft WordArt 2.0. After the program is installed, you can resume your work at the beginning of this set of steps. If WordArt 2.0 cannot be installed, you will not be able to use the program and cannot complete the steps in this section for embedding and changing a WordArt object. You should read this section and continue your work on the document with the steps in the next section.

5. Click **Microsoft WordArt 2.0** then click the **OK** button. WordArt starts and, after a few moments, displays the Enter Your Text Here dialog box on top of the Word window. The WordArt menu bar and toolbar also appear. See Figure 2-36.

Figure 2-36 WordArt dialog box, menu bar, and toolbar

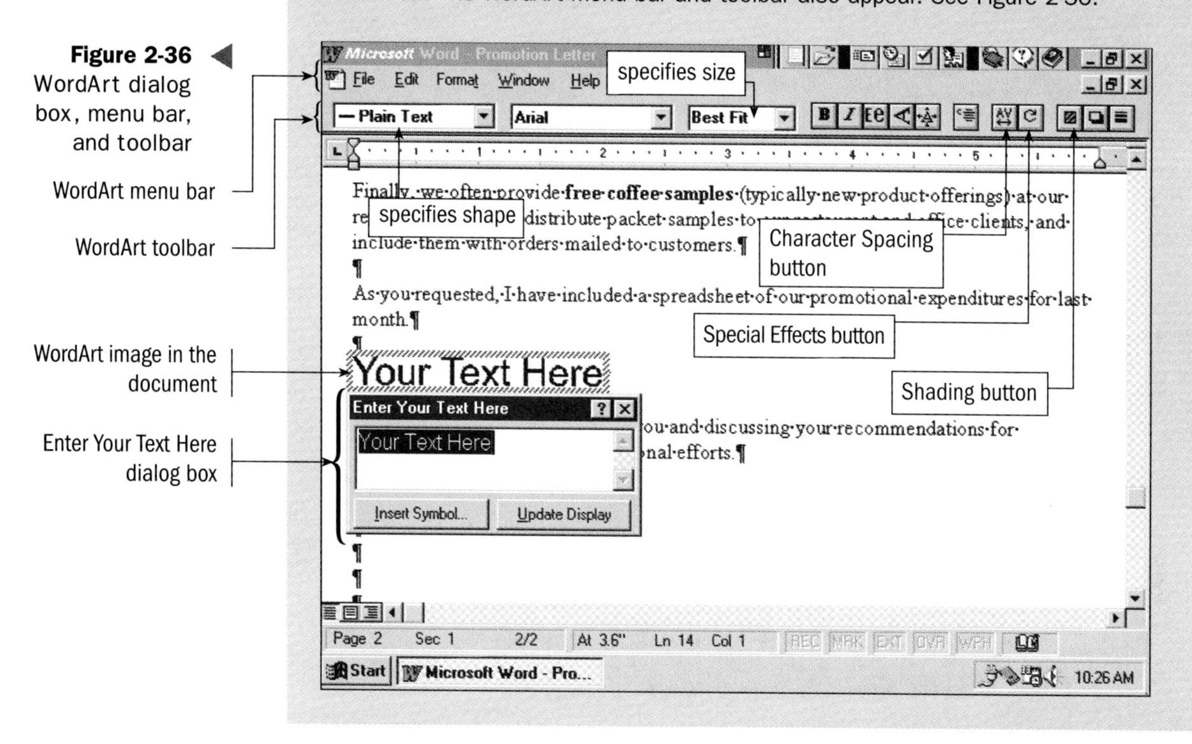

After starting WordArt, you enter the text you want to display and then apply special effects. Among the special effects available are borders and shadows; styles for curved, slanted, or waving text; expanding or compressing the spacing between characters; coloring the text and/or background; and rotating the text.

Kim wants the words "preliminary data" inserted as the WordArt text, and she asks you to select a shape for the text.

To enter the WordArt text and select a shape:

1. Type **preliminary data** then click the **Update Display** button. The text you entered in the dialog box appears inside the selection box in your document. Next, you'll view some of the shapes available in WordArt.

2. Click the list arrow next to **Plain Text** to display the Shape list box, then click the **Arch Up (Curve)** style (row 2, column 1). WordArt applies the selected style to the text. Kim decides that this style isn't really appropriate for this business letter, so she asks you to reapply the Plain Text style to the text.

3. Click the list arrow next to **Arch Up (Curve)**, then click the **Plain Text** style (row 1, column 1). WordArt applies the selected style. Next, you'll rotate the text sideways so that you can position it alongside the worksheet.

4. Click the **Special Effects** button on the WordArt toolbar. The Special Effects dialog box opens. See Figure 2-37.

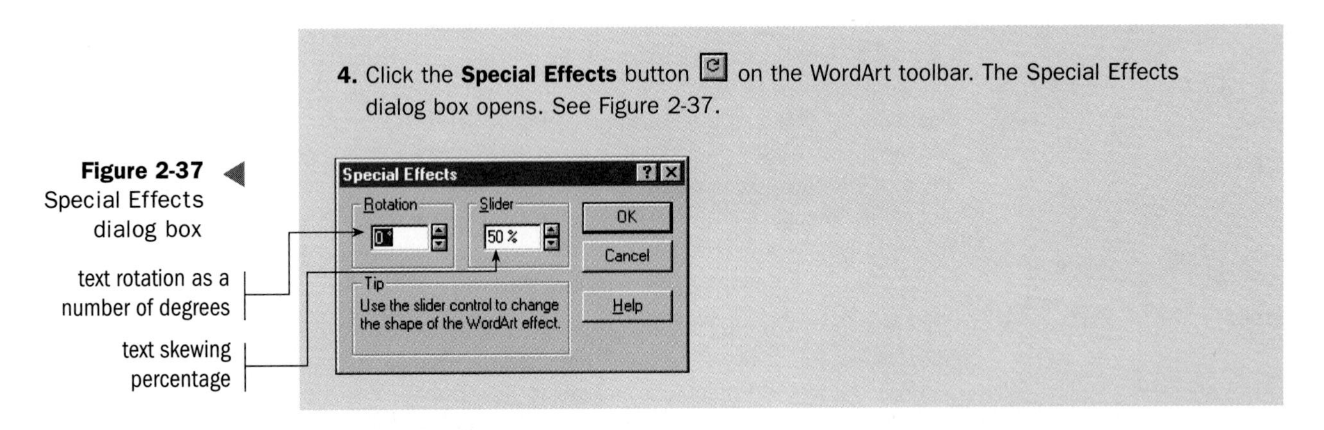

Figure 2-37 Special Effects dialog box

The Special Effects dialog box contains two spin boxes. A **spin box** is a text box with a pair of arrows you can click to increase or decrease the value in the text box. The Rotation spin box allows you to rotate text a selected number of degrees. Positive numbers rotate text in a counterclockwise direction, whereas negative numbers rotate text in a clockwise direction. The Slider spin box allows you to skew text a selected percentage. Percentages greater than 50 skew text to the left, and percentages less than 50 skew text to the right.

Kim wants the text rotated so that it is read from bottom to top, so she asks you to use a rotation value of 90 degrees.

To apply special effects to the WordArt text:

1. Type **90** then click the **OK** button. WordArt rotates the text sideways 90 degrees. The letters look a bit crowded, so Kim asks you to increase the spacing between the characters.
2. Click the **Character Spacing** button on the WordArt toolbar. The Spacing Between Characters dialog box opens. To double the normal spacing between characters, you'll change the spacing from normal (100%) to a custom value of 200%.
3. Click the **Custom** radio button, then type **200**. See Figure 2-38.

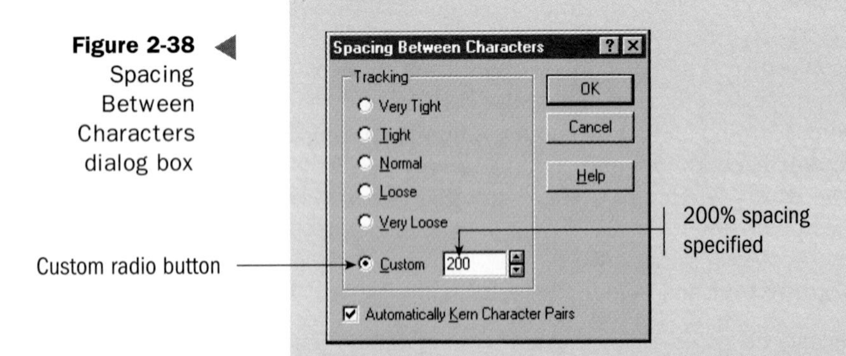

Figure 2-38 Spacing Between Characters dialog box

4. Click the **OK** button to close the Spacing Between Characters dialog box.
5. Click anywhere within the visible part of the document but outside the WordArt image and dialog box. WordArt closes and the object is inserted in your document. See Figure 2-39. Notice that the text is surrounded by a border with small black boxes called sizing handles, which indicate that the object is selected.

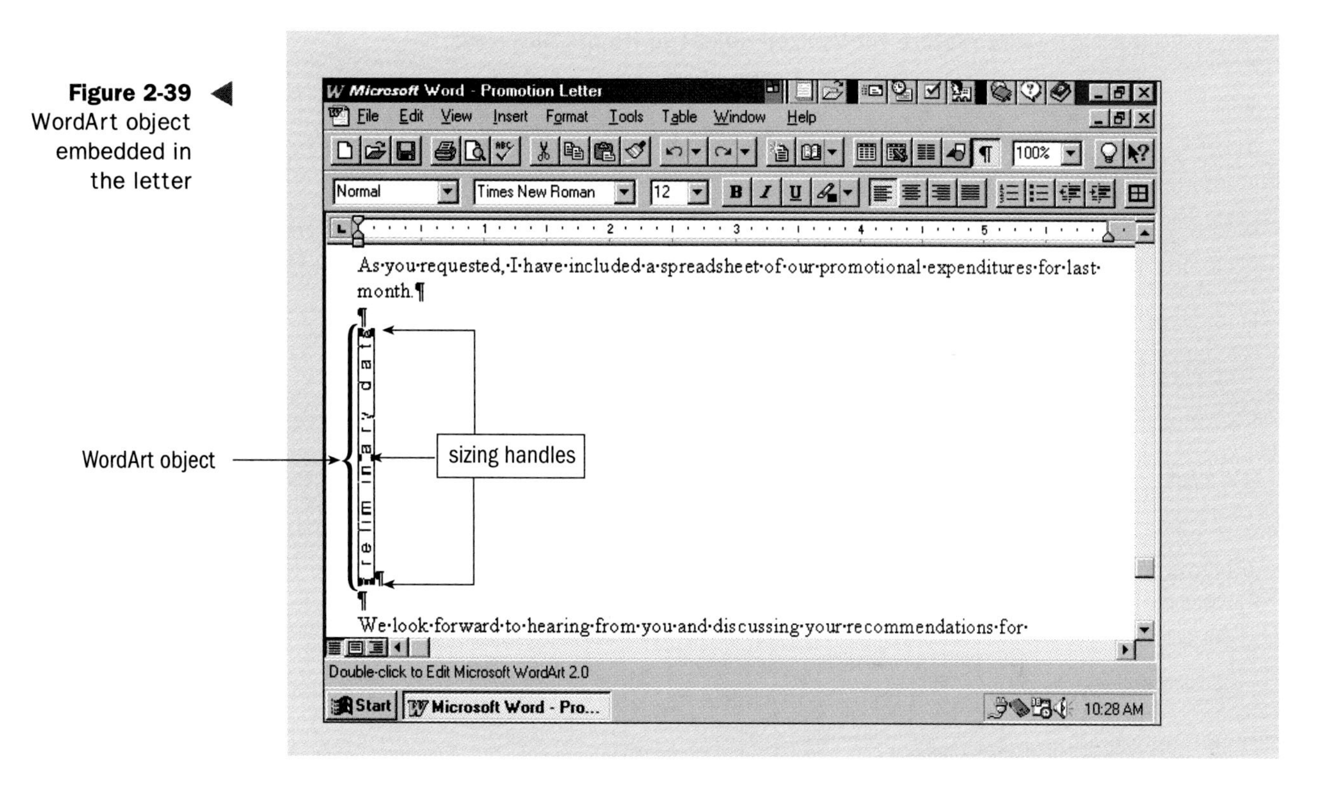

Figure 2-39 WordArt object embedded in the letter

You can use the sizing handles to resize the WordArt object.

Resizing a WordArt Object

You can edit an embedded WordArt object from within Word. One method for resizing an embedded object is to use the **sizing handles**.

Kim thinks the WordArt object might look better in a larger size, and she asks you to resize it.

To resize the embedded WordArt object using the sizing handles:

1. If the WordArt object is not selected, click the object to select it.

   TROUBLE? If WordArt starts when you click the object, simply close WordArt by clicking anywhere within the visible part of the document but outside the WordArt image and dialog box. If the object is not selected after WordArt closes, repeat Step 1.

2. Position the pointer over the sizing handle at the lower-right corner of the object. The pointer changes to ↘.

3. Click-and-drag the pointer down approximately one inch, then release the mouse button. When you start to drag the pointer, a dashed outline of the object is displayed. The dashed outline increases in dimension as you drag. When you release the mouse button, the WordArt object is resized and redisplayed.

   TROUBLE? Don't worry if you increased the size of the image more or less than one inch; you'll resize the object again in the following steps.

To return the object to its original size, you could use the sizing handles to resize the object to a size approximately equal to the original. Or, you can use an Edit menu command to restore the object to its original size.

To restore the resized object to its original size:

1. Click **Edit** on the menu bar.
2. Click **Undo Picture Formatting**. The WordArt object is restored to its original size.

In addition to using the sizing handles, you can also use the Picture option on the Format menu to resize a WordArt object. This method lets you specify exactly how much bigger or smaller to make the object.

To resize the WordArt object using the Picture option:

1. Select the WordArt object if it isn't already selected.
2. Click **Format** on the menu bar, then click **Picture**. The Picture dialog box opens. Notice that the current (original) size of the object is 0.14" by 2", as shown in the Original Size box at the bottom of the dialog box. See Figure 2-40.

Figure 2-40 Picture dialog box

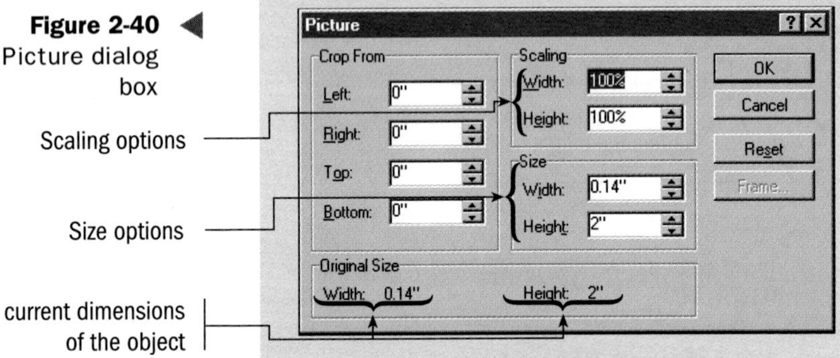

Scaling options

Size options

current dimensions of the object

TROUBLE? If the Width and Height settings in the Original Size box on your screen are slightly different from those in the figure, this is probably due to the monitor you are using.

You can resize an object to specific dimensions by changing the values for Width and Height in the Size section of the Picture dialog box. To increase or decrease the width or height of the object by a specified percentage, you change the percentages in the Scaling section of the dialog box. It's best to resize the object using proportional width and height values. If you don't, the resulting object might be distorted.

Next, you'll double the size of the object by changing the percentages in the Scaling section.

3. Click the **Width** box up arrow and continue to click it until the displayed value is 200%. Notice that when you change a Scaling value, Word changes the corresponding Sizing value.
4. Press the **Tab** key to highlight the Height value of 100%, type **200**, then press the **Tab** key. The new dimensions of the object are 0.27" by 4", the values displayed in the Size section.

   TROUBLE? The dimensions of the object on your screen might be slightly different due to the monitor you are using. This is not a problem.
5. Click the **OK** button to close the Picture dialog box. The object is resized.

When you first resized the WordArt object using the sizing handles, you were able to restore the object to its original size with the Undo Picture Formatting command on the Edit menu. When you resize an object using the Picture dialog box, the Undo Picture Formatting command will not restore the picture to its original size. In this case, if you wanted to restore the WordArt object to its original size, you would have to use the options in the Picture dialog box again, this time to reduce the dimensions to 50% of the current values.

Kim likes the appearance of the resized object. Now, she'd like you to change the color of the object to make it stand out more, because she plans to print the letter on a color printer.

Changing a WordArt Object

To perform any editing task other than resizing on a WordArt object, you must work on the object from within the WordArt program. Next, you'll change the color of the WordArt text to red so that it looks like a caution or warning.

To change the color of the WordArt object:

1. Position the pointer over the WordArt object, click the right mouse button to display the shortcut menu, then click **Edit WordArt 2.0** (or **Edit WordArt**). WordArt starts and, after a few moments, displays the Enter Your Text Here dialog box on top of the Word window. The dialog box contains the text you entered, and the WordArt menu bar and toolbar have replaced those of Word.
2. Click the **Shading** button on the WordArt toolbar. The Shading dialog box opens.

   The Shading dialog box lets you choose a style for your text from a palette that includes plain, colored, dotted, crosshatched, brick, and other patterns. In the Color section you can choose a text color from the Foreground list box and a background color from the Background list box. The background is the rectangular area that frames the text.
3. Click the **Foreground** list arrow in the Color section to display the list of available colors, then click **Red**. See Figure 2-41.

Figure 2-41 Shading dialog box

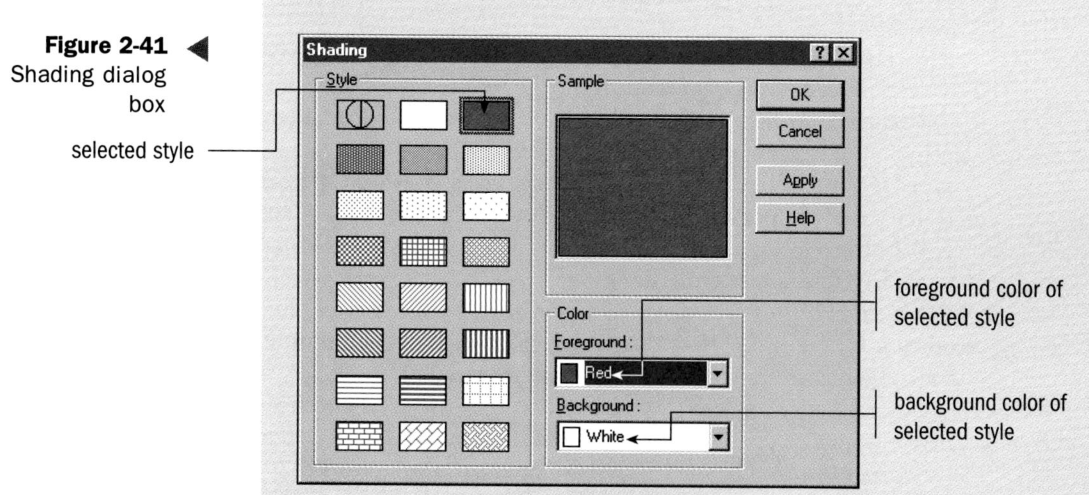

4. Click the **OK** button to close the Shading dialog box. WordArt displays the text in red letters on the default white background.
5. Close WordArt by clicking anywhere within the visible part of the document but outside the WordArt image and dialog box.
6. Click anywhere outside the WordArt image to deselect it. The edited version of the embedded WordArt object is now visible. See Figure 2-42.

Figure 2-42 Edited WordArt object in the letter

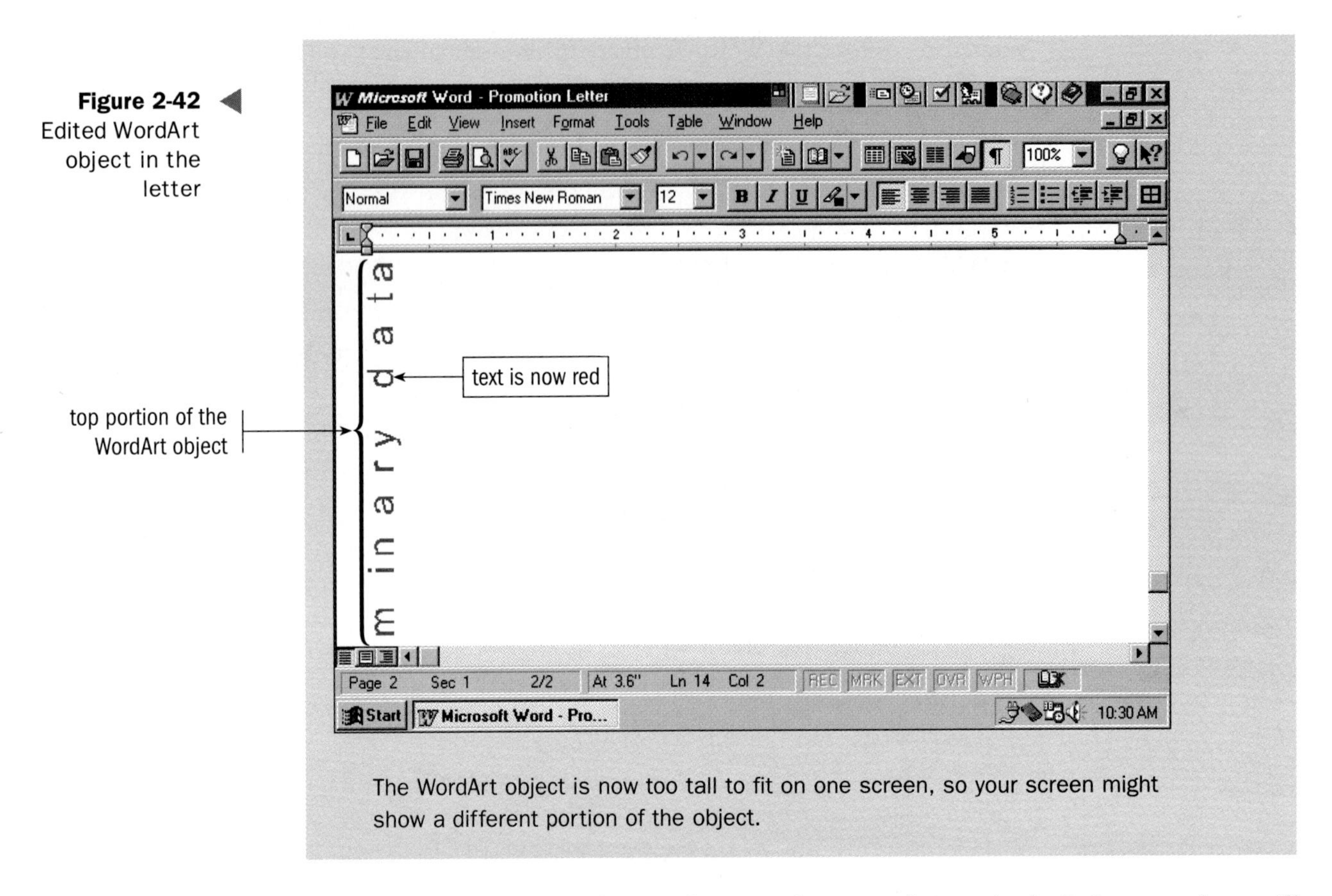

The WordArt object is now too tall to fit on one screen, so your screen might show a different portion of the object.

The letter is now complete, and you're almost ready to print it. Before you do, you'll check the spelling of the text in the document to find and correct any errors.

Checking the Spelling in a Document

You are done planning, entering, editing, and formatting the Promotion Letter document. However, before previewing and printing, you need to check the document for grammatical, spelling, and other errors. You can use Word's automated spell check to help you identify and correct spelling errors.

Word and the other Office 95 programs use a common spell check feature and share a dictionary that includes approximately 130,000 words. When you use the spell check feature, the program identifies any words not found in the dictionary and suggests possible corrections from among the dictionary entries. The spell check also identifies repeated words such as "of of." The words underlined with red wavy lines in your document are words not found in the dictionary. Many of these are proper nouns, such as the names of people and places. If you are using your own computer, you can create your own customized dictionary and add words to it so that the spell check will recognize them.

Any automated spell check feature has limitations. The Office 95 spell check will not identify inappropriately spelled words (such as "their" for "there" or "deer" for "dear") or spelling errors in objects such as WordArt text. Nor does it check for grammatical mistakes or errors in syntax. So you cannot rely solely on the spell check to catch all your errors. You still have to proofread your document as a final check.

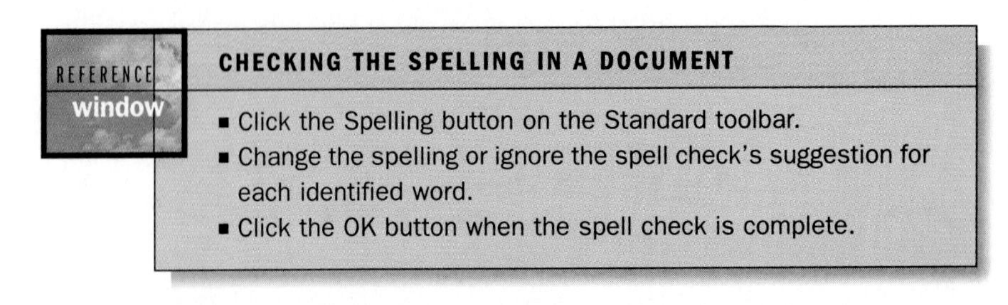

CHECKING THE SPELLING IN A DOCUMENT

- Click the Spelling button on the Standard toolbar.
- Change the spelling or ignore the spell check's suggestion for each identified word.
- Click the OK button when the spell check is complete.

You'll use the spell check feature to correct misspellings and typos in Kim's letter.

To start checking the spelling in the document:

1. Press and hold down the **Ctrl** key and press the **Home** key. (From now on, key combinations such as this one will be shown as Ctrl + Home.) The insertion point moves to the beginning of the document. Because the spell check feature begins checking your document at the insertion point location, you want the insertion point at the top of the document.

2. Click the **Spelling** button on the Standard toolbar. The Spelling dialog box opens. See Figure 2-43.

Figure 2-43 Spelling dialog box

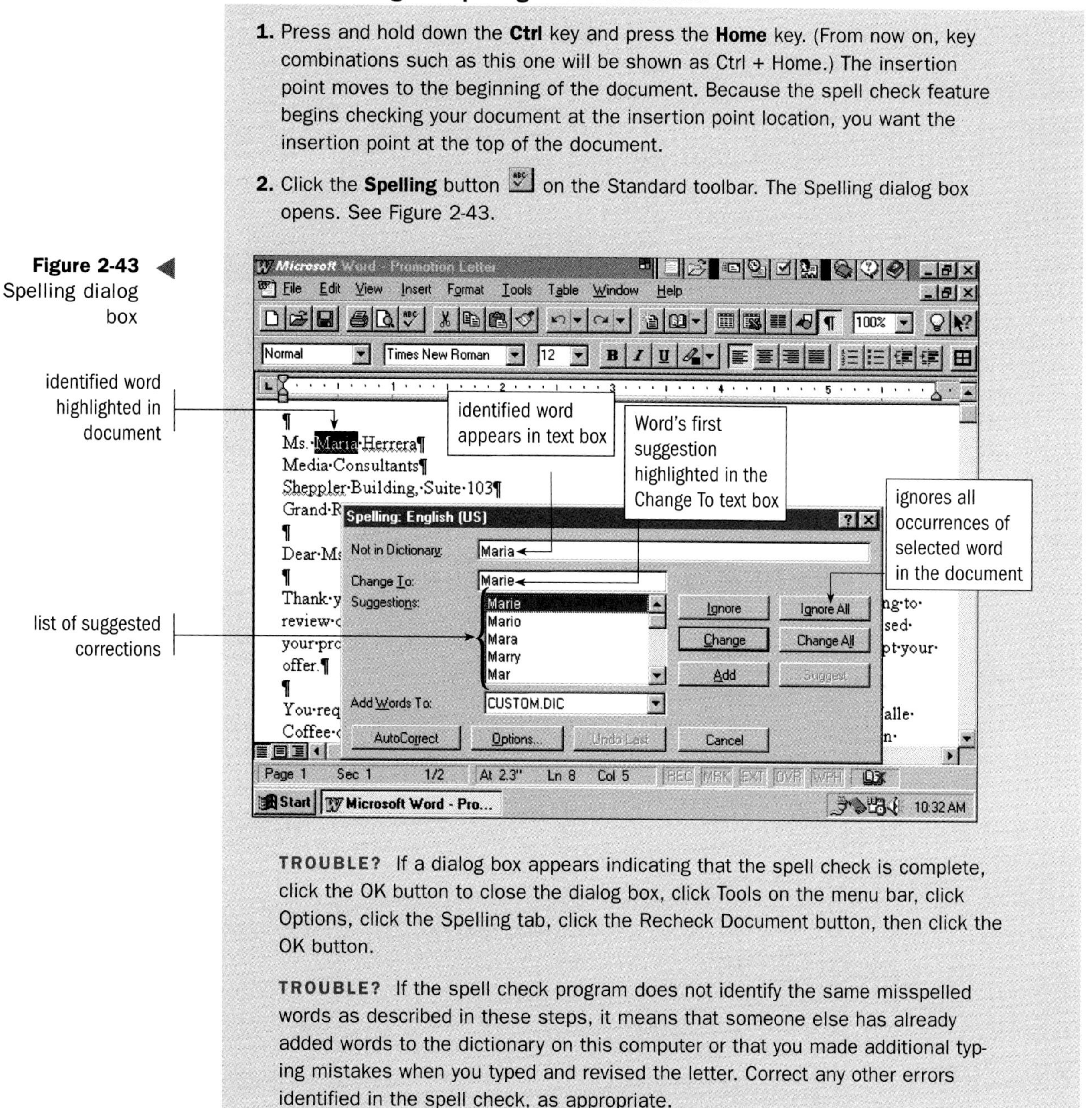

TROUBLE? If a dialog box appears indicating that the spell check is complete, click the OK button to close the dialog box, click Tools on the menu bar, click Options, click the Spelling tab, click the Recheck Document button, then click the OK button.

TROUBLE? If the spell check program does not identify the same misspelled words as described in these steps, it means that someone else has already added words to the dictionary on this computer or that you made additional typing mistakes when you typed and revised the letter. Correct any other errors identified in the spell check, as appropriate.

The word "Maria" is not in the dictionary. Notice that "Maria" is highlighted in the document and also appears in the Not in Dictionary text box of the dialog box. The spell check has several suggestions for a correct spelling, all of which are listed in the Suggestions list box. The first of those suggestions, "Marie," is highlighted and is also displayed in the Change To text box.

The word "Maria" is spelled correctly, so you can tell the spell check feature to ignore this word as well as any other occurrences of the word "Maria" in the letter.

To continue the spell check:

1. Click the **Ignore All** button in the Spelling dialog box. The spell check now stops at the word "Herrera" and again displays a list of several suggestions. The word "Herrera" is spelled correctly, so you can tell spell check to ignore all occurrences of the word.

2. Click the **Ignore All** button. Next the program identifies "Sheppler" as a word not found in its dictionary and suggests "Sheller." You check with Kim and she points out that the correct spelling is actually "Shepler." To change to a spelling that is not one of the suggested spellings, you need to type or edit the text in the Change To text box.

3. Position the insertion point between the "l" and "l" in "Sheller" in the Change To text box, press the **Backspace** key, then type **p**. See Figure 2-44.

Figure 2-44 Spelling dialog box with "Shepler" edited

Spelling: English (US)
Not in Dictionary: Sheppler
Change To: Shepler
Suggestions: Sheller
Ignore | Ignore All | Change | Change All | Add | Suggest
Add Words To: CUSTOM.DIC
AutoCorrect | Options... | Undo Last | Cancel

corrected spelling for selected word

4. Click the **Change** button. Spell check displays a dialog box telling you that the Change To word is not in its dictionary and asks you to confirm that you want to use the word.

5. Click the **Yes** button. Spell check changes "Sheppler" to "Shepler," continues the spell check, and identifies "Valle" as the next potential misspelling. Because the company name would appear in many documents, you would typically add it to the dictionary using the Add button so that the spell check would not stop at this word in the future. However, adding dictionary entries is not feasible in a computer lab, so you will instruct the spell check to ignore all occurrences of the word.

6. Click the **Ignore All** button. Spell check next identifies "onners" as a misspelled word, and displays "oneness" in the Change To text box. See Figure 2-45.

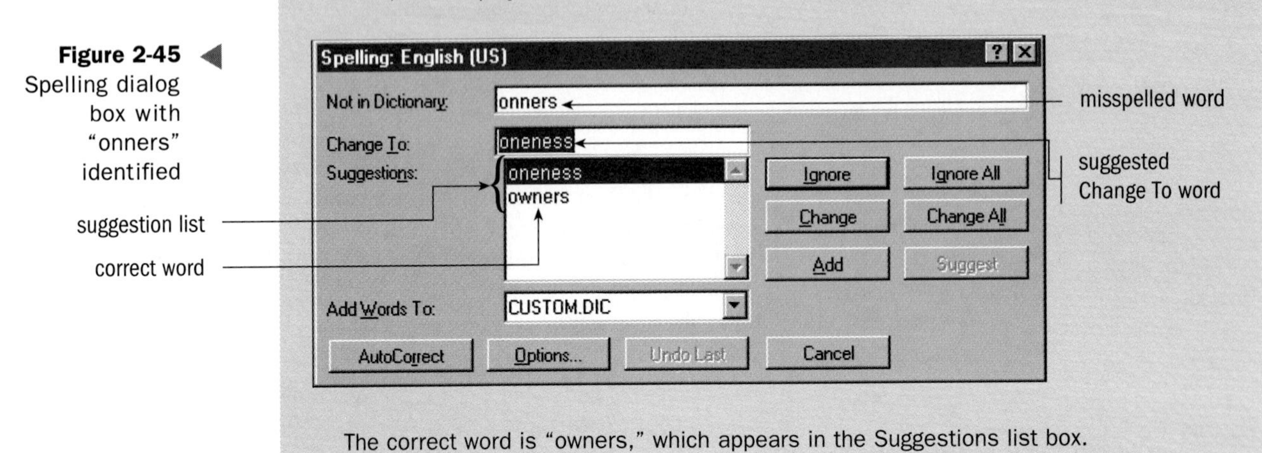

Figure 2-45 Spelling dialog box with "onners" identified

The correct word is "owners," which appears in the Suggestions list box.

7. In the Suggestions list, click **owners**, which now appears in the Change To box, then click the **Change** button. The spell check program corrects "owners," continues the spell check, identifies "potentail" as a misspelled word, and displays the correct word "potential" in the Change To text box.

   Kim points out that she frequently misspells the word "potential" as "potentail," so she suggests you use the Change All button to correct any other possible occurrences of this misspelling.

8. Click the **Change All** button. The spell check corrects all occurrences of "potentail" to "potential," continues the spell check, and identifies "the" as a repeated word. See Figure 2-46. You want to remove the word "the" highlighted in the document.

Figure 2-46 Spelling dialog box with repeated "the" identified

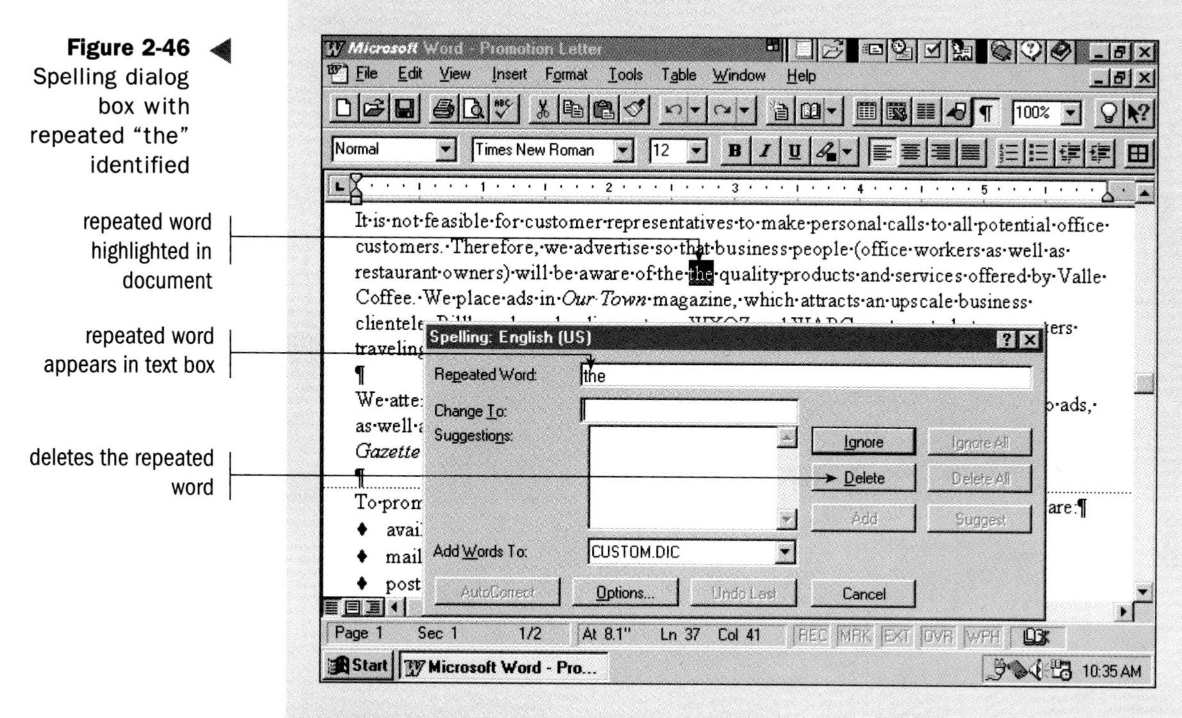

9. Click the **Delete** button. The program deletes the repeated word "the," then displays a dialog box indicating that the spell check is complete.

   TROUBLE? If you have other errors in your document, the spell check program will continue to identify them. Continue correcting all errors until the spell check program indicates that the spell check is complete.

10. Click the **OK** button to close the dialog box and end the spell check.

The letter is now finished, except for the worksheet that you'll insert in it (in Tutorial 3). Kim asks you to print the letter so she can check it before you insert the worksheet.

Previewing and Printing a Document

Word allows you to change the way it displays your document on the screen by offering six different document views, as shown and described in Figure 2-47. You can change to normal, page layout, and outline views by clicking a view button or by selecting an option on the View menu. To switch to print preview view, you must click the Print Preview button on the Standard toolbar. For full screen and master document views, you must select an option on the View menu.

Figure 2-47 Word document views

Document View	Button	View Menu Option	Usage
Normal		Normal	Enter, edit, and format text
Page Layout		Page Layout	See how objects, such as WordArt objects and frames, and other page elements, such as headers, margins, and footers, are positioned on the page
Outline		Outline	Review and reorganize the structure of complex documents
Print Preview		(none)	Check the document's layout before printing by viewing multiple pages in a reduced size
Full Screen	(none)	Full Screen	Hide all toolbars, menus, scroll bars, and other screen components so that the document fills the entire screen
Master Document	(none)	Master Document	Group several documents (for example, chapters in a book) into one document

Because normal view is best for entering, editing, and formatting text, you will do most of your work in this view. Before you print any document, it's a good idea to preview the document to see how it will look when printed. Previewing gives you a chance to make final adjustments to the document so that it will look the way you want it to when you print it. This helps you to avoid wasting paper and time. After previewing and making any final corrections, you should save the document before printing it.

To preview the document:

1. Click the **Print Preview** button on the Standard toolbar. The Print Preview window opens. See Figure 2-48.

Figure 2-48 Print Preview window

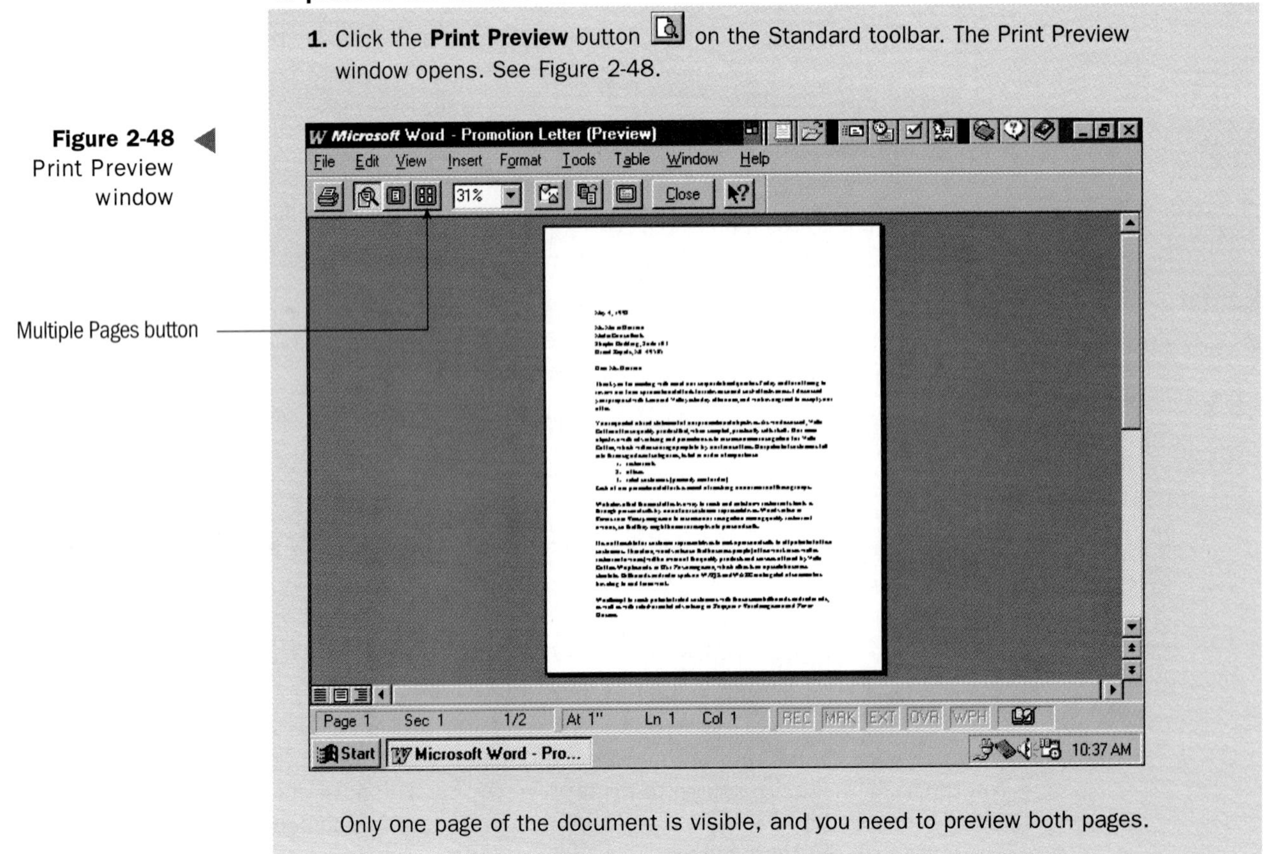

Only one page of the document is visible, and you need to preview both pages.

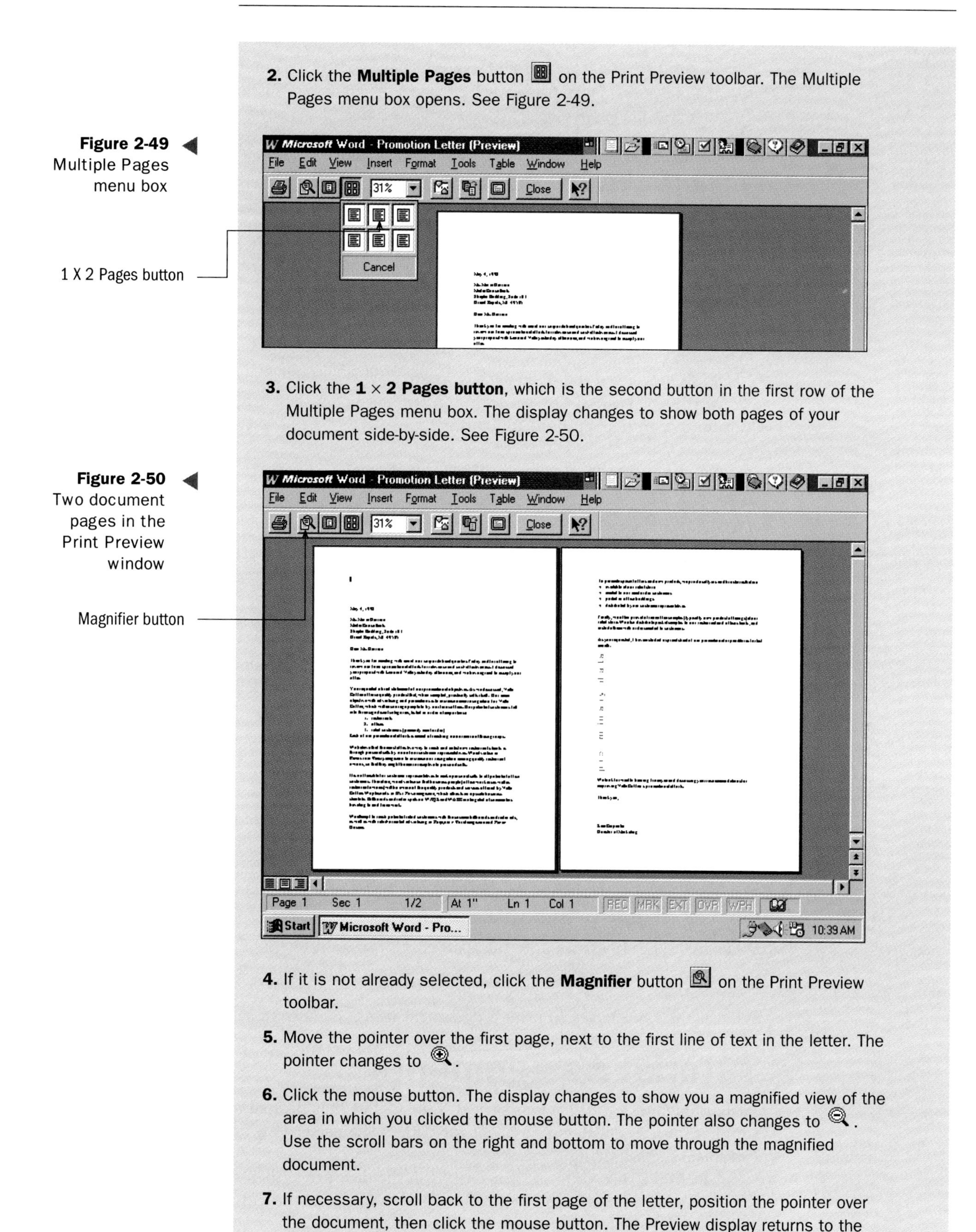

2. Click the **Multiple Pages** button on the Print Preview toolbar. The Multiple Pages menu box opens. See Figure 2-49.

Figure 2-49 Multiple Pages menu box

3. Click the **1 × 2 Pages button**, which is the second button in the first row of the Multiple Pages menu box. The display changes to show both pages of your document side-by-side. See Figure 2-50.

Figure 2-50 Two document pages in the Print Preview window

4. If it is not already selected, click the **Magnifier** button on the Print Preview toolbar.

5. Move the pointer over the first page, next to the first line of text in the letter. The pointer changes to .

6. Click the mouse button. The display changes to show you a magnified view of the area in which you clicked the mouse button. The pointer also changes to . Use the scroll bars on the right and bottom to move through the magnified document.

7. If necessary, scroll back to the first page of the letter, position the pointer over the document, then click the mouse button. The Preview display returns to the full 1 × 2 Pages view.

TROUBLE? If the first page of your document ends in a different location from the one shown in the figure, you can insert a hard page break to force the page to end at the correct location. Page 2 of the letter should begin with the paragraph that starts "To promote special offers..." (refer back to Figure 2-2, if necessary). To enter a hard page break at the correct location, click the Magnifier button on the Print Preview toolbar to turn the button off, click to place the insertion point in front of the "T" in "To," click Insert on the menu bar, click Break, make sure the Page Break radio button is selected in the Break dialog box, then click the OK button. If doing this causes some text to be placed on a third page, delete one or two of the blank lines in the signature block.

8. Click the **Close** button on the Print Preview toolbar to close the Print Preview window.

Having previewed the document, you are now ready to save and print the letter, then exit Word. The easiest way to print a document using the current settings is to use the Print button on the Standard toolbar.

To save and print the document, then exit Word:

1. Click the **Save** button on the Standard toolbar.
2. Click the **Print** button on the Standard toolbar. Word prints the entire letter.
3. Click the **Close** button on the Word title bar to close the document and exit Word.

Kim reviews the printed letter and is pleased with the results. She plans to take one more look at it and make any final changes before giving it back to you so you can embed the Excel worksheet in it (which you will do in Tutorial 3).

Quick Check

1. The process of running two or more programs at the same time is called __________.
2. Describe two methods for resizing a WordArt object.
3. In a WordArt object, the text is the __________ and the rectangular area that frames the text is the __________.
4. What two types of errors does the spell check program identify?
5. You enter, edit, and format text using Word's __________ view.
6. What is the easiest way to print a document using the current settings?

Tutorial Assignments

Barbara Hennessey, office manager at Valle Coffee, has drafted a letter to a potential supplier for a peach flavoring agent for coffee. She needs your help finishing the letter. Complete the following:

1. Make sure your Student Disk is in the disk drive, then open the document named Peach, which is in the TAssign folder of the Tutorial.02 folder.
2. Save the letter as Peach Letter in the same folder.
3. Display nonprinting characters (if necessary), position the insertion point in the paragraph mark just above the salutation, open the document named Address in the same folder, then copy the entire contents of the Address document to your Peach Letter document at the insertion point.

4. Close the Address document. If you are prompted to save changes, answer No.
5. Change the closing from "Truly yours," to "Sincerely,".

6. Select the date at the beginning of the letter, use the Answer Wizard in the Help system to find out how to insert today's date, then replace the date in the letter with today's date. (*Hint:* Type the text "today's date" in the Answer Wizard text box, click the Search button, then display the topic "Insert the date and time in a document.")
7. Delete the phrase "and Seasonings" from the inside address.
8. Change the font type for the entire letter to Century Schoolbook. If that font is not available on your computer, use Bookman Old Style. If that font is also unavailable, choose any serif font. The Font list does not indicate if a font is serif or sans serif; you simply have to try different fonts until you find a serif font that you like.
9. Change the font size for the entire letter to 12 point.
10. Locate the words "Georgia Peach" and format them as bold and italic.
11. Move the first paragraph in the body of the letter so that it follows the second paragraph. Be sure you leave one paragraph mark between paragraphs and between the salutation and the first paragraph.
12. Locate the paragraph that begins "If you are able to" and complete the following:
    a. Insert four new paragraphs immediately following this paragraph, tabbing once before entering the text for each paragraph. Enter the following text in the four paragraphs (one line per paragraph):
       your current catalog
       your current price list
       an order form
       a sample of your peach flavoring, for a taste test
    b. Format these four paragraphs as a bulleted list.
    c. Change the bullets to the open diamond format.
13. Insert three paragraph marks at the beginning of the letter, before the date line.

14. In the new first line of the letter, create and embed a WordArt object containing the text "Valle Coffee." Apply any effects you want, including shape, color, spacing, font, bold, italic, and so on, to create an attractive and readable object.

15. Underline the WordArt object you embedded in the previous step.
16. Use the spell check feature to find and correct all misspellings. Assume that all proper names are spelled correctly.
17. Preview, save, then print the letter.
18. Close the document then exit Word.

Case Problems

1. Ashbrook Mall Information Desk The Information Desk personnel at Ashbrook Mall keep track of each service they provide and how often they provide it. You need to complete a memo to be distributed to all store managers detailing the prior month's service statistics. Complete the following:

1. Make sure your Student Disk is in the disk drive, then open the document named Ashbrook, which is in the Cases folder of the Tutorial.02 folder.
2. Save the document as Ashbrook Memo in the same folder.
3. In the first paragraph of the body of the memo, insert the phrase "just concluded" between the words "month" and "are."
4. In the last line of the second paragraph in the body of the memo, change the word "people" to "applicants."
5. In the first paragraph in the body of the memo, delete the last sentence, which begins "We are sorry."
6. Change the font type and size for the entire document to Times New Roman 12.

7. Copy and paste the phrase "Mall Information" from the first line of the document to the last line between the words "The" and "Staff."
8. In the first paragraph in the body of the memo, exchange the order of the two sentences so that the second sentence precedes the first. When you are done, make sure there is one space between the two sentences and no spaces at the beginning and end of the paragraph.
9. Following "TO:," insert a tab then type "All Store Managers."
10. Following "FROM:," insert a tab then type "Information Desk."
11. Following "SUBJECT:," insert a tab then type "August Service Statistics."
12. Following "DATE:," insert a tab then type "September 3, 1998."

13. Change the font type and size of just the headings "TO:", "FROM:", "SUBJECT:", and "DATE:" to Arial 10. Do not change the text that follows the headings.
14. Add additional tabs following one or more of the four headings, if necessary, so that all the text following the headings is left-aligned.

15. The first line of the document, which consists of the four words "Ashbrook Mall Information Desk," will serve as a heading for the memo. Use WordArt to create an attractive heading consisting of some or all of these four words. Embed the object in the first line. Apply any WordArt effects you want. If you don't include all four words in the WordArt object, format the remaining words in any way you want, including font type, font size, bold, italic, and underlining.

16. Use the Word Help system to find out about paragraph formatting, specifically how to control the vertical spacing before and after paragraphs. Then select the second paragraph in the body of the memo and change its Before Spacing value to 3.5".
17. Check the spelling in the document and make any necessary corrections.
18. Preview, save, then print the document.
19. Close the document and exit Word.

2. Professional Litigation User Services Mr. Robert Seifullah of the law firm Korman, Rosen & Zek requested a detailed accounting of recent services provided to the law firm by Professional Litigation User Services. Anh Nguyen, the administrative manager at PLUS, asks you to finish a letter she has written in response to that request. Complete the following:

1. Make sure your Student Disk is in the disk drive, then open the document named PLUS, which is in the Cases folder of the Tutorial.02 folder.
2. Save the letter as PLUS Letter in the same folder.
3. Complete the inside address by inserting the following lines after the name "Mr. Robert Seifullah":
   Business Manager
   Korman, Rosen & Zek
   413 Center Avenue, NW
   Boston, MA 02102
4. Copy the text from the first line of the document to the location of the next-to-last paragraph symbol, which should be the first paragraph on the second page.
5. In the last line of the first paragraph in the body of the letter, change the phrase "will not be" to "are not."
6. In the second paragraph in the body of the letter, delete the phrase "now or in the future."
7. Change the font type and size for the entire document to Times New Roman 12.
8. The text in the first line of the document will form the letterhead. Change the font of this text to any type and size you want. Add bold and/or italic formatting. You can also change the capitalization of the words.
9. For the first paragraph in the second page of the document, apply the same formatting you just applied to the letterhead, *except* change the font size to 9.
10. In the body of the letter, exchange the order of the second and third paragraphs so that the third paragraph precedes the second paragraph.

11. At the end of the paragraph that begins "We are happpy to provide," do the following:
    a. Insert a space, then type "The accounting includes these cases:".
    b. Insert three new paragraphs immediately following this paragraph, tabbing twice before entering the text for each paragraph. Enter the following text in the three new paragraphs (one line per paragraph):
       Crocker vs. Moreno
       EPA vs. Schwartz
       Khamly Home Furnishings
    c. Format these three paragraphs as a numbered list.
    d. Change the numbered list to a bulleted list with the star bullet format.
12. In the document's last paragraph, create and embed a WordArt object with the text "confidential." Apply any effects you want to the object.

13. Use the Word Help system to find out about adding borders and shading to paragraphs. Then in the first paragraphs on both the first and second pages add a bottom border of your choice.
14. Check the spelling in the document and make any necessary corrections. Assume that all proper names are correctly spelled.
15. Preview, save, then print the document.
16. Close the document and exit Word.

3. Best Friends Beth Warnick-Moscovitch, who serves as the volunteer coordinator at Best Friends, asks you to finish a letter she has written to the Darklers, a couple who volunteered to conduct a Walk-A-Thon to raise funds for Best Friends. Complete the following:

1. Make sure your Student Disk is in the disk drive, then open the document named Darkler, which is in the Cases folder of the Tutorial.02 folder.
2. Save the letter as Darkler Letter in the same folder.
3. Display nonprinting characters (if necessary), position the insertion point in the paragraph mark immediately following the paragraph that begins "All dogs MUST" on page 2, open the document named Rules in the same folder, then copy the entire contents of the Rules document to your Darkler Letter document at the insertion point.
4. Close the Rules document. If you are prompted to save changes, answer No.
5. Type "enclosure" in the last paragraph of the document.
6. Change the font type and size for the entire document to Times New Roman 12.
7. Change the font type and size for the inside address to Arial 10, then use the Format Painter to apply the same font type and size to Beth's name and title lines near the end of the document.
8. Move the paragraph beginning "As you requested" and the blank paragraph following it to the beginning of the paragraph that starts "An event of this kind."
9. Format the list of eight rules on page 2 as a bulleted list, using the arrow bullet.

10. Use the Help button on the Standard toolbar to learn about the Increase Indent button on the Formatting toolbar. Next select the list of 11 volunteer staff duties, increase the indent once for the list, then format the list as a bulleted list (use the default round bullet).
11. Use the Picture option on the Format menu to resize the picture logo at the beginning of the letter to half its current size.
12. Italicize the first line of text in the document, which contains the name and address of Best Friends.
13. Underline the entire first line of the document, which contains the picture logo and the name and address of Best Friends.

14. Use the Word Help system's Answer Wizard to find out about replacing text. Specifically, ask "how do I replace" then display the "Finding and replacing information" topic under Tell Me About. Then replace every occurrence of the word "route" with the phrase "walk route."

15. Check the spelling in the document and make any necessary corrections. Assume all proper names are spelled correctly. ("Parvo" is also spelled correctly.)
16. Preview, save, and print the document.
17. Close the document and exit Word.

4. Herkimer Light Manufacturers Jared Klinger, the director of Customer Relations at Herkimer Light Manufacturers, recently received a letter of complaint, shown in Figure 2-51, from a customer of long-standing. He asks you to use Word to write a letter of response.

Figure 2-51

Pine Bluff Civic Theater

#10 Fountain Square Pine Bluff, ARKansas 71601

May 4, 1998

Herkimer Light Manufacturers
15365 Industrial Drive
Charleston, SC 29411

Dear Sirs:

Our theater has been purchasing #201 footlight bulbs directly from your company for 8 years. In all that time, we have never had a problem with your product... until now.

Last month I ordered a case of #201 footlight bulbs. We received them on time, and they all looked fine — not one broken bulb. However, this latest batch of bulbs all burn out after only a few hours use, and they burn out with a truly loud ***pop*** that startles everyone in the building!

I expect either to be reimbursed for the entire cost of the case of defective bulbs or sent a new case of bulbs immediately. I would appreciate your looking into this matter as soon as possible.

Awaiting your reply,

Elliott Carnaby

Elliott Carnaby
Theater Manager

In your letter, Jared asks you to mention that the Pine Bluff Civic Theater is a "valued customer," to reaffirm Herkimer's commitment to quality, and to tell the customer that a replacement case is being rushed to him immediately. Jared adds that it would be a good idea to include the company's 800 number and to suggest that the customer use it if there are any problems in the future.

First, plan the letter and organize exactly what you intend to write. Jared wants the letter to be from you, so be sure your name appears in the signature block. Complete the following:

1. Make sure your Student Disk is in the disk drive, then start a new Word document.

2. Enter the text of the letter. Before entering your name in the signature block, add an entry in the AutoCorrect dialog box—use your correct last name in the With box and a misspelling of your last name in the Replace box. When you enter your name in the signature block, purposely enter the misspelling and watch how AutoCorrect corrects it automatically.
3. Edit the letter as necessary.
4. Format the letter to make it attractive and readable.
5. Create and embed a WordArt object to serve as a letterhead.
6. Save the document as Pine Bluff Civic Theater on your Student Disk in the Cases folder of the Tutorial.02 folder.
7. Check the spelling in the document and make any necessary corrections.
8. Preview, save, then print the letter.
9. Close the document and exit Word.

Lab Assignment

This Lab Assignment is designed to accompany the interactive Course Lab called Word Processing. To start the Word Processing Lab, click the Start button on the Windows 95 taskbar, point to Programs, point to Course Labs, point to New Perspectives Applications, and then click Word Processing. If you do not see Course Labs on your Programs menu, see your instructor or lab manager.

LABS

Word Processing

Word Processing Word processing software is the most popular computerized productivity tool. In this Lab you will learn how word processing software works. When you have completed this Lab, you should be able to apply the general concepts you learned to any word processing package you use at home, at work, or in your school lab.

1. Click the Steps button to learn how word processing software works. As you proceed through the Steps, answer all of the Quick Check questions that appear. After you complete the Steps, you will see a Quick Check summary report. Follow the instructions on the screen to print this report.

2. Click the Explore button to begin. Click File, then click Open to display the Open dialog box. Click the file TIMBER.TEX then press the Enter key to open the letter to Northern Timber Company. Make the following modifications to the letter, then print it. You do not need to save the document.

a. In the first and last lines of the letter, change "Jason Kidder" to your name.
b. Change the date to today's date.
c. The second paragraph begins, "Your proposal did not include..." Move this paragraph so it is the last paragraph in the text of the letter.
d. Change the cost of a permanent bridge to $20,000.
e. Spell check the letter.

3. Using Explore, open the file STARS.TEX. Make the following modifications to the document, then print it. You do not need to save the document.

a. Center and boldface the title.
b. Change the title font to size 16 Arial.
c. Boldface the DATE, SHOWER, and LOCATION.
d. Move the January 2-3 line to the top of the list.
e. Number the items in the list 1., 2., 3., etc.
f. Add or delete tabs to realign the columns.
g. Double-space the entire document.

4. Using Explore, compose a one-page, double-spaced letter to anyone you choose. Make sure you date the letter and check your spelling. Print the letter and sign it. You do not need to save your document to a disk.

TUTORIAL 3

Excel Basics and Embedding a Worksheet

Creating a Promotional Expense Worksheet to Embed in a Word Document

OBJECTIVES

In this tutorial you will:

- Plan a worksheet
- Start, save, and close an Excel workbook
- Rename and print an Excel worksheet
- Enter and correct labels, numbers, dates, and formulas
- Navigate a worksheet and work with ranges
- Copy, move, and clear cell contents
- Change number and date formats, adjust column widths, and add and remove borders
- Split the worksheet window
- Insert and size an embedded picture
- Embed an Excel worksheet in a Word document

LABS

CASE

Valle Coffee

Maria Herrera of Media Consultants has offered to evaluate Valle Coffee's advertising and promotional efforts. At the request of Kim Carpenter, you prepared a letter of response, which Kim subsequently revised, that itemizes Valle Coffee's promotional objectives. She now asks you to prepare a detailed report of the most recent month's promotional expenditures, which you will then insert into the letter.

In this tutorial you will use Excel to create the promotional expense worksheet, which is shown in Figure 3-1. You'll learn how to plan and develop effective worksheets, and how to create, edit, navigate, and format an Excel worksheet.

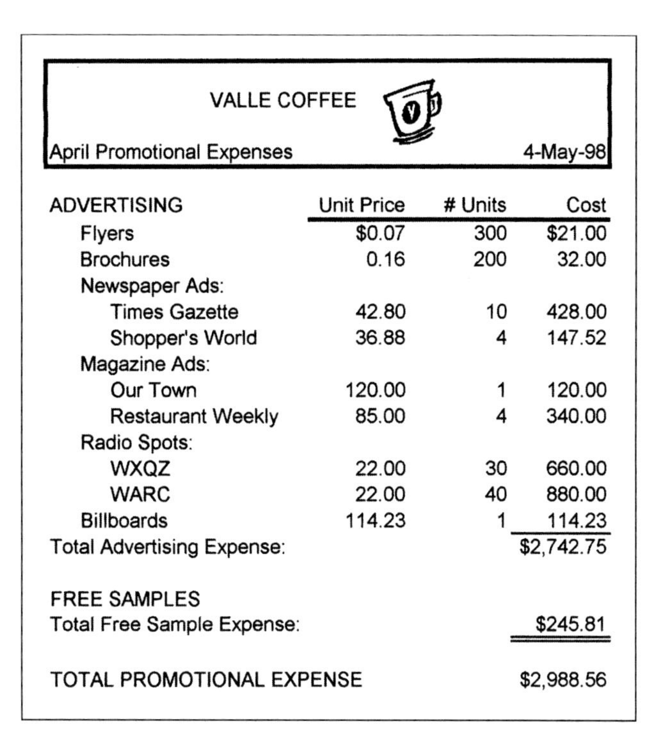

VALLE COFFEE

April Promotional Expenses			4-May-98
ADVERTISING	Unit Price	# Units	Cost
Flyers	$0.07	300	$21.00
Brochures	0.16	200	32.00
Newspaper Ads:			
Times Gazette	42.80	10	428.00
Shopper's World	36.88	4	147.52
Magazine Ads:			
Our Town	120.00	1	120.00
Restaurant Weekly	85.00	4	340.00
Radio Spots:			
WXQZ	22.00	30	660.00
WARC	22.00	40	880.00
Billboards	114.23	1	114.23
Total Advertising Expense:			$2,742.75
FREE SAMPLES			
Total Free Sample Expense:			$245.81
TOTAL PROMOTIONAL EXPENSE			$2,988.56

Figure 3-1 The completed expense report

In this session you will learn how to develop and plan effective worksheets; start a new Excel workbook; rename a worksheet; enter and correct labels, numbers, and dates; navigate a worksheet; save a new workbook; enter and correct formulas; copy cell contents; use the Function Wizard; and close a workbook and exit Excel.

Developing Effective Worksheets

Excel is a spreadsheet program that you use to manipulate, analyze, and display numerical information. A **spreadsheet** is a general term for a display of numbers in rows and columns. Typical applications for spreadsheets in business include financial reporting, budgeting, and cash flow analysis.

Spreadsheet programs offer significant advantages over traditional spreadsheets created by hand. A spreadsheet program calculates results quickly and accurately. If a value in the spreadsheet is changed, any result that depends on that changed value is immediately and automatically recalculated. Spreadsheet programs make "what-if" analyses easy to perform. In a **what-if** analysis, you change a value and then determine the impact of that change by evaluating how other values in the spreadsheet change as a result. With a spreadsheet program, you also can easily create charts based on information in a spreadsheet; if that spreadsheet information is updated, the chart is immediately and automatically updated as well.

An Excel document is called a **workbook**, which is made up of one or more individual **worksheets** (or spreadsheets). In this tutorial, you will create and work with an Excel workbook that contains a single worksheet.

The strategy for developing an effective Excel worksheet is similar to that for developing an effective Word document, as illustrated in Figure 3-2.

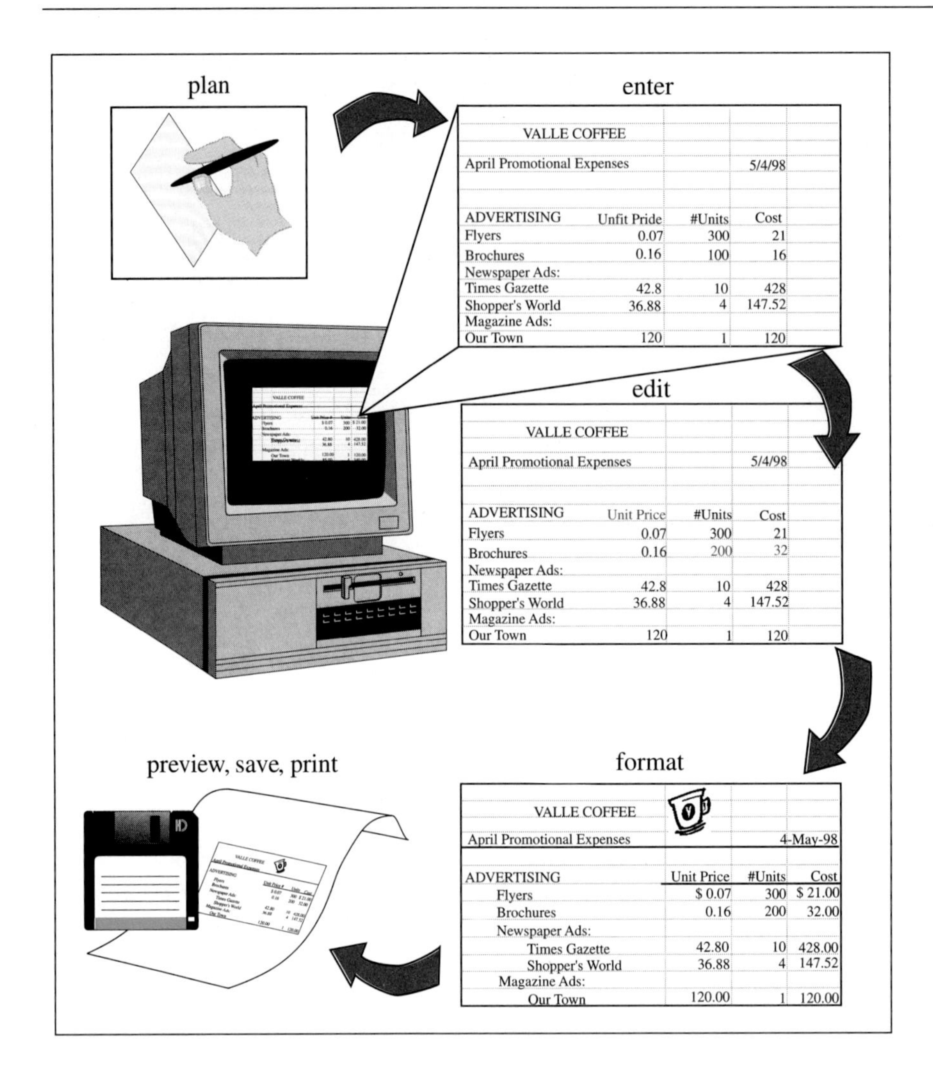

Figure 3-2 Developing an Excel worksheet

The general process for developing a worksheet is as follows:

- Plan the worksheet by determining its purpose and what it will include.
- Enter the data, which can include labels, numbers, dates, and formulas.
- Edit the worksheet to correct errors.
- Format the data to make it more attractive, readable, and usable.
- Preview, save, then print the completed worksheet.

Planning a Worksheet

The first step in effective worksheet preparation is to plan the worksheet. If you plan well first, you are less likely to omit critical data. Planning also simplifies worksheet editing and formatting. For example, you are less likely to have to move or rearrange data if you enter it in the appropriate location in the first place.

Kim wants the promotional expense worksheet to have an appropriate title at the top; the name of the company, a descriptive name for the worksheet, and the date of preparation are typically included in a worksheet title area. She also wants you to embed a picture of the Valle Coffee cup in the title area to add visual interest. A breakdown of all the promotional expenses will follow the title area. The expenses will be divided into two general classifications—advertising and free samples—with an appropriate heading and subtotal for each classification. A grand total promotional expense will appear at the bottom of the worksheet.

Within the advertising classification, you will list each individual expense category. For each such expense, you plan to include a unit price, the number of units, and a total cost (which is the product of unit price times the number of units). Figure 3-3 shows the plan for the worksheet.

Figure 3-3 The worksheet plan

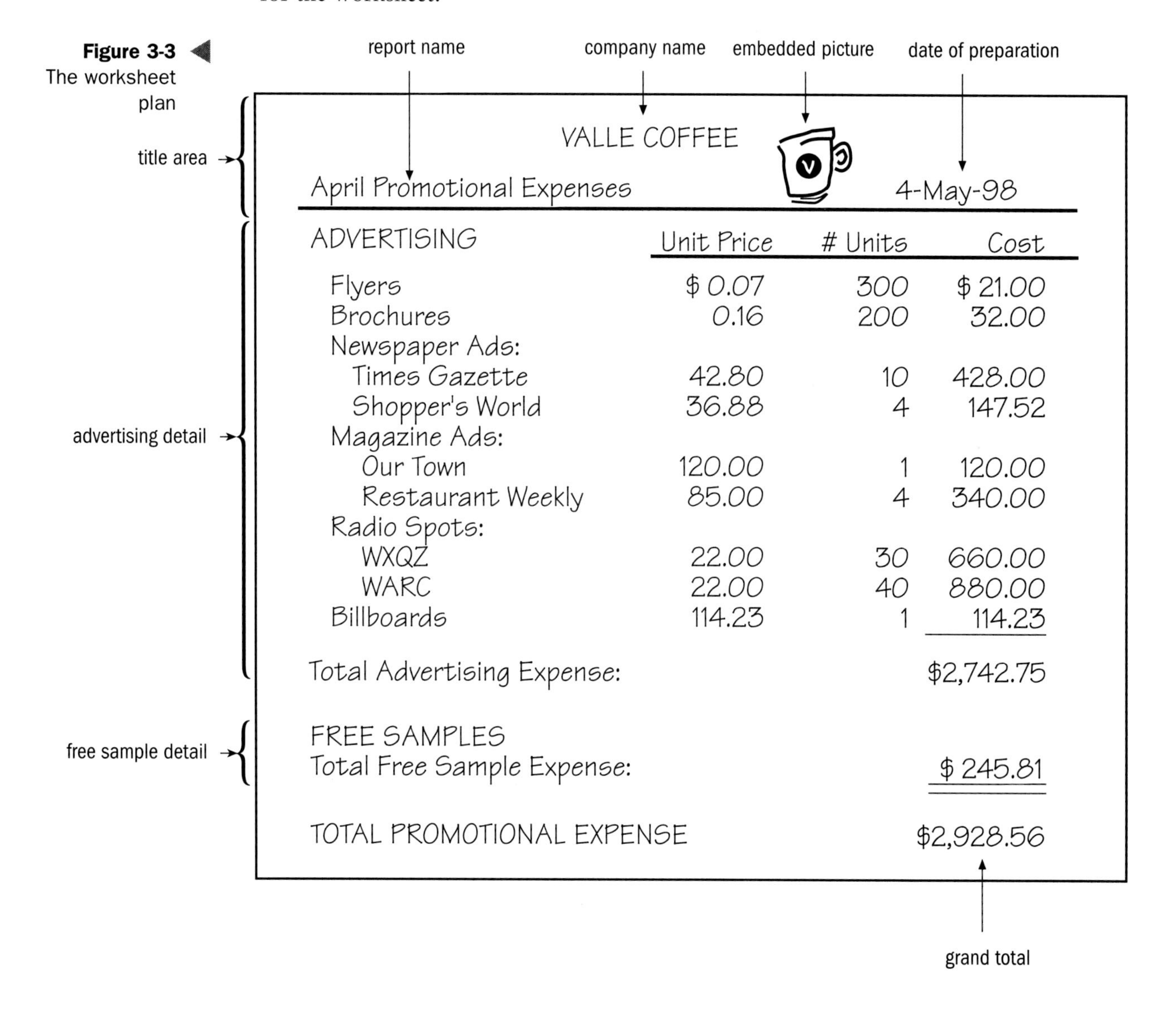

Starting a New Excel Workbook

Having planned the worksheet, you are now ready to enter the worksheet data. First, you must start a new Excel workbook.

To start a new Excel workbook:

1. Start Windows 95 and make sure the Office Shortcut Bar is displayed.

   TROUBLE? If you don't see the Office Shortcut Bar, click the Start button on the taskbar, point to Programs, then click Microsoft Office Shortcut Bar. If you don't see the Microsoft Office Shortcut Bar option on the Programs menu, ask your instructor or technical support person for assistance.

2. Insert your Student Disk in the disk drive.
3. Click the **Start a New Document** button on the Office Shortcut Bar. The New dialog box opens.
4. If necessary, click the **General** tab to make it the active tab in the New dialog box.
5. Click the **Blank Workbook** icon.
6. Click the **OK** button. The Excel window opens.
7. Make sure both the Excel program window and the workbook window are maximized. Your screen should look like Figure 3-4.

Figure 3-4 The Excel window

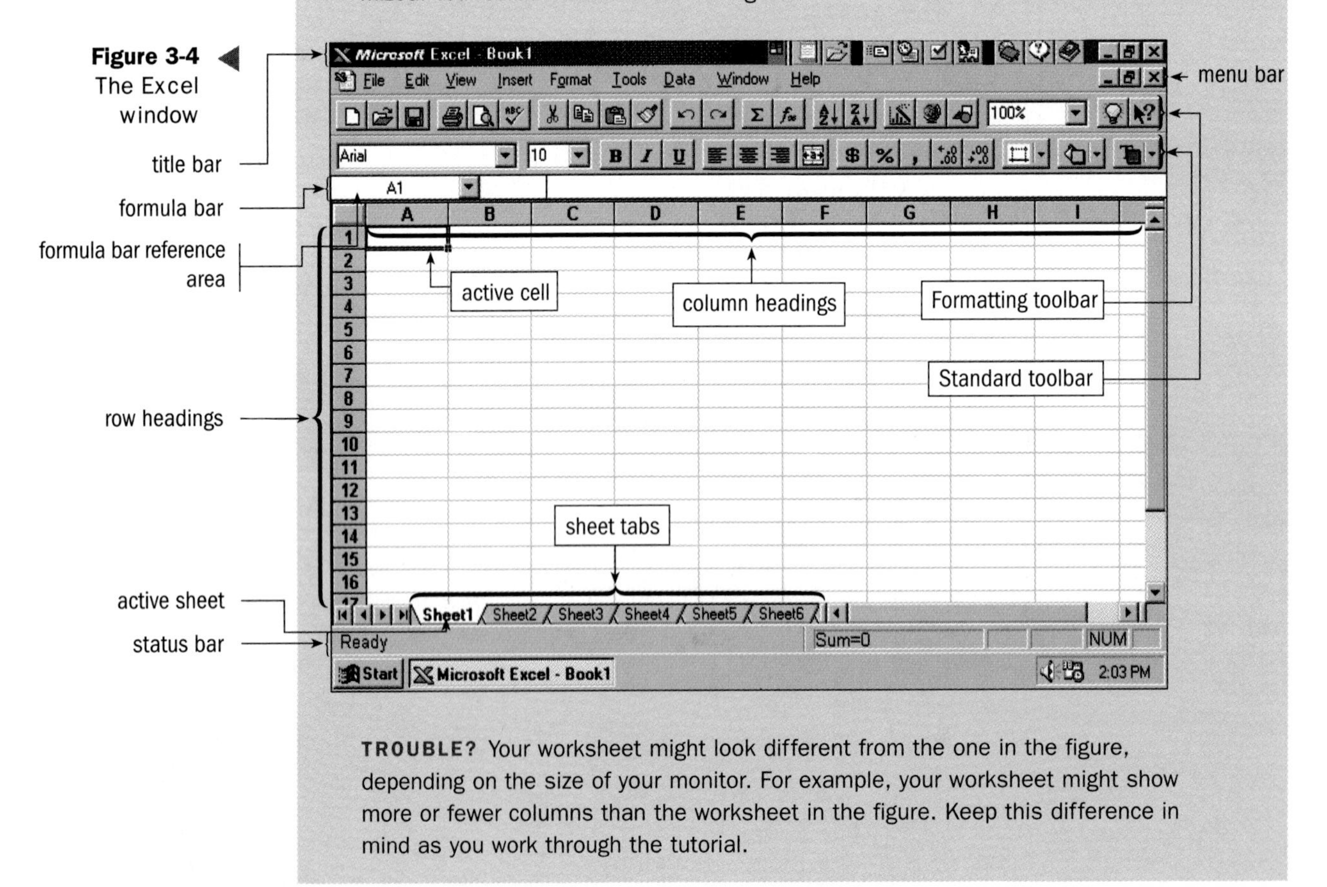

   TROUBLE? Your worksheet might look different from the one in the figure, depending on the size of your monitor. For example, your worksheet might show more or fewer columns than the worksheet in the figure. Keep this difference in mind as you work through the tutorial.

The Excel Window

The Excel window is consistent with the layout of other Office 95 programs, and it contains many common features, such as the title bar, menu bar, scroll bars, and taskbar. Carefully read through Figure 3-5 and note the location of the corresponding component on the Excel window in Figure 3-4.

Figure 3-5
Excel window components and their functions

Screen Component	Function
Title bar	Identifies the program (Microsoft Excel) and the workbook name (for example, Book1).
Menu bar	Each word on the menu bar is the name of a menu you can open to display a list of commands and options. The menu names are identical to those found on the menu bar in Word.
Standard toolbar	Provides shortcuts to common Excel commands. The left and right sides of this toolbar are identical in appearance and purpose to the Word Standard toolbar.
Formatting toolbar	Provides shortcuts to often used Excel formatting options.
Formula bar and reference area	The reference area at the left identifies the active cell. The remainder of the formula bar displays data as you enter or edit it.
Column headings	Letters that uniquely identify the columns in the worksheet. For example, column D includes every cell that appears below the "D" heading. The first 26 columns of a worksheet have column headings "A" through "Z." If more than 26 columns are used, additional columns are automatically headed "AA," "AB," and so on. Excel allows a maximum of 256 columns; the 256th column, if used, would be labeled "IV."
Active cell	The cell currently being worked on or ready to be worked on.
Row headings	Numbers that uniquely identify the rows in a worksheet. Excel allows a maximum of 16,384 rows in a worksheet.
Sheet tabs	Identify the worksheets in a workbook. Use the sheet tabs to move quickly from one worksheet to another in the open workbook.
Active sheet	The worksheet currently visible in the Excel window.
Status bar	Left side displays a brief description of the current command or task in progress. Center section displays the sum of the numeric values (if any) in the selected cells when more than one cell is selected. Right side displays the status of the Caps Lock and Num Lock keys.

"Book1" is the default name for the workbook document. You can change the name when you save the workbook. An Excel workbook consists of one or more worksheets. The default names for these worksheets are "Sheet1," "Sheet2," and so on. The **active sheet** is the worksheet you are currently working on in the Excel window. The sheet tab for the active sheet is white and the sheet name is bold; sheet tabs for all the other worksheets are gray. The maximum number of worksheets in a workbook is 255; however, the available memory on your computer might prevent you from creating that many worksheets.

A **cell** is the rectangular box at the intersection of a column and a row. A cell is identified by its **cell reference**, which consists of the cell's column heading followed by its row number. For example, the cell located in the second row under the column headed by "D" has the cell reference D2. In Figure 3-4, a dark black border surrounds cell A1, which indicates that it is the active cell. The **active cell** (or cells) is the currently selected cell (or cells) in which you are working. Notice that A1, the cell reference for the active cell, appears in the reference area of the formula bar.

Renaming a Worksheet

The active worksheet is currently named "Sheet1." When creating Valle Coffee workbooks, Kim always renames each Excel worksheet with a meaningful name that describes or indicates the purpose of the worksheet. Descriptive names are especially helpful when you are managing a workbook with many worksheets.

An Excel worksheet name can contain up to 31 characters. Special characters, numbers, blanks, and capital letters are all allowed. Kim wants you to rename the worksheet to describe its contents. You'll use the shortcut menu to name this worksheet "Promotional Expenses - April."

To rename the worksheet:

1. Right-click the **Sheet1** tab. The shortcut menu opens.
2. Click **Rename**. The Rename Sheet dialog box opens.
3. Type **Promotional Expenses - April**.
4. Click the **OK** button to close the Rename Sheet dialog box. The new sheet name appears in the active sheet tab, which has expanded to accommodate the longer name. See Figure 3-6.

Figure 3-6 Renamed worksheet

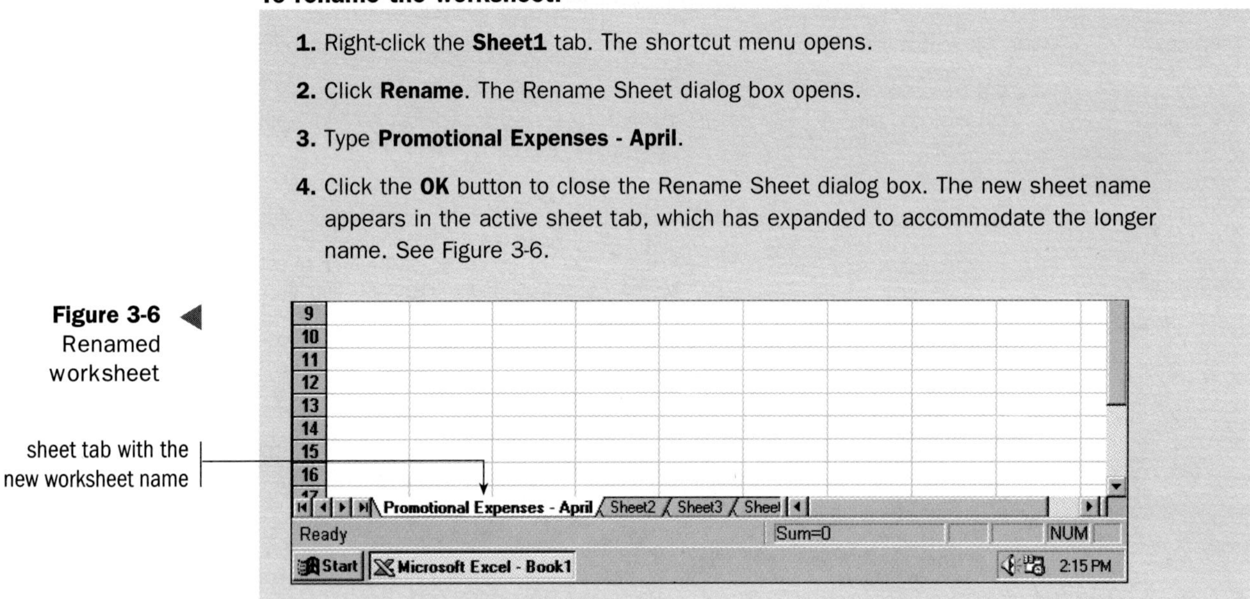

Entering and Correcting Labels

You are now ready to begin building the worksheet you have planned. As shown in Figure 3-3, the data you need to enter includes numeric values and dates, labels to identify and clarify parts of the worksheet, and formulas for calculations. Typically, you enter all the labels first; then, using the labels as a guide, you enter the values and formulas.

When entering data in a cell, you do not have to indicate if the data is a label, as opposed to a number or a date. Excel examines the data and determines its type. If a value is not a legitimate number or a date, Excel considers the data to be a **label**, which is also called text.

A value is considered to be a date if it consists only of digits, slashes or dashes, or a valid month name or abbreviation, *and* if it constitutes a valid date. Excel would recognize the following input values as dates: 3-4-98; 12/17/1998; Jan 13, 1955; March 1970; and May 30. The following are not valid dates and would be considered labels: 3-32-98; 2/3/4/98; 17/22/98; and Murch 5.

Excel interprets a value entered in a cell as a number if it contains only characters in the following set: 0 1 2 3 4 5 6 7 8 9 + - ( ) , . $ % E e. However, a value that contains only these characters but that is not a legitimate number would be considered text. For example, the following entries are not legitimate numbers and, therefore, would be considered labels: 1,23,456; 98.76.5; 55.123%4; 12+78-5; and 55$31.2.

Excel automatically aligns a label at the left side of the cell. A label that is too long to fit in the cell will spill over into the cells to the right if those cells are empty; otherwise, Excel will display as much of the label as fits in the cell. An **empty cell** is one that contains no data. A cell that contains a space inserted with the spacebar is *not* empty, even though it appears to be empty.

You'll begin by entering the worksheet title labels.

To enter the worksheet title labels:

1. Click cell **B2** to make it the active cell.
2. Type **VALLE COFFEE** then press the **Enter** key. The company name appears in cell B2 and spills over into cell C2. Cell B3 is now the active cell.

   TROUBLE? If you entered the label in the wrong cell, click the Undo button on the Standard toolbar, then repeat Steps 1 and 2.

   TROUBLE? If B3 is not the active cell, you need to change one of the edit options on your computer. Click Tools on the menu bar, click Options, then click the Edit tab in the Options dialog box. If the box next to the Move Selection after Enter option does not contain a check mark, click the box to activate the option. If the text box after Direction: does not display "Down," click the text box down arrow, then click Down. This setting will move the active cell down one cell below the cell in which you enter data. Then click the OK button to close the Options dialog box.
3. Click cell **A4**, then type **April Promotional Expenses** and press the **Enter** key. The report title spills over into cells B4 and C4. See Figure 3-7.

Figure 3-7 Entering labels

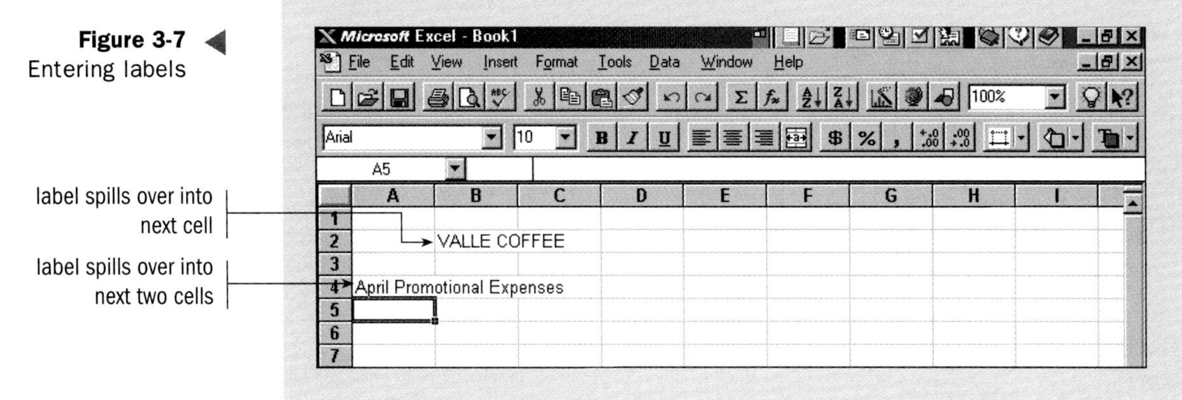

You'll continue to enter labels, following your worksheet plan. To practice correcting mistakes, you'll make a few intentional errors.

To correct a mistake before you have pressed the Enter key, you simply press the Backspace key as many times as necessary to back up and delete the incorrect characters.

To correct a mistake as you are typing:

1. Click cell **A7** to make it the active cell.
2. Type **ADVIS** to make an intentional error, *but don't press the Enter key.*
3. Press the **Backspace** key twice to delete the "S" and the "I."
4. Type **ERTISING** and press the **Enter** key to complete the ADVERTISING label.

You cannot use the Backspace key to correct the contents of a cell after you have completed the entry and pressed the Enter key. Instead, you must edit the cell contents in Edit mode using one of two techniques: editing within the formula bar or editing within the cell itself.

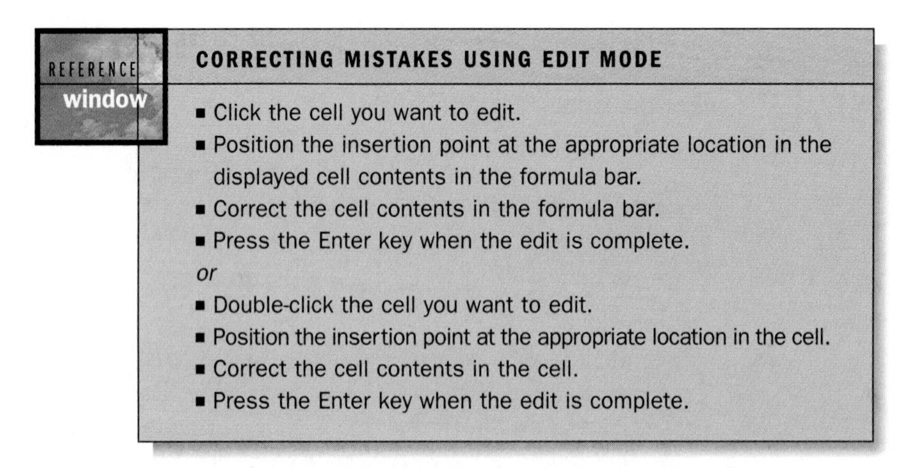

REFERENCE window

CORRECTING MISTAKES USING EDIT MODE

- Click the cell you want to edit.
- Position the insertion point at the appropriate location in the displayed cell contents in the formula bar.
- Correct the cell contents in the formula bar.
- Press the Enter key when the edit is complete.

or

- Double-click the cell you want to edit.
- Position the insertion point at the appropriate location in the cell.
- Correct the cell contents in the cell.
- Press the Enter key when the edit is complete.

You'll make two intentional errors in the next label you enter and then correct the errors in Edit mode. You'll correct the first error by editing the cell contents in the formula bar.

To edit cell contents using the formula bar:

1. Click cell **C7** to make it the active cell.
2. Type **Unfit Pride** then press the **Enter** key.
3. Click cell **C7** to make it the active cell again.
4. Move the mouse pointer into the formula bar and position it over the word "Unfit." The pointer changes to I when it enters the formula bar.
5. Position the insertion point by placing the pointer between the "n" and the "f" in "Unfit" then clicking the mouse button. The status bar now displays the word "Edit," indicating that you are in Edit mode. See Figure 3-8.

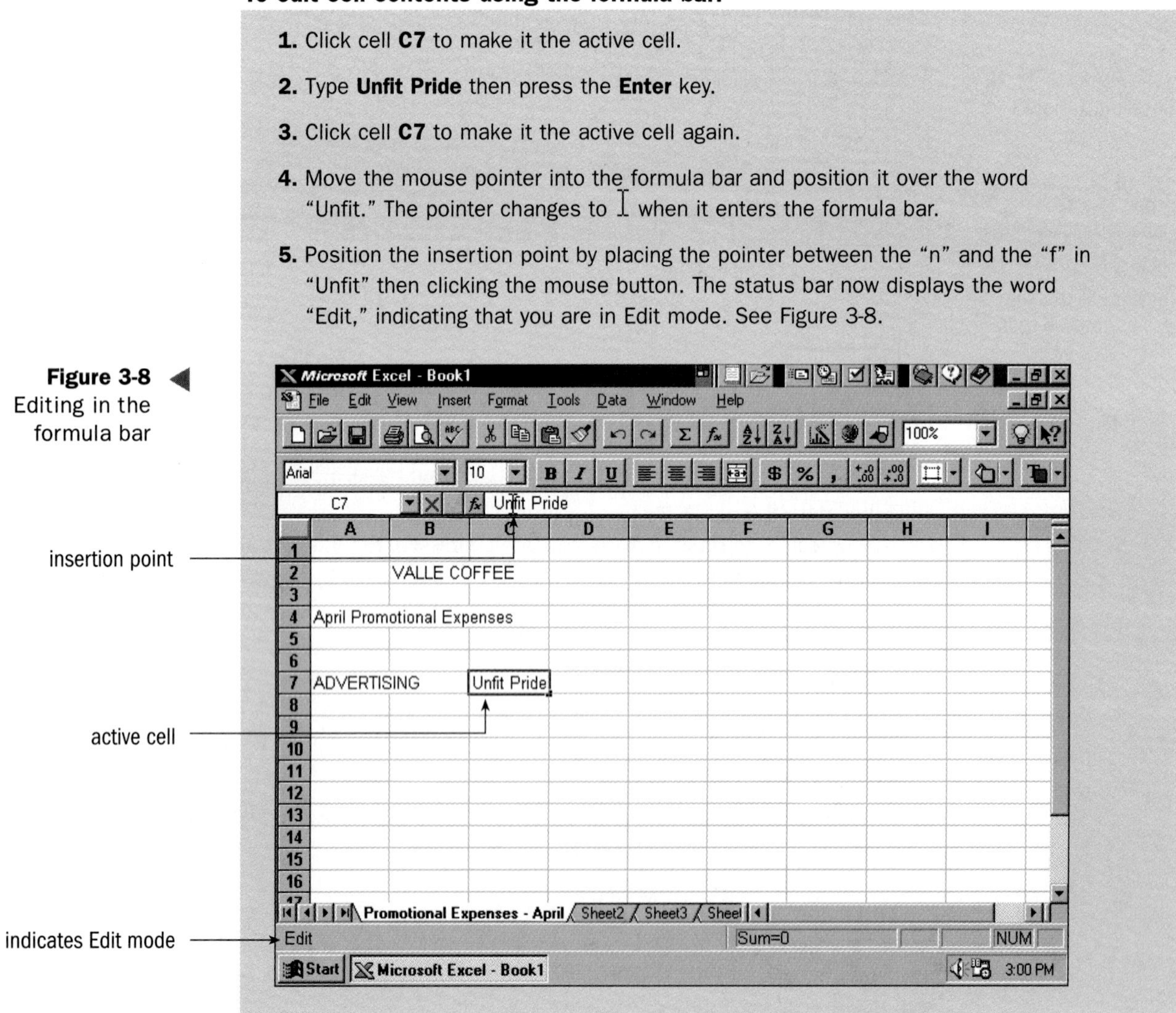

Figure 3-8 Editing in the formula bar

6. Press the **Delete** key to delete the "f." Both cell C7 and the displayed cell contents in the formula bar now contain the text "Unit Pride."
7. Press the **Enter** key to complete the edit.

Next, you'll correct the second error by editing the contents in the cell itself.

To edit cell contents in the cell:

1. Double-click cell **C7**. The pointer changes to I and the status bar displays the word "Edit," indicating that you are in Edit mode.
2. Position the insertion point by placing the pointer between the "i" and the "d" in "Pride" then clicking the mouse button. See Figure 3-9.

Figure 3-9 Editing within a cell

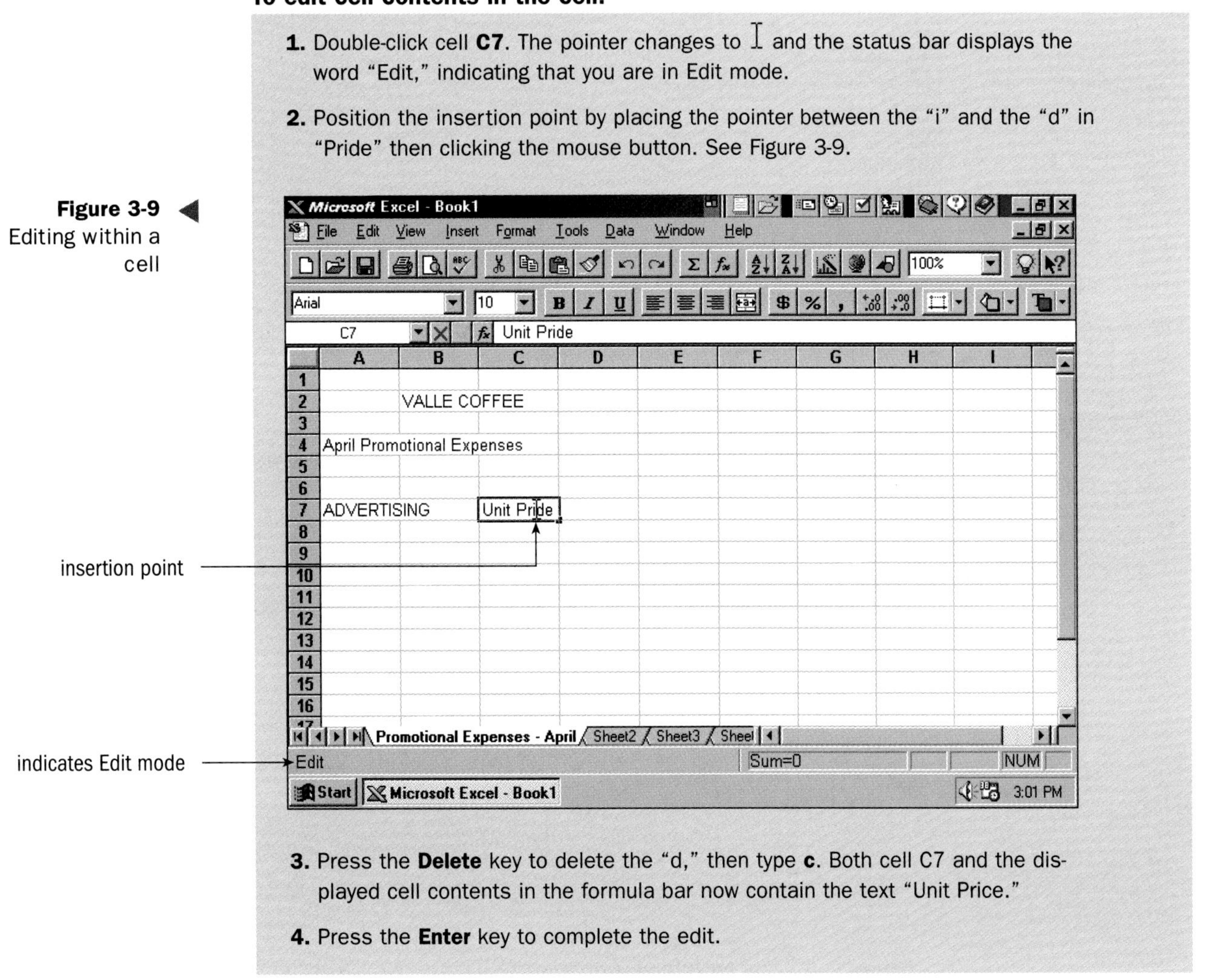

3. Press the **Delete** key to delete the "d," then type **c**. Both cell C7 and the displayed cell contents in the formula bar now contain the text "Unit Price."
4. Press the **Enter** key to complete the edit.

Next, you'll enter several more of the planned labels into your worksheet. Figure 3-10 shows how your worksheet will look after you've entered the advertising expense labels.

Figure 3-10 Advertising expense labels entered

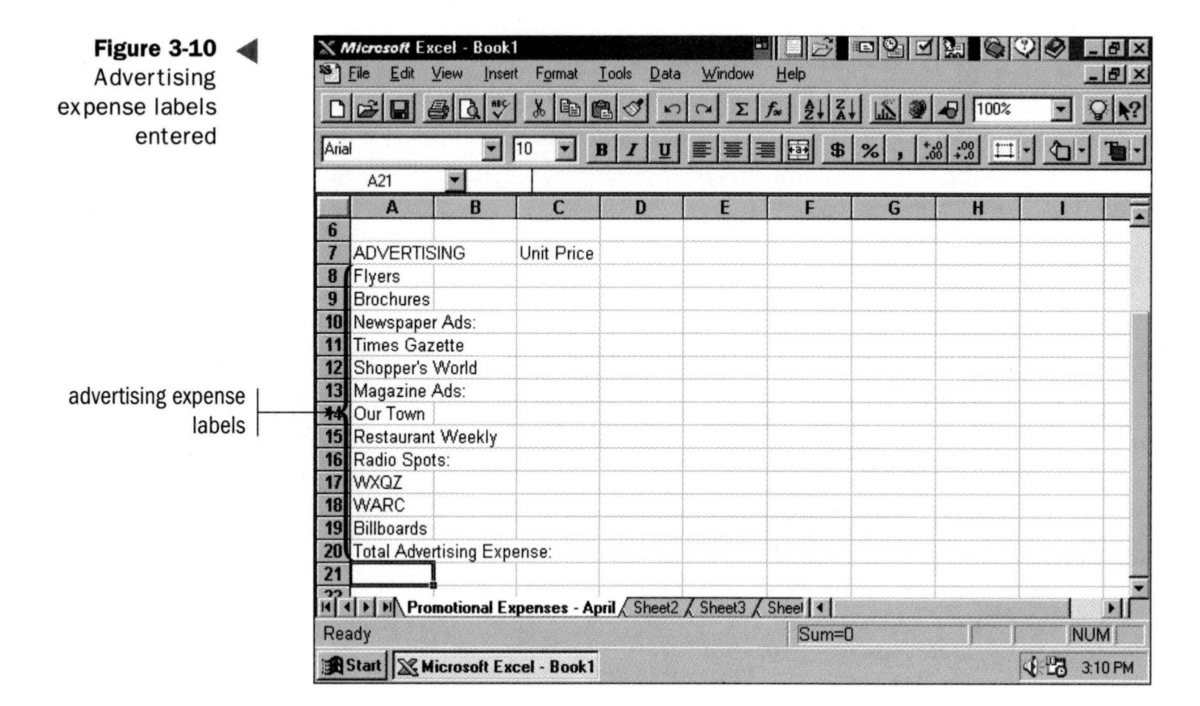

To enter the advertising expense labels:

1. Click cell **A8**, type **Flyers**, then press the **Enter** key to complete the entry and move to cell A9.
2. Type **Brochures** then press the **Enter** key to complete the entry and move to cell A10.
3. Type **Newspaper Ads:** then press the **Enter** key to complete the entry and move to cell A11.
4. Type **Times Gazette** then press the **Enter** key.
5. Type **Shopper's World** then press the **Enter** key.
6. Refer to Figure 3-10 and enter the rest of the labels in cells A13 through A20, as shown.

   TROUBLE? If any cell does not contain the correct label, edit the cell using either of the Edit mode methods to correct the entry.

Before you begin entering numbers, you'll enter the remaining two column headings in row 7.

To complete entry of the column labels:

1. Click cell **D7**, type **# Units** then press the **Enter** key.
2. Click cell **E7**, type **Cost** then press the **Enter** key.

You have now entered all the labels for the title area and the advertising detail area of your worksheet. Before you enter the remaining values in the worksheet, you'll learn how to navigate through a worksheet.

Navigating a Worksheet

You have entered labels in rows 2 and 20, as well as most of the rows in between; however, the worksheet window is not large enough to display your entire worksheet at one time. To move to or view a cell that isn't visible in the worksheet window, you need to be able to **navigate**, or move around, the worksheet.

The vertical and horizontal scroll bars provide one method of navigation. Using the vertical scroll bar, you can move the worksheet display up or down one row at a time by clicking the up or down arrow, or one full screen at a time by clicking above or below the scroll box in the vertical scroll bar. You can also drag the scroll box in the vertical scroll bar to move through the rows of the worksheet; when you do, the displayed ScrollTip shows the current row number as you scroll. You use the horizontal scroll bar to move the display left or right one column or one screen at a time. You can drag the scroll box in the horizontal scroll bar to move through the columns of the worksheet; when you do, the displayed ScrollTip shows the current column letter as you scroll. Using a scroll bar changes only what is displayed in the worksheet window; it does not change the active cell.

You can also use keyboard techniques to navigate the worksheet. Unlike the scroll bars, the keyboard navigation techniques change the active cell, but might not change which cells are displayed in the worksheet window. Figure 3-11 shows the keys you can use to change the active cell and navigate the worksheet.

Figure 3-11 Keyboard navigation techniques

Press this key or key combination:	To move:
↑	Up one cell
↓	Down one cell
←	Left one cell
→	Right one cell
Page Up	Up one full screen
Page Down	Down one full screen
Alt + Page Up	Left one full screen
Alt + Page Down	Right one full screen
Ctrl + Home	To cell A1
Home	To column A in the current row

Excel provides a third technique for rapid navigation of your worksheet. You can move directly to any cell in a worksheet by typing the cell's reference in the reference area. This technique also changes the active cell. If the cell to which you want to move is not currently visible in the worksheet window, moving directly to that cell also changes which cells are displayed in the worksheet window.

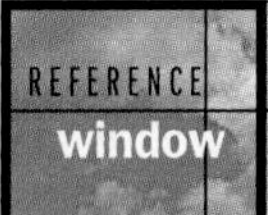

MOVING TO A CELL USING THE CELL REFERENCE

- Click the current cell reference in the reference area.
- Type the cell reference of the cell you want to move to, then press the Enter key.

Next, you'll try some of the keyboard navigation techniques and also move directly to a cell using its cell reference.

To navigate the worksheet:

1. If the active cell is not E8, click cell **E8**.
2. Press the → key. The active cell is now F8.
3. Press the ↑ key. F7 becomes the active cell.
4. Press the **Page Down** key. The display moves down one screen, changing the active cell.
5. Press the **Page Up** key. The display moves up one screen, and cell F7 is again the active cell.
6. Press the **Home** key. Cell A7 is now the active cell.
7. Press **Ctrl + Home**. The display moves up so that row 1 is visible, and cell A1 is now the active cell.
8. Click the reference area at the left side of the formula bar. The reference A1, which identifies the active cell, is highlighted.
9. Type **D20** then press the **Enter** key. The display shifts down so that row 20 is visible, and cell D20 is now the active cell.

Now that you know how to navigate the worksheet, you'll continue with the second step of the worksheet development process—entering the number and date values.

Entering and Correcting Numbers and Dates

So far you have entered only labels in your Excel worksheet. Every cell into which you entered data contains at least one character not allowed in a number or date value; therefore, Excel considers them to be labels, left-aligns the text of the labels, and allows them to spill over into empty cells to the right, if necessary.

In contrast, the default display for number and date values is right-justified within the cell. Also, numbers and dates are not allowed to spill over into other cells.

The process for entering and correcting numbers and dates is similar to that for entering and correcting labels. First, you click the cell in which you want to enter a number or date, then you enter the value. You can use the Backspace key to correct errors before the entry is complete, and you can use Edit mode to correct errors after the entry is complete.

Working with Numbers

As noted earlier, Excel automatically determines that an entry is a number if it contains only valid characters and is a legitimate number.

Now you'll enter the numbers in the Unit Price column of the worksheet.

To enter the unit prices:

1. Click cell **C8**, type **.07** then press the **Enter** key. Excel determines that you entered a number and displays the number as "0.07" at the right side of the cell. (Don't worry about the leading zero, the number of displayed decimal places, or the lack of a dollar sign for now. You will format this and other unit prices later in this tutorial.)
2. Type **.16** then press the **Enter** key. Cell C10 is now the active cell.
3. Press the **Enter** key to make cell C11 the active cell.
4. Type **42.8** then press the **Enter** key.
5. Type **36.88**, press the **Enter** key, then press the **Enter** key again. Cell C14 is now the active cell.
6. Type **120** then press the **Enter** key.
7. Type **85**, press the **Enter** key, then press the **Enter** key again. Cell C17 is now the active cell.
8. Type **22**, press the **Enter** key, type **22**, then press the **Enter** key.
9. Type **114.23** then press the **Enter** key. Your screen should now look like Figure 3-12.

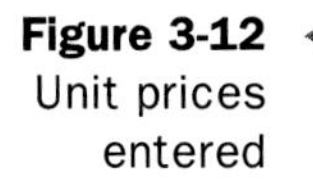

Figure 3-12
Unit prices entered

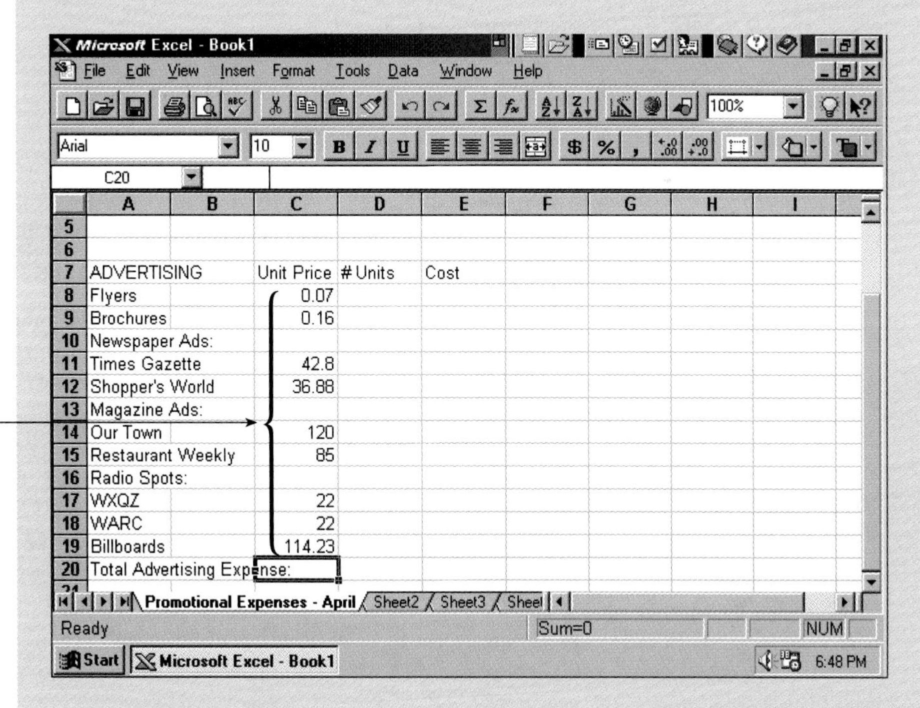

TROUBLE? If any cell value in your worksheet does not match the corresponding cell in Figure 3-12, edit the cell to change it to the correct value.

Next, you'll enter the values in the # Units column on the worksheet.

To enter the values in the # Units column:

1. Refer to Figure 3-13 and enter the values shown. Press the Enter key twice where necessary to leave a cell blank and move to the next cell.

Figure 3-13 Values entered in the # Units column

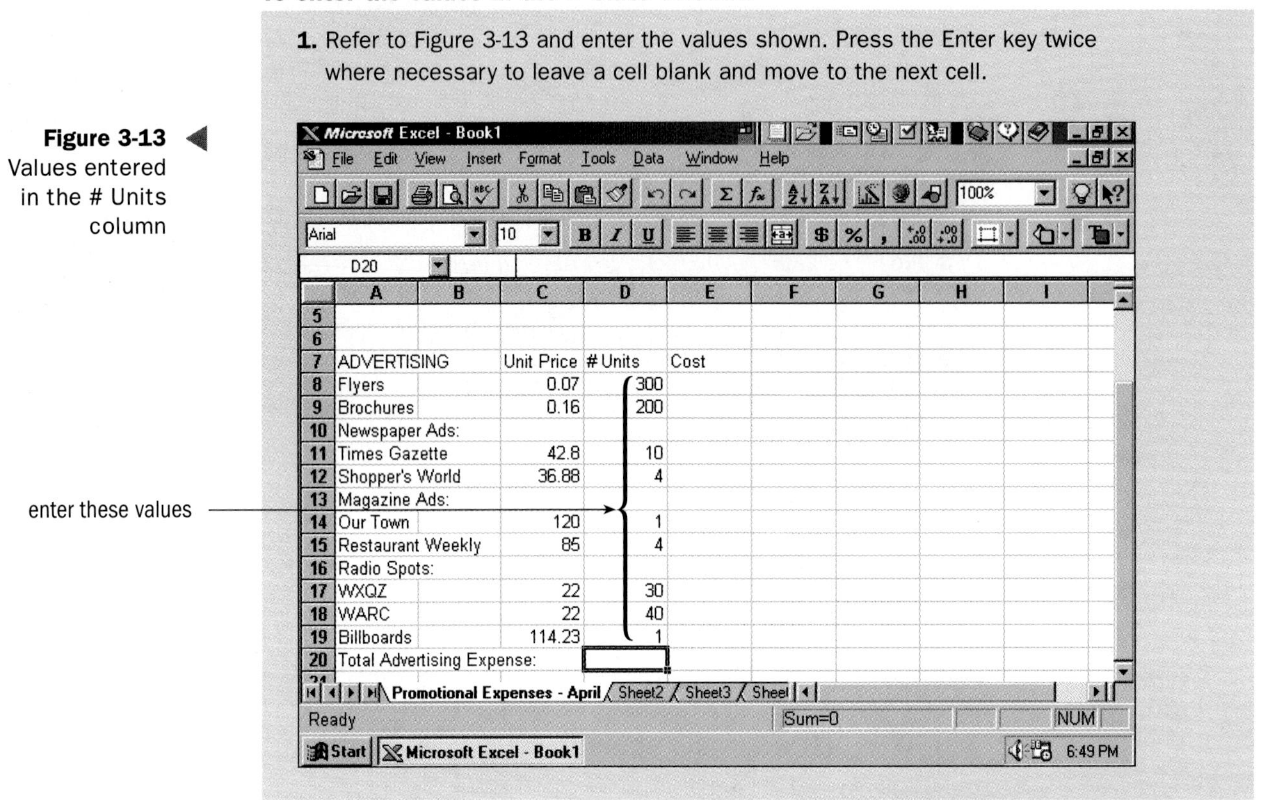

Working with Dates

When you enter a value in a cell, Excel determines if it is a valid date and, if so, stores and treats that value as a date. Excel can recognize a date input in any of several different forms, including 3/5/98, 03/05/98, 5-Mar-98, 05-Mar-98, and March 5, 1998. Excel stores all dates as serial dates, regardless of how they're entered. A **serial date** is the number of days since January 1, 1900. Storing dates as serial dates offers several advantages: Excel can sort them easily, determine the number of days between any two serial dates by simply subtracting one from the other, and quickly convert a serial date to any display format you want. For example, you might enter a date as 6/4/98. Excel would store that date internally as the serial date 35,950. You could then instruct Excel to display the date as June 4, 1998.

Your worksheet plan includes only one date, which appears in the worksheet title area. You'll enter and display the date in a simple month/day/year format.

To enter the date:

1. Navigate your worksheet so that cell E4 is visible, then click cell **E4** to make it the active cell.

2. Type **5/4/98** then press the **Enter** key. Excel recognizes this entry as a valid date and displays the date right-justified in the cell, in the same format in which you entered it.

Now that you've entered the labels, numbers, and a date in your worksheet, you need to save the workbook to your Student Disk.

Saving a New Workbook

You save a new workbook in the same way that you save any Office 95 document for the first time—you use the Save button on the Standard toolbar, then specify a name and location for the document. You'll save the current workbook as Promo Expense Report in the Tutorial.03 folder of your Student Disk.

To save the new workbook:

1. Make sure your Student Disk is in the disk drive.
2. Click the **Save** button on the Standard toolbar. Excel opens the Save As dialog box. "Book1" is highlighted in the File name text box.
3. Type **Promo Expense Report**. *Do not press the Enter key.*
4. Click the **Save in** list arrow, click the drive containing your Student Disk, click **Tutorial.03**, then click the **Open** button.
5. Click the **Save** button. Excel saves the workbook on your Student Disk and closes the Save As dialog box. The new workbook name, Promo Expense Report, is now displayed in the Excel title bar.

You'll continue with the data entry process by entering the formulas in your worksheet to perform the necessary calculations.

Entering and Correcting Formulas

According to your worksheet plan, the total cost of the flyers will be calculated as the product of the unit price times the number of flyers. That product will be displayed in your worksheet in cell E8. You could determine the product yourself by multiplying the value in cell C8 by the value in cell D8 (0.07 times 300), and then entering the result, 21, as a value in cell E8. By doing so, however, you would not be taking advantage of one of Excel's most powerful features: its ability to perform calculations. Instead, you should use an Excel formula to determine the product and store the result in cell E8.

Formulas and Functions

A **formula** specifies a calculation you want Excel to perform. An Excel formula always begins with an equal sign (=). Most often, a formula contains one or more **arithmetic operators**, such as +, –, or /. Formulas can also contain cell references and numbers. For example, the formula =B2/5 instructs Excel to divide the contents of cell B2 by 5. Other examples of formulas include =G3+G4 and =A3+E6 * 100. Figure 3-14 shows examples of the numbers, arithmetic operators, and cell references you can use in a formula.

Figure 3-14 Examples of numbers, operators, and cell references used in formulas

Formula Component	Examples	Description
Number	15 -3.6 1,256	any legitimate number value
Arithmetic operator	+ – * / ^ %	addition operator subtraction operator multiplication operator division operator exponentiation operator percentage operator
Cell reference	A1 F8	reference to a cell
	(B4:B7)	reference to the range of cells including cells B4, B5, B6, and B7
	(C:C)	reference to the entire column C
	(D:E)	reference to the entire columns D and E
	(2:2)	reference to the entire row 2
	(4:6)	reference to the entire rows 4, 5, and 6

If a formula contains more than one arithmetic operator, Excel performs the calculations in the standard order of precedence of the operators. Exponentiation has the highest rank, followed by multiplication and division, which share the next order of precedence, and then subtraction and addition. For example, because multiplication has precedence over addition, in the formula =A3+E6*100, the contents of cell E6 are multiplied by 100 first; then the contents of cell A3 are added to the product. Figure 3-15 shows the order of operations for the arithmetic operators.

Figure 3-15 Order of operations

Order	Operator	Description
1.	^	exponentiation
2.	* or /	multiplication or division
3.	+ or –	addition or subtraction

When a formula contains more than one operator with the same order of precedence, Excel performs those operations from left to right. Thus, in the formula =5*A6/9, Excel first multiplies 5 times the contents of cell A6, then divides that result by 9. You can enter parentheses in a formula to make it easier to understand or to change the order of operation. Excel always performs any calculations contained in parentheses first. In the formula =A3+E6*100, the multiplication is performed before the addition. If instead you wanted the formula to multiply 100 times the sum of A3 and E6, you would enter the formula as =(A3+E6)*100.

You can include blank spaces before and after operators in a formula to improve readability. The formula =G3+G4 is equivalent to =G3 + G4. Blank spaces have no effect on a formula. That is, the formula =A1*A2 + 50 is the same as the formula =A1 * A2+50, even though the spacing might lead you to interpret them differently.

Entering Arithmetic Formulas

You enter a formula in the cell in which you want the result displayed. Formula *results*—not the formulas themselves—are always displayed in cells. The formula bar displays the formula for the active cell (if that cell contains a formula).

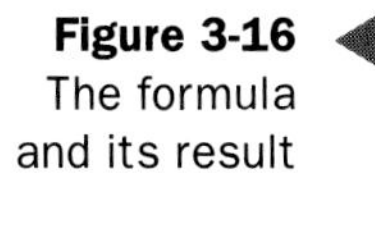

ENTERING A FORMULA

- Click the cell where you want the result to appear.
- Type = and then type the rest of the formula.
- For formulas containing cell references, type the cell reference or use the mouse to point to the cell or cells.
- Press the Enter key when the formula is complete.

As with other types of cell values, you can correct formulas during entry by backspacing and retyping. After entering a formula, you can correct it in Edit mode, either by correcting the formula in the formula bar or double-clicking the cell and correcting the formula in the cell.

First you'll enter the formulas for the flyer cost and brochure cost in cells E8 and E9.

To enter the formulas for flyer and brochure costs:

1. Click cell **E8** to make it the active cell.
2. Type **=C8*D8** then press the **Enter** key. Excel performs the calculation and displays the result in cell E8. The formula itself is no longer visible.
3. Click cell **E8** again to make it the active cell. Your screen should now look like Figure 3-16. Notice that the formula appears in the formula bar.

Figure 3-16 The formula and its result

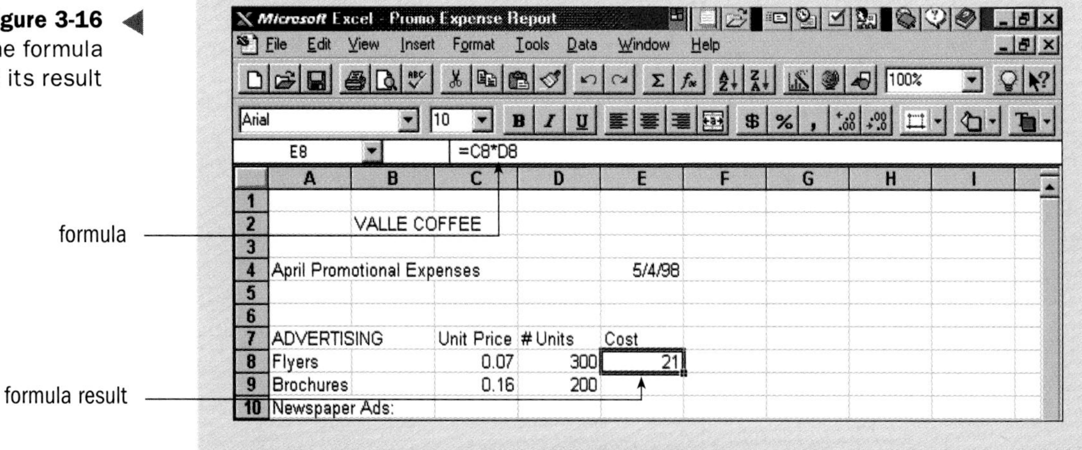

TROUBLE? If the value displayed in cell E8 is not 21, check to see that you entered the formula correctly. If the formula is incorrect, edit it in the formula bar. If the formula is correct, check the values in cells C8 and D8, which should be 0.07 and 300, respectively. Correct any incorrect value.

4. Press the ↓ key to make cell E9 the active cell.
5. Type **=C9*D9** then press the **Enter** key. The result 32 appears in cell E9.

You can enter a cell reference in a formula by typing the cell reference, as you did in the previous steps. Alternatively, you can use the mouse to point to a cell and click it to include its reference in a formula. You'll use this point-and-click technique to enter the appropriate formulas in cells E11 and E12.

To enter formulas using the point-and-click technique for cell references:

1. Click cell **E11** to make it the active cell.
2. Type **=**. The = tells Excel that you are entering a formula.
3. Position the pointer over cell C11, then click the mouse button. Excel enters the cell reference in the formula. Your screen should now look like Figure 3-17.

Figure 3-17 ◀ Entering a formula cell reference by pointing and clicking

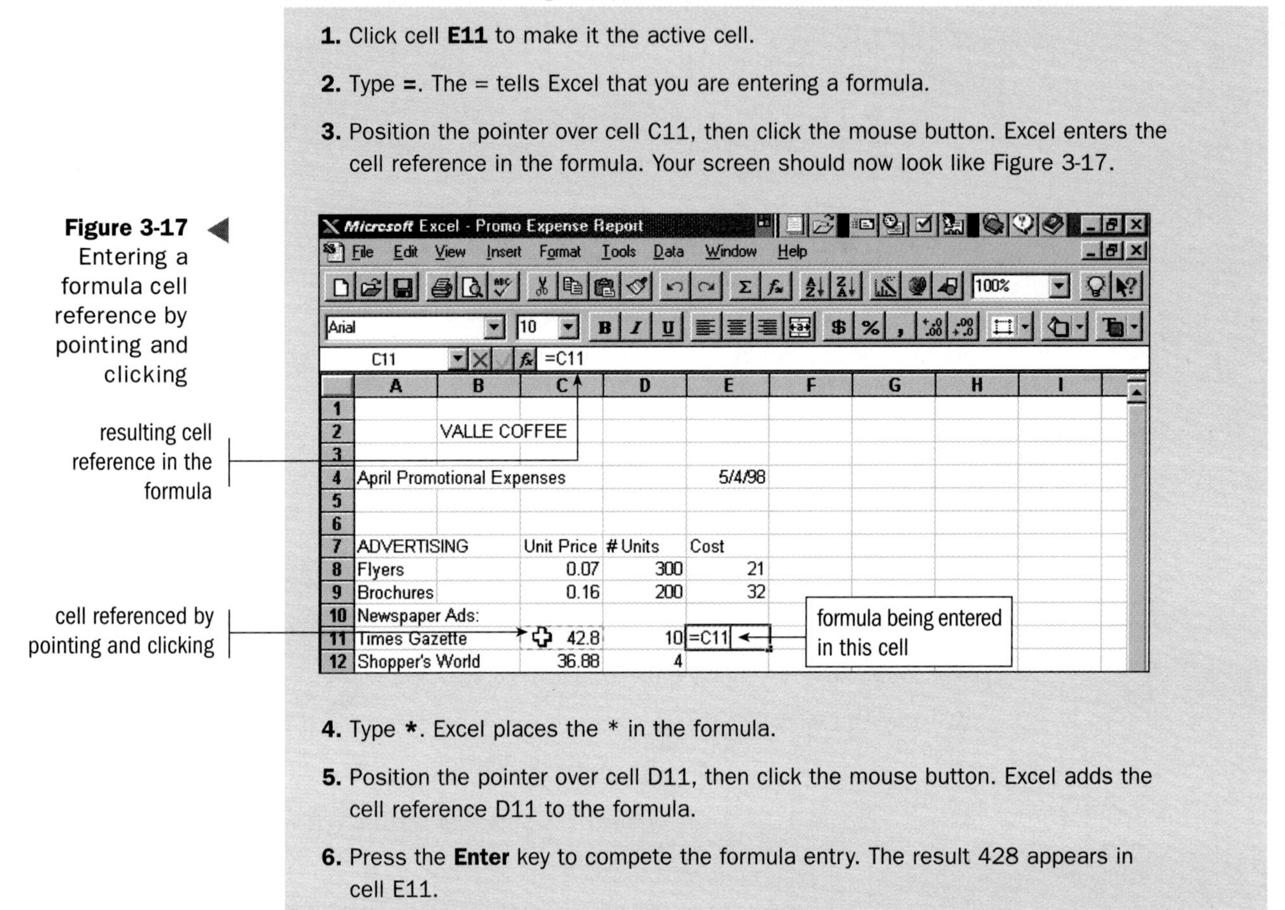

4. Type *****. Excel places the * in the formula.
5. Position the pointer over cell D11, then click the mouse button. Excel adds the cell reference D11 to the formula.
6. Press the **Enter** key to compete the formula entry. The result 428 appears in cell E11.
7. Repeat Steps 2 through 6 to enter the formula for Shopper's World cost in cell E12, but point and click at cells C12 and D12 instead of C11 and D11. The resulting formula will be =C12*D12. The result 147.52 appears in cell E12.

In the formulas for the cost of the various advertising classifications, each cost is the product of the corresponding unit price and number of units. Rather than enter the remaining formulas one at a time, you can copy and paste the formula from one cell to the others.

Copying and Pasting Formulas

In Excel, you can duplicate the contents of a cell or range of cells by making a copy of the cell or range and then pasting the copy into one or more locations in the same worksheet, another worksheet, or another workbook.

When you copy a cell or range of cells, the copied material is placed on the Clipboard and remains there until it is replaced by a subsequent copy or cut operation. In most Office 95 programs, you can access the Clipboard contents at any time. In Excel, however, you must *immediately* paste the Clipboard contents to a new location; once you perform any other operation, the Clipboard contents are no longer accessible.

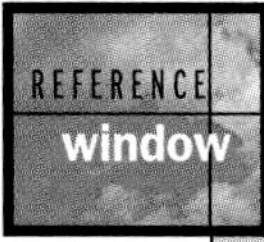

COPYING AND PASTING A CELL OR RANGE OF CELLS

- Select the cell or cells to be copied.
- With the pointer in the highlighted cells, right-click to display the shortcut menu, then click Copy (or click the Copy button on the Standard toolbar).
- Select the cell or the first cell in the range into which you want to paste the copy.
- With the pointer in the highlighted cells, right-click to display the shortcut menu, then click Paste (or click the Paste button on the Standard toolbar).
- Press the Enter key to end the operation.

You can copy labels, numbers, dates, or formulas. Because formulas almost always contain cell references, copying formulas is more complex than copying other types of cells contents. Cell references are either relative or absolute. A simple cell reference, such as D8 or C12, is called a **relative reference** because its location is relative to the cell containing the formula. When a formula with a relative cell reference is copied, the relative cell reference will be adjusted automatically to reflect the change in location. All the cell references in this worksheet are relative references. In contrast, an **absolute reference** is a reference that always points to a fixed location; it does not change when you copy the formula containing the absolute reference. (You will learn about absolute references in a later tutorial.)

You need to copy the formula in cell E12 and then paste it into cell E14. The formula in cell E12 is =C12*D12. When you paste that formula into cell E14, Excel will automatically adjust the two relative cell references from row 12 to row 14. The resulting formula in cell E14 will be =C14*D14, which is the formula you want in cell E14.

To copy the formula in cell E12 and paste it in other cells:

1. Click cell **E12** to make it the active cell.
2. Right-click to display the shortcut menu, then click **Copy**. A moving dashed line surrounds cell E12, indicating that its formula has been copied and is available to be pasted into other cells.
3. Click cell **E14** to make it the active cell.
4. Right-click to display the shortcut menu, then click **Paste**. Excel adjusts the formula and pastes it into cell E14. The formula =C14*D14 appears in the formula bar, and the result 120 appears in cell E14. The moving dashed line still surrounds cell E12, indicating that its formula is still available to be pasted into other cells.
5. Repeat Steps 3 and 4 to paste the formula into cell E15. The result 340 appears in cell E15.

   Next you'll paste the formula into two cells at once.
6. Position the pointer over cell E17, click and hold the left mouse button as you drag the mouse down until it is positioned over cell E18, then release the mouse button. Cells E17 and E18 are both selected. See Figure 3-18. Both cells are now considered to be active cells.

Figure 3-18 Multiple cell selection

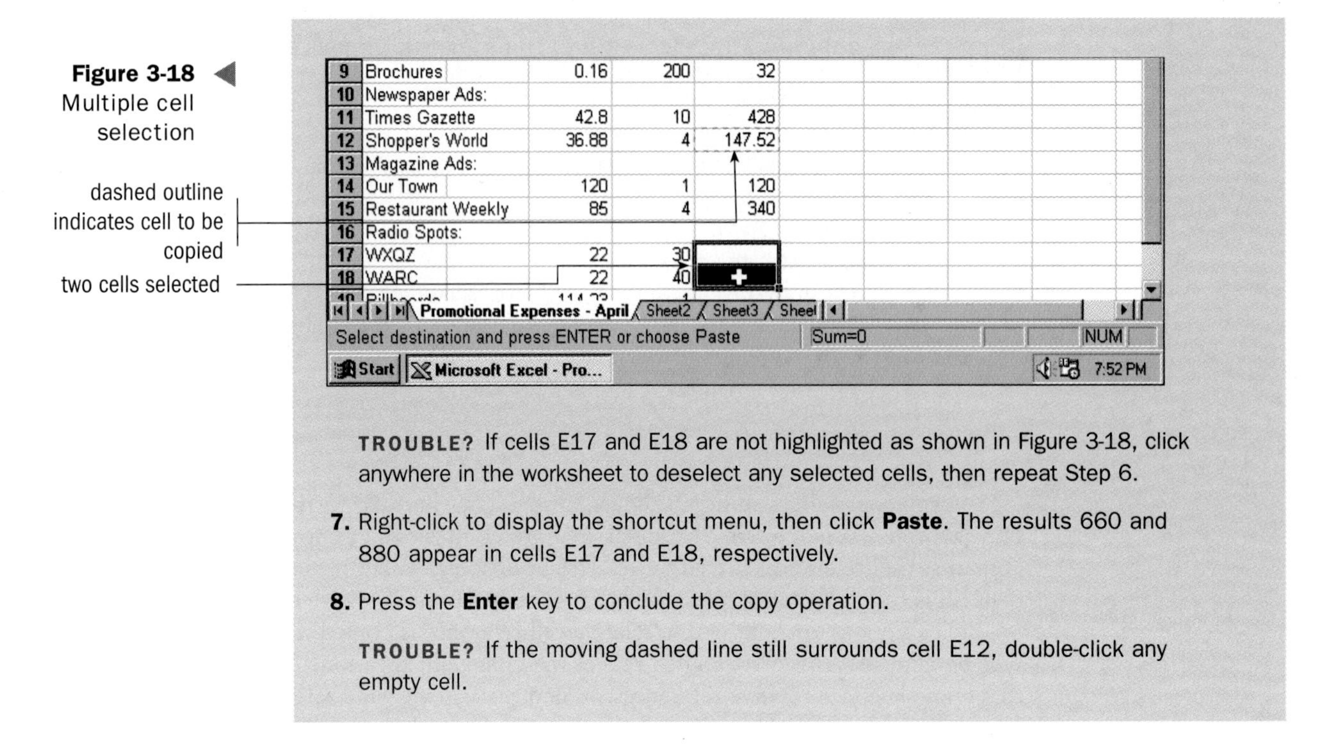

TROUBLE? If cells E17 and E18 are not highlighted as shown in Figure 3-18, click anywhere in the worksheet to deselect any selected cells, then repeat Step 6.

7. Right-click to display the shortcut menu, then click **Paste**. The results 660 and 880 appear in cells E17 and E18, respectively.

8. Press the **Enter** key to conclude the copy operation.

TROUBLE? If the moving dashed line still surrounds cell E12, double-click any empty cell.

You have now entered formulas for all the advertising costs except the billboard category. For that cost, you will use a function.

Entering Formulas Containing Functions

A **function** is a prewritten formula that takes specified values, performs a predefined operation, and then returns a value. The values you supply to a function are called the **arguments**. To use an Excel function in a formula, you specify the name of the function following an equal sign, then specify the arguments in parentheses.

For example, assume that you need the sum of the four values in cells E3, E4, E5, and E6. You could enter the formula =E3+E4+E5+E6. Or, you could use the equivalent Excel SUM function in the formula =SUM(E3:E6). The **SUM function** calculates the total value of the specified cells. The argument for the SUM function is the collection of cells for which you want the total determined. In this example, you request the sum of the values in the range of cells from E3 to E6 by entering (E3:E6). You could also have entered the argument of the formula as (E3, E4, E5, E6).

Excel provides hundreds of functions, organized into categories as shown in Figure 3-19. The SUM function is one of the most commonly used and easiest to understand. Other simple functions include MIN, which returns the smallest (minimum) value in a group; MAX, which finds the largest (maximum) value; and AVERAGE, which calculates the average value. As examples of complex functions, consider the financial function PV, which returns the present value of an investment; and the trigonometric function ATANH, which returns the inverse hyperbolic tangent of a number.

Figure 3-19 Excel function categories

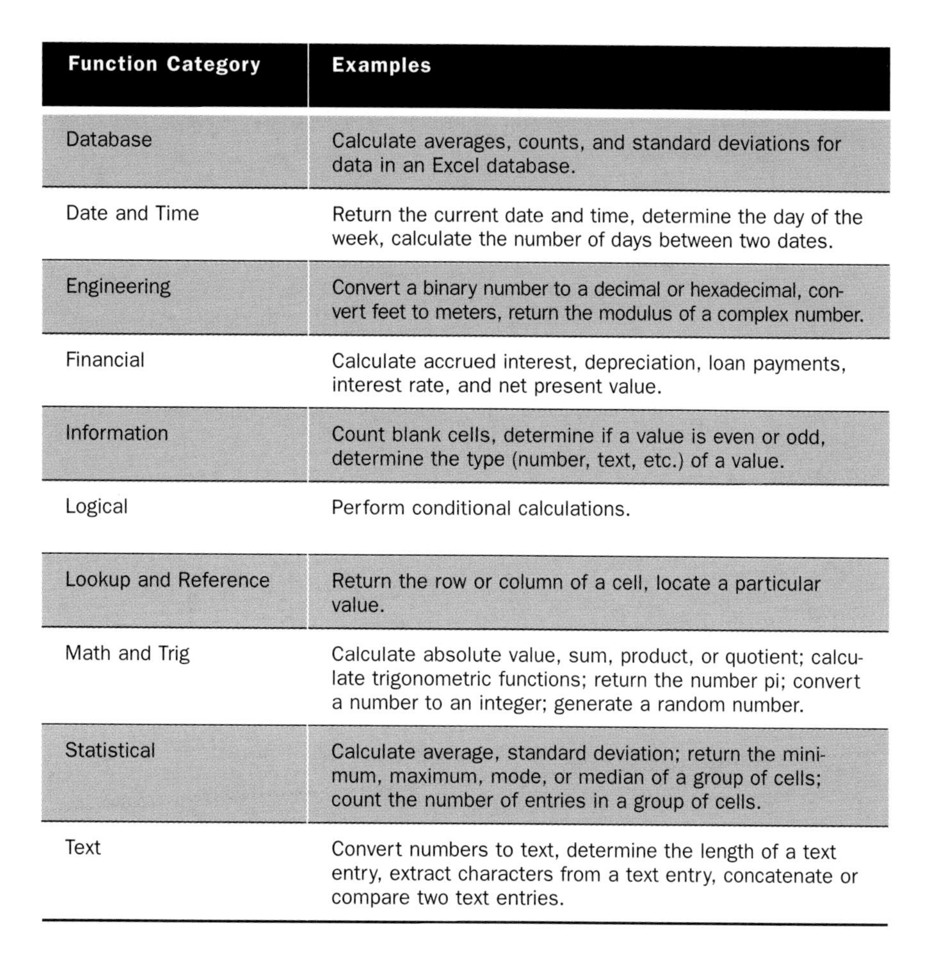

Function Category	Examples
Database	Calculate averages, counts, and standard deviations for data in an Excel database.
Date and Time	Return the current date and time, determine the day of the week, calculate the number of days between two dates.
Engineering	Convert a binary number to a decimal or hexadecimal, convert feet to meters, return the modulus of a complex number.
Financial	Calculate accrued interest, depreciation, loan payments, interest rate, and net present value.
Information	Count blank cells, determine if a value is even or odd, determine the type (number, text, etc.) of a value.
Logical	Perform conditional calculations.
Lookup and Reference	Return the row or column of a cell, locate a particular value.
Math and Trig	Calculate absolute value, sum, product, or quotient; calculate trigonometric functions; return the number pi; convert a number to an integer; generate a random number.
Statistical	Calculate average, standard deviation; return the minimum, maximum, mode, or median of a group of cells; count the number of entries in a group of cells.
Text	Convert numbers to text, determine the length of a text entry, extract characters from a text entry, concatenate or compare two text entries.

You'll use the PRODUCT function to calculate the cost for cell E19. The syntax for a formula using the PRODUCT function is =PRODUCT(argument1, argument2, ...), which indicates that the PRODUCT function requires at least two values to multiply. The ellipsis (...) in the argument list indicates that you can specify more than two values to be multiplied. Excel will multiply all the arguments and then place the result in the cell containing the formula.

To create the formula using the PRODUCT function:

1. If necessary, click cell **E19** to make it the active cell.
2. Type **=PRODUCT(C19,D19)** then press the **Enter** key. Excel performs the PRODUCT calculation and displays the result 114.23 in cell E19.

You can type functions directly, as you just typed the PRODUCT function. However, you might not always be sure what arguments are required for a specific function, or in what order those arguments must appear. The easiest and safest way to enter functions is to use Excel's **Function Wizard**, which leads you step-by-step through the process of entering a formula containing a function.

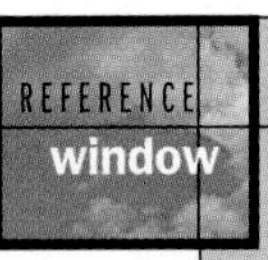

USING THE FUNCTION WIZARD

- Click the cell in which you want to display the results of the formula containing the function.
- Click the Function Wizard button on the Standard toolbar to open the Function Wizard - Step 1 of 2 dialog box.
- Click the classification of the function you want in the Function Category box.
- Click the function you want in the Function Name box.
- Click the Next button to open the Step 2 of 2 box.
- Enter values for each argument in the function.
- Click the Finish button to close the dialog box.

According to your worksheet plan, you need to calculate and display a total of all the advertising costs, which are located in cells E8 through E19. Three of the cells in this range are empty, but that will not cause a problem. Excel ignores the contents of empty cells when determining the sum.

You'll use the Function Wizard to create a formula using the SUM function, which is one of the mathematics and trigonometry functions.

To start the Function Wizard for the SUM function:

1. If necessary, click cell **E20**, the cell in which you want the total to appear, to make it the active cell.
2. Click the **Function Wizard** button on the Standard toolbar. The Function Wizard - Step 1 of 2 dialog box opens.
3. Click **Math & Trig** in the Function Category list box. The Function Name list box displays an alphabetical list of functions in the mathematics and trigonometry classification.
4. Scroll the Function Name list box until the function SUM is visible, then click **SUM**. See Figure 3-20.

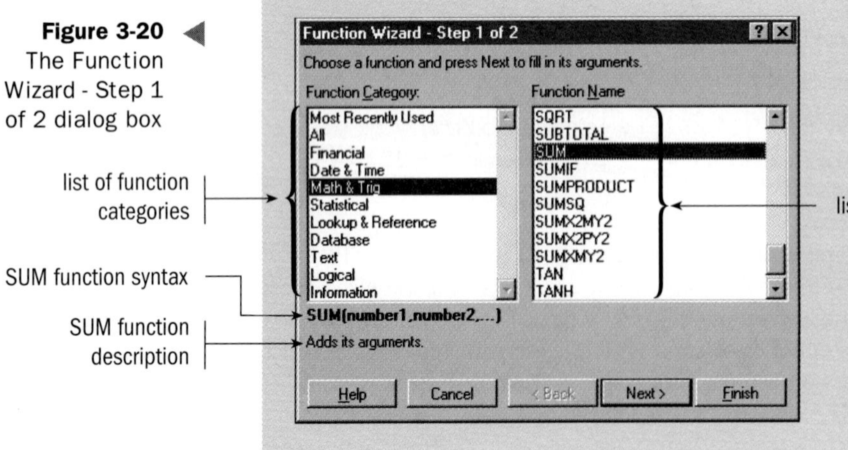

Figure 3-20 The Function Wizard - Step 1 of 2 dialog box

The syntax for the SUM function and a description of the function are displayed beneath the Function Category box. The description "Adds its arguments" tells you that all the arguments are added together. The syntax is given as SUM(number1, number2,...), which indicates that the SUM function requires at least two numbers to add; the ellipsis indicates that you can add more than two numbers.

5. Click the **Next** button to open the Function Wizard - Step 2 of 2 dialog box. See Figure 3-21.

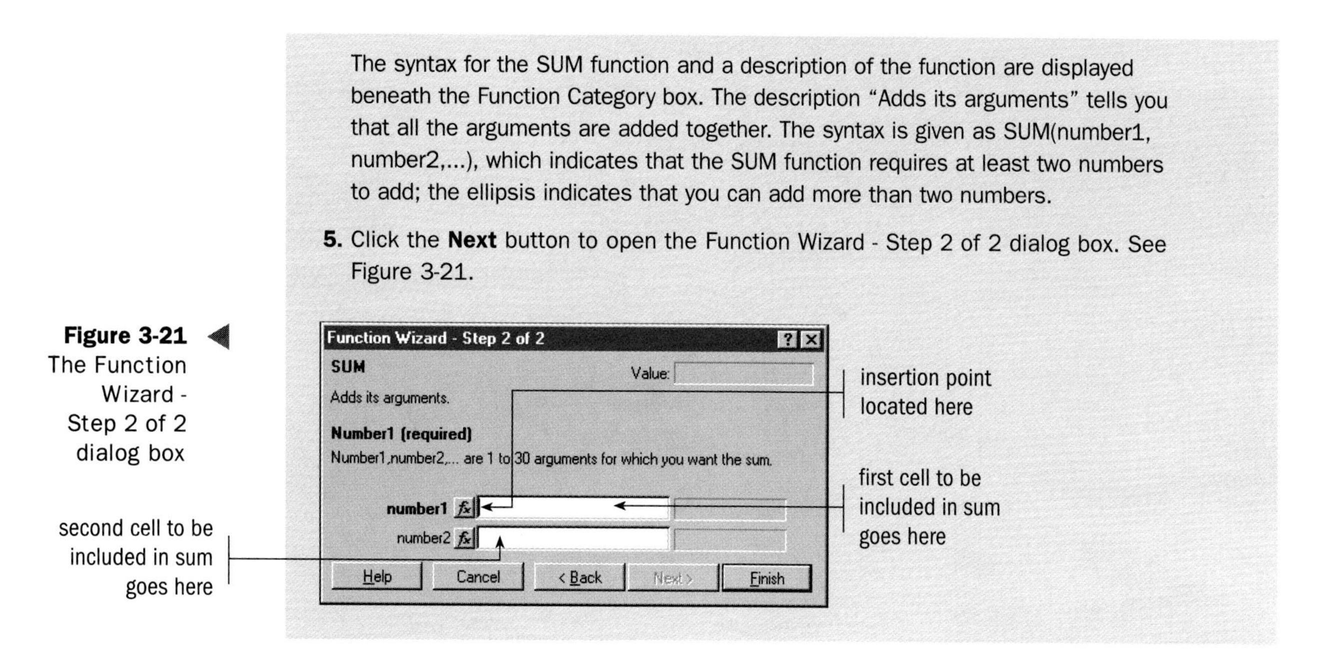

Figure 3-21 The Function Wizard - Step 2 of 2 dialog box

In this dialog box, you specify the cells whose contents you want to sum. The insertion point is originally positioned in the number1 box. To indicate the first cell you want to be included in the sum, you can either type a cell reference directly in the box or select the cell in your worksheet. After you've indicated a cell for the number1 argument, the insertion point moves into the number2 box. Again, you either type the second cell reference or select a second worksheet cell. You continue this process of adding arguments until you click the Finish button to indicate that you have specified all the cells to sum.

You can use a shortcut method to specify a range of cells to be summed. For example, when you indicate the number1 argument, you can specify an entire range of cells either by using the mouse to select the range of cells in the worksheet or by typing the cell range. This shortcut method is often easier and more accurate than entering individual cell references.

You want to add the range of cells E8 through E19, so you only need to indicate that one cell range. You'll use the mouse to select the cells, but first you must scroll the worksheet and move the cells out from underneath the dialog box.

To complete the Function Wizard specifications for the SUM function:

1. Click the right arrow on the horizontal scroll bar three times to move column E toward the left of the worksheet window.

   TROUBLE? If the dialog box still blocks part of column E, position the pointer on the dialog box's title bar, then click and drag the box to the right until you can see all of column E.

2. Position the pointer over cell E8, then click and drag to select cells E8 through E19. See Figure 3-22. A dashed outline surrounds the selected cells.

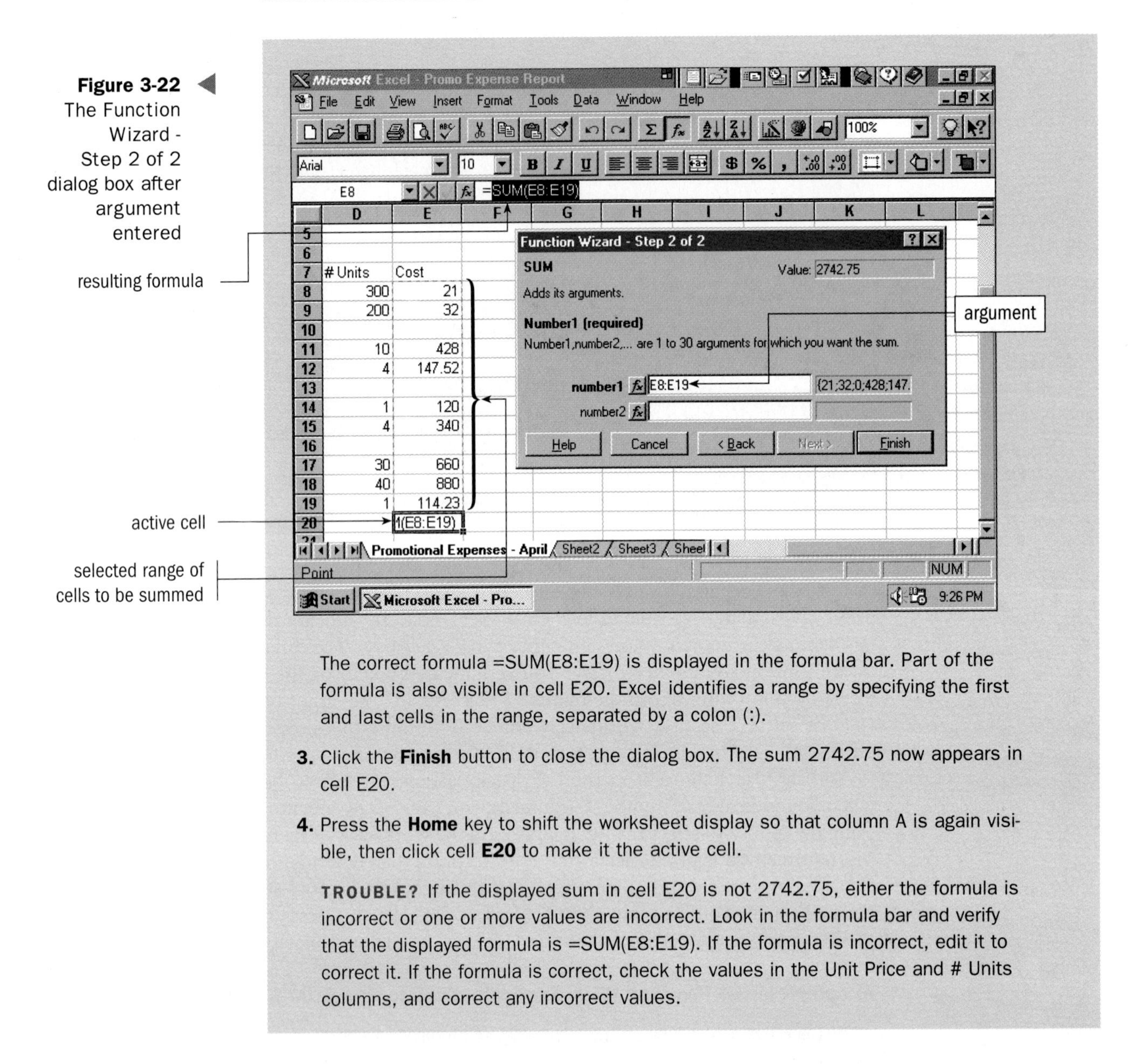

Figure 3-22 The Function Wizard - Step 2 of 2 dialog box after argument entered

The correct formula =SUM(E8:E19) is displayed in the formula bar. Part of the formula is also visible in cell E20. Excel identifies a range by specifying the first and last cells in the range, separated by a colon (:).

3. Click the **Finish** button to close the dialog box. The sum 2742.75 now appears in cell E20.

4. Press the **Home** key to shift the worksheet display so that column A is again visible, then click cell **E20** to make it the active cell.

TROUBLE? If the displayed sum in cell E20 is not 2742.75, either the formula is incorrect or one or more values are incorrect. Look in the formula bar and verify that the displayed formula is =SUM(E8:E19). If the formula is incorrect, edit it to correct it. If the formula is correct, check the values in the Unit Price and # Units columns, and correct any incorrect values.

Kim points out that the unit price for an ad in *Restaurant Weekly* magazine is not always $85. If a customer places fewer than four ads in a particular month, the price of each ad is $100; the price is $85 per ad only if four or more ads are placed in that month. You need to use a logical function in the formula in cell C15 to allow for the different prices.

Using Logical Functions

The Excel **logical functions**, which include IF, AND, OR, NOT, TRUE, and FALSE, allow you to assign values to a cell based on a conditional evaluation of the contents of other cells. In the case of the ad in *Restaurant Weekly*, an ad costs one of two amounts—$85 or $100—depending on how many ads are placed in that month. To express this condition in the formula in cell C15, you need to use the IF logical function.

The **IF function** evaluates an "if-then-else" situation to produce a value. In this case, *if* the number of ads placed in a month (cell D15) is less than 4, *then* the cost of each ad (cell C15) is $100, *else* the cost of each ad (cell C15) is $85.

You'll use the Function Wizard to enter a conditional formula for the unit price in cell C15, based on the value for the number of ads in cell D15.

To enter a conditional formula in cell C15 using the Function Wizard:

1. Click cell **C15** to make it the active cell.
2. Click the **Function Wizard** button on the Standard toolbar. The Function Wizard - Step 1 of 2 dialog box opens.
3. Click **Logical** in the Function Category box.
4. Click **IF** in the Function Name box. The syntax for an IF function is displayed below the Function Category box and also in the formula bar. The IF function has three arguments: the logical test (the *if* argument of "if-then-else"); the value to assign if the result of the test is true (the *then* argument); and the value to assign if the result of the test is false (the *else* argument). See Figure 3-23.

Figure 3-23 The Function Wizard - Step 1 of 2 dialog box for the IF function

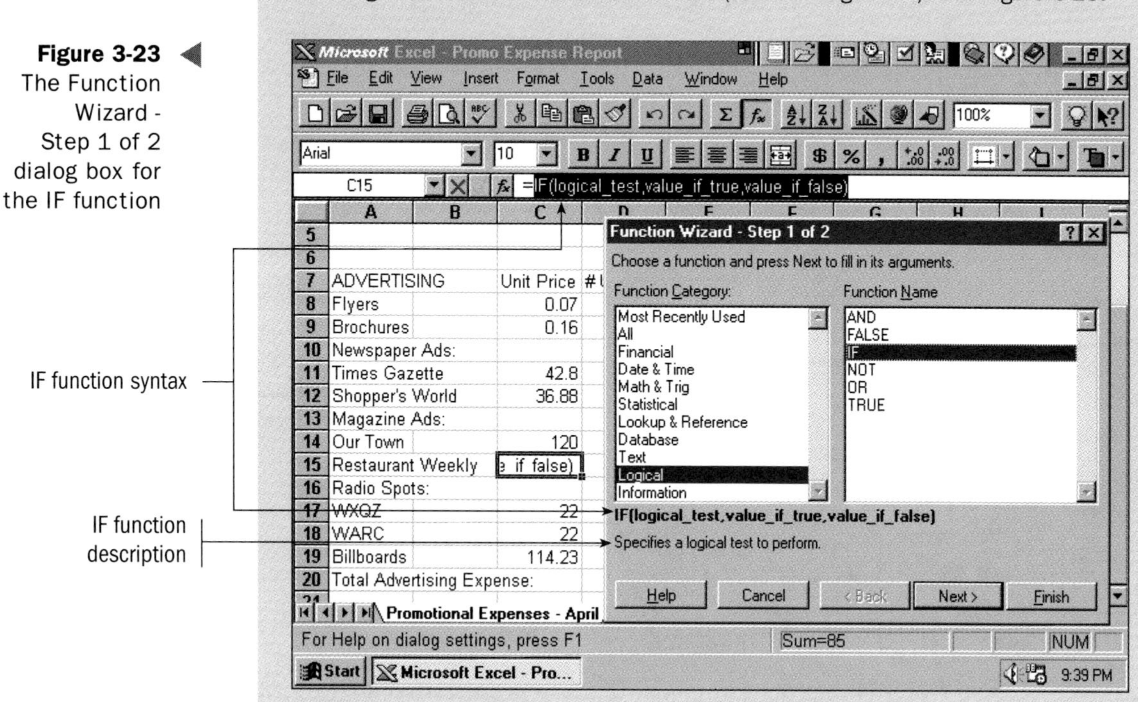

5. Click the **Next** button. The Function Wizard - Step 2 of 2 dialog box opens. This dialog box provides three text boxes to be completed, one for each of the IF function arguments.

   In this case, the logical test is to determine if the number of ads placed (cell D15) is less than 4.

6. Type **D15<4**. The word "FALSE" is displayed to the right of the logical test box, indicating that the current value in cell D15 is *not* less than 4.
7. Press the **Tab** key to advance the insertion point to the second argument.

   Next, you need to enter the value if the logical test is true. In this case, if fewer than 4 ads are placed in a month, the cost of each ad is $100.

8. Type **100** then press the **Tab** key.

   Finally, you need to enter the value if the logical test is false. In this case, if 4 or more ads are placed in a month, the cost of each ad is $85.

9. Type **85** to complete the formula. See Figure 3-24.

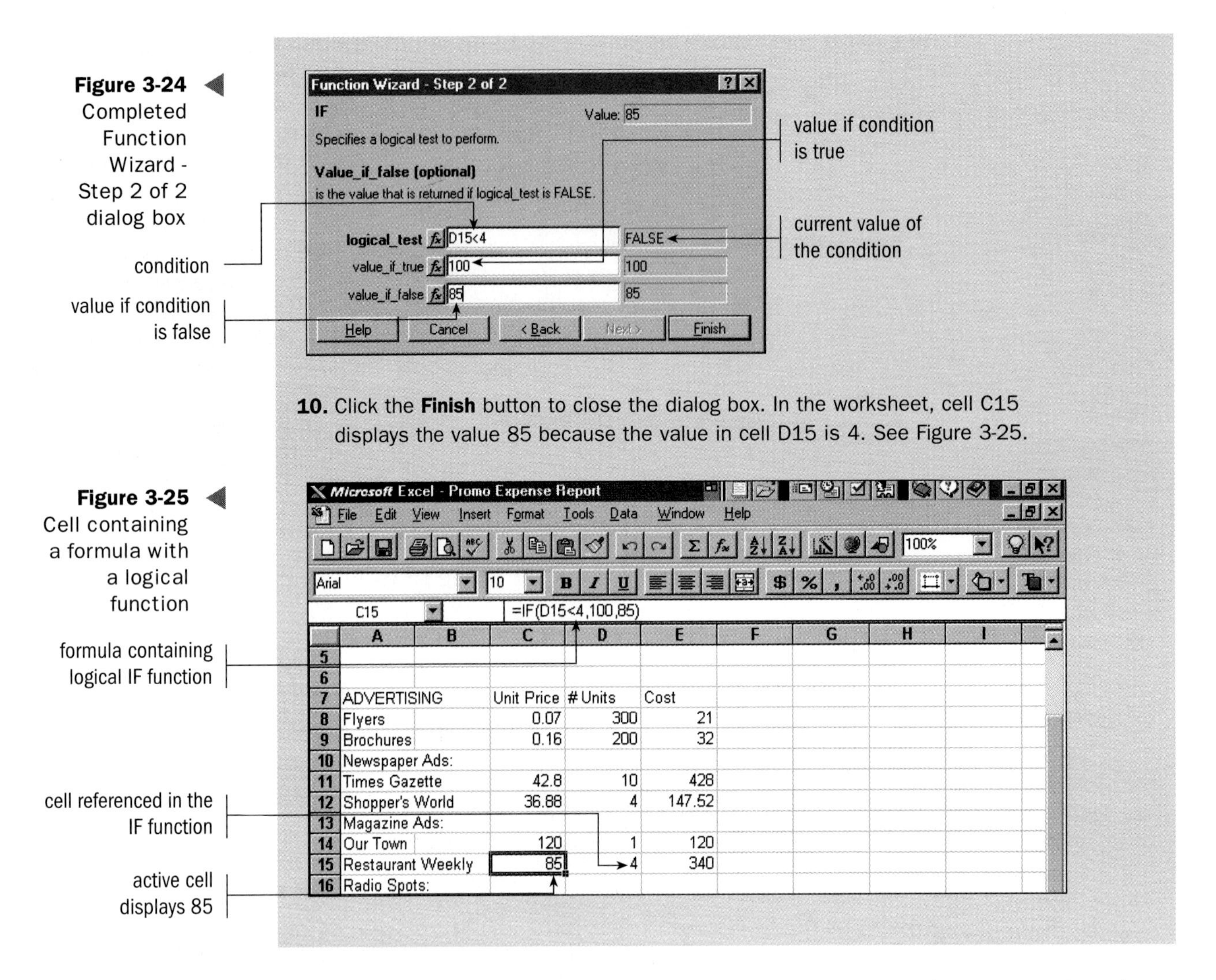

Figure 3-24 Completed Function Wizard - Step 2 of 2 dialog box

10. Click the **Finish** button to close the dialog box. In the worksheet, cell C15 displays the value 85 because the value in cell D15 is 4. See Figure 3-25.

Figure 3-25 Cell containing a formula with a logical function

To verify that the formula in cell C15 is correct, you'll test it by changing the value in cell D15.

To test the IF function in cell C15:

1. Click cell **D15** to make it the active cell.
2. Type **3** then press the **Enter** key. The value in cell C15 changes to 100, which is correct. Cell E15, which contains the formula =C15*D15, changes to 300, which is the correct product of 3 times 100.
3. Click cell **D15**, type **5**, then press the **Enter** key. Cell C15 now displays 85.
4. Click cell **D15**, type **4**, then press the **Enter** key. The value in cell D15 is now correct, cell C15 correctly displays 85, and cell E15 correctly displays 340.

Now that you've entered the labels, numbers, and formulas for the advertising section in your worksheet, you can save the workbook, then close the workbook and exit Excel.

Closing a Workbook and Exiting Excel

To close a workbook document, you can use the Close option on the File menu or the Close button on the menu bar. As with other Office 95 programs, to close a workbook document and exit Excel at the same time, you use the Close button on the title bar.

To save the workbook, then close the workbook and exit Excel:

1. Click the **Save** button on the Standard toolbar.
2. Click the **Close** button on the title bar. Excel closes, and you return to the Windows 95 desktop.

   TROUBLE? If a dialog box opens and asks if you want to save changes to Promo Expense Report, click the No button.

Quick Check

1. What is the difference between a workbook and a worksheet?
2. What are the five phases of worksheet development?
3. How do you rename a worksheet?
4. Do you need to tell Excel that a value you are entering in a cell is a date, a number, or a label? If so, how do you indicate this? If not, how does Excel determine the type of value you are entering?
5. To move directly to a cell and also make it the active cell, you type its ___________ in the ___________.
6. How does Excel recognize a formula?
7. What is the difference between a formula and a function?
8. Describe the standard order of precedence for arithmetic operators and how it affects a formula.
9. Describe the three Excel functions that you entered in this session. Explain how the if-then-else logic works in an IF function.

SESSION 3.2

In this session you will open an existing workbook; work with cell ranges; insert and delete rows and columns; move, cut, and paste cell contents; change number and date formats; adjust column widths; add and remove cell borders; and split the worksheet window.

Opening an Existing Workbook

In the previous session you created a workbook with a worksheet containing most of the elements of your worksheet plan. Now you'll continue your work on that worksheet using the workbook named PromoExp, which is stored on your Student Disk. The PromoExp workbook is similar to the workbook you created in the first session except that it includes the free sample classification labels, total free sample expense value, and total promotional expense formula.

You open an existing workbook in the same way that you open other Office 95 documents—using the Office Shortcut Bar.

To open the PromoExp workbook and start Excel:

1. Make sure your Student Disk is in the disk drive.
2. Click the **Open a Document** button on the Office Shortcut Bar. Office 95 displays the Open dialog box.

3. Click the **Look in** list arrow to display the list of devices and drives, click the drive that contains your Student Disk, click **Tutorial.03**, then click the **Open** button. The main list display changes to show you all the folders and files in the Tutorial.03 folder.
4. Click **PromoExp** then click the **Open** button. Because the document is an Excel workbook, Excel starts with PromoExp as the active workbook.

You'll create your own copy of the workbook and keep the original intact by renaming the workbook as April Promotions.

To rename the workbook:

1. Click **File** then click **Save As**.
2. Type **April Promotions**. *Do not press the Enter key.*

   If the Tutorial.03 folder is not displayed in the Save in text box, you must change the current setting.
3. If necessary, click the **Look in** list arrow to display the list of devices and drives, click the drive that contains your Student Disk, click **Tutorial.03**, then click the **Open** button.
4. Click the **Save** button.

To make it easier for you to navigate the worksheet, you'll name several cells and cell ranges in your worksheet.

Working with Ranges

A **range** is a group of two or more contiguous cells that form a rectangle. For example, cells A21, B21, and C21 constitute a range of cells that is one row high by three columns wide. Cells D17, D18, E17, and E18 define a range of cells two rows high by two columns wide. In contrast, the three cells C15, D15, and D16 are not a range because they do not form a rectangle.

You can assign a name to any cell or any range of cells in your workbook. The name must be one word and cannot contain spaces. Once you have named a cell or a range, you can use the name to move immediately to that cell or range from any location in your workbook, even from a different worksheet. When you move to a named cell or range, that cell or range becomes the active cell(s), and the worksheet display shifts, if necessary, to display the cell(s). Named cells and ranges are easier to remember than cell locations, and they allow you to navigate a workbook quickly and efficiently. Named ranges can overlap one another, and a particular cell can be a member of more than one range.

Naming Ranges and Cells

The cells in your worksheet that constitute the title area (cells A1 through E4) comprise a range of cells to which you could assign a name. Similarly, the advertising section of your worksheet (cells A7 through E20) and the free samples section (cells A22 through E23) are ranges to which you might want to move quickly. Cell E25, which contains the total promotional expense, is an important cell in your worksheet that you might want to name. These three cell ranges and the one cell are identified in Figure 3-26, along with the names you'll be assigning to each.

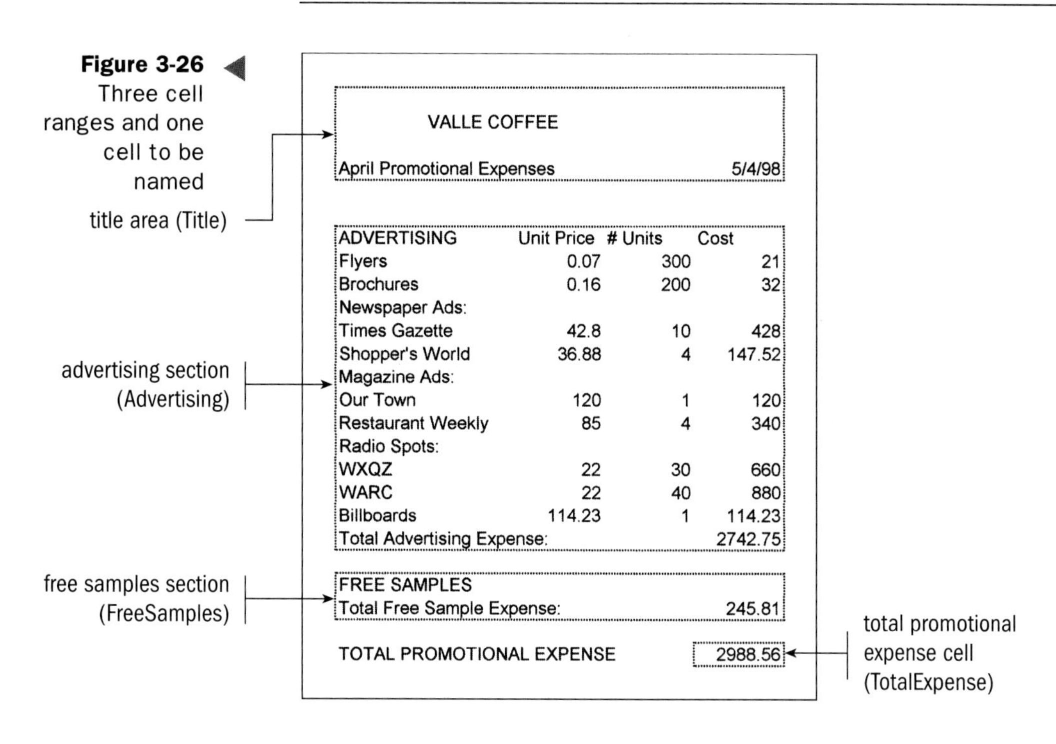

VALLE COFFEE			
April Promotional Expenses			5/4/98
ADVERTISING	Unit Price	# Units	Cost
Flyers	0.07	300	21
Brochures	0.16	200	32
Newspaper Ads:			
Times Gazette	42.8	10	428
Shopper's World	36.88	4	147.52
Magazine Ads:			
Our Town	120	1	120
Restaurant Weekly	85	4	340
Radio Spots:			
WXQZ	22	30	660
WARC	22	40	880
Billboards	114.23	1	114.23
Total Advertising Expense:			2742.75
FREE SAMPLES			
Total Free Sample Expense:			245.81
TOTAL PROMOTIONAL EXPENSE			2988.56

Figure 3-26 Three cell ranges and one cell to be named

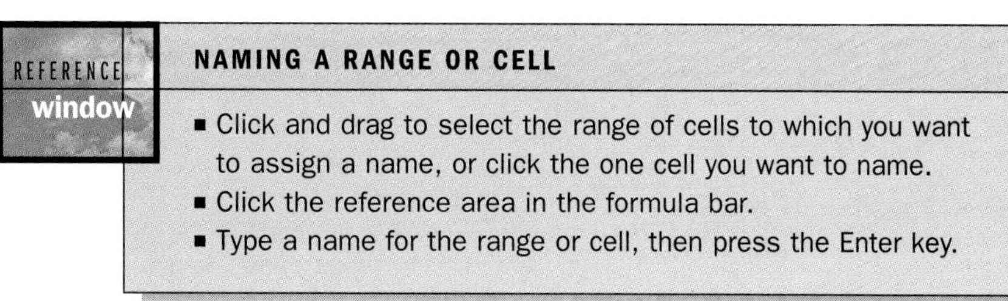

REFERENCE window

NAMING A RANGE OR CELL

- Click and drag to select the range of cells to which you want to assign a name, or click the one cell you want to name.
- Click the reference area in the formula bar.
- Type a name for the range or cell, then press the Enter key.

First, you'll name the range of cells that forms the worksheet title area.

To name the title range:

1. Position the pointer over cell A1, click and drag to select the cells from A1 through E4, then release the mouse button. The range of cells from A1 through E4 is highlighted.

   TROUBLE? If you make a mistake selecting the cells, click anywhere in the worksheet to deselect any selected cells, then repeat Step 1.

2. Click **A1** in the reference area of the formula bar. The A1 is highlighted. See Figure 3-27.

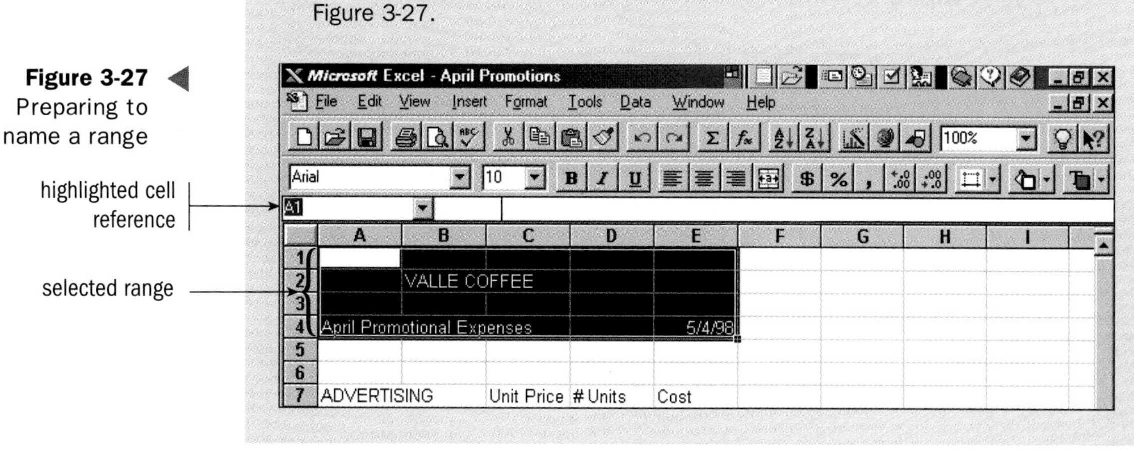

Figure 3-27 Preparing to name a range

3. Type **Title** then press the **Enter** key. The range is now named, and the word "Title" appears centered in the reference area of the formula bar.

   TROUBLE? If you make a mistake selecting the range of cells or naming the range, you should delete the range name. Click Insert on the menu bar, click Name, then click Define. In the Define Name dialog box, click the range name you want to delete, click the Delete button, then click the Close button. Then repeat Steps 1 through 3 to define and name the range correctly. Note that deleting a range name deletes the range *only*—not the contents of the cells in the range.

Next, you'll name the advertising section and the free samples section of the worksheet, as well as the cell containing the total promotional expense.

To name the two ranges and the total promotional expense cell:

1. Click and drag to select the range of cells from **A7** through **E20**.
2. Click **A7** in the reference area, type **Advertising**, then press the **Enter** key. "Advertising" is now centered in the reference area, indicating that you successfully named the range.
3. Scroll the worksheet until rows 22 and 23 are visible, then click and drag to select the range of cells from **A22** through **E23**.
4. Click **A22** in the reference area, type **FreeSamples**, then press the **Enter** key. "FreeSamples" is now centered in the reference area.

   TROUBLE? If Excel displays a message indicating that you must enter a valid reference or type a valid name, you probably typed a space between "Free" and "Samples" when you entered the range name. A legal range name must be a single word and cannot contain any spaces. Click the OK button to close the message box, then repeat Step 4.

5. Click cell **E25** to make it the active cell.
6. Click **E25** in the reference area, type **TotalExpense**, then press the **Enter** key. The total promotional expense cell is now named.

Moving to a Named Range or Cell

Excel allows you to navigate the worksheet quickly by moving directly to any named range or cell in a workbook.

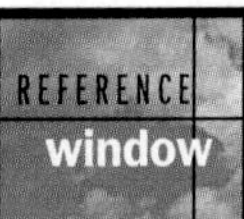

MOVING TO A NAMED RANGE OR NAMED CELL

- Click the reference area list arrow.
- Click the name of the range or cell to which you want to move, then press the Enter key.

Next, you'll practice navigating your worksheet by moving to the ranges and cells you just named.

To move to the named ranges and cell:

1. Click the **reference area** list arrow. The list box displays an alphabetical list of all the cell and range names you have defined. See Figure 3-28.

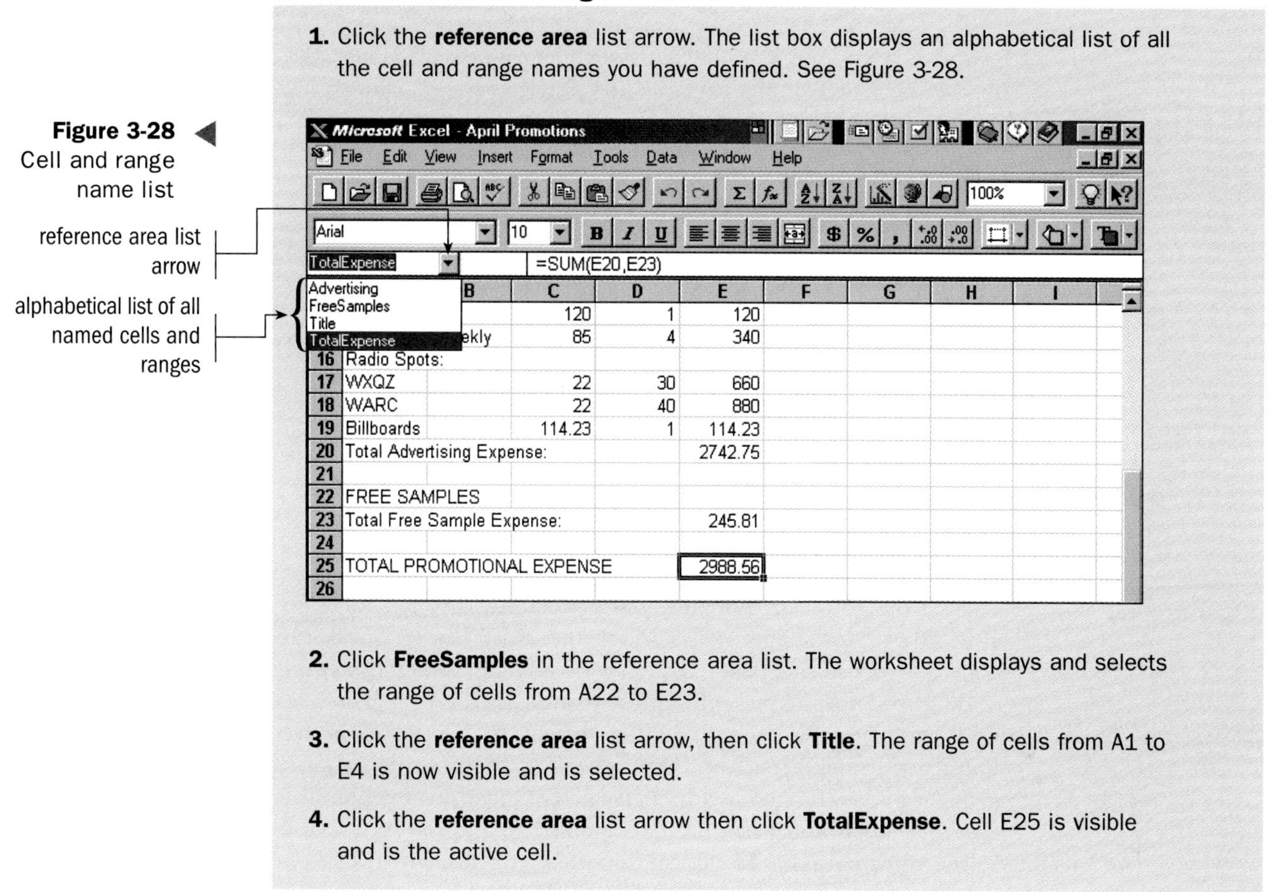

Figure 3-28 Cell and range name list

2. Click **FreeSamples** in the reference area list. The worksheet displays and selects the range of cells from A22 to E23.
3. Click the **reference area** list arrow, then click **Title**. The range of cells from A1 to E4 is now visible and is selected.
4. Click the **reference area** list arrow then click **TotalExpense**. Cell E25 is visible and is the active cell.

Now that you've entered and corrected all the worksheet data, you can begin formatting the worksheet to make it more attractive, readable, and usable.

Inserting and Deleting Columns and Rows

Sometimes you might need to add a column or row to a worksheet to accommodate additional data or to improve the worksheet's appearance or readability. Or, you might want to delete a column or row to remove data or to improve the worksheet's layout. You can insert or delete columns or rows in an Excel worksheet at any time.

Inserting Columns and Rows

The process for inserting either columns or rows is similar; you select the same number of columns or rows as the number you want to insert, then use the Insert menu or the Insert command on the shortcut menu to insert the columns or rows.

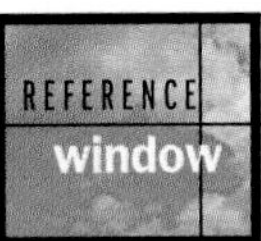

INSERTING COLUMNS OR ROWS

To insert columns:
- Select the same number of columns as the number of columns you want to insert, immediately to the right of where you want the new column or columns to be inserted.
- With the pointer in the highlighted area, right-click to display the shortcut menu, then click Insert (or click Insert on the menu bar, then click Columns).

To insert rows:
- Select the same number of rows as the number of rows you want to insert, immediately below where you want the new row or rows to be inserted.
- With the pointer in the highlighted area, right-click to display the shortcut menu, then click Insert (or click Insert on the menu bar, then click Rows).

The advertising section of your worksheet is located in rows 7 through 20. Cell A7 contains the label that identifies this section (ADVERTISING), and cell A20 contains the label that ends this section (Total Advertising Expense). The expense category labels are located between cells A7 and A20 in cells A8 through A19. Six of these labels—Flyers, Brochures, Newspaper Ads, Magazine Ads, Radio Spots, and Billboards—relate to general expense categories. The other six labels, which are specific newspaper, magazine, and radio station names, all represent subdivisions of a general expense category. With all 14 labels aligned in column A, it is difficult to distinguish between the general categories and the subcategories. Kim thinks the worksheet would be more readable if the labels in cells A7 and A20 remained in their current locations in column A, the six general expense category labels appeared in the next column, and the six specific expense labels appeared in the third column. To accomplish this, you need to insert two new columns between columns A and B.

To insert two columns between columns A and B:

1. Position the pointer over the B in the column headings area, click and hold down the mouse button as you move the pointer into the C column heading, then release the mouse button. Both columns B and C are highlighted, indicating that they are selected.

   TROUBLE? If both columns B and C are not highlighted, or if some other column is highlighted, you did not correctly select columns B and C. Click in any empty cell to remove the current highlighting, then repeat Step 1.

2. With the pointer in the highlighted area, right-click to display the shortcut menu.
3. Click **Insert** on the shortcut menu. Because you selected two columns, two new columns, now labeled B and C, are inserted and the existing columns shift to the right.

   Excel automatically adjusts the cell definitions in the ranges you have named to reflect the added columns. For example, you originally defined the range Advertising as cells A9 through E20. That named range now encompasses cells A9 through G20. Similarly, the TotalExpense cell, which was originally defined as cell E25, is now cell G25.

4. Click the **reference area** list arrow, then click **TotalExpense**. Cell G25 is visible and is selected. See Figure 3-29.

Figure 3-29 Inserting columns

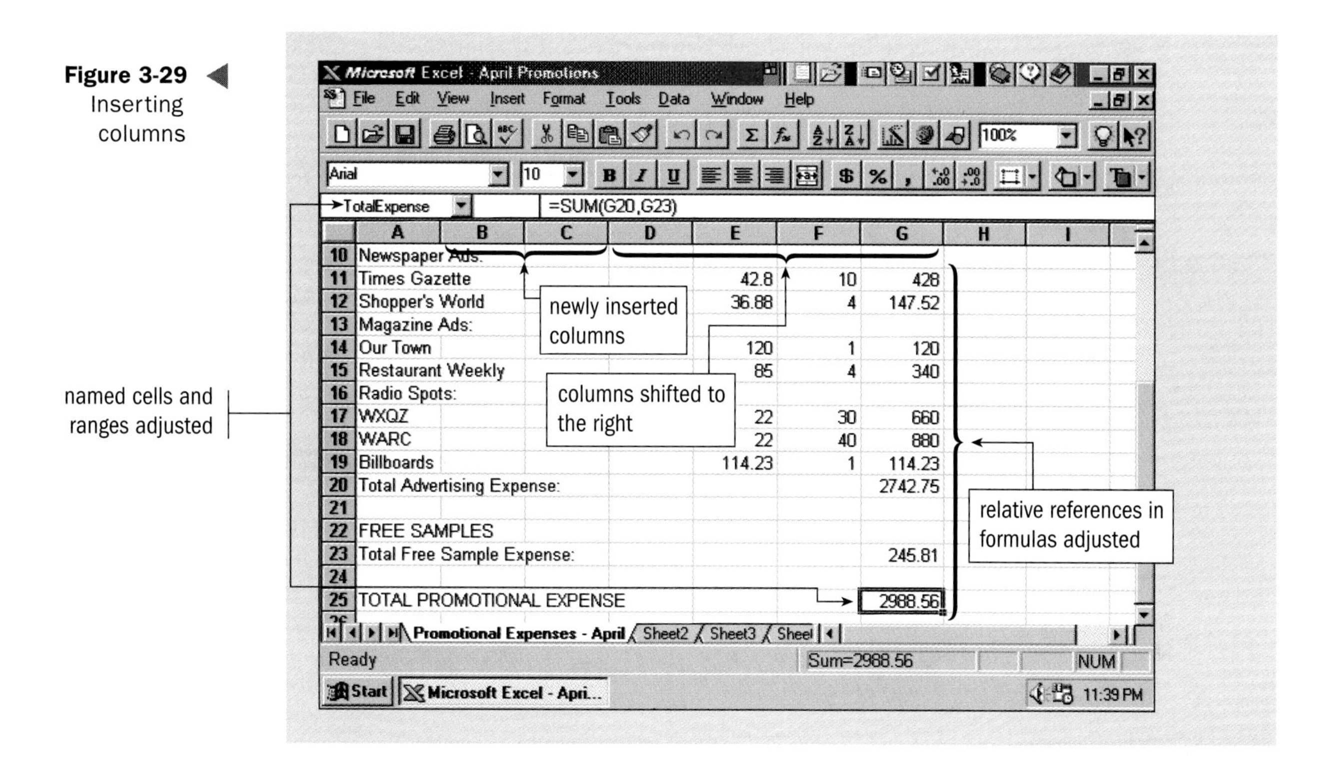

Notice that the displayed values in those cells that contain formulas did not change. When you added the two columns, Excel automatically adjusted all the relative cell references in the shifted columns to reflect the new column locations. All your worksheet formulas, therefore, are still correct.

Deleting Columns and Rows

To remove all the cells and their contents from a column or row, you use the Delete command on the Edit menu or the shortcut menu.

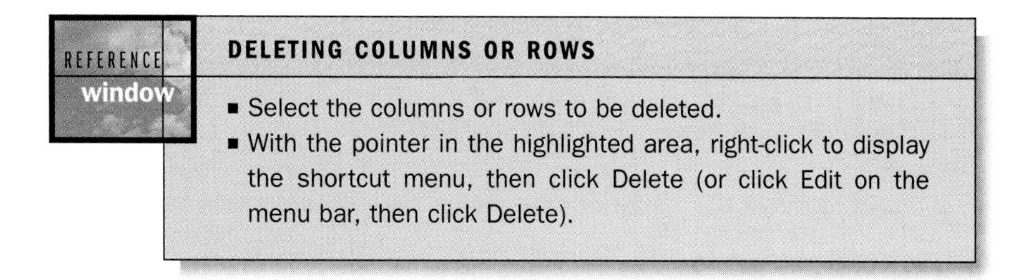
REFERENCE window

DELETING COLUMNS OR ROWS

- Select the columns or rows to be deleted.
- With the pointer in the highlighted area, right-click to display the shortcut menu, then click Delete (or click Edit on the menu bar, then click Delete).

Kim thinks that one blank row between the title area and the advertising section of the worksheet is sufficient. Currently both rows 5 and 6 are blank, so you need to delete one of the two rows using the Delete command.

To delete row 6:

1. Click the **reference area** list arrow, then click **Title**. Excel moves to and selects the title area, which now includes cells A1 through G4.
2. Select row 6 by clicking the **6** that identifies the row. The entire blank row 6 is highlighted.
3. With the pointer in the highlighted area, right-click to display the shortcut menu, then click **Delete**. The highlighted row is removed, and all the following rows are moved up one row.

Just as when you insert rows or columns, relative cell references in formulas and cell definitions in named cells and ranges are adjusted automatically when you delete rows or columns.

Now you can move the advertising labels into the two columns you added to your worksheet.

Moving the Contents of Cells

Moving cells is not the same as copying cells. When you copy cells, the original cells remain intact. In contrast, when you move cells, the original cell locations are cleared. You move cells to rearrange a worksheet; you copy cells to duplicate them on the worksheet.

Cutting and Pasting Cell Contents

To move the contents of a cell or range of cells to another location, you can use the cut-and-paste technique. You first cut the cell or range. The cut material is placed on the Clipboard and remains there until it is replaced by a subsequent cut or copy operation. In most Office 95 programs, you can access the Clipboard contents at any time. In Excel, however, you must *immediately* paste the Clipboard contents to a new location; once you perform any other operation, the Clipboard contents are no longer accessible.

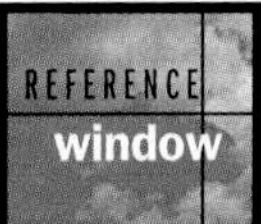

CUTTING AND PASTING CELL CONTENTS

- Select the cell or cells to be cut.
- With the pointer in the selected cell or cells, right-click to display the shortcut menu, then click Cut (or click the Cut button on the Standard toolbar).
- Select the cell or the first cell in the range into which you want to paste the cell contents.
- With the pointer in the selected cell, right-click to display the shortcut menu, then click Paste (or click the Paste button on the Standard toolbar).

Using the cut-and-paste technique, you'll move the labels in cells A7 through A18 to column B, into cells B7 through B18.

To move the range of cells using the cut-and-paste technique:

1. Select cells **A7** through **A18**. The cells in column A from "Flyers" through "Billboards" are highlighted.
2. With the pointer in the highlighted area, right-click to display the shortcut menu, then click **Cut**. A rotating dashed line surrounds the highlighted cells.
3. Click cell **B7**, right-click to display the shortcut menu, then click **Paste**. Excel removes the selected labels from their original location and places them in cells B7 through B18. See Figure 3-30.

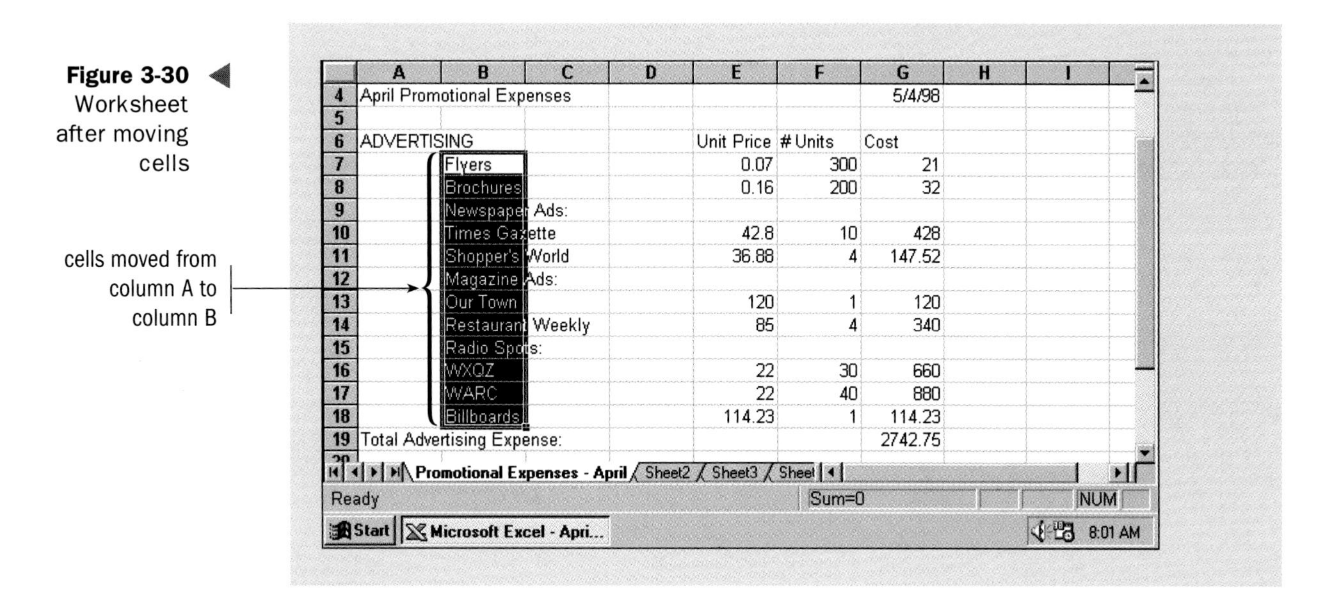

Figure 3-30 Worksheet after moving cells

You moved 12 labels from column A to column B. Six of these labels are subcategories, which you want to place in column C.

Dragging Cell Contents

Excel provides a second technique for moving cell contents. You can use the mouse to drag cell contents to a new location. Using the mouse to move cells is called **drag and drop**.

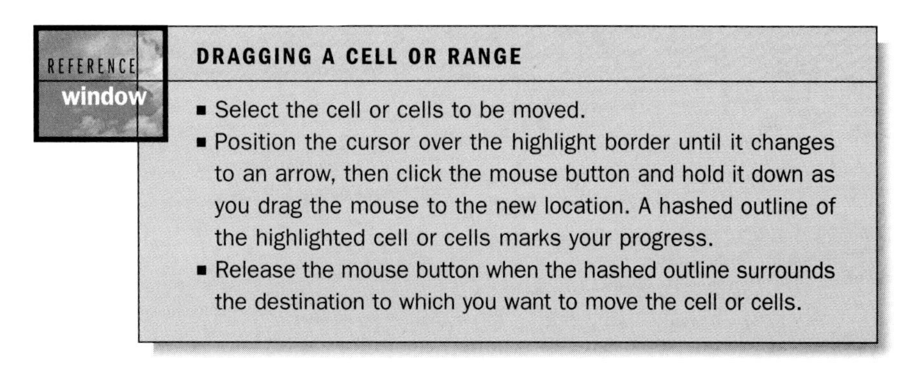
REFERENCE window

DRAGGING A CELL OR RANGE

- Select the cell or cells to be moved.
- Position the cursor over the highlight border until it changes to an arrow, then click the mouse button and hold it down as you drag the mouse to the new location. A hashed outline of the highlighted cell or cells marks your progress.
- Release the mouse button when the hashed outline surrounds the destination to which you want to move the cell or cells.

You'll use the drag-and-drop technique to move the six cells containing the advertising expense subcategories—Times Gazette, Shopper's World, Our Town, Restaurant Weekly, WXQZ, and WARC—from column B to column C.

To move the cell range using the drag-and-drop technique:

1. Select cells **B10** and **B11**.
2. Position the pointer over the right edge of the selection. The pointer changes to ↖. See Figure 3-31.

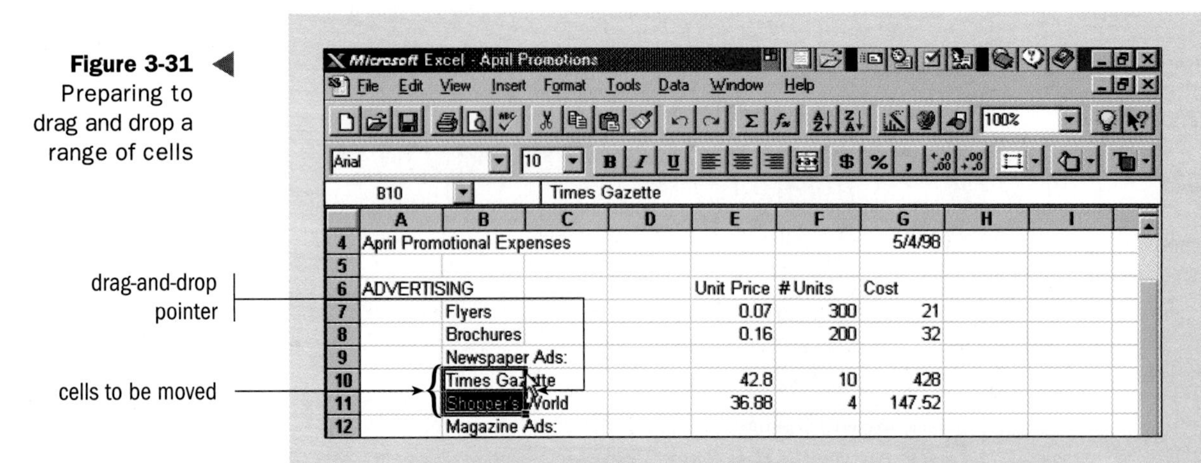

Figure 3-31 Preparing to drag and drop a range of cells

3. Click the mouse button and hold the button down as you move the mouse one column to the right. A hashed outline of the highlighted cells surrounds cells C10 through C11. See Figure 3-32.

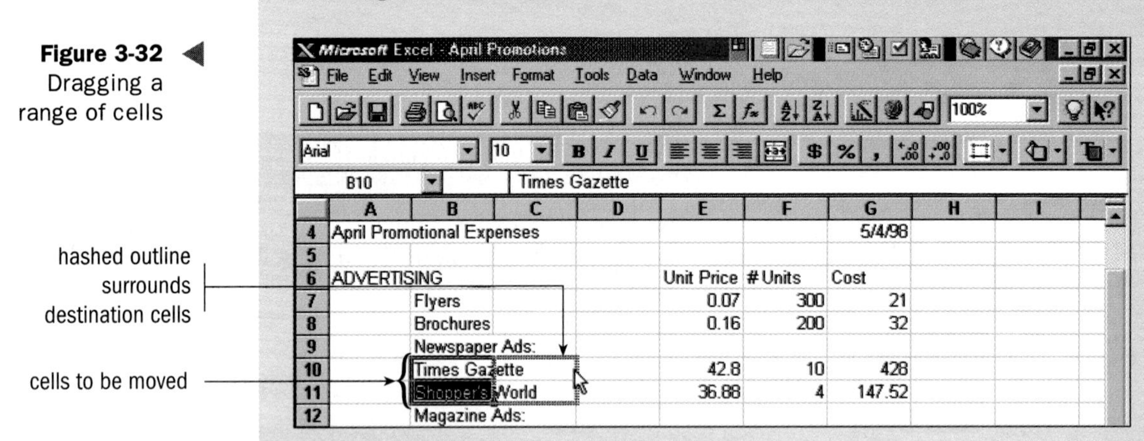

Figure 3-32 Dragging a range of cells

4. Release the mouse button. Excel moves the two selected cells into cells C10 and C11.
5. Select cells **B13** and **B14**.
6. Drag and drop the selected cells to move them one column to the right.
7. Select cells **B16** and **B17**.
8. Drag and drop the selected cells to move them one column to the right.
9. Click cell **D19** to remove the highlight from the cells you just moved. Your screen should now look like Figure 3-33.

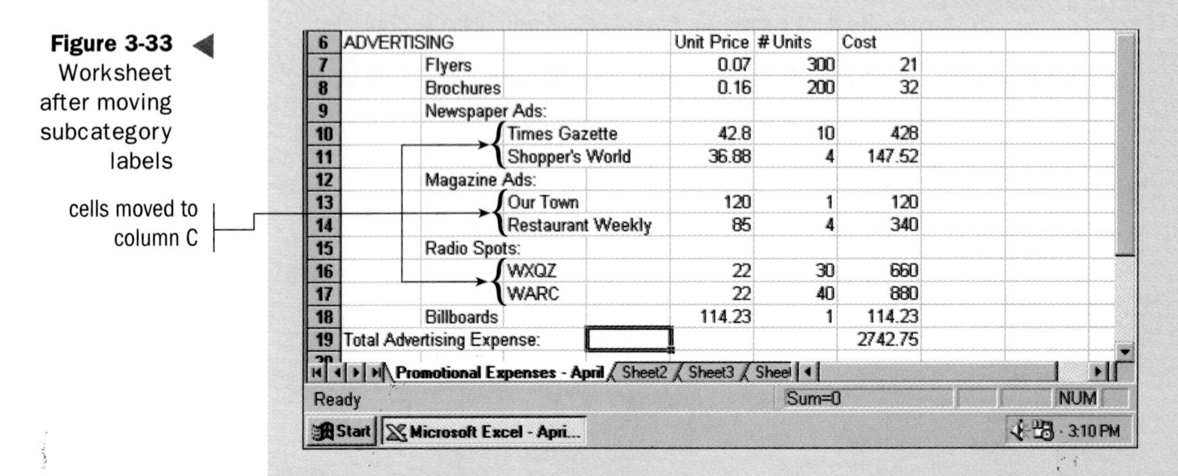

Figure 3-33 Worksheet after moving subcategory labels

You typically use the drag-and-drop method to move cell contents within the same worksheet, and the cut-and-paste method to move cell contents to another worksheet or even another workbook.

Changing Number and Date Formats

In the first session you entered the unit price values, which are now located in cells E7 through E18. In every case, you typed only as much of the value as was required to correctly represent the value. You were not concerned with how the value appeared in the worksheet. However, you can format values to specify how they should look. Typical formatting attributes for number values include a dollar sign, commas, a decimal point, and decimal digits.

The values in the cells in the Cost column of your worksheet (cells G7 through G19) were calculated by Excel using formulas you supplied. These values, like the values in the Unit Price column, are dollar amounts and need to be formatted accordingly.

Excel provides style buttons on the Formatting toolbar for many formatting tasks. You'll use the Formatting buttons to format the cells in the Cost column of the advertising section so that they display two decimal places. Typically, you display a dollar sign on the first value in a list of money values and on all subtotals and totals. You'll also add a dollar sign to the value in cell G7 using a Formatting toolbar button.

To format the advertising cost numbers using the Formatting toolbar:

1. Select cells **G7** through **G19**. Notice that this range includes some blank cells; these will also be formatted. If you enter a value in one of the blank cells later on, the value will be automatically formatted.

   Some values in the range display two decimal places; others display none. You want to display two decimal places for all the values so that they align consistently.

   Clicking the Increase Decimal button adds one decimal place to a selected cell. If you have selected a range, clicking this button adds one decimal place to the *first* cell in the range; the remaining cells in the range are adjusted to display the same number of decimal places as the first cell. Because the value in cell G7, the first cell in the selected range, has no decimal places, you need to click the Increase Decimal button twice to display two decimal places.

2. Click the **Increase Decimal** button on the Formatting toolbar. All the values in the range now display one decimal digit.

3. Click the **Increase Decimal** button again. All values in the range are displayed with two decimal digits.

   Next you'll add a dollar sign to the value in cell G7.

4. Click cell **G7**.

5. Click the **Currency Style** button on the Formatting toolbar. The value in cell G7 is displayed with a dollar sign. See Figure 3-34.

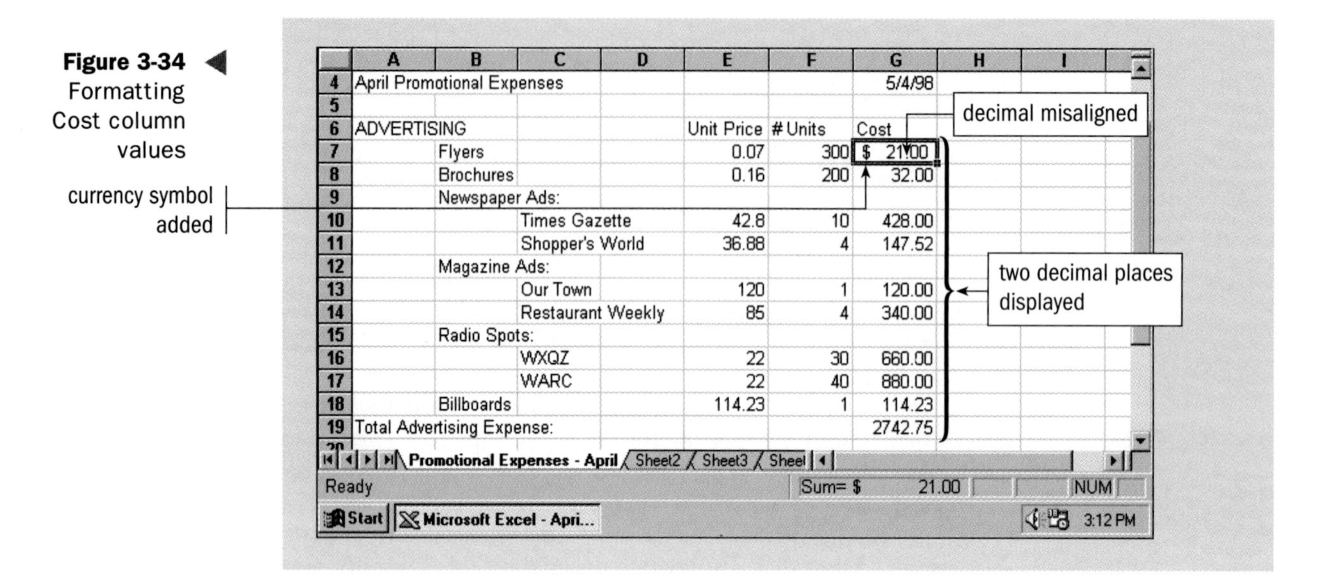

	A	B	C	D	E	F	G
4	April Promotional Expenses						5/4/98
5							
6	ADVERTISING				Unit Price	# Units	Cost
7		Flyers			0.07	300	$ 21.00
8		Brochures			0.16	200	32.00
9		Newspaper Ads:					
10			Times Gazette		42.8	10	428.00
11			Shopper's World		36.88	4	147.52
12		Magazine Ads:					
13			Our Town		120	1	120.00
14			Restaurant Weekly		85	4	340.00
15		Radio Spots:					
16			WXQZ		22	30	660.00
17			WARC		22	40	880.00
18		Billboards			114.23	1	114.23
19	Total Advertising Expense:						2742.75

Figure 3-34 Formatting Cost column values

Did you notice that the decimal points in column G are no longer aligned? The value in cell G7 moved slightly to the left when you added the dollar sign. When you clicked the Currency Style button, Excel changed the category of the value in cell G7 from "General" (the default category for a number field) to "Accounting." A negative number in the General category is indicated with a minus-sign prefix; a negative number in the Accounting category is indicated by enclosing the number in parentheses. Excel shifted the value in G7 slightly to the left to leave room to place a right parenthesis, if necessary.

Excel classifies all cells into one of 12 categories. Your worksheet currently includes four different cell categories. Cell G7 is now assigned to the Accounting category. All the other number values in your worksheet, and all blank cells in the worksheet as well, are categorized as General. The date in cell G4 is categorized as a Date. Finally, all the labels in the worksheet are categorized as Text.

Another cell category is Currency, which is the category that Kim prefers for worksheet dollar values. To assign the Currency category to a cell, you must use the Format Cells dialog box, which is available from the Format menu or the shortcut menu. The Format Cells dialog box provides many formatting options that are not available on the Formatting toolbar.

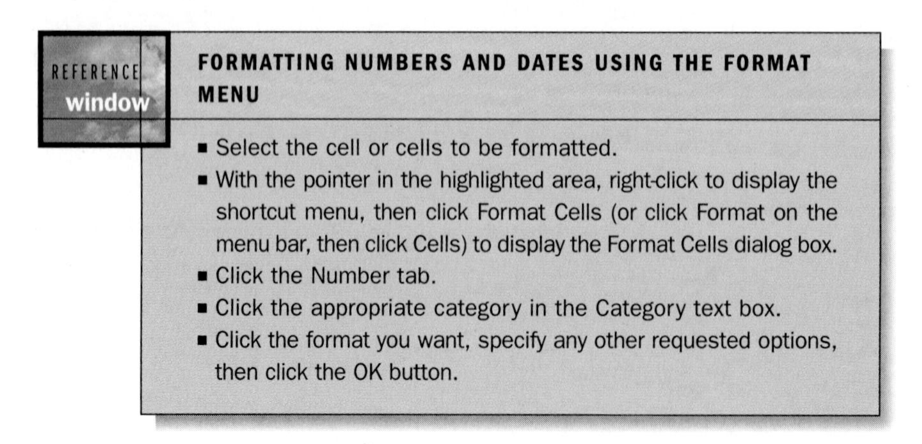

REFERENCE window

FORMATTING NUMBERS AND DATES USING THE FORMAT MENU

- Select the cell or cells to be formatted.
- With the pointer in the highlighted area, right-click to display the shortcut menu, then click Format Cells (or click Format on the menu bar, then click Cells) to display the Format Cells dialog box.
- Click the Number tab.
- Click the appropriate category in the Category text box.
- Click the format you want, specify any other requested options, then click the OK button.

You'll use the Format Cells dialog box to reformat cell G7 as a Currency cell.

To format the cost in cell G7 as Currency:

1. If cell G7 is not selected, click cell **G7**.

2. With the pointer in the selected cell, right-click to display the shortcut menu, then click **Format Cells**. The Format Cells dialog box opens.

3. If necessary, click the **Number** tab. The 12 categories are listed in the Category list box. "Accounting" is currently highlighted, indicating that cell G7 is assigned to that category.

4. Click **Currency** in the Category list box. The dialog box now looks like Figure 3-35.

Figure 3-35 Number tab of the Format Cells dialog box

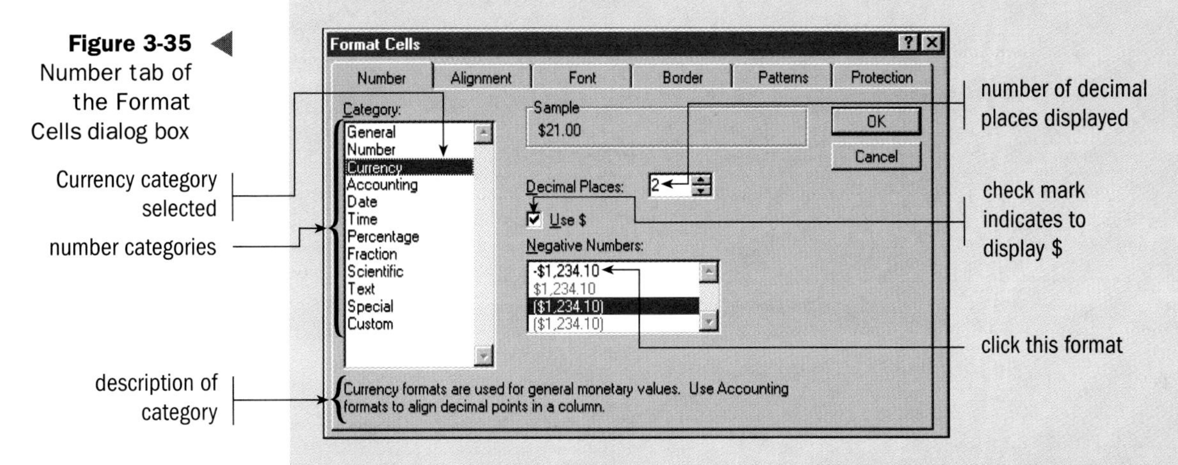

The number of decimal places is set at 2, which is what you want. The Use $ check box contains a check mark, indicating that cell G7 is displayed with a dollar sign. The Negative Numbers list box includes optional formats for displaying negative numbers, and the option to enclose a negative number in parentheses is currently selected. To match the decimal alignment of the other cells in the Cost column, you need to change this option so that negative numbers will be displayed with a minus sign.

5. Click the first display format in the Negative Numbers list box. See Figure 3-35.

6. Click the **OK** button to close the Format Cells dialog box. The value in G7 is displayed as "$21.00," and the decimal point aligns with the decimal points in the other values in the column.

The format you have defined for cell G7 is also the appropriate format for the first Unit Price value in cell E7, as well as the subtotals and totals in cells G19, G22, and G24. The fastest way to apply the format in cell G7 to those other cells is to use the Format Painter, which works exactly the same way in Excel as it does in Word. To apply a format to more than one cell or range, you must double-click the Format Painter button on the Standard toolbar.

To use the Format Painter to apply the formatting in cell G7 to other cells:

1. Make sure cell G7 is selected.

2. Double-click the **Format Painter** button on the Standard toolbar. The pointer changes to and a moving dashed line appears around cell G7.

3. Click cell **E7**. The formatting for cell G7 is applied to cell E7, which now displays $0.07.

   TROUBLE? If the value "$0.07" is not displayed in cell E7, you either used the format of the wrong cell or you applied the Format Painter to the wrong cell. Click the Undo button on the Standard toolbar to undo your last action, then repeat Steps 1 through 3.

4. Click cell **G19**. The formatting for cell G7 is applied to cell G19.

TROUBLE? If cell G19 is not reformatted, you might have clicked rather than double-clicked the Format Painter button in Step 1. Click cell G7 to make it the active cell, double-click the Format Painter button, then repeat Step 4.

5. Scroll the worksheet so that rows 22 and 24 are visible, then click cell **G22** to apply the format to that cell.

6. Click cell **G24**. The formatting for cell G7 is applied to cell G24.

   You applied the G7 format to all the appropriate cells, so you need to turn off the Format Painter. You can press the Enter key or click the Format Painter button to turn off the option.

7. Click the **Format Painter** button on the Standard toolbar to turn off the Format Painter.

Now you'll format the rest of the values in the Unit Price column as Currency values with two decimal places and no dollar signs.

To format the remaining Unit Price values:

1. Scroll the worksheet so that rows 4 through 18 are visible.

2. Select cells **E8** through **E18**.

3. With the pointer in the highlighted area, right-click to display the shortcut menu, then click **Format Cells**. The Format Cells dialog box opens.

4. Click **Currency** in the Category list box.

   You don't want a dollar sign displayed in these cells, so you need to turn off the Use $ option.

5. Click the **Use $** check box to remove the check mark.

6. If the first formatting option in the Negative Numbers list box is not selected, click that first option.

7. Make sure the Decimal Places option is set to 2.

8. Click the **OK** button to close the Format Cells dialog box. The values in cells E8 through E18 are correctly formatted. See Figure 3-36.

Figure 3-36 Formatted Unit Price and Cost values

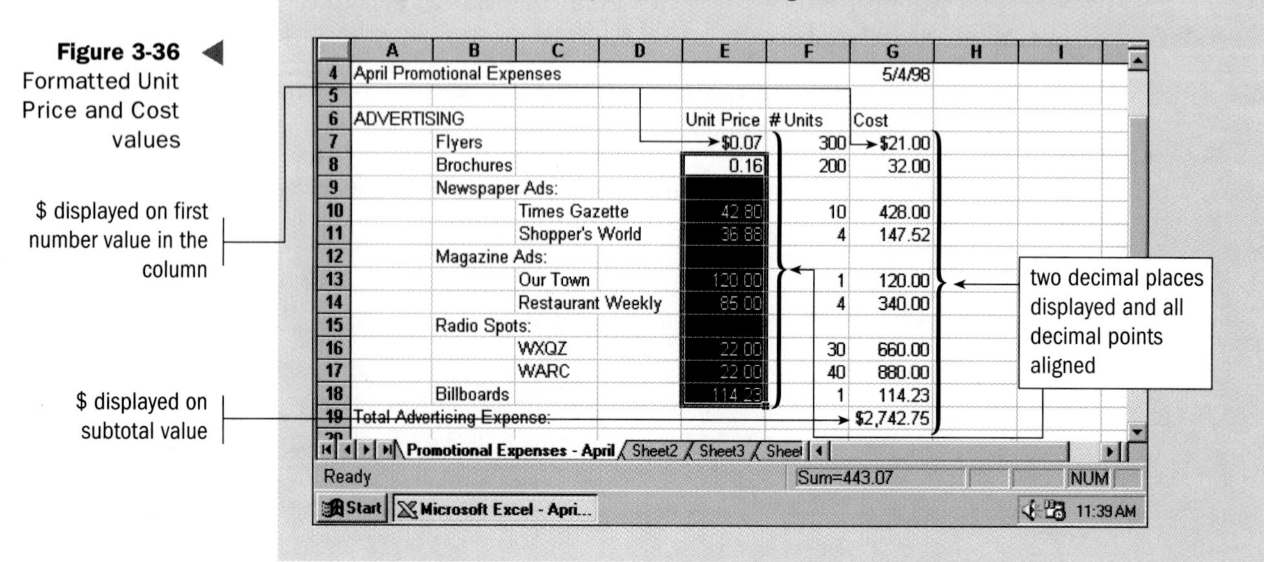

You'll now use the Format Cells dialog box to change the format of the date in cell G4.

To format the date:

1. Click cell **G4** to make it the active cell.
2. With the pointer in the selected cell, right-click to display the shortcut menu, then click **Format Cells** to open the Format Cells dialog box. The Date category is already selected, because the selected cell (G4) contains a date, and the Type list box shows optional date display formats.
3. Click the fifth option in the Type list box. The value "4-May-98" is displayed in the Sample section at the top of the dialog box.
4. Click the **OK** button to close the Format Cells dialog box. Cell G4 now displays 4-May-98.

Next, Kim wants you to adjust the width of certain columns to improve the appearance of the worksheet.

Adjusting Column Widths

Changing the width of a column is another formatting option. You might decide to increase or decrease the width of one or more columns to improve the appearance of a worksheet or to increase its readability.

Sometimes changing the width of a column is necessary to correctly display a value in that column. If a number or date is too large to be displayed in its cell, Excel displays a series of #s to indicate that the cell is too small. When this happens, you need to increase the width of the column containing the value so that the entire value can be displayed.

The standard width for an Excel cell is 8.43 characters, which means that, on average, just over eight characters in the default font (Arial 10) can be displayed in a cell. You can change cell widths to any value from 0 through 255.

Excel provides several ways to adjust the width of a column. One way is to use the **AutoFit** feature, which allows Excel to determine how wide the column must be in order to display all the values in the column.

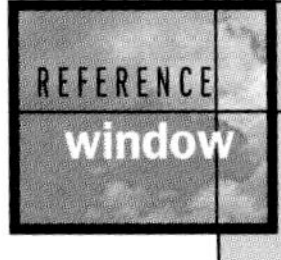

ADJUSTING COLUMN WIDTH USING AUTOFIT

- Position the pointer on the column line between the column you want to adjust and the next column to the right until the pointer changes to ✛.
- Double-click the mouse button.

You can also specify an exact width for a column using the Format menu.

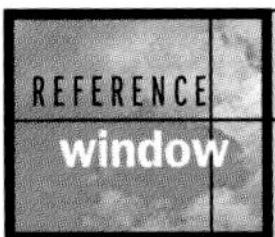

ADJUSTING COLUMN WIDTH USING THE FORMAT MENU

- Select the column to be adjusted.
- Click Format, point to Column, then click Width to display the Column Width dialog box.
- Type the width you want, then click the OK button.

Kim wants you to decrease the width of column A, so that the advertising category labels in column B will appear to be indented under the ADVERTISING heading. Similarly, she wants you to decrease the width of column B so that the subcategory labels in column C will appear indented under their corresponding advertising categories. Columns A, B, and C contain only labels, and column D is empty. When you decrease the width of columns A and B, all the labels in those columns will still be visible because they'll spill over into empty cells to the right.

You'll change the width of columns A and B from the standard 8.43 to 2 characters.

To adjust the width of columns A and B using the Format menu:

1. Click the **A** in the column headings area, hold down the mouse button as you move the mouse into the column B heading, then release the mouse button. Columns A and B are selected and highlighted.

   TROUBLE? If both columns A and B are not highlighted, click any cell to remove the highlight, then repeat Step 1.

2. Click **Format**, point to **Column**, then click **Width**. The Column Width dialog box opens and displays the standard 8.43 column width in the text box. See Figure 3-37.

Figure 3-37 Column Width dialog box

Column Width
Column Width: 8.43
OK
Cancel

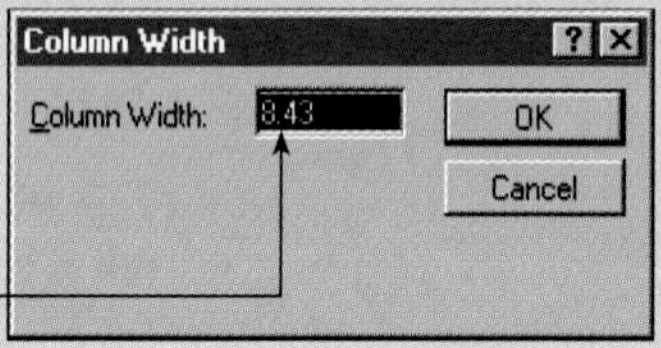

standard column width

3. Type **2** to replace the current entry of 8.43, then click the **OK** button to close the Column Width dialog box. The widths of columns A and B are decreased to 2 characters each.

4. Click cell **F4** to remove the highlight from columns A and B. All labels are visible, and the advertising category and subcategory labels appear appropriately indented in the advertising section of your worksheet. Your screen should now look like Figure 3-38.

Figure 3-38 Adjusted column widths

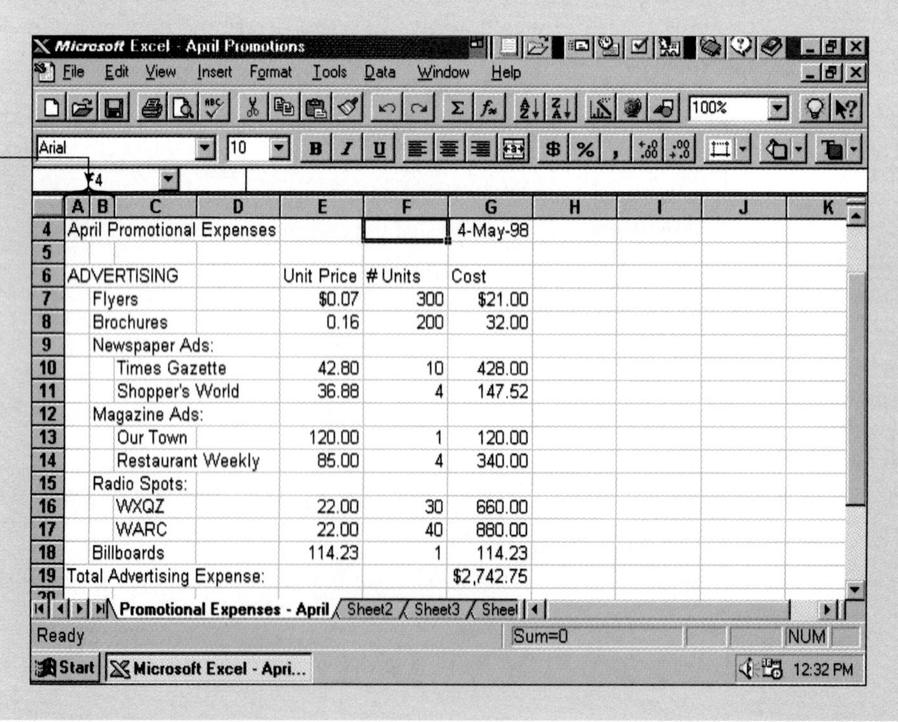

column widths changed to 2

Next, Kim wants you to add borders to the worksheet to improve its appearance.

Adding and Removing Borders

Lines in a worksheet, called **borders**, can add visual interest to a worksheet, separate worksheet sections from one another, highlight particular cells, or provide visual clues to the information in the worksheet. You can add a border to a single cell or a group of cells. The border can be any combination of lines at the top, bottom, left, or right of the selected cell(s).

Excel provides two methods for creating borders: the Borders button on the Formatting toolbar and the Border tab in the Format Cells dialog box. The Borders button allows you to choose from 12 border styles and positions. The Border tab in the Format Cells dialog box provides a wider selection of border positions, line thicknesses, and line styles, including solid, dashed, double, and colored lines.

REFERENCE window

ADDING A BORDER

- Select the cell or cells to which you want to add a border.
- With the highlighted area selected, right-click to display the shortcut menu, then click Format Cells (or click Format on the menu bar then click Cells) to display the Format Cells dialog box, then click the Border tab.
- Click the Outline, Left, Right, Top, and/or Bottom box to indicate where you want the border.
- Select the border Style and Color.
- Click the OK button.

or

- Select the cell or cells to which you want to add a border.
- Click the down arrow next to the Borders button on the Formatting toolbar, then click the type of border you want.

To set off the title area of the worksheet, you'll use the Borders button to outline those cells.

To place a border around the title area:

1. Click the **reference area** list arrow in the formula bar, then click **Title** to move to and select cells A1 through G4.
2. Click the down arrow next to the **Borders** button on the Formatting toolbar. The Borders palette opens. See Figure 3-39.

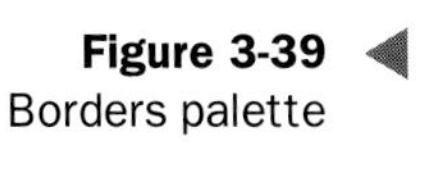

Figure 3-39 Borders palette

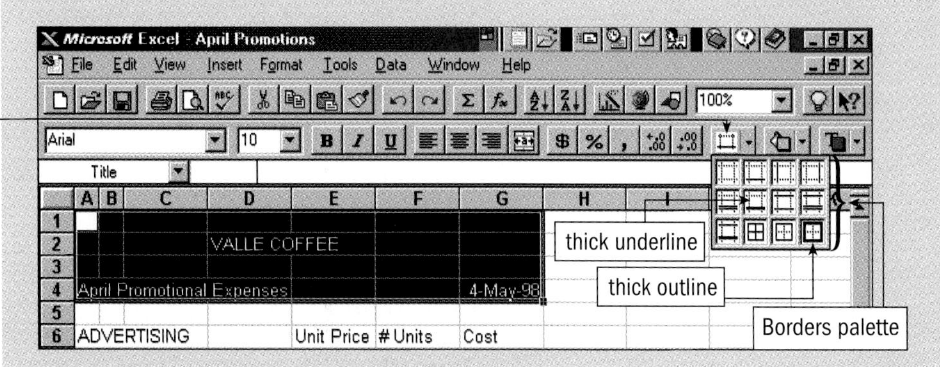

TROUBLE? If you click the Borders button instead of the down arrow next to the button, the Borders palette will not open, and the type of border most recently applied will be placed on the selected cell or cells. To remove the outline, click the down arrow next to the Borders button to open the palette, then click the first button in the first row of the palette. Then repeat Step 2.

3. Click the thick outline button at the far right in the bottom row of the Borders palette.
4. Click any empty cell to remove the highlight and view the border. The top and left sides of the border are not visible because they abut the column and row headings areas. You can use Print Preview to verify that the entire title area is outlined.
5. Click the **Print Preview** button on the Standard toolbar, verify that the worksheet title area is outlined on all four sides, then click the **Close** button on the Print Preview toolbar.

   The preview screen shows your worksheet will be printed with the Excel default settings for margins, paper orientation, worksheet positioning, headers, and footers. Don't worry about these settings for now. You'll learn about changing the page setup in a later tutorial.

Kim also wants an underline below the total promotional expense cell to call attention to that cell.

To underline the total promotional expense cell.

1. Click the **reference area** list arrow in the formula bar, then click **TotalExpense** to move to and select cell G24.
2. Click the down arrow next to the **Borders** button on the Formatting toolbar to open the Borders palette.

   TROUBLE? If you click the Borders button instead of the down arrow next to the button, the Borders palette will not open and a thick black outline (the type of border most recently applied) will be placed around cell G24. To remove the outline, click the down arrow next to the Borders button to open the palette, then click the first button in the first row of the palette. Then repeat Step 2.
3. Click the thick underline button in the second column, second row of the Borders palette.
4. Click any empty cell to remove the highlight and view the border.

Kim thinks that a line under the three column labels in cells E6 through G6 would help highlight the column headings. She would like the text in these three cells to be right-justified to better align with the values below those headings.

To underline and right justify the column heading cells:

1. Select cells **E6** through **G6**.

   The Borders button currently displays a thick black underline, which was the last Borders button style you applied. This is the style you want for these cells, so it is not necessary to open the Borders palette to make a different selection.
2. Click the **Borders** button on the Formatting toolbar. The selected cells are now underlined.
3. Click the **Align Right** button on the Formatting toolbar to right justify the text in the three selected cells.
4. Click any empty cell to remove the highlight and view the applied border.

Cell G19 contains the sum of the column of values in cells G7 through G18. Typically, in a column of such numbers on paper, a line is drawn below the last number in the column as a visual clue to identify the number below the line as a sum. You'll place such a line at the bottom of cell G18 to visually identify the total in cell G19 as a sum. Similarly, cells G19 and G22 are summed to produce the grand total value displayed in G24. A grand total value is often marked off with a double line, so you'll place a double line beneath the value in cell G22 as a visual clue.

To underline cells G18 and G22 using the Format Cells dialog box:

1. Click cell **G18**.
2. With the pointer in the selected cell, right-click to display the shortcut menu, click **Format Cells** to display the Format Cells dialog box, then click the **Border** tab. All the border boxes in the left Border section are blank, indicating that the active cell currently does not have a border.
3. Click the **Bottom** text box to specify a bottom border.
4. If necessary, click the thin solid line in the second box, first column under Style. See Figure 3-40.

Figure 3-40 Border tab of the Format Cells dialog box

selects a border along the bottom of the cell

thin solid line style is selected

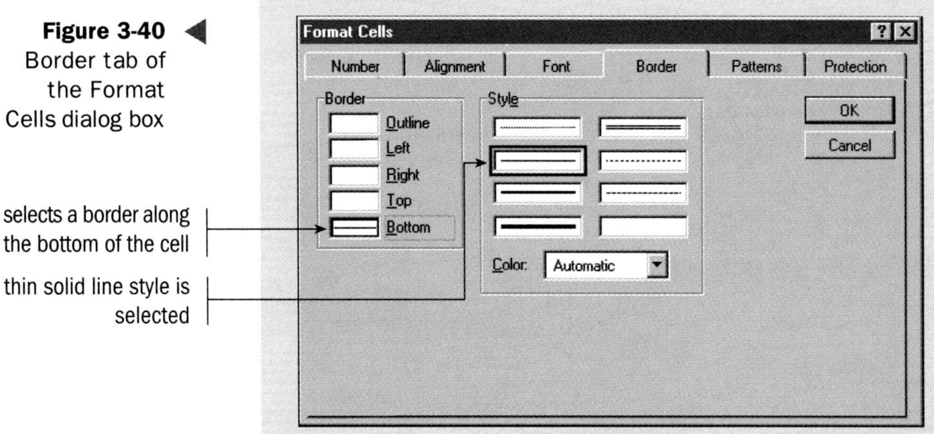

5. Click the **OK** button to close the dialog box, then click any empty cell to remove the highlight and view the underlined cell.

   Next, you'll add the double line to the bottom of cell G22 to mark off the grand total value in cell G24.

6. Click cell **G22**.
7. With the pointer in the selected cell, right-click to display the shortcut menu, then click **Format Cells**. The Format Cells dialog box opens. Note that the Border tab is already selected, because it's the tab you accessed most recently.
8. Click the **Bottom** text box to specify a bottom border, then click the double line in the first box, second column under Style.
9. Click the **OK** button to close the dialog box, then click any empty cell to remove the highlight and view the underlined cell.

Kim thinks that the dark line below cell G24 conflicts with the underlines in cells G18 and G22 and could confuse someone viewing the worksheet. She asks you to remove this dark line. To remove a border, you again use the Border tab in the Format Cells dialog box.

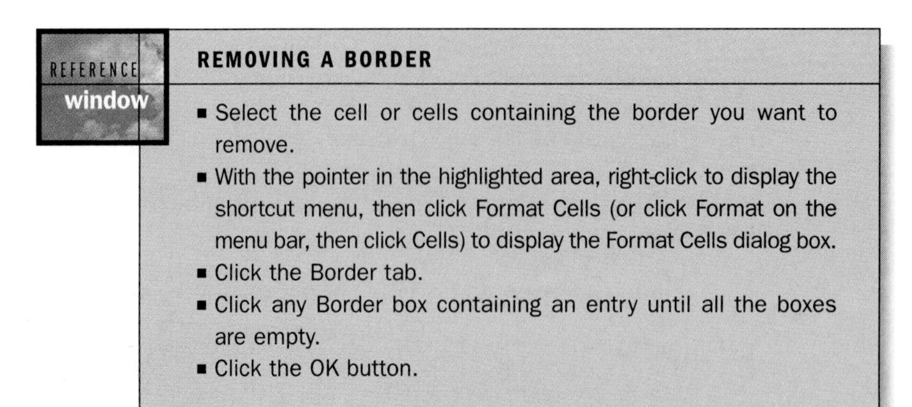

REFERENCE window

REMOVING A BORDER

- Select the cell or cells containing the border you want to remove.
- With the pointer in the highlighted area, right-click to display the shortcut menu, then click Format Cells (or click Format on the menu bar, then click Cells) to display the Format Cells dialog box.
- Click the Border tab.
- Click any Border box containing an entry until all the boxes are empty.
- Click the OK button.

You need to remove the dark line border applied to the bottom of cell G24.

To remove the border from the total promotional expense cell:

1. Click cell **G24**.
2. With the pointer in the selected cell, right-click to display the shortcut menu, then click **Format Cells**. The Format Cells dialog box opens. In the Border section of the dialog box, the line in the box next to Bottom indicates the presence of a bottom border.
3. Click the **Bottom** text box to remove the line from the box.
4. Click the **OK** button to close the dialog box, then click any empty cell to remove the highlight on cell G24. Cell G24 no longer has a border. See Figure 3-41.

Figure 3-41 Bottom borders

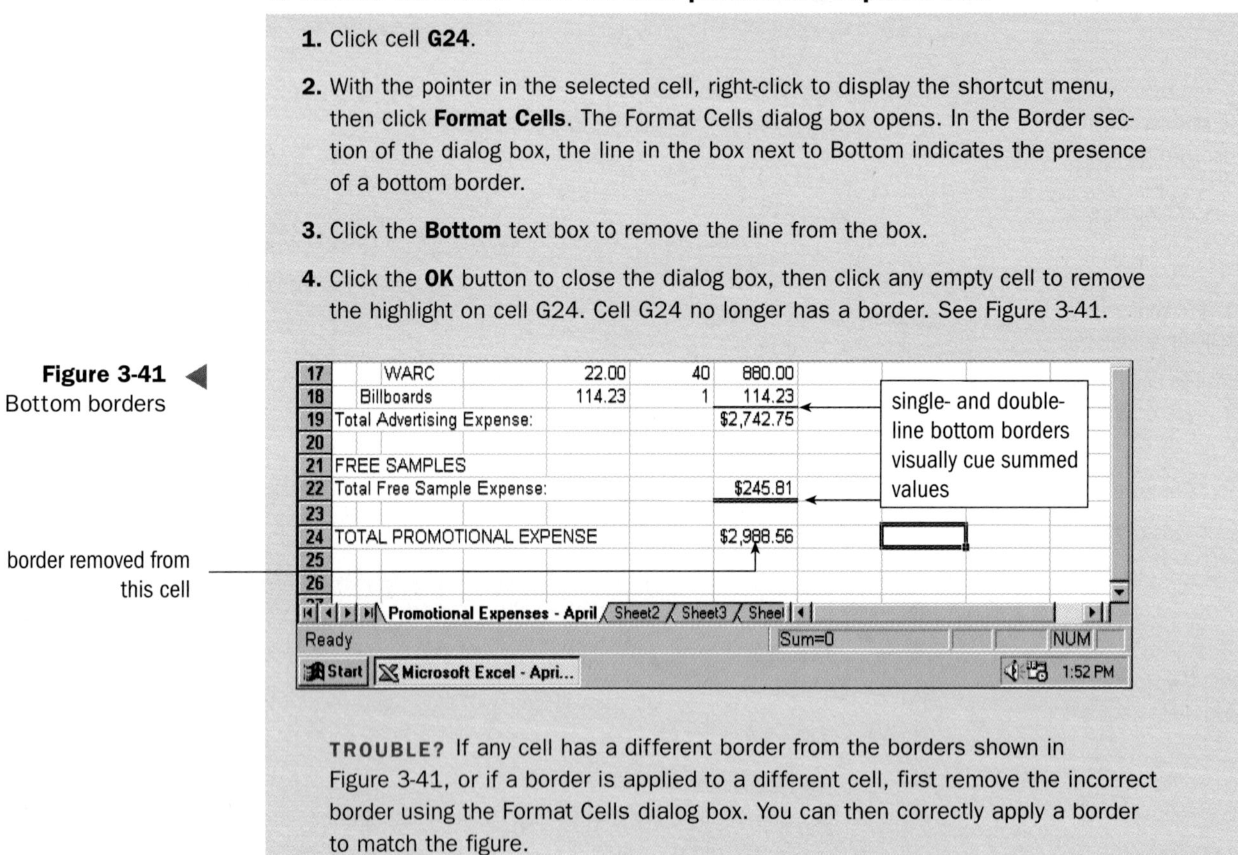

TROUBLE? If any cell has a different border from the borders shown in Figure 3-41, or if a border is applied to a different cell, first remove the incorrect border using the Format Cells dialog box. You can then correctly apply a border to match the figure.

Splitting the Worksheet Window

The worksheet window can display only a section of your entire worksheet. The April Promotions worksheet is not particularly large, yet you've had to scroll it many times to view and work in different sections of the worksheet. A larger worksheet presents an even greater problem.

In your worksheet, the column headings in row 6 apply to the values displayed in rows 7 through 18. The specific heading in cell G6 also applies to values in rows 19, 22, and 24. Because the worksheet window might not display rows 6 through 24 on a single screen, you might not be able to view the headings and all the associated values at the same time. Suppose that you had twice as many advertising expense categories and twice as many columns of data; then it would be even more difficult to identify the meaning of values that are more than a screen below the column headings. To determine which column is which, you would have to scroll up the worksheet to see the headings again.

Excel allows you to split the worksheet window so that you can view two different parts of the worksheet at the same time, as shown in Figure 3-42.

Figure 3-42 Splitting the worksheet window

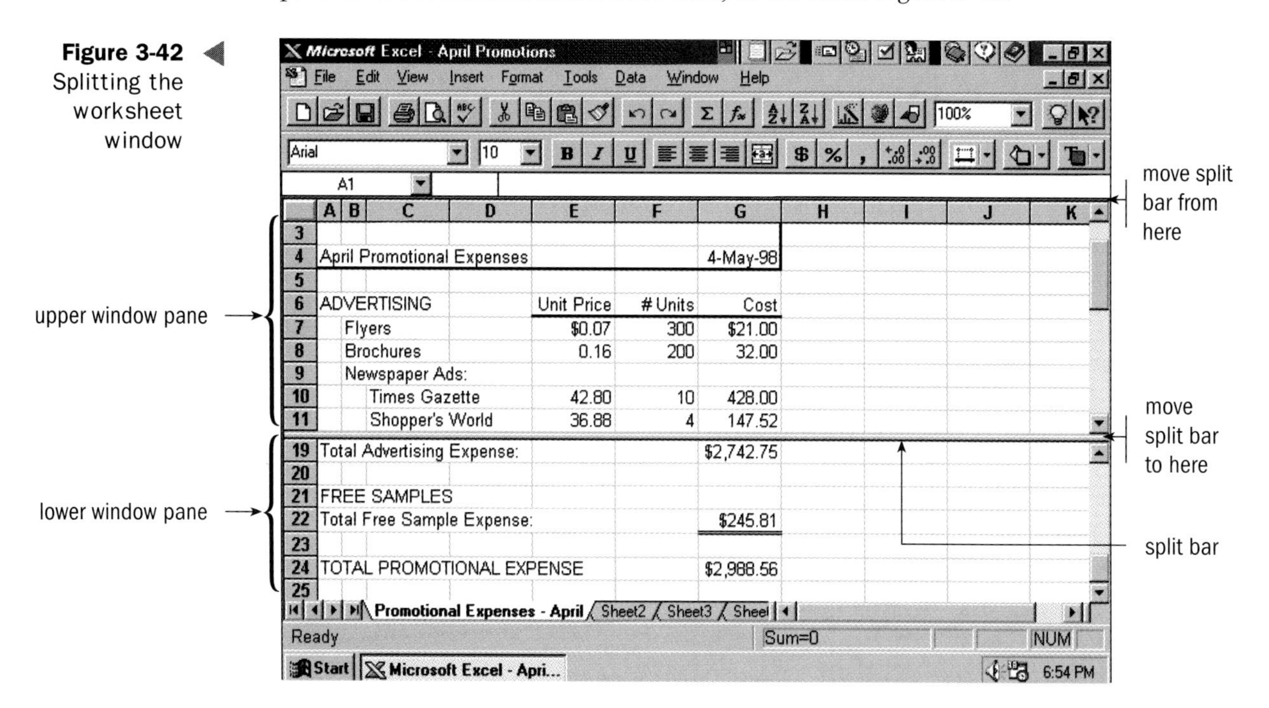

A **window pane** is a subdivision of the worksheet window that you can scroll independently to display a separate section of a worksheet. Figure 3-42 shows your worksheet split into two horizontal window panes, each with its own vertical scroll bar.

Excel provides several techniques for splitting worksheet windows. The easiest way is to use the horizontal split bar. You'll split your worksheet window as shown in Figure 3-42.

To split the worksheet window into two horizontal window panes:

1. Click the reference area at the left side of the formula bar, then type **A1** to move to the top of the worksheet.
2. Move the pointer into the vertical scroll bar area at the right of the screen. The pointer changes to ↖.
3. Position the pointer over the small rectangle at the top of the scroll bar until it changes to ╪, click and hold down the mouse button as you drag the split bar down to just below row 9, then release the mouse button. The worksheet window splits into two window panes, with rows 1 through 9 visible in the upper pane and row 9 visible at the top of the lower pane.

   TROUBLE? If the split bar didn't end up just below row 9, place the pointer on the split bar and then drag it up or down until it is correctly positioned.
4. Scroll the lower window pane until row 19 appears at the top of that window pane. You can now see the worksheet title area and the total promotional expense (cell G24) on the screen at the same time.
5. Scroll the upper window pane until rows 3 though 11 are visible. Your screen should now look like Figure 3-42.

To remove the split, you either drag the split bar back to the top of the scroll bar or double-click the split bar.

To remove the split window:

1. Move the pointer over the split bar until it changes to ÷.
2. Click the mouse button and hold it down as you drag the split bar to the top of the worksheet window, then release the mouse button.

You've finished making the necessary formatting changes to your worksheet, and you should now save the workbook.

To save the workbook:

1. Click the **Save** button on the Standard toolbar to save the changes you've made to the workbook.

Quick Check

1. How do you move quickly to a named cell in a worksheet?
2. What happens to formulas and named cells and ranges when you add or delete columns or rows?
3. How have you used the Clipboard in this tutorial? What is different about the way the Clipboard works in Excel versus the other Office 95 programs?
4. The fastest way to apply the formatting in one cell to other cells is to use the ___________.
5. Why might a cell display a series of #s?
6. ___________ can add visual interest, separate worksheet sections, highlight particular cells, or provide visual clues to information.
7. A(n) ___________ is a subdivision of the worksheet window that can be scrolled independently.

Now that you've completed Session 3.2, you can exit Excel or you can continue to the next session.

SESSION 3.3

In this session you will insert and size an embedded picture, clear cells, print a worksheet, embed an Excel worksheet in a Word document, and then resize and edit the embedded worksheet.

Inserting and Sizing an Embedded Picture

To add some visual interest to the worksheet, Kim wants you to embed a picture of the Valle Coffee cup in the title area.

REFERENCE window

EMBEDDING A PICTURE

- Select a cell in an empty area of your worksheet.
- Click Insert then click Picture to open the Picture dialog box.
- Make sure the Look in text box shows the folder that contains the picture you want to embed.
- Click the filename you want, then click the OK button.

The picture of the Valle Coffee cup is called ValleCup and is located in the Tutorial.03 folder on your Student Disk. You'll embed the picture in an empty cell to the right of your worksheet data.

To embed the ValleCup picture:

1. Click cell **I5**, click **Insert**, then click **Picture**. The Picture dialog box opens.
2. Click the **Look in** list arrow, then click the drive containing your Student Disk.
3. Click **Tutorial.03** in the Name list box, then click the **Open** button.
4. Click **ValleCup**.
5. Click the **OK** button to close the dialog box and insert the picture in your worksheet. See Figure 3-43.

Figure 3-43 Embedded picture

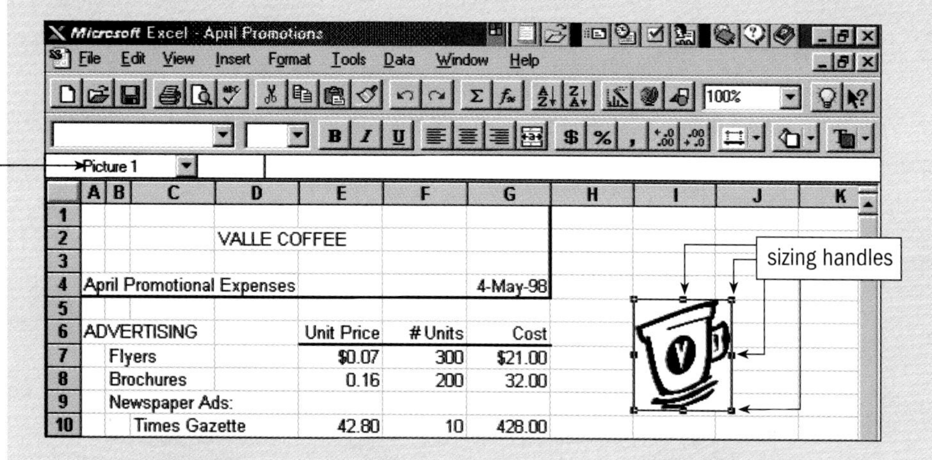

Eight sizing handles appear around the border of the picture, and the reference area displays "Picture 1," both of which indicate that the picture is selected.

6. Click an empty cell to deselect the picture.

The picture occupies more than the one cell (I5) in which you inserted it. You inserted the picture in an empty area of the worksheet so that it would not cover any of your worksheet data. If the picture did overlap cells containing data, however, those cells would not be affected, and you could simply move the picture to another location.

Notice that Excel automatically added a border around the picture. You'll remove the border so that only the coffee cup appears in the worksheet.

To remove the border around the picture:

1. Right-click the picture to select it and display its shortcut menu, then click **Format Object**. The Format Object dialog box opens.
2. Click the **Patterns** tab, if necessary. See Figure 3-44.

Figure 3-44 Format Object dialog box

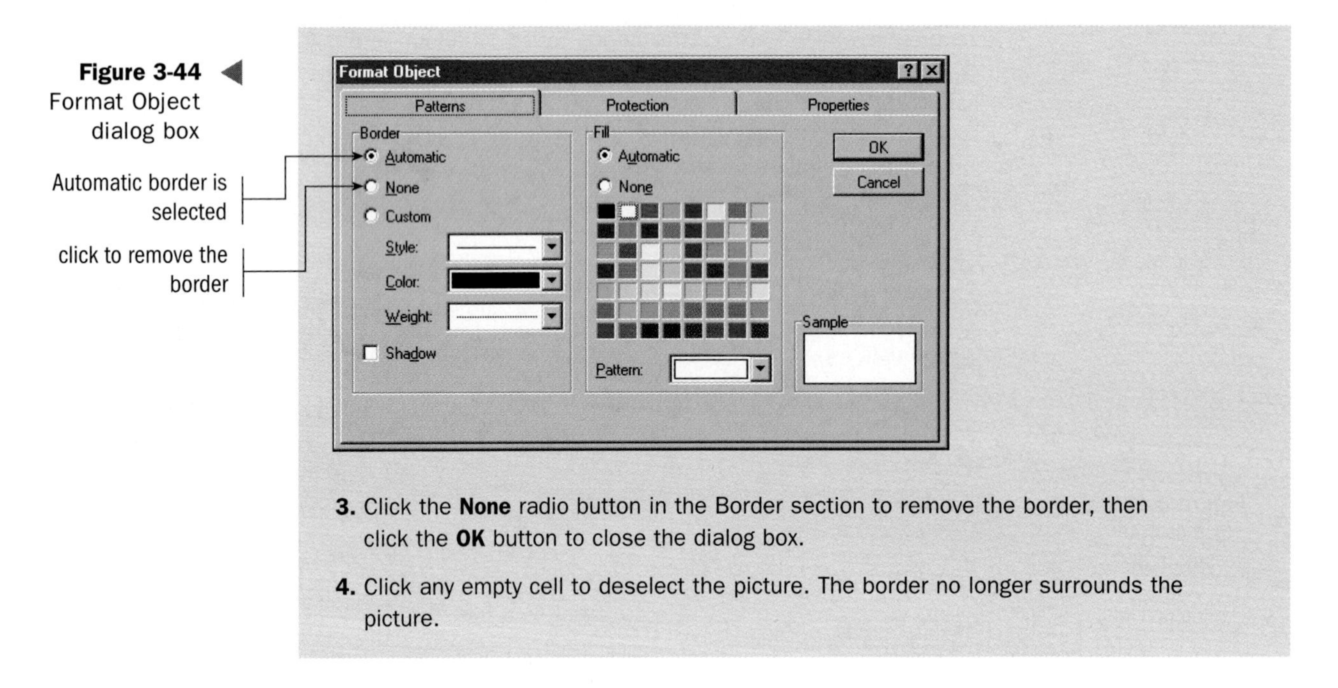

3. Click the **None** radio button in the Border section to remove the border, then click the **OK** button to close the dialog box.
4. Click any empty cell to deselect the picture. The border no longer surrounds the picture.

The Valle Coffee cup picture is currently too large to fit into the title area where you planned to place it. You need to resize the picture to make it smaller.

To resize the picture:

1. Click the picture to select it. The sizing handles are visible around the picture.
2. Move the pointer over the sizing handle at the lower-right corner of the picture until the pointer changes to ↘.
3. Click the mouse button and hold it down as you move the mouse diagonally up and to the left until the pointer is approximately in the middle of cell I7, then release the mouse button. See Figure 3-45.

Figure 3-45 Resizing a picture

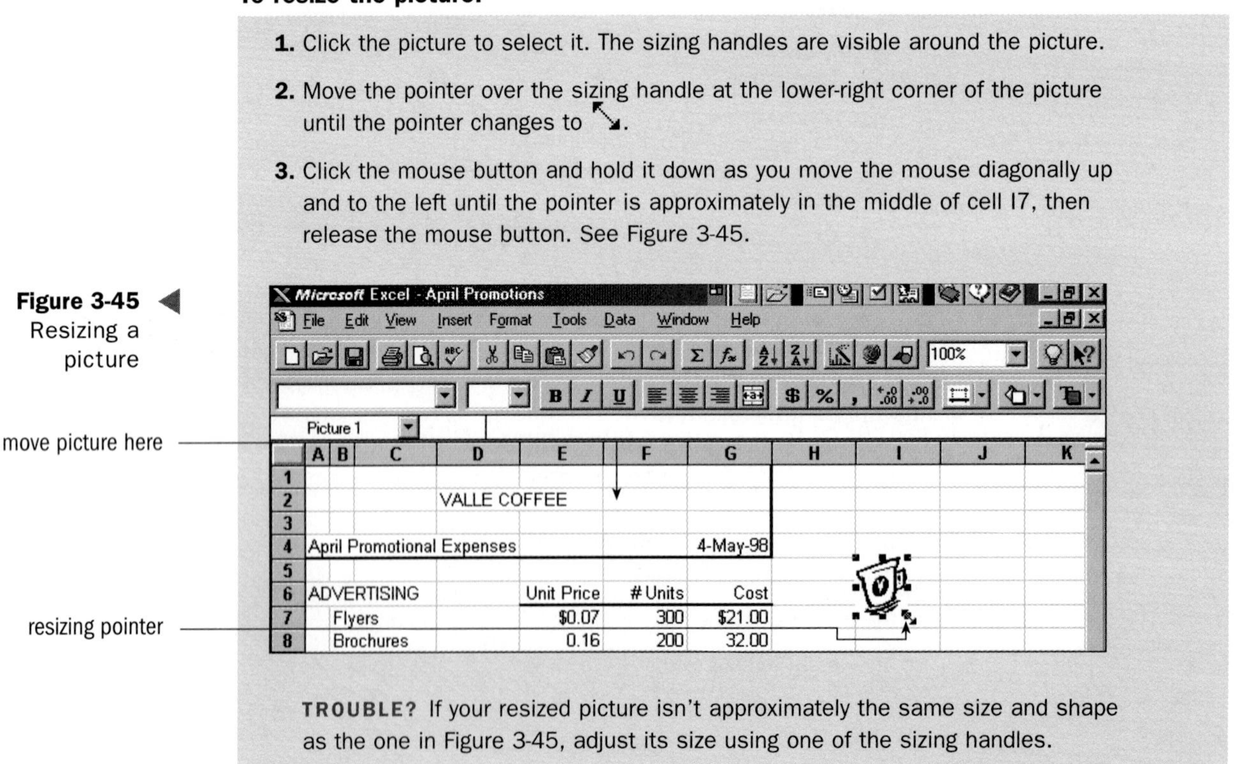

TROUBLE? If your resized picture isn't approximately the same size and shape as the one in Figure 3-45, adjust its size using one of the sizing handles.

Now that the picture is the size you want it, you can move it to the title area, as indicated in Figure 3-45.

To move the Valle Coffee cup picture:

1. If necessary, scroll your screen so that both the picture and the location you're moving it to are visible. See Figure 3-45.
2. If the picture isn't still selected, click the picture.
3. Position the pointer over the picture. The pointer changes to ↖.
4. Click the mouse button and hold it down as you drag the outline of the picture up and to the left until it is positioned to the right of the text "VALLE COFFEE," then release the mouse button. See Figure 3-46.

Figure 3-46 Picture correctly positioned

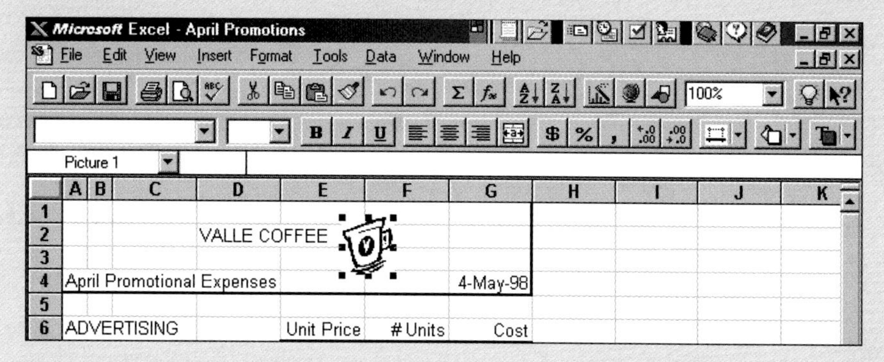

TROUBLE? If the picture isn't positioned as shown in Figure 3-46, repeat Steps 3 and 4 to reposition the picture.

5. Click any empty cell to deselect the picture.

You have now completed formatting the worksheet. Before you print the worksheet or embed it in the Word document, however, you need to complete one important task—clearing the cells around your worksheet.

Clearing Cell Contents

Before you print the worksheet or embed it into another document, you must make sure that the cells around the worksheet data are, in fact, empty. If you embed the worksheet in a Word document, for example, Word will display the worksheet from column A through the last column with a cell containing a value, formula, format, or note; and from row 1 through the last row with a cell containing a value, formula, format, or note. When you embed your current worksheet in Word (which you will do later in this session), you want Word to display columns A through G and rows 1 through 24. However, you might have accidentally entered something in a cell beyond those limits. For example, when deselecting a cell you might have clicked an empty cell in row H and then inadvertently pressed the spacebar; if you then inserted that worksheet into Word, columns A through H, rather than A though G, would be displayed.

If you enter data into the wrong cell or enter the wrong data into a cell, you can clear the cell contents using the Delete key, the Clear Contents command on the shortcut menu, or the Clear option on the Edit menu. Do *not* press the spacebar to enter a blank character in an attempt to clear a cell's contents. A blank character is considered text, so even though the cell appears empty, it is not.

Pressing the Delete key or choosing Clear Contents from the shortcut menu clears only the contents of a cell. The Clear option on the Edit menu allows you to clear the cell contents, cell formatting, cell notes (text comments attached to a cell), or all three.

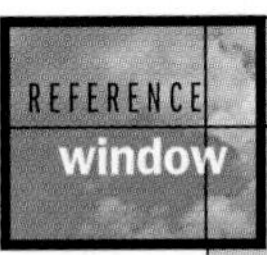

CLEARING CELL CONTENTS

- Select the cell or cells to be cleared.
- Press the Delete key.

or

- With the pointer in the highlighted area, right-click to display the shortcut menu, then click Clear Contents.

or

- Click Edit, point to Clear, then click Contents to erase only the contents of the cell, or click All to completely clear the cell contents, formatting, and notes.

As a precaution, you should completely clear at least the 8 columns and 15 rows that immediately follow the last significant column and row in your worksheet.

To completely clear the rows and columns around the worksheet data:

1. Select columns **H** through **O**.
2. Click **Edit**, point to **Clear**, then click **All**.
3. Scroll the horizontal scroll bar so that column A is visible.
4. Select rows **25** through **40**.
5. Click **Edit**, point to **Clear**, then click **All**.

The worksheet is now ready to be printed. Kim wants to review the printed worksheet before you embed it in her letter to Media Consultants.

Printing a Worksheet

You can print an Excel worksheet using either the Print button on the Standard toolbar or the Print option on the File menu. As in other Office 95 programs, the Print button prints one copy of the worksheet with the current settings, and the Print option displays a dialog box with settings you can specify. For example, in a multisheet workbook, you can specify which worksheets to print, or you can choose to print the entire workbook.

Before printing the worksheet, you should preview it first to see how it will look when printed. By default, Excel prints a worksheet with landscape orientation, positions the worksheet in the upper-left corner of the page, and prints standard page headers and footers. In **landscape orientation**, the paper is positioned so that it is wider than it is tall. A **header** is text printed in the top margin of every page of a worksheet. The default Excel header is the worksheet name centered in the top margin. A **footer** is text printed in the bottom margin of every worksheet page. Excel's default footer is a centered page number.

To preview the worksheet and check the page setup:

1. Click the **Print Preview** button on the Standard toolbar. Excel displays the worksheet in the Print Preview window. See Figure 3-47.

Figure 3-47 Worksheet displayed in Print Preview

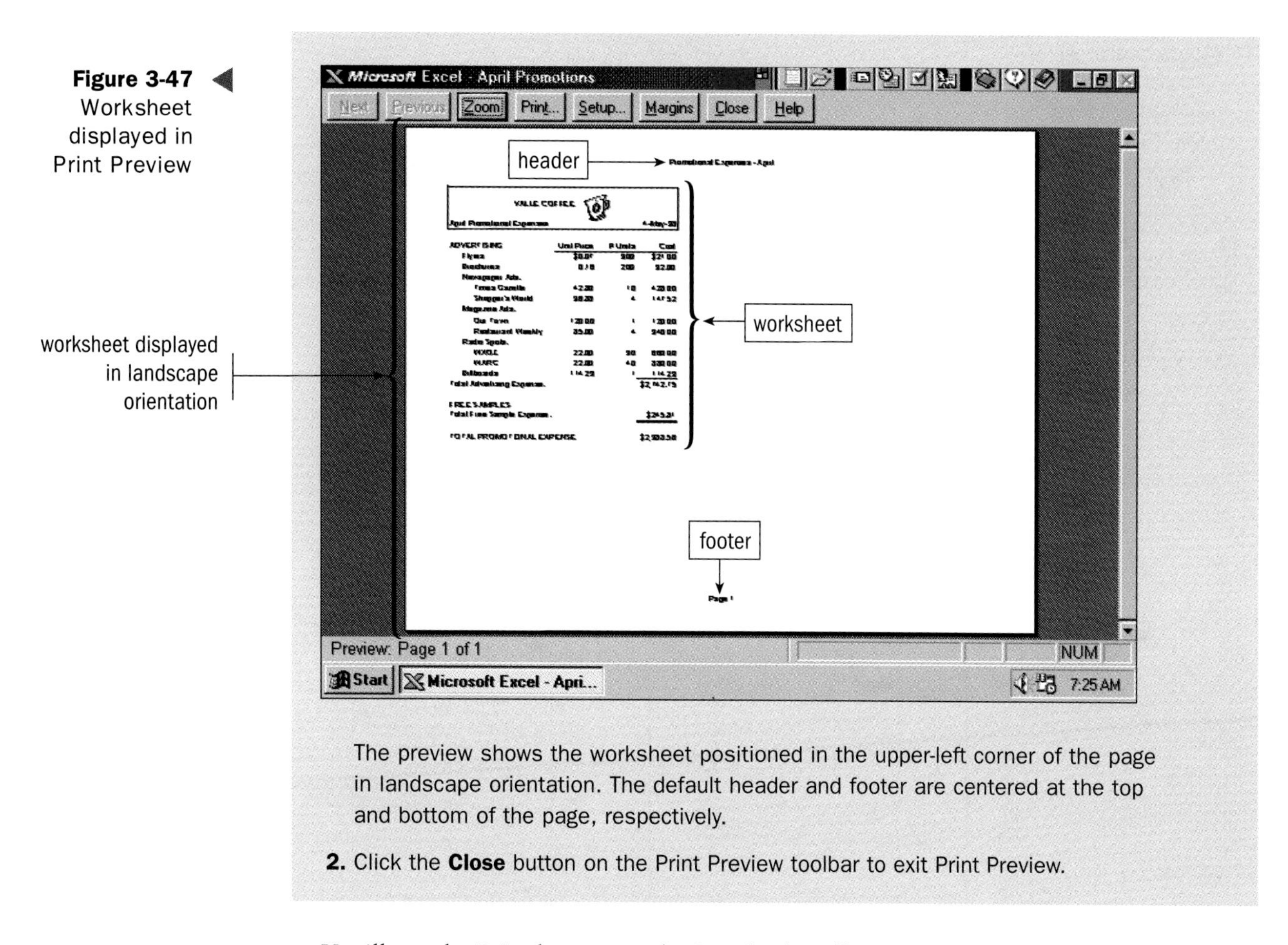

The preview shows the worksheet positioned in the upper-left corner of the page in landscape orientation. The default header and footer are centered at the top and bottom of the page, respectively.

2. Click the **Close** button on the Print Preview toolbar to exit Print Preview.

You'll use the Print button on the Standard toolbar to print one copy of the worksheet with the current settings. As with other documents, it's a good idea to save the worksheet before printing it.

To save and print the worksheet:

1. Click the **Save** button on the Standard toolbar.
2. Click the **Print** button on the Standard toolbar.

Kim reviews the printed worksheet and is satisfied with its appearance. Now she wants you to embed the worksheet in the letter to Media Consultants.

Embedding an Excel Worksheet in a Word Document

There are two ways to embed Excel data in a Word document. You can use the Insert Object command in Word to embed a copy of an entire Excel worksheet. If you want to embed only a section of an Excel worksheet, you can use the Copy command in Excel to place a copy of the selected worksheet section on the Clipboard, then switch to Word, where you use the Paste Special command to paste the Clipboard contents into the Word document. See Figure 3-48.

Figure 3-48 Inserting versus Copy and Paste Special

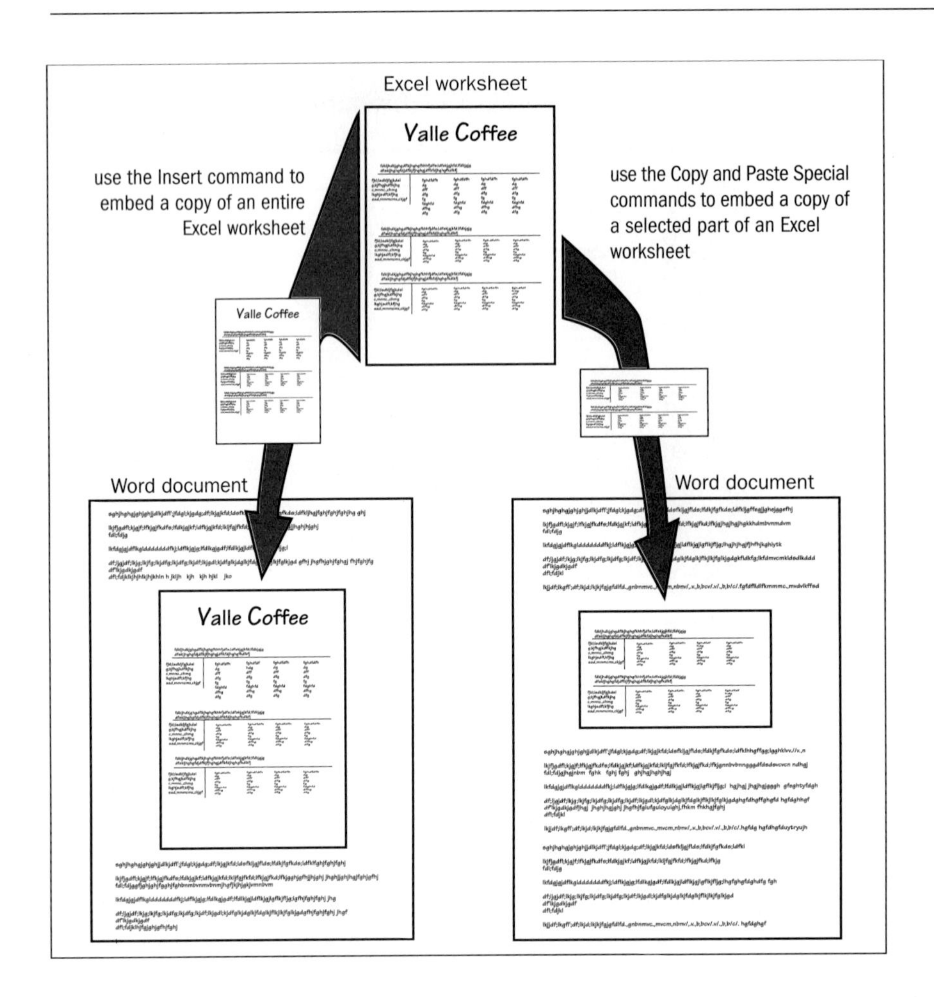

No matter which method you use to embed the Excel data in your Word document, Word contains only a *copy* of the Excel data. If you edit the embedded worksheet, only the worksheet in Word is changed; the original Excel worksheet remains intact.

REFERENCE window

EMBEDDING AN EXCEL WORKSHEET IN WORD

- In Word, place the insertion point where you want to insert the embedded worksheet.
- Click Insert on the menu bar, click Object, then click the Create from File tab in the Object dialog box.
- In the File Name box, type the name of the file containing the worksheet you want to embed, or click Browse and then locate and select the workbook file you want.
- Click the OK button to close the Object dialog box.

or

- In Excel, select the cells to be embedded, then click the Copy button on the Standard toolbar.
- In Word, place the insertion point where you want to embed the selected worksheet cells, click Edit on the menu bar, then click Paste Special to open the Paste Special dialog box.
- Click Microsoft Excel Worksheet Object.
- Click the OK button to close the Paste Special dialog box.

You need to open Kim's final version of the letter document, which is called PLetter in the Tutorial.03 folder of your Student Disk, and start Word. You can do this without first exiting Excel.

To open the letter document and start Word:

1. Click the **Open a Document** button on the Office Shortcut Bar. Office 95 opens the Open dialog box.
2. Click the **Look in** list arrow, click the drive containing your Student Disk, click **Tutorial.03**, then click the **Open** button.
3. Click **PLetter** then click the **Open** button. Word starts with PLetter as the active document.

You'll immediately save the document with a new name, so that you don't alter the original document.

To save the letter with a different filename:

1. Click **File** on the menu bar, then click **Save As** to display the Save As dialog box.
2. Type **Final Promotion Letter** then click the **Save** button. Word saves the letter as Final Promotion Letter in the Tutorial.03 folder.

If you use the Copy and Paste Special commands to embed Excel worksheet cells into Word, it is easier to do so if both Word and Excel are running so that you can switch easily between the two programs. If you use the Insert command to insert an Excel worksheet, the workbook *must* be closed, because Office 95 will not allow you to access an open file. (It doesn't matter if Excel is running or not.)

You'll use the Insert command to embed the entire worksheet in the letter; therefore, you need to close the Excel workbook. Also, because you're finished working in Excel, you'll exit the Excel program.

To close your workbook and exit Excel:

1. Click the **Microsoft Excel** button on the taskbar to switch to Excel.
2. Click the **Close** button on the title bar to close the workbook and exit Excel. You return to the Word document.

   TROUBLE? If a dialog box appears asking if you want to save changes, click the No button, because any changes made since you've printed the worksheet would be accidental.

Now you can insert the Excel worksheet into the letter.

To embed the worksheet in the letter:

1. Scroll the letter until the bottom of the WordArt image is visible on page 2, then place the insertion point to the left of the paragraph mark next to the WordArt image, as shown in Figure 3-49.

Figure 3-49 Preparing to embed the Excel worksheet

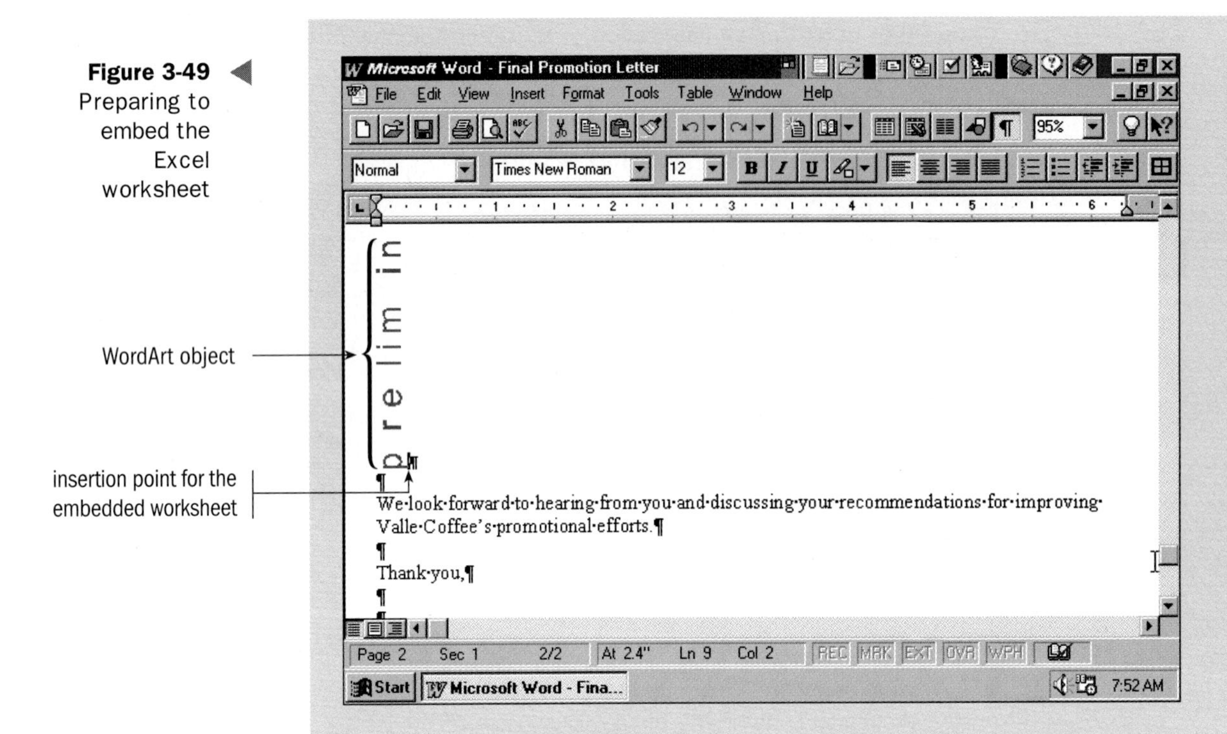

TROUBLE? If the paragraph marks are not visible on your screen, click the Show/Hide button ¶ on the Standard toolbar to display nonprinting characters.

To allow for some spacing between the WordArt object and the embedded worksheet, you'll tab to the right before inserting the worksheet.

2. Press the **Tab** key three times to move the insertion point over to the 1.5-inch mark.

   TROUBLE? Your document might have scrolled up after you pressed the Tab key the first time. When you press the Tab key the second time, your window should automatically return to its previous position. If the document continues to scroll up after you press the Tab key a total of three times, scroll the document down so that you can see the bottom of the WordArt object and the three tab indicators.

3. Click **Insert** on the menu bar, then click **Object**. The Object dialog box opens.
4. Click the **Create from File** tab, then click the **Browse** button. The Browse dialog box opens.
5. If Tutorial.03 is not displayed in the Look in text box, click the **Look in** list arrow, click the drive containing your Student Disk, click **Tutorial.03**, then click the **Open** button.
6. Click **April Promotions** then click the **OK** button to close the Browse dialog box. The filename now appears in the File Name text box of the Object dialog box.
7. Click the **OK** button to close the Object dialog box. After a few moments, the worksheet is embedded in your document. See Figure 3-50. If necessary, scroll your screen so that it looks like Figure 3-50.

Figure 3-50 ◀ Worksheet embedded in the Word document

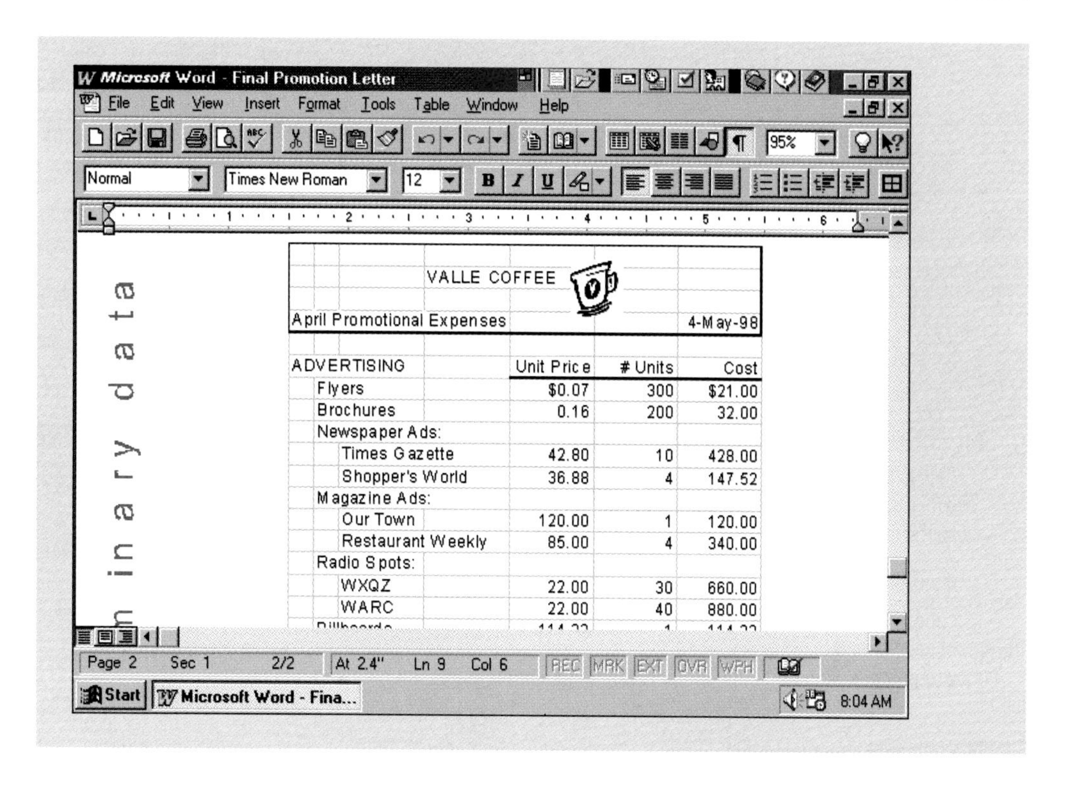

To see how the letter appears now that you've embedded the worksheet, you'll display the letter in Print Preview.

To preview the letter and the embedded worksheet:

1. Click the **Print Preview** button on the Standard toolbar.

   Kim thinks the worksheet is too close to the paragraphs both above and below it. Also, she thinks the WordArt text and the worksheet would look better indented from the left margin of the document. You can make these changes right in Print Preview.

2. Click the **Magnifier** button on the Print Preview toolbar to turn off the magnifier pointer. The pointer changes to I when you move it into the document area.

3. At the top of page 2, click to position the pointer at the end of the paragraph immediately above the embedded worksheet, then press the **Enter** key to add an additional blank line before the worksheet.

4. Click to position the pointer directly below the embedded worksheet, then press the **Enter** key to add an additional blank line after the worksheet.

5. Click to position the pointer in front of the sideways "p" in the WordArt object, then press the **Tab** key. The WordArt object and the worksheet both move one-half inch to the right.

6. Click the **Close** button on the Print Preview toolbar to exit Print Preview.

7. Click the **Save** button on the Standard toolbar to save the document.

Kim thinks that the cell gridlines visible in the worksheet are distracting and should be eliminated. To remove the gridlines you need to edit the embedded worksheet.

Editing an Embedded Excel Worksheet

As you learned in Tutorial 1, you can edit an embedded Excel worksheet from within Word. When you do, the features and commands of the source program—Excel, in this case—are available to you.

To remove the gridlines from the embedded worksheet:

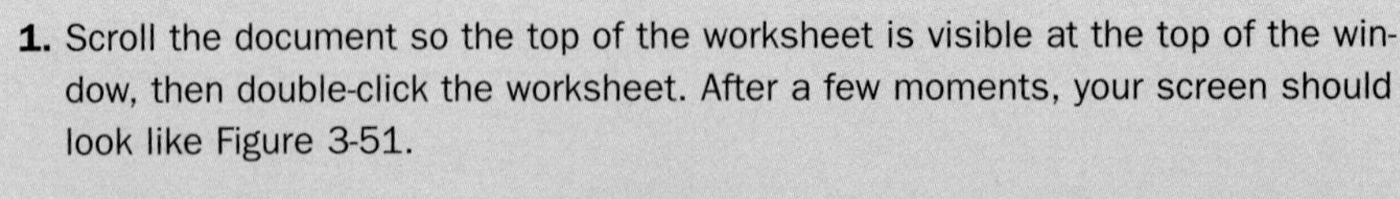

1. Scroll the document so the top of the worksheet is visible at the top of the window, then double-click the worksheet. After a few moments, your screen should look like Figure 3-51.

Figure 3-51 Editing the embedded worksheet

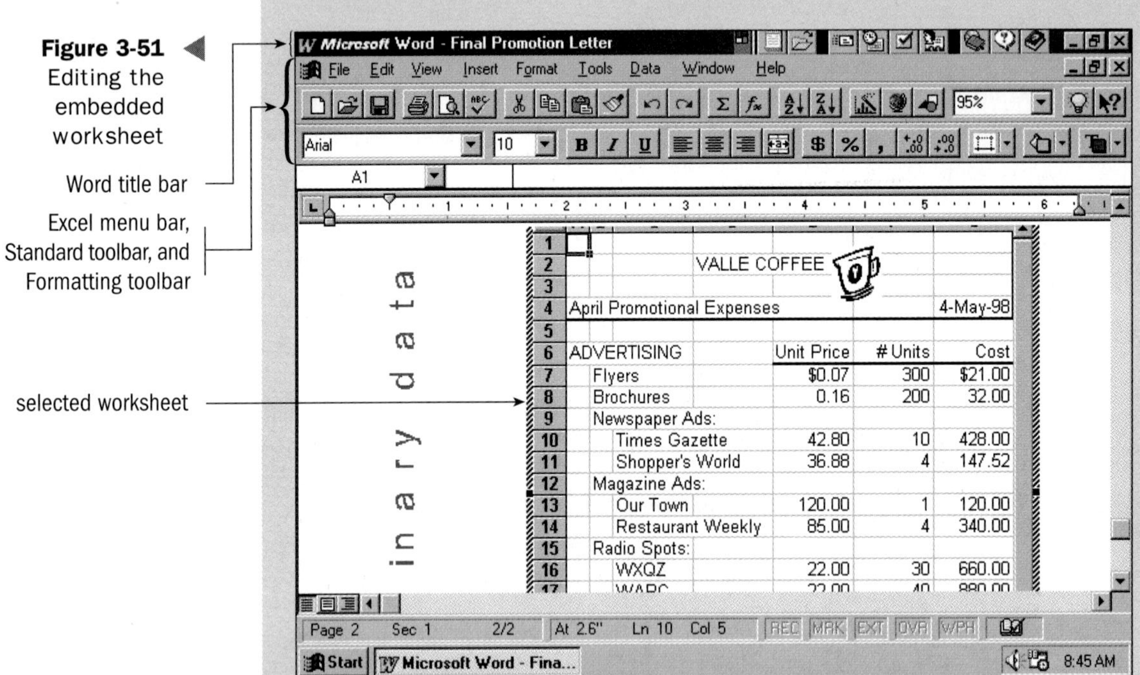

TROUBLE? If you see a series of number signs (######) in the worksheet, just continue with the steps. When you are editing a worksheet, the columns are temporarily displayed with different widths.

The title bar still displays "Microsoft Word," but the Standard and Formatting toolbars change to those of Excel, not Word. Although you can't tell by looking at it, the menu bar is also Excel's. Word has initiated Excel so that you can edit the worksheet.

2. Click **Tools** on the menu bar, click **Options** to open the Options dialog box, then click the **View** tab, if necessary.
3. Click the **Gridlines** check box in the Window Options section of the dialog box to remove the check mark, then click the **OK** button to close the Options dialog box. The worksheet is displayed without gridlines.
4. Click in the blank area to the left of the worksheet to end the edit. The Word screen returns.
5. Click in the blank area to deselect the worksheet.

After viewing the worksheet without the gridlines, Kim decides that the entire worksheet would look better with a border around it to distinguish the worksheet as a separate entity. You'll use the Borders button in Word to outline the worksheet. This button displays the Borders toolbar, which provides options for adding borders in a Word document.

To place a border around the embedded worksheet:

1. Click the worksheet to select it.
2. Click the **Borders** button on the Formatting toolbar to display the Borders toolbar. See Figure 3-52.

Figure 3-52 Placing a border around the embedded worksheet

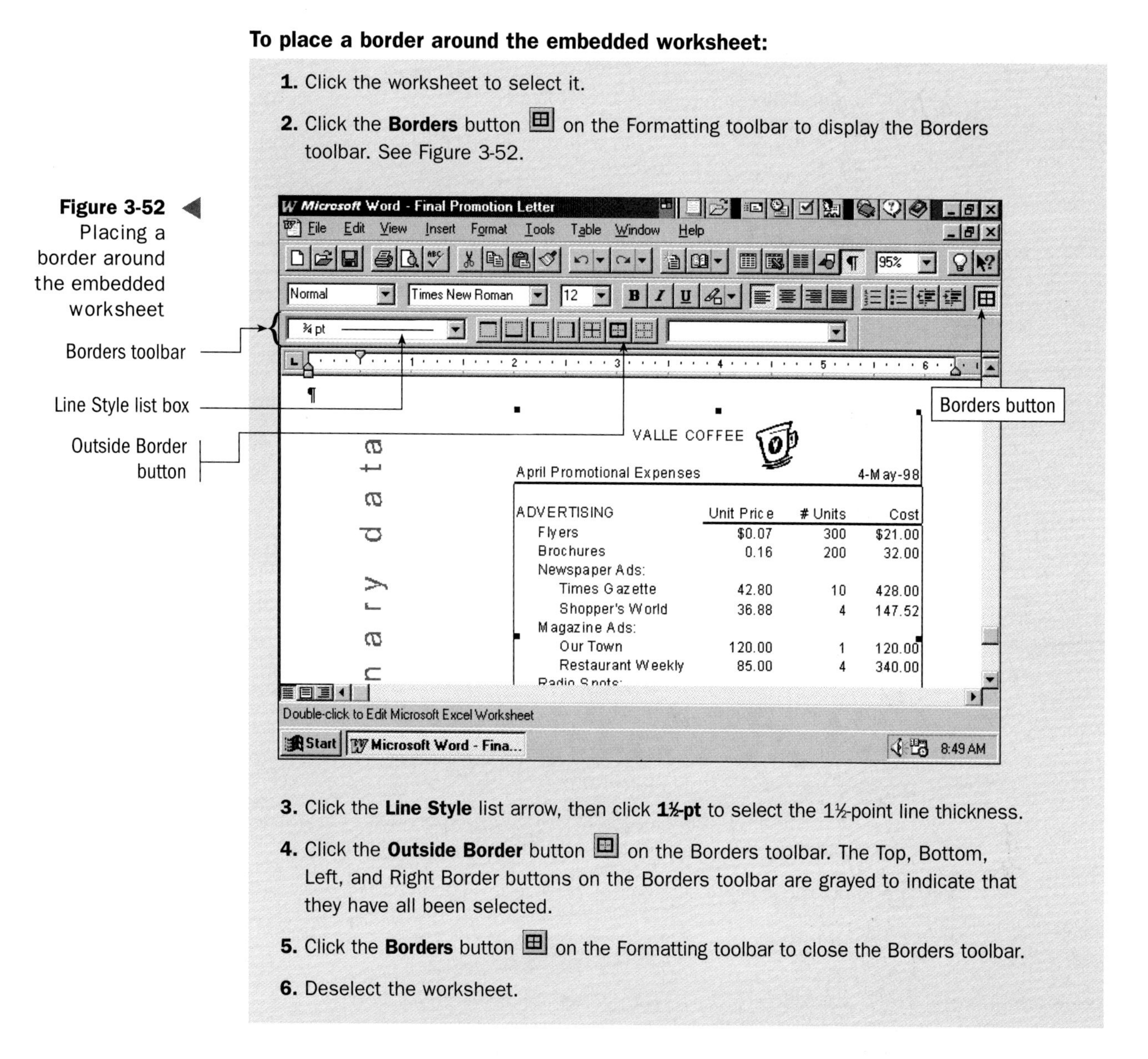

3. Click the **Line Style** list arrow, then click **1½-pt** to select the 1½-point line thickness.
4. Click the **Outside Border** button on the Borders toolbar. The Top, Bottom, Left, and Right Border buttons on the Borders toolbar are grayed to indicate that they have all been selected.
5. Click the **Borders** button on the Formatting toolbar to close the Borders toolbar.
6. Deselect the worksheet.

You'll preview the document once again to check the effects of the changes you've made. If the document looks fine, you will save and then print the letter.

To preview, save, and print the finished letter:

1. Click the **Print Preview** button on the Standard toolbar.

   Kim approves this final document preview, and asks you to save and print the letter.

   TROUBLE? If the first page of your letter ends somewhere within the bulleted list and breaks the list across pages, you can insert a hard page break by positioning the insertion point to the left of the first word in the line preceding the bulleted list (beginning "To promote..."); then click Insert on the menu bar, click Break, make sure the Page Break radio button is selected in the Break dialog box, then click the OK button. If doing this causes some text to be placed on a third page, delete one or more of the blank lines in the signature block.

2. Click the **Close** button on the Print Preview toolbar to exit Print Preview.
3. Click the **Save** button on the Standard toolbar to save the final version of the letter.
4. Click the **Print** button on the Standard toolbar.

With the letter complete, you can now close the document and exit Word.

To close the document and exit Word.

1. Click the **Close** button on the title bar. Word closes, and you return to the Windows 95 desktop.

   TROUBLE? If a dialog box opens asking if you want to save changes to the document, click the No button because any changes you might have made since last saving would be unintentional.

Kim is satisfied with the finished letter and sends it to Maria at Media Consultants. She is also pleased with the design and contents of the promotional expense worksheet, which she plans to use to evaluate Valle Coffee's promotional expenditures on a monthly basis.

Quick Check

1. To embed a picture, you use the ____________ command on the ____________ menu.
2. What is the difference between clearing a cell and deleting a cell? For which of these two tasks can you use the Delete key?
3. When you print an Excel worksheet using default settings, a(n) ____________ is printed in the top margin, and a(n) ____________ is printed in the bottom margin.
4. What two methods can you use to embed an Excel worksheet in a Word document, and when is each method appropriate?
5. When you are editing an Excel worksheet embedded in a Word document, to which application does the Formatting toolbar belong? The menu bar? The title bar?
6. Label the parts of the window shown in Figure 3-53.

Figure 3-53

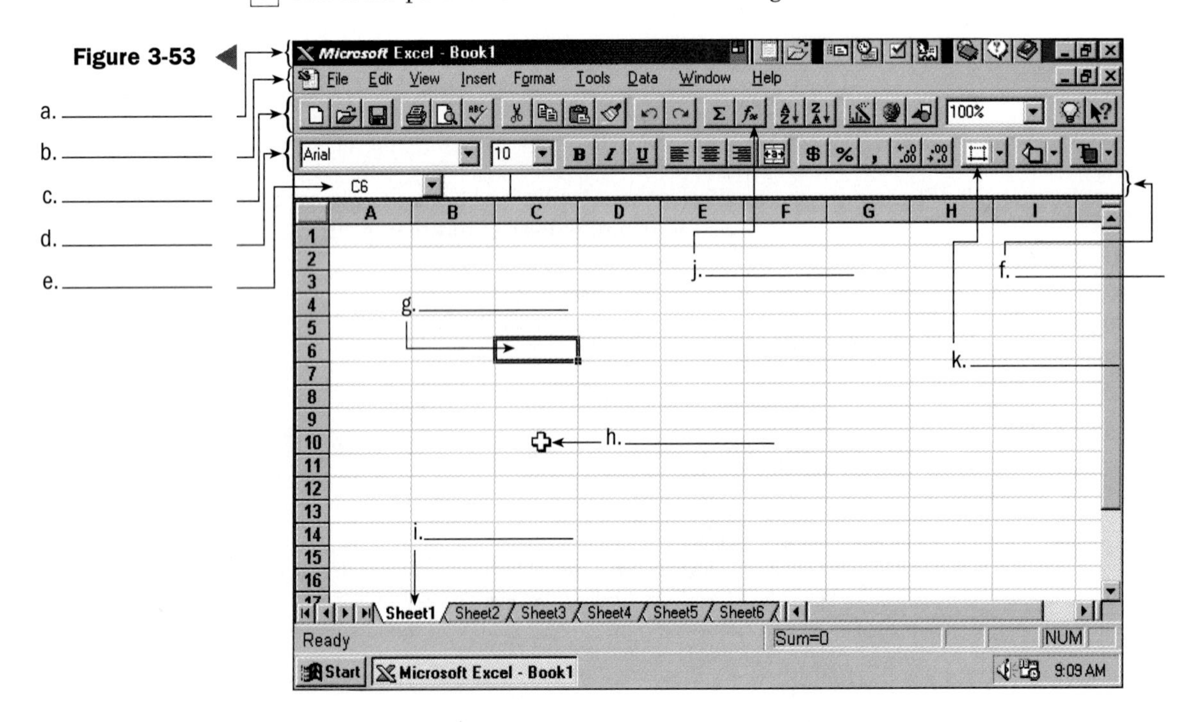

Tutorial Assignments

Belinda Jones asks you to complete a Valle Coffee cash forecast workbook that she has started. Complete the following:

1. Make sure your Student Disk is in the disk drive. Open the file named Forecast in the TAssign folder within the Tutorial.03 folder.
2. Save the workbook as Cash Forecast.
3. Rename the first sheet as Cash Budget.
4. Enter the following labels in the cells indicated:
   A10: Expected Cash Sales
   A11: Expected Collections
   A12: Other Money Expected
5. Enter the following numbers in the cells indicated:
   E10: 278401.57
   E11: 638844.31
   E12: 3940.33
6. Enter the following date in cell E4: 5/5/98.
7. Move the contents of cell F6 to cell E7.
8. Assign the name "TitleSection" to the range of cells from cell A1 through cell E4.
9. Enter a formula in cell E9 so that the cell displays the sum of cells E7 and E8.
10. Enter a formula in cell E13 so that the cell displays the sum of the three cells above it.

11. Enter a formula in cell E18 to subtract the contents of cell E16 from the contents of cell E14.
12. Move to the range TitleSection, and outline the entire range with a double-line border.
13. To improve the worksheet's readability, insert a new row between rows 13 and 14; insert another row between rows 9 and 10.
14. Format cells E7 through E20 as Currency, with a displayed dollar sign and two decimal places.

15. Use AutoFit to change the width of column E.
16. Change the width of column D to 2.5.
17. Format cell E4 as a Date, using the "March 4, 1995" type.
18. Place a single thin-line bottom border on cell E8; do the same for cell E13; place a double-underline bottom border in cell E18.
19. Insert the picture named Dollar, which is located in the TAssign folder in the Tutorial.03 folder on your Student Disk. Resize the picture so that it is slightly less than two rows tall. Remove the automatic border, then place the picture in the title area, immediately below "VALLE COFFEE."
20. Completely clear the cells to the right of and beneath your worksheet.
21. Open the document named Barbara, which is located in the TAssign folder in the Tutorial.03 folder of your Student Disk. Find the words "I have" in the document and replace them with your name and the word "has," then save the document as Barbara Memo.
22. Switch to Excel, save and close your workbook, then exit Excel.
23. Embed the Cash Forecast worksheet in the last paragraph mark in the memo document, then edit the worksheet to remove the gridlines and to apply a bold style to the "VALLE COFFEE" text.

24. Center the embedded worksheet, then apply an outline border around it. (*Hint:* center the worksheet just as you would center any object in Word.)
25. Preview, save, then print the memo.
26. Close the document and exit Word.

Case Problems

1. Ashbrook Mall Information Desk The Information Desk staff at Ashbrook Mall compiles statistics on the services they provide and how often each is provided. You are asked to complete a worksheet detailing the prior month's service statistics. Then you'll embed the worksheet into a memo to be distributed to all the mall store managers.

Complete the following:

1. Make sure your Student Disk is in the disk drive. Open the document named Services in the Cases folder within the Tutorial.03 folder.
2. Open the document named StatMemo located in that same folder on your Student Disk.
3. Save the memo as Service Statistics Memo in the Cases folder of the Tutorial.03 folder.
4. Using the taskbar, switch to Excel.
5. Save the workbook as Ashbrook Services in the Cases folder of the Tutorial.03 folder.
6. Rename the active worksheet "August Statistics."
7. Insert a new row between rows 2 and 3.
8. Delete column D.
9. Enter the following labels in the cells indicated:
   A18: First Aid:
   C18: Customers
   C19: Mall employees
10. Enter the following numbers in the cells indicated:
    E18: 58
    E19: 13
11. Place a double-line border under cells A2 through D2.
12. Move cells E4 through E27 into column D so they occupy cells D4 through D27.
13. Reformat cells D4 through D27 to eliminate the commas (1000 separator).

14. Use AutoFit to change the width of columns C and D.
15. Right-justify the text in cells A4, A8, A14, A18, A21, and A25. Then move each of these six cells one cell to the right.
16. Place a formula in cell D29 so that it displays the total number of different services.

17. Use the Excel Help system's Answer Wizard to find out about coloring text. Specifically, ask "how do I color text," then display the "Change the color of text" topic. Then color the final total in cell D29 a dark green; also apply a bold style to that cell.
18. Check the spelling and correct all misspellings. (Note: USPS is correct.)
19. Completely clear cells to the right of and below the worksheet.
20. Save the workbook and close Excel.
21. In Word, place the insertion point immediately to the left of the third paragraph mark following the paragraph that begins "The Information Desk service statistics," then press the Tab key three times.
22. Without moving the insertion point, insert the August Statistics worksheet from the Ashbrook Services workbook into the memo.
23. Edit the embedded worksheet to eliminate gridlines.
24. Delete all but two of the blank paragraphs between the embedded worksheet and the paragraph that begins "A reminder."
25. Preview, save, then print the memo document.
26. Close the document and exit Word.

2. Professional Litigation User Services Robert Seifullah of the law firm Korman, Rosen & Zek requested a detailed accounting by case and type of the services provided by Professional Litigation User Services (PLUS) during the first three months of the year. You are asked to complete a worksheet in response to that request, then embed the worksheet into a letter.

Complete the following:

1. Make sure your Student Disk is in the disk drive. Open the document named KRZ in the Cases folder within the Tutorial.03 folder.
2. Open the document named KRZ-PLUS located in that same folder on your Student Disk.
3. Save the letter as Seifullah Letter in the Cases folder of the Tutorial.03 folder.
4. Using the taskbar, switch to Excel.
5. Save the workbook as KRZ Services in the Cases folder of the Tutorial.03 folder.
6. Rename the worksheet as Jan-Mar Charges.
7. Enter KORMAN, ROSEN & ZEK in cell D3.
8. Enter 4800 in cell G27.
9. Enter an appropriate formula in cell E28 to sum the four cells directly above this cell.
10. Copy the formula in cell E28 to cells F28 and G28.
11. Use the Function Wizard to enter a formula in cell E31 that sums the values in cells E14, E20, and E28.
12. Copy the formula in cell E31 into cells F31 through G31.
13. Change the width of column A to 2.5 and the width of column D to 5.8.
14. Place a thin solid border around cells A23 through D23.

15. Activate the Drawing toolbar and apply a drop shadow to cells A23 through D23. (*Hint:* Use the View menu to activate the toolbar, then use the appropriate button on the toolbar to apply the drop shadow.)
16. Copy the formula in cell H20, which sums the three cells to the left, into the range of cells from H24 through H28; also copy that formula into cell H31.
17. Select the range of cells from E12 through H31, which includes all the numeric values and sums, and apply the Currency format that displays a dollar sign, displays no decimal places, and uses the third of the format choices for negative numbers.

18. Use AutoFit to change the width of columns E, F, G, and H.
19. Insert a blank column between each of the columns currently labeled E, F, G, and H. Make the three new columns (now labeled F, H, and J) very narrow by changing the column width to 0.5 for each of these columns.
20. Place a double-underline border, similar to the one in the cell containing the label "January," into the "February," "March," and "Total" cells.
21. Place a thin single-underline border, similar to the one in cell E19, into cells G19, G27, and I27.
22. Insert a new column between the current columns D and E, and change the column width of the new column to 2.5.
23. Place a thick black outline border around cells A1 through L7.

24. Use the Excel Help system's Answer Wizard to find out about adding color to a range of cells. Specifically, ask "how do I shade a cell" and then display the topic "Shade cells with solid colors." Then color cells A1 through L7 a very light gray.
26. Save the workbook.

27. Use the Copy and Paste Special commands to embed the worksheet at the end of the Word document.
28. Edit the embedded worksheet to remove the gridlines.
29. Preview, save, then print the letter.
30. Close the document and exit Word.
31. Close the workbook and exit Excel.

3. Best Friends Norma and Ivan Darkler have requested information about organizing a Dog Walk-A-Thon to raise funds for Best Friends. You are asked to complete a worksheet detailing the income and expenses for a similar fund-raising event held in Burley, Idaho. Then you'll embed the worksheet into a letter.

Complete the following:

1. Make sure your Student Disk is in the disk drive. Open the document named Burley in the Cases folder within the Tutorial.03 folder.
2. Open the document named Darkler located in that same folder on your Student Disk.
3. Save the memo as Darkler Letter in the Cases folder of the Tutorial.03 folder.
4. Using the taskbar, switch to Excel.
5. Save the workbook as Burley WalkAThon in the Cases folder of the Tutorial.03 folder.
6. Rename the worksheet as Walk-A-Thon Accounting.
7. Enter the date 9/14/97 in cell G2.
8. Insert a new row to accommodate a "Radio ads" expense entry, which should fall in alphabetical order among the other expenses (not counting "Other" at the end of the list).
9. Enter "Radio ads" in column B of the new row, enter "27" in column E of the new row, and enter "50% discount donated by KBUR" in column G of the new row.
10. Format cell E6 as Currency with two decimal places and a displayed dollar sign, and select the first choice for negative number display.
11. Use the Format Painter to copy the formatting for cell E6 into cells E8 through E26.
12. Copy cell E7 into cells E9, E13 through E16, and E18.
13. Place a double-underline border in cells A2 through G2.
14. Place a single thick underline border in cells E19 and E25.
15. Enter a formula in cell E20 that sums all the expense values above it, and enter a formula in cell E26 that sums the two income values above it.

16. Enter a formula in cell E29 to subtract the contents of cell E20 from the contents of cell E26.
17. Change the width of column A to 3.3, column F to 2.5, and column G to 62.
18. Format the date in cell G2 with the "March 4, 1995" option.

19. Use the Excel Help system's Answer Wizard to find out about drawing. Specifically ask "how do I draw an ellipse" and then display the topic "Draw a line, rectangle, ellipse, arc, or arrow." Draw an ellipse around the contents of cell E29 to highlight the net proceeds value. If necessary, resize and reposition the ellipse as you would any selected object. Close the Drawing toolbar when you are finished.

20. Reselect (if necessary) the ellipse you drew in the previous step, then format that drawing object as follows:
    a. Change the Border Color to bright pink (seventh position of the first row of the color palette).
    b. Change the Border Weight to a medium line thickness.
21. Save the workbook, then close the workbook and exit Excel.
22. In Word, position the insertion point at the end of the document and enter two blank paragraphs.
23. Insert the Burley WalkAThon worksheet into the document.
24. Edit the embedded worksheet to remove the gridlines.

25. Position the insertion point to the left of the last paragraph mark before the embedded document, then change the paper orientation to Landscape and apply that orientation *from this point forward.* (*Hint:* "Orientation" and "Apply To" are options on the Paper Size tab of the Page Setup dialog box, which is available from the File menu.)

26. Select the embedded worksheet, change the Zoom Control on the Standard toolbar to "Page Width," then resize the embedded worksheet by dragging the lower-right corner sizing handle until the dashed line marking the right edge is at the 9-inch mark on the ruler.
27. Preview, save, then print the letter.
28. Close the document and exit Word.

4. Johnson Scales Johnson Scales, a manufacturer of all kinds of weighing equipment, is in the midst of an intensive effort to develop a prototype for a new scale currently called the X-350. Sandra Amidon has asked to you prepare a worksheet detailing and comparing the development costs for the last two months. Specifically, she wants to know by how much last month's cost in each expense category exceeded the corresponding previous month's cost.

The relevant total base salaries were $11,248.55 in both May and June. Nobody worked overtime in May, but there were $2,307.68 in overtime charges in June. The June charges for lab equipment, computer usage, materials, telephone and postage, and special machining requests were $1,700.98, $9,844.40, $3,109.33, $612.88, and $5,016.00, respectively. The corresponding May costs were $1,691.72, $9,488.25, $1,420.12, $609.31, and $917.55.

Complete the following:

1. Plan the worksheet.
2. Make sure your Student Disk is in the disk drive. From the Windows 95 desktop, click the Start a New Document button on the Office Shortcut Bar, click the General tab, click Blank Workbook, then click the OK button to open a new Excel workbook.
3. Name the worksheet.
4. Enter the worksheet values.
5. Enter appropriate formulas where needed.
6. Check the worksheet values and correct them as necessary.
7. Format the displayed values.
8. Embed and resize the ClipArt picture named Scales, which is located in the Cases folder within the Tutorial.03 folder on your Student Disk.
9. Save the workbook as "Johnson X-350" on your Student Disk in the Cases folder of the Tutorial.03 folder.
10. Preview, save, then print the worksheet.
11. Close the workbook and exit Excel.

Lab Assignment

This Lab Assignment is designed to accompany the interactive Course Lab called Spreadsheets. To start the Spreadsheets Lab, click the Start button on the Windows 95 taskbar, point to Programs, point to Course Labs, point to New Perspectives Applications, and click Spreadsheets. If you do not see Course Labs on your Programs menu, see your instructor or lab manager.

LABS

Spreadsheets

Spreadsheets Spreadsheet software is used extensively in business, education, science, and the humanities to simplify tasks that involve calculations. In this Lab you will learn how spreadsheet software works. You will use spreadsheet software to examine and modify worksheets, as well as to create your own worksheets.

1. Click the Steps button to learn how spreadsheet software works. As you proceed through the Steps, answer all of the Quick Check questions that appear. After you complete the Steps, you will see a Quick Check Report. Follow the instructions on the screen to print this report.

2. Click the Explore button to begin this assignment. Click OK to display a new worksheet. Click File, then click Open to display the Open dialog box. Click the file INCOME.XLS, then press the Enter key to open the Income and Expense Summary worksheet. Notice that the worksheet contains labels and values for income from consulting and training. It also contains labels and values for expenses such as rent and salaries. The worksheet does not, however, contain formulas to calculate Total Income, Total Expenses, or Profit. Do the following:

a. Calculate the Total Income by entering the formula =SUM(C4:C5) in cell C6.
b. Calculate the Total Expenses by entering the formula =SUM(C9:C12) in cell C13.

c. Calculate Profit by entering the formula =C6-C13 in cell C15.
d. Manually check the results to make sure you entered the formulas correctly.
e. Print your completed worksheet showing your results.

3. You can use a spreadsheet to keep track of your grade in a class. Click the Explore button to display a blank worksheet. Click File, then click Open to display the Open dialog box. Click the file GRADES.XLS to open the Grades worksheet. This worksheet contains all the labels and formulas necessary to calculate your grade based on four test scores.

Suppose you receive a score of 88 out of 100 on the first test. On the second test, you score 42 out of 48. On the third test, you score 92 out of 100. You have not taken the fourth test yet. Enter the appropriate data in the GRADES.XLS worksheet to determine your grade after taking three tests. Print your worksheet.

4. Worksheets are handy for answering "what if" questions. Suppose you decide to open a lemonade stand. You're interested in how much profit you can make each day. What if you sell 20 cups of lemonade? What if you sell 100? What if the cost of lemons increases?

In Explore, open the file LEMONS.XLS and use the worksheet to answer questions a through d, then print the worksheet for item e:

a. What is your profit if you sell 20 cups a day?
b. What is your profit if you sell 100 cups a day?
c. What is your profit if the price of lemons increases to $.07 and you sell 100 cups?
d. What is your profit if you raise the price of a cup of lemonade to $.30? (Lemons still cost $.07 and assume you sell 100 cups.)
e. Suppose your competitor boasts that she sold 50 cups of lemonade in one day and made exactly $12.00. On your worksheet adjust the cost of cups, water, lemons, and sugar, and the price per cup to show a profit of exactly $12.00 for 50 cups sold. Print this worksheet.

5. It is important to make sure the formulas in your worksheet are accurate. An easy way to test this is to enter 1's for all the values on your worksheet, then check the calculations manually. In Explore, open the worksheet RECEIPT.XLS, which calculates sales receipts. Enter 1 as the value for Item 1, Item 2, and Item 3. Enter .01 for the Sales Tax rate. Now, manually calculate what you would pay for three items that cost $1.00 each in a state where sales tax is 1% (.01). Do your manual calculations match those of the worksheet? If not, correct the formulas in the worksheet and print a formulas report of your revised worksheet.

6. In Explore, create your own worksheet showing your household budget for one month. You may use real or made-up numbers. Make sure you put a title on the worksheet. Use formulas to calculate your total income and your total expenses for the month. Add another formula to calculate how much money you were able to save. Print a formulas report of your worksheet. Also, print your worksheet showing realistic values for one month.

TUTORIAL 4

Access Basics and Importing an Excel Worksheet

Creating Customer and Order Tables with Forms, Reports, and Queries

OBJECTIVES

In this tutorial you will:

- Define the terms field, table, record, database, primary key, and foreign key
- Learn the rules for designing databases and Access tables
- Create a database and the fields for its tables
- Select a table's primary key, save the table structure, and add records to a table
- Import Excel data to create a new table
- Create a new table and populate it with data
- Create forms automatically using the AutoForm and Form Wizards
- Create reports automatically using the Report Wizard
- Create new queries using one or more tables

LABS

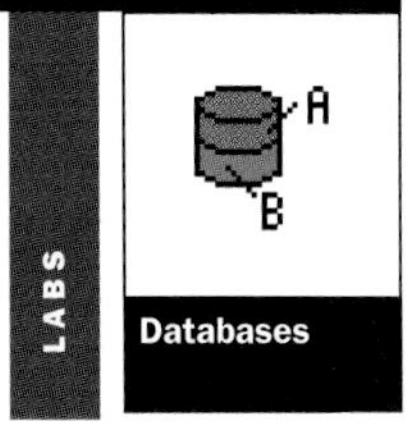

Databases

Valle Coffee

Barbara Hennessey, office manager at Valle Coffee, and her staff handle all company paperwork, such as customer orders and billing, coffee supplier orders and payments, and advertising placements and payments. Barbara asks you to create a database named Restaurant Business to track the company's restaurant customers, their orders, and related data such as the products they order.

Initially, Barbara wants order and customer data included in the new database. For instance, she wants to track each customer's name, address, and phone number, and each order's billing date and invoice amount. Because the database will provide information that will be used by Carlos Sangris, director of production, and his staff, it must eventually contain product data such as coffee names, types, and prices. Once the data is stored in the database, Barbara will be able to print customer lists and order reports, and Carlos will be able to print product price lists and other reports. Both Barbara and Carlos and their staff members will be able to query the database to display specific information, such as customer data, sales by state or by date, and selected coffee types.

Some of the order data Barbara needs is already stored in another Valle Coffee database, and an existing Excel worksheet contains the required customer data. You'll use Access to integrate this data easily into the new database, which you will create. You will also learn about database concepts and how to use the features of Access to work with tables, forms, reports, and queries.

SESSION 4.1

In this session you will learn how data is organized in a database and learn the guidelines for designing databases and Access tables. You'll also learn how to create a database, create a table, define the fields for a table, select the primary key for a table, save the table structure, and add records to a table datasheet.

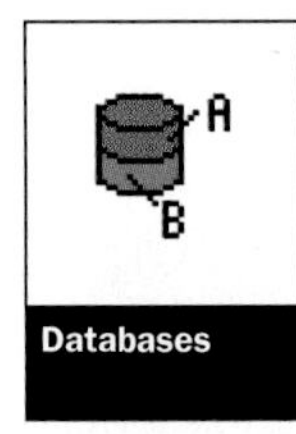

Introduction to Database Concepts

Before you begin working on Barbara's database and using Access, you need to understand a few key terms and concepts associated with databases.

Organizing Data

Data is a valuable resource to any business. At Valle Coffee, for example, important data includes customers' names and addresses, and order dates and amounts. Organizing, storing, maintaining, retrieving, and sorting this type of data are critical activities that enable a business to find and use information effectively. Before storing such data on a computer, however, you first must organize the data.

Your first step in organizing data is to identify the individual fields. As noted in Tutorial 1, a **field** is a single characteristic or attribute of a person, place, object, event, or idea. For example, some of the many fields that Valle Coffee tracks are customer number, customer name, customer address, customer phone number, order number, billing date, and invoice amount.

Next, you group related fields together into tables. A **table** is a collection of fields that describes a person, place, object, event, or idea. For example, Figure 4-1 shows a Customer table and an Order table. The Customer table consists of four fields: Customer Number, Customer Name, Customer Address, and Phone Number. The Order table also contains four fields: Order Number, Customer Number, Billing Date, and Invoice Amount.

Figure 4-1 Fields organized in two tables

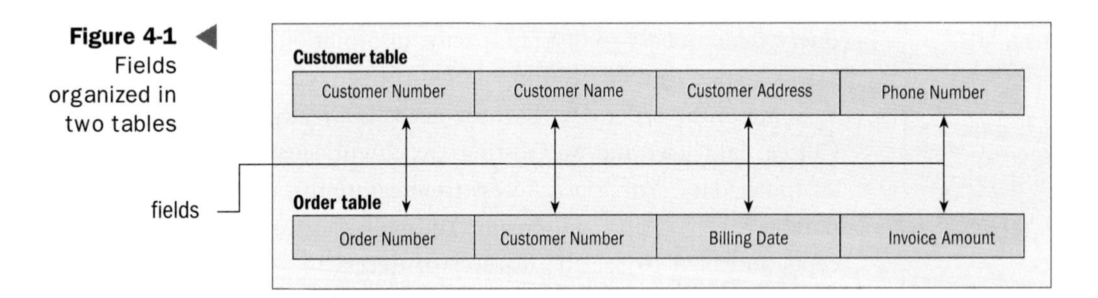

The specific value, or content, of a field is called the **field value**. For example, Figure 4-2 shows a Customer table. The first set of field values for Customer Number, Customer Name, Customer Address, and Phone Number are, respectively, 104; Meadows Restaurant; Pond Hill Road, Monroe MI 48161; and (313) 792-3546. This set of field values is called a **record**. In this Customer table, the data for each customer is stored as a separate record. Six records are shown in Figure 4-2; each row of field values is a record.

Figure 4-2 Data organization for a table of customers

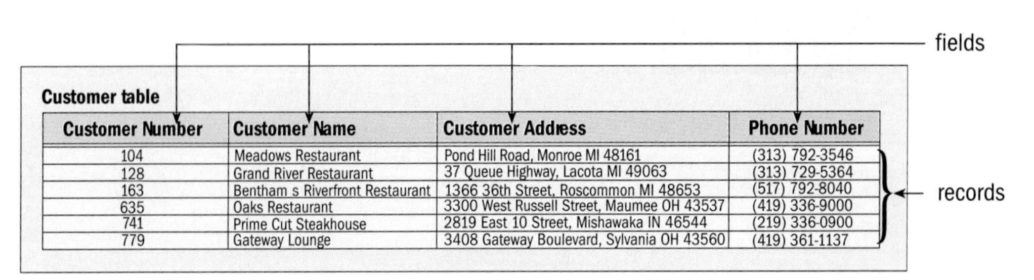

Customer Number	Customer Name	Customer Address	Phone Number
104	Meadows Restaurant	Pond Hill Road, Monroe MI 48161	(313) 792-3546
128	Grand River Restaurant	37 Queue Highway, Lacota MI 49063	(313) 729-5364
163	Bentham s Riverfront Restaurant	1366 36th Street, Roscommon MI 48653	(517) 792-8040
635	Oaks Restaurant	3300 West Russell Street, Maumee OH 43537	(419) 336-9000
741	Prime Cut Steakhouse	2819 East 10 Street, Mishawaka IN 46544	(219) 336-0900
779	Gateway Lounge	3408 Gateway Boulevard, Sylvania OH 43560	(419) 361-1137

Databases and Relationships

A collection of related tables is called a **database**, or **relational database**. The initial database you will create for Valle Coffee, for example, will contain two related tables: the Customer table and the Order table. Sometimes you might want information about customers and the orders they placed. To obtain this information you must have a way to connect records in the Customer table to records in the Order table. You connect the records in the separate tables through a **common field** that appears in both tables. In the database in Figure 4-3, for example, each record in the Customer table has a field named Customer Number, which is also a field in the Order table. For example, Oaks Restaurant is the fourth customer in the Customer table and has a Customer Number of 635. This same Customer Number field value, 635, appears in three records in the Order table. Therefore, Oaks Restaurant is the customer that placed these three orders.

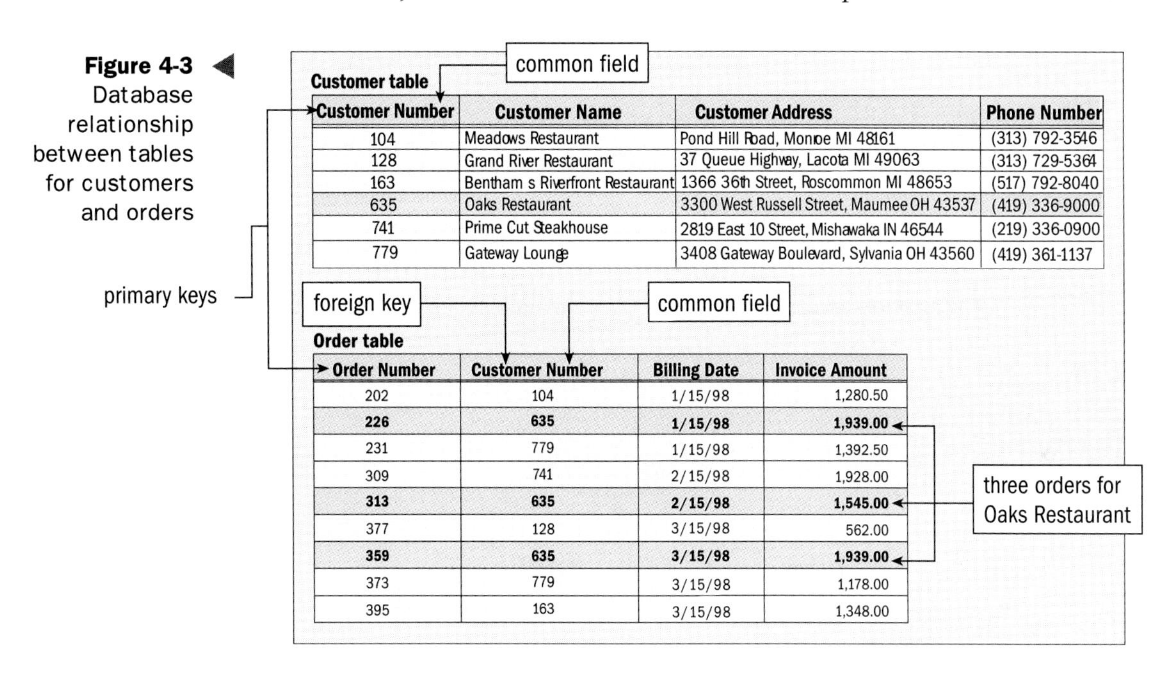

Customer table

Customer Number	Customer Name	Customer Address	Phone Number
104	Meadows Restaurant	Pond Hill Road, Monroe MI 48161	(313) 792-3546
128	Grand River Restaurant	37 Queue Highway, Lacota MI 49063	(313) 729-5364
163	Bentham s Riverfront Restaurant	1366 36th Street, Roscommon MI 48653	(517) 792-8040
635	Oaks Restaurant	3300 West Russell Street, Maumee OH 43537	(419) 336-9000
741	Prime Cut Steakhouse	2819 East 10 Street, Mishawaka IN 46544	(219) 336-0900
779	Gateway Lounge	3408 Gateway Boulevard, Sylvania OH 43560	(419) 361-1137

Order table

Order Number	Customer Number	Billing Date	Invoice Amount
202	104	1/15/98	1,280.50
226	**635**	**1/15/98**	**1,939.00**
231	779	1/15/98	1,392.50
309	741	2/15/98	1,928.00
313	**635**	**2/15/98**	**1,545.00**
377	128	3/15/98	562.00
359	**635**	**3/15/98**	**1,939.00**
373	779	3/15/98	1,178.00
395	163	3/15/98	1,348.00

Figure 4-3 Database relationship between tables for customers and orders

Each Customer Number in the Customer table must be unique, so that you can distinguish one customer from another and identify the customer's specific orders in the Order table. The Customer Number field is referred to as the primary key of the Customer table. A **primary key** is a field, or a collection of fields, whose values uniquely identify each record in a table. In the Order table, Order Number is the primary key.

When you include the primary key from one table as a field in a second table to form a relationship between the two tables, it is called a **foreign key** in the second table, as shown in Figure 4-3. For example, Customer Number is the primary key in the Customer table and a foreign key in the Order table. Although the primary key Customer Number has unique values in the Customer table, the same field as a foreign key in the Order table does not have unique values. The Customer Number value 635, for example, appears three times in the Order table, because the Oaks Restaurant placed three orders. Each foreign key value, however, must match one of the field values for the primary key in the other table. In the example in Figure 4-3, each Customer Number value in the Order table must match a Customer Number value in the Customer table. The two tables are related, enabling users to tie together the facts about customers with the facts about orders.

Relational Database Management Systems

To manage its databases, a company purchases a database management system. A **database management system (DBMS)** is a software program that lets you create databases and then manipulate data in the databases. Most of today's database management systems, including Access, are called relational database management systems. In a **relational database management system**, data is organized as a collection of related tables.

As stated earlier, a relationship between two tables in a relational DBMS is formed through a common field. A relational DBMS controls the storage of databases on disk by carrying out data creation and manipulation requests. Specifically, a relational DBMS provides the following functions, which are illustrated in Figure 4-4:

- It allows you to create database structures containing fields, tables, and table relationships.
- It lets you easily add new records, change field values in existing records, and delete records.
- It contains a built-in query language, which lets you obtain immediate answers to the questions you ask about your data.
- It contains a built-in report generator, which lets you produce professional-looking, formatted reports from your data.
- It provides protection of databases through security, control, and recovery facilities.

Figure 4-4 A relational database management system

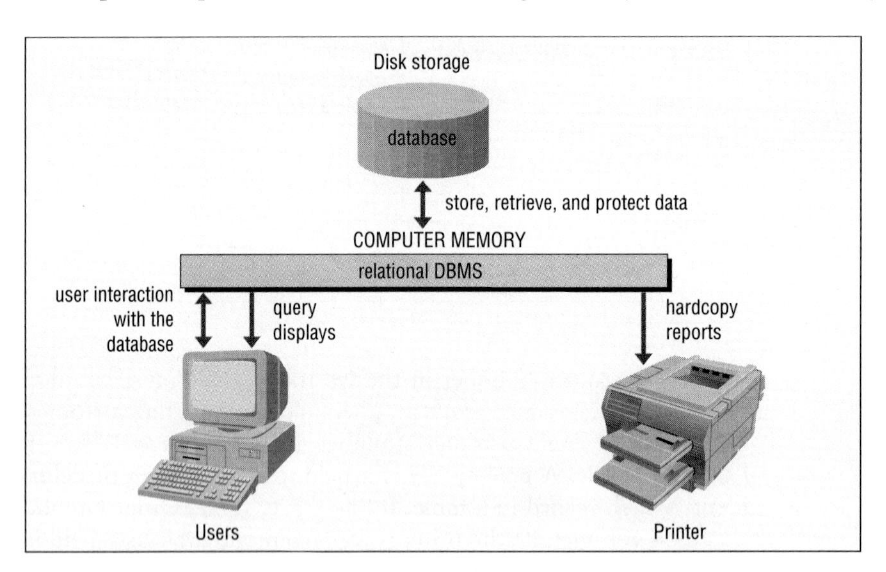

A company like Valle Coffee will benefit from a relational DBMS because it allows several users working in different departments to share the same data. More than one user can enter data into a database, and more than one user can retrieve and analyze data that was entered by others. For example, Valle Coffee will keep only one copy of the Customer table, and all employees will be able to use it to meet their specific needs for customer information.

Finally, unlike other software programs, such as worksheets, a DBMS can handle massive amounts of data and can easily form relationships among multiple tables. Each Access database, for example, can be up to one gigabyte in size and can contain up to 32,768 tables.

Guidelines for Designing Databases

A database management system can be a useful tool, but only if you first carefully design the database so that it meets the needs of those who will use it. In database design, you determine the fields, tables, and relationships needed to satisfy the data and processing requirements. When you design a database, you should follow the guidelines described in this section:

- **Identify all the fields needed to produce the required information.** For example, Barbara needs information about customers and orders, so she lists the fields that satisfy those information requirements, as shown in Figure 4-5.

Figure 4-5 Barbara's data requirements

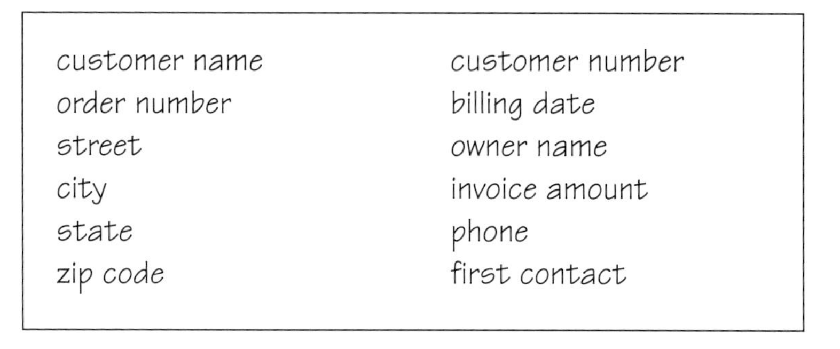

- **Group related fields into tables.** For example, Barbara's fields can be logically grouped into a Customer table and an Order table, as shown in Figure 4-6.

Figure 4-6 Barbara's fields grouped into Customer and Order tables

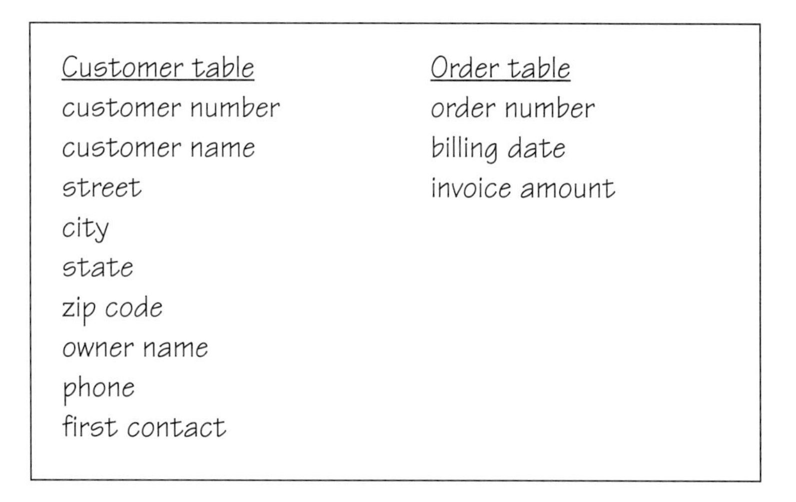

- **Determine each table's primary key.** Recall that a primary key uniquely identifies each record in a table. Although a primary key is not mandatory in Access, it's usually a good idea to include one in each table. Without a primary key, selecting the exact record you want can be a problem. For some tables, one of the fields, such as a Social Security number or credit card number, naturally serves the function of a primary key. For other tables, two or more fields might be needed to function as the primary key. In these cases, the primary key is referred to as a **composite key.** For example, a school grade table would use a combination of student number and course code to serve as the primary key. For a third category of tables, no single field or combination of fields can uniquely identify a record in a table. In these cases, you need to add a field whose sole purpose is to serve as the primary key.

  For Barbara's tables, Customer Number will be the primary key for the Customer table, and Order Number will be the primary key for the Order table.

- **Include a common field in related tables.** You use the common field to connect one table logically with another table. For example, Barbara's Customer and Order tables will include the Customer Number field as a common field. With this common field, Barbara can find all orders placed by a customer; she can use the Customer Number value for a customer and search the Order table for all orders with that Customer Number value. Likewise, she can determine which customer placed a particular order by searching the Customer table to find the one record with the same Customer Number value as the corresponding value in the Order table.

- **Avoid data redundancy.** Data redundancy occurs when you store the same data in more than one place. With the exception of common fields to connect tables, you should avoid redundancy because it wastes storage space and can cause inconsistencies, if, for instance, you type a field value one way in one table and a different way in the same table or in a second table. Figure 4-7 shows an example of incorrect database design that illustrates data redundancy in the Order table: the Customer Name field is redundant and one value was entered incorrectly in three different ways.

Figure 4-7 Incorrect database design with data redundancy

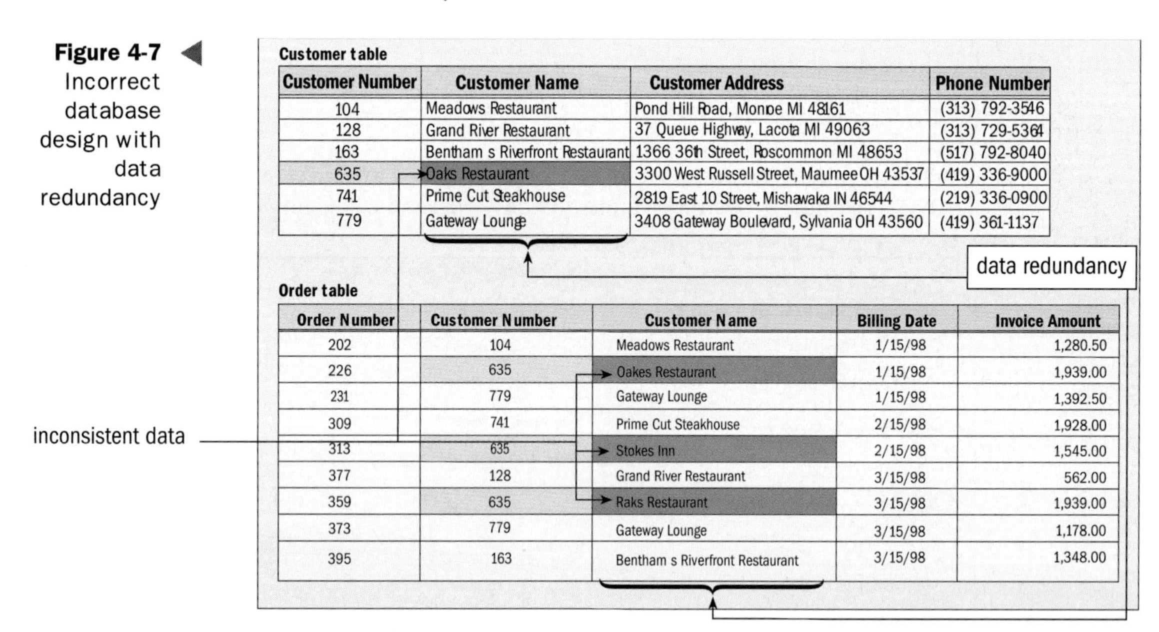

Customer table

Customer Number	Customer Name	Customer Address	Phone Number
104	Meadows Restaurant	Pond Hill Road, Monroe MI 48161	(313) 792-3546
128	Grand River Restaurant	37 Queue Highway, Lacota MI 49063	(313) 729-5364
163	Bentham s Riverfront Restaurant	1366 36th Street, Roscommon MI 48653	(517) 792-8040
635	Oaks Restaurant	3300 West Russell Street, Maumee OH 43537	(419) 336-9000
741	Prime Cut Steakhouse	2819 East 10 Street, Mishawaka IN 46544	(219) 336-0900
779	Gateway Lounge	3408 Gateway Boulevard, Sylvania OH 43560	(419) 361-1137

Order table

Order Number	Customer Number	Customer Name	Billing Date	Invoice Amount
202	104	Meadows Restaurant	1/15/98	1,280.50
226	635	Oakes Restaurant	1/15/98	1,939.00
231	779	Gateway Lounge	1/15/98	1,392.50
309	741	Prime Cut Steakhouse	2/15/98	1,928.00
313	635	Stokes Inn	2/15/98	1,545.00
377	128	Grand River Restaurant	3/15/98	562.00
359	635	Raks Restaurant	3/15/98	1,939.00
373	779	Gateway Lounge	3/15/98	1,178.00
395	163	Bentham s Riverfront Restaurant	3/15/98	1,348.00

- **Determine the properties of each field.** You need to identify the **properties**, or characteristics, of each field, so that the DBMS knows how to store, display, and process the field. These properties include the field name, the field's maximum number of characters or digits, the field's description, the field's valid values, and other field characteristics. You will learn more about field properties later in this tutorial.

Keeping the database design guidelines in mind, Barbara developed the design for the Restaurant Business database, as shown in Figure 4-8.

Figure 4-8 Barbara's design of the Restaurant Business database

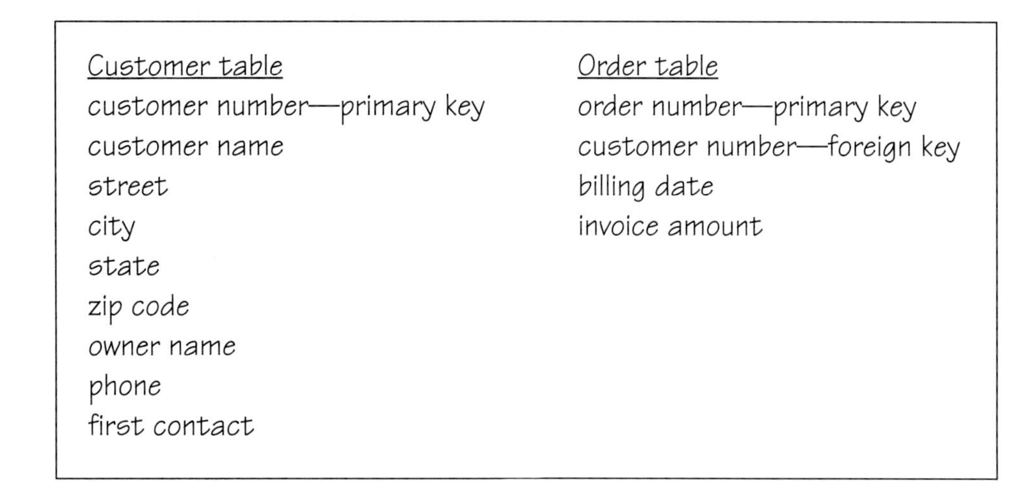

You'll create the two tables of the Restaurant Business database according to Barbara's design.

Creating a Database

A new Access database requires approximately 80KB of disk space. Most of this space is used when you add the first tables, fields, and other objects.

You'll begin by creating the Restaurant Business database.

To create the database:

1. Start Windows 95 and make sure the Office Shortcut Bar is displayed.

   TROUBLE? If you don't see the Office Shortcut Bar, click the Start button on the taskbar, point to Programs, then click Microsoft Office Shortcut Bar. If you don't see the Microsoft Office Shortcut Bar option on the Programs menu, ask your instructor or technical support person for assistance.

2. Place your Student Disk in the disk drive.

3. From the Windows 95 desktop, click the **Start a New Document** button on the Office Shortcut Bar. The New dialog box opens.

4. If necessary, click the **General** tab. See Figure 4-9.

Figure 4-9 New dialog box

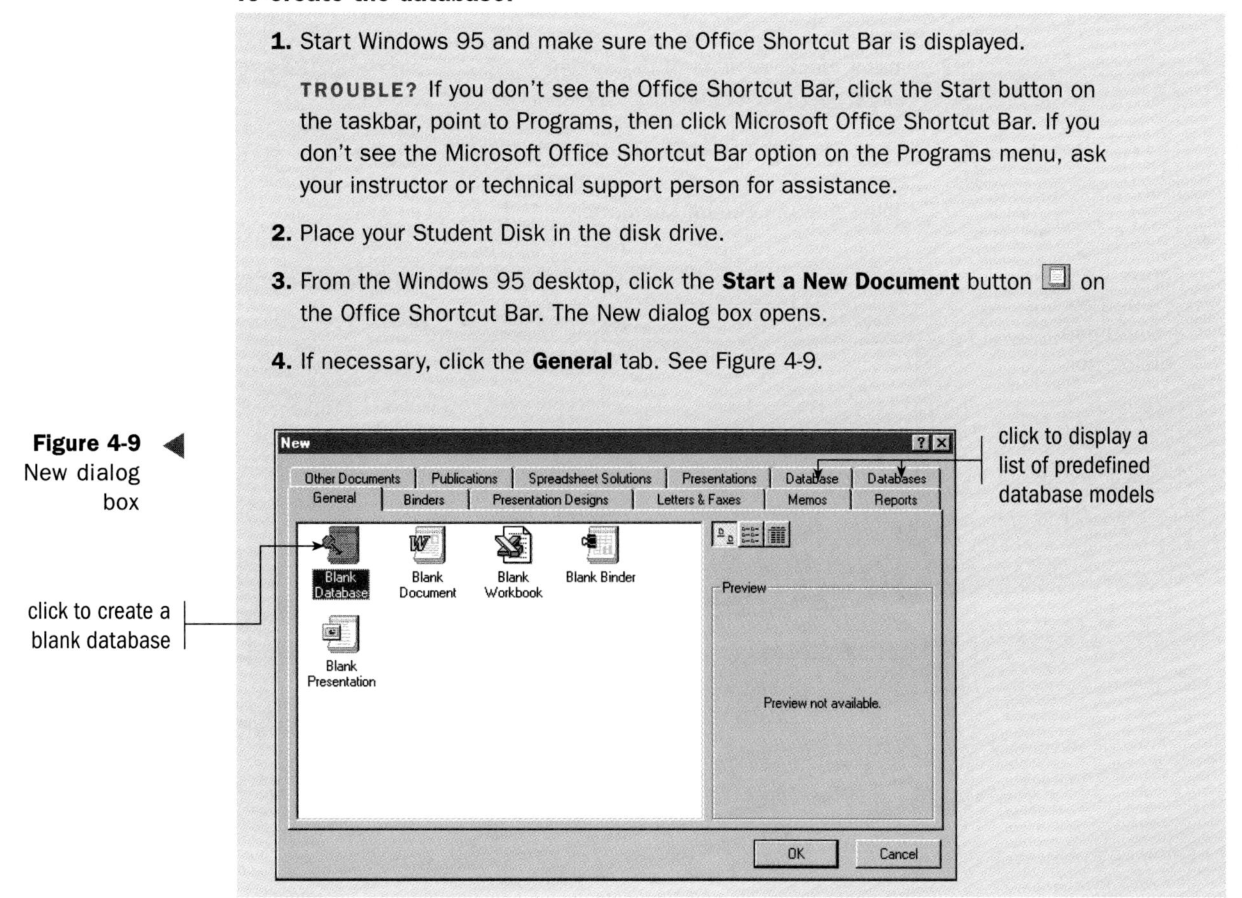

Access provides two ways to create a new database. If you use the Blank Database icon, Access creates a new database with no tables or other objects defined. If you click the Database or Databases tab, Access displays a list of predefined databases you can use as models for creating your own.

5. Click the **Database** tab. Access displays a list of available predefined database models. See Figure 4-10.

Figure 4-10 Database tab in the New dialog box

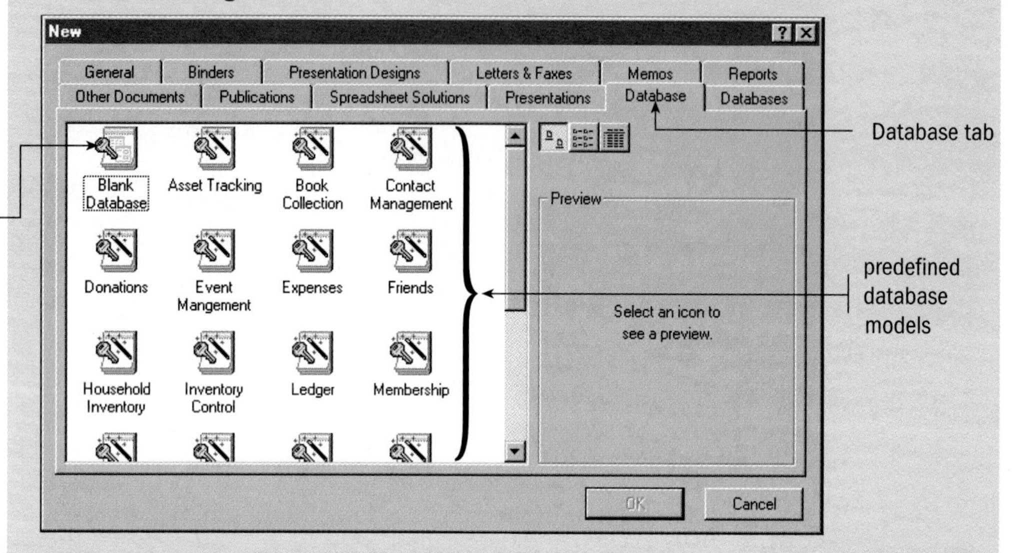

Each predefined database model contains tables and other objects. If one of the models is appropriate, you can select it to simplify the task of creating a database. Because none of the models is appropriate for the Restaurant Business database, you'll define the database yourself.

6. Click the **Blank Database** icon, then click the **OK** button. Access starts, then the File New Database dialog box opens. See Figure 4-11. The File name text box highlights the default name, db1.

Figure 4-11 File New Database dialog box

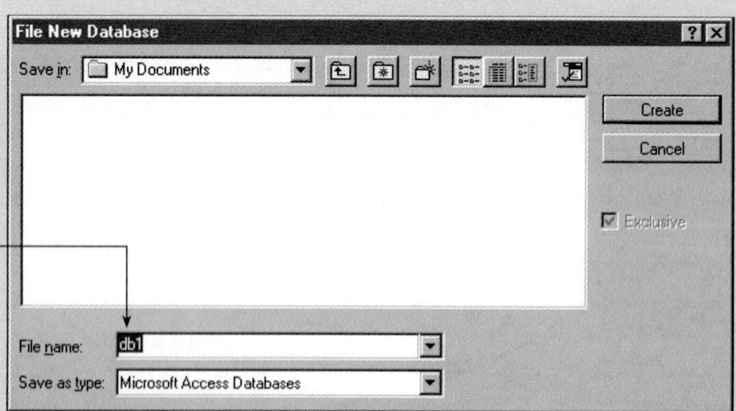

TROUBLE? Your screen might show files listed in the list box for the My Documents folder, depending on the computer you are using.

7. Type **Restaurant Business** in the File name text box.

TROUBLE? If the contents of the File name text box do not show Restaurant Business, the text box might not have been highlighted when you began typing. If this is the case, highlight the contents of the text box, then type Restaurant Business.

8. Click the **Save in** list arrow, click the drive containing your Student Disk, click **Tutorial.04**, then click the **Open** button.

9. Click the **Create** button. Access creates the Restaurant Business database and opens the Database window. See Figure 4-12. Because this is a new database, no tables appear in the Tables list box.

Figure 4-12 Access and Database windows

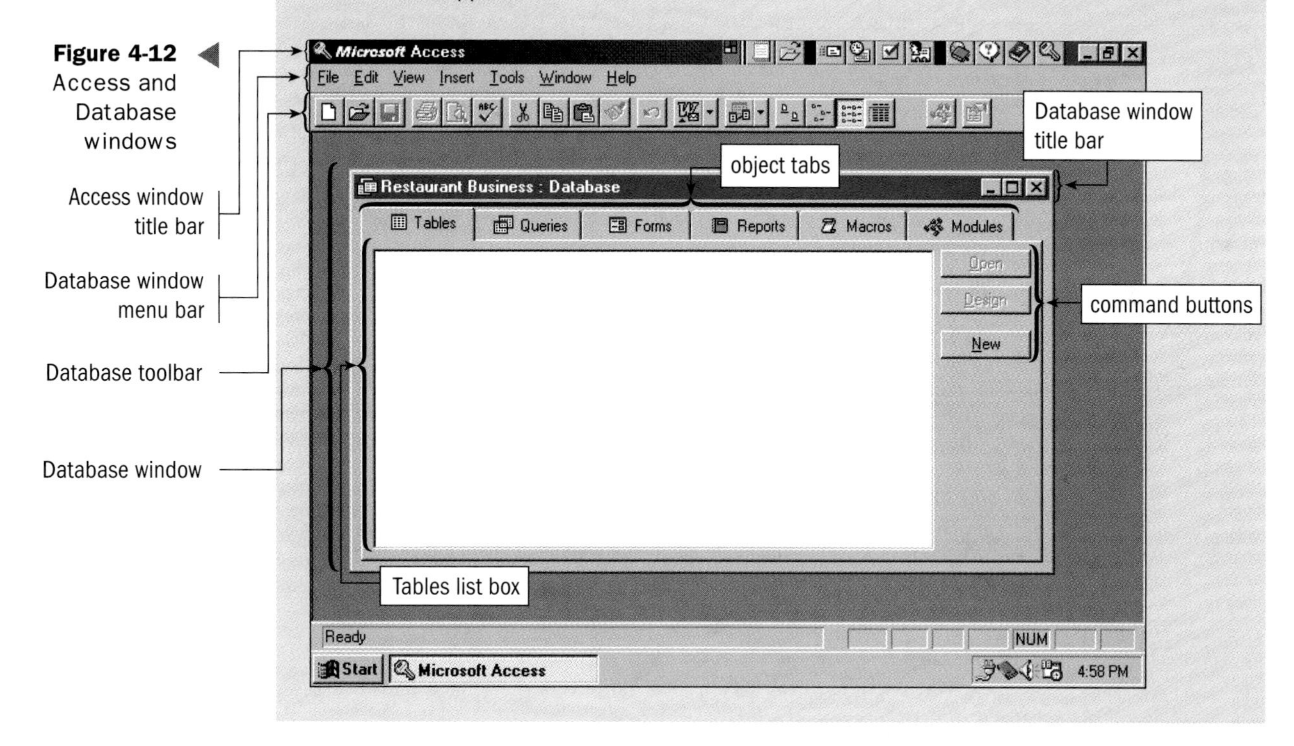

Barbara's database design includes the Customer and Order tables. The first table you will create is the Order table. However, you first have to learn about the properties of a field.

Guidelines for Designing Access Tables

As you learned earlier in this session, the last step of database design is to determine the properties, such as the name and data type, of each field. Access has rules for naming fields, choosing data types, and defining other properties of fields.

Naming Fields and Objects

You must name each field, table, and other object in an Access database. Access then stores these items in the database using the names you supply. It's best to choose a field or object name that describes the purpose or contents of the field or object, so that later you can easily remember what the name represents. For example, Barbara wants the two tables to be named Customer and Order, because these names suggest their contents.

The following rules apply to naming fields and objects:

- A name can be up to 64 characters long.
- A name can contain letters, numbers, spaces, and special characters except a period (.), exclamation mark (!), accent grave (`), and square brackets ([]).
- A name cannot start with a space.
- A table or query name must be unique within a database. A field name must be unique within a table, but it can be used again in another table.

In addition, experienced users of databases have the following tips for naming fields and objects:

- Capitalize the first letter of each word in the name.
- Avoid extremely long names because they are difficult to remember and refer to.
- Use standard abbreviations such as Num for Number, Amt for Amount, and Qty for Quantity.
- Do not use spaces in field names because these names will appear in column headings on datasheets and labels on forms and reports. By not using spaces you'll be able to show more fields on these objects at one time.

Assigning Field Data Types

You must assign a data type for each field. The **data type** determines what field values you can enter for the field and what other properties the field will have. For example, the Order table will include a BillingDate field, so you will assign the date/time data type to this field because it will store date values. Access will allow you to enter only dates or times as values for the field and will allow you to manipulate a value only as a date or time.

Figure 4-13 lists the nine data types available in Access, describes the field values allowed with each data type, explains when each data type should be used, and indicates the field size of each data type.

Figure 4-13 Data types for fields

Data Type	Description	Field Size
Text	Allows field values containing letters, digits, spaces, and special characters. Use for names, addresses, descriptions, and fields containing digits that are not used in calculations.	1 to 255 characters; 50 characters default
Memo	Allows field values containing letters, digits, spaces, and special characters. Use for long comments and explanations.	1 to 64,000 characters; exact size is determined by entry
Number	Allows positive and negative numbers as field values. Numbers can contain digits, a decimal point, commas, a plus sign, and a minus sign. Use for fields that you will use in calculations, except calculations involving money.	1 to 15 digits
Date/Time	Allows field values containing valid dates and times from January 1, 100 to December 31, 9999. Dates can be entered in mm/dd/yy (month, day, year) format, several other date formats, or a variety of time formats such as 10:35 PM. You can perform calculations on dates and times and you can sort them. For example, you can determine the number of days between two dates.	8 digits
Currency	Allows field values similar to those for the number data type. Unlike calculations with number data type decimal values, calculations performed using the currency data type are not subject to round-off error.	15 digits
AutoNumber	Consists of integers with values controlled by Access. Access automatically inserts a value in the field as each new record is created. You can specify sequential numbering or random numbering. This guarantees a unique field value, so that such a field can serve as a table's primary key.	9 digits
Yes/No	Limits field values to yes and no, or true and false. Use for fields that indicate the presence or absence of a condition, such as whether an order has been filled, or if an employee is eligible for the company dental plan.	1 character
OLE Object	Allows field values that are created in other programs as objects, such as photographs, video images, graphics, drawings, sound recordings, voice-mail messages, spreadsheets, and word-processing documents. These objects can be linked or embedded.	1 gigabyte maximum; exact size depends on object size
Lookup Wizard	Creates a field that lets you look up a value in another table or in a predefined list of values.	Same size as the primary key field used to perform the lookup

Assigning Field Sizes

The **field size** property defines a field value's maximum storage size for text and number fields only. The other data types have no field size property, because their storage size is either a fixed, predetermined amount or is determined automatically by the field value itself, as shown in Figure 4-13. A text field has a default field size of 50 characters. You set its field size by entering a number in the range 1 to 255. For example, the OrderNum and CustomerNum fields in the Order table will be text fields with sizes of 3 each.

Barbara documents the design for the Order table by listing each field's name, data type, size (if applicable), and description, as shown in Figure 4-14. OrderNum, the table's primary key, and CustomerNum, a foreign key to the Customer table, will be assigned the text data type. BillingDate will have the date/time data type, and InvoiceAmt will have the currency data type.

Figure 4-14 Design for the Order table

Field Name	Data Type	Field Size	Description
OrderNum	Text	3	primary key
CustomerNum	Text	3	foreign key
BillingDate	Date/TIme		
InvoiceAmt	Currency		

With Barbara's design, you are ready to create the Order table.

Creating a Table

You have created the Restaurant Business database, so you can now create its tables. Creating a table consists of naming the fields and defining the properties for the fields, selecting a primary key for the table, then saving the table structure. You will use Barbara's design (Figure 4-14) as a guide to creating the Order table.

To begin creating the Order table:

1. Click the **New** button in the Database window. The New Table dialog box opens. See Figure 4-15.

Figure 4-15 New Table dialog box

In Access, you can create a table from entered data (Datasheet View), define your own table (Design View), use Table Wizard to automate the table creation process (Table Wizard), or use a wizard to import or link data from another database or other data source (Import Table and Link Table). For the Order table, you will define your own table.

2. Click **Design View** in the list box, then click the **OK** button. The Table window opens in Design view. See Figure 4-16.

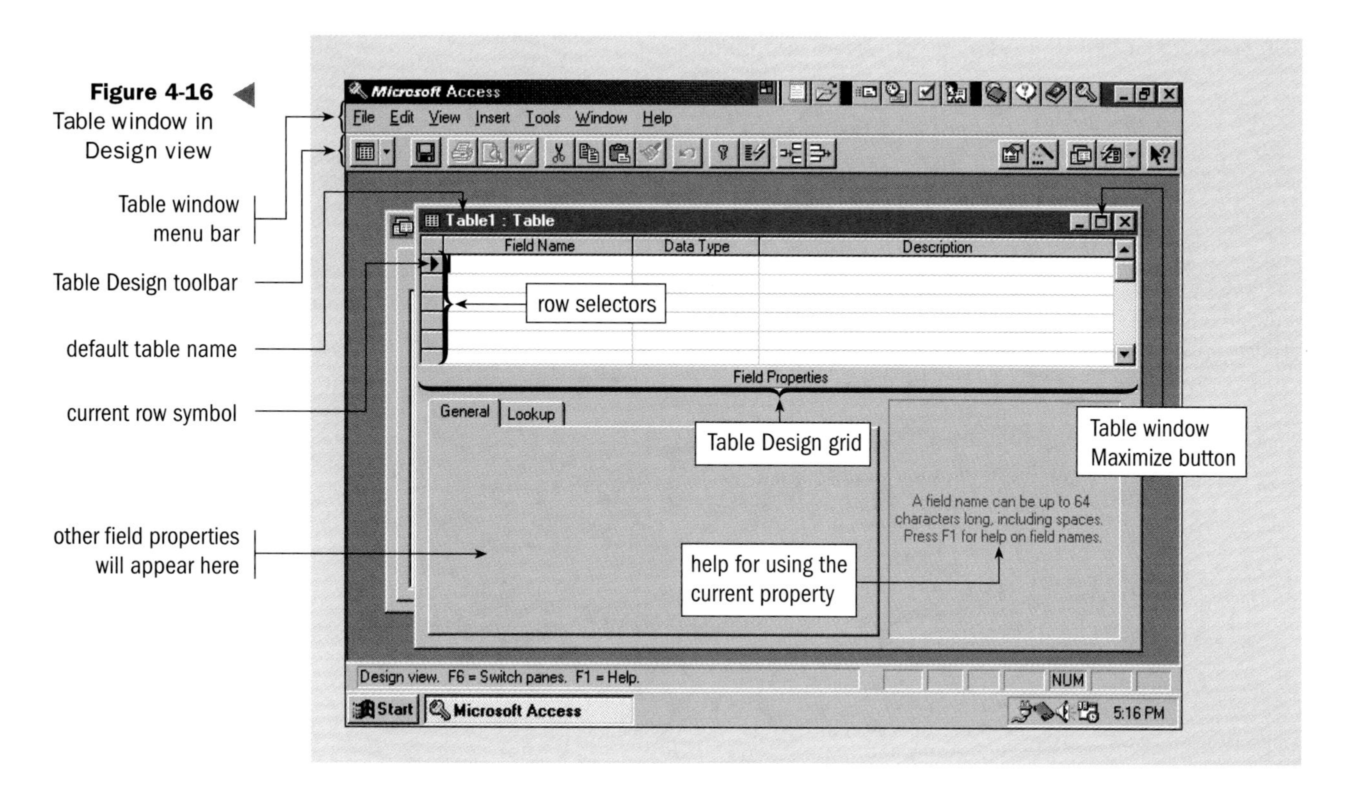

You use Design view to define or modify a table structure or the properties of the fields in a table. If you create a table without using a wizard, you enter the fields and their properties for your table directly in this window.

Defining Fields

Initially, Table1, the default table name, appears in the Table window title bar; the current row symbol is positioned in the first row selector of the Table Design grid; and the insertion point is located in the first row's Field Name box. The purpose or characteristics of the current property (Field Name, in this case) appear in the lower-right of the Table window. You can display more complete information about the current property by pressing the F1 key.

You enter values for the Field Name, Data Type, and Description field properties in the upper-half of the Table window. You select values for all other field properties in the lower-half of the window. These other properties will appear when you move to the first row's Data Type text box.

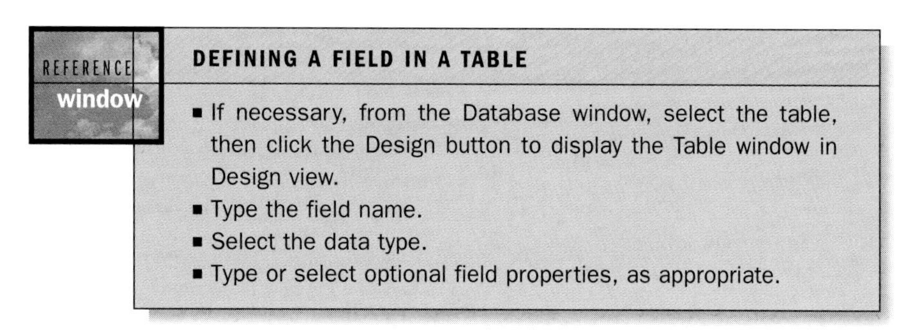

DEFINING A FIELD IN A TABLE

- If necessary, from the Database window, select the table, then click the Design button to display the Table window in Design view.
- Type the field name.
- Select the data type.
- Type or select optional field properties, as appropriate.

The first field you need to define is OrderNum.

To define the OrderNum field:

1. Type **OrderNum** in the first row's Field Name text box, then press the **Tab** key (or press the **Enter** key) to advance to the Data Type text box. The default data type, "Text," appears highlighted in the Data Type text box, which now also contains a down arrow, and field properties for a text field appear in the lower-half of the window. See Figure 4-17.

Figure 4-17 Table window after entering the first field name

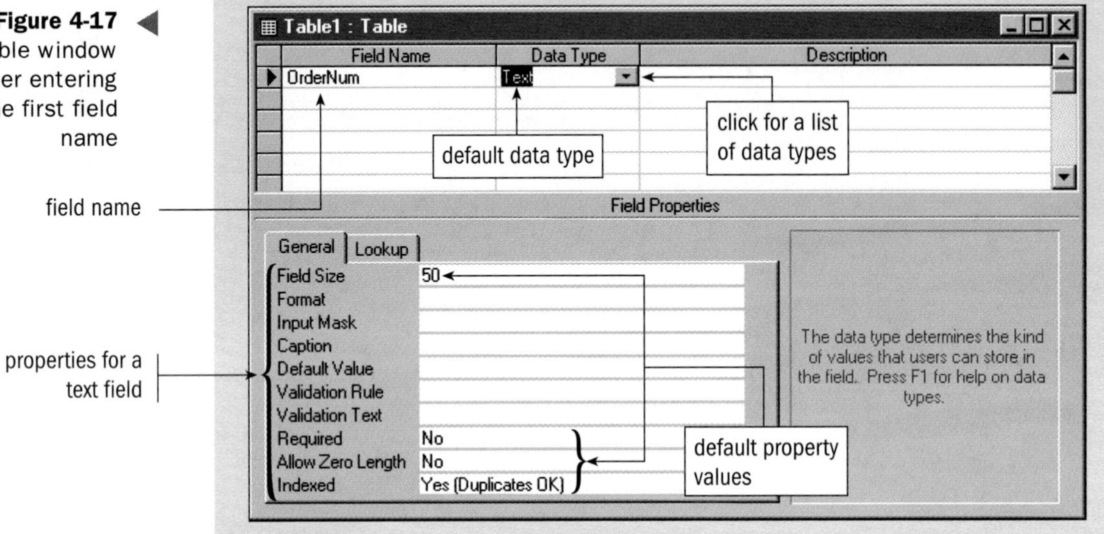

field name

properties for a text field

Notice that the lower-right of the window now provides an explanation for the current Data Type property.

TROUBLE? If you make a typing error, you can correct it by using any of the text correction methods you've already learned for the other Office 95 programs.

Because order numbers will not be used for calculations, you will assign the text data type to it instead of the number data type, then enter the Description property value as "primary key." You can use the Description property to enter an optional description for a field to explain its purpose or usage. A field's Description property can be up to 255 characters long, and its value appears in the status bar when you view the table datasheet.

2. Press the **Tab** key to accept Text as the field's Data Type and move to the Description text box, then type **primary key** in the Description text box.

   The Field Size property has a default value of 50, which you will change to a value of 3, because order numbers at Valle Coffee contain 3 digits. The Required property has a default value of No, which means that a value does not need to be entered for the field. Because Barbara doesn't want an order entered without an order number, you will change the Required property to Yes. The Allow Zero Length property has a default value of No, meaning that a value *must* be entered for the field, as is appropriate for the OrderNum field. Finally, the Indexed property has a value of "Yes (Duplicates OK)," which means that a list of index entries will be created to speed up operations using the OrderNum field.

3. Select **50** in the Field Size text box either by dragging the pointer or double-clicking the mouse, then type **3**.
4. Click the **Required** text box to position the insertion point there. A list arrow appears on the right side of the Required text box.
5. Click the **Required** list arrow. Access displays the Required list. See Figure 4-18.

Figure 4-18 ◀
Defining the OrderNum field

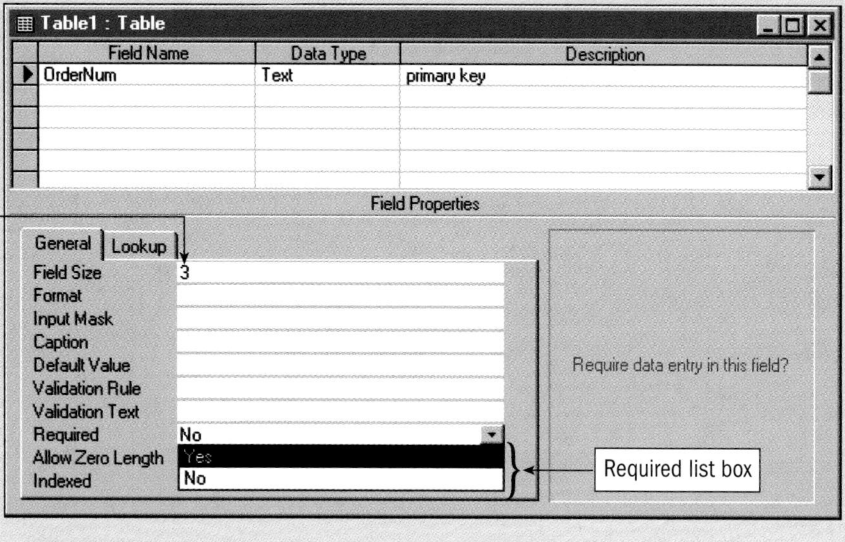

changed from default value of 50

Required list box

When you position the insertion point or select text in many Access text boxes, Access displays a list arrow, which you can click to display a list box with options. You can display the list arrow *and* the list box simultaneously if you click the text box near its right side.

6. Click **Yes** in the list box. The list box disappears, and Yes is now the value for the Required property. The definition of the first field is complete.

Barbara's Order table design shows CustomerNum as the second field. You will define CustomerNum as a text field with a Description of "foreign key" and a Field Size of 3, because customer numbers at Valle Coffee contain 3 digits. Because it's possible that a record for an order might need to be entered for a customer not yet added to the database, Barbara asks you to leave the Required property at its default value of No and to change the Allow Zero Length property value to Yes.

To define the CustomerNum field:

1. Place the insertion point in the second row's Field Name text box, type **CustomerNum** in the text box, then press the **Tab** key to advance to the Data Type text box.

   Customer numbers are not used in calculations, so you'll assign the text data type to the field, then enter its Description value as "foreign key."

2. Press the **Tab** key to accept Text as the field's Data Type and move to the Description text box, then type **foreign key** in the Description text box.

   Finally, change the Field Size property to 3 and the Allow Zero Length property to Yes.

3. Select **50** in the Field Size text box, type **3**, click the right side of the Allow Zero Length text box, then click **Yes**. You have completed the definition of the second field. See Figure 4-19.

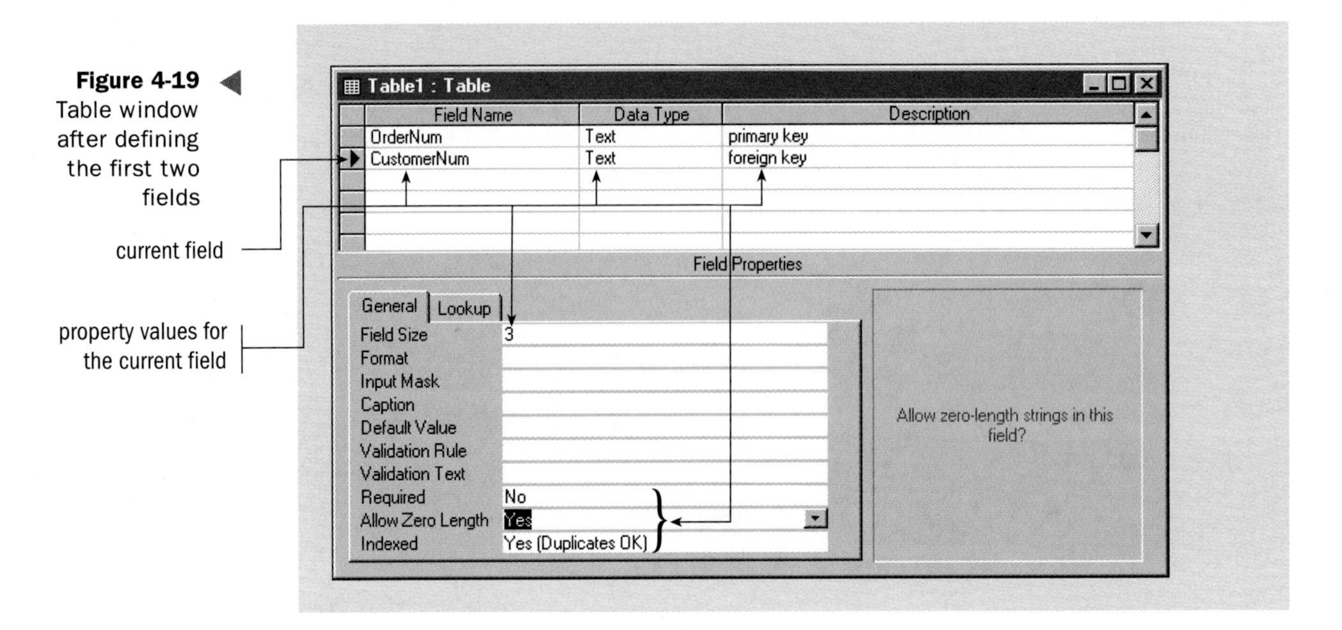

Figure 4-19 Table window after defining the first two fields

Using Barbara's Order table design in Figure 4-14, you can now complete the remaining field definitions: BillingDate with the date/time data type, and InvoiceAmt with the currency data type.

To define the BillingDate and InvoiceAmt fields:

1. Place the insertion point in the third row's Field Name text box, type **BillingDate** in the text box, then press the **Tab** key to advance to the Data Type text box.

2. Click the **Data Type** list arrow, click **Date/Time** in the list box, then press the **Tab** key to advance to the Description text box.

   If you've assigned a descriptive field name and the field does not fulfill a special function (for example, primary key), you usually do not enter a value for the optional Description property. BillingDate is a field that does not require a value for its Description property.

   Barbara does not want to require that a value be entered for the BillingDate field, nor does she want an index for the field. So, you do not need to change any of the default property values for the BillingDate field. Neither do you need to enter any new property values. Because you have finished defining the BillingDate field, you can now define the InvoiceAmt field.

3. Press the **Tab** key to advance to the fourth row's Field Name text box.

4. Type **InvoiceAmt** in the Field Name text box, then press the **Tab** key to advance to the Data Type text box.

   You can select a value from the Data Type list box as you did for the BillingDate field. Alternatively, you can type the property value in the text box or type just the first character of the property value.

5. Type **c**. The value in the fourth row's Data Type text box changes to "currency," with the letters "urrency" highlighted. See Figure 4-20.

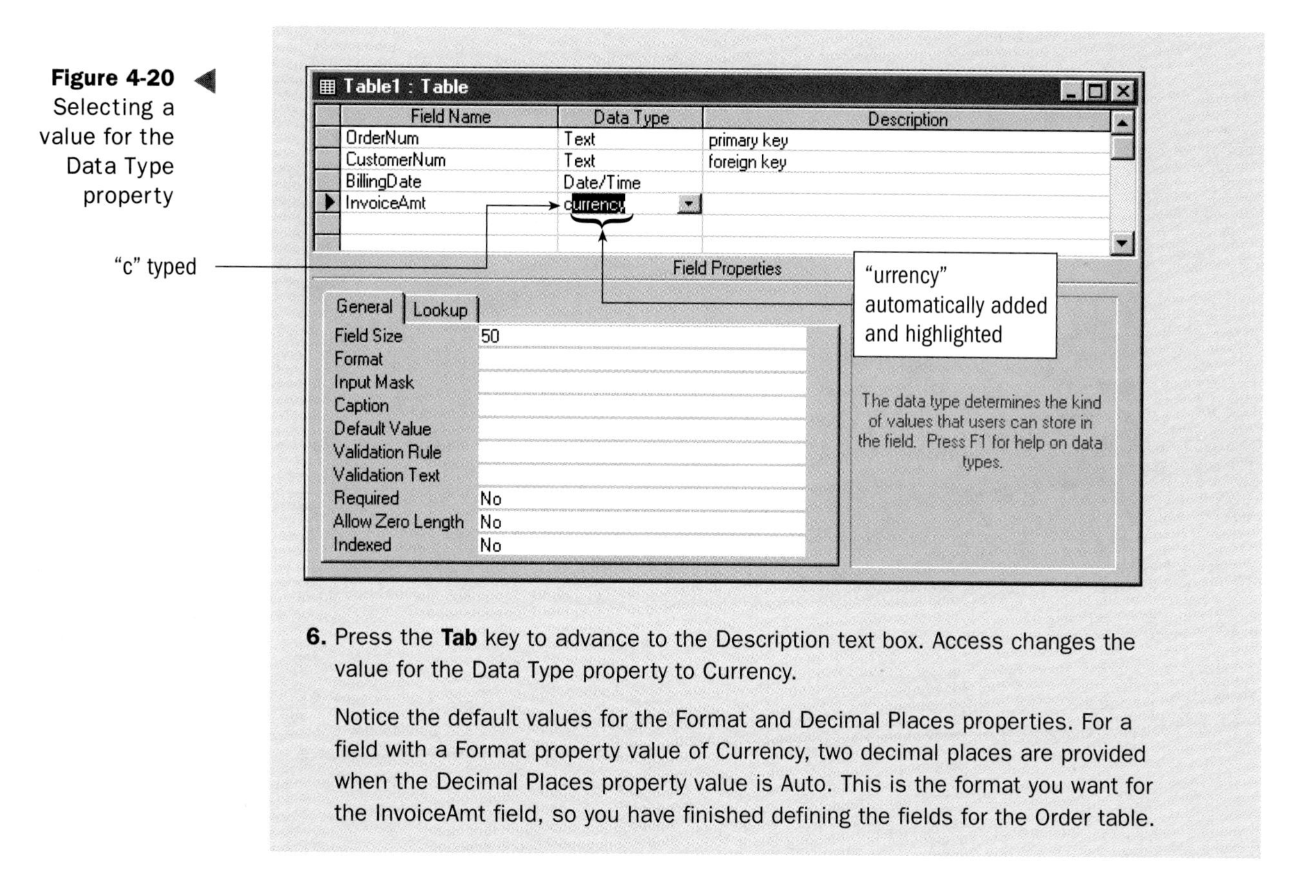

Figure 4-20 Selecting a value for the Data Type property

6. Press the **Tab** key to advance to the Description text box. Access changes the value for the Data Type property to Currency.

   Notice the default values for the Format and Decimal Places properties. For a field with a Format property value of Currency, two decimal places are provided when the Decimal Places property value is Auto. This is the format you want for the InvoiceAmt field, so you have finished defining the fields for the Order table.

Next, you need to specify the primary key for the Order table.

Specifying the Primary Key

Although Access does not require a table to have a primary key, including a primary key offers several advantages:

- A primary key uniquely identifies each record in a table.
- Access does not allow duplicate values in the primary key field. If a record already exists with an OrderNum value of 143, for example, Access prevents you from adding another record with this same value in the OrderNum field. Preventing duplicate values ensures the uniqueness of the primary key field and helps to avoid data redundancy.
- Access forces you to enter a value for the primary key field in every record in the table. This is known as **entity integrity**. If you do not enter a value for a field, you have actually given the field what is known as a **null value**. You cannot give a null value to the primary key field, because entity integrity prevents Access from accepting and processing that record.
- Access stores records on disk in the same order as you enter them but displays them in order by the field values of the primary key. If you enter records in no specific order, you are ensured that you will later be able to work with them in a more meaningful, primary key sequence.
- Access responds faster to your requests for specific records based on the primary key.

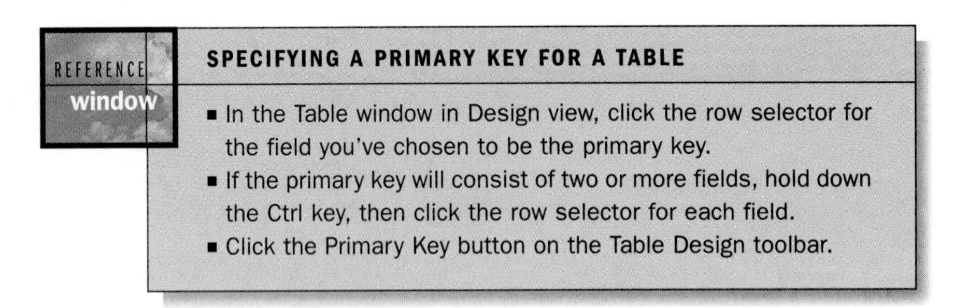

SPECIFYING A PRIMARY KEY FOR A TABLE

- In the Table window in Design view, click the row selector for the field you've chosen to be the primary key.
- If the primary key will consist of two or more fields, hold down the Ctrl key, then click the row selector for each field.
- Click the Primary Key button on the Table Design toolbar.

According to Barbara's design, you need to specify OrderNum as the primary key for the Order table.

To specify OrderNum as the primary key:

1. Move the pointer to the row selector for the OrderNum field until the pointer changes to ➡. See Figure 4-21.

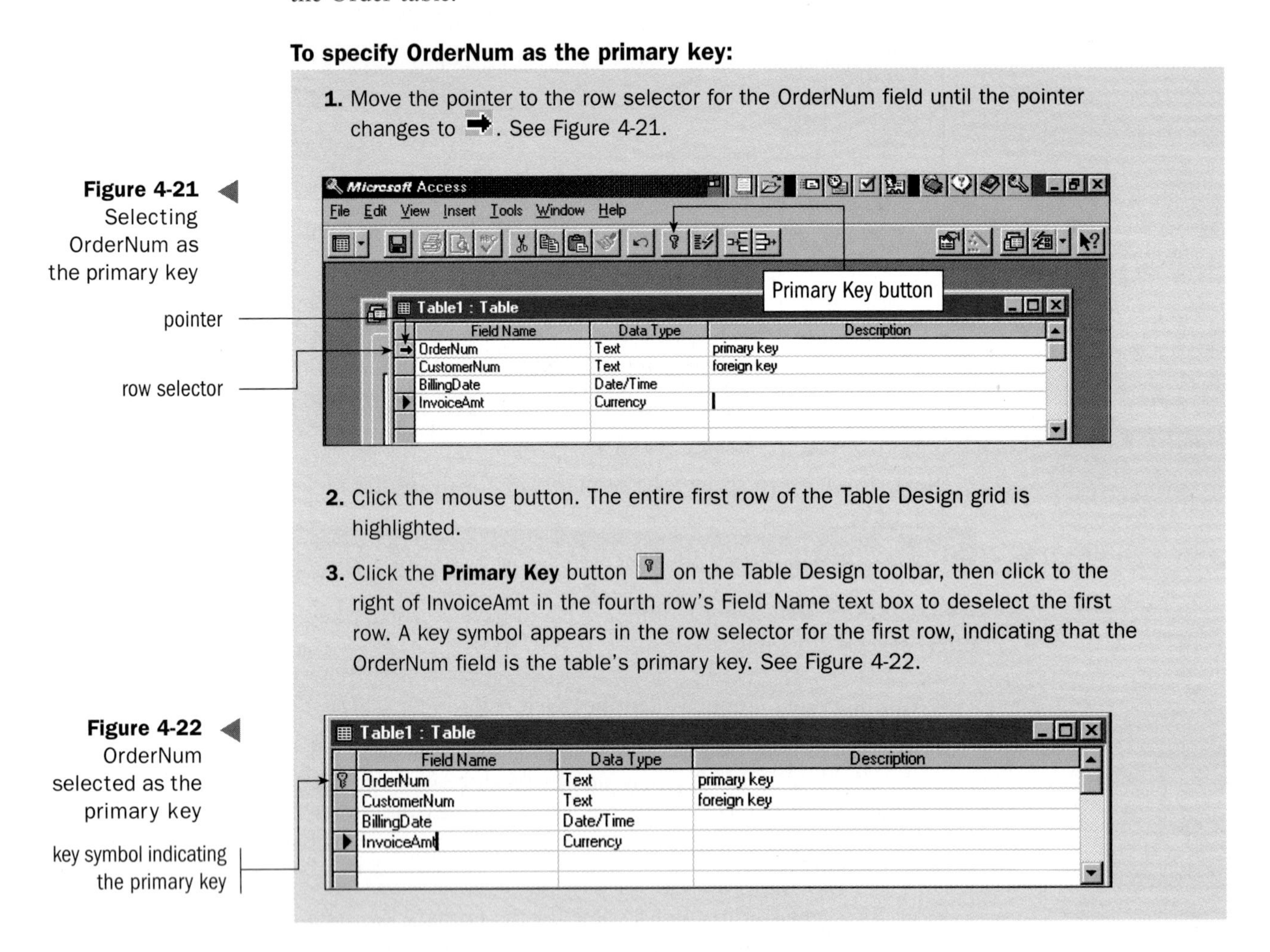

Figure 4-21 Selecting OrderNum as the primary key

2. Click the mouse button. The entire first row of the Table Design grid is highlighted.

3. Click the **Primary Key** button on the Table Design toolbar, then click to the right of InvoiceAmt in the fourth row's Field Name text box to deselect the first row. A key symbol appears in the row selector for the first row, indicating that the OrderNum field is the table's primary key. See Figure 4-22.

Figure 4-22 OrderNum selected as the primary key

You've defined the fields for the Order table and selected its primary key, so you can now save the table structure.

Saving the Table Structure

The last step in creating a table is to name the table and save the table's structure on disk. Once the table is saved, you can use it to enter data in the table.

You'll use the name Order for the table you've defined.

To name and save the Order table:

1. Click the **Save** button on the Table Design toolbar. The Save As dialog box opens.

2. Type **Order** in the Table Name text box, then press the **Enter** key. Access saves the table with the name Order in the Restaurant Business database on your Student Disk. Notice that Order appears instead of Table1 in the Table window title bar.

Barbara asks you to add two records, shown in Figure 4-23, to the Order table.

Figure 4-23 Records to be added to the Order table

OrderNum	CustomerNum	BillingDate	InvoiceAmt
323	624	2/15/98	$1,986.00
201	107	1/15/98	$854.00

Adding Records to a Table

You can add records to an Access table in several ways. A table datasheet provides a simple way for you to add records. A **datasheet** shows a table's contents in rows and columns, similar to a table or worksheet. Each row is a separate record in the table, and each column contains the field values for one field in the table. To view a table datasheet, you first must change from Design view to Datasheet view.

You'll add the two records in the Order table datasheet.

To add records in the Order table datasheet:

1. Click the **Table View** button for Datasheet view on the Table Design toolbar. The Table window opens in Datasheet view. See Figure 4-24.

Figure 4-24 Table window in Datasheet view

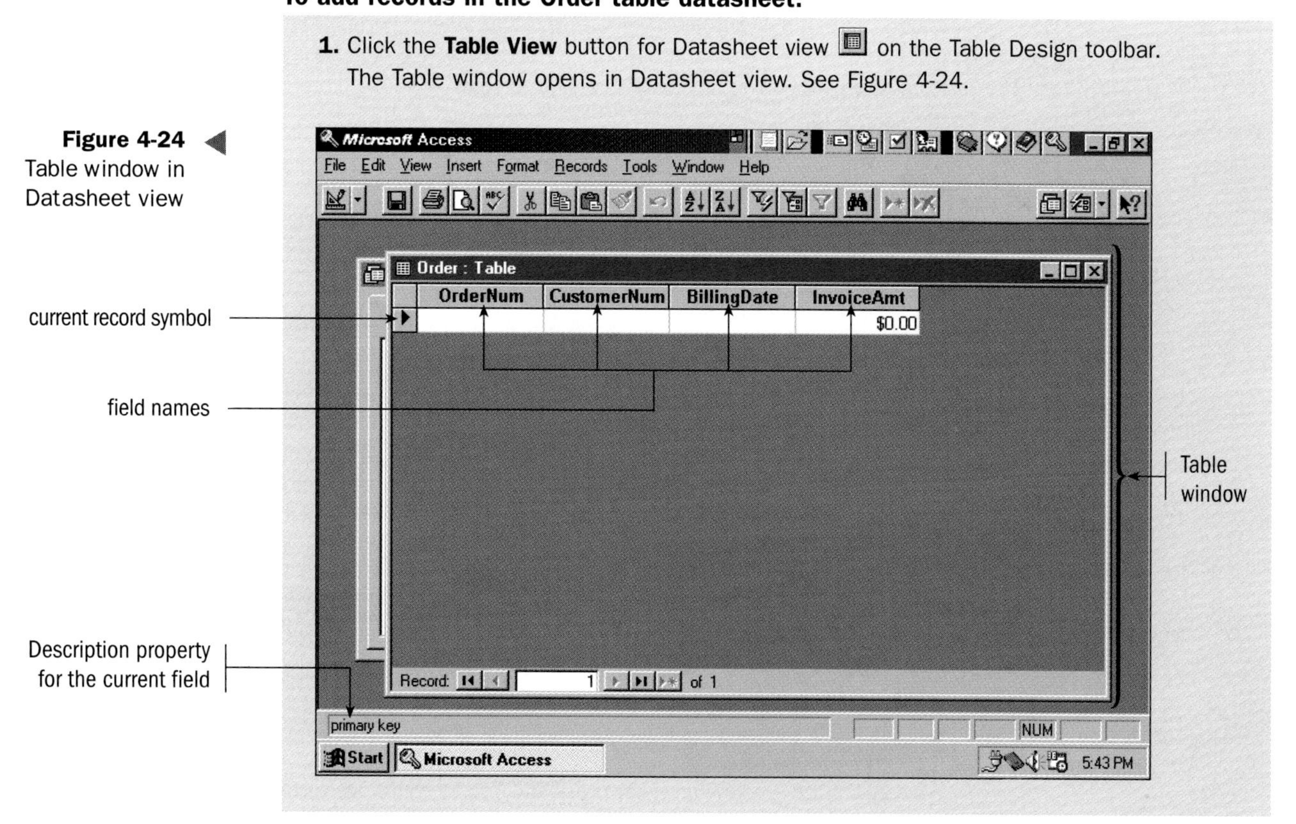

The table's four field names appear at the top of the datasheet. The current record symbol in the first row's record selector identifies the currently selected record, which contains no data until you enter the first record. The insertion point is located in the first row's OrderNum field, whose Description property appears in the status bar when the pointer is in the Table window.

2. Type **323**, which is the first record's OrderNum field value, then press the **Tab** key. Each time you press the Tab key, the insertion point moves to the right to the next field in the record. See Figure 4-25.

Figure 4-25 Datasheet for Order table after entering the first field value

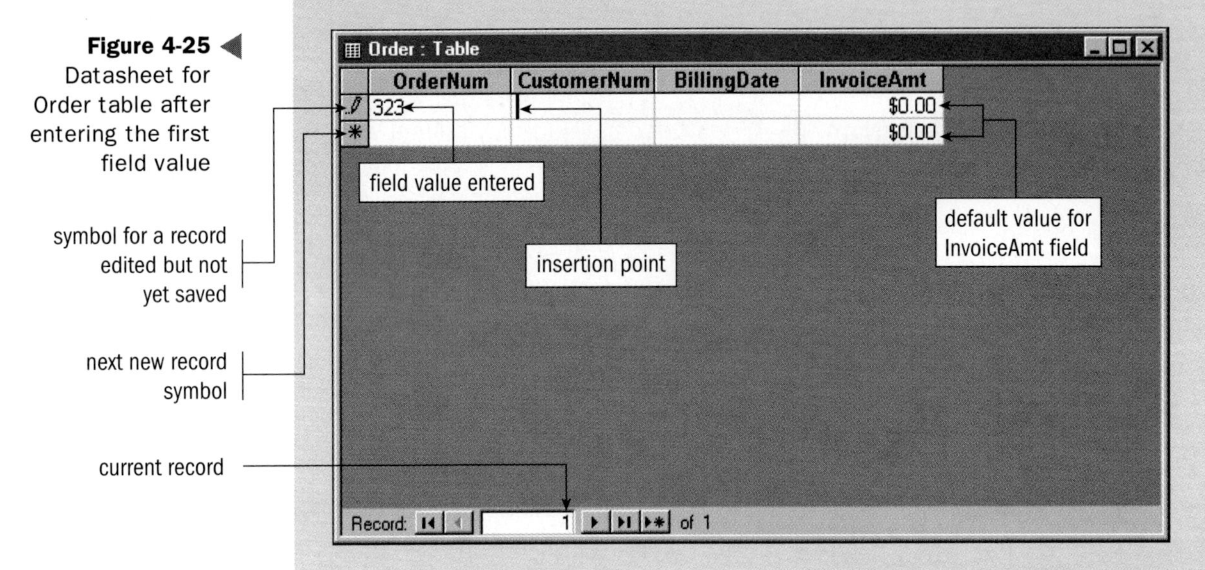

The pencil symbol in the first row's record selector indicates the record is being edited but has not yet been saved to the database. The star symbol in the second row's record selector identifies the second row as the next one available for a new record. The InvoiceAmt column displays "$0.00," the default value for the field.

3. Type **624** then press the **Tab** key. The insertion point moves to the BillingDate field.

4. Type **2/15/98** then press the **Tab** key. The insertion point moves to the InvoiceAmt field, whose field value is highlighted.

   Notice that field values for text fields are left-aligned in their boxes and field values for date/time and currency fields are right-aligned in their boxes. If the default value of $0.00 is correct for the InvoiceAmt field, you can press the Tab key to accept the value and advance to the beginning of the next record. Otherwise, type the field value for the InvoiceAmt field. You do not need to type the dollar sign, commas, or decimal point (for whole dollar amounts), because Access adds these symbols automatically for you.

5. Type **1986** then press the **Tab** key. Access displays $1,986.00 for the InvoiceAmt field, stores the first completed record in the Order table, removes the pencil symbol from the first row's record selector, advances the insertion point to the second row's OrderNum text box, and places the current record symbol in the second row's record selector.

   Now you can enter the values for the second record.

6. Type **201** in the OrderNum field, press the **Tab** key to move to the CustomerNum field, type **107** in the CustomerNum field, then press the **Tab** key. The insertion point moves to the BillingDate field.

7. Type **1/15/98** then press the **Tab** key. The value in the InvoiceAmt field is now highlighted.

8. Type **854** then press the **Tab** key. Access changes the InvoiceAmt field value to $854.00, saves the record in the Order table, and moves the insertion point to the beginning of the third row. See Figure 4-26.

Figure 4-26 Order table datasheet after entering the second record

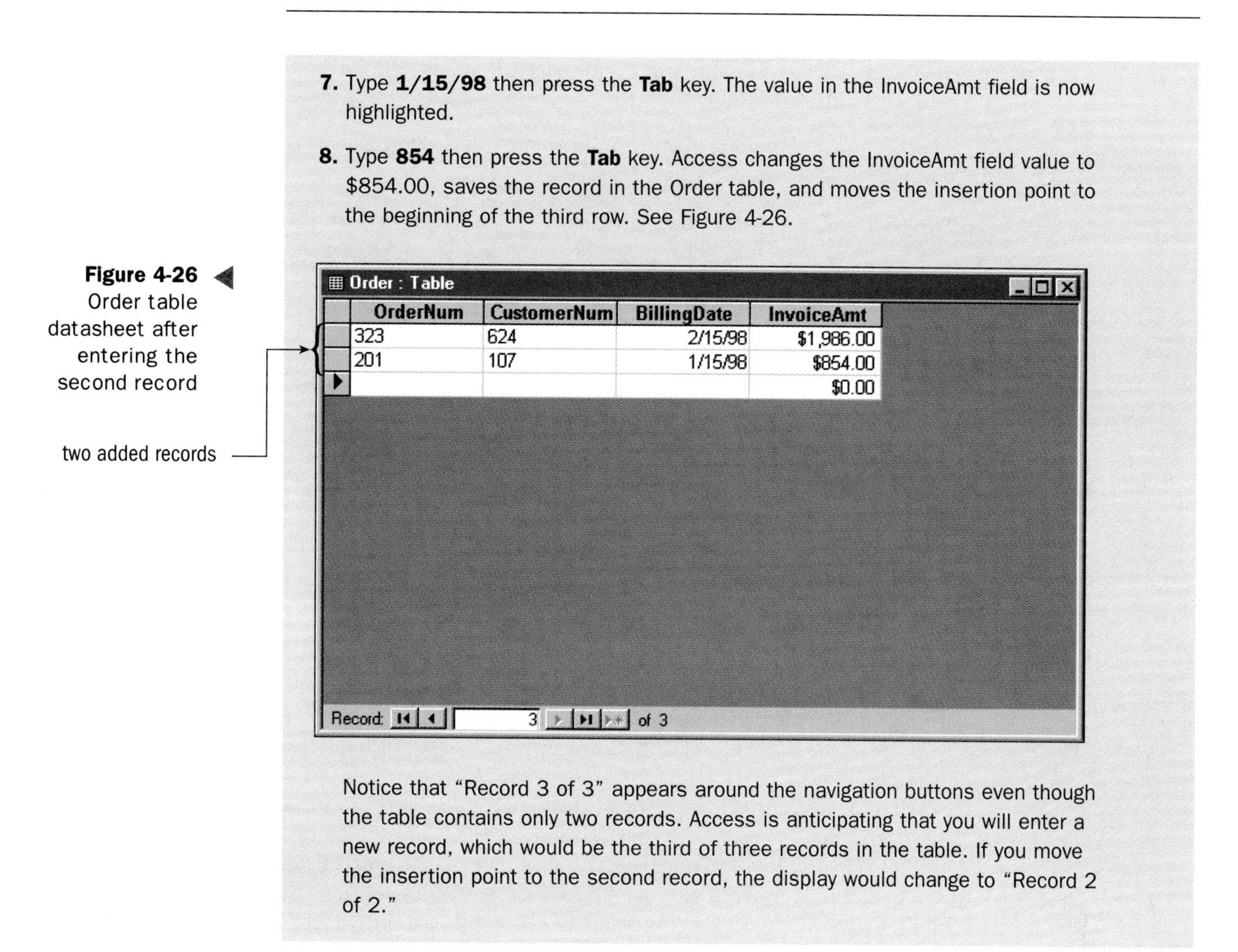

Notice that "Record 3 of 3" appears around the navigation buttons even though the table contains only two records. Access is anticipating that you will enter a new record, which would be the third of three records in the table. If you move the insertion point to the second record, the display would change to "Record 2 of 2."

You have created the Restaurant Business database and its Order table and added two records to the Order table, which Access saved to the database on your Student Disk.

Saving a Database

Notice the Save button on the Table Datasheet toolbar. This Save button, unlike the Save buttons in the other Office 95 programs, does not save the active document, or database, to your disk. Instead, you use the Save button to save the design of a table, query, form, or report, or to save datasheet format changes. Access does not have a button or option you can use to save the active database.

Access saves the active database to your disk automatically, both on a periodic basis and whenever you close the database. This means that if your database is stored on a disk in drive A or drive B, you should never remove the disk while the database file is open. If you do remove the disk, Access will encounter problems when it tries to save the database; this might damage the database.

Quick Check

1. A(n) __________ is a single characteristic of a person, place, object, event, or idea.
2. The __________, whose values uniquely identify each record in a table, is called a __________ when it is placed in a second table to form a relationship between the two tables.
3. What guidelines should you follow when you design a database?
4. What is the purpose of the data type property for a field?

5. Why were the OrderNum and CustomerNum fields defined as text fields instead of number fields?

6. A(n) __________ value, which results when you do not enter a value for a field, is not permitted for a primary key.

7. What does a pencil symbol in a datasheet's row selector represent? a star symbol?

Now that you've completed Session 4.1, you can exit Access or you can continue to the next session.

SESSION 4.2

In this session you will learn how to modify the structure of a table, copy records from another Access database, update a database, import Excel data to create a new table, and print a datasheet.

Modifying the Structure of an Access Table

Even a well-designed table might need to be modified. For example, the government at all levels and the competition place demands on a company to track more data and to modify the data it already tracks. Access allows you to modify a table's structure in Design view: you can add and delete fields, change the order of fields, and change the properties of the fields.

After reviewing the structure of the Order table and the format of the field values in the datasheet, Barbara has several changes she wants you to make to the table. She decides that the InvoiceAmt field should remain a currency field, but she wants the dollar signs removed from the displayed field values in the datasheet. She also wants the BillingDate field moved to the end of the table, as shown in Figure 4-27. Finally, she wants you to add a yes/no field, named Paid, to the table to indicate whether the invoice has been paid for the order. The Paid field will be inserted between the CustomerNum and InvoiceAmt fields.

Figure 4-27 Modified design for the Order table

Field Name	Data Type	Field Size	Description
OrderNum	Text	3	primary key
CustomerNum	Text	3	foreign key
Paid	Yes/No		
InvoiceAmt	Currency		
BillingDate	Date/Time		

Moving a Field

To move a field, you use the mouse to drag it to a new location in the Table window in Design view. You'll begin modifying the Order table structure by moving the BillingDate field to the end of the table, as Barbara requested.

To move the BillingDate field:

1. Click the **Table View** button for Design view on the Table Datasheet toolbar. The Table window for the Order table opens in Design view.

2. Click the row selector for the BillingDate field to select the entire row.

3. Place the pointer in the row selector for the BillingDate field, click the pointer, then drag the pointer to the row selector below the InvoiceAmt row selector. See Figure 4-28.

Figure 4-28 Moving a field in the table structure

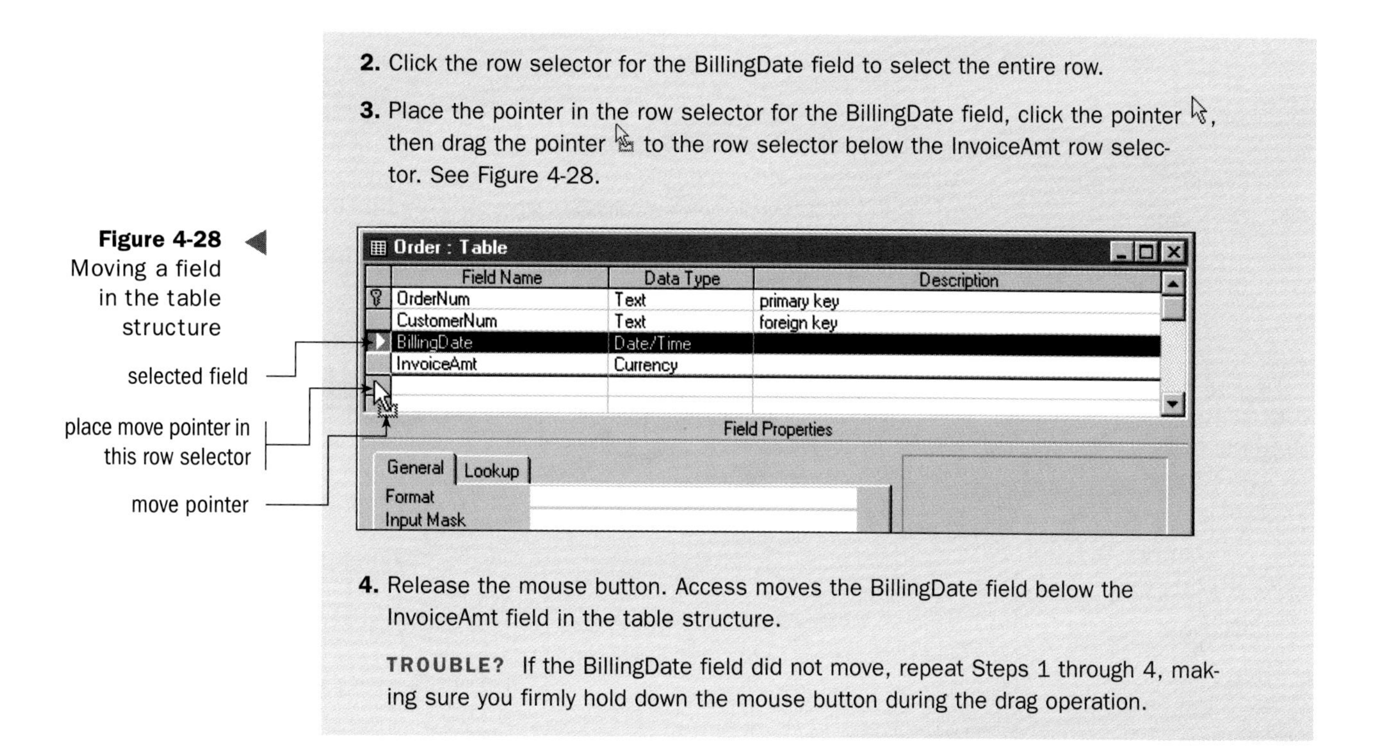

4. Release the mouse button. Access moves the BillingDate field below the InvoiceAmt field in the table structure.

   TROUBLE? If the BillingDate field did not move, repeat Steps 1 through 4, making sure you firmly hold down the mouse button during the drag operation.

You have moved the BillingDate field in the Table window, but the move doesn't take place in the table on disk until you save the table structure. Because you have other modifications to make to the table, you'll wait until you finish them all before saving the modified table structure to disk.

Adding a Field

Next, you need to add the Paid field to the table structure between the CustomerNum and InvoiceAmt fields. To add a new field between existing fields, you must insert a row. You begin by selecting the field *above* which you want to insert the new field.

To add the Paid field to the Order table:

1. Right-click the row selector for the InvoiceAmt field to select this field and display the shortcut menu, then click **Insert Field**. Access adds a new, blank row between the CustomerNum and InvoiceAmt fields. See Figure 4-29.

Figure 4-29 After inserting a row in the table structure

Order : Table

Field Name	Data Type	Description
OrderNum	Text	primary key
CustomerNum	Text	foreign key
InvoiceAmt	Currency	
BillingDate	Date/Time	

   You'll define the Paid field in the new row for the Order table. Access will add this new field to the Order table structure between the CustomerNum and InvoiceAmt fields.

2. Click the **Field Name** text box for the new row, type **Paid**, then press the **Tab** key.

   The Paid field will be a yes/no field that will specify whether an invoice has been paid.

3. Type **y**. Access completes the data type as "yes/No."

4. Press the **Tab** key to select the yes/no data type and move to the Description field.

   Notice that Access changes the value in the Data Type text box from "yes/No" to "Yes/No." Barbara wants the Paid field to have a Default Value property value of "no." When you select or enter a value for a property, you *set* the property.

5. Click the **Default Value** text box, type **no**, then click the **Description** text box for the Paid field. Notice that Access changes the Default Value property value from "no" to "No." See Figure 4-30.

Figure 4-30
Paid field added to the Order table

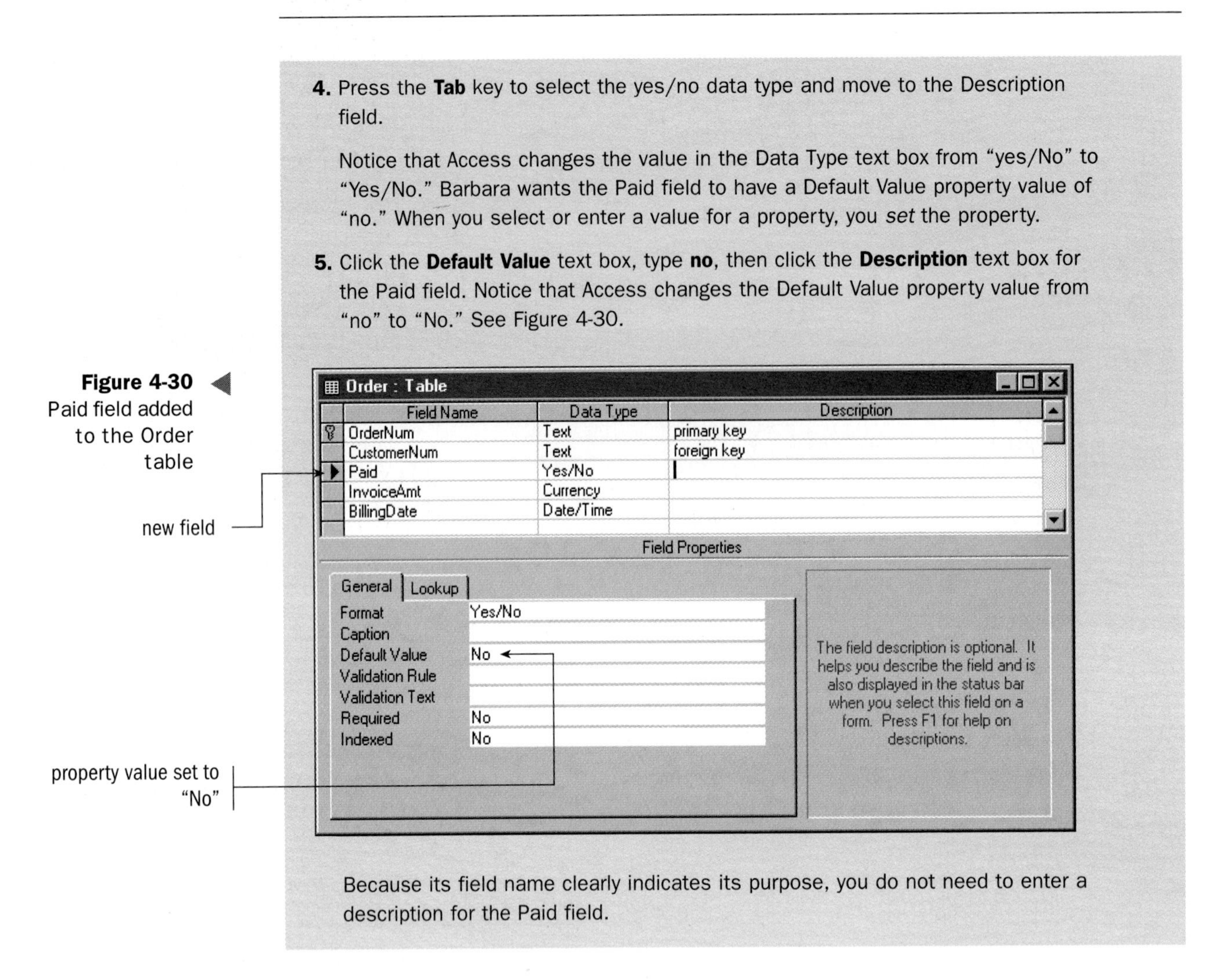

Because its field name clearly indicates its purpose, you do not need to enter a description for the Paid field.

You've completed adding the Paid field to the Order table in Design view. Until you save the table changes, however, the Paid field is not added to the Order table in the Restaurant Business database.

Changing Field Properties

Barbara's last modification to the table structure is to remove the dollar signs from the InvoiceAmt field values displayed in the datasheet, because repeated dollar signs are unnecessary and clutter the datasheet. You use the **Format property** to control the display of a field value.

To change the Format property of the InvoiceAmt field:

1. Click the **Description** text box for the InvoiceAmt field. The InvoiceAmt field is now the current field.

2. Click the **Format** text box in the Field Properties section, then click the **Format** list arrow to display the Format list box. See Figure 4-31.

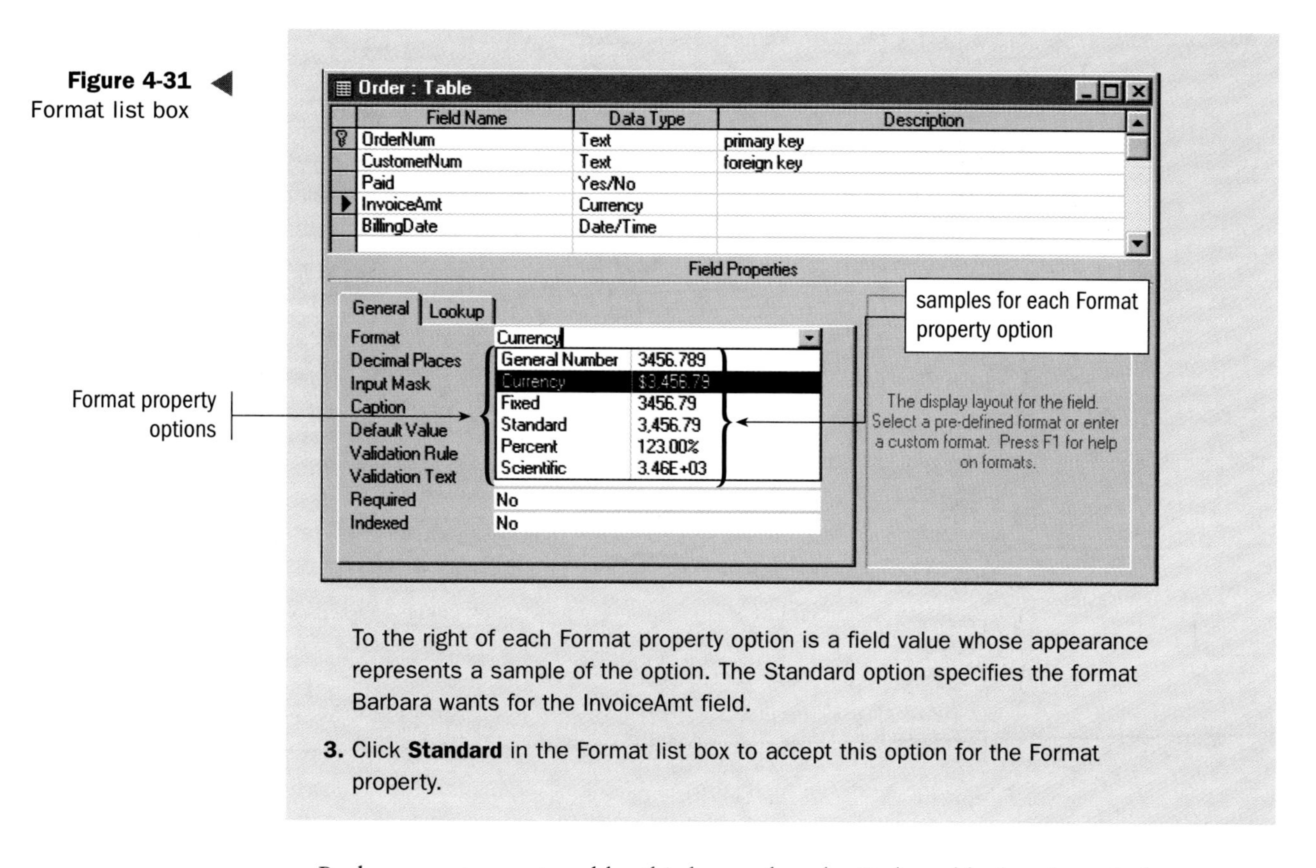

Figure 4-31 Format list box

To the right of each Format property option is a field value whose appearance represents a sample of the option. The Standard option specifies the format Barbara wants for the InvoiceAmt field.

3. Click **Standard** in the Format list box to accept this option for the Format property.

Barbara wants you to add a third record to the Order table datasheet. Before you can add the record, you must save the modified table structure, then switch to the Order table datasheet.

To save the modified table structure, then switch to the datasheet:

1. Click the **Save** button on the Table Design toolbar. The modified table structure for the Order table is stored in the Restaurant Business database.
2. Click the **Table View** button for Datasheet view on the Table Design toolbar. The Order table opens in Datasheet view. See Figure 4-32.

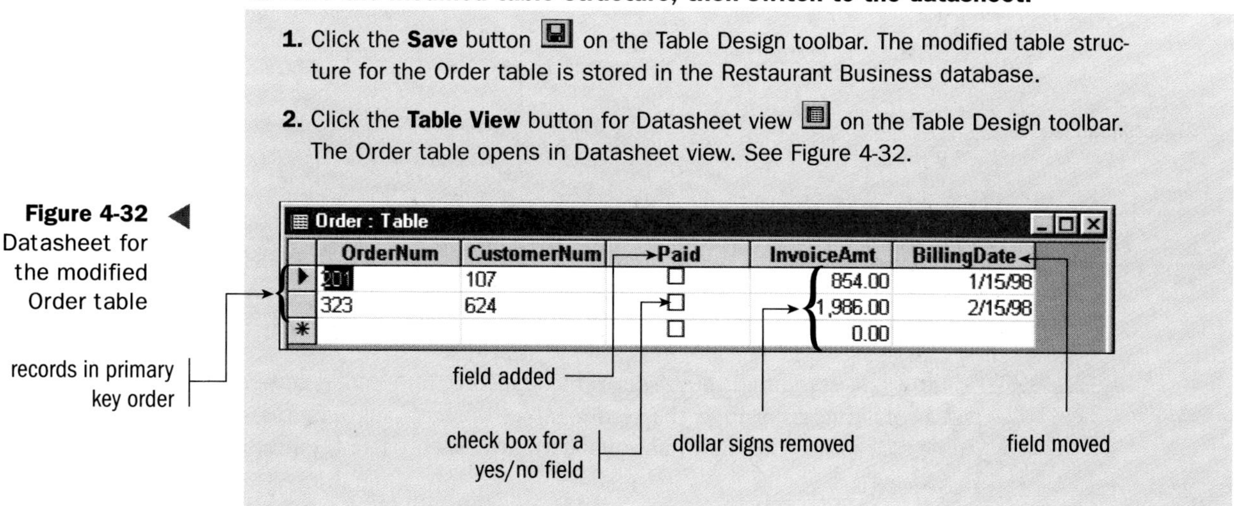

Figure 4-32 Datasheet for the modified Order table

Notice that the BillingDate field is now the rightmost column, the InvoiceAmt field values do not contain dollar signs, and the Paid field appears between the CustomerNum and InvoiceAmt fields. The Paid column contains check boxes to represent the yes/no field values. Empty check boxes signify "No," which is the default value for the Paid field. A "Yes" value is indicated by a check mark in the check box. Also notice that the records appear in ascending order based on the value in the OrderNum field, the Order table's primary key, even though you did not enter the records in this order.

Barbara asks you to add a third record to the table. This record is for an order that has been paid.

To add the record to the modified Order table:

1. Click the **New Record** button on the Table Datasheet toolbar. The insertion point is located in the OrderNum field for the third row, which is the next row available for a new record.
2. Type **211**. The pencil symbol appears in the row selector for the third row, and the star appears in the row selector for the fourth row. Recall that these symbols represent a record being edited but not yet saved and the next available record, respectively.
3. Press the **Tab** key. The insertion point moves to the CustomerNum field.
4. Type **201** then press the **Tab** key. The insertion point moves to the Paid field.

   Recall that the default value for this field is "No," which means the check box is initially empty. For yes/no fields with check boxes, you press the Tab key to leave the check box unchecked; you press the spacebar or click the check box to add or remove a check mark in the check box. Because the invoice for this order has been paid, you need to insert a check mark in the check box.
5. Press the **spacebar**. A check mark appears in the check box.
6. Press the **Tab** key. The value in the InvoiceAmt field is now highlighted.
7. Type **703.5** then press the **Tab** key. The insertion point moves to the BillingDate field.
8. Type **1/15/98** then press the **Tab** key. Access saves the record in the Order table and moves the insertion point to the beginning of the fourth row. See Figure 4-33.

Figure 4-33 Order table datasheet with third record added

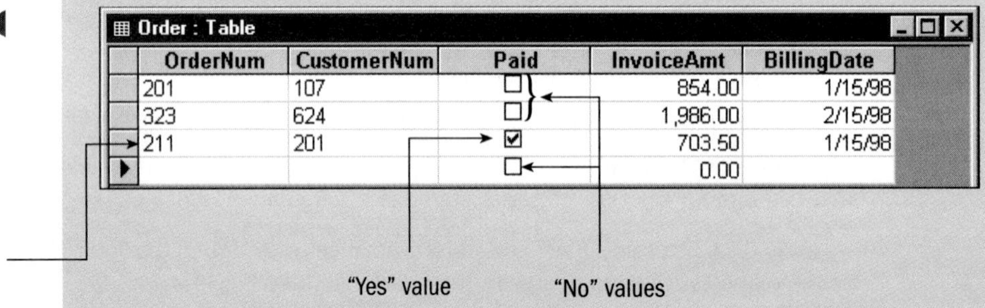

Order : Table

OrderNum	CustomerNum	Paid	InvoiceAmt	BillingDate
201	107	☐	854.00	1/15/98
323	624	☐	1,986.00	2/15/98
211	201	☑	703.50	1/15/98
		☐	0.00	

record added

"Yes" value

"No" values

As you add records, Access places them at the end of the datasheet. If you switch to Design view then return to the datasheet or if you close the table then open the datasheet, Access will display the records in primary key sequence.

You have modified the Order table structure and added one record. Instead of typing the remaining records in the Order table, Barbara suggests that you copy them from a table that already exists in another database, then paste them into the Order table.

Copying Records from Another Access Database

You can copy and paste records from a table in the same database or in a different database, but only if the tables have the same table structure. Barbara's Valle database in the Tutorial.04 folder on your Student Disk has a table named Restaurant Order, which has the same table structure as the Order table. The records in the Restaurant Order table are the records Barbara wants you to copy into the Order table.

Other Office 95 programs, such as Word and Excel, allow you to have two or more documents open at a time. However, you can have only one Access database open at a time. Therefore, you need to close the Restaurant Business database, open the Restaurant Order table in the Valle database, select and copy the table records, close the Valle database, reopen the Order table in the Restaurant Business database, then paste the copied records.

To copy the records from the Restaurant Order table:

1. Click the **Close** button on the Table window title bar to close the Order table, then click the **Close** button on the Database window title bar to close the Restaurant Business database.
2. Click the **Open Database** button on the Access window toolbar. The Open dialog box opens.
3. If necessary, display the list of files on your Student Disk, then open the **Tutorial.04** folder.
4. Open the file named **Valle**. The Database window opens, showing the tables for the Valle database.

   Notice that the Valle database contains two tables: the Restaurant Customer table and the Restaurant Order table. The Restaurant Order table contains the records you need to copy.
5. Click **Restaurant Order** in the Tables list box, then click the **Open** button. The datasheet for the Restaurant Order table opens. See Figure 4-34. Note that this table contains a total of 102 records.

Figure 4-34 Datasheet for the Valle database's Restaurant Order table

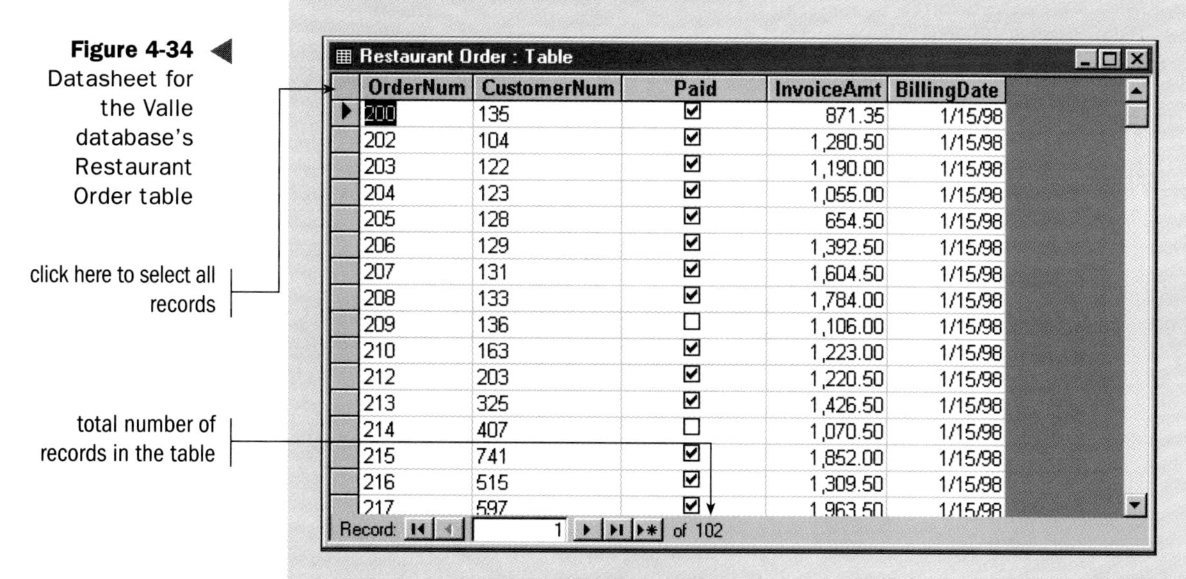

OrderNum	CustomerNum	Paid	InvoiceAmt	BillingDate
200	135	☑	871.35	1/15/98
202	104	☑	1,280.50	1/15/98
203	122	☑	1,190.00	1/15/98
204	123	☑	1,055.00	1/15/98
205	128	☑	654.50	1/15/98
206	129	☑	1,392.50	1/15/98
207	131	☑	1,604.50	1/15/98
208	133	☑	1,784.00	1/15/98
209	136	☐	1,106.00	1/15/98
210	163	☑	1,223.00	1/15/98
212	203	☑	1,220.50	1/15/98
213	325	☑	1,426.50	1/15/98
214	407	☐	1,070.50	1/15/98
215	741	☑	1,852.00	1/15/98
216	515	☑	1,309.50	1/15/98
217	597	☑	1,963.50	1/15/98

Barbara wants you to copy all the records in the Restaurant Order table. You can select all records by clicking the row selector for the field name row.

6. Click the **row selector** for the field name row (see Figure 4-34). All the records in the table are now highlighted, which means that Access has selected all of them.
7. Click the **Copy** button on the Table Datasheet toolbar. All the records are copied to the Clipboard.
8. Click the **Close** button on the Table window title bar. A dialog box opens asking if you want to save the data you copied on the Clipboard.
9. Click the **Yes** button in the dialog box. The dialog box closes, then the table closes.
10. Click the **Close** button on the Database window title bar to close the Valle database.

To finish copying and pasting the records, you must open the Order table and paste the copied records into the table.

To paste the copied records into the Order table:

1. Click **File** on the menu bar, then click **Restaurant Business** in the list of recently opened databases. The Database window opens, showing the tables for the Restaurant Business database. Note that the Order table is already selected, because it is the only table in the database.
2. Click the **Open** button. The datasheet for the Order table opens.

   You must paste the records at the end of the table.
3. Click the **row selector** for row four, which is the next row available for a new record.
4. Click the **Paste** button on the Table Datasheet toolbar. All the records are pasted from the Clipboard, and a dialog box appears, asking if you are sure you want to paste the records.
5. Click the **Yes** button. The pasted records remain highlighted. See Figure 4-35. Notice that the table now contains a total of 105 records—the three original records plus the 102 copied records.

Figure 4-35 After copying and pasting records

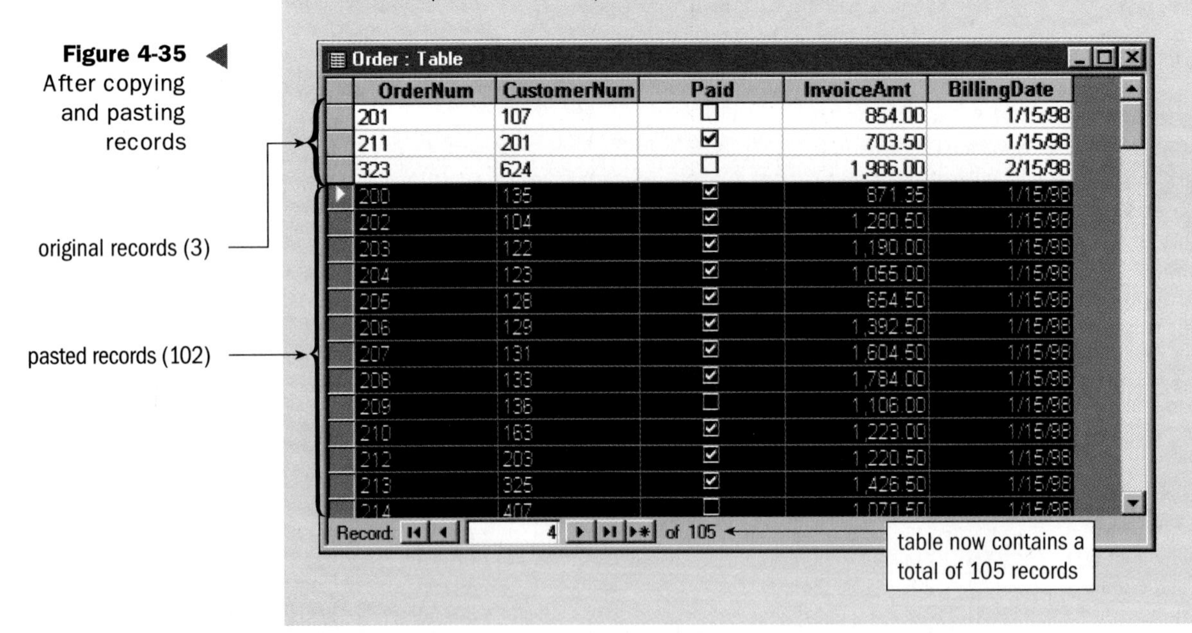

Order : Table

OrderNum	CustomerNum	Paid	InvoiceAmt	BillingDate
201	107	☐	854.00	1/15/98
211	201	☑	703.50	1/15/98
323	624	☐	1,986.00	2/15/98
200	135	☑	871.35	1/15/98
202	104	☑	1,280.50	1/15/98
203	122	☑	1,190.00	1/15/98
204	123	☑	1,055.00	1/15/98
205	128	☑	654.50	1/15/98
206	129	☑	1,392.50	1/15/98
207	131	☑	1,604.50	1/15/98
208	133	☑	1,784.00	1/15/98
209	136	☐	1,106.00	1/15/98
210	163	☑	1,223.00	1/15/98
212	203	☑	1,220.50	1/15/98
213	325	☑	1,426.50	1/15/98
214	407	☐	1,070.50	1/15/98

Record: 4 of 105

You've completed copying and pasting the records between the two tables. Now that you have all the records in the Order table, Barbara examines the records to make sure they are correct. She finds one record that she wants you to delete and another record that needs changes to its field values.

Updating a Database

Updating, or **maintaining,** a database is the process of adding, changing, and deleting records in database tables to keep them current and accurate. You've already added records to the Order table. Now Barbara wants you to delete and change records.

Deleting Records

To delete a record, you need to select the record in Datasheet view, then delete it using the Cut option on the shortcut menu (or the Edit menu). Barbara asks you to delete the record whose OrderNum is 200 because this record was entered in error; it represents an order from an office customer, not a restaurant customer, and therefore does not belong in the Restaurant Business database. The fourth record in the table has an OrderNum value of 200. This is the record you need to delete.

To delete the record:

1. Right-click the **row selector** for row four. Access selects the fourth record and displays the shortcut menu. See Figure 4-36.

Figure 4-36 Deleting a record

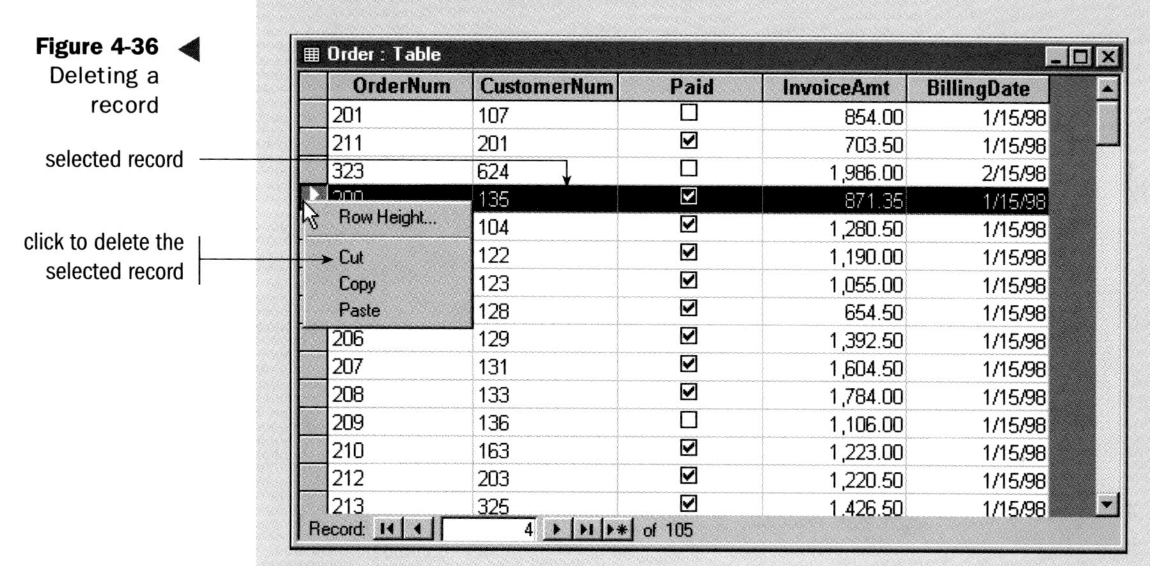

OrderNum	CustomerNum	Paid	InvoiceAmt	BillingDate
201	107	☐	854.00	1/15/98
211	201	☑	703.50	1/15/98
323	624	☐	1,986.00	2/15/98
200	135	☑	871.35	1/15/98
	104	☑	1,280.50	1/15/98
	122	☑	1,190.00	1/15/98
	123	☑	1,055.00	1/15/98
	128	☑	654.50	1/15/98
206	129	☑	1,392.50	1/15/98
207	131	☑	1,604.50	1/15/98
208	133	☑	1,784.00	1/15/98
209	136	☐	1,106.00	1/15/98
210	163	☑	1,223.00	1/15/98
212	203	☑	1,220.50	1/15/98
213	325	☑	1,426.50	1/15/98

2. Click **Cut** on the shortcut menu. Access deletes the record and opens a dialog box asking you to confirm the deletion.

3. Click the **Yes** button to confirm the deletion and close the dialog box.

Barbara's last update to the Order table involves changes to field values in one of the records.

Changing Records

To change the field values in a record, you first must make the record the current record. Then you position the insertion point in the field value to make minor changes or select the field value to replace it entirely. In Tutorial 1, you used the mouse with the scroll bars and the navigation buttons to navigate through the records in a datasheet. You can also use keystroke combinations and the F2 key to navigate a datasheet and to select field values.

The **F2 key** is a toggle that you use to switch between navigation mode and editing mode:

- In **navigation mode**, Access selects an entire field value. If you type while you are in navigation mode, your typed entry replaces the highlighted field value.
- In **editing mode**, you can insert or delete characters in a field value based on the location of the insertion point.

The navigation mode and editing mode keystroke techniques are shown in Figure 4-37.

Figure 4-37 Navigation mode and editing mode keystroke techniques

Press	To Move the Selection in Navigation Mode	To Move the Insertion Point in Editing Mode
←	Left one field value at a time	Left one character at a time
→	Right one field value at a time	Right one character at a time
Home	Left to the first field value in the record	To the left of the first character in the field value
End	Right to the last field value in the record	To the right of the last character in the field value
↑ or ↓	Up or down one record at a time	Up or down one record at a time and switch to navigation mode
Tab or Enter	Right one field value at a time	Right one field value at a time and switch to navigation mode
Ctrl + Home	To the first field value in the first record	To the left of the first character in the field value
Ctrl + End	To the last field value in the last record	To the right of the last character in the field value

The record Barbara wants you to change has an OrderNum field value of 397. Some of the values were entered incorrectly for this record, and you need to enter the correct values.

To modify the record:

1. Press **Ctrl + End**. Access displays records from the end of the table and selects the last field value in the last record. This field value is for the BillingDate field.
2. Press the **Home** key. The first field value in the record is now selected. This field value is for the OrderNum field.
3. Press the ↑ key. The OrderNum field value for the previous record is selected. This is the record Barbara wants you to change.

   Barbara wants you to change these field values in the record: OrderNum to 398, CustomerNum to 165, Paid to "Yes" (checked), and InvoiceAmt to 1426.5. The BillingDate does not need to be changed.
4. Type **398**, press the **Tab** key, type **165**, press the **Tab** key, press the **spacebar** to insert a check mark in the Paid check box, press the **Tab** key, then type **1426.5**. This completes the changes to the record.
5. Press the ↓ key to save the changes to the record and make the next record the current record. See Figure 4-38.

Figure 4-38 After changing field values in a record

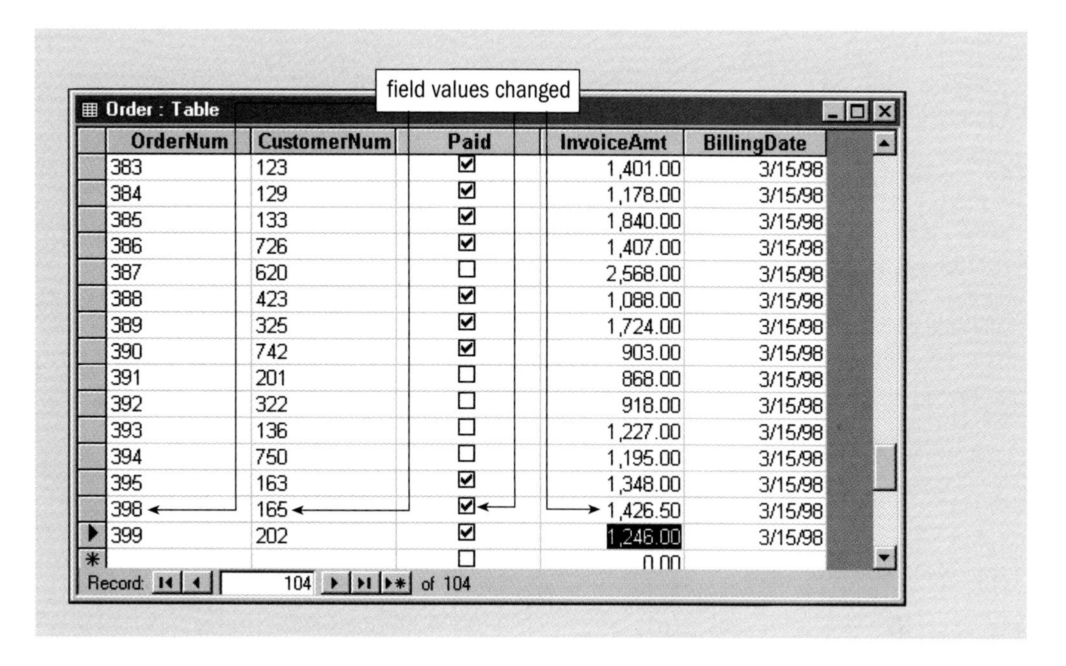

Barbara next wants you to create the Customer table by importing an Excel workbook, which contains data about restaurant customers, to the Restaurant Business database.

Importing Excel Data to a New Table

Importing data creates a copy of data from a source that is external to the open database, then places the copy in a new table in the open Access database. The original data is not changed by the import operation. You can import data from tables in another Access database; from worksheet programs, such as Excel and Lotus 1-2-3; from other database management systems, such as Paradox, dBASE, and FoxPro; and from delimited or fixed-width text files.

The data you need to import to your Restaurant Business database is contained in the Customer workbook, which is a Microsoft Excel file that is located in the Tutorial.04 folder on your Student Disk.

To select the Customer workbook for importing:

1. Click the **Close** button [X] on the Table window title bar to close the Order table.
2. Click the **New** button in the Database window to open the New Table dialog box.
3. Click **Import Table** in the dialog box, then click the **OK** button. The Import dialog box opens.
4. If necessary, open the **Tutorial.04** folder on your Student Disk.

   The Files of type list box contains a list of the different types of data sources you can import to an Access database. You have to change the data source from Microsoft Access to Microsoft Excel.
5. Click the **Files of type** list arrow, then click **Microsoft Excel**. The Look in list box displays the folders and Excel workbook files in the Tutorial.04 folder. See Figure 4-39. (The list of folders and files on your screen might be different.)

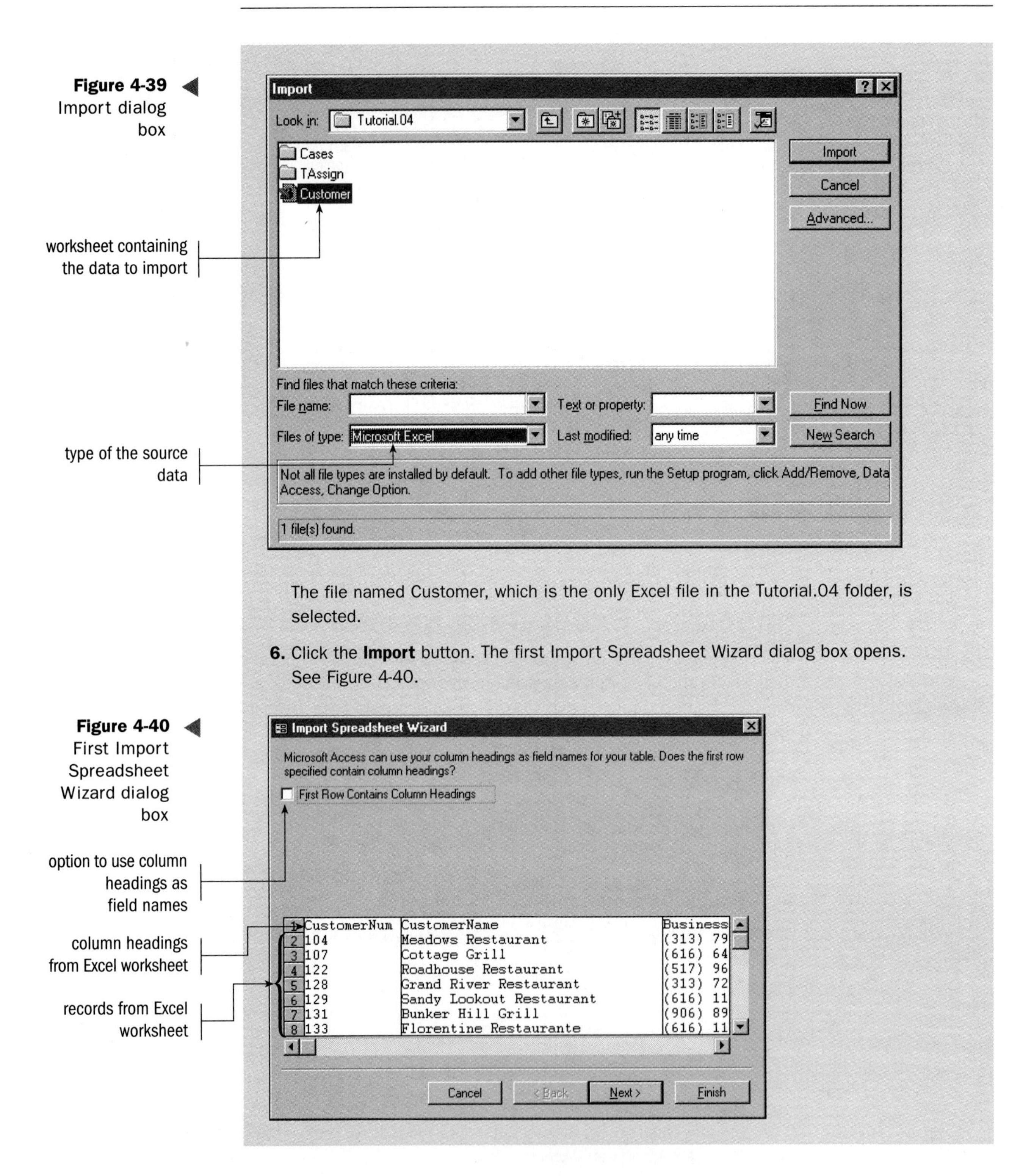

Figure 4-39 Import dialog box

The file named Customer, which is the only Excel file in the Tutorial.04 folder, is selected.

6. Click the **Import** button. The first Import Spreadsheet Wizard dialog box opens. See Figure 4-40.

Figure 4-40 First Import Spreadsheet Wizard dialog box

The first Import Spreadsheet Wizard dialog box displays the first few rows and columns from the active worksheet in the Customer workbook. The check box allows you to use the column headings in the worksheet's first row as field names in the table you are creating.

To import the worksheet using the Import Spreadsheet Wizard:

1. Click the **First Row Contains Column Headings** check box to place a check mark in it. The worksheet display changes to show the first row as column headings.

2. Click the **Next** button. The second Import Spreadsheet Wizard dialog box opens. See Figure 4-41.

Figure 4-41
Second Import Spreadsheet Wizard dialog box

field name

field properties

exclude the field

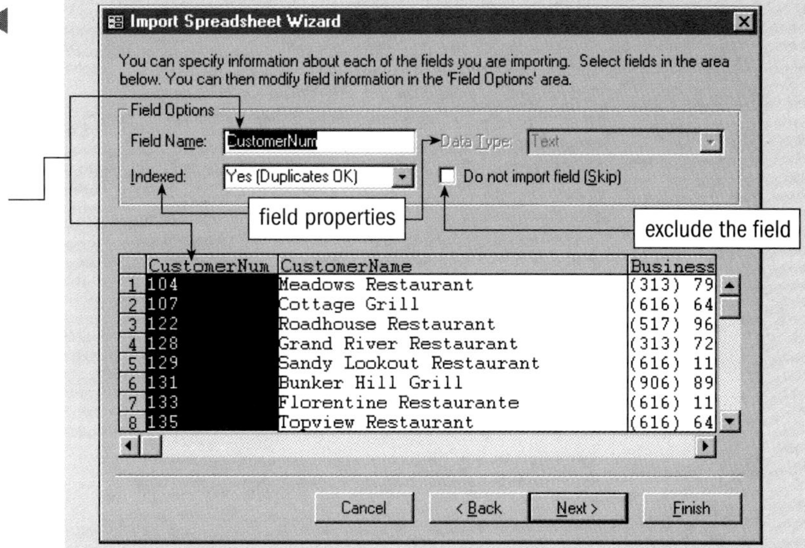

In this dialog box you can change field names, change the data type and indexed property value chosen by the wizard, and exclude fields from the new table. You will accept the wizard's choices for the imported data.

3. Click the **Next** button to open the third Import Spreadsheet Wizard dialog box, in which you choose the primary key for the table.
4. Click the **Choose my own Primary Key** radio button. CustomerNum, the first field in the worksheet, appears in the text box to the right of the radio button. You want CustomerNum to be the table's primary key.
5. Click the **Next** button to open the final Import Spreadsheet Wizard dialog box, in which you choose a name for the table.
6. Type **Customer** in the Import to Table text box, then click the **Finish** button. Access imports the data from the Customer workbook, closes the dialog box, displays the Customer and Order tables in the Database window's Tables list box, then displays a message indicating that the importing process is complete.
7. Click the **OK** button to close the message dialog box.

Now, Barbara wants you to display the records in the Customer table.

To open the Customer table datasheet:

1. If necessary, click **Customer** in the Tables list box, then click the **Open** button in the Database window. The Table window opens in Datasheet view.
2. Click the **Maximize** button on the Table window title bar. See Figure 4-42.

Figure 4-42 Datasheet for the Customer table

click here to select all records

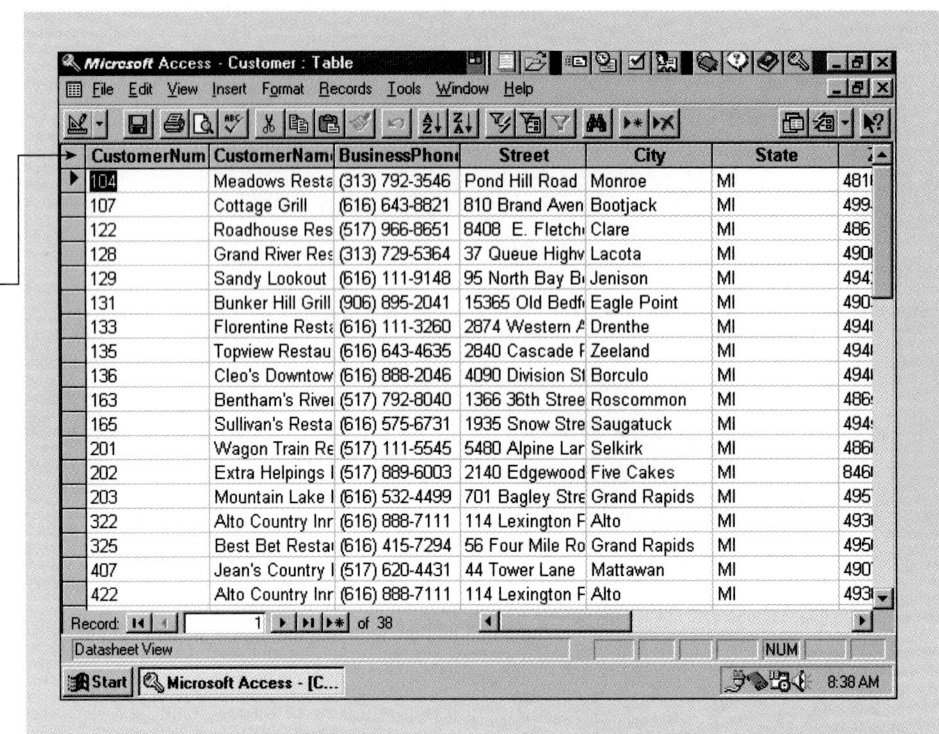

CustomerNum	CustomerNam	BusinessPhon	Street	City	State	
104	Meadows Resta	(313) 792-3546	Pond Hill Road	Monroe	MI	481
107	Cottage Grill	(616) 643-8821	810 Brand Aven	Bootjack	MI	499
122	Roadhouse Res	(517) 966-8651	8408 E. Fletch	Clare	MI	486
128	Grand River Re	(313) 729-5364	37 Queue Highw	Lacota	MI	490
129	Sandy Lookout	(616) 111-9148	95 North Bay B	Jenison	MI	494
131	Bunker Hill Grill	(906) 895-2041	15365 Old Bedf	Eagle Point	MI	490
133	Florentine Rest	(616) 111-3260	2874 Western A	Drenthe	MI	494
135	Topview Restau	(616) 643-4635	2840 Cascade F	Zeeland	MI	494
136	Cleo's Downtow	(616) 888-2046	4090 Division St	Borculo	MI	494
163	Bentham's Rive	(517) 792-8040	1366 36th Stree	Roscommon	MI	486
165	Sullivan's Resta	(616) 575-6731	1935 Snow Stre	Saugatuck	MI	494
201	Wagon Train Re	(517) 111-5545	5480 Alpine Lar	Selkirk	MI	486
202	Extra Helpings I	(517) 889-6003	2140 Edgewood	Five Cakes	MI	846
203	Mountain Lake I	(616) 532-4499	701 Bagley Stre	Grand Rapids	MI	495
322	Alto Country Inr	(616) 888-7111	114 Lexington F	Alto	MI	493
325	Best Bet Resta	(616) 415-7294	56 Four Mile Ro	Grand Rapids	MI	495
407	Jean's Country I	(517) 620-4431	44 Tower Lane	Mattawan	MI	490
422	Alto Country Inr	(616) 888-7111	114 Lexington F	Alto	MI	493

Notice that the columns are too narrow to allow the full display of all field names and field values. You can use a combination of a smaller font size and wider columns to allow all names and values to be displayed.

3. Click the **row selector** for the field name row to select all the records in the table.

4. Click **Format** on the menu bar, then click **Font** to open the Font dialog box. The current font size is 10.

5. Click **8** in the Size list box, then click the **OK** button. The field names and field values are now displayed in the smaller font size.

6. Move the pointer to the right edge of the CustomerNum field selector. When the pointer changes to ✛, double-click to resize the column to its best fit. Note that the column is resized for only the visible field values. You need to scroll the datasheet to make sure all field values are completely displayed. If any are not, double-click the pointer ✛ as necessary to resize the column until all field values are completely displayed.

7. Repeat Step 6 for each column in the datasheet. Be sure you scroll to the right to resize all columns.

8. Click the vertical scroll box to display the ScrollTip, "Record: 1 of 38," then drag the scroll box to the bottom of the scroll bar. Notice how the ScrollTip changes to "New Record" when you go beyond the last record in the table.

9. Drag the vertical scroll box toward the top of the scroll bar until the last record in the table appears at the bottom of the datasheet, then resize any column that still does not fully display all field values.

Barbara notices that the BusinessPhone and Phone fields contain the same field values, so she asks you to delete the BusinessPhone field from the table structure.

Deleting a Field from a Table Structure

After you've defined a table structure and added records to the table, you can delete a field from the table structure. When you delete the field, you also delete all the field values for the field from the table. Therefore, you should make sure you need to delete a field and that you delete the correct field.

You need to delete the BusinessPhone field from the Customer table structure.

To delete the field from the table structure:

1. Click the **Table View** button for Design view on the Table Datasheet toolbar to display the table in Design view.
2. Right-click the **row selector** for the BusinessPhone field, then click **Delete Field** on the shortcut menu. A dialog box opens asking you to confirm the deletion.
3. Click the **Yes** button to close the dialog box and to delete the field and its data from the table. See Figure 4-43.

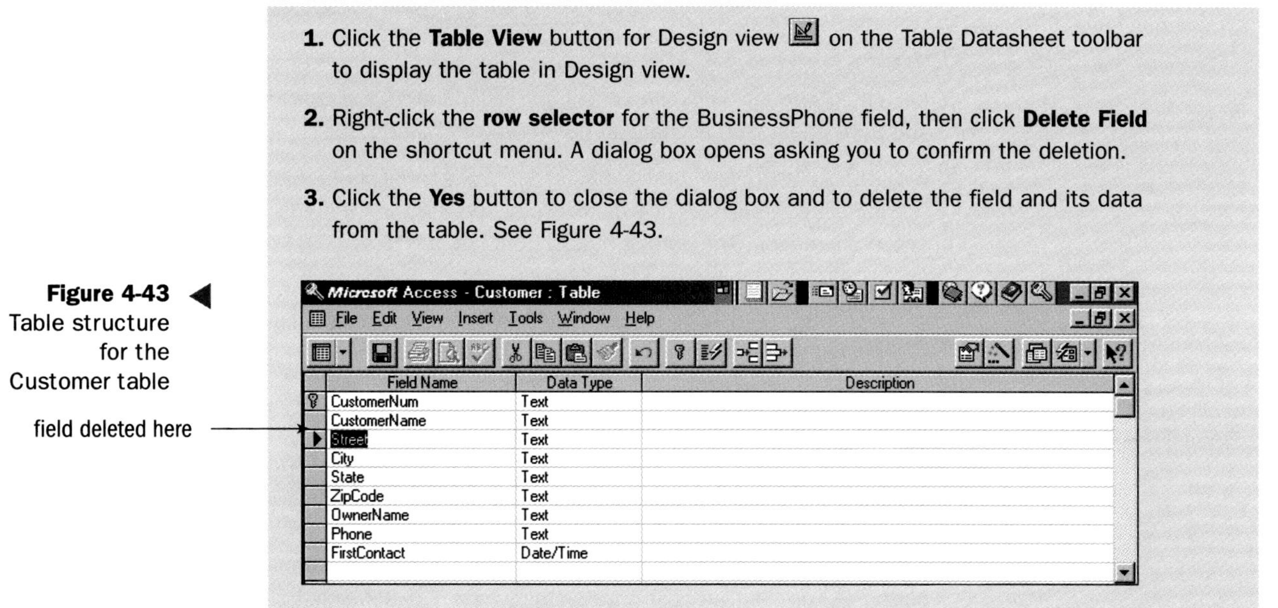

Figure 4-43 Table structure for the Customer table

When you import data from Excel to a new Access table, each text field is assigned the maximum value of 255 for the Field Size property. Because Access uses this property value to determine the amount of room a field value uses on forms and reports, you should set each field's Field Size property to the actual number of characters it needs.

To set each field's Field Size property:

1. Click the CustomerNum **Field Name** text box to select the field as the current field.
2. Select **255** in the Field Size text box in the Field Properties section, then type **3**.
3. Repeat Steps 1 and 2 for the remaining text fields in the table. Change the Field Size property value of these fields: **CustomerName** to **35**, **Street** to **30**, **City** to **20**, **State** to **2**, **ZipCode** to **5**, **OwnerName** to **25**, and **Phone** to **14**.
4. Click the **Save** button on the Table Design toolbar. Access displays a dialog box informing you that some data may be lost. Because any data lost would be data exceeding the field sizes you just set and none of the field values exceeds them, you can safely continue.
5. Click the **Yes** button in the dialog box to save the modified table structure.

Barbara asks you to print a copy of the Customer datasheet so she can examine the data in the table.

Printing a Datasheet

The Customer datasheet is wider than it is long, so you need to change the page orientation from portrait to landscape before you preview then print the datasheet.

To change the page orientation, preview, then print the datasheet:

1. Click the **Table View** button for Datasheet view on the Table Design toolbar to switch to Datasheet view.
2. Click **File** on the menu bar, then click **Page Setup**. The Page Setup dialog box opens.
3. Click the **Page** tab, click the **Landscape** radio button, then click the **OK** button. The page orientation is changed from portrait to landscape.
4. Click the **Print Preview** button on the Table Datasheet toolbar. The Print Preview window opens, showing the datasheet for the Customer table in landscape orientation. The default header contains the table name and date, and the default footer contains the page number.
5. Click the **Print** button on the Print Preview toolbar. One copy of the datasheet is printed.
6. Click the **Close** button on the Print Preview toolbar. The Print Preview window closes, and you return to the table in Datasheet view.

   You have finished your work with the Customer datasheet, so you can close it and restore the Database window.

7. Click the **Close** button on the Table window menu bar, then click the **Restore** button on the Database window menu bar. The datasheet closes and you return to the Database window.

Quick Check

1. Use the __________ property to control the display appearance of a field value.
2. A field with the __________ data type can appear in the table datasheet as a check box.
3. Why must you close an open database when you want to copy records to it from a table in another database?
4. What is the difference between navigation mode and editing mode?
5. Name three sources that can be used to import data into an open Access database.
6. What is the effect of deleting a field from a table structure?
7. Which page orientations are available in the Page Setup dialog box?

Now that you've completed Session 4.2, you can exit Access or you can continue to the next session.

SESSION 4.3

In this session you will learn how to create forms automatically using the AutoForm and Form Wizards, find data using a form, print a selected form record, change a form's AutoFormat, maintain data using a form, define a table relationship, and create a form containing a main form and a subform.

Barbara has some updates she wants you to make to the Order table, and she suggests you use a form to make the updates.

Creating a Form with an AutoForm Wizard

A **form** is an object you use to maintain, view, and print records in a database. For example, Barbara can create a form for others to use that displays one customer record at a time. In Access, you can design your own forms or use Form Wizards to create forms for you automatically. A **Form Wizard** is an Access tool that asks you a series of questions, then creates a form based on your answers. Whether you use a Form Wizard or design your own form, you can change the form's design after you create it.

The quickest way to create a form is to use an AutoForm Wizard. An **AutoForm Wizard** places all the fields from a selected table or query on a form automatically, without asking you any questions, then displays the form on the screen.

You'll use the AutoForm: Columnar Wizard to create a form for the Order table. This wizard creates a form that will display fields in a columnar format, one record at a time, from the Order table.

To create a form using the AutoForm: Columnar Wizard:

1. Click the **Forms** tab in the Database window to display the Forms list box. You have not created any forms, so the list box is empty.
2. Click the **New** button in the Database window. The New Form dialog box opens. See Figure 4-44.

Figure 4-44 New Form dialog box

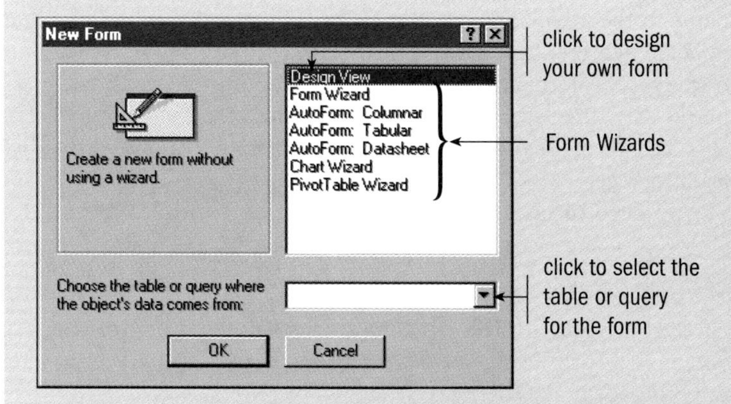

In the top list box, you choose the Design View option to design your own form or one of the six Form Wizard options to help you create the form. In the bottom list box, you choose the table or query that will supply the data for the form. (You'll learn more about queries later in this tutorial.)

3. Click **AutoForm: Columnar** to select this method for creating the form.
4. Click the list arrow for choosing the table or query on which to base the form, click **Order** to select this table as the source for the form, then click the **OK** button. The Form Wizard creates the form, then displays the form in Form view.

Figure 4-45 Form created by the AutoForm: Columnar Wizard

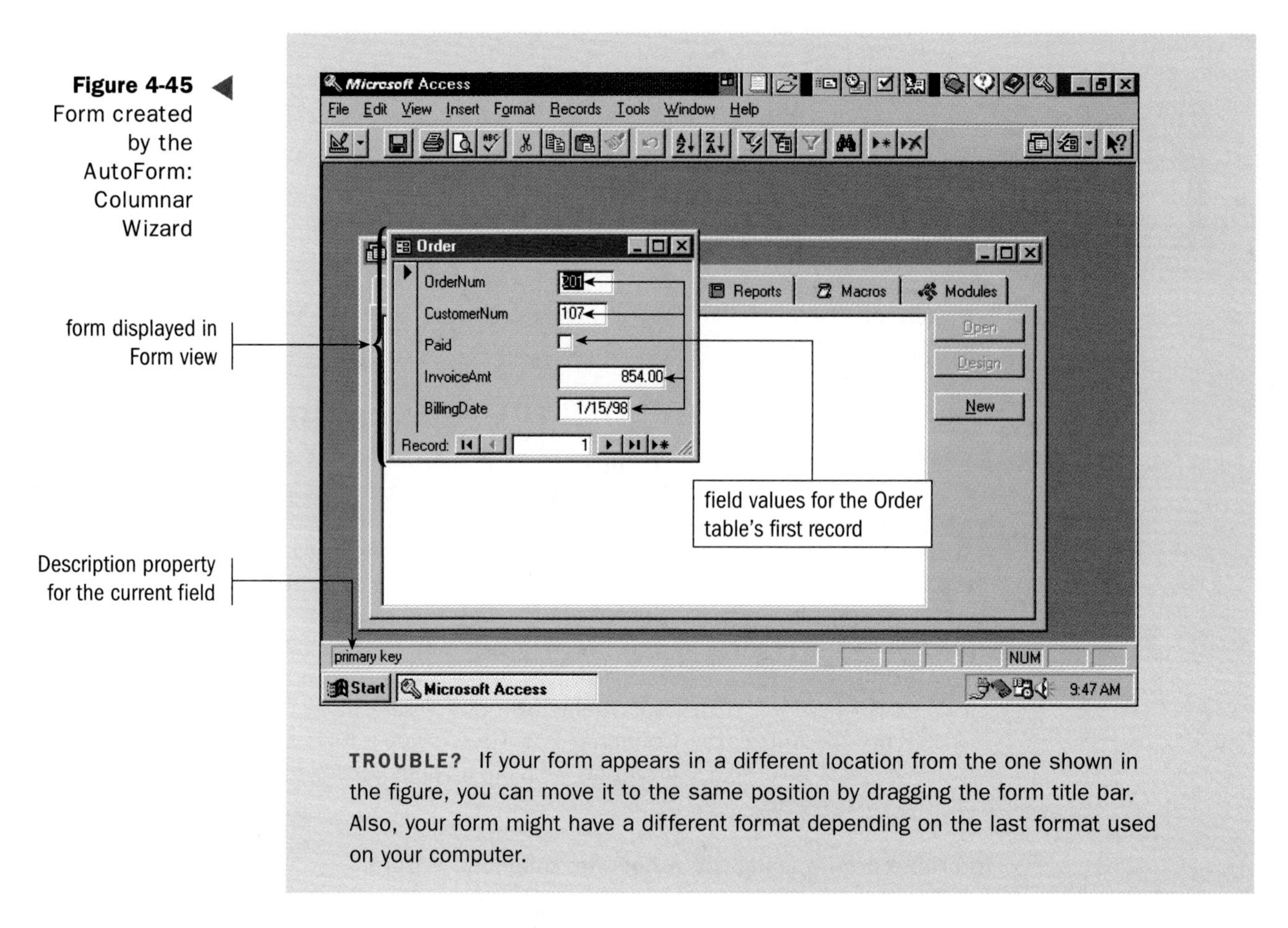

TROUBLE? If your form appears in a different location from the one shown in the figure, you can move it to the same position by dragging the form title bar. Also, your form might have a different format depending on the last format used on your computer.

The form displays one record at a time in the Order table. Access displays the field values for the first record in the Order table and selects the first field value, whose Description property value (if the field has one) appears in the status bar. In this case, the OrderNum field is selected, and the description "primary key" appears in the status bar. Each field name in the table appears on a separate line and on the same line as its field value, which appears in a box. The widths of the boxes are different to accommodate the different sizes of the displayed field values; for example, compare the small box for the Paid field's check mark with the larger box for the BillingDate field's value. The AutoForm: Columnar Wizard automatically placed the field names and values on the form and supplied the background style.

You need to save the form before working with it.

Saving a Form

After you create a form, it's a good idea to save it before you work with it. The first time you save a form using the Save button on the toolbar, Access asks for a filename. You'll save this form as Order Data.

To save the form created by the AutoForm: Columnar Wizard:

1. Click the **Save** button on the Form View toolbar. The Save As dialog box opens.
2. Type **Order Data** in the Form Name text box, then press the **Enter** key. Access saves the form as Order Data in your Restaurant Business database and closes the dialog box.

Barbara wants to view some data in the Order table using the form. To view data, you need to navigate through the form.

Navigating a Form

To maintain and view data using a form, you must know how to move from field to field and from record to record. The mouse movement, selection, and placement techniques to navigate a form are the standard Windows 95 techniques you've used to navigate a table datasheet and documents in Word and Excel. Also, the navigation mode and editing mode keystroke techniques are the same as those you used previously for datasheets (see Figure 4-37).

To navigate through the form:

1. Press the **Tab** key to move to the CustomerNum field value, press the **End** key to move to the BillingDate field value, then press the **Home** key to move back to the OrderNum field value. The first record in the Order table still appears on the form.
2. Press **Ctrl + End** to move to the BillingDate field value in record 104, which is the last record in the table. The record number for the current record appears between the navigation keys at the bottom of the form.
3. Click the **Previous record** navigation button ◀ to move to the BillingDate field value in record 103.
4. Press the ↑ key to move to the InvoiceAmt field value in record 103.
5. Position the insertion point between the numbers "2" and "6" in the InvoiceAmt field value, press the **Home** key to move the insertion point to the beginning of the field value, then press the **End** key to move the insertion point to the end of the field value.
6. Click the **First record** navigation button |◀ to move to the InvoiceAmt field value in the first record. The entire field value is highlighted because you have switched from editing mode to navigation mode.
7. Click the **Next record** navigation button ▶ to move to the InvoiceAmt field value in record 2, which is the next record.

Barbara asks you to display the records for Jean's Country Restaurant, whose customer number is 407, because she wants to review the recent orders for this customer.

Finding Data Using a Form

The **Find** command allows you to search the data in a form and to display only those records you want to view. You choose a field to serve as the basis for the search by making that field the current field, then you enter the value you want Access to match in the Find in field dialog box. You can use the Find command for a form or datasheet, and you can activate the command from the Edit menu or by clicking the toolbar Find button.

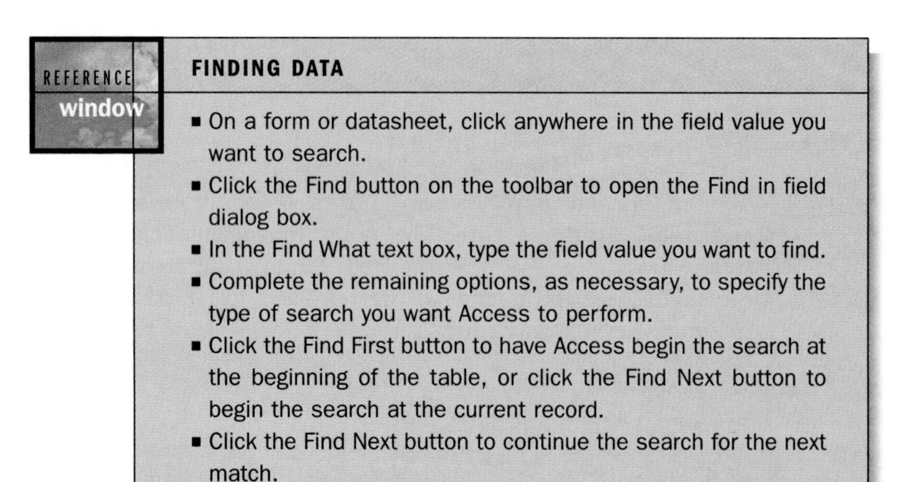

REFERENCE window

FINDING DATA

- On a form or datasheet, click anywhere in the field value you want to search.
- Click the Find button on the toolbar to open the Find in field dialog box.
- In the Find What text box, type the field value you want to find.
- Complete the remaining options, as necessary, to specify the type of search you want Access to perform.
- Click the Find First button to have Access begin the search at the beginning of the table, or click the Find Next button to begin the search at the current record.
- Click the Find Next button to continue the search for the next match.
- Click the Close button to stop the search operation.

You need to find all records in the Order table for Jean's Country Restaurant, whose customer number is 407.

To find the records using the Order Data form:

1. Position the insertion point in the CustomerNum field value box. This is the field for which you will find matching values.
2. Click the **Find** button on the Form View toolbar to open the Find in field dialog box. Note that the title bar of the dialog box specifies the first part of the name of the field that Access will search, in this case, the CustomerNum field.
3. If the Find in field dialog box covers any part of the form, move the dialog box by dragging its title bar. See Figure 4-46.

Figure 4-46 Find in field dialog box

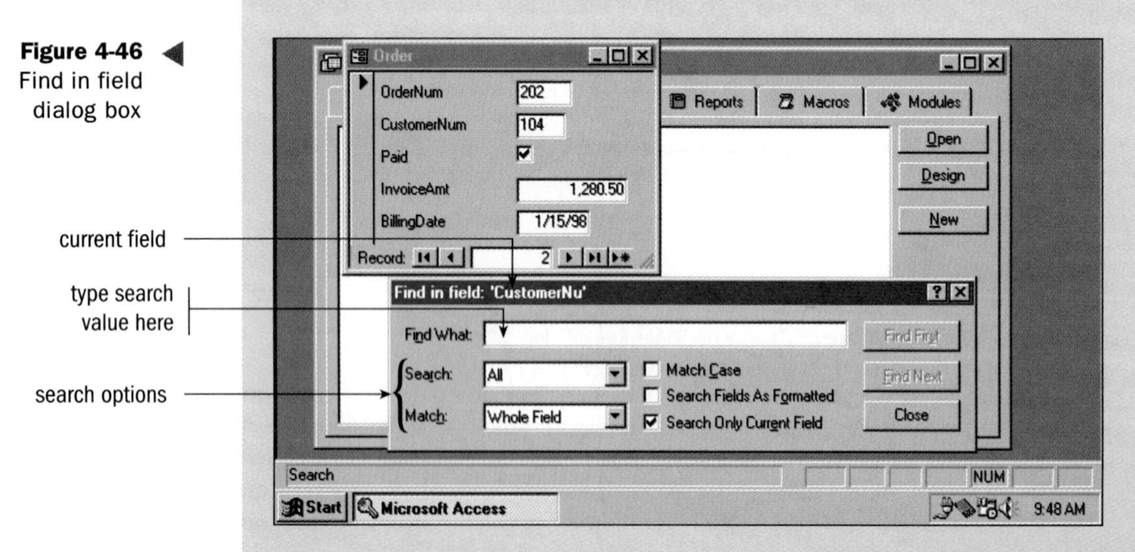

4. In the Find What text box, type **407** then click the **Find First** button. Access displays record 14, which is the first record for CustomerNum 407.
5. Click the **Find Next** button. Access displays record 51, which is the second record for CustomerNum 407.
6. Click the **Find Next** button. Access displays record 88, which is the third record for CustomerNum 407.

7. Click the **Find Next** button. Access opens a dialog box informing you that the search is finished.

8. Click the **OK** button to close the dialog box.

The search value you enter can be an exact value, such as the customer number 407 you just entered, or it can include wildcard characters. A **wildcard character** is a placeholder you use when you know only part of a value or when you want to start or end with a specific character or match a certain pattern. Figure 4-47 shows the wildcard characters you can use when finding data.

Figure 4-47 Wildcard characters

Wildcard Character	Purpose	Example
*	Match any number of characters. It can be used as the first or last character in the character string.	th* finds *the, that, this, therefore,* and so on
?	Match any single alphabetic character.	a?t finds *act, aft, ant,* and *art*
[ ]	Match any single character within the brackets.	a[fr]t finds *aft* and *art* but not *act* and *ant*
!	Match any character not within brackets.	a[!fr]t finds *act* and *ant* but not *aft* and *art*
-	Match any one of a range of characters. The range must be in ascending order (a to z, not z to a).	a[d-p]t finds *aft* and *ant* but not *act* and *art*
#	Match any single numeric character.	#72 finds *072, 172, 272, 372,* and so on

To check if their orders have been paid, Barbara wants to view the order records for two customers: Cheshire Restaurant (CustomerNum 515) and Around the Clock Restaurant (CustomerNum 597). You'll use the * wildcard character to search for these customers' orders.

To find the records using the Order Data form:

1. Double-click **407** in the Find What text box to select the entire value, then type **5***.

   Access will match any field value in the CustomerNum field that starts with the digit 5.

2. Click the **Find First** button. Access displays record 16, which is the first record for CustomerNum 515.

3. Click the **Find Next** button. Access displays record 17, which is the first record for CustomerNum 597.

4. Click the **Find Next** button. Access displays record 39, which is the second record for CustomerNum 597.

5. Click the **Find Next** button. Access displays record 68, which is the second record for CustomerNum 515.

6. Click the **Find Next** button. Access displays record 82, which is the third record for CustomerNum 515.

7. Click the **Find Next** button. Access opens a dialog box informing you that the search is finished.

8. Click the **OK** button to close the dialog box.
9. Click the **Close** button to close the Find in field dialog box.

All five orders have been paid, but Barbara wants to make sure Valle Coffee has a record of payment for order number 375. She asks you to print the data displayed on the form for record 82, which is for order number 375, so she can ask a staff member to look for the payment record for this order.

Printing Selected Form Records

Access prints as many form records as can fit on a printed page. If only part of a form record fits on the bottom of a page, the remainder of the record prints on the next page. Like Word and Excel, Access allows you to print all pages or a range of pages. In addition, you can print the currently selected form record.

Before printing record 82, you'll preview the form record to see how it will look when printed.

To preview the form, then print the data for record 82:

1. Click the **Print Preview** button on the Form View toolbar. The Print Preview window opens, showing the form records for the Order table in miniature.
2. Click the **Maximize** button on the form title bar.
3. Click the **Zoom** button on the Print Preview toolbar, then use the vertical scroll bar to view the contents of the window. See Figure 4-48.

Figure 4-48 Print Preview window

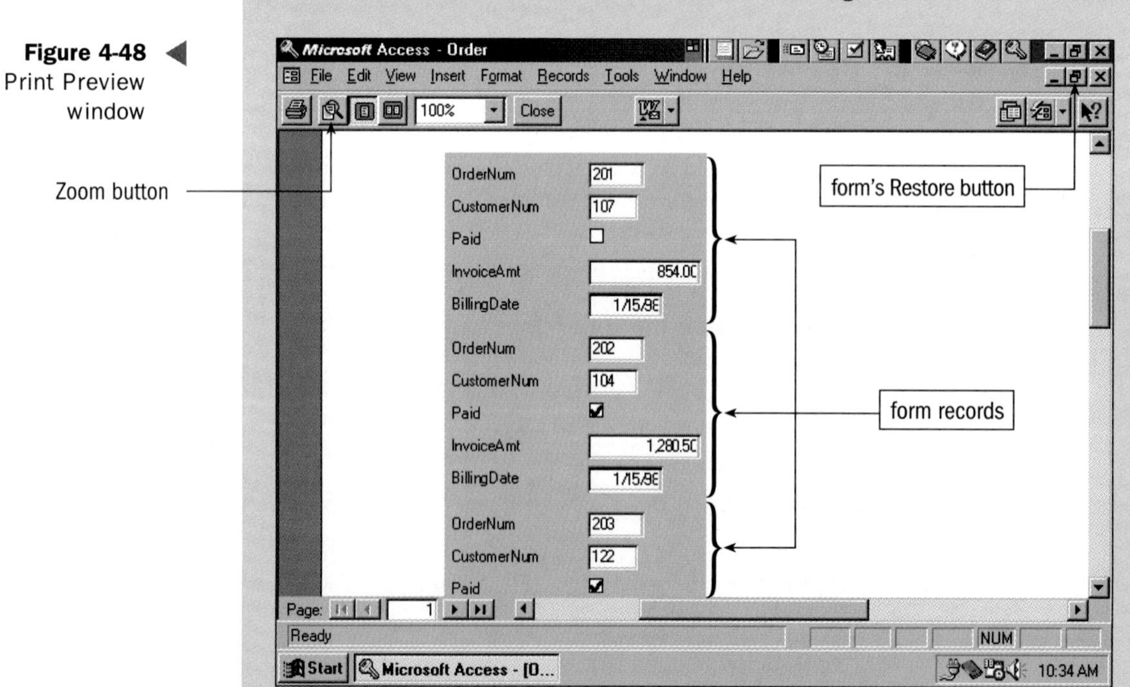

Each record from the Order table appears in a separate form. Access places as many forms as will fit on each page.

4. Click the **Restore** button on the Print Preview menu bar, then click the **Close** button on the Print Preview toolbar to close the window and return to the table in Form view.
5. Click **File** on the menu bar, then click **Print**. The Print dialog box opens.

6. Click the **Selected Record(s)** radio button to print only the current form record (record 82).
7. Click the **OK** button to close the dialog box and print the selected record.

   You have finished your work with the Order Data form, so you can close it.
8. Click the **Close** button on the form title bar. The form closes and you return to the Database window.

   Notice that the Order Data form is now listed in the Forms list box.

Barbara has several updates she wants you to make to the Customer table. She wants you to create a new form to use for the updates. To create this form, you'll use the Form Wizard.

Creating a Form Using the Form Wizard

Instead of using an AutoForm Wizard, which creates a form automatically using all the fields in the selected table or query, you'll use the Form Wizard to create a columnar form for data in the Customer table. The Form Wizard allows you to choose some or all of the fields in the selected table or query, choose fields from other tables and queries, and display the chosen fields in any order on the form. You can also choose a style for the form.

To activate the Form Wizard:

1. Click the **New** button in the Database window. The New Form dialog box opens.
2. Click **Form Wizard**, click the list arrow for choosing a table or query, click **Customer** to select this table as the source for the form, then click the **OK** button. The first Form Wizard dialog box opens. See Figure 4-49.

Figure 4-49 First Form Wizard dialog box

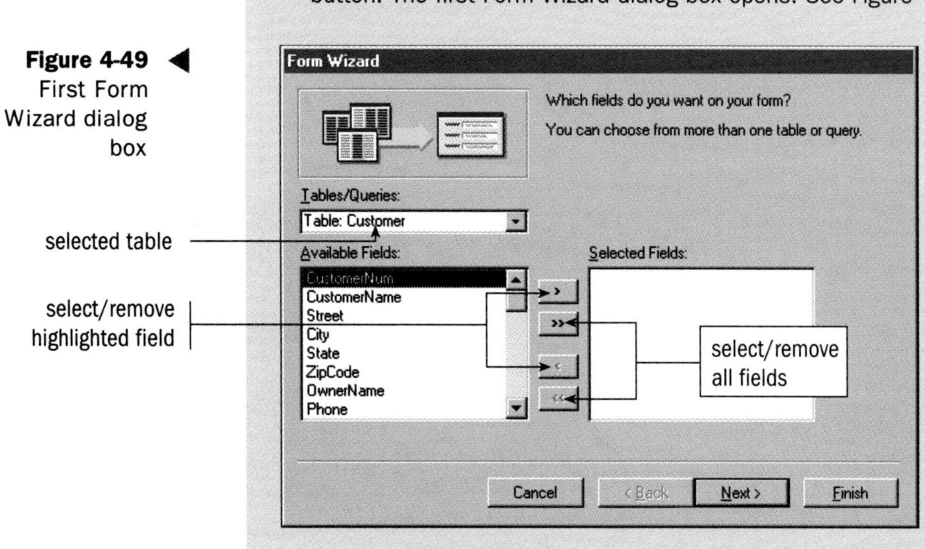

In the first Form Wizard dialog box, you select fields in the order you want them to appear on the form. To select fields one at a time, highlight a field by clicking it, then click the > button. To select all fields, click the >> button. The selected fields move from the Available Fields list box on the left to the Selected Fields list box on the right. If you make a mistake, click the << button to remove all fields from the Selected Fields list box, or highlight a field and click the < button to remove fields one at a time.

Each Form Wizard dialog box displays buttons on the bottom that allow you to move quickly to the other Form Wizard dialog boxes. You can go to the previous (Back button) or next (Next button) Form Wizard dialog box, and you can cancel the form creation process (Cancel button) to return to the Database window. You can also finish the form (Finish button) and accept the Form Wizard defaults for the remaining form options.

Barbara wants the form to display all the fields in the Customer table in the order in which they appear in the table.

To finish creating the form using the Form Wizard:

1. Click the **>>** button. Access removes all the fields from the Available Fields list box and places them in the same order in the Selected Fields list box.

2. Click the **Next** button to display the second Form Wizard dialog box, in which you select a layout for the form. See Figure 4-50.

Figure 4-50 Choosing a layout for the form

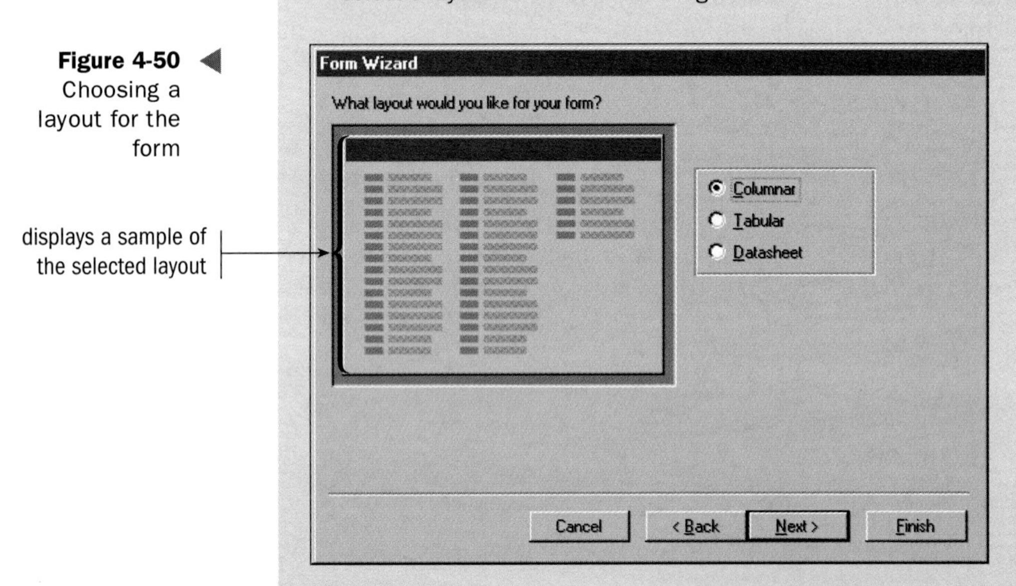

The layout choices are columnar, tabular, and datasheet. A sample of the selected layout appears on the left side of the dialog box.

3. Click each of the radio buttons and review the corresponding sample layout.

The tabular and datasheet layouts display the fields from multiple records at one time, whereas the columnar layout displays the fields from one record at a time. Because the columnar layout is the appropriate arrangement for displaying and updating data in a table, you'll choose this layout.

4. If necessary, click the **Columnar** radio button, then click the **Next** button. Access displays the third Form Wizard dialog box, in which you choose a style for the form. See Figure 4-51.

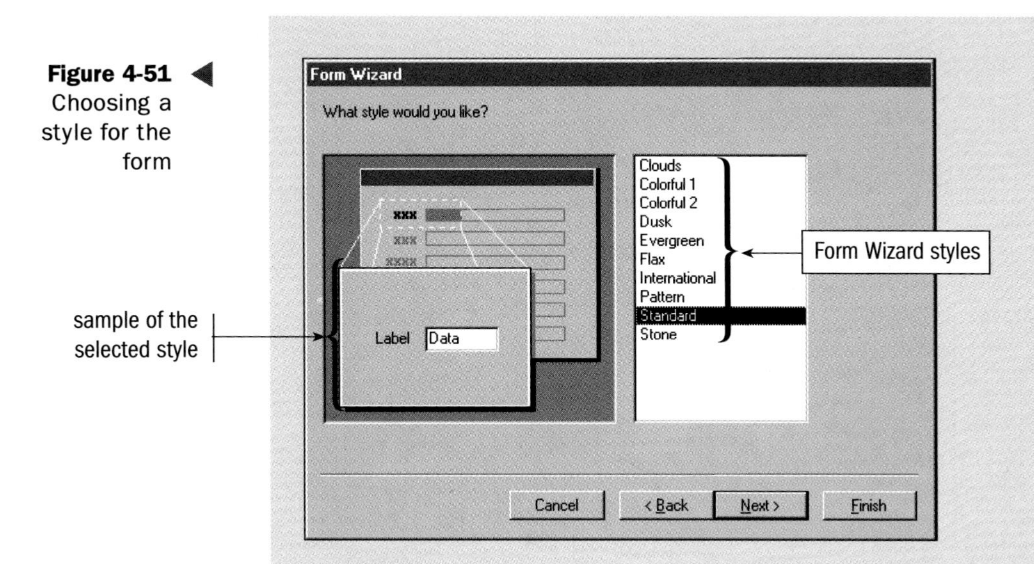

Figure 4-51 Choosing a style for the form

A sample of the selected style appears in the box on the left. If you choose a style, which is called an *AutoFormat*, and decide you'd prefer a different one after the form is created, you can change it.

5. Click each of the radio buttons and review the corresponding sample style. Barbara likes the Evergreen style and asks you to use it for the form.

6. Click **Evergreen** then click the **Next** button. Access displays the final Form Wizard dialog box and shows the table name as the default for the form name and for the title that will appear in the form title bar. See Figure 4-52.

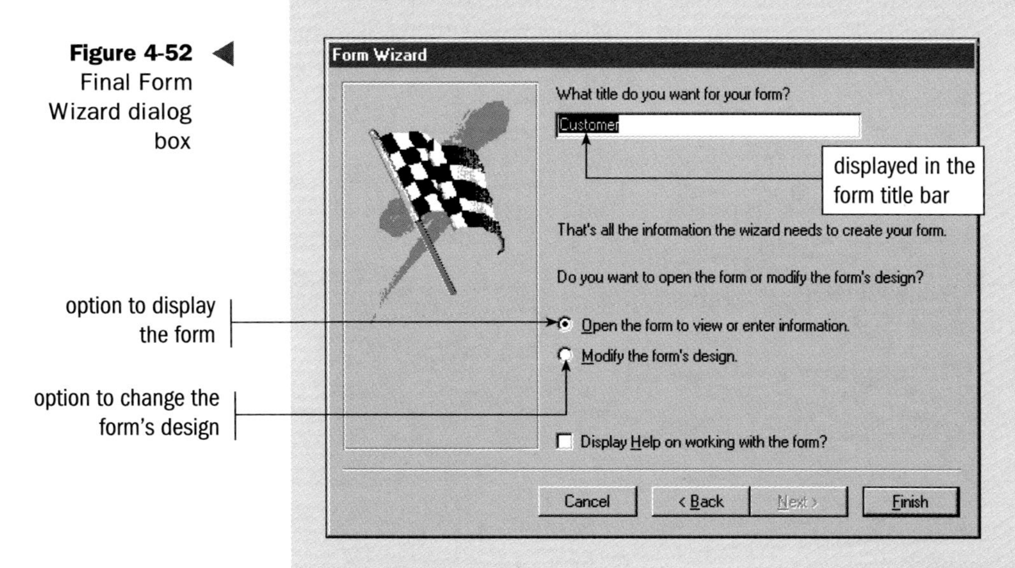

Figure 4-52 Final Form Wizard dialog box

You'll use Customer Data as the form name and, because you don't need to change the form's design at this point, you'll display the form.

7. Position the insertion point to the right of Customer in the text box, press the **spacebar**, type **Data**, then click the **Finish** button. The completed form is displayed in Form view. See Figure 4-53.

Figure 4-53 Completed form for the Customer table

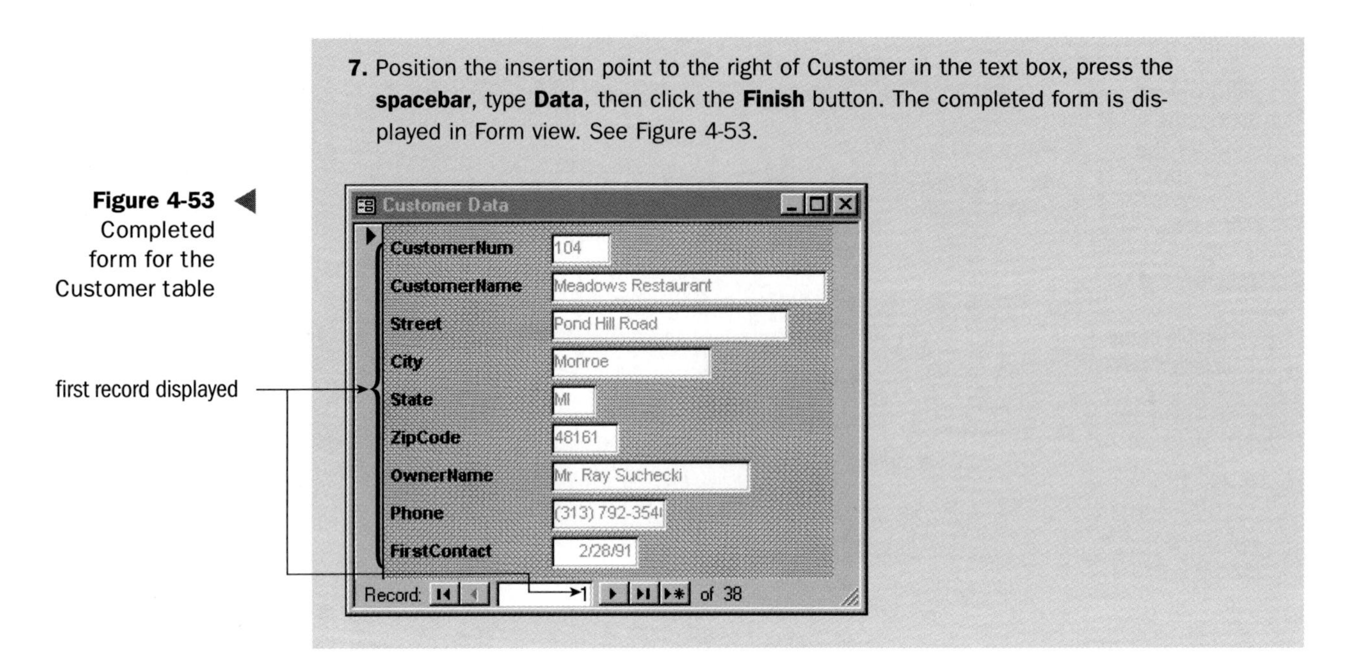

Barbara doesn't like the form's style—the field names are difficult to read and the green color clashes with the blue on the title bar. She asks you to change the form's style.

Changing a Form's AutoFormat

You can change a form's appearance by choosing a different AutoFormat for the form. As you learned when you created the Customer Data form, an **AutoFormat** is a predefined style for a form (or report). The AutoFormats available for a form are the ones you saw when you selected the form's style using the Form Wizard. To change an AutoFormat, you must switch to Design view.

To change the AutoFormat for the Customer Data form:

1. Click the **Form View** button for Design view on the Form View toolbar. The form is displayed in Design view. See Figure 4-54.

Figure 4-54 Form displayed in Design view

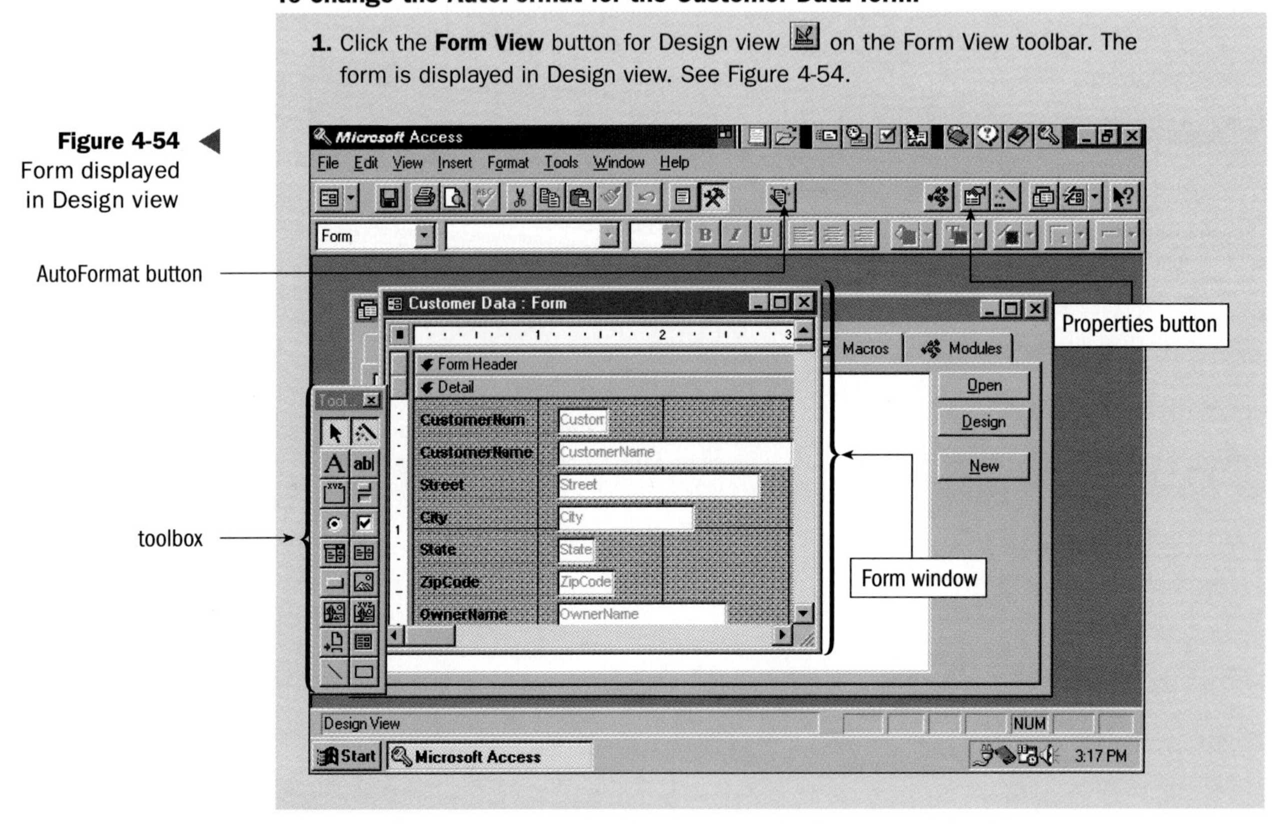

TROUBLE? If the property sheet appears on your screen, click the Properties button on the Form Design toolbar to close it.

You use Design view to create and modify forms. You will create your own forms in a later tutorial. For now, you need to change the AutoFormat for the Customer Data form.

2. Click the **AutoFormat** button on the Form Design toolbar. The AutoFormat dialog box opens.
3. Click the **Options** button to display the AutoFormat options. See Figure 4-55.

Figure 4-55 AutoFormat dialog box

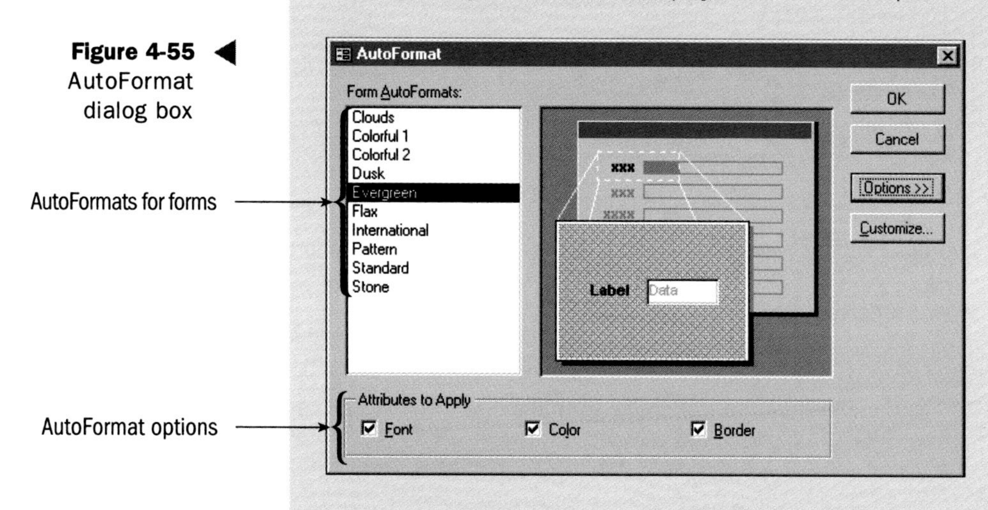

A sample of the selected AutoFormat appears to the right of the Form AutoFormats list box. You can choose to apply the selected AutoFormat or just its font, color, or border. Barbara wants to view each of the available AutoFormats.

4. Click each AutoFormat in the Form AutoFormats list box, pausing after each to examine its sample.

Barbara decides that she prefers the Standard AutoFormat, because its field names are easy to read and its color doesn't clash with the blue on the title bar.

5. Click **Standard** in the Form AutoFormats list box, then click the **OK** button. The AutoFormat dialog box closes, the AutoFormat is applied to the form, and the Form window in Design view becomes the active window.
6. Click the **Form View** button on the Form Design toolbar. The form is displayed in Form view with the new AutoFormat. See Figure 4-56.

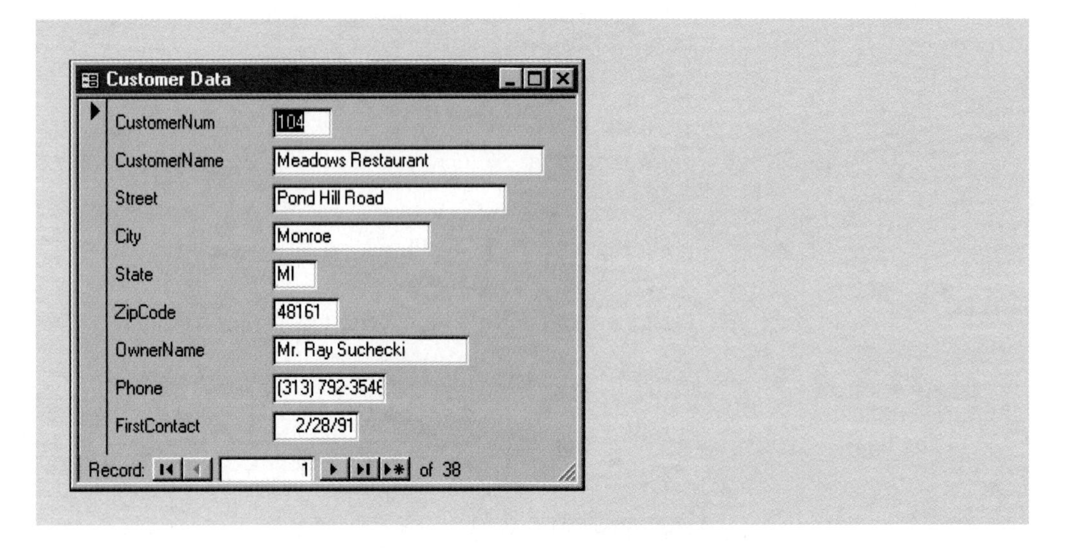

Figure 4-56 Form displayed with the new AutoFormat

You have finished modifying the format of the form and can now save and close it.

To save and close the form:

1. Click the **Save** button on the Form View toolbar to save the modified form.
2. Click the **Close** button on the form title bar. The form closes and the Database window becomes the active window.

Barbara has identified several updates she wants you to make to the Customer table using the Customer Data form, as shown in Figure 4-57.

Figure 4-57 Updates to the Customer table

Customer Number	Update Action
202	Change City to Five Lakes
	Change ZipCode to 48446
422	Delete record
123	Add record for Bridge Inn, 400 Salmon Street,
	Ada MI 49301
	Mr. Wayne Bouwman, (616) 888-9827, 4/17/91

Maintaining Table Data Using a Form

Maintaining data using a form is often easier than using a datasheet, because you can concentrate on all the changes required to a single record at a time. You already know how to navigate a form and find specific records. Now you'll make the changes Barbara requested to the Customer table using the Customer Data form.

First, you'll update the record for CustomerNum 202.

To change the record using the Customer Data form:

1. If it's not already selected, click **Customer Data** in the Forms list box.
2. Click the **Open** button. The Customer Data form opens in Form view.

The current record number appears between the sets of navigation buttons at the bottom of the form. If you know the number of the record you want to change, you can type the number and press the Enter key to go directly to the record. When she reviewed the customer data to identify possible corrections, Barbara noted that 13 is the record number for customer 202.

3. Position the insertion point to the right of the 1 that appears between the navigation buttons, type **3**, then press the **Enter** key. Record 13 is now the current record.

   You must change the City field value of "Five Cakes" to "Five Lakes" and the ZipCode field value of "84664" to "48446."

4. Position the insertion point between the letters "C" and "a" in the City field value, press the **Backspace** key, then type **L**.
5. Press the **Tab** key twice to move to the ZipCode field value, then type **48446**. See Figure 4-58.

Figure 4-58 Customer record after changing field values

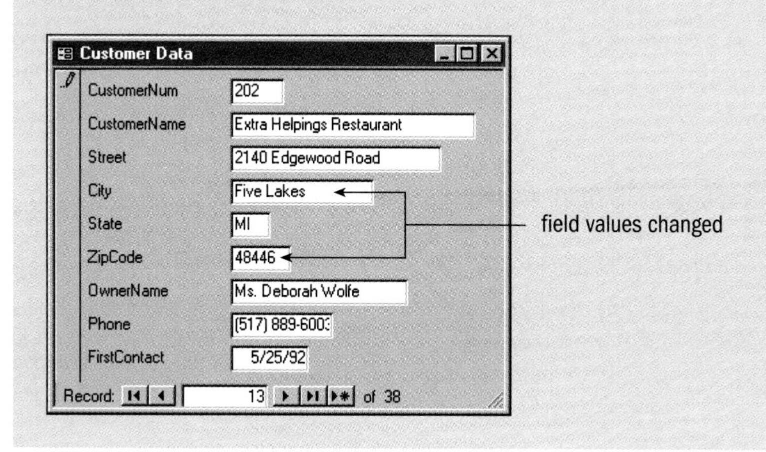

You have completed the changes for customer 202. Barbara's next update involves the Alto Country Inn. By mistake, a member of Barbara's staff added this customer as customer 422 after someone else had already added the same customer as customer 322. With the exception of the customer numbers, the two records are identical. To eliminate the data redundancy, one record must be deleted. Because orders for the Alto Country Inn already exist for customer number 322 but none exist for 422, you need to find and delete the record for customer 422.

To delete the record using the Customer Data form:

1. Click anywhere in the CustomerNum field value to make it the current field.
2. Click the **Find** button on the Form View toolbar. The Find in field dialog box opens.
3. Type **422**, click the **Find First** button, then click the **Close** button. The record for Alto Country Inn with the CustomerNum value of 422 is now the current record.

   To select the entire record, you can click anywhere in the large rectangular area surrounding the record selector.

4. Click the **record selector** in the upper-left of the form to select the entire record. See Figure 4-59.

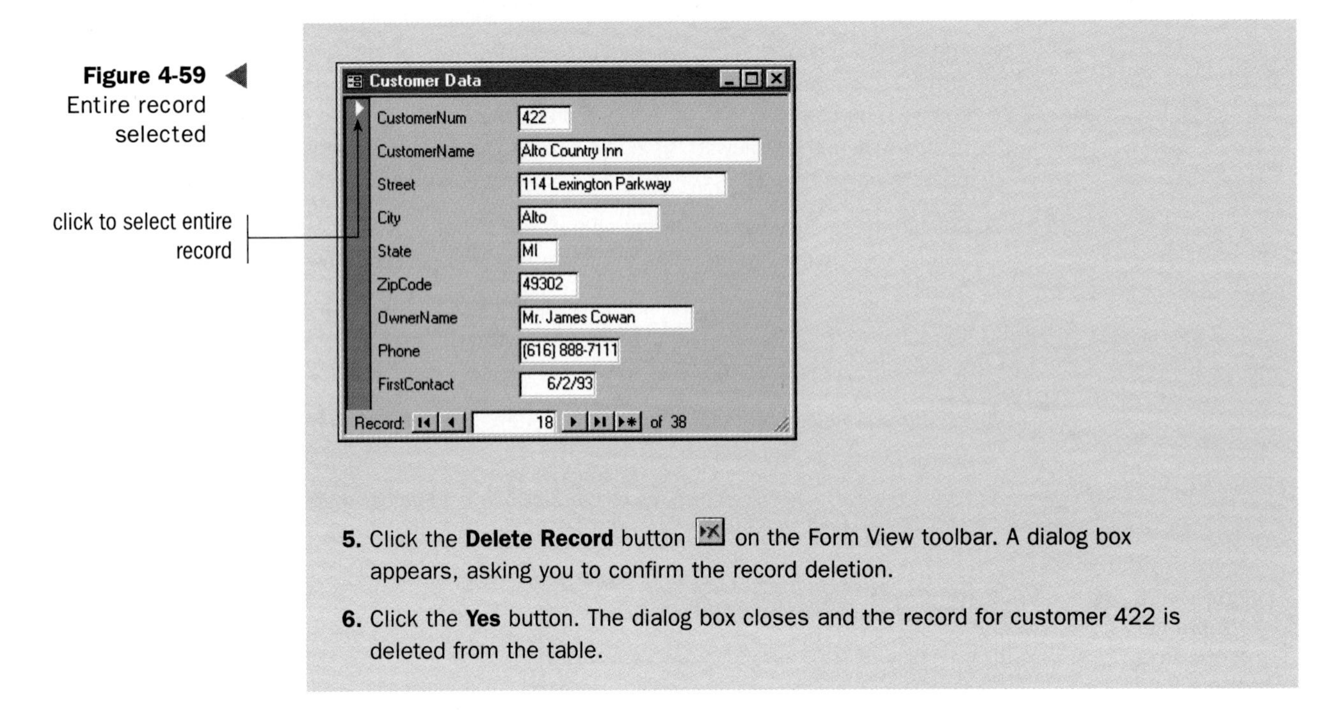

Figure 4-59 Entire record selected

5. Click the **Delete Record** button on the Form View toolbar. A dialog box appears, asking you to confirm the record deletion.
6. Click the **Yes** button. The dialog box closes and the record for customer 422 is deleted from the table.

Barbara's final maintenance change is to add a record for a new customer, Bridge Inn.

To add the record using the Customer Data form:

1. Click the **New Record** button on the Form View toolbar. Record 38, the next record available for a new record, becomes the current record. All field value boxes are empty, and the insertion point is positioned at the beginning of the field value for CustomerNum.
2. Refer to Figure 4-60 and enter the values shown for each field, pressing the Tab key to move from field to field.

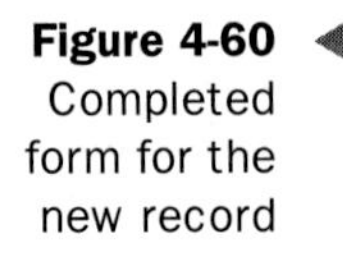

Figure 4-60 Completed form for the new record

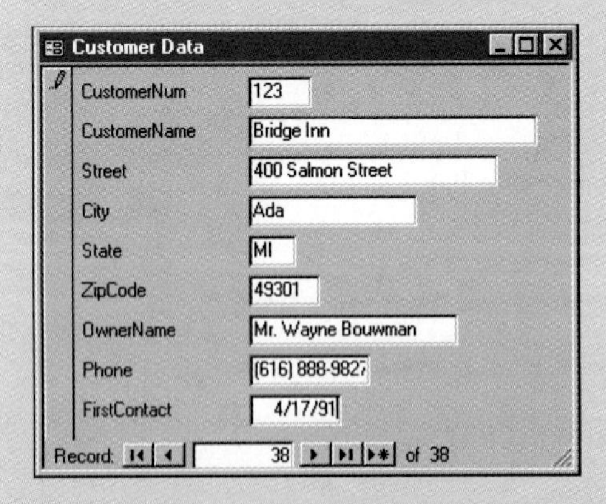

Notice that the Phone field value is not entirely visible because its box is too narrow. The last digit in the number, 7, is partially obscured. This is one example of why it's often necessary to modify, or customize, forms created by the Form Wizard. You will customize forms in a later tutorial. Also notice the FirstContact field value of 4/17/91; this represents the first time a Valle Coffee representative talked with Bridge Inn's management about using the company's coffee products.

TROUBLE? Compare your screen to Figure 4-60. If any field value is wrong, correct it now using the methods described earlier for editing field values.

3. After entering the value for FirstContact, press the **Tab** key again (if necessary). Record 39, the next record available for a new record, becomes the current record, and the record for customer 123 is saved in the Customer table.

   You've completed Barbara's changes to the Customer table, so you can close the form.

4. Click the **Close** button [X] on the form title bar. The form closes, and the Database window becomes the active window.

Barbara would like you to create a form so that she can view the data for each customer and all the orders for the customer at the same time. To accomplish this, you need to define a relationship between the Customer and Order tables.

Defining Table Relationships

One of the most powerful features of a relational database management system is its ability to define relationships between tables. You use a common field to relate one table to another. The process of relating tables is often called performing a **join**. When you join tables that have a common field, you can extract data from them as if they were one larger table. For example, you can join the Customer and Order tables by using the CustomerNum field in both tables as the common field. You then can use a form, query, or report to extract selected data from each table, even though the data is contained in two separate tables, as shown in Figure 4-61. In the Orders query shown in Figure 4-61, the OrderNum, Paid, and InvoiceAmt columns are fields from the Order table; and the CustomerName and State columns are fields from the Customer table. The joining of records is based on the common field of CustomerNum. The Customer and Order tables have a type of relationship called a one-to-many relationship.

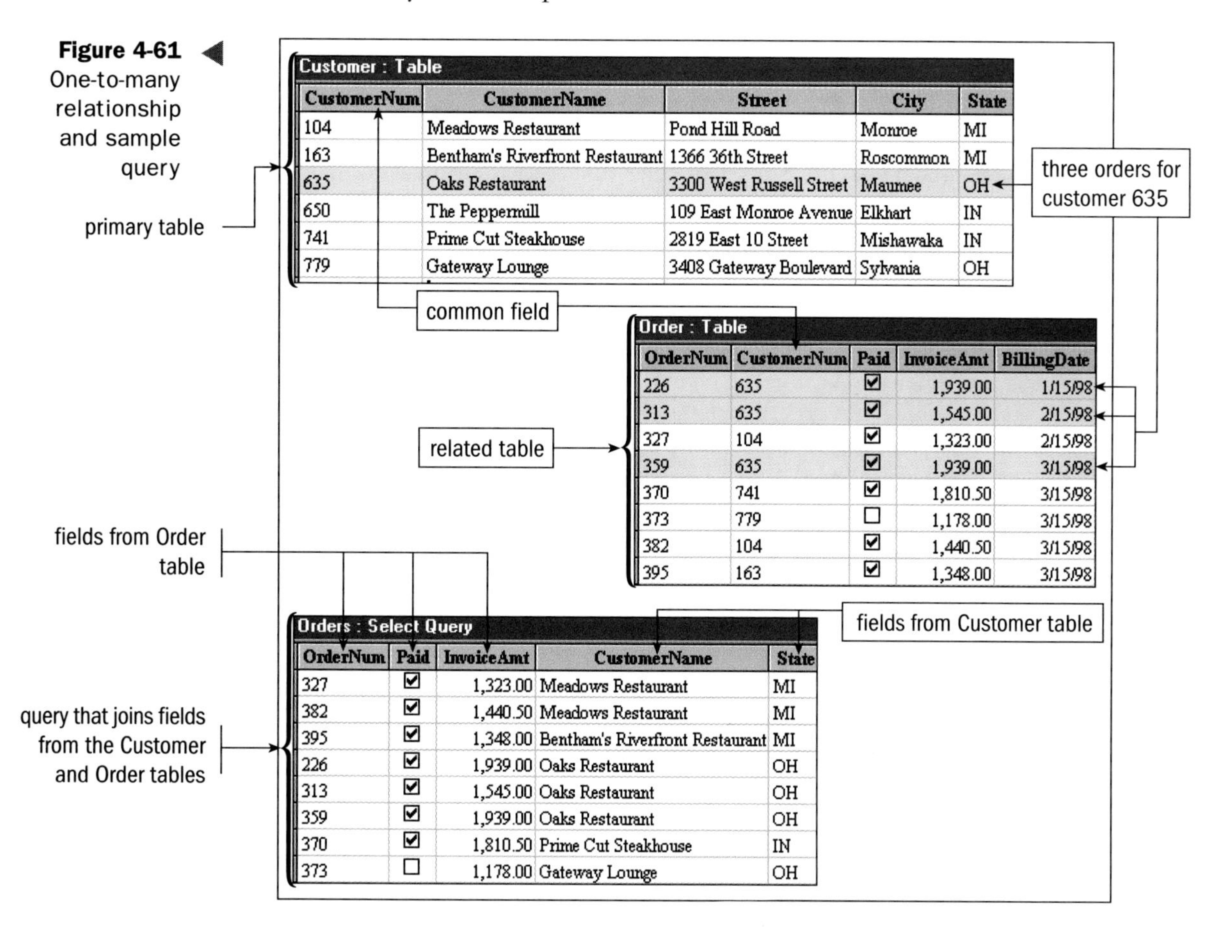

Customer : Table

CustomerNum	CustomerName	Street	City	State
104	Meadows Restaurant	Pond Hill Road	Monroe	MI
163	Bentham's Riverfront Restaurant	1366 36th Street	Roscommon	MI
635	Oaks Restaurant	3300 West Russell Street	Maumee	OH
650	The Peppermill	109 East Monroe Avenue	Elkhart	IN
741	Prime Cut Steakhouse	2819 East 10 Street	Mishawaka	IN
779	Gateway Lounge	3408 Gateway Boulevard	Sylvania	OH

Order : Table

OrderNum	CustomerNum	Paid	InvoiceAmt	BillingDate
226	635	☑	1,939.00	1/15/98
313	635	☑	1,545.00	2/15/98
327	104	☑	1,323.00	2/15/98
359	635	☑	1,939.00	3/15/98
370	741	☑	1,810.50	3/15/98
373	779	☐	1,178.00	3/15/98
382	104	☑	1,440.50	3/15/98
395	163	☑	1,348.00	3/15/98

Orders : Select Query

OrderNum	Paid	InvoiceAmt	CustomerName	State
327	☑	1,323.00	Meadows Restaurant	MI
382	☑	1,440.50	Meadows Restaurant	MI
395	☑	1,348.00	Bentham's Riverfront Restaurant	MI
226	☑	1,939.00	Oaks Restaurant	OH
313	☑	1,545.00	Oaks Restaurant	OH
359	☑	1,939.00	Oaks Restaurant	OH
370	☑	1,810.50	Prime Cut Steakhouse	IN
373	☐	1,178.00	Gateway Lounge	OH

Figure 4-61 One-to-many relationship and sample query

One-to-Many Relationships

A **one-to-many relationship** exists between two tables when one record in the first table matches zero, one, or many records in the second table, and when one record in the second table matches exactly one record in the first table. For example, as shown in Figure 4-61, customer 635 has three orders; customer 650 has zero orders; customers 163, 741, and 779 each have one order; and customer 104 has two orders. Every order has a single matching customer.

Access refers to the two tables that form a relationship as the primary table and the related table. The **primary table** is the "one" table in a one-to-many relationship; in Figure 4-61, the Customer table is the primary table because there is only one customer for each order. The **related table** is the "many" table; in Figure 4-61, the Order table is the related table because there can be many orders for each customer.

Because related data is stored in two tables, inconsistencies between the tables can occur. Consider the following scenarios:

- Barbara adds an order to the Order table for customer 107, Cottage Grill. This order does not have a matching record in the Customer table. The data is inconsistent, and the order record is considered to be an **orphaned** record.
- Barbara changes Oaks Restaurant from customer number 635 to 997 in the Customer table. Three orphaned records for customer 635 now exist in the Order table, and the database is inconsistent.
- Barbara deletes the record for Meadows Restaurant, customer 104, in the Customer table because this customer is no longer a Valle Coffee customer. The database is again inconsistent; two records for customer 104 in the Order table have no matching record in the Customer table.

You can avoid these problems by specifying referential integrity between tables when you define their relationships.

Referential Integrity

Referential integrity is a set of rules that Access enforces to maintain consistency between related tables when you update data in a database. Specifically, the referential integrity rules are as follows:

- When adding a record to a related table, a matching record must already exist in the primary table.
- When attempting to change the value of the primary key in the primary table, Access prevents this change if matching records exist in a related table. However, if you choose the **cascade updates** option, Access permits the change in value to the primary key and changes the appropriate foreign key values in the related table.
- When you delete a record in the primary table, Access prevents the deletion if matching records exist in a related table. However, if you choose the **cascade deletes** option, Access deletes the record in the primary table and all records in related tables that have matching foreign key values.

Now you'll define a one-to-many relationship between the Customer and Order tables so that you can use fields from both tables to create the form Barbara wants.

Defining a Relationship Between Two Tables

When two tables have a common field, you can define a relationship between them in the Relationships window. The **Relationships window** illustrates the relationships among a database's tables. In this window you can view or change existing relationships, define new relationships between tables, and rearrange the layout of the tables.

You need to open the Relationships window and define the relationship between the Customer and Order tables. As noted earlier, you'll define a one-to-many relationship between the two tables, with Customer as the primary table and Order as the related table, and with CustomerNum as the common field (the primary key in the Customer table and a foreign key in the Order table).

To define a one-to-many relationship between the two tables:

1. Click the **Relationships** button on the Database toolbar. Access displays the Show Table dialog box on top of the Relationships window. See Figure 4-62.

Figure 4-62 Show Table dialog box

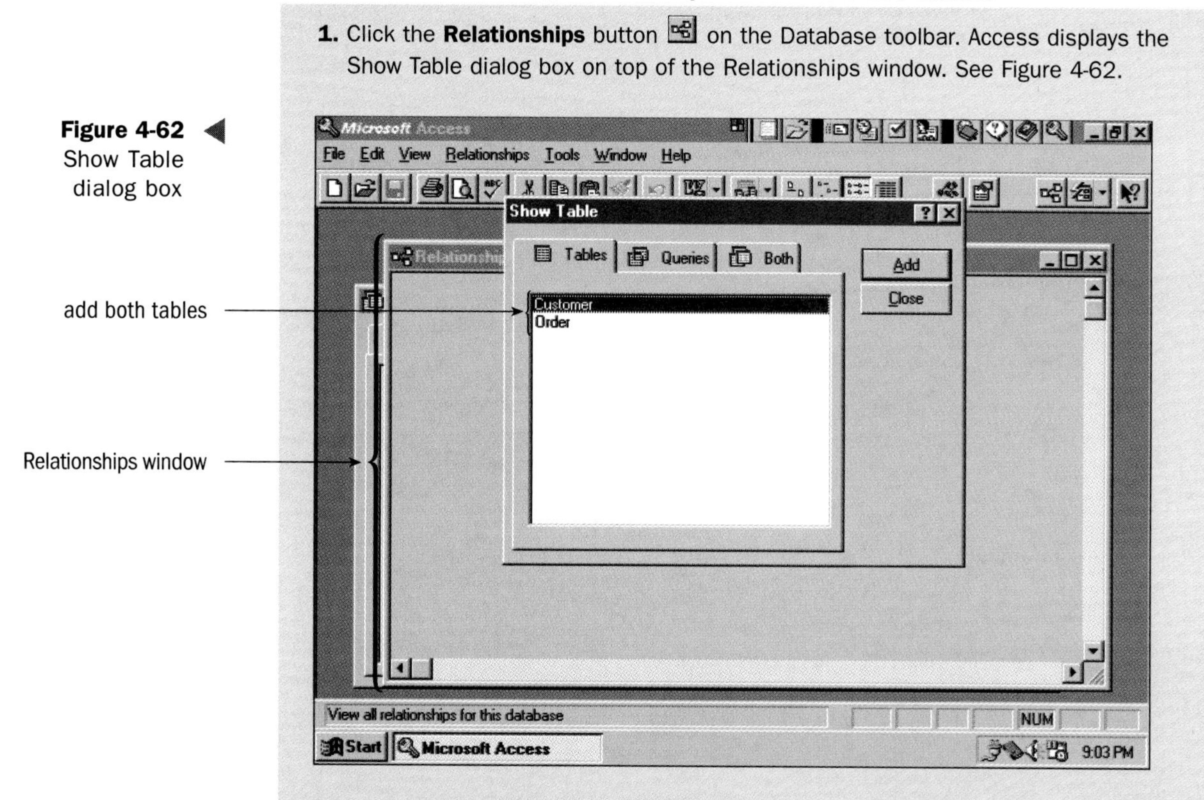

Each table participating in a relationship must be added to the Relationships window.

2. Click **Customer** then click the **Add** button. The Customer table is added to the Relationships window.

3. Click **Order** then click the **Add** button. The Order table is added to the Relationships window.

4. Click the **Close** button in the Show Table dialog box. Access closes the dialog box and reveals the entire Relationships window.

   To form the relationship between the two tables, you drag the common field of CustomerNum from the primary table to the related table. Access then opens the Relationships dialog box, in which you select the relationship options for the two tables. Notice that the table lists do not have horizontal scroll bars. This is one example of why it's best to keep field names relatively short; longer names would not be fully visible in these table lists.

5. Click **CustomerNum** in the Customer table list and drag it to **CustomerNum** in the Order table list. When you release the mouse button, Access opens the Relationships dialog box. See Figure 4-63.

Figure 4-63 Relationships dialog box

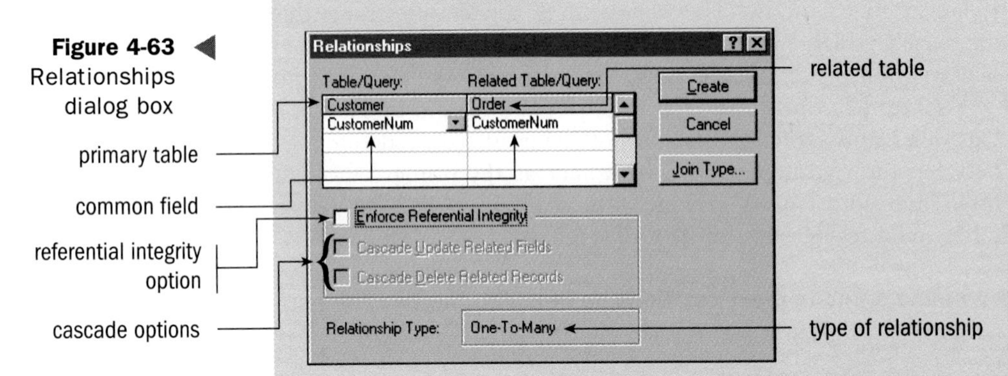

The primary table, related table, and common field appear at the top of the dialog box. The type of relationship, one-to-many, appears at the bottom of the dialog box. When you click the Enforce Referential Integrity check box, the two cascade options become available. With the Cascade Update Related Fields option, Access will change the appropriate foreign key values in the related table when you change a primary key value in the primary table. With the Cascade Delete Related Records option, when you delete a record in the primary table, Access will delete all records in the related table that have a matching foreign key value.

6. Click the **Enforce Referential Integrity** check box, click the **Cascade Update Related Fields** check box, then click the **Cascade Delete Related Fields** check box. You have now selected all the necessary relationship options.

7. Click the **Create** button to define the one-to-many relationship between the two tables and close the dialog box. The completed relationship appears in the Relationships window. See Figure 4-64.

Figure 4-64 Defined relationship in the Relationships window

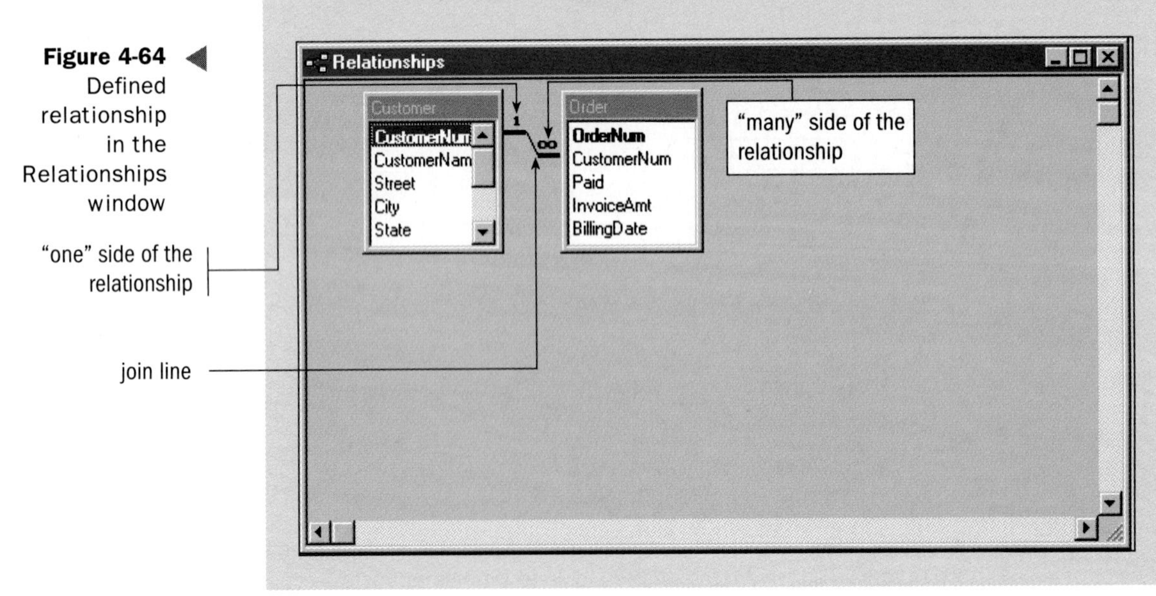

The *join line* connects the CustomerNum fields, which are common to the two tables. The common field joins the two tables, which have a one-to-many relationship. The join line is thick at both ends; this signifies that you have chosen the option to enforce referential integrity. If you do not select this option, the join line is thin at both ends. The "one" side of the relationship has the digit 1 at its end, and the "many" side of the relationship has the infinity symbol (∞) at its end. The two tables are still separate tables, but you can use the data in them as if they were one table.

8. Click the **Save** button on the Relationships toolbar to save the layout in the Relationships window.

9. Click the **Close** button on the Relationships window title bar. Access closes the Relationships window and returns you to the Database window.

Now that you have joined the Customer and Order tables, you can create a form that shows data from both tables. The type of form you will create will include a main form and a subform.

Creating a Form with a Main Form and a Subform

When you create a form containing data from two tables that have a one-to-many relationship, you actually create a main form for data from the primary table and a subform for data from the related table. Access uses the defined relationship between the tables to automatically join the tables through the common field that exists in both tables.

Barbara and her staff will use the form when contacting customers about the status of their order payments. Consequently, the main form will contain the customer number and name, owner name, and phone number; the subform will contain the order number, paid status, invoice amount, and billing date.

You'll use the Form Wizard to create the form.

To activate the Form Wizard to create the form:

1. Click the **Forms** tab (if necessary) in the Database window, then click the **New** button in the Database window. The New Form dialog box opens.

2. Click **Form Wizard**, click the list arrow for choosing a table or query, click **Customer** to select this table as the source for the main form, then click the **OK** button. The first Form Wizard dialog box opens, in which you select fields in the order you want them to appear on the form.

   Barbara wants only the CustomerNum, CustomerName, OwnerName, and Phone fields from the Customer table on the form.

3. Click **CustomerNum** in the Available Fields list box, then click the **>** button to move the field to the Selected Fields list box.

4. Repeat Step 3 for the **CustomerName**, **OwnerName**, and **Phone** fields.

   The CustomerNum field will appear in the main form, so you do not have to include it in the subform. Otherwise, Barbara wants all the fields from the Order table on the subform.

5. Click the **Tables/Queries** list arrow, then click **Table: Order**. The fields from the Order table appear in the Available Fields list box. The quickest way to add the fields you want to include is to move all the fields to the Selected Fields list box, then remove only the field you don't want to include (CustomerNum).

6. Click the **>>** button to move all the fields from the Order table to the Selected Fields list box.
7. Click **Order.CustomerNum** in the Selected Fields list box, then click the **<** button to move the field back to the Available Fields list box.
8. Click the **Next** button. The next Form Wizard dialog box opens. See Figure 4-65.

Figure 4-65 Choosing a main/subform format

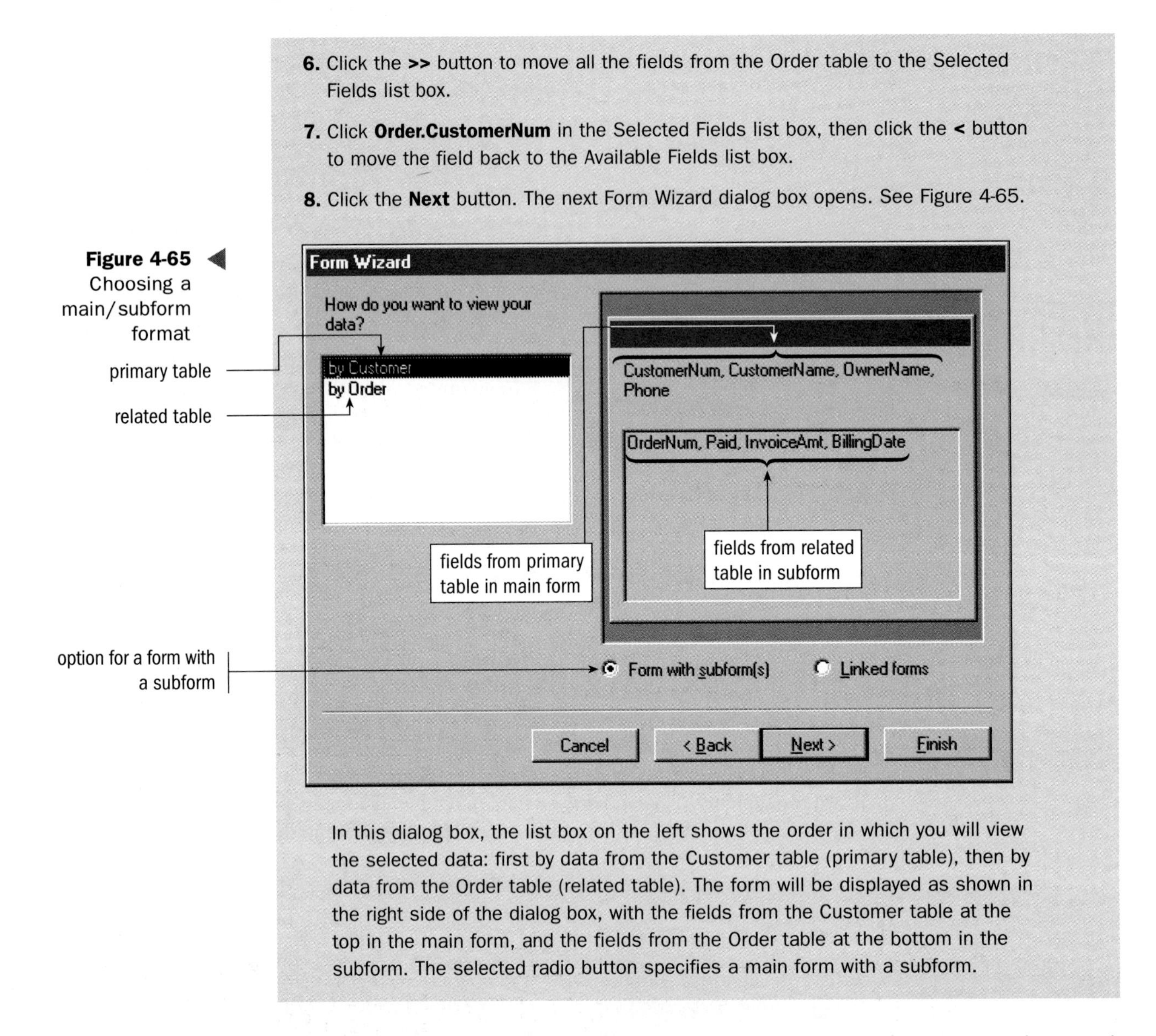

In this dialog box, the list box on the left shows the order in which you will view the selected data: first by data from the Customer table (primary table), then by data from the Order table (related table). The form will be displayed as shown in the right side of the dialog box, with the fields from the Customer table at the top in the main form, and the fields from the Order table at the bottom in the subform. The selected radio button specifies a main form with a subform.

The default options shown in Figure 4-65 are correct for creating a form with Customer data in the main form and Order data in the subform.

To finish creating the form:

1. Click the **Next** button. The next Form Wizard dialog box opens, in which you choose the subform layout.

   The tabular layout displays subform fields as a table, whereas the datasheet layout displays subform fields as a table datasheet. The layout choice is a matter of personal preference. You'll use the datasheet layout.

2. Click the **Datasheet** radio button (if necessary), then click the **Next** button. The next Form Wizard dialog box opens, in which you choose the form's AutoFormat.

   Barbara wants all forms to have the same style, so you will choose the Standard AutoFormat, which is the same AutoFormat you used to create the Customer Data form earlier.

3. If necessary, click **Standard**, then click the **Next** button. The next Form Wizard dialog box opens, in which you choose names for the main form and the subform.

You will use Customer Orders as the main form name and Order Subform as the subform name.

4. Position the insertion point to the right of the last letter in the Form text box, press the **spacebar,** then type **Orders**. The main form name is now Customer Orders. Note that the default subform name, Order Subform, is the name you want, so you don't need to change it.

   You have answered all the Form Wizard questions.

5. Click the **Finish** button. The completed form is displayed in Form view. See Figure 4-66.

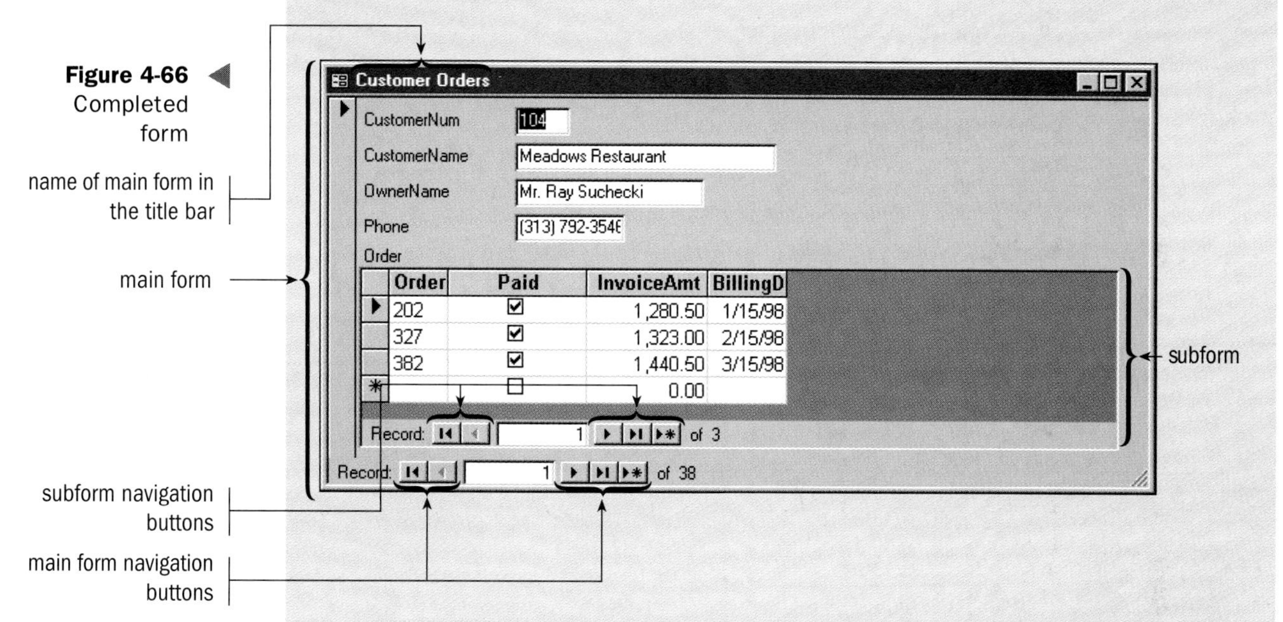

Figure 4-66 Completed form

In the main form, Access displays the fields from the first record in the Customer table in columnar format. The records in the main form appear in primary key sequence. Customer 104 has three related records in the Order table; these records are shown at the bottom in a datasheet format. The form shows that Meadows Restaurant has placed three orders with Valle Coffee.

Two sets of navigation buttons appear near the bottom of the form. You use the top set of navigation buttons to select records from the related table in the subform and the bottom set to select records from the primary table in the main form.

You'll use the navigation buttons to view different records.

To navigate to different main form and subform records:

1. Click the **Last record** navigation button in the main form. Record 38 in the Customer table for Embers Restaurant becomes the current record in the main form. The subform shows that this customer placed three orders with Valle Coffee.

2. Click the **Last record** navigation button in the subform. Record 3 in the Order table becomes the current record in the subform.

3. Click the **Previous record** navigation button in the main form. Record 37 in the Customer table for The Empire becomes the current record in the main form.

   You have finished your work with the form, so you can close it.

4. Click the **Close** button on the form title bar. The form closes, and the Database window becomes the active window.

Quick Check

1. The quickest way to create a form is to use a(n) __________.
2. Which table record is displayed on a form when you press Ctrl + End?
3. You can use the Access Find command to search for data in a form or __________.
4. Which wildcard character matches any single alphabetic character?
5. How many form records does Access print by default on a page?
6. What action does the Form Wizard >> button accomplish? the < button?
7. What is an AutoFormat?
8. How do you select an entire form record?
9. What is a one-to-many relationship?
10. __________ is a set of rules that Access enforces to maintain consistency between tables when you update data in a database.
11. How are a related and a primary table associated with a form that contains a main form and a subform?

Now that you have completed Session 4.3, you can exit Access or continue to the next session.

SESSION 4.4

In this session you will create a report using the Report Wizard, create queries for a single table and for two joined tables, sort data in a query, and update data in a query.

Creating a Report Using the Report Wizard

A **report** is a formatted hardcopy of the contents of one or more tables in a database. For example, Barbara might create a report to generate a printed list that shows selected customer and order information. In Access, you can create your own reports or use the Report Wizard to create them for you. Like the Form Wizard, the **Report Wizard** asks you a series of questions, then creates a report based on your answers. Whether you use the Report Wizard or design your own report, you can change the report's design after you create it.

Barbara wants you to create a report that includes selected customer data from the Customer table and all the orders from the Order table for each customer. Barbara sketched a design of the report she wants (Figure 4-67). Just like the form you created in the previous session, which included a main form with a subform, the report will be based on both tables, which are joined in a one-to-many relationship through the common field of CustomerNum. As shown in the sketch in Figure 4-67, the selected customer data from the primary Customer table includes the customer number, name, city, state, owner name, and phone. Below the data for each customer, the report will include the order number, paid status, invoice amount, and billing date from the related Order table. The set of field values for each order is called a **detail record.**

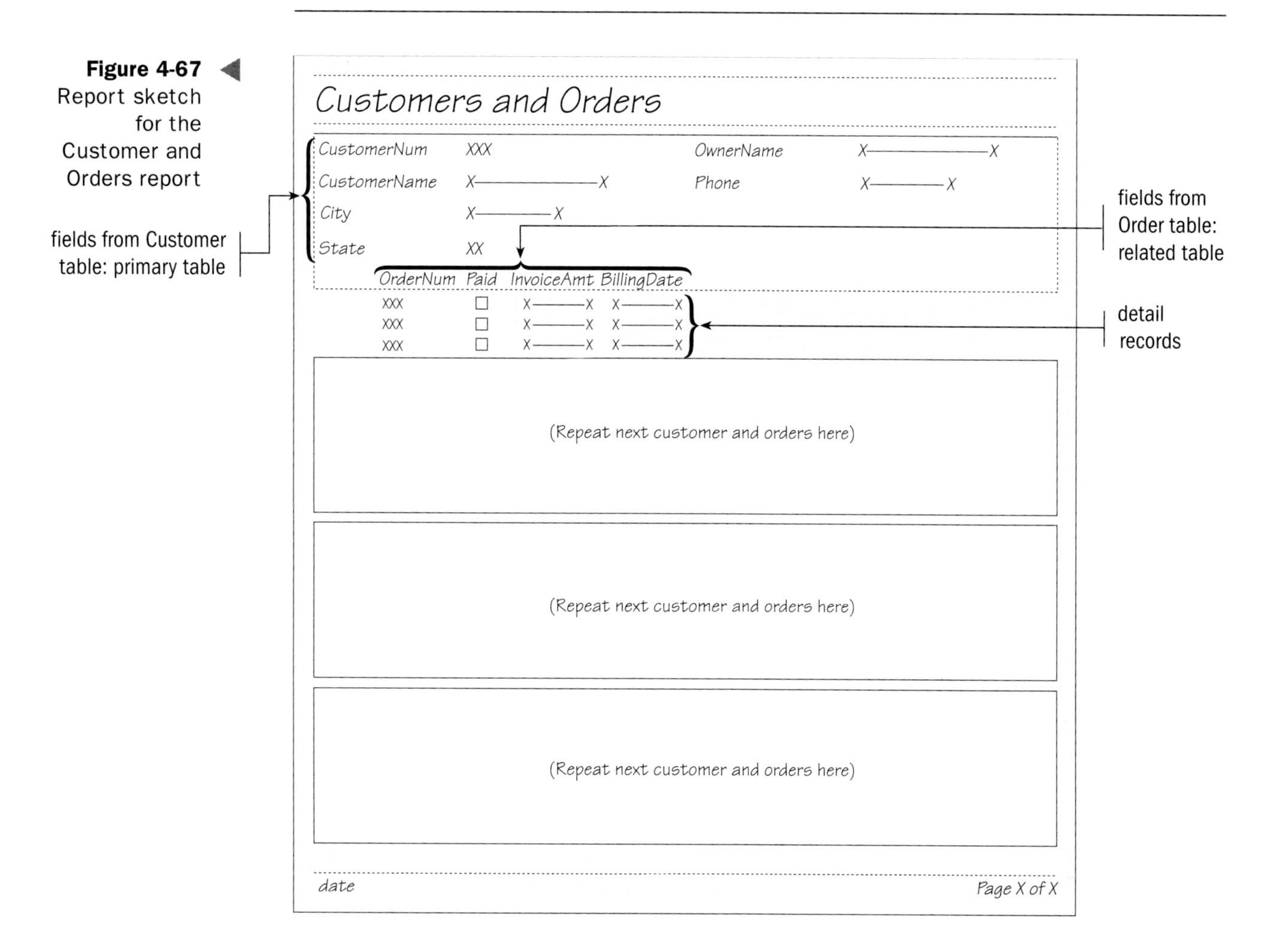

Figure 4-67 Report sketch for the Customer and Orders report

You'll use the Report Wizard to create the report according to the design in Barbara's sketch.

To activate the Report Wizard and select the fields to include in the report:

1. Click the **Reports** tab in the Database window to display the Reports list box. You have not created any reports, so the list box is empty.
2. Click the **New** button in the Database window. The New Report dialog box opens.

   Although the data for the report exists in two tables (Customer and Order), you can choose only one table or query to be the data source for the report in the New Report dialog box. However, in the Report Wizard dialog boxes you can include data from other tables. You will select the primary Customer table in the New Report dialog box.
3. Click **Report Wizard**, click the list arrow for choosing a table or query, then click **Customer**. See Figure 4-68.

Figure 4-68
Completed New Report dialog box

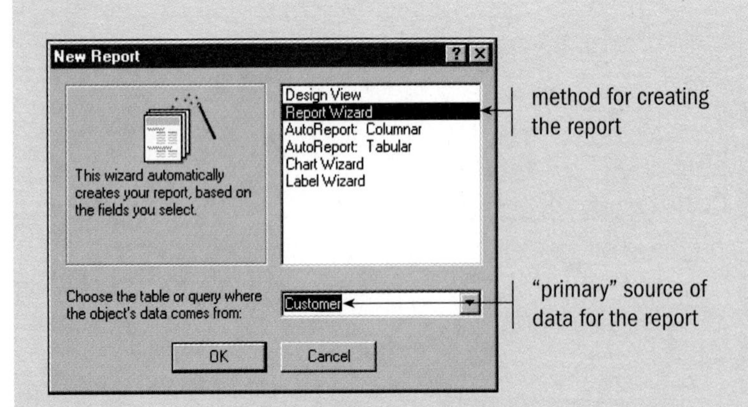

4. Click the **OK** button. The first Report Wizard dialog box opens.

   In the first Report Wizard dialog box, you select fields in the order you want them to appear on the report. Barbara wants the CustomerNum, CustomerName, City, State, OwnerName, and Phone fields from the Customer table to appear on the report.

5. Click **CustomerNum** in the Available Fields list box, then click the **>** button. The field moves to the Selected Fields list box.

6. Repeat Step 5 for **CustomerName**, **City**, **State**, **OwnerName**, and **Phone**.

7. Click the **Tables/Queries** list arrow, then click **Table: Order**. The fields from the Order table appear in the Available Fields list box.

   The CustomerNum field will appear on the report with the customer data, so you do not have to include it in the detail records for each order. Otherwise, Barbara wants all the fields from the Order table to be included in the report. The easiest way to include the necessary fields is to add all the Order table fields to the Selected Fields list box, then to remove the only field you don't want to include—CustomerNum.

8. Click the **>>** button to move all the fields from the Available Fields list box to the Selected Fields list box.

9. Click **Order.CustomerNum** in the Selected Fields list box, click the **<** button to move the selected field back to the Available Fields list box, then click the **Next** button. The second Report Wizard dialog box opens. See Figure 4-69.

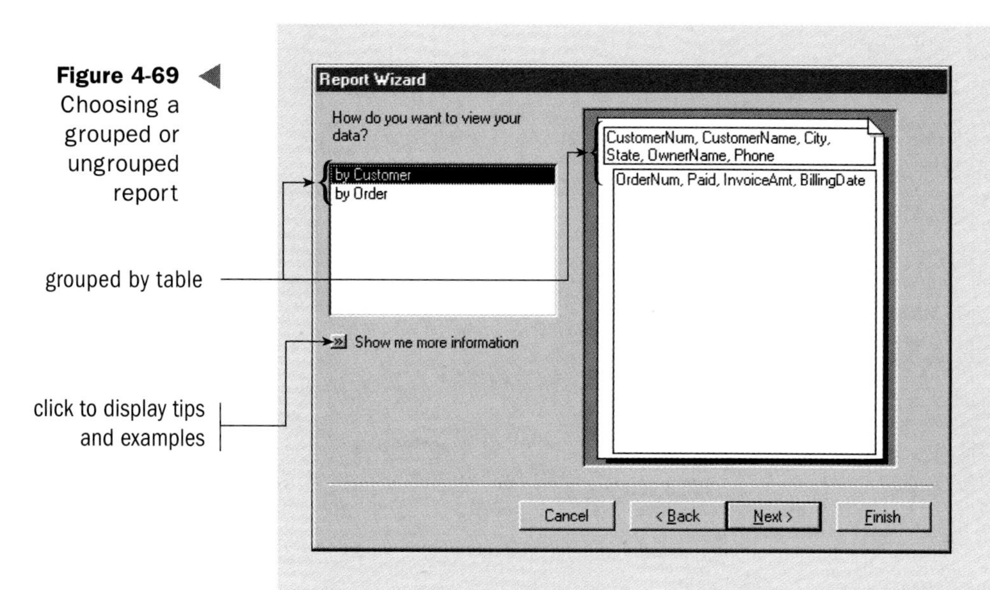

Figure 4-69 Choosing a grouped or ungrouped report

You can choose to arrange the selected data grouped by table, which is the default, or ungrouped. For a grouped report, the data from a record in the primary table appears as a group, followed by the joined records from the related table. In the case of the report you are creating, data from a record in the Customer table appears in a group, followed by the records for the customer from the Order table. An example of an ungrouped report would be a report of records from the Customer and Order tables in order by OrderNum. Each order and its associated customer data would appear together; the data would not be grouped by table.

You can display tips and examples about the choices in the first Report Wizard dialog box by clicking the >> button ("Show me more information").

To display tips about the first Report Wizard dialog box:

1. Click the **>>** button. The Report Wizard Tips dialog box opens. Read the displayed information in the dialog box.

   You can display examples of different grouping methods by clicking the >> button ("Show me examples").

2. Click the **>>** button. The Report Wizard Examples dialog box opens. See Figure 4-70.

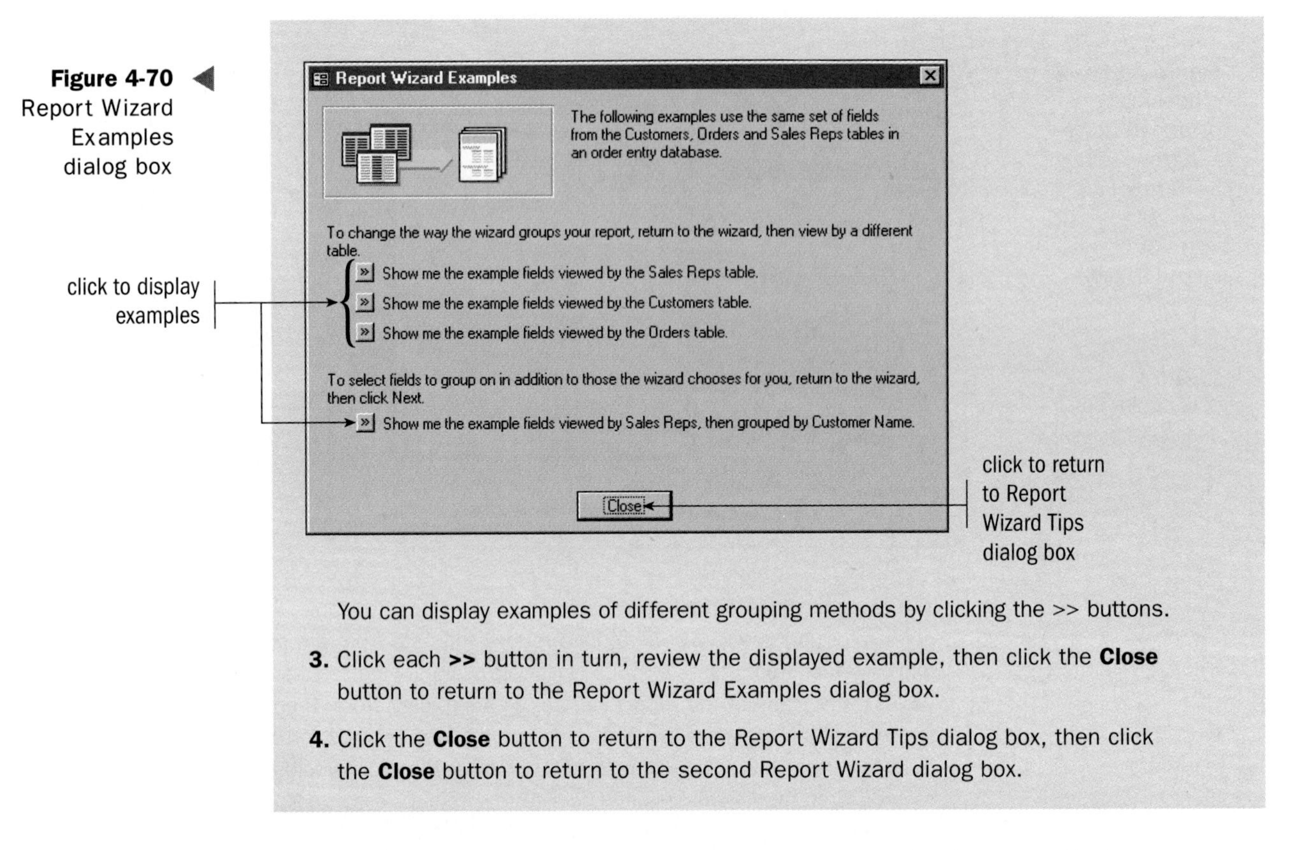

Figure 4-70 Report Wizard Examples dialog box

You can display examples of different grouping methods by clicking the >> buttons.

3. Click each **>>** button in turn, review the displayed example, then click the **Close** button to return to the Report Wizard Examples dialog box.

4. Click the **Close** button to return to the Report Wizard Tips dialog box, then click the **Close** button to return to the second Report Wizard dialog box.

The default options shown on your screen are correct for the report Barbara wants, so you can continue responding to the Report Wizard questions.

To finish creating the report using the Report Wizard:

1. Click the **Next** button. The next Report Wizard dialog box opens, in which you choose additional grouping levels.

   Two grouping levels are shown: one for each customer's data, the other for a customer's orders. Grouping levels are useful for reports with multiple levels, such as those containing month, quarter, and annual totals; or containing city and country groups. Barbara's report contains no further grouping levels, so you can accept the default options.

2. Click the **Next** button. The next Report Wizard dialog box opens, in which you choose the sort order for the detail records. See Figure 4-71.

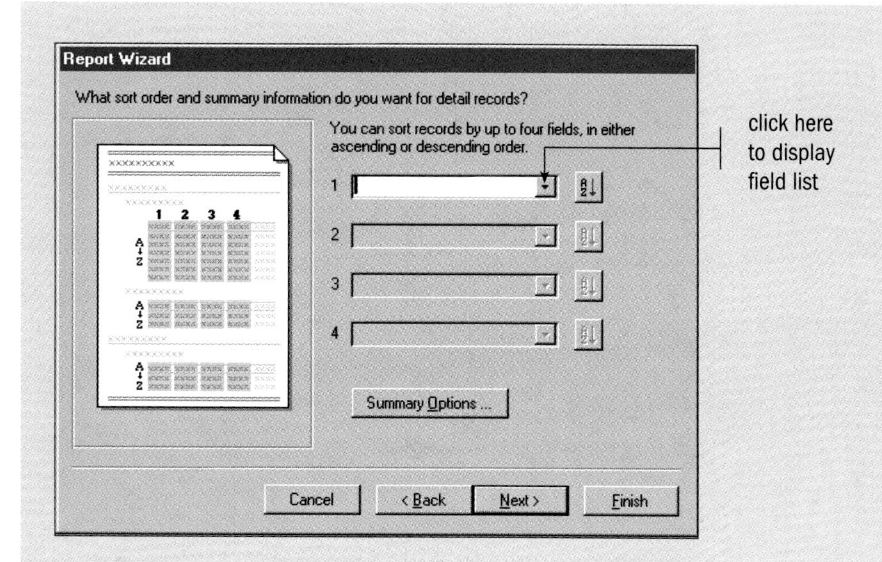

Figure 4-71 Choosing the sort order for detail records

The records from the Order table for a customer represent the detail records for Barbara's report. She wants these records to appear in increasing, or ascending, order by the value in the OrderNum field.

3. Click the **1** list arrow, click **OrderNum**, then click the **Next** button. The next Report Wizard dialog box opens, in which you choose a layout and page orientation for the report. See Figure 4-72.

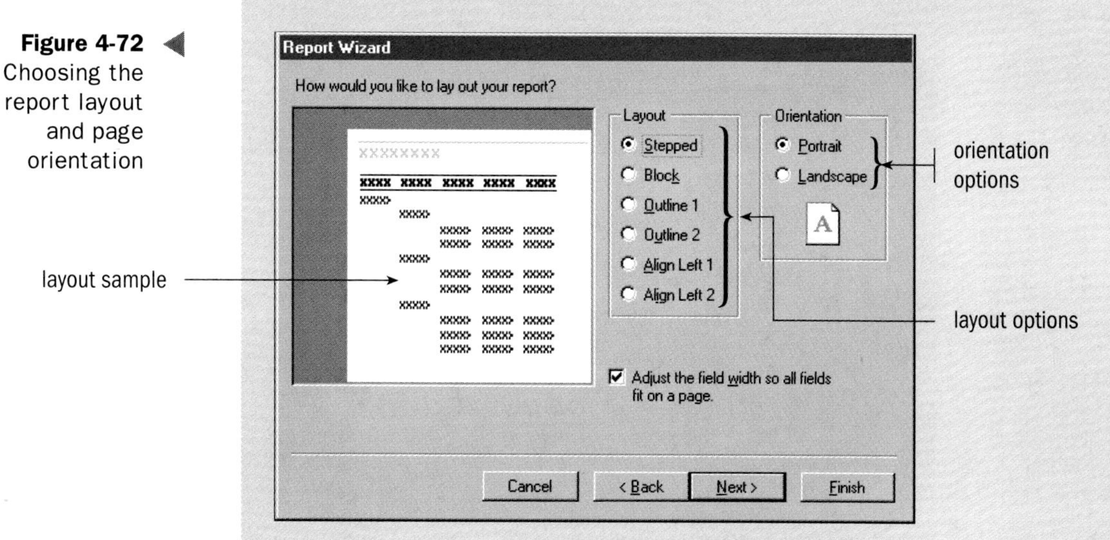

Figure 4-72 Choosing the report layout and page orientation

A sample of each layout appears in the box on the left.

4. Click each layout option and examine each sample that appears. You'll use the Outline 2 layout option because it resembles the layout shown in Barbara's sketch of the report.

5. Click the **Outline 2** radio button, then click the **Next** button. The next Report Wizard dialog box opens, in which you choose a style for the report.

   A sample of each style option, or AutoFormat, appears in the box on the left. You can always choose a different AutoFormat after you create the report, just as you could when creating a form. Barbara likes the appearance of the Corporate AutoFormat, so you'll choose this one for your report.

6. Click **Corporate** then click the **Next** button. The last Report Wizard dialog box opens, in which you choose a report name, which also serves as the printed title on the report.

   According to Barbara's sketch, the report title you need to specify is "Customers and Orders."

7. Type **Customers and Orders** then click the **Finish** button. The Report Wizard creates the report based on your answers and saves it to your Student Disk. Then Access opens the Customers and Orders report in Print Preview.

   To better view the report, you need to maximize the report window.

8. Click the **Maximize** button on the Customers and Orders title bar.

   To view the entire page, you need to change the Zoom Control setting.

9. Click the **Zoom Control** list arrow on the Print Preview toolbar, then click **Fit**. The first page of the report is displayed in Print Preview. See Figure 4-73.

Figure 4-73 Completed report in the Print Preview window

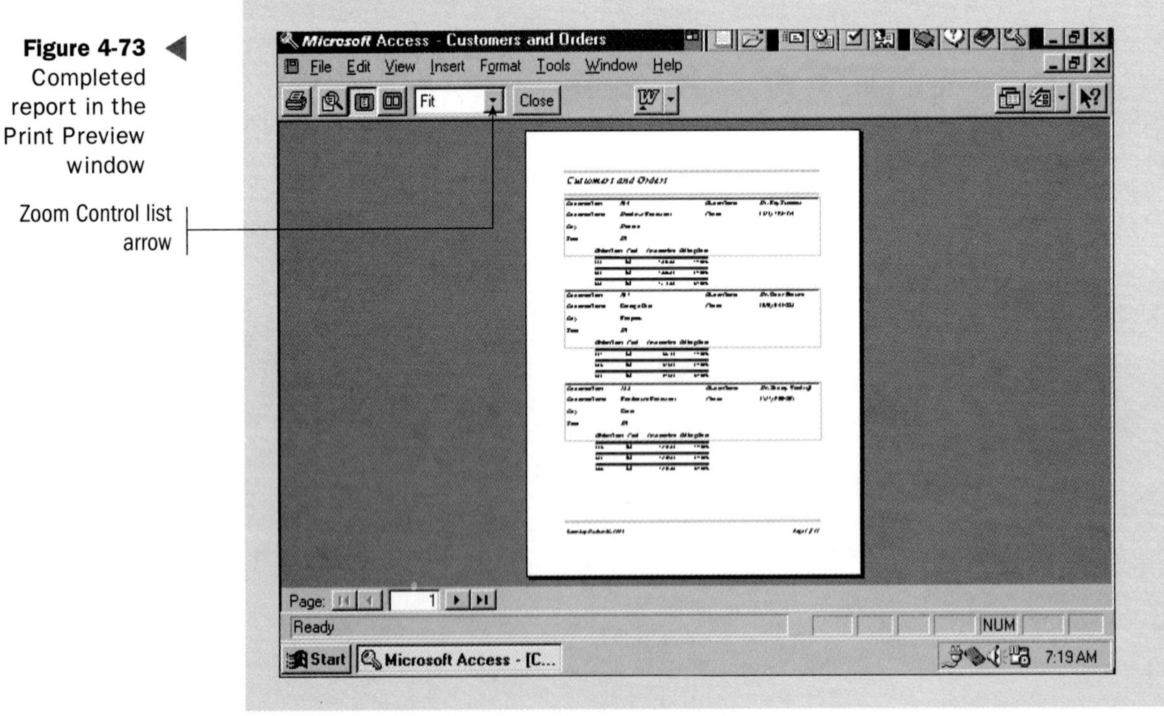

The report is now complete. You'll print a hardcopy of just one page of the report so that Barbara can review the report layout.

To print page 1 of the report:

1. Click **File** on the menu bar, then click **Print**. The Print dialog box opens.

2. In the Print Range section, click the **Pages** radio button. The insertion point now appears in the From text box so that you can specify the range of pages to print.

3. Type **1** in the From text box, press the **Tab** key to move to the To text box, then type **1**. These settings specify that only page 1 of the report will be printed.

4. Click the **OK** button. The Print dialog box closes, and the first page of the report is printed. See Figure 4-74.

Figure 4-74
First page of the Customers and Orders report

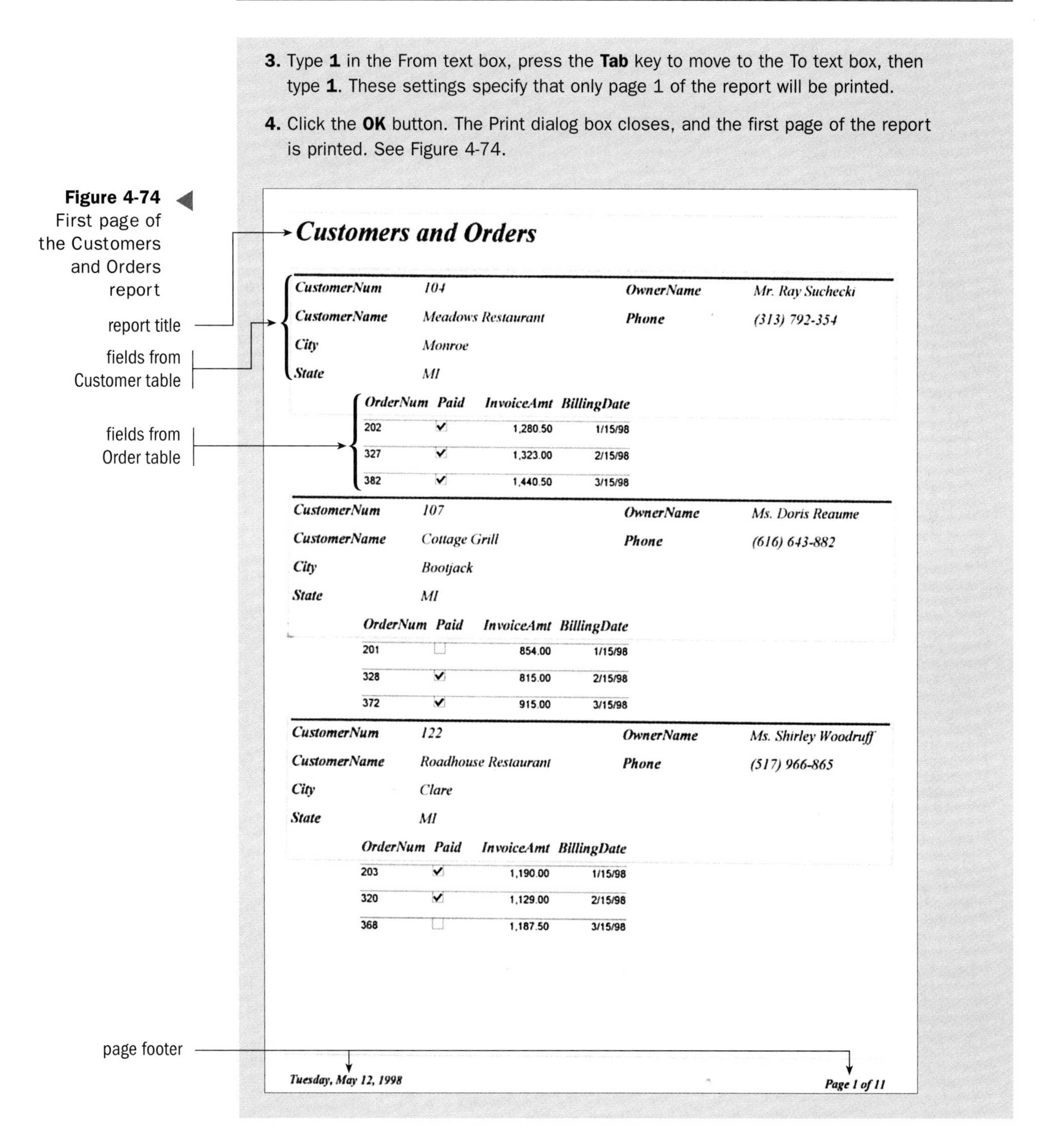

Customers and Orders

CustomerNum	*104*	*OwnerName*	*Mr. Ray Suchecki*
CustomerName	*Meadows Restaurant*	*Phone*	*(313) 792-354*
City	*Monroe*		
State	*MI*		

OrderNum	Paid	InvoiceAmt	BillingDate
202	☑	1,280.50	1/15/98
327	☑	1,323.00	2/15/98
382	☑	1,440.50	3/15/98

CustomerNum	*107*	*OwnerName*	*Ms. Doris Reaume*
CustomerName	*Cottage Grill*	*Phone*	*(616) 643-882*
City	*Bootjack*		
State	*MI*		

OrderNum	Paid	InvoiceAmt	BillingDate
201	☐	854.00	1/15/98
328	☑	815.00	2/15/98
372	☑	915.00	3/15/98

CustomerNum	*122*	*OwnerName*	*Ms. Shirley Woodruff*
CustomerName	*Roadhouse Restaurant*	*Phone*	*(517) 966-865*
City	*Clare*		
State	*MI*		

OrderNum	Paid	InvoiceAmt	BillingDate
203	☑	1,190.00	1/15/98
320	☑	1,129.00	2/15/98
368	☐	1,187.50	3/15/98

Tuesday, May 12, 1998 *Page 1 of 11*

Barbara approves of the report layout and contents, so you can close the report.

To close the report:

1. Click the **Close** button ☒ on the menu bar to close the report and return to the Database window.

   TROUBLE? If you click the Close button on the Print Preview toolbar by mistake, Access displays the report in Design view. Click the Close button ☒ on the menu bar to close the report and return to the Database window.

You no longer need to have the Database window maximized, so you can restore it now.

2. Click the **Restore** button on the menu bar.

Next, Barbara wants you to create queries to find specific information she needs.

Introduction to Queries

A **query** is a question you ask about data stored in a database. For example, Barbara might create a query to find records in the Customer table for only those customers in a specific state. When you create a query, you tell Access which fields you need and what criteria Access should use to select the records. Access then displays only the information you want, so you don't have to scan through the entire database for the information.

Access provides powerful query capabilities that allow you to:

- display selected fields and records from a table
- sort records
- perform calculations
- generate data for forms, reports, and other queries
- update data in the tables in a database
- find and display data from two or more tables

Most questions about data take the forms of generalized queries in which you specify the fields and records you want Access to select. These common requests for information, such as "Which customers have unpaid bills?" or "Which type of coffee sells best in Ohio?" are called **select queries.** The answer to a select query is returned in the form of a datasheet.

More specialized, technical queries, such as finding duplicate records in a table or orphaned records in related tables, are best formulated through a Query Wizard. In a **Query Wizard**, Access prompts you for information through a set of questions and then creates the appropriate query based on your answers. For common, informational queries, it is easier for you to design your own query rather than use a Query Wizard.

Barbara wants you to create a query to display the customer number, customer name, city, owner name, and phone for each record in the Customer table, which the marketing staff needs for a survey they are conducting. You'll open the Query window to create Barbara's first query.

The Query Window

You use the Query window in Design view to create a query. In Design view you specify the data you want to view by constructing a query by example. Using **query by example (QBE)**, you give Access an example of the information you are requesting. Access then retrieves the information that precisely matches your example.

For Barbara's first query, you need to display data from the Customer table. Specifically, Barbara wants to view the customer number, customer name, city, owner name, and phone number for each record in the Customer table. You'll begin by displaying the Query window in Design view.

To open the Query window in Design view:

1. Click the **Queries** tab in the Database window, then click the **New** button. The New Query dialog box opens. See Figure 4-75.

Figure 4-75 New Query dialog box

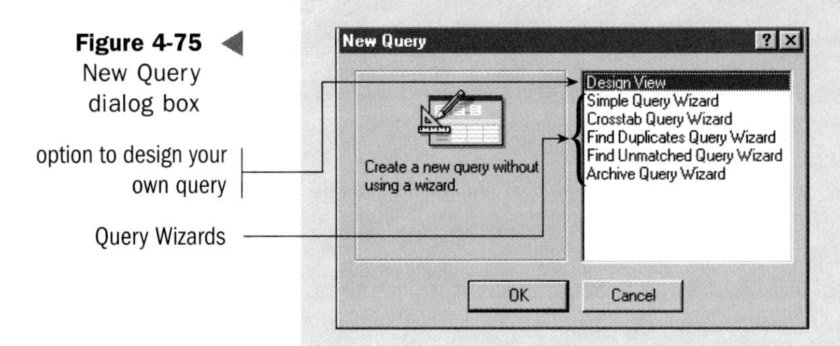

You'll design your own query instead of using a Query Wizard.

2. If necessary, click **Design View** in the list box.
3. Click the **OK** button. Access opens the Show Table dialog box on top of the Query window. Notice that the title bar of the window shows that you are creating a select query. The query you are creating will retrieve data from the Customer table, so you need to add this table to the Select Query window.
4. Click **Customer** in the Tables list box, click the **Add** button, then click the **Close** button. Access places the Customer table field list in the Select Query window and closes the dialog box.

   To display more of the fields you'll be using for Barbara's queries, you'll maximize the Select Query window.

5. Click the **Maximize** button on the Select Query window title bar. See Figure 4-76.

Figure 4-76 Select Query window in Design view

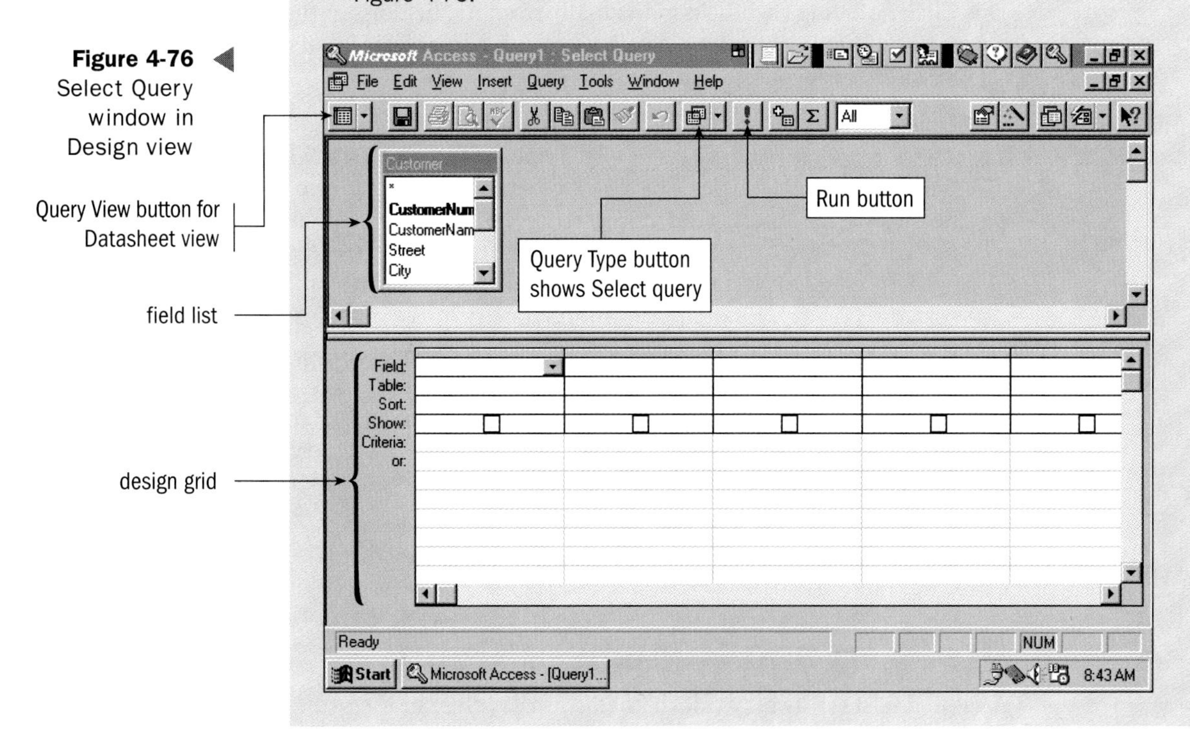

In Design view, the Select Query window contains the standard title bar, menu bar, toolbar, and status bar. On the toolbar, the Query Type button shows a select query; the icon on this button changes according to the type of query you are creating. The title bar on the Select Query window displays the query type, Select Query, and the default query name, Query1. You'll change the default query name to a more meaningful one later when you save the query.

The Select Query window in Design view contains a field list and the design grid. The **field list**, which appears in the upper-left area of the window, contains the fields for the table you are querying. The table name appears at the top of the list box, and the fields are listed in the order in which they appear in the table. If you've chosen two or more tables for your query, each table's field list appears in this upper portion of the Select Query window.

In the **design grid**, you include the fields and record selection criteria for the information you want to see. Each column in the design grid contains specifications about a field you will use in the query. You can choose a single field for your query by dragging its name from the field list to the design grid in the lower portion of the window. Alternatively, you can double-click a field name to place it in the next available column in the design grid.

When you are constructing a query, you can see the query results at any time by clicking the Query View button or the Run button on the toolbar. In response, Access displays the datasheet, which contains the set of fields and records that result from answering, or **running**, a query. The order of the fields in the datasheet is the same as the order of the fields in the design grid. Although the datasheet looks just like a table datasheet and appears in Datasheet view, a query datasheet is temporary and its contents are based on the criteria you establish in the design grid. In contrast, a table datasheet shows the permanent data in a table. However, you can update data while viewing a query datasheet, just as you can when working in a table datasheet or a form.

If the query you are creating includes all the fields from the specified table, you could use one of the following three methods to transfer all the fields from the field list to the design grid:

- Click and drag each field individually from the field list to the design grid. Use this method if you want the fields in your query to appear in an order that is different from the order in the field list.
- Double-click the asterisk in the field list. Access places the table name followed by a period and an asterisk (as in "Customer.*") in the design grid. This signifies that the order of the fields will be the same in the query as it is in the field list. Use this method if the query does not need to be sorted or to have conditions for the records you want to select. The advantage of using this method is that you do not need to change the query if you add or delete fields from the underlying table structure. They will all appear automatically in the query.
- Double-click the field list title bar to highlight all the fields, then click and drag one of the highlighted fields to the design grid. Access places each field in a separate column and arranges the fields in the order in which they appear in the field list. Use this method rather than the previous one if your query needs to be sorted or to include record selection criteria.

Now you'll create and run Barbara's first query to display selected fields from the Customer table.

Creating and Running a Query

A table datasheet displays all the fields in the table, in the same order as they appear in the table. In contrast, a query datasheet can display selected fields from a table, and the order of the fields can be different from that of the table.

For Barbara's query, she wants the CustomerNum, CustomerName, City, OwnerName, and Phone fields to appear in the query results. You'll add each of these fields to the design grid.

To select the fields for the query, then run the query:

1. Drag **CustomerNum** from the Customer field list to the design grid's first column Field text box. See Figure 4-77.

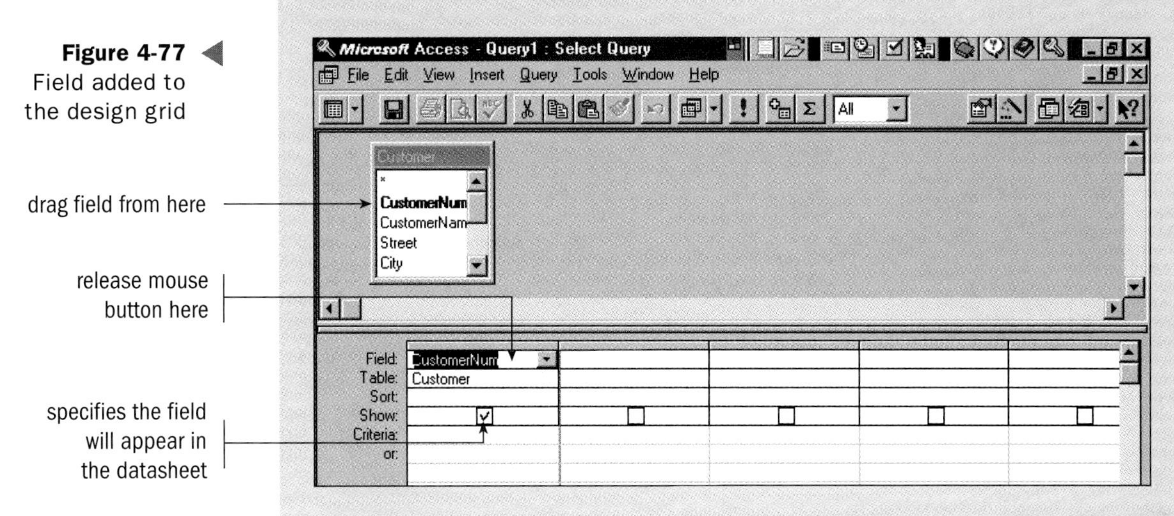

Figure 4-77 Field added to the design grid

In the design grid's first column, the field name, CustomerNum, appears in the Field text box; the table name, Customer, appears in the Table text box; and the check mark in the Show check box indicates that the field will be displayed in the datasheet when you run the query. There are times when you might choose not to display a field and its values in the query results. For example, if you are creating a query to show all the customers located in Michigan and you assign the name "Customers in Michigan" to the query, you would not need to include the State field value for each record in the query results. Even if you choose not to include a field in the display of the query results, you can still use the field as part of the query to select specific records or to specify a particular sequence for the records in the datasheet.

2. Double-click **CustomerName** in the Customer field list. Access adds this field to the second column of the design grid.

3. Scrolling the Customer field list as necessary, repeat Step 2 for the **City**, **OwnerName**, and **Phone** fields to add these fields to the design grid, in that order. The Phone field is added to the fifth column, which might not appear on your screen.

   Having selected the fields for Barbara's query, you can now run the query.

4. Click the **Run** button [!] on the Query Design toolbar. Access runs the query and displays the results in Datasheet view. See Figure 4-78.

Figure 4-78 Datasheet displayed after running the query

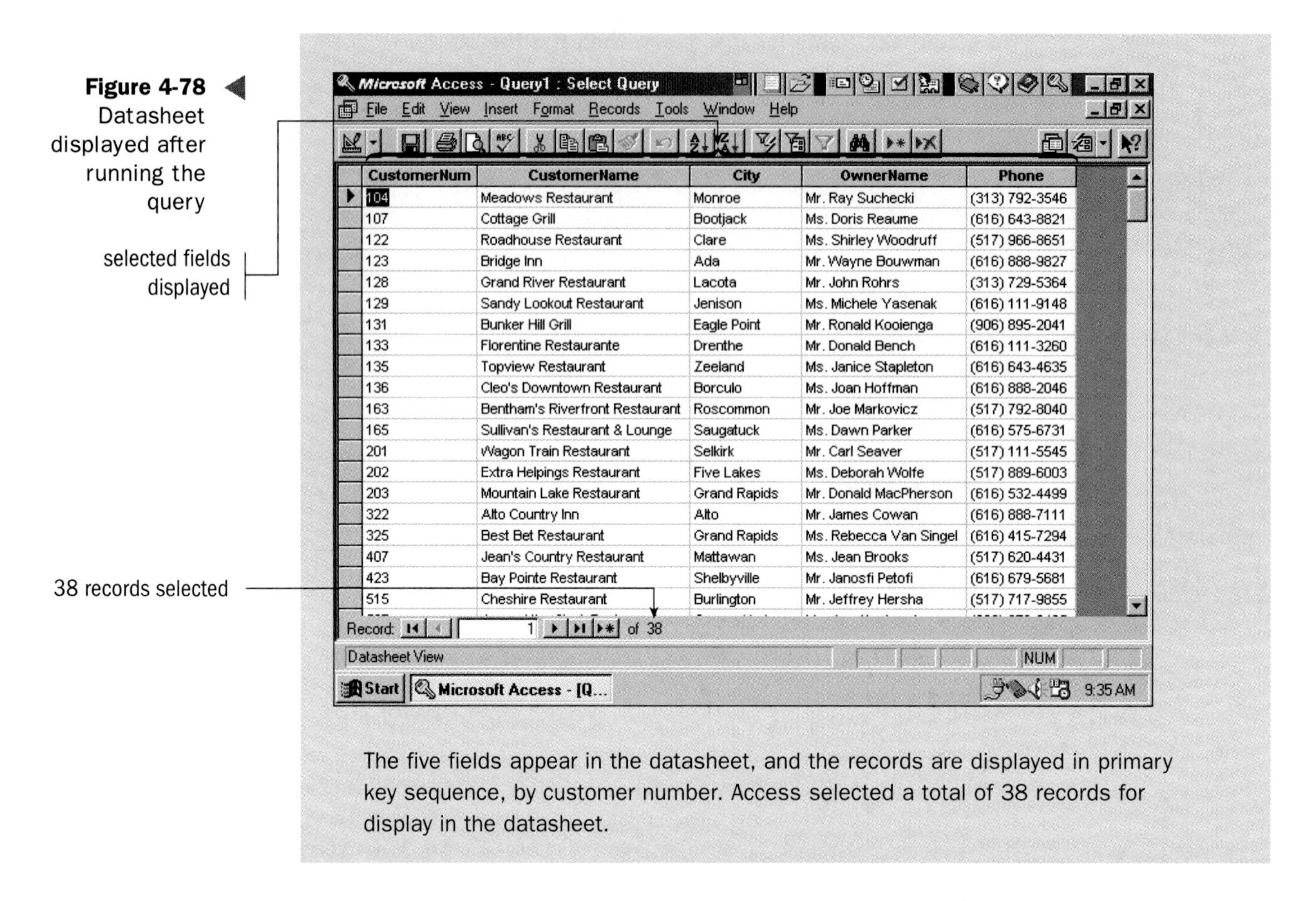

CustomerNum	CustomerName	City	OwnerName	Phone
104	Meadows Restaurant	Monroe	Mr. Ray Suchecki	(313) 792-3546
107	Cottage Grill	Bootjack	Ms. Doris Reaume	(616) 643-8821
122	Roadhouse Restaurant	Clare	Ms. Shirley Woodruff	(517) 966-8651
123	Bridge Inn	Ada	Mr. Wayne Bouwman	(616) 888-9827
128	Grand River Restaurant	Lacota	Mr. John Rohrs	(313) 729-5364
129	Sandy Lookout Restaurant	Jenison	Ms. Michele Yasenak	(616) 111-9148
131	Bunker Hill Grill	Eagle Point	Mr. Ronald Kooienga	(906) 895-2041
133	Florentine Restaurante	Drenthe	Mr. Donald Bench	(616) 111-3260
135	Topview Restaurant	Zeeland	Ms. Janice Stapleton	(616) 643-4635
136	Cleo's Downtown Restaurant	Borculo	Ms. Joan Hoffman	(616) 888-2046
163	Bentham's Riverfront Restaurant	Roscommon	Mr. Joe Markovicz	(517) 792-8040
165	Sullivan's Restaurant & Lounge	Saugatuck	Ms. Dawn Parker	(616) 575-6731
201	Wagon Train Restaurant	Selkirk	Mr. Carl Seaver	(517) 111-5545
202	Extra Helpings Restaurant	Five Lakes	Ms. Deborah Wolfe	(517) 889-6003
203	Mountain Lake Restaurant	Grand Rapids	Mr. Donald MacPherson	(616) 532-4499
322	Alto Country Inn	Alto	Mr. James Cowan	(616) 888-7111
325	Best Bet Restaurant	Grand Rapids	Ms. Rebecca Van Singel	(616) 415-7294
407	Jean's Country Restaurant	Mattawan	Ms. Jean Brooks	(517) 620-4431
423	Bay Pointe Restaurant	Shelbyville	Mr. Janosfi Petofi	(616) 679-5681
515	Cheshire Restaurant	Burlington	Mr. Jeffrey Hersha	(517) 717-9855

The five fields appear in the datasheet, and the records are displayed in primary key sequence, by customer number. Access selected a total of 38 records for display in the datasheet.

For her next query, Barbara wants to view the data for only those customers who are not located in Michigan. To produce these results, you need to specify a condition in the query.

Specifying a Condition in a Query

Just as you can display selected fields from a table in a query datasheet, you can display selected records. To tell Access which records you want to select, you must specify a condition. A **condition** is a criterion, or rule, that determines which records are selected. For example, Barbara wants records selected only if they meet the condition that a customer's state is not Michigan. To define a condition for a field, you place the condition in the field's Criteria text box in the design grid. For example, to create the query Barbara wants, you can enter "not MI" (without the quotation marks) for the State field in the Criteria row of the design grid. You will learn more about conditions in a later tutorial.

To produce the query Barbara wants, you need to add the State field and its condition to the design grid. Barbara does not want the State field values to appear in the query results, because she knows that the customers are all located somewhere other than Michigan. Therefore, you must uncheck the State field's Show check box.

To select the records for the query, then run the query:

1. Click the **Query View** button for Design View on the Query Datasheet toolbar. Access closes the window and opens the query in Design view.
2. Drag **State** from the Customer field list to the design grid's first column Field text box. The State field now appears in the first column, and all the other fields have shifted one column to the right.
3. Click the State field's **Show** check box to remove the check mark. The State field and its values will not appear in the datasheet when you run the query.

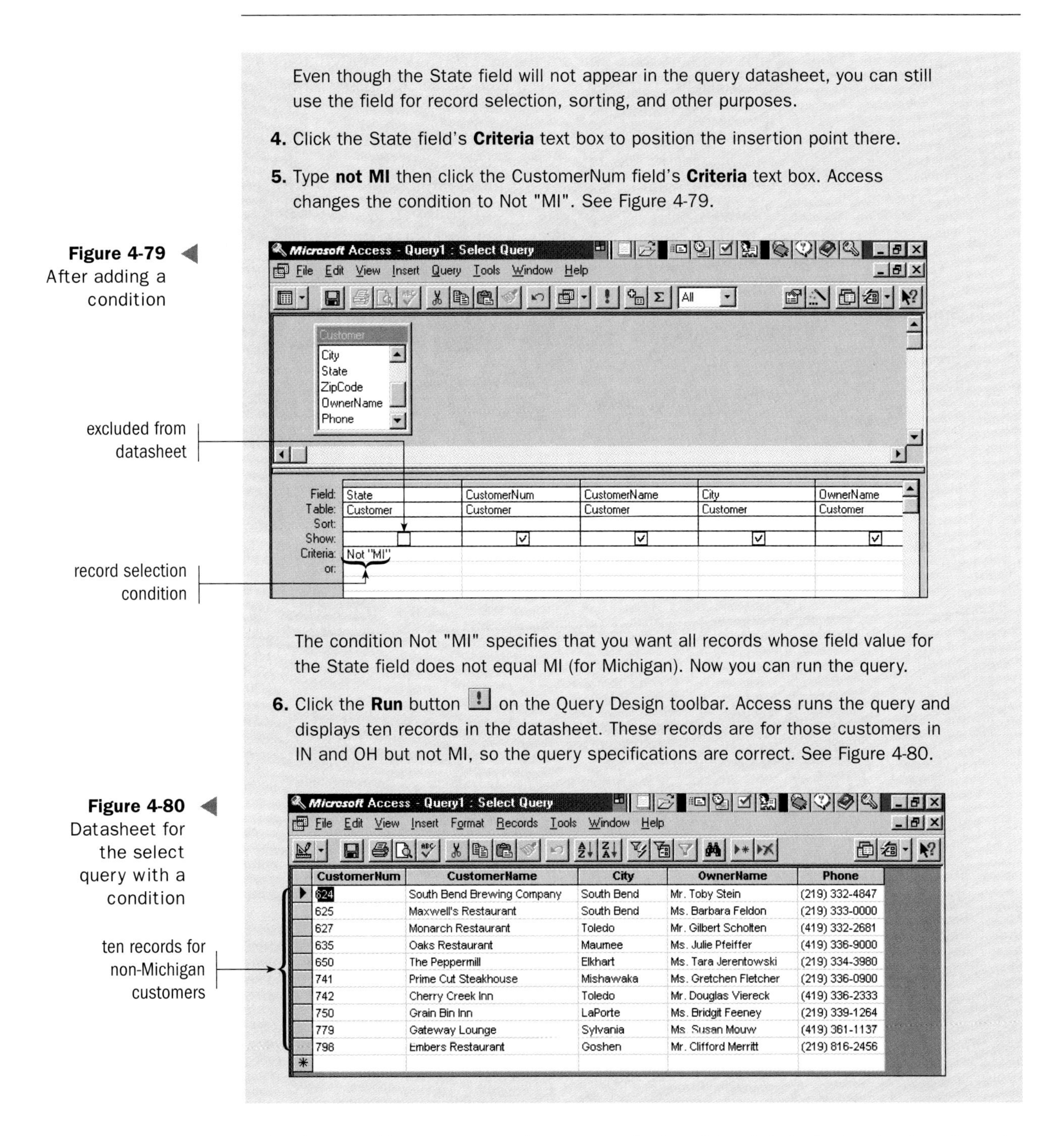

Even though the State field will not appear in the query datasheet, you can still use the field for record selection, sorting, and other purposes.

4. Click the State field's **Criteria** text box to position the insertion point there.

5. Type **not MI** then click the CustomerNum field's **Criteria** text box. Access changes the condition to Not "MI". See Figure 4-79.

Figure 4-79
After adding a condition

The condition Not "MI" specifies that you want all records whose field value for the State field does not equal MI (for Michigan). Now you can run the query.

6. Click the **Run** button on the Query Design toolbar. Access runs the query and displays ten records in the datasheet. These records are for those customers in IN and OH but not MI, so the query specifications are correct. See Figure 4-80.

Figure 4-80
Datasheet for the select query with a condition

Barbara decides she wants the records displayed in alphabetical order based on the field value of the CustomerName field.

Sorting Data in a Query

Because your query displays data in order by the field value of CustomerNum, the primary key for the Customer table, you need to sort the records by CustomerName to display the data in the order Barbara wants. **Sorting** is the process of rearranging records in a specified order or sequence. Often you need to sort data before displaying or printing it to meet a specific request. For example, Barbara might want to review order information arranged by the Paid field because she is interested in which orders are still unpaid. On the other hand, Leonard Valle might want to view order information arranged by the InvoiceAmt totals for each customer because he tracks company sales.

When you sort data in a database, Access does not change the sequence of the records in the underlying tables. Only the records in the query datasheet are rearranged according to your specifications.

To sort records, you must select the **sort key**, which is the field used to determine the order of records in the datasheet. For example, Barbara wants the customer data sorted by the customer name, so the CustomerName field will be the sort key. Sort keys can be text, number, date/time, currency, AutoNumber, or yes/no fields, but not memo or OLE object fields. You sort records in either ascending (increasing) or descending (decreasing) order. Figure 4-81 shows the results of each type of sort for each data type.

Figure 4-81 Sorting results for each data type

Data Type	Ascending Sort Results	Descending Sort Results
Text	A to Z	Z to A
Memo	cannot sort using a memo field	cannot sort using a memo field
Number	lowest to highest numeric value	highest to lowest numeric value
Date/Time	oldest to most recent date	most recent to oldest date
Currency	lowest to highest numeric value	highest to lowest numeric value
AutoNumber	lowest to highest numeric value	highest to lowest numeric value
Yes/No	yes (check mark in check box) then no values	no then yes values
OLE Object	cannot sort using an OLE object field	cannot sort using an OLE object field
Lookup Wizard	depends on the data type of the field in the other table or of the predefined list	depends on the data type of the field in the other table or of the predefined list

You need to specify an ascending sort order for the CustomerName field in the design grid so that the records will be sorted alphabetically by customer name.

To select the sort key for the query, then run the query:

1. Click the **Query View** button for Design View on the Query Datasheet toolbar. Access displays the query in Design view.
2. Click the CustomerName's **Sort** text box, click the **Sort** list arrow, then click **Ascending**.
3. Click the **Run** button on the Query Design toolbar. Access runs the query and displays ten records in the datasheet. These records now appear in ascending sort order based on the field value for the CustomerName field. See Figure 4-82.

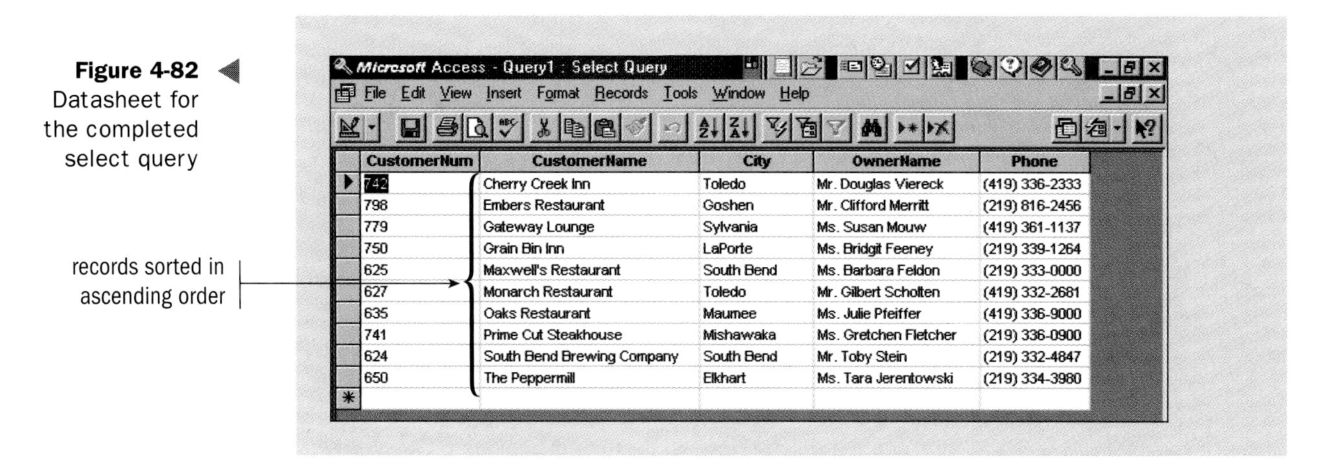

CustomerNum	CustomerName	City	OwnerName	Phone
742	Cherry Creek Inn	Toledo	Mr. Douglas Viereck	(419) 336-2333
798	Embers Restaurant	Goshen	Mr. Clifford Merritt	(219) 816-2456
779	Gateway Lounge	Sylvania	Ms. Susan Mouw	(419) 361-1137
750	Grain Bin Inn	LaPorte	Ms. Bridgit Feeney	(219) 339-1264
625	Maxwell's Restaurant	South Bend	Ms. Barbara Feldon	(219) 333-0000
627	Monarch Restaurant	Toledo	Mr. Gilbert Scholten	(419) 332-2681
635	Oaks Restaurant	Maumee	Ms. Julie Pfeiffer	(419) 336-9000
741	Prime Cut Steakhouse	Mishawaka	Ms. Gretchen Fletcher	(219) 336-0900
624	South Bend Brewing Company	South Bend	Mr. Toby Stein	(219) 332-4847
650	The Peppermill	Elkhart	Ms. Tara Jerentowski	(219) 334-3980

Figure 4-82 Datasheet for the completed select query

Barbara wants to monitor the activity of customers outside of Michigan on a regular basis. Therefore, she wants you to save this query so that she won't need to recreate it each time she wants to retrieve the necessary data.

Saving a Query

When a query produces results that you want to view repeatedly, it's a good idea to save the query so that you don't have to recreate it. You'll save your query as Non-Michigan Customers, then close the query.

To save and close the query:

1. Click the **Save** button on the Query Datasheet toolbar. The Save As dialog box opens.
2. Type **Non-Michigan Customers** in the Query Name text box, then press the **Enter** key. Access saves the query with the specified name on your Student Disk, and displays the name in the title bar.
3. Click the **Close** button on the menu bar to close the query and return to the Database window.

Next, Barbara wants you to create a query that displays data from both the Customer table and the Order table.

Querying More Than One Table

When two or more tables are joined in a relationship, such as the one-to-many relationship between the Customer and Order tables, you can create a query that displays data from both tables. You use the same techniques in Design view that you've already used, except you include the field lists for both tables.

Barbara needs a query that displays the CustomerName, Street, City, and State fields from the Customer table and the BillingDate and InvoiceAmt fields from the Order table. She wants the records sorted in ascending order by the value in the CustomerName field.

To create, run, and save the query using the Customer and Order tables:

1. Click the **New** button in the Database window to open the New Query dialog box, click **Design View** in the dialog box, then click the **OK** button. Access opens the Show Table dialog box on top of the Query window in Design view.

   You need to add both tables to the Query window.

2. Click **Customer** in the Tables list box, click the **Add** button, click **Order**, click the **Add** button, then click the **Close** button. Access places the Customer and Order field lists in the Query window and closes the Show Table dialog box. Note that the one-to-many relationship that exists between the two tables is shown in the Query window.

   You need to place the CustomerName, Street, City, and State fields from the Customer field list into the design grid, then place the BillingDate and InvoiceAmt fields from the Order field list into the design grid.

3. Double-click **CustomerName** in the Customer field list. Access places CustomerName in the design grid's first column Field text box.

4. Repeat Step 3 to add the **Street**, **City**, and **State** fields from the Customer table, then add the **BillingDate** and **InvoiceAmt** fields from the Order table, so that these fields are placed in the second through sixth columns of the design grid.

   Next you need to specify the sort order for the query.

5. Click the CustomerName's **Sort** text box, click the **Sort** list arrow, then click **Ascending**. The query results will be sorted in ascending order by the value in the CustomerName field.

   The query specifications are complete, and you can now run the query.

6. Click the **Run** button on the Query Design toolbar. Access runs the query and displays the results in the datasheet. See Figure 4-83.

Figure 4-83
Datasheet for the query based on the Customer and Order tables

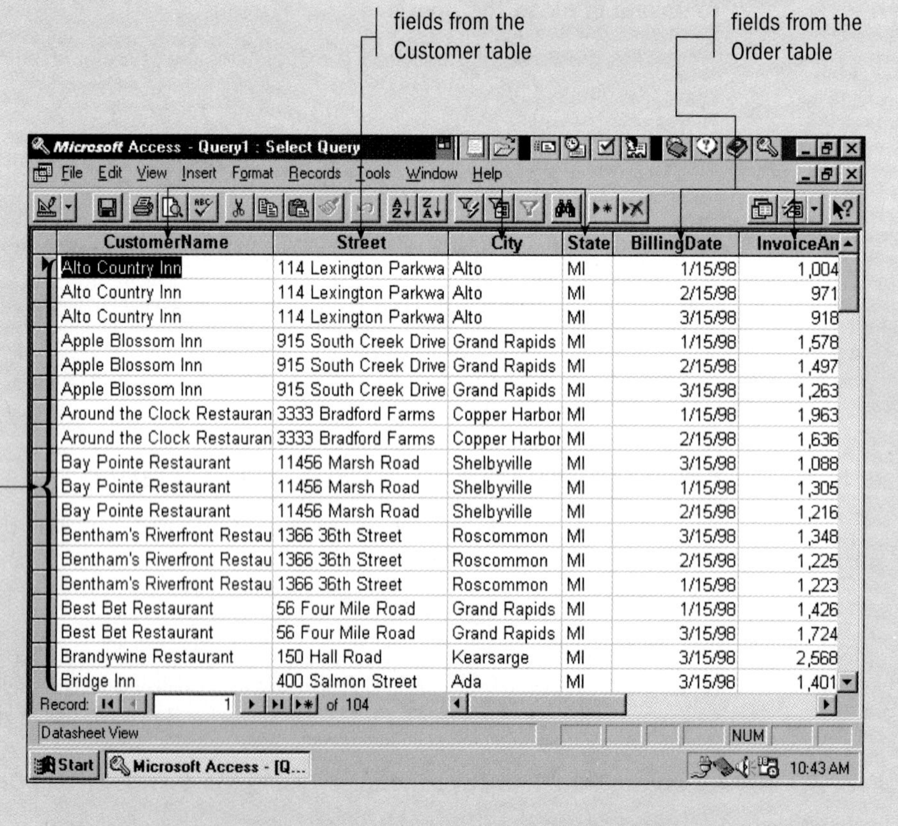

CustomerName	Street	City	State	BillingDate	InvoiceAn
Alto Country Inn	114 Lexington Parkwa	Alto	MI	1/15/98	1,004
Alto Country Inn	114 Lexington Parkwa	Alto	MI	2/15/98	971
Alto Country Inn	114 Lexington Parkwa	Alto	MI	3/15/98	918
Apple Blossom Inn	915 South Creek Drive	Grand Rapids	MI	1/15/98	1,578
Apple Blossom Inn	915 South Creek Drive	Grand Rapids	MI	2/15/98	1,497
Apple Blossom Inn	915 South Creek Drive	Grand Rapids	MI	3/15/98	1,263
Around the Clock Restauran	3333 Bradford Farms	Copper Harboı	MI	1/15/98	1,963
Around the Clock Restauran	3333 Bradford Farms	Copper Harboı	MI	2/15/98	1,636
Bay Pointe Restaurant	11456 Marsh Road	Shelbyville	MI	3/15/98	1,088
Bay Pointe Restaurant	11456 Marsh Road	Shelbyville	MI	1/15/98	1,305
Bay Pointe Restaurant	11456 Marsh Road	Shelbyville	MI	2/15/98	1,216
Bentham's Riverfront Restau	1366 36th Street	Roscommon	MI	3/15/98	1,348
Bentham's Riverfront Restau	1366 36th Street	Roscommon	MI	2/15/98	1,225
Bentham's Riverfront Restau	1366 36th Street	Roscommon	MI	1/15/98	1,223
Best Bet Restaurant	56 Four Mile Road	Grand Rapids	MI	1/15/98	1,426
Best Bet Restaurant	56 Four Mile Road	Grand Rapids	MI	3/15/98	1,724
Brandywine Restaurant	150 Hall Road	Kearsarge	MI	3/15/98	2,568
Bridge Inn	400 Salmon Street	Ada	MI	3/15/98	1,401

records sorted in ascending order

The records are displayed in ascending order according to the field values in the CustomerName field. Only the six selected fields from the Customer and Order tables appear in the datasheet.

7. Click the **Save** button on the Query Datasheet toolbar. The Save As dialog box opens.

8. Type **Customer Orders** in the Query Name text box, then press the **Enter** key. Access saves the query with the specified name and displays the name in the Query window title bar.

Barbara remembers that one of Valle Coffee's customers, the Cottage Grill restaurant, has moved to a different location in the same town. She asks you to change the value of the Street field in the Customer table for this customer. To make this change, you'll use the query datasheet.

Changing Data Using a Query

When viewing the results of a query, you can use the query datasheet to maintain data in a database. You need to change the Street field value for the Cottage Grill customer. The new street address for this customer is 82 Mix Avenue.

To change the field value using the query:

1. Scroll the vertical scroll bar until the three datasheet records for the Cottage Grill are visible on your screen.

2. Highlight **10 Brand** in the Street field value for the first of the three Cottage Grill records. See Figure 4-84.

Figure 4-84 Changing data using the query datasheet

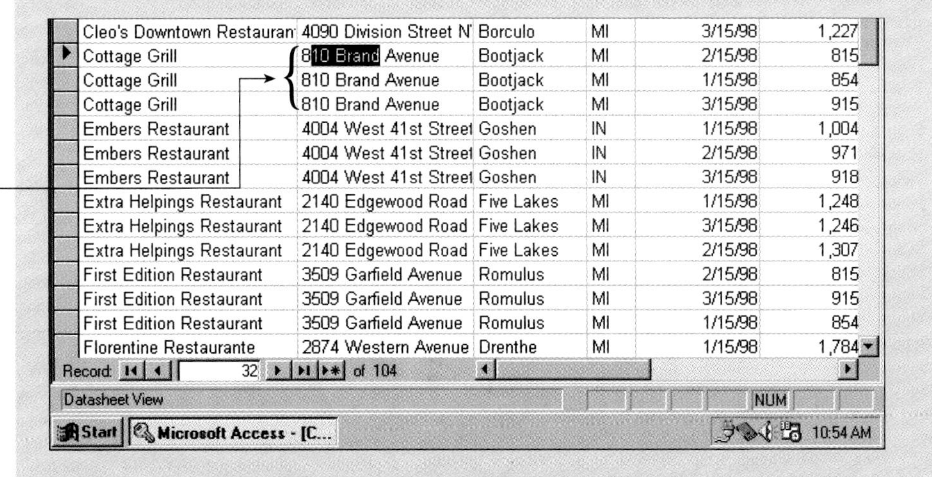

Cleo's Downtown Restauran	4090 Division Street N	Borculo	MI	3/15/98	1,227
Cottage Grill	810 Brand Avenue	Bootjack	MI	2/15/98	815
Cottage Grill	810 Brand Avenue	Bootjack	MI	1/15/98	854
Cottage Grill	810 Brand Avenue	Bootjack	MI	3/15/98	915
Embers Restaurant	4004 West 41st Street	Goshen	IN	1/15/98	1,004
Embers Restaurant	4004 West 41st Street	Goshen	IN	2/15/98	971
Embers Restaurant	4004 West 41st Street	Goshen	IN	3/15/98	918
Extra Helpings Restaurant	2140 Edgewood Road	Five Lakes	MI	1/15/98	1,248
Extra Helpings Restaurant	2140 Edgewood Road	Five Lakes	MI	3/15/98	1,246
Extra Helpings Restaurant	2140 Edgewood Road	Five Lakes	MI	2/15/98	1,307
First Edition Restaurant	3509 Garfield Avenue	Romulus	MI	2/15/98	815
First Edition Restaurant	3509 Garfield Avenue	Romulus	MI	3/15/98	915
First Edition Restaurant	3509 Garfield Avenue	Romulus	MI	1/15/98	854
Florentine Restaurante	2874 Western Avenue	Drenthe	MI	1/15/98	1,784

3. Type **2**, press the **spacebar**, type **Mix**, then position the insertion point anywhere in the previous record's Street field value.

   The Street field value for Cottage Grill appears just once in the database, specifically in the Customer table. The change you made in the query datasheet is actually made in the Customer table. Because all three records for Cottage Grill take their value for the Street field from the one value in the Customer table, they each change to "82 Mix Avenue" when you change only one occurrence of the Street value in the datasheet.

   Barbara wants a printed copy of the query results to take with her to a meeting with her staff members.

4. Click the **Print** button on the Query Datasheet toolbar to print one copy of the datasheet with the current settings.

Barbara has no further requests for information, so you can now exit Access.

5. Click the **Close** button [X] on the Access window title bar to close the query and the Restaurant Business database, and to exit Access.

Barbara is pleased with the design and contents of the Restaurant Business database. The three forms you created—Order Data, Customer Data, and Customer Orders—will make it easy for her staff members to find and update data in the Order and Customer tables. And, the Customers and Orders report will allow her to print and distribute important customer and order data to other Valle Coffee employees. Barbara also knows that her staff members, as well as Carlos and other production staff personnel, can easily query the database to display specific information they want to view.

Quick Check

1. When you use the Report Wizard, the report name is also used as the ________.
2. What is a select query?
3. Describe the rows that appear in the design grid for a query.
4. How are a table datasheet and a query datasheet similar? How are they different?
5. A(n) ________ is a criterion, or rule, that determines which records are selected for a query datasheet.
6. For a date/time field, what is ascending sort order?

Tutorial Assignments

Barbara needs a database to track the coffee products offered by Valle Coffee. She asks you to create the database by completing the following:

1. Make sure your Student Disk is in the disk drive, then create a database named Valle Products in the TAssign folder within the Tutorial.04 folder on your Student Disk.
2. Create a table named Product using the table design shown in Figure 4-85.

Figure 4-85

Field Name	Data Type	Description	Field Size	Other Properties
ProductCode	Text	primary key	4	
CoffeeCode	Text	foreign key	4	
Price	Currency	price for this product		Format: Fixed Decimal Places: 2
Decaf	Text	D if decaf, Null if regular	1	Default Value: D
BackOrdered	Yes/No	back-ordered from supplier?		

3. Add the product records shown in Figure 4-86 to the Product table.

Figure 4-86

ProductCode	CoffeeCode	Price	Decaf	BackOrdered
2316	JRUM	8.99		Yes
9754	HAZL	40.00	D	No
9309	COCO	9.99	D	No

4. Make the following changes to the structure of the Product table:
   a. Add a new field between the CoffeeCode and Price fields, using these properties:
      Field Name: WeightCode
      Data Type: Text
      Field Size: 1
      Description: foreign key
   b. Move the BackOrdered field so that it appears between the WeightCode and Price fields.
5. Use the Product datasheet to update the database as follows:
   a. Enter these WeightCode values for the three records: A for ProductCode 2316, A for ProductCode 9309, and E for ProductCode 9754.
   b. Add a record to the Product datasheet with these field values:
      ProductCode: 9729
      CoffeeCode: COLS
      WeightCode: E
      BackOrdered: No
      Price: 37.50
      Decaf: D
6. Barbara created a database with her name as the database name. The Coffee Product table in that database has the same format as the Product table you created. Copy all the records from the Coffee Product table in the Barbara database to the end of your Product table.
7. Delete the record with the ProductCode 2333 from the Product table.
8. Delete the BackOrdered field from the Product table.
9. Resize all columns in the datasheet for the Product table. Scroll the datasheet to make sure all field values are fully displayed. For any field values that are not fully displayed, make sure the field values are visible on the screen, then resize the appropriate columns again.
10. Print the first page of data from the Product table datasheet.
11. Create a table named Weight based on the data shown in Figure 4-87.

EXPLORE

Figure 4-87

WeightCode	Weight/Size
A	1 lb pkg
B	6 lb case
C	24 ct 1.5 oz pkg
D	44 ct 1.25 oz pkg
E	44 ct 1.5 oz pkg
F	88 ct 1.25 oz pkg
G	88 ct 1.5 oz pkg

   a. Select Datasheet View in the New Table dialog box.
   b. Enter the seven records shown in Figure 4-87.
   c. Switch to Design view, supply the table name, then answer No if asked if you want to create a primary key.
   d. Type the field names and set the properties as follows:

      WeightCode
      Field Size: 1
      Description: primary key

      Weight/Size
      Field Size: 17
      Description: weight in pounds or size in packages (number and weight) per case

e. Select the primary key, save the table structure changes, then switch back to Datasheet view. If you receive any warning messages, answer Yes to continue.
f. Resize both datasheet columns to fit the data; then save, print, and close the datasheet.

12. Create a table named Coffee using the Import Table wizard. The table you need to import is named Coffee.dbf and is located in the TAssign folder within the Tutorial.04 folder on your Student Disk. This table has a dBASE 5 file type. After importing the table, complete the following:
    a. Change all field names to use the Valle Coffee convention of uppercase and lowercase letters, then enter the following Description property values:
       CoffeeCode: primary key
       Decaf: Is decaf available for this coffee?
    b. Change the Format property of the Decaf field to Yes/No.
    c. Select the primary key, then save the table structure changes.
    d. In response to the warning about duplicate indexes, click the OK button, click the Indexes button on the toolbar, delete the PRIMARYKEY row in the Indexes dialog box, close the dialog box, then save the table structure.
    e. Switch to Datasheet view, then resize all columns in the datasheet to fit the data.
    f. Save, print, then close the datasheet.
13. Use the AutoForm: Tabular Wizard to create a form based on the Weight table. Save the form as "Weight Data" then print and close the form.
14. Use the Form Wizard to create a form based on the Product table. Select all fields for the form, the Columnar layout, the Stone style, and the title name of Product Data.
15. Using the form you created in the previous step, print the fifth form record, change the AutoFormat to Standard, save the changed form, then print the fifth form record again.
16. Use the Product Data form to update the Product table as follows:
    a. Navigate to the record with the ProductCode 2310. Change the field values for CoffeeCode to BRUM, WeightCode to A, Price to 8.99, and Decaf to Null for this record.
    b. Use the Find command to move to the record with the ProductCode 4306, then delete the record.
    c. Add a new record with the following field values:
       ProductCode: 2306
       CoffeeCode: AMAR
       WeightCode: A
       Price: 8.99
       Decaf: Null

       Print only this form record.
17. Define a one-to-many relationship between the primary Coffee table and the related Product table, and then define a one-to-many relationship between the primary Weight table and the related Product table. Select the referential integrity option and both cascade options for both relationships.
18. Use the Form Wizard to create a form containing a main form and a subform. Select the CoffeeName and CoffeeType fields from the Coffee table for the main form, and select all fields except CoffeeCode from the Product table for the subform. Use the Tabular layout and the Standard style. Specify the title Coffee Products for the main form and the title Product Subform for the subform. Print the fourth main form record and its subform records.

19. Use the Report Wizard to create a report based on the primary Coffee table and the related Product table. Select the CoffeeName field from the Coffee table, and select the ProductCode, WeightCode, Price, and Decaf fields from the Product table. View the data by the CoffeeName field in the Coffee table, and do not add any grouping levels. Select an ascending sort based on the ProductCode field, the Align Left 1 layout, the Soft Gray style, and the title Coffee Products. Print the first page of the report.
20. Create a select query based on the Product table. Display the ProductCode, WeightCode, and Price fields; sort in descending order based on the Price field values; and select only those records whose CoffeeCode equals KENP. Save the query as KENP Coffee, then run the query. For the record with the ProductCode 2322, change the WeightCode to A and the Price to 8.99, then print the query datasheet.

21. Create a select query based on the Coffee, Product, and Weight tables. Display the CoffeeType, CoffeeName, ProductCode, Price, and Weight/Size fields, in this order. Sort in ascending order based on the CoffeeType field values, then sort in ascending order based on the CoffeeName field values. Select only those records whose CoffeeType equals "Special Import." Resize all columns in the datasheet to fit the data. Save the query as Special Imports, print the datasheet, then close the query.

Case Problems

1. Ashbrook Mall Information Desk Leticia Perez, director of the Mall Operations Office at Ashbrook Mall, oversees all mall operations, including the work performed by the Information Desk staff. To streamline the work performed by the Information Desk staff, she wants you to create a database for the catalog of current job openings at stores within the mall. Create the database by completing the following:

1. Make sure your Student Disk is in the disk drive, then create a database named Ashbrook Job Openings in the Cases folder within the Tutorial.04 folder on your Student Disk.
2. Create a table named Store using the table design shown in Figure 4-88.

Figure 4-88

Field Name	Data Type	Description	Field Size
Location	Text		3
Store	Text	primary key	3
StoreName	Text		30

3. Add the store records shown in Figure 4-89 to the Store table.

Figure 4-89

Location	Store	StoreName
A1	PS	Pinson Shoes
C1	WT	White's
D1	BR	Brennan's Cafe
C2	TH	Theatricks
B2	BE	Broiler Express
D3	TC	Taco City
C5	OI	Original Imports
B5	JB	Julie's Boutique
A2	SW	Sports World

4. Resize all columns in the datasheet for the Store table to their best fit.
5. Change the structure of the Store table by moving the Location field so that it follows the StoreName field.
6. Use the Store datasheet to update the database as follows:
   a. For Store BE, change the StoreName to Book Emporium and the Location to A3. Resize the StoreName column to its best fit.
   b. Add a record to the Store datasheet with the following field values:
      Store: JP
      StoreName: Just Purses
      Location: D2
   c. Delete the record for Store OI.
7. Print the entire Store table datasheet.
8. Create a table named Job using the Import Table wizard. The table you need to import is named Jobs.DB and is located in the Cases folder within the Tutorial.04 folder on your Student Disk. This table has a Paradox file type. After importing the table, complete the following:
   a. In Design view, enter the following Description property values:
      Job: primary key
      Store: foreign key
   b. Select the primary key, then save the table structure changes.
   c. Switch to Datasheet view, then resize all columns in the datasheet to fit the data.
   d. Save, print, then close the table.
   e. Rename the table as Job. (*Hint:* use the shortcut menu for the table in the Database window.)
9. Use the Form Wizard to create a form based on the Store table. Select all fields for the form, the Columnar layout, and the Clouds style. Specify the title Store Data for the form.
10. Use the Store Data form to add a new record with the following field values:
    Store: BC
    StoreName: Big Cookies
    Location: B4

    Print only this form record.
11. Define a one-to-many relationship between the primary Store table and the related Job table. Select the referential integrity option and both cascade options for the relationship.
12. Create a select query based on the Store and Job tables. Display the StoreName, Location, Position, and Hours/Week fields, in this order. Sort in ascending order based on the StoreName field values. Save the query as Store Jobs, print the datasheet, then close the query.

13. Use the Report Wizard to create a report based on the Store Jobs query. Select the Location, StoreName, Position, and Hours/Week fields, in this order, from the query. View the data by Job, do not add any grouping levels, then sort in ascending order based on the StoreName field values. Select the Tabular layout, the Bold style, and the title Available Jobs. Print the entire report.

2. Professional Litigation User Services Raj Jawahir, a new employee at PLUS, is now responsible for tracking the daily payments received from the firm's clients. He asks you to create a database by completing the following:

1. Make sure your Student Disk is in the disk drive, then create a database named PLUS Payments in the Cases folder within the Tutorial.04 folder on your Student Disk.

2. Create a table named Payment using the table design shown in Figure 4-90.

Figure 4-90 

Field Name	Data Type	Description	Field Size	Other Properties
Payment#	Text	primary key	5	
Deposit#	Text		3	
Firm#	Text	foreign key	4	
AmtPaid	Currency			Format: Standard Decimal Places: 2 Default Value: 0
DatePaid	Date/Time			Format: Medium Date

3. Add the payment records shown in Figure 4-91 to the Payment table.

Figure 4-91 

Payment#	Deposit#	Firm#	AmtPaid	DatePaid
10031	103	1147	2435.00	6/3/98
10002	100	1100	1300.00	6/1/98
10015	101	1142	2000.00	6/1/98

4. Raj created a database named PlusPays that contains recent payments in the Payment Records table. The Payment table you created has the same format as the Payment Records table. Copy all the records from the Payment Records table in the PlusPays database to the end of your Payment table.
5. Resize all columns in the datasheet for the Payment table to their best fit.
6. Print the first page of data from the Payment table datasheet.

7. Create a table named Firm using the Import Table wizard. The table you need to import is named Firm.dbf and is located in the Cases folder within the Tutorial.04 folder on your Student Disk. This table has a Microsoft FoxPro file type. After importing the table, complete the following:
   a. Change the field names to Firm# and FirmName, enter a Description property value of "primary key" for the Firm# field, select the primary key, then save the table structure changes.
   b. Switch to Datasheet view, then resize the columns in the datasheet to fit the data.
   c. Save, print, then close the table.
8. Define a one-to-many relationship between the primary Firm table and the related Payment table. Select the referential integrity option and both cascade options for the relationship.
9. Use the Form Wizard to create a form containing a main form and a subform. Select the Firm# and FirmName fields from the Firm table for the main form, and select all fields except Firm# from the Payment table for the subform. Use the Datasheet layout and the Flax style. Specify the title Firm Payments for the main form and the title Payment Subform for the subform. Print the first main form record and its displayed subform records.
10. For the form you just created, change the AutoFormat to Colorful 2, save the changed form, then print the first main form record and its displayed subform records.
11. Use the Report Wizard to create a report based on the Firm and Payment tables. Select the Firm# and FirmName fields from the Firm table, and select the Payment#, Deposit#, AmtPaid, and DatePaid fields from the Payment table. Use the defaults for viewing the data and for grouping levels. Select an ascending sort based on the Payment# field, choose the Align Left 1 layout and the Casual style, and enter the title Firm Payments. Print the first page of the report.

12. Create a select query based on the Firm and Payment tables. Display the Firm#, FirmName, AmtPaid, and DatePaid fields, in this order. Sort in descending order based on the AmtPaid field values. Select only those records whose AmtPaid is greater than 2,400.00. Save the query as Large Payments, print the datasheet, then close the query.

3. Best Friends Because of the growing popularity in Dog Walk-A-Thons, Richard Moscovitch has asked you to create a database to track walker and pledge data for Best Friends. Complete the following:

1. Make sure your Student Disk is in the disk drive, then create a database named Walk-A-Thon in the Cases folder within the Tutorial.04 folder on your Student Disk.
2. Create a table named Walker using the table design shown in Figure 4-92.

Figure 4-92

Field Name	Data Type	Description	Field Size	Other Properties
WalkerID	Text	primary key	3	
WalkerName	Text		25	Required: Yes
Phone	Text		8	

3. Add the participant records shown in Figure 4-93 to the Walker table.

Figure 4-93

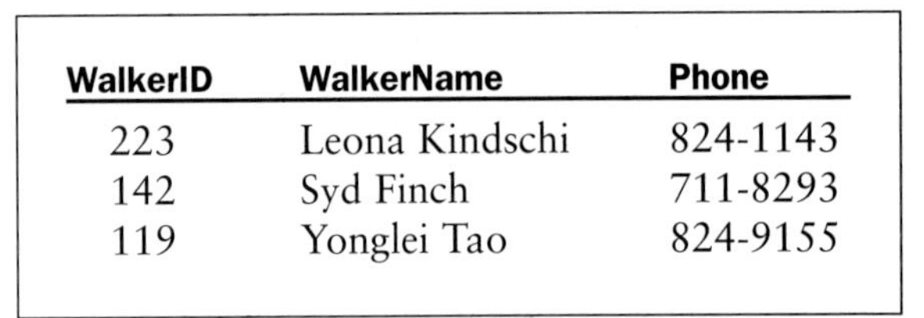

WalkerID	WalkerName	Phone
223	Leona Kindschi	824-1143
142	Syd Finch	711-8293
119	Yonglei Tao	824-9155

4. Make the following changes to the Walker table:
   a. Change the table structure by adding two fields between the WalkerName and Phone fields. The first field, named LastName, is a 15-character text field; set its Required property to Yes. The second field, named FirstName, is a 12-character text field.
   b. Save the table structure. (Answer Yes if you receive any warning messages in this step or any subsequent step.) Use the values for the WalkerName field to enter the appropriate field values for the two new fields in the table datasheet.
   c. Delete the WalkerName field from the table structure.
   d. Add a field named Distance to the end of the table structure; assign the following property values to the Distance field:
      Data Type: Number
      Description: distance walker covered
      Field Size: Single
      Format: Fixed
      Decimal Places: 1
   e. Use the Access Help system to learn about the Validation Rule and Validation Text properties. For the Distance field, enter a Validation Rule property value to prevent the entry of negative numbers, then set the Validation Text property to "Must not be a negative number."
   f. Save the table structure, then enter the following values for the Distance field:
      Tao: 2.3
      Finch: 2.3
      Kindschi: 0.7

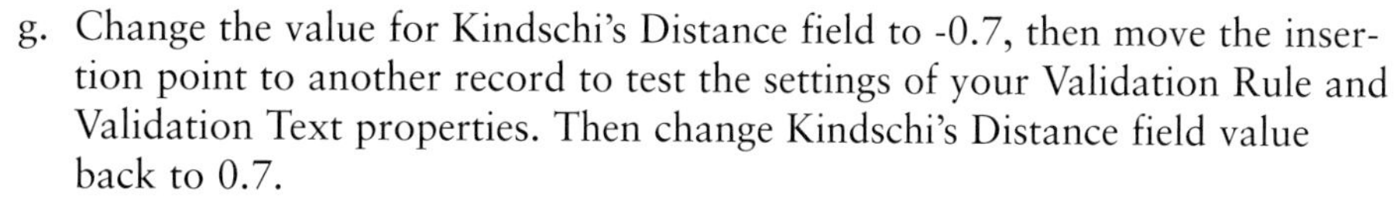

g. Change the value for Kindschi's Distance field to -0.7, then move the insertion point to another record to test the settings of your Validation Rule and Validation Text properties. Then change Kindschi's Distance field value back to 0.7.

h. Resize all columns in the datasheet for the table to their best fit.

5. Create a table named Pledge using the Import Table wizard. The table you need to import is named Pledge.DB and is located in the Cases folder within the Tutorial.04 folder on your Student Disk. This table has a Paradox file type. After importing the table, complete the following:
   a. In Design view, enter the following Description property values:
      Pledge#: primary key
      WalkerID: foreign key
      PerMile: amount pledged per mile
   b. Select the primary key, then save the table structure changes.
   c. Switch to Datasheet view, then resize all columns in the datasheet to fit the data.
   d. Save, print, then close the table.
6. Use the AutoForm: Tabular Wizard to create a form based on the Walker table. Save the form as Walker Data then use the form to update the Walker table as follows:
   a. For the record with the WalkerID 223, change the LastName to King and the Distance to 0.
   b. Add a new record with the following values:
      WalkerID: 101
      LastName: Wattros
      FirstName: Gretchen
      Phone: 824-1880
      Distance: 2.0
   c. Delete the record with the WalkerID field value of 119.
7. Use the Walker Data form to print all the records in the Walker table.
8. Change the AutoFormat of the Walker Data form to Dusk, save the changed form, then use the form to print all the records in the Walker table.
9. Define a one-to-many relationship between the primary Walker table and the related Pledge table. Select the referential integrity option and both cascade options for the relationship.

10. Use the Find Unmatched Query Wizard to find all records in the Walker table that have no matching records in the Pledge table. Display all fields from the Walker table in the query datasheet, and enter a query name of Walkers Without Pledges. Print the query datasheet.

11. Create a select query based on the Walker table. Display all fields from the Walker table in the same order as they appear in the table. Save the query as Walker Data, run the query, then add a new record with the following values:
    WalkerID: 224
    LastName: Young
    FirstName: Albert
    Phone: 881-9827
    Distance: 2.3
    Print the query datasheet.

4. Balanced Businesses Balanced Businesses is a national service organization that maintains and balances the financial records of small businesses. You'll create a database to track the outstanding checks for the organization's clients. The data in your database consists of business ID, business name, bank account number, bank ID, bank name, check number, check amount, check date, and a field to indicate whether the check has cleared or is still outstanding. Complete the following to create the database:

1. Design the database. For each table, list the fields and their properties, such as field names, data types, descriptions, field sizes, and formats.
2. Create a new Access database named Balanced Businesses, then create the tables.
3. Define one-to-many relationships between appropriate tables.
4. Create forms to maintain data on businesses, banks, bank accounts, and checks.
5. Create test data for each table in the database and add the data, using the forms you created in Step 4.
6. Create a report that lists all cleared checks by business. For each cleared check print the business name, bank name, bank ID, bank account number, check number, check amount, and check date. Print the entire report.
7. Create a report that lists outstanding checks by business. For each outstanding check print the business name, bank name, bank ID, bank account number, check number, check amount, and check date. Print the entire report.

Lab Assignment

This Lab Assignment is designed to accompany the interactive Course Lab called Databases. To start the Databases Lab, click the Start button on the Windows 95 taskbar, point to Programs, point to Course Labs, point to New Perspectives Applications, and click Databases. If you do not see Course Labs on your Programs menu, see your instructor or lab manager.

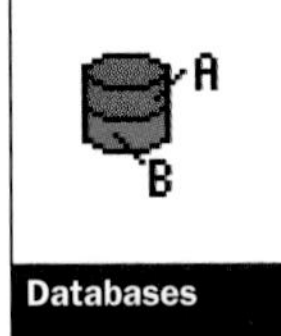

Databases

Databases This Databases Lab demonstrates the essential concepts of file and database management systems. You will use the Lab to search, sort, and report the data contained in a file of classic books.

1. Click the Steps button to review basic database terminology and to learn how to manipulate the classic books database. As you proceed through the Steps, answer the Quick Check questions that appear. After you complete the Steps, you will see a Quick Check Report. Follow the instructions on the screen to print this report.

2. Click the Explore button. Make sure you can apply basic database terminology to describe the classic books database by answering the following questions:

a. How many records does the file contain?
b. How many fields does each record contain?
c. What are the contents of the Catalog # field for the book written by Margaret Mitchell?
d. What are the contents of the Title field for the record with Thoreau in the Author field?
e. Which field has been used to sort the records?

3. In Explore, manipulate the database as necessary to answer the following questions:

a. When the books are sorted by title, what is the first record in the file?
b. Use the Search button to search for all the books in the West location. How many do you find?
c. Use the Search button to search for all the books in the Main location that are checked in. What do you find?

4. In Explore, use the Report button to print out a report that groups the books by Status and sorted by Title. On your report, circle the four field names. Draw a box around the summary statistics showing which books are currently checked in and which books are currently checked out.

TUTORIAL 5

PowerPoint Basics and Embedding an Excel Chart in a Presentation

Creating a Seminar Presentation with an Embedded Chart Showing Sales Data

OBJECTIVES

In this tutorial you will:

- Create a presentation using a design template
- Work in slide, outline, slide sorter, and notes pages views to add, edit, delete, and rearrange slides
- Use the Drawing toolbar to add and change shapes
- Insert, resize, and recolor a clip art picture
- Add animation effects
- Embed an Excel chart in a presentation
- Insert slides from another presentation
- View a slide show and annotate slides during the slide show
- Create speaker's notes
- Print a presentation and its notes pages

Valle Coffee

Valle Coffee currently offers three seminars open to the public: Coffee I, Coffee II, and Espresso. Belinda Jones, who conducts many of the seminars, has already created a PowerPoint presentation for the Coffee I seminar. Now she wants you to create a PowerPoint presentation for the Coffee II seminar.

Belinda isn't certain of all the slides she needs for the presentation. She gives you the note cards she uses when she conducts the Coffee II seminar. She suggests that you use the note cards to begin developing an initial set of slides. Then she'll review and revise the slides as necessary.

SESSION 5.1

In this session you will start a new PowerPoint presentation using a design template, enter and edit text on slides, view the slide show, add and delete slides, and save the presentation.

Developing Effective PowerPoint Presentations

PowerPoint is a presentation program that allows you to create effective presentations in the form of black-and-white or color overheads, 35-mm photographic slides, or on-screen slides. On-screen slide shows can even include sounds, music, photos, media clips, and special animation effects.

A PowerPoint **presentation** is a document, or file, that contains a related collection of slides, audience handouts, speaker's notes, and an outline. You can use PowerPoint to create all these presentation components.

A **slide** is a single image or picture that is part of the visual presentation. PowerPoint provides 24 predefined slide layouts: 1 title slide layout and 23 non-title slide layouts. A title slide usually contains one or more headings that introduce the presentation. Examples of non-title slide layouts include bulleted lists, graphs, and tables.

Two **masters** together control the formatting for all slides in a given presentation, thus making it easier to maintain a consistent "look" throughout the presentation. The **title master** contains any text and graphics that appear on all title slides in the presentation, as well as style definitions for title slide text. The **slide master**, which controls all non-title slides, includes text and graphics that appear on all non-title slides, as well as style definitions for all types and levels of slide text. The title master and slide master are provided in the **design template**, which also specifies a predefined color scheme and background layout for all the slides in a presentation. PowerPoint supplies a wide variety of professionally designed templates that you can use as given or modify to create a custom look—for example, to incorporate company colors or a company logo. If you don't want to use any of the supplied design templates, you can start with a **blank presentation**, for which you must design a background, color schemes, and text styles.

The following guidelines can help you develop effective PowerPoint presentations:

- Establish a single "look" for the presentation, and use a consistent color scheme and text style throughout the presentation.
- Identify the goal of the presentation and make sure each slide works toward that goal.
- Present one concept or idea per slide.
- Keep slides uncluttered. Too many words or graphics detract from the main point.
- Present information consistently. For example, if one item in a bulleted list is a complete sentence, all items in the list should be complete sentences.
- Display the same type of information in the same location on each slide. For example, bulleted items should appear in the same location on each slide in the presentation. Information that appears to "jump" from slide to slide can be jarring and confusing to viewers.
- Don't include too many slides in a presentation. As a general rule, 7 to 10 slides are sufficient for a medium-length presentation. If your presentation includes more than 12 slides, consider removing any slide that is not absolutely necessary.
- Keep in mind that the purpose of presentation slides is to supplement, clarify, or highlight the speaker's words, not replace them.

Planning a Presentation

Planning the presentation before you create it will save you time and effort, and will improve the quality of the resulting presentation. As you develop your presentation plan, keep in mind the goal of the presentation and the needs of the audience.

The first step in planning is to decide what slides you will include and what each slide will contain. Then, you sketch on paper how you want each slide to look. If you plan to include a special image such as a drawing, picture, graph, or table on a particular slide, sketch a simple outline of the image; at this point, you are more concerned with the content, positioning, and approximate size of any images than with specific image details.

Based on Belinda's seminar notes, your initial design consists of six slides, as shown in Figure 5-1. Note that the last slide is blank. As you learned in Tutorial 1, a blank slide is often placed as the last slide to signal the end of the presentation.

Figure 5-1 Initial sketch of presentation slides

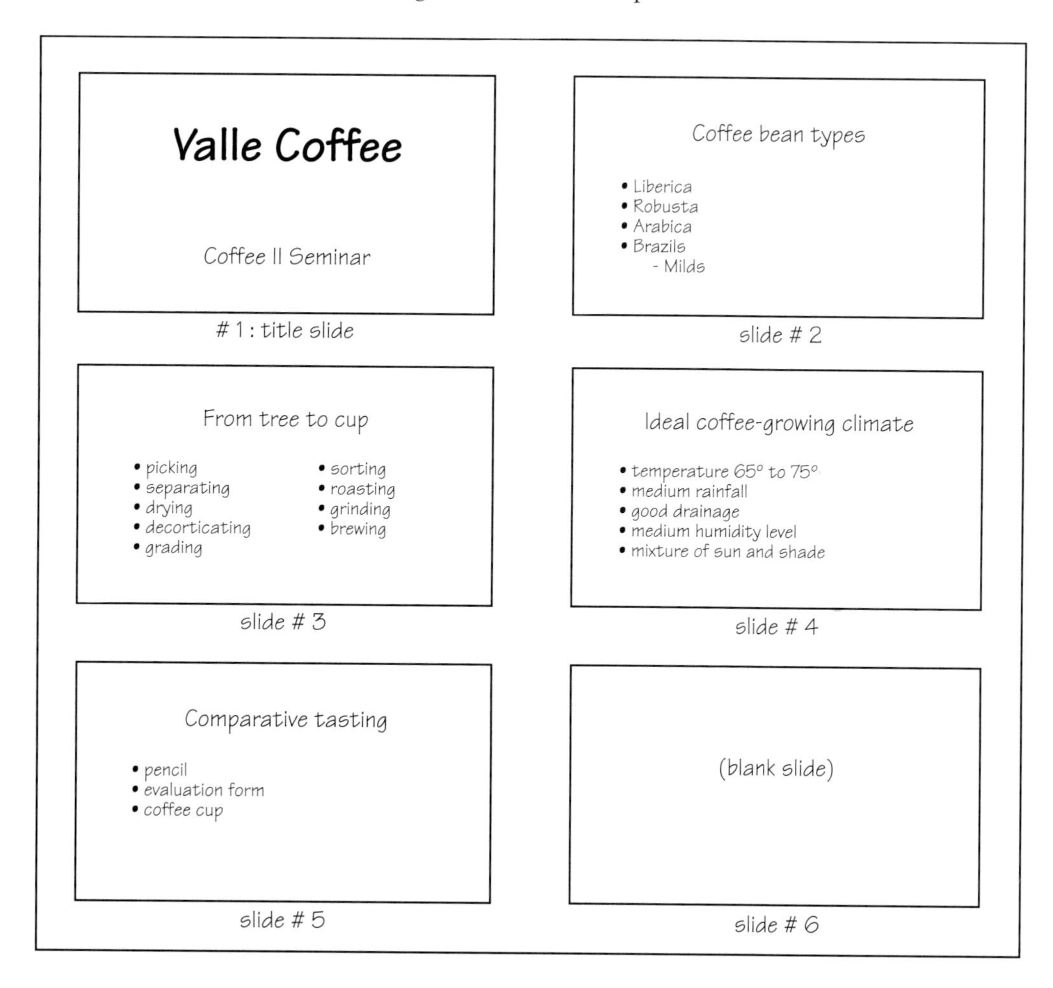

Next, you should consider the "look" you want for the presentation. Do you plan to include a significant object, such as a logo or company name, on every slide? Most design templates have a background image, shape, or lines that could conflict with such an object. In that case, you might want to consider using a blank presentation and designing your own slide background, title and slide master layouts, color schemes, and text styles. If you start with a blank presentation, you can easily switch to a design template at any time.

In most cases you will choose to use a predefined design template. The PowerPoint design templates have been professionally designed to be attractive and aesthetically pleasing, and they greatly simplify the task of preparing slides. If you decide to use a design template, PowerPoint can display slide samples for each template to help you choose an appropriate one for your presentation. After you choose a design template, you can easily change to any other design template at any time.

Belinda wants the presentation as soon as possible, so you'll use a design template, and you will not include a graphic or logo on each slide.

Starting a New Presentation

Having completed your presentation plan, you are now ready to start creating the Coffee II seminar presentation for Belinda. The first step is to start a new presentation.

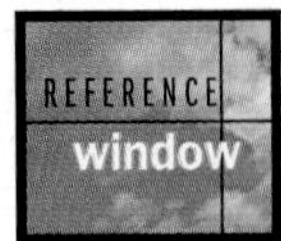

STARTING A NEW PRESENTATION

- Click the Start a New Document button on the Office Shortcut Bar.
- Click the Presentation Designs tab, then click a design template icon to select a design template.
- Click the OK button to close the New dialog box and start PowerPoint.

or

- Click the Start a New Document button on the Office Shortcut Bar.
- Click the General tab, then click the Blank Presentation icon to select a blank presentation.
- Click the OK button to close the New dialog box and start PowerPoint.

You plan to use one of PowerPoint's design templates for the Coffee II seminar, so you'll select a design template when you start a new presentation.

To start a new presentation using a design template:

1. Start Windows 95 and make sure the Office Shortcut Bar is displayed.

   TROUBLE? If you don't see the Office Shortcut Bar, click the Start button on the taskbar, point to Programs, then click Microsoft Office Shortcut Bar. If you don't see the Microsoft Office Shortcut Bar option on the Programs menu, ask your instructor or technical support person for help.

2. Insert your Student Disk in the disk drive.
3. Click the **Start a New Document** button on the Office Shortcut Bar. The New dialog box opens.
4. Click the **Presentation Designs** tab, then click the **Azure** icon to select that design template. A preview of the Azure design template is displayed in the Preview box. See Figure 5-2.

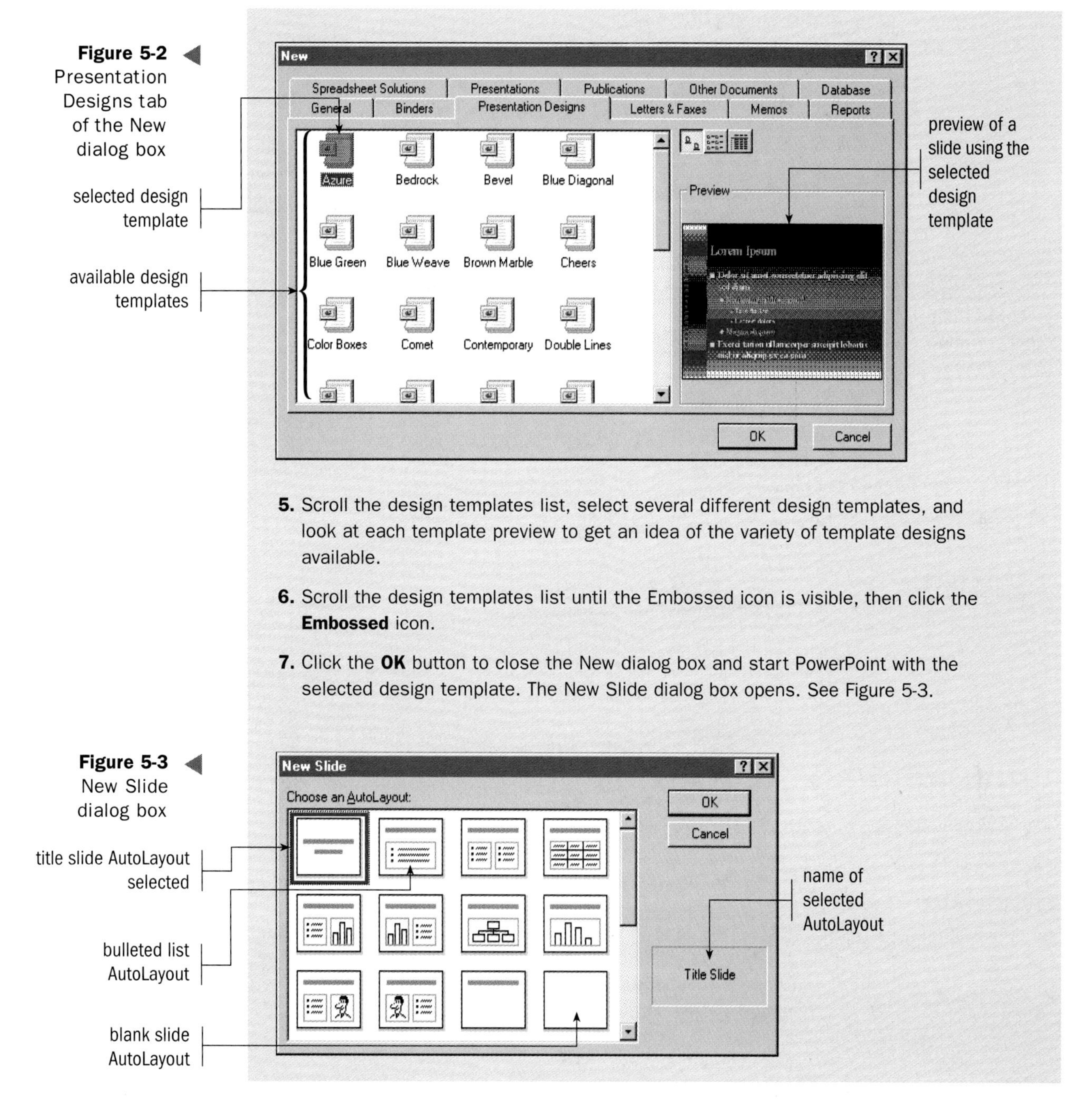

Figure 5-2 Presentation Designs tab of the New dialog box

5. Scroll the design templates list, select several different design templates, and look at each template preview to get an idea of the variety of template designs available.
6. Scroll the design templates list until the Embossed icon is visible, then click the **Embossed** icon.
7. Click the **OK** button to close the New dialog box and start PowerPoint with the selected design template. The New Slide dialog box opens. See Figure 5-3.

Figure 5-3 New Slide dialog box

You select a layout for a new slide using the New Slide dialog box, which presents the 24 available slide AutoLayouts. The first of these is for a title slide; the remaining AutoLayouts all relate to non-title slides. You would select the third AutoLayout in the second row, for example, if you wanted to create a new slide with an organization chart.

According to your presentation plan (Figure 5-1), slides 2 through 5 will contain bulleted lists, so the second or third layout in the top row would be appropriate for these slides. Slide 6 will be a blank slide like the last slide layout in the third row. The first slide in the presentation will be a title slide. You'll create this slide first.

To create the title slide:

1. If it is not already selected, click the first icon in the top row of the Choose an AutoLayout list box. The name of this AutoLayout, "Title Slide," is displayed in the lower-right corner of the dialog box.
2. Click the **OK** button to close the New Slide dialog box. The entire PowerPoint window is now visible, and the newly created title slide is displayed. By default, PowerPoint opens in slide view, which is one of the four available views. See Figure 5-4.

Figure 5-4 PowerPoint window

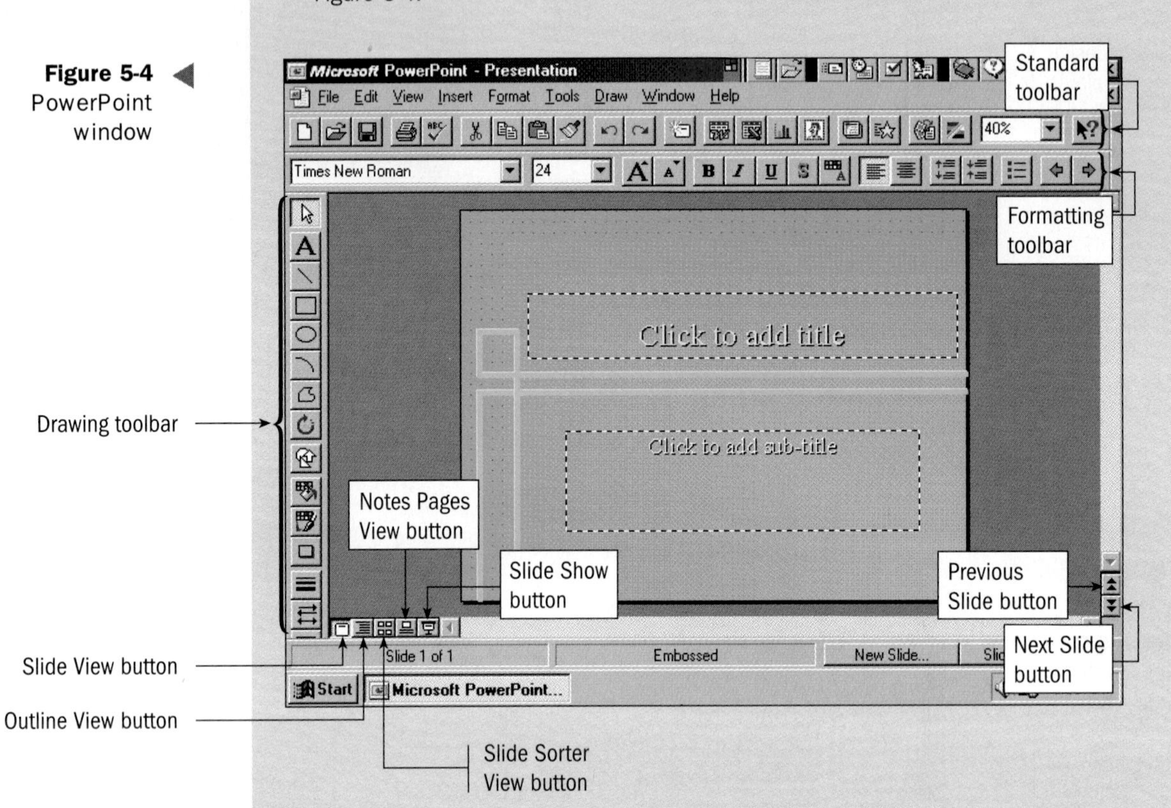

Review the components of the PowerPoint window, as identified in Figure 5-4. Your window might look slightly different from Figure 5-4, depending on the characteristics of your monitor. For example, you might be able to see one more button at the bottom of the Drawing toolbar.

Entering Text on a Slide

The title slide, the first slide in your presentation, is currently displayed in the PowerPoint window, but you have not yet entered any text on the slide. The window includes two **placeholders**, or areas of the slide reserved for entering text or graphics: one for the title and one for the subtitle.

As indicated in your slide plan, the words "Valle Coffee" will appear at the top of the slide as the slide title. The words "Coffee II Seminar" will be the slide subtitle.

To enter the text on the title slide:

1. Click the **title placeholder** then type **Valle Coffee**.

   TROUBLE? If you make a typing error while entering this or any other slide text, correct it as you would correct text in any other Office 95 program. Place the insertion point at the location of the mistake, use the Backspace or Delete key to remove any incorrect characters, then type the correct text.

2. Click the **subtitle placeholder** then type **Coffee II Seminar**. Your screen should now look like Figure 5-5.

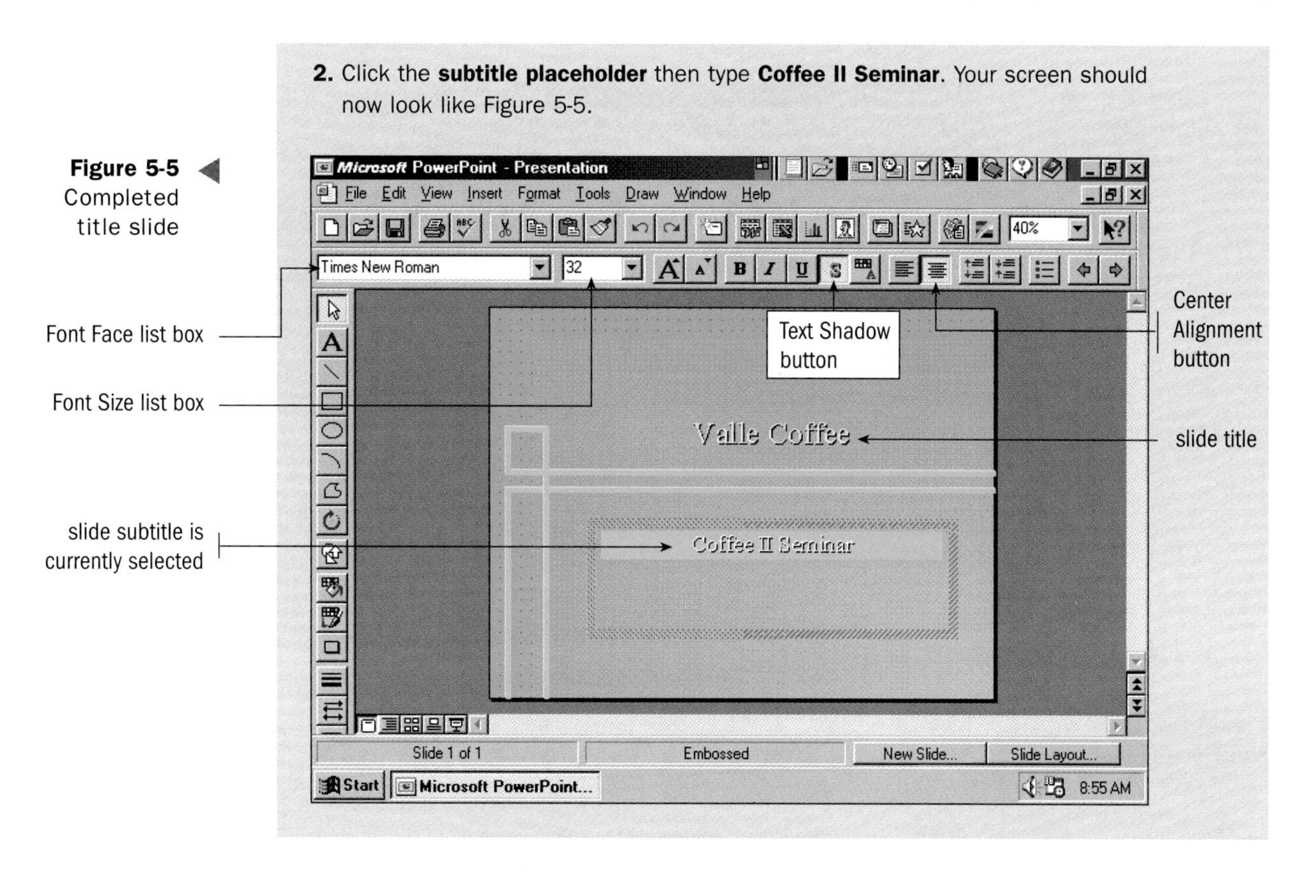

Figure 5-5 Completed title slide

Notice that the title text is yellow and is slightly larger than the subtitle text, which is white and is currently selected. The font of the subtitle is Times New Roman, as shown in the Font Face list box, and the font size of the subtitle is 32, as shown in the Font Size list box on the Formatting toolbar. Also on the Formatting toolbar, the Text Shadow button and Center Alignment button both appear pushed in and lighter, indicating that both are selected. Therefore, the text of the subtitle has a shadow effect and appears centered in the slide. The specific choices for text color, font face, font size, text shadow, and alignment for both the title slide's title and subtitle are specified in the title master of the selected design template.

You decide to make the "Valle Coffee" title slightly larger. You could select the title text on this slide and change its font size. Instead, you'll change the title master, so that any changes you make will also apply to any other title slides you might add to this presentation.

To edit the title master:

1. Click **View** on the menu bar, point to **Master**, then click **Title Master**. The title master is displayed. Five placeholders are visible on the title master, and the explanatory text in each is displayed in the format defined for that placeholder. Two of the placeholders, those for the master title and the master subtitle, correspond to the two placeholders that appeared on the title slide you created. The other three placeholders define areas for displaying optional slide information: a date, footer text, and a slide number.

2. Click the **master title style placeholder**. The Formatting toolbar display changes to show the current styles for the master title.

3. Click the **Font Size** list arrow on the Formatting toolbar, then click **48**. The font size of the master title style placeholder text changes from 44 to 48. See Figure 5-6.

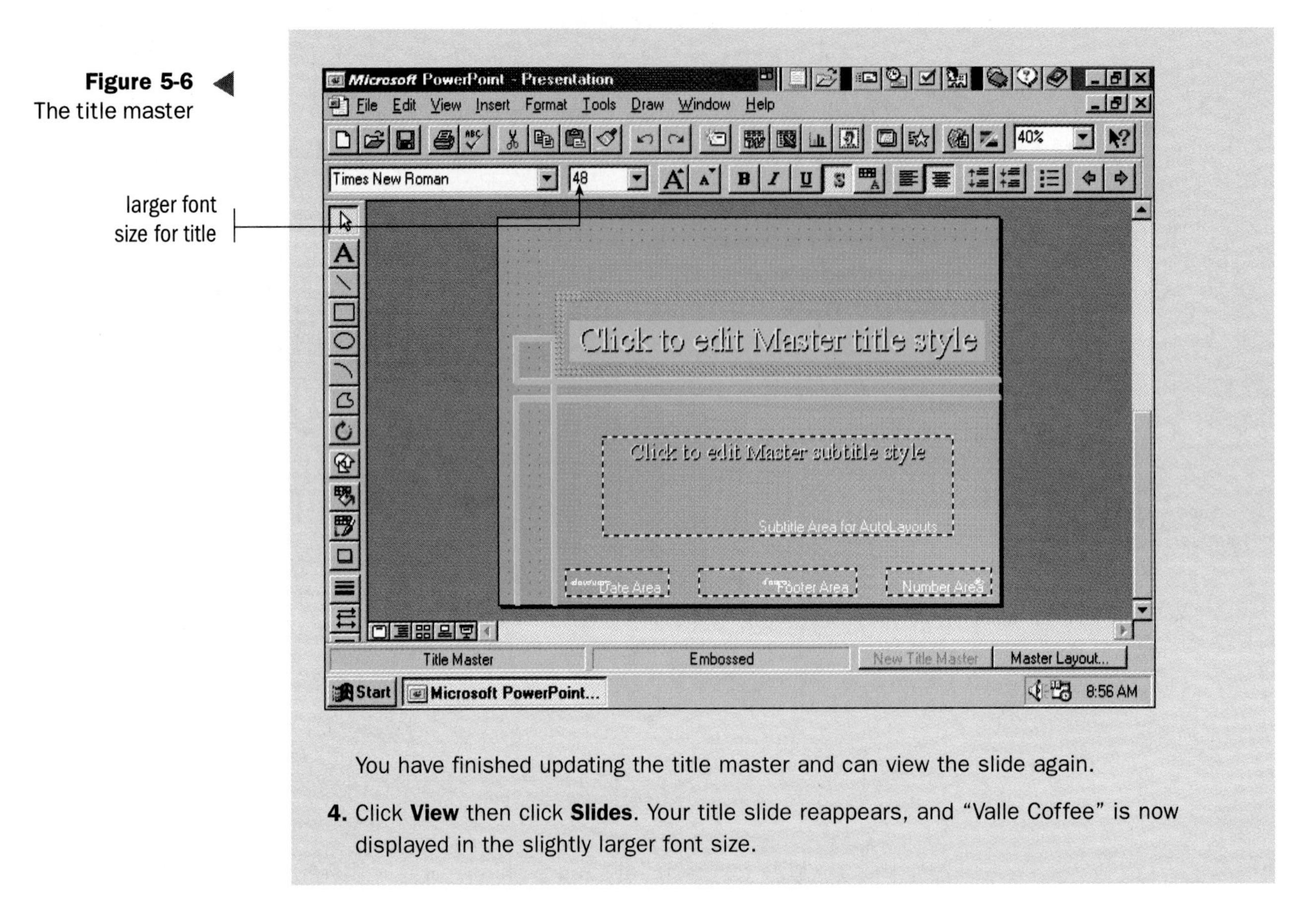

Figure 5-6 The title master

You have finished updating the title master and can view the slide again.

4. Click **View** then click **Slides**. Your title slide reappears, and "Valle Coffee" is now displayed in the slightly larger font size.

Adding Slides

Now that the title slide is finished, you are ready to add a second slide and enter the text for that slide. You can add slides in any view. You'll remain in slide view to add the next several slides.

Adding Slides in Slide View

To add a new slide to follow the current slide, you can either click the Insert New Slide button on the Standard toolbar or click the New Slide button on the status bar.

To add the second slide:

1. Click the **New Slide** button on the status bar. The New Slide dialog box opens.
2. If it is not already selected, click the second box in the first row to select the Bulleted List AutoLayout, then click the **OK** button. A new slide appears, with a placeholder for the slide title and a main text placeholder for the bulleted list. One bullet appears in the main text placeholder.
3. Click the **title placeholder** then type **Coffee bean types**.
4. Click the **main text placeholder**, type **Liberica**, then press the **Enter** key. A bullet appears for the next item in the list.
5. Type **Robusta** then press the **Enter** key.
6. Type **Arabica** then press the **Enter** key.
7. Type **Brazils** then press the **Enter** key.

The next text item to be entered is "Milds." Your plan shows this item as a second-level, or indented, item. To indent an item to the next level, you must *demote* the item.

8. Click the **Demote (Indent more)** button on the Formatting toolbar. The square bullet changes to a dash and is indented.
9. Type **Milds**.
10. Click anywhere in the blank area of the screen to deselect the main text placeholder. See Figure 5-7.

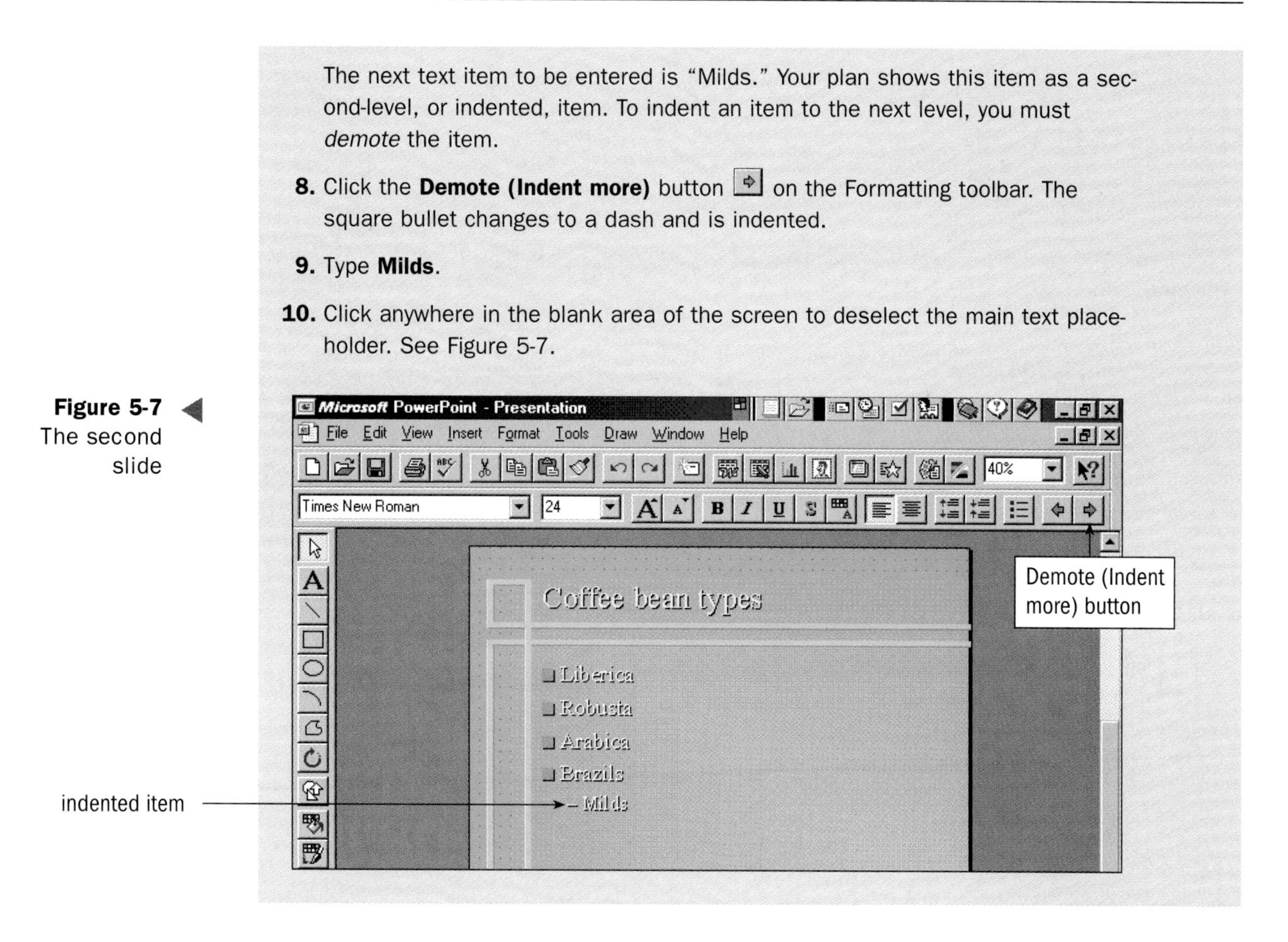

Figure 5-7 The second slide

Take a moment to examine the completed second slide. Did you notice the background for this non-title slide is slightly different from the title slide background? The horizontal embossing lines are positioned in the middle of the title slide; those same lines are nearer the top on this second slide. The text styles and the background and text colors are consistent, however. Many of the PowerPoint design templates feature some minor variation in the backgrounds for title slides versus non-title slides. Such a subtle difference adds a special interest to the title slide without undermining the presentation's overall consistent look.

Next you'll add the third slide, which contains a two-column bulleted list.

To add the third slide:

1. Click the **New Slide** button on the status bar. The New Slide dialog box opens.
2. Click the third box in the first row to select the 2 Column Text AutoLayout, then click the **OK** button. A new slide with the selected layout is displayed.
3. Click the **title placeholder** then type **From tree to cup**.
4. Click the leftmost **main text placeholder**, then type **picking**.
5. Press the **Enter** key then type **separating**.
6. Repeat Step 5 three times to enter **drying**, then **decorticating**, then **grading**. Do not press the Enter key after typing "grading."

   TROUBLE? If you accidentally pressed the Enter key after typing "grading," an extra bullet was added in the line following "grading." Press the Backspace key to remove the bullet.

7. Click the rightmost **main text placeholder**, then type **sorting**.
8. Press the **Enter** key then type **roasting**.

9. Repeat Step 8 two more times to enter **grinding**, then **brewing**. Do not press the Enter key after typing "brewing."

10. Click anywhere in the blank area of the screen to deselect the main text placeholder. See Figure 5-8.

Figure 5-8 The third slide

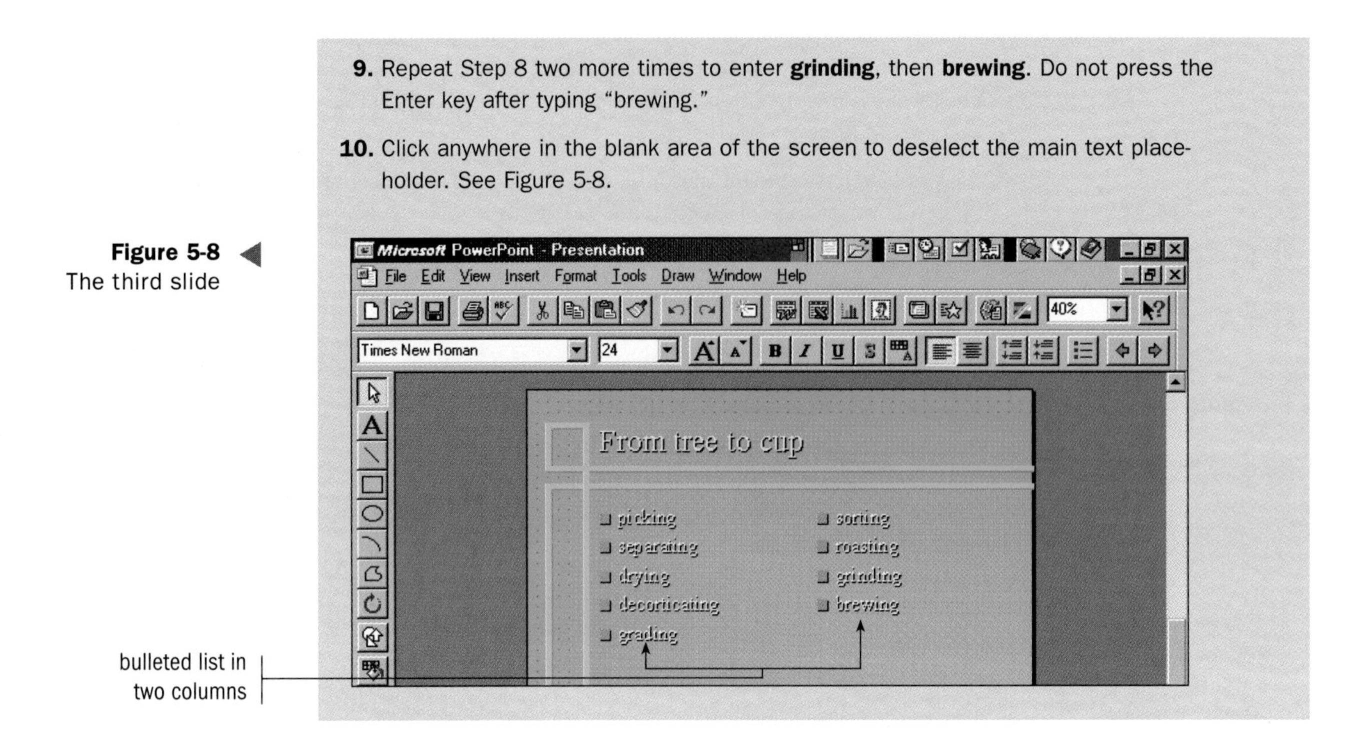

Belinda might not like the two-column format of the third slide. You'll add another slide similar to the current slide, but with a single-column bulleted list. Then Belinda can choose the one she prefers, and you can delete the other one. To add this new slide you'll work in outline view.

Adding Slides in Outline View

So far in this session, you've been working in slide view, which is only one of the several views provided by PowerPoint. Because you can add new slides in outline view as easily as in slide view, you'll change to outline view to add the new slide that will contain the same text as in slide 3.

To switch to outline view:

1. Click the **Outline View** button on the horizontal scroll bar. The window changes to outline view.

2. If necessary, scroll to the top of the outline, so that your screen looks like Figure 5-9.

Figure 5-9 Presentation in outline view

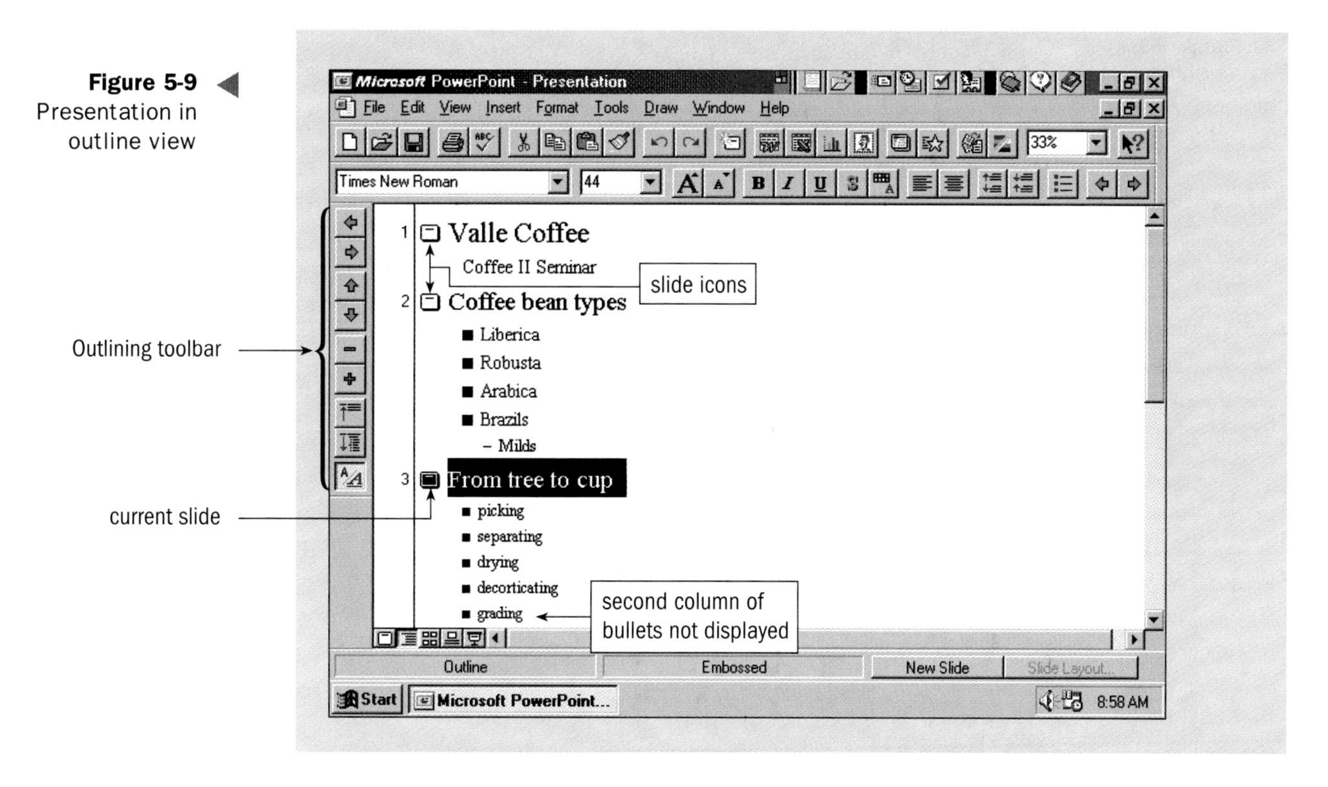

In outline view, your presentation appears as an outline made up of the titles and body text from each slide. There is one significant exception: text entered in the second column of a slide using the 2 Column Text AutoLayout is not displayed in the outline. Therefore, you won't see the last four bulleted items you entered on the third slide, even though these items are on the slide.

By default, outline view displays all text in the same font and font size in which it appears on the slides. Each slide title appears next to a slide number and a slide icon, as shown in Figure 5-9. The slide icon for the selected slide appears highlighted, as does the title of the selected slide.

Along the left side of the window, notice the Outlining toolbar, which automatically replaces the Drawing toolbar whenever you enter outline view. The Outlining toolbar buttons are described in Figure 5-10. The first two Outlining toolbar buttons, Promote (Indent less) and Demote (Indent more), also appear on the Formatting toolbar.

Figure 5-10 Outlining toolbar buttons

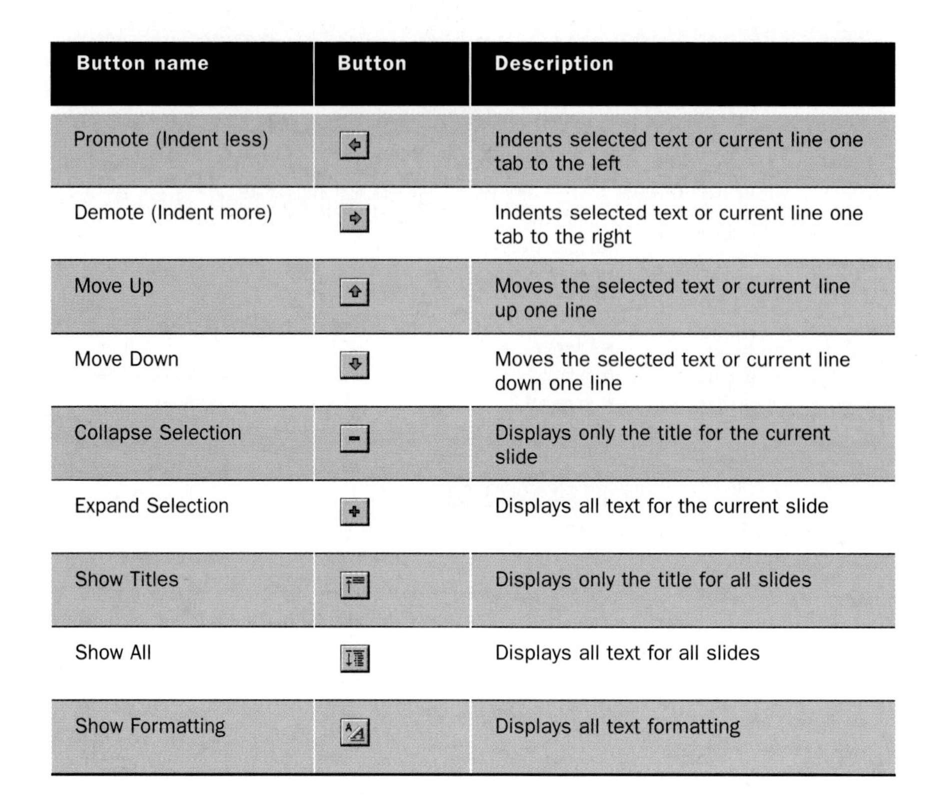

Button name	Button	Description
Promote (Indent less)		Indents selected text or current line one tab to the left
Demote (Indent more)		Indents selected text or current line one tab to the right
Move Up		Moves the selected text or current line up one line
Move Down		Moves the selected text or current line down one line
Collapse Selection		Displays only the title for the current slide
Expand Selection		Displays all text for the current slide
Show Titles		Displays only the title for all slides
Show All		Displays all text for all slides
Show Formatting		Displays all text formatting

Now you'll add a new slide, then enter the same text from slide 3 but in a single-column bulleted list.

To add the new slide in outline view:

1. Click the **New Slide** button on the status bar. A new slide 4 is added.
2. Type **From tree to cup** then press the **Enter** key. The pointer moves to the next line and a new slide, numbered 5, is added on that line. When you add slides or text in outline view, PowerPoint adds a new entry at the same level as the previous entry when you press the Enter key. Because the previous entry was a slide title, the new line is another slide title.

   In order to enter the bulleted items for the new slide you added, you must first demote (indent) the newest line from a slide title to body text.
3. Click the **Demote (Indent more)** button on the Outlining toolbar. The current line changes to a body text line with a bullet.

   To avoid having to retype the first five entries in the bulleted list, you'll copy them from slide 3 and paste them into slide 4.
4. Use the mouse to select the five bulleted items on slide 3 by positioning the pointer in front of the "p" in "picking," and then clicking and holding down the mouse button as you drag down beyond the final "g" in "grading."
5. Click the **Copy** button on the Standard toolbar, position the insertion point after the bullet for slide 4, then click the **Paste** button on the Standard toolbar. The five bulleted items are added to slide 4. See Figure 5-11.

Figure 5-11 Outline view after adding slide 4

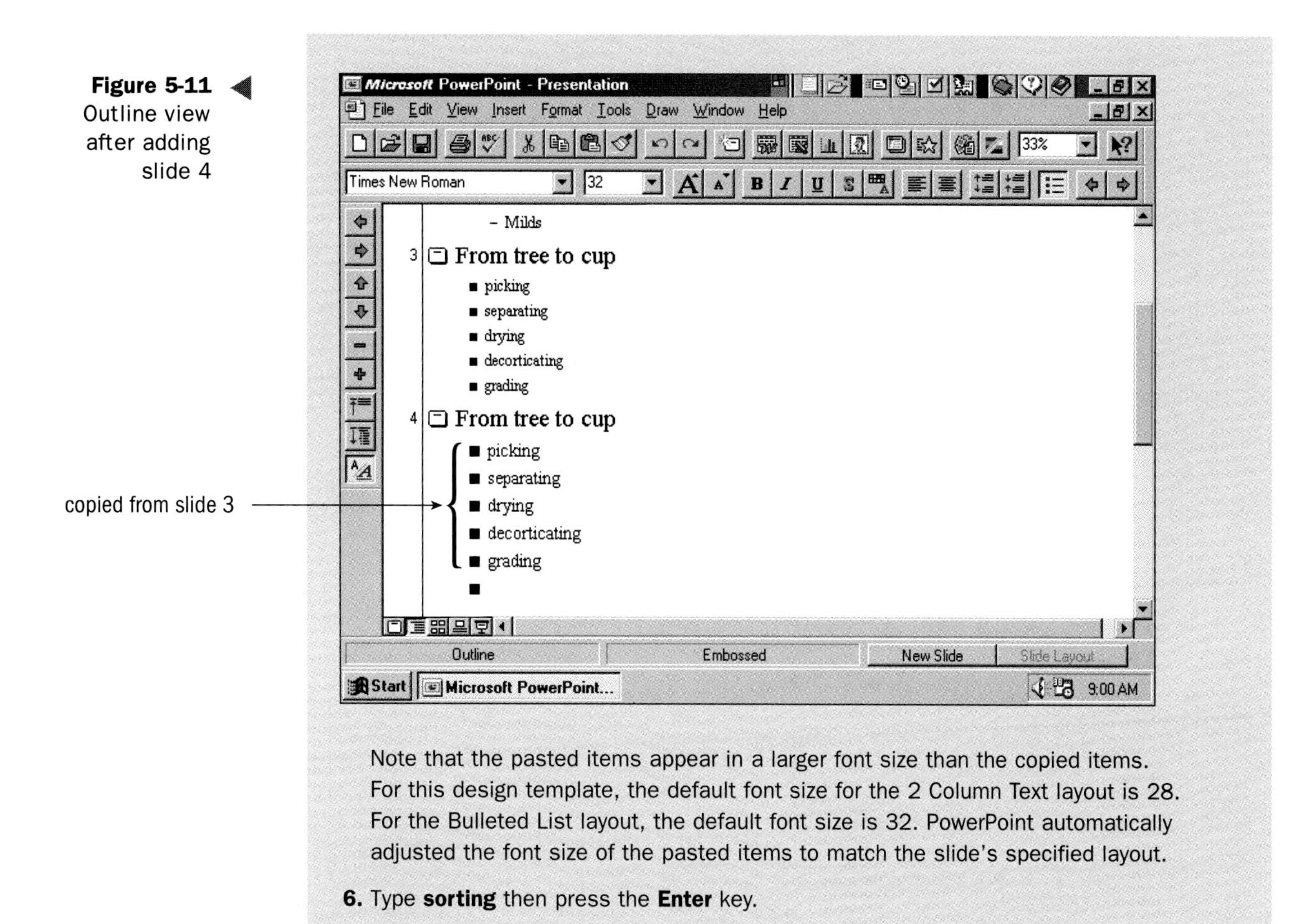

Note that the pasted items appear in a larger font size than the copied items. For this design template, the default font size for the 2 Column Text layout is 28. For the Bulleted List layout, the default font size is 32. PowerPoint automatically adjusted the font size of the pasted items to match the slide's specified layout.

6. Type **sorting** then press the **Enter** key.
7. Repeat Step 6 twice to add bulleted entries for **roasting** and **grinding**.
8. Type **brewing**. This completes the entry for slide 4, the single-column version of slide 3.

According to your presentation plan, you have just three slides left to enter. You'll add them now.

To add the last three slides:

1. Click the **New Slide** button on the status bar, type **Ideal coffee-growing climate** then press the **Enter** key.
2. Click the **Demote (Indent more)** button on the Outlining toolbar to demote the current line to body text.
3. Type **temperature 65 to 75 degrees** then press the **Enter** key.
4. Repeat Step 3 four times to create bulleted entries for the following items: **medium rainfall**, **good drainage**, **medium humidity**, and **mixture of sun and shade**.

   Pressing the Enter key after the last item creates another body text line. To create a title line on a new slide, you need to *promote* the item to increase its outline level.

5. Click the **Promote (Indent less)** button on the Outlining toolbar. The body text line is promoted to a slide title line on a new slide.
6. Type **Comparative tasting** then press the **Enter** key.

7. Click the **Demote (Indent more)** button, type **pencil**, press the **Enter** key, type **evaluation form**, press the **Enter** key, type **coffee cup**, then press the **Enter** key.

8. Click the **Promote (Indent less)** button to change the last bullet to a new slide, which will be the blank final slide. See Figure 5-12.

Figure 5-12 Outline view after all slides have been added

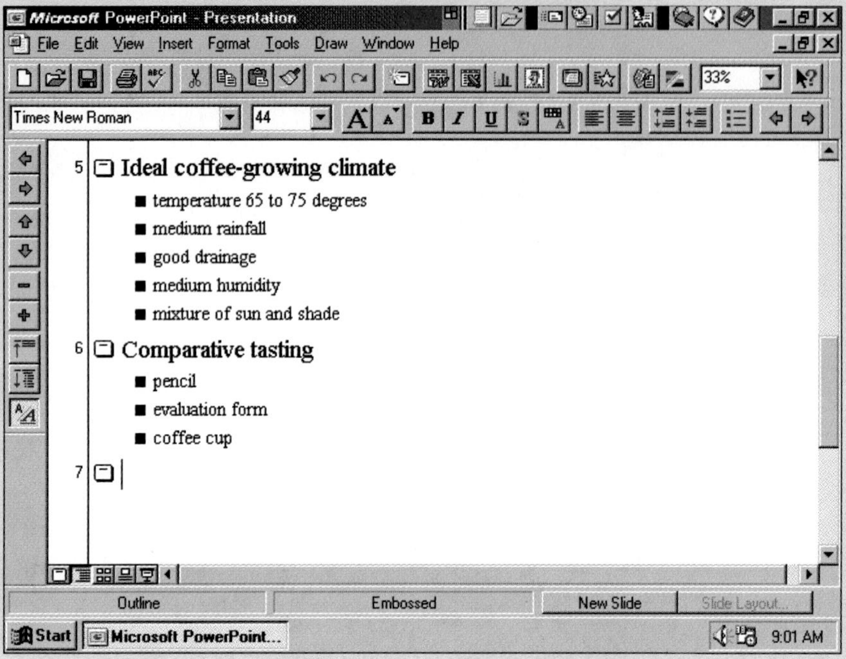

Did you notice that the New Slide dialog box was not displayed when you added these last four slides? When you add a slide in any view *except* outline view, the New Slide dialog box opens for you to select an AutoLayout. When you add a slide in outline view, the slide is automatically assigned the Bulleted List AutoLayout. This layout is appropriate for the first three of the four slides you just added. The final blank slide, however, does not include a bulleted list. This is not a problem. You can change the layout of any slide when you are in either slide or slide sorter view by clicking the Slide Layout button. You will reassign an appropriate AutoLayout for the final slide later, when you change to another view.

You have now created all the slides in your presentation plan, as well as one extra slide, so you should save the presentation. You'll save the presentation with the name "Coffee II Seminar."

To save the presentation:

1. Make sure your Student Disk is in the disk drive.
2. Click **File** then click **Save As**. The File Save dialog box opens.
3. Type **Coffee II Seminar**.
4. Save the presentation file in the Tutorial.05 folder on your Student Disk.

Now you'll view the slide show of your presentation.

Viewing a Slide Show

You can view a slide show at any time by clicking the Slide Show button on the horizontal scroll bar. It's a good idea to view the slide show periodically as you're building a presentation so that you can see how the final slide show will look.

You'll run the slide show and have Belinda view it as well. When you run a slide show, the first slide that appears on the screen is the slide that is currently selected. To start the presentation at the beginning, you must select slide 1.

To view the slide show:

1. Scroll to the top of the outline, then click the title on the first slide. The first slide is now the current slide.
2. Click the **Slide Show** button on the horizontal scroll bar to start the slide show. The title slide appears and fills the screen.

   TROUBLE? If the Office Shortcut Bar is still visible on your screen, you have to minimize it. Click the four colored boxes in the top left of the Office Shortcut Bar to display its menu, then click Minimize. The Office Shortcut Bar disappears. Later, when you finish the slide show and return to the PowerPoint window, the Office Shortcut Bar will be represented by a button on the taskbar.
3. When you have completed viewing the first slide, click the mouse button to advance to slide 2.
4. Click the mouse button to advance to slide 3.
5. Advance to the fourth slide. Notice that most of the last bulleted item is off the bottom of the screen. Belinda points out that grading and sorting are not really two separate steps, but are done concurrently. Therefore, the slide needs to show only eight bulleted items, all of which would fit on a slide. She asks if you can show the previous slide again.
6. Right-click to display the shortcut menu, then click **Previous**. Slide 3 is displayed.
7. Continue viewing the slide show, clicking the mouse button when you want to advance to the next slide. Clicking the mouse button when the last slide is displayed ends the slide show.

When the slide show ends, PowerPoint returns you to outline view, which is the same view you were using when you started the slide show.

Working in Outline View

Belinda prefers the two-column layout in slide 3 instead of the single-column layout in slide 4. You need to delete slide 4, which you'll do in outline view.

Deleting a Slide

You can delete a selected slide in any view by clicking Edit on the Standard toolbar, then clicking Delete Slide. In outline and slide sorter views, you can also delete a slide by first selecting the slide and then pressing the Delete key.

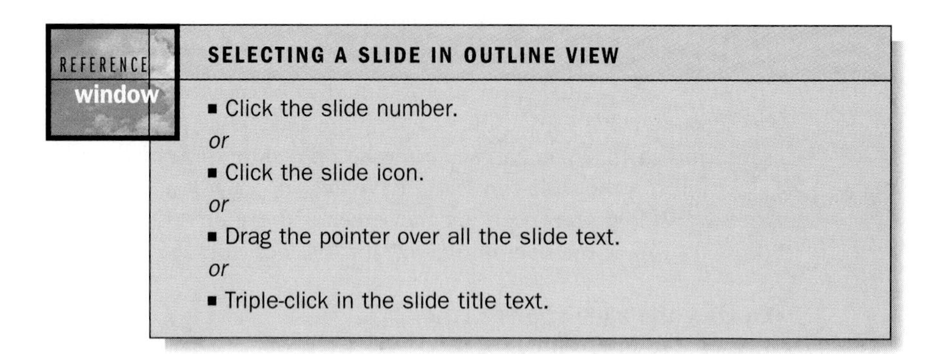

REFERENCE window

SELECTING A SLIDE IN OUTLINE VIEW

- Click the slide number.

or

- Click the slide icon.

or

- Drag the pointer over all the slide text.

or

- Triple-click in the slide title text.

Now you'll delete slide 4.

To select and delete slide 4 in outline view:

1. Scroll the outline until slide 4 is visible, then position the pointer on the icon for slide 4. The pointer changes to ✥.
2. Click the mouse button. The entire fourth slide is highlighted.
3. Press the **Delete** key. The selected slide is deleted, and the following slides are renumbered.

Moving Text Up and Down

Belinda wants you to reorder the items in the bulleted list on the slide that is now slide 4 so that "medium humidity" immediately precedes "good drainage." You can move the item up using the Move Up button on the Outlining toolbar.

To move the item in outline view:

1. Position the pointer to the left of the text "medium humidity." The pointer changes to ✥. See Figure 5-13.

Figure 5-13 Selecting text in outline view

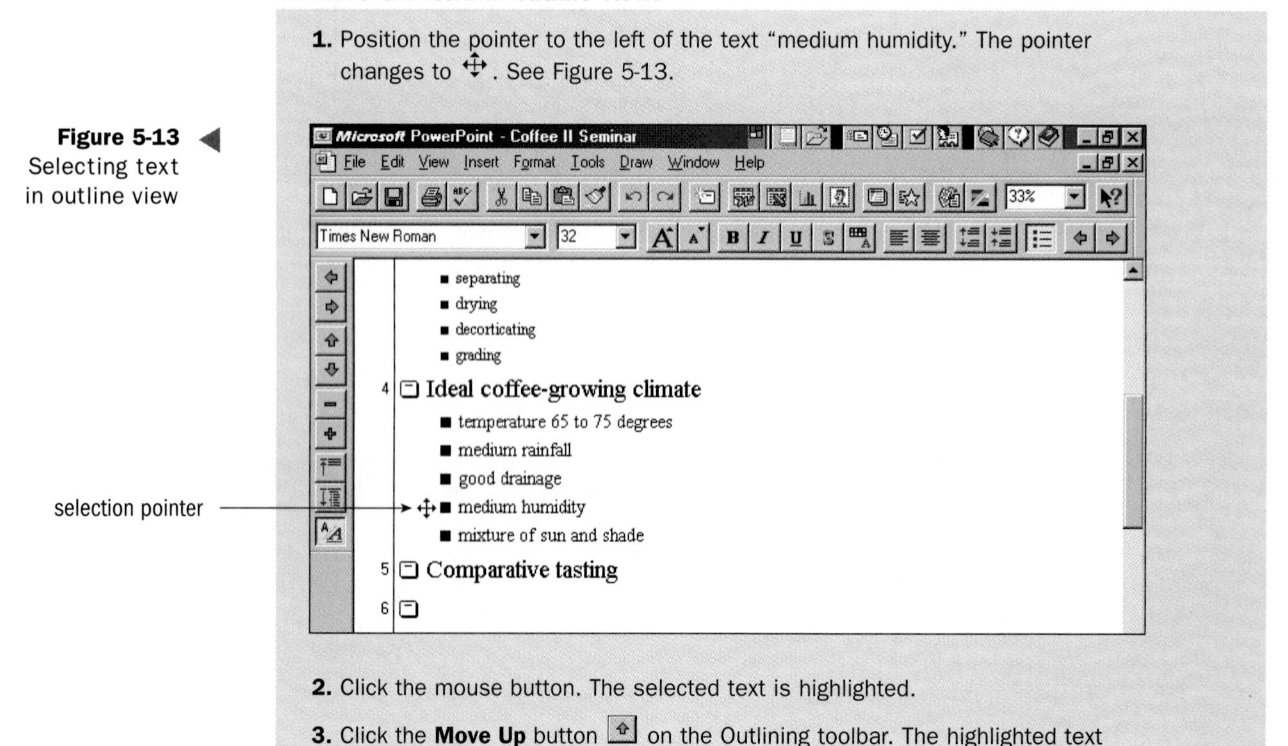

2. Click the mouse button. The selected text is highlighted.
3. Click the **Move Up** button on the Outlining toolbar. The highlighted text moves up one position in the list and is now located in the correct position.

To move selected text down rather than up, you use the Move Down button. You can use the same Move Up/Move Down technique to move entire slides.

Promoting and Demoting Text

Belinda noticed an error in the second slide. Brazils, like Milds, are types of Arabica beans. Therefore, the item "Brazils" appears at the wrong level. To correct this, you must select and demote the item "Brazils." As you learned earlier when entering text on the slides, **demoting** an item means decreasing its outline level. In contrast, **promoting** an item means increasing its outline level.

If you try to select the item "Brazils" by positioning the pointer to the left of the item and then clicking, both "Brazils" and "Milds" will be selected. Selecting text using the pointer ✥ causes the indicated line of text *plus* all subsidiary items to be selected. To select only the item "Brazils," you must either double-click the item or drag the pointer across it.

To demote the item "Brazils" in outline view:

1. Scroll the outline so that slide 2 is visible, then double-click "Brazils" to select just that item.
2. Click the **Demote (Indent more)** button on the Outlining toolbar.
3. Click in the blank area to the right of "Brazils" to remove the highlighting. Your screen should now look like Figure 5-14, with Brazils and Milds presented at equal levels, subsidiary to Arabica.

Figure 5-14 Demoting text

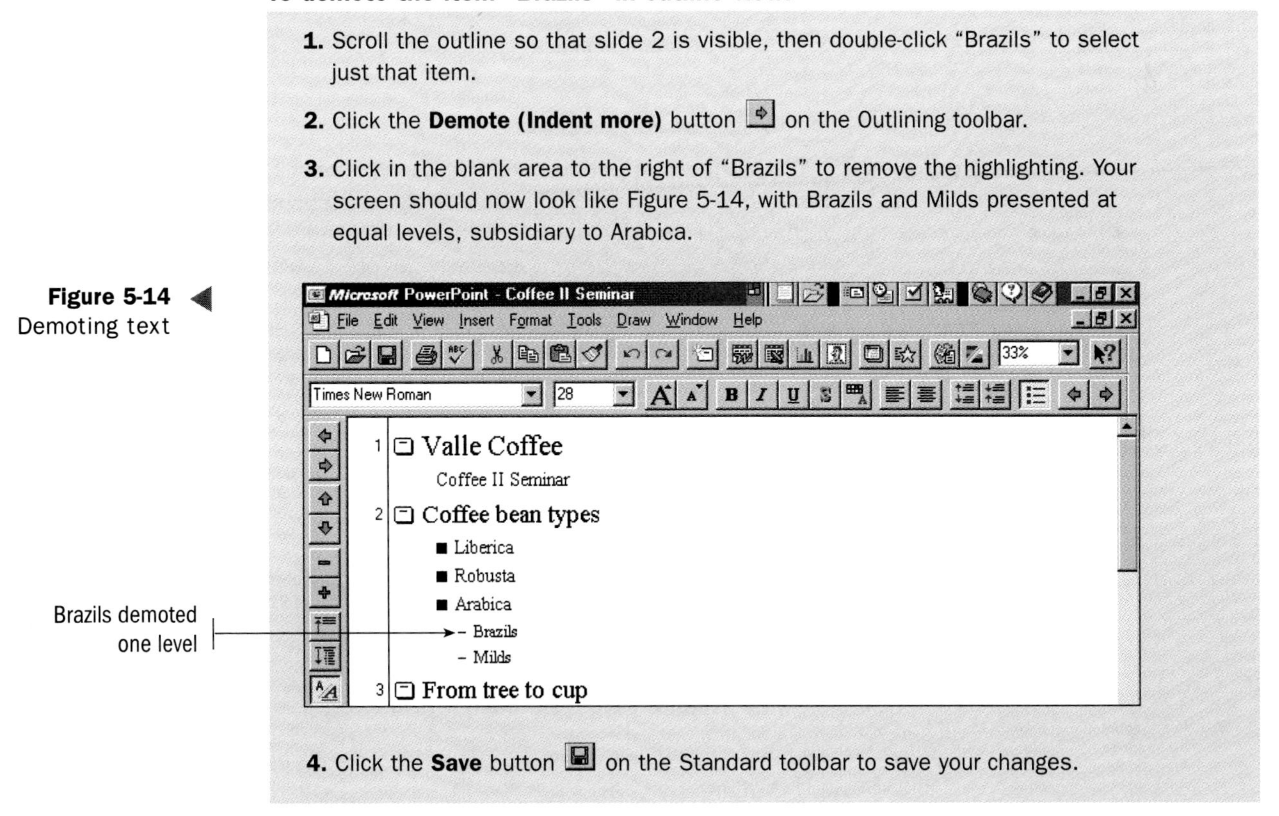

4. Click the **Save** button on the Standard toolbar to save your changes.

Quick Check

1. How does a title slide differ from a non-title slide? Why is the distinction important?
2. Describe at least four guidelines for designing effective presentations.
3. For what reasons might you choose a blank presentation rather than a design template when creating a presentation?
4. What does it mean to demote an item on a slide? What can be demoted? When might you need to demote a slide item? (*Hint:* Consider the two separate occasions when you used the Demote (Indent more) button in this session.)
5. What components of a slide are displayed in outline view? What slide features cannot be displayed in outline view?

6 What significant difference exists between adding a slide in outline view versus adding a slide in any other view?

7 During a slide show, how do you return to the previous slide?

8 Can you change the order of slides in outline view? If so, explain how you would make the slide that is currently the fourth slide become the second slide.

Now that you've completed Session 5.1, you can exit PowerPoint or you can continue to the next session.

SESSION 5.2

In this session you will change a presentation's design template; add, delete, rearrange and format text; use the Drawing toolbar to create and change shapes; change a slide layout; insert slides from another presentation; insert clip art; and add animation effects to a slide.

Changing the Template

After reviewing the presentation, Belinda looked at several of the other predefined design templates. She thinks that the Double Lines template would be more appropriate for the Coffee II seminar, because it has a "rich" look that reflects the richness of Valle Coffee's products. She asks you to change the template of your presentation to Double Lines.

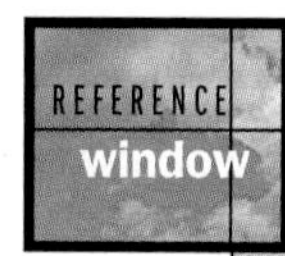

CHANGING A DESIGN TEMPLATE

- Click the Apply Design Template button on the Standard toolbar.
- Select the new template you want.
- Click the Apply button.

You can apply a new design template from any view, including outline view. However, in outline view you can't see the effects of changing the template, so you need to switch to slide view.

To switch to slide view, then change the design template:

1. Click the **Slide View** button on the horizontal scroll bar to change from outline view to slide view.

   You'll want to see the effect of changing the design template on all your slides, including the title slide. So you'll move to the title slide now.

2. If necessary, click the **Previous Slide** button at the bottom of the vertical scroll bar to move to the first slide.

   Now you'll change the design template, as Belinda requested.

3. Click the **Apply Design Template** button on the Standard toolbar. The Apply Design Template dialog box opens.

4. Scroll the Name list box until "Double Lines" is visible, then click **Double Lines**. A sample slide using that design template appears in the preview window. See Figure 5-15.

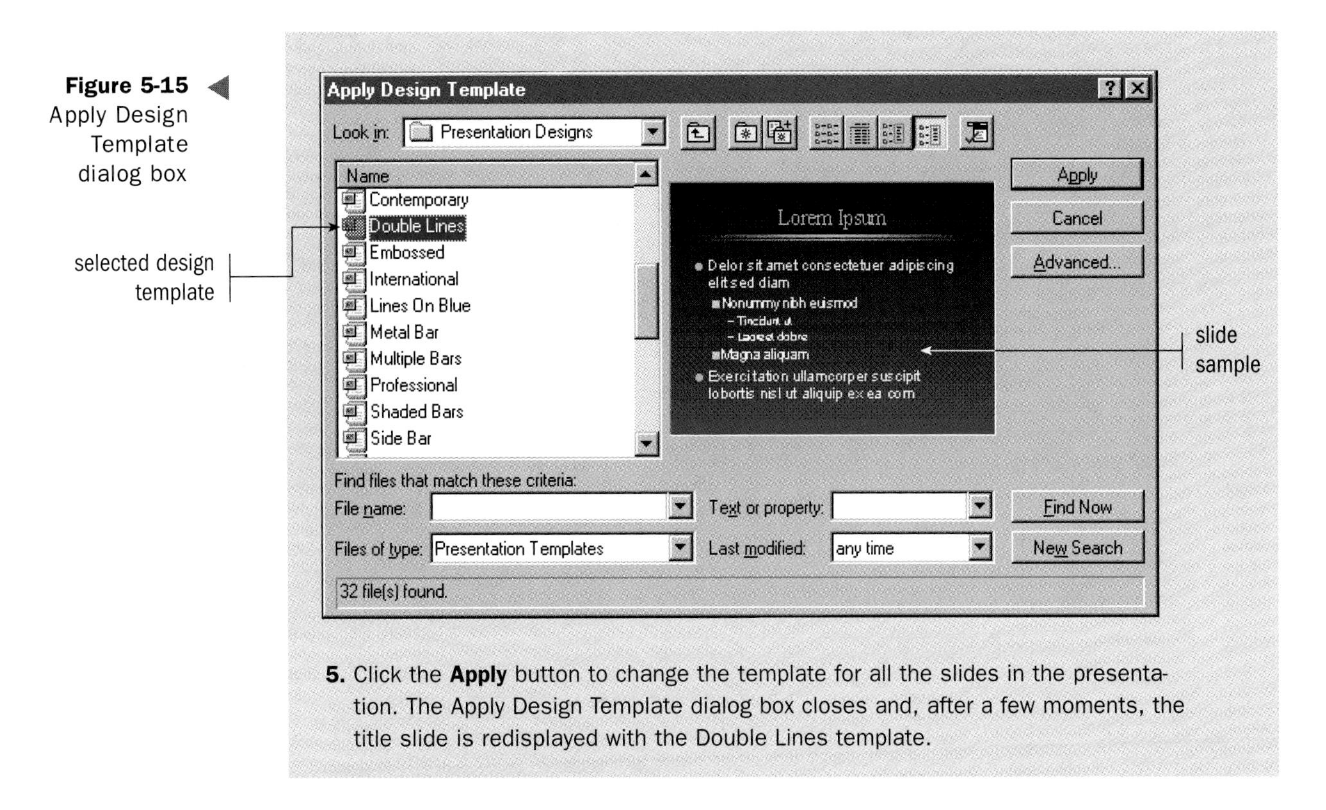

Figure 5-15 Apply Design Template dialog box

5. Click the **Apply** button to change the template for all the slides in the presentation. The Apply Design Template dialog box closes and, after a few moments, the title slide is redisplayed with the Double Lines template.

Working in Slide View

Belinda has some additional editing and formatting changes she wants you to make to the Coffee II Seminar presentation. You'll make these changes in slide view so that you can see the results of the changes immediately on the slides.

Adding and Deleting Text

You can add and delete text on slides using the same techniques you used to edit text in Word. Belinda has one change to the "Ideal coffee-growing climate" slide (slide 4)—she wants you to add the word "full" before the word "sun." To move to this slide, you'll use the scroll box in the vertical scroll bar. This scroll box enables you to move quickly through the slides in your presentation.

To add the word "full" on slide 4:

1. Position the pointer on the scroll box in the vertical scroll bar, then press and hold the mouse button. A ScrollTip appears and displays the slide number and slide title. See Figure 5-16.

Figure 5-16
Using the scroll box to move to a slide

2. Drag the scroll box down until the ScrollTip for slide 4 is displayed, then release the mouse button. Slide 4 is now displayed.

3. Position the pointer immediately to the left of the "s" in "sun" in the last bulleted item, then click the mouse to set the insertion point. A selection box appears around the bulleted items and the entire bulleted list text is highlighted. See Figure 5-17.

Figure 5-17
Adding text to a slide

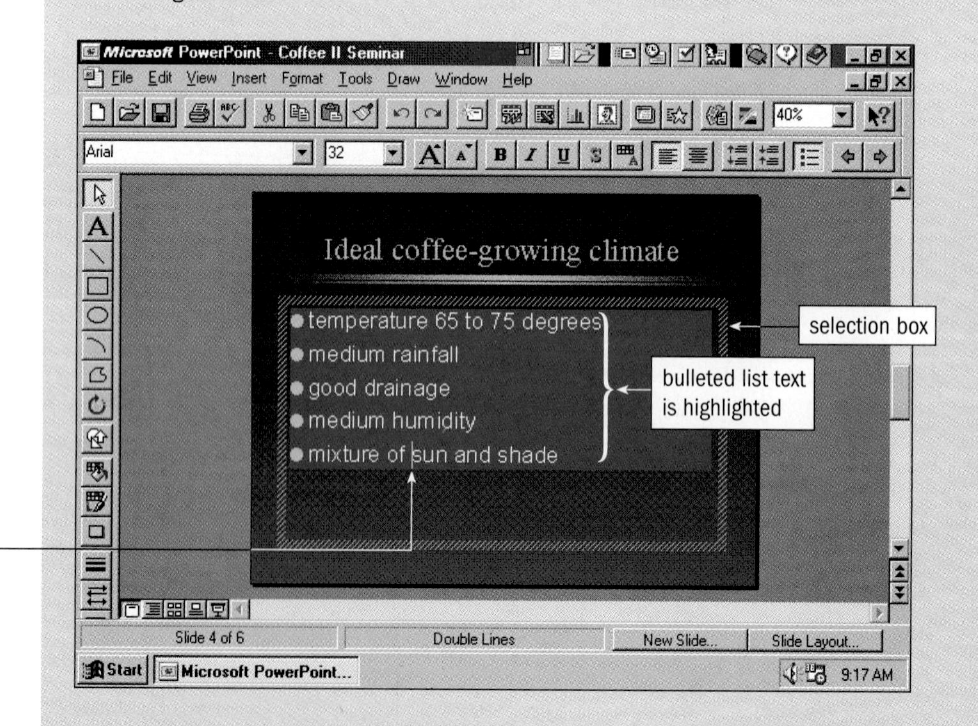

4. Type **full** then press the **spacebar**.

5. Click the blank area next to the slide to deselect the bulleted list.

The bulleted list on slide 3 is incorrect: grading and sorting should be a single step. To correct this, you must delete one bulleted item and change another.

To delete one bulleted item and add text to another item on slide 3:

1. Click the **Previous Slide** button on the vertical scroll bar to move to the "From tree to cup" slide.
2. Click the bullet to the left of "grading," then press the **Delete** key. The bulleted item is deleted.
3. Position the pointer to the left of the "s" in sorting, click the mouse to set the insertion point, type **grading and** then press the **spacebar**.
4. Click the blank area next to the slide to deselect the bulleted list. Your screen should now look like Figure 5-18.

Figure 5-18
Corrected list

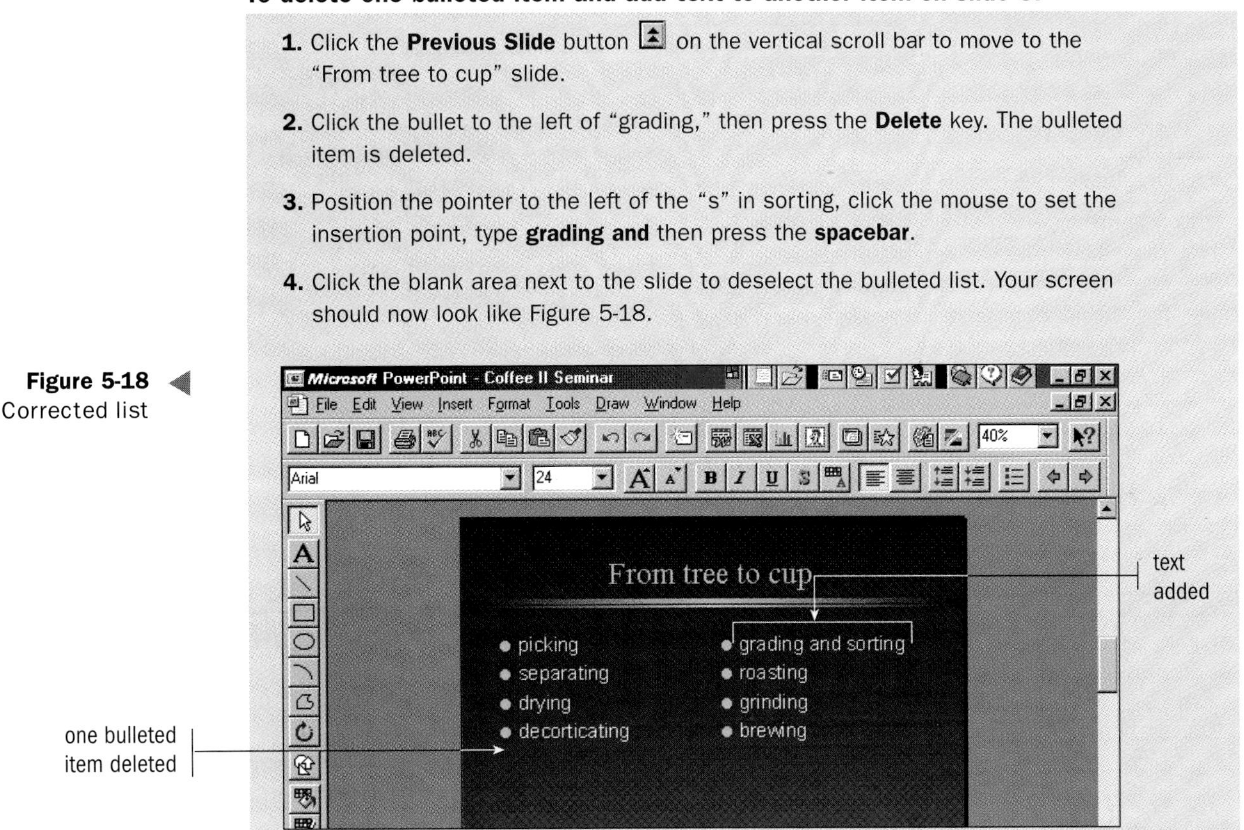

Rearranging Text

You can rearrange text on slides while in slide view. To move text, you can use the same drag-and-drop technique that you used in Tutorial 2 to move text in a Word document. Recall that with this technique, you select the text to be moved, drag it to its new location, then release the mouse button to drop the text in the new location.

The second slide, "Coffee bean types," lists the three classifications of coffee beans along with two subclassifications. When delivering the seminar, Belinda usually discusses Robusta beans before Liberica and Arabica beans. Therefore, you need to rearrange the order of items in the bulleted list on slide 2.

To rearrange the bulleted items on slide 2:

1. Click the **Previous Slide** button on the vertical scroll bar to move to the "Coffee bean types" slide.
2. Click the bullet to the left of "Robusta" to select the item. A highlighted boxed area appears around the word "Robusta."
3. Move the pointer within the highlighted area, press and hold the mouse button, then drag the mouse pointer up until the dashed vertical line of the pointer appears to the left of "Liberica." See Figure 5-19.

Figure 5-19 Moving "Robusta" to the top of the list

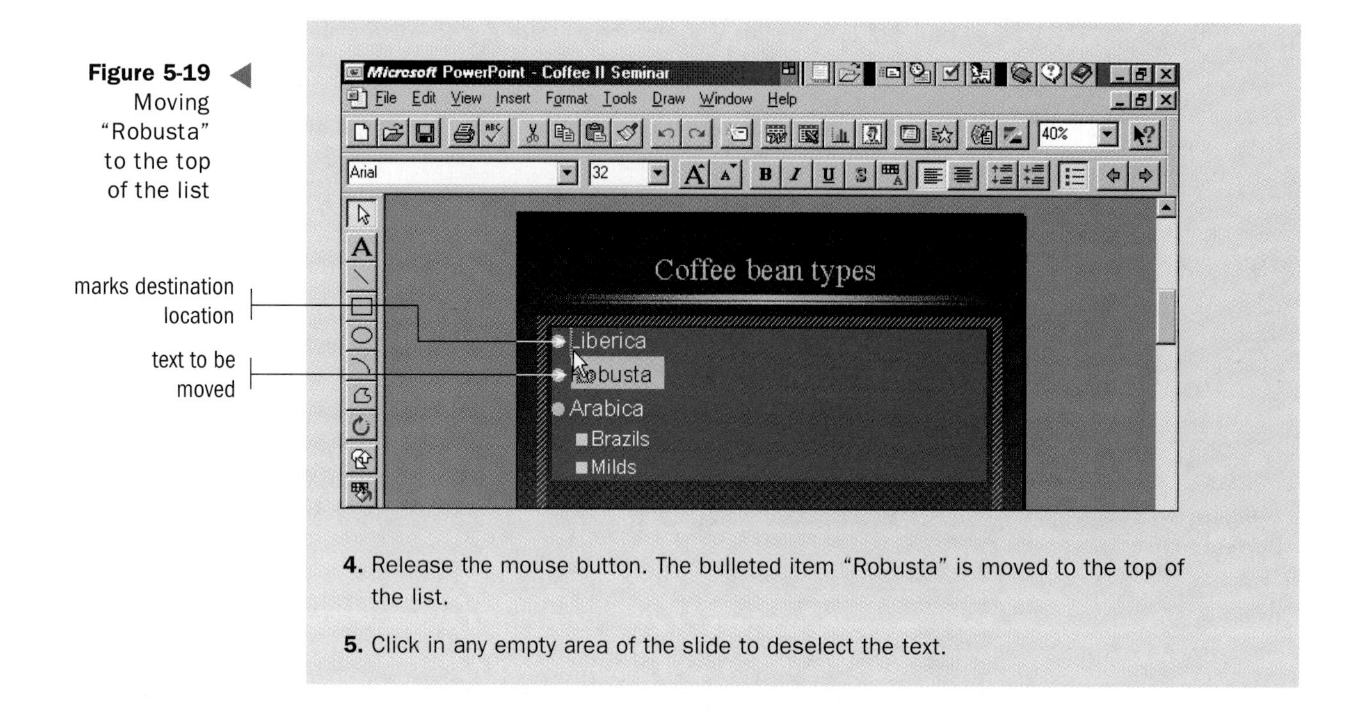

4. Release the mouse button. The bulleted item "Robusta" is moved to the top of the list.
5. Click in any empty area of the slide to deselect the text.

Formatting Text

You can format text on a slide using the buttons on the Formatting toolbar or the options on the Format menu.

Belinda has two text formatting changes that she wants you to make. First, on slide 2 she wants you to remove the capitalization on all the words in the bulleted list, so this slide will be consistent with the other slides in the presentation. You could select each capital letter, then delete the letter and type a lowercase letter. Or, you could use the Change Case command on the Format menu to correct all the items at once.

To change the case of the bulleted items on slide 2:

1. Select all five words in the bulleted list by dragging from the beginning of the first word through to the end of the last word.
2. Click **Format** on the menu bar, then click **Change Case**. The Change Case dialog box opens. See Figure 5-20.

Figure 5-20 Change Case dialog box

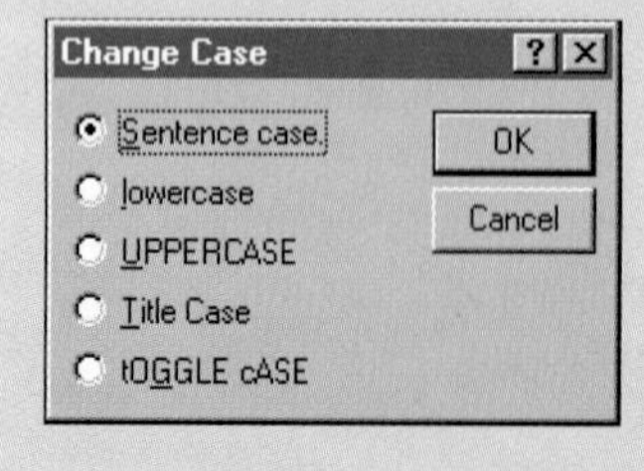

3. Click the **lowercase** radio button, then click the **OK** button. All five words are now lowercase.

The second text formatting change involves the two-column bulleted list on the "From tree to cup" slide (slide 3). Belinda wants the listed items to have a larger font size to match the size of the text on the rest of the slides, which is 32 point.

To change the font size of the bulleted items on slide 3:

1. Click the **Next Slide** button on the vertical scroll bar to move to slide 3.
2. Select all the items in the bulleted list on the left side of the slide. The Font Size list box on the Formatting toolbar displays the size 28. You need to change this size to 32.
3. Click the **Font Size** list arrow, then click **32**.
4. Repeat Steps 2 and 3 for the items in the rightmost bulleted list.

The item "grading and sorting" now requires two lines. Belinda would prefer that item to appear on a single line, if possible. If you widen the placeholder for the second list, the item "grading and sorting" will fit on one line.

To resize the placeholder for the rightmost bulleted list:

1. If necessary, click anywhere within the rightmost bulleted list to display the selection box around the bulleted list.
2. Click the selection box border to activate the sizing handles on the selection box.
3. Position the pointer over the sizing handle in the middle of the right side. The pointer changes to ↔. See Figure 5-21.

Figure 5-21 Resizing the placeholder

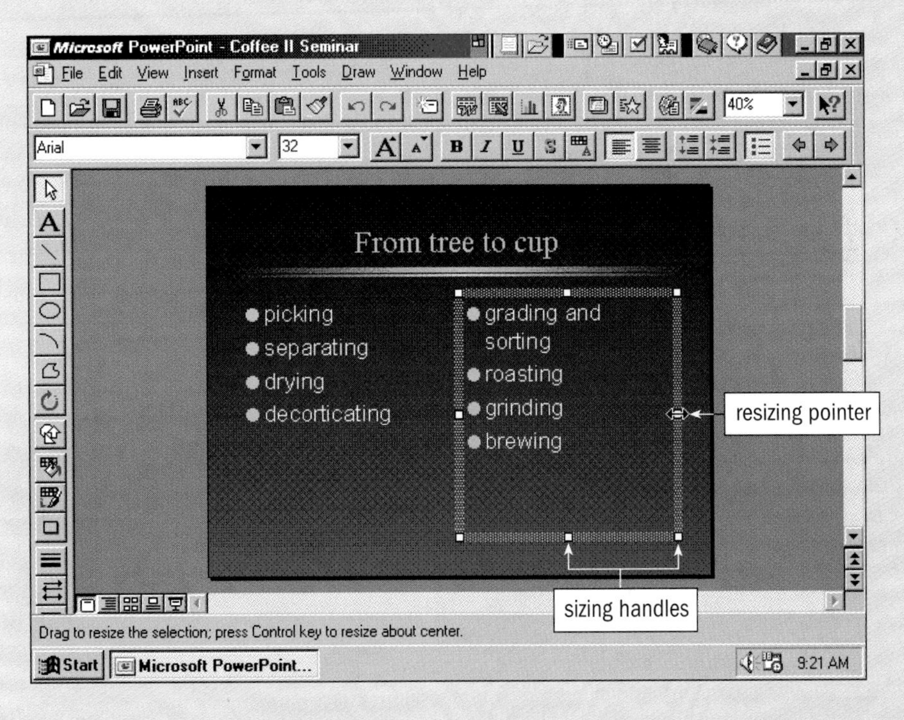

4. Click and drag the pointer to the right edge of the slide, then release the mouse button. The item "grading and sorting" now appears on a single line.

Now you'll view the slide show to see the results of the changes you've made so far. First you'll save the presentation.

To save the presentation, then view the slide show from the beginning:

1. Click the **Save** button on the Standard toolbar to save the changes you've made to the presentation.

2. Click the **Previous Slide** button on the vertical scroll bar twice to move to the first slide.

3. Click the **Slide Show** button on the horizontal scroll bar to start the slide show.

4. Click the mouse button to advance to the second slide. Because all the items in the bulleted list are short words, this slide appears unbalanced. In the next section, you'll add a graphic to the right side of this slide to help balance it.

5. Click the mouse button to advance through the rest of the slides in the presentation until you return to slide view.

When delivering the Coffee II seminar, Belinda highlights the fact that Arabica Milds are the finest, highest-quality coffee beans, and the only beans used by Valle Coffee. To emphasize the importance of these coffee beans, Belinda wants you to add a star next to this item on slide 2. You can draw a star shape using the Drawing toolbar.

Working with Objects on the Drawing Toolbar

PowerPoint's drawing capabilities allow you to draw and modify lines, arcs, and shapes to enhance your presentation. Shapes can be drawn freehand, or you can draw one of PowerPoint's 24 predefined AutoShapes such as a rectangle, diamond, ellipse, triangle, star, or arrow.

You can draw lines and arcs in any of ten different widths and styles, and in any color. You can fill and outline shapes with any color, using the same or different colors for the fills and outlines. The fill color can be solid, patterned, shaded, or textured. Also, you can apply a shadow to any line, arc, or shape.

Creating and Changing a Shape

The AutoShapes button on the Drawing toolbar allows you to use the mouse to draw one of the 24 predefined AutoShapes. To draw a shape with perfect proportions, you must press and hold the Shift key as you drag the mouse to draw the shape on your slide. Figure 5-22 illustrates several AutoShapes drawn with and without the Shift key.

Figure 5-22 AutoShape drawing methods

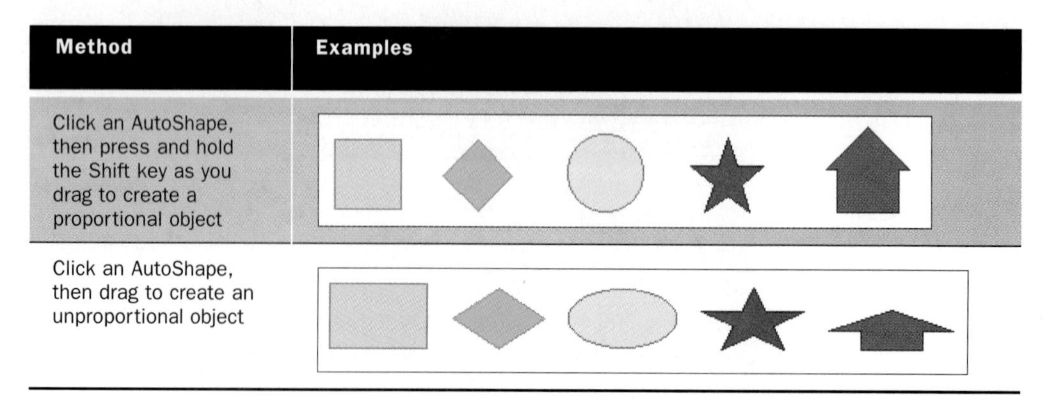

Method	Examples
Click an AutoShape, then press and hold the Shift key as you drag to create a proportional object	
Click an AutoShape, then drag to create an unproportional object	

Belinda wants you to place a star shape to the right of the word "milds" on slide 2 to emphasize the importance of these coffee beans and to better balance the slide.

To draw the star AutoShape:

1. Click the **Next Slide** button on the vertical scroll bar to move to slide 2.

2. Click the **AutoShapes** button on the Drawing toolbar. The AutoShapes toolbar appears. See Figure 5-23.

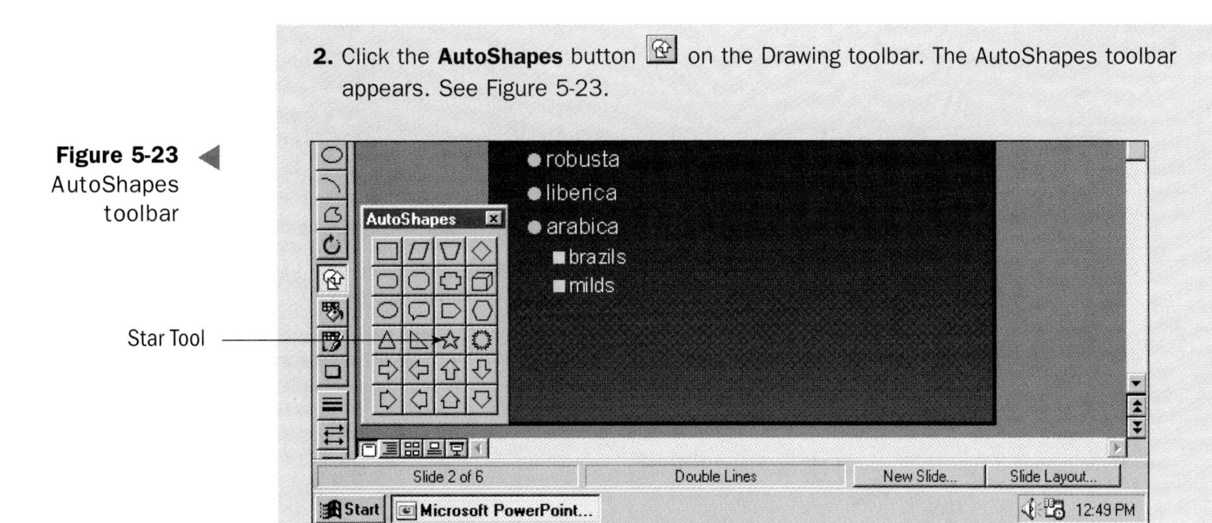

Figure 5-23 AutoShapes toolbar

3. Click the **Star Tool** button (see Figure 5-23).
4. Position the pointer to the right of and above the "s" in "milds," as shown in Figure 5-24.

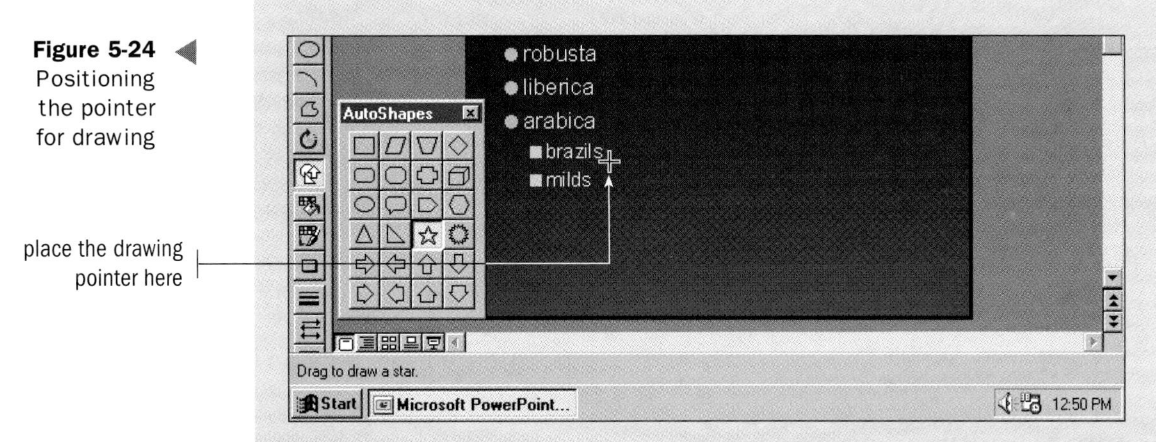

Figure 5-24 Positioning the pointer for drawing

5. Press and hold down the **Shift** key, click and hold the mouse button as you drag the pointer down until the pointer's horizontal crossbar is just below the bottom of the word "milds," then release the mouse button and then the Shift key.
6. Click anywhere in an empty area to deselect the shape. See Figure 5-25.

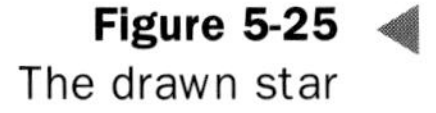

Figure 5-25 The drawn star

TROUBLE? Don't worry if your star is larger, smaller, or positioned differently from the star in Figure 5-25. You will resize and reposition the shape later.

7. Click the **Close** button on the AutoShapes toolbar to close it.

PowerPoint automatically colors a shape, using a fill color and an outline color selected from the design template's color scheme. The medium rose fill and lighter rose outline that PowerPoint used to color the star coordinate with the slide colors. But you decide to change the fill color to a two-color shaded effect using the blue in the title text along with the medium rose color. The shape's outline should be a darker rose color. Finally, you'll add a shadow effect to the star.

To change the colors of the star:

1. Click the star to select it.
2. Click the **Fill Color** button on the Drawing toolbar, then click **Shaded** in the displayed box. The Shaded Fill dialog box opens. The star's current fill color is displayed in the color box.
3. Click the **Two Color** radio button, click the **Color 2** list arrow, then click the second color box in the second row to select the blue of the title text. The Shaded Fill dialog box now looks like Figure 5-26.

Figure 5-26 Shaded Fill dialog box

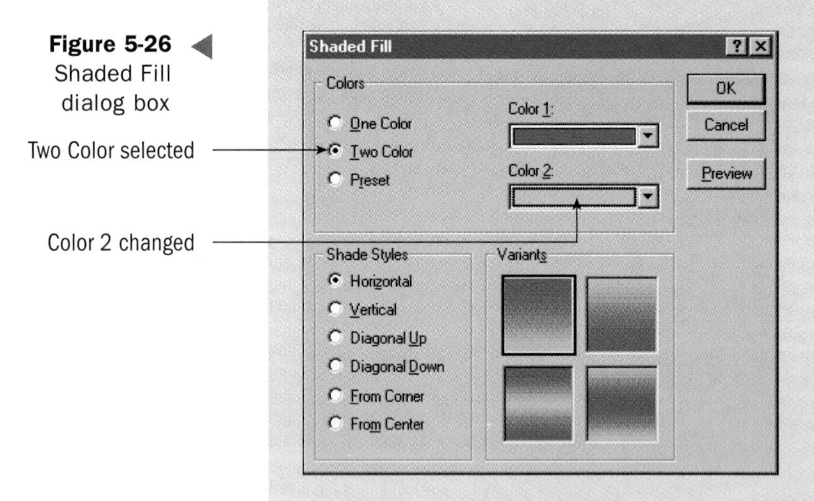

4. Click the **OK** button to close the Shaded Fill dialog box. The star is now displayed with the shaded two-color fill.

   Next you'll change the outline color.

5. Click the **Line Color** button on the Drawing toolbar, then click the dark rose color in the first position of the first row in the displayed box.
6. Click the **Shadow On/Off** button on the Drawing toolbar to apply a shadow effect to the star.
7. Click anywhere in an empty area to deselect the shape. The star is now recolored and shadowed. See Figure 5-27.

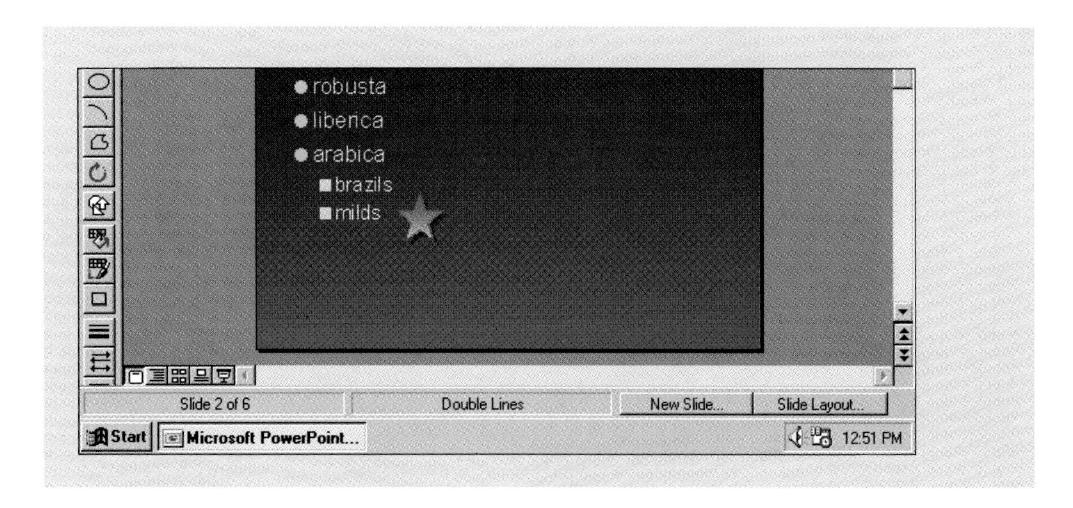

Figure 5-27 Recolored star with shadow effect

To see how this slide and the star look in the full-screen slide show, you'll start the slide show from this slide.

To view just slide 2 in a slide show:

1. Click the **Slide Show** button on the horizontal scroll bar. The current slide fills the screen, and the modified star appears next to the item "milds."
2. Right-click to display the shortcut menu, then click **End Show**. You return to slide view.

Belinda has created two new slides to be added to the presentation, but first she has some additional changes she'd like you to make. First, she wants you to increase the size of the star you added to the second slide.

Recall that you had to use the Shift key to create a shape with perfect proportions. You must also use the Shift key when resizing to maintain the perfect star shape. To make it easier to work with the drawing object, you'll magnify the image by increasing the zoom percentage.

To change the zoom, resize, and reposition the star:

1. Click the star to select it.
2. Click the **Zoom Control** list arrow on the Standard toolbar, then click **150%**. The slide image is magnified, and the selected star object appears centered in the window.
3. Press and hold the **Shift** key as you drag the lower-right sizing handle until your star is about the same size as the star in Figure 5-28.

Figure 5-28 Resizing and repositioning using 150% magnification

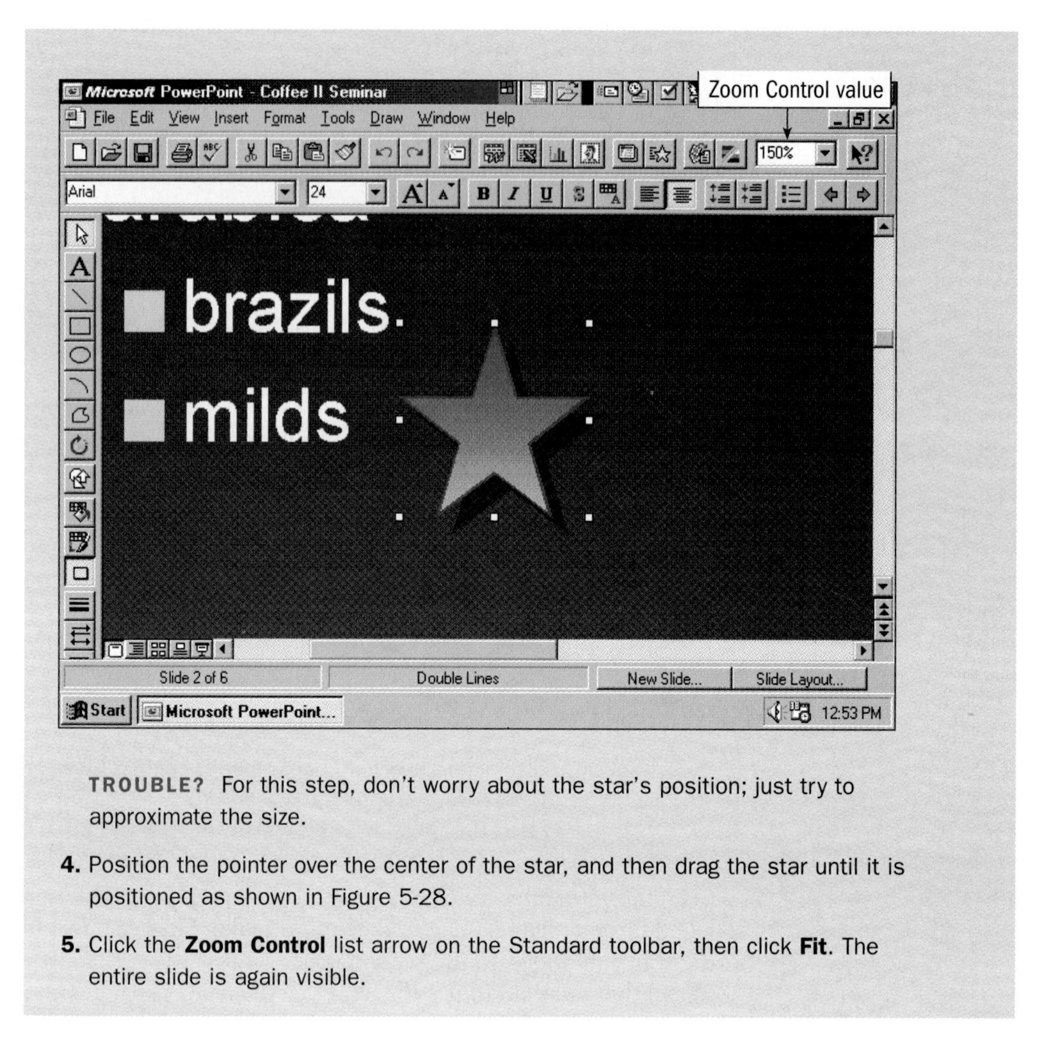

TROUBLE? For this step, don't worry about the star's position; just try to approximate the size.

4. Position the pointer over the center of the star, and then drag the star until it is positioned as shown in Figure 5-28.

5. Click the **Zoom Control** list arrow on the Standard toolbar, then click **Fit**. The entire slide is again visible.

Changing the Slide Layout

Recall that the final blank slide was automatically assigned the Bulleted List AutoLayout when you created it in outline view. When you are working in slide view, this slide displays two placeholders that you don't need. This is potentially confusing, so you'll change the layout for the final slide to the Blank AutoLayout.

To change the layout of slide 6:

1. Use the scroll box in the vertical scroll bar to move to slide 6. This slide will be the blank slide at the end of the presentation. It currently displays placeholders for a title and a bulleted list.

2. Click the **Slide Layout** button on the status bar. The Slide Layout dialog box opens. This dialog box is essentially the same as the New Slide dialog box.

3. Click the last AutoLayout in the third row to select the Blank layout, then click the **Apply** button. The slide is changed to a blank layout, and the two place-holders are removed.

Now you can insert the two additional slides that Belinda already created for the presentation.

Inserting Slides from Another Presentation

PowerPoint allows to you insert slides from one presentation into another, thus saving you the effort of recreating a slide from scratch.

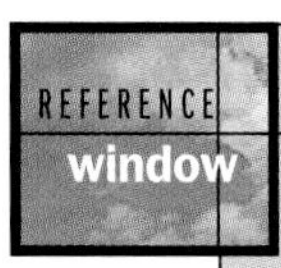

INSERTING SLIDES FROM ANOTHER PRESENTATION

- Display the slide after which you want to insert existing slides.
- Click Insert on the menu bar, then click Slides from File.
- Select the presentation file containing the existing slides.
- Click the Insert button.

Belinda already created a PowerPoint presentation file containing two slides for use in the Coffee II Seminar presentation. She asks you to insert these two slides into your presentation before the "Comparative tasting" slide (slide 5).

To insert the slides from Belinda's presentation:

1. Click the **Previous Slide** button on the vertical scroll bar twice to move to slide 4. The inserted slides will be positioned following slide 4.
2. Click **Insert** on the menu bar, then click **Slides from File**. The Insert File dialog box opens. The slides Belinda created are in the presentation document named NewSlide, which is located in the Tutorial.05 folder on your Student Disk.
3. Click **NewSlide** then click the **Insert** button. The two slides in the NewSlide file are inserted into your presentation as slides 5 and 6, and all subsequent slides are renumbered. The first of the added slides, which is now displayed, is a Bulleted List slide to which Belinda added double-headed arrows using the Drawing toolbar. See Figure 5-29.

Figure 5-29 The first inserted slide

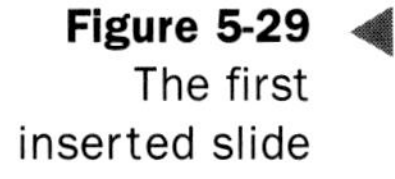

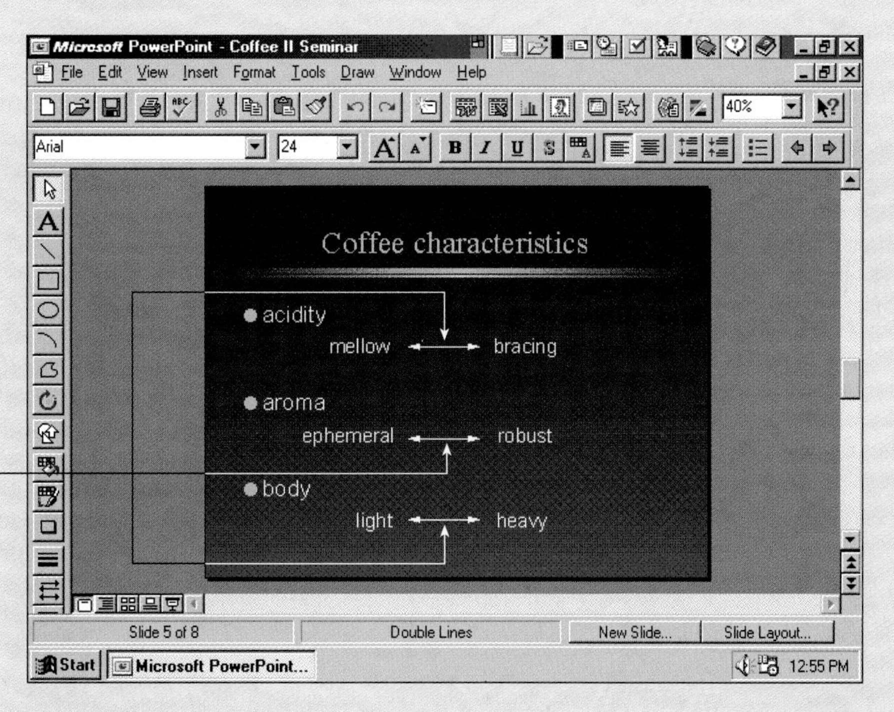

4. Click the **Next Slide** button on the vertical scroll bar to move to the second of the new slides. See Figure 5-30. This slide currently contains only a title. Belinda wants you to embed an Excel chart on this slide (which you will do in the next session).

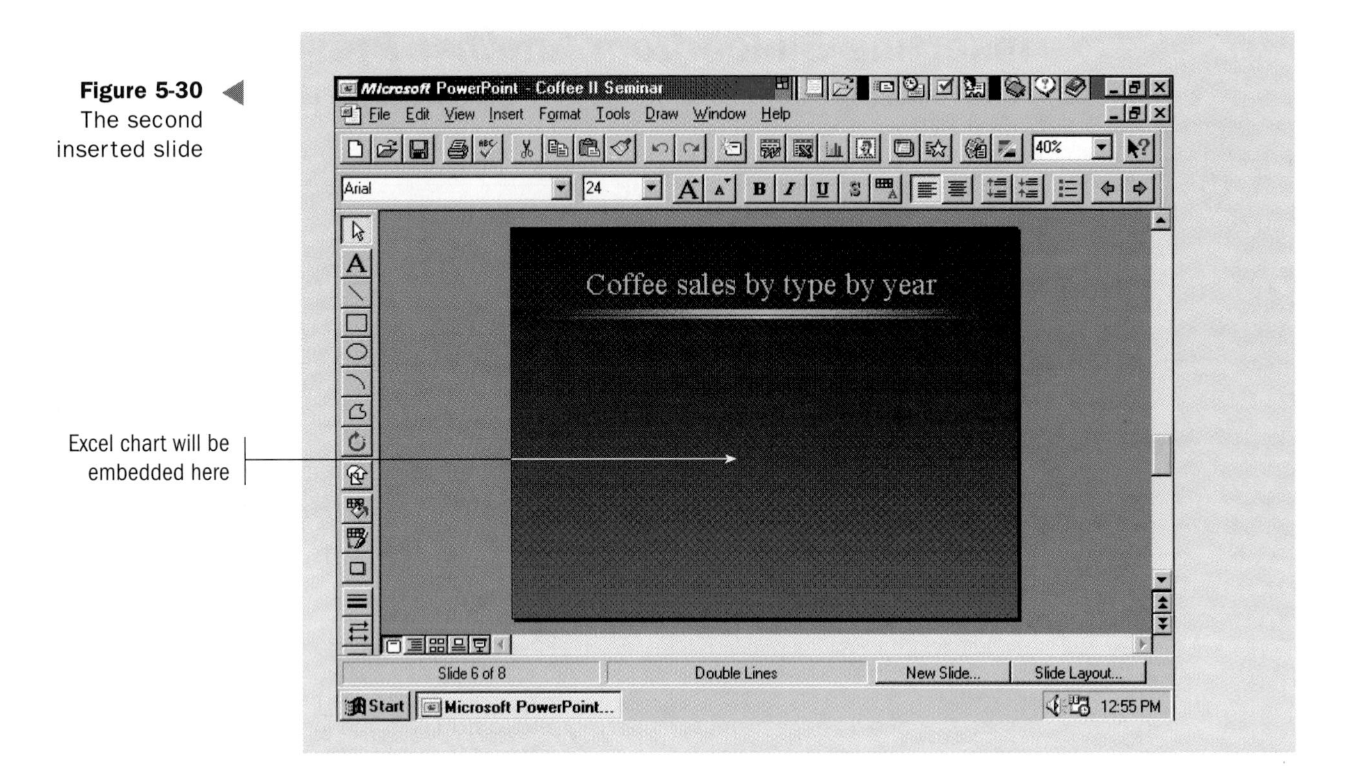

Figure 5-30 The second inserted slide

Belinda created the two added slides using the same Double Lines design template, but this is not a requirement. PowerPoint automatically applies the current presentation's design template to any inserted slides.

When you insert slides from another presentation, all the slides from that presentation are inserted. If you don't want to keep all the slides from that file, you must delete those slides that you don't need.

Inserting Clip Art

Belinda wants you to add some clip art to slide 7, "Comparative tasting," to make the slide more interesting. Before you add the clip art, however, you need to remove the bullets, which would conflict with the clip art, and then adjust the spacing and position of the three items on the slide.

To remove the bullets and adjust the items on slide 7:

1. Click the **Next Slide** button on the vertical scroll bar to move to slide 7.
2. Select the three items in the bulleted list, then click the **Bullet On/Off** button on the Formatting toolbar to remove the bullets.
3. Click at the end of the word "pencil" to position the insertion point at the end of that word, then press the **Enter** key twice.
4. Click at the end of the word "form" to position the insertion point, then press the **Enter** key twice.

   To move the three items to the right, you need to resize the placeholder.
5. Click the placeholder border. Sizing handles appear on the placeholder border.
6. Position the pointer over the middle sizing handle on the left side, then click and drag to the right until the placeholder is sized as shown in Figure 5-31.

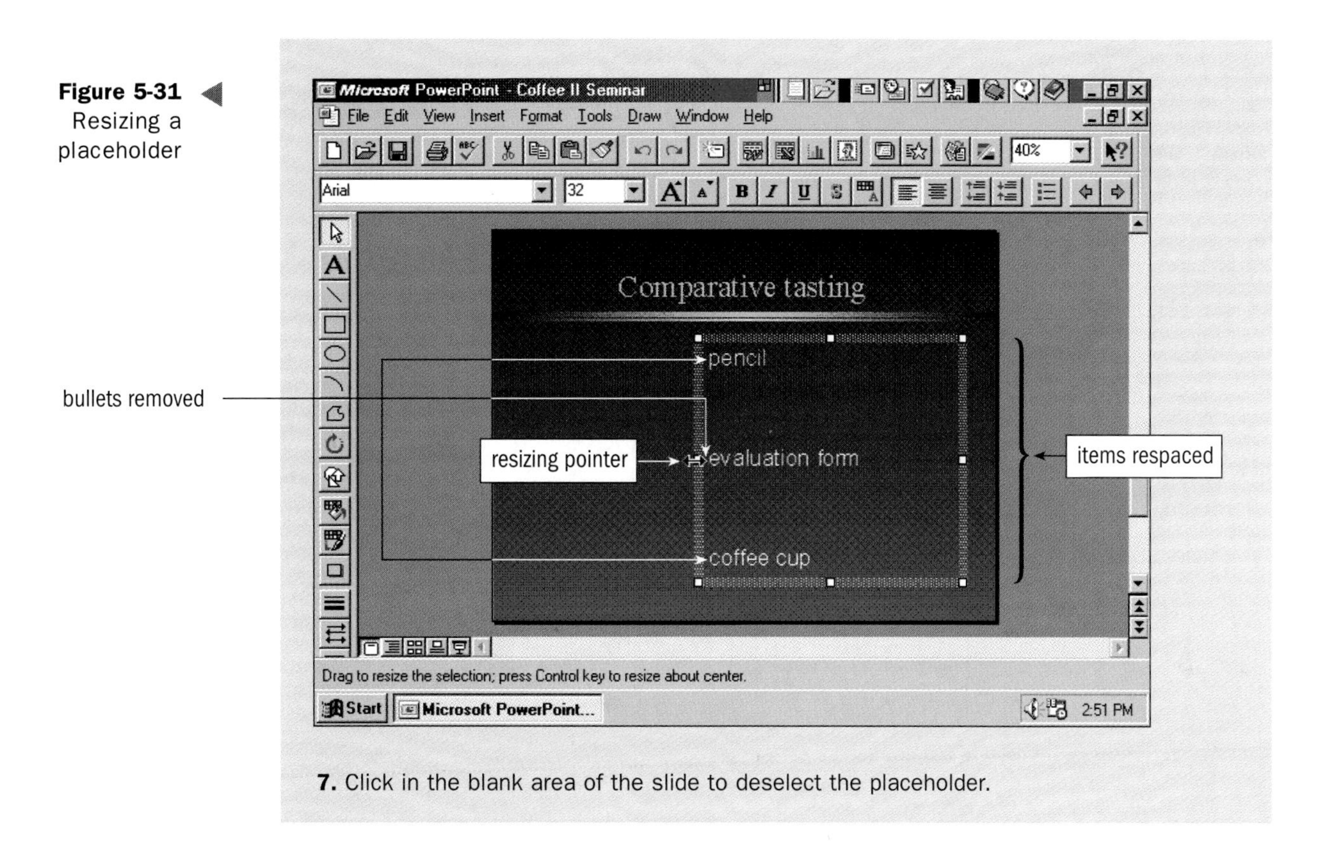

Figure 5-31 Resizing a placeholder

7. Click in the blank area of the slide to deselect the placeholder.

Now you'll add a clip art picture of a check mark to the slide.

To insert the clip art picture on slide 7:

1. Click the **Insert Clip Art** button on the Standard toolbar. The Microsoft ClipArt Gallery 2.0 dialog box opens.
2. Scroll the Categories list until the category named "Shapes" is visible, then click **Shapes**.
3. Scroll the Pictures list until you see the picture of the check mark, then click that picture. See Figure 5-32.

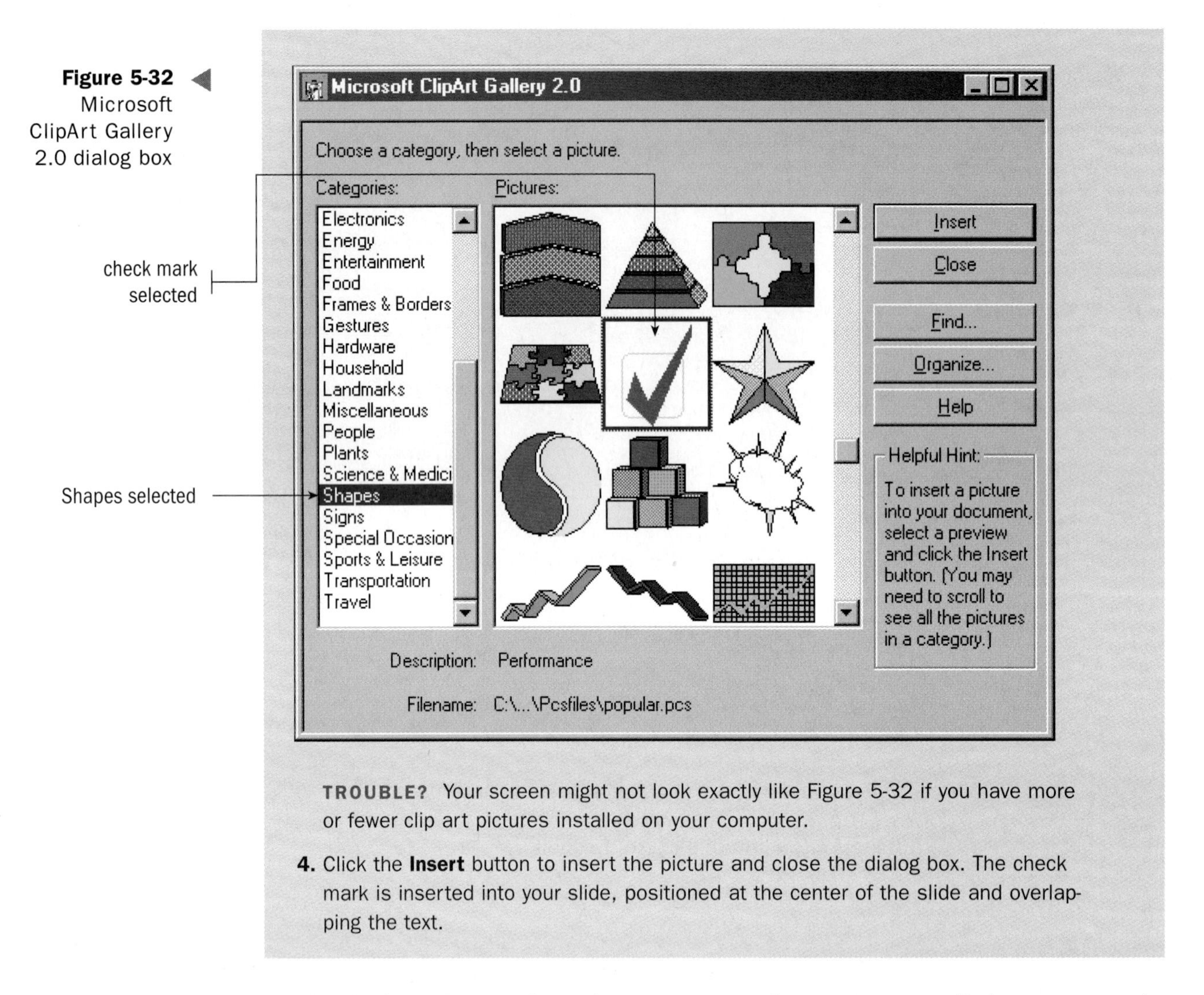

Figure 5-32 Microsoft ClipArt Gallery 2.0 dialog box

TROUBLE? Your screen might not look exactly like Figure 5-32 if you have more or fewer clip art pictures installed on your computer.

4. Click the **Insert** button to insert the picture and close the dialog box. The check mark is inserted into your slide, positioned at the center of the slide and overlapping the text.

The check mark is much too large, so you need to resize it. You'll also reposition the check mark so that it is just to the left of the word "pencil." You resize and reposition clip art images the same way you resize and reposition any object.

To resize and reposition the clip art picture:

1. Position the pointer over the sizing handle in the upper-right corner of the check mark, then click and drag the resizing pointer until the picture is the same size as the one shown in Figure 5-33.

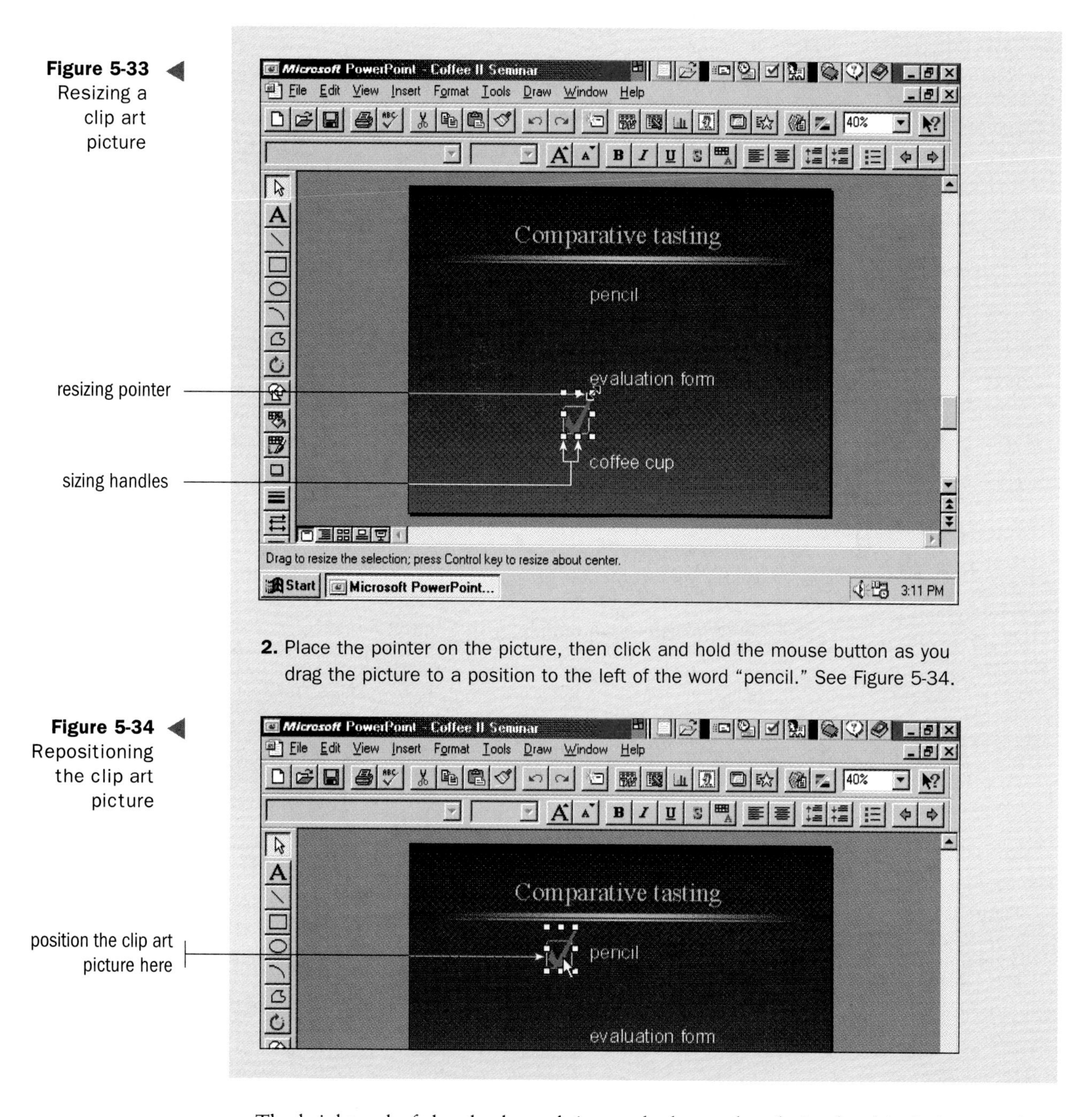

Figure 5-33 Resizing a clip art picture

2. Place the pointer on the picture, then click and hold the mouse button as you drag the picture to a position to the left of the word "pencil." See Figure 5-34.

Figure 5-34 Repositioning the clip art picture

The bright red of the check mark is not the best color choice for this design template. PowerPoint allows you to recolor clip art pictures using colors from the template palette or any other color you want. You'll recolor the check mark to change the red to the medium pink in the template palette.

To recolor the clip art picture:

1. Right-click the check mark to display the shortcut menu, then click **Recolor**. The Recolor Picture dialog box opens.

2. Click the list arrow next to the red color in the New section, then click the medium pink color box in the third position of the first row. See Figure 5-35.

Figure 5-35
Recolor Picture dialog box

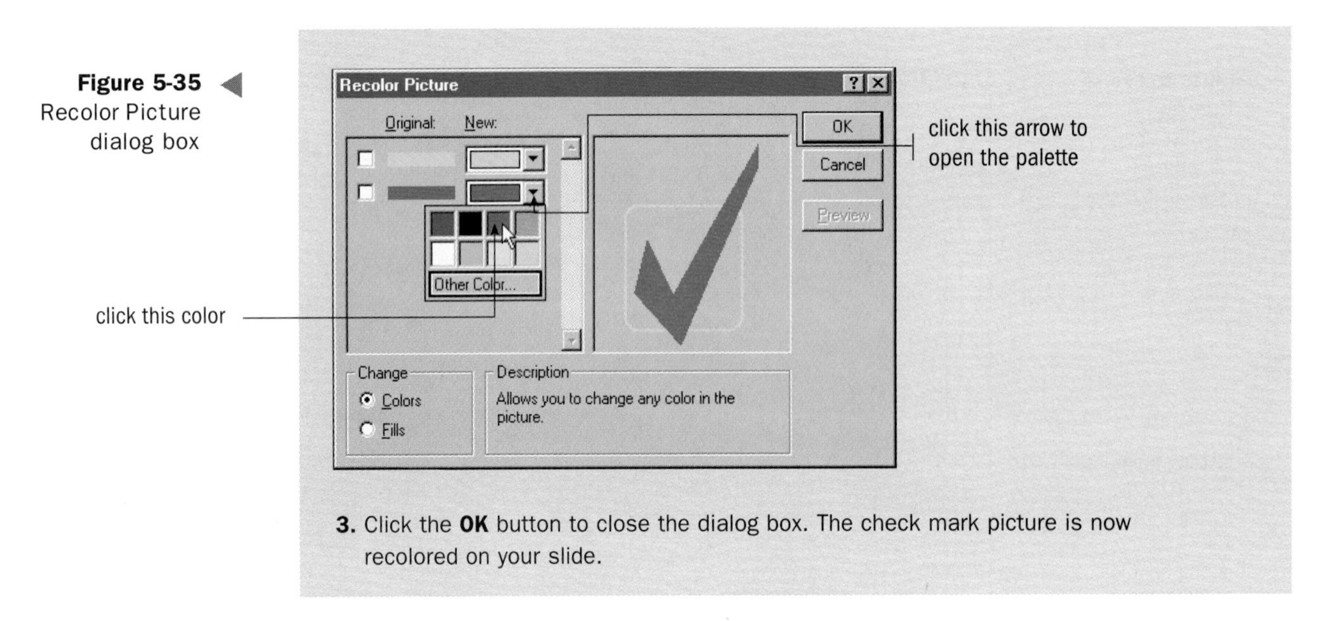

3. Click the **OK** button to close the dialog box. The check mark picture is now recolored on your slide.

Next, you'll copy the resized and recolored check mark, paste it twice, and then position the two copies to the left of the other two text items on this slide.

To make and position two copies of the check mark:

1. With the check mark selected, click the **Copy** button on the Standard toolbar, then click the **Paste** button two times. Two copies of the check mark are placed on the slide.
2. Move the currently selected copy to a position to the left of the words "coffee cup."
3. Click the other copy of the clip art picture to select it, then move it to a position to the left of the words "evaluation form." See Figure 5-36.

Figure 5-36
Correctly positioned copies of the clip art picture

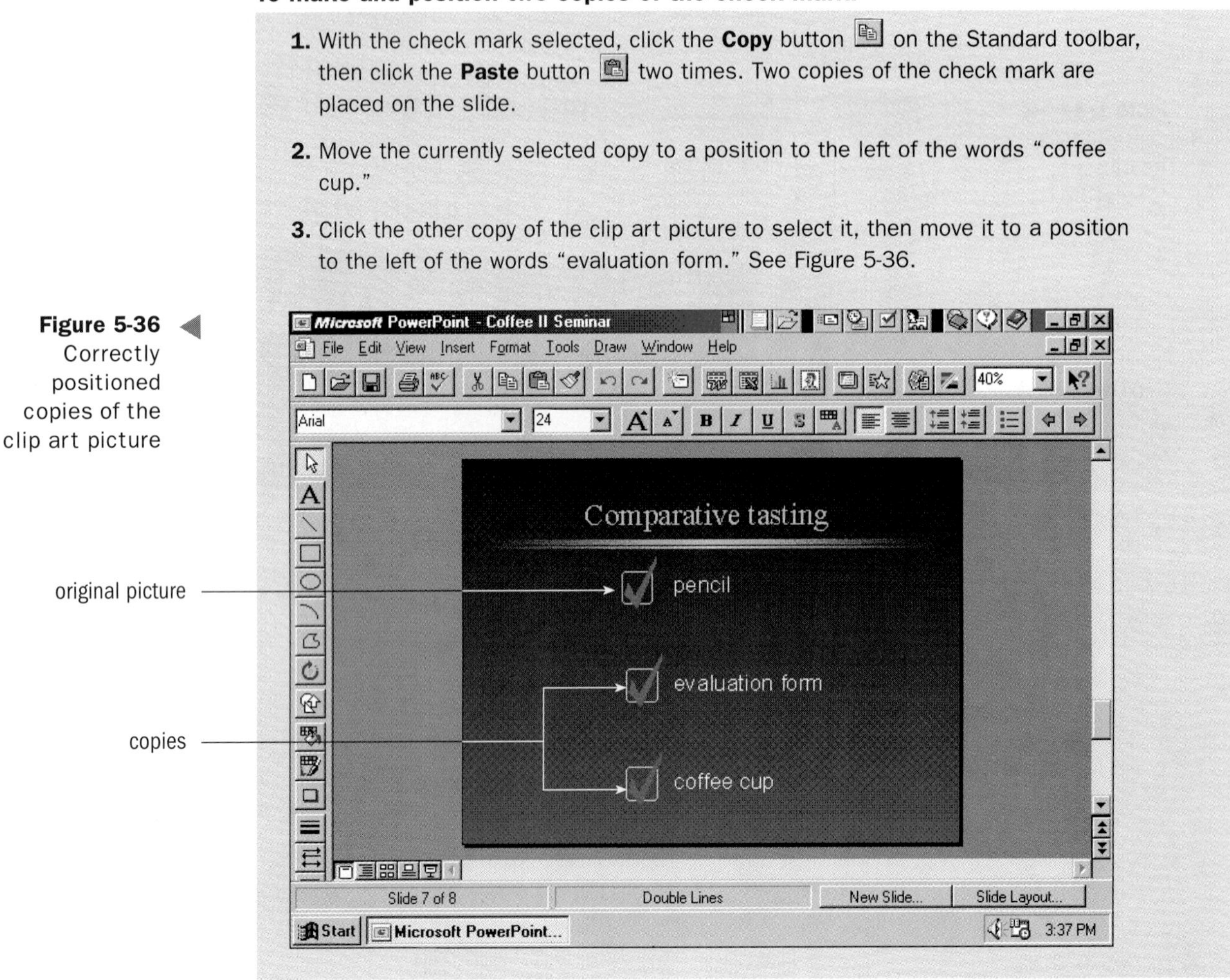

TROUBLE? If the three clip art pictures aren't in the approximate positions as those in Figure 5-36, reposition them. Don't worry about the exact vertical alignment of the three pictures; you will adjust the vertical alignment in the next step.

PowerPoint provides a feature for exactly aligning multiple objects. To use this option, you must first select all the objects to be aligned.

4. Click the first check mark picture to select it, then press and hold the **Shift** key as you click the second and third pictures. All three check mark pictures are now selected.
5. Click **Draw** on the menu bar, point to **Align**, then click **Lefts**. PowerPoint aligns the left edges of the three selected pictures.

Belinda likes how the check marks look and thinks that the slide will be even more interesting if they appear one at a time as she is speaking during the seminar. To achieve this effect, you need to animate the slide.

Adding Animation Effects

With PowerPoint's animation effects options, you can specify that the text and graphics on a slide appear independently of one another during a slide show. For example, you can have the items in a bulleted list appear one at a time, which is called **building**. You can also specify the way you want each text or graphics item to appear. You might choose to have an item "fly in" from the left side of the screen, for example. You can also select a sound effect to accompany the appearance of a text item or graphic. However, the computer on which you run the slide show must have speakers attached in order for any sound effects to be heard.

For slide 7, Belinda wants all the text items to appear when the slide is first shown. Then she wants to add the check marks one at a time, with each check mark flying in from the upper-left corner of the screen. Because Belinda will be talking at this point in the slide show, she doesn't want any sound effects.

To add animation effects to slide 7:

1. If necessary, select the three check mark pictures by clicking the top picture, then holding down the **Shift** key as you click the second and third pictures.
2. With the pointer positioned on the third check mark, right-click to display the shortcut menu, then click **Animation Settings**. The Animation Settings dialog box opens.
3. Click the list arrow in the Build Options section, then click **Build**.
4. Click the list arrow next to "No Build Effect" in the Effects section, then click **Fly From Top-Left**.

   If a sound effect has been selected, you must change that option to "[No Sound]."
5. If "[No Sound]" is not displayed in the last list box in the Effects section, click the list arrow next to that list box, scroll the list to the top, if necessary, then click **[No Sound]**. The dialog box should now look like Figure 5-37.

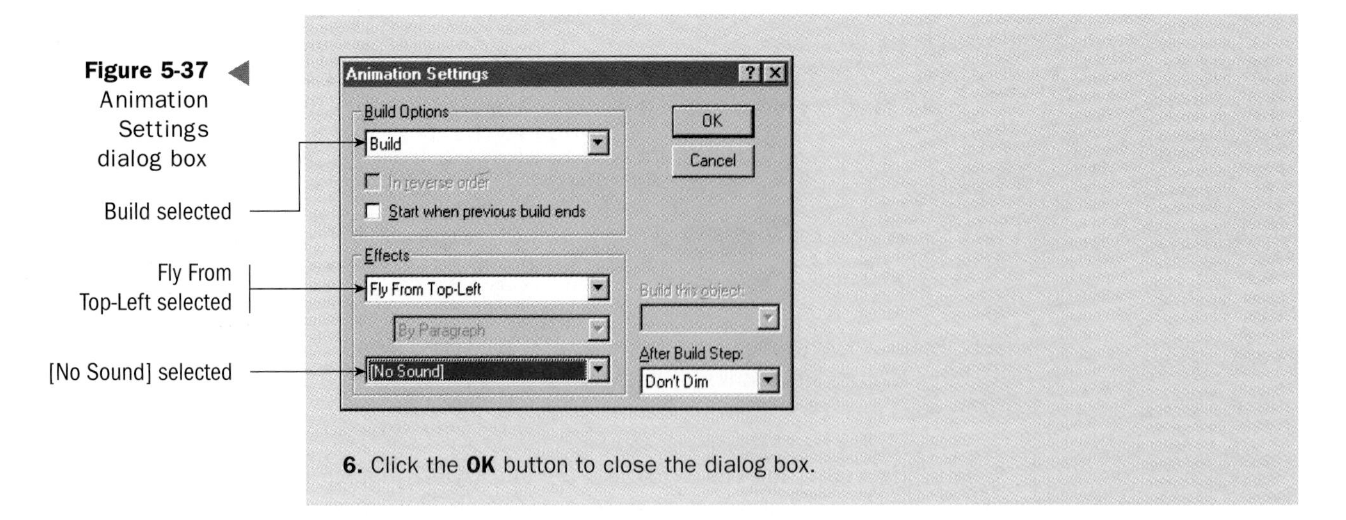

Figure 5-37 Animation Settings dialog box

6. Click the **OK** button to close the dialog box.

To see the animation effects, you'll run the slide show after you save the presentation.

To save the presentation and check the animation effects on slide 7:

1. Click the **Save** button on the Standard toolbar.
2. Click the **Slide Show** button on the horizontal scroll bar to start the slide show with the current slide. When the slide show starts, only the title and the three text items on slide 7 are displayed.
3. Click the mouse button once. The first check mark appears in the upper-left corner of the slide and then flies into position to the left of the word "pencil."
4. Click the mouse button. The second check mark flies into position.
5. Click the mouse button. The third check mark flies into position.
6. Right-click to display the shortcut menu, then click **End Show**. The slide show ends and you return to slide view.

Quick Check

1. From what views can you change to another design template? Are there any restrictions on when or how often you change design templates?
2. Explain how you would rearrange the items in a five-item bulleted list so that the second item becomes the fourth item.
3. How does the process of drawing a perfect square on a slide differ from that for drawing a rectangle? Does that difference also apply when you resize the square?
4. How do you change a slide's layout to another AutoLayout? Is there any restriction on where or when you can change a slide's layout?
5. You want to insert the third slide from a four-slide presentation into your own presentation. How would you accomplish this?
6. Which of the following can you do with an inserted clip art picture: resize it, reposition it, recolor it, copy it.
7. Describe some of the options available when you use animation effects on a slide.

Now that you've completed Session 5.2, you can exit PowerPoint or you can continue to the next session.

SESSION 5.3

In this session you will embed an Excel chart, rearrange slides, annotate slides during a slide show, insert speaker's notes, check the spelling in the presentation, and print the presentation and notes pages.

Embedding an Excel Chart

The Excel chart that Belinda created, which she wants you to include in slide 6, is located on the Sales Chart worksheet of the Excel workbook named Sales. The worksheet contains a table of sales data for the last five years for each of the four classifications of coffee, along with a bar chart of the data. You'll embed rather than link this chart because Belinda does not expect changes to the data on which the chart is based.

Because you don't want to embed the entire worksheet on the slide, you need to open the Excel workbook and copy only the chart. Earlier in this session, you might have minimized the Office Shortcut Bar so that it wasn't visible while you viewed the slide show. If so, you need to restore it now so you can open the Sales workbook and start Excel.

To start Excel, open the Sales workbook, and copy the chart to be embedded:

1. If necessary, click the **Microsoft Office Shortcut** button on the taskbar to restore the Office Shortcut Bar.
2. Click the **Open a Document** button on the Office Shortcut Bar. The Open dialog box appears.
3. Open the **Sales** workbook in the Tutorial.05 folder on your Student Disk.
4. Click the chart to select it, then click the **Copy** button on the Standard toolbar.

Now that you have copied the chart, you can embed it in your presentation. You'll leave the Excel workbook open until you have successfully embedded the chart.

To embed the Excel chart:

1. Click the **Microsoft PowerPoint** button on the taskbar to switch to your presentation.
2. Use the vertical scroll bar to move to slide 6, "Coffee sales by type by year."
3. Click **Edit** on the menu bar, then click **Paste Special**. The Paste Special dialog box opens. See Figure 5-38.

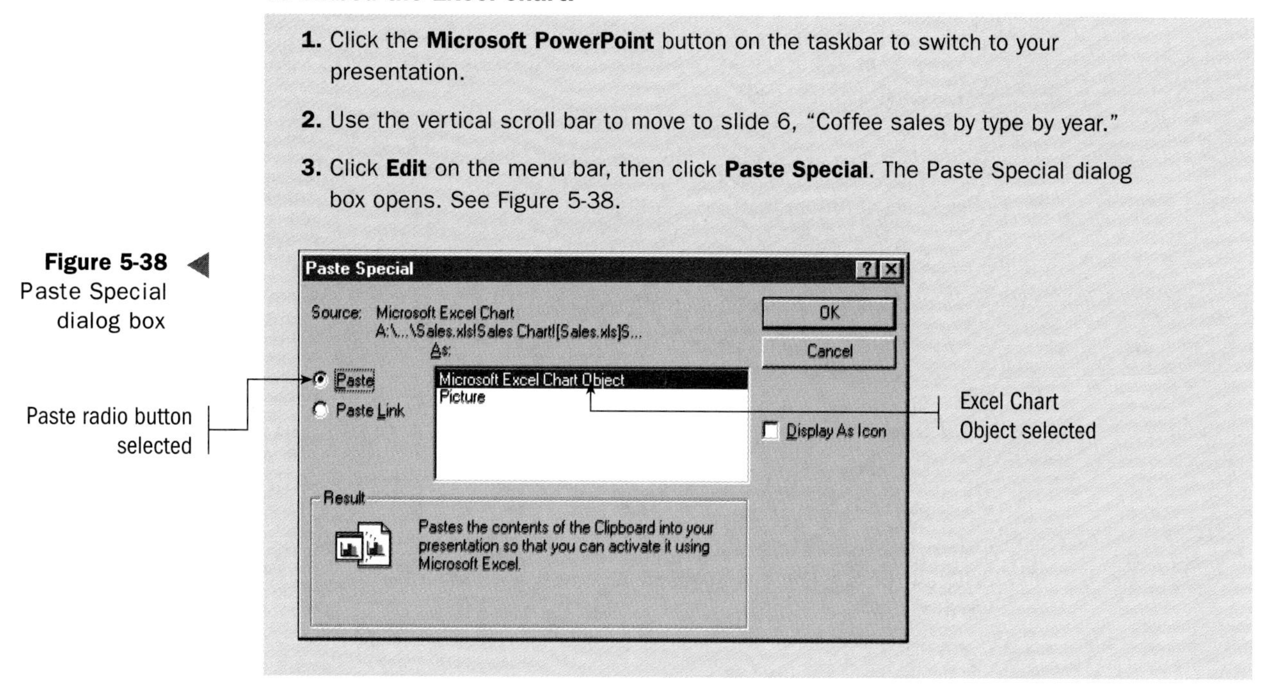

Figure 5-38 Paste Special dialog box

4. If necessary, click the **Paste** radio button, then click **Microsoft Excel Chart Object**, so that the dialog box looks like Figure 5-38.
5. Click the **OK** button to embed the copied chart. After a few moments, the embedded chart is displayed on the slide. The chart is too small, so you need to resize it.
6. Resize and reposition the chart so that it is the same size and in the same position as the chart in Figure 5-39.

Figure 5-39 The embedded Excel chart

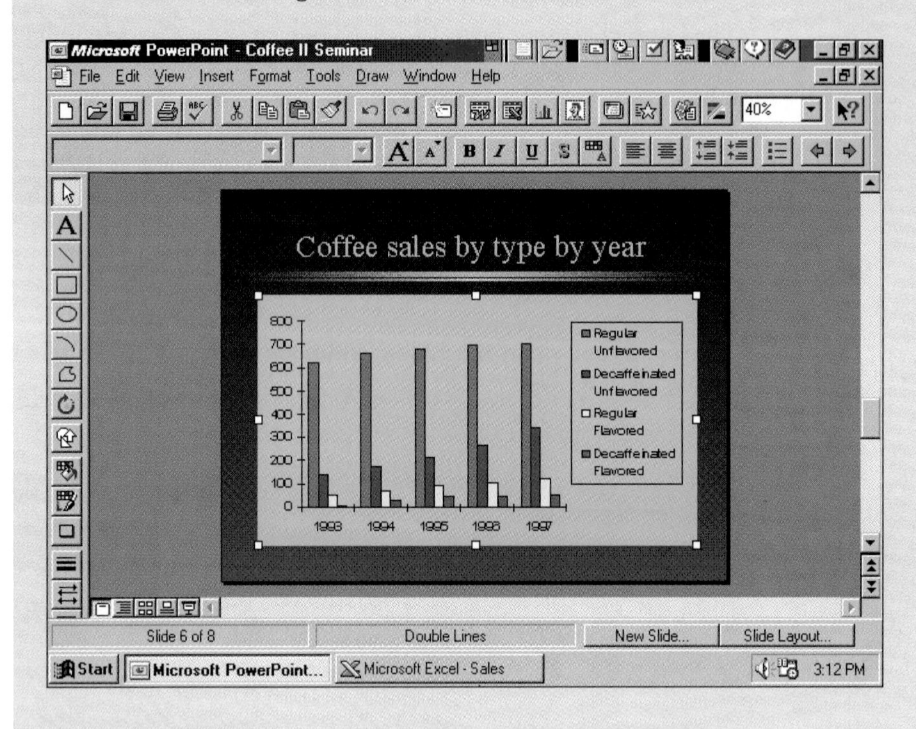

TROUBLE? To resize the chart, drag a sizing handle. To reposition the chart, position the pointer on the selected chart and then click and drag it to a new location.

Now that you have successfully embedded the Excel chart, you can close the workbook and exit Excel.

To switch to Excel, close the workbook, and exit Excel:

1. Click the **Microsoft Excel - Sales** button on the taskbar.
2. Click the **Close** button on the Excel title bar.
3. If a message box appears asking if you want to save changes in the Sales workbook, click the **No** button.

Next, Belinda wants you to change the order of two slides in the presentation.

Rearranging Slides

When delivering the Coffee II seminar, Belinda prefers to discuss the climate before the coffee-growing process, so she asks you to switch slides 3 and 4. You can change the order of slides in either outline view or slide sorter view.

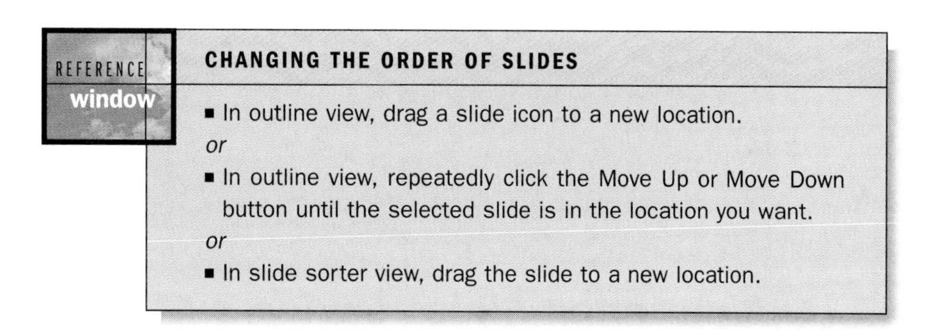

REFERENCE window

CHANGING THE ORDER OF SLIDES

- In outline view, drag a slide icon to a new location.

or

- In outline view, repeatedly click the Move Up or Move Down button until the selected slide is in the location you want.

or

- In slide sorter view, drag the slide to a new location.

You'll switch the third and fourth slides in slide sorter view.

To switch to slide sorter view and rearrange the slide order:

1. Click the **Slide Sorter View** button on the horizontal scroll bar. The first six slides in your presentation are displayed in miniature on the screen.

   TROUBLE? Your screen might display more or fewer than six slides, depending on the size of your monitor. In any case, if slides 3 and 4 are not displayed on your screen, use the vertical scroll bar to shift the display until both of these slides are visible.

   To switch slides 3 and 4, you can move slide 3 so that it falls between slides 4 and 5.

2. Click **slide 3**. A heavy black box appears around slide 3 to indicate that it is selected.

3. Click **slide 3** and hold down the mouse button as you drag the pointer to a position between slides 4 and 5. As you drag the pointer, it changes to . When the pointer is correctly positioned between slides 4 and 5, a vertical solid black line is displayed between those two slides. See Figure 5-40.

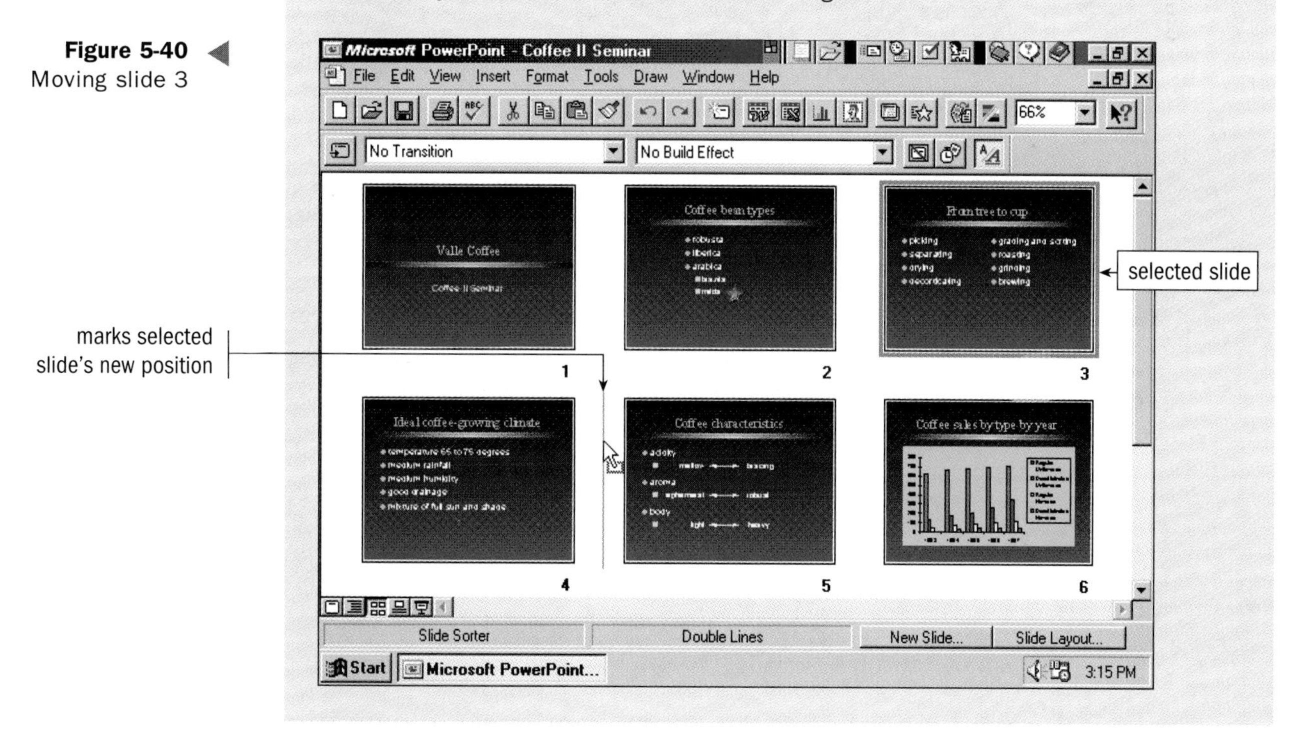

Figure 5-40
Moving slide 3

TROUBLE? If your screen shows four slides in each row, rather than three as shown in Figure 5-40, to move slide 3 between slides 4 and 5, you need to drag the pointer until the vertical solid black line is displayed to the left of slide 5.

4. Release the mouse button. Slide 3, "From tree to cup," is moved and becomes slide 4; and slide 4, "Ideal coffee-growing climate," is now slide 3.

Annotating Slides During a Slide Show

When you are delivering a presentation, it is often helpful to use a pointer to focus audience attention on a particular slide feature. PowerPoint makes it easy to initiate and use a pointer during a slide show, both to direct the audience's attention and to annotate slides by writing or drawing on them. You'll start the slide show and use the pointer.

To use the pointer during a slide show:

1. Click the **Slide Show** button on the horizontal scroll bar to start the slide show with the current slide. The slide show starts, and the "From tree to cup" slide is displayed.

   TROUBLE? If the Office Shortcut Bar is still visible on your screen, you have to minimize it. Click the four colored boxes in the top left of the Office Shortcut Bar to display its menu, then click Minimize. The Office Shortcut Bar disappears. Later, when you finish the slide show and return to the PowerPoint window, the Office Shortcut Bar will be represented by a button on the taskbar.

2. Move the mouse until the pointer is displayed. You can now use as a pointer by simply moving the mouse.

   When the pointer appears, two buttons also appear in the lower-left corner of the screen. You can click either button or right-click the mouse to display the shortcut menu.

3. Right-click to display the shortcut menu, then click **End Show** to end the slide show and return to slide sorter view.

Belinda mentioned that she might want to write or draw on the slides during the seminar. You'll investigate the annotation feature using the Answer Wizard in PowerPoint's Help system.

To use the Answer Wizard to find out about annotating slides:

1. Click **Help** on the menu bar, then click **Answer Wizard**. The Help Topics: Microsoft PowerPoint dialog box opens.
2. Type **write on slides** then click the **Search** button. The Answer Wizard displays a list of topics related to your request.
3. Click **Write or draw (annotate) on slides during a slide show**, then click the **Display** button. The dialog box shown in Figure 5-41 opens.

Figure 5-41 Help information on annotating slides

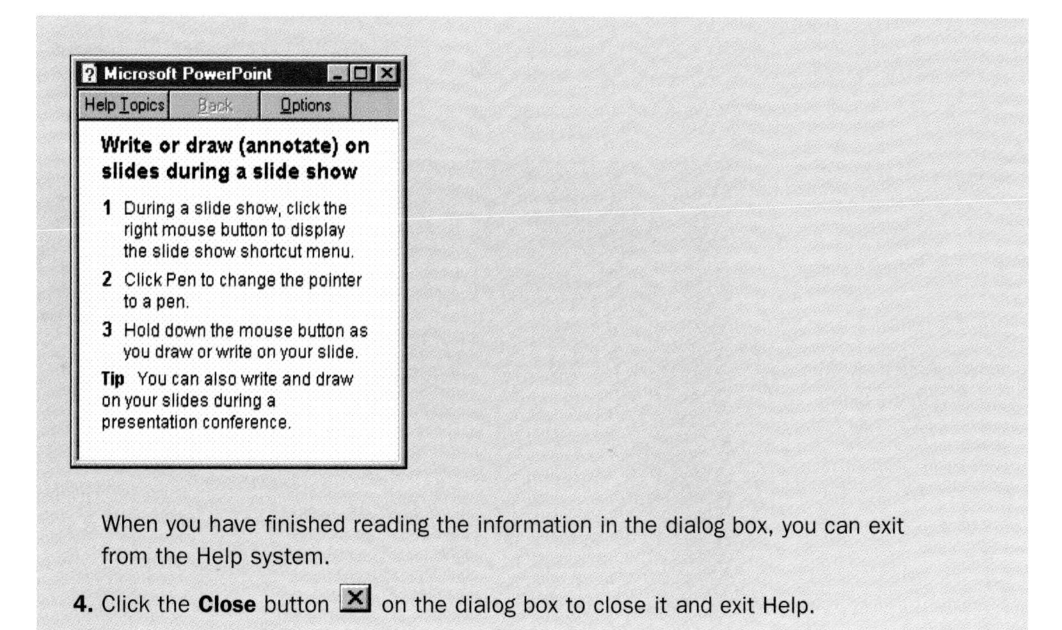

When you have finished reading the information in the dialog box, you can exit from the Help system.

4. Click the **Close** button on the dialog box to close it and exit Help.

Next, you'll start the slide show with slide 3 and practice making freehand marks on that slide.

To annotate slide 3 during a slide show:

1. Click **slide 3** to select it.
2. Click the **Slide Show** button on the horizontal scroll bar to start the slide show with the selected slide. The slide show starts, and the "Ideal coffee-growing climate" slide is displayed.
3. Right-click to display the shortcut menu, then click **Pen**. A pen pointer appears on the screen.

   You can move the pen around the screen, using it as a simple pointer to direct the audience's attention to a particular slide feature. Or, you can use the pen to draw something on the screen. Any marks you make on the screen affect only the current viewing of the slide; they are not part of the slide itself. To see how the pen works, you'll make a check mark over the first bullet.

4. Position the pen pointer to the left of the first bullet, hold the mouse button down as you trace a check mark shape over the bullet, then release the mouse button. The pen mark is only temporary and does not become a permanent part of the slide.

   TROUBLE? Don't worry if your check mark isn't perfect. Developing skill at free-hand slide annotation takes practice. It's a good idea, in general, to avoid drawing diagonal lines. You will find that drawing horizontal or vertical lines is much easier.

   You can also change the color of the "ink" in the pen, which you might need to do depending on the colors of the presentation template you're using. You'll change the color of the pen to yellow.

5. Right-click to display the shortcut menu, point to **Pointer Options**, point to **Pen Color**, then click **Yellow**.

   To see if the pen now writes in yellow, you'll try underlining the words "full sun" to emphasize them.

6. Position the pointer beneath the beginning of the word "full," hold the mouse button down as you drag the pointer to the right to underline "full sun," then release the mouse button. See Figure 5-42.

Figure 5-42 Annotating slide 3

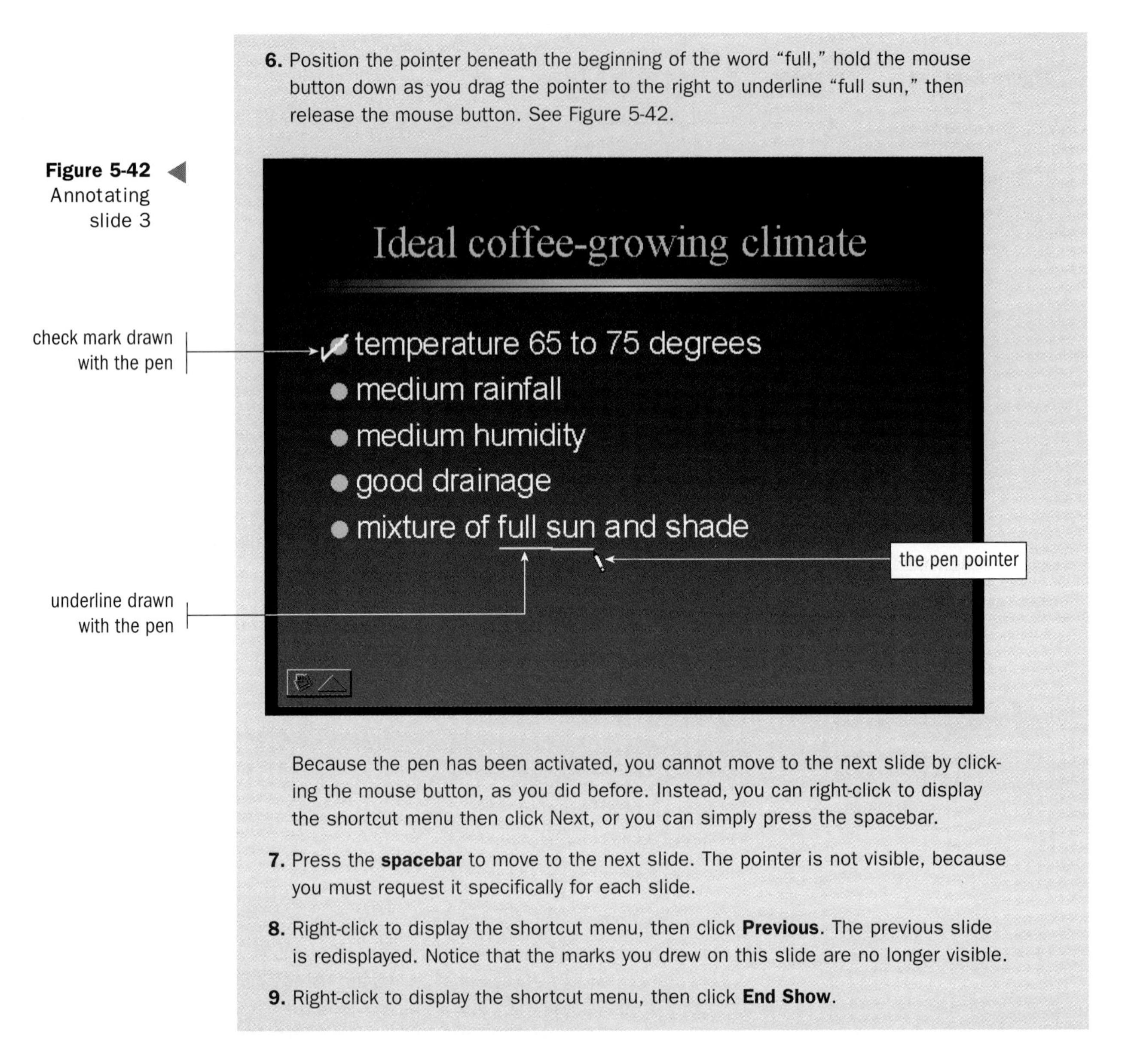

Because the pen has been activated, you cannot move to the next slide by clicking the mouse button, as you did before. Instead, you can right-click to display the shortcut menu then click Next, or you can simply press the spacebar.

7. Press the **spacebar** to move to the next slide. The pointer is not visible, because you must request it specifically for each slide.
8. Right-click to display the shortcut menu, then click **Previous**. The previous slide is redisplayed. Notice that the marks you drew on this slide are no longer visible.
9. Right-click to display the shortcut menu, then click **End Show**.

If you want to learn more about running a slide show, use the Help system to read about annotations, slide shows, slide show controls, and using keyboard shortcuts during a slide show.

Working with Speaker's Notes

Each PowerPoint slide has an accompanying notes page that includes a smaller copy of the slide along with room for notes you type. You can print the notes pages, also called **speaker's notes**, and use them to remember key points as you give a presentation.

Inserting Speaker's Notes

You use the notes pages view to enter, edit, or view speaker's notes. To create speaker's notes, you type the text as you would enter text in any Office 95 program.

You still have Belinda's note cards, which she gave you when she first asked you to create this presentation. You'll enter speaker's notes using Belinda's notes as a guide.

To change to notes pages view and insert speaker's notes:

1. Click the **Notes Pages View** button on the horizontal scroll bar to switch to notes pages view. PowerPoint displays the notes page for the current slide.
2. Use the vertical scroll bar to scroll until the notes page for the first slide is displayed. The entire page is displayed, with a copy of the slide at the top of the page and a blocked area for notes at the bottom of the page. See Figure 5-43.

Figure 5-43
Slide 1 in notes pages view

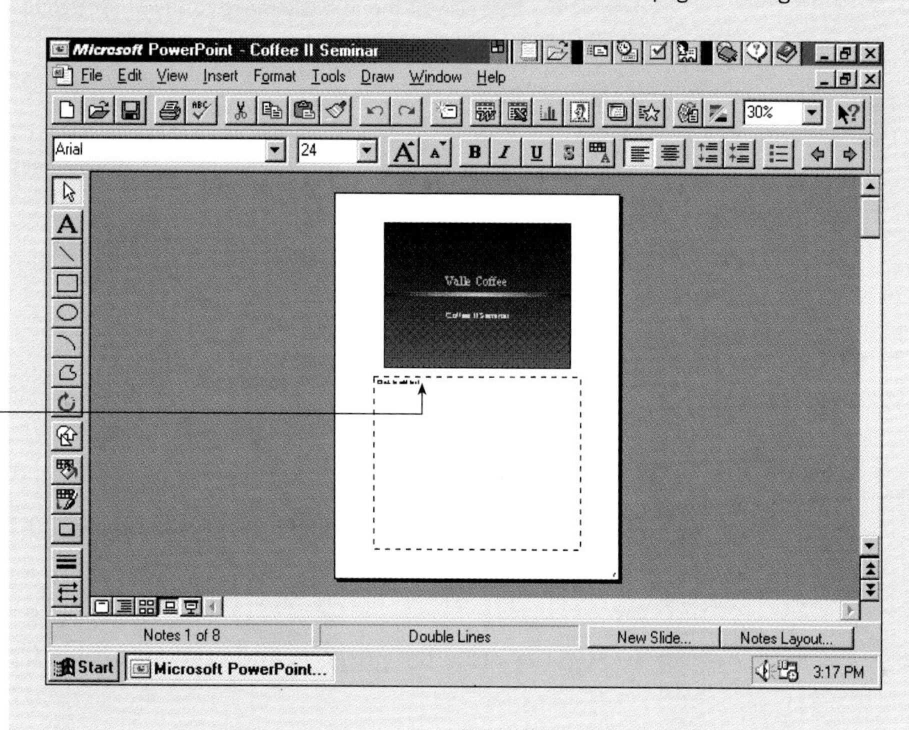

TROUBLE? If the entire page is not visible, click the Zoom Control list arrow on the Standard toolbar, then click Fit.

Next you'll increase the magnification to make it easier to see the text area of the notes page.

3. Click the **Zoom Control** list arrow on the Standard toolbar, then click **100%**. The bottom of the slide and the top of the text area are now visible.
4. Click the text box, type **Welcome the audience and introduce myself.**, then press the **Enter** key.

   TROUBLE? If you make a typing error, correct it as you would correct text in any Office 95 program.

5. Type **Briefly state the purpose and content of this Coffee II seminar.**, press the **Enter** key, then type **Give a very brief history of Valle Coffee.**

You can format the text of speaker's notes just as you format text in any Office 95 program. Belinda had underlined the words "very brief" in her notes to emphasize these words. You'll italicize them on the notes page for emphasis and make some other formatting changes to the text to make it easier to read.

To format the text of the speaker's notes:

1. Select the words "very brief," then click the **Italic** button on the Formatting toolbar.

2. Select all three lines of text, then click the **Bullet On/Off** button on the Formatting toolbar. Bullets are inserted to the left of each line.

3. With the three lines of text still selected, click the **Increase Paragraph Spacing** button on the Formatting toolbar twice. The spacing between the three lines is increased, helping to visually separate the three items.

   Increasing the font size of the text will make it easier for Belinda to see the notes during the presentation.

4. With the three lines of text still selected, click the **Font Size** list arrow, then click **18**.

5. Click the mouse in a blank area to deselect the text. Your screen should now look like Figure 5-44.

Figure 5-44 Speaker's notes entered for slide 1

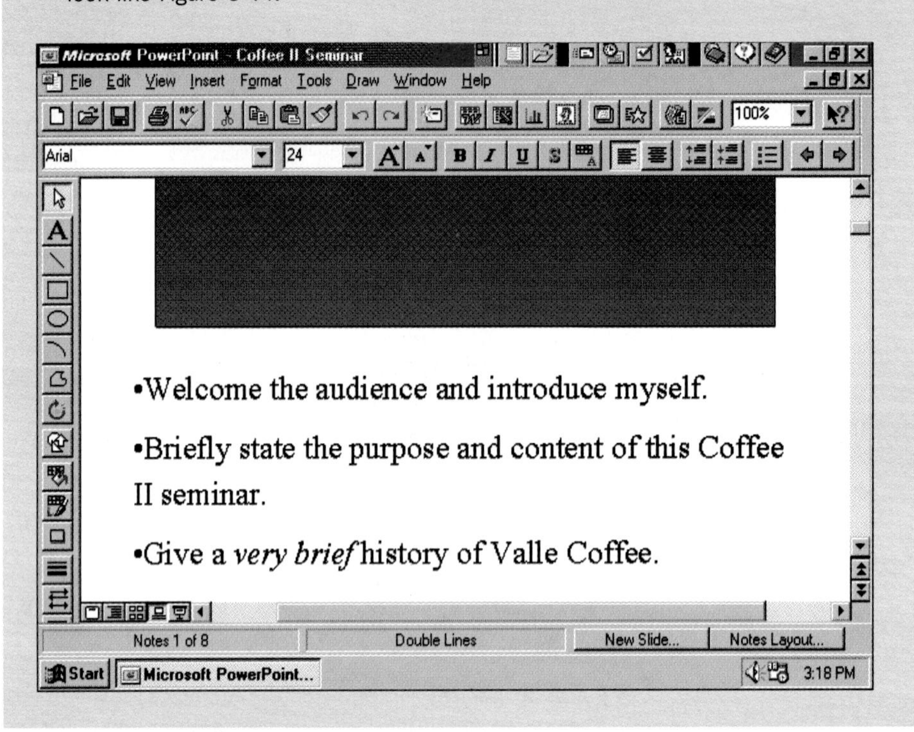

Checking Spelling

As you near completion of a presentation, it is always a good idea to check the spelling. You should also proofread your slides carefully to find and correct punctuation and capitalization errors as well as any misuses of words that the spell check would not catch.

You check spelling in PowerPoint in exactly the same way as you check spelling in any Office 95 document, by clicking the Spelling button on the Standard toolbar. All the words that appear on your slides will be checked. If you have entered any speaker's notes, these too will be checked. However, words that are part of an object, such as an embedded Excel worksheet or a WordArt image, will not be checked.

To spell check the presentation:

1. Click the **Spelling** button on the Standard toolbar. The spell check begins to check your slides and notes from the beginning of the presentation.

2. Continue the spell checking process, choosing Ignore or Change, as appropriate, until a message appears indicating that the spell check has finished checking the entire presentation. The spell check will stop on the words "Valle," "robusta," "liberica," "arabica," and "milds." If you have spelled these words correctly, click the Ignore All button. If the spell check detects any other word not in its dictionary, correct the word.
3. Click the **OK** button to close the dialog box containing the message.

Printing a Presentation

Now that the presentation is complete, you'll print a copy of it to show to Belinda. You'll also print the speaker's notes page for slide 1 so that she can check the notes and how you formatted them. Then she'll enter notes for the remaining slides.

Printing Multiple Slides per Page

PowerPoint provides several options for printing the slides in a presentation. You can print one slide per page, with each slide filling a page. Or you can print **handouts**, on which two, three, or six slides are printed on a page. Handouts are useful if you want to distribute copies of your presentation slides to the audience so they can follow along as you make your presentation.

To print the presentation as handouts:

1. Click **File** on the menu bar, then click **Print**. The Print dialog box opens.
2. Click the **Print what** list arrow, scroll the list until "Handouts (6 slides per page)" is visible, then click **Handouts (6 slides per page)**.
3. To print on a black-and-white printer, click the **Black & White** check box.
4. Click the **OK** button.

Printing Speaker's Notes

You can choose to print just the speaker's notes for one or more slides in a presentation. Belinda wants to see how you formatted the notes for slide 1, and she asks you to print the notes page for this slide.

To print the notes page for the first slide:

1. Make sure slide 1 is the current slide.
2. Click **File** on the menu bar, then click **Print**. The Print dialog box opens.
3. Click the **Print what** list arrow, scroll the list until "Notes Pages" is visible, then click **Notes Pages**.
4. Click the **Current Slide** radio button to select printing of the notes page for only the current slide (slide 1).
5. To print on a black-and-white printer, click the **Black & White** check box.
6. Click the **OK** button to print the notes page for slide 1.

You have now completed your work on the Coffee II Seminar presentation, so you will save the presentation and exit PowerPoint.

To save and close the presentation, then exit PowerPoint:

1. Click the **Save** button on the Standard toolbar.

   Earlier in this session you might have minimized the Office Shortcut Bar so that it wasn't visible while you viewed the slide show. If so, you must restore it now.

2. If necessary, click the **Microsoft Office Shortcut** button on the taskbar.
3. Click the **Close** button on the PowerPoint title bar to close PowerPoint. PowerPoint closes, and you return to the Windows 95 desktop.

You give Belinda the presentation file and the printouts. After reviewing the material, Belinda is very pleased with the results and feels sure that the presentation will be well received by the seminar participants.

Quick Check

1. Describe the procedure you used to embed the Excel chart into your presentation.
2. Describe two different techniques you can use to move a slide.
3. During a slide show, how do you activate a pointer? A pen?
4. What are speaker's notes? In what view can you access them? How might they be used?
5. When you spell check a presentation, what parts of the presentation are checked? What parts are not checked?
6. What are handouts? What options are available for printing handouts?

Tutorial Assignments

Belinda asks you to assist her in preparing a sales presentation for Valle Coffee. Complete the following:

1. Make sure your Student Disk is in the disk drive.
2. Start a new PowerPoint presentation using the Lines On Blue design template.
3. Add slides 1 through 4, and type the slide text as shown in Figure 5-45. Use the AutoLayout indicated below each slide. Then add a blank slide as slide 5.

Figure 5-45

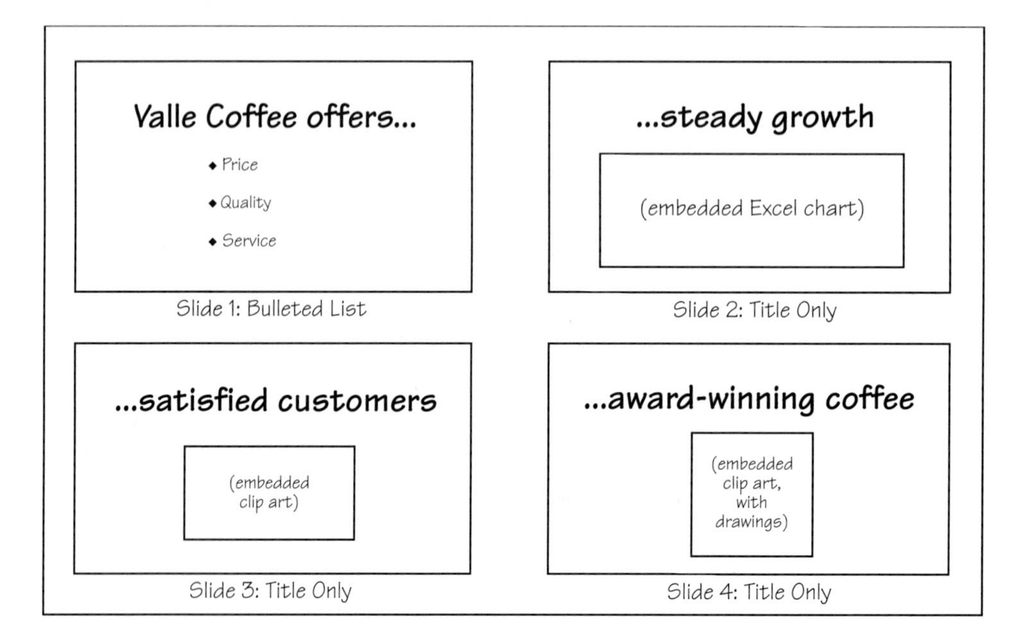

4. Save the presentation as Sales Presentation in the TAssign folder in the Tutorial.05 folder on your Student Disk.
5. On slide 1, click the bulleted list to activate the placeholder, click the placeholder border to display the sizing handles, then resize the placeholder so that the bulleted list is positioned as shown in Figure 5-45.

6. Select the bulleted list items on slide 1, then apply animation effects to build By 1st Level Paragraphs. Then use a Build Effect of your own choosing.
7. Move to slide 3, then insert the picture of the clapping hands, which is available in the Gestures category in the Microsoft ClipArt Gallery 2.0 dialog box.

8. Select the clip art on slide 3 and apply animation effects. Choose Build, then select the Clapping sound effect. (*Note:* The computer you're using must have speakers attached in order for you to hear any sound effects during the slide show.)

9. Edit slide 4 as follows:
   a. Insert the picture of the gold medal with blue ribbons, which is available in the Entertainment category in the Microsoft ClipArt Gallery 2.0 dialog box.
   b. Click the Help button on the Standard toolbar, click the Text Tool button on the Drawing toolbar, then read the displayed Help information.
   c. Activate the Text Tool, position the pointer in the lower-right portion of the medal, click the mouse to set the insertion point, click the Text Color button on the Formatting toolbar, select the medium-blue color choice, then type "1st Place."
   d. Reposition the text box, if necessary, so that "1st Place" is centered in the bottom half of the medal.
   e. Draw a perfect star AutoShape to fit in the top half of the medal, then reposition the star, if necessary, so that it is centered in the top half of the medal.
   f. Change the Fill Color for the star to a Shaded, Two Color fill, using the yellow choice for Color 1, and the medium-blue choice for Color 2.
   g. Change the Line Color for the star to the medium-blue choice.
10. Edit slide 1 and move the bulleted item Price to the bottom of the bulleted list.
11. Move to slide 3, then insert the slides from the file Slides2, which is located in the TAssign folder within the Tutorial.05 folder on your Student Disk.
12. Open the AllSales document in the TAssign folder within the Tutorial.05 folder on your Student Disk, and then copy the selected chart.
13. Switch to PowerPoint, move to slide 2, embed the chart on that slide, then resize the chart so it is large enough to be readable. Position the chart so that it is centered on the slide.
14. Switch to slide sorter view, then move the slide that is currently slide 4 so that it becomes slide 1.

15. Use the Index feature in the on-line Help in PowerPoint to look up the topic "transitions." Read the topic "Add transitions to a slide show," then add a transition effect of your choosing to all the slides in the presentation.
16. View the slide show. Activate and use the pointer to point to each of the three bulleted items on slide 2.
17. Enter brief speaker's notes for slide 3, indicating the points you want to make about the chart.
18. Spell check your presentation, correcting spelling errors as necessary.
19. Save the presentation, then print the entire presentation as Handouts (6 slides per page). Print the notes page for slide 3.
20. Close PowerPoint.
21. Close Excel. (If you are asked if you want to save changes, answer No.)

Case Problems

1. Ashbrook Mall Information Desk Rita Galvez, who works in the Mall Operations Office, requests your assistance in preparing a presentation to promote the mall's meeting facilities. Complete the following:

1. Make sure your Student Disk is in the disk drive.
2. Start a new PowerPoint presentation using the Soaring design template.
3. Add slides 1 through 6, and type the slide text as shown in Figure 5-46. Use the AutoLayout indicated below each slide. Then add a blank slide at the end.

Figure 5-46

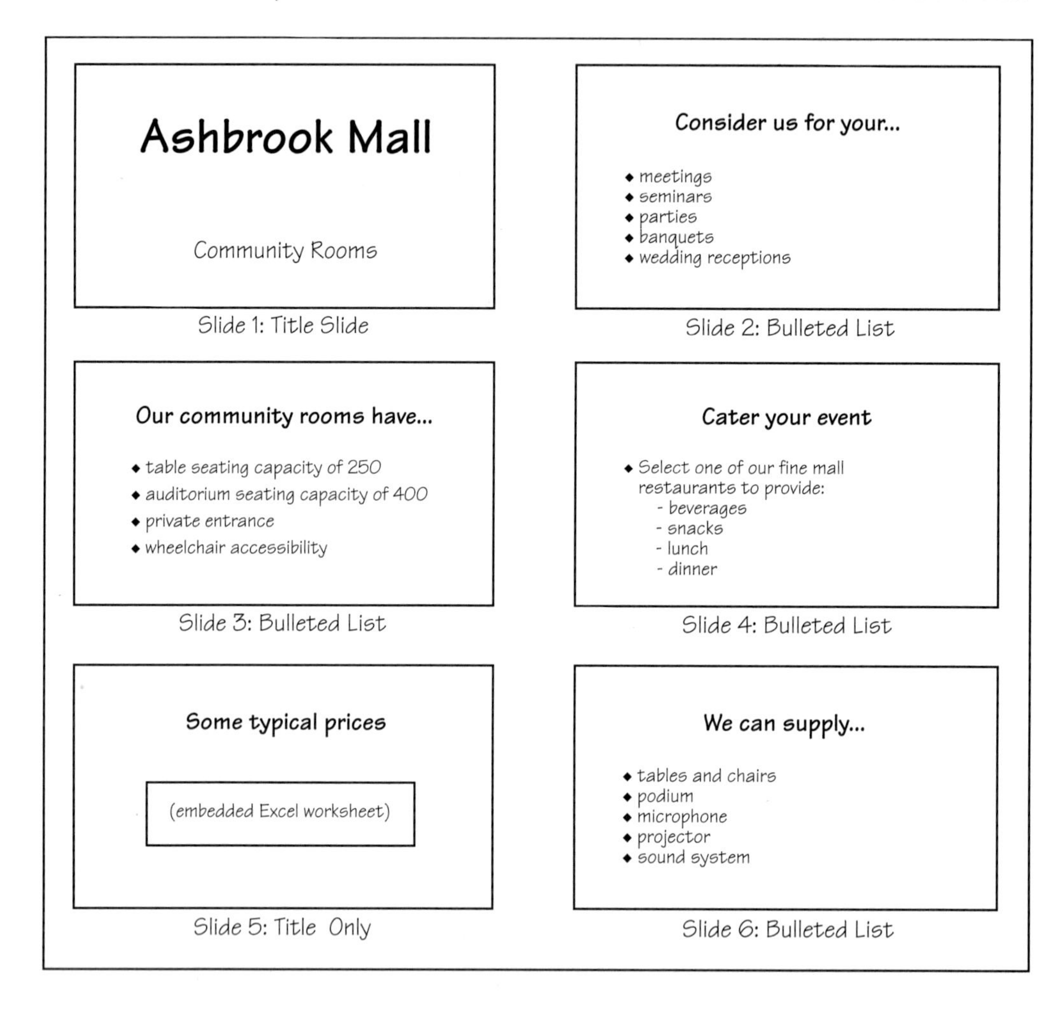

4. Save the presentation as Community Rooms in the Cases folder within the Tutorial.05 folder on your Student Disk.
5. Select the four second-level bulleted items on slide 4, then Demote them one level to indent them to the third level. Change the font size for those four items to 28.
6. On slide 2, move "banquets" so it becomes the third item in the bulleted list.

7. Select the five bulleted items on slide 2, then apply animation effects to build By 1st Level Paragraphs. Select the Box Out build effect and the Camera sound effect.
8. Change the design template to Tridots.
9. Edit the title master to change the font size for the title to 60, and the font size for the subtitle to 40.

10. Move to slide 5, then do the following:
    a. Open the document Catering in the Cases folder within the Tutorial.05 folder on your Student Disk.
    b. Select cells A5 through D8, then copy the selection.
    c. Switch back to PowerPoint, then use the Paste Special command to embed the Excel worksheet object.
    d. Resize and reposition the embedded worksheet object so that there is approximately a one-inch margin on the left and right sides of the object.

    e. Position the pointer over the worksheet, then right-click to display the shortcut menu. Click Recolor, change the darker green color box in the New column to gray, change the lighter green color box in the New column to medium orange (second column of the second row), then click the OK button.

    f. Click the Help button on the Standard toolbar, click the Text Tool button on the Drawing toolbar, then read the displayed Help information. Activate the Text Tool, change the font size to 18, position the pointer beneath the last column of the embedded worksheet, then type "Prices as of 4/1/98".
    g. Reposition the text you just entered so that it is slightly below the embedded worksheet object, with its right edge even with the right edge of the embedded object.
11. Change to slide sorter view, and move slide 6 so that it becomes slide 3.
12. Add appropriate speaker's notes to one slide of your choosing.
13. Spell check your presentation, then save it.
14. View the slide show. Activate the pointer and use it to point at items in a bulleted list.
15. Print the presentation as Handouts (6 slides per page). Then print the notes page for the slide to which you added speaker's notes.
16. Close PowerPoint.
17. Close Excel. (If you are asked if you want to save changes, answer No.)

2. Professional Litigation User Services Diana Bullard, a graphic artist at PLUS, is preparing a manual and supplementary presentation to be used for new-employee training in her department. She asks you to help her create the presentation by completing the following:

1. Make sure your Student Disk is in the disk drive.
2. Start a new PowerPoint presentation using the Side Fade design template.
3. Add slides 1 through 5, and type the slide text as shown in Figure 5-47. Use the AutoLayout indicated below each slide. Then add a blank slide as slide 6.

Figure 5-47

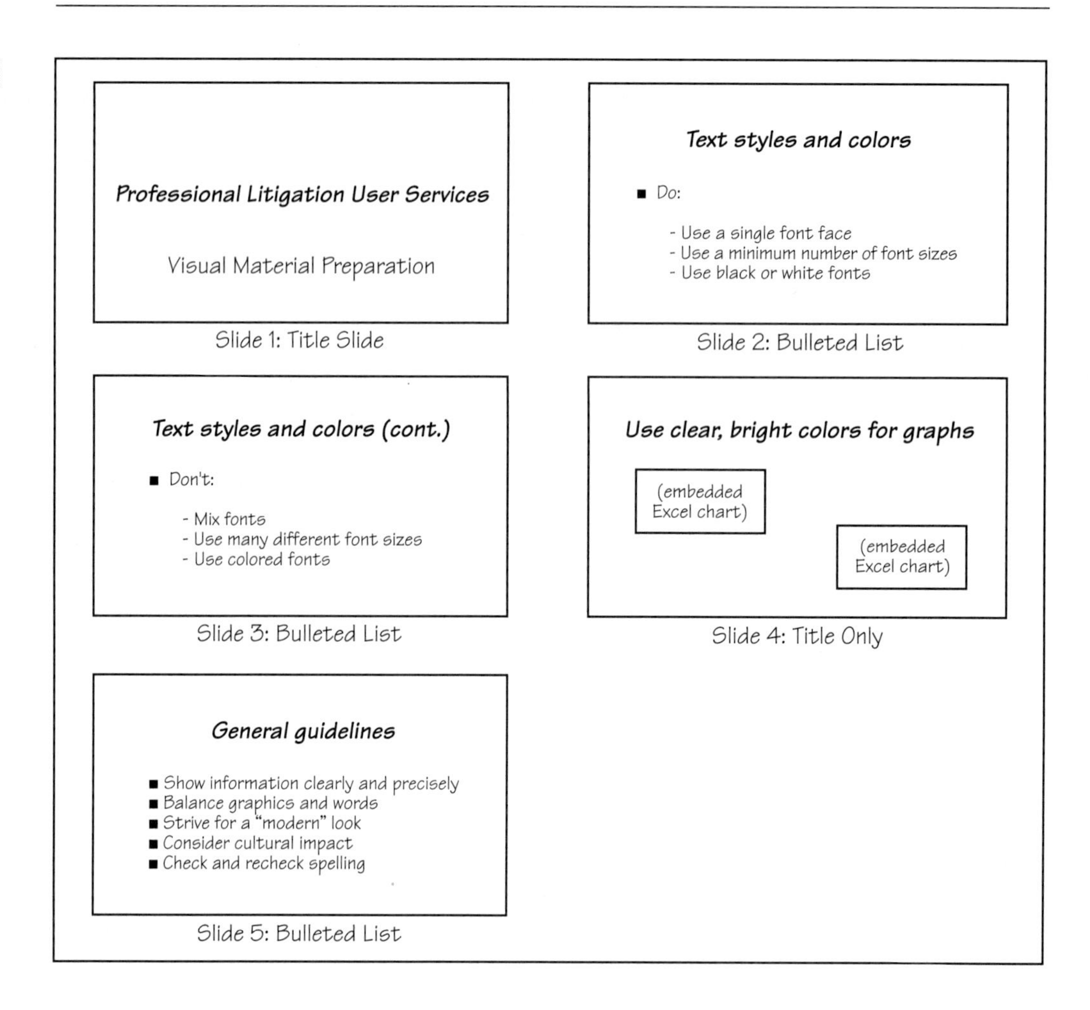

4. Save the presentation as PLUS Presentation in the Cases folder within the Tutorial.05 folder on your Student Disk.
5. For both slides 2 and 3, select the second-level bulleted items, then increase the paragraph spacing using the Increase Paragraph Spacing button on the Formatting toolbar. For slide 5, select the entire bulleted list and then increase the paragraph spacing.
6. Resize the title placeholders on slides 1 and 4 so that the titles fit on a single line.
7. Edit slide 3 as follows:
   a. Select the word "fonts" in the "Mix fonts" item, then change its Font Face to Britannic Bold (or choose any font other than Arial if Britannic Bold isn't available).
   b. Change the font size for the word "many" to 36.
   c. Change the font size for the word "sizes" to 24.
   d. Select the word "colored," click the Text Color button on the Formatting toolbar, then click the third color sample in the second row.

8. Select all four bulleted items on slide 3, then apply animation effects to build By 2nd Level Paragraphs using the Blinds Horizontal effect. Then do the same for slide 2.
9. Change the design template to Shaded Bars. (If that design template isn't available, use any other template of your choice. In that case, your color choices will be different from those specified in step 11.)

10. Embed a chart on slide 4 as follows:
    a. Open the Commuter document in the Cases folder within the Tutorial.05 folder on your Student Disk.
    b. Click the chart to select it, then click the Copy button.
    c. Switch back to PowerPoint, then use the Paste Special command to embed the Microsoft Excel Chart Object onto the slide.
    d. Resize the embedded chart so it is approximately 1½ times its current size, then reposition the chart at the upper left, as indicated in the presentation plan in Figure 5-47.
    e. With the embedded chart still selected, click the Copy button, then click the Paste button.
    f. Reposition the selected chart copy in the lower-right corner of the slide, as shown in the presentation plan.

11. Edit slide 4 as follows:
    a. Right-click the selected chart copy, then click Recolor. Change the original colors for the chart as follows: change the blue to the pink sample in the first row; change the green to the pink sample in the second row; change the red to the pale blue sample in the second row; and change the yellow to the gray sample in the second row.
    b. Click the Help button on the Standard toolbar, click the Text Tool button on the Drawing toolbar, then read the displayed Help information.
    c. Click the Text Tool button on the Drawing toolbar, click the Text Color button on the Formatting toolbar, click the second color in the second row, position the pointer to the right of the first chart, approximately one-third of the way down, then type "Do".
    d. Repeat the previous step, except position the pointer to the left of the second chart, approximately two-thirds of the way down, then type "Don't".
    e. Click the Line Tool button on the Drawing toolbar, then draw a horizontal line directly beneath the word "Do." Click the Line Color button on the Drawing toolbar, then click the second color in the second row. Click the Arrowheads button on the Drawing toolbar, then click the large left-pointing arrow.
    f. With the arrow still selected, click the Copy button, click the Paste button, then position the selected arrow copy beneath the word "Don't." Click the Arrowheads button on the Drawing toolbar, then click the large right-pointing arrow.
12. Insert the slide from the file NewPLUS, which is in the Cases folder within the Tutorial.05 folder on your Student Disk.
13. Move the slide you just added so that it becomes slide 6. Then move slide 5 ("General guidelines") so it becomes slide 2.
14. Add appropriate speaker's notes to any one slide of your choosing.
15. Check the spelling in your presentation, correcting misspellings if necessary. Then save the presentation.
16. View the slide show. Use the pointer and pen as you go through the slide show.
17. Print your presentation as Handouts (6 slides per page). Print the notes page for the slide to which you added speaker's notes.
18. Close PowerPoint.
19. Close Excel. (If you are asked if you want to save changes, answer No.)

3. Best Friends Richard Moscovitch, one of the directors at Best Friends, is preparing a recruitment presentation for field trainers. He asks you to help him create the presentation by completing the following:

1. Make sure your Student Disk is in the disk drive.
2. Start a new PowerPoint presentation using the Comet design template.
3. Add slides 1 through 5, and type the slide text as shown in Figure 5-48. Use the AutoLayout indicated below each slide. Then add a blank slide at the end of the presentation.

Figure 5-48

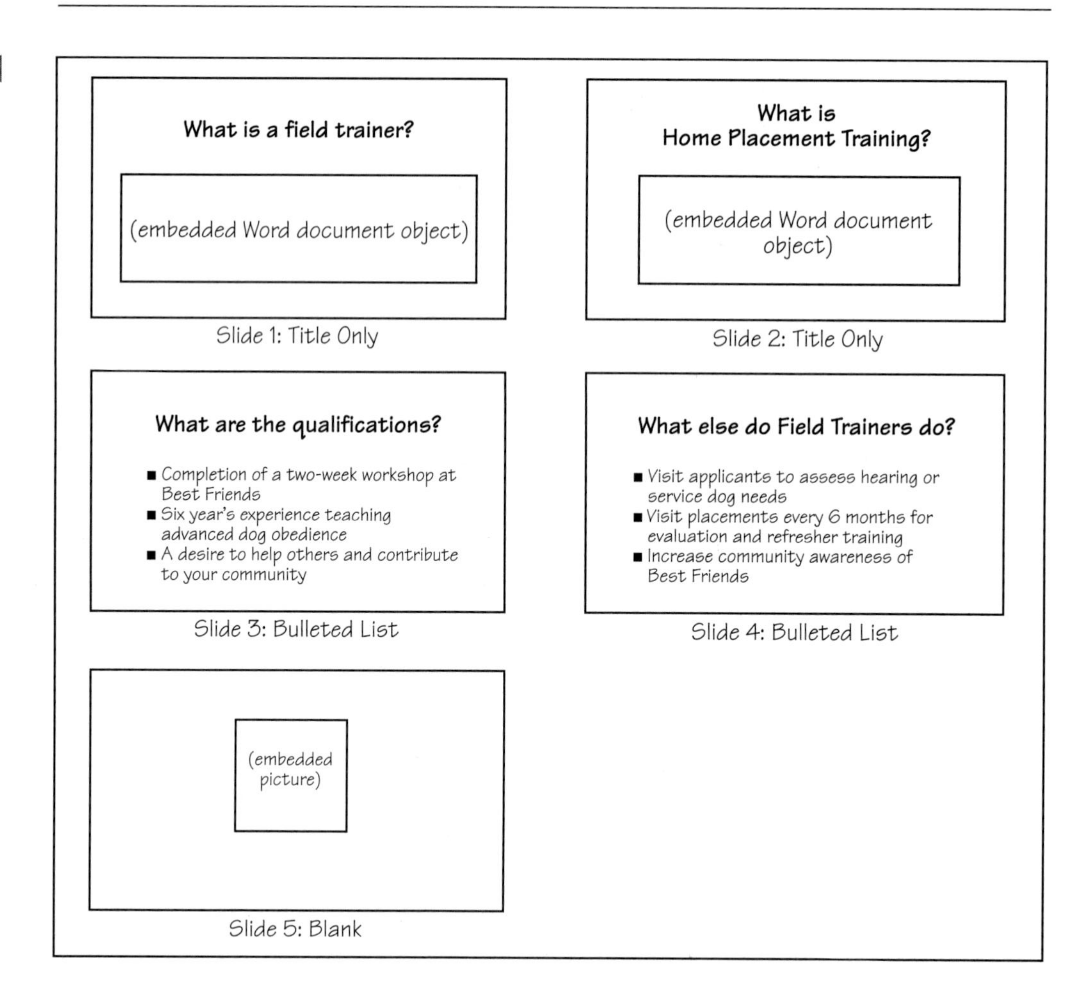

4. Save the presentation as Field Trainers in the Cases folder within the Tutorial.05 folder on your Student Disk.

5. Edit slide 5 as follows:
   a. Click the Help button on the Standard toolbar, click the Text Tool button on the Drawing toolbar, then read the displayed Help information. Click the Text Tool button on the Drawing toolbar, click anywhere near the left edge of the slide to position the insertion point, then type "Join the Best Friends team... today!"
   b. Change the font size for the text you just typed to 32.
   c. Select the text "Best Friends," change the font size to 36, italicize the text, and apply a Text Shadow.
   d. Position the text so that it is horizontally centered and positioned about three-fourths of the way down the slide.
   e. Click Insert on the menu bar, click Picture, then insert the picture named Heart, which is located in the Cases folder within the Tutorial.05 folder on your Student Disk.
   f. Resize the embedded picture so that it is approximately twice as large, then reposition it so that it is centered above the text message.

6. Select the picture on slide 5, then apply animation effects to Build, using the Dissolve build effect and the Chime sound effect. (*Note:* The computer you're using must have speakers attached in order for you to hear any sound effects during the slide show.)
7. Change the design template to Blue Green.

8. Edit slide 4 as follows:
   a. Italicize the text "Best Friends."
   b. Insert enough blank spaces to the left of the word "Best" so that "Best Friends" appears together on a second line.

   c. Select all the bulleted items, then apply animation effects to build By 1st Level Paragraphs, using the Split Horizontal Out build effect.
9. Edit slide 3 as follows:
   a. Move the first bulleted item so that it becomes the second item in the list.
   b. Italicize the text "Best Friends."

   c. Select all the bulleted items, then apply animation effects to build By 1st Level Paragraphs, using the Split Horizontal Out build effect.
10. Edit slide 1 as follows:
    a. Open the document named Trainers, which is located in the Cases folder within the Tutorial.05 folder of your Student Disk.
    b. Select and copy the first seven lines of the document.
    c. Switch to PowerPoint and use the Paste Special command to embed the Word Document Object into your presentation.
    d. Right-click the embedded object, then click Edit Document Object.
    e. Select all the text in the edit window and change the font size to 32. (*Hint:* click the Font Size list box, type "32," then press the Enter key.)
    f. Select and resize the edit window so that all the text is visible and so that the text occupies just seven lines, then click outside the edit window to close it.
    g. Right-click the embedded text, click Recolor, then change the original black color to white, and the gray color to the pink in the second row of color choices.
    h. Reposition the embedded text so it is centered beneath the title.

11. Edit slide 2 as follows:
    a. Switch to Word, then select and copy the last four lines of the document.
    b. Switch to PowerPoint and use the Paste Special command to embed the Word Document Object into your presentation.
    c. Right-click the embedded object, then click Edit Document Object.
    d. Select all the text in the edit window, then change the font size to 32. (*Hint:* click the Font Size list box, type "32," then press the Enter key.)
    e. Resize the edit window so that all the text is visible and so that the text occupies just five lines, then click outside the edit window to close it.
    f. Right-click the embedded text, click Recolor, then change the original black color to white.
    g. Reposition the embedded text so it is centered beneath the title.
12. Insert the slide from the file Title, which is located in the Cases folder within the Tutorial.05 folder of your Student Disk.
13. In either outline or slide sorter view, move the title slide you just inserted so it becomes the first slide, then move the current slide 5 so it becomes slide 4.
14. Enter appropriate speaker's notes to any one slide of your choosing.
15. Check the spelling of your presentation, correcting it as needed. Then save the presentation.
16. View the slide show. Use the pointer to point to items on the slides as you view the slide show.
17. Print your presentation as Handouts (6 slides per page). Print the notes page for the slide to which you added speaker's notes.
18. Close PowerPoint.
19. Close Word. (If you are asked if you want to save changes, answer No.)

4. Carlson Containers Tom Carlson is seeking venture capital in the amount of $1.2 million for his startup company, Carlson Containers. Tom started his company after he had developed a new child-resistant cap. When the cap was tested with children, adults, and senior citizens, it passed with flying colors—children could not open it, but adults and senior citizens had few problems. So Tom decided to manufacture pill containers using his new cap.

Tom has sketched a presentation to give to executives at a local investment banking firm and asks for your help in preparing the presentation slides.

Complete the following:

1. Make sure your Student Disk is in the disk drive.
2. Start a new presentation, using the Color Boxes design template.
3. Add and enter text for each of the six slides shown in Figure 5-49. Use the AutoLayout indicated below each slide. Then add a final, blank slide.

Figure 5-49

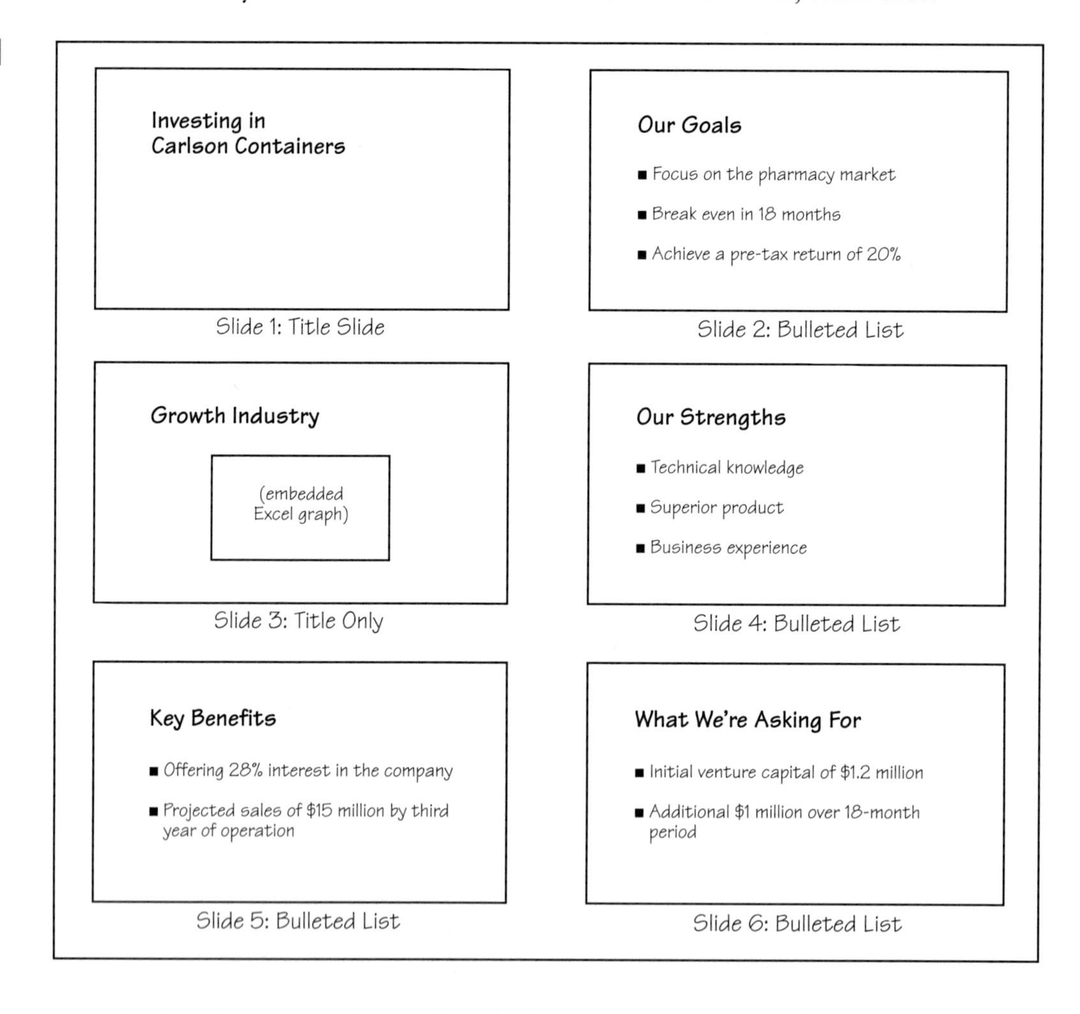

4. Save the presentation as Carlson Containers in the Cases folder within the Tutorial.05 folder on your Student Disk.
5. On slide 3, embed the chart found in the Excel workbook named Carlson, which is located in the Cases folder within the Tutorial.05 folder on your Student Disk. Resize the chart so it is readable, and reposition the chart so it is slightly left of center.

6. Use the Drawing toolbar to create an upward pointing arrow to the right of the chart. Make the arrow red with a black outline. Resize the arrow so it is exactly as tall as the embedded chart.
7. Edit slide 4 to move the second bulleted item to the first position in the list.
8. Use the Increase Paragraph Spacing button on the Formatting toolbar to increase the paragraph spacing for all bulleted lists, so that all the text doesn't appear crowded into the top halves of the slides.

9. Move slide 4 so it becomes slide 3.

10. Click the Help button on the Standard toolbar, click the Text Tool button on the Drawing toolbar, then read the displayed Help information. Click the Text Tool button on the Drawing toolbar, then type two lines of text centered beneath the embedded Excel chart. Type "Forecast Industry Growth" as the first line, and "(Source: 1997 Pharmaceutical Industry Research)" as the second line. Use a font size of 24 for the first line, and a font size of 18 for the second line.

11. On each slide with a bulleted list, select all the bulleted items and then add animation effects to build By 1st Level Paragraphs. Select a build effect you like and use that same effect for all the bulleted list slides.

12. On the slide with the embedded Excel chart, select the arrow and apply animation effects to build the arrow using the Wipe Up build effect.
13. Add appropriate speaker's notes to any one slide of your choosing.
14. Spell check the presentation, then save it.
15. View the slide show. Use the pointer or the pen to draw attention to particular slide items.
16. Print your presentation as Handouts (6 slides per page). Print the notes page for the slide to which you added speaker's notes.
17. Close all programs. (Do not save changes to the Excel workbook.)

TUTORIAL 6

Enhancing an Excel Workbook and Creating and Linking a Chart to Word

Enhancing and Charting Sales Information

OBJECTIVES

In this tutorial you will:

- Learn how to organize multisheet workbooks and create a documentation sheet
- Use the Excel AutoFill, AutoSum, and AutoFormat features
- Enhance a worksheet's appearance and usefulness
- Test a worksheet
- Learn how to plan and develop effective charts
- Plan, create, and modify two charts
- Link a chart to a Word document

CASE

Valle Coffee

Kim Carpenter, director of marketing at Valle Coffee, has compiled sales totals, in pounds, for each of the last five years for each of the four general coffee classifications. She has also collected five-year total sales data by state. She plans to use this data to analyze Valle Coffee sales trends.

Kim has started an Excel workbook and asks you to complete it for her. She wants you to use the table of sales by coffee type to calculate values for four additional tables: sales of unflavored coffee versus flavored coffee for each of the five years, sales of regular coffee versus decaffeinated coffee for each of the five years, percentage increase in sales over the prior year for each of the four coffee types, and percentage increase in sales over 1993 sales for each of the four coffee types.

Kim also asks you to chart the sales data. She would like a chart to visually dramatize the increasing total coffee sales over the last five years. She plans to include this chart in a memo to Valle Coffee customer representatives to highlight this positive trend. Kim also wants a second chart that illustrates the proportion of 1997 sales attributable to each coffee type.

SESSION 6.1

In this session you will learn how to organize workbooks effectively, use the TODAY date function, create a series with AutoFill, use AutoSum, use the fill handle to copy formulas, enter text notes, test a worksheet, apply percentage formats, and sort worksheet rows.

Effective Workbook Organization

As you learned in Tutorial 3, planning is the first step in effective worksheet preparation. The workbook you created in that tutorial consisted of a single worksheet, which you planned and designed before you entered, edited, and printed data in the worksheet. Because workbooks can contain more than one worksheet, you must often plan workbooks as well.

The most critical aspect of workbook planning is the organization of individual worksheets. If a workbook is not organized logically, locating information in it can be difficult. In addition, charting data is more complicated when the data to be charted is scattered throughout the workbook. Logical workbook organization makes it easier for you to create a workbook and ensures that the resulting workbook is easy for others to use and understand.

Typically, all the input values are organized on a single worksheet. Standard supplementary values, such as interest rate tables or depreciation schedules, are usually entered on separate worksheets. Also, each chart is typically placed on its own worksheet.

When you are working with multiple worksheets, you should include a documentation sheet as the first worksheet. All the workbook documentation, which includes the information others will need to understand, use, and revise the workbook, is then located in a single place.

Kim wants her workbook to include a documentation sheet, a worksheet for the input values of five-year sales by coffee type, a worksheet for the five-year sales values by state, a sheet for a chart of five-year total coffee sales, and a sheet for a chart of 1997 sales by coffee type. Kim's workbook plan is shown in Figure 6-1.

Figure 6-1 Workbook plan

Workbook Plan for the Valle Coffee Five-Year Sales Data Workbook

My Goal:

To develop a workbook to be used by Kim Carpenter of Valle Coffee for trend analyses of coffee sales by year, by type, and by location.

What worksheets will I use?

Type	Name	Contents
Worksheet	Documentation	Workbook documentation
Worksheet	Sales Values	5-year sales values by coffee type, used as input for the charts
Worksheet	State Sales	5-year sales values by state
Chart	Sales Chart	5-year chart of total coffee sales
Chart	1997 Sales	Chart of 1997 sales by coffee type

Kim has already completed much of the initial data entry for the workbook. You'll begin by opening Kim's workbook, which is named SaleData, and starting Excel.

To open the SaleData workbook and start Excel:

1. Start Windows 95 and make sure the Office Shortcut Bar is displayed.

   TROUBLE? If you don't see the Office Shortcut Bar, click the Start button on the taskbar, point to Programs, then click Microsoft Office Shortcut Bar. If you don't see the Microsoft Office Shortcut Bar option on the Programs menu, ask your instructor or technical support person for help.

2. Insert your Student Disk in the disk drive.
3. Click the **Open a Document** button on the Office Shortcut Bar. Office 95 displays the Open dialog box.
4. Display the list of files in the Tutorial.06 folder on your Student Disk, then open the **SaleData** file. Excel starts with SaleData as the active workbook.

Three sheets in the workbook have already been named: Documentation, Sales Values, and State Sales. You'll begin by examining and completing the Documentation sheet.

Completing the Documentation Sheet

A typical documentation sheet specifies information that applies to the entire workbook as well as information that relates to individual worksheets in the workbook. General workbook information that you should specify in a documentation sheet includes the workbook name, the name of the person who created it, the date the workbook was created, the date it was last updated, and the purpose for which the workbook was created. For each worksheet, you should include, at a minimum, the name and a brief description of the worksheet contents.

To view the contents of the Documentation sheet:

1. If the Documentation sheet is not the active worksheet, click the **Documentation** tab.
2. Scroll the worksheet until you see rows 7 through 20. See Figure 6-2.

Figure 6-2 Documentation sheet

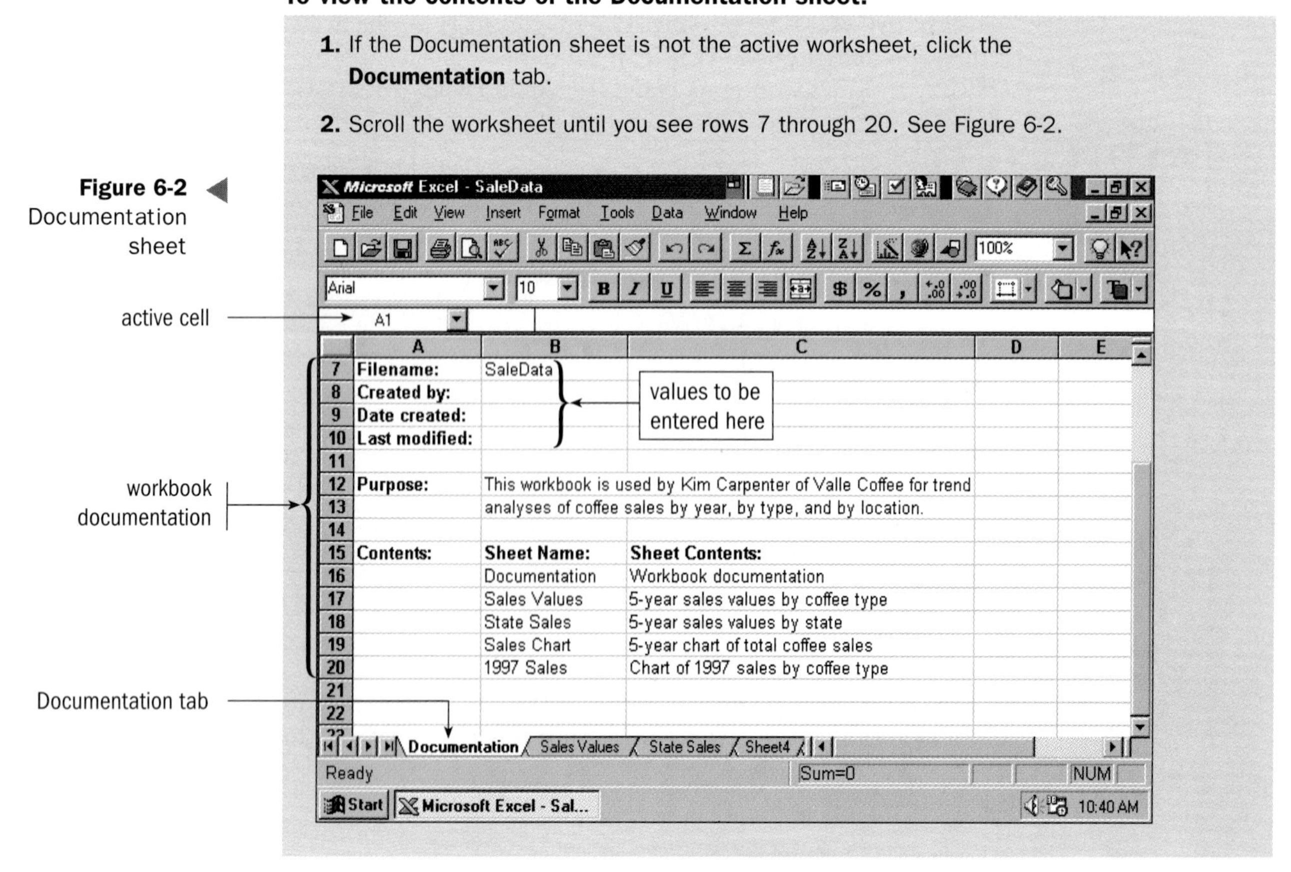

Notice that the information entered into the Documentation sheet follows the workbook plan shown in Figure 6-1. The worksheet purpose in rows 12 and 13 is consistent with the worksheet goal, as stated in the plan. Rows 15 through 20 of the Documentation sheet list the planned worksheet names and describe their contents.

Before you make any changes to the workbook, you'll first save the workbook with a different name so your changes will not alter the original file. When working with multiple worksheets, it's helpful to make A1 the active cell in each worksheet before saving or closing the workbook. By making A1 the active cell in all worksheets, it's easier to know where you are when you switch between sheets.

To save the workbook as Five-Year Sales:

1. If A1 is not the active cell, as indicated in the reference area, scroll to the top of the Documentation sheet, then click cell **A1**.
2. Click **File** on the menu bar, then click **Save As** to open the Save As dialog box.
3. Save the workbook as **Five-Year Sales** in the Tutorial.06 folder on your Student Disk.

Rows 7 through 10 of the Documentation sheet will contain the name of the workbook file, the name of the person who created the workbook, the date the workbook was originally created, and the date it was last modified, as shown in Figure 6-2. You need to enter this information to complete the Documentation sheet.

To enter the new filename, and the created by and date created information:

1. Click cell **B7**, edit the cell entry in the formula bar to change the filename to **Five-Year Sales**, then press the **Enter** key. The active cell becomes cell B8.

   TROUBLE? If cell B8 is not the active cell, you need to change one of the edit options on your computer. Click Tools on the menu bar, click Options, then click the Edit tab in the Options dialog box. If the box to the left of the Move Selection after Enter option does not contain a check mark, click the box to activate the option. If the text box after Direction: does not display "Down," click the text box down arrow, then click Down. This setting will move the active cell down one cell below the cell in which you enter data. Click the OK button to close the Options dialog box. Then click cell B8 to make it the active cell.
2. Type your name in cell B8, then press the **Enter** key.
3. Type today's date in a month/day/year format (for example, 5/18/98), then press the **Enter** key.

The date of the workbook's original creation (cell B9) is a constant value for which you typed a specific date. In contrast, the date on which the workbook was last modified (cell B10) will change every time the workbook is updated. It is impractical to expect users of this workbook to remember to change this date whenever they use or modify the workbook. Instead, you'll use a date function that instructs Excel to determine the date each time the workbook is opened.

Displaying and Formatting the Date Using the TODAY Function

The **TODAY function** is an Excel function that reads the computer system clock and displays the current date in the cell that contains the function. The cell will be updated with the current date automatically whenever the workbook is opened.

To enter the TODAY function in cell B10:

1. Click the **Function Wizard** button on the Standard toolbar to open the Function Wizard - Step 1 of 2 dialog box.
2. Click **Date & Time** in the Function Category list box, click **TODAY** in the Function Name list box, then click the **Next** button to open the Function Wizard - Step 2 of 2 dialog box.

   As shown in the dialog box, the TODAY function returns today's date, and requires no arguments, so you do not need to specify any further information.
3. Click the **Finish** button to close the dialog box. Today's date is now displayed in cell B10.

You can change the display format for a cell containing the TODAY function, in the same way you change the format of any date. You'll change the display format to 04-Mar-95 for both dates (cells B9 and B10) at the same time.

To format the dates:

1. Select cells **B9** and **B10**.
2. Right-click in the selected area to display the shortcut menu, then click **Format Cells**. The Format Cells dialog box opens.
3. If necessary, click the **Number** tab.
4. If necessary, click **Date** in the Category list box.
5. Click **04-Mar-95** in the Type list box to select that format for the dates.
6. Click the **OK** button to close the dialog box.

The Documentation sheet is now complete. Next, Kim wants you to complete the Sales Values sheet. To enter data in this sheet, you'll use an Excel feature called AutoFill.

Creating a Series with AutoFill

AutoFill is an Excel feature that automatically fills areas of a worksheet with a series of values. AutoFill is activated when you use the **fill handle**, which is the small black square in the lower-right corner of the border that surrounds the active cell or cells. To use AutoFill, you first type one or, in some cases, two initial values, then you drag the fill handle to define the cells to be filled. AutoFill evaluates the initial entry or entries, determines the most likely sequence to follow, and completes the remaining entries in the range of cells you specify.

REFERENCE window

USING AUTOFILL TO COMPLETE A SERIES

- Type one or two values, as necessary, to start the series.
- Select the initial cell or cells.
- Drag the fill handle to outline the cells to be filled with the series continuation.
- Release the mouse button.

Before you can add values using AutoFill, you need to move to and view the Sales Values sheet.

To view the contents of the Sales Values sheet:

1. Click cell **A1**.

   TROUBLE? The picture overlaps much of cell A1 on the Documentation sheet, so you might accidentally activate the picture when you try to activate cell A1. To activate cell A1, position the pointer over the far left, visible portion of the cell, so that the pointer appears as ✚. Then click the mouse to select the cell.

2. Click the **Sales Values** tab. The Sales Values worksheet is now displayed. Notice that cell A1, the active cell, contains the worksheet title: "Sales Values by Type by Year -- 1993-1997."

3. If necessary, scroll the worksheet until rows 3 through 17 are visible. Your screen should now look like Figure 6-3.

Figure 6-3 ◀ Sales Values sheet

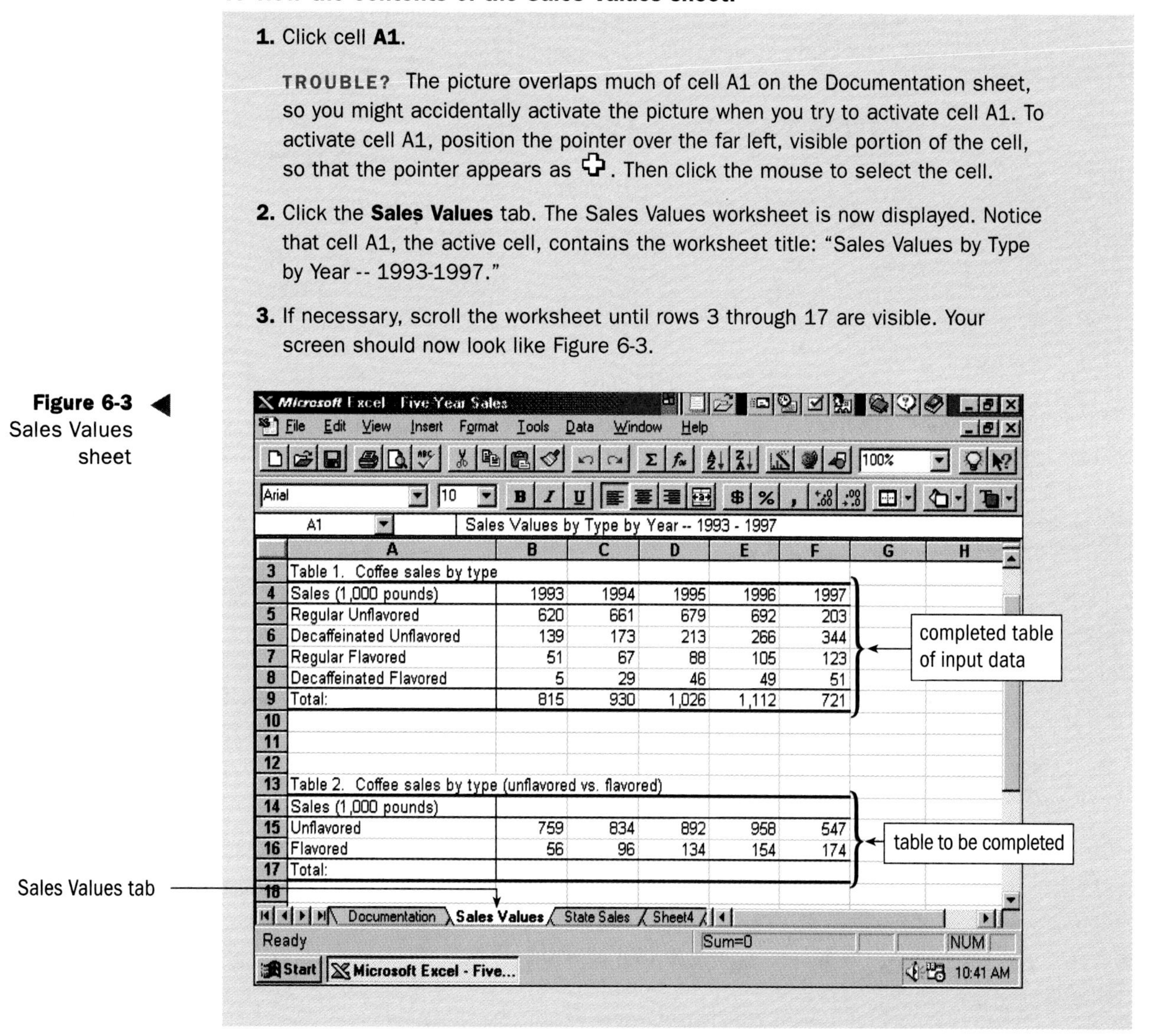

The data values for Table 1 have already been entered in cells A3 through F9. Table 2, in rows 13 through 17, is incomplete. You will use AutoFill to complete much of Table 2.

AutoFill recognizes series of numbers, dates, times, and certain labels. Figure 6-4 shows examples of some of the types of series that AutoFill recognizes and completes.

Figure 6-4 Series completed by AutoFill

Initial Entry or Entries	Extended Series
7:00	8:00, 9:00, 10:00, . . .
Mon	Tue, Wed, Thu, . . .
Monday	Tuesday, Wednesday, Thursday, . . .
Jan	Feb, Mar, Apr, . . .
Jan, Mar	May, Jul, Sep, . . .
Jan-98, Apr-98	Jul-98, Oct-98, Jan-99, . . .
1991	1991, 1991, 1991, . . .
1991, 1992	1993, 1994, 1995, . . .
1, 2	3, 4, 5, . . .
1, 3	5, 7, 9, . . .
100, 95	90, 85, 80, . . .
Qtr3	Qtr4, Qtr1, Qtr2, . . .
1st Period	2nd Period, 3rd Period, 4th Period, . . .
Product 1	Product 2, Product 3, Product 4, . . .

In most cases, AutoFill needs only a single entry to complete the series correctly. However, in two situations you must enter at least two values in the series. The first is a situation in which you want to skip parts of a standard set of values; in this case, two entries are required to define the series. For example, to create an alternating month series such as "Jan," "Mar," "May," "Jul," and so on, you must enter two values. The second situation involves integers. If you enter "1" and then extend the series with AutoFill, the extended series would be "1," "1," "1," and so on. To create the series "1," "2," "3," and so on, you must enter two values. Note that years are integers, and thus require two initial values for a correct AutoFill.

You can begin a repeating series, such as months or days of the weeks, anywhere in the series. If cells must be filled after the series ends, AutoFill repeats the series starting at the beginning. For example, if your initial entry is "November," AutoFill would extend the series as "December," "January," and so on.

You'll enter the year values in Table 2, using AutoFill to complete the entry. As just noted, you need to enter the first two values when entering years.

To enter the series of years using AutoFill:

1. Click cell **B14** then type **1993**.
2. Click cell **C14** then type **1994**.

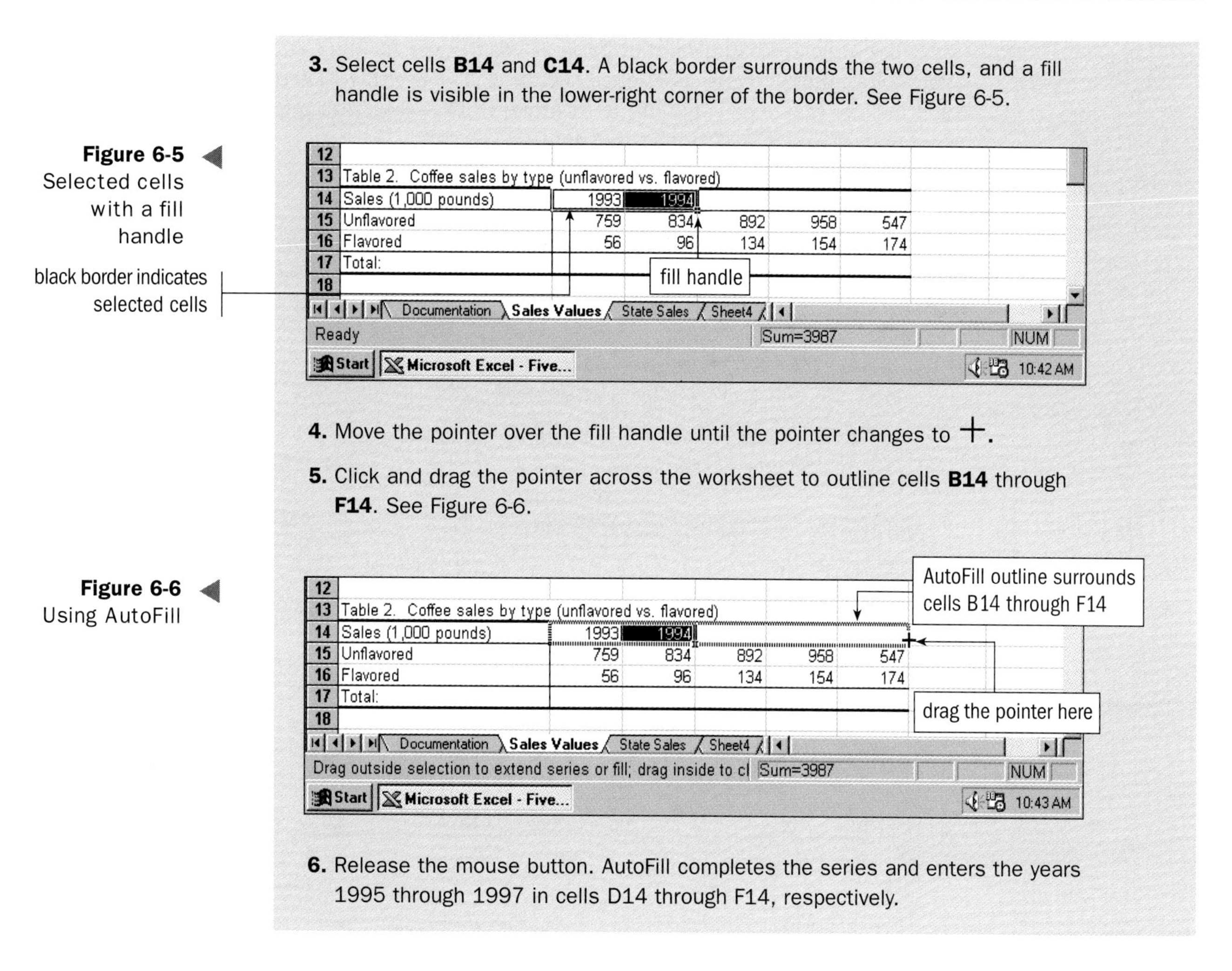

3. Select cells **B14** and **C14**. A black border surrounds the two cells, and a fill handle is visible in the lower-right corner of the border. See Figure 6-5.

Figure 6-5 Selected cells with a fill handle

4. Move the pointer over the fill handle until the pointer changes to +.

5. Click and drag the pointer across the worksheet to outline cells **B14** through **F14**. See Figure 6-6.

Figure 6-6 Using AutoFill

6. Release the mouse button. AutoFill completes the series and enters the years 1995 through 1997 in cells D14 through F14, respectively.

Next, you need to enter the necessary formulas in the Sales Values sheet.

Working with Formulas

As you learned in Tutorial 3, a **formula** specifies a calculation you want Excel to perform; the result of the calculation is displayed in the cell containing the formula. All formulas begin with an equal sign (=). A typical formula contains one or more arithmetic operators along with numbers or cell references, or both. A **function** is a prewritten formula that takes values, performs a predefined operation, and then returns a value. One example of an Excel function is the TODAY function, which you used earlier in this session.

Using the AutoSum Button

Kim points out that cells B17 through F17 in your worksheet should each display the total of the two values that appear directly above those cells. To display the correct total in cell B17, for example, you could type =B15+B16 in that cell. Or, you could select cell B17, activate Excel's Function Wizard, and respond to a series of dialog boxes to create the formula =SUM(B15:B16).

Because summing values that appear in cells to the left or above a given cell is a common task, Excel provides a quick method, AutoSum, for creating an appropriate formula. **AutoSum** automatically creates formulas that contain the SUM function. When you click the AutoSum button on the Standard toolbar, Excel looks at the cells adjacent to the active cell, then displays a best guess for the appropriate formula. To accept the formula as presented, you press the Enter key. If the cells used in the formula must be adjusted, you can use the mouse to select a different range of cells.

Most often AutoSum's initial guess is exactly the formula you want. However, when you use a numeric value as a label, such as the year value "1993" in cell B14, AutoSum will include that year value in the formula. In that case, you must adjust the formula to eliminate the reference to the unwanted cell.

To use AutoSum to create the formula for cell B17:

1. Click cell **B17** then click the **AutoSum** button on the Standard toolbar. AutoSum displays the formula =SUM(B14:B16) in cell B17 and in the formula bar, and a rotating dashed line surrounds cells B14 through B16, the cells used in the formula. To accept the formula, you would press the Enter key. In this case, however, the formula is not correct because the year is included in the sum. So you must first adjust the formula.

2. Select cells **B15** and **B16**. The displayed formula changes to =SUM(B15:B16), and the rotating dashed line surrounds those two cells. See Figure 6-7.

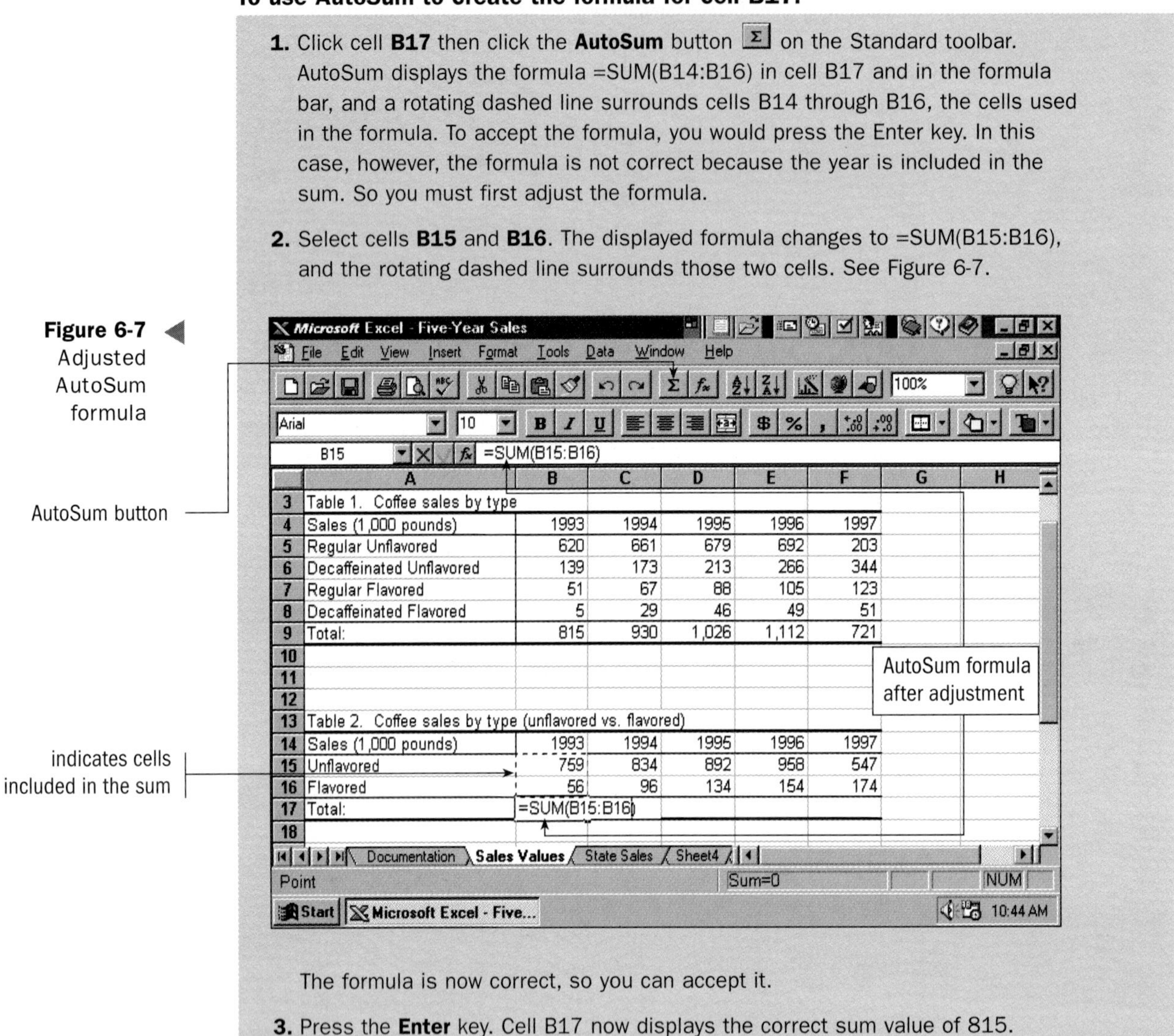

Figure 6-7 Adjusted AutoSum formula

The formula is now correct, so you can accept it.

3. Press the **Enter** key. Cell B17 now displays the correct sum value of 815.

Using the Fill Handle to Copy a Formula

The fill handle, which you used in conjunction with AutoFill to complete a series, can also be used to copy the contents of a cell to one or more adjacent cells. You can also copy values, labels, and formulas using the fill handle.

When you select one or more cells and then use the fill handle to highlight additional cells, Excel first determines if the contents of the originally selected cell or range of cells fit one of the series illustrated in Figure 6-4. If so, Excel uses AutoFill to extend the series, as previously described. If not, Excel treats the action as a copy operation.

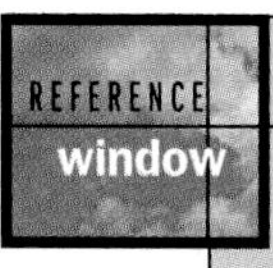

COPYING CELL CONTENTS WITH THE FILL HANDLE

- Select the cell whose contents you want to copy.
- Drag the fill handle to outline the cells where you want the copies to appear.
- Release the mouse button.

Now that you have the correct formula in cell B17, you can use the fill handle to copy that formula into the remaining cells in the row.

To copy the formula from cell B17 to cells C17 through F17:

1. Click cell **B17** to make it the active cell.
2. Position the pointer over the fill handle until the pointer changes to +.
3. Drag the pointer to the right to outline cells **B17** through **F17**, then release the mouse button. The formula is copied into cells C17 through F17, and the appropriate sums are displayed in those cells. See Figure 6-8.

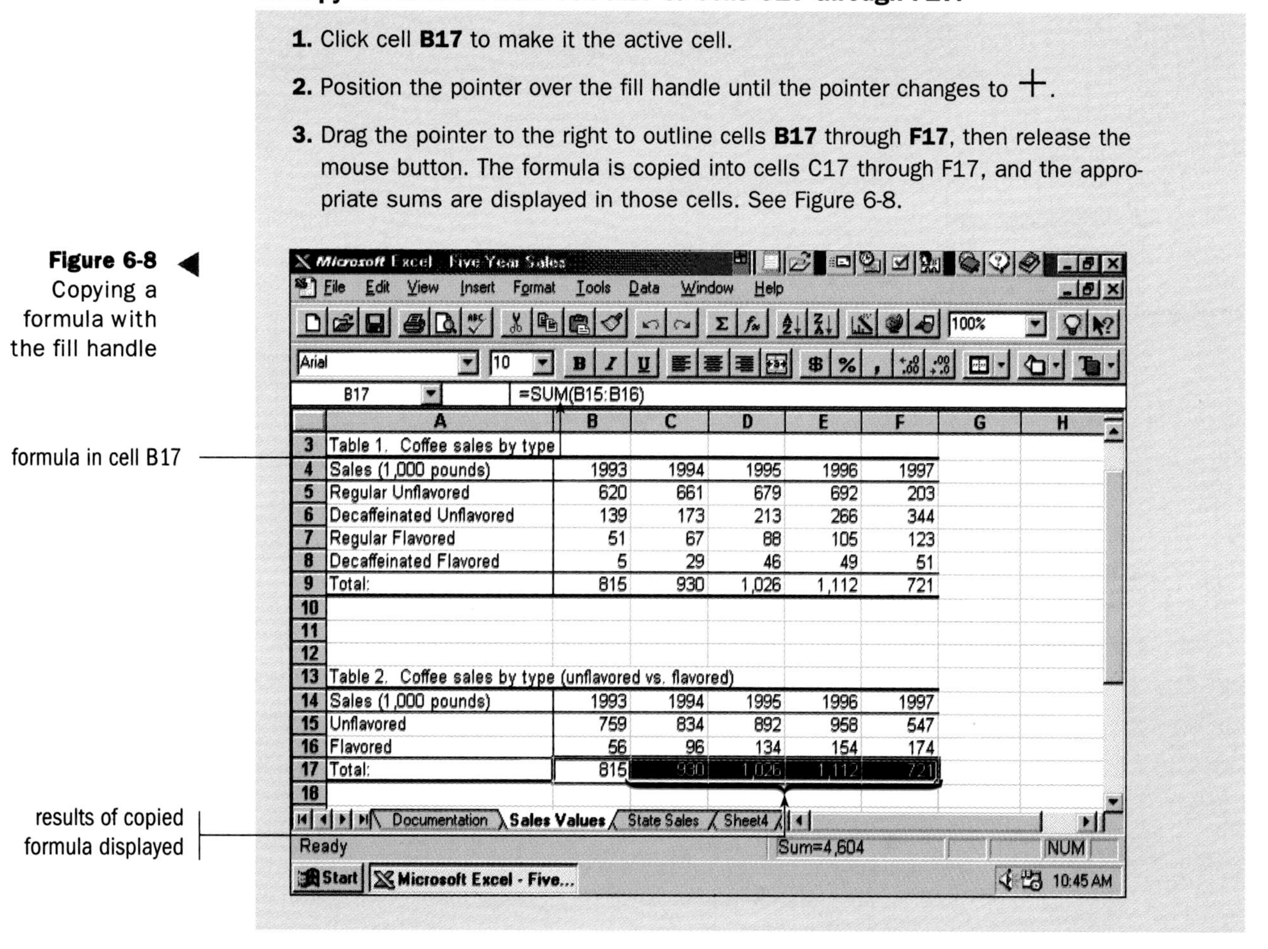

	A	B	C	D	E	F
3	Table 1. Coffee sales by type					
4	Sales (1,000 pounds)	1993	1994	1995	1996	1997
5	Regular Unflavored	620	661	679	692	203
6	Decaffeinated Unflavored	139	173	213	266	344
7	Regular Flavored	51	67	88	105	123
8	Decaffeinated Flavored	5	29	46	49	51
9	Total:	815	930	1,026	1,112	721
10						
11						
12						
13	Table 2. Coffee sales by type (unflavored vs. flavored)					
14	Sales (1,000 pounds)	1993	1994	1995	1996	1997
15	Unflavored	759	834	892	958	547
16	Flavored	56	96	134	154	174
17	Total:	815	930	1,026	1,112	721
18						

Figure 6-8 Copying a formula with the fill handle

The formula in cell B17 is =SUM(B15:B16). When you copied the contents of cell B17 to the other cells, the cells did not receive *exact* copies of that formula. Instead, Excel adjusted each cell reference in the formula to reflect the formula's new location. Thus, cell C17 correctly contains the adjusted formula =SUM(C15:C16), not the original formula =SUM(B15:B16). As noted in Tutorial 3, whenever you copy or move a formula, Excel automatically adjusts all relative cell references.

Relative and Absolute References

In a formula, a simple cell reference such as B17 or A1 is called a relative cell reference. A **relative reference** tells Excel which cell to use based on its location *relative* to the cell containing the formula. When you copy a formula to another cell, Excel changes a cell reference in the formula copy so that it refers to a cell in the same location *relative* to the cell containing the copy of the formula. Figure 6-9 shows how a relative reference in a formula changes when the formula is copied to a cell in a different column, a different row, and a different column *and* row.

Figure 6-9 Copying a formula with a relative cell reference

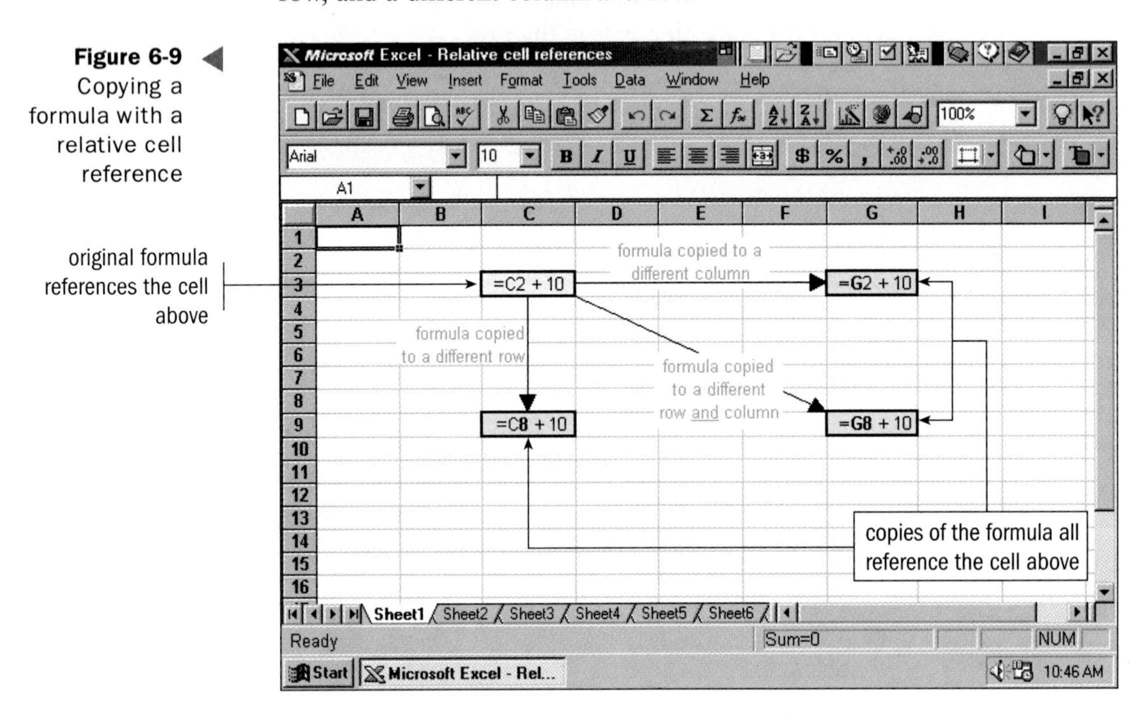

When the formula in cell C3 is copied to cell G3, for example, the relative reference in the formula is adjusted to reflect the new location. The original formula refers to cell C2, which is one row above and in the same column as the cell containing the formula. The copied formula also refers to the cell that is one row above and in the same column as the cell containing the formula. In other words, the copied formula uses the cell in the same relative location.

Occasionally, you might need to create a formula that refers to a cell in a fixed location on the worksheet. A reference that always points to the same row, column, or cell is called an **absolute reference**. Absolute references contain a dollar sign before the column letter, the row number, or both. Examples of absolute cell references include $C1, E$7, and $A$3.

When you copy a formula with an absolute cell reference, a row reference preceded by the symbol $ is not changed, and a column reference preceded by $ is not changed. For example, if you copy a formula containing the absolute reference =$C$4, the copied formula will always contain the reference =$C$4, no matter where it is located. When you copy a formula containing the absolute reference =$C4, the column letter is fixed, but the row number might change to reflect the new location of the copied formula. In contrast, in the cell reference C$4, the row number is fixed, while the column letter can change. Figure 6-10 shows how an absolute cell reference in a formula is affected when you copy the formula; examples are shown for an absolute cell reference with a fixed row *and* column, one with a fixed column only, and one with a fixed row only.

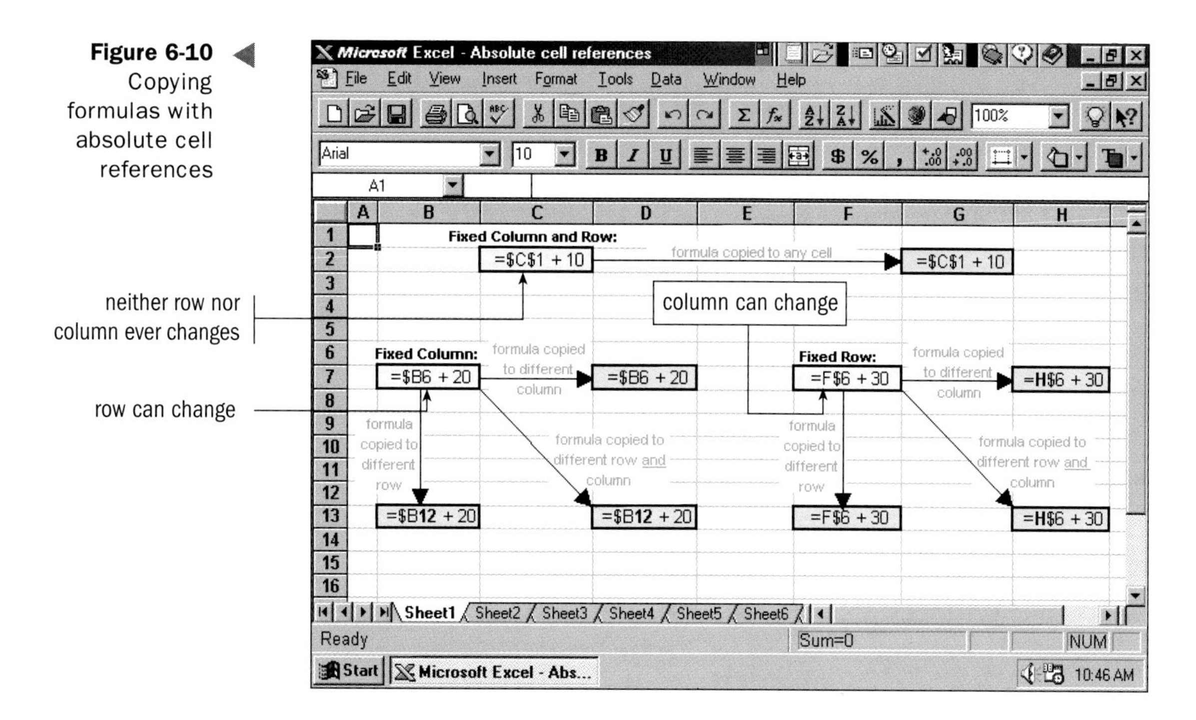

Figure 6-10 Copying formulas with absolute cell references

Now you can complete the Sales Values sheet as Kim wants it. Strictly speaking, only the 20 values in cells B5 through F8 are true input values. Except for the labels, all the other values in this worksheet are calculated from those 20 cells. As examples, the value in cell C9 is the sum of the four values above it, and the value in B15 is calculated using the formula =B5+B6.

Kim wants to include a new table in the worksheet that is similar to Table 2 but that compares regular coffee sales to decaffeinated coffee sales. The easiest way to create this table, Table 3, is to copy Table 2, then change labels and formulas where appropriate.

To create Table 3 by copying Table 2, and to change the appropriate labels:

1. Select cells **A13** through **F17**.
2. With the pointer in the highlighted area, right-click to display the shortcut menu, then click **Copy**.
3. Scroll down eight rows, then click cell **A21**.
4. With the pointer in the highlighted cell, right-click to display the shortcut menu, then click **Paste**. Cells A21 through F25 now contain a copy of Table 2.
5. Press the **Enter** key to remove the dashed line around the selected cells.
6. Click cell **A21**, then edit the text in the formula bar to change 2 to **3** and the label (unflavored vs. flavored) to **(regular vs. decaffeinated)**.
7. Click cell **A23** then type **Regular**.
8. Click cell **A24** then type **Decaffeinated**.
9. Click cell **B23** to make it the active cell. See Figure 6-11.

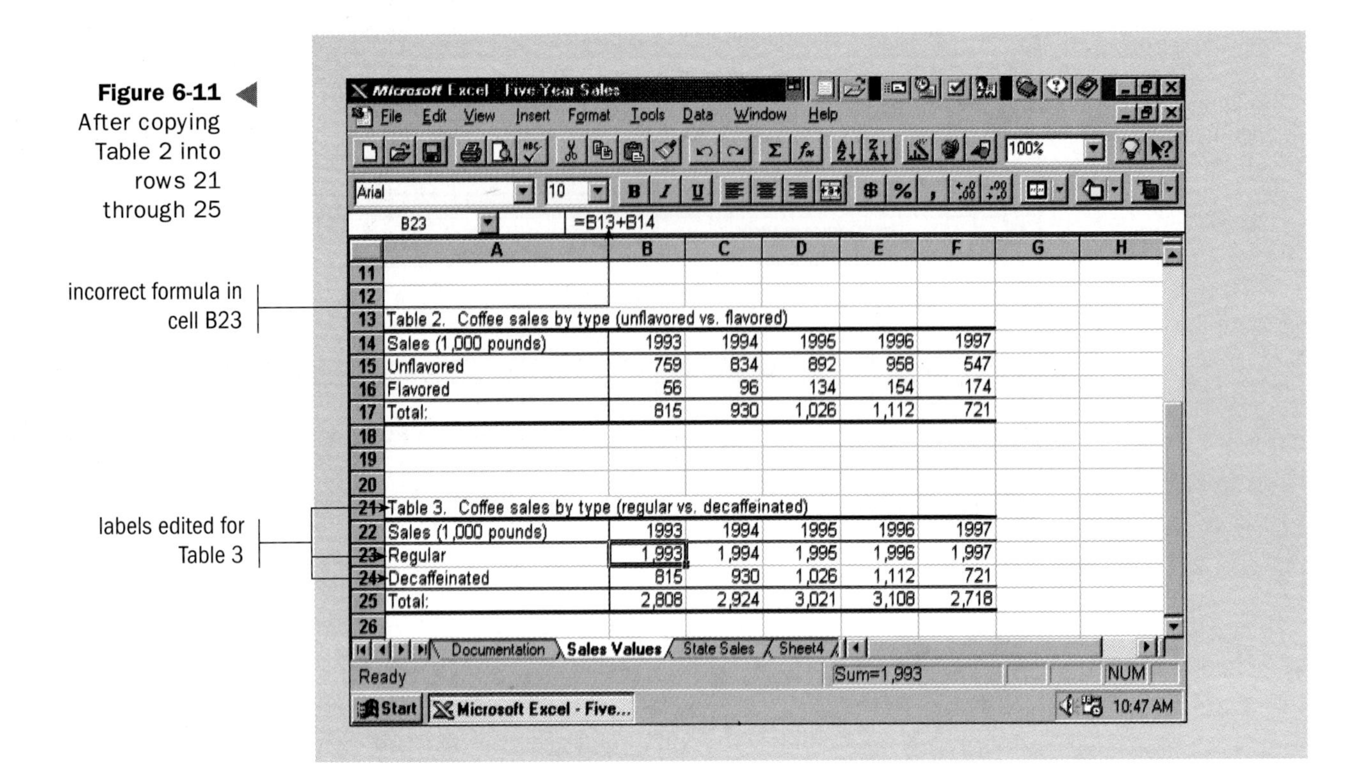

Figure 6-11 After copying Table 2 into rows 21 through 25

The formula currently in cell B23 is the same as the formula in cell B15, adjusted for the new location. The actual formula you want for this cell is =B5+B7, referring to the input items in Table 1. After you enter the correct formula in cell B23, you can use the fill handle to copy the formula into the rest of the cells in the table.

To enter the correct formula in cell B23, then copy the formula to the other cells:

1. Type **=B5+B7** then press the **Enter** key. The correct result 671 is displayed in cell B23.
2. Click cell **B23** then use the fill handle to copy the formula from that cell to cells C23 through F23. The five cells B23 through F23 are all selected, and a fill handle appears in the lower-right corner of cell F23.

   So far you've used the fill handle to copy formulas to adjacent cells to the right. You can also copy formulas to cells below the selected cells by dragging the fill handle down.
3. Drag the fill handle down to cell F24, so that cells **B23** through **F24** are outlined, then release the mouse button. The formulas in cells B23 through F23 are copied into cells B24 through F24. Your screen should now look like Figure 6-12.

Figure 6-12 Table 3 after the formulas have been corrected

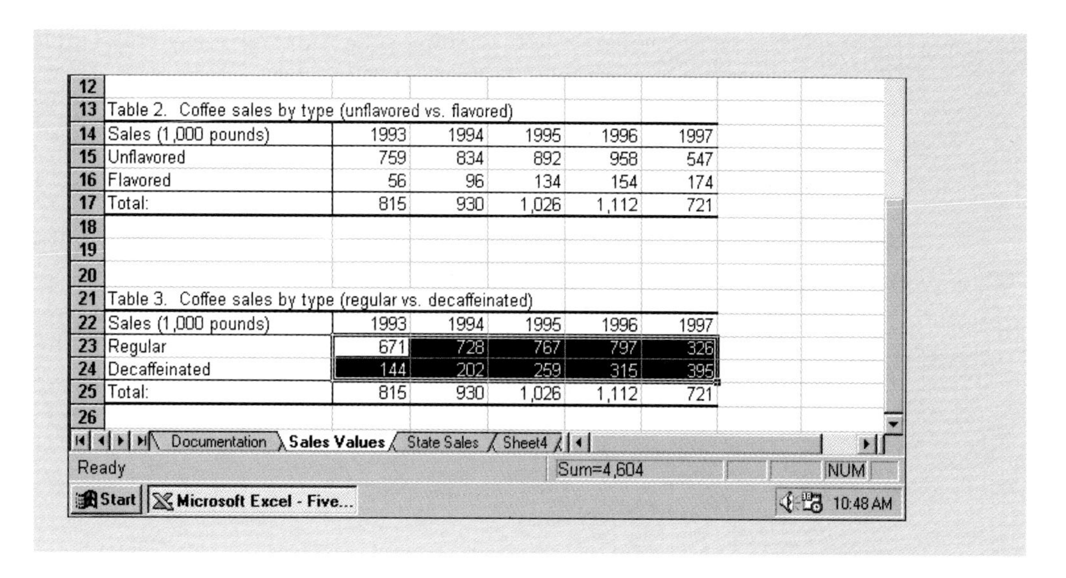

12						
13	Table 2. Coffee sales by type (unflavored vs. flavored)					
14	Sales (1,000 pounds)	1993	1994	1995	1996	1997
15	Unflavored	759	834	892	958	547
16	Flavored	56	96	134	154	174
17	Total:	815	930	1,026	1,112	721
18						
19						
20						
21	Table 3. Coffee sales by type (regular vs. decaffeinated)					
22	Sales (1,000 pounds)	1993	1994	1995	1996	1997
23	Regular	671	728	767	797	326
24	Decaffeinated	144	202	259	315	395
25	Total:	815	930	1,026	1,112	721
26						

The totals displayed in row 25 now match the totals in row 17, which they should. You do not have to correct the formulas in row 25 because they simply sum the two values immediately above the given cell, as do the formulas in row 17, which you copied.

Kim wants two more tables in the Sales Values worksheet. The first table, Table 4, will show the percentage of increase in sales over the prior year's sales for each coffee type. The second table, Table 5, will show the percentage of increase in sales over the 1993 figures for each coffee type. The tables will be similar, so once you create one table, you can copy it and then adjust it to create the other. The plan for Table 4 is shown in Figure 6-13.

Figure 6-13 The plan for Table 4

Table 4. Coffee sales by type -- % increase over prior year

Sales	1993	1994	1995	1996	1997
Regular Unflavored		*	*	*	*
Decaffeinated Unflavored		*	*	*	*
Regular Flavored		*	*	*	*
Decaffeinated Flavored		*	*	*	*
Total:		*	*	*	*

* = (current sales – prior year sales)/ prior year sales

The plan for Table 4 looks like Table 1's layout. So you can copy and paste Table 1 to create an initial version of Table 4, then edit the labels and formulas, as necessary. To streamline the copy-and-paste process, you'll split the worksheet window. Also, since you last saved the workbook, you've completed Table 2 and created Table 3, so it's a good idea to save the file again.

To save the file then split the worksheet window:

1. Scroll to the top of the worksheet and select cell **A1**.
2. Click the **Save** button on the Standard toolbar.
3. Position the pointer over the small rectangle at the top of the vertical scroll bar until it changes to ÷, click and hold down the mouse button as you drag the split bar down to just below row 8, then release the mouse button. The worksheet window splits into two panes.
4. Scroll the upper pane down one row so that rows 2 through 9 are visible.
5. Scroll the lower pane down until row 29 appears at the top of that pane.

With the worksheet window split, you can easily copy Table 1 in the top pane and paste it in the bottom pane to create Table 4.

To create Table 4 by copying and pasting Table 1, and then to edit the labels:

1. Select cells **A3** through **F9** in the upper pane.
2. With the pointer in the highlighted area, right-click to display the shortcut menu, then click **Copy**.
3. Right-click cell **A29** in the lower pane to display the shortcut menu, then click **Paste**.
4. Press the **Enter** key.
5. Click cell **A29**, edit the cell contents in the formula bar to change the 1 to **4**, position the pointer at the end of the word "type" in the formula bar, press the **spacebar**, then type **-- % increase over prior year**.
6. Click cell **A30** then delete the text "(1,000 pounds)" in the formula bar.

   Cells B31 through B35, which relate to 1993, should not contain values, because the worksheet does not contain prior year data (for 1992) to use for calculations. You need to clear these cells.

7. Select cells **B31** through **B35**, right-click to display the shortcut menu, then click **Clear Contents**. Your screen should now look like Figure 6-14.

Figure 6-14 After copying Table 1 to rows 29 through 35

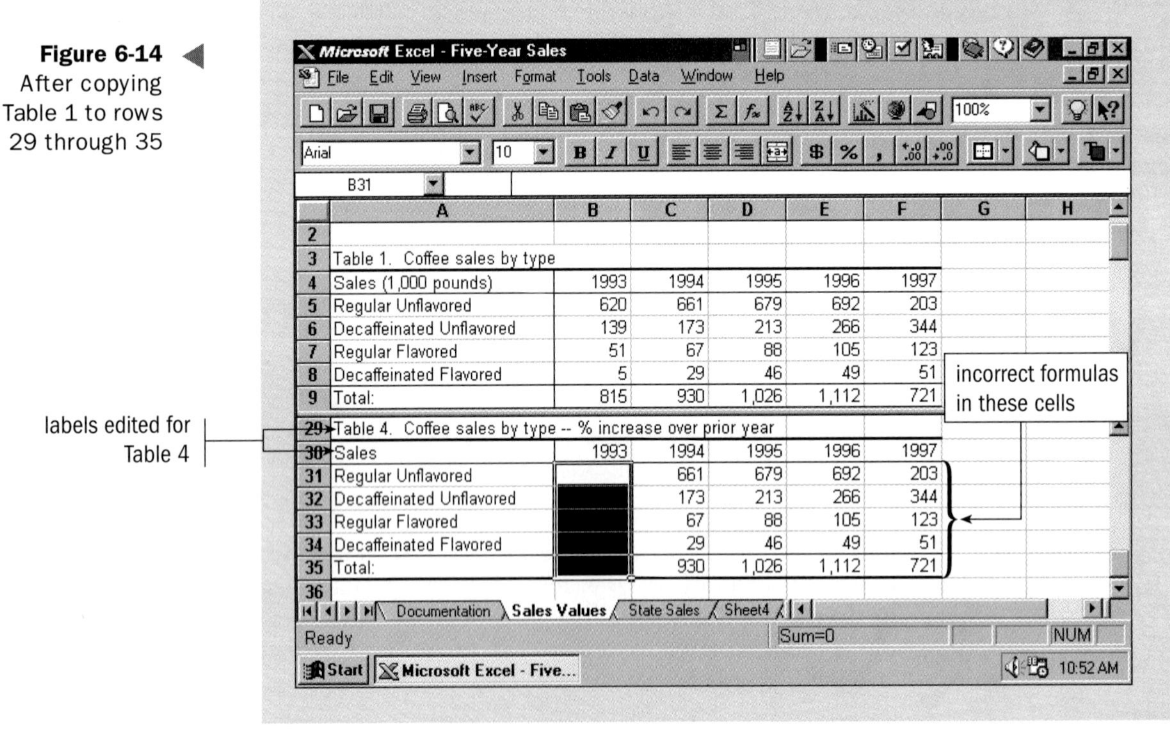

Table 4 is now formatted and labeled according to the plan. The next step is to enter the correct formulas in cells C31 through F35. As before, you need to enter a formula for only one cell, then use the fill handle to copy the formula into the rest of the cells.

To enter formulas for Table 4:

1. Click cell **C31**, type **=(C5-B5)/B5**, then press the **Enter** key. The value "0" is displayed. The actual value is 0.066129, but the default display format shows the value to the nearest whole number, which is 0.
2. Click cell **C31** then click the **Increase Decimal** button on the Formatting toolbar. The value "0.1" is now displayed.
3. Click the **Increase Decimal** button one more time. The value "0.07" is now displayed.
4. Use the fill handle to copy the contents of cell C31 to cells D31 through F31.
5. With cells C31 through F31 still highlighted, use the fill handle to copy the contents of these cells to cells C32 through F35.
6. Click cell **G36** to deselect the highlighted cells.

When you copy a cell, whether you use the fill handle or one of the other copy techniques, you copy *all* the characteristics of the cell. In the previous set of steps, you formatted cell C31 with two decimal places before you copied it, so that the format would be copied to all the other cells in the range C31 through F35. By formatting that one cell before copying it, you avoid having to format all the cells after copying them.

Notice, however, that the border separating rows 34 and 35 and the darker border under row 35 have both disappeared in rows C through F. Because cell C31 had no borders, that characteristic was copied to all the other cells in the range C31 through F35. Typically, you enter all data and formulas before applying borders, so this is usually not a problem. In this case, however, you have a legitimate reason for having the borders in place before you entered and copied the formulas—because you copied a completed, formatted table as a basis for the new table.

To fix the table format, you need to reapply the borders to cells C35 through F35.

To reapply the borders to cells C35 through F35:

1. Select cells **C35** through **F35**.
2. Click the **down arrow** next to the **Borders** button on the Formatting toolbar.
3. Click the first sample in the third row to apply a thin top border and a thicker bottom border to the selected cells.
4. Click cell **G36** to deselect the cells. Your screen should now look like Figure 6-15.

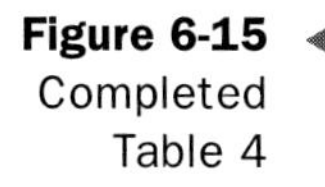

Figure 6-15
Completed Table 4

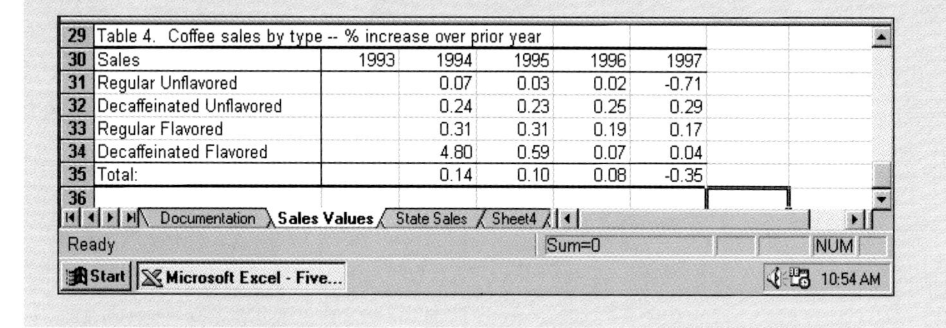

29	Table 4. Coffee sales by type -- % increase over prior year					
30	Sales	1993	1994	1995	1996	1997
31	Regular Unflavored		0.07	0.03	0.02	-0.71
32	Decaffeinated Unflavored		0.24	0.23	0.25	0.29
33	Regular Flavored		0.31	0.31	0.19	0.17
34	Decaffeinated Flavored		4.80	0.59	0.07	0.04
35	Total:		0.14	0.10	0.08	-0.35
36						

The only difference between the completed Table 4 and Table 5, which you still have to create, is that Table 5 will show the percentage of increase in sales over 1993 rather than over the prior year. To create Table 5, you'll first copy Table 4. Because you no longer need the split window, you'll remove the split before copying Table 4.

To remove the split, copy Table 4 to create Table 5, and correct the title:

1. Drag the split bar to the top of the worksheet window.
2. Scroll the window until row 29 is at the top of the worksheet window.
3. Select cells **A29** through **F35**, right-click to display the shortcut menu, then click **Copy**.
4. Right-click cell **A39** to display the shortcut menu, then click **Paste**.
5. Press the **Enter** key. Notice that some cells contain the message "#DIV/0!", which alerts you that you are attempting to divide by 0. You will correct the formulas in this table later, so you can ignore the messages for now.
6. Click cell **A39**, then edit the contents in the formula bar to change the 4 to **5**, and "prior year" to **1993**.

If you enter the formula =(C5-B5)/B5 in cell C41, that cell will display the percentage of increase in sales over the 1993 values. But what happens if you copy that formula to cell D41? The relative cell references will change, and the formula will be =(D5-C5)/C5. This is not the formula you need. To correctly calculate the percentage of increase in sales over the 1993 values for cell D41, you need the formula =(D5-B5)/B5 in cell D41. Can you enter an appropriate formula in cell C41 that will also produce correct results when copied to the remaining cells? Yes, by using an absolute cell reference.

In order to maintain the references to column B, the 1993 values, when you copy the formula, you'll enter the formula =(C5-$B5)/$B5 in cell C41. The $ symbol preceding the two B's in the formula makes each $B5 an absolute reference with a fixed column; when the formula is copied to any other column, the two absolute references to column B will not change.

To enter the formulas for Table 5:

1. Click cell **C41**, type **=(C5-$B5)/$B5** in the cell, then press the **Enter** key. The value "0.07" is displayed. When you copied Table 4 to Table 5, you also copied cell formats; so the value in this cell is already formatted to display two decimal places, the same as cell C31.
2. Click cell **C41** then use the fill handle to copy the contents of cell C41 to cells D41 through F41.
3. With cells C41 through F41 still highlighted, use the fill handle to copy the contents of those cells to cells C42 through F45.

   As before, the borders on cells C45 through F45 were lost when you copied the formula into these cells. You need to reapply the borders.
4. Select cells **C45** through **F45**.

   The border you need to apply is still displayed on the Borders button, so you can simply click the button.
5. Click the **Borders** button on the Formatting toolbar.
6. Click cell **F41**. Your screen should now look like Figure 6-16.

Figure 6-16 Completed Table 5

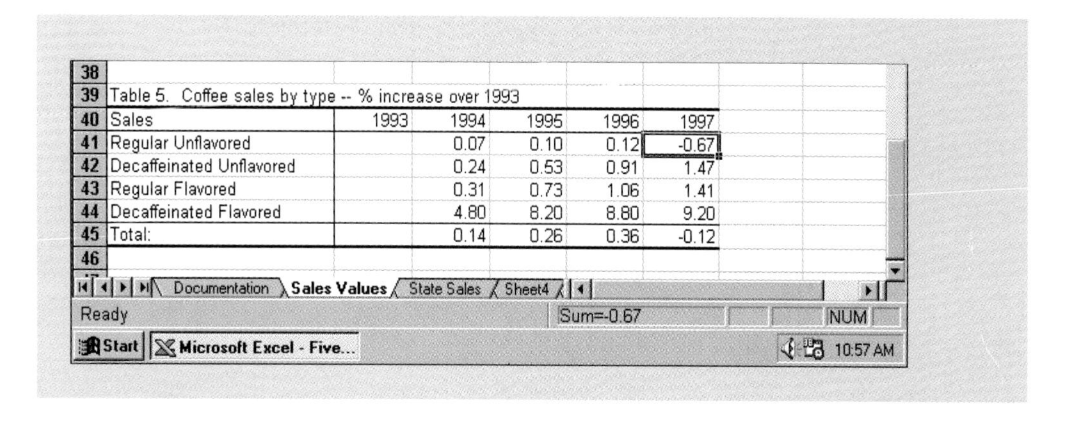

As you look at Table 5, notice the value -0.67 displayed in cell F41. This value means that the sales of regular unflavored coffee *decreased* by 67% from 1993 to 1997. Kim points out that sales have increased each year for all coffee types. She concludes that there is an error somewhere in the worksheet. You need to find and correct the error, then Excel will recalculate the formulas automatically.

Automatic Recalculation

In your search for the error in the worksheet, you first need to verify the formula in cell F41. That formula is =(F5-$B5)/$B5, which is correct. The error, therefore, must be in either cell F5 or cell B5.

To locate and correct the error:

1. Scroll to the top of the worksheet. The value in cell F5 is 203. Kim tells you this value should be 703. Before you enter the correct value, you'll split the worksheet window so that you can see cells F5 and F41 at the same time.
2. Split the worksheet window so that eight rows are visible in the upper pane, then scroll the upper pane to show rows 3 through 10.
3. Scroll the lower pane so that row 36 is at the top of the lower pane.
4. Click cell **F5**, type **703**, then press the **Enter** key. The total in cell F9 is recalculated immediately. The value displayed in cell F41 is also recalculated, and is now 0.13.

The values in cells F9 and F41 were not the only values that changed when you changed the value in cell F5. The values in cells F15, F17, F23, F25, F31, F35, and F45 were also recalculated. All these cells either contain a formula that references cell F5 or contain a sum function involving a cell that references cell F5. When you change a value in a worksheet, Excel automatically recalculates every cell that depends on that value. This **automatic recalculation** is one of the most significant features of a computerized spreadsheet program such as Excel.

You've created Tables 4 and 5 since you last saved the workbook, so you should save it again now.

To remove the split and save the workbook:

1. Drag the split bar to the top of the worksheet window to remove the split.
2. Scroll to the top of the worksheet, then click cell **A1**.
3. Click the **Save** button on the Standard toolbar.

Kim wants you to add a text note to the first sales value, which is located in cell B5, stating that the sales values are in thousands of pounds. The label in cell A4 already states this fact, but the label could accidentally be edited or deleted.

Adding a Text Note

A **text note** is text that is attached to a cell. The note is visible on the worksheet only when you point to the cell to which it is attached. A text note is not visible when you point to or select any other cell, nor is it visible when the worksheet is printed. A cell that contains a text note displays a small red square in the upper-right corner of the cell.

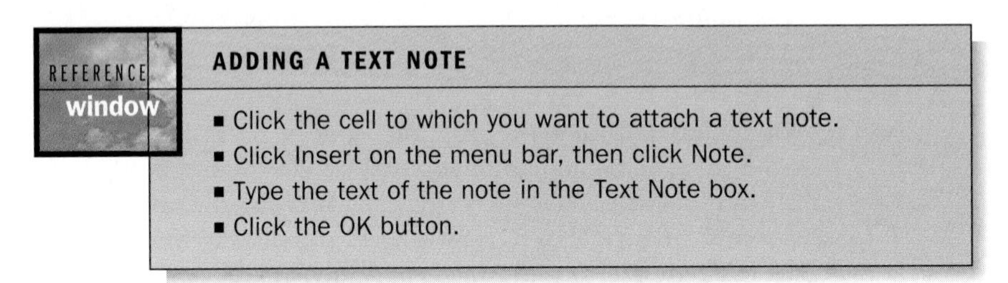
REFERENCE window

ADDING A TEXT NOTE

- Click the cell to which you want to attach a text note.
- Click Insert on the menu bar, then click Note.
- Type the text of the note in the Text Note box.
- Click the OK button.

You enter the note's text as you would enter text in any Office 95 program. To start a new line, for example, press the Enter key. You'll now add the text note to cell B5.

To add the text note to cell B5:

1. Click cell **B5**.
2. Click **Insert** on the menu bar, then click **Note** to open the Cell Note dialog box.
3. In the Text Note box, type the following: **This sales figure, as well as all other sales figures in this table, is given in thousands of pounds.** See Figure 6-17.

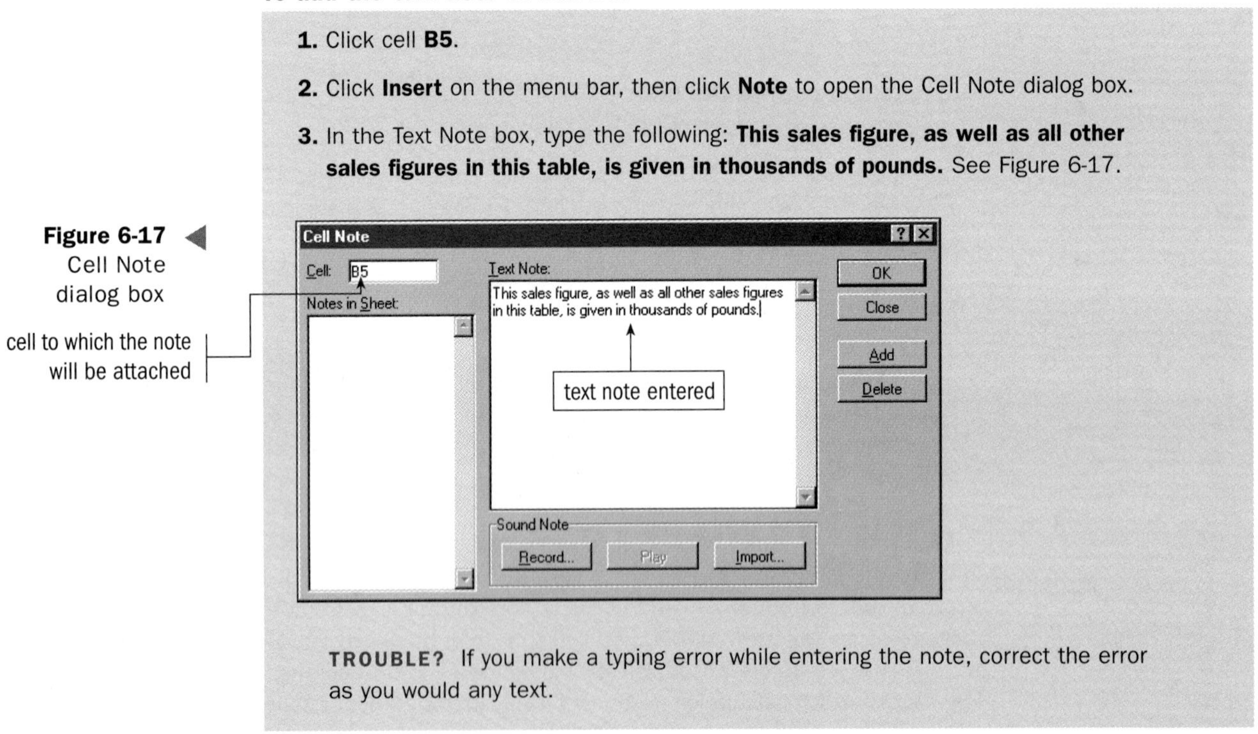

Figure 6-17 Cell Note dialog box

TROUBLE? If you make a typing error while entering the note, correct the error as you would any text.

4. Click the **OK** button to close the Cell Note dialog box.

5. Click cell **A1** to remove the highlighting from cell B5. A small red square is visible in the upper-right corner of cell B5.

6. Position the pointer over cell B5. The text note appears, as shown in Figure 6-18.

Figure 6-18 Displayed text note

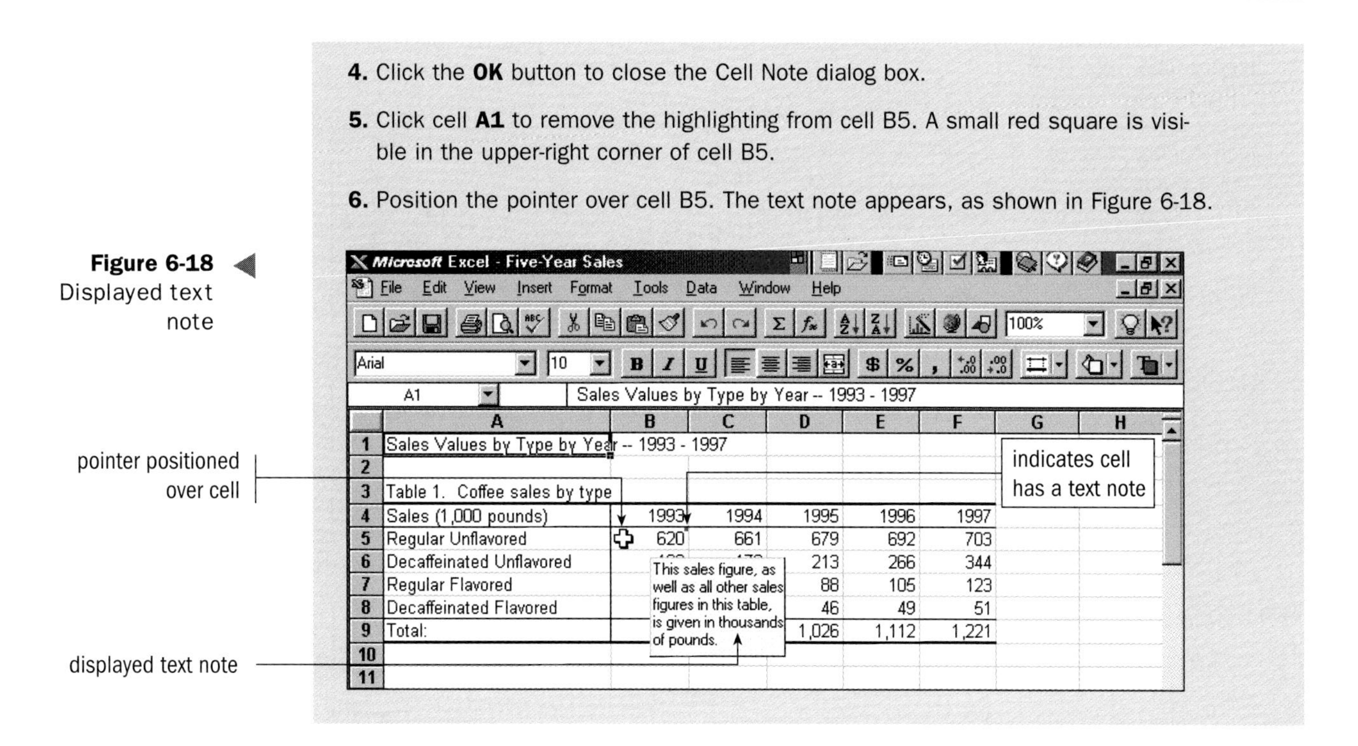

To edit a note, you follow the same steps you used to create the note: display the Cell Note dialog box, then edit the text of the note.

Kim will be using this worksheet for sales analyses, and she wants to be certain that all the formulas are accurate. One way to verify a worksheet is to enter test values for the input data.

Testing a Worksheet

Test values are numbers that generate a known or easily calculated result. Using test values to verify that the formulas in a worksheet are correct helps to ensure the accuracy of the worksheet.

You'll test the worksheet with simple input values of 1 for the 1993 values, 2 for the 1994 values, and so forth. Then you can easily verify the worksheet formulas. It is best to predict the results before you enter test values. Otherwise, it might be easy to convince yourself that a displayed result is correct. The predicted results using the test values are shown in Figure 6-19.

Figure 6-19 Predicted worksheet results using test input values

Table 1. Coffee sales by type

Sales (1,000 pounds)	1993	1994	1995	1996	1997
Regular Unflavored	1	2	3	4	5
Decaffeinated Unflavored	1	2	3	4	5
Regular Flavored	1	2	3	4	5
Decaffeinated Flavored	1	2	3	4	5
Total:	4	8	12	16	20

Table 2. Coffee sales by type (unflavored vs. flavored)

Sales (1,000 pounds)	1993	1994	1995	1996	1997
Unflavored	2	4	6	8	10
Flavored	2	4	6	8	10
Total:	4	8	12	16	20

Table 3. Coffee sales by type (regular vs. decaffeinated)

Sales (1,000 pounds)	1993	1994	1995	1996	1997
Regular	2	4	6	8	10
Decaffeinated	2	4	6	8	10
Total:	4	8	12	16	20

Table 4. Coffee sales by type -- % increase over prior year

Sales	1993	1994	1995	1996	1997
Regular Unflavored		1.00	0.50	0.33	0.25
Decaffeinated Unflavored		1.00	0.50	0.33	0.25
Regular Flavored		1.00	0.50	0.33	0.25
Decaffeinated Flavored		1.00	0.50	0.33	0.25
Total:		1.00	0.50	0.33	0.25

Table 5. Coffee sales by type -- % increase over 1993

Sales	1993	1994	1995	1996	1997
Regular Unflavored		1.00	2.00	3.00	4.00
Decaffeinated Unflavored		1.00	2.00	3.00	4.00
Regular Flavored		1.00	2.00	3.00	4.00
Decaffeinated Flavored		1.00	2.00	3.00	4.00
Total:		1.00	2.00	3.00	4.00

Before you change the input values, you should save the current version of the workbook with the actual input values. After you have verified that the formulas in the worksheet are correct, or have identified which formulas must be corrected, you can close the test version *without saving changes* and then reopen the saved workbook with the actual input values.

To test the worksheet:

1. Click cell **A1** then click the **Save** button on the Standard toolbar to save the workbook with the actual input values.

   Now you can enter the test input values.

2. Click cell **B5** then type **1**.

3. Click cell **C5** then type **2**.
4. Select cells **B5** and **C5**, then use the fill handle to complete the series in cells D5 through F5.
5. With cells B5 through F5 still selected, use the fill handle to fill cells B6 through F8. The displayed totals in row 9 (4, 8, 12, 16, and 20) are correct.
6. Scroll the worksheet until Tables 2 and 3 are visible. Note that all the displayed values are correct.
7. Scroll the worksheet until Tables 4 and 5 are visible. Compare the results with the predicted results in Figure 6-19. Note that all the displayed values are correct. See Figure 6-20.

Figure 6-20 Testing the worksheet

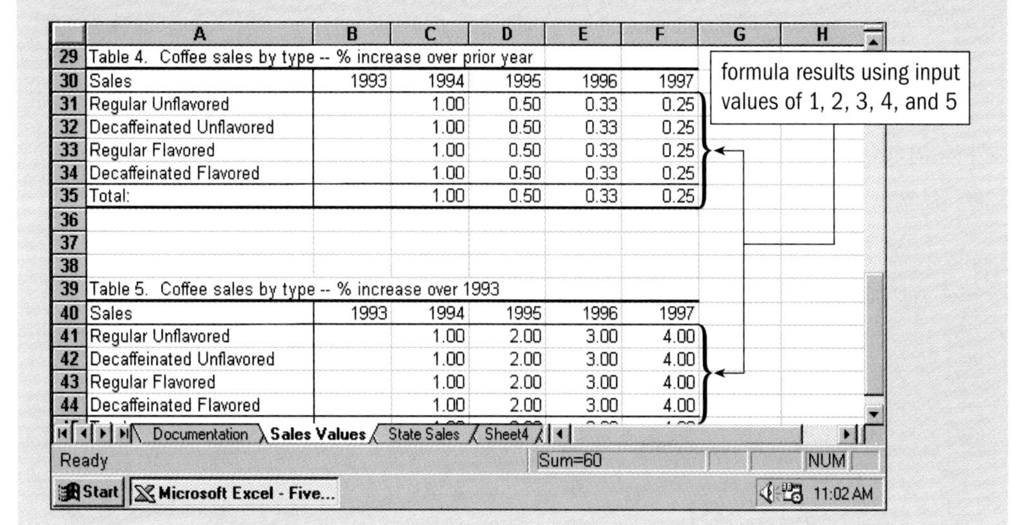

	A	B	C	D	E	F
29	Table 4. Coffee sales by type -- % increase over prior year					
30	Sales	1993	1994	1995	1996	1997
31	Regular Unflavored		1.00	0.50	0.33	0.25
32	Decaffeinated Unflavored		1.00	0.50	0.33	0.25
33	Regular Flavored		1.00	0.50	0.33	0.25
34	Decaffeinated Flavored		1.00	0.50	0.33	0.25
35	Total:		1.00	0.50	0.33	0.25
36						
37						
38						
39	Table 5. Coffee sales by type -- % increase over 1993					
40	Sales	1993	1994	1995	1996	1997
41	Regular Unflavored		1.00	2.00	3.00	4.00
42	Decaffeinated Unflavored		1.00	2.00	3.00	4.00
43	Regular Flavored		1.00	2.00	3.00	4.00
44	Decaffeinated Flavored		1.00	2.00	3.00	4.00

TROUBLE? If the values displayed on your screen don't match those shown in Figures 6-19 and 6-20, first check the values in cells B5 through F8. If any of these values are incorrect, correct them now. Then, if any of the remaining cells still display incorrect values, write down the cell references. *Do not correct those cells now.* At the conclusion of this set of steps, when you've reopened the original worksheet with the actual input values, you can verify and correct the formulas in the cells you noted.

Now that you have tested the worksheet and verified that all formulas produce the expected results, you need to close the workbook *without saving changes.*

8. Click the **Close** button on the menu bar, then click the **No** button when asked if you want to save changes.

Now you'll open the saved workbook with the actual input values. Because you just closed the workbook, you can use the list of recently accessed files on the File menu to reopen it.

To reopen the Five-Year Sales workbook:

1. Click **File** on the menu bar. The File menu opens with the most recently accessed files listed at the bottom. The Five-Year Sales workbook will be at the top of that list, preceded by the number 1.
2. Click **1 Five-Year Sales** in the filename list to open the Five-Year Sales workbook.

If you had detected any erroneous formulas, you would now correct them. If the corrections are extensive, you should repeat the testing process until you have verified that all formulas are correct.

Using Percentage Formats

After viewing the Sales Values sheet, Kim asks you to change the display format for all the calculated values in Tables 4 and 5. Instead of decimal numbers, she would prefer to see percentages. For example, "0.50" should be displayed as 50%.

You could use a Format command to specify a percentage format. But it is easier and faster to use the Percent Style button on the Formatting toolbar.

To format the values in Tables 4 and 5 as percentages:

1. Select cells **C31** through **F35**.
2. Click the **Percent Style** button on the Formatting toolbar. The values are displayed in a percentage format.

   Kim asks you to show the percentages with one decimal place.

3. Click the **Increase Decimal** button on the Formatting toolbar. The values are displayed to show one decimal place.

   Next you'll format Table 5 in the same way.

4. Select cells **C41** through **F45**.
5. Click the **Percent Style** button on the Formatting toolbar, then click the **Increase Decimal** button on the Formatting toolbar.
6. Click cell **F37** to deselect the highlighted cells. Your screen should now look like Figure 6-21.

Figure 6-21
After applying the percent style

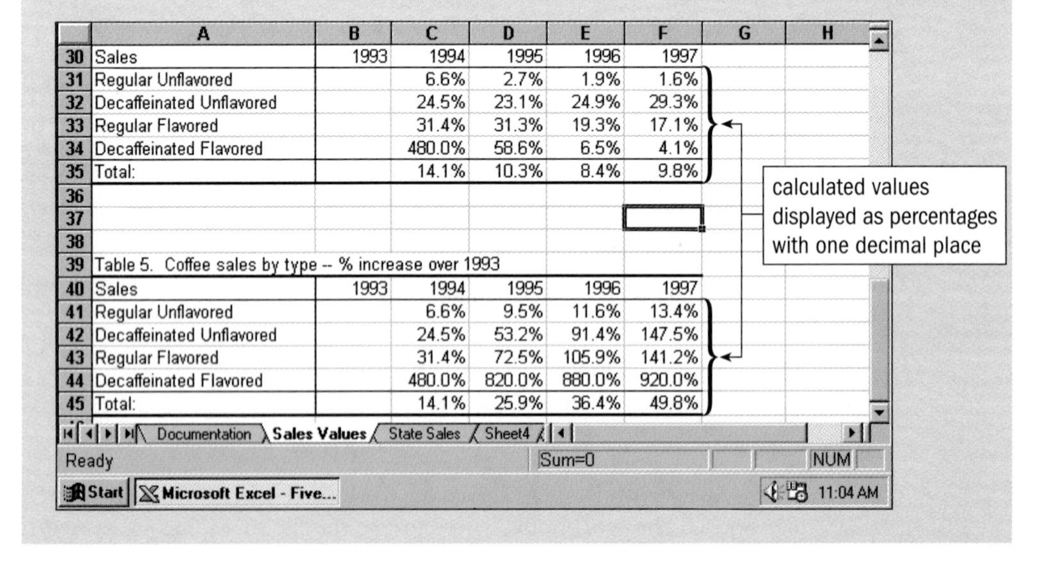

	A	B	C	D	E	F	G	H
30	Sales	1993	1994	1995	1996	1997		
31	Regular Unflavored		6.6%	2.7%	1.9%	1.6%		
32	Decaffeinated Unflavored		24.5%	23.1%	24.9%	29.3%		
33	Regular Flavored		31.4%	31.3%	19.3%	17.1%		
34	Decaffeinated Flavored		480.0%	58.6%	6.5%	4.1%		
35	Total:		14.1%	10.3%	8.4%	9.8%		
36								
37								
38								
39	Table 5. Coffee sales by type -- % increase over 1993							
40	Sales	1993	1994	1995	1996	1997		
41	Regular Unflavored		6.6%	9.5%	11.6%	13.4%		
42	Decaffeinated Unflavored		24.5%	53.2%	91.4%	147.5%		
43	Regular Flavored		31.4%	72.5%	105.9%	141.2%		
44	Decaffeinated Flavored		480.0%	820.0%	880.0%	920.0%		
45	Total:		14.1%	25.9%	36.4%	49.8%		

You have entered all the input values, labels, and formulas in the Sales Values sheet, formatted all the data values appropriately, and tested the formulas. Now you'll work on the third sheet in the workbook, State Sales.

To view the contents of the State Sales sheet:

1. Click cell **A1** to make it the active cell in the Sales Values sheet.
2. Click the **State Sales** tab. The State Sales worksheet is now displayed.

Row 2 contains table heading information, similar to the heading information for Tables 1 through 5 on the Sales Values sheet. The cells in row 6 are totals. Rows 3 through 5 contain sales data for each of the three states in which Valle Coffee operates. These three rows do not appear to be presented in any logical order. Kim wants you to sort these three rows.

Sorting Rows

Excel can sort rows in ascending or descending order, based on the contents of any one or more columns. For example, you could sort the three rows containing sales data in ascending order on column A. This would produce an alphabetical list, with the Indiana data in row 3, Michigan data in row 4, and Ohio data in row 5. You specify the rows to be sorted and the sort order in the Sort dialog box.

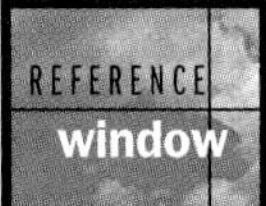

SORTING ROWS

- Select the rows to be sorted.
- Click Data on the menu bar, then click Sort to display the Sort dialog box.
- Select the column on which you want to sort.
- Click either the Ascending or Descending radio button.
- If you want to sort on a second column, click the first Then By box, select the column, then click either the Ascending or Descending radio button.
- If you want to sort on a third column, click the second Then By box, select the column heading, then click either the Ascending or Descending radio button.
- Click the OK button to sort the rows.

Kim wants Michigan, the state with the highest sales each year, to appear first, followed by Indiana and then Ohio. To produce this order, you could do a descending sort on any one of the columns B through F. You'll sort on column B.

To sort the rows in descending order by sales:

1. Position the pointer over the number "3" that identifies row 3, click and hold the mouse as you drag the mouse down to select rows 4 and 5, then release the mouse button. Rows 3 through 5 are now selected.
2. Click **Data** on the menu bar, then click **Sort** to open the Sort dialog box.
3. Click the **Sort By** list arrow, then click **Column B**.
4. If necessary, click the **Descending** radio button. See Figure 6-22.

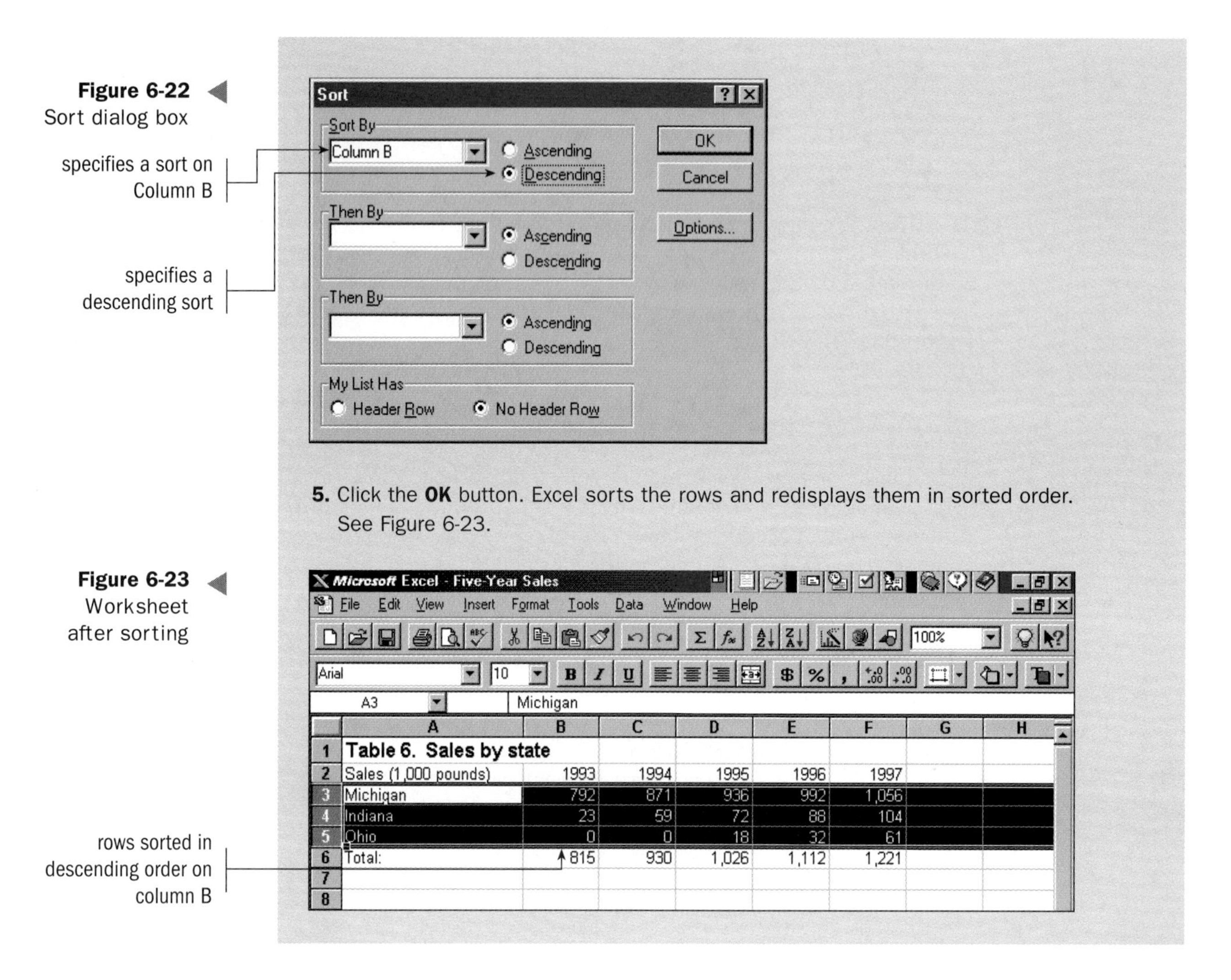

Figure 6-22 Sort dialog box

5. Click the **OK** button. Excel sorts the rows and redisplays them in sorted order. See Figure 6-23.

Figure 6-23 Worksheet after sorting

In addition to the ascending and descending sorts, Excel can also sort rows in order by month name or day name. To request a month or day name sort, you click the Options button on the Sort dialog box.

This completes your work for the first session, so you need to save the workbook.

To save the workbook:

1. Click cell **A1** to make it the active cell.
2. Click the **Documentation** tab to move to the Documentation sheet. By making the Documentation sheet active before saving, when you close the workbook and later reopen it, the Documentation sheet will be displayed.
3. Click the **Save** button on the Standard toolbar to save the current version of the workbook.

Quick Check

1. What general guidelines were offered for effectively organizing a multisheet workbook?
2. What information is included on the Documentation sheet for the workbook you used in this session?
3. What Excel function returns the current date?
4. What is the fill handle? How did you use the fill handle in this session?

5. Cell B5 contains the formula =B1 + $B2 + B$3 + $B$4. If you copy the contents of cell B5 to cell E7, what formula will cell E7 contain?
6. A worksheet has values in cells C1 through C7. Describe the quickest way to place a formula for the sum of those values in cell C8.
7. How can you tell if a cell has an associated text note? How do you display a cell's text note?
8. What does it mean to test a worksheet? What are test values?
9. How can you change the format for a cell that currently displays "0.85" so that it displays "85%" instead?
10. Briefly describe the steps you must take to sort a set of worksheet rows.

Now that you've completed Session 6.1, you can exit Excel or you can continue to the next session.

SESSION 6.2

In this session you will continue to develop the Five-Year Sales workbook. You will learn how to change character font types and font sizes; use bold, italic, and underlining; apply patterns and colors; adjust row heights; change cell alignments; center text across columns; use AutoFormat; change the orientation, centering, headers, and footers for printing a worksheet; and display and print formulas.

Changing Character Formats

Formatting is the process of changing the appearance of the data in the cells of a worksheet to make the worksheet easier to understand and more attractive, and to draw attention to important points. You've already used some of the Excel formatting options to format numbers and dates, add borders to cells or groups of cells, and apply the percentage format. Many of the other Excel formatting options parallel Word's formatting options, so you'll be able to apply your Word experience to Excel.

Kim wants you to format the Five-Year Sales workbook to improve its appearance.

Changing Font Type and Font Size

You have changed both character font types and font sizes in Word. You can use the same techniques and the same toolbar buttons to format cell contents in Excel.

Kim wants to emphasize the text in the title area of the Documentation sheet to draw attention to it, and she asks you to change the font type and font size of the title text.

To change the font type and font size of the title text:

1. On the Documentation sheet, click cell **B2**, which contains the label "VALLE COFFEE."
2. Click the **Font** list arrow on the Formatting toolbar to open the font list. All the fonts available in Excel are listed in alphabetical order in the font list.
3. Scroll the font list until you see the font named Impact, then click **Impact**.

   TROUBLE? If your font list does not include Impact, then select Arial Narrow instead.
4. Click the **Font Size** list arrow on the Formatting toolbar to open the font size list.

5. Click **36**. The text changes from 10 point to 36 point, and the height of row 2 is automatically increased to accommodate the larger text.
6. Click cell **B4** to select the subtitle text.
7. Click the **Font Size** list arrow to open the font size list.
8. Click **14**. The text changes from 10 point to 14 point, and the height of row 4 is automatically increased to accommodate the larger text.

Using Bold, Italic, and Underlining

Three additional formatting techniques for emphasizing text are to display the text in boldface, to italicize it, or to underline it. You can apply each of these styles with a button on Excel's Formatting toolbar. You'll apply the italic style to the title.

To italicize the title:

1. Click cell **B2**.
2. Click the **Italic** button on the Formatting toolbar.

Next, Kim wants you to format the Sales Values worksheet. To make the sheet title and all the table titles stand out, you'll bold and increase the font size of each.

To bold and increase the font size of the Sales Values sheet titles:

1. Click the **Sales Values** tab to display the Sales Values sheet. Cell A1, which contains the sheet title, is already selected.
2. Click the **Bold** button on the Formatting toolbar.
3. Click the **Font Size** list arrow, then click **14**.
4. Click cell **A3** to select the cell containing the Table 1 title, click the **Bold** button, click the **Font Size** list arrow, then click **11**.

   To format the remaining table titles, you can use the Format Painter.

5. Double-click the **Format Painter** button on the Standard toolbar. A dashed rotating line appears around cell A3, indicating its format can be applied to other cells.
6. Click cells **A13**, **A21**, **A29**, then **A39**. Excel applies the format for cell A3 to the other four cells.
7. Click the **Format Painter** button on the Standard toolbar to turn the option off.
8. Scroll to the top of the Sales Values sheet.

After looking at Table 1, Kim suggests that two text items, "Sales (1,000 pounds)" and "Total:," should also be boldfaced, and that the five year values should be italicized. She asks you to make these changes to all five tables on this sheet.

To bold and italicize the labels:

1. Click cell **A4** then click the **Bold** button on the Formatting toolbar.
2. Select cells **B4** through **F4**, then click the **Italic** button on the Formatting toolbar.
3. Click cell **A9** then click the **Bold** button on the Formatting toolbar.
4. Repeat Steps 1 through 3 for Tables 2 through 5.
5. Scroll to the top of the sheet, then click cell **A1**. Your screen should now look like Figure 6-24.

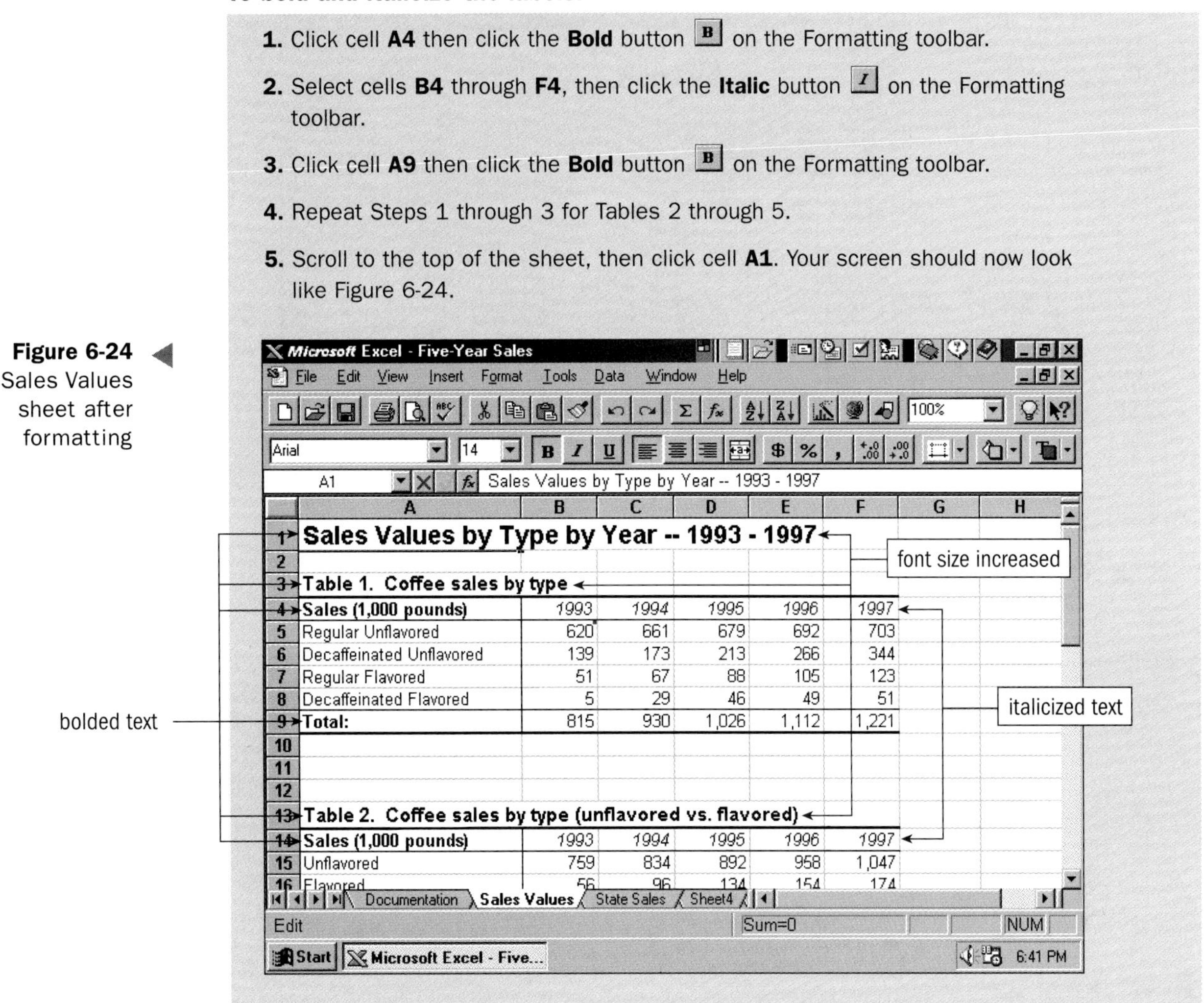

Figure 6-24 Sales Values sheet after formatting

Applying Patterns and Colors

Excel provides a variety of patterns and colors you can apply to cells to add visual interest. You can apply a color, a pattern, or both to any cell. Patterns are most useful if you are using a printer without color capabilities. When you print in black and white, Excel translates all colors to shades of gray; some colors are translated to dark grays that make it difficult to read any values or text printed in a colored cell.

Kim suggests applying a pattern to the sheet title on the Sales Values sheet.

To apply a pattern to the title:

1. Select cells **A1** through **F1**.
2. Right-click a selected cell to display the shortcut menu, then click **Format Cells**. The Format Cells dialog box opens.
3. Click the **Patterns** tab.
4. Click the **Pattern** list arrow to display the color and pattern palette. See Figure 6-25.

Figure 6-25 Applying a pattern to cells

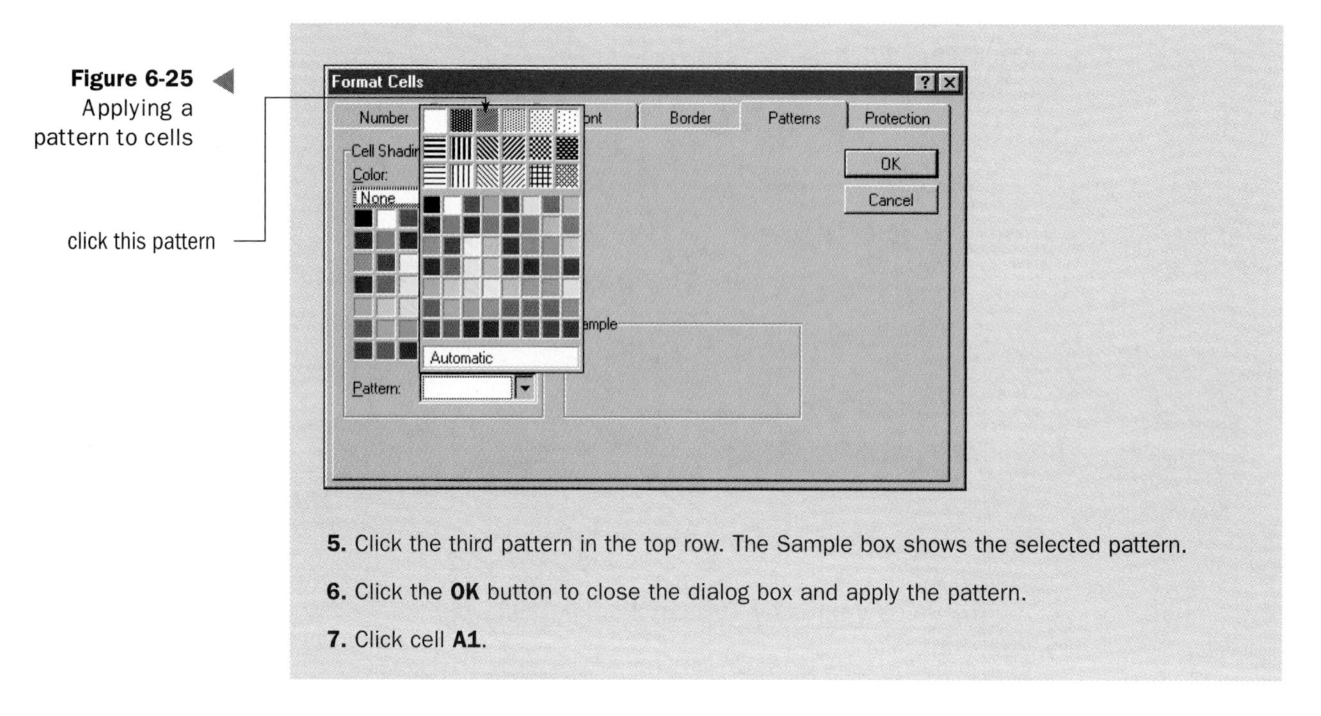

5. Click the third pattern in the top row. The Sample box shows the selected pattern.
6. Click the **OK** button to close the dialog box and apply the pattern.
7. Click cell **A1**.

The title area of the Documentation sheet includes a title and subtitle along with an inserted picture of the Valle Coffee logo. The background of that logo is blue. Kim thinks that the title area would look best if its cells were colored the same blue.

You can apply color to a cell or cells just as you apply a pattern, by opening the Format Cells dialog box and choosing an option on the Patterns tab. It is easier, however, to use the Color button on the Formatting toolbar.

To color the title area cells of the Documentation sheet:

1. Click the **Documentation** tab to display the Documentation sheet.
2. Select cells **A1** through **C5**.
3. Click the **down arrow** next to the **Color** button on the Formatting toolbar. The cell color palette opens. See Figure 6-26.

Figure 6-26 Applying color to cells

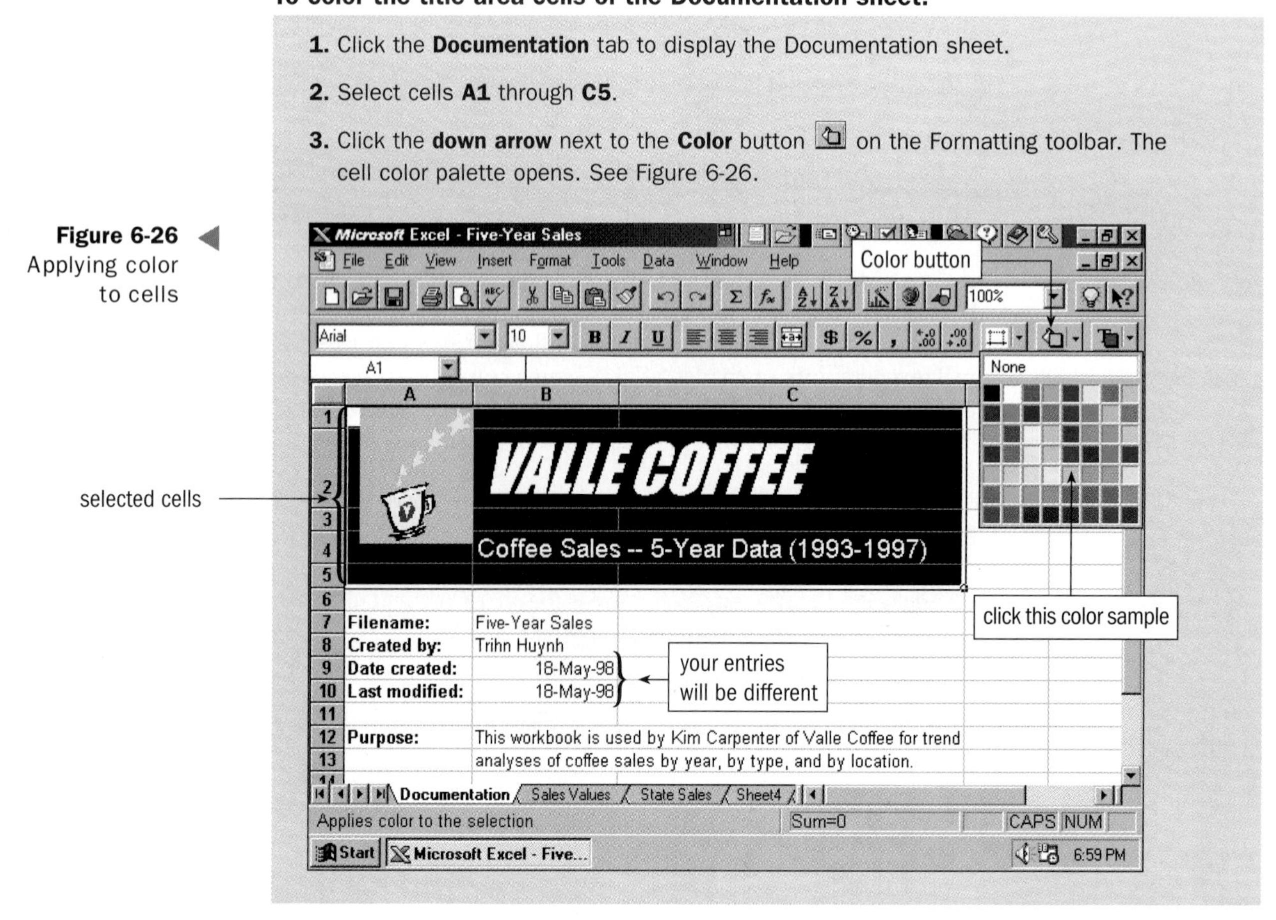

4. Click the **blue color** in the fifth position of the fifth row of color samples.
5. Click cell **C7** to remove the highlight from the title area cells. You can now see that the cells in the title area are colored blue and the logo blends in.

Adjusting Row Heights

The standard height of a row in an Excel worksheet is 12.75 points, where a point is 1/72 of an inch. Excel will automatically adjust a row's height to accommodate text with a large font size in that row. You can also click and drag the bottom border of a row heading to change that row's height, usually to improve readability or to increase or decrease the separation between adjacent rows. Excel allows row heights from 0 to 409.5 points. A row height of 0 means that the row is hidden.

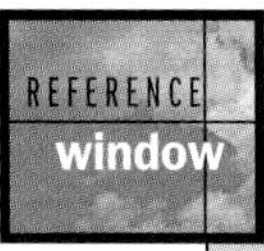

CHANGING ROW HEIGHT WITH THE ROW RESIZING POINTER

- Position the pointer at the bottom border of the row heading until the pointer changes to ✢.
- Click and drag the border until the row is the height you want, then release the mouse button.

When you resize a row by clicking and dragging its border, Excel displays the changing row height in the box at the far left of the formula bar as you drag the row resizing pointer.

The rows in the Documentation sheet that list the sheet names and sheet contents might be easier to read if the entries were more separated. You'll increase the height of the row containing the first entry to check the effect.

To increase the height of row 16:

1. If necessary, scroll the worksheet until rows 15 through 20 are visible.
2. Position the pointer over the bottom of the row 16 number so that it changes to the row resizing pointer ✢.
3. Click and drag the pointer down until a row height of 15.00 is displayed in the formula bar. See Figure 6-27.

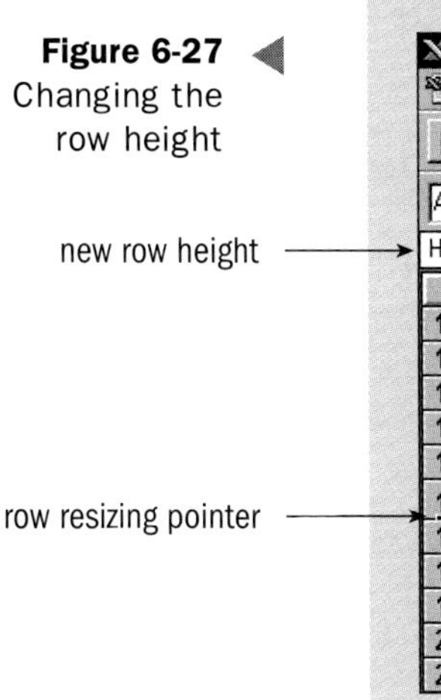

Figure 6-27 Changing the row height

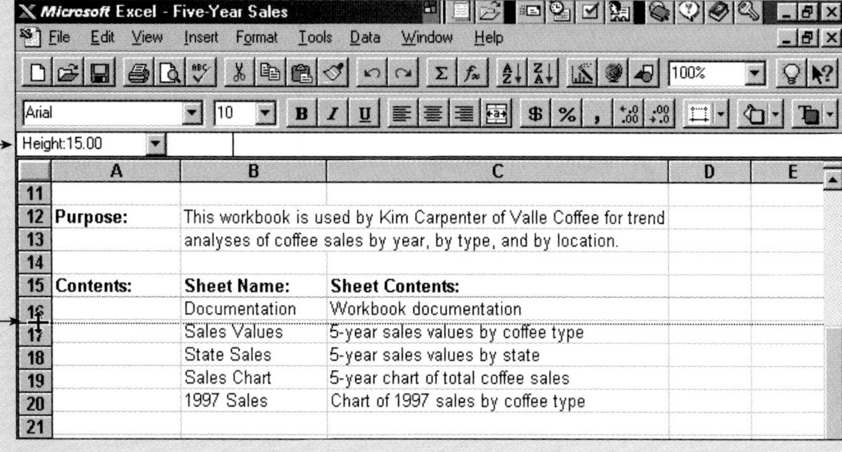

4. Release the mouse button.

Kim thinks the increased row height improves the readability. You could now change the row heights for the remaining rows individually. Or, you can use the same technique to change the height of several adjacent rows at once. First you select the rows to be resized, then use the row resizing pointer to resize one of the selected rows. When you complete the resizing and release the mouse button, the heights of all the selected rows are changed.

Using the row resizing pointer allows you to change the row height to a multiple of 0.75 points. For example, you can increase the row height to 14.25 points, or 15.00 points, or 15.75 points. However, this technique will not allow you to change the row height to a value such as 14.80 or 15.50 points. The Row Height dialog box allows you to change the row height to any value.

REFERENCE window

CHANGING ROW HEIGHT WITH THE ROW HEIGHT DIALOG BOX

- Select the row or rows whose height you want to change.
- Right-click to display the shortcut menu, then click Row Height (or click Format, point to Row, then click Height) to display the Row Height dialog box.
- Type the row height you want.
- Click the OK button to close the dialog box.

You'll use the shortcut menu method to change the heights of rows 17 through 20 to 15 points.

To change the heights of rows 17 through 20:

1. Select rows **17** through **20**.
2. Right-click a selected row to display the shortcut menu, then click **Row Height**. The Row Height dialog box opens.
3. Type **15** then click the **OK** button. The heights of the selected rows are changed to 15 points.

Changing Alignments

The **alignment** of data in a cell is the position of the data relative to the right and left edges of the cell. You can align data on the left or right side of a cell, centered in a cell, or centered across several adjacent cells. By default, Excel left-aligns text entries and right-aligns numbers and dates.

Changing Cell Alignment

You can change a cell's alignment using the Format Cells dialog box. However, it is often quicker and easier to use one of the alignment buttons on Excel's Formatting toolbar. You'll use a Formatting toolbar button to change the alignment of the two dates on the Documentation sheet.

To change the alignment of the date cells:

1. Scroll up the worksheet then select cells **B9** and **B10**. The dates in these cells are both right-aligned, by default. They would look better if left-aligned to match the alignment of the text in cells B7 and B8.
2. Click the **Align Left** button on the Formatting toolbar.

Centering Text Across Columns

Excel also provides a Formatting toolbar button to center the contents of a cell across more than one column. This feature is most useful for centering titles at the top of a worksheet.

Kim asks you to center the Sales Values sheet title across the top of that worksheet.

To center the Sales Values title across columns:

1. Click cell **A1** then click the **Sales Values** tab to display the Sales Values sheet.

   When you use the center across columns option, you must first select the columns across which you want to center the text.

2. Select cells **A1** through **F1**.

3. Click the **Center Across Columns** button on the Formatting toolbar. The worksheet title is centered across columns A through F. See Figure 6-28.

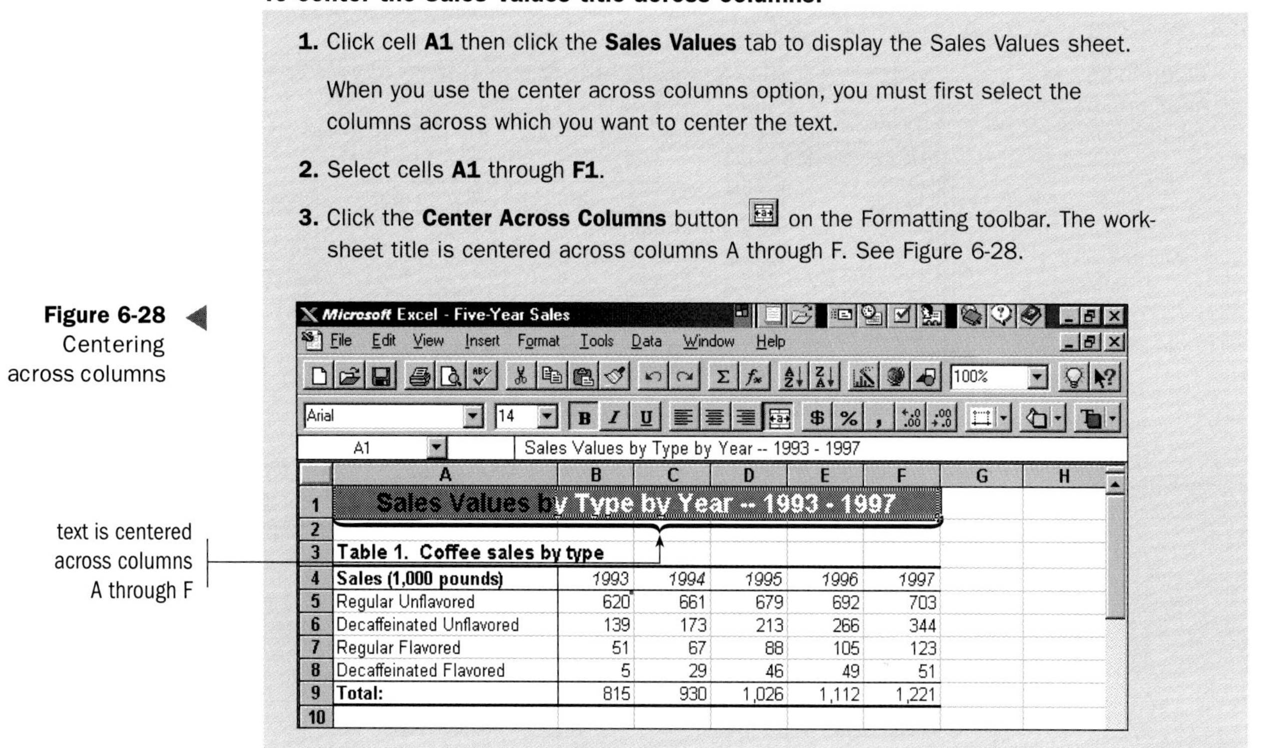

Figure 6-28 Centering across columns

For proper centering, text to be centered across columns should be entered in the leftmost column. For example, if you plan to center text across columns C through G, you would enter the text in column C. You can also center numbers and dates across columns, but centering text is much more common.

Using AutoFormat

You formatted the tables in the Sales Values worksheet by changing font sizes and applying bold and italic where appropriate. These tables were already formatted with borders and changed column widths. You could also apply patterns and colors to cells within these tables, or change one or more row heights.

To simplify the process of formatting a table, Excel provides a collection of predesigned table formats. Each format combines a choice of font types and font sizes, borders, colors, shading, column widths, row heights, and text alignment to create an attractive table layout. You use the **AutoFormat** command to apply one of the predesigned table formats to a selected table or tables.

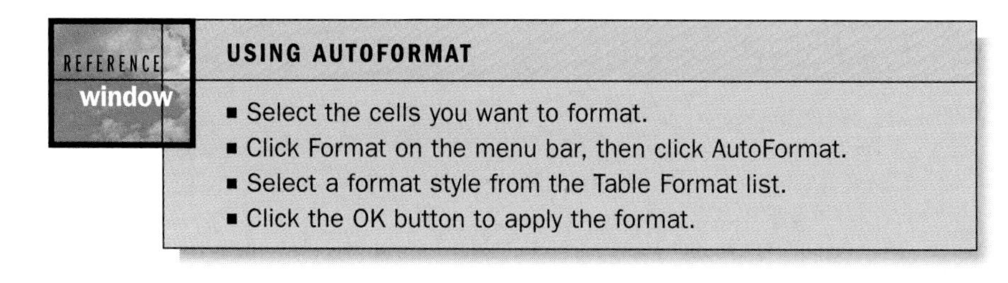
REFERENCE window

USING AUTOFORMAT

- Select the cells you want to format.
- Click Format on the menu bar, then click AutoFormat.
- Select a format style from the Table Format list.
- Click the OK button to apply the format.

The table in the State Sales sheet has not been formatted. You'll use the AutoFormat command to format this table.

To format Table 6 using AutoFormat:

1. Click cell **A1** then click the **State Sales** tab to display the State Sales sheet.
2. Select cells **A2** through **F6**, click **Format** on the menu bar, then click **AutoFormat**. The AutoFormat dialog box opens. See Figure 6-29.

Figure 6-29 AutoFormat dialog box

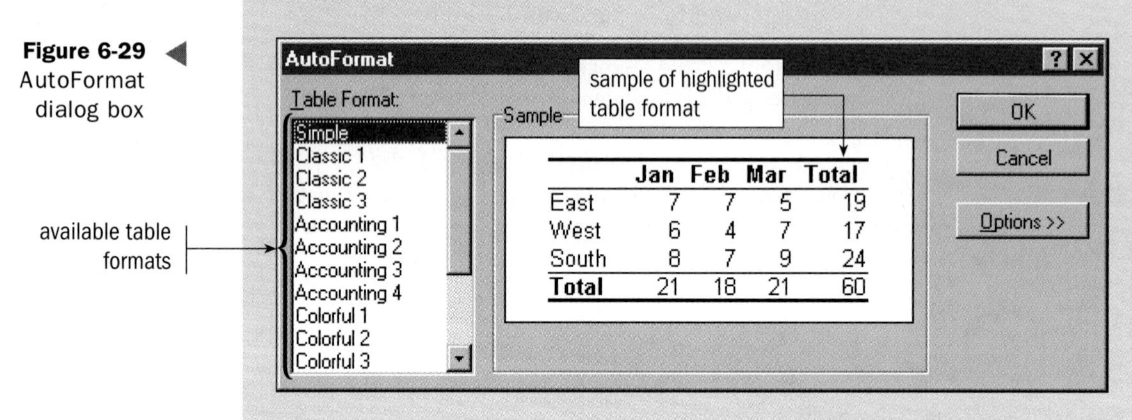

3. Click each of the table formats in the Table Format list, and look at the displayed sample for each. Notice that the Classic 1 format closely resembles the formatting used for the tables in the Sales Values sheet. However, Kim wants Table 6 to have a different format because it's on a different sheet. She asks you to apply the Classic 3 format to this table.
4. Scroll the list until you see Classic 3, click **Classic 3**, then click the **OK** button to close the AutoFormat dialog box and apply the selected format.
5. Click cell **A1** to remove the highlighting from the table. The title line of the table is now shown in white type on a deep blue background. The row labels (cells A3 through A6) are boldfaced, and the column labels (cells B2 through F2) are italicized. The body of the table (rows 3 through 5) has a gray background. A deep blue color is used for the type for the data values in the table body.

   One of the many formatting changes applied to the table involves the column widths. Excel sized each column to be only as wide as necessary to display the cell values. The table would be more readable if columns B through F were wider. As you learned in Tutorial 3, column width is measured in characters. A column width of 5, for example, means that 5 characters in the default Arial 10-point font can fit in the column. You'll increase this default width to 7.
6. Select columns **B** through **F** by selecting their column letters.
7. Right-click a selected column to display the shortcut menu, click **Column Width**, type **7**, then click the **OK** button.
8. Click cell **A1** to remove the highlighting from columns B through F. Your screen should now look like Figure 6-30.

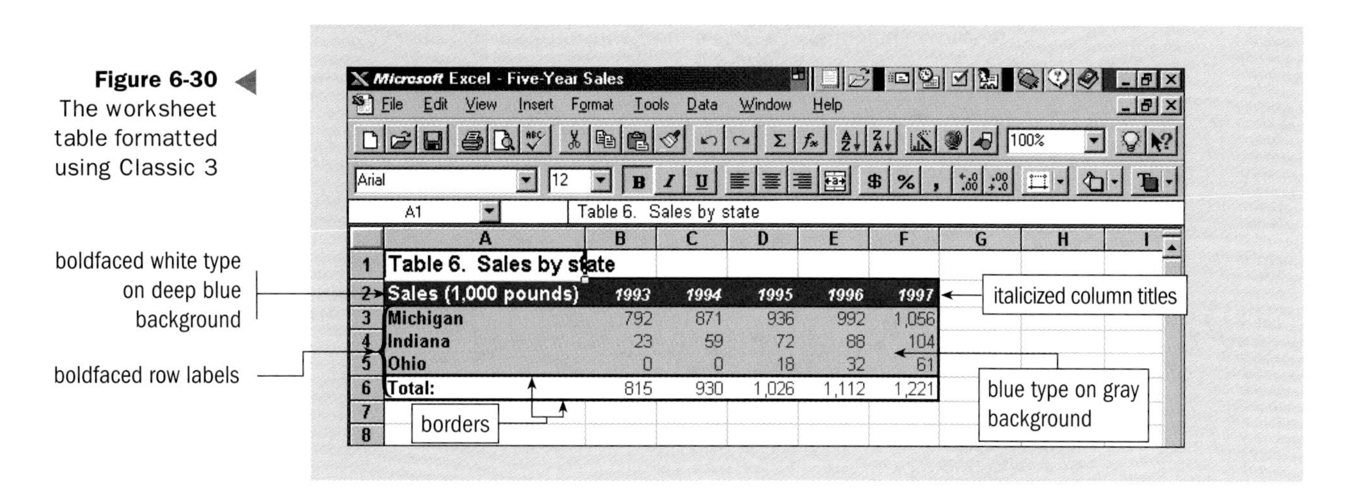

Figure 6-30 The worksheet table formatted using Classic 3

Kim is satisfied with the AutoFormat results for this table. If you wanted to change to another format, you would reselect the table cells, click Format, click AutoFormat, and then select another format. You can remove an AutoFormat by selecting "None" in the Table Format list.

Changing the Printed Appearance of a Worksheet

The printed appearance of a worksheet involves many factors: the paper orientation (lengthwise or widthwise); the size of the left, right, top, and bottom margins; the worksheet positioning (positioned at the far left or horizontally centered, positioned at the top or vertically centered); the information printed in the header and footer; and the presence or absence of printed gridlines.

By default, Excel prints a worksheet in landscape orientation with 1-inch top and bottom margins and ¾-inch left and right margins. Headers and footers are printed ½-inch from the top and bottom of the page, respectively. The sheet name is displayed in the header, and the page number is displayed in the footer. The worksheet is positioned in the upper-left corner of the print area, and gridlines are not printed. You can change any of these default characteristics in the Page Setup dialog box, which you open by clicking the Page Setup command on the File menu or by clicking the Setup button on the Print Preview toolbar.

The page setups for worksheets in a workbook are independent. If you change a page setup characteristic for one worksheet, that change is *not* applied to the other worksheets in the workbook.

Kim has already specified the page setup characteristics for all the worksheets in this workbook *except* the Sales Values sheet. She asks you to check and change, where appropriate, the page setup characteristics for that worksheet so that it is consistent with the rest of the sheets in the workbook.

Portrait and Landscape Orientations

Excel provides two paper orientations, portrait and landscape. The **portrait** orientation prints a worksheet with the paper positioned so it is taller than it is wide. In contrast, the **landscape** orientation prints the worksheet with the paper positioned so it is wider than it is tall. If your worksheet is wider than it is tall, a landscape orientation is appropriate.

The Sales Values worksheet is taller than it is wide, so a portrait orientation would be appropriate.

To preview the Sales Values sheet and change the sheet orientation:

1. Click the **Sales Values** tab to display the Sales Values sheet.
2. Click the **Print Preview** button on the Standard toolbar. The Print Preview window opens. See Figure 6-31.

Figure 6-31 Print preview of the Sales Values sheet

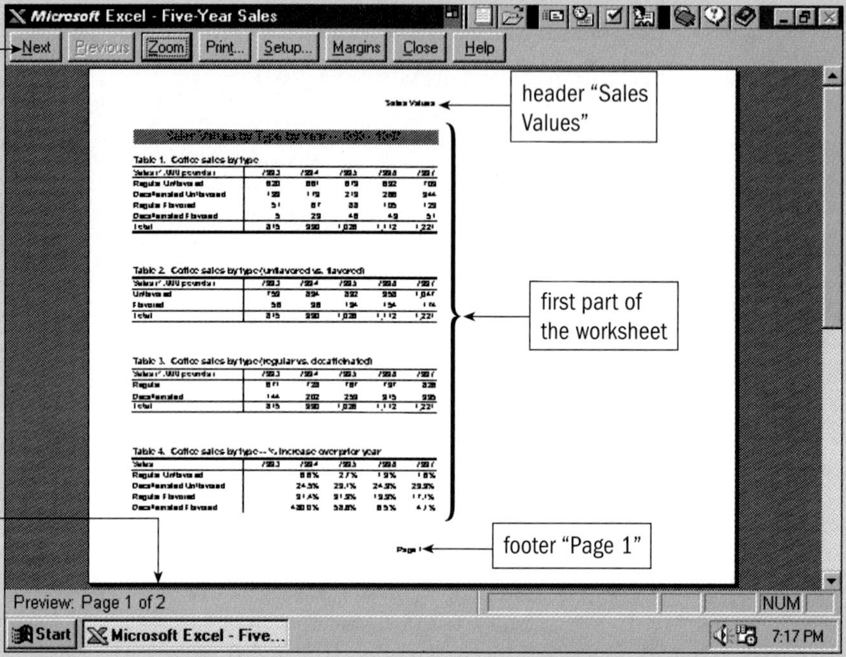

click to preview the next page

number of pages required for printout

header "Sales Values"

first part of the worksheet

footer "Page 1"

Microsoft Excel - Five-Year Sales

Next Previous Zoom Print... Setup... Margins Close Help

Preview: Page 1 of 2

Notice the default landscape orientation and the default header and footer text.

TROUBLE? If you have difficulty reading the header and footer text, position the pointer over the header, then click the mouse button to zoom the picture. Read the header, then click the mouse to return to the full-page view. To view the footer, repeat this process, but position the pointer over the footer text.

3. Click the **Next** button on the Print Preview toolbar to preview the second page of the worksheet.
4. Click the **Previous** button on the Print Preview toolbar to display the first page again.
5. Click the **Setup** button on the Print Preview toolbar to open the Page Setup dialog box, then (if necessary) click the **Page** tab.
6. Click the **Portrait** radio button in the Orientation section, then click the **OK** button to close the dialog box. The preview display changes to show the worksheet in portrait orientation. The Sales Values worksheet now fits on a single printed page.
7. Click the **Close** button on the Print Preview toolbar to close the Print Preview window.

Changing Headers and Footers

As you learned earlier in Tutorial 3, a **header** is text that is printed in the top margin of every page of a worksheet. A **footer** is text that is printed in the bottom margin of every page of a worksheet. Instead of printing a centered worksheet name in the header or a centered page number in the footer (the Excel defaults), you can customize a header or footer to include other information and to place it in a different position. You can even choose to not print a header or footer.

When you create a custom header or footer, you indicate what you want to print by clicking a button on the Page Setup dialog box. Excel then inserts a code to represent the item you want to print. The buttons, their names, their codes, and their purposes are shown in Figure 6-32.

Figure 6-32 Header and footer formatting buttons

Button	Button Name	Code	Purpose
	Font	none	set font and font size
	Page Number	&[Page]	print page number
	Total Pages	&[Pages]	print total number of pages
	Date	&[Date]	print current date
	Time	&[Time]	print current time
	Filename	&[File]	print workbook name
	Sheet Name	&[Tab]	print worksheet name

Kim asks you to create a custom header with the workbook name and worksheet name separated by a period in the upper-left corner, and the current date in the upper-right corner. You closed the Page Setup dialog box after you changed the orientation so you could see the effect of the change in the Print Preview window. You need to open this dialog box again to change the header. This time you'll use the Page Setup command on the File menu.

To customize the header for the Sales Values sheet:

1. Click **File** on the menu bar, then click **Page Setup** to open the Page Setup dialog box.
2. Click the **Header/Footer** tab in the Page Setup dialog box.
3. Click the **Custom Header** button to open the Header dialog box. See Figure 6-33.

Figure 6-33 Header dialog box

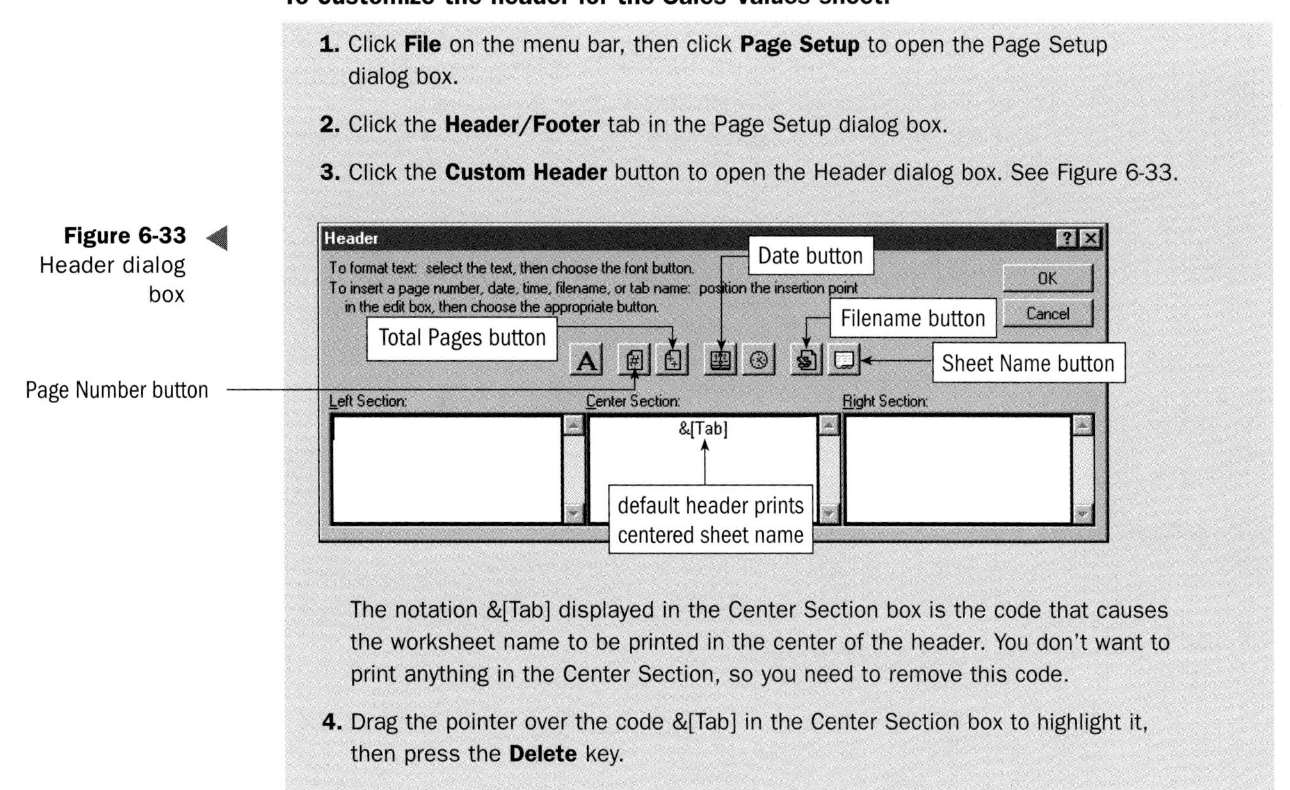

The notation &[Tab] displayed in the Center Section box is the code that causes the worksheet name to be printed in the center of the header. You don't want to print anything in the Center Section, so you need to remove this code.

4. Drag the pointer over the code &[Tab] in the Center Section box to highlight it, then press the **Delete** key.

5. Click the **Left Section** box to move the insertion point to that section.

6. Click the **Filename** button in the Header dialog box, type a period, then click the **Sheet Name** button.

7. Click the **Right Section** box to move the insertion point to that section. The insertion point is right-aligned in the Right Section.

8. Click the **Date** button in the Header dialog box. See Figure 6-34.

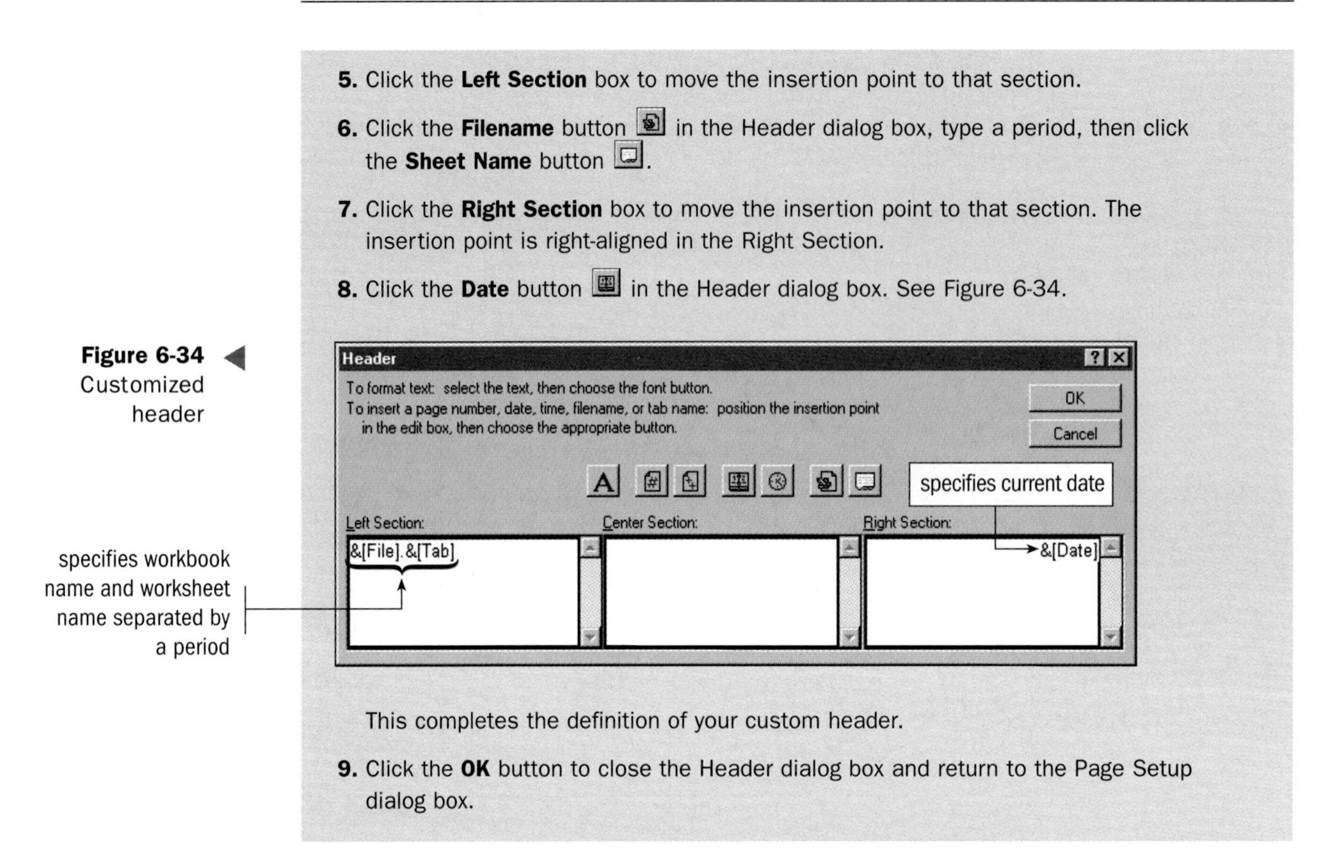

Figure 6-34 Customized header

This completes the definition of your custom header.

9. Click the **OK** button to close the Header dialog box and return to the Page Setup dialog box.

Kim wants the footer to show the page number and the total number of pages, presented in the form "Page m of n" and centered at the bottom of the page. When page numbers are printed in this form, it is easier to verify that you have all the pages of a worksheet printout. The footer "Page 1 of 2," for example, tells you that a worksheet is printed on two pages, and that the other page is labeled "Page 2 of 2." You also know that there is no need to look for a third page.

Excel offers a selection of optional headers and footers that you can select from the Header list box and Footer list box in the Page Setup dialog box. None of the optional headers matched the format Kim wanted, so you had to customize the header. A centered footer in the form "Page m of n" is available, however, so you only need to select that footer (which Excel calls "Page 1 of ?") in the Footer list.

To select the footer:

1. In the Page Setup dialog box, click the **Footer** list arrow to display the optional footers list.

2. Scroll the list, if necessary, then click **Page 1 of ?** to select that footer.

You also need to change the placement of the worksheet on the page, so you'll leave the Page Setup dialog box open.

Centering a Printed Worksheet

By default, Excel prints a worksheet at the top left of the page print area. You can specify that the worksheet be centered vertically or horizontally, or both. Kim asks you to center the Sales Values worksheet both horizontally and vertically on the printed page.

To center the Sales Values sheet printout:

1. Click the **Margins** tab in the Page Setup dialog box. Notice that the Preview box displays a worksheet positioned in the upper left of the page.

   TROUBLE? If you closed the Page Setup dialog box at the conclusion of the previous steps, reopen the dialog box by clicking File, then Page Setup. Then complete Step 1.

2. Click the **Horizontally** check box in the Center on Page section. The preview changes to show a worksheet centered horizontally.
3. Click the **Vertically** check box in the Center on Page section. The preview changes to show a worksheet centered vertically as well as horizontally. This is the placement that you need for this worksheet.
4. Click the **Sheet** tab in the Page Setup dialog box.

You'll leave the Page Setup dialog box open so you can examine the options on the Sheet tab.

Working with Printed Gridlines

The fourth tab in the Page Setup dialog box is the Sheet tab. The Print Area option allows you to specify a range of cells to be printed, rather than printing the entire worksheet. The Print Titles options are useful if you have a worksheet that is both too wide and too long to fit on a single printed page. You can choose to repeat particular rows and/or particular columns, so that your row headings and/or column labels appear on every page of the worksheet printout.

The Print section includes options for printing gridlines, cell notes, or row and column headings, as well as options for selecting draft quality or black-and-white print. The default is to select none of these options.

Sometimes you might want to see the gridlines as well as the row and column headings on a worksheet printout. These options are most commonly used when you print a worksheet while you are still in the process of creating it. Figure 6-35 shows a portion of the Sales Values worksheet printed with and without row and column headings and gridlines.

Figure 6-35 Printing with and without row and column headings and gridlines

With:

	A	B	C	D	E	F
1	**Sales Values by Type by Year -- 1993 - 1997**					
2						
3	**Table 1. Coffee sales by type**					
4	**Sales (1,000 pounds)**	*1993*	*1994*	*1995*	*1996*	*1997*
5	Regular Unflavored	620	661	679	692	703
6	Decaffeinated Unflavored	139	173	213	266	344
7	Regular Flavored	51	67	88	105	123
8	Decaffeinated Flavored	5	29	46	49	51
9	**Total:**	815	930	1,026	1,112	1,221
10						
11						

Without:

Sales Values by Type by Year -- 1993 - 1997

Table 1. Coffee sales by type

Sales (1,000 pounds)	*1993*	*1994*	*1995*	*1996*	*1997*
Regular Unflavored	620	661	679	692	703
Decaffeinated Unflavored	139	173	213	266	344
Regular Flavored	51	67	88	105	123
Decaffeinated Flavored	5	29	46	49	51
Total:	815	930	1,026	1,112	1,221

Kim thinks that the printout looks better without the headings and gridlines, so you do not need to change any options on the Sheet tab.

Printing Worksheets

Now you'll print the Documentation, Sales Values, and State Sales worksheets.

To preview and print the three sheets:

1. Click the **OK** button to close the Page Setup dialog box.
2. Click the **Documentation** tab to display that worksheet.
3. Click the **Print Preview** button on the Standard toolbar. The Documentation sheet is centered horizontally in portrait orientation, with the headers and footers Kim defined.
4. Click the **Close** button to close the Print Preview window.
5. Click the **Print** button on the Standard toolbar. Excel prints the active worksheet. See Figure 6-36.

Figure 6-36
Printout of the Documentation worksheet

Five-Year Sales.Documentation 5/18/98

Filename: Five-Year Sales
Created by: Trihn Huynh
Date created: 18-May-98
Last modified: 18-May-98

Purpose: This workbook is used by Kim Carpenter of Valle Coffee for trend analyses of coffee sales by year, by type, and by location.

Contents:

Sheet Name:	**Sheet Contents:**
Documentation	Workbook documentation
Sales Values	5-year sales values by coffee type
State Sales	5-year sales values by state
Sales Chart	5-year chart of total coffee sales
1997 Sales	Chart of 1997 sales by coffee type

Page 1 of 1

TROUBLE? If your Windows 95 setup specifies that filename extensions are shown, your header will include the text "Five-Year Sales.xls.Documentation" rather than "Five-Year-Sales.Documentation" in the upper-left corner.

6. Click the **Sales Values** tab to switch to that worksheet.

7. Repeat Steps 3 through 5 to preview and print the Sales Values worksheet. See Figure 6-37.

Figure 6-37 Printout of the Sales Values worksheet

Five-Year Sales.Sales Values 5/18/98

Sales Values by Type by Year -- 1993 - 1997

Table 1. Coffee sales by type

Sales (1,000 pounds)	1993	1994	1995	1996	1997
Regular Unflavored	620	661	679	692	703
Decaffeinated Unflavored	139	173	213	266	394
Regular Flavored	51	67	88	105	123
Decaffeinated Flavored	5	29	46	49	51
Total:	815	930	1,026	1,112	1,271

Table 2. Coffee sales by type (unflavored vs. flavored)

Sales (1,000 pounds)	1993	1994	1995	1996	1997
Unflavored	759	834	892	958	1,097
Flavored	56	96	134	154	174
Total:	815	930	1,026	1,112	1,271

Table 3. Coffee sales by type (regular vs. decaffeinated)

Sales (1,000 pounds)	1993	1994	1995	1996	1997
Regular	671	728	767	797	826
Decaffeinated	144	202	259	315	445
Total:	815	930	1,026	1,112	1,271

Table 4. Coffee sales by type -- % increase over prior year

Sales	1993	1994	1995	1996	1997
Regular Unflavored		6.6%	2.7%	1.9%	1.6%
Decaffeinated Unflavored		24.5%	23.1%	24.9%	48.1%
Regular Flavored		31.4%	31.3%	19.3%	17.1%
Decaffeinated Flavored		480.0%	58.6%	6.5%	4.1%
Total:		14.1%	10.3%	8.4%	14.3%

Table 5. Coffee sales by type -- % increase over 1993

Sales	1993	1994	1995	1996	1997
Regular Unflavored		6.6%	9.5%	11.6%	13.4%
Decaffeinated Unflavored		24.5%	53.2%	91.4%	183.5%
Regular Flavored		31.4%	72.5%	105.9%	141.2%
Decaffeinated Flavored		480.0%	820.0%	880.0%	920.0%
Total:		14.1%	25.9%	36.4%	56.0%

Page 1 of 1

8. Click the **State Sales** tab to switch to that worksheet.

9. Repeat Steps 3 through 5 to preview and print the State Sales worksheet. See Figure 6-38.

Figure 6-38
Printout of the State Sales worksheet

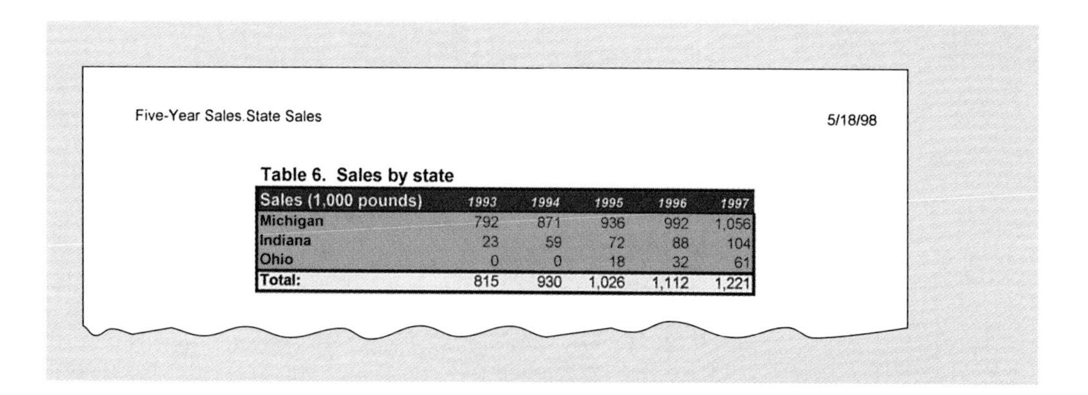

Five-Year Sales.State Sales 5/18/98

Table 6. Sales by state

Sales (1,000 pounds)	1993	1994	1995	1996	1997
Michigan	792	871	936	992	1,056
Indiana	23	59	72	88	104
Ohio	0	0	18	32	61
Total:	815	930	1,026	1,112	1,221

Displaying and Printing Formulas

Excel provides an option that allows you to see the actual formulas you have entered in cells rather than the results of the formulas. Printing the worksheet with the formulas displayed provides a valuable documentation record.

You should always save your workbook immediately before you display and print formulas. You will often want to change cell formats or page setup settings to improve the formulas printout. You don't want such changes to be permanent, and you don't want to have to remember and then undo all the changes you make. If you have saved the workbook first, you can later recover the unchanged version of that workbook.

Kim wants you to display and print the formulas for the Sales Values worksheet.

To display and print the formulas:

1. Click the **Save** button on the Standard toolbar.
2. Click the **Sales Values** tab to switch to that worksheet.
3. Click **Tools** on the menu bar, then click **Options** to open the Options dialog box.
4. Click the **View** tab, if necessary, then click the **Formulas** check box in the Window Options section to place a check mark in the box.
5. Click the **OK** button to close the Options dialog box. The worksheet columns have widened to accommodate the longer formula lengths. This change is only temporary; if you turn off the formula display, the columns will return to their previous widths. See Figure 6-39.

Figure 6-39
Displaying formulas

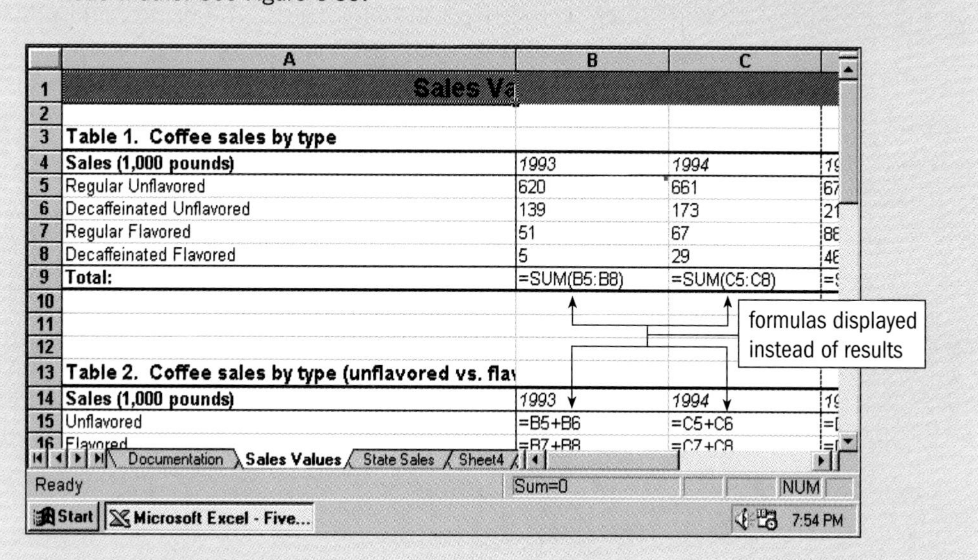

Notice that the complete Table 2 title is not visible. This is a typical occurrence when displaying formulas, so you needn't be concerned. The worksheet title and all the table titles were entered in column A and allowed to overlap into the following columns. In order to display the formulas, Excel increased the width of column A to 24, which is sufficient to print most, but not all, of the table titles. The worksheet title, which is centered across columns A through F, is barely visible, however. To show more of the worksheet title, you need to left-justify it.

6. Click the **Align Left** button on the Formatting toolbar. Most of the worksheet title is now visible.

   TROUBLE? If you left-justified a cell other than A1, click the Undo button on the Standard toolbar, click cell A1, then repeat Step 6.

7. Click the **Print** button on the Standard toolbar. Because of the wide columns, the printout will require two pages.

As noted earlier, you need to close the workbook *without saving changes* so that the display of formulas is removed and the previous version of the worksheet remains intact.

To close the workbook without saving changes:

1. Click **File** on the menu bar, then click **Close**. Excel displays a dialog box asking if you want to save changes to the file.
2. Click the **No** button to close the workbook without saving changes.

Quick Check

1. Describe two methods for adjusting the height of a row.
2. How would you center a label in cell A3 across columns A through D? Be specific.
3. Describe how you would apply a predesigned table format to a table. What is the name of this Excel feature?
4. What are the two page orientations, and how do they differ?
5. When you customize a header, what items of information could you include in the header by clicking a button in the Header dialog box?
6. Why should you save a workbook before you display and print worksheet formulas?

Now that you've completed Session 6.2, you can exit Excel or you can continue to the next session.

SESSION 6.3

In this session you will continue to develop the Five-Year Sales workbook. You will learn how to develop effective Excel charts, and then you will plan, create, modify, and print an Excel column chart.

Developing Effective Charts

An Excel chart is a graphical representation of your data. An effective chart conveys information more readily than a series of number values. Because charts can illustrate, emphasize, or dramatize data, they can usefully supplement the values in an Excel workbook.

To develop effective charts, it is important to understand the Excel chart terminology. Figure 6-40 shows the elements of a typical Excel chart.

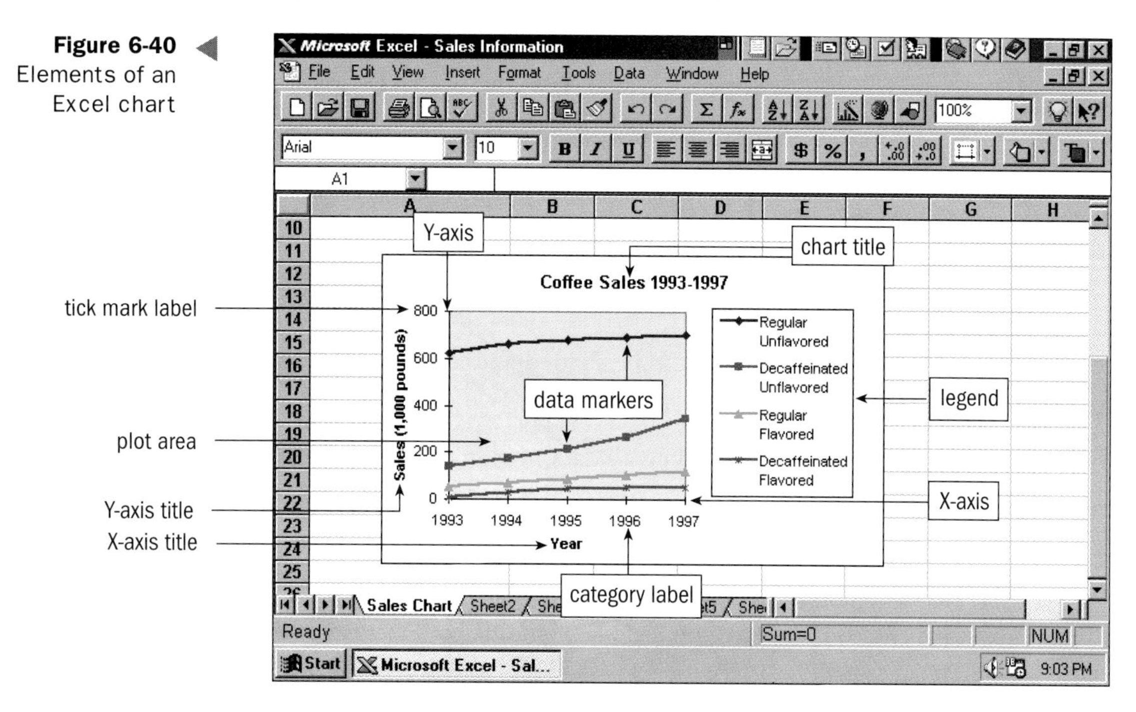

Figure 6-40 Elements of an Excel chart

The **chart title** identifies the chart. The horizontal axis is called the **X-axis.** The X-axis is divided into sections called **categories**, and the X-axis labels are called **category labels.** The vertical axis is called the **Y-axis. Tick mark labels** mark the scale for the Y-axis. The **X-axis title** and the **Y-axis title** identify the two axes. The **plot area** is the rectangular area defined by the axes, with the Y-axis forming the left side and the X-axis forming the base; in Figure 6-40, the plot area is gray.

A **data point** is a single value in a cell in the worksheet. A **data marker** is a symbol that marks a single data point on a chart; depending on the type of chart, a data marker can be a small symbol, a bar, a column, an area, or a pie wedge. A **data series** is a group of related data points. In the chart in Figure 6-40, a data series is represented as a set of data markers connected by a line. When you have more than one data series, your chart will contain more than one set of data markers. The chart in Figure 6-40 has four data series, each represented by a line on the chart. A **legend** identifies which data series is represented by which data marker.

Excel charts are often linked to or embedded in documents created in other programs. Even within a workbook, you often place a chart in a different worksheet from the one that contains its supporting data. So an Excel chart must be able to stand on its own to be useful. That is, an effective chart must be clearly titled and labeled, and include a legend when appropriate.

When you create a chart, Excel selects the colors and symbols used in the chart. You should evaluate the colors and symbols in a chart and change them to improve the appearance of the chart, if necessary.

The size of a chart is also related to its effectiveness. The graph area should be large enough to include a reasonable number of category and tick mark labels on the axes, and to ensure that the data points can be discerned easily. At the same time, the graph area should not be so large that it overwhelms the titles and legend or generates an excessive number of category and tick mark labels that unnecessarily clutter the chart. You should resize a chart, or any portion of a chart, until you are satisfied with the balance of chart elements.

Using the right kind of chart to represent data is a critical factor in creating effective charts. Excel provides many different chart types, each with a different purpose. You will learn more about the different chart types later in this tutorial.

A final guideline for developing an effective chart is to plan the chart before you create it.

Planning a Chart

It is important to plan a chart before you create it. Planning a chart includes the following steps:

1. Identify the data points to be charted and locate them in your worksheet.
2. Determine the purpose of the chart and choose an appropriate chart type.
3. Sketch the chart, including all data points, axes, titles, labels, and legend.
4. Identify any titles, labels or legend text that will come from the worksheet and locate them in your worksheet.

The sketch you make in step 3 does not have to be a perfect drawing—a simple sketch is sufficient. Making sure you include all the chart elements in your sketch is more important than creating a perfect sketch. The effort you put into preparing the sketch, along with completing each of the other planning steps, will pay off later by saving you the time and effort necessary to redo or correct the chart.

Creating an Excel Chart

To create an Excel chart, you use the ChartWizard. The **ChartWizard** automates the chart-making process by guiding you through a sequence of five steps to create a chart.

REFERENCE window

USING THE CHARTWIZARD

- Select the cells you want to chart.
- Click the ChartWizard button on the Standard toolbar.
- Drag the pointer to outline the area in the worksheet where you want the chart to appear.
- Follow the ChartWizard instructions to complete the chart.

Excel Chart Types

In the second of the five ChartWizard steps, you select the type of chart you want to create. Figure 6-41 shows the Step 2 of 5 dialog box for the ChartWizard, which displays samples of each Excel chart type.

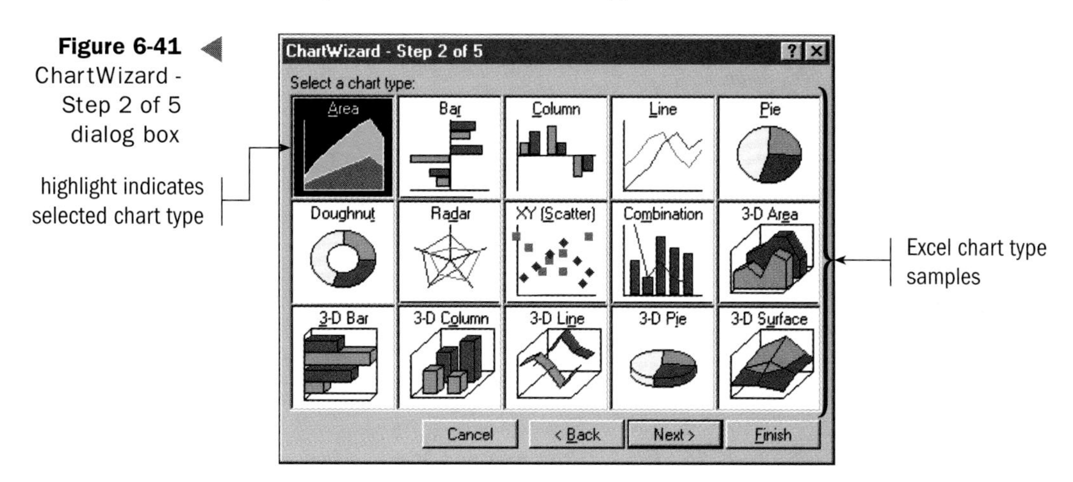

Figure 6-41 ChartWizard - Step 2 of 5 dialog box

There are 14 basic types of Excel charts, each with at least one chart subtype, or variation of the chart type. The two-dimensional (2-D) and three-dimensional (3-D) versions of a particular chart form are considered separate chart types. A fifteenth chart type, the Combination chart, mixes two or more basic chart types on a single chart. Figure 6-42 lists the 15 chart types and briefly describes the purpose for each.

Figure 6-42 Excel chart types and their purposes

Chart Type	Chart Purpose
2-D Area 3-D Area	Shows trends in data over a period of time, at even intervals, emphasizing the magnitude of change.
2-D Bar 3-D Bar	Shows variation over time, emphasizing comparisons among items.
2-D Column 3-D Column	Shows variation over time, emphasizing the variation among items.
2-D Line 3-D Line	Shows trends in data over a period of time, at even intervals, emphasizing the rate of change.
2-D Pie 3-D Pie	Shows the relationship or proportions of parts to the whole, in a pie shape.
Doughnut	Shows the relationship or proportions of parts to the whole, in a doughnut shape.
Radar	Shows differences in data relative to a series of axes that radiate from a center point.
XY (Scatter)	Shows the pattern or relationship between sets of points; most often used for scientific data.
Combination	Shows data in different ways in the same chart.
3-D Surface	Shows a topographic map useful for finding optimum combinations between two sets of data.

Creating a Column Chart

Kim wants a chart showing total coffee sales for the five years from 1993 to 1997. This data is available in the Five-Year Sales workbook you have been working on.

To open the workbook:

1. Make sure your Student Disk is in the disk drive.
2. Click the **Open a Document** button on the Office Shortcut Bar.
3. If necessary, display the list of files in the Tutorial.06 folder on your Student Disk, then open the file **Five-Year Sales**.

   You need to check the Documentation sheet to verify the plan for the new chart.
4. Make sure the Documentation sheet is the active worksheet.
5. If necessary, scroll the Documentation worksheet until rows 15 through 20 are visible, then review the entries in row 19.

According to the workbook plan, the chart will be located on the fourth worksheet, which you will name "Sales Chart." You need to rename the fourth sheet and then plan the chart. To rename a worksheet you right-click its sheet tab, then choose the Rename option.

To rename the fourth sheet:

1. Right-click the **Sheet4** tab to display the shortcut menu, then click **Rename** to open the Rename Sheet dialog box.
2. Type **Sales Chart** then click the **OK** button.
3. Click the **Sales Values** tab to display that worksheet.

Note that cells B9 through F9 of the Sales Values sheet contain the total coffee sales amounts you need for the chart. These cells will constitute the data points for the chart.

The purpose of the chart is to illustrate the five sales totals in such a way that they can be compared to one another. Kim wants the chart to emphasize the fact that total sales have increased every year. A two-dimensional column chart would be appropriate in this case.

If you were to sketch the chart, you would produce a sketch like the one shown in Figure 6-43. Notice that the sketch includes all the different chart elements except a legend, which is not really necessary for this chart.

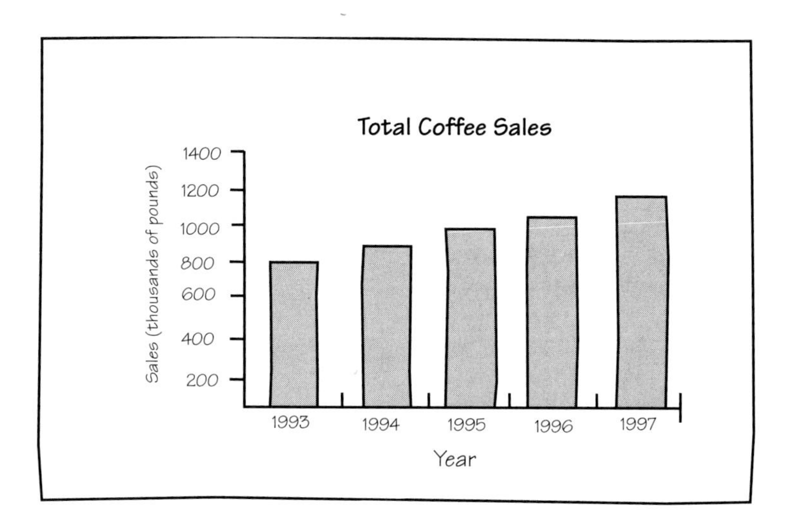

Figure 6-43 Sketch of the column chart

The five years that appear as X-axis labels are located in your worksheet in cells B4 through F4. None of the other labels or titles will come from the worksheet. The chart will not include a legend, so you don't need to identify any cells for supplying legend text. Therefore, you have identified all the worksheet cells you need for the chart: B4 through F4 and B9 through F9.

Now that you have finished the plan for the chart, you can begin to create it. Before you activate the ChartWizard, you need to select all the cells to be charted. The two cell ranges you need to select are not adjacent. To select non-adjacent cells, you select the first cell or range of cells, then press and hold the Ctrl key while you select additional cells.

REFERENCE window

SELECTING NON-ADJACENT CELLS

- Click the first cell or highlight the first range of cells you want to select.
- Press and hold the Ctrl key while you click additional cells or highlight additional ranges.
- When you have selected all the cells, release the Ctrl key.

You need to select two ranges for the chart: cells B4 through F4 and cells B9 through F9.

To select the two cell ranges for the chart:

1. Select cells **B4** through **F4**.
2. Press and hold the **Ctrl** key while you select cells **B9** through **F9**, then release the Ctrl key. Two cell ranges are highlighted: B4:F4 and B9:F9. See Figure 6-44.

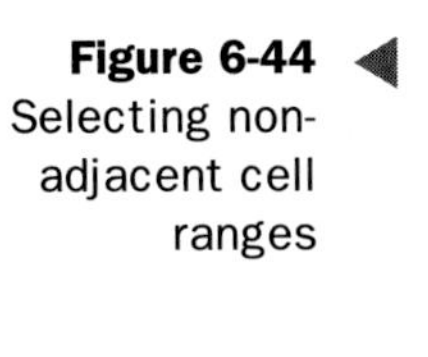

Figure 6-44 Selecting non-adjacent cell ranges

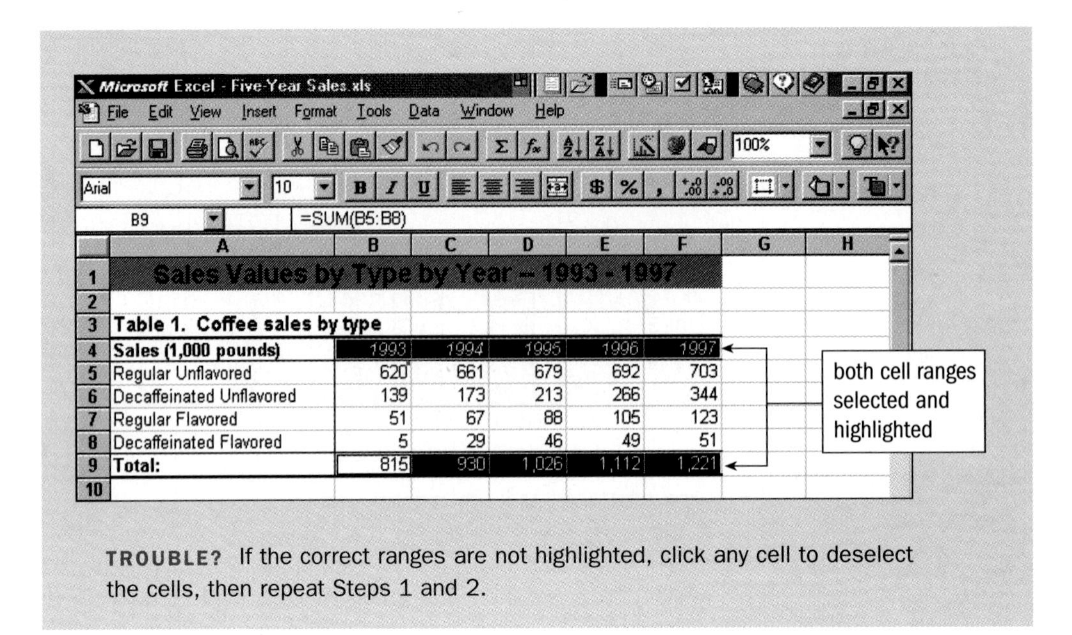

TROUBLE? If the correct ranges are not highlighted, click any cell to deselect the cells, then repeat Steps 1 and 2.

Now you can initiate the ChartWizard and create the chart.

To create the column chart:

1. Click the **ChartWizard** button on the Standard toolbar. Rotating dashed lines surround the selected cell ranges, the pointer changes to +, and the prompt "Drag in document to create a chart" appears in the status bar.

2. Click the **Sales Chart** tab to display the sheet where you want the chart to appear.

   You need to create a chart outline that is approximately 5 columns wide and 14 columns tall. Don't worry about placement; you'll have a chance to reposition the chart later.

3. Move the pointer to the location that will be the upper-left corner of your chart, click and hold down the mouse button as you drag the pointer to create a chart that is roughly 5 columns wide and 14 rows tall, then release the mouse button. The ChartWizard - Step 1 of 5 dialog box appears over the Sales Values sheet so you can correct the range address if necessary. See Figure 6-45.

Figure 6-45 ChartWizard - Step 1 of 5 dialog box

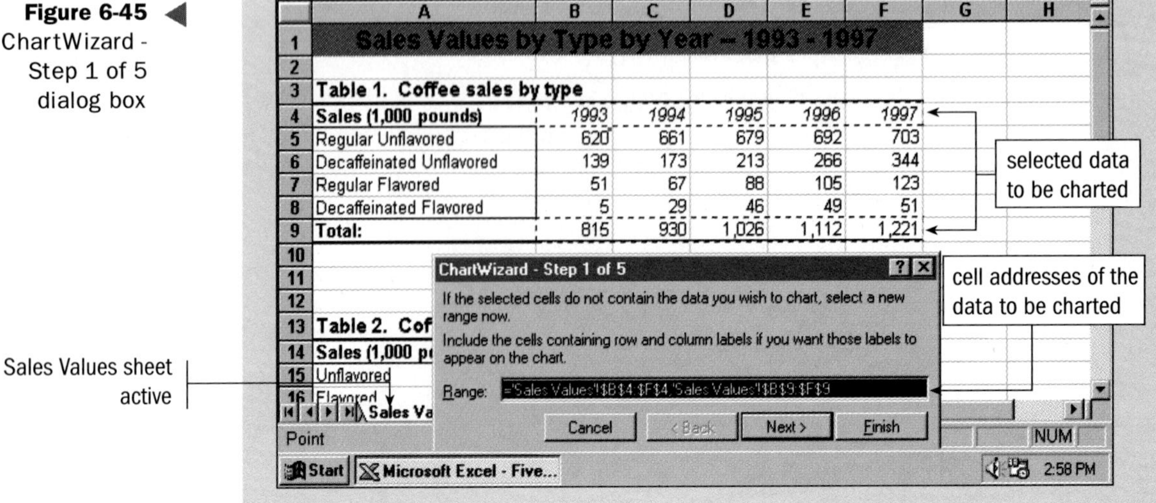

Verify that the range is ='Sales Values'!$B$4:$F$4, 'Sales Values'!$B$9:$F$9. These cell references are the absolute references for the two ranges you selected in the previous set of steps. Note that the cell references also include the name of the sheet where the cells are located.

TROUBLE? If the range displayed on your screen is not correct, type the necessary corrections in the Range box or reselect the correct cells. If the dialog box blocks your view of the cells, position the pointer on the dialog box title bar, then drag the dialog box to move it out of the way.

4. Click the **Next** button to display the ChartWizard - Step 2 of 5 dialog box.
5. If necessary, click the **Column** chart type in the center of the first row to select it, then click the **Next** button to display the ChartWizard - Step 3 of 5 dialog box. See Figure 6-46.

Figure 6-46
ChartWizard - Step 3 of 5 dialog box

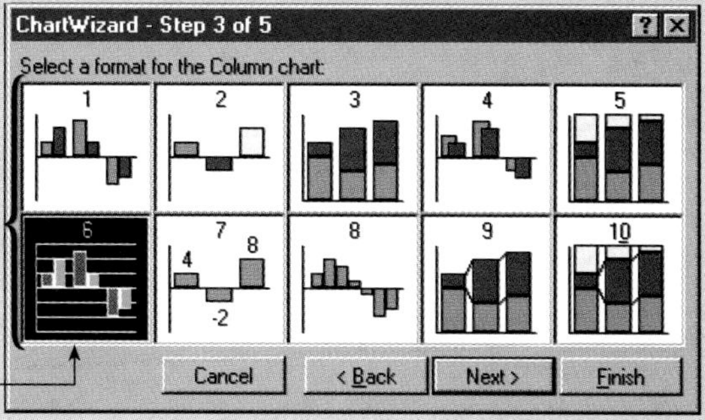

ten column chart subtype samples

highlight indicates currently selected format

This dialog box displays samples of the ten Excel column chart subtypes. You'll use format 1.

6. Click the first sample to select it, then click the **Next** button to display the ChartWizard - Step 4 of 5 dialog box. See Figure 6-47.

Figure 6-47
ChartWizard - Step 4 of 5 dialog box

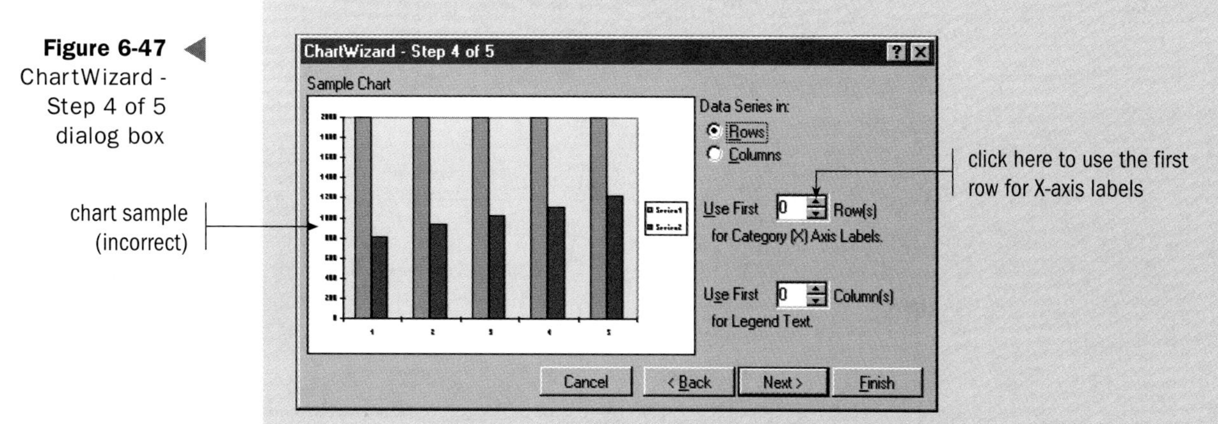

chart sample (incorrect)

click here to use the first row for X-axis labels

This dialog box displays a sample of the completed chart, which does not look at all like the sketch you had prepared. The problem is that both of the cell ranges you specified for this chart are being plotted as data points. Instead you want the first row of selected data cells, B4 through B9, to be used for the X-axis labels (years). So you need to specify this change.

7. Click the up arrow on the list box for **Use First 0 Row(s) for Category (X) Axis Labels**. The 0 changes to 1, the first row is now used for the X-axis labels, and the chart sample now looks like your sketch.
8. Click the **Next** button to move to the ChartWizard - Step 5 of 5 dialog box. You use this dialog box to remove the legend and to enter the text for the chart title and the two axis labels.

9. Click the **No** radio button to remove the legend, click the **Chart Title** text box, type **Total Coffee Sales**, click the Axis Title **Category (X)** text box, type **Year**, click the Axis Title **Value (Y)** text box, then type **Sales (thousands of pounds)**. See Figure 6-48.

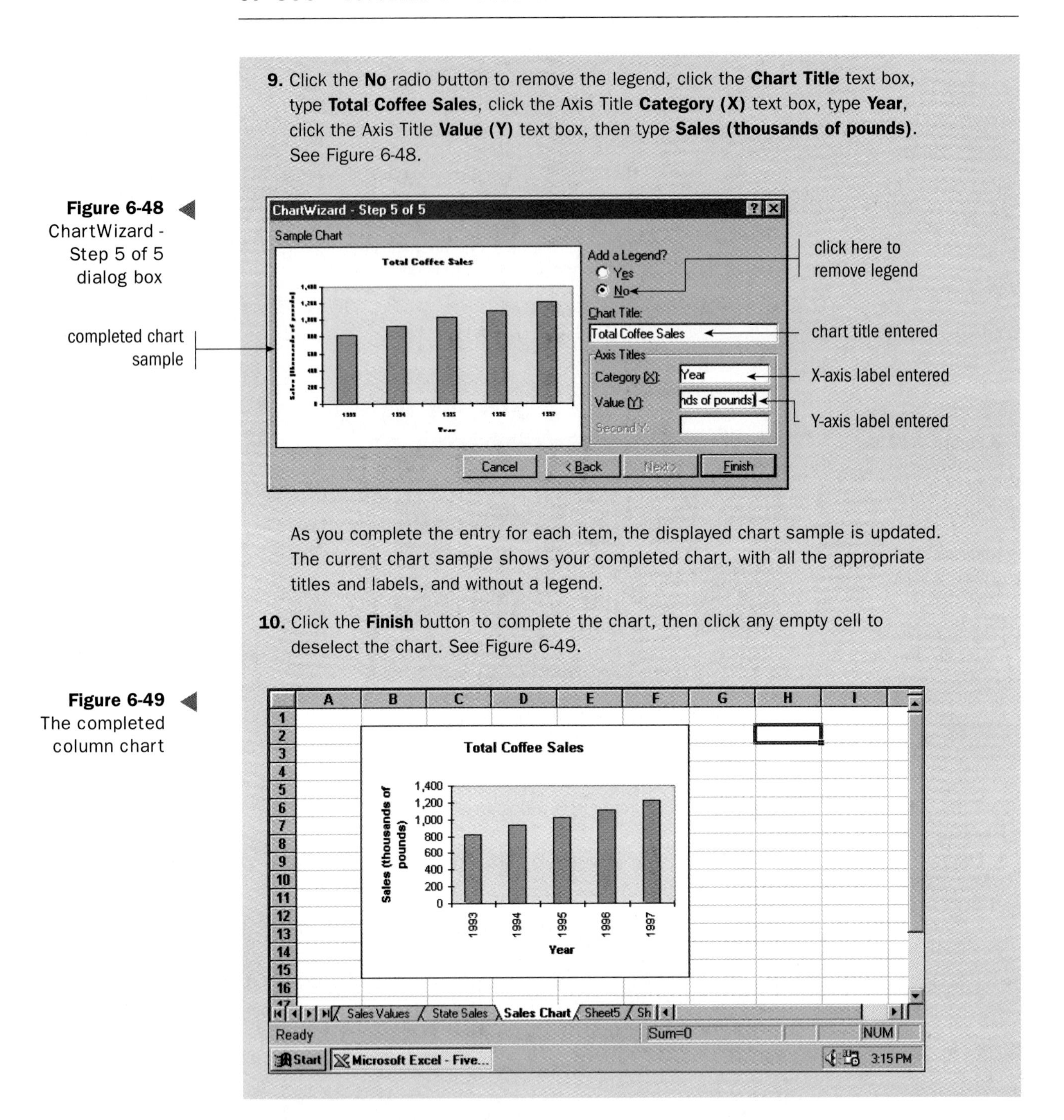

Figure 6-48 ChartWizard - Step 5 of 5 dialog box

As you complete the entry for each item, the displayed chart sample is updated. The current chart sample shows your completed chart, with all the appropriate titles and labels, and without a legend.

10. Click the **Finish** button to complete the chart, then click any empty cell to deselect the chart. See Figure 6-49.

Figure 6-49 The completed column chart

The chart is associated with the data cells used to create it. If you change a value in any cell in the chart data series, Excel automatically updates the chart to reflect the change.

Revising the Chart Data Series

After you create a chart, you might discover that you have specified the wrong data range, or you might decide that your chart should display a different data series. In either event, you do not have to start over and create a new chart from scratch. You can use the ChartWizard to change the data series for the existing chart. In this case, the ChartWizard provides two dialog boxes instead of five.

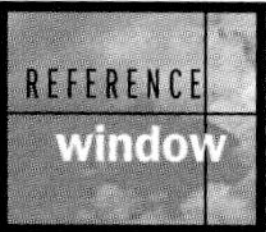

REVISING THE CHART DATA SERIES

- Click the chart to select it.
- Click the ChartWizard button to display the ChartWizard - Step 1 of 2 dialog box.
- Select the range(s) of cells you want to include in the revised chart (or edit the Range entry in the dialog box), then click the Next button.
- Make any necessary revisions in the ChartWizard - Step 2 of 2 dialog box, then click the OK button.

You show the chart to Kim, who is generally pleased with the results. She does have several suggestions for improving the chart, however, and asks you to modify it.

Modifying an Excel Chart

You can make many modifications to a chart, including changing the plot area, changing the text of the titles or labels, moving and resizing the chart, and so on. To modify a chart, you must first select the chart and then activate it.

Selecting and Activating a Chart

You click once anywhere within the borders of a chart to select the chart. When a chart is selected, Excel displays eight sizing handles at the corners and along the sides of the chart border. The Chart toolbar is also displayed when a chart is selected. You can move and resize a selected chart. After you select a chart, you must activate it in order to edit it.

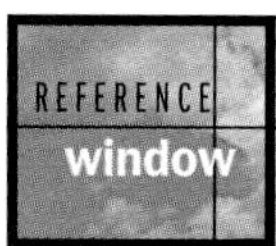

ACTIVATING A SELECTED CHART

- Right-click to display the shortcut menu, then click Edit Object.

or

- Click Edit on the menu bar, then click Object.

When a chart is activated, the chart border changes to a hashed border, and the horizontal and vertical scroll bars disappear. Activating a chart gives you access to the chart commands on the menu bar and the shortcut menu. You can click any object within an activated chart to select and modify that chart object. Chart objects include the entire chart area, the chart title, both axis titles, both axes, the plot area, the entire data series, or an individual data marker.

To select and activate the chart:

1. Click within the chart border to select the chart. The Chart toolbar and sizing handles appear.
2. Right-click to display the shortcut menu, then click **Edit Object** to activate the chart. A hashed border surrounds the chart, indicating that the entire chart area is selected within the activated chart. See Figure 6-50.

Figure 6-50 Activated chart

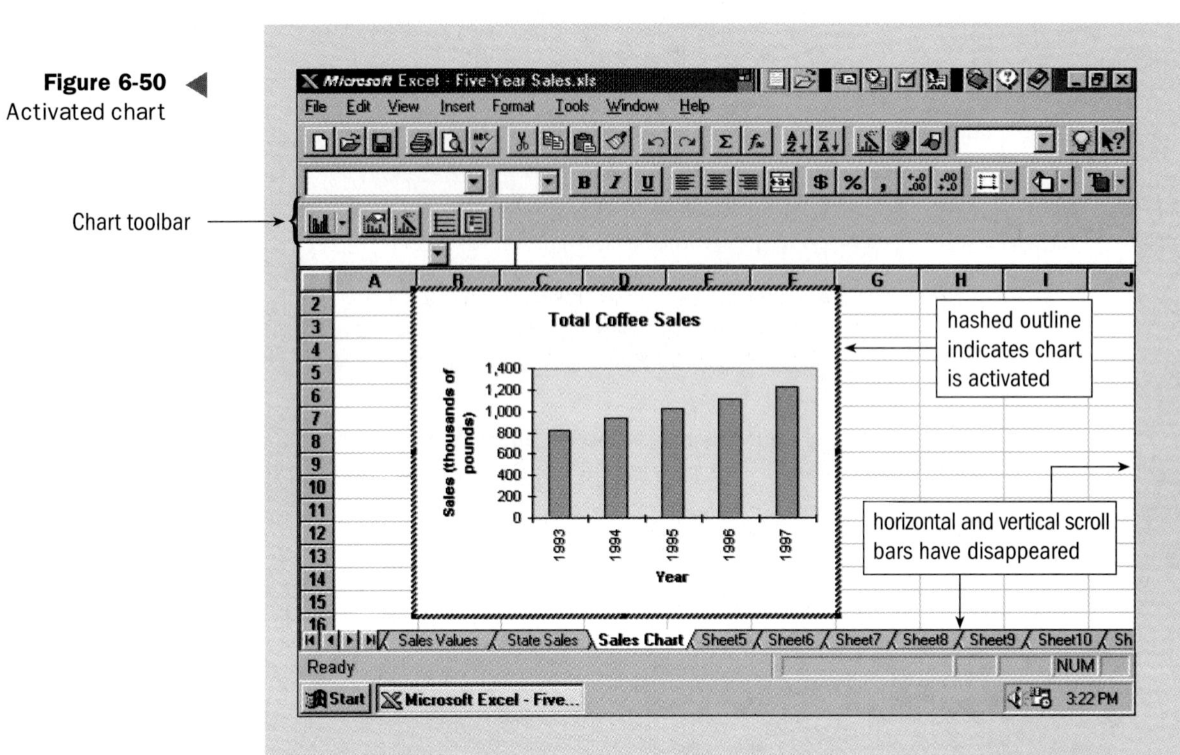

TROUBLE? Your Chart toolbar might be floating rather than docked. If your Chart toolbar is floating, it will have a title bar saying "Chart" and will appear somewhere over the worksheet area. The Chart toolbar in Figure 6-50 has been docked beneath the Formatting toolbar. It isn't necessary to dock the Chart toolbar, but if you want to do so, drag the toolbar's title bar over to the reference area of the formula bar.

TROUBLE? You might see additional large black handles inside the hashed border when you activate a chart. The presence or absence of these squares has no significance.

3. Click **Format** on the menu bar. The Format menu displays chart formatting options. Click **Format** again to close the Format menu.
4. Position the pointer over the chart, then right-click to display the shortcut menu. Chart formatting options are displayed on the shortcut menu.
5. Click anywhere within the chart area to close the shortcut menu.
6. Position the pointer over the chart title, then click the mouse button. The chart title object is now selected within the activated chart, and sizing handles appear around the border of the chart title.
7. Click anywhere outside the chart border to deactivate the chart.
8. Click again outside the chart border to deselect the chart.

Now that you know how to select and activate a chart and how to select specific objects within a chart, you can make the modifications Kim wants. Kim's first request is to remove the border around the shaded plot area and the gray shading within the plot area. She thinks the chart would be clearer without them.

Changing the Plot Area

To change the plot area of a selected chart, you use the Format Plot Area dialog box. The option for opening this dialog box is available on the shortcut menu.

To modify the chart plot area:

1. Right-click within the chart border to select the chart and display the shortcut menu, then click **Edit Object** to activate the chart.
2. Position the pointer over the gray plot area, right-click to display the shortcut menu, then click **Format Plot Area**. The Format Plot Area dialog box opens. See Figure 6-51.

Figure 6-51 Format Plot Area dialog box

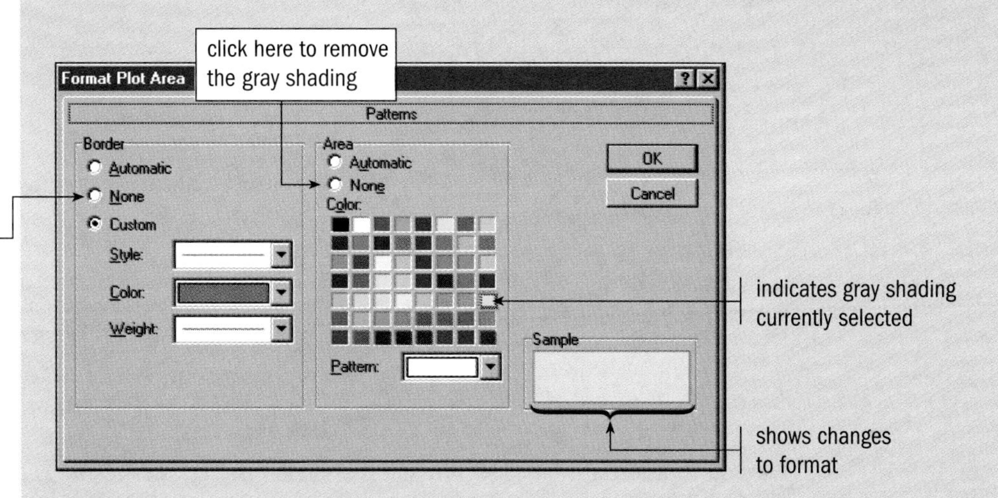

3. Click the **None** radio button in the Border section to remove the border around the plot area. The Sample box changes to reflect the change.
4. Click the **None** radio button in the Area section to remove the gray shading in the plot area.
5. Click the **OK** button to close the Format Plot Area dialog box.
6. Click anywhere within the white space inside the chart border to deselect the plot area. The gray shading and the plot area border have been removed from the chart.

Kim asks you to edit the Y-axis title so that the word "Sales" is on one line and the text "(thousands of pounds)" is on the second line.

Editing, Adding, and Removing Chart Text

You can edit the text of existing chart titles and labels, and you can add or remove titles and labels to clarify a chart or improve its appearance. You need to edit the text of the Y-axis title to improve the appearance of the chart.

To edit the Y-axis title:

1. Position the pointer over the Y-axis title, then click the mouse button to select the object. A selection box appears around the title, and the pointer changes to I.
2. With the pointer positioned inside the object selection box, click the mouse button. The selection box disappears and the text is displayed in a normal horizontal position so that you can edit it.

3. Position the pointer immediately to the left of the opening parenthesis, click to position the insertion point, then press the **Enter** key. The text display changes to show "Sales" alone on the first line and the entire parenthetical phrase on the second line.

4. Click any blank area inside the chart to deselect the title object. The Y-axis title is again displayed sideways, with the line split where you want it.

Kim thinks that the X-axis title "Year" is unnecessary because the X-axis labels "1993," "1994," and so on are obviously years. She asks you to delete the X-axis title.

To delete the X-axis title:

1. Position the pointer over the word "Year" and then click to select the object.

2. Press the **Delete** key. The X-axis title object is deleted.

You can add any text object that does not already appear on the chart. A text object might be missing because you have deleted it (as you just deleted the X-axis title) or because you did not supply the text for that object when you created the chart. In either case, you can choose the Insert Titles option on the shortcut menu, choose the type of title you want to add (chart, X-axis, or Y-axis), then type the title text.

You also might want to include data labels on your chart to identify the value of each data point. Only one chart subtype for a column chart includes the display of data labels. Format 7 in the ChartWizard - Step 3 of 5 dialog box (Figure 6-46) includes labels for the actual data values; however, you selected the format 1 column chart subtype. Kim asks you to add data labels to the chart, which you can do at any time using the Insert Data Labels option.

To add data labels to your chart:

1. With the pointer positioned within the chart, right-click to display the shortcut menu, then click **Insert Data Labels** to display the Data Labels dialog box.

2. Click the **Show Value** radio button to activate that option.

3. Click the **OK** button to close the dialog box.

4. Click any blank cell outside the chart to deactivate the chart. See Figure 6-52.

Figure 6-52 The updated chart

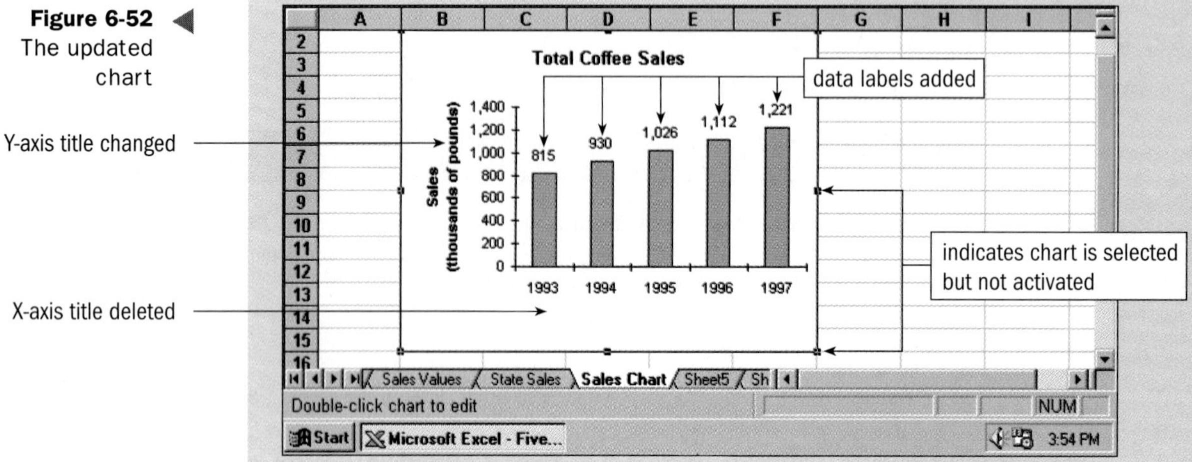

Y-axis title changed

X-axis title deleted

data labels added

indicates chart is selected but not activated

Next, Kim asks you to move the chart almost to the very top of the sheet, so it will be visible whenever she opens this worksheet. She also wants the chart lengthened one-half cell and widened so that the Y-axis title doesn't crowd the Y-axis labels.

Moving and Resizing a Chart

To move or resize a chart, the chart must be selected but not activated. You move a chart by clicking anywhere inside the chart border and dragging the chart to a new location; a dashed outline marks the changing position of the chart as you drag it. You resize a chart by dragging one of the sizing handles.

To move and resize the chart:

1. Position the pointer over a blank area within the chart, click and hold the mouse button as you drag the chart up as high as it will go, drag the chart down just until you can see the dashed outline at the top, then drag the chart, if necessary, so that its left edge is on the border between columns A and B.
2. Release the mouse button. The chart is moved to the new position.
3. Position the pointer over the sizing handle in the lower-right corner of the chart. The pointer changes to ↘.
4. Hold down the mouse button and drag the mouse to the right until the right edge of the dashed outline is positioned on the border between rows G and H, then drag down until the bottom of the dashed outline falls in the middle of row 15.
5. Release the mouse button. The chart is resized, as shown in Figure 6-53.

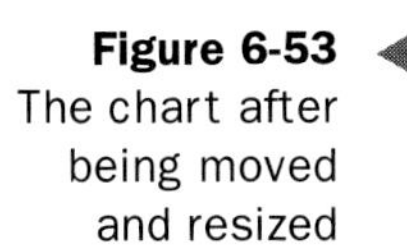

Figure 6-53 The chart after being moved and resized

TROUBLE? If your chart is not the same size or in the same position as the chart in Figure 6-53, adjust the size or position or both so it looks like Figure 6-53.

Kim still isn't completely satisfied with the chart. The Y-axis title is too close to the Y-axis labels, and there's too much white space at the bottom of the chart. She asks you to resize the plot area to make it narrower and taller.

To resize the plot area and reposition the Y-axis title:

1. Right-click within the chart area, then click **Edit Object** on the shortcut menu to activate the chart.
2. Click in an area between two bars to select the plot area. A selection box with sizing handles surrounds the plot area.

3. Position the pointer over the middle sizing handle at the bottom of the selection box, click and hold the mouse button down as you drag the bottom border down as far as it will go, then release the mouse button.
4. Position the pointer over the middle sizing handle at the left side of the selection box, click and hold the mouse button as you drag the mouse to the right until the inner dashed line is even with the left edge of the first bar, then release the mouse button. The plot area is resized. The Y-axis title has also moved to the right. You need to move the Y-axis title object back to the left.
5. Position the pointer over the Y-axis title, then click to select the object.
6. Position the pointer on the left border of the selection box until the pointer changes to ↖, click and drag to the left until the dashed outline has moved half the distance to the left chart border, then release the mouse button. The Y-axis title object is repositioned and no longer crowds the Y-axis labels.
7. Click any blank area within the chart to deselect the Y-axis title object. Your chart should now look like Figure 6-54.

Figure 6-54 The chart after resizing the plot area and moving the Y-axis title

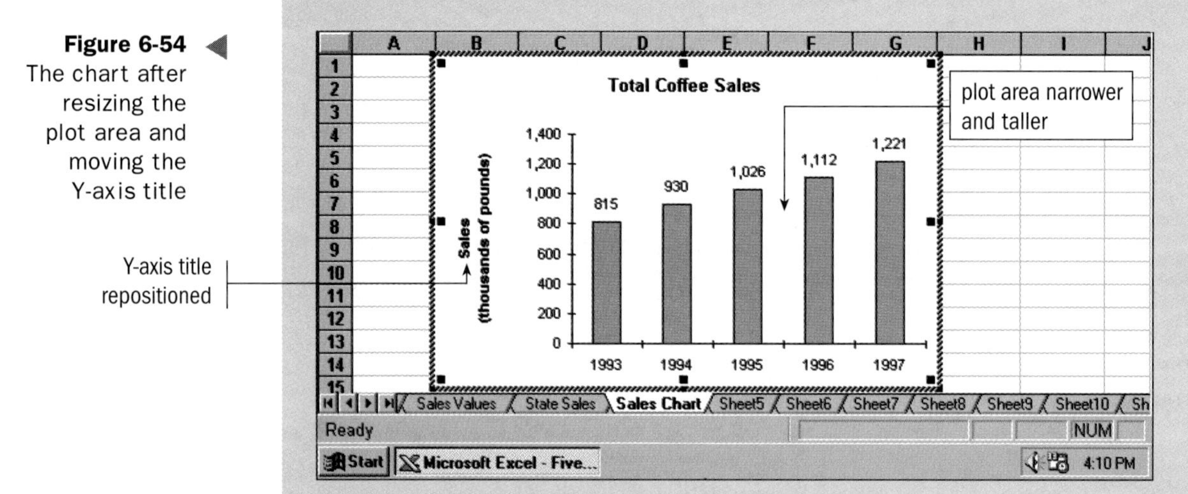

TROUBLE? If your chart doesn't look like Figure 6-54, resize the plot area or reposition the Y-axis title object, or do both, to change your chart to the approximate size and position shown in the figure.

8. Click any cell outside the chart border to deactivate the chart.
9. Click any cell outside the chart border to deselect the chart.

Kim is now satisfied with the appearance of the chart, including the size and position of the various chart elements. Because Kim will be including this chart in a memo to Valle Coffee customer representatives, however, she wants it to have as much visual appeal as possible. She remembers reading something about using pictures rather than colored bars for Excel bar charts and column charts. She asks you to try using the picture of the Valle Coffee cup in this chart instead of the colored bars.

Using Pictures in a Column Chart

When you create a column or bar chart with the ChartWizard, a simple bar is used as the data marker. You can add visual interest to a column or bar chart by using a picture as a data marker. The picture can be stretched or shrunk to indicate the magnitude of the chart value, or you can stack pictures to indicate the chart values.

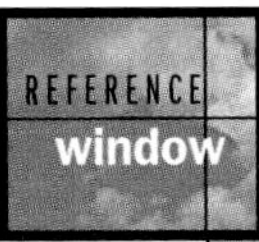

USING A PICTURE IN A COLUMN OR BAR CHART

- Insert the picture in the worksheet.
- Click the Copy button on the Standard toolbar to place the picture on the Clipboard.
- Activate the chart and select the data marker or data series you want to replace with the picture.
- Click the Paste button on the Standard toolbar.
- When you have finished editing the chart, delete the original inserted picture.

Kim wants you to use the coffee cup from the Valle Coffee logo in the chart. This picture file is located in the Tutorial.06 folder on your Student Disk.

To insert the picture in your worksheet:

1. Click cell **A1** to make it the active cell.
2. Make sure your Student Disk is in the disk drive.
3. Click **Insert** on the menu bar, then click **Picture**. The Picture dialog box opens.
4. Make sure Tutorial.06 is the folder shown in the Look in box, click **ValleCup**, then click the **OK** button to insert the picture in your worksheet in cell A1, the active cell.

   TROUBLE? Don't worry if the picture overlaps your chart. This will not cause a problem, and you will delete the picture when you have finished with it.

   Excel automatically places a border around the picture, which you want to remove.
5. Right-click the picture then click **Edit Object** to open the Format Object dialog box.
6. If necessary, click the **Patterns** tab.
7. Click the **None** radio button in the Border section, then click the **OK** button to close the dialog box.
8. With the picture still selected, click the **Copy** button on the Standard toolbar to place the picture on the Clipboard.

Now that you have placed the picture on the Clipboard, you can activate the chart and use the picture in the chart.

To include the picture in the column chart:

1. Right-click within the chart border to select the chart and display the shortcut menu, then click **Edit Object** to activate the chart.
2. Click one of the data markers (columns) to select the data series object. A small square appears inside each of the five data markers indicating that the data series object is selected.

   TROUBLE? If only the one data marker you clicked is selected and shows sizing handles on its perimeter, click anywhere in the white area to deselect that data marker, then repeat Step 2.

3. Click the **Paste** button on the Standard toolbar. The five column bars are each replaced by the coffee cup picture. Each picture is stretched to fit the shape of the column bar it replaced. See Figure 6-55.

Figure 6-55 The chart with stretched pictures

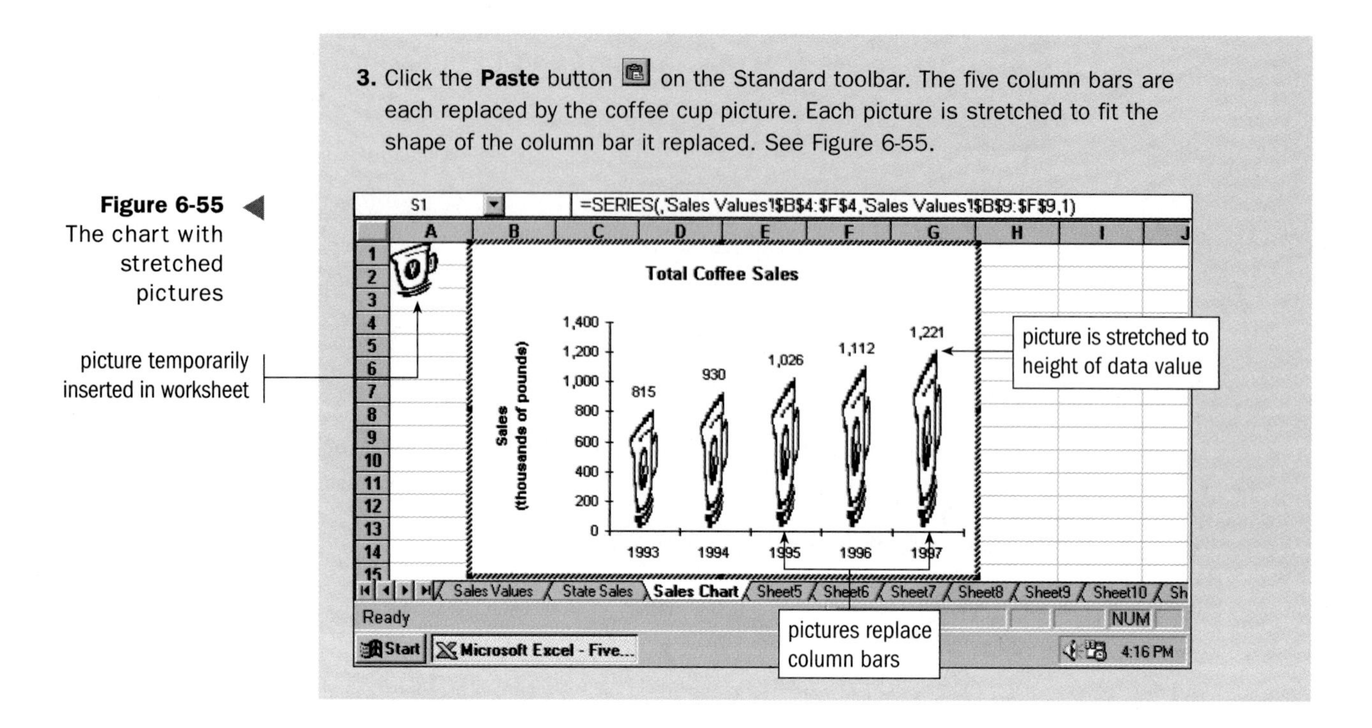

The picture you use as the data marker is automatically stretched or shrunk to represent the height of the column or width of the bar it replaced. Some pictures stretch well, but other pictures become too abstract and unrecognizable when distorted. The coffee cup picture is an example of a picture that is unrecognizable when stretched; you can't even tell it is the cup from the Valle Coffee logo.

Stacking Pictures

As an alternative to stretching a picture, you can stack it so that it appears repeatedly in columns, reaching as high as the original bars in the chart. You'll stack the coffee cup picture in your chart to improve its appearance.

The Y-axis scale has tick mark labels at 200, 400, 600, and so on. To match the Y-axis labels, you'll stack one coffee cup for each 200 units.

To stack the picture:

1. With the pointer positioned over any one of the five data markers, right-click to display the shortcut menu, then click **Format Data Series** to open the Format Data Series dialog box.

2. If necessary, click the **Patterns** tab.

3. Click the **Stack and Scale to** radio button, type **200** (if necessary), then click the **OK** button to close the Format Data Series dialog box. The chart is displayed with stacked coffee cups, with each complete cup representing 200 units (sales of 200,000 pounds). Some columns have a portion of a cup at the top of the column; a half-cup, for example, would represent 100 units (100,000 pounds).

4. Click any worksheet cell to deactivate the chart, then click the cell again to deselect the chart. Your chart should now look like Figure 6-56.

Figure 6-56 The chart with stacked pictures

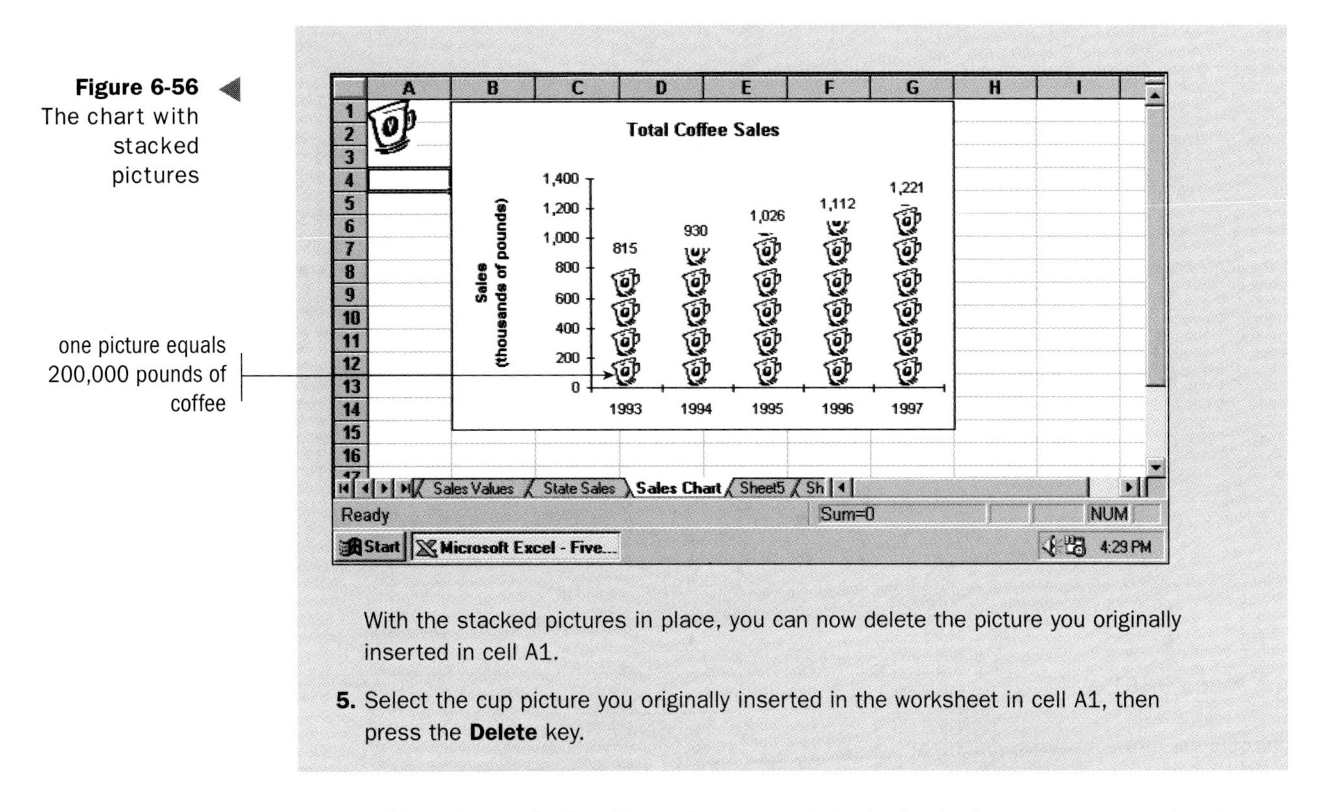

With the stacked pictures in place, you can now delete the picture you originally inserted in cell A1.

5. Select the cup picture you originally inserted in the worksheet in cell A1, then press the **Delete** key.

Kim likes the stacked Valle Coffee cups. If she had asked you to remove the pictures and return to the original columns for the data markers, you would select the data series, click Edit, click Clear, and then click Formats.

Displaying the Title in a Colored Box with a Shadow

Kim has two final suggestions: to add some color and visual interest to the chart and to highlight the chart title, she wants you to fill the title area with the same blue you used for the Documentation sheet title area and to add a border with a shadow around the title.

To display the title in a colored box with a shadow:

1. Right-click within the chart border to select the chart and display the shortcut menu, then click **Edit Object** to activate the chart.
2. Position the pointer over the chart title, right-click to select the chart title object and display the shortcut menu, then click **Format Chart Title**. The Format Chart Title dialog box opens.
3. If necessary, click the **Patterns** tab.
4. Click the **blue color** in the fifth position of the fifth row of color samples. The Sample box shows the results of each change you make.
5. Click the **Weight** list arrow to display the list of border weights, then click the third line in the list.
6. Click the **Shadow** check box to select that option. See Figure 6-57.

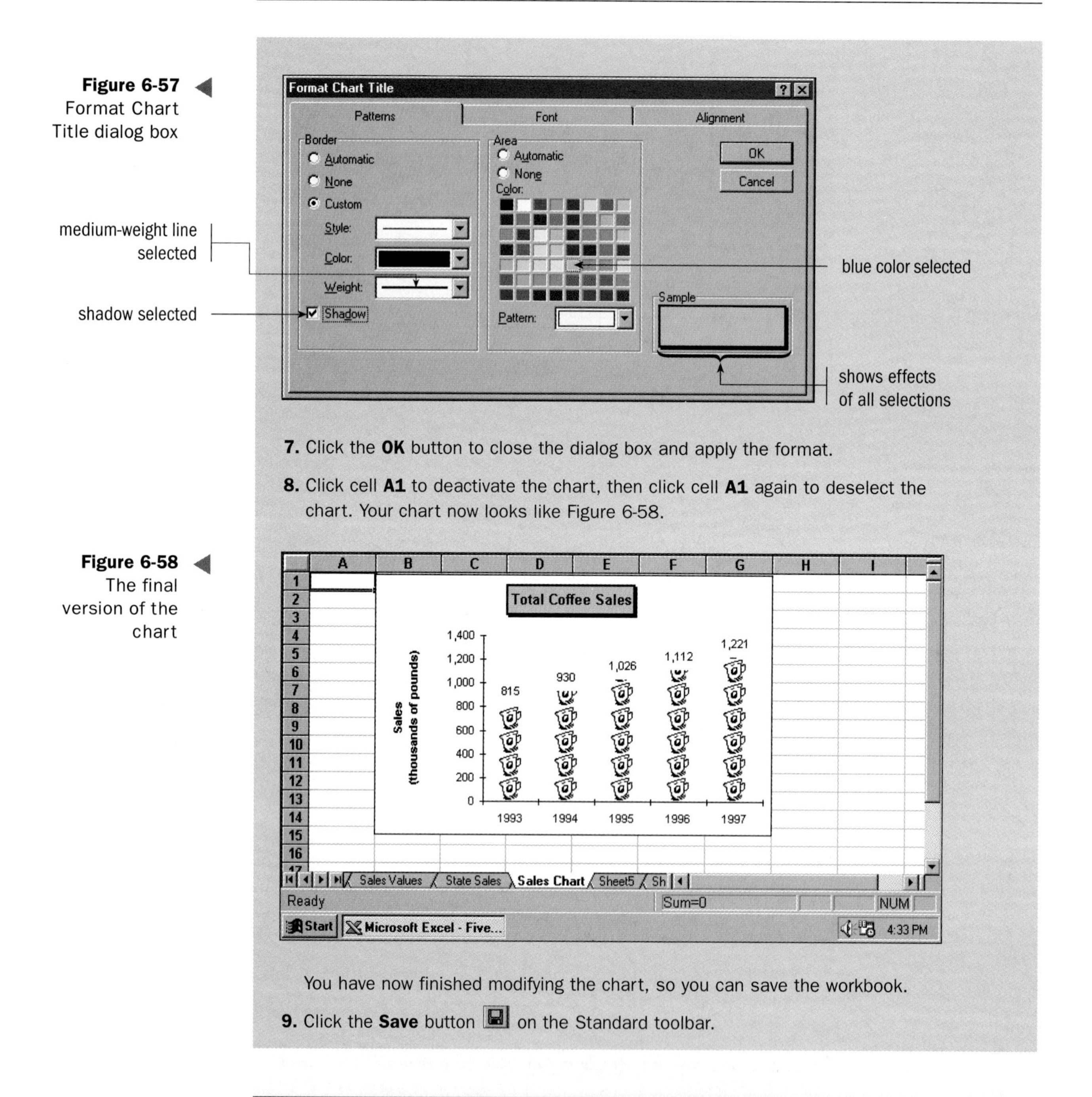

Figure 6-57 Format Chart Title dialog box

7. Click the **OK** button to close the dialog box and apply the format.
8. Click cell **A1** to deactivate the chart, then click cell **A1** again to deselect the chart. Your chart now looks like Figure 6-58.

Figure 6-58 The final version of the chart

You have now finished modifying the chart, so you can save the workbook.

9. Click the **Save** button on the Standard toolbar.

Previewing and Printing a Worksheet and Chart

You have completed the sales chart, so you can print the finished Sales Chart worksheet. Before you print, you should preview the worksheet to check how it will appear on the printed page.

To preview and print the worksheet:

1. Click the **Print Preview** button on the Standard toolbar to open the Print Preview window. Kim had previously changed several of the default page setup options for this worksheet, so the page setup is the way she wants it—with a portrait orientation and the chart positioned in the center of the page. Kim customized the header and footer the same way you customized the header and footer for the Sales Values worksheet.

2. Click the **Print** button on the Print Preview toolbar to print the worksheet. The Print dialog box opens.

3. Click the **OK** button. The worksheet is printed and the Print Preview window is automatically closed.

Quick Check

1 Label the parts of the window shown in Figure 6-59.

Figure 6-59

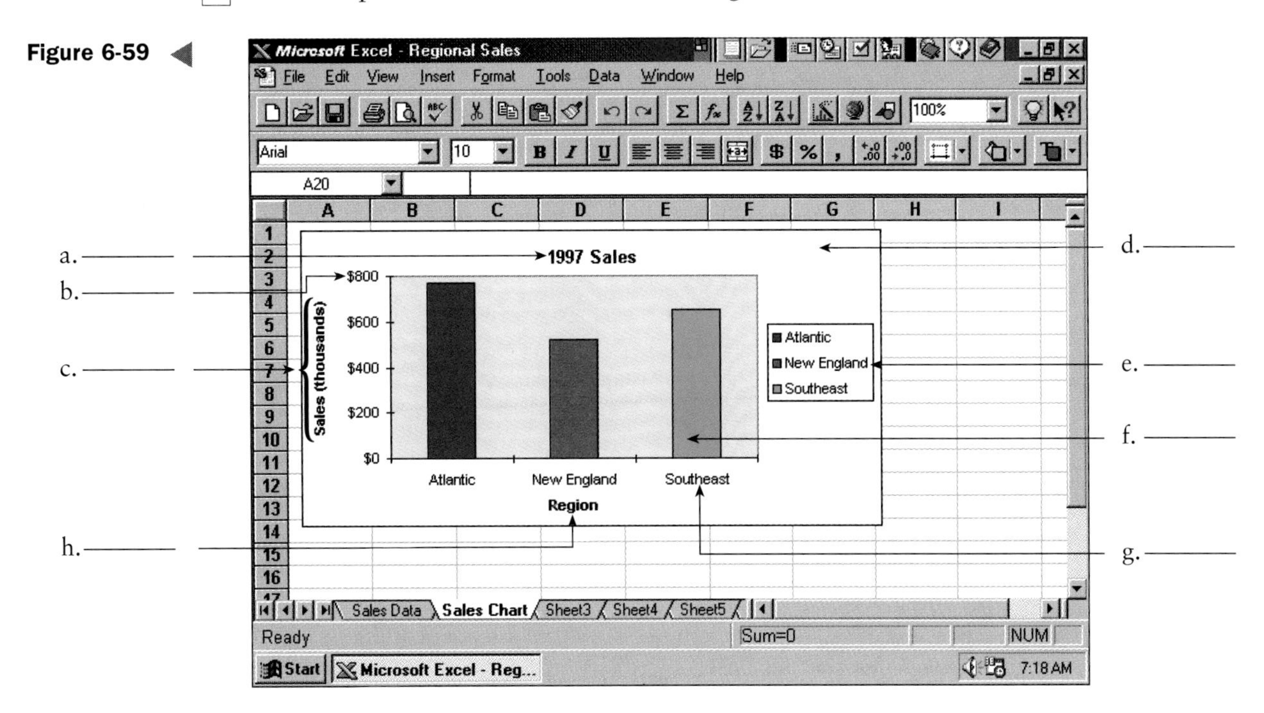

2 What are the four steps you should follow to plan a chart?

3 How many different Excel chart types are there? How many chart types are three-dimensional?

4 How do you select non-adjacent cells?

5 What is the difference between selecting a chart and activating a chart? How do you do each?

6 In what two ways can a picture in a column chart indicate the magnitude of a data point value?

Now that you've completed Session 6.3, you can exit Excel or you can continue to the next session.

SESSION 6.4

In this session you will complete the Five-Year Sales workbook. You will create and modify a pie chart, link an Excel chart to a Word document, and update the linked chart.

Analyzing Data with Charts

A chart is a visual representation of data. An *effective* chart is one that makes it easier to recognize and analyze relationships. A chart cannot be effective, no matter how attractive it is, if it doesn't portray the data appropriately. Creating the right type of chart is critical to its analytical value.

Kim's original workbook plan includes a second chart, which she asks you to plan and create now. Before you begin, you'll check Kim's Documentation sheet entry for the second chart.

To check the Documentation sheet entry:

1. Click the **Documentation** tab to display that sheet.
2. Scroll the worksheet until rows 15 through 20 are visible. The entries in row 20 tell you that the second chart Kim wants you to create is a chart of 1997 sales by coffee type. This chart will be located on the fifth workbook sheet, which you will name 1997 Sales.

The documentation does not specify the type of chart. You will determine the appropriate chart type as part of your chart planning process.

First, you need to rename the fifth worksheet. Recall that to rename a worksheet, you right-click its sheet tab to display the shortcut menu, then choose the Rename command. The Sheet5 tab, however, might not be visible, depending on the size of the monitor you're using. Only the first three sheet tabs and part of the fourth sheet tab might be visible on your screen. To display a tab for a sheet that's not currently visible, you must use one of the tab scrolling buttons located to the left of the sheet tabs. Figure 6-60 describes the four tab scrolling buttons and their effects.

Figure 6-60 Sheet tab scrolling buttons

Button	Button Name	Action
◀◀	First Tab	Shifts the sheet tab display so the tab for the first sheet is visible.
◀	Previous Tab	Shifts the sheet tab display one sheet tab to the left.
▶	Next Tab	Shifts the sheet tab display one sheet tab to the right.
▶▶	Last Tab	Shifts the sheet tab display so the tab for the last sheet is visible.

Note that clicking any of the four tab scrolling buttons does *not* close the worksheet that is currently open; it changes only the sheet tab display.

To rename Sheet5:

1. If the Sheet5 tab is not visible on your screen, click the **Next Tab** button ▶ to shift the sheet tab display one tab to the right.

2. Right-click the **Sheet5** tab to display the shortcut menu, click **Rename**, type **1997 Sales**, then click the **OK** button.

3. Click the **Sales Values** tab to display that worksheet.

The first step in planning a chart is to identify the data points to be charted and locate them in your worksheet. Kim wants a chart of 1997 sales by coffee type. The data points to be charted are the four values in cells F5 through F8 in the Sales Values worksheet.

In the second planning step, you evaluate the purpose of the chart and determine the appropriate chart type. The new chart's purpose is to depict the proportion of total coffee sales attributable to each of the four coffee types. The 2-D pie charts, 3-D pie charts, and doughnut charts all show the proportions of parts to the whole. You'll create a 2-D pie chart.

For the third planning step, you need to sketch the chart, including all data points, all necessary titles and labels, and a legend. The sketch of the pie chart is shown in Figure 6-61.

Figure 6-61
Sketch of the 1997 sales pie chart

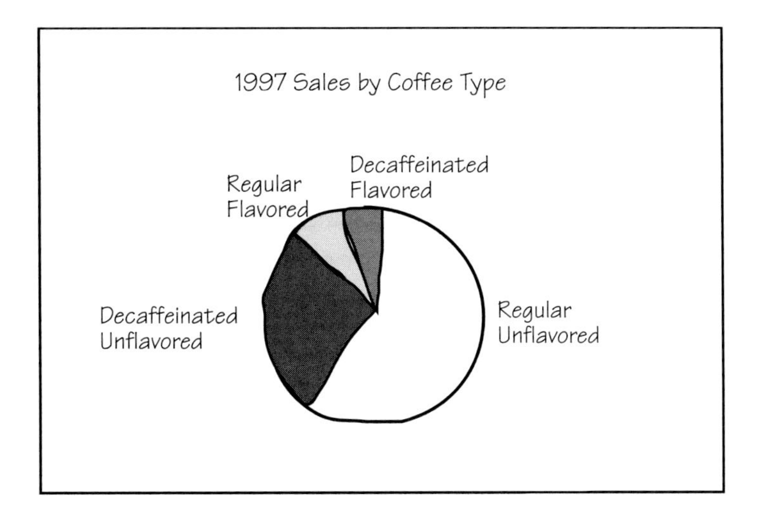

In the final planning step, you identify any titles, labels or legend text that will come from the worksheet and locate them in your worksheet. The four data labels you need are located in cells A5 through A8 of the Sales Values worksheet.

Creating a Pie Chart

To create the pie chart, you use the ChartWizard. You'll begin the process by selecting the cells to be charted.

To select the pie chart cell ranges:

1. Select cells **A5** through **A8**, then release the mouse button.

2. Press and hold the **Ctrl** key while you select cells **F5** through **F8**, then release the Ctrl key and the mouse button. Two cell ranges are highlighted: A5:A8 and F5:F8.

   TROUBLE? If the correct ranges are not highlighted, click any cell to remove the highlighting, then repeat Steps 1 and 2.

Now you can initiate the ChartWizard and create the chart.

To create the pie chart:

1. Click the **ChartWizard** button on the Standard toolbar. Rotating dashed lines surround the selected cell ranges, the pointer changes to , and the prompt "Drag in document to create a chart" appears in the status bar.
2. Click the **1997 Sales** tab to display the sheet where you want the chart to appear.
3. Move the pointer to the center of cell A1, click and hold down the mouse button as you drag the pointer to the center of cell G16, then release the mouse button. The ChartWizard - Step 1 of 5 dialog box appears over the Sales Values sheet so you can correct the range address if necessary.

   Verify that the range is ='Sales Values'!$A$5:$A$8,'Sales Values'!$F$5:$F$8.

   TROUBLE? If the range displayed on your screen is not correct, type the necessary corrections in the Range box or select the correct cells. If the dialog box blocks your view of the cells, position the pointer on the dialog box title bar, then drag the dialog box to move it out of the way.
4. Click the **Next** button to display the ChartWizard - Step 2 of 5 dialog box.
5. Click the **Pie** chart type at the end of the first row to select it, then click the **Next** button to display the ChartWizard - Step 3 of 5 dialog box. See Figure 6-62.

Figure 6-62 ChartWizard - Step 3 of 5 dialog box

seven pie chart subtypes

ChartWizard - Step 3 of 5
Select a format for the Pie chart:
1 2 3 4 5 6 7
Cancel < Back Next > Finish

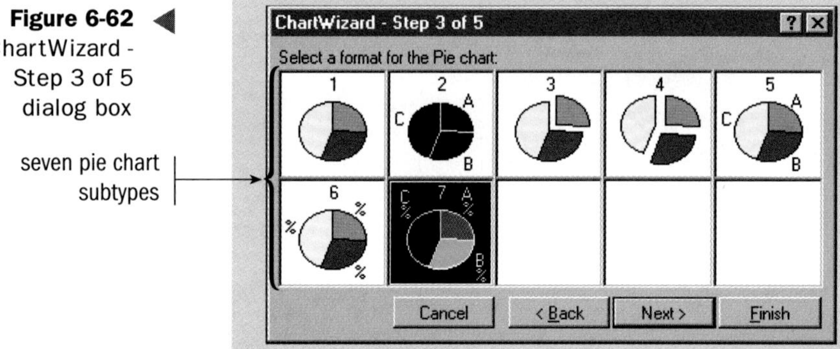

   This dialog box displays samples of the seven Excel pie chart subtypes. Your pie chart sketch resembles format 5. Format 7 is similar to format 5, but it also displays percentages that would be helpful for anyone viewing the chart. You'll use format 7.
6. If necessary, click the seventh sample to select it, then click the **Next** button to display the ChartWizard - Step 4 of 5 dialog box. The sample of the completed chart looks correct, so you do not need to change any of the options.
7. Click the **Next** button to display the ChartWizard - Step 5 of 5 dialog box. You use this dialog box to remove the legend and to enter the text for the chart title.

8. If necessary, click the **No** radio button to remove the legend, then click the **Chart Title** text box, type **1997 Sales by Coffee Type**, then click the **Finish** button. Your finished pie chart is displayed on the 1997 Sales worksheet.

9. Click any empty cell to deselect the chart. Your screen should now look like Figure 6-63.

Figure 6-63 Completed pie chart

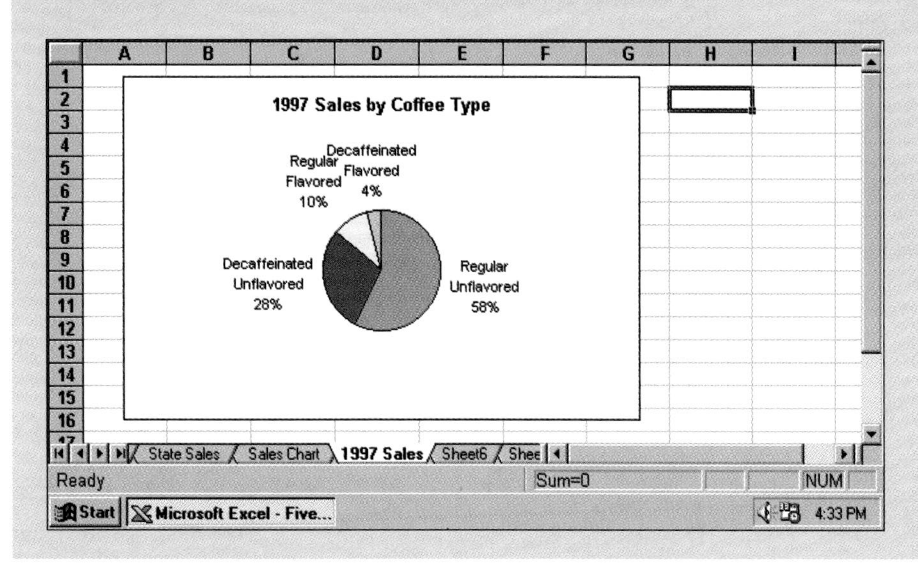

The chart needs some modifications. The color choices for the data points are not the best. Also, there should be more contrast between adjacent pie sections. The data labels overlap, so at least one of them should be moved. In addition, Kim suggests that you change the chart to a 3-D pie chart, which she thinks would be more visually interesting. You'll make this change first.

Changing the Chart to a 3-D Pie Chart

To change a chart from one type to another, you use the Chart Type button on the Chart toolbar, then select one of the 14 samples that correspond to the 14 basic Excel chart types.

To change the chart to a 3-D pie chart:

1. Select the chart by clicking anywhere inside the chart area. The Chart toolbar opens.

2. Click the **down arrow** next to the **Chart Type** button on the Chart toolbar to display the chart type list. See Figure 6-64.

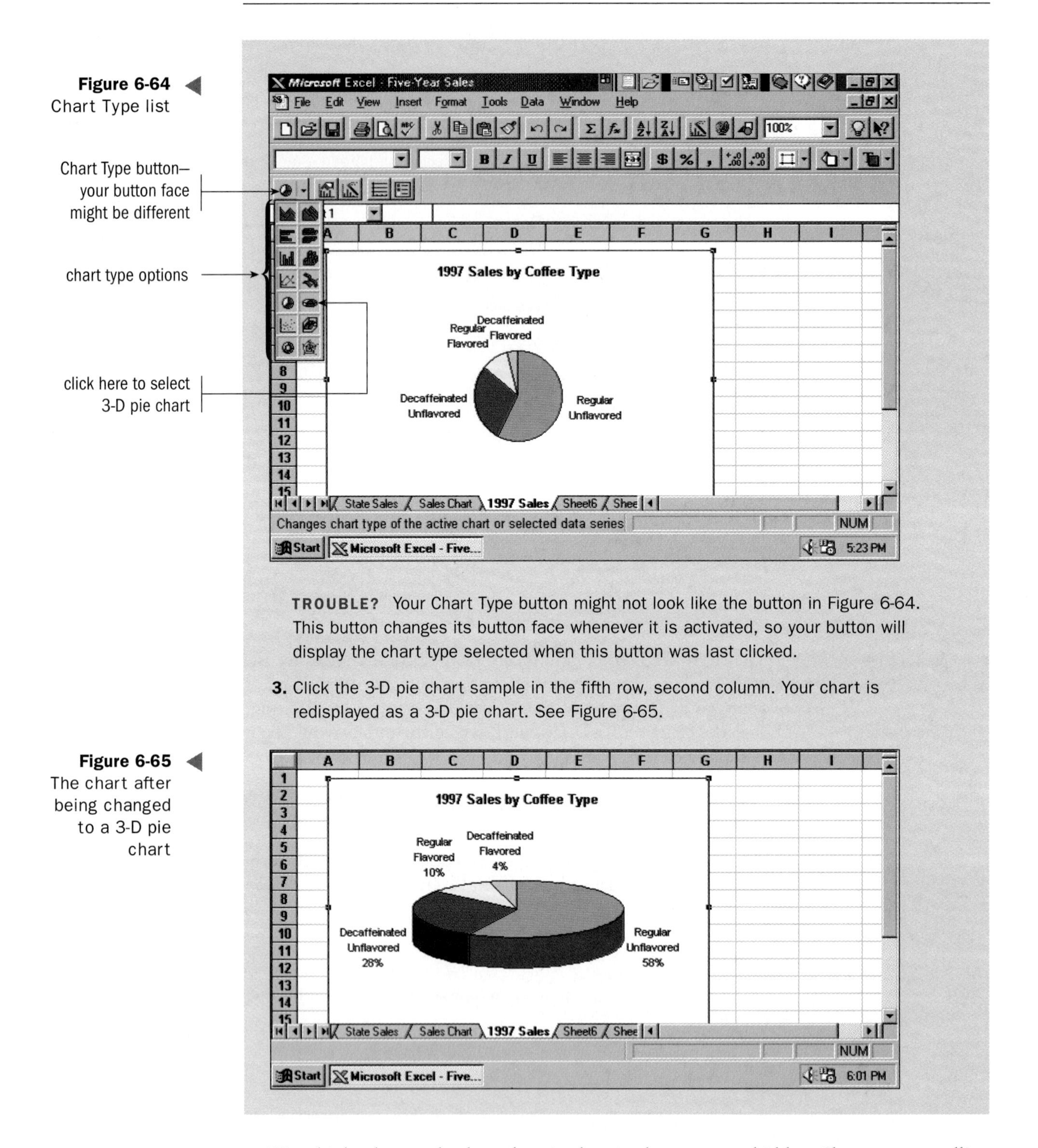

Figure 6-64 Chart Type list

Chart Type button—your button face might be different

chart type options

click here to select 3-D pie chart

TROUBLE? Your Chart Type button might not look like the button in Figure 6-64. This button changes its button face whenever it is activated, so your button will display the chart type selected when this button was last clicked.

3. Click the 3-D pie chart sample in the fifth row, second column. Your chart is redisplayed as a 3-D pie chart. See Figure 6-65.

Figure 6-65 The chart after being changed to a 3-D pie chart

Kim thinks the two back wedges in the pie chart are too hidden. She suggests pulling the Regular Unflavored wedge forward to expose more of the back wedges.

Pulling Out a Wedge on a 3-D Pie Chart

A 3-D pie chart wedge is simply a data marker that you can edit and manipulate like any other data marker. When you select a single wedge, sizing handles appear to indicate that the wedge is selected. You can then drag the wedge out of the circle.

To pull out the wedge that represents Regular Unflavored sales:

1. Right-click within the selected chart to display the shortcut menu, then click **Edit Object** to activate the chart. The chart appears in a chart window. See Figure 6-66.

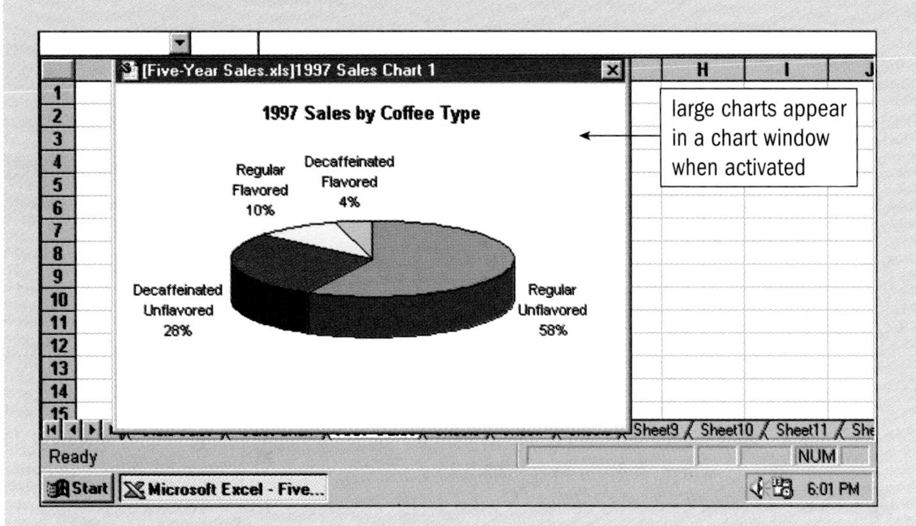

Figure 6-66 Activated chart

When you activated the column chart in the previous session, a hashed border surrounded the chart. If your chart is too large to fit in the worksheet window, Excel displays the activated chart in a chart window.

TROUBLE? Depending on the size of the monitor you are using, your chart might fit in the worksheet window. If so, your chart will not appear in a chart window, as shown in Figure 6-66 and later figures.

2. Click the blue wedge corresponding to Regular Unflavored sales. Four sizing handles appear around the upper perimeter of the pie, indicating that the entire data series is selected.

3. Click the blue wedge a second time. Six sizing handles appear around the upper perimeter of the blue wedge, indicating that only that data point is selected.

4. Position the pointer on the blue wedge, then click and hold down the mouse button as you drag the wedge away from the center of the pie. A wedge-shaped outline marks your progress. Note that the wedge will only slide directly in or out; you cannot move the wedge up or down.

5. When the outline indicates the wedge is positioned as shown in Figure 6-67, release the mouse button.

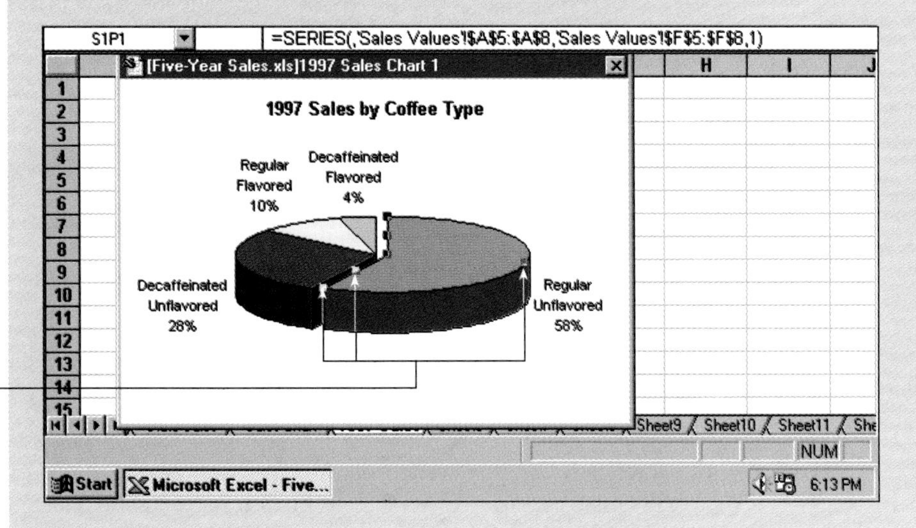

Figure 6-67 Pulling out a wedge

TROUBLE? If your wedge is pulled out too little or too much, repeat Steps 4 and 5 to reposition the wedge.

Pulling out the blue wedge did make the back two wedges slightly more noticeable. But the blue wedge still dominates the chart. Kim asks you to try rotating the blue wedge to the back. She also asks you to decrease the elevation.

Changing the Elevation and Rotation of a 3-D Chart

You can change the elevation or the rotation for any 3-D chart. **Elevation** refers to the apparent angle from which you view the chart. When the elevation is 0, you can see only the sides of the pie, as if you were looking straight ahead at the edges of the pie chart. If the elevation is 90, you can see only the top of the pie, as if you were looking straight down at the pie chart.

You can change the **rotation** angle to turn the pie in a clockwise or counterclockwise direction. The rotation angle of the 3-D pie chart is currently 0 degrees. If you change the rotation angle to 180 (half a circle), for example, the point on the pie chart that was originally in the center back of the chart would be rotated to the center front of the chart; in other words, a point at 12 o'clock would be rotated to the 6 o'clock position.

To change the elevation and rotation of the 3-D pie chart:

1. Right-click in the blank area of the activated chart to display the shortcut menu, then click **3-D View**. The Format 3-D view dialog box opens. See Figure 6-68.

Figure 6-68 Format 3-D View dialog box

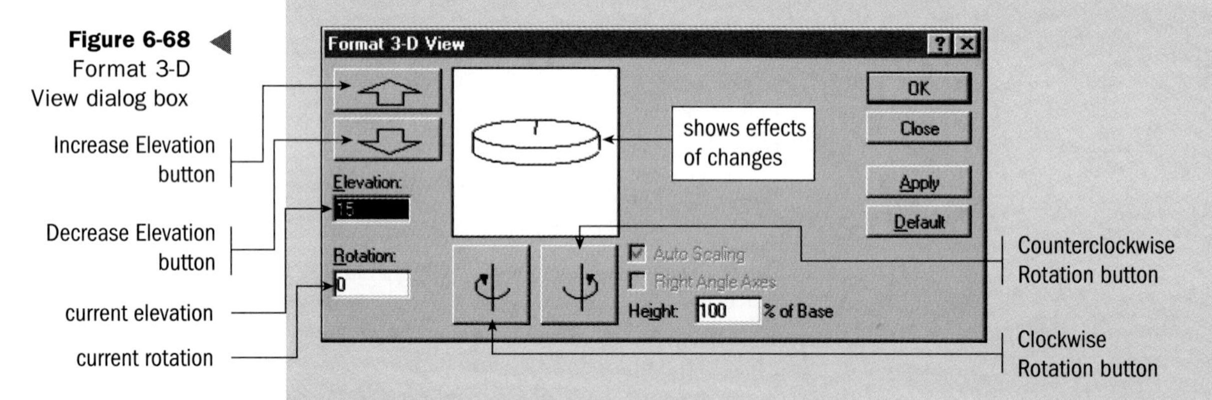

The current elevation is 15 degrees, and the rotation is 0 degrees. You can use the arrow buttons to increase or decrease the elevation angle by five-degree increments, or you can type a specific elevation angle in the Elevation text box. Similarly, you can use the rotation buttons to rotate the chart clockwise or counterclockwise in ten-degree increments, or you can type a specific rotation angle in the Rotation text box.

2. Click the **Decrease Elevation** button once to decrease the elevation angle to 10 degrees. The outline of the chart in the 3-D view dialog box changes to show the effect of the changed elevation.

   Now you'll change the rotation angle to 200 degrees.

3. Click the **Counterclockwise Rotation** button until the Rotation box shows 200. As you click the button, notice how the outline of the chart in the Format 3-D View dialog box rotates to show the effects of your changes.

4. Click the **OK** button to apply the changes. The small wedges are now in front, where they won't be overlooked. However, two of the data labels overlap. You'll fix the labels after you've made all other changes to the chart.

Kim thinks that rotating the chart and changing the elevation has improved its appearance. Next, she asks you to recolor the wedges to add more contrast.

Changing the Colors on a Chart

You can change any color used in a chart to any of the other colors in the 56-color Excel palette. To change the color of a wedge, you select the data marker and then format the data point. You'll change the four wedge colors to yellow, red, blue-green, and purple.

To change the colors of the pie wedges:

1. Click the large blue wedge to select the data series, then click the wedge a second time to select only that data point.
2. Right-click the wedge to display the shortcut menu, click **Format Data Point** to open the Format Data Point dialog box, then, if necessary, click the **Patterns** tab. See Figure 6-69.

Figure 6-69 Format Data Point dialog box

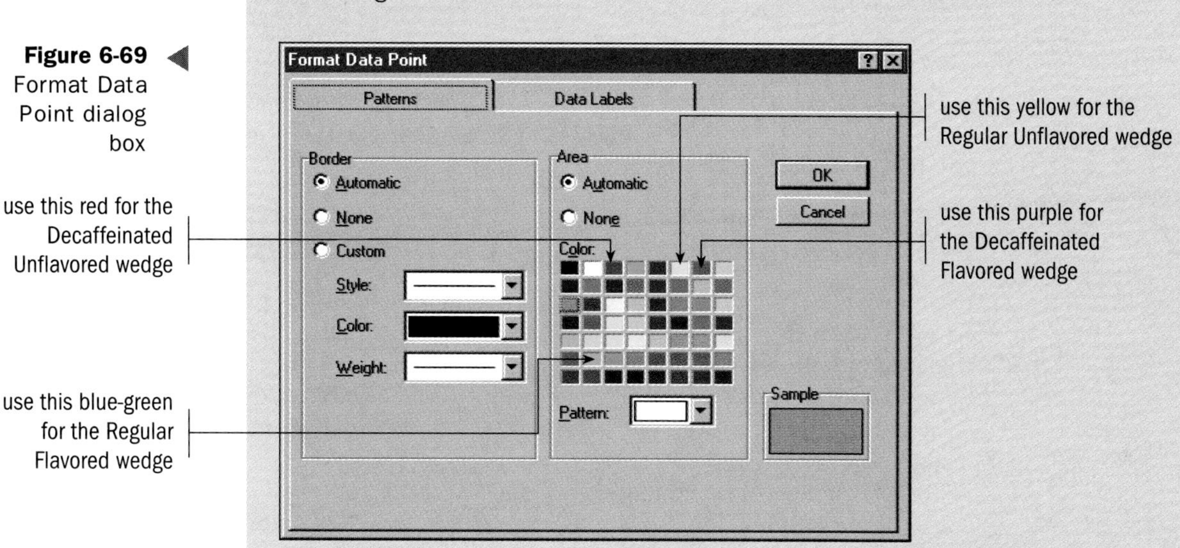

3. Click the yellow color sample in the top row of the displayed palette, then click the **OK** button to apply the color.
4. Click the dark purple wedge corresponding to Decaffeinated Unflavored to select that data point, right-click the wedge to display the shortcut menu, click **Format Data Point** to open the Format Data Point dialog box, click the red color sample in the top row, then click the **OK** button to apply the color.
5. Repeat Step 4 to apply the blue-green color indicated in Figure 6-69 to the beige wedge corresponding to Regular Flavored.
6. Repeat Step 4 to apply the purple color indicated in Figure 6-69 to the light blue wedge corresponding to Decaffeinated Flavored.
7. Click any blank area in the chart to deselect the last wedge. Your chart now looks like Figure 6-70.

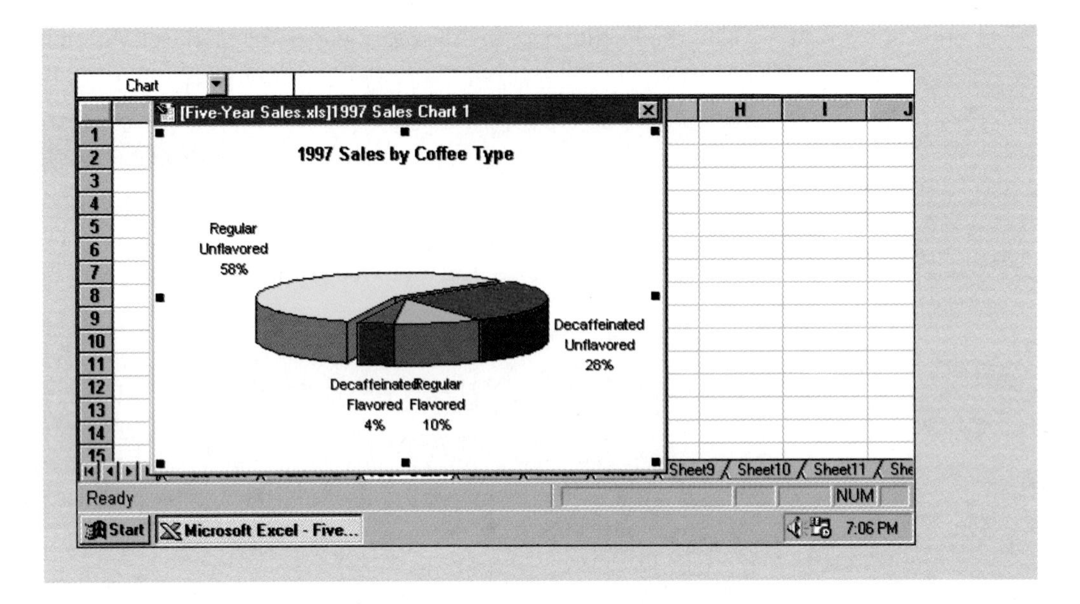

Figure 6-70 The chart after changing elevation, rotation, and colors

While you were changing chart colors, Kim noticed the Pattern list box on the Format Data Point dialog box. She asks you to apply a pattern to one wedge so she can see the effect.

Changing Chart Patterns

Excel provides 17 patterns you can apply to data markers. A pattern adds visual interest to a chart. More importantly, patterns help distinguish the different data markers when a colored chart is not printed in color. If you are printing in black and white, Excel translates each color to a shade of gray. The differences in gray shades can often be subtle. Applying a different pattern to each data marker makes a gray chart more readable.

To apply a pattern to a data marker, you select the data marker and then use the same Format Data Point dialog box you used to change the data marker color.

To apply a pattern to a wedge in the pie chart:

1. Click the large yellow wedge to select the data series, then click the wedge a second time to select only that data point.
2. Right-click the wedge to display the shortcut menu, then click **Format Data Point** to open the Format Data Point dialog box.
3. Click the **Pattern** list arrow to display the combination pattern/color palette. See Figure 6-71.

Figure 6-71 The pattern/color palette

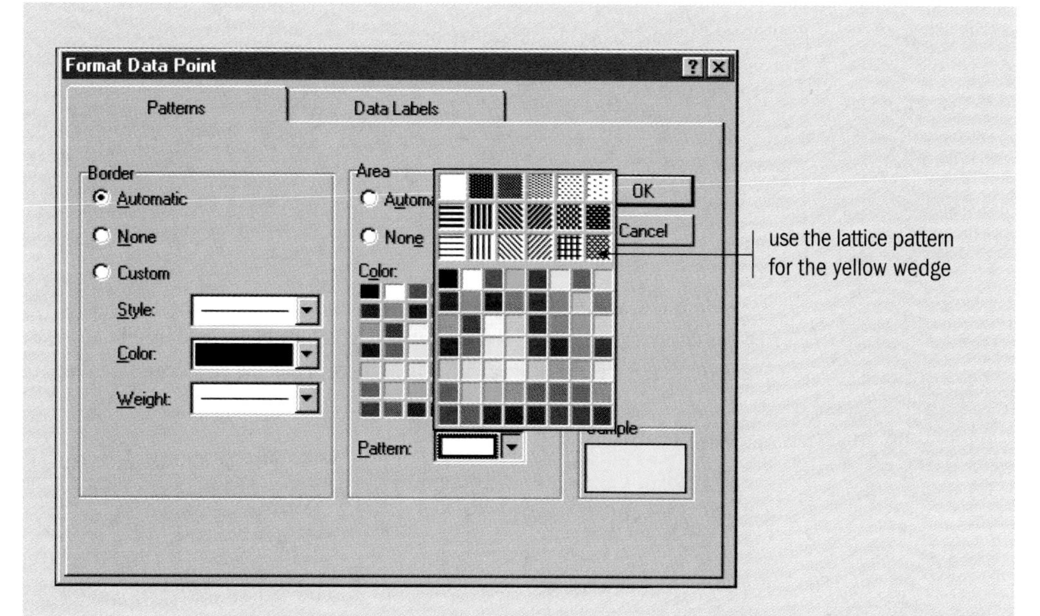

4. Click the lattice pattern in the last column of the third row of the pattern samples, then click the **OK** button to apply the pattern.

   Kim decides she prefers the wedge without the pattern, especially because she usually prints on a color printer, so patterned data markers aren't necessary.

5. Click the **Undo** button on the Standard toolbar to remove the lattice pattern from the yellow wedge.

   TROUBLE? If clicking the Undo button doesn't remove the pattern, repeat Steps 2 through 4, except this time select the blank pattern in the first column of the first row of patterns.

6. Click a blank area in the chart to deselect the data point.

Kim now asks you to work on the chart labels. The two front data labels are slightly overlapped, and should be moved apart. She would also like the label font to be larger. Finally, Kim asks if you can add one decimal place to the percentages.

Formatting the Chart Labels

To change the font type, font size, color, style (bold or italic or both), or alignment of label text, or to change the number format of label percentages, you use the Format Data Labels dialog box.

The label text is currently formatted in the Arial font type with a font size of 8. Increasing the font size will make it even harder to find room for the two front labels near their small wedges. So you'll also change the font type to Arial Narrow, which can fit larger letters into a smaller width.

To change the data label font type, font size, and number format:

1. Click one of the four data labels to select all the data labels.

2. Right-click one of the selected data labels to display the shortcut menu, click **Format Data Labels** to open the Format Data Labels dialog box, then click the **Font** tab.

3. Scroll the Font list box until Arial Narrow is visible, then click **Arial Narrow**.

4. Click **10** in the **Size** list box.
5. Click the **Number** tab.
6. Click the up arrow on the **Decimal Places** spin box to change the number of decimal places to **1**.
7. Click the **OK** button to close the Format Data Labels dialog box.

Kim decides the labels are more readable with the new font type and font size. So now you can move the labels. You'll move the two front labels to remove the overlap. And, to better balance the chart, you'll also reposition the other two data labels.

To reposition the data labels:

1. Click the **Regular Unflavored** data label to select it. A hashed selection box appears around the text.
2. Position the pointer on the selection box border, click and hold the mouse button as you drag the label until it is positioned as shown in Figure 6-72, then release the mouse button. (Note that the figure shows the chart after all four labels have been repositioned.)

Figure 6-72 Reformatted and repositioned data labels

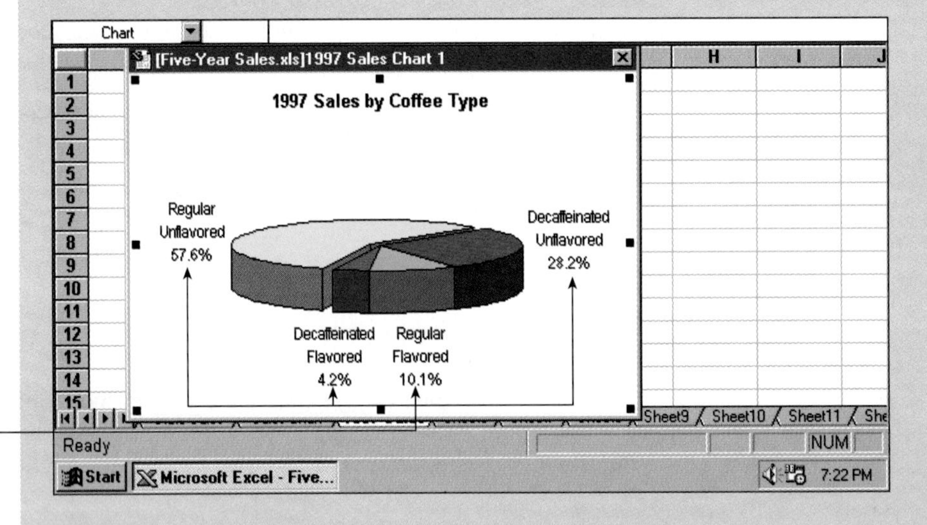

all four data labels are repositioned

3. Repeat Steps 1 and 2 for each of the other three data labels.
4. Click the blank area of the chart to deselect the data label. Your chart should now look like Figure 6-72.

Kim thinks that the font type for the title should also be changed to Arial Narrow so that two different fonts are not mixed in the chart. She also asks you to increase the font size at the same time.

You can change the font type and font size for any chart text using the buttons on the Formatting toolbar. You'll use these buttons to change the chart title.

To change the font type and font size of the chart title:

1. Click the chart title to select it. A selection box appears around the title.
2. Click the **Font** list arrow on the Formatting toolbar, then click **Arial Narrow**.
3. Click the **Font Size** list arrow on the Formatting toolbar, then click **16**.

Kim has one final request. She asks you to add a shadowed border around the chart.

Adding a Border Around a Chart

To balance the large, bright elements in the chart, you'll add a heavy, shadowed black border around the entire chart.

To add a heavy shadowed border to the chart:

1. Click any empty cell to deactivate the chart.
2. Right-click in a blank area of the chart to display the shortcut menu, then click **Format Object** to open the Format Object dialog box.
3. Click the **Weight** list arrow in the Border section to open the Weight list, then click the thickest of the four lines.
4. Click the **Shadow** radio button to select a shadow.
5. Click the **OK** button to apply the border and shadow.
6. Click cell **A1** to deselect the chart. Your finished chart should now look like Figure 6-73.

Figure 6-73 The finished 3-D pie chart

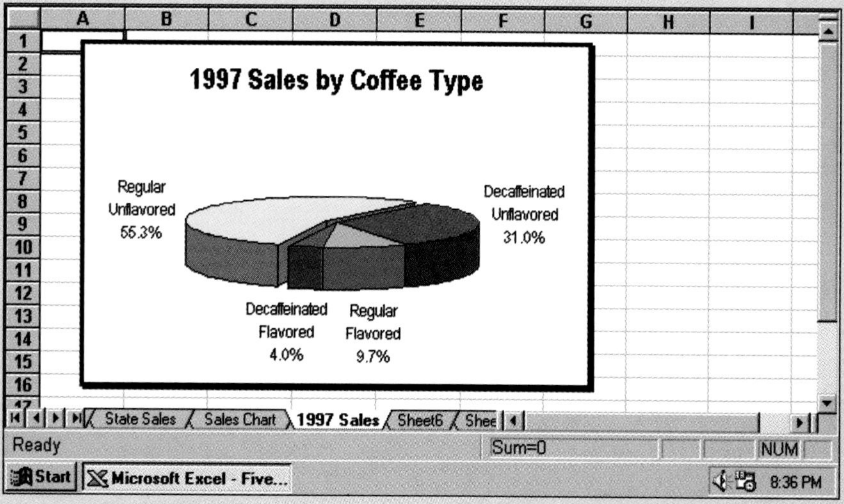

Now that the 3-D pie chart is finished, Kim asks you to save the current version of the workbook and print a copy of the chart. She has already set the page setup characteristics the way she wants them for this worksheet, so you do not need to check or change the page setup before you save and print.

To save the workbook and print the 3-D pie chart:

1. Click the **Save** button on the Standard toolbar.
2. Click the **Print** button on the Standard toolbar to print the 1997 Sales worksheet.

Kim has prepared a memo using Word to be distributed to the Valle Coffee customer representatives. She asks you to link the column chart you created earlier to that memo.

Linking an Excel Chart to a Word Document

Kim wants you to link the chart rather than embed it so that any changes made to the Excel chart or the data used to create the chart will be reflected in the memo. Before you can link the chart to the Word document, you need to open Kim's document, which is called KimMemo and is located in the Tutorial.06 folder on your Student Disk.

To open Kim's memo:

1. Click the **Open a Document** button on the Office Shortcut bar. The Open dialog box appears.
2. Click **KimMemo** in the list box, then click the **Open** button. Word starts and opens the KimMemo document.
3. Scroll the document until your screen looks like Figure 6-74.

Figure 6-74 Kim's memo

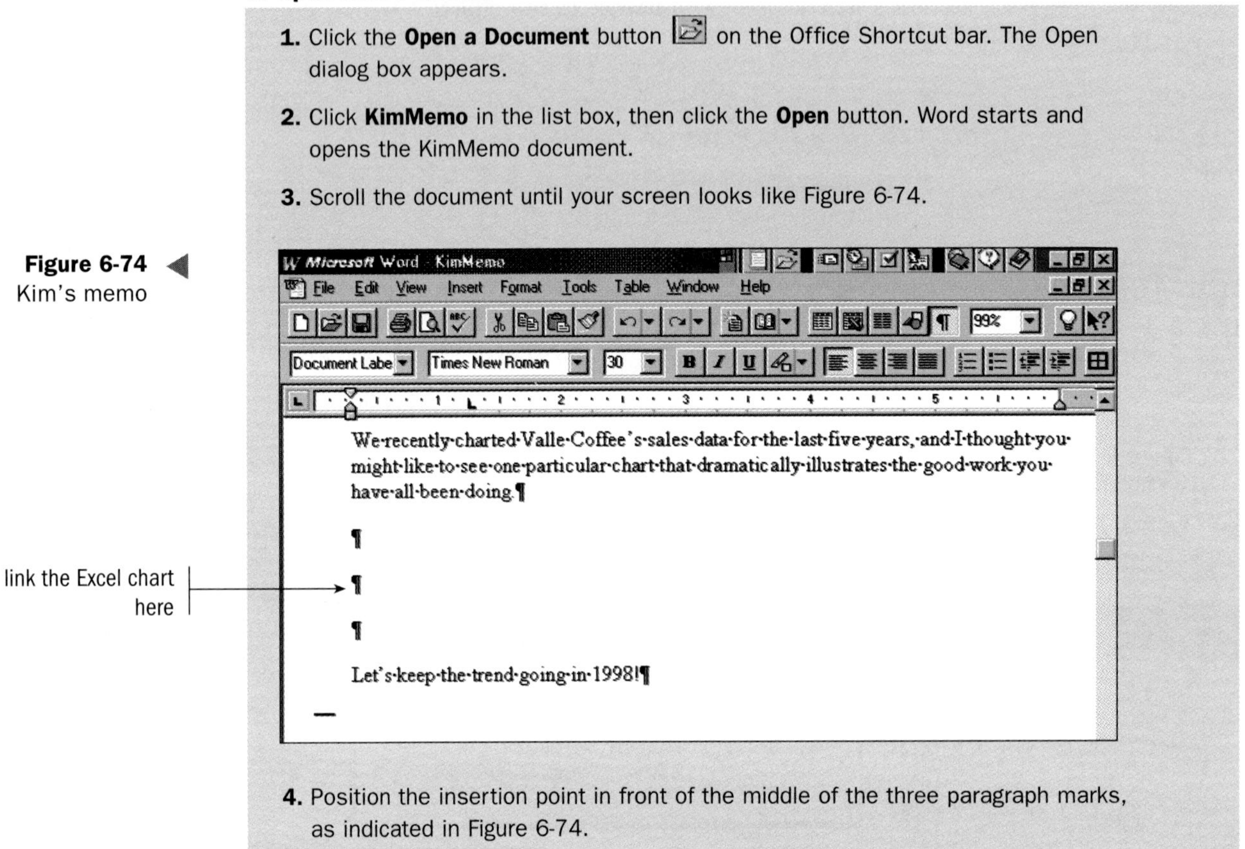

4. Position the insertion point in front of the middle of the three paragraph marks, as indicated in Figure 6-74.

You do not need to link the entire Five-Year Sales workbook to Kim's Word document. Instead, you want to link just the column chart. Therefore, you will copy the chart in Excel, and then use the Paste Special command in Word to link the chart.

To link the column chart to the memo document:

1. Click the **Microsoft Excel - Five Ye...** button on the taskbar. The Excel window is now active and the 1997 Sales sheet is open.
2. Click the **Sales Chart** tab to display the Sales Chart worksheet.
3. Select the chart then click the **Copy** button on the Standard toolbar.
4. Click the **Microsoft Word - KimMemo** button on the taskbar. The Word window is now active on the screen.
5. Click **Edit** on the menu bar, then click **Paste Special**. The Paste Special dialog box opens. See Figure 6-75.

Figure 6-75
Paste Special dialog box

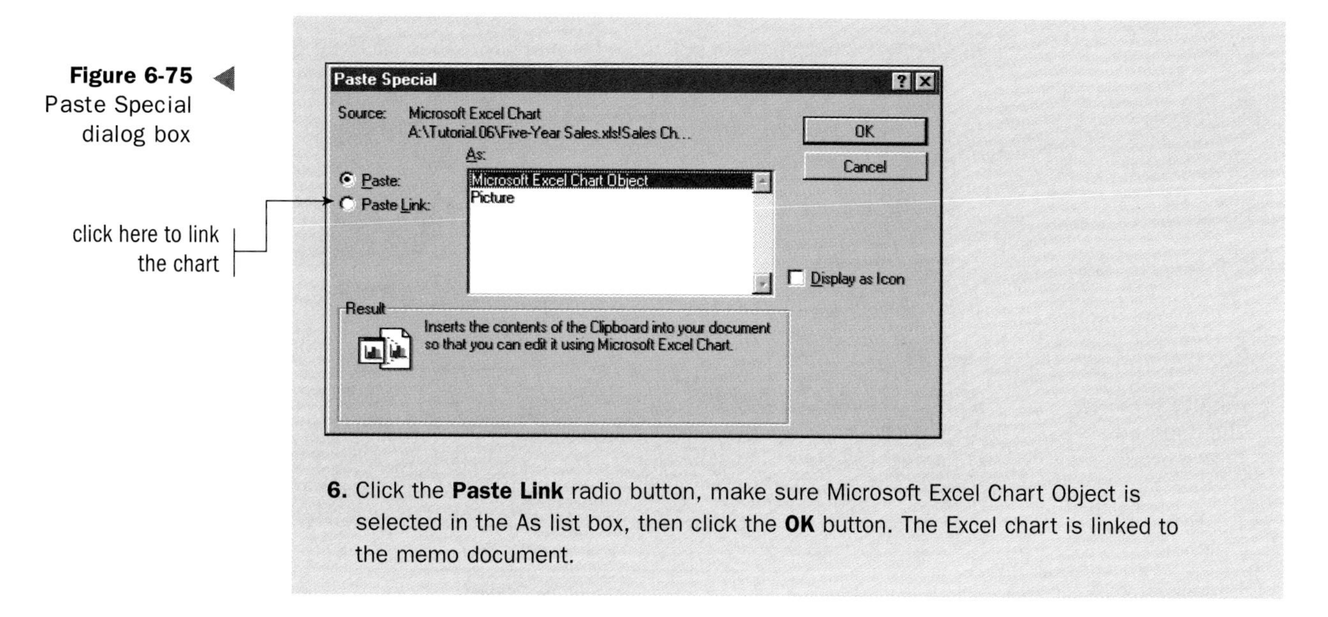

6. Click the **Paste Link** radio button, make sure Microsoft Excel Chart Object is selected in the As list box, then click the **OK** button. The Excel chart is linked to the memo document.

The link was successful, but Kim asks you to make several changes. You need to make two of the changes in Word: centering the chart and editing the memo text to include your name.

To center the chart and edit the text:

1. Position the pointer in the left margin next to the chart, then click to select the chart. The selected chart is displayed in reverse video, with white text on a black background.
2. Click the **Center** button on the Formatting toolbar, then click the blank area to the right of the chart to deselect the chart.
3. Scroll up a few lines until you can see the entire paragraph that begins "We recently."
4. Select the word "We" then type your first and last name.

Kim asks you to add a border and shadow to the original chart to match the border and shadow already applied to the chart title.

Updating a Linked Chart

To add a border and shadow to the original chart, you must switch to Excel and then make the changes.

To change the linked Excel chart:

1. Click the **Microsoft Excel - Five-Ye...** button on the taskbar to switch to Excel.
2. Right-click the chart to select it and display the shortcut menu, then click **Edit Object** to activate the chart.
3. Right-click any white area of the chart, then click **Format Chart Area** to open the Format Chart Area dialog box.
4. Click the **Weight** list arrow, then click the third line sample to select a medium-weight border.

5. Click the **Shadow** check box to select a shadow, then click the **OK** button to apply the formatting changes.

6. Click cell **A1** to deactivate the chart, then click cell **A1** again to deselect the chart.

   Now, switch back to Word to verify that the linked chart has been changed.

7. Click the **Microsoft Word - KimMemo** button on the taskbar to switch to Word.

8. Scroll the document until you can see the entire chart. The chart now appears with a border and shadow. See Figure 6-76.

Figure 6-76 The updated linked chart

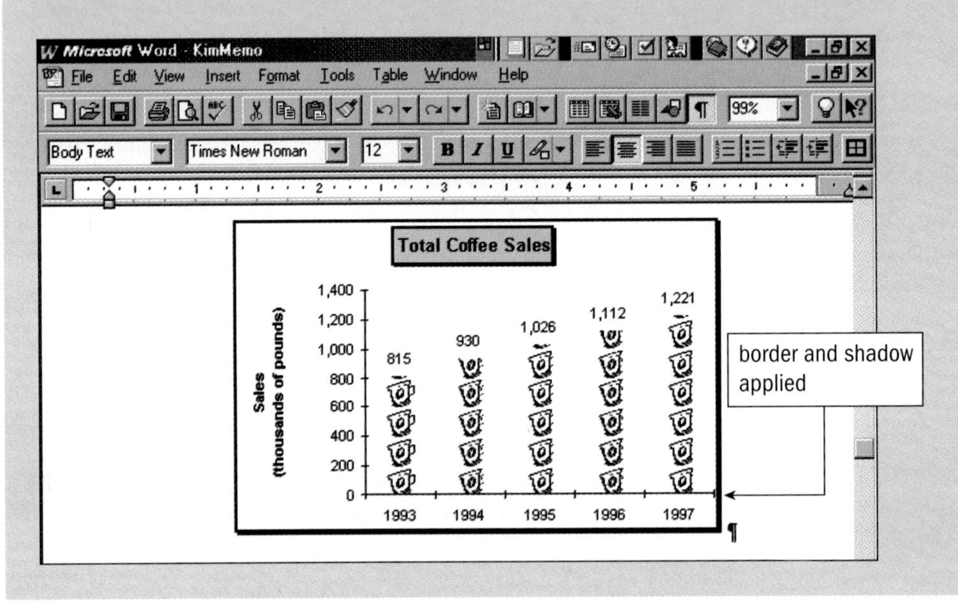

Kim has just learned that she entered the wrong value for 1997 sales of decaffeinated unflavored coffee. The figure should be 394,000 pounds rather than 344,000 pounds. She asks you to change this value in the Five-Year Sales workbook. The change in this value will also be reflected in the two charts in the workbook and in the linked chart in the Word memo document.

To change the sales value:

1. Click the **Microsoft Excel - Five-Ye...** button on the taskbar to switch to Excel.

2. Click the **Sales Values** tab to display the Sales Values worksheet.

3. Click cell **F6**, type **394**, then press the **Enter** key. Excel automatically recalculates all affected values in the Sales Values worksheet. For example, the total in cell F9 is now 1,271.

4. Click cell **A1** to make it the active cell.

5. Click the **1997 Sales** tab to display the 1997 Sales worksheet. The 3-D pie chart has been changed to reflect the change in its input data. For example, decaffeinated unflavored coffee now accounts for 31% of 1997 sales rather than 28.2%.

6. Click the **Sales Chart** tab to display the Sales Chart worksheet. The column chart has also been updated. For example, the column representing 1997 total sales is now taller, and the label has changed from 1,221 to 1,271.

7. Click the **Microsoft Word - KimMemo** button on the taskbar to switch to Word. Because the chart was linked to the Word document, the change in the chart is reflected automatically in the memo and the total sales value for 1997 is now shown as 1,271.

Kim asks you to save the memo with the name Chart Memo and to print one copy of the memo. You will then have completed your work with the memo, so you can exit Word.

To save and print the memo, then exit Word:

1. Click **File** on the menu bar, then click **Save As**.
2. Type **Chart Memo** then click the **Save** button to save the file with the new name.
3. Click the **Print** button on the Standard toolbar to print a copy of the memo.
4. Click the **Close** button on the title bar. Word closes and you return to the Excel window.

   TROUBLE? If a dialog box opens with the message "Do you want to save changes to Chart Memo?" click the No button. You have made no intentional changes since you last saved the file.

This completes your work for this session. You can now save the workbook file and exit Excel.

To save the workbook then exit Excel:

1. If necessary, click cell **A1** to make it the active cell.
2. Click the **Documentation** tab to switch to that worksheet. When Kim later opens the workbook, it will open to the first worksheet in the workbook.
3. Click the **Save** button on the Standard toolbar to save the workbook.
4. Click the **Close** button on the title bar. The workbook is closed, Excel closes, and you return to the Windows 95 desktop.

Kim is pleased with the contents and organization of the finished workbook. The completed tables will make it easy for her to analyze data and sales trends at Valle Coffee, and the charts will help her to convey the data effectively to other employees.

Quick Check

1. How do you change an existing chart from one type to another?
2. Explain the process of pulling a wedge out of a 3-D pie chart.
3. Exactly how would you change a pie chart so that the wedge in front is moved to the back?
4. How do you select and recolor a data point on a 3-D pie chart?
5. For what reasons might you add patterns to a chart's data markers?
6. How did you link the column chart into Kim's memo? How would that process have been different if you had wanted to embed rather than link the chart?
7. What happens when you change a data value in an Excel workbook?

Tutorial Assignments

Kim started an Excel workbook for analyzing dollar coffee sales by year and by type, but she had to go out of town before she could complete it. She needs your help finishing the workbook and asks you to complete the following:

1. Make sure your Student Disk is in the disk drive, then open the document named $Sales, which is in the TAssign folder of the Tutorial.06 folder.
2. Save the workbook as Five-Year Dollar Sales in the same folder.

3. Use the Help system's Answer Wizard to learn about adding a worksheet, then insert a new worksheet in front of the Input Values worksheet, name the sheet Documentation, change the width of column A to 14, then enter data in the cells to match Figure 6-77.

Figure 6-77

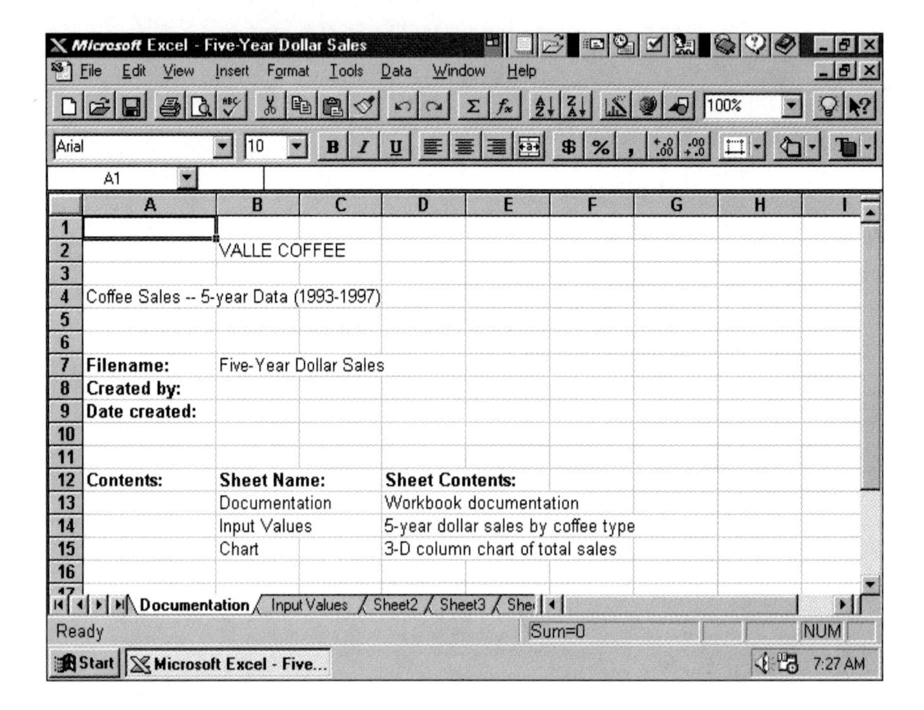

4. Type your name in cell B8, enter a function that will display the current date in cell B9, then left-justify the contents of cell B9.
5. On the Input Values sheet, use AutoFill to complete the entries for cells D4 through F4.
6. In cell B9, use AutoSum to create a formula that totals the four values above that cell, then use the fill handle to copy the formula to cells C9 through F9.
7. Copy cells A4 through F9 and paste them in cell A13, then delete the contents of cells B14 through B18.
8. Replace the contents of cell C14 with the formula =(C5-B5)/B5, apply a percent style to the cell, then use the fill handle to copy the formula to the rest of the cells in the range C14 through F18.
9. In cell B8, add a cell note with the text "First offered May, 1993".
10. Change the contents of cell E8 to 2 and of F8 to 3, verify that cell F17 has been automatically recalculated and now contains 50%, then change the contents of cell E8 to 465 and of F8 to 511.

11. Format cells as follows:
    a. Bold cells A1, A3, and A12.
    b. Change the font size for cell A1 to 12 and center its contents across columns A through F.
    c. Switch to the Documentation sheet, change the font type and size for cell B2 to Impact 28, apply the italic style, then center the cell's contents across columns B through F.
    d. On the Documentation sheet, change the font size for cell A4 to 12, bold the cell, then center its contents across columns A through F.
12. On the Documentation sheet, decrease the height of row 5 to 9.00, select cells A1 through F5, then format the cells to apply a sparse dot pattern and a black outline of medium thickness.
13. Switch to the Input Values sheet, apply the List 3 AutoFormat to cells A13 through F18, apply the same AutoFormat to cells A4 through F9, then change the width of columns B through F to 7.
14. Switch to the Documentation sheet, change to a portrait orientation, center the printout horizontally on the page, customize the header to add the filename and a period in front of the sheet name, then change the footer to the Page 1 of ? form.
15. Rename Sheet2 as Chart, switch to the Input Values sheet, select cells B4 through F4 and B9 through F9, then use the ChartWizard to create a 2-D column chart of format 4 on the Chart sheet. The chart should be 5 rows wide and 13 rows deep; it should be titled "Coffee Sales -- 1993-1997," include the Y-axis title "Sales ($1000)," and have no legend or X-axis title.

16. Modify the chart as follows:
    a. Change the chart to a 3-D column chart.
    b. Change the elevation to 20 and the rotation to 30.
    c. Change the data markers to red.
    d. Delete the axis in the lower right of the chart (labeled "S1").
    e. Format the plot area to change the color to "None" and the border to "None."
    f. Format the walls to apply a light gray color.
    g. Format the Z-axis (the vertical axis) to change the scale maximum to 12,000 and the major unit to 4,000.
    h. Add horizontal gridlines (using a button on the Chart toolbar).
    i. Resize the plot area to make it as large as possible without overlapping the chart title.
17. Open the document named KimFax, which is in the TAssign folder of the Tutorial.06 folder, then complete the following:
    a. Save the document as Fax With Chart in the same folder.
    b. Type your name following the tab after "From:."
    c. Link the chart you created to the document at the last paragraph mark.
    d. Center the chart.
    e. Preview, save, then print the document.
    f. Close the document and exit Word.
18. Preview each worksheet, save the workbook, then print all worksheets.
19. Close the workbook and then exit Excel.

Case Problems

1. Ashbrook Mall Information Desk Janet Nez, an Information Desk supervisor, has started to create a workbook containing data on mall usage statistics for services provided by the Information Desk. She asks you to finish the workbook by completing the following:

1. Make sure your Student Disk is in the disk drive, then open the document named UseStats, which is in the Cases folder of the Tutorial.06 folder.
2. Save the workbook as Mall Usage Statistics in the same folder.

3. Complete the Documentation sheet entry by typing your name in cell C10 and entering a formula in cell C11 that will display the current date.
4. Format the Documentation sheet as follows:
   a. Underline the contents of cell D5.
   b. Apply a light gray color to cells A1 through G6.
   c. Select the Ashbrook Mall WordArt object, then format the object to apply the same light gray color fill.
   d. Change the height of rows 17 through 19 to 14.25.
5. Format the Tables sheet as follows:
   a. Change cell A1 to font size 14, then center the contents of cell A1 across columns A through I.
   b. Change cell A3 to font size 11, then bold the cell.
   c. Use the cell B4 fill handle to complete the series in cells C4 through H4.
   d. Apply a bold italic style to cells B4 through I4, and right-justify the contents of those cells.
   e. Bold cells A5 through A7.
6. Use AutoSum to enter an appropriate sum formula in cell I5, then use the fill handle to copy the formula into cells I6 and I7.
7. Create Table 2 by completing the following:
   a. Copy cells A3 through H7, then paste the copied cells into cell A10.
   b. Change the label in cell A10 to "Table 2: Average daily usage."
   c. Enter a formula in cell B12 to calculate the average Sunday stroller usage, given that there were five Sundays in August 1998.
   d. Use the fill handle to copy the formula in cell B12 into the remaining cells in the range B12 through H14.
   e. Format cells B12 through H14 to display one decimal place.
   f. Correct the formula in cell D12 to account for the fact that there were only four Tuesdays in August 1998.
   g. Use the fill handle to copy the formula in cell D12 into the remaining cells in the range D12 through G14.
8. Select cells A11 through H12, then use the ChartWizard to create a 2-D column chart at the top of Sheet3 that is 6 columns wide and 11 columns tall. Use the format 7 chart subtype, then specify "August Daily Stroller Usage" as the chart title. Do not add a legend or any axis titles.
9. Edit the chart as follows:
   a. Resize the plot area to make it as wide and tall as possible without overlapping the chart title.
   b. Format the plot area to change the color to white and to remove the border.

10. Create a second chart by selecting and copying the stroller chart, then pasting it in the cell in column A that is three rows below the bottom of the stroller chart. Paste again three rows below the second chart to create a third chart.

11. Edit the second chart as follows:
    a. Select the second chart, activate the ChartWizard, then specify the non-adjacent range of cells A11 through H11 and A13 through H13 as the input data range.
    b. Edit the chart title to change "Stroller" to "Wheelchair."
    c. Format the data series to change the data marker color to the green color in the third position of the sixth row of the color samples.
12. Edit the third chart as follows:

    a. Select the third chart, activate the ChartWizard, then specify the non-adjacent range of cells A11 through H11 and A14 through H14 as the input data range.
    b. Edit the chart title to change "Stroller" to "Motorized Cart."
    c. Format the data series to change the data marker color to the color in the sixth position of the last row of the color samples.
13. Rename Sheet3 as "Bar Charts."

14. Change the page setup for the Bar Charts worksheet as follows:
    a. Use a portrait orientation.
    b. Center the printout horizontally.
    c. Create a custom heading by adding the date in the left section and the filename in the right section.
    d. Select the centered footer of the form "Page 1 of ?."
15. Preview each worksheet, save the workbook, then print each worksheet.
16. Close the workbook and exit Excel.

2. Professional Litigation User Services Carl Nghiep, the administration manager at Professional Litigation User Services (PLUS), needs your help to finish a workbook he has started. The workbook contains data about cases currently in litigation. Complete the following:

1. Make sure your Student Disk is in the disk drive, then open the document named Clients, which is in the Cases folder of the Tutorial.06 folder.
2. Save the workbook as Active Cases in the same folder.
3. Change the filename in cell B13 of the Documentation sheet to the new filename, change the name in cell B14 to your name, and enter the current date in cell B15.
4. Format the Documentation sheet as follows:
    a. Format the contents of cell A10 as bold Arial 14, center the cell contents across rows A through G, then change the font color to white.
    b. Select cells A1 through G11 and apply a black color.
    c. Increase the height of rows 21 through 23 to 18.00.
5. Complete the Data sheet as follows:
    a. Use AutoFill to complete the series beginning in cell B4 through column G.
    b. Use AutoSum to calculate an appropriate sum in cell B8, then use the fill handle to copy the formula into cells C8 through G8.
6. Format the Data sheet as follows:
    a. Apply the Simple AutoFormat to cells A4 through G8.
    b. Change the width of column A to 14, and the width of columns B through G to 5.
    c. Format cell A1 as bold with a font size of 14, then center the cell contents across columns A through G.
    d. Bold the contents of cell A3.
    e. Change the font size for cell A3 to 11.
7. Select cells A4 through G7, then use the ChartWizard to create a 3-D column chart on Sheet3. Make the chart 6 columns wide and 13 rows tall, use the format 5 chart subtype, add a legend, and add "Active Cases -- 1998" as the chart title.
8. Modify the chart as follows:

    a. Select the axis along the right side of the figure that is labeled with the three stages, format its scale to present the series in reverse order, then delete that axis.
    b. Edit the 3-D view to change the elevation to 20 and the rotation to 30.
    c. Resize the plot area so it is as wide and tall as possible without blocking the chart title or legend.

    d. Add horizontal gridlines (using a button on the Chart toolbar).
    e. Change the color for the Appeal stage data series to the peach color in the sixth column of the third row of color samples.
9. Modify Sheet3 as follows:
    a. Rename the sheet as Chart.
    b. Change the page setup to a portrait orientation, and center the worksheet contents both horizontally and vertically.

   c. Customize the heading to insert the workbook name and a period immediately in front of the centered worksheet name.
   d. Create a custom footer with the date in the left section, and the word "Page," a space, the page number, a space, the word "of," a space, and the total pages in the right section.
10. Format the chart object to add the thickest possible black border and a shadow.
11. Copy the chart, then paste it six rows below the chart.

12. Edit the second chart as follows:
   a. Change the chart to a 2-D bar chart. (*Hint:* The bar chart is the sample in the second row, first column of the chart type list.)
   b. Activate the ChartWizard. In the Step 2 of 2 dialog box, indicate that the Data Series is in columns.
   c. Change the color of the April data series to red.
   d. Change the color of the March data series to yellow.
   e. Move the legend to the right so it doesn't overlap the last gridline.

   f. Remove the horizontal gridlines (which are now vertical).
   g. Format the Y-axis (now horizontal) to change the scale maximum to 16 and the major unit to 4.
13. Open the document PLUSMemo, which is in the Cases folder of the Tutorial.06 folder.
14. Save the document as PLUS Chart Memo in the same folder.
15. Edit the document as follows:
   a. Locate the text "FROM:" then type your name after the tab.
   b. Locate the text "DATE:" then type the current date following the tab.
   c. Link the 3-D column chart into the document at the first of the two centered paragraph marks.
   d. Link the 2-D bar chart into the document at the second of the two centered paragraph marks.
16. Preview, save, then print the memo.
17. Close the document and exit Word.
18. Preview each of the three worksheets, save the workbook, then print the three worksheets.
19. Close the workbook and exit Excel.

3. Best Friends Richard Moscovitch, one of the directors at Best Friends, has started to create a workbook containing data about dog placements made by Best Friends. He asks you to finish the workbook by completing the following:

1. Make sure your Student Disk is in the disk drive, then open the document named Dogs, which is in the Cases folder of the Tutorial.06 folder.
2. Save the workbook as Placements in the same folder.
3. Make the following changes in the Documentation sheet:
   a. Format cell B2 as italicized Arial Black with a font size of 20, then center the cell contents across columns B through F. (If Arial Black is not available, select any sans serif font, preferably another type of Arial font, if possible.)
   b. Format cell B4 as Arial Black with a font size of 12, then center the cell contents across columns B through F. (If Arial Black is not available, use the same font type you selected in the previous step.)
   c. Select cells A1 through F4, apply a light gray color, then apply a dark outline border.
   d. Type your name in cell B8, type the current date in cell B9 in mm/dd/yy format, then insert a formula in cell B10 that will display the current date.
4. Switch to the Placements worksheet, then format cell A1 as Arial 16, bold the cell contents, then center the cell contents across columns A through I.
5. Use AutoFill to complete the entries in cells D3 through I3.

6. Use AutoSum to place a formula in cell B6 that sums the two values above that cell, then use the fill handle to copy the formula into cells C6 through I6.
7. Select cells A3 through I6, then apply the Classic 2 AutoFormat.
8. Change the width of columns B through I to 6.
9. Select cells A3 through I5, then use the ChartWizard to create a line chart that is 5 columns wide and 13 rows tall on Sheet3. Use the format 2 subtype, specify the first row for category labels and the first column for legend text, and enter "Best Friends Placements" as the chart title.
10. Rename Sheet3 as Charts.
11. Format the chart object to give it a medium-weight border.
12. Format the Hearing dogs data series to change the line weight from the light choice to the medium choice, then format the Service dogs data series to change to the same medium-weight line and to change its color to red.

13. Copy the line chart and paste it three cells below the bottom of the line chart.

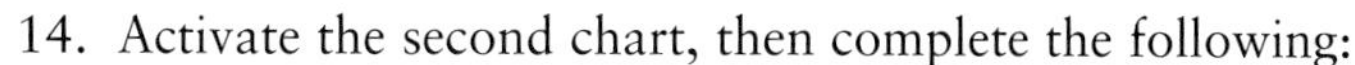

14. Activate the second chart, then complete the following:
    a. Change the chart type to 2-D bar chart.
    b. Format the chart type, click Options, then select the second subtype.
    c. Format the Hearing dogs data series to change the area color to dark blue. Use the same dark blue as the border color shown in the Border section of the Format Data Series dialog box.
    d. Format the Service dogs data series to change the area color to red. Use the same red as the border color shown in the Border section of the Format Data Series dialog box.
    e. Format the horizontal axis to change the scale maximum to 24 and the major unit to 6.
    f. Resize the plot area so it is as wide and tall as possible without overlapping the chart title or the legend.
    g. Deactivate and deselect the chart.
15. Change the page setup for the Charts sheet as follows:
    a. Use portrait orientation.
    b. Center the printout horizontally on the page.
    c. Create a custom header with the workbook name in the left section and the worksheet name in the right section.
    d. Create a custom footer with the date in the right section and the word "Page," a space, the page number, a space, the word "of," a space, then the total number of pages in the left section.
16. Open the document Memo, which is in the Cases folder of the Tutorial.06 folder.
17. Save the document as Placements Memo in the same folder.
18. Edit the document as follows:

    a. Locate the text "DATE:" then use the Insert Date and Time command to insert the current date as an automatically updated field in a "monthname day, year" format following the tab.
    b. Select the displayed date and change the font type and size to Times New Roman 12.
    c. Locate the text "Student Name" and replace it with your name.
    d. Link the line chart to the document at the first of the two centered paragraph marks.
    e. Link the bar chart to the document at the second of the two centered paragraph marks.
19. Preview, save, then print the memo.
20. Close the document and exit Word.
21. Preview each worksheet, save the workbook, then print each worksheet.
22. Close the workbook and exit Excel.

4. De Longpre Furniture Lowell De Longpre owns and operates a furniture store. Although the vast majority of his customers pay by credit card or check, some cash is received every day. Lowell has kept track of the cash receipts by "week within month" for the last four months, as shown in Figure 6-78. This figure also shows the number of workdays for each of the four months.

Figure 6-78

Table 1: Cash receipts by week

	February	March	April	May
Week 1	$2,808	$2,674	$1,422	$701
Week 2	$2,145	$2,668	$2,701	$3,250
Week 3	$3,009	$1,977	$2,020	$2,752
Week 4	$2,550	$2,526	$2,999	$2,455
Week 5	$0	$880	$1,609	$2,828

Table 2: Workdays per month

February	March	April	May
24	26	26	26

Lowell asks you to create a workbook he can use to analyze this cash receipt data. The workbook should contain the two tables in Figure 6-78 plus a third table of calculated average daily receipts for each of the four months. (*Hint*: sum the month's receipts, then divide each sum by the corresponding number of workdays.) The average daily receipts for each month should be used to create a 2-D column chart.

First plan the workbook organization. Then complete the following:

1. Make sure your Student Disk is in the disk drive, then start a new blank Excel workbook.
2. Rename each of the worksheets you plan to use.
3. Enter and format the documentation information and input values.
4. Enter formulas to generate the necessary calculations. Use AutoSum where appropriate.
5. Sketch the 2-D column chart of average daily receipts.
6. Create the 2-D column chart using the format 7 chart subtype, then modify the chart to improve its appearance. (*Hint:* format the Y-axis scale to use a minimum value of 400, a maximum value of 475, and a major unit of 25.)
7. In the worksheet containing the chart, temporarily insert the picture MoneyBag, which is located in the Cases folder in the Tutorial.06 folder. Remove the outline, copy the picture, then paste it into the chart's data series. Stack and scale the picture as 10 units per picture. Delete the picture when you are finished working with it.
8. Preview each worksheet and change the page setups as appropriate. Customize the header for each worksheet to include the workbook name as well as the sheet name.
9. Save the workbook as De Longpre Cash, then print each of the worksheets.
10. Close the workbook and exit Excel.

TUTORIAL 7

Querying and Enhancing an Access Database

Displaying Specific Data and Creating Custom Forms

OBJECTIVES

In this tutorial you will:

- Create queries using single and multiple record selection criteria
- Sort data
- Filter data
- Use calculated fields, record calculations, and record group calculations in a query
- Create parameter, top values, and action queries
- Create a custom form
- Add a graphic to a form
- Use Paint to modify a graphic
- Compact a database

Valle Coffee

Valle Coffee maintains a database that contains data about recent orders from their restaurant customers. This database is similar to the Restaurant Business database, which you worked with in Tutorial 4, except that it includes more tables. Among the tables in the database are the Customer and Order tables you worked with earlier, and the Coffee table, which contains data about the different types of coffees the company sells.

Barbara Hennessey, office manager, and Carlos Sangris, director of production at Valle Coffee, often need information from the database. For example, Barbara needs to find information about all the orders for which bills were sent out on a specific date so that she can track whether the bills have been paid. Carlos needs to find information about all orders for a specific type of coffee, such as Colombian, so that he can monitor its demand and inventory level. While he is reviewing the information about all orders for one type of coffee, Carlos wants to be able to check the demand for a specific weight and size to make sure that enough coffee has been packaged to meet the demand. In addition, Barbara's staff members frequently need to contact customers in a specific state or whose invoice amounts exceed a specific amount, so that they can question the customers about their level of satisfaction with the company's service and product quality. All these informational needs can be satisfied by queries you will create in this tutorial.

Carlos and his staff have been using a form to maintain data about the coffee products the company sells. The existing form, which was created with the Form Wizard, is difficult for the staff members to use. In this tutorial you'll create a custom form that is more attractive and easier to use. This custom form will contain special list boxes that users can display to choose the various codes they need when maintaining product data. The form will also group and emphasize data to make the form easier to work with and draw attention to the important data on the form.

SESSION 7.1

In this session you will work with a database containing one-to-many and many-to-many relationships, define conditions for queries, change a datasheet's appearance, use the And and Or logical operators, sort data, and filter data.

Viewing the Relationships of Database Tables

Before you begin creating the queries and form for the Valle Coffee database, you need to become familiar with the data it contains. You'll first make a copy of the database, which is named Valle, then rename the copied file as Restaurant Coffee Orders in order to keep the original database file intact. Then you'll review the tables and relationships among the tables in the database.

To copy and rename the Valle database:

1. Right-click the **Start** button on the taskbar, then click **Explore** on the shortcut menu. The Exploring window opens.
2. Scrolling as necessary, click the plus symbol to the left of the drive that contains your Student Disk in the All Folders list box, then click **Tutorial.07**. The list of files in the Tutorial.07 folder on your Student Disk appears in the Contents of 'Tutorial.07' list box.
3. Right-click **Valle** in the list box, then click **Copy** on the shortcut menu.

   The filename on your screen might be Valle.mdb instead of Valle, depending on the default settings on your computer.
4. Right-click **Tutorial.07** in the All Folders list box, then click **Paste** on the shortcut menu. A copy of the Valle database with the default filename "Copy of Valle" is added to the Contents of 'Tutorial.07' list box.
5. Right-click **Copy of Valle** in the Contents of 'Tutorial.07' list box, then click **Rename** on the shortcut menu. The filename appears highlighted inside a box to indicate that it is selected for editing.
6. Type **Restaurant Coffee Orders** then press the **Enter** key. The filename is now Restaurant Coffee Orders, which remains highlighted.

   TROUBLE? If a dialog box appears warning you that you are changing a filename extension, click the No button, type .mdb at the end of the filename, then press the Enter key.

   TROUBLE? If only a portion of the filename is visible, drag the right edge of the Name column heading in the Contents of 'Tutorial.07' list box to the right until the entire filename is visible.
7. Click the **Close** button on the Exploring title bar to close the Exploring window.

Next, you'll open the Restaurant Coffee Orders database on your Student Disk.

To start Access and open the Restaurant Coffee Orders database:

1. Click the **Open a Document** button on the Office Shortcut Bar.
2. Display the list of folders and files in the Tutorial.07 folder on your Student Disk, then open the **Restaurant Coffee Orders** file. Access starts and displays the Restaurant Coffee Orders database in the Database window. See Figure 7-1.

Figure 7-1 Tables in the Restaurant Coffee Orders database

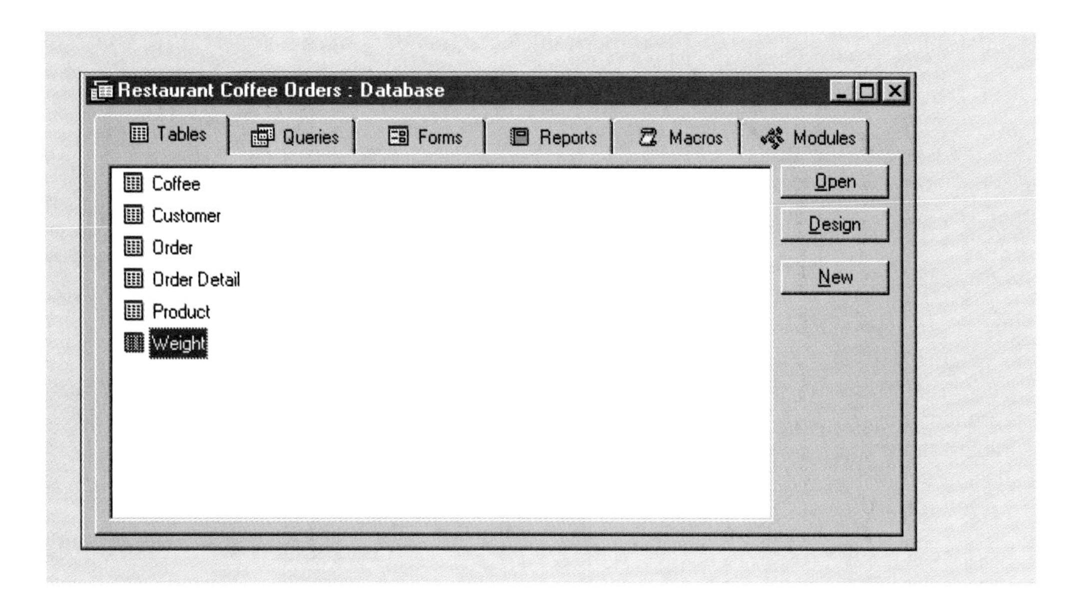

The database contains six tables, which are listed in the Database window. Barbara has already defined the relationships among the database tables. To view these relationships you need to open the Relationships window.

To view the table relationships in the Restaurant Coffee Orders database:

1. Click the **Relationships** button on the Database toolbar. Access opens the Relationships window. See Figure 7-2.

Figure 7-2 Table relationships in the Restaurant Coffee Orders database

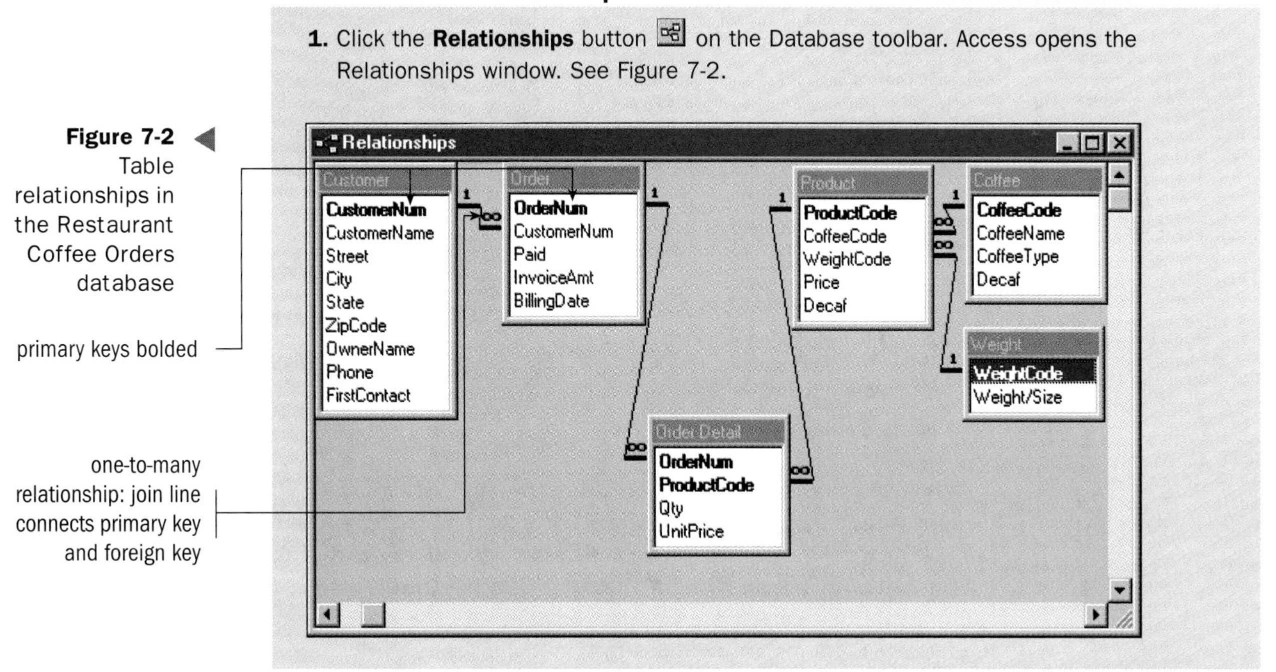

Each table has a relationship with at least one other table. In some cases, the relationship is a one-to-many relationship; in others the relationship is a many-to-many relationship.

One-To-Many Relationships

As you learned in Tutorial 4, a **one-to-many relationship** exists between two tables when one record in the first table matches zero, one, or many records in the second table, and when one record in the second table matches exactly one record in the first table.

The Customer table contains data about Valle Coffee's restaurant customers, and the Order table contains data about the restaurant customers' orders. (These are the tables you worked with in Tutorial 4.) Because each order is placed by exactly one customer and each customer places many orders, the Customer and Order tables have a one-to-many relationship, abbreviated 1:M, as shown in Figure 7-3. CustomerNum is the primary key of the Customer table, and OrderNum is the primary key of the Order table. CustomerNum in the Order table serves as a foreign key to join the two tables. For example, the records in the Order table with OrderNum field values of 227, 325, and 367 are for The Peppermill restaurant, which has a CustomerNum of 650.

Figure 7-3 Query results produced by joining tables having a 1:M relationship

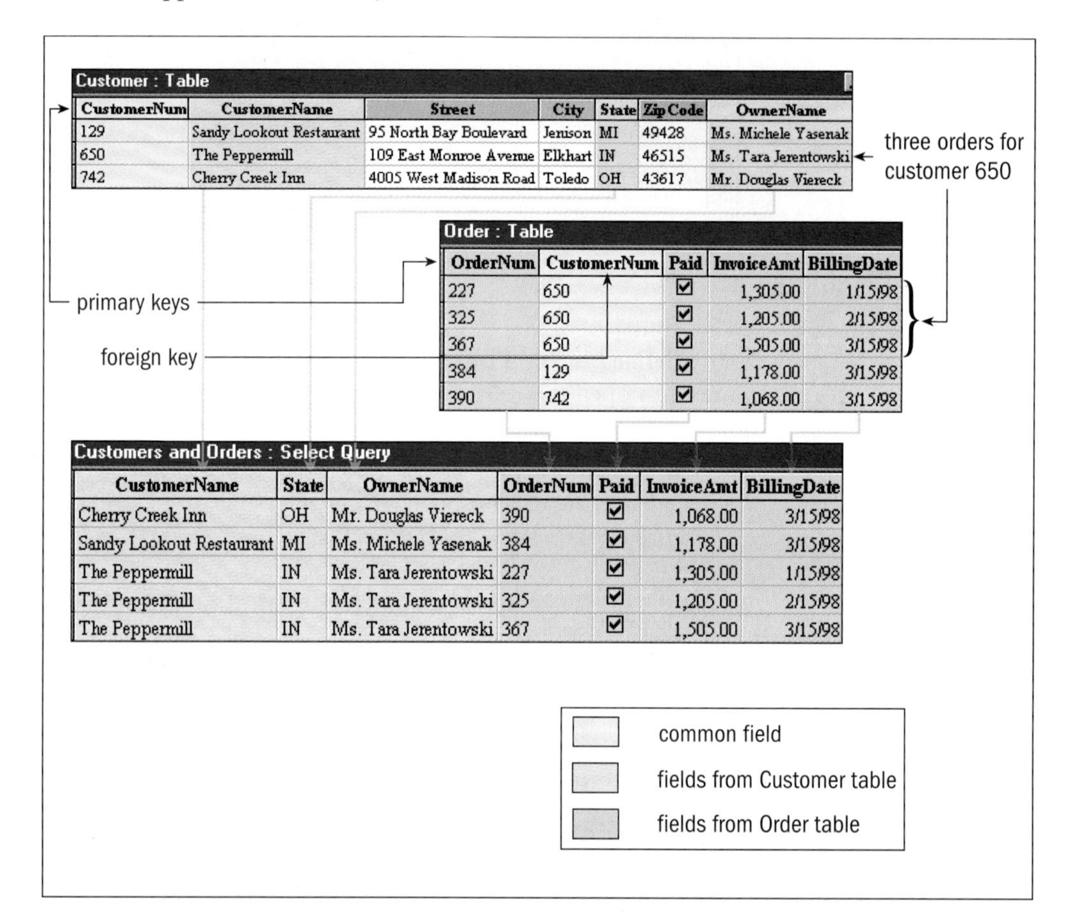

Customer : Table

CustomerNum	CustomerName	Street	City	State	Zip Code	OwnerName
129	Sandy Lookout Restaurant	95 North Bay Boulevard	Jenison	MI	49428	Ms. Michele Yasenak
650	The Peppermill	109 East Monroe Avenue	Elkhart	IN	46515	Ms. Tara Jerentowski
742	Cherry Creek Inn	4005 West Madison Road	Toledo	OH	43617	Mr. Douglas Viereck

Order : Table

OrderNum	CustomerNum	Paid	InvoiceAmt	BillingDate
227	650	☑	1,305.00	1/15/98
325	650	☑	1,205.00	2/15/98
367	650	☑	1,505.00	3/15/98
384	129	☑	1,178.00	3/15/98
390	742	☑	1,068.00	3/15/98

Customers and Orders : Select Query

CustomerName	State	OwnerName	OrderNum	Paid	InvoiceAmt	BillingDate
Cherry Creek Inn	OH	Mr. Douglas Viereck	390	☑	1,068.00	3/15/98
Sandy Lookout Restaurant	MI	Ms. Michele Yasenak	384	☑	1,178.00	3/15/98
The Peppermill	IN	Ms. Tara Jerentowski	227	☑	1,305.00	1/15/98
The Peppermill	IN	Ms. Tara Jerentowski	325	☑	1,205.00	2/15/98
The Peppermill	IN	Ms. Tara Jerentowski	367	☑	1,505.00	3/15/98

When you join tables that have a one-to-many relationship, you can extract data from them as if they were one larger table. For example, you can join the Customer and Order tables using the CustomerNum field in both tables to create the Customers and Orders query shown in Figure 7-3. In the query the CustomerName, State, and OwnerName columns are fields from the Customer table, and the OrderNum, Paid, InvoiceAmt, and BillingDate columns are fields from the Order table.

Many-To-Many Relationships

A **many-to-many relationship** exists between two tables when one record in the first table matches many records in the second table and one record in the second table matches many records in the first table.

The Coffee table contains data about each type of coffee marketed by Valle Coffee, and the Weight table contains data about the size and weight options for packaging each coffee. Because each coffee can be packaged in many ways, and each packaging option applies to many coffees, the Coffee and Weight tables have a many-to-many relationship, abbreviated M:N, as shown in Figure 7-4.

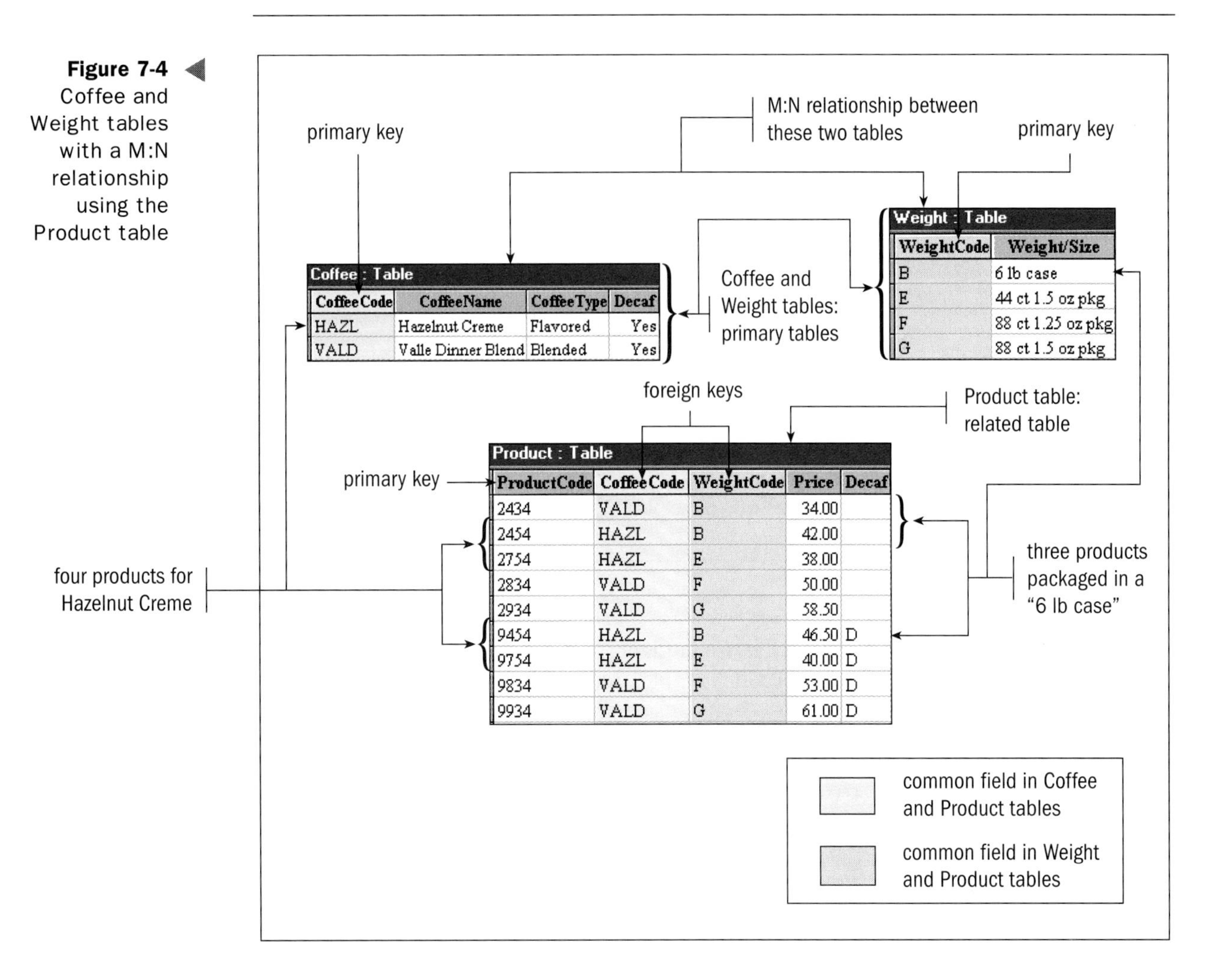

Coffee : Table

CoffeeCode	CoffeeName	CoffeeType	Decaf
HAZL	Hazelnut Creme	Flavored	Yes
VALD	Valle Dinner Blend	Blended	Yes

Weight : Table

WeightCode	Weight/Size
B	6 lb case
E	44 ct 1.5 oz pkg
F	88 ct 1.25 oz pkg
G	88 ct 1.5 oz pkg

Product : Table

ProductCode	CoffeeCode	WeightCode	Price	Decaf
2434	VALD	B	34.00	
2454	HAZL	B	42.00	
2754	HAZL	E	38.00	
2834	VALD	F	50.00	
2934	VALD	G	58.50	
9454	HAZL	B	46.50	D
9754	HAZL	E	40.00	D
9834	VALD	F	53.00	D
9934	VALD	G	61.00	D

Figure 7-4 Coffee and Weight tables with a M:N relationship using the Product table

When you have a many-to-many relationship between two tables, you must create a third table and form one-to-many relationships between the two tables and the new table. For instance, the Product table exists because the Coffee and Weight tables have a many-to-many relationship. Each record in the Product table contains two foreign keys: the CoffeeCode field is a foreign key that allows you to join the Product table to the Coffee table; and the WeightCode field is a foreign key that allows you to join the Product table to the Weight table. Thus, you define a many-to-many relationship between two tables by defining two one-to-many relationships between each table and a third table. For example, the third record in the Product table represents Hazelnut Creme, a flavored coffee, in the "44 ct 1.5 oz pkg" size. Hazelnut Creme, which has a CoffeeCode of HAZL, appears in four records in the Product table; these four Product records have two different WeightCode field values. Also, three Product records are packaged in a "6 lb case," represented by a WeightCode of B; these three Product records have two different CoffeeCode field values.

When two tables have a many-to-many relationship, why must a third table be used? Suppose the Weight and Coffee Product tables shown in Figure 7-5 were used for the many-to-many relationship between coffees and weights. In the Coffee Product table, the ProductCode field is the primary key, and the WeightCode field is a foreign key. The many-to-many relationship between the Weight and Coffee tables (in Figure 7-4) has been changed to a one-to-many relationship between the primary Weight table and the related Coffee Product table.

Figure 7-5 Redundant data resulting from an incorrect definition of a M:N relationship

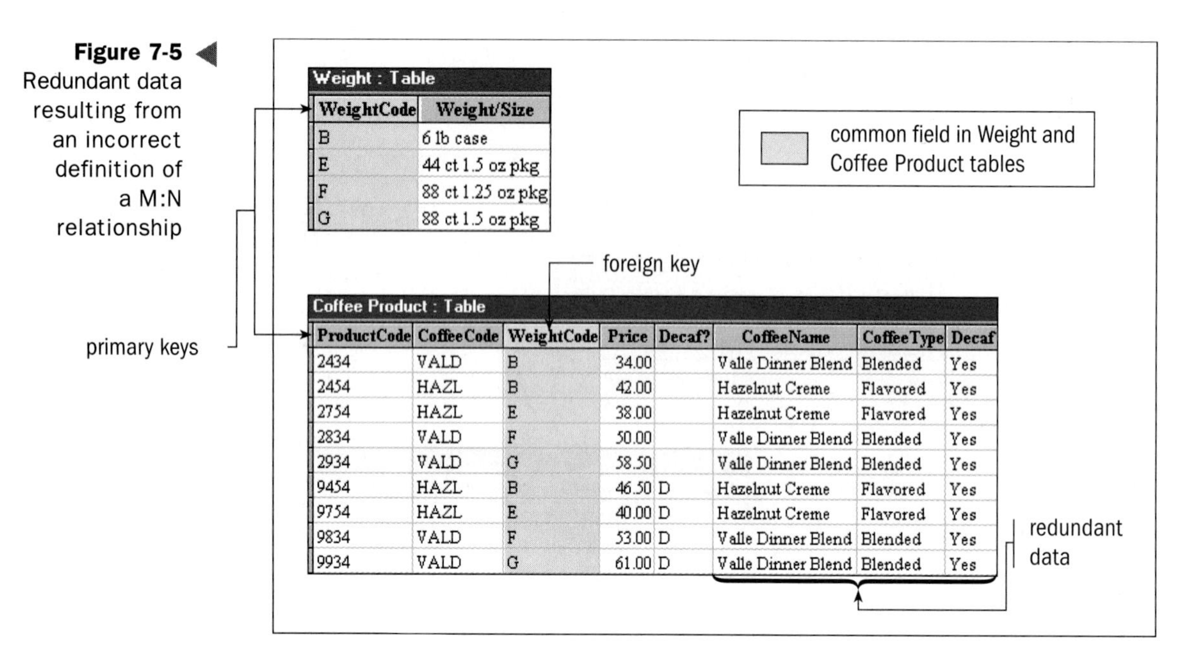

Weight : Table

WeightCode	Weight/Size
B	6 lb case
E	44 ct 1.5 oz pkg
F	88 ct 1.25 oz pkg
G	88 ct 1.5 oz pkg

Coffee Product : Table

ProductCode	CoffeeCode	WeightCode	Price	Decaf?	CoffeeName	CoffeeType	Decaf
2434	VALD	B	34.00		Valle Dinner Blend	Blended	Yes
2454	HAZL	B	42.00		Hazelnut Creme	Flavored	Yes
2754	HAZL	E	38.00		Hazelnut Creme	Flavored	Yes
2834	VALD	F	50.00		Valle Dinner Blend	Blended	Yes
2934	VALD	G	58.50		Valle Dinner Blend	Blended	Yes
9454	HAZL	B	46.50	D	Hazelnut Creme	Flavored	Yes
9754	HAZL	E	40.00	D	Hazelnut Creme	Flavored	Yes
9834	VALD	F	53.00	D	Valle Dinner Blend	Blended	Yes
9934	VALD	G	61.00	D	Valle Dinner Blend	Blended	Yes

Notice that data redundancy exists in the CoffeeName, CoffeeType, and Decaf fields in the Coffee Product table. As you learned in Tutorial 4, redundancy wastes storage space and can cause inconsistencies if, for instance, you type a field value one way in one record and a different way in another record. For example, it's possible that one of the records in the Coffee Product table with a CoffeeCode field value of VALD, which is the blended Valle Dinner Blend coffee, could be identified as the flavored Hazelnut Creme coffee if the value was entered incorrectly. Because of this data redundancy, the three-table design (Figure 7-4) is better than the two-table design (Figure 7-5) when a many-to-many relationship exists between two tables.

When you join tables that have a many-to-many relationship, you can extract data from them as if they were one larger table. For example, you can join the Coffee, Weight, and Product tables to create the Product Data query shown in Figure 7-6.

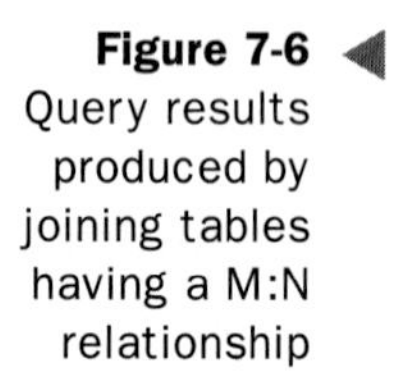

Figure 7-6 Query results produced by joining tables having a M:N relationship

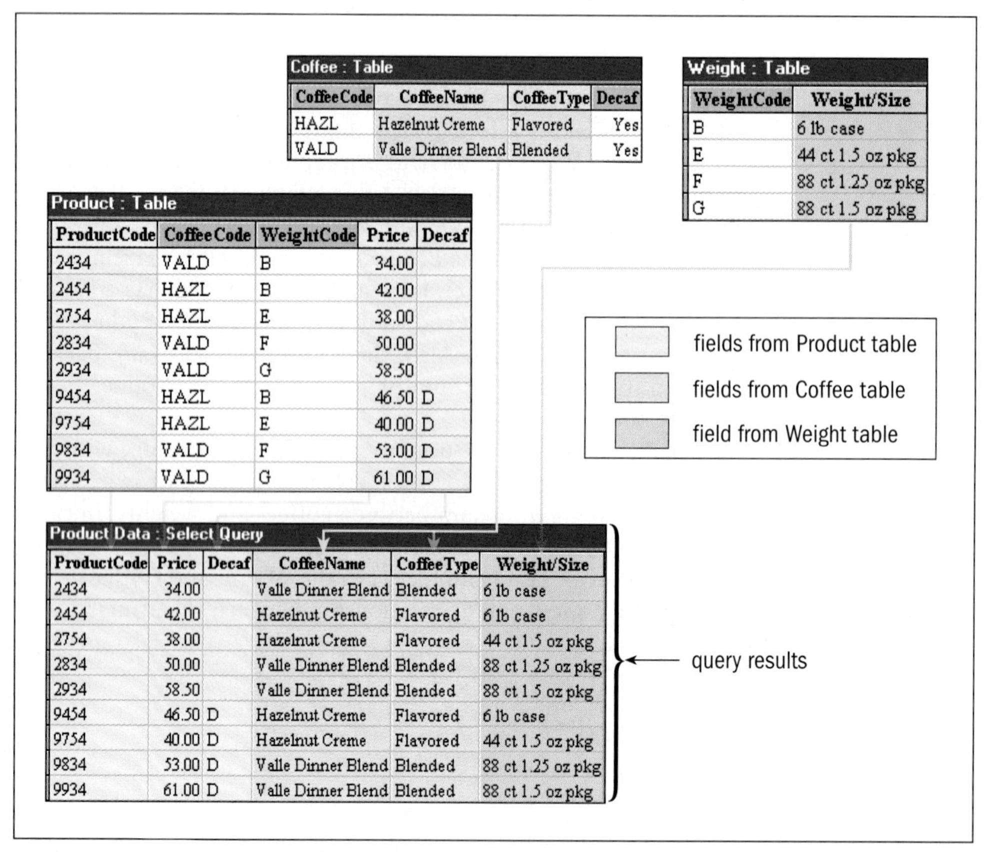

Coffee : Table

CoffeeCode	CoffeeName	CoffeeType	Decaf
HAZL	Hazelnut Creme	Flavored	Yes
VALD	Valle Dinner Blend	Blended	Yes

Weight : Table

WeightCode	Weight/Size
B	6 lb case
E	44 ct 1.5 oz pkg
F	88 ct 1.25 oz pkg
G	88 ct 1.5 oz pkg

Product : Table

ProductCode	CoffeeCode	WeightCode	Price	Decaf
2434	VALD	B	34.00	
2454	HAZL	B	42.00	
2754	HAZL	E	38.00	
2834	VALD	F	50.00	
2934	VALD	G	58.50	
9454	HAZL	B	46.50	D
9754	HAZL	E	40.00	D
9834	VALD	F	53.00	D
9934	VALD	G	61.00	D

Product Data : Select Query

ProductCode	Price	Decaf	CoffeeName	CoffeeType	Weight/Size
2434	34.00		Valle Dinner Blend	Blended	6 lb case
2454	42.00		Hazelnut Creme	Flavored	6 lb case
2754	38.00		Hazelnut Creme	Flavored	44 ct 1.5 oz pkg
2834	50.00		Valle Dinner Blend	Blended	88 ct 1.25 oz pkg
2934	58.50		Valle Dinner Blend	Blended	88 ct 1.5 oz pkg
9454	46.50	D	Hazelnut Creme	Flavored	6 lb case
9754	40.00	D	Hazelnut Creme	Flavored	44 ct 1.5 oz pkg
9834	53.00	D	Valle Dinner Blend	Blended	88 ct 1.25 oz pkg
9934	61.00	D	Valle Dinner Blend	Blended	88 ct 1.5 oz pkg

The CoffeeCode field is used to join the Coffee and Product tables, and the WeightCode field is used to join the Weight and Product tables. In the query the ProductCode, Price, and Decaf columns are fields from the Product table; the CoffeeName and CoffeeType columns are fields from the Coffee table; and the Weight/Size column is a field from the Weight table. The third record in the query results shows data from the third record in the Product table joined with data from the matching first record in the Coffee table and with data from the matching second record in the Weight table.

In Valle Coffee's Restaurant Coffee Orders database, the Order and Product tables also have a many-to-many relationship, as shown in Figure 7-7, because each order placed can be for more than one product, and each product can appear in more than one order. The Order Detail table ties together the Order and Product tables. Each record in the Order Detail table contains two common fields: the OrderNum field is a foreign key in the Order Detail table and is the primary key in the Order table; and the ProductCode field is a foreign key in the Order Detail table and is the primary key in the Product table. For example, OrderNum 384 in the Order table appears in four records in the Order Detail table; these four Order Detail records have four different ProductCode field values. Also, ProductCode 9834 in the Product table appears in five records in the Order Detail table; these five Order Detail records have five different OrderNum field values.

Figure 7-7 Order and Product tables with a M:N relationship using the Order Detail table

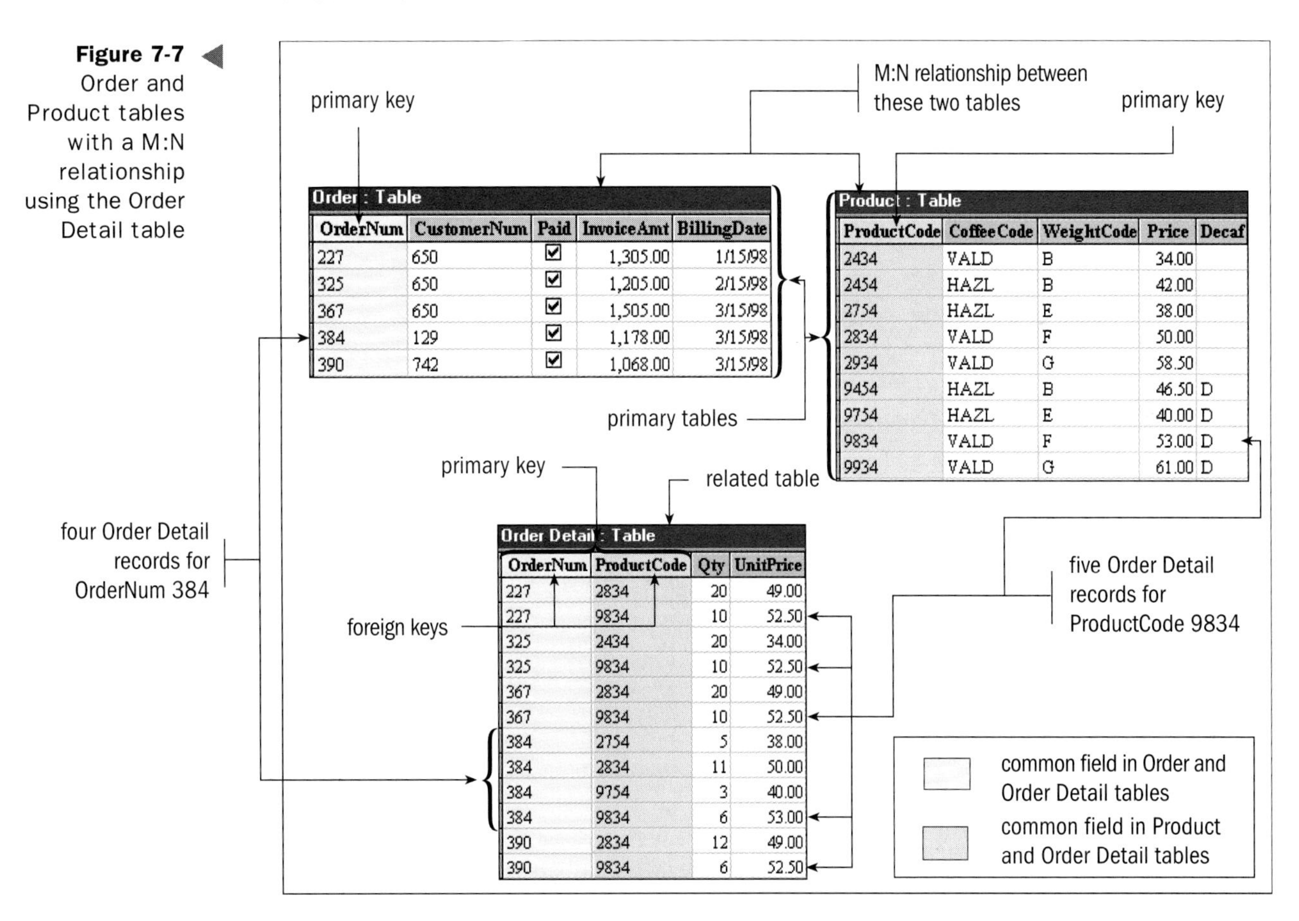

OrderNum	CustomerNum	Paid	InvoiceAmt	BillingDate
227	650	☑	1,305.00	1/15/98
325	650	☑	1,205.00	2/15/98
367	650	☑	1,505.00	3/15/98
384	129	☑	1,178.00	3/15/98
390	742	☑	1,068.00	3/15/98

ProductCode	CoffeeCode	WeightCode	Price	Decaf
2434	VALD	B	34.00	
2454	HAZL	B	42.00	
2754	HAZL	E	38.00	
2834	VALD	F	50.00	
2934	VALD	G	58.50	
9454	HAZL	B	46.50	D
9754	HAZL	E	40.00	D
9834	VALD	F	53.00	D
9934	VALD	G	61.00	D

OrderNum	ProductCode	Qty	UnitPrice
227	2834	20	49.00
227	9834	10	52.50
325	2434	20	34.00
325	9834	10	52.50
367	2834	20	49.00
367	9834	10	52.50
384	2754	5	38.00
384	2834	11	50.00
384	9754	3	40.00
384	9834	6	53.00
390	2834	12	49.00
390	9834	6	52.50

The OrderNum and ProductCode fields together serve as the primary key for the Order Detail table because both fields are needed to uniquely identify each record in the table. This is because each order placed can be for more than one product, and each product can appear in more than one order. For example, the first record in the Order Detail table represents OrderNum 227 and ProductCode 2834; the second record is also for OrderNum 227, but for ProductCode 9834. Therefore, the order placed for OrderNum 227 was for two products: 2834 and 9834.

You can extract data from the Order, Product, and Order Detail tables as if they were one larger table, as shown in Figure 7-8. The OrderNum field is used to join the Order and Order Detail tables, and the ProductCode field is used to join the Product and Order Detail tables. In the query the OrderNum, ProductCode, Qty, and UnitPrice columns are fields from the Order Detail table; the InvoiceAmt and BillingDate columns are fields from the Order table; and the CoffeeCode and WeightCode columns are fields from the Product table. The first record in the query results shows data from the first record in the Order Detail table joined with data from the matching first record in the Order table and with data from the matching fourth record in the Product table.

Figure 7-8 Query results produced by joining tables having a M:N relationship

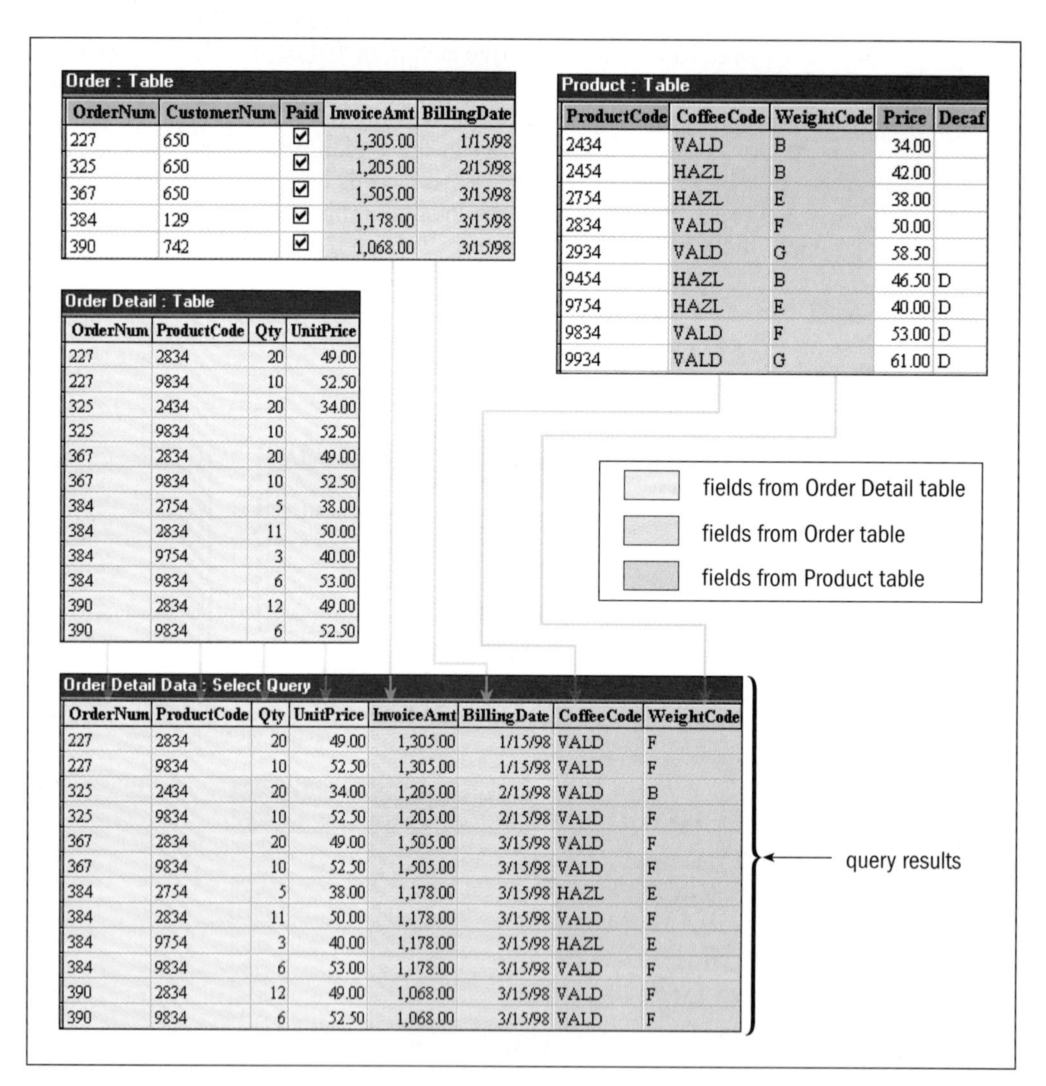

Order : Table

OrderNum	CustomerNum	Paid	InvoiceAmt	BillingDate
227	650	☑	1,305.00	1/15/98
325	650	☑	1,205.00	2/15/98
367	650	☑	1,505.00	3/15/98
384	129	☑	1,178.00	3/15/98
390	742	☑	1,068.00	3/15/98

Product : Table

ProductCode	CoffeeCode	WeightCode	Price	Decaf
2434	VALD	B	34.00	
2454	HAZL	B	42.00	
2754	HAZL	E	38.00	
2834	VALD	F	50.00	
2934	VALD	G	58.50	
9454	HAZL	B	46.50	D
9754	HAZL	E	40.00	D
9834	VALD	F	53.00	D
9934	VALD	G	61.00	D

Order Detail : Table

OrderNum	ProductCode	Qty	UnitPrice
227	2834	20	49.00
227	9834	10	52.50
325	2434	20	34.00
325	9834	10	52.50
367	2834	20	49.00
367	9834	10	52.50
384	2754	5	38.00
384	2834	11	50.00
384	9754	3	40.00
384	9834	6	53.00
390	2834	12	49.00
390	9834	6	52.50

Order Detail Data : Select Query

OrderNum	ProductCode	Qty	UnitPrice	InvoiceAmt	BillingDate	CoffeeCode	WeightCode
227	2834	20	49.00	1,305.00	1/15/98	VALD	F
227	9834	10	52.50	1,305.00	1/15/98	VALD	F
325	2434	20	34.00	1,205.00	2/15/98	VALD	B
325	9834	10	52.50	1,205.00	2/15/98	VALD	F
367	2834	20	49.00	1,505.00	3/15/98	VALD	F
367	9834	10	52.50	1,505.00	3/15/98	VALD	F
384	2754	5	38.00	1,178.00	3/15/98	HAZL	E
384	2834	11	50.00	1,178.00	3/15/98	VALD	F
384	9754	3	40.00	1,178.00	3/15/98	HAZL	E
384	9834	6	53.00	1,178.00	3/15/98	VALD	F
390	2834	12	49.00	1,068.00	3/15/98	VALD	F
390	9834	6	52.50	1,068.00	3/15/98	VALD	F

Barbara, Carlos, and their staff members, need to view specific data retrieved from the Restaurant Coffee Orders database on a regular basis. To find the data they want to view, you need to query the database. First, Barbara wants to display customer and order information for all orders billed on 3/15/98 so she can see which orders have been paid. For this request you need to create a query that displays selected fields from the Order and Customer tables and selected records that satisfy a condition.

Defining Record Selection Criteria for Queries

As you learned in Tutorial 4, to display specific records from a database, you need to enter a condition as part of the query. A **condition** is a criterion, or rule, that determines which records are selected. A condition usually consists of an operator, often a comparison operator, and a value. A **comparison operator** asks Access to compare the values of a database field to the condition value and to select all the records for which the relationship is true. For example, the condition >8.99 for the Price field selects all records in the Product table having Price field values greater than 8.99. The Access comparison operators are shown in Figure 7-9.

Figure 7-9 Access comparison operators

Operator	Meaning
<	less than
<=	less than or equal to
>	greater than
>=	greater than or equal to
<>	not equal to

Specifying an Exact Match

For Barbara's first request, you need to create a query that will display only those records in the Order table with the value 3/15/98 in the BillingDate field. This type of condition is called an **exact match** because the value in the specified field must match the condition exactly in order for the record to be included in the query results.

First you need to close the Relationships window, then start a new query using the Simple Query Wizard. This Query Wizard prompts you through the steps to create a query.

To create the query using the Simple Query Wizard:

1. Click the **Close** button on the Relationships window title bar, click the **Queries** tab in the Database window, then click the **New** button. The New Query dialog box opens.
2. Click **Simple Query Wizard** then click the **OK** button. Access opens the first Simple Query Wizard dialog box, in which you select the tables and fields for the query.
3. Click the **Tables/Queries** list arrow, then click **Table: Order**. The fields in the Order table appear in the Available Fields list box. See Figure 7-10.

Figure 7-10 First Simple Query Wizard dialog box

selected table

move needed fields here

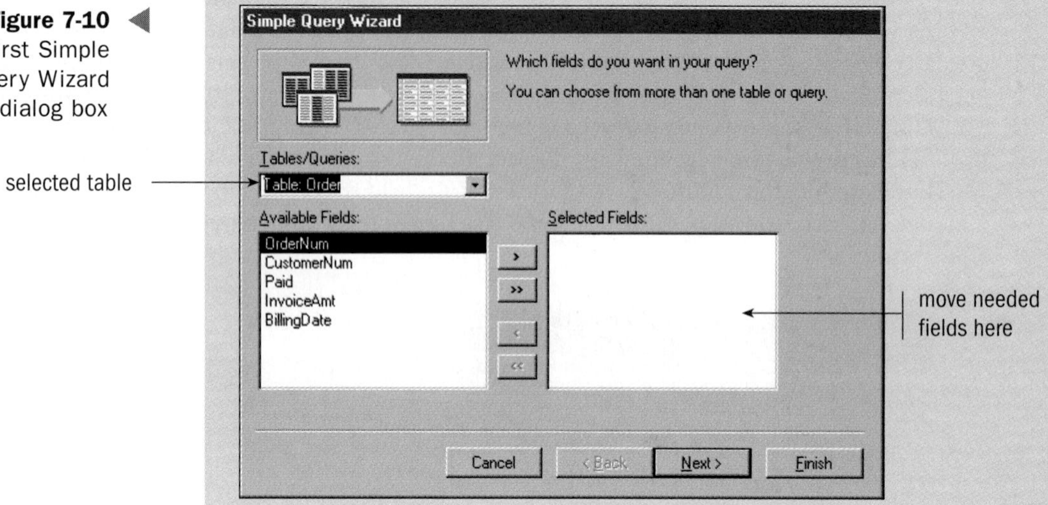

Except for the CustomerNum field, you will include all fields from the Order table in the query.

4. Click the **>>** button. Access removes all the fields from the Available Fields list box and places them in the same order in the Selected Fields list box.
5. Click **CustomerNum** in the Selected Fields list box, click the **<** button to move the CustomerNum field back to the Available Fields list box, then click **BillingDate** in the Selected Fields list box.

   Barbara also wants certain information from the Customer table included in the query results.
6. Click the **Tables/Queries** list arrow, then click **Table: Customer**. The fields in the Customer table now appear in the Available Fields list box.
7. Click **CustomerName** in the Available Fields list box, then click the **>** button to move CustomerName to the Selected Fields list box.
8. Repeat Step 7 for the **State**, **OwnerName**, and **Phone** fields.
9. Click the **Next** button to open the second Simple Query Wizard dialog box, in which you choose whether the query will display records from the selected tables or a summary of those records. Barbara wants to view the details for the records, not a summary.
10. Make sure the Detail radio button is selected, then click the **Next** button to open the last Simple Query Wizard dialog box, in which you choose a name for the query and complete the wizard. You need to enter a condition for the query, so you'll want to modify the query's design.
11. Type **March Orders**, click the **Modify the query design** radio button, then click the **Finish** button. Access saves the query as March Orders, then opens the query in Design view. See Figure 7-11.

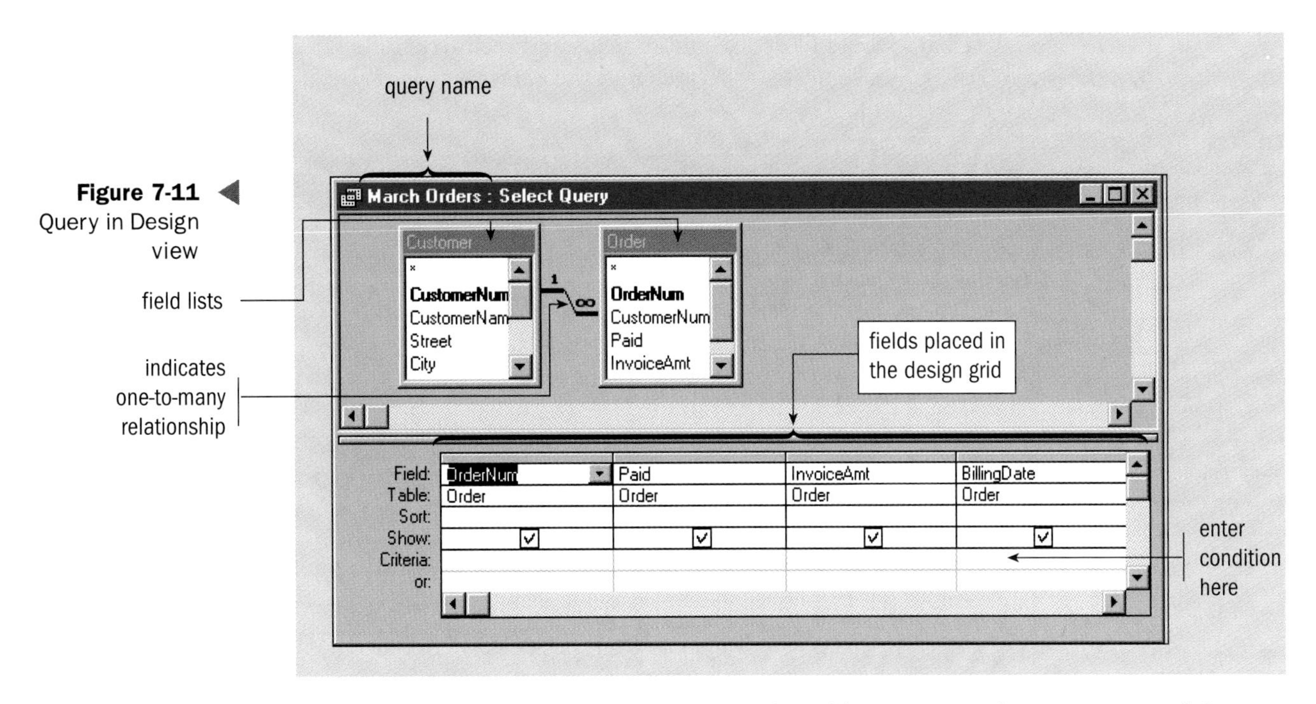

Figure 7-11 Query in Design view

The field lists for the Customer and Order tables appear in the top portion of the window, and the join line indicating a one-to-many relationship connects the two tables. The selected fields appear in the design grid. Not all the fields are visible in the grid; to see the other selected fields, you need to scroll to the right using the horizontal scroll bar.

To display the information Barbara wants, you need to enter the condition for the BillingDate field in its Criteria text box. Recall that Barbara wants to display only those records with a billing date of 3/15/98.

To enter the exact match condition, then run the query:

1. Click the **BillingDate Criteria** text box, type **3/15/98**, then click the **InvoiceAmt Criteria** text box. Access changes the condition to #3/15/98#.

   Access automatically placed number signs (#) before and after the condition. You must place date and time values inside number signs. If you omit the number signs, however, Access will include them automatically.

2. Click the **Run** button on the Query Design toolbar. Access runs the query and displays the selected field values for only those records with a BillingDate field value of 3/15/98. A total of 36 records are selected and displayed in the datasheet. See Figure 7-12.

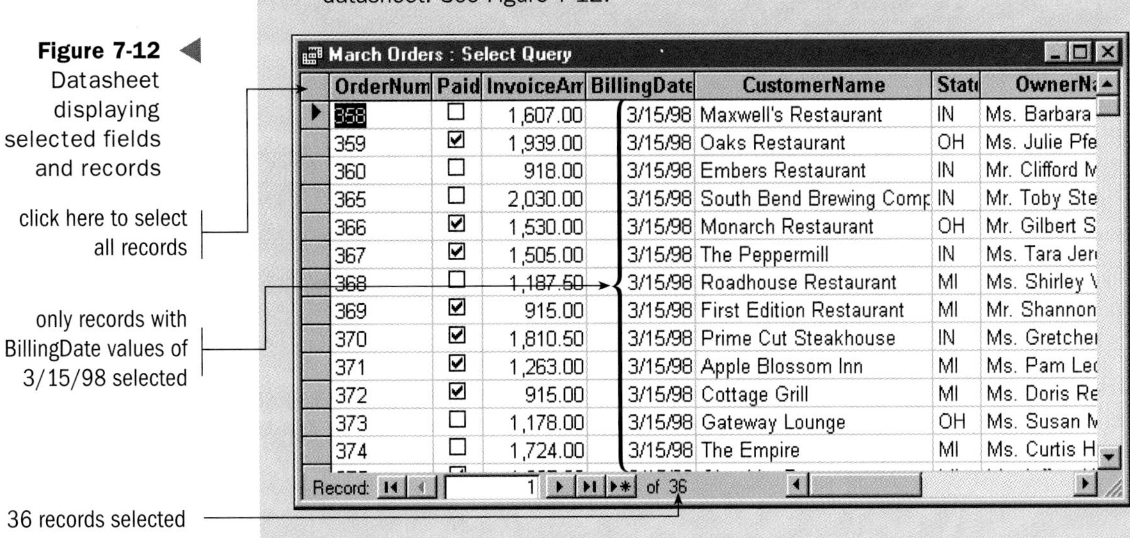

OrderNum	Paid	InvoiceAm	BillingDate	CustomerName	Stat	OwnerN
358	☐	1,607.00	3/15/98	Maxwell's Restaurant	IN	Ms. Barbara
359	☑	1,939.00	3/15/98	Oaks Restaurant	OH	Ms. Julie Pfe
360	☐	918.00	3/15/98	Embers Restaurant	IN	Mr. Clifford M
365	☐	2,030.00	3/15/98	South Bend Brewing Comp	IN	Mr. Toby Ste
366	☑	1,530.00	3/15/98	Monarch Restaurant	OH	Mr. Gilbert S
367	☑	1,505.00	3/15/98	The Peppermill	IN	Ms. Tara Jer
368	☐	1,187.50	3/15/98	Roadhouse Restaurant	MI	Ms. Shirley \
369	☑	915.00	3/15/98	First Edition Restaurant	MI	Mr. Shannon
370	☑	1,810.50	3/15/98	Prime Cut Steakhouse	IN	Ms. Gretche
371	☑	1,263.00	3/15/98	Apple Blossom Inn	MI	Ms. Pam Lec
372	☑	915.00	3/15/98	Cottage Grill	MI	Ms. Doris Re
373	☐	1,178.00	3/15/98	Gateway Lounge	OH	Ms. Susan M
374	☐	1,724.00	3/15/98	The Empire	MI	Ms. Curtis H

Figure 7-12 Datasheet displaying selected fields and records

Barbara would like to see more fields and records on the screen at one time. She asks you to maximize the datasheet, change the datasheet's font size, and resize all the columns to their best fit.

Changing a Datasheet's Appearance

You can change the characteristics of a datasheet, including the font type and size of text in the datasheet, to improve its appearance or readability—just as you can make these types of changes in the other Office 95 programs. You can also resize the datasheet columns to view more columns on the screen at the same time.

You'll maximize the datasheet, change the font from the default Arial 10 to Arial 8, then resize the datasheet columns.

To change the font size and resize columns in the datasheet:

1. Click the **Maximize** button on the Query window.
2. Click the **record selector** to the left of the field names at the top of the datasheet (see Figure 7-12). The entire datasheet is selected.
3. Click **Format** on the menu bar, then click **Font** to open the Font list box.
4. Scroll the Size list box, click **8**, then click the **OK** button. The font size for the entire datasheet changes to 8.

   Next you need to resize the columns to their best fit—that is, so each column is just wide enough to fit the longest value in the column.

5. Position the pointer in the OrderNum field selector. When the pointer changes to ⬇, click to select the entire column.
6. If necessary, click the horizontal scroll right arrow until the Phone field appears, and position the pointer in the Phone field selector until the pointer changes to ⬇.
7. Press and hold the **Shift** key, then click the mouse button. All the columns are selected. Now you can resize all of them at once.
8. Position the pointer at the right edge of the Phone field selector until the pointer changes to ✛. See Figure 7-13.

all columns selected

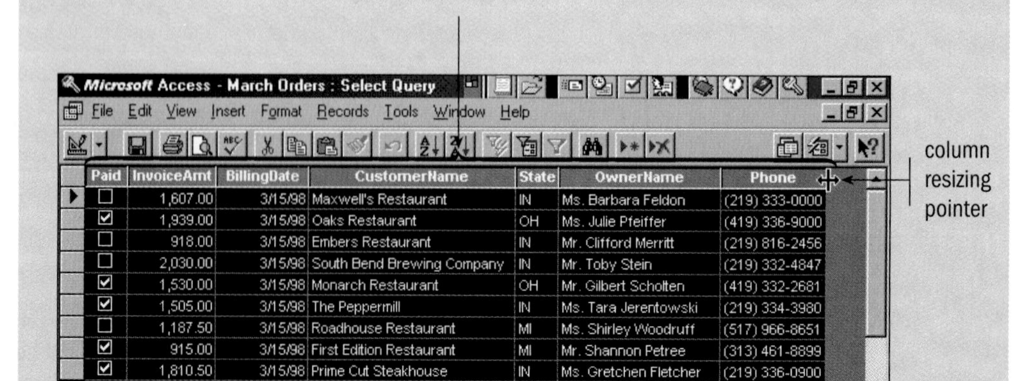

Paid	InvoiceAmt	BillingDate	CustomerName	State	OwnerName	Phone
☐	1,607.00	3/15/98	Maxwell's Restaurant	IN	Ms. Barbara Feldon	(219) 333-0000
☑	1,939.00	3/15/98	Oaks Restaurant	OH	Ms. Julie Pfeiffer	(419) 336-9000
☐	918.00	3/15/98	Embers Restaurant	IN	Mr. Clifford Merritt	(219) 816-2456
☐	2,030.00	3/15/98	South Bend Brewing Company	IN	Mr. Toby Stein	(219) 332-4847
☑	1,530.00	3/15/98	Monarch Restaurant	OH	Mr. Gilbert Scholten	(419) 332-2681
☑	1,505.00	3/15/98	The Peppermill	IN	Ms. Tara Jerentowski	(219) 334-3980
☐	1,187.50	3/15/98	Roadhouse Restaurant	MI	Ms. Shirley Woodruff	(517) 966-8651
☑	915.00	3/15/98	First Edition Restaurant	MI	Mr. Shannon Petree	(313) 461-8899
☑	1,810.50	3/15/98	Prime Cut Steakhouse	IN	Ms. Gretchen Fletcher	(219) 336-0900

Figure 7-13 Preparing to resize all columns to their best fit

9. Double-click the mouse button. All columns are resized to their best fit, which makes each column just large enough to fit the longest visible field value in the column, including the field name at the top of the column. Scroll through the datasheet and resize the columns as necessary to completely display all field values.

10. If necessary, scroll to the left so that the OrderNum field is visible, then click any field value box to deselect all columns. See Figure 7-14.

Figure 7-14
Datasheet after changing font size and column widths

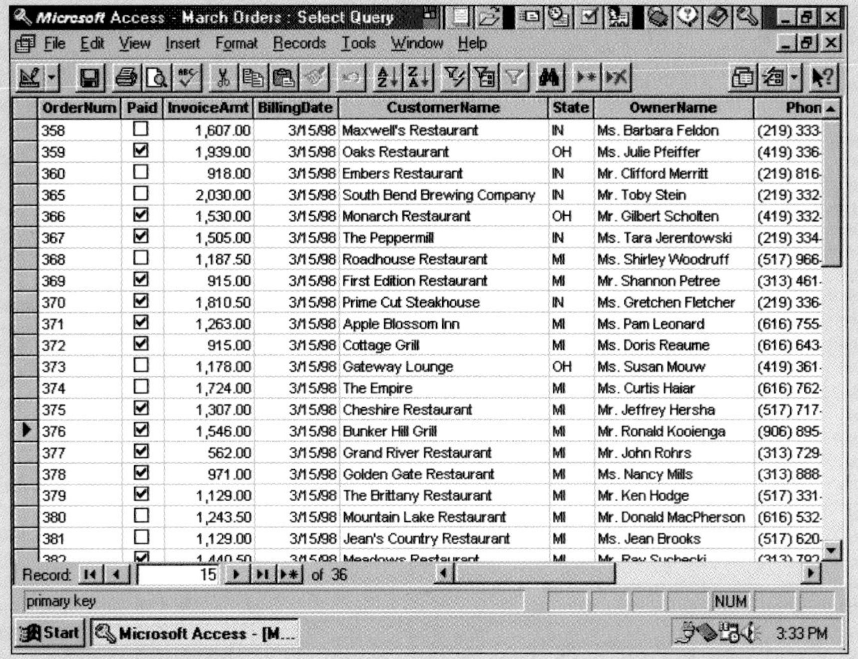

OrderNum	Paid	InvoiceAmt	BillingDate	CustomerName	State	OwnerName	Phon
358	☐	1,607.00	3/15/98	Maxwell's Restaurant	IN	Ms. Barbara Feldon	(219) 333-
359	☑	1,939.00	3/15/98	Oaks Restaurant	OH	Ms. Julie Pfeiffer	(419) 336-
360	☐	918.00	3/15/98	Embers Restaurant	IN	Mr. Clifford Merritt	(219) 816-
365	☐	2,030.00	3/15/98	South Bend Brewing Company	IN	Mr. Toby Stein	(219) 332-
366	☑	1,530.00	3/15/98	Monarch Restaurant	OH	Mr. Gilbert Scholten	(419) 332-
367	☑	1,505.00	3/15/98	The Peppermill	IN	Ms. Tara Jerentowski	(219) 334-
368	☐	1,187.50	3/15/98	Roadhouse Restaurant	MI	Ms. Shirley Woodruff	(517) 966-
369	☑	915.00	3/15/98	First Edition Restaurant	MI	Mr. Shannon Petree	(313) 461-
370	☑	1,810.50	3/15/98	Prime Cut Steakhouse	IN	Ms. Gretchen Fletcher	(219) 336-
371	☑	1,263.00	3/15/98	Apple Blossom Inn	MI	Ms. Pam Leonard	(616) 755-
372	☑	915.00	3/15/98	Cottage Grill	MI	Ms. Doris Reaume	(616) 643-
373	☐	1,178.00	3/15/98	Gateway Lounge	OH	Ms. Susan Mouw	(419) 361-
374	☐	1,724.00	3/15/98	The Empire	MI	Ms. Curtis Haiar	(616) 762-
375	☑	1,307.00	3/15/98	Cheshire Restaurant	MI	Mr. Jeffrey Hersha	(517) 717-
376	☑	1,546.00	3/15/98	Bunker Hill Grill	MI	Mr. Ronald Kooienga	(906) 895-
377	☑	562.00	3/15/98	Grand River Restaurant	MI	Mr. John Rohrs	(313) 729-
378	☑	971.00	3/15/98	Golden Gate Restaurant	MI	Ms. Nancy Mills	(313) 888-
379	☑	1,129.00	3/15/98	The Brittany Restaurant	MI	Mr. Ken Hodge	(517) 331-
380	☐	1,243.50	3/15/98	Mountain Lake Restaurant	MI	Mr. Donald MacPherson	(616) 532-
381	☐	1,129.00	3/15/98	Jean's Country Restaurant	MI	Ms. Jean Brooks	(517) 620-

TROUBLE? Your screen might show more or fewer columns depending on the monitor you are using.

11. Click the **Save** button on the Query Datasheet toolbar, then click the **Close** button on the menu bar. Access saves and closes the query, and you return to the Database window.

After viewing the query results and determining which orders had been paid, Barbara decided that she would like to see the same fields but only for those records whose InvoiceAmt exceeds $2,000. She wants to note this information and pass it along to the accounting department so that they can contact those customers with higher outstanding invoices. To create the query needed to produce these results, you need to use a comparison operator to match a range of values—in this case, any InvoiceAmt value greater than $2,000.

Using a Comparison Operator to Match a Range of Values

Once you create and save a query, you can click the Open button to run it again or you can click the Design button to change its design. Because the design of the query you need to create next is similar to the March Orders query, you will change its design, run the query to test it, then save the query with a new name, keeping the March Orders query intact.

To change the March Orders query design to create a new query:

1. In the Database window, click the **Design** button. Access opens the March Orders query in Design view.

2. Click the **InvoiceAmt Criteria** text box, type **>2000**, then press the **Tab** key. See Figure 7-15.

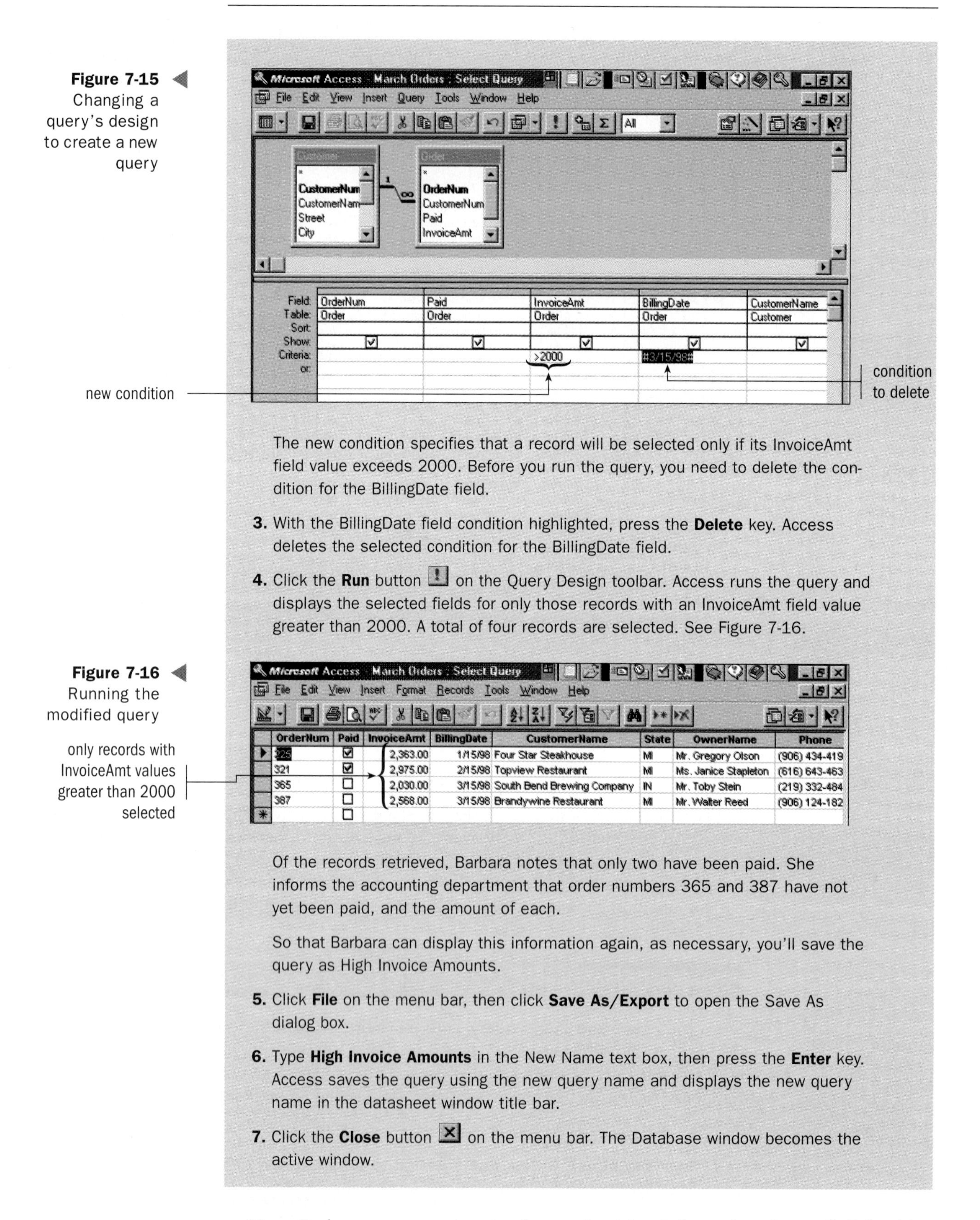

Figure 7-15 Changing a query's design to create a new query

The new condition specifies that a record will be selected only if its InvoiceAmt field value exceeds 2000. Before you run the query, you need to delete the condition for the BillingDate field.

3. With the BillingDate field condition highlighted, press the **Delete** key. Access deletes the selected condition for the BillingDate field.

4. Click the **Run** button on the Query Design toolbar. Access runs the query and displays the selected fields for only those records with an InvoiceAmt field value greater than 2000. A total of four records are selected. See Figure 7-16.

Figure 7-16 Running the modified query

Of the records retrieved, Barbara notes that only two have been paid. She informs the accounting department that order numbers 365 and 387 have not yet been paid, and the amount of each.

So that Barbara can display this information again, as necessary, you'll save the query as High Invoice Amounts.

5. Click **File** on the menu bar, then click **Save As/Export** to open the Save As dialog box.

6. Type **High Invoice Amounts** in the New Name text box, then press the **Enter** key. Access saves the query using the new query name and displays the new query name in the datasheet window title bar.

7. Click the **Close** button on the menu bar. The Database window becomes the active window.

Next, Barbara wants to view product and pricing information about all Colombian coffee products. Valle Coffee's costs for purchasing Colombian coffees are increasing, and Barbara wants to make sure that the pricing and packaging of these products are appropriate, given this trend. To find the information Barbara wants, you need to use a pattern match in a query.

Using a Pattern Match

Access provides several special operators you can use in conditions. Figure 7-17 describes the most commonly used special operators. The comparison and special operators are not case-sensitive; you can enter them in any combination of uppercase and lowercase letters. For example, you can enter Like "Colombian*" or liKe "Colombian*" for the third operator listed in Figure 7-17 to find all records beginning with the word "Colombian." The field values also do not have to match in case; for example, you can enter Like "colombian*" or Like "COLOMBIAN*" to perform the same pattern match. A **pattern match** uses the Like operator to select records by matching field values to a specific pattern that includes one or more wildcard characters (* ? [ ] ! - #). As you learned in Tutorial 4, a **wildcard character** is a placeholder you use when you know only part of a value or when you want to start or end with a specific character or match a certain pattern. For example, you can use the asterisk (*) wildcard character as the first or last character in a character string to match any number of characters.

Figure 7-17 Access special operators

Operator	Records Selected If the Specified Field Value	Example
Between...And	Is between the two values, inclusively	Between 1500 And 2000
In ( )	Matches any one of the listed values	In (7.99, 8.99, 9.99)
Like	Matches a pattern that includes wildcard characters of * ? [ ] ! - #	Like "Colombian*"
Not	Does not match the condition	Not =#3/15/98#

To display the information Barbara wants to view, you'll again use the Simple Query Wizard to select the fields for the query.

To create the query using the Simple Query Wizard:

1. In the Database window, click the **New** button to open the New Query dialog box, click **Simple Query Wizard** in the list box, then click the **OK** button. Access opens the first Simple Query Wizard dialog box, in which you select the tables and fields for the query.

   Barbara wants to view the ProductCode, Price, and Decaf field values from the Product table; the CoffeeName and CoffeeType field values from the Coffee table; and the Weight/Size field values from the Weight table.

2. Click the **Tables/Queries** list arrow, then click **Table: Product**. The fields in the Product table appear in the Available Fields list box.
3. Click **ProductCode** then click the **>** button to move the ProductCode field from the Available Fields list box to the Selected Fields list box.
4. Repeat Step 3 for the **Price** and **Decaf** fields.
5. Click the **Tables/Queries** list arrow, then click **Table: Coffee**. The fields in the Coffee table now appear in the Available Fields list box.
6. Repeat Step 3 for the **CoffeeName** and **CoffeeType** fields.
7. Repeat Steps 5 and 6 for the **Table: Weight** table and the **Weight/Size** field.

8. Click the **Next** button to open the second Simple Query Wizard dialog box, make sure the Detail radio button is selected, then click the **Next** button to open the last Simple Query Wizard dialog box, in which you choose a name for the query and complete the wizard. You need to enter a condition for the query, so you'll want to modify the query's design.

9. Type **Colombian**, click the **Modify the query design** radio button, then click the **Finish** button. Access saves the query as Colombian, then displays the query in Design view. See Figure 7-18.

Figure 7-18 Design view displaying three joined tables

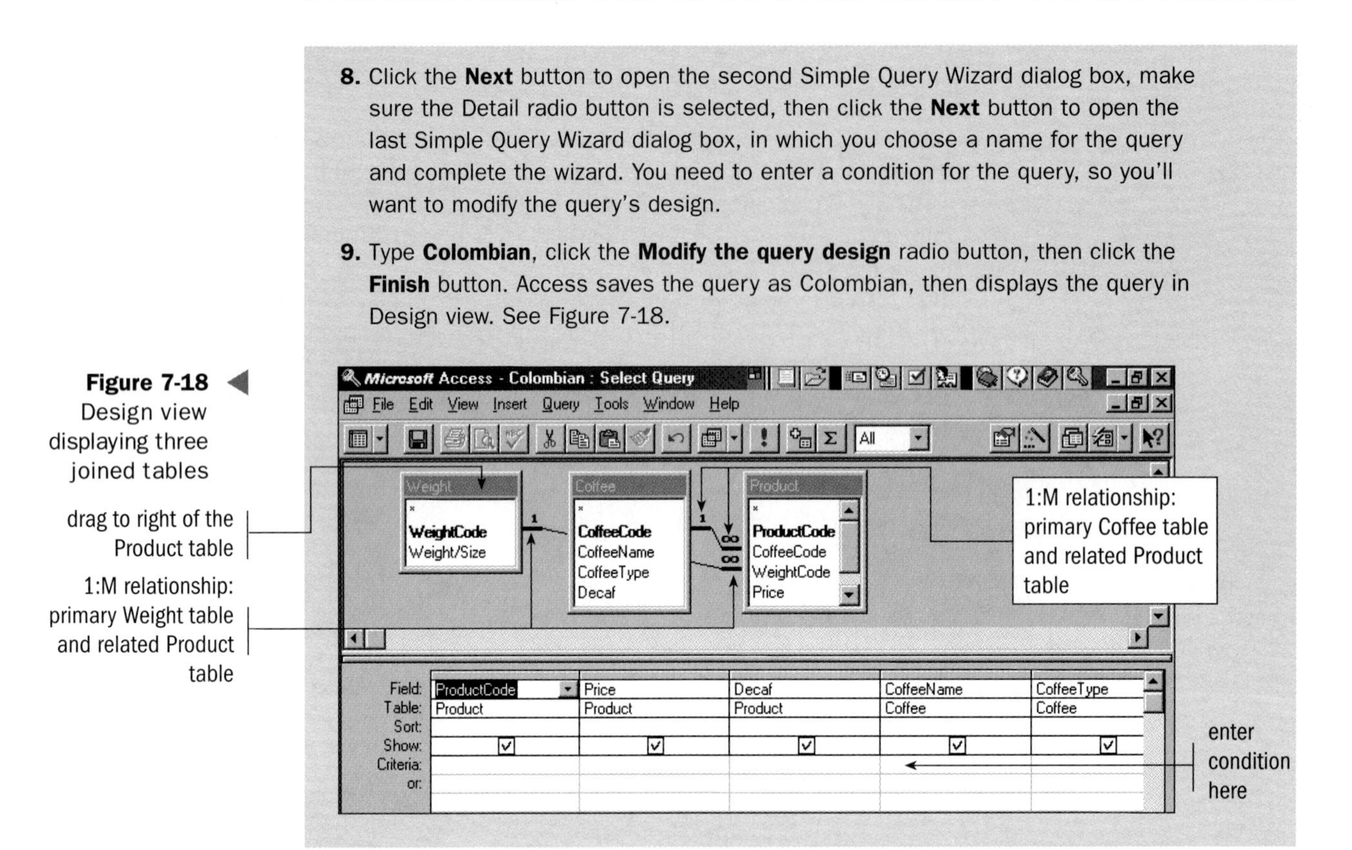

The field list for the Product table, the first table selected in the Simple Query Wizard, appears as the rightmost table in Design view; and the field list for the Weight table, the last table selected in the Simple Query Wizard, appears as the leftmost table. One join line connects the CoffeeCode fields in the Coffee and Product field lists and depicts a one-to-many relationship between the primary Coffee table (1) and the related Product table (∞). A second join line connects the WeightCode fields in the Weight and Product field lists and depicts a one-to-many relationship between the primary Weight table (1) and the related Product table (∞).

Because the Coffee field list was placed between the Weight and Product field lists, the second join line is partially obscured. You'll move the Weight field list to the right of the Product field list to display the entire join line between them. Then you will enter the condition for the CoffeeName field to specify that only Colombian coffee records will be included in the query results.

To move the Weight field list, enter the pattern match condition, and run the query:

1. Click the **Weight field list title bar**, then drag the field list to the right of the Product field list. Release the mouse button when the join line and its symbols are clearly visible.

   Barbara wants to view just Colombian coffee products, which all have CoffeeName field values starting with the word "Colombian." You'll enter the pattern match *like Colombian**—the * wildcard character matches any number of characters that follow the word "Colombian" in a CoffeeName field value.

2. Click the **CoffeeName Criteria** text box, type **like Colombian***, then click the **Decaf Criteria** text box. Access changes the condition to Like "Colombian*". See Figure 7-19.

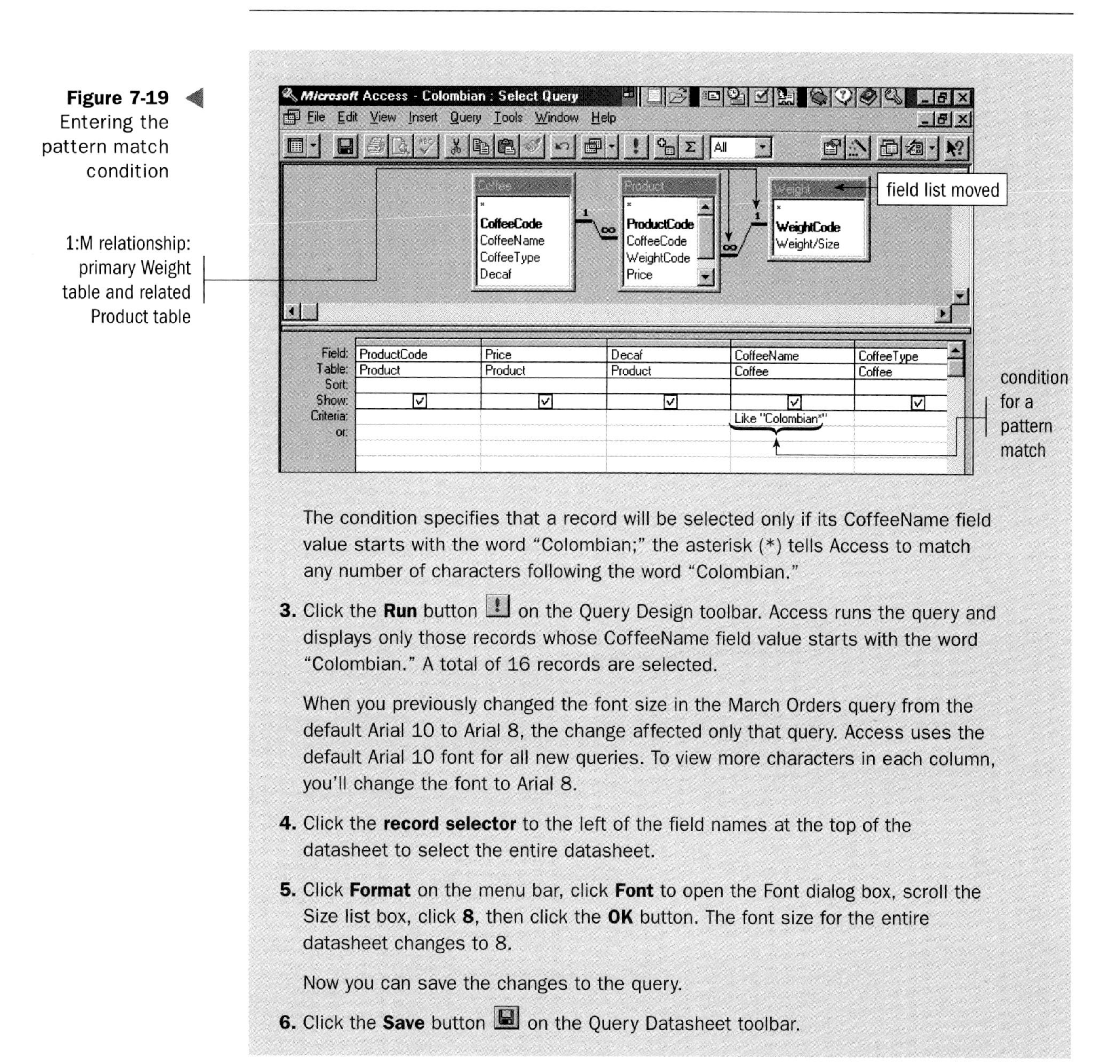

Figure 7-19 Entering the pattern match condition

The condition specifies that a record will be selected only if its CoffeeName field value starts with the word "Colombian;" the asterisk (*) tells Access to match any number of characters following the word "Colombian."

3. Click the **Run** button on the Query Design toolbar. Access runs the query and displays only those records whose CoffeeName field value starts with the word "Colombian." A total of 16 records are selected.

   When you previously changed the font size in the March Orders query from the default Arial 10 to Arial 8, the change affected only that query. Access uses the default Arial 10 font for all new queries. To view more characters in each column, you'll change the font to Arial 8.

4. Click the **record selector** to the left of the field names at the top of the datasheet to select the entire datasheet.

5. Click **Format** on the menu bar, click **Font** to open the Font dialog box, scroll the Size list box, click **8**, then click the **OK** button. The font size for the entire datasheet changes to 8.

   Now you can save the changes to the query.

6. Click the **Save** button on the Query Datasheet toolbar.

Valle Coffee's profit margin for decaf Colombian coffees is lower than for regular Colombian coffees, so Barbara wants to review the pricing and packaging of the decaf Colombian coffees. This query involves two conditions.

Defining Multiple Selection Criteria for Queries

Multiple conditions require you to use **logical operators** to combine two or more conditions. When you want a record selected only if two or more conditions are met, you need to use the **And logical operator**. For example, if you want to select records only for the CoffeeName field values of "Valle Dinner Blend" *and* "Valle Gourmet Blend," you would enter the condition "Like "Valle*" And Like "*Blend"." If you place conditions in separate fields in the *same* Criteria row of the design grid, all the conditions in that row must be met in order for a record to be included in the query results. However, if you place conditions in *different* Criteria rows, Access selects a record if at least one of the conditions is met. If none of the conditions is met, then Access does not select the record. This is known as the **Or logical operator**. The difference between these two logical operators is illustrated in Figure 7-20.

Figure 7-20 Logical operators And and Or for multiple selection criteria

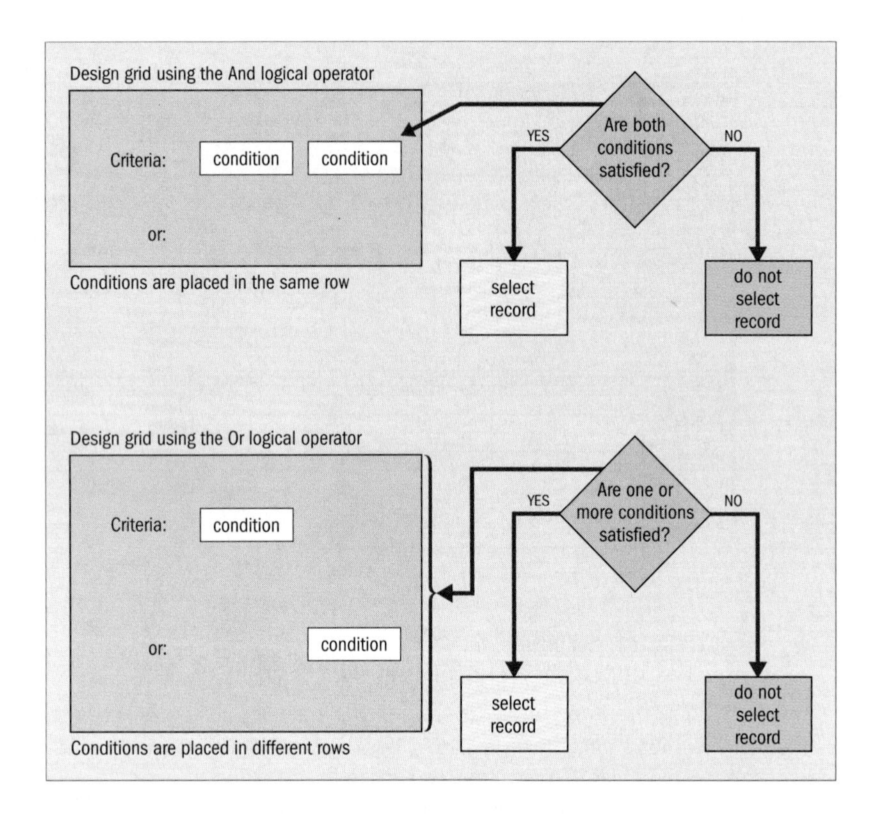

The And Logical Operator

You need to change the Colombian query to display only the decaf Colombian coffees. For the modified query, you must place two conditions in the same Criteria row. The condition *"D"* for the Decaf field finds records for decaf coffees, and the condition *Like "Colombian*"* finds records with coffee names starting with the word "Colombian." Because the conditions appear in the same Criteria row, Access selects records only if both conditions are met.

To modify the query and use the And logical operator:

1. Click the **Query View** button for Design view on the Query Datasheet toolbar to switch back to Design view.
2. Click the **Decaf Criteria** text box, then type **"D"**. See Figure 7-21.

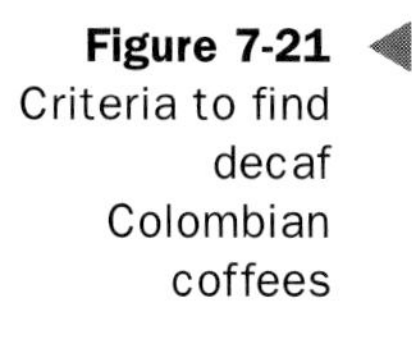

Figure 7-21
Criteria to find decaf Colombian coffees

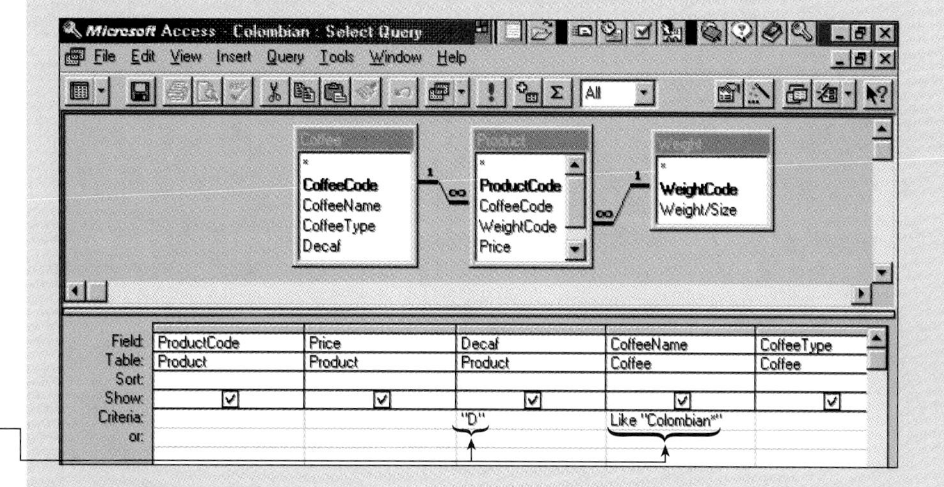

The condition for the CoffeeName field is already entered, so you can run the query.

3. Click the **Run** button on the Query Design toolbar. Access runs the query and displays in the datasheet only those records that meet both conditions: a Decaf field value D and a CoffeeName field value starting with the word "Colombian." A total of eight records are selected. See Figure 7-22.

Figure 7-22
Results of query using the And logical operator

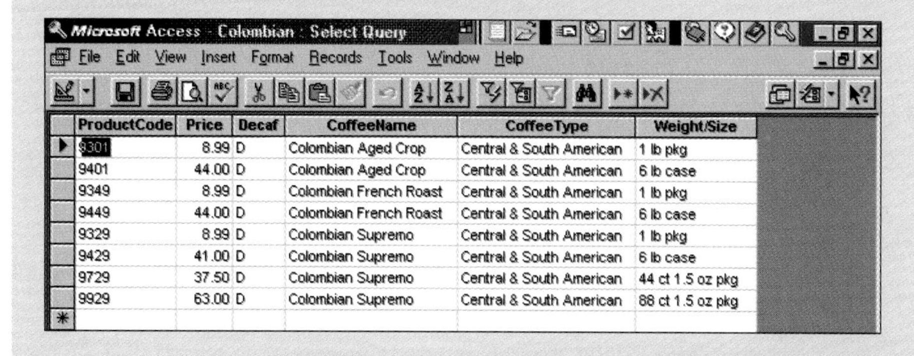

ProductCode	Price	Decaf	CoffeeName	CoffeeType	Weight/Size
9301	8.99	D	Colombian Aged Crop	Central & South American	1 lb pkg
9401	44.00	D	Colombian Aged Crop	Central & South American	6 lb case
9349	8.99	D	Colombian French Roast	Central & South American	1 lb pkg
9449	44.00	D	Colombian French Roast	Central & South American	6 lb case
9329	8.99	D	Colombian Supremo	Central & South American	1 lb pkg
9429	41.00	D	Colombian Supremo	Central & South American	6 lb case
9729	37.50	D	Colombian Supremo	Central & South American	44 ct 1.5 oz pkg
9929	63.00	D	Colombian Supremo	Central & South American	88 ct 1.5 oz pkg

Now you can save the changes to the query, then rename the query.

4. Click the **Save** button on the Query Datasheet toolbar, then click the **Close** button on the menu bar.

5. Right-click **Colombian** in the Queries list box, then click **Rename** on the shortcut menu.

6. Position the insertion point to the right of Colombian.

7. Press the **spacebar**, type **Decaf**, then press the **Enter** key. The query name is now Colombian Decaf.

Carlos also needs information from the Restaurant Coffee Orders database. First, he wants to verify that Valle Coffee's inventory includes all the different packaging options for Kenya AA coffee and the Special Import coffee types. Customer demand for these products is lower and less predictable than other Valle Coffee products, so the company special orders them once every six weeks after Carlos has verified current inventory levels. To create this query, you need to use the Or logical operator.

The Or Logical Operator

For Carlos's request, you need a query that selects records when either one of two conditions is satisfied, or when both conditions are satisfied. That is, a record is selected if CoffeeName equals "Kenya AA" or CoffeeType equals "Special Import." You will enter the condition for the CoffeeName field in one Criteria row and the condition for the CoffeeType field in another Criteria row.

The fields that Carlos wants to view are the same as those in the Colombian Decaf query with the exception of the Price field, which Carlos does not want to view. So you'll modify the design of this query, run the query, then rename it.

To modify the query and use the Or logical operator:

1. Make sure that Colombian Decaf is selected in the Queries list box, then click the **Design** button on the Database window. Access opens the Query window in Design view.

   You need to remove the Price field from the design grid.

2. Click the **Price field selector**, which is the narrow gray box just above the field name in the design grid, to select the entire column, then press the **Delete** key. Access deletes the Price column from the design grid.

   Next, you need to remove the conditions for the Decaf and CoffeeName fields before entering the new conditions.

3. Select **"D"** in the Decaf Criteria text box, press the **Delete** key, press the **Tab** key to select the condition in the CoffeeName field's Criteria text box, then press the **Delete** key. The two conditions are deleted from the design grid.

   Now you need to enter the condition for the CoffeeName field.

4. Type **Kenya AA** then press the **Tab** key.

   Because you want records selected if either of the conditions for the CoffeeName or CoffeeType fields is satisfied, you must enter the condition for the CoffeeType field in the "or" row of the design grid.

5. Press the ↓ key, type **Special Import**, then press the ↑ key. See Figure 7-23.

Figure 7-23 Query window with the Or logical operator

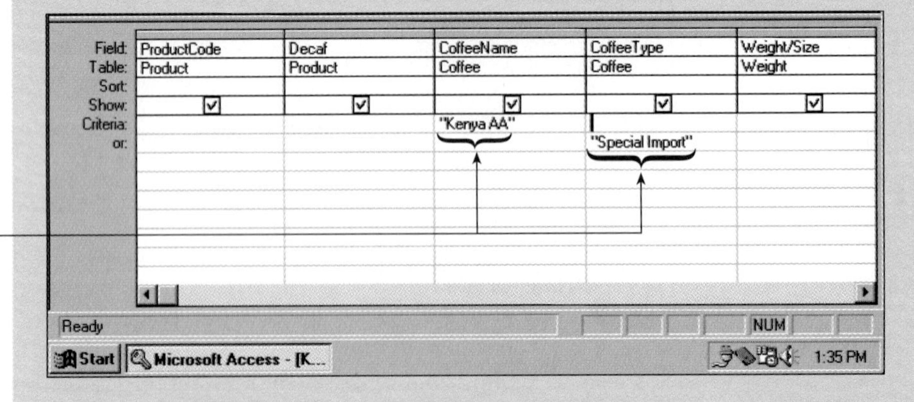

6. Click the **Run** button on the Query Design toolbar. Access runs the query and displays only those records that meet either condition: a CoffeeName field value equal to "Kenya AA" or a CoffeeType field value equal to "Special Import." A total of 16 records are selected. See Figure 7-24.

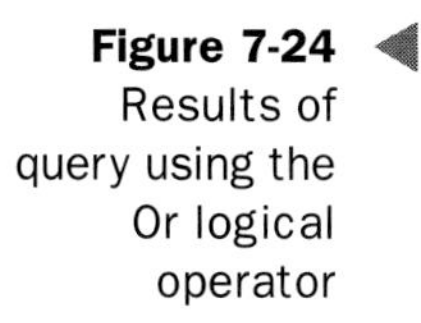

Figure 7-24 Results of query using the Or logical operator

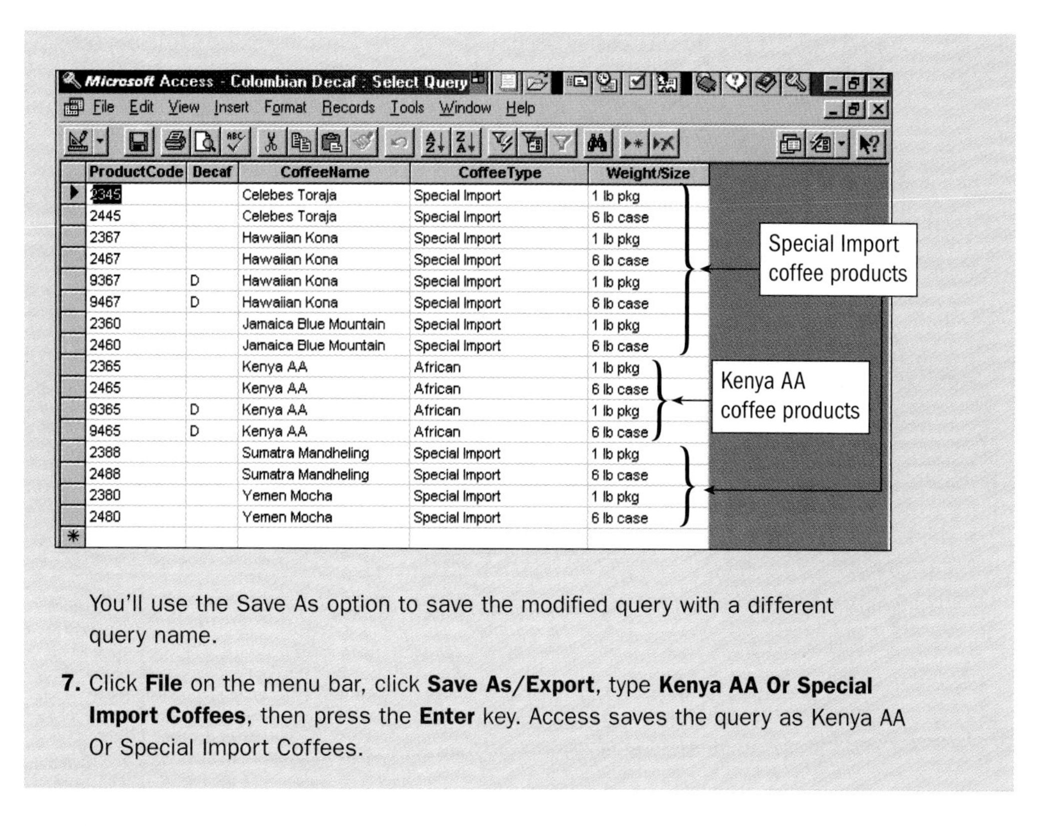

ProductCode	Decaf	CoffeeName	CoffeeType	Weight/Size
2345		Celebes Toraja	Special Import	1 lb pkg
2445		Celebes Toraja	Special Import	6 lb case
2367		Hawaiian Kona	Special Import	1 lb pkg
2467		Hawaiian Kona	Special Import	6 lb case
9367	D	Hawaiian Kona	Special Import	1 lb pkg
9467	D	Hawaiian Kona	Special Import	6 lb case
2360		Jamaica Blue Mountain	Special Import	1 lb pkg
2460		Jamaica Blue Mountain	Special Import	6 lb case
2365		Kenya AA	African	1 lb pkg
2465		Kenya AA	African	6 lb case
9365	D	Kenya AA	African	1 lb pkg
9465	D	Kenya AA	African	6 lb case
2388		Sumatra Mandheling	Special Import	1 lb pkg
2488		Sumatra Mandheling	Special Import	6 lb case
2380		Yemen Mocha	Special Import	1 lb pkg
2480		Yemen Mocha	Special Import	6 lb case

You'll use the Save As option to save the modified query with a different query name.

7. Click **File** on the menu bar, click **Save As/Export**, type **Kenya AA Or Special Import Coffees**, then press the **Enter** key. Access saves the query as Kenya AA Or Special Import Coffees.

Before you close the datasheet, Carlos asks for a printout of the query you just completed to show his staff. Because Carlos wants a printout of the entire query datasheet, you can print it using either the Print option on the File menu or the Print button on the toolbar.

To print then close the query datasheet:

1. Click the **Print** button on the Query Datasheet toolbar. Access prints the entire datasheet.

2. Click the **Close** button on the menu bar to return to the Database window.

The March Orders query that you completed earlier in this session displays records in increasing OrderNum sequence. Barbara wants the records displayed in increasing order by the State field, so that she can see which orders have been paid, with the data grouped by state. To display the results Barbara wants, you need to sort the records in the March Orders query datasheet.

Sorting Data

As you learned in Tutorial 4, when you sort data in a database, Access does not change the sequence of the records in the underlying tables. Only the records displayed in a table datasheet, query datasheet, or form are rearranged according to your specifications.

Access provides several methods for sorting data in a table or query datasheet and in a form. One method, clicking the toolbar sort buttons, lets you quickly sort the displayed records.

Sorting One Field Using a Toolbar Sort Button

The **Sort Ascending** and **Sort Descending** buttons on the toolbar allow you to sort records immediately, based on the selected field. First you select the column on which you want to base the sort, then click the appropriate sort button on the toolbar to rearrange the records in either ascending or descending order. Unless you save the datasheet or form after you've sorted the records, the rearrangement of records is temporary.

You need to open the March Orders query, then sort the query datasheet records in ascending order by the State field.

To open the March Orders query, then sort the records using a toolbar sort button:

1. Click **March Orders** in the Queries list box, then click the **Open** button. Access opens the Query window in Datasheet view.
2. Click any visible State field value to establish the State field as the current field.
3. Click the **Sort Ascending** button on the Query Datasheet toolbar. Access rearranges the records in ascending order by state. See Figure 7-25.

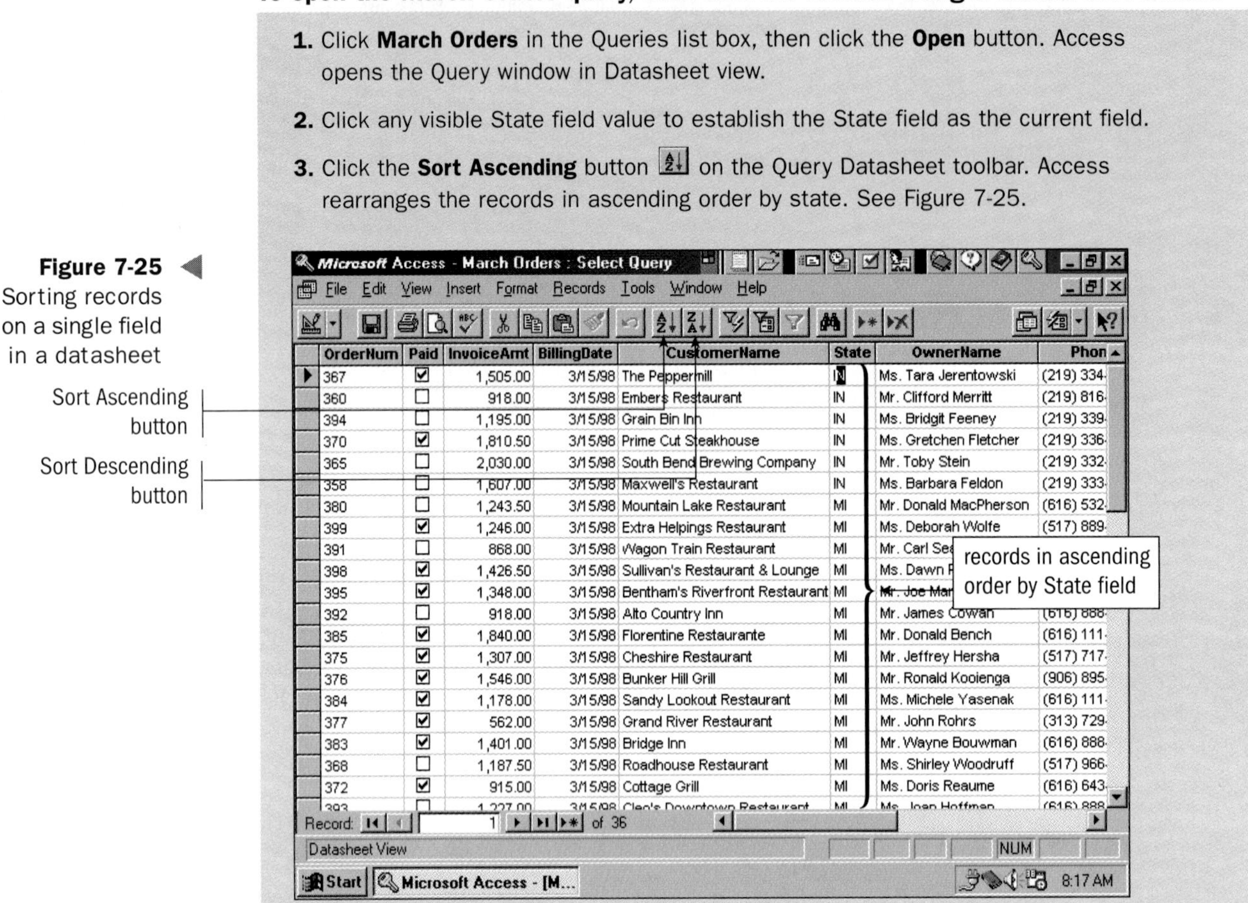

Figure 7-25 Sorting records on a single field in a datasheet

You can restore the records to their original order by using the Remove Filter/Sort option on the Records menu.

To restore the records to their original order:

1. Click **Records** on the menu bar, then click **Remove Filter/Sort**. Access restores the records to their original order.

Suppose that Barbara instead wanted to view all the unpaid invoices before the paid invoices (descending order for the Paid field, which is a yes/no field), then display the records within each group in decreasing value of the InvoiceAmt field. To do this you need to sort using two fields.

Sorting Multiple Fields Using a Toolbar Sort Button

Sort keys can be unique or nonunique. A sort key is **unique** if the value of the sort key field for each record is different. The ProductCode field in the Product table is an example of a unique sort key because each product has a different value in the ProductCode field. A sort key is **nonunique** if more than one record can have the same value for the sort key field. The Paid field in the Product table is a nonunique sort key because more than one record has the same Paid value.

When the sort key is nonunique, records with the same sort key value are grouped together, but they are not in a specific order within the group. To arrange these grouped records in a specific order, you can specify a **secondary sort key**, which is a second sort key field. The first sort key field is called the **primary sort key**. Note that the primary sort key is not the same as a table's primary key field. A table has at most one primary key, which must be unique, whereas any field in a table can serve as a primary sort key.

Access lets you select up to 10 different sort keys. When you use the toolbar sort buttons, the sort key fields must be in adjacent columns in the datasheet. You highlight the columns, and Access sorts first by the first column and then by each other highlighted column in order from left to right. Because you click either the Sort Ascending or the Sort Descending button, each of the multiple sort key fields is arranged in either ascending or descending sort order.

You need to select the adjacent fields Paid and InvoiceAmt and sort them in descending order.

To select and sort the two adjacent fields in the datasheet:

1. Click the **Paid field selector**, which is the gray box containing the field name at the top of the column, and, while holding down the mouse button, drag the pointer ⬇ to the right until both the Paid and InvoiceAmt columns are highlighted. Then release the mouse button.

2. Click the **Sort Descending** button on the Query Datasheet toolbar. Access rearranges the records to place them in descending order by Paid field values and, when the Paid field values are the same, in descending order by the InvoiceAmt field values. See Figure 7-26.

Figure 7-26 Sorting a datasheet on two adjacent fields

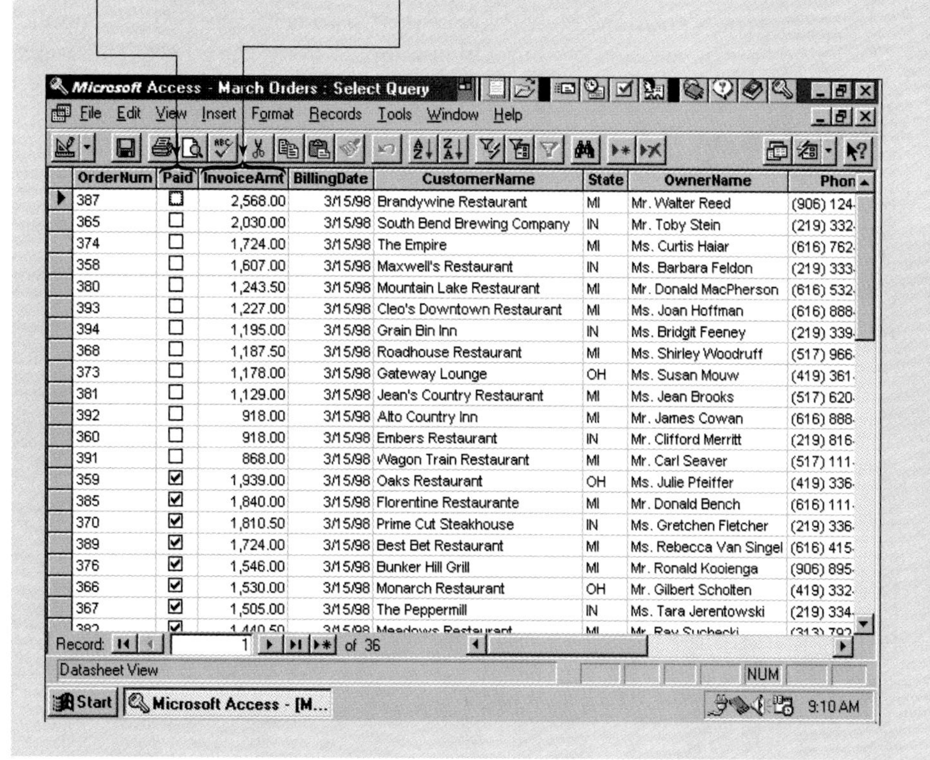

OrderNum	Paid	InvoiceAmt	BillingDate	CustomerName	State	OwnerName	Phon
387	☐	2,568.00	3/15/98	Brandywine Restaurant	MI	Mr. Walter Reed	(906) 124-
365	☐	2,030.00	3/15/98	South Bend Brewing Company	IN	Mr. Toby Stein	(219) 332-
374	☐	1,724.00	3/15/98	The Empire	MI	Ms. Curtis Haiar	(616) 762-
358	☐	1,607.00	3/15/98	Maxwell's Restaurant	IN	Ms. Barbara Feldon	(219) 333-
380	☐	1,243.50	3/15/98	Mountain Lake Restaurant	MI	Mr. Donald MacPherson	(616) 532-
393	☐	1,227.00	3/15/98	Cleo's Downtown Restaurant	MI	Ms. Joan Hoffman	(616) 888-
394	☐	1,195.00	3/15/98	Grain Bin Inn	IN	Ms. Bridgit Feeney	(219) 339-
368	☐	1,187.50	3/15/98	Roadhouse Restaurant	MI	Ms. Shirley Woodruff	(517) 966-
373	☐	1,178.00	3/15/98	Gateway Lounge	OH	Ms. Susan Mouw	(419) 361-
381	☐	1,129.00	3/15/98	Jean's Country Restaurant	MI	Ms. Jean Brooks	(517) 620-
392	☐	918.00	3/15/98	Alto Country Inn	MI	Mr. James Cowan	(616) 888-
360	☐	918.00	3/15/98	Embers Restaurant	IN	Mr. Clifford Merritt	(219) 816-
391	☐	868.00	3/15/98	Wagon Train Restaurant	MI	Mr. Carl Seaver	(517) 111-
359	☑	1,939.00	3/15/98	Oaks Restaurant	OH	Ms. Julie Pfeiffer	(419) 336-
385	☑	1,840.00	3/15/98	Florentine Restaurante	MI	Mr. Donald Bench	(616) 111-
370	☑	1,810.50	3/15/98	Prime Cut Steakhouse	IN	Ms. Gretchen Fletcher	(219) 336-
389	☑	1,724.00	3/15/98	Best Bet Restaurant	MI	Ms. Rebecca Van Singel	(616) 415-
376	☑	1,546.00	3/15/98	Bunker Hill Grill	MI	Mr. Ronald Kooienga	(906) 895-
366	☑	1,530.00	3/15/98	Monarch Restaurant	OH	Mr. Gilbert Scholten	(419) 332-
367	☑	1,505.00	3/15/98	The Peppermill	IN	Ms. Tara Jerentowski	(219) 334-

After viewing the sorted March Orders query, Barbara decides that the records in each state group should be displayed in order by increasing values of the CustomerName field. This would let her quickly find a specific customer in a state. Although the CustomerName and State fields are adjacent, they are in the wrong order. If you used a toolbar sort button, the CustomerName field would be the primary sort key instead of the State field. In this case, you need to specify the sort keys in Design view.

Selecting Multiple Sort Fields in Design View

When you have two or more nonadjacent sort keys or when the fields to be used for sorting are in the wrong order, you must specify the sort keys in the Query window in Design view. Access first uses the sort key that is leftmost in the design grid. Therefore, you must arrange the fields you want to sort from left to right in the design grid with the primary sort key being the leftmost sort key field.

SORTING A QUERY DATASHEET

- In the query datasheet, select the field or adjacent fields on which you want to sort.
- Click the Sort Ascending button or the Sort Descending button on the toolbar.

or

- In Design view, position the fields serving as sort keys from left (primary sort key) to right, then select the sort order for each sort key.

Barbara wants the CustomerName field displayed in the datasheet to the left of the State field; this is the way the fields are currently arranged. However, the State field is the primary sort key and, therefore, it must be positioned to the left of the secondary sort key of CustomerName. You'll add the State field to the design grid a second time, positioning it to the left of the CustomerName field. Then you'll select this duplicate State field as a sort key and uncheck its Show check box to hide the field in the datasheet. Because it is positioned to the left of the CustomerName field, the duplicate State field will be the primary sort key but will not appear in the datasheet. The original State field will appear in the datasheet but will not be used for sorting.

To add the field to the design grid and select the multiple sort keys:

1. Click the **Query View** button for Design view on the Query Datasheet toolbar. Access closes the window and opens the query in Design view.

   First, you'll scroll the design grid horizontally so you can clearly see the fields you'll be working with.

2. Click the horizontal right scroll arrow until BillingDate is the leftmost field in the design grid.

   Next, you'll drag the State field in the Customer field list to a position between the BillingDate and CustomerName fields in the design grid.

3. Scroll the Customer field list if necessary, then click and drag **State** in the Customer field list to the CustomerName column in the design grid until the pointer changes to . See Figure 7-27.

Figure 7-27 Dragging a field to the design grid

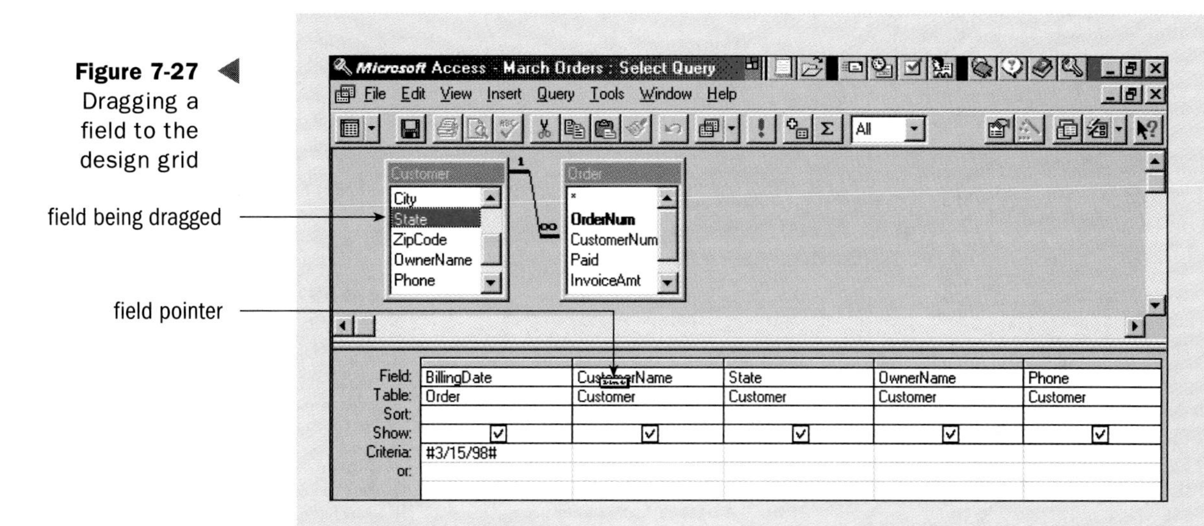

4. Release the mouse button. Access places the State field between the BillingDate and CustomerName fields.

   The State field now appears twice in the design grid. You'll use the leftmost State field as the primary sort key and the rightmost State field for display in the datasheet. The CustomerName field, which is between the two State fields, will be the secondary sort key.

5. Click the leftmost **State Sort** text box, click the **Sort** list arrow, click **Ascending**, then click the leftmost **State Show** check box. You've selected an ascending sort order for the State field, which will be the primary sort key. The State field values for this occurrence of the field will not be displayed in the query results.

6. Click the **CustomerName Sort** text box, click the **Sort** list arrow, then click **Ascending**. You've selected an ascending sort order for the CustomerName field, which will be the secondary sort key. See Figure 7-28.

Figure 7-28 Selecting two sort keys in Design view

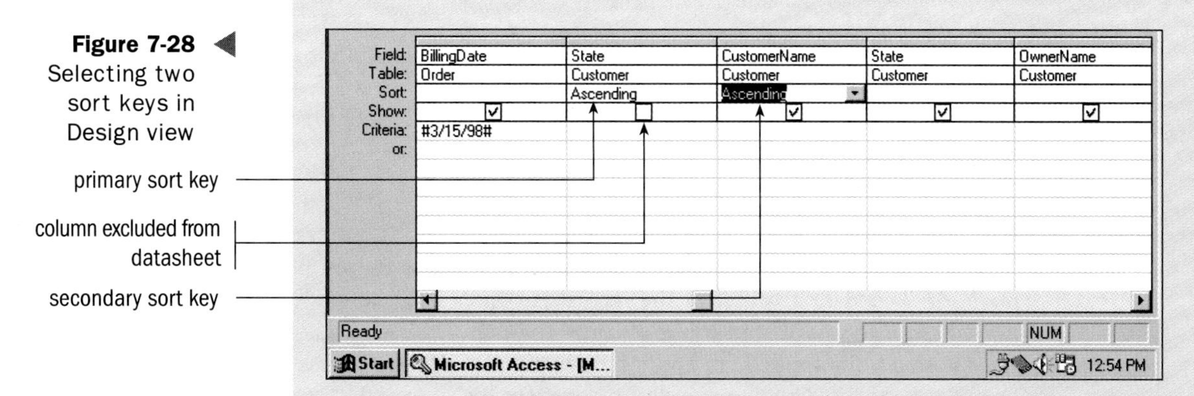

You have finished your query changes, so now you can run the query, then save the modified query with the same query name.

7. Click the **Run** button on the Query Design toolbar. Access runs the query and displays the query datasheet. The records appear in ascending order, based on the values of the State field. Within groups of records with the same State field value, the records appear in ascending order by the values of the CustomerName field. See Figure 7-29.

Figure 7-29 Datasheet sorted on two fields

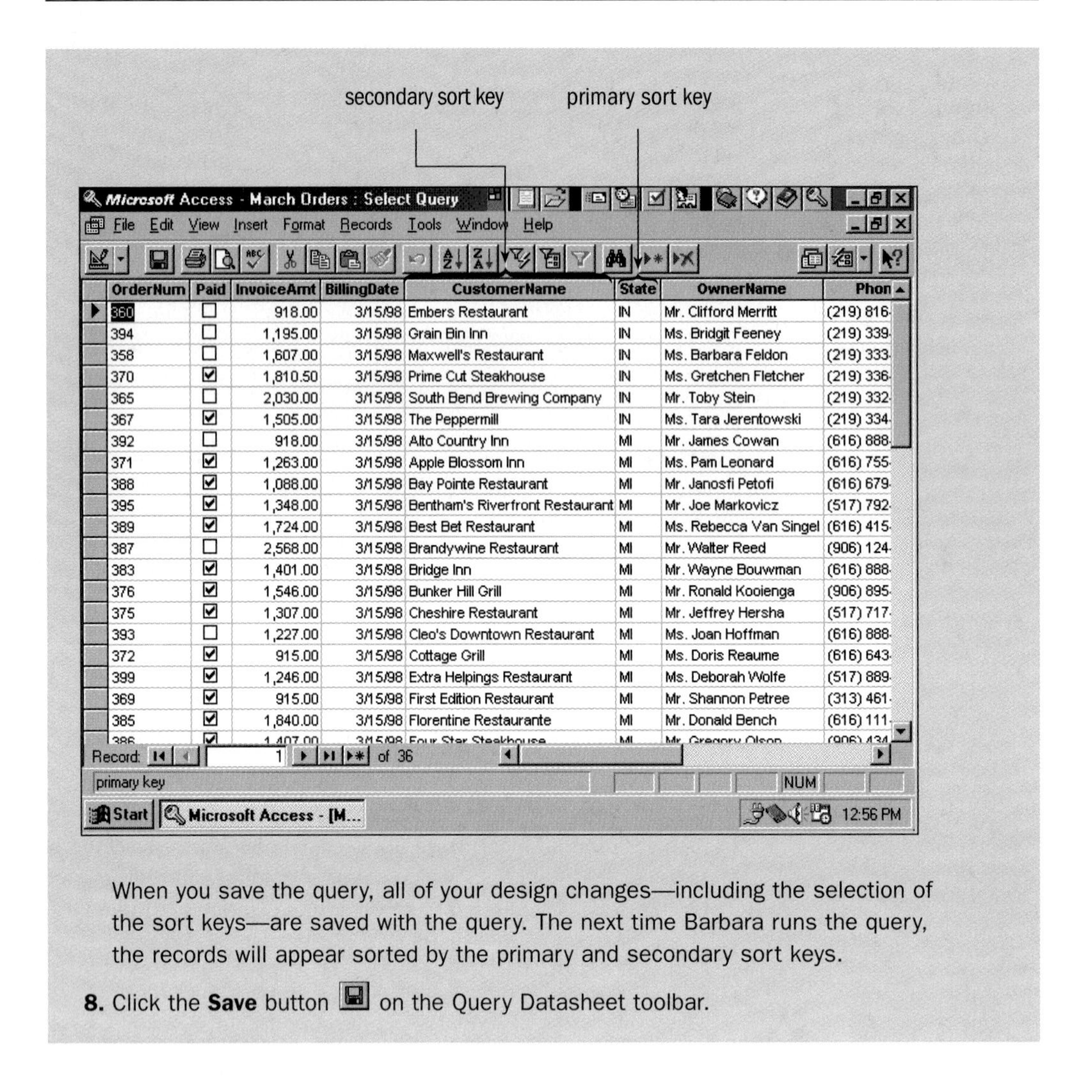

OrderNum	Paid	InvoiceAmt	BillingDate	CustomerName	State	OwnerName	Phon
360	☐	918.00	3/15/98	Embers Restaurant	IN	Mr. Clifford Merritt	(219) 816-
394	☐	1,195.00	3/15/98	Grain Bin Inn	IN	Ms. Bridgit Feeney	(219) 339-
358	☐	1,607.00	3/15/98	Maxwell's Restaurant	IN	Ms. Barbara Feldon	(219) 333-
370	☑	1,810.50	3/15/98	Prime Cut Steakhouse	IN	Ms. Gretchen Fletcher	(219) 336-
365	☐	2,030.00	3/15/98	South Bend Brewing Company	IN	Mr. Toby Stein	(219) 332-
367	☑	1,505.00	3/15/98	The Peppermill	IN	Ms. Tara Jerentowski	(219) 334-
392	☐	918.00	3/15/98	Alto Country Inn	MI	Mr. James Cowan	(616) 888-
371	☑	1,263.00	3/15/98	Apple Blossom Inn	MI	Ms. Pam Leonard	(616) 755-
388	☑	1,088.00	3/15/98	Bay Pointe Restaurant	MI	Mr. Janosfi Petofi	(616) 679-
395	☑	1,348.00	3/15/98	Bentham's Riverfront Restaurant	MI	Mr. Joe Markovicz	(517) 792-
389	☑	1,724.00	3/15/98	Best Bet Restaurant	MI	Ms. Rebecca Van Singel	(616) 415-
387	☐	2,568.00	3/15/98	Brandywine Restaurant	MI	Mr. Walter Reed	(906) 124-
383	☑	1,401.00	3/15/98	Bridge Inn	MI	Mr. Wayne Bouwman	(616) 888-
376	☑	1,546.00	3/15/98	Bunker Hill Grill	MI	Mr. Ronald Kooienga	(906) 895-
375	☑	1,307.00	3/15/98	Cheshire Restaurant	MI	Mr. Jeffrey Hersha	(517) 717-
393	☐	1,227.00	3/15/98	Cleo's Downtown Restaurant	MI	Ms. Joan Hoffman	(616) 888-
372	☑	915.00	3/15/98	Cottage Grill	MI	Ms. Doris Reaume	(616) 643-
399	☑	1,246.00	3/15/98	Extra Helpings Restaurant	MI	Ms. Deborah Wolfe	(517) 889-
369	☑	915.00	3/15/98	First Edition Restaurant	MI	Mr. Shannon Petree	(313) 461-
385	☑	1,840.00	3/15/98	Florentine Restaurante	MI	Mr. Donald Bench	(616) 111-
386	☑	1,407.00	3/15/98	Four Star Steakhouse	MI	Mr. Gregory Olson	(906) 434-

When you save the query, all of your design changes—including the selection of the sort keys—are saved with the query. The next time Barbara runs the query, the records will appear sorted by the primary and secondary sort keys.

8. Click the **Save** button on the Query Datasheet toolbar.

Barbara wants to focus her attention for a few minutes on the orders in the datasheet that are unpaid. Because selecting only the unpaid orders is a temporary change Barbara wants in the datasheet, you do not need to switch to Design view and change the query. Instead, you can apply a filter.

Filtering Data

A **filter** is a set of restrictions you place on the records in an open datasheet or form to *temporarily* isolate a subset of the records. A filter lets you view different subsets of displayed records so you can focus on only the data you need. Unless you save a query or form with a filter applied, an applied filter is not available the next time you run the query or open the form. The two simplest techniques for filtering records are Filter By Selection and Filter By Form.

Using Filter By Selection

Filter By Selection lets you select all or part of a field value in a datasheet or form, then display only those records that contain the selected value in the field.

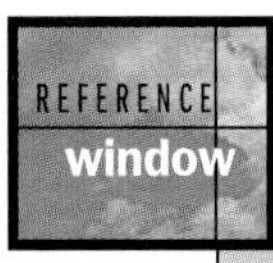

USING FILTER BY SELECTION

- In the datasheet or form, select all or part of the field value that will be the basis for the filter.
- Click the Filter By Selection button on the toolbar.

For Barbara's request, you need to select an unchecked box in the Paid field, which represents an unpaid order, then use Filter By Selection to display only those query records with this value.

To display the records using Filter By Selection:

1. Click any check box that is unchecked in the Paid column. When you click the check box, you select the field value but you also change the check box from unchecked to checked. Because you've changed an unpaid order to a paid order, you need to click the same check box a second time.
2. Click the same check box a second time. The field value changes back to unchecked, which is now the selected field value.
3. Click the **Filter By Selection** button on the Query Datasheet toolbar. Access displays the filtered results. Only the 13 query records that have an unchecked Paid field value appear in the datasheet; these records are the unpaid order records. Note that the status bar display and the selected Remove Filter button on the toolbar both indicate that records have been filtered. See Figure 7-30.

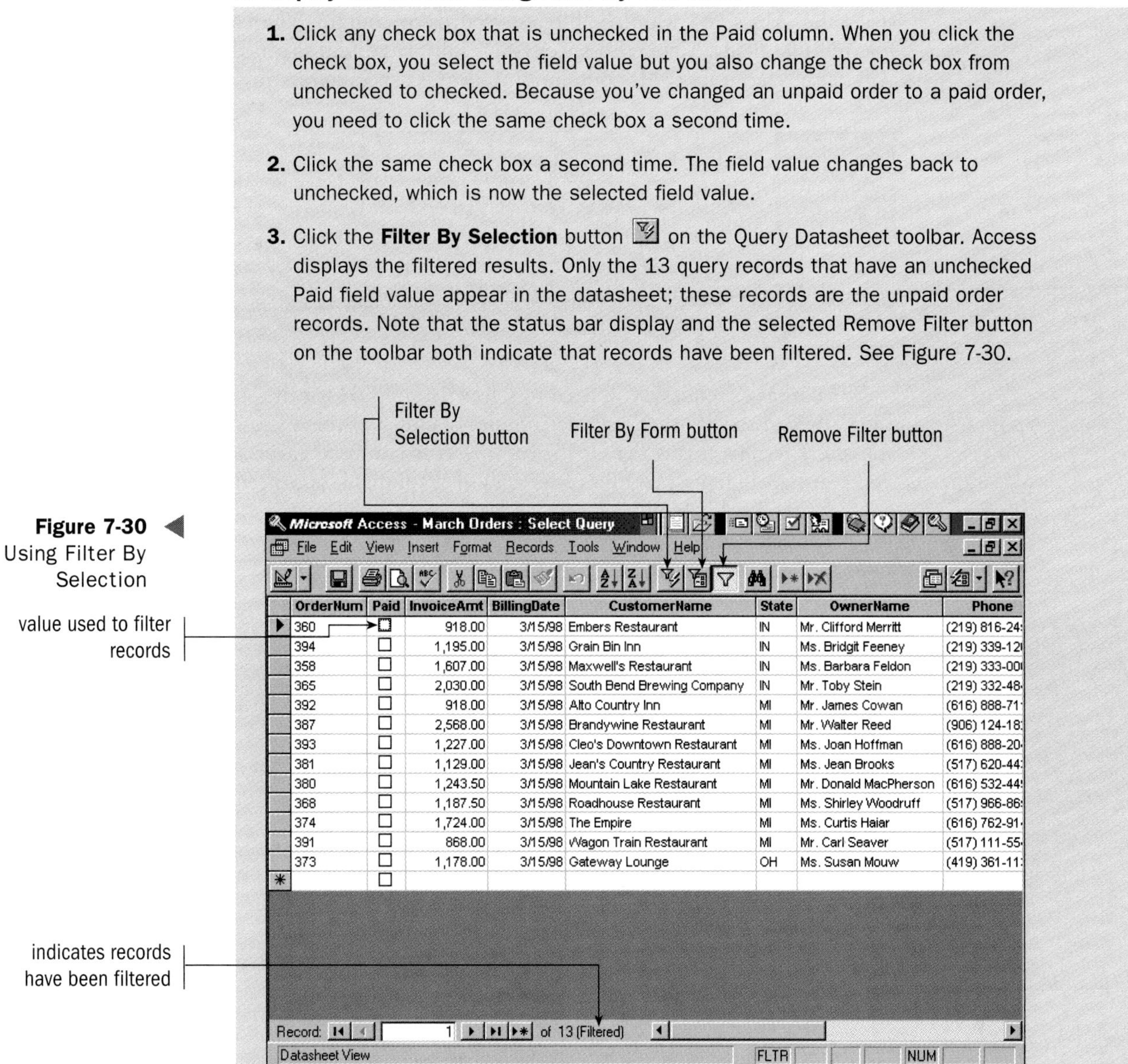

OrderNum	Paid	InvoiceAmt	BillingDate	CustomerName	State	OwnerName	Phone
360	☐	918.00	3/15/98	Embers Restaurant	IN	Mr. Clifford Merritt	(219) 816-24
394	☐	1,195.00	3/15/98	Grain Bin Inn	IN	Ms. Bridgit Feeney	(219) 339-12
358	☐	1,607.00	3/15/98	Maxwell's Restaurant	IN	Ms. Barbara Feldon	(219) 333-00
365	☐	2,030.00	3/15/98	South Bend Brewing Company	IN	Mr. Toby Stein	(219) 332-48
392	☐	918.00	3/15/98	Alto Country Inn	MI	Mr. James Cowan	(616) 888-71
387	☐	2,568.00	3/15/98	Brandywine Restaurant	MI	Mr. Walter Reed	(906) 124-18
393	☐	1,227.00	3/15/98	Cleo's Downtown Restaurant	MI	Ms. Joan Hoffman	(616) 888-20
381	☐	1,129.00	3/15/98	Jean's Country Restaurant	MI	Ms. Jean Brooks	(517) 620-44
380	☐	1,243.50	3/15/98	Mountain Lake Restaurant	MI	Mr. Donald MacPherson	(616) 532-44
368	☐	1,187.50	3/15/98	Roadhouse Restaurant	MI	Ms. Shirley Woodruff	(517) 966-86
374	☐	1,724.00	3/15/98	The Empire	MI	Ms. Curtis Haiar	(616) 762-91
391	☐	868.00	3/15/98	Wagon Train Restaurant	MI	Mr. Carl Seaver	(517) 111-55
373	☐	1,178.00	3/15/98	Gateway Lounge	OH	Ms. Susan Mouw	(419) 361-11
*	☐						

Figure 7-30 Using Filter By Selection

You can redisplay all the query records by clicking the Remove Filter button on the toolbar.

To redisplay all query records:

1. Click the **Remove Filter** button on the Query Datasheet toolbar. Access redisplays all the records in the query datasheet.

Barbara decides she wants to focus on only the unpaid orders from Indiana and Ohio, which have State field values of IN and OH. For more complicated filters such as this one, you must use Filter By Form instead of Filter By Selection.

Using Filter By Form

Filter By Form displays a copy of your datasheet or form with blank fields and lets you select the values you want the filtered records to contain. You can select multiple values for multiple fields. Similar to specifying multiple conditions in the design grid, a record will be selected if its fields contain all the values specified in any filter row.

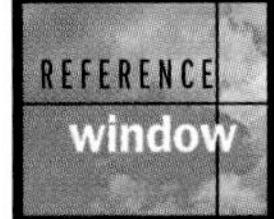

USING FILTER BY FORM

- Click the Filter By Form button on the toolbar.
- Select the field values you want to use as the basis for the filter, using the Or tabs to define multiple filter rows.
- Click the Apply Filter button on the toolbar.

For Barbara's request, you need to select IN and OH for the State field in two different filter rows to specify that records containing either of these values should be included in the query results; this is the Or logical operator you used earlier in Design view. Because you want an Indiana or Ohio order only if it's unpaid, you need to select an unchecked value for the Paid field in both rows. Because each row has two conditions, you'll be using the And logical operator in each row. A record will be selected if it's unpaid *and* from Indiana, *or* if it's unpaid *and* from Ohio.

To display the records using Filter By Form:

1. Click the **Filter By Form** button on the Query Datasheet toolbar. Access displays a copy of the query datasheet with blank fields. See Figure 7-31.

Figure 7-31 Using Filter By Form

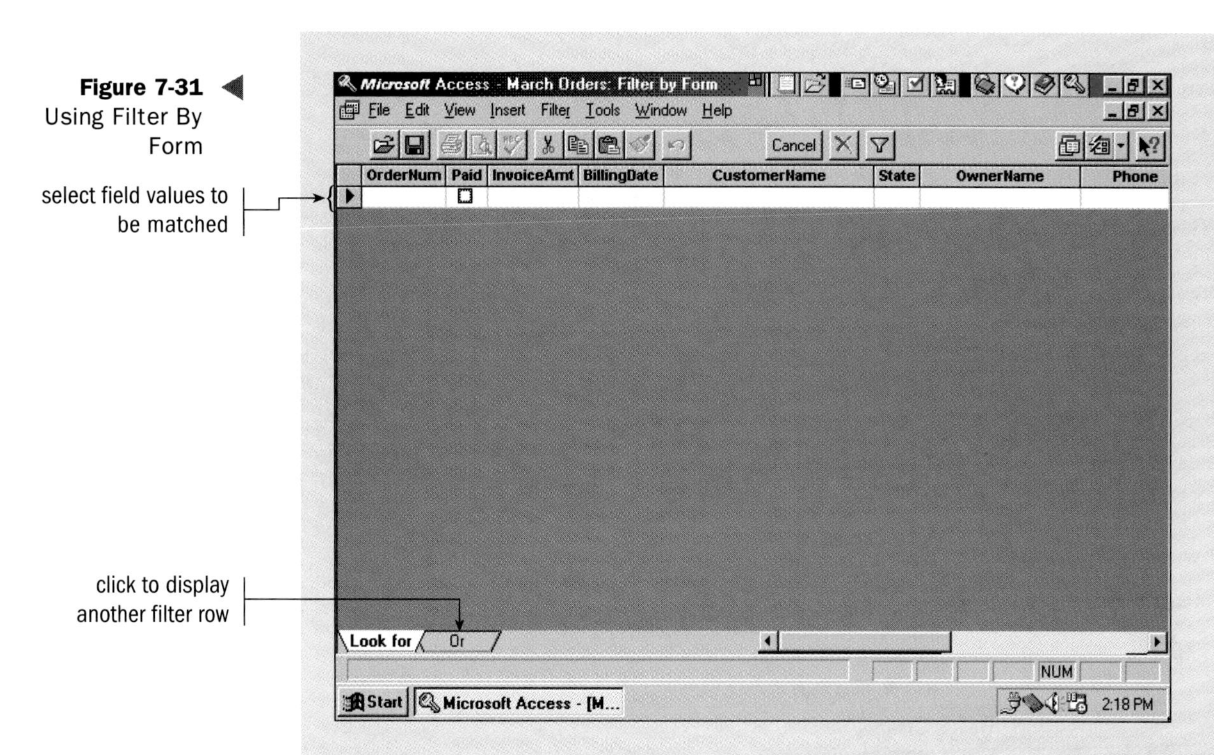

The Paid column already has an unchecked check box, because it was your filter criterion when you used the Filter By Selection option.

First you need to select one of the two states.

2. Click the right side of the **State** text box to display the list, then click **IN**. Because the State field is a text field, Access displays the state within quotation marks.

   You've completed the first filter row. To display a second filter row, you click the Or tab, which is just above the status bar.

3. Click the **Or** tab to display a second filter row. Access displays a check box in the Paid text box and an arrow on the right side of the State text box. These were the two fields used in the first filter row.

   TROUBLE? If the Paid check box is checked, click it to remove the check mark.

4. Click the right side of the **State** text box, then click **OH**.

   TROUBLE? If you make a mistake and want to start over, click the Clear Grid button on the toolbar, then reselect the field values.

   If you need to review the first filter row, click the Look for tab. Now you can apply the filter.

5. Click the **Apply Filter** button on the Filter/Sort toolbar. Access displays the filtered results. Only the query records that contain the selected values appear in the datasheet. See Figure 7-32.

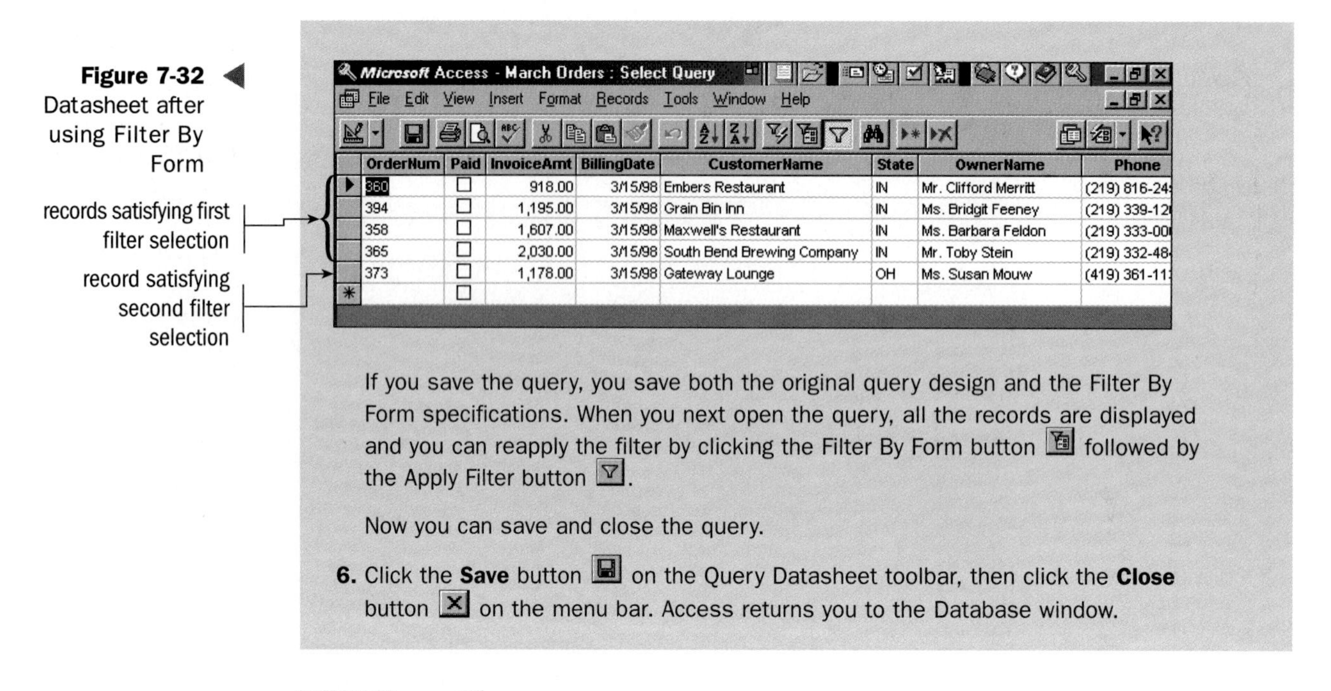

OrderNum	Paid	InvoiceAmt	BillingDate	CustomerName	State	OwnerName	Phone
360	☐	918.00	3/15/98	Embers Restaurant	IN	Mr. Clifford Merritt	(219) 816-24
394	☐	1,195.00	3/15/98	Grain Bin Inn	IN	Ms. Bridgit Feeney	(219) 339-12
358	☐	1,607.00	3/15/98	Maxwell's Restaurant	IN	Ms. Barbara Feldon	(219) 333-00
365	☐	2,030.00	3/15/98	South Bend Brewing Company	IN	Mr. Toby Stein	(219) 332-48
373	☐	1,178.00	3/15/98	Gateway Lounge	OH	Ms. Susan Mouw	(419) 361-11
*	☐						

Figure 7-32 Datasheet after using Filter By Form

If you save the query, you save both the original query design and the Filter By Form specifications. When you next open the query, all the records are displayed and you can reapply the filter by clicking the Filter By Form button followed by the Apply Filter button.

Now you can save and close the query.

6. Click the **Save** button on the Query Datasheet toolbar, then click the **Close** button on the menu bar. Access returns you to the Database window.

Quick Check

1. When two tables have a(n) ________ relationship, you must use a third table to join them.
2. What is the difference between the condition "In (20, 30)" and the condition "Between 20 And 30"?
3. What operator do you use for a pattern match?
4. In the design grid, where do you place the conditions for two different fields when you use the Or logical operator?
5. When must you define multiple sort keys in Design view instead of in the query datasheet?
6. What are the differences between Filter By Selection and Filter By Form? When would you use each?

Now that you've completed Session 7.1, you can exit Access or you can continue to the next session.

SESSION 7.2

In this session you will learn how to perform calculations in a query; change query field properties; use record and record group calculations; and create parameter, top values, and action queries.

Leonard Valle has asked Barbara if the Restaurant Coffee Orders database can be used to perform the calculations necessary in preparing customer invoices. These calculations include determining the total price of each product ordered for each order. Barbara asks you to create a query to perform these calculations, so that her staff doesn't have to do them manually; this will reduce errors and improve productivity.

Performing Calculations in a Query

In addition to using queries to retrieve, sort, and filter data in a database, you can use a query to perform calculations. To perform a calculation, you define an **expression** containing a combination of database fields, constants, and operators. For numeric expressions, the data types of the database fields must be number, currency, or date/time; the constants are numbers such as 1.06; and the operators can be arithmetic operators (+ - * /) or other specialized operators. In complex expressions you can use parentheses ( ) to indicate which calculation should be performed first. In expressions without parentheses, Access calculates in the following order of precedence: multiplication and division before addition and subtraction. Access calculates operators that have equal precedence in order from left to right.

To perform a calculation in a query, you add a calculated field to the query. A **calculated field** is a field that displays the results of an expression. A calculated field appears in a query datasheet but does not exist in a database. When you run a query that contains a calculated field, Access evaluates the expression defined by the calculated field and displays the resulting value in the datasheet.

Using Calculated Fields

Barbara's first calculation request is to display all the fields from the Order Detail table and to calculate the total price charged to customers for each product they order. You need to create a new query that displays all the fields from the Order Detail table, then add a calculated field for each product's total price. The expression for the calculated field involves multiplying the quantity ordered by the unit price, then multiplying the result by 1.06 to account for a 6% sales tax rate.

You'll begin by creating a new query and adding all the fields from the Order Detail table.

To create a new query displaying all the fields from the Order Detail table:

1. Make sure the Queries tab is selected in the Database window and the Database window is maximized.
2. Click the **New** button to open the New Query dialog box, click **Design View** (if necessary), then click the **OK** button. Access opens the Show Table dialog box on top of the Query window in Design view.
3. Click **Order Detail**, click the **Add** button, then click the **Close** button. Access adds the Order Detail field list to the top of the Query window and closes the dialog box.
4. Double-click the **field list title bar** to select all fields in the table, then drag the highlighted fields to the first column of the design grid. Access adds the four fields to the design grid in the same order in which they appear in the table.

To enter an expression for a calculated field, you can type it directly in a Field text box. Alternatively, you can open the Zoom dialog box or Expression Builder from the Field text box shortcut menu and use either one to enter the expression. The **Zoom dialog box** is a large text box for entering text, expressions, or other values. **Expression Builder** is an Access tool that contains an expression box for entering the expression, buttons for common operators, and one or more lists of expression elements, such as table and field names. Unlike a Field text box, which is too small to show an entire expression at one time, the Zoom dialog box and Expression Builder are large enough to display lengthy expressions. You'll almost exclusively use the Zoom dialog box or Expression Builder to enter expressions. If you know the exact expression you need to enter, you might use the Zoom dialog box. In most cases Expression Builder is easier and faster to use than either of the other two methods for entering expressions.

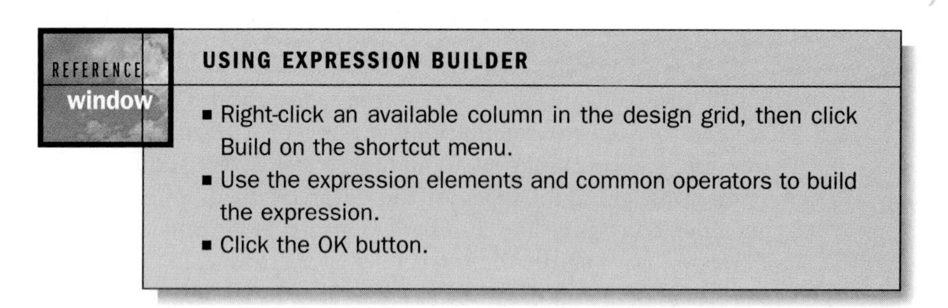
REFERENCE window

USING EXPRESSION BUILDER

- Right-click an available column in the design grid, then click Build on the shortcut menu.
- Use the expression elements and common operators to build the expression.
- Click the OK button.

You'll use Expression Builder to enter the calculated field to determine the total price of each product.

To enter the calculated field using Expression Builder, then run the query:

1. Position the pointer in the first available Field text box, just to the right of the UnitPrice field, right-click the **Field** text box, then click **Build** on the shortcut menu. The Expression Builder dialog box opens. See Figure 7-33.

Figure 7-33 Initial Expression Builder dialog box

expression box

common operators

expression elements

   You use the common operators and expression elements to help you build an expression. Because the expression requires fields from the Order Detail table, you need to display the tables in the database, then display the fields in the Order Detail table.

2. Double-click **Tables** to display the database's table names, then click **Order Detail**. Access displays the field names for the Order Detail table in the middle box. See Figure 7-34.

Figure 7-34 Displaying tables and fields in the Expression Builder dialog box

Restaurant Coffee Orders database tables

click to place selected field in the expression

Order Detail fields

Next you enter the expression for the calculated field. The expression will multiply the Qty field values by the UnitPrice field values times the numeric constant 1.06 (which represents a 6% tax rate). To include a field in the expression, you select the field then click the Paste button. To include a numeric constant, you simply type the constant in the expression.

3. Click **Qty** then click the **Paste** button. Access places [Order Detail]![Qty] in the expression box.

   The notation [Order Detail]![Qty] indicates that the expression contains the Qty field from the Order Detail table. Whenever an expression includes a field name, such as Qty, or a table name, such as Order Detail, the brackets indicate that the name is one that has been defined in the open database.

   To include the multiplication operator in the expression, you click the asterisk (*) button.

4. Click the * button in the row of common operators, click **UnitPrice**, click the **Paste** button, click the * button, then type **1.06**. You have completed the entry of the expression. See Figure 7-35.

Figure 7-35 Completed expression for the calculated field

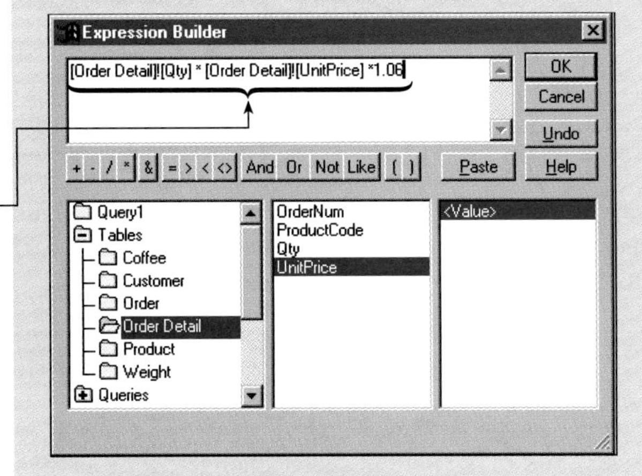

5. Click the **OK** button. Access closes the Expression Builder dialog box and adds the expression to the design grid. The expression is too long to fit in the field, so only the end of the expression is visible.

6. Click the **Run** button on the Query Design toolbar. Access runs the query and displays the query datasheet, which contains the four fields from the Order Detail table and the calculated field. See Figure 7-36.

Figure 7-36 Datasheet displaying the calculated field

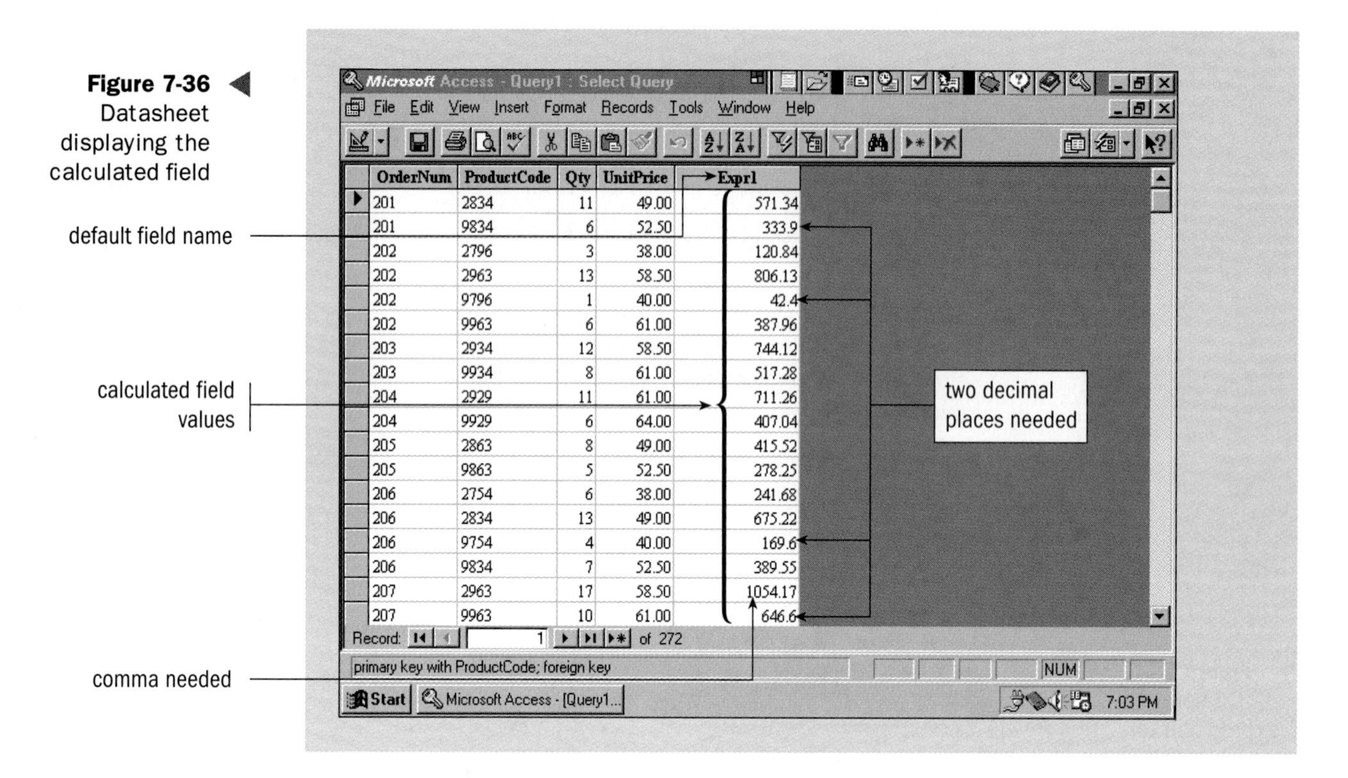

OrderNum	ProductCode	Qty	UnitPrice	Expr1
201	2834	11	49.00	571.34
201	9834	6	52.50	333.9
202	2796	3	38.00	120.84
202	2963	13	58.50	806.13
202	9796	1	40.00	42.4
202	9963	6	61.00	387.96
203	2934	12	58.50	744.12
203	9934	8	61.00	517.28
204	2929	11	61.00	711.26
204	9929	6	64.00	407.04
205	2863	8	49.00	415.52
205	9863	5	52.50	278.25
206	2754	6	38.00	241.68
206	2834	13	49.00	675.22
206	9754	4	40.00	169.6
206	9834	7	52.50	389.55
207	2963	17	58.50	1054.17
207	9963	10	61.00	646.6

Expr1 is the default name for the calculated field. Barbara wants you to change the name to TotalPrice, which is more descriptive of the field's contents, and to make sure each calculated field value displays two decimal places and includes commas for thousands separators.

Changing Query Field Properties

You can change the properties for a query's fields, just as you can change the properties for a table's fields. You make field property changes, such as the field name and the number of decimals places, in Design view.

To change the properties of the calculated field in the query:

1. Click the **Query View** button for Design view on the Query Datasheet toolbar to switch to Design view.
2. Right-click the **Expr1 Field** text box, then click **Properties** on the shortcut menu. The Field Properties dialog box opens.

   The Expr1 field has the default General Number format, which does not display commas. You'll change the field's format to Standard, which displays commas.
3. Click the right side of the **Format** text box to display the list of available formats with examples, then click **Standard**.
4. Click the right side of the **Decimal Places** text box to display the list, then click **2**. See Figure 7-37.

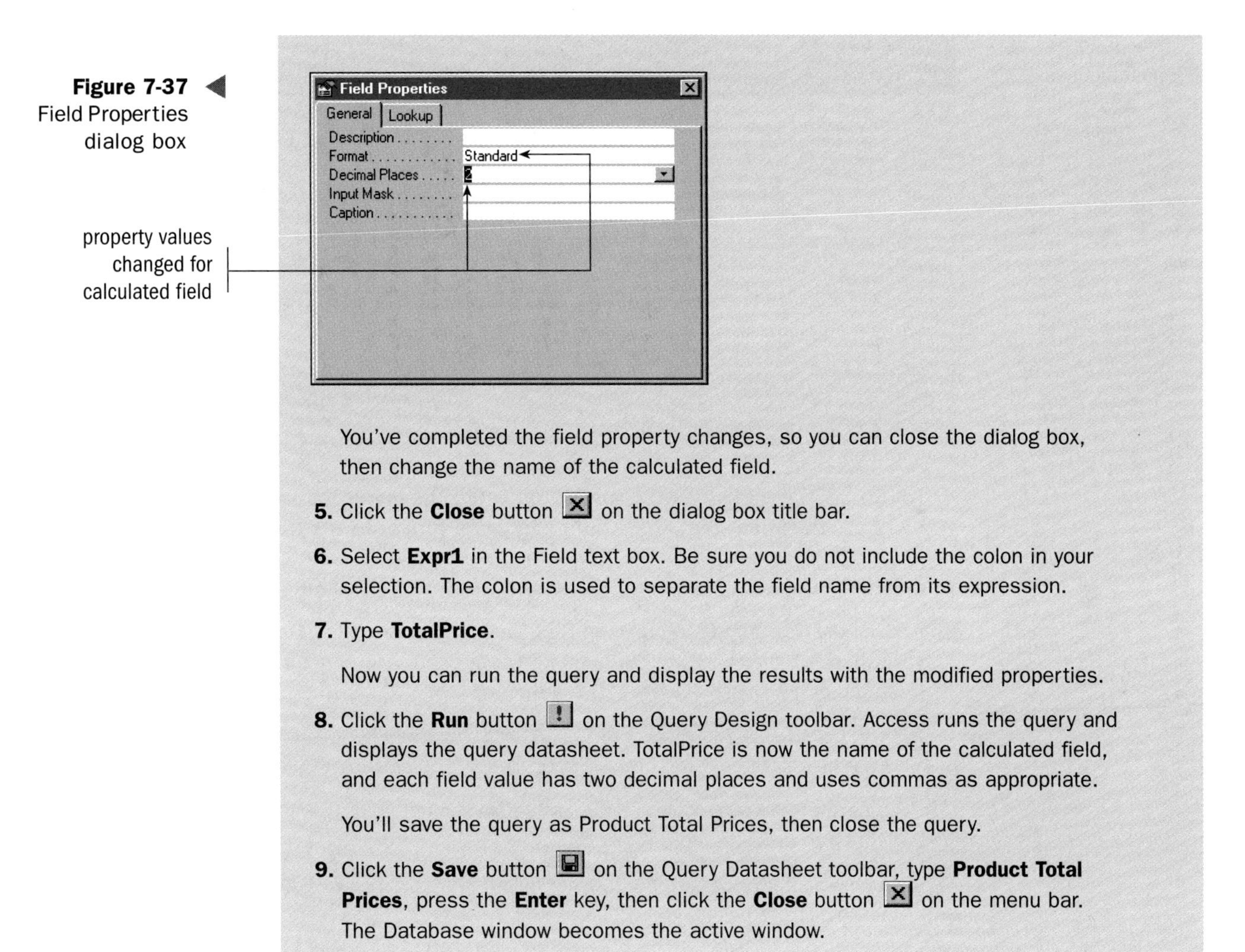

Figure 7-37 Field Properties dialog box

You've completed the field property changes, so you can close the dialog box, then change the name of the calculated field.

5. Click the **Close** button on the dialog box title bar.
6. Select **Expr1** in the Field text box. Be sure you do not include the colon in your selection. The colon is used to separate the field name from its expression.
7. Type **TotalPrice**.

   Now you can run the query and display the results with the modified properties.

8. Click the **Run** button on the Query Design toolbar. Access runs the query and displays the query datasheet. TotalPrice is now the name of the calculated field, and each field value has two decimal places and uses commas as appropriate.

   You'll save the query as Product Total Prices, then close the query.

9. Click the **Save** button on the Query Datasheet toolbar, type **Product Total Prices**, press the **Enter** key, then click the **Close** button on the menu bar. The Database window becomes the active window.

Once each quarter Barbara prepares a report of Valle Coffee's restaurant business for Leonard. The information in the report includes a summary of the restaurant orders for the quarter. Barbara lists the total invoice amount for all orders, the average invoice amount, and the total number of orders. She asks you to create a query to determine these statistics from data in the Order table.

Using Record Calculations

You can calculate statistical information, such as totals and averages, on the records selected in a query. To do this, you use the Access aggregate functions. **Aggregate functions** perform arithmetic operations on selected records in a database. Figure 7-38 lists the most frequently used aggregate functions. Aggregate functions operate on the records that meet a query's selection criteria. You specify an aggregate function for a specific field, and the appropriate operation applies to that field's values for the selected records.

Figure 7-38 Frequently used aggregate functions

Aggregate Function	Determines	Data Types Supported
Avg	Average of the field values for the selected records	AutoNumber, Currency, Date/Time, Number
Count	Number of records selected	AutoNumber, Currency, Date/Time, Memo, Number, OLE Object, Text, Yes/No
Max	Highest field value for the selected records	AutoNumber, Currency, Date/Time, Number, Text
Min	Lowest field value for the selected records	AutoNumber, Currency, Date/Time, Number, Text
Sum	Total of the field values for the selected records	AutoNumber, Currency, Date/TIme, Number

To display the total, average, and count of all the invoice amounts in the Order table, you will use the Sum, Avg, and Count aggregate functions for the InvoiceAmt field.

To calculate the total, average, and count of all invoice amounts:

1. Click the **New** button to open the New Query dialog box, click **Design View** (if necessary), then click the **OK** button. Access opens the Show Table dialog box on top of the Query window in Design view.

2. Click **Order**, click the **Add** button, then click the **Close** button. Access adds the Order field list to the top of the Query window and closes the dialog box.

   To perform the three calculations on the InvoiceAmt field, you need to add the field three times to the design grid.

3. Double-click **InvoiceAmt** in the Order field list three times to add three copies of the field to the design grid.

   You need to select an aggregate function for each InvoiceAmt field. When you click the Totals button on the Query Design toolbar, Access adds a row labeled "Total" to the design grid. The Total row provides a list of the aggregate functions that can be selected.

4. Click the **Totals** button Σ on the Query Design toolbar. Access inserts a row labeled "Total" between the Table and Sort rows in the design grid. See Figure 7-39.

Figure 7-39 Total row inserted in the design grid

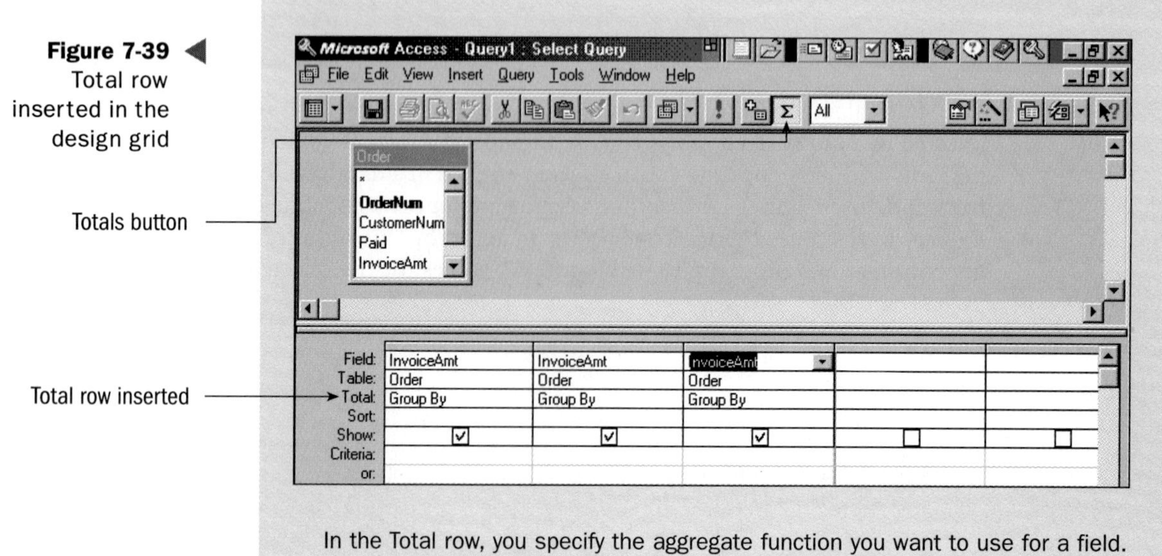

In the Total row, you specify the aggregate function you want to use for a field.

5. Click the right side of the first column's **Total** text box, then click **Sum**. This field will calculate the total of all the InvoiceAmt field values.

   Access automatically assigns a datasheet column name of "SumOfInvoice Amount" for this field. You can change the datasheet column name to a more descriptive or readable name by entering the name you want in the Field text box. However, you must also keep InvoiceAmt in the Field text box because it identifies the field whose values will be summed. The Field text box will contain the datasheet column name you specify followed by the field name (InvoiceAmt) with a colon separating the two names.

6. Position the pointer to the left of InvoiceAmt in the first column's Field text box, then type **Total of Quarter's Invoices:**. Be sure you include the colon at the end.

7. Click the right side of the second column's **Total** text box, then click **Avg**. This field will calculate the average of all the InvoiceAmt field values.

8. Position the pointer to the left of InvoiceAmt in the second column's Field text box, then type **Average of Quarter's Invoices:**.

9. Click the right side of the third column's **Total** text box, then click **Count**. This field will calculate the total number of invoices (orders).

10. Position the pointer to the left of InvoiceAmt in the third column's Field text box, then type **Number of Invoices:**.

    The columns in the design grid are too narrow to display the entire values in the Field text boxes, but you can resize the columns to see the entire entries.

11. Position the pointer at the right edge of the second column's field selector until the pointer changes to ↔, then double-click the mouse button. The column is resized to its best fit. See Figure 7-40.

Figure 7-40 Aggregate functions selected for the query

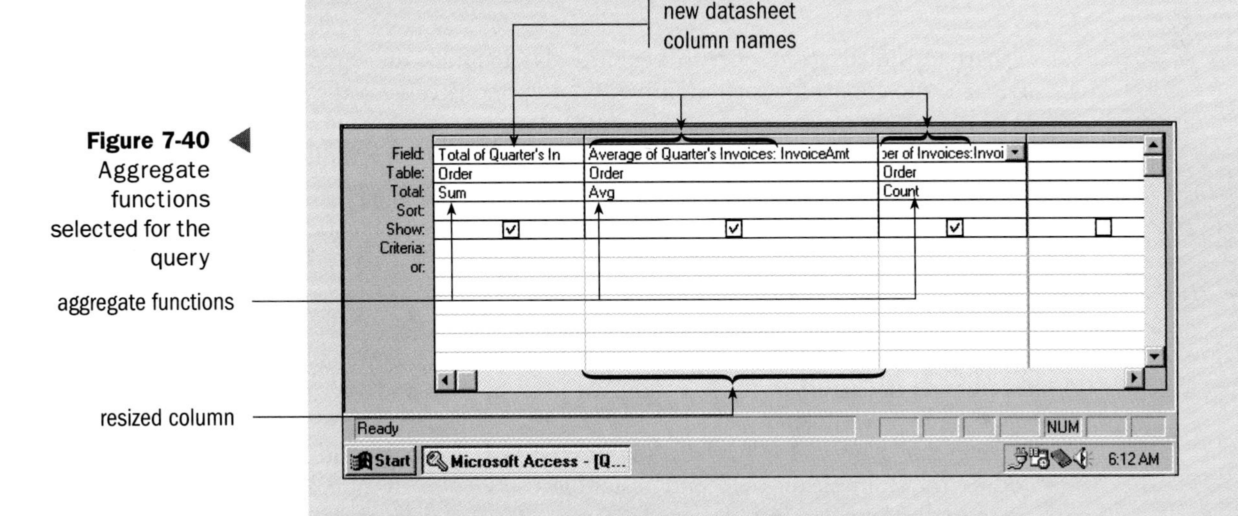

12. Repeat Step 11 to resize the first column and the third column.

The query design is complete, so you can run and save the query.

To run and save the query with aggregate functions:

1. Click the **Run** button on the Query Design toolbar. Access runs the query and displays one record containing the three aggregate function values. The one row of summary statistics represents calculations based on the 104 records selected in the query.

You need to resize the three columns to their best fit to see the column names.

2. Position the pointer in the first column's field selector. When the pointer changes to ↓, click to select the entire column.
3. Position the pointer in the third column's field selector until the pointer changes to ↓.
4. Press and hold the **Shift** key, then click the mouse button. All the columns are selected. Now you can resize all of them at once.
5. Position the pointer at the right edge of the third column's field selector until the pointer changes to ↔, then double-click the mouse button. All columns are resized to their best fit.

   To deselect the three columns you can position the insertion point anywhere in the displayed record.

6. Position the pointer at the start of the field value in the first column to deselect the three columns. See Figure 7-41.

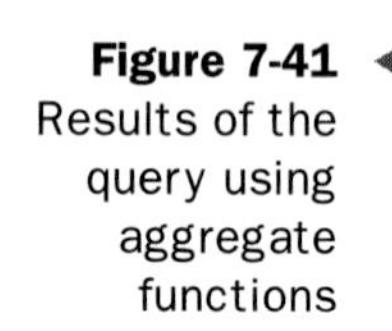

Figure 7-41 Results of the query using aggregate functions

Microsoft Access - Query1 : Select Query

File Edit View Insert Format Records Tools Window Help

Total of Quarter's Invoices	Average of Quarter's Invoices	Number of Invoices
$136,715.00	$1,314.57	104

You'll save the query as Quarterly Invoice Statistics.

7. Click the **Save** button on the Query Datasheet toolbar, type **Quarterly Invoice Statistics**, then press the **Enter** key.

Barbara's quarterly report to Leonard also includes the same invoice statistics (total, average, and count) for each month in the quarter. Because Valle Coffee sends invoices to their restaurant customers once a month, each invoice in a month has the same billing date. Barbara asks you to display the invoice statistics for each different billing date in the Order table, so that she will no longer have to calculate them.

Using Record Group Calculations

In addition to calculating statistical information on all or selected records in selected tables, you can calculate statistics for groups of records. For example, you can determine the number of customers in each state, the average sales by coffee type, or the total invoice amounts by billing date.

To create a query for Barbara's latest request, you can modify the current query by adding the BillingDate field and assigning the Group By operator to it. The **Group By operator** divides the selected records into groups based on the values in that field. Those records with the same value for the field are grouped together, and the datasheet displays one record for each group. Aggregate functions, which appear in the other columns of the design grid, provide statistical information for each group.

You need to modify the current query to add the Group By operator for the BillingDate field. This will display the statistical information grouped by billing date for the 104 selected records in the query.

To add the BillingDate field with the Group By operator, then run the query:

1. Click the **Query View** button for Design view on the Query Datasheet toolbar to switch to Design view.
2. Scroll the Order field list, then double-click **BillingDate** to add the field to the design grid. Group By, which is the default option in the Total row, appears for the BillingDate field.

   You've completed the query changes, so you can run the query.
3. Click the **Run** button on the Query Design toolbar. Access runs the query and displays three records, one for each BillingDate group. Each record contains the three aggregate function values and the BillingDate field value for the group. Again, the summary statistics represent calculations based on the 104 records selected in the query. See Figure 7-42.

Figure 7-42 Aggregate functions grouped by BillingDate

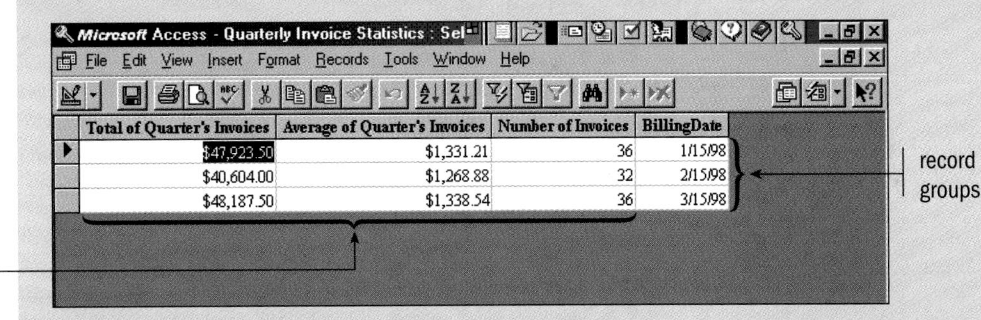

   You'll save the query as Quarterly Invoice Statistics by Billing Date, then close the query.
4. Click **File** on the menu bar, then click **Save As/Export**.
5. Position the insertion point to the right of the last character in the New Name text box, press the **spacebar**, type **by Billing Date**, then press the **Enter** key.
6. Click the **Close** button on the menu bar. The Database window becomes the active window.

Once every two weeks Kim Carpenter from the marketing department calls each restaurant customer to ask about the customer's satisfaction with Valle Coffee's service and coffee quality and to promote specials and new coffee products. When making these calls, Kim focuses on a single state. Therefore, she asks you to create a query that will display the customer name, city, state, owner name, and phone for all customers in a specific state, arranged in ascending order by customer name. You could create a query that uses a condition for the State field to select records in the specified state; then Kim could change the condition to view the data for a different state. A better approach, however, is to create a parameter query.

Creating a Parameter Query

With a **parameter query**, Access displays a dialog box and prompts you to enter your criteria, or parameters, each time you run the query. Access then displays the records in the datasheet that match the parameters just as if you had changed the criteria in Design view.

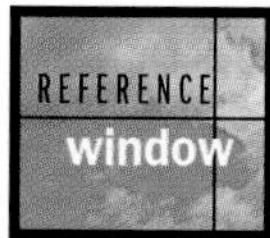

CREATING A PARAMETER QUERY

- Create a select query that includes all the fields that will appear in the datasheet. Also choose the sort keys and set the criteria that do not change when you run the query.
- Decide on the fields that will have prompts when you run the query. For each of them, type the prompt you want in the field's Criteria text box and enclose each prompt in brackets.
- Highlight the prompt, but do not highlight the brackets. Click the Copy button on the Query Design toolbar to copy the prompt to the Clipboard.
- Click Query on the menu bar, click Parameters, press Ctrl + V to paste the contents of the Clipboard into the Parameter text box, press the Tab key, then select the field's data type.
- Click the OK button.

You'll create a select query for Kim's request, then change it to a parameter query so that anyone running the query can enter the appropriate State field value to view the records for a particular state.

To create the parameter query:

1. Click the **New** button to open the New Query dialog box, click **Design View** (if necessary), then click the **OK** button. Access opens the Show Table dialog box on top of the Query window.

2. Click **Customer**, click the **Add** button, then click the **Close** button. Access adds the Customer field list to the Query window and closes the dialog box.

3. Scrolling as necessary in the Customer field list, double-click **CustomerName**, double-click **City**, double-click **State**, double-click **OwnerName**, then double-click **Phone** to add these five fields to the design grid, in that order.

   Next, you need to specify CustomerName as a sort key, because Kim wants the records to appear in ascending order by the CustomerName field values.

4. Click the right side of the **CustomerName Sort** text box, then click **Ascending**.

   Now you need to enter the prompt that will appear each time someone runs this query. The prompt will direct the user to enter the appropriate State field value to view its records.

5. Click the **State Criteria** text box, then type **[Enter a State:]**. You must include the brackets around the prompt to identify it as the prompt text.

6. Select the prompt, including the colon, but do not select the brackets. The parameter query will not work unless you highlight only the text "Enter a State:" because this is the text that you want to appear in a dialog box when you run the query. See Figure 7-43.

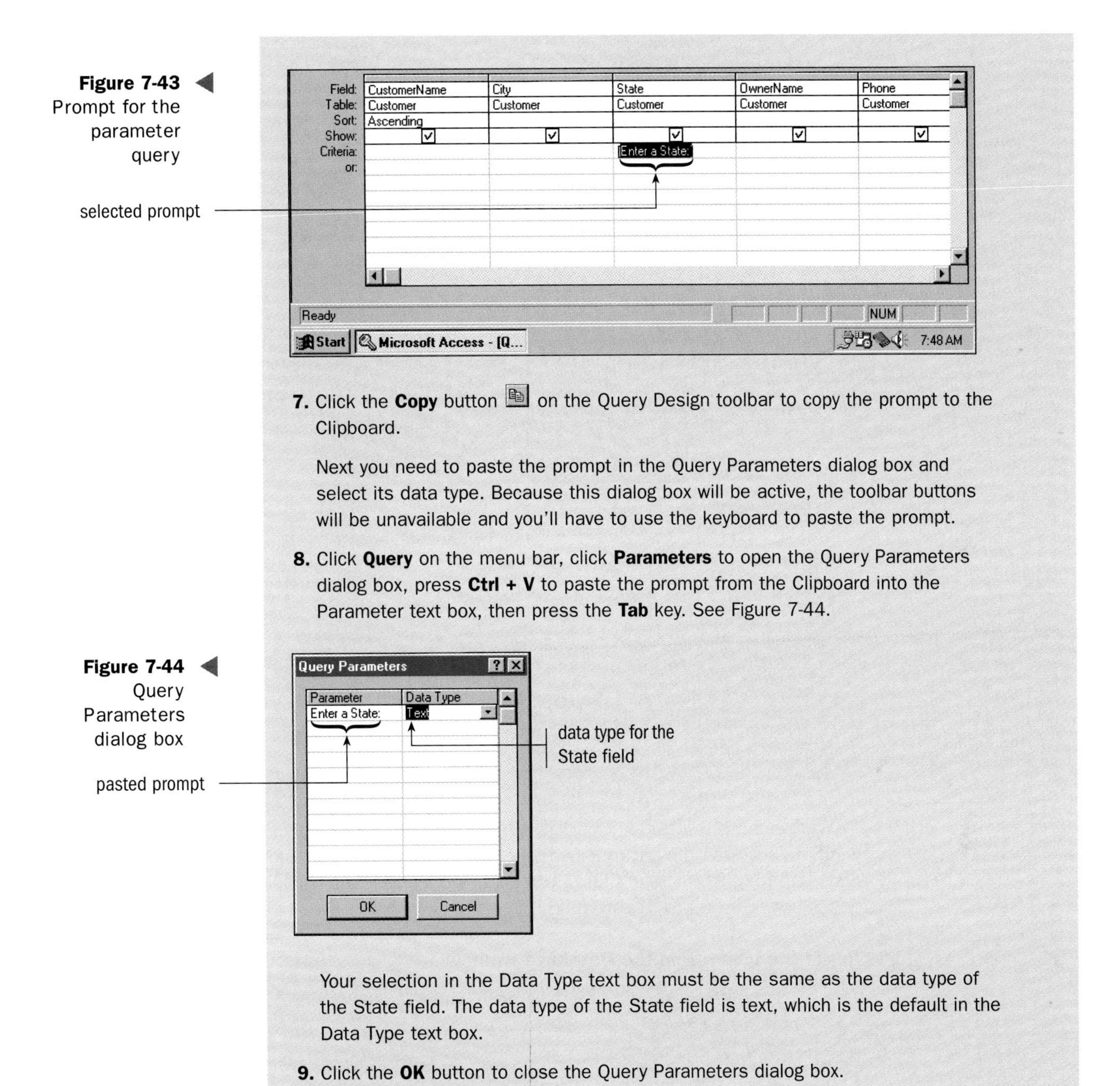

Figure 7-43 Prompt for the parameter query

7. Click the **Copy** button on the Query Design toolbar to copy the prompt to the Clipboard.

   Next you need to paste the prompt in the Query Parameters dialog box and select its data type. Because this dialog box will be active, the toolbar buttons will be unavailable and you'll have to use the keyboard to paste the prompt.

8. Click **Query** on the menu bar, click **Parameters** to open the Query Parameters dialog box, press **Ctrl + V** to paste the prompt from the Clipboard into the Parameter text box, then press the **Tab** key. See Figure 7-44.

Figure 7-44 Query Parameters dialog box

   Your selection in the Data Type text box must be the same as the data type of the State field. The data type of the State field is text, which is the default in the Data Type text box.

9. Click the **OK** button to close the Query Parameters dialog box.

You've completed the parameter query, so you can save it as "Customers in a Selected State" and then run it.

To save and run the parameter query:

1. Click the **Save** button on the Query Design toolbar, type **Customers in a Selected State**, then press the **Enter** key.

2. Click the **Run** button on the Query Design toolbar. The Enter Parameter Value dialog box appears with your prompt above the text box.

   The State field in the Customer table is defined as a two-character text field. To select customers in a specified state, you must enter the two-character State abbreviation for the state in any combination of lowercase and uppercase letters.

3. To display all the customers in the state of Indiana, type **IN** in the text box. See Figure 7-45.

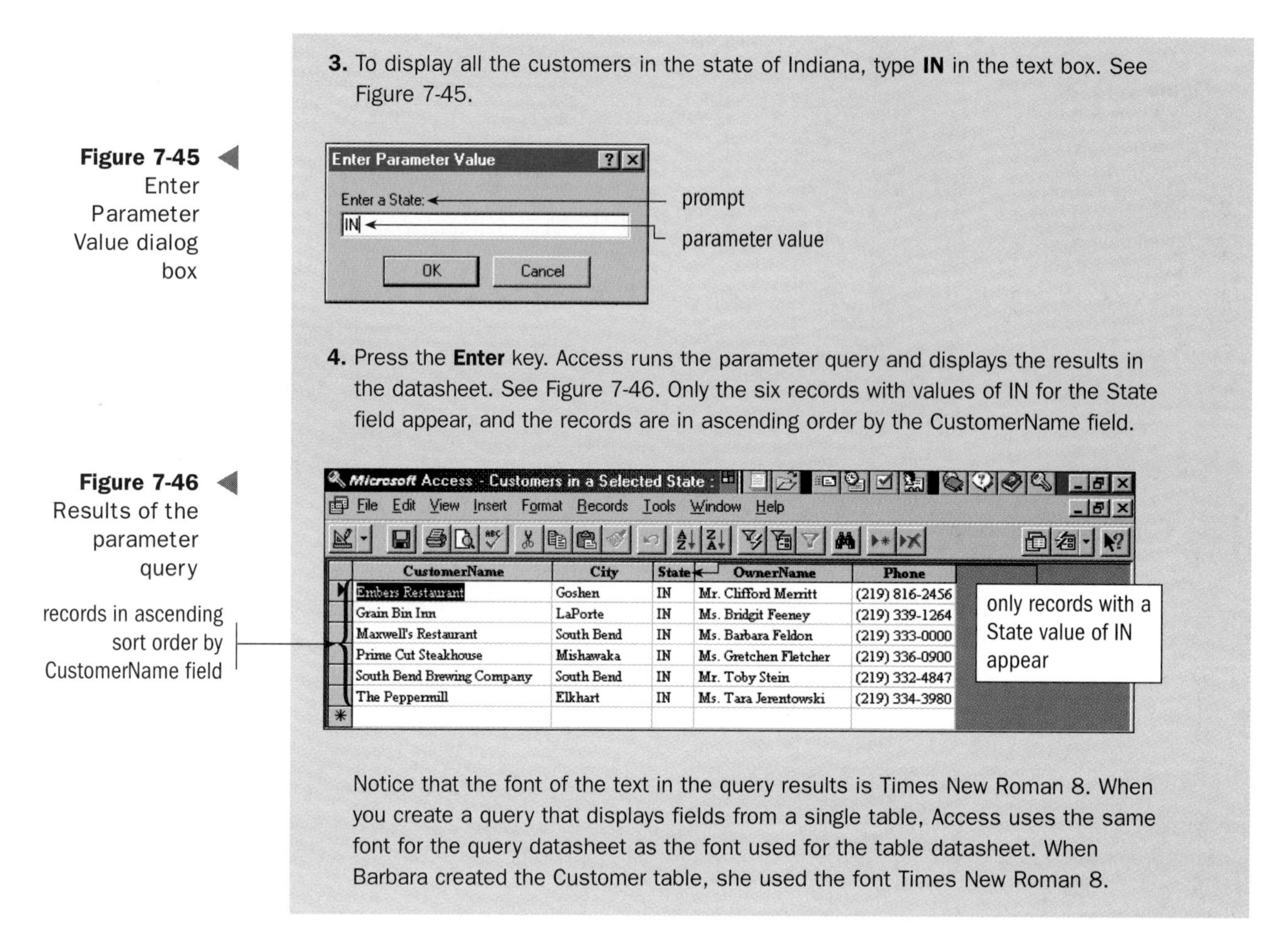

Figure 7-45 Enter Parameter Value dialog box

4. Press the **Enter** key. Access runs the parameter query and displays the results in the datasheet. See Figure 7-46. Only the six records with values of IN for the State field appear, and the records are in ascending order by the CustomerName field.

Figure 7-46 Results of the parameter query

Notice that the font of the text in the query results is Times New Roman 8. When you create a query that displays fields from a single table, Access uses the same font for the query datasheet as the font used for the table datasheet. When Barbara created the Customer table, she used the font Times New Roman 8.

You've completed the query that Kim can use when she places her customer calls. Kim wants to see how the parameter query works, and she asks you to run the query to display data for customers in Ohio. You'll run the query from the Database window because this is how Kim plans to run queries.

To run the query from the Database window:

1. Click the **Close** button on the menu bar to close the query and return to the Database window.

   To run a query from the Database window, you click the query name then click the Open button (or double-click the query name).

2. Click **Customers in a Selected State**, then click the **Open** button. The Enter Parameter Value dialog box appears with your prompt above the text box.

   Kim wants to see all customers located in Ohio.

3. Type **OH** then press the **Enter** key. The four customers located in Ohio appear in the datasheet.

4. Click the **Close** button on the menu bar to close the query and return to the Database window.

When she contacts restaurant customers about their unpaid invoices, Barbara prefers to concentrate on those invoices with the highest invoice amounts. She asks you to display the top 25% of unpaid orders based on the values of their invoice amounts and in decreasing order by their invoice amounts. For this request, you need to create a top values query.

Creating a Top Values Query

If you have a query that displays thousands of records, you might want to limit the number to a more manageable size; for example, you might choose to show just the first 20 records. The **Top Values property** for a query lets you limit the number of records displayed in the query datasheet. For the Top Values property you enter either an integer (such as 20, to show the first 20 records) or a percentage (such as 25%, to show the first quarter of the records). For example, suppose you have a query that displays 45 records. If you want the datasheet to show only the first five records, you can change the query by entering a Top Values property of either the number 5 or the percentage 10%. If you have specified a sort for the query, Access will display the records in order by the primary sort key. For the last record included in the display, if two or more records have the same value for the primary key, Access will include all these records in the query results.

For Barbara's request you need to select only the unpaid orders from the Order table. Because she wants to see the selected records in decreasing order by invoice amount, you'll add a sort so that the unpaid orders appear in order from highest to lowest invoice amount. When you select 25% for the query's Top Values property, Access will display one-quarter of the unpaid orders; these will have the highest invoice amounts.

To create the top values query:

1. Click the **New** button to open the New Query dialog box, click **Design View** (if necessary), then click the **OK** button.
2. In the Show Table dialog box, click **Order**, click the **Add** button, then click the **Close** button. Access adds the Order field list to the Query window and closes the dialog box.
3. Double-click the **Order field list title bar** to select all the fields in the table, then drag the highlighted fields to the first column's Field text box. Access adds all the fields from the table to the design grid.

   To select only the unpaid orders, you need to enter the condition "no" for the Paid field.
4. Click the **Paid Criteria** text box, then type **no**.

   Next, you need to choose InvoiceAmt as the sort key, using a descending sort order.
5. Click the right side of the **InvoiceAmt Sort** text box, then click **Descending**. Notice that the condition for the Paid field changes to "No."

   Now you need to change the value of the Top Values property. The Top Values text box appears to the right of the Totals button on the Query Design toolbar. You can select a value from the Top Values list or type an integer or percent value in the Top Values text box.
6. Click the **Top Values** list arrow on the Query Design toolbar, then click **25%**. See Figure 7-47.

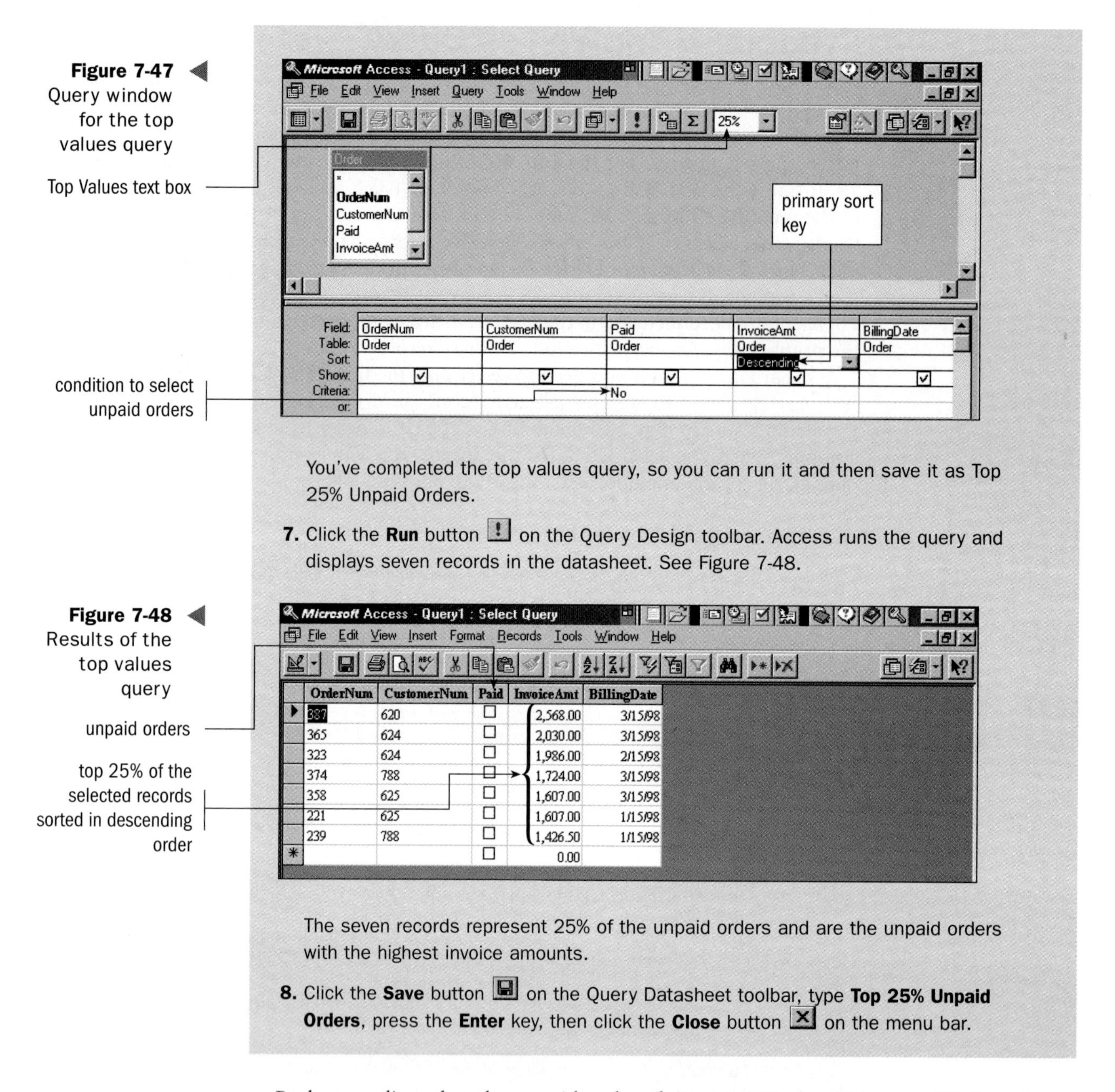

Figure 7-47 Query window for the top values query

You've completed the top values query, so you can run it and then save it as Top 25% Unpaid Orders.

7. Click the **Run** button on the Query Design toolbar. Access runs the query and displays seven records in the datasheet. See Figure 7-48.

Figure 7-48 Results of the top values query

The seven records represent 25% of the unpaid orders and are the unpaid orders with the highest invoice amounts.

8. Click the **Save** button on the Query Datasheet toolbar, type **Top 25% Unpaid Orders**, press the **Enter** key, then click the **Close** button on the menu bar.

Barbara realizes that the unpaid orders from 1/15/98 should have a 5% late charge applied to the invoice amounts. She asks you to create an update query to add the late charge amounts to the invoice amounts.

Creating an Action Query

Queries enable you to do more than display, sort, select, join, change, and filter data; you can also run queries to perform actions on the data in a database. For example, you can create queries, called action queries, to delete or update selected records in a database. An **action query** is a query that adds, changes, or deletes multiple database records at one time. Action queries save time and eliminate the chance for error when compared with modifying the records individually; however, because they modify many records at a time, you should design and test them carefully before running them.

Access provides four types of action queries: the make-table query, the append query, the update query, and the delete query.

- Use a **make-table query** to create a new table from one or more existing tables. The new table can be an exact copy of an existing table, a subset of the fields and records of an existing table, or a combination of the fields and records from two or more tables. Access does not delete the selected fields and records from the existing tables. You can use make-table queries, for example, to create backup copies of tables or to create customized tables for others to use.
- Use an **append query** to add records from an existing table or query to the end of one or more tables. Access does not delete the selected data from the original tables. You can use append queries, for example, when some of the records in one table don't exist in the other table.
- Use an **update query** to change selected fields and records in one or more tables. You choose the fields and records you want to change by entering the selection criteria and update rules. You can use update queries, for example, to increase the salaries of selected employee groups by a specified percentage or to change the coffee type from one value to another.
- Use a **delete query** to delete a group of records from one or more tables. You choose which records you want to delete by entering the selection criteria. Once the records are deleted, they are removed permanently from the database. You can use delete queries, for example, to remove data about discontinued products or inactive customers.

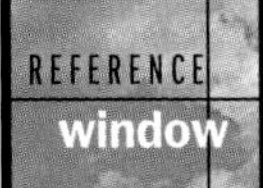

CREATING AND RUNNING AN ACTION QUERY

- Create a select query that includes all the fields that will be involved in the action query.
- Click the Query Type list arrow on the Query Design toolbar, then click the appropriate action query.
- Complete the entries in the design grid.
- Click the Query View button for Datasheet view to preview the fields and records in the datasheet without running the query, then click the Query View button for Design view.
- Click the Run button to execute the action query.

For Barbara's request you will create an update query to add a 5% late charge to the invoice amounts for all unpaid invoices billed on 1/15/98. When you run the update query, Access will change the invoice amount in each selected record.

To create the update query:

1. Click the **New** button to open the New Query dialog box, click **Design View** (if necessary), then click the **OK** button.
2. In the Show Table dialog box, click **Order**, click the **Add** button, then click the **Close** button. Access adds the Order field list to the Query Design window and closes the dialog box.

   Because the query will update the invoice amounts for all unpaid orders billed on 1/15/98, you need to add the Paid, InvoiceAmt, and BillingDate fields to the query. You will enter conditions for the Paid and BillingDate fields on which to base record selection, and the InvoiceAmt field values will be updated.
3. In the Order field list, double-click **Paid**, double-click **InvoiceAmt**, scroll the field list, then double-click **BillingDate**.

   Next, you need to enter the conditions to select records for only the unpaid orders billed on 1/15/98.

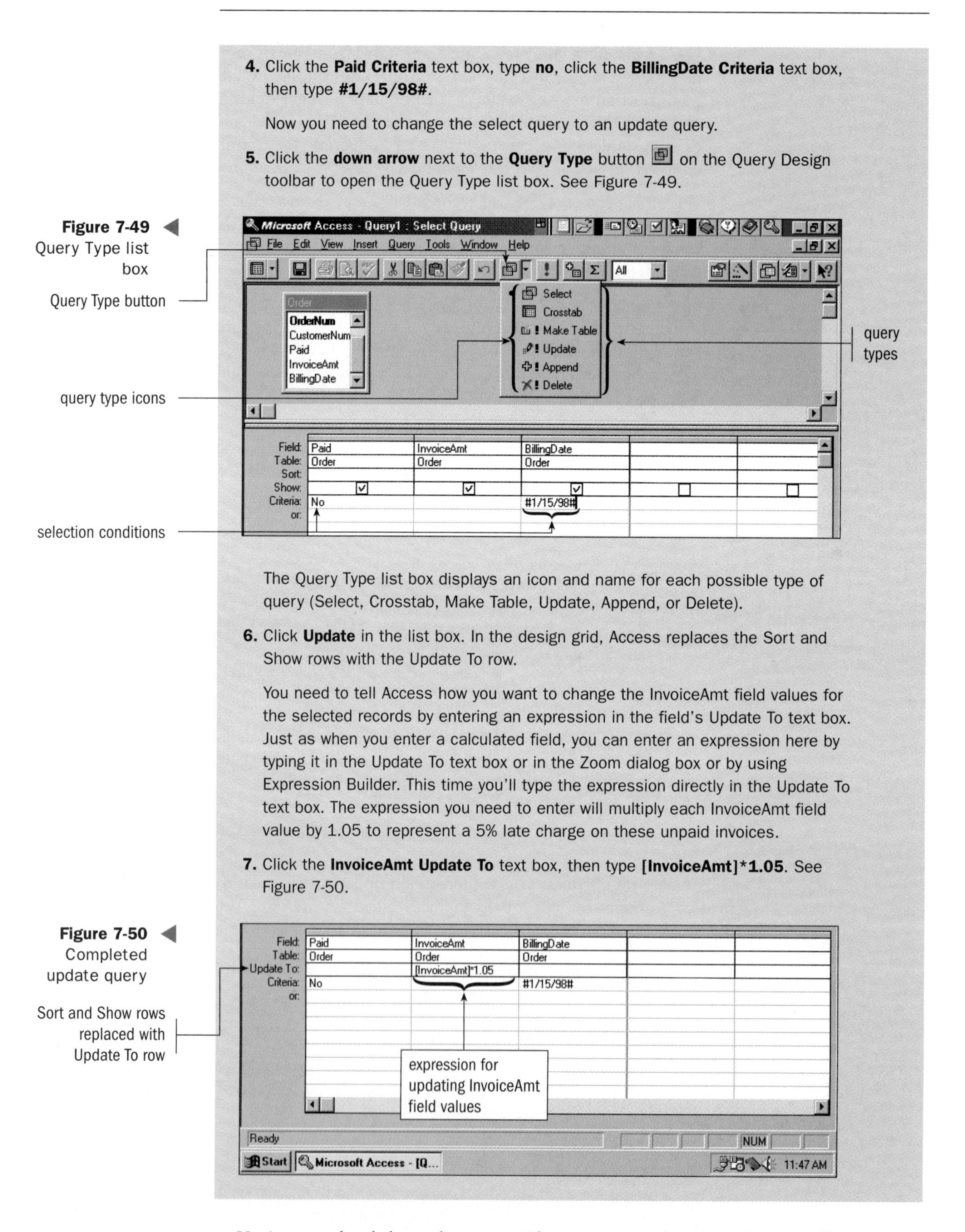

4. Click the **Paid Criteria** text box, type **no**, click the **BillingDate Criteria** text box, then type **#1/15/98#**.

   Now you need to change the select query to an update query.

5. Click the **down arrow** next to the **Query Type** button on the Query Design toolbar to open the Query Type list box. See Figure 7-49.

Figure 7-49 Query Type list box

   The Query Type list box displays an icon and name for each possible type of query (Select, Crosstab, Make Table, Update, Append, or Delete).

6. Click **Update** in the list box. In the design grid, Access replaces the Sort and Show rows with the Update To row.

   You need to tell Access how you want to change the InvoiceAmt field values for the selected records by entering an expression in the field's Update To text box. Just as when you enter a calculated field, you can enter an expression here by typing it in the Update To text box or in the Zoom dialog box or by using Expression Builder. This time you'll type the expression directly in the Update To text box. The expression you need to enter will multiply each InvoiceAmt field value by 1.05 to represent a 5% late charge on these unpaid invoices.

7. Click the **InvoiceAmt Update To** text box, then type **[InvoiceAmt]*1.05**. See Figure 7-50.

Figure 7-50 Completed update query

You've completed the update query. If you now run the query, Access will update the invoice amounts for the selected records, whether or not you've created the query correctly. Therefore, as a precaution before running the query, you should view the datasheet for the selected records. If the wrong records have been selected, you can change the selection criteria then view the datasheet again. When the query is correct, you then can run the query.

To display the datasheet then run the update query:

1. Click the **Query View** button for Datasheet view on the Query Design toolbar. In the datasheet Access displays the InvoiceAmt field values for the six records that meet the criteria: unpaid invoices for 1/15/98. The field values displayed are the current values before you run the update query. See Figure 7-51.

Figure 7-51 InvoiceAmt field values before running the update query

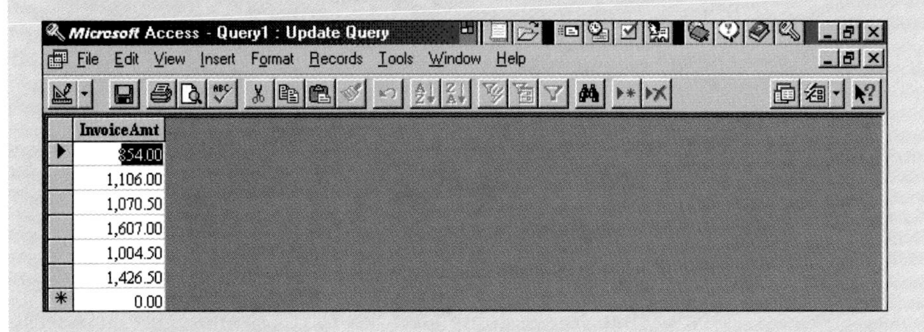

   For an update query, Access displays only those fields that will be updated, so only the InvoiceAmt field appears in the datasheet. The Paid and BillingDate fields, which are needed to select the correct Order table records, do not appear in the datasheet.

2. Click the **Query View** button for Design view on the Query Datasheet toolbar to switch back to Design view.

3. Click the **Run** button on the Query Design toolbar. Access opens a dialog box asking you to confirm the update for the six records. This is a precaution Access takes because the query will be changing multiple records in the database.

4. Click the **Yes** button. Access runs the update query and leaves the Query window displayed in Design view.

   To verify the update, you'll switch to the datasheet.

5. Click the **Query View** button for Datasheet view on the Query Design toolbar. The six values for the InvoiceAmt field have been increased by 5%. See Figure 7-52.

Figure 7-52 InvoiceAmt field values after running the update query

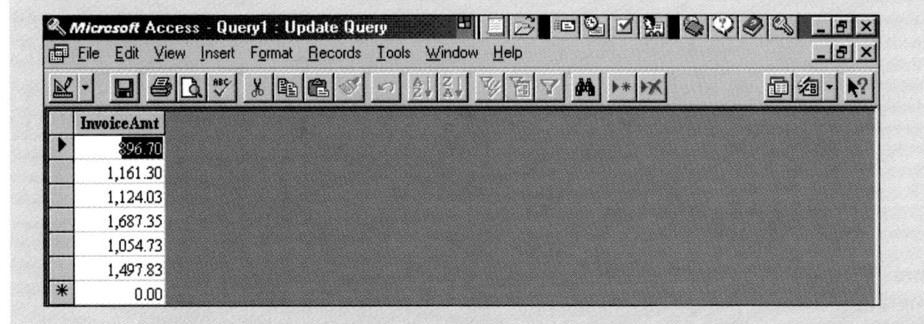

   Action queries usually serve a one-time need to change the data in a database for a specific purpose. Because you usually run an action query only once, you do not normally need to save it.

6. Click the **Close** button on the menu bar. Access opens a dialog box asking if you want to save the query.

7. Click the **No** button to return to the Database window without saving the query.

Quick Check

1. How does a table field differ from a calculated field?
2. Where do you find the name of a calculated field?
3. What is an aggregate function?
4. The __________ operator divides selected records into groups based on the values in a field.
5. Before the datasheet is displayed, what special action must you take when you run a parameter query?
6. What two types of values can you use for a top values query?
7. What is the difference between a select and an action query?

Now that you've completed Session 7.2, you can exit Access or you can continue to the next session.

SESSION 7.3

In this session you will learn how to create a custom form, add fields to a form, resize and move form controls, select and align multiple form controls, use captions, add a combo box to a form, add a graphic image to a form, modify a graphic image in Paint, and compact a database.

Customizing Forms

Barbara's staff members use several forms created with the Access Form Wizards to maintain the data in the Restaurant Coffee Orders database. Although the forms were easy to create, some staff members are having difficulty using them. For example, staff members spend too much time looking up different codes, such as the values for the CoffeeCode and WeightCode fields, when entering data using the forms. Also, the fields on the forms are not well organized; Barbara thinks they should be separated into groups in order to draw attention to important data and allow her staff to find specific data more easily.

Barbara has designed a new form that she and her staff will use to maintain data in the Product table (Figure 7-53). You'll create this new form following Barbara's design.

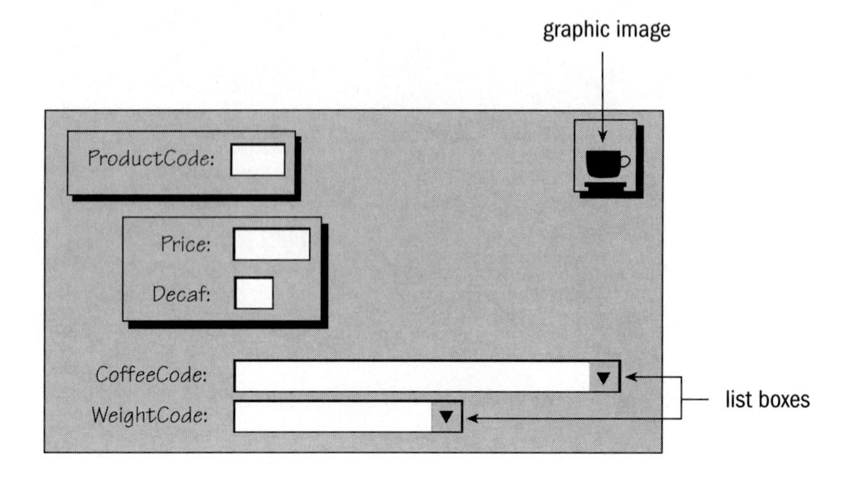

Figure 7-53 Design of a custom form to maintain Product table data

The ProductCode field, which is the primary key of the Product table, is boxed separately from all the other data on the form. The Price and Decaf fields are grouped together in another box. Two list boxes will display the CoffeeCode and CoffeeName fields and the WeightCode and Weight/Size fields, respectively. Although the CoffeeName and Weight/Size fields are not in the Product table, their presence on the form will help Barbara's staff to select the correct CoffeeCode and WeightCode field values when using the form to enter data in the table. Finally, Barbara wants you to include a graphic image of a coffee cup in the upper-right of the form for visual interest.

You will create a custom form to implement the form's design. A **custom form** is either a form you create without using a Form Wizard or a form created by a Form Wizard that you modify. The following guidelines for designing forms will help you to create a form that presents information in an attractive way and allows those who use the form to work more productively:

- Arrange the fields on the screen in an order that is meaningful to users of the form. For instance, if a user enters data from a printed document, use that document as a guide for arranging the data on the form.
- Group together logically related fields. Leave space between groups or use lines and boxes to separate groups.
- Use properties such as font, style, color, and graphics to improve the appearance of the form and to emphasize important areas and controls. However, keep these visual effects to a minimum; too many visual effects tire the eyes and draw attention to too many areas at one time.
- Make the form self-explanatory by using controls such as list boxes, check boxes, radio buttons, and push buttons instead of codes and lengthy explanations.

The Form Window in Design View

You use the Form window in Design view to create custom forms and to modify all forms. To create Barbara's custom form, you will create a blank form based on the Product table in Design view.

To create a blank form in the Form window:

1. Click the **Forms** tab in the Database window, then click the **New** button. The New Form dialog box opens.
2. If necessary, click **Design View** in the list box to select this method for creating a form.
3. Click the list arrow for selecting a table or query on which to base the form, scroll the list box, click **Product**, then click the **OK** button. The Form window opens in Design view.
4. If the Form window is maximized, click the **Restore** button on the menu bar. See Figure 7-54.

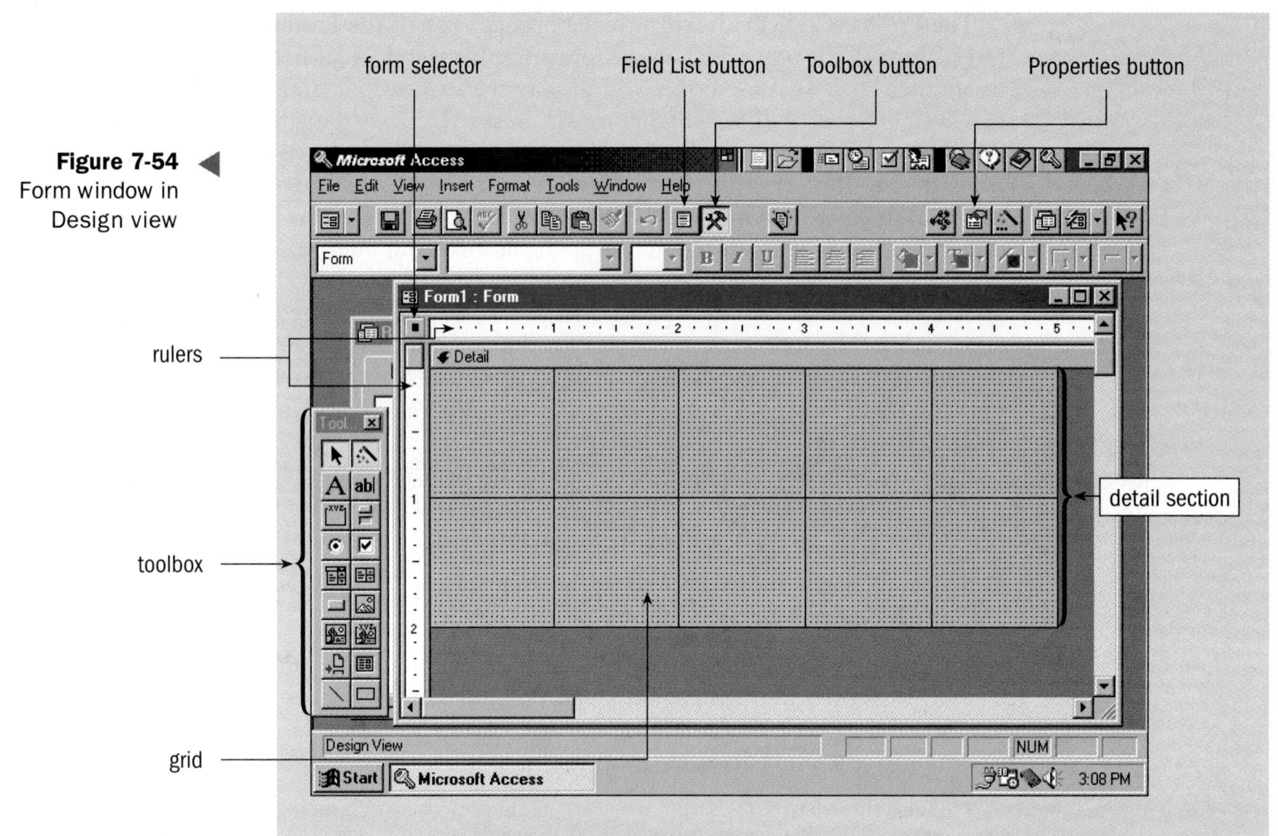

Figure 7-54 Form window in Design view

TROUBLE? If the rulers, grid, or toolbox do not appear on your screen, click View on the menu bar, then click Ruler, Grid, or Toolbox to display the missing component. A check mark appears in front of these View menu commands when the components are displayed in the Form window. If the grid is still invisible or if the grid on your screen contains fewer dots than shown in Figure 7-54, click the Properties button on the Form Design toolbar, scroll the property sheet, select the Grid X property value, type 24, select the Grid Y property value, type 24, then click the Properties button again. If the Properties button is selected, click it to close the property sheet. If the toolbox appears in a location different from the one shown in Figure 7-54, drag its title bar until it is in the same location.

Controls

The Form window in Design view contains a horizontal ruler along the top and a vertical ruler along the left side. The **rulers** assist you in determining the horizontal and vertical dimensions of a form and serve as a guide to the placement of controls on a form. A **control** is an object, such as a text box, list box, rectangle, line, or command button, that you place on a form to display data, perform an action, or make the form easier to read and use. Access has three types of controls—bound controls, unbound controls, and calculated controls.

- A **bound control** is linked, or bound, to a field in a table or query. You use a bound control to display or update a table field value. The most common type of bound control is a text box.
- An **unbound control** is not linked to a field in a table or query. You use an unbound control to display text, such as a form title or instructions, rectangles and lines, and graphics and pictures from other programs. If you use an unbound control to display text, the unbound control is called a **label**.

- A **calculated control** displays a value calculated from an expression based on data from one or more fields in a database.

When you want to create a bound control, click the Field List button on the Form Design toolbar to display the field list for the underlying table or query. You can then drag fields from the field list to the Form window, placing the bound controls where you want them to appear on the form.

To place other controls on a form, you use the buttons, called **tools**, on the toolbox. The **toolbox** is a special toolbar containing buttons that represent the tools you use to place controls on a form. If you want to display or hide the toolbox, click the Toolbox button on the Form Design toolbar. A summary of the more commonly used tools available in the toolbox is shown in Figure 7-55.

Figure 7-55 Commonly used tools available in the toolbox

Icon	Tool Name	Control Purpose on a Form
	Bound Object Frame	Display a picture, graph, or other OLE object stored in an Access database; a bound control
	Combo Box	Display a drop-down list box, so that you can either type a value or select a value from the list; can use a Control Wizard to create
	Command Button	Display a command button that runs a macro or calls a Visual Basic for Applications event procedure when the button is clicked; can use a Control WIzard to create
	Control Wizards	When selected, activates Control Wizards for certain other toolbox tools
A	Label	Display text, such as a title or instructions; an unbound control
	Line	Display a horizontal, vertical, or diagonal line
	List Box	Display a list of values from which you can choose one value; can use a Control Wizard to create
	Option Group	Display a group frame containing toggle buttons, option buttons, or check boxes; can use a Control Wizard to create
	Rectangle	Display a rectangle
	Select Objects	Select, move, size, and edit controls or deselect other tools
	Subform/Subreport	Display both a main form from a primary table and a subform from a related table; can use a Control Wizard to create
ab|	Text Box	Display a label attached to a text box that contains a bound control or a calculated control
	Unbound Object Frame	Display a graph, spreadsheet, or other OLE object created in another program; an unbound control

To open and close the property sheet for a selected control, a section of the form, or the entire form, you use the Properties button on the Form Design toolbar. You use the **property sheet** to modify the appearance, behavior, and other characteristics of the overall form, a section of the form, or the controls on the form. For example, you can change a control's size or position on the form using the control's property sheet. The properties listed in the property sheet differ depending on the type of control selected. You select a control by clicking it, a section by clicking in any blank area in the section, and an entire form by clicking the **form selector**.

Form Sections

The form's **detail section** is the area in which you place the fields, labels, and most other controls for the form. You can change the default detail section size by dragging the edges of the section. The **grid** consists of the dots that appear in a section. These dots help you to position controls precisely on a form. When you position or move a control, its top or bottom edge and its left or right edge always line up exactly on the grid dots.

You can add four other sections to a form by using the View menu. The other four sections are the form header, form footer, page header, and page footer. You can use the **form header** and **form footer sections** for special information, such as titles, dates, and instructions, that you want to appear only at the top or bottom of a form on the screen or in print. Use the **page header** and **page footer sections** for information, such as column headings or page numbers, that you want to appear at the top or bottom of each page in the printed form.

Adding Fields to a Form

Based on Barbara's form design, you need to add the ProductCode, Price, and Decaf fields from the Product table to the form. To do this, you must open the field list for the Product table, then drag the fields to the grid. When you add a field in this way, Access adds a bound control to the form. The bound control consists of a label and, to its right, a text box that will contain the field value when you use the form.

Now you'll add the three fields to the grid.

To add the three fields as bound controls to your form:

1. Click the **Field List** button on the Form Design toolbar. Access opens the field list for the Product table.

2. Drag **ProductCode** from the field list to the grid. When you move the pointer to the grid, it changes to . See Figure 7-56.

Figure 7-56 Dragging the ProductCode field to the grid

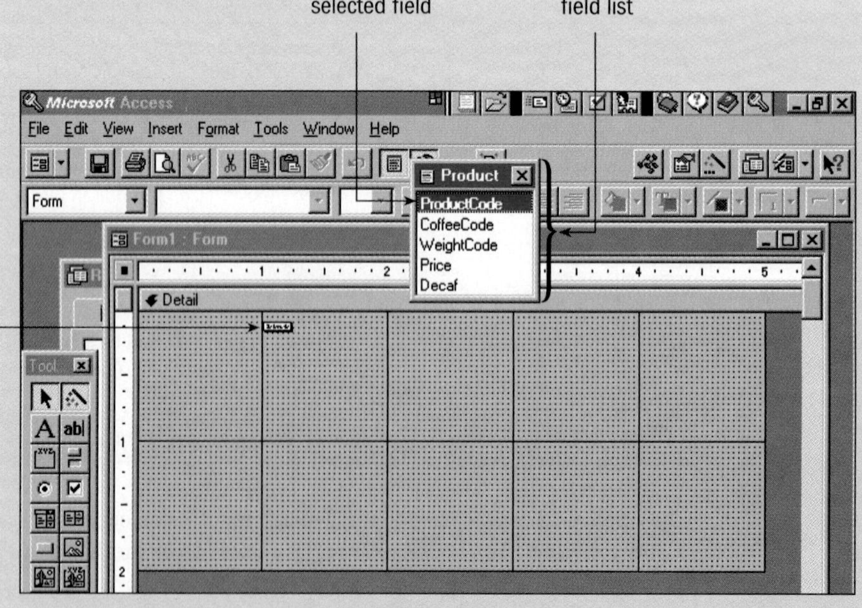

3. When the pointer is positioned as shown in Figure 7-56, release the mouse button. Access adds a bound control, which consists of a label and a text box, to the grid. The top and left edges of the text box are placed in a position similar to that of the field pointer, and the label is positioned to the left of the text box.

4. Repeat Steps 2 and 3 for the **Price** and **Decaf** fields, positioning the controls as shown in Figure 7-57.

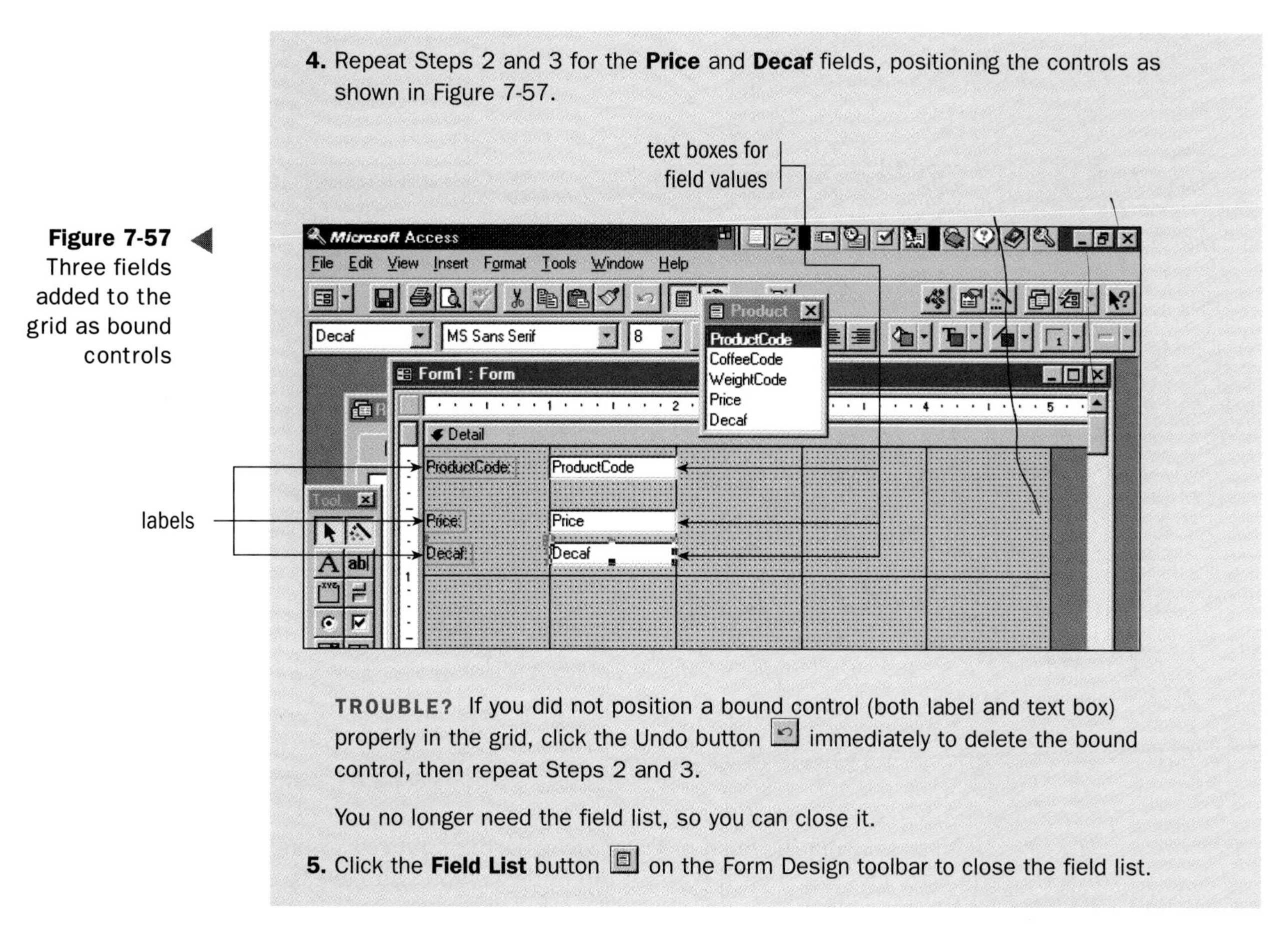

Figure 7-57 Three fields added to the grid as bound controls

TROUBLE? If you did not position a bound control (both label and text box) properly in the grid, click the Undo button immediately to delete the bound control, then repeat Steps 2 and 3.

You no longer need the field list, so you can close it.

5. Click the **Field List** button on the Form Design toolbar to close the field list.

Performing operations in the Form Design window might seem awkward for you at first. With practice you will become comfortable with creating a custom form. Remember that you can always click the Undo button immediately after you make a form adjustment that produced results you don't like. Also, you should save the form frequently and view your progress creating the form periodically in Form view.

Viewing and Saving a Form

When you create a custom form, you should check your progress in Form view to see the evolving form with actual field values from the database. You might see adjustments you need to make to the form. You should also save the form frequently, especially after you have completed a series of form modifications successfully. If you then make a series of form changes incorrectly, you can close the form without saving the changes and open the last saved version of the form.

Next, you'll switch to Form view to see how the new form looks and then save the form as Pricing.

To switch to Form view, then save the form:

1. Click the **Form View** button on the Form Design toolbar. Access closes the Form window in Design view and opens it in Form view.
2. Click the **Save** button on the Form View toolbar. The Save As dialog box opens.
3. Type **Pricing** then press the **Enter** key. Access saves the form as Pricing, which appears in the form's title bar. See Figure 7-58.

Figure 7-58 Form window in Form view

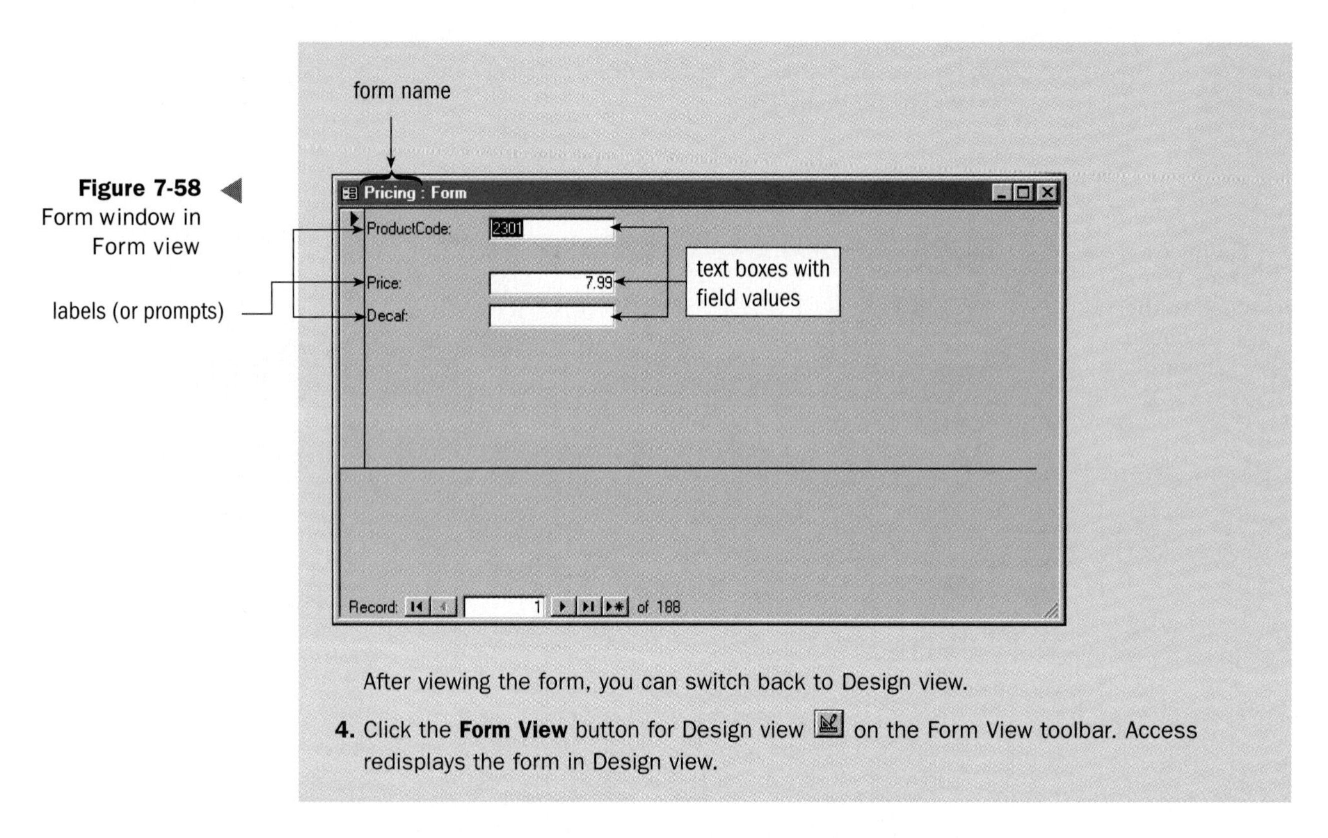

After viewing the form, you can switch back to Design view.

4. Click the **Form View** button for Design view on the Form View toolbar. Access redisplays the form in Design view.

When viewing the form in Form view, Barbara noticed several changes she wants you to make. First, the text boxes are too large, so you will have to resize them. Second, the labels, also called **prompts**, are too far from their related text boxes, which makes it difficult to identify the text boxes. Barbara wants you to move the labels closer to the text boxes and align them on the right instead of the left. Finally, she wants you to change the title of the form, which appears in the title bar, to Product Data.

Resizing Controls

When you click a control, such as a text box or label, sizing handles appear on the border of the control indicating it is selected and can be modified. You use the sizing handles to change the dimensions of a control in the same way that you modify objects in other Office 95 programs. Sometimes when you select a control, controls that were selected previously remain selected too. Therefore, you first should deselect any controls you don't want to modify by clicking an open area in the grid.

The first of Barbara's changes to the form is to resize all three text boxes to make them smaller.

To resize the three text box controls:

1. Click an open area in the grid to deselect all controls.
2. Click the **ProductCode** text box to select it. Sizing handles appear around the text box, and move handles appear in the upper-left corner of the text box and its related label.
3. Move the pointer to the right side of the ProductCode text box over the middle handle. See Figure 7-59.

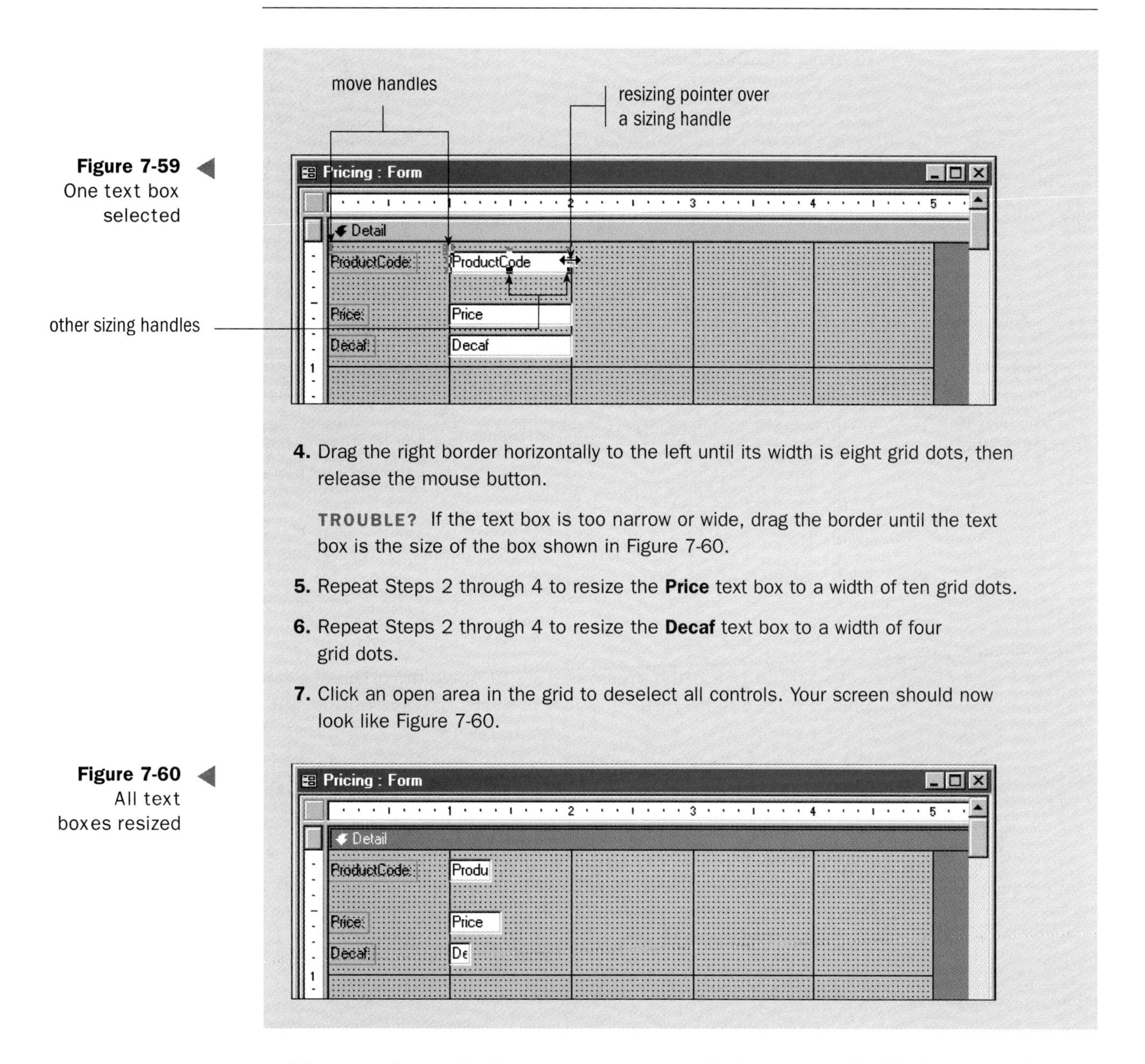

Figure 7-59 One text box selected

4. Drag the right border horizontally to the left until its width is eight grid dots, then release the mouse button.

   TROUBLE? If the text box is too narrow or wide, drag the border until the text box is the size of the box shown in Figure 7-60.

5. Repeat Steps 2 through 4 to resize the **Price** text box to a width of ten grid dots.
6. Repeat Steps 2 through 4 to resize the **Decaf** text box to a width of four grid dots.
7. Click an open area in the grid to deselect all controls. Your screen should now look like Figure 7-60.

Figure 7-60 All text boxes resized

The next change Barbara wants you to make is to move the labels so that they are closer to their text boxes on the form.

Moving Controls

You can move a text box and its related label together. To move them, you first select them both by clicking the text box. Then place the pointer anywhere on the border of the text box, but *not* on a move or sizing handle. When the pointer changes to ✋, drag the text box and its related label to the new location. As you move the boxes, their outlines move to show you the changing position.

You can also move either the text box or its label individually. For example, if you want to move the text box but not its label, place the pointer on the text box's move handle. When the pointer changes to ☝, drag the text box to the new location. You use the label's move handle in a similar way to move just the label.

You can also delete a text box and its label or delete just the label. To delete both boxes together, click the text box to select both boxes, right-click the text box to open its shortcut menu, then click Cut on the menu. To delete just the label, perform the same steps, clicking the label instead of the text box.

As Barbara requested, you need to move the Decaf label to the right so that it is closer to its text box.

To move the Decaf label:

1. Click the **Decaf** label to select it.
2. Position the pointer on the Decaf label's move handle. When the pointer changes to , drag the label horizontally to the right, until there's one column of grid dots between the label and the text box. Release the mouse button. The label and text box should not touch each other, and there should be one column of grid dots between the two controls.
3. Click an open area in the grid to deselect the Decaf label. Your screen should now look like Figure 7-61.

Figure 7-61 Form window after moving the Decaf label

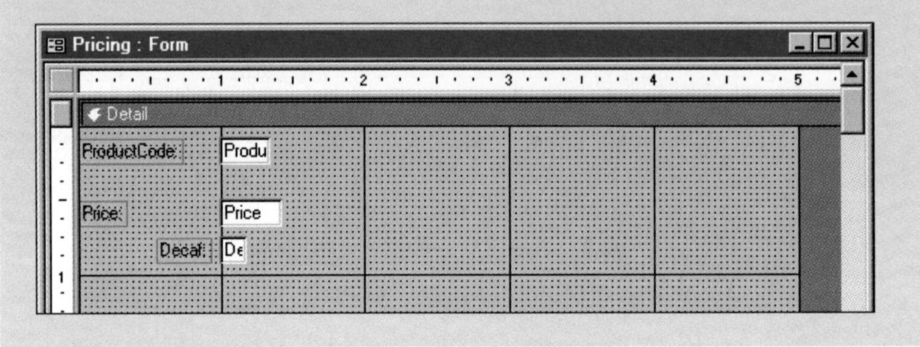

You could repeat the previous steps to move the other two labels, so that all three are aligned on the right. Instead, you will select all three objects and align them on the right at the same time.

Selecting and Aligning Multiple Controls

So far you've worked with one control at a time. However, you can often work more productively if you select and manipulate multiple controls at the same time. To select multiple controls you click each control while holding down the Shift key. The next operation you perform on one of the controls applies to all the selected controls.

To align the three labels, you'll select them and align all of them at the same time.

To select and align the three labels:

1. Click the **Decaf** label to select it.
2. Press and hold down the **Shift** key, then click the **ProductCode** and **Price** labels.
3. Release the **Shift** key. Handles appear around all three controls.

   TROUBLE? If any label is not selected, press and hold down the Shift key, then click that label.

4. Click **Format** on the menu bar, point to **Align**, then click **Right**. Access aligns the labels on their right edges. See Figure 7-62.

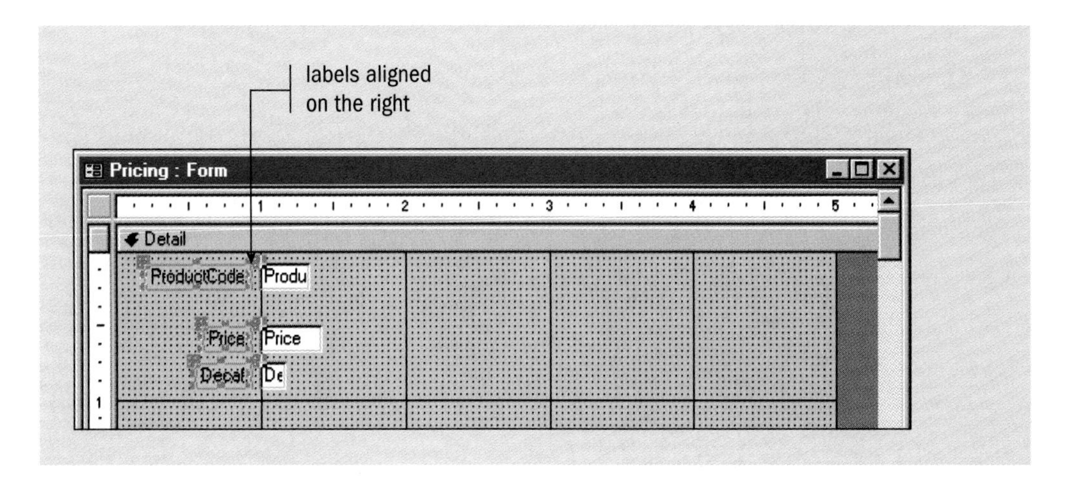

Figure 7-62 Form after aligning labels

Next, Barbara wants you to change the form title in the title bar from "Pricing" to "Product Data." To make this change you need to use a caption.

Using Captions

In Access you can use the **Caption property** to provide a **caption**, or identifying text, in the following situations:

- For an entire form, the caption is the identifying text that appears in the title bar of the form.
- For labels and command buttons, the caption is the identifying text that appears on those controls.
- For table fields, the caption is the identifying text that appears as the column heading in the table or query datasheet and as the label on the form.

To change the text in the title bar to Product Data, you need to set the form's Caption property.

To set the form's Caption property:

1. Click the **form selector**, which is the box where the rulers meet. See Figure 7-63. A small black box appears inside the form selector, indicating that the entire form is selected.
2. Click the **Properties** button on the Form Design toolbar, then click the **All** tab, if necessary. The property sheet for the form opens.

   TROUBLE? If the property sheet is in a different position from the one in Figure 7-63, drag the property sheet title bar to the position shown in the figure.
3. Scroll the list of properties, if necessary, click the **Caption** text box, then type **Product Data**. See Figure 7-63.

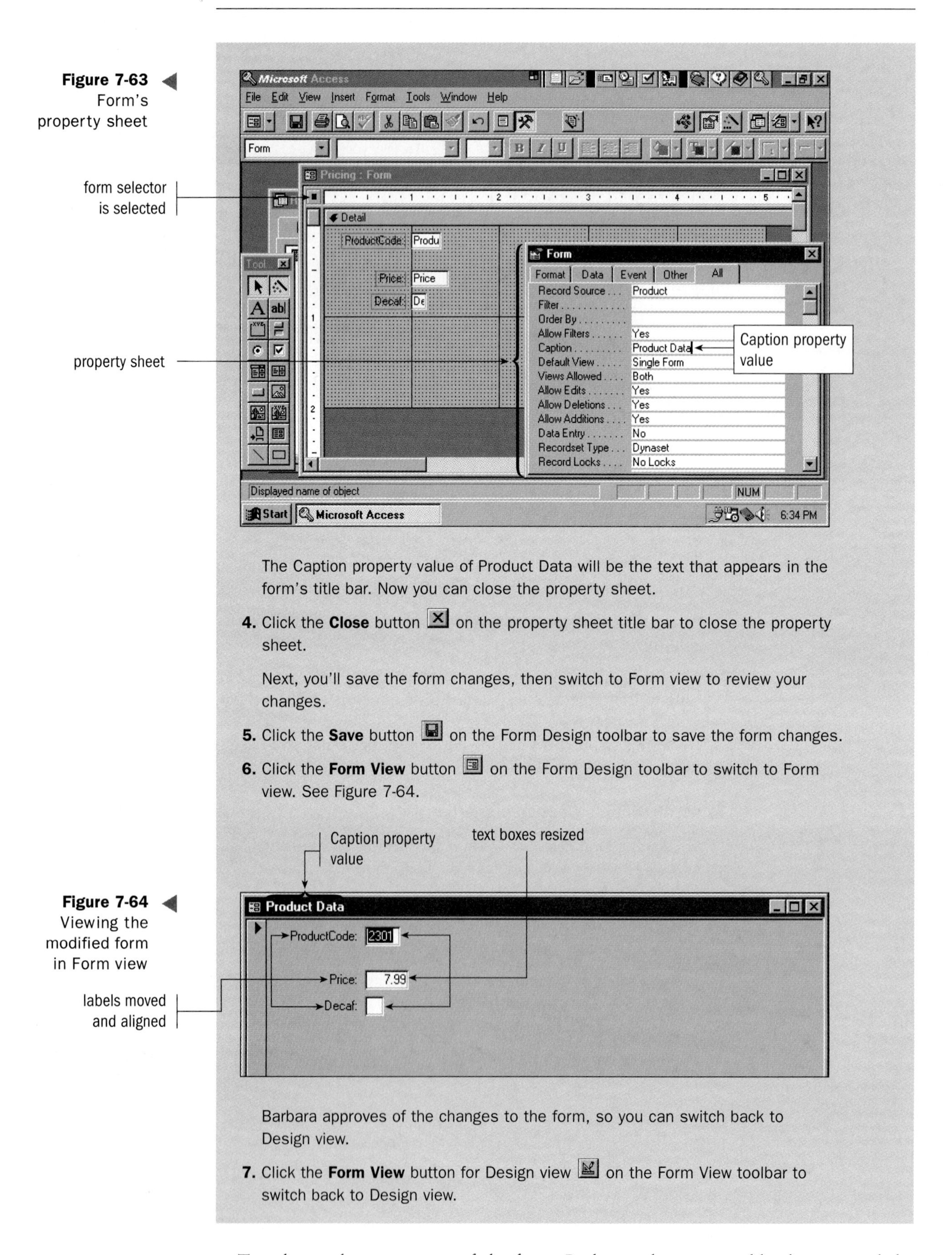

Figure 7-63 Form's property sheet

The Caption property value of Product Data will be the text that appears in the form's title bar. Now you can close the property sheet.

4. Click the **Close** button on the property sheet title bar to close the property sheet.

   Next, you'll save the form changes, then switch to Form view to review your changes.

5. Click the **Save** button on the Form Design toolbar to save the form changes.

6. Click the **Form View** button on the Form Design toolbar to switch to Form view. See Figure 7-64.

Figure 7-64 Viewing the modified form in Form view

Barbara approves of the changes to the form, so you can switch back to Design view.

7. Click the **Form View** button for Design view on the Form View toolbar to switch back to Design view.

To enhance the appearance of the form, Barbara asks you to add a box around the ProductCode bound control and a second box around the Price and Decaf bound controls. Placing boxes around these areas will help them to stand out from the rest of the form.

Placing a Rectangle Around Controls

Access provides rectangle and line tools that allow you to add visual effects to a form and to emphasize the form's data. You draw a line using the toolbox **Line tool** and a rectangle using the toolbox **Rectangle tool**. After drawing a rectangle, you can use the Special Effect and Back Style properties to change its appearance. As shown in Figure 7-65, the **Special Effect property** choices are flat, raised, sunken, etched, shadowed, and chiseled. The **Back Style property** choices are transparent and normal.

Figure 7-65 Options for the Special Effect and Back Style properties

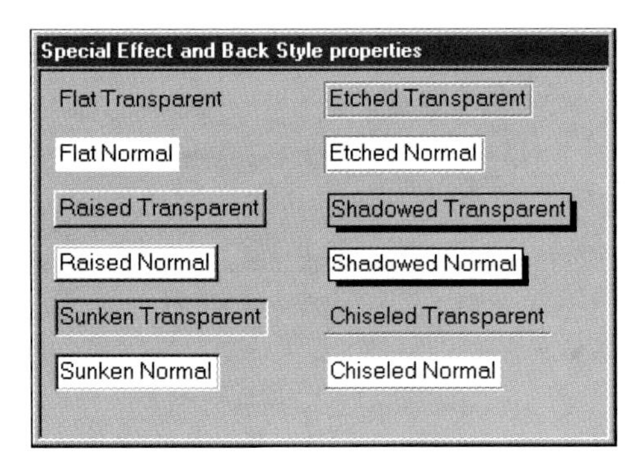

You need to draw two rectangles—one around the ProductCode bound control and one around both the Price and Decaf bound controls. For each of these rectangles, Barbara wants you to choose the shadowed Special Effect property, then set the Border Color property to blue to match the color of the coffee cup graphic you will add to the form later.

To draw the two rectangles and set their properties:

1. Click the **Rectangle** tool on the toolbox, position the pointer + in the third column of grid dots from the left and along the top edge of the detail section, click and hold the mouse button, then drag a rectangle down and to the right, releasing the mouse button when the pointer + is positioned two grid-dot rows below the ProductCode boxes and two grid-dot columns to their right. See Figure 7-66.

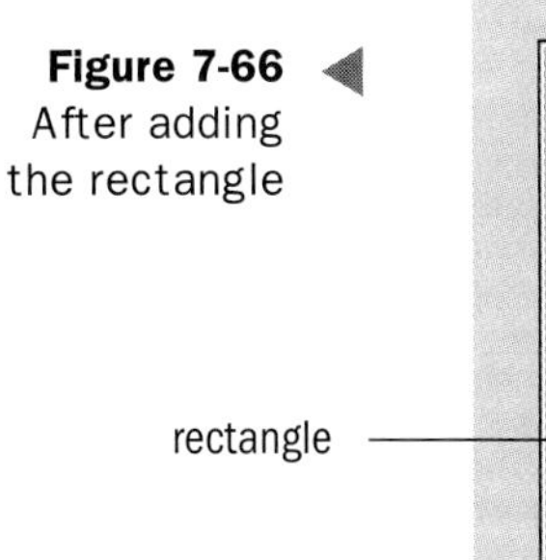

Figure 7-66 After adding the rectangle

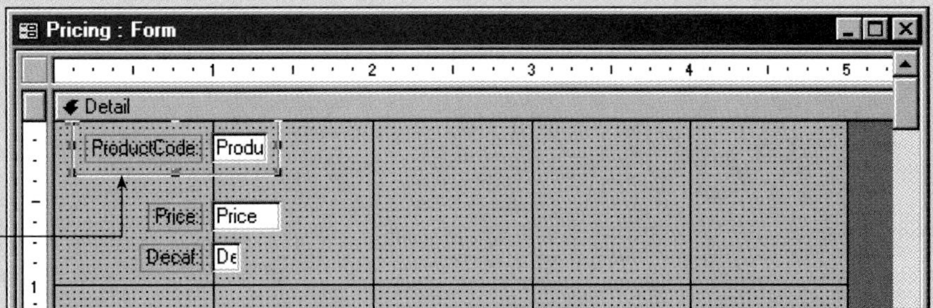

TROUBLE? If your rectangle is not positioned correctly, you can click the Undo button and repeat Step 1, or you can use the sizing handles to resize the rectangle and the move handle to reposition the rectangle.

Note that "Pricing" appears in the title bar even though you've changed the form's Caption property to "Product Data." After you set a form's Caption property, the Caption property value appears in the form title bar in Form view, but the form name continues to appear in the title bar in Design view. After you finish creating the form, you'll change the form name to "Product Data" so that this name will appear in Design view as well.

2. Click the **Properties** button on the Form Design toolbar to open the property sheet for the selected rectangle.

   Note that the title bar of the property sheet includes the notation "Rectangle: Box4," which indicates that the rectangle object is selected. "Box4" also appears in the Select Object box on the Formatting toolbar. You can use the Select Object box to select objects instead of clicking them.

   TROUBLE? Access might not have assigned the name "Box4" to your rectangle. Don't be concerned if Access assigned a number other than 4; this has no effect on your form design.

3. Click the right side of the **Special Effect** text box in the property sheet, then click **Shadowed**. Access adds the shadowed special effect to the rectangle.

   You can also use the Special Effect button on the Formatting toolbar to set a rectangle's Special Effect property. Likewise, you can use the property sheet or Formatting toolbar to set a rectangle's Border Color property.

4. Click the down arrow next to the **Border Color** button on the Formatting toolbar. The palette of border colors appears. See Figure 7-67.

Figure 7-67 Displaying the Border Color palette

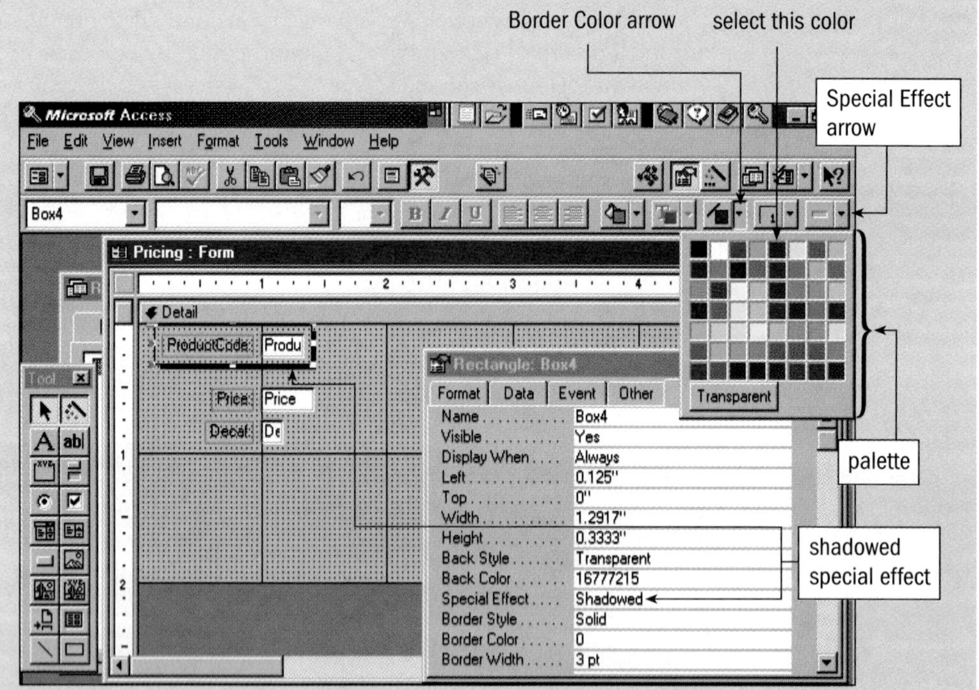

   You use the *palette* to change the color of the rectangle's border and to choose between the normal and transparent Back Style property. You also use the palette to choose the foreground and background color and appearance of controls.

   Barbara wants you to change the border color of the form to a blue color similar to the blue color in the coffee cup graphic, which you will add to the form later.

5. Click the **blue** color, which is the fourth color from the right in the top row of the palette (see Figure 7-67). Access changes the shadowed border color from black to blue. Notice that the blue color now appears on the Border Color button.

   TROUBLE? If your palette looks different from the one shown in Figure 7-67, the appropriate blue color might be in a different position. If this is the case, reopen the palette, then click the blue color that most closely matches the blue color shown in the figure.

Next, you'll add the rectangle around the Price and Decaf boxes.

6. Click the **Rectangle** tool on the toolbox, position the pointer + three grid-dot columns to the left of the Price boxes and two grid-dot rows above them, click and hold the mouse button, then drag a rectangle down and to the right, releasing the mouse button when the pointer + is positioned two grid-dot columns to the right of the Price text box and two grid-dot rows below the Decaf boxes. Notice that the title bar of the property sheet now displays "Rectangle: Box5" (a digit other than 5 might appear on your screen) and the Select Object box displays "Box5."
7. Repeat Step 3 to apply the shadowed effect to the rectangle.
8. Click the **Border Color** button on the Formatting toolbar to apply the same blue color to the rectangle.
9. Click the **Properties** button on the Form Design toolbar to close the property sheet. See Figure 7-68.

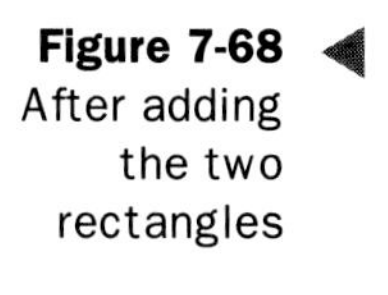
Figure 7-68 After adding the two rectangles

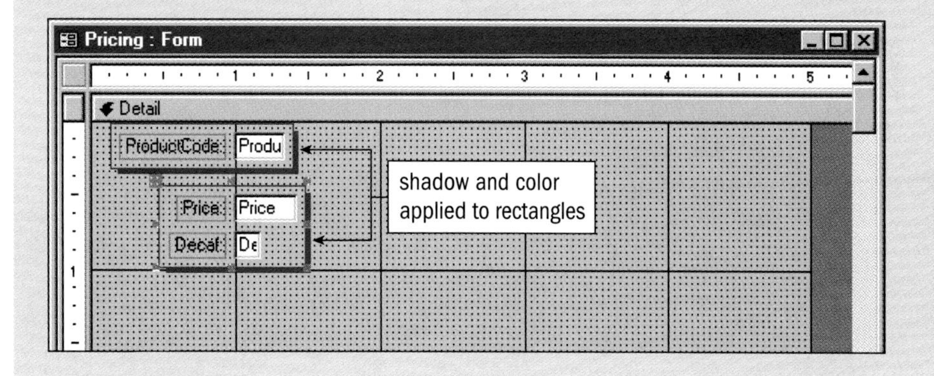

The CoffeeCode and WeightCode fields will also be included in the Product Data form. For these fields Barbara asks you to add combo boxes to make it easier for her staff to enter the correct values for them.

Adding a Combo Box Using Control Wizards

A **combo box** is a control that displays a drop-down list box, so that you can either type a value for the field or select its value from the list box. You can use a combo box when a field, such as the CoffeeCode field, is a coded value that might not be easy to remember. In the combo box you can display a list of all the acceptable values for the CoffeeCode field, and the corresponding values for the CoffeeName field, from the Coffee table. You then scroll the list box until you find the proper CoffeeName field value and click that row to assign the corresponding CoffeeCode field value to the CoffeeCode field in the Product table. When you add a combo box to a form, Access adds a label to its left to identify the combo box.

You use the toolbox **Combo Box tool** to add a combo box to a form. Depending on whether the toolbox Control Wizards tool is selected, you can add a combo box with or without using Control Wizards. A **Control Wizard** is an Access tool that asks you a series of questions, then creates a control on a form based on your answers.

You will use the Combo Box Wizard to add two combo boxes to the form—one for the CoffeeCode field and one for the WeightCode field. First, you'll add the combo box for the CoffeeCode field.

To add the CoffeeCode combo box using the Combo Box Wizard:

1. If necessary, click the **Control Wizards** tool on the toolbox. Make sure this tool is selected.

   TROUBLE? If the detail section on your form is not 2" high, you need to change it. Position the pointer at the bottom edge of the detail section. When the pointer changes to ╋, click and drag the bottom edge of the detail section to the 2" mark on the vertical ruler.

2. Click the **Combo Box** tool on the toolbox. When you move the pointer into the form, the pointer changes to . See Figure 7-69.

Figure 7-69 Positioning the combo box

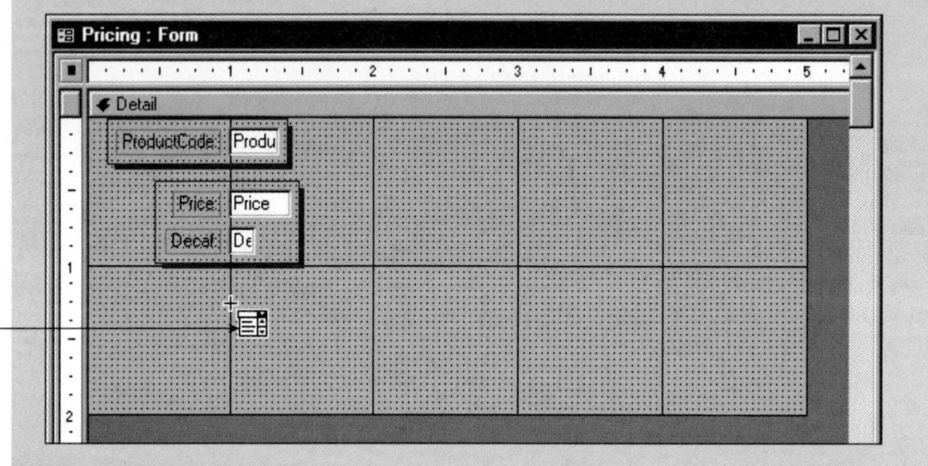

3. Click the combo box pointer at the position shown in Figure 7-69. After a few seconds, the first Combo Box Wizard dialog box opens. In this dialog box, you specify how the combo box will get its values. In this case, you want the combo box to look up certain values in the Coffee table.
4. Click the top radio button, if necessary, then click the **Next** button. Access opens the second Combo Box Wizard dialog box, in which you select the table or query that contains the values for the combo box.
5. Click **Coffee** in the list box, if necessary, then click the **Next** button. Access opens the third Combo Box Wizard dialog box, in which you choose the fields for the combo box. You will include the CoffeeCode and CoffeeName fields, because Barbara wants to easily identify which coffee is represented by each coffee code.
6. Click the **>** button twice to move CoffeeCode and CoffeeName to the Selected Fields list box, then click the **Next** button. Access opens the fourth Combo Box Wizard dialog box, in which you adjust the column widths for the combo box columns.

   Only the CoffeeName column appears and you need both the CoffeeCode and CoffeeName columns for the combo box.

7. Click the **Hide key column** check box to deselect the option and display the CoffeeCode column.
8. Size both columns to their best fit, making sure you scroll the list to check that all the values are completely visible. Recall that when you size columns to their best fit only the visible values are sized properly. You need to scroll the list then resize a column if you see values too wide for the column.

9. Click the **Next** button. Access opens the fifth Combo Box dialog box, in which you choose the field you want updated in the database when you make a selection in the combo box.

10. Click **CoffeeCode**, if necessary, then click the **Next** button. Access opens the sixth Combo Box dialog box, in which you choose whether you want to store the selected CoffeeCode value in the database.

11. Click the **Store that value in this field** radio button, click the list box arrow, click **CoffeeCode**, then click the **Next** button. Access opens the last Combo Box dialog box, in which you choose the caption for the label related to the combo box.

12. Type **CoffeeCode:** then click the **Finish** button. Access closes the Combo Box Wizard dialog box and displays the completed combo box on the form. See Figure 7-70.

Figure 7-70 After adding the combo box to the form

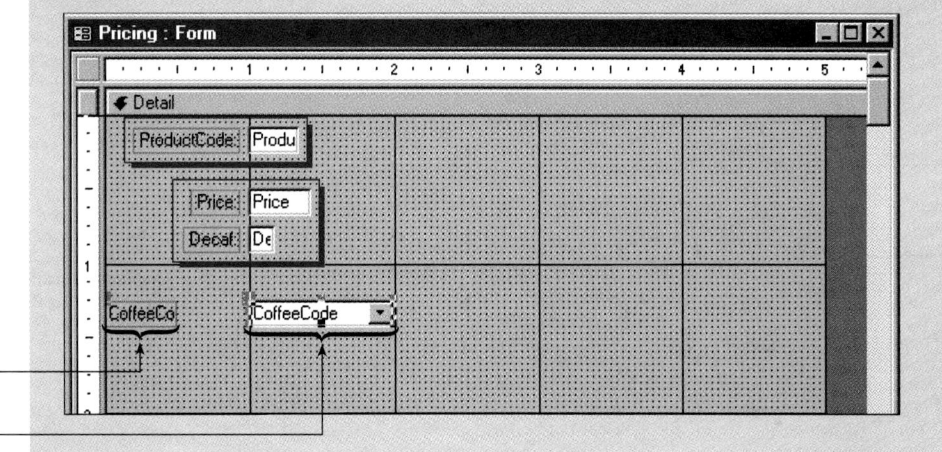

The combo box appears so that its upper-left corner is in the same location where you earlier clicked the + in the combo box pointer, and the label for the combo box appears to its left. Note that the label caption is not fully visible in the box, so you'll need to resize the box.

You have to make several adjustments to the combo box and its related label. First you'll increase the width of the label and align it on the right with the other labels.

To resize and align the CoffeeCode label:

1. Click the **CoffeeCode** label, click **Format** on the menu bar, point to **Size**, then click **to Fit**. The label widens so that the entire caption is visible.

2. Press and hold the **Shift** key, click the **Decaf** label, then release the **Shift** key. Both the Decaf and CoffeeCode labels are selected.

3. Right-click the **CoffeeCode** label, point to **Align** on the shortcut menu, then click **Right**. The CoffeeCode label shifts to the right to align on the right with the Decaf label, the other selected label.

Now you'll save the form changes then switch to Form view to review those changes.

To save the form then switch to Form view:

1. Click the **Save** button on the Form Design toolbar to save the form changes.

2. Click the **Form View** button on the Form Design toolbar to switch to Form view.

3. Click the **CoffeeCode** list arrow to display the contents of the combo box. See Figure 7-71.

Figure 7-71 Combo box open on the form

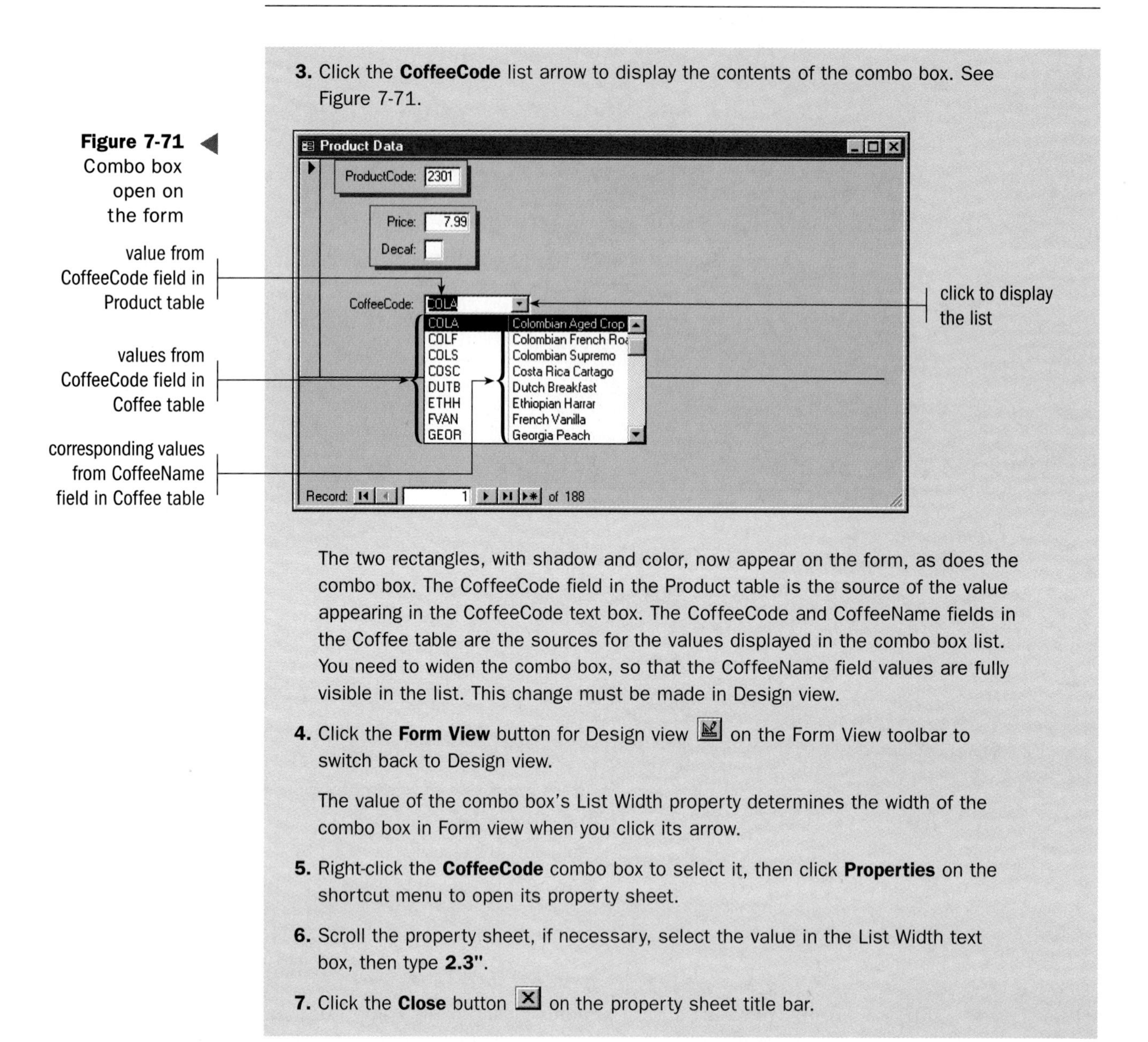

The two rectangles, with shadow and color, now appear on the form, as does the combo box. The CoffeeCode field in the Product table is the source of the value appearing in the CoffeeCode text box. The CoffeeCode and CoffeeName fields in the Coffee table are the sources for the values displayed in the combo box list. You need to widen the combo box, so that the CoffeeName field values are fully visible in the list. This change must be made in Design view.

4. Click the **Form View** button for Design view on the Form View toolbar to switch back to Design view.

   The value of the combo box's List Width property determines the width of the combo box in Form view when you click its arrow.

5. Right-click the **CoffeeCode** combo box to select it, then click **Properties** on the shortcut menu to open its property sheet.
6. Scroll the property sheet, if necessary, select the value in the List Width text box, then type **2.3"**.
7. Click the **Close** button on the property sheet title bar.

The second combo box you need to add is for the WeightCode field. The WeightCode text box will contain the value of the WeightCode field in the Product table, and the combo box list will contain the WeightCode and Weight/Size field values in the Weight table. You will add this combo box to the form in the Tutorial Assignments at the end of this tutorial.

The final change Barbara wants you to make is to add the graphic image of a coffee cup to the form. She thinks the graphic image will enhance the visual interest of the form.

Embedding and Changing a Graphic Image on a Form

Barbara wants you to embed a graphic image of a coffee cup on the form. Sources of graphic images include Microsoft Paint, other drawing programs, and scanners.

To embed a graphic image on a form, you position an unbound object frame on the design screen where you want the graphic to appear. An **unbound object frame** is a control on a form that displays an OLE object not stored in a table in an Access database. You use this control to create and change the graphic from within the form using the program in which the object was originally created. For example, you can embed the coffee cup graphic image on the form and change it, if necessary, using Paint. To create an unbound object frame you use the toolbox Unbound Object Frame tool.

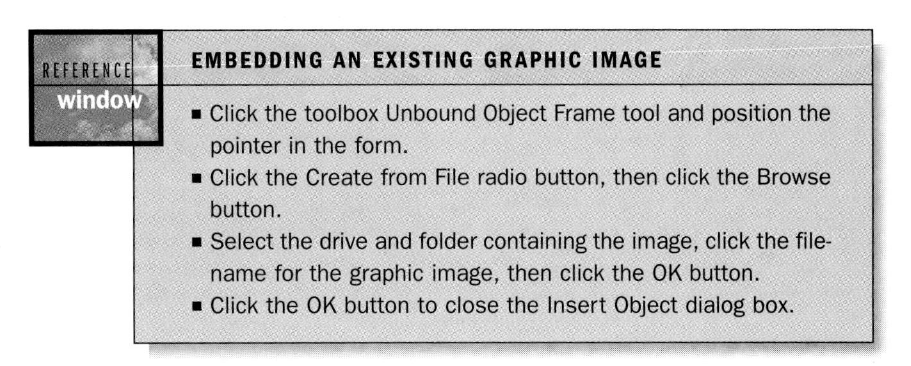

REFERENCE window

EMBEDDING AN EXISTING GRAPHIC IMAGE

- Click the toolbox Unbound Object Frame tool and position the pointer in the form.
- Click the Create from File radio button, then click the Browse button.
- Select the drive and folder containing the image, click the filename for the graphic image, then click the OK button.
- Click the OK button to close the Insert Object dialog box.

You'll embed the graphic image of the coffee cup in an unbound object frame on the form. The file containing the coffee cup image, which is named BlueCup, is stored on your Student Disk.

To embed the graphic image on the form:

1. Click the **Unbound Object Frame** tool on the toolbox.
2. Move the pointer to the form, then click the pointer when it is positioned as shown in Figure 7-72. The Insert Object dialog box opens.

position pointer here

Figure 7-72 Positioning the unbound object frame

3. Click the **Create from File** radio button, then click the **Browse** button to open the Browse dialog box.
4. Click the **Drives** list arrow, then select the drive containing your Student Disk.
5. Double-click **Tutorial.07** in the Directories list box.
6. Click **BlueCup.bmp** in the File Name list box, click the **OK** button to close the Browse dialog box, then click the **OK** button to close the Insert Object dialog box. After several seconds, Access embeds the graphic image in an unbound object frame. See Figure 7-73.

Figure 7-73 Graphic image inserted in an unbound object frame

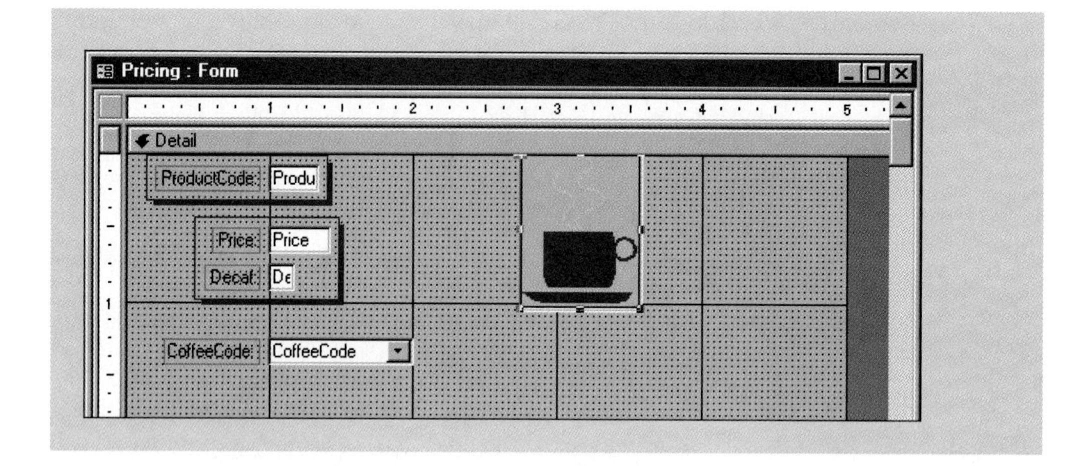

You need to reduce the size of the graphic image. To do so, you set the unbound object frame's Size Mode property to Stretch. The **Stretch Size Mode property** lets you size a graphic image to fit the control, the unbound object frame. That is, changing the size of the control also changes the size of the graphic image with minimum distortion.

You also will choose the shadowed special effect and the blue border color for the unbound object frame.

To modify the unbound object frame:

1. Right-click the **graphic image** then click **Properties** on the shortcut menu to open the property sheet.
2. Click the right side of the **Size Mode** text box, then click **Stretch.**
3. Click the **Close** button on the property sheet to close the property sheet.
4. Click the **Border Color** button on the Formatting toolbar to apply the same blue color to the border of the graphic image.
5. Click the **down arrow** next to the **Special Effect** button on the Formatting toolbar to display a set of icons representing choices for the Special Effect property, then click the **Shadowed** icon.
6. Use the lower-right corner sizing handle to resize the unbound object frame until it looks like the one shown in Figure 7-74.

Figure 7-74 After modifying and resizing the graphic image

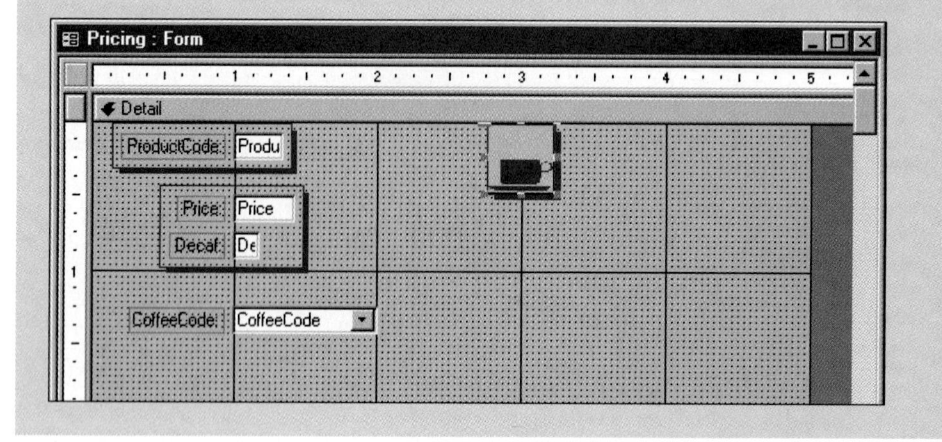

Next, you'll save the form changes then switch to Form view to review them.

To save then view the form in Form view:

1. Click the **Save** button on the Form Design toolbar to save the form changes.
2. Click the **Form View** button on the Form Design toolbar to switch to Form view. See Figure 7-75.

Figure 7-75 Viewing the graphic image in Form view

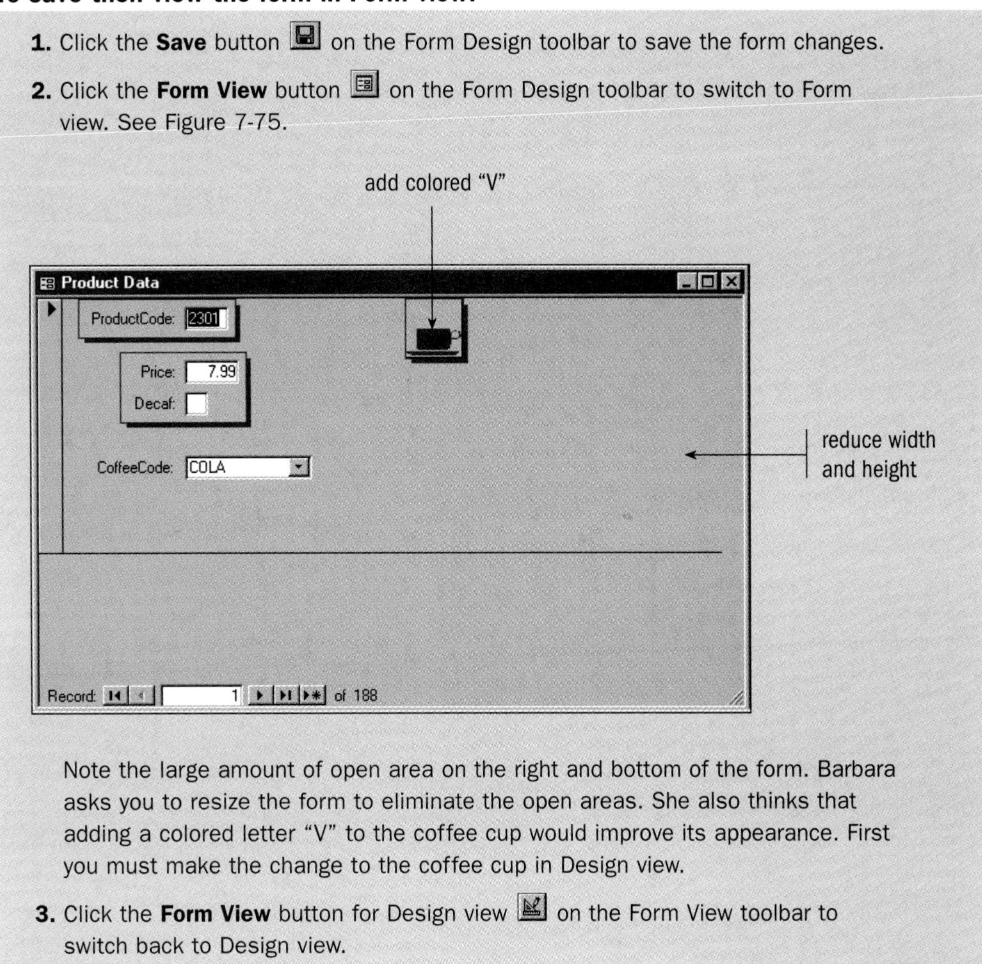

Note the large amount of open area on the right and bottom of the form. Barbara asks you to resize the form to eliminate the open areas. She also thinks that adding a colored letter "V" to the coffee cup would improve its appearance. First you must make the change to the coffee cup in Design view.

3. Click the **Form View** button for Design view on the Form View toolbar to switch back to Design view.

You'll use the Paint program to add a colored letter "V" (for "Valle") to the coffee cup.

Modifying a Graphic Image in Paint

The **Paint** program enables you to view, create, and modify graphic images. You can embed a graphic image created in Paint into another program. As happens when you embed any object, the file containing the original graphic image will remain unchanged when you change the embedded copy of it.

To change the embedded graphic image using Paint:

1. Right-click the graphic image to select it and display the shortcut menu, point to **Bitmap Image Object**, then click **Edit**. The Paint program starts, then displays the graphic image in the Paint window on top of the Form window. See Figure 7-76.

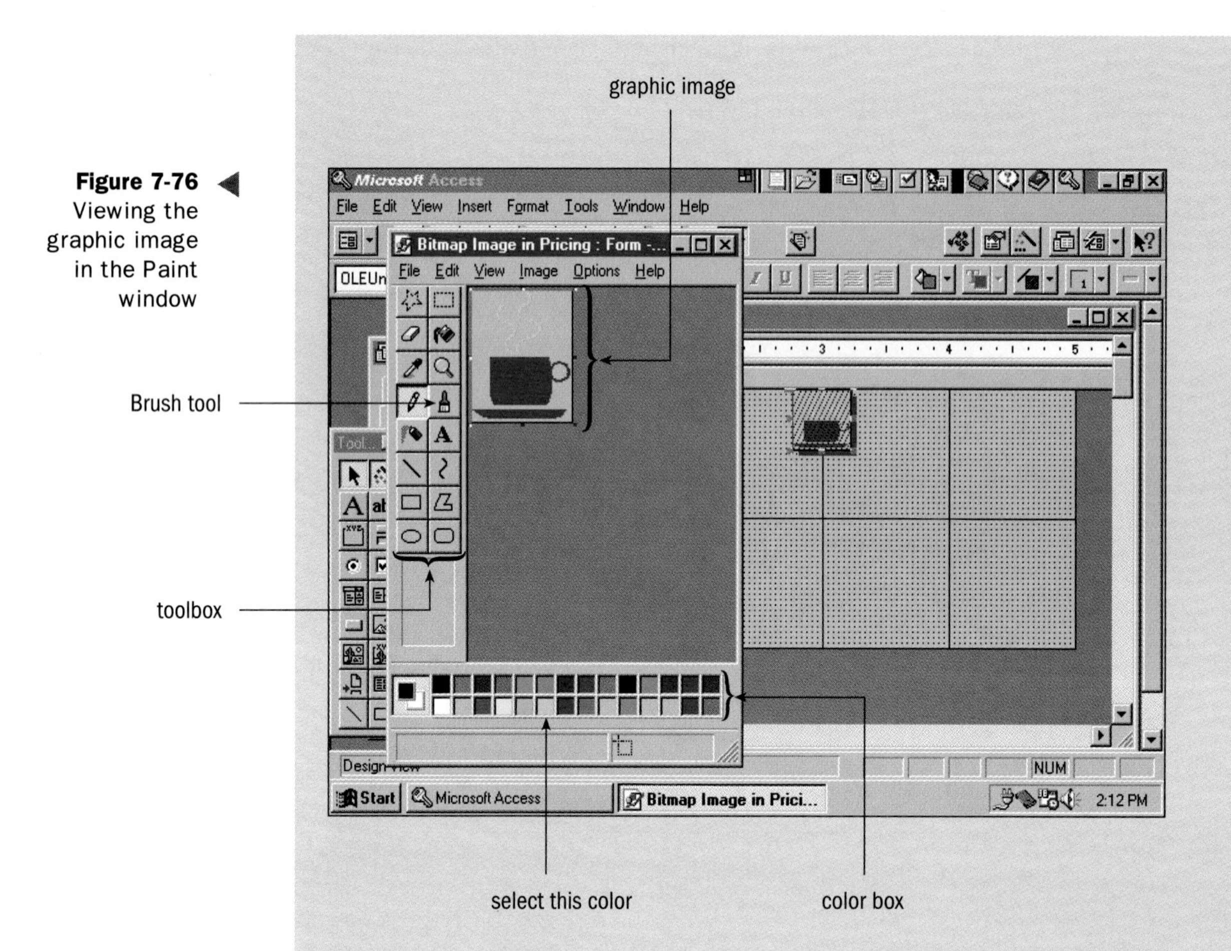

Figure 7-76 Viewing the graphic image in the Paint window

TROUBLE? The Paint window might appear on your screen in a different location or might be smaller or larger than the Paint window shown in Figure 7-76. As long as the Paint window displays the graphic image, toolbox, and color box, you'll be able to make the needed change. If you need to resize the Paint window, drag appropriate edges of the window until you can see all the components.

You'll use the Brush tool to paint a letter "V" on the coffee cup. First you select a foreground color from the color box. Barbara wants you to use the same color that's used for the steam rising from the top of the coffee cup.

2. Click the **aqua** color, which is the sixth color from the left in the bottom row. The color key at the left end of the color box displays the aqua foreground color on top of the white background color. When you brush the letter "V" on the coffee cup, Paint will use the aqua foreground color.

3. Click the **Brush** tool on the toolbox, then move the pointer to the coffee cup where it changes to +.

You brush the foreground color on the graphic image by dragging the pointer where you want the color applied. After brushing on the color, you can release the mouse button, then move the pointer to another location on the graphic image without applying any color. If you make a brush stroke by mistake, click Undo on the Edit menu immediately to remove the last brush stroke you applied.

4. Use two separate semi-diagonal brush strokes to apply the letter "V" to the coffee cup, similar to the letter "V" shown in Figure 7-77.

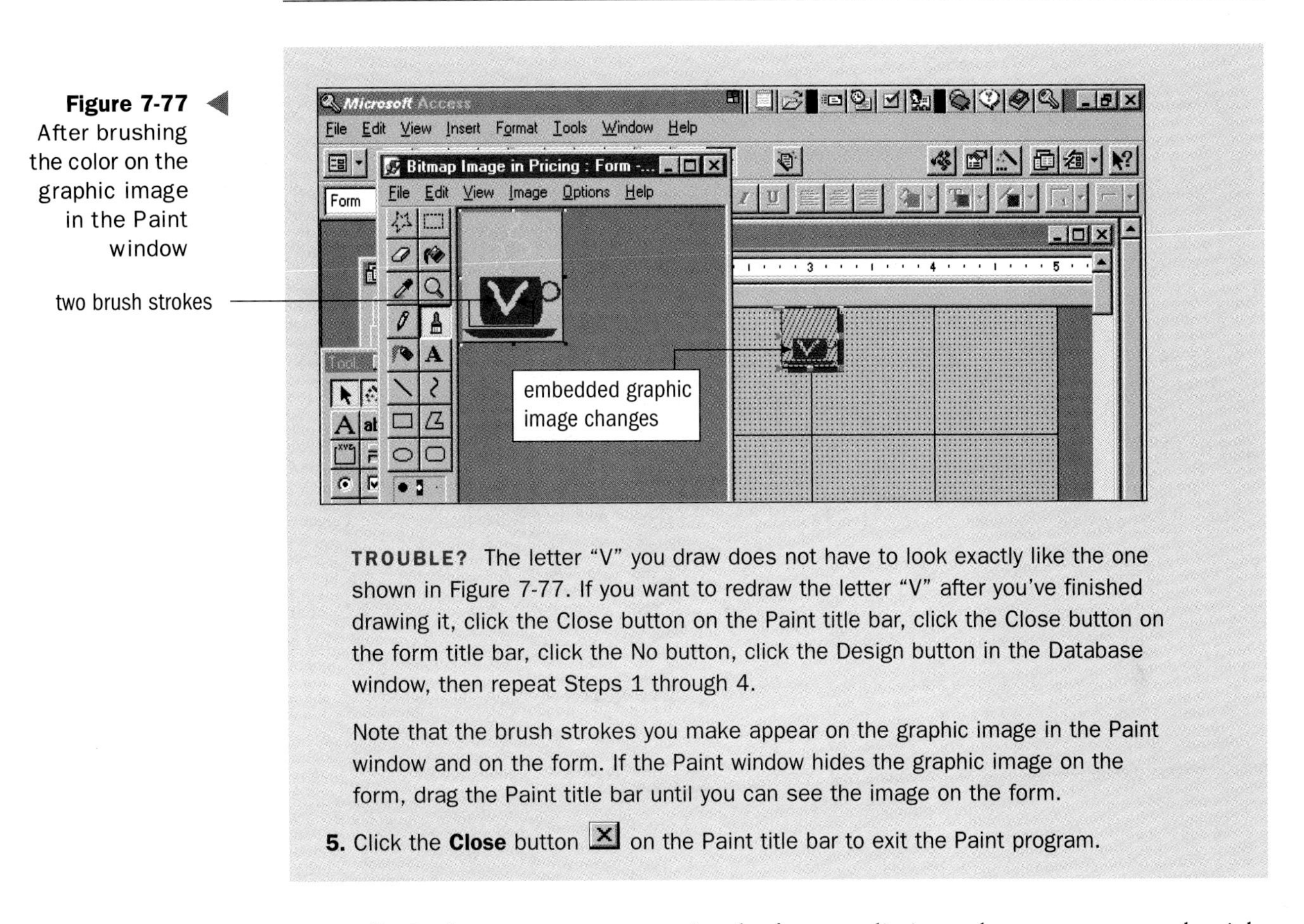

Figure 7-77 After brushing the color on the graphic image in the Paint window

TROUBLE? The letter "V" you draw does not have to look exactly like the one shown in Figure 7-77. If you want to redraw the letter "V" after you've finished drawing it, click the Close button on the Paint title bar, click the Close button on the form title bar, click the No button, click the Design button in the Database window, then repeat Steps 1 through 4.

Note that the brush strokes you make appear on the graphic image in the Paint window and on the form. If the Paint window hides the graphic image on the form, drag the Paint title bar until you can see the image on the form.

5. Click the **Close** button on the Paint title bar to exit the Paint program.

Finally, Barbara wants you to resize the form to eliminate the open areas on the right and bottom of the form. You'll reduce the width of the form detail section, resize and position the form in Form view, then save and close the form.

Resizing a Form

You can change the width and height of the form detail section in Design view. However, to resize and position the form, you must display the form in Form view.

To decrease the width of the detail section and resize and position the form:

1. Position the pointer at the right edge of the detail section. When the pointer changes to ✛, click and drag the right edge of the form to the left, to the position shown in Figure 7-78.

Figure 7-78 Reducing the width of the detail section

detail section width

Resizing the form in Design view does not affect the form in Form view. Now you need to switch to Form view to resize and position the form.

2. Click the **Form View** button on the Form Design toolbar to switch to Form view.

3. Resize the form by using the right and bottom edge resizing pointers, and move the form by dragging the form title bar until the form is positioned as shown in Figure 7-79.

Figure 7-79 Completed form resized and positioned

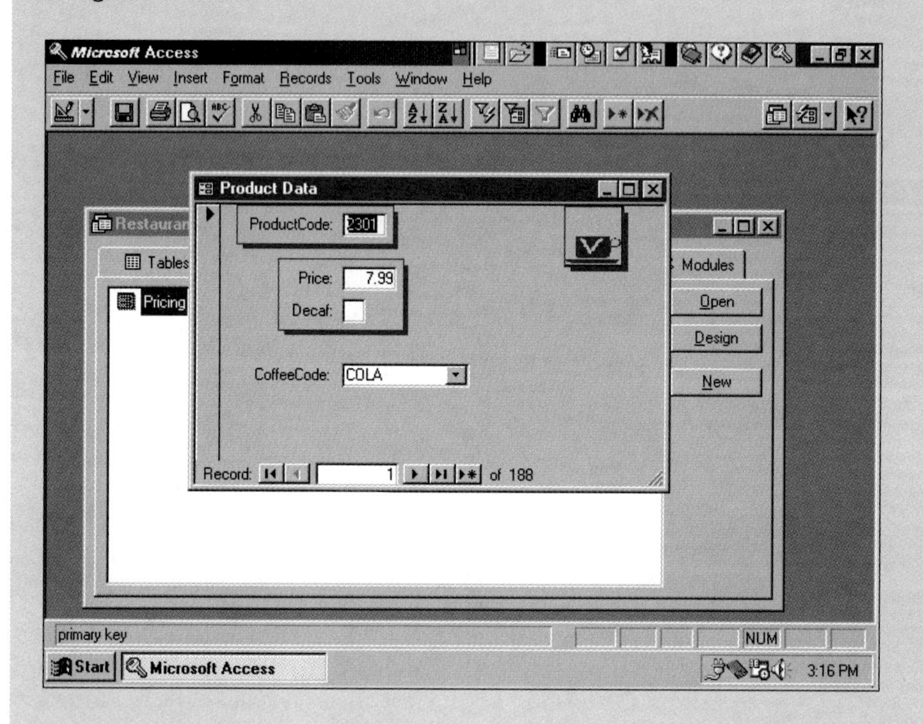

TROUBLE? If your form includes horizontal and vertical scroll bars, ignore them for now. The scroll bars will disappear after you save and close the form, then reopen it in Form view.

You now can save the form, close it, then rename it as Product Data.

4. Click the **Save** button on the Form View toolbar, then click the **Close** button on the form title bar.

5. Right-click **Pricing** in the Forms list box, click **Rename** on the shortcut menu, type **Product Data**, then press the **Enter** key.

Barbara recently learned that the cost of macadamia nuts has increased, and she wants you to use the Product Data form to change the price of the Macadamia Nut coffee from $9.49 to $9.99 then print the form record for the change.

To change the coffee price using the Product Data form then print the form record:

1. Make sure that Product Data is still selected in the Forms list box, then click the **Open** button to open the Product Data form in Form view.

   You'll use the Find command to display the Macadamia Nut coffee priced at $9.49; it has a CoffeeCode of MNUT.

2. Position the insertion point in the CoffeeCode field value box. This is the field for which you will find matching values.

3. Click the **Find** button on the Form View toolbar to open the Find in field dialog box.
4. If the Find in field dialog box covers the fields on the form, move the dialog box out of the way by dragging its title bar.
5. In the Find What text box, type **mnut** then click the **Find First** button. Access displays the record for ProductCode 2320, priced at 9.49.
6. Click the **Close** button to close the dialog box.
7. Select the **4** in the Price field value box, then type **9** to change the value to 9.99.

   Next you'll print the selected form record.

8. Click **File** on the menu bar, click **Print**, click the **Selected Record(s)** radio button, then click the **OK** button. Access prints the selected record whose Price field value you just changed.

   You can now close the form.

9. Click the **Close** button on the form title bar.

Before you exit Access, Barbara recommends that you compact the Restaurant Coffee Orders database to free up disk space.

Compacting a Database

When you delete records in an Access table, the space occupied by the deleted records on disk does not become available for other records. The same is true if you delete an object, such as a table, query, or form. To make the space available, you must compact the database. **Compacting** a database rearranges the data and objects in a database and creates a smaller copy of the database. Unlike making a copy of a database file, which you do to protect your database against loss or damage, you compact the database to make it smaller, thereby making more space available on your disk. Before compacting a database, you must close it.

To compact the Restaurant Coffee Orders database:

1. Click the **Close** button on the Database window title bar.
2. Click **Tools** on the menu bar, point to **Database Utilities**, then click **Compact Database**. Access opens the Database to Compact From dialog box, in which you select the database you want to compact.
3. Make sure Tutorial.07 appears in the Look in list box, click **Restaurant Coffee Orders** in the list box, then click the **Compact** button. Access opens the Compact Database Into dialog box, in which you enter the filename for the compacted copy of the database and select its drive and folder location.

   Usually you would back up the database as a safeguard before compacting. Here, you'll save the compacted database with a different name, delete the original database file, then rename the compacted database to the original database name.

4. Type **Compacted Restaurant Coffee Orders** in the File name text box, make sure Tutorial.07 appears in the Look in list box, then click the **Save** button. Access compacts the Restaurant Coffee Orders database, creating the copied file named Compacted Restaurant Coffee Orders, and returns you to the Access window.

Now you need to exit Access, delete the original Restaurant Coffee Orders database, then rename the compacted database as Restaurant Coffee Orders.

5. Click the **Close** button [X] on the Access window title bar. Access closes and you return to the Windows 95 desktop.
6. Open the Exploring window, then verify that both database files—the original Restaurant Coffee Orders database and the Compacted Restaurant Coffee Orders database—are included in the window. Note the difference in size of the two files.

   Now you need to delete the original (uncompacted) database file, then rename the compacted file.
7. Delete the Restaurant Coffee Orders file, then rename Compacted Restaurant Coffee Orders as Restaurant Coffee Orders.
8. Click the **Close** button [X] on the Exploring title bar.

Barbara, Kim, and Carlos now have several queries they can use to do their work with the Restaurant Coffee Orders database. Before they can begin fully using the Product Data form, you'll need to add the WeightCode combo box to it. You'll do this in the Tutorial Assignments.

Quick Check

1. Describe at least two guidelines for designing a custom form.
2. What is the difference between a bound control and an unbound control?
3. What are the five sections you can include on a form?
4. What type of control is placed on a form when you drag a table field to the form grid?
5. Another name for a label is a(n) __________.
6. How do you move a text box and its related label at the same time?
7. How do you select multiple controls?
8. To change the text in the title bar of a form, you set the form's __________ property.
9. Flat, raised, sunken, etched, shadowed, and chiseled are choices for a control's __________ property.
10. What is a combo box?
11. To add a graphic image to a form, you place it in a(n) __________ object frame.

Tutorial Assignments

Barbara has several additional queries she wants you to create. She also wants you to complete the Product Data form and to create a second form. Complete the following steps, making sure you display the fields in the same order as they are listed in the assignments and that you change the font and resize columns to their best fit, when necessary.

1. Make sure your Student Disk is in the disk drive, then copy the database named Valle in the TAssign folder within the Tutorial.07 folder on your Student Disk. Rename the document as Valle Coffee in the same folder.
2. For all flavored coffee types, display the CoffeeType, CoffeeName, CoffeeCode, and Decaf fields from the Coffee table. Save the query as Flavored, then print the query results.
3. For all non-flavored coffee types, display the CoffeeType, CoffeeCode, and CoffeeName fields. Save the query as Non-Flavored, then print the query results.
4. For all customers first contacted in 1993, display the CustomerName,

OwnerName, FirstContact, City, and State fields. Save the query as 1993 Customers, then print the query results.

5. For all customers with 313 or 517 phone area codes, display the OwnerName, Phone, CustomerName, City, and State fields. Save the query as Area Codes 313 Or 517, then print the query results.

6. For all customers who have 313 or 517 phone area codes *or* who were first contacted in 1993, display the OwnerName, Phone, CustomerName, City, State, and FirstContact fields. Save the query as Area Codes Or 1993, then print the query results. Change the query to select all customers who have 313 or 517 phone area codes *and* who were first contacted in 1993, save the query as Area Codes And 1993, then print the query results.
7. For all unpaid orders, display the BillingDate, InvoiceAmt, CustomerName, Phone, and OwnerName fields. Display the results in ascending order by BillingDate, then in descending order by InvoiceAmt. Save the query as Unpaid Orders, then print the query results. Change the query by displaying the results in descending order by InvoiceAmt, then in ascending order by CustomerName. Print the query results but do not save the query.
8. For all unpaid orders, display the BillingDate, InvoiceAmt, CustomerName, Phone, and OwnerName fields. Then do the following:
   a. Display the results in descending order by BillingDate. Save the query as Unpaid Order Filters, then print the query results.
   b. Use Filter By Selection to select just those records with 1/15/98 billing dates, then print the query results.
   c. Remove the filter, then use Filter By Form to select just those records for Embers Restaurant or Cottage Grill, print the query results, then save the query.
9. For all products that do not have a WeightCode field value of A or B, display all the fields from the Product table. Create a calculated field named NewPrice that displays the results of increasing the product price by 4%. Display the results in descending order by NewPrice and display two decimal places and a dollar sign for NewPrice. Save the query as New Prices, then print the query results.
10. For all products that do not have a WeightCode field value of A or B, create an update query to increase the Price field by 4%, then run the query. Do not save this query. However, run the New Prices query, then print the query results.

11. Use the Access Help system to learn about the standard deviation and variance aggregate functions and the Where operator, which is also described with the aggregate functions. Then use the Order table to display the sum, standard deviation, and variance of the InvoiceAmt field for all paid orders and the lowest and highest InvoiceAmt field values for the paid orders. Set the Format property for each displayed column to Currency, save the query as Paid Order Statistics, then print the query results in landscape orientation. Change the query to display the sum, average, lowest, and highest InvoiceAmt field values by CustomerName for all paid orders, save the query as Paid Order Statistics by Customer, then print the query results.
12. For products with a specific coffee type, create a parameter query to display the ProductCode, Price, CoffeeName, CoffeeType, and Weight/Size fields. Display the results in ascending order by CoffeeName. Save the query as Specify a Coffee Type, run the query using a parameter value of "Central & South American," then print the query results.
13. For all orders display the InvoiceAmt, BillingDate, OrderNum, and CustomerName fields. Display the results in descending order by InvoiceAmt and display the top 15 orders. Save the query as Top 15 Orders, then print the query results.

14. Open the Product Data form in Design view, then complete the following:
    a. Add a combo box three grid dots below the CoffeeCode combo box. The new combo box includes the WeightCode and Weight/Size fields from the Weight table; the selected WeightCode value is to be stored in the Product table. Specify WeightCode as the label caption.
    b. Right align the label with the other labels on the form and, if necessary, resize the combo box.
    c. Save the form then add a new record with the following field values:

ProductCode:	2545
Price:	31.00
Decaf:	Null
CoffeeCode:	CELT
WeightCode:	C

    Use the form to print just this new record.

15. Design and create a custom form that includes all the fields from the Order table. Use a combo box that includes the CustomerNum and CustomerName fields from the Customer table. Group fields logically and use rectangles to separate each group. Use the BlueCup.bmp graphic image in an appropriate position on the form. Save the form as Order Data. Use the form to display the record for OrderNum 205, change the InvoiceAmt to $645.00, then print just this record.
16. Compact the Valle Coffee database; name the copy of the database "Compacted Valle Coffee." After the compacting process is complete, delete the original Valle Coffee database, then rename Compacted Valle Coffee as "Valle Coffee."

Case Problems

1. Ashbrook Mall Information Desk Arthur Harrington, supervisor of maintenance at Ashbrook Mall, has a database that tracks the special maintenance jobs performed by his group at the mall. The database contains three tables: the Job table contains data about each job, the Location table contains data about each mall location, and the Rate table contains data about the per hour rates for maintenance workers. One-to-many relationships exist between the Location and Job tables based on the Location field, and between the Rate and Job tables based on the RateCode field.

Arthur has a form and several queries he wants you to create. Complete the following steps, making sure you display the fields in the same order as they are listed in the steps and that you change the font and resize the columns to their best fit, as necessary.

1. Make sure your Student Disk is in the disk drive, then copy the database named Ashbrook in the Cases folder within the Tutorial.07 folder on your Student Disk. Rename the document as Ashbrook Maintenance Jobs in the same folder.
2. Review the database design by opening the Relationships window, then open each table in Design view. Be careful not to change the relationships or table structures.
3. For all *store* locations, display the Job#, Location, Reported, Rate, and JobDescription fields. Save the query as Store Jobs, then print the query results.
4. For all jobs with job rates less than or equal to $30, display the Job#, LocationName, JobDescription, Rate, and RateDescription fields. Save the query as $30 Or Less Jobs, then print the query results.

5. For all jobs that require between 1.5 and 4.5 hours of effort, display the LocationName, Rate, Completed, Effort, and JobDescription fields. Save the query as Medium Length Jobs, then print the query results.
6. For all jobs beginning with the words Repair or Replace, display the Job#, LocationName, RateDescription, JobDescription, and Status fields. Save the query as Repair Or Replace Jobs, then print the query results.

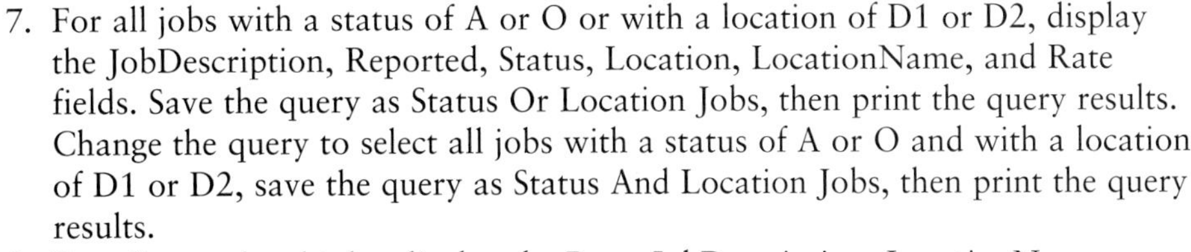

7. For all jobs with a status of A or O or with a location of D1 or D2, display the JobDescription, Reported, Status, Location, LocationName, and Rate fields. Save the query as Status Or Location Jobs, then print the query results. Change the query to select all jobs with a status of A or O and with a location of D1 or D2, save the query as Status And Location Jobs, then print the query results.
8. For all completed jobs, display the Rate, JobDescription, LocationName, Reported, Completed, Effort, and Status fields. Display the results in descending order by Rate, then in ascending order by JobDescription. Save the query as Completed Jobs, then print the query results. Change the query by displaying the results in ascending order by Reported, then in ascending order by Completed. Print the query results but do not save the query.
9. For all completed jobs, display the Rate, JobDescription, LocationName, Reported, Completed, Effort, and Status fields. Then do the following:
   a. Display the results in ascending order by Completed, save the query as Completed Job Filters, then print the query results.
   b. Use Filter By Selection to select just those records with $30.00 rates, then print the query results.

   c. Remove the filter, then use Filter By Form to select just those records completed on 4/30/98 and reported on either 4/29/98 or 4/30/98; print the query results, then save the query.
10. For all completed jobs, display the RateDescription, LocationName, JobDescription, Effort, and Rate fields. Create a calculated field named JobCost that displays the results of multiplying the rate and the effort. Format the calculated field as currency. Display the results in ascending order by RateDescription, then in ascending order by LocationName. Save the query as Job Cost, then print the query results.

11. For all uncompleted jobs, create a make-table query. The new table is named Uncompleted Job and contains the Job#, Location, Reported, RateCode, Status, and JobDescription fields. Run the query, save the query as Make Uncompleted Job Table, open the Uncompleted Job table datasheet, resize all columns to their best fit, then print the datasheet.
12. Use the Job table to display the sum, average, and count of the Effort field for all completed jobs. Then do the following:
   a. Specify column names of Total Effort, Average Effort, and Number of Jobs. Change properties so that the values in the Total Effort column display one decimal place and the fixed format; change properties so that the values in the Average Effort column display two decimal places and the fixed format. Save the query as Effort Statistics, then print the query results.

   b. Change the query to display the sum, average, and count of the Effort field for all completed jobs by RateDescription. Save the query as Effort Statistics by Rate, then print the query results.
13. For jobs with a specific rate code, create a parameter query to display the Job#, LocationName, Rate, Reported, Completed, JobDescription, and RateCode fields. Display the results in ascending order by JobDescription. Save the query as Specify a Rate Code, run the query using a parameter value of "S2," then print the query results.
14. For all jobs display the Job#, Location, Reported, Completed, Effort, and JobDescription fields. Display the results in descending order by Effort and display the top 5 jobs. Save the query as Top 5 Effort Jobs, then print the query results.
15. Use Figure 7-80 to create a form based on the Job table. Save the form as Job Data. Use the following guidelines to create the form:
   - The graphic image in the upper-left is named trio.bmp; the graphic image in the upper-right is named wrench.bmp. The files for these images are located in the Cases folder within the Tutorial.07 folder on your Student Disk.

- The Location combo box displays the Location and LocationName fields from the Location table. The RateCode combo box displays the RateCode, Rate, and RateDescription fields from the Rate table.
- The two rectangles, the line under the Job# field, and the frames around the graphic images use a Border Width property of 2.

Figure 7-80

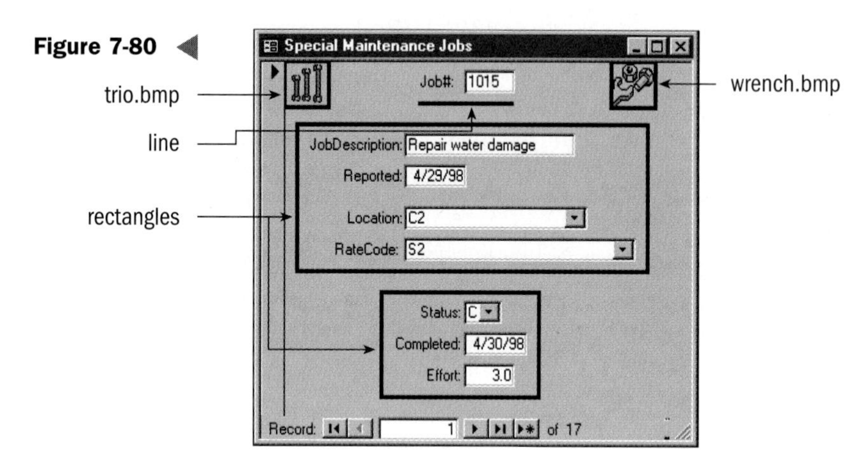

16. Use the Job Data form you just created to update the Job# 1030 record with the following field values:
    Status: C
    Completed: 5/3/98
    Effort: 1.5

    Use the form to print only this updated record.
17. Compact the Ashbrook Maintenance Jobs database; name the copy of the database "Compacted Ashbrook Maintenance Jobs." After the compacting process is complete, delete the original Ashbrook Maintenance Jobs database, then rename the compacted version as "Ashbrook Maintenance Jobs."

2. Professional Litigation User Services Raj Jawahir, a new employee at Professional Litigation User Services, has been tracking the daily payments received from the firm's clients using a database you created. The database includes two tables: the Payment table contains data about each payment, and the Firm table contains data about each firm making payments. A one-to-many relationship exists between the Firm and Payment tables based on the Firm# field.

Raj wants you to create a form and several queries. Complete the following steps, making sure you display the fields in the same order as they are listed in the steps.

1. Make sure your Student Disk is in the disk drive, then copy the database named PLUS in the Cases folder within the Tutorial.07 folder on your Student Disk. Rename the document as PLUS Payments in the same folder.
2. Review the database design by opening the Relationships window, then open each table in Design view. Be careful not to change the relationships or table structures.
3. For all payments on 6/2/98, display the Payment#, AmtPaid, DatePaid, and FirmName fields. Save the query as June 2 Payments, then print the query results.
4. For all payments with amounts greater than $2,500, display the AmtPaid, DatePaid, FirmName, City, and State fields. Save the query as Over $2500 Payments, then print the query results.

5. For all firms that are not in the states of Georgia (GA), Massachusetts (MA), and Ohio (OH), display the City, State, FirmName, and Firm# fields. Save the query as Selected States, then print the query results.

6. For all payments from the states of GA, MA, or OH or with payment amounts over $2,500, display the FirmName, City, State, AmtPaid, and DatePaid fields. Save the query as Selected State Or Over $2500, then print the query results. Change the query to select all payments from the states of GA, MA, or OH and with payment amounts over $2,500, save the query as Selected State And Over $2500, then print the query results. Finally, change the query to select all payments from states other than GA, MA, and OH and with payment amounts over $2,500, save the query as Over $2500 And Not Selected State, then print the query results.
7. For all payments made on 6/11/98 or 6/12/98, display the DatePaid, AmtPaid, FirmName, State, and City fields. Display the results in ascending order by DatePaid, then in descending order by AmtPaid. Save the query as Selected Dates, then print the query results. Change the query by displaying the results in ascending order by State, then City. Print the query results but do not save the query.
8. Use the Payment table to display the highest, lowest, total, average, and count of the AmtPaid field for all payments. Then do the following:
   a. Specify column names of HighestPayment, LowestPayment, TotalPayments, AveragePayment, and #Payments. Resize all datasheet columns to their best fit, save the query as Payment Statistics, then print the query results.
   b. Change the query to display the same statistics by DatePaid, save the query as Payment Statistics by Date, then print the query results.

   c. Change the Payment Statistics by Date query to display the same statistics by DatePaid then by Deposit#, save the query as Payment Statistics by Date by Deposit, then print the query results using landscape orientation.
9. For payments made on a specific date, create a parameter query to display the DatePaid, AmtPaid, FirmName, City, and State fields. Display the results in ascending order by AmtPaid. Save the query as Select a Date Paid, run the query using a parameter value of 6/1/98, then print the query results.

10. Use Figure 7-81 to create a form based on the Firm table and save the form as Firm and Payment Data. Use the following guidelines to create the form:
    - Before creating the main form, use the Form Wizard to create a subform based on the Payment table. Select all the fields from the Payment table, choose the tabular layout, the Standard AutoFormat, and the title Payment Subform.
    - Create the main form, adding the fields from the Firm table to the form, then select the back colors shown in Figure 7-81.
    - Use the Subform/Subreport tool, along with the Control Wizards tool, to place the Payment Subform form at the bottom of the main form.
    - Resize and reposition the subform in Design view.
    - Resize and reposition the main form in Design view, then in Form view.
    - From Form view, save the form, then print the first record using the form.

Figure 7-81

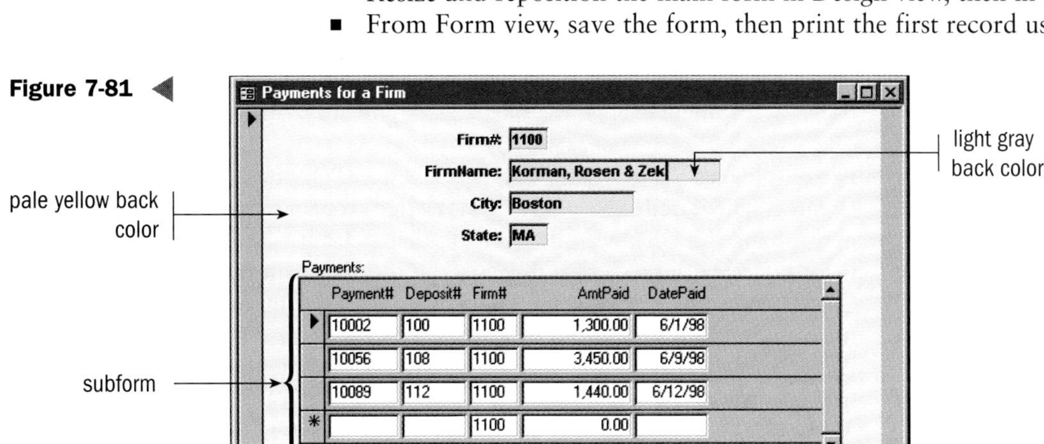

11. Use the Firm and Payment Data form you just created to update the Firm# 1131 record with the following field values:
    FirmName: Syracuse Municipal Court
    City: Syracuse

    Use the form to print only this updated record.
12. Compact the PLUS Payments database; name the copy of the database "Compacted PLUS Payments." After the compacting process is complete, delete the original PLUS Payments database, then rename the compacted version as "PLUS Payments."

3. Best Friends The staff members at Best Friends maintain a database for tracking walker, pledge, and payment data for the dog Walk-A-Thons they conduct. The database includes three tables: the Walker table contains data about each walker, the Pledge table contains data about each pledge, and the Payment table contains data about payments received. The database currently contains data for one Walk-A-Thon. One-to-many relationships exist between the Walker and Pledge tables based on the WalkerID field, and between the Pledge and Payment tables based on the Pledge# field.

You've been asked to create several queries for the staff members. Complete the following steps, making sure you display the fields in the same order as they are listed in the steps.

1. Make sure your Student Disk is in the disk drive, then copy the database named Pledges in the Cases folder within the Tutorial.07 folder on your Student Disk. Rename the document as Best Friends Pledges in the same folder.
2. Review the database design by opening the Relationships window, then open each table in Design view. Be careful not to change the relationships or table structures.
3. For all walkers who completed the 2.3-mile route, display the FirstName, LastName, Phone, WalkerID, and Distance fields. Save the query as Went the Distance, then print the query results.

4. For all pledge amounts not between $10 and $25, display the Pledger, PledgeAmt, Pledge#, and WalkerID fields. Save the query as High And Low Pledges, then print the query results.

5. For all walkers who do not have phone numbers starting with 711, display the FirstName, LastName, Phone, WalkerID, and Distance fields. Save the query as Not 711 Phones, then print the query results.

6. For all walkers who pledged between $10 and $12 or between $20 and $23 or who pledged $5 per mile, display the Pledger, PledgeAmt, PerMile, LastName, and FirstName fields. Save the query as Pledged Or Per Mile, then print the query results. Change the query to select all walkers who pledged between $10 and $12 or between $20 and $23 and who pledged $5 per mile, save the query as Pledged And Per Mile, then print the query results.
7. For all payments, display the Pledger, PledgeAmt, Payment#, and PaidAmt fields. Display the results in ascending order by Pledger, then in descending order by Payment#. Save the query as Payments by Pledger, then print the query results.

8. For all pledges, display the Pledger, Distance, PerMile, and PledgeAmt fields. Create a calculated field named CalcPledgeAmt that displays the results of multiplying the Distance and PerMile fields. Then create a second calculated field named Difference that displays the results of subtracting the CalcPledgeAmt field from the PledgeAmt field. Format the calculated fields as fixed with two decimal places. Display the results in ascending order by PledgeAmt. Resize all datasheet columns for the calculated fields to their best fit, save the query as Difference, then print the query results.

9. Use the Pledge table to display the total, average, and count of the PledgeAmt field for all pledges. Then do the following:
   a. Specify column names of TotalPledge, AveragePledge, and NumberOfPledges. Change properties so that the values in the TotalPledge and AveragePledge columns display two decimal places and the fixed format. Resize all datasheet columns to their best fit, save the query as Pledge Statistics, then print the query results.

   b. Change the query to display the sum, average, and count of the PledgeAmt field for all pledges by LastName. Save the query as Pledge Statistics by Walker, then print the query results.
10. For all payments display the Pledger, PaidAmt, LastName, and FirstName fields. Display the results in descending order by PaidAmt, run the query, then write down the number of records displayed in the datasheet. Change the query to display the top 40% payments. Save the query as Top 40% Payments, then print the query results. How many records appeared in the datasheet and why?
11. Compact the Best Friends Pledges database; name the copy of the database "Compacted Best Friends Pledges." After the compacting process is complete, delete the original Best Friends Pledges database, then rename the compacted version as "Best Friends Pledges."

4. Lopez Used Cars Maria and Luis Lopez own a chain of used-car lots throughout Texas. They have a database to track their used-car inventory. The database includes four tables: the Vehicle table contains data about used cars, the Location table contains data about each used-car location, the Class table contains data about each type of vehicle, and the Transmission table contains data about the each type of transmission. One-to-many relationships exist between the Vehicle table and each of the other three tables.

Maria wants you to create a form and several queries. Complete the following steps, making sure you display the fields in the same order as they are listed in the steps and that you change the font and resize columns to their best fit, as necessary.

1. Make sure your Student Disk is in the disk drive, then copy the database named UsedCars in the Cases folder within the Tutorial.07 folder on your Student Disk. Rename the document as Lopez Used Cars in the same folder.
2. Review the database design by opening the Relationships window, then open each table in Design view. Be careful not to change the relationships or table structures.
3. For all Ford vehicles, display the Manufacturer, Model, Year, and SellingPrice fields. Save the query as Fords, then print the query results.
4. For all vehicles manufactured prior to 1989, display the Manufacturer, Model, Year, Cost, SellingPrice, and LocationName fields. Save the query as Older Than 1989, then print the query results.
5. For all vehicles having a manufacturer that starts with the letter C or the letter N, display the Manufacturer, Model, Year, Cost, SellingPrice, and LocationName fields. Save the query as C Or N Manufacturers, then print the query results.
6. For all vehicles located in Houston or Waco or with a transmission of L3 or L4, display the Manufacturer, Model, Year, Cost, SellingPrice, TransmissionDesc, LocationCode, and LocationName fields. Save the query as Location Or Trans, then print the query results using landscape orientation. Change the query to select all vehicles located in Houston or Waco and with a transmission of L3 or L4, save the query as Location And Trans, then print the query results.

7. For all vehicles, display the Manufacturer, Model, Year, SellingPrice, ClassDescription, LocationName, and ManagerName fields. Display the results in ascending order by LocationName, then in descending order by SellingPrice. Save the query as Vehicles by Location Then Price; preview the query results; change to landscape orientation, if necessary; then print the query results. Change the query by displaying the results in ascending order by Manufacturer, then Model. Print the query results but do not save the query.
8. For all vehicles, display the Manufacturer, Model, Class, Year, Cost, and Selling Price fields. Then do the following:
   a. Display the results in ascending order by SellingPrice, save the query as Vehicle Filters, then print the query results.
   b. Use Filter By Selection to select just those records with S2 classes, then print the query results.
   c. Remove the filter, then use Filter By Form to select just those records with S2 classes and for the year 1991, print the query results, then save the query.
9. For all vehicles, display the Manufacturer, Model, Year, Cost, and Selling Price fields. Create a calculated field named Profit that displays the difference between the vehicle's selling price and cost. Display the results in descending order by Profit. Save the query as Profit, then print the query results.
10. Use the Used Car table to display for all vehicles the total cost, total selling price, total profit, average profit, and total number of vehicles. Rename datasheet columns, save the query as Vehicle Statistics, then print the query results. Change the query to display the same statistics for all vehicles by year, save the query as Vehicle Statistics by Year, then print the query results.
11. Create a parameter query to display all the fields from the Used Car table based on a selected manufacturer. Display the query results in ascending order by SellingPrice. Save the query as Selected Manufacturer, run the query using a parameter value of Dodge, then print the query results.
12. Use Figure 7-82 to create a form based on the Used Car table. Save the form as Used Car Data. Use the following guidelines to create the form:
    - The graphic image in the upper-left is named lopez.bmp and is located in the Cases folder within the Tutorial.07 folder on your Student Disk.
    - The LocationCode combo box displays the LocationCode, LocationName, and ManagerName fields from the Location table. The Class combo box displays the Class and ClassDescription fields from the Class table. The TransmissionType combo box displays the TransmissionType and TransmissionDesc fields from the Transmission table.
    - To add the Profit label and text box to the form, use the Text Box tool on the toolbox. In the text box create a calculated field by setting the Control Source property to "=[SellingPrice]-[Cost]" and then setting the Format and Decimal Places properties.
    - Resize and reposition the form in Design view, then in Form view.
    - From Form view, save the form, display record 22 in the form, then print record 22 using the form.

Figure 7-82

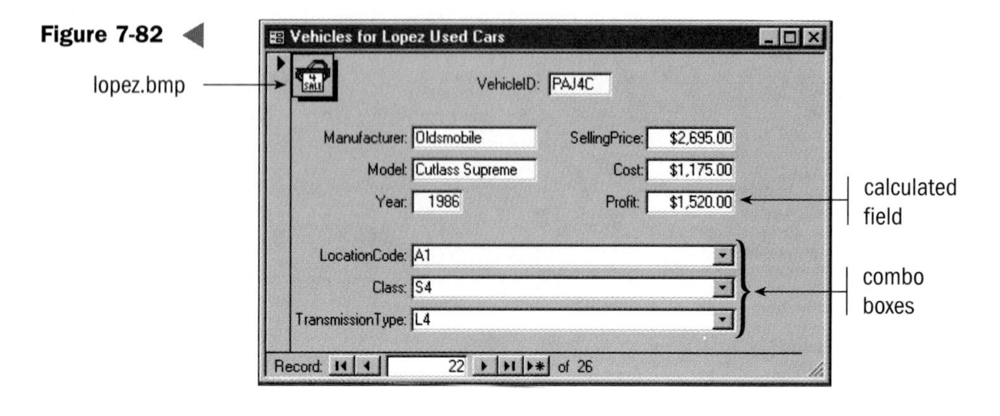

13. Use the Used Car Data form you just created to update record 22 with the following field values:
    SellingPrice: 2400.00
    LocationCode: L1

    Use the form to print only this updated record.
14. Compact the Lopez Used Cars database; name the copy of the database "Compacted Lopez Used Cars." After the compacting process is complete, delete the original Lopez Used Cars database, then rename the compacted version as "Lopez Used Cars."

Answers to Quick Check Questions

SESSION 1.1

1 Word, Excel, Access, and PowerPoint

2 Office Shortcut Bar

3 ToolTip

4 Tutorial.01 (for Tutorial 1), TAssign, and Cases

5 a. Office Shortcut Bar b. title bar c. menu bar d. Standard toolbar e. Formatting toolbar f. ruler g. insertion point h. end mark i. workspace j. vertical scroll bar

6 The existing file is replaced by the saved file.

7 the character to the left of the insertion point; the character to the right of the insertion point

8 For the cut-and-paste technique, you click the Cut button instead of the Copy button, and the selected text is deleted from its original location instead of remaining in its original location.

9 Common formatting options are font type, font size, font style, and paragraph alignment; all are applied by clicking buttons on the Formatting toolbar.

10 The Contents tab contains topics within books; you use this documentation just like you use a normal book. The Index tab contains an alphabetical list of topics, similar to an index in the back of a book; you select a topic to display information about the topic. The Find tab lets you enter words you're interested in, then displays topics that contain those words. The Answer Wizard provides a list of topics that answer a question you enter.

11 The Print button on the Standard toolbar prints one copy of the entire document immediately using the current settings. The Print command on the File menu displays a dialog box that lets you specify which pages of the document you want to print, the number of copies you want to print, and the printer you will use.

12 Clicking the Exit option on the File menu or clicking the Close button on the title bar allows you to exit Word.

SESSION 1.2

1 records, fields

2 right-click a screen component

3 navigation buttons

4 current record symbol

5 Both linking and embedding use the source program to change the object. For embedding, a copy of the object is stored in the destination program; for linking, just a link to the object is stored in the destination program. For embedding, changes to the object in either the source or destination program are not reflected in the object in the other program; for linking, changes to the object in either program are reflected in the object in the other program. Copying is similar to embedding except that the destination program, rather than the source program, is used when you make changes to a copied object.

6 Embedding would be better if, for example, you want to show sales data as of the end of last month. The data in the source program would continue to change after the end of the month, but these changes would not affect the data embedded in the destination program.

7 workbook, worksheets

8 menu and toolbars change to those of the source program

9 cell

SESSION 1.3

1 Right-click the My Computer icon on the Windows 95 desktop, then click Open on the shortcut menu. Repeat for the drive, folders, then the existing document you want to open.

2 Slide view displays one slide at a time for you to view, enter, and edit your slides. Slide Sorter view displays miniaturized images of several slides at a time for you to change the slide order and set special features for a slide show. Slide Show view displays one slide at a time that fills the screen and shows a presentation's special effects.

3 In Slide Shorter view drag the slide to its new position.

4 AutoLayout

5 an area of a window reserved for entering text or graphics

6 Use the Paste option to embed an object and use the Paste Link option to link an object.

7 a special effect that adds the text list one point at a time or one group at a time

SESSION 2.1

1 Plan the document by determining its purpose and what it will include; enter the text; edit the document by inserting, deleting, and moving text; format the document; and preview, save, then print the completed document.

2 Click the Start a New Document button on the Office Shortcut Bar, click the General tab in the New dialog box, click the Blank Document icon, then click the OK button.

3 The Show/Hide button on the Standard toolbar controls the display of nonprinting characters. It is a toggle because you click the same button to turn the display on and off.

4 AutoCorrect can make these corrections to text entries automatically: correctly spell commonly misspelled words, capitalize the first letter in a sentence, capitalize the first letter of a day's name, and correct capitalization if you type two capital letters at the beginning of a word.

5 Use the Undo button to cancel one or more changes made since opening a document. Use the Redo button to restore one or more changes you've undone since opening a document.

6 An open document is a document you've just started in RAM or a saved document that you've transferred from disk to RAM. The active document is the open document that is visible in the active program's window.

7 Position the pointer at the start of the text you want to select, click and drag the mouse to the end of the text, release the mouse button, then press the Delete key.

8 The selection bar is the area along the left margin of a document. Clicking the mouse button in the selection bar allows you to select entire paragraphs and documents quickly.

SESSION 2.2

1 In general, serif fonts are used for the body of text, and sans serif fonts are used for titles and other headings.

2 point

3 toggle

4 boldface, italics, and underlining

5 left, center, right, and decimal

6 The Cut, Copy, and Paste buttons on the Standard toolbar are associated with the Clipboard. The Cut button deletes the selected text and places it on the Clipboard. The Copy button places a copy of the selected text on the Clipboard. The Paste button inserts a copy of the text from the Clipboard at the insertion point.

7 Drag and drop works best when you need to move text only a short distance.

8 Use a numbered list rather than a bulleted list when the items specify a sequence of steps or other ordered group, such as items listed in order by size, age, or importance.

SESSION 2.3

1 multitasking

2 You can use the sizing handles or the Picture option on the Format menu to resize a WordArt object.

3 foreground, background

4 The spell check program identifies any words not found in its dictionary and any occurrences of repeated words.

5 Normal

6 Click the Print button on the Standard toolbar.

SESSION 3.1

1 A workbook is an Excel document, which is made up of one or more worksheets.

2 planning; entering data; editing; formatting; previewing, saving, and printing

3 right-click the worksheet tab, click Rename, then type the new name

4 Excel determines the type of an entered value by examining the characters in the data. If the value is a legitimate date, it is considered a date. If the value is a legitimate number, it is considered a number. Otherwise, it is considered a label.

5 cell reference, reference area

6 by the = that precedes it

7 A formula specifies a calculation you want Excel to perform. A function is a prewritten formula that takes specified values, performs a predefined operation, and then returns a value.

8 The standard order of precedence determines the order in which calculations are performed in a formula. Exponentiation has the highest order of precedence; multiplication and division have the next order of precedence; addition and subtraction have the lowest order of precedence.

9 The PRODUCT function multiplies a range of cells or two or more specified cells or ranges. The SUM function adds a range of cells or two or more specified cells or ranges. The IF function specifies a logical test to perform, and requires three arguments: the logical test, the value if true, and the value if false. If the specified logical test is true, then the function result is set to the value if true. Else, if the specified condition is false, the function result is set to the value if false.

SESSION 3.2

1 Click the formula bar reference area list arrow, then click the name of the cell.

2 Excel automatically adjusts formulas and named cells and ranges.

3 You used the Clipboard to move cell contents by the cut-and-paste technique. When you cut the cell contents, they were temporarily stored on the Clipboard; when you pasted the cell contents, they were copied from the Clipboard. If you want to paste cell contents that you have cut in Excel, you must do so immediately; once any other operation is performed, the Clipboard contents are no longer accessible.

4 Format Painter

5 the value is too large to be displayed in the cell

6 borders

7 window pane

SESSION 3.3

1 Insert, Standard

2 You can remove the contents of a cell with the Delete key; that operation does not remove any formatting or notes associated with the cell. When you clear a cell, you can specify that you want to clear the contents, the formatting, the cell notes, or all three. You can actually delete a cell only by deleting the entire row or the entire column containing that cell.

3 header, footer

4 You use the Object command on the Insert menu to embed the entire worksheet. You use the Copy and Paste Special commands to embed a selected part of a worksheet.

5 The Formatting toolbar and menu bar belong to Excel. The title bar belongs to Word.

6 a. title bar b. menu bar c. Standard toolbar d. Formatting toolbar e. formula bar reference area f. formula bar g. cell h. pointer i. sheet tab (or active sheet) j. Function Wizard button k. Borders button

SESSION 4.1

1 field

2 primary key, foreign key

3 Identify all the fields needed to produce the required information; group related fields into tables; determine each table's primary key; include a common field in related tables; avoid data redundancy; determine the properties of each field.

4 The data type determines what field values you can enter for the field and what other properties the field will have.

5 Their values will not be used for calculations.

6 null

7 A pencil symbol indicates that the record is being edited but has not yet been saved to the database. A star symbol identifies the next available row for a new record.

SESSION 4.2

1 Format

2 yes/no

3 Access allows you to have only one database open at a time.

4 If you type in navigation mode, your typed entry replaces the highlighted field value. If you type in editing mode, you can insert or delete characters in a field value based on the location of the insertion point.

5 another Access database, worksheet programs, other DBMSs, or delimited or fixed-width text files

6 You delete the field from the table structure and all its field values from the table.

7 portrait and landscape

SESSION 4.3

1 AutoForm

2 last record

3 datasheet

4 ? character

5 as many records as can fit on a page

6 selects all available fields; removes the selected field

7 predefined style for a form or report

8. Click anywhere in the large rectangular area surrounding the record selector.
9. A one-to-many relationship exists between two tables when one record in the first table matches zero, one, or many records in the second table, and when one record in the second table matches exactly one record in the first table.
10. referential integrity
11. The main form contains fields from the primary table and the subform contains fields from the related table.

SESSION 4.4

1. printed title on the report
2. A select query asks a question about the data stored in a database and returns the answer as a datasheet.
3. The QBE grid contains these rows: Field, Table, Sort, Show, Criteria, and or. Each Field box indicates the database field selected for the query, and the Table box indicates which table contains the field. The Sort box identifies whether the field is used as the basis for an ascending or descending sort or no sort at all. The Show box indicates if the field appears in the query datasheet. The Criteria and or boxes contain conditions used to select records for the query results.
4. Both look the same, appearing in Datasheet view, and can be used to update data in a database. A table datasheet shows the permanent data in a table, whereas a query datasheet is temporary and its contents are based on the criteria you establish in the QBE grid.
5. condition
6. oldest date to most recent date

SESSION 5.1

1. A title slide, whose formatting is controlled by the title master, usually contains one or more headings, and is typically used as the first slide in a presentation. The slide master controls the formatting for all types of non-title slides. A non-title slide might contain, for example, a bulleted list, a chart, a picture, or nothing at all. Many design templates have a slightly different design for the title slide than for non-title slides.
2. Establish a single look and use a consistent color scheme and text style throughout the presentation; identify the presentation goal and make sure each slide works toward that goal; present one concept or idea per slide; keep slides uncluttered; present information consistently; display the same type of information in the same location on each slide; don't include too many slides in a presentation; remember that the purpose of a presentation is to supplement, clarify, or highlight the speaker's words, not replace them.
3. You might choose a blank presentation if you want every slide to include a significant object, such as a company logo or name, that would conflict with a design template's background design.
4. To demote an item means to lower its position in an outline hierarchy. Items on a slide or even entire slides can be demoted. You would need to demote when you are adding items to a bulleted list in either slide view or outline view in order to add an item at a lower level than the previous item. When you are adding slides in outline view, pressing the Enter key always adds a new item at the same level as the previous item, so you will often have to demote (or promote) to establish the appropriate levels.
5. Titles and body text are displayed in outline view. Embedded or linked objects and items entered in the rightmost column of a 2-column bulleted list are not displayed.
6. In outline view, the New Slide dialog box is not displayed. Instead, a new slide is automatically assigned the Bulleted List AutoLayout.
7. Click the right mouse button, then click Previous.
8. Yes. Select the fourth slide, then click the Move Up button as many times as necessary.

SESSION 5.2

1. any view; no
2. In slide view, click the second item's bullet to select that item, then click and drag until the dashed vertical line appears in front of the fifth item.

3 To draw a perfect square instead of a rectangle, you must hold down the Shift key while dragging the pointer. You must also use the Shift key to resize a perfect square.

4 Click the Slide Layout button on the status bar, then select the desired slide layout. You cannot change a slide's layout while in outline view.

5 You must insert all four slides, using the Insert Slides from File command on the Insert menu, then delete the three slides you don't want.

6 All of the actions are allowed.

7 You can build items on a slide one at a time using a number of effects, such as fly from right and dissolve, and you can add sound effects.

SESSION 5.3

1 With both PowerPoint and Excel active, you selected and copied the chart in Excel, then used the Paste Special command in PowerPoint to embed the chart in the presentation.

2 You can move a slide in slide sorter view by dragging it to a new location. You can move a slide in outline view by selecting the slide and then clicking the Move Up or Move Down button until the slide is in the location you want.

3 Move the mouse to activate a pointer. To activate the pen, right-click and then click Pen.

4 Speaker's notes are another name for notes pages, and are accessed in notes pages view. Speaker's notes are most often used to guide the speaker during a presentation. Printed speaker's notes could also be distributed to the audience, so that audience members wouldn't have to take detailed notes.

5 All words entered directly on your slides and all speaker's notes are spell checked. Any words that are part of an object are not checked.

6 Handouts are slide printouts that show either 2, 3, or 6 slides per page.

SESSION 6.1

1 The first sheet should be a documentation sheet; all the input values should be organized on a single worksheet; standard supplementary values, such as an interest rate table or a depreciation schedule, should be entered on a separate worksheet; each chart should be placed on its own worksheet.

2 This Documentation sheet includes a title area, the filename, the name of the person who created the workbook, the date the workbook was created, the date the workbook was last modified, a statement of the purpose of the workbook, and a table that includes an entry for each sheet. An entry in the sheet table includes the name of a sheet and a short description of that sheet's contents.

3 the TODAY function

4 The fill handle is the small black square in the lower-right corner of the border that surrounds the active cell or cells. You can use a fill handle in an AutoFill process to create cell entries that complete a series, or to copy a formula to an adjacent cell or cells.

5 Cell E7 will contain the formula =E3 + $B4 + E$3 + $B$4.

6 Click cell C8, click the AutoSum button, then press the Enter key.

7 A cell that contains a text note displays a small red square in the upper-right corner of the cell. To display a cell's text note, point to the cell.

8 To test a worksheet means to verify that all formulas are accurate by using test values as the input values. Test values are numbers that generate a known or easily calculated result.

9 Select the cell, then click the Percent Style button on the Formatting toolbar.

10 Select the rows to be sorted, click Data, click Sort, specify the column(s) on which to sort, specify ascending or descending, then click the OK button.

SESSION 6.2

1. You can adjust a row's height with the row resizing pointer or by typing a value in the Row Height dialog box.
2. To center text in cell A3 across columns A through D, you select cells A3 through D3, then click the Center Across Columns button on the Formatting toolbar.
3. You use AutoFormat to apply a predesigned table format to selected cells. You select the cells you want to format, click Format on the menu bar, click AutoFormat, select a format style from the Table Format list, then click the OK button.
4. Portrait orientation prints a worksheet with the paper positioned so it is taller than it is wide. Landscape orientation prints the worksheet with the paper positioned so it is wider than it is tall.
5. When you customize a header or a footer, buttons are available for printing page number, total pages, date, time, filename (workbook name), and sheet name.
6. When you display and print worksheet formulas, you might have to change worksheet cell formats or page setup settings. You save first so that you can recover the original, unchanged workbook.

SESSION 6.3

1. a. chart title b. tick mark label or Y-axis label c. Y-axis title d. plot area e. legend f. data marker g. category label or X-axis label h. X-axis title
2. Identify the data points to be charted and locate them in your worksheet; assess the purpose of the chart and determine the appropriate chart type; sketch the chart, including all data points, axes, titles, labels, and legend; identify any titles, labels or legend text that will come from the worksheet and locate them in your worksheet.
3. Excel has 14 basic chart types plus a Combination chart, for a total of 15 different chart types. There are six three-dimensional chart types: 3-D area, 3-D bar, 3-D column, 3-D line, 3-D pie, and 3-D surface.
4. To select non-adjacent cells, you first select a cell or range of cells. Then you press and hold the Ctrl key as you select additional cells or cell ranges. You release the Ctrl key after all the desired cells have been selected.
5. A selected chart is surrounded by a simple border with sizing handles. An activated chart is surrounded by a hashed border. A selected chart can be moved, resized, or activated. To modify any chart object, the chart must be activated. To select a chart, you click anywhere within the chart border. To activate a selected chart, you right-click to open the shortcut menu and then click Edit Object, or you click Edit on the menu bar and then click Object.
6. A picture can be either stretched or stacked to a height that represents the magnitude of a data value.

SESSION 6.4

1. Click the Chart Type button on the Chart toolbar, then select one of the 14 samples that correspond to the 14 basic Excel chart types.
2. In an activated pie chart, click a wedge until only that wedge is selected, then click and drag to pull out the wedge.
3. Rotate the pie chart using the Format 3-D View dialog box. You click either the Clockwise Rotation or the Counterclockwise Rotation button until the pie wedges have been rotated to the desired position.
4. In an activated chart, click the data series, click the data point, right-click to display the shortcut menu, click Format Data Point, select the Patterns tab, then select the desired color.
5. Patterns can add visual interest to a chart. Because pattern differences are often easier to discern than differences between color shades, patterns can also make a printed chart more readable, especially one printed in black and white.
6. To link an Excel chart to a Word document, you copy the chart in Excel, then use Word's Paste Special command, specifying a Paste Link. To embed rather than link the chart, you would activate the Paste rather than the Paste Link radio button.

7 Excel automatically recalculates the workbook. Any cell with a formula involving the changed data value is changed, and the change propagates throughout the workbook. If the data value is used in a chart, the chart is updated to reflect the change. If the data value is a part of a linked object or is used as a basis for a linked object, the program containing the link to the object will automatically display the updated object.

SESSION 7.1

1 many-to-many (M:N)

2 match field values of 20 or 30; match field values in the range of 20 to 30

3 Like operator

4 different Criteria rows

5 when the sort keys are nonadjacent, when the fields to be sorted are in the wrong order, or when the sorts are a mixture of ascending and descending

6 Use Filter By Selection to select all or part of a single field value in a datasheet or form, then display only those records that contain the selection. Use Filter By Form to select multiple values for multiple fields.

SESSION 7.2

1 A table field exists in a database, whereas a calculated field does not exist in a database and displays the results of an expression.

2 to the left of the colon in the Field text box

3 performs arithmetic operations on selected records in a database

4 Group By

5 You must enter your criteria, or parameters, in the dialog box.

6 integer or percent

7 Select queries display data from a database; action queries update multiple records in a database at one time.

SESSION 7.3

1 Arrange the fields on the screen in an order that is meaningful to users of the form; group together logically related fields; use properties such as font, style, color, or graphics to improve the appearance of the form and to emphasize important areas and controls but keep these to a minimum; make the form self-explanatory by using controls such as list boxes, check boxes, radio buttons, and push buttons instead of codes and lengthy explanations.

2 A bound control is linked, or bound, to a field in a table or query, whereas an unbound control is not.

3 detail, form header, form footer, page header, page footer

4 bound control

5 prompt

6 Click the text box; place the pointer anywhere on the border of the text box, but not on a move or sizing handle; then drag the text box and its related label to the new location.

7 Click each control while holding down the Shift key.

8 Caption

9 Special Effect

10 a control that displays a drop-down list box, so that you can either type a value for the field or select its value from the list box

11 unbound

Index

Special Characters
  · (blank space marker), OF 85
  > (greater than operator), OF 433
  < (less than operator), OF 433
  ! (exclamation point), OF 241
  # (hash mark), OF 241
  % (percentage operator), OF 150
  ¶ (paragraph mark), OF 85
  ** (tab character), OF 105
  ** (tab marker), OF 85
  * (asterisk), OF 150, OF 241, OF 439
  + (plus sign), OF 150
  - (hyphen/minus sign), OF 150, OF 241
  / (slash), OF 150
  >= (greater than or equal to operator), OF 433
  <= (less than or equal to operator), OF 433
  ? (question mark), OF 241
  [ ] (square brackets), OF 241
  < > (not equal to operator), OF 433
  ^ (caret), OF 150

A

absolute references, OF 153, OF 350–357
Access, OF 5, OF 8, OF 37–48. *See also* databases; datasheets; fields; forms; queries; records; reports; tables
  changing data copied from, OF 37–38
  exiting, OF 48
  objects, OF 39–40
Access window, OF 8, OF 43
action queries, OF 468–471
activating charts, OF 391–392
active cells, OF 54, OF 139
active document, OF 90–91
active programs, exiting, OF 56
active sheet, OF 138, OF 139
adding. *See also* inserting
  borders to worksheets, OF 177–179, OF 193
  combo boxes to forms, OF 485–488
  fields. *See* adding fields
  records. *See* adding records to tables
  slides to presentations. *See* adding slides to presentations
  text. *See* adding text
adding fields
  forms, OF 476–477
  tables, OF 223–224
adding records to tables, OF 46, OF 219–221, OF 226
  using forms, OF 250–251
adding slides to presentations, OF 62–66, OF 292–298
  outline view, OF 295–298
  slide view, OF 292–294
adding text
  charts, OF 394
  slides, OF 63–65, OF 303–305
  text notes in worksheets, OF 358–359
addition operator (+), OF 150
aggregate functions, OF 459–463
  record groups, OF 462–463
alignment
  controls, OF 480–481
  paragraphs, OF 28
  tabs, OF 106
  worksheet cells, OF 370–371
AND function, OF 158
And logical operator, OF 441–443
animation effects, slides, OF 319–320
Animation Settings dialog box, OF 320
annotating slides, OF 324–326
Answer Wizard, OF 32, OF 33–34
  annotating slides, OF 324–325
append queries, OF 469
Apply Design Template dialog box, OF 303
arithmetic operators
  queries, OF 455
  worksheets, OF 149–150
Arrange All option, Window menu, OF 91–92
asterisk (*)
  multiplication operator, OF 150
  wildcard character, OF 241, OF 439
ATANH function, OF 154
AutoCorrect dialog box, OF 87
AutoCorrect feature, OF 87–88
AutoFill, completing series, OF 344–347
AutoFit feature, adjusting column width, OF 175
AutoFormat dialog box, OF 247, OF 372
AutoFormats, OF 245–248, OF 371–373
  changing, OF 246–248
AutoForm Wizards, OF 237–238
AutoLayouts, OF 63, OF 298
automatic recalculation, OF 357
AutoNumber data type
  fields, OF 211
  sorting results, OF 272
AutoSave feature, OF 19
AutoShapes
  changing, OF 310–312
  creating, OF 308–310
  drawing methods, OF 308
AutoShapes toolbar, OF 309
AutoSum, OF 347–348
AVERAGE function, OF 154
Avg function, OF 460, OF 461

B

Backspace key, OF 24, OF 25, OF 86–87
Back Style property, OF 483
Between...And operator, OF 439
blank lines, inserting in documents, OF 84
blank presentations, OF 286
blank space marker (y), OF 85
blocks, text. *See* text blocks
bold font style
  documents, OF 30, OF 103–104
  worksheets, OF 366
Border Color palette, OF 484
borders
  charts, OF 413
  removing from embedded pictures, OF 183–184
  worksheets, OF 177–180, OF 193
Borders button, OF 177
Borders palette, OF 177
Border tab, OF 177
  Format Cells dialog box, OF 179
bound controls, OF 474
Bound Object Frame tool, OF 475
building slide shows, OF 319
build slides, OF 72
Bulleted List AutoLayout, OF 298
bulleted lists, OF 111–113
bullets, OF 111
Bullets and Numbering dialog box, OF 113
buttons. *See also specific buttons*
  navigation, OF 45
  open windows, OF 58
  ToolTips, OF 13

C

calculated controls, OF 475
calculated fields, OF 455–459
  changing properties, OF 458–459
calculations. *See* calculations in queries; formulas; functions; record calculations
calculations in queries, OF 455–463
  calculated fields. *See* calculated fields
  record calculations, OF 459–462
  record group calculations, OF 462–463
canceling actions, OF 88, OF 89
capitalization, error correction, OF 87
Caption property, OF 481–482
captions, forms, OF 481–482
caret (^), exponentiation operator, OF 150
cascade deletes, OF 252
cascade updates, OF 252
Cases folder, OF 15
categories, charts, OF 383
category labels, charts, OF 383
Cell Note dialog box, OF 358
cell ranges, OF 162–165
  moving to, OF 164–165
  naming, OF 162–164
cell references, OF 139
  absolute, OF 153, OF 350–357
  navigating, OF 146
  relative, OF 153, OF 350

cells
- active, OF 54
- empty, OF 140
- selecting for charts, OF 387–388
- tables, OF 37
- worksheets. *See* worksheet cells

centered alignment, OF 28
centering
- linked charts, OF 415
- text in worksheet cells, OF 371
- worksheets, OF 377

Change Case dialog box, OF 306
chart labels, formatting, OF 411–412
charts, OF 67, OF 383–417
- borders, OF 413
- ChartWizard, OF 384
- column. *See* column charts
- developing, OF 383–384
- editing, OF 69–71
- elements, OF 383
- embedding in presentations, OF 321–322
- formatting labels, OF 411–412
- linking to slides, OF 66–71
- linking to Word documents, OF 414–417
- modifying. *See* modifying charts
- opening, OF 66–67
- pie. *See* pie charts; 3-D pie charts
- planning, OF 384
- plot area, OF 383, OF 393
- previewing, OF 400
- printing, OF 401
- resizing, OF 68–69
- selecting and activating, OF 391–392
- selecting cells, OF 387–388
- 3-D pie charts. *See* 3-D pie charts
- titles. *See* chart titles
- types, OF 385

chart titles, OF 383
- color and shadow, OF 399–400
- formatting, OF 412

Chart toolbar, OF 392
Chart Type list, OF 406
ChartWizard, OF 384–391
- changing data series, OF 390–391
- creating pie charts, OF 403–405
- dialog boxes, OF 385, OF 388, OF 389, OF 390, OF 404

Clear Contents command, OF 185, OF 186
Clear option, OF 185, OF 186
click-and-drag technique, OF 97
clip art
- color, OF 317–318
- inserting on slides, OF 314–319
- moving, OF 317, OF 318–319
- sizing, OF 316–317

ClipArt Gallery, OF 10
Clipboard, OF 108, OF 152
Close button, OF 36
- Access, OF 48
- Excel, OF 160

Close option, Excel, OF 160
closing
- documents, OF 93
- queries, OF 273
- reports, OF 265–266
- workbooks, OF 160–161

Collapse Selection button, OF 296
color
- chart titles, OF 399–400
- clip art, OF 317–318
- pie chart wedges, OF 409–410
- WordArt objects, OF 121–122
- worksheets, OF 368–369

column charts, OF 386–390
- pictures, OF 396–399

column headings, Excel window, OF 139
columns
- resizing in datasheets, OF 436–437
- worksheets. *See* worksheet columns

column selector, OF 44
Column Width dialog box, OF 176
combo boxes, adding to forms, OF 485–488
Combo Box tool, OF 475
Combo Box Wizard, OF 485–488
command buttons, Database window, OF 43
Command Button tool, OF 475
common fields, OF 203
- designing databases, OF 206
- joining tables, OF 251

compacting databases, OF 495–496
comparison operators
- matching ranges of values, OF 437–438
- queries, OF 433, OF 437–438

composite key, OF 205
conditions, queries, OF 270–271, OF 433
Contents tab, Help system, OF 31, OF 32
context menus, OF 41, OF 42
context-sensitive Help, OF 34–35
controls, OF 474–475
- bound and unbound, OF 474
- calculated, OF 475
- drawing rectangles around, OF 483–485
- moving, OF 479–480
- resizing, OF 478–479
- selecting and aligning, OF 480–481

Control Wizards, adding combo boxes to forms, OF 485–488
Control Wizards tool, OF 475
copy-and-paste technique, OF 25–26
- entering formulas, OF 152–154
- records from another database, OF 226–228

Copy button, OF 108
Copy command, OF 108, OF 187
copying
- databases, OF 40–42
- formulas. *See* copying formulas
- records from another database, OF 226–228
- text blocks, OF 108
- text in documents, OF 25–26

copying formulas, OF 55, OF 152–154
- absolute cell references, OF 350–357
- AutoSum, OF 347–348
- fill handles, OF 348–349

Count function, OF 460, OF 461
criteria, queries, OF 441–445
currency data type
- fields, OF 211
- sorting results, OF 272

current record symbol, OF 45
customizing forms, OF 472–476
- Form window, OF 473–476

Custom radio button, Spacing Between Characters dialog box, OF 118
cut-and-paste technique, OF 26–27
- moving worksheet cell contents, OF 168–169

D

data
- avoiding redundancy, OF 206
- finding using forms, OF 239–242
- integrating, OF 5, OF 6
- organizing, OF 202
- series. *See* data series

database functions, OF 155
database management system (DBMS), OF 38, OF 204. *See also* Access
databases. *See also* Access
- compacting, OF 495–496
- copying, OF 40–42
- copying records between, OF 226–228
- creating, OF 207–209
- defined, OF 38–39, OF 203
- deleting records, OF 229
- designing, OF 205–207
- fields. *See* fields
- opening, OF 42–43
- queries. *See* queries
- records. *See* records
- renaming, OF 42
- reports. *See* reports

saving, OF 221
tables. *See* tables
updating (maintaining). *See* updating databases
Database tab, New dialog box, OF 208
Database toolbar, OF 43
Database window, OF 43
running parameter queries, OF 466
data integration, OF 5, OF 6
data labels
adding to charts, OF 394
moving, OF 412
Data Map, OF 10
data markers, charts, OF 383
data points, charts, OF 383
data series
charts, OF 383, OF 390–391
completing using AutoFill, OF 344–347
datasheets, OF 44, OF 219
changing appearance, OF 436–437
navigating, OF 45
printing, OF 236
Datasheet view, OF 44
Table window, OF 219
data types, fields, OF 210–211, OF 216, OF 217
sorting results, OF 272
date and time functions, OF 155
Date button, Page Setup dialog box, OF 375
dates
entering in worksheets, OF 148
serial, OF 148
TODAY function, OF 343–344
worksheets, formatting, OF 175
date/time data type, OF 211
sorting results, OF 272
DBMS (database management system), OF 38, OF 204. *See also* Access
defining
fields, OF 213–217
table relationships, OF 251–255
Delete key, OF 86, OF 99
clearing cell contents, OF 185, OF 186
deleting text, OF 24, OF 25
delete queries, OF 469
deleting
borders. *See* deleting borders
columns and rows in worksheets, OF 167–168
fields from table structure, OF 235
records. *See* deleting records
text. *See* deleting text
deleting borders
embedded objects, OF 183–184
worksheets, OF 180
deleting records
databases, OF 229
forms, OF 249–250
referential integrity, OF 252
tables, OF 46
deleting text
charts, OF 394
documents, OF 24–25, OF 99–100
slides, OF 305
Demote button, Outlining toolbar, OF 295, OF 296
demoting text, slides, OF 295, OF 296, OF 301
design grid, OF 268
design templates, OF 286, OF 288–289
changing, OF 302–303
Design view
forms, OF 246
Form window, OF 473–476
joined tables, OF 440
multiple sort fields, OF 448–450
queries, OF 435
Select Query window, OF 267–268
Table window, OF 213
destination program, OF 48, OF 50
detail records, OF 258
detail section, forms, OF 476
disks, OF 14
displaying. *See also* viewing
chart titles, OF 399–400
dates using TODAY function, OF 343–344
documentation sheets, OF 342
formulas, OF 381–382
nonprinting characters, OF 85
toolbars, OF 11–13
ToolTips, OF 13
worksheets, OF 345
division operator (/), OF 150
docking toolbars, OF 11, OF 13
documentation sheets, OF 342–343
document-centric approach, OF 5, OF 6
documents. *See also* presentations
active, OF 90–91
checking spelling, OF 122–125
closing, OF 93
deleting text, OF 24–25, OF 99–100
developing, OF 79–80
editing. *See* editing documents
embedding WordArt objects, OF 114–119
embedding worksheets. *See* embedded worksheets
entering text. *See* entering text in documents
filenames, OF 19–21, OF 31
formatting. *See* formatting documents
inserting blank lines, OF 84
integrated, OF 13–18
linking charts to, OF 414–417
locating and storing, OF 14–16
naming, OF 93
navigating, OF 22–23, OF 94–96
opening, OF 16–18, OF 89–90
planning, OF 80–81
previewing, OF 125–128
printing, OF 35, OF 128
saving, OF 19–21, OF 31, OF 93
scrolling, OF 95
selecting, OF 98
starting, OF 81–83
switching between, OF 90–91
document view buttons, OF 19
PowerPoint, OF 60
Word window, OF 18
document views, OF 126
document window buttons, OF 18, OF 19
document windows, OF 19
organizing, OF 89–93
tiling, OF 91–92
drag-and-drop technique
moving text in documents, OF 109–111
moving text on slides, OF 305–306
moving worksheet cell contents, OF 169–171
Drawing toolbar, OF 60, OF 290, OF 308–312

E

editing
charts, OF 69–71
documents. *See* editing documents
embedded worksheets, OF 192–193
linked charts, OF 415
text. *See* editing documents; editing text
title masters, OF 291–292
worksheets, OF 54–56, OF 69–71
editing documents, OF 23–27, OF 94–100
copying text, OF 25–26
deleting text, OF 24–25, OF 99–100
inserting text, OF 23–24, OF 96
moving text, OF 26–27
navigating, OF 94–96
selecting and replacing text, OF 96–99
editing mode
keystroke techniques, OF 230
switching between navigation mode and, OF 229
editing text. *See also* editing documents
charts, OF 393–394
undoing changes, OF 88–89
Edit mode, editing worksheet labels, OF 141–142
elevation, 3-D pie charts, OF 408
embedded objects, OF 48–49
on forms, OF 488–491
modifying in Paint, OF 491–493

moving, OF 185
resizing, OF 184
Word Art, OF 116–119
in worksheets, OF 182–185
worksheets. *See* embedded worksheets
embedded worksheets, OF 187–194
editing, OF 192–193
empty cells, OF 140
engineering functions, OF 155
entering
dates in worksheets, OF 148
formulas in worksheets, OF 151–152, OF 154–158
text. *See* entering text in documents; entering text on slides
values in worksheets, OF 146–148
WordArt images, OF 117–118
worksheet labels, OF 141, OF 144
entering text in documents, OF 23–24, OF 83–89, OF 96
canceling actions, OF 88–89
displaying nonprinting characters, OF 85
error correction, OF 86–88
typing text, OF 83–86
entering text on slides, OF 290–292
Enter Parameter Value dialog box, OF 466
Enter Your Text Here dialog box, OF 117
entity integrity, OF 217
Equation Editor, OF 10
error correction
AutoCorrect feature, OF 87–88
capitalization, OF 87
spelling errors. *See* spell checking
text, OF 86–88
worksheet labels, OF 141–144
exact matches, queries, OF 433–435
Excel, OF 5, OF 7, OF 50–56, OF 135
charts. *See* charts
importing data to Access table, OF 231–234
workbooks. *See* workbooks
worksheets. *See* worksheets
Excel window, OF 7, OF 53, OF 138–139
exclamation point (!), wildcard character, OF 241
exiting
Access, OF 48
active programs, OF 56
Word, OF 36
Expand Selection button, Outlining toolbar, OF 296
exponentiation operator (^), OF 150
Expression Builder, OF 455–458
Expression Builder dialog box, OF 456
expressions, calculations, OF 455

F

FALSE function, OF 158
field list, OF 268
field properties
calculated fields, changing, OF 458–459
determining, OF 206
Field Properties dialog box, OF 459
fields, OF 39, OF 202
adding. *See* adding fields
assigning sizes, OF 212, OF 235
calculated. *See* calculated fields
changing properties, OF 224–226
common. *See* common fields
composite key, OF 205
data types. *See* data types, fields
defining, OF 213–217
deleting from table structure, OF 235
designing databases, OF 205
foreign key, OF 203
grouping into tables, OF 205
moving, OF 222–223
naming, OF 209–210
primary key. *See* primary key
properties. *See* field properties
selecting. *See* selecting fields
sorting. *See* sorting
field selector, OF 44
field values, OF 202
changing using queries, OF 275–276
Filename button, Page Setup dialog box, OF 375
filename extensions, OF 15
filenames, OF 14
documents, OF 19–21, OF 31
presentations, OF 58, OF 59
File New Database dialog box, OF 208
fill handles, OF 344
copying formulas, OF 348–349
Filter By Form, OF 452–454
Filter By Selection, OF 450–453
filtering records, OF 450–454
financial functions, OF 155
Find button, OF 239
Find command, OF 239
Find in field dialog box, OF 240
finding. *See also* queries
data using forms, OF 239–242
Find tab, Help system, OF 32
F2 key, switching between navigation mode and editing mode, OF 229
folders, OF 14, OF 15
Font button, Page Setup dialog box, OF 375
Font list box, Word, OF 101
fonts, OF 101–102
printer, OF 101
sans serif, OF 100–101
screen, OF 101
serif, OF 100
size. *See* font size
styles. *See* font style
TrueType, OF 101
type. *See* font type
font size
chart labels, OF 412
chart titles, OF 412
datasheets, OF 436
documents, OF 29–30, OF 101–103, OF 109–111
slides, OF 291, OF 307
worksheets, OF 365–366
font style
documents, OF 30, OF 103–105
worksheets, OF 366–367
font type
chart labels, OF 411
chart titles, OF 412
documents, OF 29–30, OF 100–101, OF 103
worksheets, OF 365–366
footers
forms, OF 476
worksheets, OF 186, OF 374–376
foreign key, OF 203
Format Cells dialog box, OF 173, OF 179
Format Chart Area dialog box, OF 70
Format Chart Title dialog box, OF 400
Format Data Point dialog box, OF 409
Format list box, OF 225
Format menu, adjusting column width, OF 175, OF 176
Format Object dialog box, OF 184
Format Painter, OF 105
worksheets, OF 173–174
Format Plot Area dialog box, OF 393
Format property, changing, OF 224–225
formatting
chart labels, OF 411–412
chart titles, OF 412
dates using TODAY function, OF 344
documents. *See* formatting documents
templates, OF 84
text. *See* formatting documents; formatting text
worksheets. *See* formatting worksheets
formatting documents, OF 27–30, OF 100–113
copying and pasting text, OF 108
font size, OF 101–103, OF 109–111
font style, OF 30, OF 103–105
font type, OF 29–30, OF 100–101, OF 103
moving text, OF 109–111
numbered and bulleted lists, OF 111–113
paragraph alignment, OF 28
tabs, OF 105–107
formatting text. *See also* formatting documents

- slides, OF 306–308
- speaker's notes, OF 327–328

Formatting toolbar
- Excel window, OF 139
- PowerPoint window, OF 59, OF 290, OF 291
- Word window, OF 18, OF 19

formatting worksheets, OF 365–373
- adjusting row heights, OF 369–370
- AutoFormat, OF 371–373
- borders, OF 177–180
- cell alignment, OF 370–371
- colors, OF 368–369
- column widths, OF 175–176
- dates, OF 175
- font style, OF 366–367
- font type and size, OF 365–366
- headers and footers, OF 375–376
- numbers, OF 171–174
- patterns, OF 367–368

form footer sections, OF 476

form header sections, OF 476

forms, OF 39, OF 237–257, OF 472–491
- adding fields, OF 476–477
- AutoFormat. *See* AutoFormats
- blank, creating, OF 473–474
- controls. *See* controls
- creating with AutoForm Wizards, OF 237–238
- creating with Form Wizard, OF 243–246
- creating with main form and subform, OF 255–257
- customizing, OF 472–476
- defined, OF 237
- defining table relationships, OF 251–255
- Design view, Design viewforms OF 246
- embedding and changing graphic images, OF 488–491
- finding data, OF 239–242
- Form window, OF 473–476
- maintaining table data, OF 248–251
- navigating, OF 239, OF 257
- printing selected form records, OF 242–243
- resizing, OF 493–495
- saving, OF 238, OF 477–478, OF 487–488
- sections, OF 476
- selecting fields, OF 244
- viewing, OF 477

form selector, OF 475

formula bar, OF 138, OF 139
- editing worksheet labels, OF 142–143

formula bar reference area, OF 138, OF 139

formulas, OF 52, OF 149–160, OF 347–357
- arithmetic, OF 151–152
- arithmetic operators, OF 149–150
- automatic recalculation, OF 357
- containing functions, OF 154–158
- copying and pasting. *See* copying formulas
- displaying, OF 381–382
- entering, OF 151–152, OF 154–158
- logical, OF 158–160
- order of precedence, OF 150
- percentage, OF 362–363
- prewritten. *See* functions
- printing, OF 381–382
- relative and absolute references, OF 350–357

Form view, OF 478
- switching to, OF 488

Form window, OF 473–476, OF 478, OF 480

Form Wizard dialog box, OF 256

Form Wizards, OF 237, OF 243–246
- activating, OF 243
- creating forms with main form and subform, OF 255–257
- dialog boxes, OF 243, OF 245

full screen view, OF 126

functions, OF 154–158. *See also specific functions*
- aggregate. *See* aggregate functions
- categories, OF 155
- formulas containing, OF 154–158

Function Wizard, OF 155–160
- dialog boxes, OF 156, OF 157, OF 158, OF 159, OF 160
- logical functions, OF 158–160

G

General tab, New dialog box, OF 82

Graph, OF 10

graphic images. *See also* clip art; pictures
- embedding on forms, OF 488–491
- modifying in Paint, OF 491–493

greater than operator (>), OF 433

greater than or equal to operator (>=), OF 433

gridlines
- removing from embedded worksheets, OF 192
- worksheets, OF 377–378

grids, forms, OF 476

Group By Operator, OF 462–463

H

hash mark (#), wildcard character, OF 241

Header dialog box, OF 375

headers
- forms, OF 476
- worksheets, OF 186, OF 374–376

Help system
- context-sensitive Help, OF 34–35
- Word, OF 31–35

Help Topics: Microsoft Word window, OF 31–32

hyphen (-), wildcard character, OF 241

I

IF function, OF 158–160

Import dialog box, OF 232

importing Excel data to new table, OF 231–234

Import Spreadsheet Wizard dialog boxes, OF 232, OF 233

Index tab, Help system, OF 32

information functions, OF 155

IN ( ) operator, OF 439

Insert command, OF 187, OF 188

inserting. *See also* adding; adding fields; adding records to tables; adding slides to presentations; adding text
- blank lines in documents, OF 84
- clip art on slides, OF 314–319
- columns and rows in worksheets, OF 165–167
- rows in worksheets, OF 55
- slides from another presentation, OF 313–314
- speaker's notes in presentations, OF 326–328
- tabs, OF 106–107
- text in documents, OF 23–24, OF 96

insertion point, OF 21
- moving, OF 94–96
- positioning, OF 22

Insert New Slide button, OF 62

integrated documents, OF 13–18

integrating data, OF 5, OF 6

integration, OF 48

italic font style
- documents, OF 30, OF 104–105
- worksheets, OF 366, OF 367

J

joins, OF 251

justified alignment, OF 28

K

key
- foreign, OF 203
- primary. *See* primary key

L

labels, OF 140–144
- charts. *See* data labels
- editing, OF 141–144
- entering, OF 141, OF 144
- forms, OF 474
- tick mark, charts, OF 383

Label tool, OF 475

landscape orientation, OF 186, OF 373, OF 374

left alignment, OF 28

legends, charts, OF 383

less than operator (?), OF 433

less than or equal to operator (?=), OF 433

Like operator, OF 439

lines (of text), selecting, OF 98

Line tool, OF 475, OF 483

linking objects, OF 49–50
- charts to slides, OF 66–71
- charts to Word documents, OF 414–417

List Box tool, OF 475

lists
 bulleted, OF 111–113
 numbered, OF 111–112
logical formulas, OF 158–160
logical functions, OF 155
logical operators, OF 441–445
lookup and reference functions, OF 155
Lookup Wizard data type
 fields, OF 211
 sorting results, OF 272

M

Magnifier button, Print Preview window, OF 127
maintaining. *See* updating; updating databases; updating tables
make-table queries, OF 469
many-to-many relationships, OF 428–432
master document view, OF 126
masters, OF 286
math and trig functions, OF 155
MAX function, OF 154
Max function, OF 460
memo data type
 fields, OF 211
 sorting results, OF 272
menu bar
 Database window, OF 43
 Excel window, OF 139
 Word window, OF 18, OF 19
menus. *See also specific menus*
 shortcut, OF 41, OF 42
Microsoft ClipArt Gallery 2.0 dialog box, OF 316
MIN function, OF 154
Min function, OF 460
minus sign (–), subtraction operator, OF 150
misspellings. *See* spell checking
modifying charts, OF 391–400
 moving and resizing charts, OF 395–396
 pictures in column charts, OF 396–399
 plot area, OF 393
 selecting and activating charts, OF 391–392
 text, OF 393–394
 titles, OF 399–400
Move Down button, Outlining toolbar, OF 296
Move Up button, Outlining toolbar, OF 296
moving. *See also* navigating
 charts, OF 395
 clip art, OF 317, OF 318–319
 controls, OF 479–480
 data labels, OF 412
 embedded pictures, OF 185
 fields, OF 222–223
 insertion point, OF 22, OF 94–96
 to named range or cell, OF 164–165
 slides in presentations, OF 61–62
 text. *See* moving text
 worksheet cell contents, OF 168–171
moving text
 documents, OF 26–27
 slides, OF 300–301, OF 305–306
 text blocks, OF 109–111
Multiple Pages button, Print Preview window, OF 126
Multiple Pages menu box, OF 127
multiplication operator (*), OF 150
multitasking, OF 116
My Computer icon, opening presentations, OF 57–59

N

naming. *See also* filenames
 databases, OF 42
 documents, OF 93
 workbooks, OF 162
 worksheet cells and ranges, OF 162–164
 worksheets, OF 140, OF 402–403
navigating
 datasheets, OF 45
 documents, OF 22–23, OF 94–96
 forms, OF 239, OF 257
 worksheets, OF 145–146
navigation buttons, OF 45
navigation mode
 keystroke techniques, OF 230
 switching between editing mode and, OF 229
New dialog box, OF 82, OF 207, OF 208, OF 289
New Form dialog box, OF 237
New Query dialog box, OF 267
New Report dialog box, OF 260
New Slide command, OF 62
New Slide dialog box, OF 63, OF 289, OF 298
New Table dialog box, OF 212
Next Slide button, OF 60, OF 290
nonprinting characters, displaying, OF 85
nonunique sort keys, OF 446–447
Normal template, OF 84
normal view, OF 126
Normal View button, OF 83
not equal to operator (), OF 433
notes pages view, OF 60
 inserting speaker's notes in presentations, OF 327
Notes Pages View button, OF 290
NOT function, OF 158
Not operator, OF 439
null value, OF 217
number data type
 fields, OF 211
 sorting results, OF 272
numbered lists, OF 111–112
numbers. *See also* values
 worksheets, formatting, OF 171–174
Number tab, Format Cells dialog box, OF 173

O

Object dialog box, OF 116
Object Linking and Embedding (OLE), OF 48, OF 49
objects. *See also specific objects*
 Access, OF 39–40
 databases, naming, OF 209–210
 embedded. *See* embedded objects
 linking. *See* linking objects
 WordArt. *See* WordArt objects
object tabs, Database window, OF 43
Office 95. *See also* Access; Excel; PowerPoint; Word
 overview, OF 5–11
 tools, OF 9–11
Office Shortcut Bar, OF 11–13
OLE (Object Linking and Embedding), OF 48, OF 49
OLE object data type
 fields, OF 211
 sorting results, OF 272
one-to-many relationships, OF 251–252, OF 427–428
 defining, OF 253–255
1 X 2 Pages button, Multiple Pages menu box, OF 127
Open a Document button, OF 57
Open dialog box, OF 17
opening
 charts, OF 66–67
 databases, OF 42–43
 documents, OF 89–90
 presentations, OF 57–59
 Query window, OF 267
 tables, OF 44
 workbooks, OF 53–54, OF 161–162
Option Group tool, OF 475
order
 operations in formulas, OF 150
 slides in presentations, OF 61–62, OF 322–324
OR function, OF 158
Organization Chart, OF 10
organizing data, OF 202
orientation, paper, OF 186, OF 373–374
Or logical operator, OF 441, OF 444–445
orphaned records, OF 252
outline view, OF 299–301
 adding slides to presentations, OF 295–298
 deleting slides, OF 299–300
 documents, OF 126
 moving text on slides, OF 300–301
 PowerPoint, OF 60
 promoting and demoting text on sides, OF 301
 selecting text, OF 300
 switching to, OF 294–295

Outline View button, OF 290
Outlining toolbar, PowerPoint window, OF 295–296

P

page footer sections, forms, OF 476
page header sections, forms, OF 476
page layout view, OF 126
Page Number button, Page Setup dialog box, OF 375
Page Setup dialog box, OF 375, OF 377
Paint, OF 10
 modifying graphic images, OF 491–493
paper orientation, OF 186, OF 373–374
paragraph mark (**), OF 85
paragraphs
 alignment, OF 28
 selecting, OF 98
parameter queries, OF 463–466
Paste button, OF 108
Paste command, OF 108
Paste Special command, OF 187, OF 188
Paste Special dialog box, OF 321, OF 415
 linking charts to slides, OF 67–68
pattern matches, queries, OF 439–441
patterns, worksheets, OF 367–368
percentage formulas, OF 362–363
percentage operator (%), OF 150
Picture dialog box, OF 120–121
pictures
 column charts, OF 396–399
 stacking, OF 398–399
pie charts
 applying patterns to wedges, OF 410–411
 changing to 3-D pie chart, OF 405–406
 color of wedges, OF 409–410
 creating, OF 403–405
 3-D. *See* 3-D pie charts
placeholders, OF 63, OF 290
 resizing, OF 307, OF 315
planning
 charts, OF 384
 documents, OF 80–81
 presentations, OF 287
 worksheets, OF 136
plot area, charts, OF 383, OF 393
plus sign (+), addition operator, OF 150
point-and-click technique, entering formulas, OF 152
pointers, slide shows, OF 324
points, OF 101
portrait orientation, OF 373–374
pound sign (#), wildcard character, OF 241
PowerPoint, OF 5, OF 8–9, OF 56–73. *See also* presentations; slides
PowerPoint window, OF 9, OF 58, OF 59–60, OF 290
presentation graphics program. *See* PowerPoint; presentations; slides
presentations, OF 57
 adding slides. *See* adding slides to presentations
 blank, OF 286
 checking spelling, OF 328–329
 design templates. *See* design templates
 developing, OF 286
 embedding Excel charts, OF 321–322
 filenames, OF 58, OF 59
 inserting slides from another presentation, OF 313–314
 opening, OF 57–59
 planning, OF 287
 printing, OF 329–330
 saving, OF 59, OF 298
 slides. *See* slides
 speaker's notes, OF 326–328, OF 329
 starting, OF 288–290
 viewing. *See* viewing presentations
Presentation tab, New dialog box, OF 289
presentation window, OF 58, OF 60
previewing. *See* Print Preview
Previous Slide button, OF 60, OF 290
primary key, OF 39, OF 203
 determining, OF 205
 sorting, OF 447
 specifying, OF 217–218
primary table, OF 252
Print button
 Access, OF 47
 Word, OF 35
Print command
 Access, OF 47
 Word, OF 35
Print dialog box, PowerPoint, OF 72
printer fonts, OF 101
printing
 charts, OF 401
 datasheets, OF 236
 documents, OF 35, OF 128
 formulas, OF 381–382
 presentations, OF 329–330
 reports, OF 264–265
 selected form records, OF 242–243
 slides, OF 72–73
 speaker's notes, OF 329
 tables, OF 47
 3-D pie charts, OF 413
 worksheets. *See* printing worksheets
printing worksheets, OF 186–187, OF 373–382
 centering worksheets, OF 377
 formulas, OF 381–382
 gridlines, OF 377–378
 headers and footers, OF 374–376
 paper orientation, OF 373–374
Print Preview
 charts, OF 400
 documents, OF 125, OF 126–128
 forms, OF 242
 reports, OF 264
 worksheets, OF 186–187
Print Preview window, OF 126, OF 127
PRODUCT function, OF 155
Promote button, OF 295, OF 296
promoting text, slides, OF 295, OF 296, OF 301
prompts, Form view, OF 478
properties, fields. *See* field properties
property sheet, OF 475
PV function, OF 154

Q

QBE (query by example), OF 266
queries, OF 39, OF 266–276, OF 433–471
 action, OF 468–471
 calculations. *See* calculations in queries
 changing datasheet appearance, OF 436–437
 changing data using, OF 275–276
 comparison operators, OF 433, OF 437–438
 creating, OF 268–269
 exact matches, OF 433–435
 filtering data, OF 450–454
 multiple selection criteria, OF 441–445
 multiple tables, OF 273–275
 parameter, OF 463–466
 pattern matches, OF 439–441
 Query window, OF 266–268
 running, OF 269–270, OF 271, OF 435, OF 438, OF 441
 saving, OF 273
 select, OF 266
 sorting data, OF 271–273, OF 445–450
 specifying conditions, OF 270–271
 Top Values property, OF 467–468
query by example (QBE), OF 266
Query parameters dialog box, OF 465
Query Type button, OF 268
Query Type list box, OF 470
Query window, OF 266–268, OF 468
 opening, OF 267
 Or logical operator, OF 444
Query Wizards, OF 266
 exact matches, OF 433–435
question mark (?), wildcard character, OF 241

R

ranges, cells. *See* cell ranges
recalculation, automatic, OF 357
Recolor Picture dialog box, OF 318

record calculations, OF 459–463
  aggregate functions, OF 459–462
  groups of records, OF 462–463
records, OF 39, OF 202
  adding to tables. *See* adding records to tables
  calculations. *See* record calculations
  changing, OF 229–231, OF 248–249
  copying from another database, OF 226–228
  deleting. *See* deleting records
  detail, OF 258
  filtering, OF 450–454
  orphaned, OF 252
  printing selected form records, OF 242–243
  selecting for queries, OF 270–271
  sorting using queries, OF 271–273
record selector, OF 44
Rectangle tool, OF 475, OF 483
Redo button, OF 88, OF 89
redundancy, data, avoiding, OF 206
Reference Windows, OF 4
referential integrity, OF 252
related table, OF 252
relational database management systems, OF 204
relational databases, defined, OF 203
Relationships dialog box, OF 254
Relationships window, OF 253
relative references, OF 153, OF 350
removing. *See also* deleting
  gridlines from embedded worksheets, OF 192
renaming. *See* naming
replacing text, OF 98–99
reports, OF 40, OF 258–266
  closing, OF 265–266
  creating, OF 259–264
  printing, OF 264–265
Report Wizard, OF 258
  activating, OF 259–260
  displaying tips about dialog boxes, OF 261–262
Report Wizard Examples dialog box, OF 262
resizing. *See* sizing
restoring actions, OF 88, OF 89
right alignment, OF 28
rotation, 3-D pie charts, OF 408
row headings, Excel window, OF 138, OF 139
Row Height dialog box, OF 370
rows. *See* worksheet rows
row selector, OF 44
rulers
  forms, OF 474
  Word window, OF 18, OF 19
running queries, OF 269–270, OF 271, OF 435, OF 438, OF 441

S

sans serif fonts, OF 100–101
Save As command, OF 20
Save As dialog box, OF 21
Save command, OF 20
saving
  databases, OF 221
  documents, OF 19–21, OF 31, OF 93
  forms, OF 238, OF 477–478, OF 487–488
  presentations, OF 59, OF 298
  queries, OF 273
  table structure, OF 225
  workbooks, OF 54, OF 149, OF 161, OF 343, OF 364
  worksheets, OF 187
screen fonts, OF 101
ScreenTips, OF 34–35
scrolling documents, OF 95
ScrollTips, OF 94
secondary sort key, OF 447
selecting
  cells for charts, OF 387–388
  charts, OF 391–392
  controls, OF 480–481
  fields. *See* selecting fields
  text. *See* selecting text
  WordArt images, OF 117–118
  worksheets, OF 51
selecting fields
  forms, OF 244
  queries, OF 269
  reports, OF 260–261
selecting text, OF 96–99
  documents, OF 96–99
  outline view, OF 300
selection bar, OF 97
selection box, OF 51
Select Objects tool, OF 475
select queries, OF 266
Select Query window, OF 267–268
sentences, selecting, OF 98
serial dates, OF 148
series. *See* data series
serif fonts, OF 100
Shaded Fill dialog box, OF 310
Shading dialog box, OF 121
shadows, chart titles, OF 399–400
shapes. *See* AutoShapes
Sheet Name button, Page Setup dialog box, OF 375
sheet tabs
  Excel window, OF 139
  Page Setup dialog box, OF 377
  scrolling buttons, OF 402
shortcut menus, OF 41, OF 42
Show All button, Outlining toolbar, OF 296
Show Formatting button, Outlining toolbar, OF 296
Show/Hide button, OF 85
Show Table dialog box, OF 253
Show Titles button, Outlining toolbar, OF 296
Simple Query Wizard
  dialog boxes, OF 434
  exact matches, OF 433–435
  pattern matches, OF 439–440
size
  fields, OF 212, OF 235
  fonts. *See* font size
sizing
  charts, OF 68–69, OF 395–396
  clip art, OF 316–317
  controls, OF 478–479
  datasheet columns, OF 436–437
  embedded pictures, OF 184
  forms, OF 493–495
  placeholders, OF 307, OF 315
  WordArt objects, OF 119–121
sizing handles, OF 119
slash (/), division operator, OF 150
slide master, OF 286
slides, OF 286. *See also* presentations; viewing presentations
  adding text, OF 63–65, OF 303–305
  animation effects, OF 319–320
  annotating, OF 324–326
  changing layout, OF 312
  deleting text, OF 305
  entering text, OF 290–292
  formatting text, OF 306–308
  inserting clip art, OF 314–319
  inserting from another presentation, OF 313–314
  linking charts to slides, OF 66–71
  masters, OF 286
  moving text, OF 300–301, OF 305–306
  multiple, printing, OF 329
  order, OF 61–62, OF 322–324
  printing, OF 72–73
  promoting and demoting text, OF 301
  rearranging, OF 322–324
  single, viewing, OF 310
  title, OF 290
slide show view, OF 60
slide sorter view, OF 60
  rearranging slides, OF 323–324
  viewing presentations, OF 61
Slide Sorter View button, OF 290
slide view, OF 303–308
  adding slides to presentations, OF 292–294
  adding text to slides, OF 303–305
  deleting text on slides, OF 305

formatting text on slides, OF 306–308
PowerPoint, OF 60
rearranging text on slides, OF 305–306
switching to, OF 302
viewing presentations, OF 60
Slide View button, OF 290
Sort Ascending button, OF 445, OF 446
sort buttons
sorting multiple fields, OF 446–447
sorting one field, OF 445–446
Sort Descending button, OF 445, OF 446
sorting, OF 445–450
multiple fields in Design view, OF 448–450
multiple fields using toolbar Sort buttons, OF 446–447
one field using toolbar Sort buttons, OF 445–446
records using queries, OF 271–273
worksheet rows, OF 363–364
sort keys, OF 272
primary and secondary, OF 447
selecting, OF 272–273
unique and nonunique, OF 446–447
source program, OF 48, OF 49, OF 50
Spacing Between Characters dialog box, OF 118
speaker's notes, OF 326–328
printing, OF 329
Special Effect property, OF 483
Special Effects dialog box, OF 118
special operators, Access, OF 439
spell checking
documents, OF 122–125
presentations, OF 328–329
Spelling dialog box, OF 123, OF 124, OF 125
spin boxes, OF 118
splash screen, OF 17
splitting worksheet windows, OF 180–182
spreadsheets, OF 135. *See also* worksheets
square brackets ([ ]), wildcard character, OF 241
stacking pictures, OF 398–399
Standard toolbar
Excel window, OF 139
PowerPoint window, OF 59, OF 290
Word window, OF 18, OF 19
starting WordArt, OF 116–117
statistical functions, OF 155
status bar
Database window, OF 43
Excel window, OF 138, OF 139
Word window, OF 18, OF 19
Stretch Size Mode property, OF 490
style, forms. *See* AutoFormats
subfolders, OF 15
subforms, OF 255–257
Subform/Subreport tool, OF 475
subtraction operator (–), OF 150
suite, OF 5
SUM function, OF 154
Function Wizard, OF 156–158
Sum function, OF 460, OF 461
switching
between documents, OF 90–91
to Form view, OF 488
between navigation mode and editing mode, OF 229
to outline view, OF 294–295
to slide view, OF 302

T

tab character (**), OF 105
table relationships, OF 251–255, OF 426–432
defining, OF 251–255
many-to-many, OF 428–432
one-to-many. *See* one-to-many relationships
tables, OF 37, OF 43–47, OF 202
adding records, OF 46, OF 219–221, OF 226
changing values, OF 38
creating, OF 212–219
fields. *See* fields
grouping fields into, OF 205
importing Excel data, OF 231–234
joined, OF 440
modifying structure, OF 222–226
multiple, querying, OF 273–275
opening, OF 44
primary, OF 252
printing, OF 47
related, OF 252
relationships. *See* table relationships
reports. *See* reports
specifying primary key, OF 217–218
structure. *See* table structure
updating (maintaining). *See* updating tables
table structure
deleting fields, OF 235
modifying, OF 222–226
saving, OF 218–219, OF 225
Table window
Datasheet view, OF 219
Design view, OF 213
tab marker (**), OF 85
tabs, OF 105–107
alignment, OF 106
inserting, OF 106–107
tab stops, OF 105
taskbar, Word window, OF 18, OF 19
TAssign folder, OF 15
templates, OF 84
design. *See* design templates
testing worksheets, OF 359–362
test values, OF 359
text. *See also* documents; editing documents; formatting documents
adding to slides, OF 63–65, OF 303–305
blocks. *See* text blocks
centering in worksheet cells, OF 371
charts, OF 393–394
copying in documents, OF 25–26
deleting. *See* deleting text
entering. *See* entering text in documents; entering text on slides
formatting on slides, OF 306–308
moving. *See* moving text
promoting and demoting on slides, OF 301
replacing, OF 98–99
selecting. *See* selecting text
WordArt, applying special effects, OF 118–119
worksheet cells. *See* labels
text blocks, OF 107–111
copying and pasting, OF 108
moving, OF 109–111
Text Box tool, OF 475
text data type
fields, OF 211
sorting results, OF 272
text functions, OF 155
text notes, adding to worksheets, OF 358–359
3-D pie charts
changing 2-D pie charts to, OF 405–406
elevation and rotation, OF 408
printing, OF 413
pulling out wedges, OF 406–408
tick mark labels, charts, OF 383
tiling document windows, OF 91–92
time. *See* date and time functions; date/time data type
Time button, Page Setup dialog box, OF 375
TipWizards, OF 18, OF 86
title bar
Access window, OF 43
Database window, OF 43
Excel window, OF 138, OF 139
Word window, OF 18, OF 19
title masters, OF 286
editing, OF 291–292
titles, charts, OF 383
title screen, OF 17
title slides, creating, OF 290
TODAY function, OF 343–344
toolbars
docking, OF 11, OF 13
Office Shortcut Bar, OF 11–13
toolbox, forms, OF 475
tools, forms, OF 475

ToolTips, OF 13
Top Values property, queries, OF 467–468
Total Pages button, Page Setup dialog box, OF 375
TROUBLE? paragraphs, OF 4
TRUE function, OF 158
TrueType fonts, OF 101
tutorials, effective use, OF 4–5
type. *See* fonts; font size; font style; font type

U

unbound controls, OF 474
unbound object frame, OF 488–491
Unbound Object Frame tool, OF 475
underlined font style
  documents, OF 30
  worksheets, OF 178–179
Undo button, OF 88, OF 89
Undo Picture Formatting command, OF 120–121
unique sort keys, OF 446
update queries, OF 469–471
updating
  databases. *See* updating databases
  linked charts, OF 415–417
  tables. *See* updating tables
  worksheets, OF 50–53
updating databases, OF 228–231
  queries, OF 275–276
updating tables, OF 46–47
  forms, OF 248–251

V

values. *See also* numbers
  entering in worksheets, OF 146–148
  fields, OF 202
  null, OF 217
  test, OF 359
viewing. *See also* displaying
  forms, OF 477
  presentations. *See* viewing presentations
  single slides, OF 310
viewing presentations, OF 71–72, OF 299, OF 308
  slide sorter view, OF 61
  slide view, OF 60

W

wedges. *See* 3-D pie charts
what-if analysis, OF 135
wildcard characters, OF 241, OF 439
window panes, OF 181
windows. *See also specific windows*
  open, buttons identifying, OF 58
Word, OF 5, OF 6–7, OF 78–128. *See also* documents
  exiting, OF 36
  Help system, OF 31–35
WordArt, OF 10
  starting, OF 116–117
WordArt dialog box, OF 117
WordArt objects, OF 114–122
  applying special effects, OF 118–119
  changing, OF 121–122
  embedding, OF 116–118
  resizing, OF 119–121
word-processing program. *See* Word
words, selecting, OF 98
Word window, OF 7, OF 18–19, OF 83
Word window buttons, OF 18, OF 19
word wrap, OF 88
workbooks, OF 135
  closing, OF 160–161
  documentation sheets, OF 342–343
  opening, OF 53–54, OF 161–162
  organization, OF 341–342
  renaming, OF 162
  saving, OF 54, OF 149, OF 161, OF 343, OF 364
  sheets. *See* worksheet cells; worksheet columns; worksheet rows; worksheets
  starting, OF 138
  TODAY function, OF 343–344
worksheet cells, OF 54, OF 139
  centering text, OF 371
  changing alignment, OF 370–371
  clearing contents, OF 185–186
  editing contents, OF 143–144
  moving contents, OF 168–171
  moving to, OF 164–165
  naming, OF 162–164
  underlining, OF 178–179
worksheet columns
  deleting, OF 167–168
  inserting, OF 165–167
  widths, OF 175–176
worksheet program. *See* Excel
worksheet rows
  changing height, OF 369–370
  deleting, OF 167–168
  inserting, OF 55, OF 165–167
  sorting, OF 363–364
worksheets. *See also* workbooks
  adding text notes, OF 358–359
  automatic recalculation, OF 357
  cells. *See* worksheet cells
  centering, OF 377
  clearing cell contents, OF 185–186
  columns. *See* worksheet columns
  completing series with AutoFill, OF 344–347
  copying formulas, OF 55
  deleting columns and rows, OF 167–168
  developing, OF 135–137
  displaying, OF 345
  editing, OF 54–56, OF 69–71
  embedded pictures, OF 182–185
  embedding in Word documents. *See* embedded worksheets
  entering dates, OF 148
  entering values, OF 146–148
  formatting. *See* formatting worksheets
  formulas. *See* formulas
  gridlines, OF 377–378
  importing into tables, OF 231–234
  inserting columns and rows, OF 55, OF 165–167
  labels. *See* labels
  moving cell contents, OF 168–171
  navigating, OF 145–146
  planning, OF 136
  printing. *See* printing worksheets
  ranges. *See* cell ranges
  renaming, OF 140, OF 402–403
  rows. *See* worksheet rows
  saving, OF 187
  selecting, OF 51
  sorting rows, OF 363–364
  testing, OF 359–362
  updating, OF 50–53
worksheet window, splitting, OF 180–182
workspace, Word window, OF 18, OF 19

X

X-axis, OF 383
X-axis title, OF 383
  deleting, OF 394

Y

Y-axis, OF 383
Y-axis title, OF 383
  editing, OF 393–394
yes/no data type
  fields, OF 211
  sorting results, OF 272

Z

Zoom dialog box, OF 455

Task Reference

TASK	PAGE #	RECOMMENDED METHOD	NOTES
Aggregate functions, use	OF 460	Click Σ	Access
Animation effects, add	OF 319	Right-click the selection, click Animation Settings	PowerPoint
AutoCorrect options, view	OF 87	Click Tools, click AutoCorrect	
AutoFill, activate	OF 344	Drag fill handle to highlight the cells to be filled	Excel
AutoFormat, change	OF 246	From Form view, click	Access
AutoFormat, change	OF 371	Click Format, click AutoFormat	Excel
AutoShape, draw	OF 308	Click	PowerPoint
AutoSum, activate	OF 348	Click Σ	Excel
Border, add	OF 177	Click down arrow	Excel
Border, remove	OF 180	Right-click the selection, click Format Cells, click the Border tab, clear all entries	Excel
Bulleted list, create	OF 113	Click	Word
Cell, clear contents of	OF 186	Click Edit, point to Clear, select the option	Excel
Cell, move to a named	OF 165	Click the reference area list arrow, click the cell name	Excel
Cell, name	OF 163	Select the cell, click the reference area in the formula bar, type cell name	Excel
Chart, activate	OF 391	Right-click the chart, click Edit Object	Excel
Chart, create	OF 388	Select the cells, click	Excel
Clip art, insert	OF 315	Click	PowerPoint
Column, adjust width of	OF 176	Double-click the right border of the column heading	Access, Excel
Column, delete	OF 167	Select column(s), right-click column(s), click Delete	Access, Excel, Word
Column, insert	OF 166	Select column(s), right-click column(s), click Insert	Access, Excel, Word
Data, find	OF 240	Click Edit, click Find, select options	
Database, compact	OF 495	Close the database, click Tools, click Database Utilities, click Compact Database	Access
Database, copy	OF 41	From the Exploring window, right-click the database, click Copy, click File, click Paste	Access

Task Reference

TASK	PAGE #	RECOMMENDED METHOD	NOTES
Database, rename	OF 42	Right-click the database name, click Rename	Access
Database, save	OF 221	Click [X]	Access
Decimal position, add or remove	OF 171	Click [icon] or [icon]	Excel
Document, close	OF 93	Click [X] on the document window	
Document, open	OF 16	Click [icon], select the drive and folder, click the document name, click Open	
Document, print	OF 41	Click [icon] to print one copy of document; otherwise, click File, click Print, select print options, click OK	
Document, print preview	OF 126	Click [icon]	
Document, save with a new filename	OF 21	Click File, click Save As, type the filename, select the drive and folder, click Save	Excel, PowerPoint, Word
Document, save with the same filename	OF 38	Click [icon]	Excel, PowerPoint, Word
Document, start a new	OF 81	Click [icon], click a tab, click an icon, click OK	
Document, switch to another open	OF 91	Click Window, click the document name	Excel, PowerPoint, Word
Document, tile each open	OF 91	Click Window, click the tile option	
Embedded object, insert	OF 188	Select the object, click [icon], position the insertion point, click Edit, click Paste Special, click Paste, click OK	
Embedded worksheet, edit	OF 51	Right-click the object, click Edit Worksheet	
Expression Builder, activate	OF 456	Right-click the Field text box, click Build	Access
Field, define	OF 213	Type the field name, select the data type, type or select optional field properties	Access
Field, delete	OF 235	Right-click the row selector, click Delete Field	Access
Filter By Form, activate	OF 452	Click [icon], select the field values, click [icon]	Access
Filter By Selection, activate	OF 451	Select the field value, click [icon]	Access
Font size, select	OF 102	Click the Font Size list arrow, click the desired font size	
Font type, select	OF 103	Click the Font list arrow, click the desired font	
Footer, edit	OF 376	Click File, click Page Setup, click Header/Footer	Excel
Form Wizard, activate	OF 237	Click Forms tab, click New, select the wizard	Access

Task Reference

TASK	PAGE #	RECOMMENDED METHOD	NOTES
Format Painter, apply formatting using	OF 105	Select the text with the format you want to copy, click [Format Painter button], select the text you want to format	
Format, bold	OF 103	Click [B]	
Format, currency	OF 172	Click [$]	Excel
Format, italic	OF 104	Click [I]	
Format, percentage	OF 362	Click [%]	Excel
Formula, enter	OF 151	Select the cell, type =, type the formula	Excel
Formulas, display	OF 381	Click Tools, click Options, click View tab, click Formulas check box	Excel
Function Wizard, activate	OF 156	Click [fx]	Excel
Gridlines, add or remove from printout	OF 377	Click File, click Page Setup, click Sheet tab, click Gridlines check box	Excel
Header, edit	OF 374	Click File, click Page Setup, click Header/Footer tab	Excel
Help, Answer Wizard	OF 33	Click the Answer Wizard tab, type the question, click Search	
Help, context-sensitive	OF 34	Click [Help button], click the window component	
Linked object, edit	OF 415	Right-click the object, click Edit Object	
Linked object, insert	OF 67	Select the object, click [Copy button], position the insertion point, click Edit, click Paste Special, click Paste Link, click OK	
Linked worksheet, edit	OF 69	Right-click the object, click Edit Worksheet Link	
Nonprinting characters, display	OF 85	Click [¶]	Word
Numbered list, create	OF 112	Click [Numbering button]	Word
Object, move	OF 395	Click the object, drag the object outline	
Object, open	OF 44	Click the object tab, click the object name, click Open	Access
Object, resize	OF 69	Click the object, drag the sizing handles	
Object, save	OF 219	Click [Save button]	Access
Office Shortcut Bar, open	OF 11	Click the Start button, point to Programs, click Microsoft Office Shortcut Bar	

Task Reference

TASK	PAGE #	RECOMMENDED METHOD	NOTES
Outline text, demote (indent more)	OF 301	Select the paragraph, click	PowerPoint
Outline text, move	OF 300	Click the slide icon or the bullet, click or	PowerPoint
Outline text, promote (indent less)	OF 301	Select the paragraph, click	PowerPoint
Outline View, switch to	OF 294	Click	PowerPoint
Picture, embed	OF 182	Click Insert, click Picture	
Primary key, select	OF 218	Select the field row(s), click	Access
Printout, center	OF 377	Click File, click Page Setup, click Margins tab, click the Horizontally and/or Vertically check boxes	Excel
Printout, landscape (sideways) orientation	OF 236	Click File, click Page Setup, click Page tab, click Landscape	Access, Excel
Printout, portrait (normal) orientation	OF 374	Click File, click Page Setup, click Page tab, click Portrait	Access, Excel
Program, exit	OF 36	Click	
Query, define	OF 267	Click Queries tab, click New, click Design View	Access
Query, run	OF 270	Click	Access
Range, move to a named	OF 164	Click the reference area list arrow, click the range name	Excel
Range, name	OF 163	Select the range of cells, click the reference area in the formula bar	Excel
Record, add	OF 219	Click	Access
Record, delete	OF 46	Select the record, press Delete	Access
Records, redisplay all	OF 452	Click	Access
Report Wizard, activate	OF 259	Click Reports tab, click New, select wizard	Access
Row, delete	OF 167	Select row(s), right-click row(s), click Delete	Excel
Row, insert	OF 166	Select row(s), right-click row(s), click Insert	Excel
Slide Show, view	OF 299	Click , press spacebar or click left mouse button to advance	PowerPoint
Slide Sorter view, switch to	OF 61	Click	PowerPoint

Task Reference

TASK	PAGE #	RECOMMENDED METHOD	NOTES
Slide, add	OF 62	Click	PowerPoint
Slide, annotate	OF 325	In Slide Show view, right-click the slide, click Pen	PowerPoint
Slide, go to next	OF 307	Click	PowerPoint
Slide, go to previous	OF 305	Click	PowerPoint
Slide, insert another presentation's	OF 313	Click Insert, click Slides from File	PowerPoint
Spelling, check	OF 122	Click	
Table, create	OF 212	Click Tables tab, click New	Access
Table, define relationship	OF 253	Click	Access
Table, import	OF 231	Click New, click Import Table	Access
Table, open Access	OF 45	Click table name, click Open	Access
Template, change a design	OF 302	Click	PowerPoint
Text note, add	OF 358	Click Insert, click Note	Excel
Text, center	OF 28	Click	Word
Text, center across columns	OF 371	Click	Excel
Text, copy	OF 108	Select the text, click , position the insertion point, click	
Text, delete	OF 99	Select the text, press Delete	
Text, insert	OF 24	Position the insertion point, type the text	
Text, justify	OF 28	Click	Word
Text, left-align	OF 28	Click	Word
Text, move	OF 109	Select the text, click , position the insertion point, click	
Text, replace	OF 98	Select the text, type the text	
Text, right-align	OF 28	Click	Word
Text, select all	OF 102	Click Edit, click Select All	Word, PowerPoint
ToolTip, display	OF 13	Position pointer over the tool	
Undo action, select	OF 88	Click	

Task Reference

TASK	PAGE #	RECOMMENDED METHOD	NOTES
Undo action, reverse an	OF 89	Click	
Window, split	OF 181	Drag small rectangle at top of the vertical scroll bar	Excel, Word
WordArt object, edit	OF 121	Right-click the object, click Edit WordArt 2.0	
WordArt object, embed	OF 116	Click Insert, click Object, click Create New, click Microsoft WordArt 2.0	
Worksheet, rename	OF 140	Right-click worksheet tab, click Rename	Excel